D.3. McDowell

iii / 2012

CARRYING ON

FETTES COLLEGE, WAR AND THE WORLD 1870-2010

DAVID MCDOWELL

For my family

Matador
9 Priory Business Park,
Wistow Road, Kibworth Beauchamp,
Leicestershire. LE8 0RX
Tel: (+44) 116 279 2299
Fax: (+44) 116 279 2277
Email: books@troubador.co.uk
Web: www.troubador.co.uk/matador

ISBN 978 1780880 327

British Library Cataloguing in Publication Data.
A catalogue record for this book is available from the British Library.

Typeset in 11pt Bembo by Troubador Publishing Ltd, Leicester, UK

Matador is an imprint of Troubador Publishing Ltd

Printed and bound in the UK by TJ International, Padstow, Cornwall

Contents

Introduction   iv

Acknowledgements   vii

1. Sir William Fettes, Enlightenment war profiteer   1

2. Public schools and Empire   24

3. Adventures overseas   63

4. The pupils of Fettes and the study of war   108

5. Life at Fettes during the First World War   146

6. Fettesians on the Western Front in the First World War   185

7. Fettesians on other fronts in the First World War   235

8. The Aftermath of the First World War   279

9. The Road to the Second World War   339

10. Life at Fettes during the Second World War   379

11. Fettesians at the front in the Blitzkrieg era, 1939-41   421

12. Fettesians as liberators, 1942-45   456

13. Fettesian Prisoners of War   500

14. Fettes and Bondage   542

15. The post-war school   576

16. National Service   626

17. The end of the British Empire   659

18. The sixties fail to swing at Fettes   696

19. The seventies and Northern Ireland   735

20. The eighties and the Falklands   775

21. Fettes in the New World Order   814

22. Fettes warriors in the new century   844

Introduction

It is currently fashionable to claim, in the title of a book, that its subject was responsible for inventing the modern world, changing the course of history, or revolutionising our way of life. These claims will not be made of Fettes College, but it can be said that this Edinburgh boarding school did have a pretty good ringside seat at the great events of the last century and a half. This book is a study of a small community's relationship with the world, focusing primarily on war, empire and international politics, beginning with its founder and carrying on, to use a popular phrase at the school, through to the twenty-first century.

William Fettes was born in 1750 and was a friend of some of the leading figures of the Scottish Enlightenment; he also helped publish Burns' poetry. It was an age when many looked forward to a new era of reason, peace and prosperity. When prosperity came to William Fettes, however, it was as a war profiteer, and for much of his life the British Army was fighting around the world, and not always to save it from the French.

By the time the school he founded was opened in 1871, the British Empire had become a global concern and Fettes College was one of the institutions which sent muscular Christians out to govern it. Inspired by the Bible, the Classics and sport, they conquered and administered vast territories across the world. Their younger brothers at home absorbed these messages eagerly and wrote patriotic verse in the school magazine.

Fettesians played a vigorous role in the two World Wars, though one, Sir John Simon, became better known to history as an arch-appeaser of fascist aggression. Although the average Old Fettesian was a junior infantry officer (hence the school's considerable losses) there were also fighter pilots, prisoners of war, and even spies – some of whom may have inspired the idea that James Bond went to Fettes.

During the Cold War Fettes prepared its pupils well for their obligatory National Service, but in parallel with this came the dismantling of the Empire which Fettesians had proudly served – a process partly accelerated by two OFs in the government, Selwyn Lloyd and Iain Macleod.

Since the sixties, the school, like British society, became more liberal and more questioning of war. The numbers entering the armed forces, and indeed other branches of public service, were lower than those in Victorian days. This book will examine the new opportunities for service which appeared in the post-war world and were often more appealing than military adventures. Although these activities flourish, the cadet corps continues to the present day, as does its proud remembrance of fallen Old Fettesians. Former pupils continued to serve wherever the British Army fought – including in the wars associated with Fettesian sixties rebel Tony Blair.

This book began life as a suggestion from the then Fettes Chaplain, the Rev Brian McDowell, that a souvenir booklet be created to mark the anniversaries of the foundation of the school corps (1908-2008) and of the cadet movement in general (1860-2010). It expanded into a much bigger project in the five years of its creation as research uncovered a fascinating variety of untold stories, veterans' memories and sometimes disturbing insights. It aims to tell the story of the pupils and staff of Fettes College as they looked out on a world from which at one level they were rather detached, but for which they were also being trained. Fettes, at any rate in its early decades, self-consciously set out to mould empire-building leaders of men. Its first intake of 53 boys in 1870 included future generals and imperial administrators as well as the traditional Scots output of clergymen, lawyers and doctors. Classically-educated, as befitted the heirs of Greece and Rome, 24 of them spent all or part of their careers in far-flung 'regions Caesar never knew' and 17 died overseas. The Victorian school magazine, which has provided the bulk of the source material for the early chapters, is a treasure-trove of tales of former pupils' military derring-do and their younger brothers' breathless imperialist poetry. As the world changed, Fettes changed too, and these features of the magazine gradually disappeared; by the twenty-first century, public-spirited Fettesians were more likely to be helping out in a Costa Rican village than taking part in a cavalry charge on the North-West Frontier (though there were, of course, Fettesians and the products of plenty of other British schools still to be found in uniform in that part of the world). The culture they left behind them at the school changed enormously, but there was still room for the old sense of duty and patriotism.

Some of this story is undoubtedly tragic. To look over the dreadful lists of the Fettes College war dead is to see the loss of many talented young men who, had they lived, would have given much to Britain in general and Scotland in particular. The obituaries crammed into the post-Somme edition of the school magazine feature excellent sportsmen, ferociously clever scholarship boys and gifted classicists who were gunned down in their late teens or early twenties before they could ever realise the potential their masters saw in them. Those of the Second World War, although less frequent, are still above the national average, and include victims characteristic of that era – shot down in air-raids on German cities, worked to death in Japanese camps, murdered by the Gestapo.

Some, like Maitland Hardyman, the school's Wilfred Owen, became cynical about the causes for which they were asked to die. Most Fettesians, however, fought in wars which Britain did not start, and in which they fervently believed they faced a foe whose victory would be disastrous to humanity. The survivors – and, of course, most Britons who join the armed forces do survive – are generally of this opinion. In the language of post-modernist discourse, this is one particular 'narrative' of the period of history concerned. Many will undoubtedly find my view of the Indian Army and Civil Service unnecessarily sunny, and some Old Fettesians (such as the one quoted in *A Nest of Singing Birds*) have noted the ambiguity of the 'Carry On' inscription on the War Memorial. I have attempted to reflect all viewpoints but there will undoubtedly be those who feel that some have received greater attention than others.

This book will primarily interest what is now referred to as the 'Fettes family' – the pupils, former pupils, common room and others connected with the school. However, those without any links to Fettes should still find it a useful resource for understanding the complex relationship which the British have had with warfare in the last two centuries. I have included politics and culture as part of the military-imperial tapestry because they cannot be woven out of it, so not all of this book is about soldiering – some of it is about the alternatives. Wherever possible, the characters in this book speak for themselves, through letters, articles, memoirs, poetry, emails and interviews. Here we have the voices of Victorian imperialists, young officers in the trenches, bomber pilots and cold warriors, with an often strident chorus of pupils in the background. They are worth listening to.

David McDowell
History Department
Fettes College
June 2011

Acknowledgments

Many current and recent members of staff at Fettes have given invaluable help during the writing of this book. Dr Diana Henderson began the process, some years ago, of collecting the wartime memories of Old Fettesians, whilst the late Miss Alexa Lindsay presided over the school archive for many years and ensured that the historical documents were all in one place, assisted by Mrs Mary McDowell. Mr John Lang of the school Foundation was generous with time and ideas, and Mr George Preston has done an incredible job in creating a database of former pupils. Lt-Col Ronnie Guild has been a gold-mine of stories and observations about the school in the second half of the twentieth century. The support of his most recent successor, Lt-Col Andrew Alexander, has been greatly appreciated, and the school's finance office, especially Miss Sharon Ross, have been very tolerant of my erratic approach to organising visits and buying books. Mr Robert Philp, author of *A Keen Wind Blows*, has been very kind – anyone who attempts a second book about the same institution will be conscious that he is standing on the shoulders of giants. Maj Jeremy Morris, Miss Alexandra Layman, Mr Tony Reeves, Mr David Kennedy, and the Headmaster, Mr Michael Spens, have made much-appreciated contributions. The reminiscences of RSM Willie Ross have been delightful, and Mr Lucas Von Hoff and Mr James Weatherby kept the flag flying for ANZAC Day. Our chaplains, the Revs Brian McDowell and David Campbell, have been assiduous in their celebration of the school's military heritage. Above all, Wing-Cdr Andrew Murray, former OC of the CCF, Head of History and now Archivist, and Mrs Dawn Beaumont of the Old Fettesian Association have been wonderful, and the book simply could not have existed without them.

The *Fettesian* magazine, from which I have drawn freely for information, is a wonderful resource, and really does provide a window into a vanished world. Of course, it can never provide the whole story, circumscribed as it is by what the headmaster of the day considers fit to print and by what the pupils of the day can be bothered to write. To collect further material for this book, requests were made for reminiscences from Old Fettesians in the pages of their magazine, and selected groups of OFs were also directly mailed or emailed. Specifically, I wanted to know about their experiences at school, primarily as cadets but also whether or not they had known much about the international military and political situation of the day, and of course what their adult careers in the services had been like. More than a hundred Old Fettesians, several, sadly, no longer with us, responded to this appeal and also to Dr Henderson's earlier request for detailed memories of the Second World War which were added to the school archive, or to the pleas of editors of the *Old Fettesian Newsletter* for material. This book is, of course, their story, and I regret that it has not been possible to include all of their memories. They include:

James Allan, Tim Alston, Robert Anderson, David Arbuthnott, Andrew Ayre, Mickey Bain, Tib Beament, Andrew Betts-Brown, Ollie Blake, Bob Bleakley, Mark Boyes, Brian Brown, Fergus Brownlee, Lindsay Buchan, Roger Christian, Barry Clegg, Bill Clark, Lindsay Clubb, Andrew Collister, Patric Colquhon, John Cormack, A.R.H. Cumming, Tim Daniels, Richard Davidson, Robin Donald, Gordon Dowell, R.H. Douglas, Rob Douglas, Hugh Dunford, Jonathan Dunlop, Peter Dunnett, Robin Durham, Robin Fairlie, David Fairweather, David Whigham Ferguson, Duncan Ferguson, John Ferguson, Donald Filshill, John Foot, Alastair Fox, Alexander Knox Gallie, Willie Geddes, Ian Gardiner, Ronald Gardiner, Tony Gilroy, Sandy Glen, Caroline Graham-Brown, Charles Gray, Rob Greaves, Neil Griffiths, Ian Hamilton, Matty Hand, R. de G. Hanson, Nigel Herdman, Alastair Heron, Allan Herriot, Charles Herzberg, Justin Holt, John Humphries, Andrew Hunter, Ian Hutchinson, Willy Inglis, Donald Jamieson, Allan Jardine, John Jeff, Andrew Ker, Lindsay Keith, David Kilpatrick, Gordon Kirkwood, James Kirsop, Charlie Lang, Christopher Lawrence, Robert Lawrence, Alexandra Layman, Matt Leary, Hamish Liddell, Ian Lowles, M.C. Lyons, Douglas MacGregor, Angus Macintosh, Alastair Maclaren, Raymond Maclean, Rhoderick Macleod, Neil Macnaughtan, Sir Thomas and Lady Macpherson, Ian Mair, M.J. Mair, Robin Mallinson, Grant Mathew, Tim McAdam, Kenneth McCallum, David McCollum, John McGlashan, Charles McKean, Ian McKee, Raymond McLennan, Ken Millar, Iain Miller, Keith Miller, Colin Mitchell-Rose, Angus Morrison, Mary Mure, Christopher Normand, Dick Normand, Trina Noyes, Sam Park, Sandy Park, Chris Parker, John Purser, Andrew Purves, Douglas Rae, Ian Rae, John Rankin, Harry Reid, E.G. Richards, Iain Ritchie, Alasdair Samson, Neil Sanders, Robert Sanders, Freddie Scott, William Sharp, Ronnie Shaw, Chris

Shennan, Ian Stewart, Chris Sutton, Urosh Teodorovich, Gilmour Thom, Hamish Thomson, David Vann, Robin Webster, Matthew Wells, John Wenger, John Weston Smith, Struan Wiley, Nicol Wilson, Gordon Wylie, Gar Yates, Neil Fyfe, Mike North, John Urquhart, J.B.A. Smyth, Bingham Kirk, Neil Irvine, Alyster Jackson, Anthony Jacobsen, Ruairidh Watters and John Younie.

There are almost certainly others and I must apologise if I have left anyone out; several accounts were lost when computers 'died'. Several Old Fettesians also kindly reviewed chapters covering the war years to check that I had not committed any serious blunders. Their generosity with both time and information has been appreciated more than I can say. Any historian looking for primary sources on war, empire and the public school experience of the twentieth century will find this book packed with them; even before it was finished, we were using excerpts in lessons in the Fettes history department.

There are, of course, omissions — a number of distinguished OFs serving or recently retired from Her Majesty's Forces did not get in touch, but perhaps seeing contemporaries in print may encourage them to do so. Any former pupil or member of staff who has a story to tell or who feels there has been a serious omission is very welcome to write to the history department at Fettes, and contribute to the paperback edition.

Outside Fettes, a number of people provided much-appreciated help. Hans Riehle gave me the story of his father's escape after being shot down by an Old Fettesian, and Kjell Sørensen and Tor Helge Solli of the Surnadal Kommune in Norway supplied information about the fate of another Old Fettesian's Spitfire, including photographs of the wreckage. Alasdair Roberts, author of *Ties that bind*, gave interesting insights, Andrew Collins helped clarify an issue regarding 1930s fascism, and Robin-Scott Elliott kindly allowed me to quote from his family's letters. A number of academics were kind enough to look at chapters or provide helpful advice and clarification, and my thanks go out to them: Mr Philip Waller, Prof Hew Strachan, Prof Graham Walker, Prof Tom Devine, Dr Dan Todman and Dr John Regan. Any remaining errors are mine alone.

The illustrations in this book come mostly from the school archives or were supplied by Old Fettesians. In addition, Fred Larimore kindly gave permission to use his picture of Maj Barnes. The majority of the colour plates were taken by Allan Forbes, who has been the school 'snapper' for as long as I can remember. I am very grateful for his generosity in allowing me to use these wonderful images.

A number of people kindly gave me permission to quote from their books and articles. Robert Philp, from *A Keen Wind Blows*, Richard Thorpe from *Selwyn Lloyd*, Lt Robert Lawrence MC, from *When the Fighting is Over*, Michel Byrne, from *George Campbell Hay*, Warren Hope, from *Norman Cameron: his life and letters*, John Humphries, from *A Lifetime of Verse*, Mark Peel from *The Land of Lost Content*, Brig Ian Gardiner, from his books, online reports and articles, and Neil 'Gurkha' Griffiths from his. I am extremely grateful to Kerry Black from the *Scotsman* who kindly gave permission to quote from that paper and from the *Edinburgh Evening News* and *Scotland on Sunday*. Selwyn Lloyd's executor and nephew, Anthony Shone, kindly allowed me to quote from that great Old Fettesian's letter to his parents before D-Day. I am informed that the works by very Old Fettesians promiscuously quoted in the first half-dozen chapters are now out of copyright, but should there be any issue with this I can be contacted directly at the school.

This book was mostly written in the History Department of Fettes, in Kimmerghame House, where I spent three years as resident tutor, on holiday visits to my family at Elie Manse, and in the Cumberland Bar, whose staff deserve thanks for tolerating my creation of a paper-strewn 'office' in the small snug. Both my teaching colleagues and my pupils, particularly the boys of Kimmerghame, have provided great encouragement, and I am very grateful to them all.

I earnestly recommend Fettes' official publications, *A Keen Wind Blows* by Robert Philp and *A Nest of Singing Birds: an anthology of Fettes Poets*, edited by Gordon Jarvie. Fettesians who were rather more famous as poets made it into the latter publication, whereas this book tends to concentrate on schoolboy material.

Finally, as will soon become apparent, this book reflects its author's idiosyncrasies and as such should not be taken as the official narrative of the school itself, nor that of the current and former staff and pupils whose stories make up the book.

Chapter One

'I did not wish my son should be a soldier'

Sir William Fettes, Enlightenment War Profiteer

Remembrance Sunday at Fettes

Each Remembrance Sunday, the pupils of Fettes College gather in the school chapel, accompanied by their teachers and a group of retired gentlemen in bemedalled blazers, and take part in a service to honour their fallen brethren. Afterwards, they troop outside, passing the exuberant Gothic gargoyles and intricate carved pillars designed by David Bryce, and line up quietly around the war memorial. This is an austere stone box at the end of the east drive into the school, on top of which lies a mortally wounded young officer in a kilt. He is larger than life size, cast in bronze in a style which, a thousand miles away to the east, would be called socialist realist – though in this environment, he is unlikely to be a socialist and modern sensibilities would also deny that such depictions are especially realistic. His hand is raised to Heaven to implore his men to follow the message carved on the stone: 'CARRY ON'. On the back and sides of the memorial are bronze tablets listing 246 names of Old Fettesians (OFs) who died in the First World War, including two Victoria Cross winners; surrounding it is a low wall with 118 more who were lost in the Second. When all are gathered in neat rows, wreaths are placed by the head boy and girl and the head of the Old Fettesian Association. The two-minute silence is politely observed, punctuated only by the wails of police sirens which float like airborne banshees above the city; the chaplain reads the act of remembrance and a piper plays a Scots lament. The ceremony over, the pupils scamper back to their boarding houses, the more loquacious bursting to continue a chatter about teenage matters which was so inconsiderately interrupted by the demands of history and tradition for silence. The bemedalled Old Fettesians join the staff and prefects for a drink and reminiscences about the old days.

During the subsequent week, when lessons are over, most pupils will put on military uniforms and take part in a variety of activities, from drill to map-reading and from weapon safety to knot-tying, which are designed to give the youth of today some idea of life in the armed services. Others will be found clad in kilts and playing the bagpipes as they practice for the next performance. Schoolmaster-officers will scurry about, offering encouragement and correction to the sixth-formers who are doing the bulk of the instruction, before retiring to bread and jam in the common room. In the evening, there is every possibility that a retired soldier or politician will be giving a talk about military or strategic issues. In some academic subjects, analysis of war poetry, the ideology of struggle or the causes of conflict will be a feature of lessons. When the holidays come, some will spend part of their holidays at an army camp or shooting at Bisley; others will be visiting battlefields across Europe with the history department. War, then, is everywhere at Fettes College.

William Fettes and the Enlightenment

As the OF veterans descend the stairs, they pass a bust of the school's founder, Sir William Fettes. The bust's imposingly classical appearance is slightly marred by a reconstructed nose, for some years ago pupils whose identity is still unknown attempted to 'abduct' the great man, but, ignorant of the density of marble, found him harder to lift than they had expected and dropped him on his face. There are those who argue that, in many ways, the school's disrespect to its founder has gone much further than this. Fettes College had scarcely been built before outraged Edinburgh citizens were denouncing the nature of its recruitment. The founder's objective was clear enough:

…young people whose parents have either died without leaving sufficient funds for that purpose, or who from innocent misfortune during their lives, are unable to give suitable education to their children.[1]

Even the school's most loyal friends would have difficulty finding large numbers of this type of pupil in the twenty-first century Fettes College. In addition, it is occasionally argued – admittedly by heavily refreshed liberal intellectuals at Burns suppers – that Fettes, as a child of the Enlightenment, would hardly have approved of the school's intimate involvement with war and imperialism. He was born in 1750 when the old highland clan system, which prized martial prowess above all else, already weakened by the corrosive influence of economic and social modernity, had finally been shattered by a vengeful state following the

1745 Jacobite rebellion. Fettes had been trading for several years on the High Street when Samuel Johnson observed of the 'animating rabble' of the highlands that 'the Chief has lost his formidable retinue; and the Highlander walks his heath unarmed and defenceless, with the peaceable submission of a French peasant or English cottager.'[2] Not only were Jacobitism and the traditional Scottish way of warfare taboo, but the intellectuals of Enlightenment Scotland, or at any rate Glasgow and Edinburgh, looked forward to an age when global liberty, reason and free trade would abolish war for good. Although not exactly pacifist in outlook, many Enlightenment writers did not regard war as a proper activity for a civilised society, and looked forward to its eventual demise. The historian William Robertson, with whose family Fettes was friendly, had this to say:

Among uncivilised nations, there is but one profession honourable, that of arms… Commerce tends to wear off those prejudices which maintain distinction and animosity between nations. It softens and polishes the manners of men. It unites them by one of the strongest of all ties, the desire of supplying their mutual wants. It disposes them to peace, by establishing in every state an order of citizens bound by their interest to be the guardians of public tranquility.[3]

In his crowded classroom at the High School of Edinburgh, the young Fettes may well have looked forward to a world of enlightened self-interest and generally amiable sentiments, in which there would surely be no need whatsoever for a school to have as part of its activities the training of boys and girls in martial skills. Certainly, the schools set up in that era do not seem to have gone it for much in the way of drill. The Belfast Academy, founded in 1785 on the Scottish model by Dr Crombie of St Andrew's, the former tutor to the Earl of Moray, promised 'languages, logick, rhetorick, moral philosophy, jurisprudence, civil government, history, mathematicks and experimental philosophy'[4] but nothing so brutal and licentious as amateur soldiery. As a boy, William Fettes was undoubtedly exposed to the fashionable theories which were making his city, in terms of ideas if not climate, the Athens of the North. His best-known teacher was Dr Alexander Adam, who wholeheartedly embraced the liberal ideals of the age, partly through political conviction and partly because he was too absent-minded efficiently to exert brutality. He came under suspicion for his habit of asking boys the Latin for 'King': 'Rex', would be the reply.

3

'Another word?'

'Tyrannus.'

'Right, boy.'

'The conception of Alexander Adam as a potential sans-culotte suggests a sad lack of humour in the City Chamber,' observed the school's historian.[5] Fettes himself was not an unreflective man; although he left school in his mid-teens and devoted his life largely to the acquisition of money, his circle of friends included several prominent intellectuals and he seems to have had many liberal sentiments. Appropriately, he wrote down some of his own thoughts on the value of education in his account book:

Study is not a toil but a recreation to the great. It prepares the mind for the encountering of dangers, it relieves us from many a pang which prejudice had inflicted. It teaches us the means of happiness. It fills up in an interesting manner the vacuity of leisure. It impresses us with serious and useful truths. It is a treasure that repays us for all misfortunes, and it renders us not only happy in ourselves, but also the pleasing companions of others.[6]

As with every other aspect of eighteenth century Scotland, however, it would be wrong to exaggerate how liberal Fettes' Edinburgh was. Fettes' neighbour Lord Cockburn recalled that new boys 'approached the High School with trembling'; it was 'notorious for its severity and violence', with a Latin teacher, 'as bad a schoolmaster as it is possible to fancy', who drove his boys 'by constant and indiscriminate harshness.'[7] Cockburn believed that 'out of the four years of my attendance there were probably not ten days in which I was not flogged, at least once.' It was not especially surprising that the Edinburgh Academy was to emerge as a fee-paying (but still cheap) and civilised alternative to the High School in the early nineteenth century.

The young Fettes went into business in 1768. He and his old mother were tea and spirit merchants 'in a tiny shop at the head of Baillie Fife's Close' on the High Street where 'a trapdoor and ladder led to their small house above.'[8] He saw an opening in the fact that whisky, which sold for 2s 6d in Edinburgh, retailed for 5s 6d in London. It was illegal to export whisky to England, so he disguised it as volatile alkali by mixing it with hartshorn; his contact in London would add green vitriol to separate the ingredients. Fettes admitted that he had never actually seen this done and 'seemed to doubt the legality'. His recipe for brandy included aquavite, tartar, salt, raisins, orris root, white ginger, bitter almonds, apples and bay leaves; given the state's increasing interest in regulating consumption, Fettes prudently began referring to himself merely as a merchant. Fettes justified his potentially lethal experiments in a patriotic fulmination at the government's tax on stills – the Scots, he wrote, 'cannot be said to be on the footing of their English brethren as was intended at the Union.'[9] Although in Fettes' schooldays 'an English boy was so rare that his accent was openly laughed at'[10] he was not a nationalist as that term is now understood – like the American colonists and Irish Presbyterians who rebelled against the crown in the late eighteenth century, he simply wanted the supposed benefits of the British constitution to be applied equally throughout the Empire, or at any rate to himself. About a century later, a poem in a Victorian *Fettesian* magazine deplored the fact that 'in ancient days' England and Scotland were enemies, and invented for Sir William the statement that 'they ne'er again shall be':

> *And on that fateful borderland*
> *He built our palace high;*
> *Where North and South set hand to hand*
> *In peaceful rivalry.*
> *One zeal inspires both house and clan,*
> *One self-same country's lot*
> *To Scotland binds the Englishman,*
> *To England binds the Scot.*[11]

Whilst, as one contemporary master in the Fettes English department observed, the only good thing about the Victorian pupils' poetry was their meticulous command of metre, these are not entirely fanciful sentiments. It is not unreasonable to assume that Sir William would have been happy with the label, happily used by his contemporaries Smith and Hume, of 'North Briton' rather than 'Scot'. The Enlightenment thinkers, and indeed many other loyal Scots, saw themselves as part of part of a blessed Union between nations which had, as Robertson put it,

> *...incorporated the two nations, and rendered them one people, the distinctions which had subsisted for many generations gradually wear away; the same manners prevail in both parts of the island; the same authors are read and admired; the same entertainments are frequented by the elegant and polite; and the same standard of taste and of purity in language is established.*[12]

Sir William Fettes, painted in the early nineteenth century

Fettes was determined that his family should be at the centre of Scotland's elegant and polite society. From his schooldays he developed useful connections, joining the prestigious Lodge of Edinburgh (Mary's Chapel) No 1 in 1766, the Royal Company of Archers in 1781, the Honourable Company of Golfers in 1783, and the Revolution Club in 1787. This last was intended to celebrate the legacy of the overthrow in 1688 of James II and his replacement with William III – that is, to be a social club for those who supported the existing establishment. In Scotland, this meant Sir Harry Dundas, another product of the High School, to whom Fettes looked for advancement. In the same year that he joined the Revolution Club, Fettes married Maria Malcolm. The Malcolms, originally the McColmes, were a respectable Ayrshire gentry family; Maria's grandfather David had been minister of Duddingston and a noted scholar of 'Erse', as Gaelic was then known, whilst her father John was a noted doctor who had been commissioned in 1744 as Senior Surgeon of the 2nd Company, 1st Royals.[13] One of Maria's brothers, 'Fighting Bob' (so called because of his frequent duelling) was killed in battle in 1796, whilst another served in the East Indies and was known for the incorruptibility of his nature. Both of Maria's sisters married into the military, Susan's family gaining posts of great prominence in the East India Company and Charlotte's husband, until his death in service, serving as Brigade Major to the Guards Battalion under the Duke of York. Maria's brothers had helped the young Robert Burns with books during his erratic schooling in

Ayrshire, and he later wrote that 'my young superiors never insulted the clouterly appearance of my ploughboy carcass, the two extremes of which were often exposed to all the inclemency of the seasons.'[14] Fettes seems to have made his own acquaintance of the poet independently of his wife, probably in the context of the Masonic lodges which feted Burns in Edinburgh in 1787. 'Mr. William Fettes, Merchant, Edinburgh' was a subscriber to Burns' *Poems, Chiefly In The Scottish Dialect*.[15] Fettes also entered the pages of history when he served on jury which convicted Deacon Brodie (the model for Stevenson's Dr Jekyll) and later administered the bankruptcy of Sir Walter Scott. Through Dundas, the Malcolms and his own sheer dedication, Fettes worked his way up a ladder of wealth and social influence, gaining promotion through the 1790s to various posts on the city council. Although he would probably have continued to develop his position anyway, events overseas gave Fettes' fortunes an extraordinary boost.

War and William Fettes

The French Revolution began in economic protest when an over-taxed, inefficiently governed populace took to the streets, but escalated into an ideological crusade for a new Enlightenment order which would strip away every last vestige of the past and build a perfect society – an Age of Reason – as quickly as possible. Revolutionary France was attacked by its reactionary neighbours, but also tried to export its beliefs. Across the British Isles, organisations were created in which sympathetic individuals might correspond with the French and express their support for the noble ideas of liberty, equality and fraternity. The overthrow by the people of France of a despotic government and superstitious religion struck even some conservative Britons as admirable. Many middle-class people, and not just the usual suspects (querulous lawyers, romantic poets and schoolmasters, and muckraking journalists) were keen. William Robertson (whose son was to be one of Fettes' neighbours in Charlotte Square[16]) and Dugald Stewart were among the prominent intellectuals initially impressed, whilst the 'Reform Burgesses of Aberdeen' pledged their support. As Devine comments, Edmund Burke, whose writings would form a conservative manifesto against radical change for the next two centuries, 'was almost a lone voice crying in the wilderness.'[17] Dark hints of what might happen if French ideas spread across the sea came from Belfast, where some of the 'sons of gentlemen', boarders at Dr Crombie's Academy, took the spirit of liberty to its logical conclusion

7

and staged an armed rebellion against their 'tyrannical' new headmaster, Dr William Bruce. When not only Bruce, but also his wife and the Sovereign (Provost) of the city had narrowly escaped death, and roofers sent to smoke the boys out were driven off 'by the threats and balls of the insurgents', troops were called in.[18] Although, as a former High School pupil, Fettes would have been familiar with the idea of a schoolboy 'barring out' (a similar incident in Edinburgh in 1595 had seen Bailie Macmoran killed) the ideological overtones of this event were both unmistakeable and widespread. Dr Richard Price, a Welsh-born Unitarian clergyman and philosopher, preached that France was living out properly all the ideals which the British claimed for themselves, and that the self-satisfied ruling class had forgotten the values of their own revolution of 1688, 'a defect in the constitution so gross and palpable as to vitiate legitimate government and make of the existing government 'nothing but an usurpation.'[19] Along with Tom Paine, whose *Rights of Man* became a virtual Bible for assorted British radicals, Price challenged the state to become democratic. Democratic, however, it neither was nor had any intention of becoming. Devine estimates that around 0.2 per cent of 'enlightened' Scotland's population could vote, around 4,000 people – roughly the same number of voters as in 'oppressed' Dublin.[20] Harry Dundas was Scotland's 'manager' — officially Lord Advocate but with powers of patronage over 34 of Scotland's 41 Westminster MPs. The fiery radicalism of the more troublesome type of Scot had been channelled, for much of the eighteenth century, into interminable disputes within the Kirk, whilst Dundas was usually able to find seats on the gravy train for those with more earthly political ambitions, but the late eighteenth century changed that.[21] Discontent had been growing in the aftermath of the American Revolution, which had acted as political ginger to the public as well as harming Scotland's huge tobacco industry (William Fettes must have rejoiced in his choice of career in the tea trade and connections to the East India Company).

A Society of United Scotsmen was set up, along with the Scottish Friends of the People, and on the streets of Dundee trees of liberty were erected in imitation of the French. There were frequent riots, such as the three-day rampage in June 1792 which saw Dundas' house attacked by a mob. When, in 1793, the French Revolution became more violent – and began to be opposed by the British state – many bourgeois radicals in Britain and Ireland turned against it. It finally became what Edmund Burke had always said it would be, an increasingly bizarre attempt to reorder the universe by force. It acquired totalitarian characteristics, as demonstrated by a declaration by the Committee for Public Safety:

We will show this Fatherland to the citizen ceaselessly, in his laws, in his games, in his home, in his loves, in his festivities. We will never leave him to himself alone. We will by this continual coercion awaken ardent love for the Fatherland. We will direct his inclination towards this single passion.[22]

The talk was no longer of reforming Catholicism, but of a new civic religion which created new months and days and held weird, cultish ceremonies in the Champ de Mars. It also began to use the guillotine with great enthusiasm and sought to export its ideals via 'armed missionaries' as 'Reason militant went on the march'.[23] The British prided themselves on being reasonable, which was not the same as worshipping abstract Reason. They went to war with France and kept up the struggle for almost twenty bitter years, during which time those who still professed an interest in French affairs (and there were many more than popular histories claim) found themselves in very deep trouble. So far as the authorities were concerned, the French Revolution's claims of 'liberty' and 'reason' were propaganda to justify the destruction of property, decency, piety and common sense. The government 'could brand its opponents as atheists and (at least potential) traitors, and could prosecute them for sedition, a crime unknown to Scottish law until 1795.'[24] The full rigour of the law was applied even more brutally in Scotland than in England, with autocratic judges such as Lord Braxfield rarely allowing the accused off on technicalities such as the fact that they were not actually plotting revolution. As Cockburn commented, 'Scotch Jacobinism did not exist. But Scotch Toryism did, and with a vengeance.'[25] Robert Burns was required to apologise for some of his more radical verses and came up, by way of ingratiating himself, with 'Does Haughty Gaul Invasion Threat?' His membership of the Dumfries Volunteers seems to have ensured that the mildly subversive messages of one verse were overlooked:

Who will not sing "God save the King,"
Shall hang as high's the steeple;
But while we sing "God save the King,"
We'll ne'er forget The People!

Burns was lucky; perhaps he was too prominent a cultural figure (despite his rackety finances) to be got rid of, and he had undoubtedly acquired some useful contacts in Edinburgh. Middle-class types, particularly the lawyers, journalists and schoolmasters considered liable to political eccentricity, were hounded for their radicalism, whilst working-class troublemakers, like Gerrald, Skirving and Palmer, were transported to Botany Bay. Robert Watt, a smuggler who offered to spy on the Friends of the People but was converted to their vision, was executed in 1794 for plotting to suborn troops and seize Edinburgh Castle. The most high-profile victim of the purge was Henry Erskine, who seems to have been a friend of Fettes; he was dismissed as Dean of the Faculty of Advocates 'on account of his obnoxious political sentiments.'[26] Despite poor harvests in mid-decade, the Scots remained quiet following Dundas' crackdown, presumably because the vaguely reformist had been scared off or rallied round the flag, the troublesome squashed and the really dangerous – always a minority – were in hiding. Most were loyal – Cockburn noted that in 1798 Edinburgh Council, of which Fettes was now First Bailie, passed a 'self-denying ordnance' to 'ruin France by abstaining from claret' which lasted a week.[27] Some revolutionaries popped up again at the end of the 1790s to exploit discontent, for instance, over the unpopular Militia Act, which led to riots in which a dozen died. United Scotsman George Mealmaker, a Dundee weaver, was sentenced to 14 years for sedition, though in fairness he does genuinely appear to have been trying to organise a revolution. Devine believes, however, that the United Scotsmen never had the slightest chance of taking over a country which was keen to show its loyalty and in which the kind of high-spirited, troublesome younger sons of the better-off could find gainful employment in the Empire.[28]

William Fettes stayed out of the politics of the revolutionary wars, but managed to become heavily involved in their economics. The wars with France saw a huge expansion in the scale and scope of British military operations, with a fleet of over 500 heavily-armed vessels (40 per cent of which were captured) and an enormous, by traditional standards, land army. Volunteering – joining the part-time, self-financing militias for home defence – was all the rage. Cockburn dismissed them as 'selected on account of their station in the world, and the intensity of their public intolerance... an assiduous and well fed corps'[29] but he joined when the threat became stronger in 1804. Not that, even then, he was able to take it terribly seriously; his descriptions of Sir Walter Scott's attempts to drill his men into attacking turnips as substitutes for Frenchmen still make entertaining reading.[30] Fettes initially joined the Volunteers, as indeed did most of the middle classes, but either became disillusioned or, more likely given his eye for the main chance, saw opportunities elsewhere. A recent Fettes College booklet comments euphemistically that 'his talents lay in feeding the army, not being part of it.'[31] He himself was perfectly frank, referring to these ventures as 'not unprofitable concerns, as they have greatly increased my fortune.'[32] It was in the period 1795–1800 that Fettes' fortunes climbed meteorically as a supplier and underwriter to the military, and we have no reason to doubt that he did this honourably, making a fortune 'from his own perseverance and honest industry'[33] as a school publication put it. Fettes' connections with the armed forces began in 1795 with a contract from the Scottish Commander-in-Chief, Lord Gordon, to supply army camps in 'North Britain'. This was developed the following year into a contract for foreign oats – as Johnson had observed, this was a grain which in Scotland supported the people, so the army's horses had to get their fodder from elsewhere. In 1797 he began supplying the large garrisons at Forts George, William, Charlotte and Augustus with salt beef, meal and biscuits. The outbreak of rebellion across the east of Ireland in 1798 did not stop him turning the sister island into his major source of beef; his quarter shares in two ships, the *Greyhound* and *Lovely Mary*, kept the supplies coming. Fettes' additional role as Admiral of the Firth of Forth and Naval Stores Contractor enabled him, Mary Cosh notes in her recent history of Edinburgh, to evade customs duty and smuggle tobacco.[34] He also bought the estate of Wamphry in Dumfriesshire and felled many of its trees to provide employment for indigent locals and timber for the Royal Navy. By April 1800 he was making a profit of £2,950 – the captains on the boats he part-owned would, for comparison, have been getting about £7 a month, and ordinary sailors about 20 per cent of that. Burns thought himself lucky to be earning roughly £40 a year as an exciseman. It was not all plain sailing for Fettes; poor weather and bad harvests in Ireland led to serious losses in 1801.[35] On the whole, however, whilst he may not have been a hard-faced man, he undoubtedly did very well out of the war.

Fettes' original (1770s) premises on the High Street, left, and his grand home in Charlotte Square (1806)

Given the inequalities which persisted in England, the cruelty of persecution in Ireland, and Dundas' feudal rule of Scotland, many have been inclined to forget the awfulness of the revolutionary, and later Napoloeonic, regimes against which the British fought. Paul Kennedy paints a stark picture of the realities of life under French conquest:

By confiscation of crown and feudal properties in defeated countries; by spoils taken directly from the enemy's armies, garrisons, museums and treasuries; by imposing war indemnities in money and in kind; and by quartering French regiments upon satellite states and requiring the latter to supply contingents, Napoleon not only covered his enormous military expenditures, he actually produced quite considerable profits for France – and himself.[36]

On this account, in which Napoleon foreshadowed Hitler's rape of occupied Europe, William Fettes and those like him were not merely smug, self-interested reactionaries. They were working for what they considered to be a better cause and, moreover, were not without a sense of duty. At the turn of the century, William Fettes became Lord Provost –

effectively mayor – of Edinburgh. As figurehead of the city, Provost Fettes acted as an important focal point for its population, and his reputation as an honest man of business, and someone genuinely committed to the improvement of the condition of the people, must surely have been a useful symbol of the fact that ordinary Scots would not necessarily have been better off under an alternative French regime. His baronetcy came as a pleasant surprise, for Provosts normally got knighthoods; he concluded that it was his 'exertions in preserving the quiet and peace of the city in the dear years 1800 and 1801 when there was generally over the country discontent and a disposition to rioting.'[37] There is much to be said for this judgment. Napoleon, like Hitler after him, wanted to starve Britain into submission, and the demands of the now enormous armed forces acted as a further drain on the food supply and thus an incitement to unrest. Sir William had done much to avert serious trouble in the city by establishing soup kitchens for the poor and making wheat available when oats ran low. He organized a public collection from the better-off to the tune of £9,700, which paid for meal and coal for the poor, and when this proved inadequate applied to Parliament to have Edinburgh assessed for a further £10,000.[38] This paternalistic concern for the poor marked him out both as a shrewder and a more compassionate figure than the bone-headed reactionaries at whose attitudes Cockburn rails in his memoirs; had one of the more blinkered Tories been at the helm, the hunger-maddened poor of Edinburgh might well have created more havoc than they did. Sir William left public life in 1807 after a series of what he considered to be snubs from Dundas (now Lord Melville) and Captain Hope, the local MP (despite securing Mrs Hope seats in church, Fettes got no more than a nod from her husband until election time). He noted in his diary: 'Resolve to withdraw myself initirely from attendance and all further connexion with city politics for ever.'[39] He bought a grand house at 13 Charlotte Square, characteristically congratulating himself that he had paid £3,100 for his whereas his neighbour John Marjoribanks paid £3,420 for No 12, and applied himself to becoming a landowner. Taking advantage of the peace, which he believed 'promises universal peace and concord… the golden age is to revive'[40] Sir William's son set off on his much-delayed Grand Tour at the end of 1814. Whilst he was away, his parents were alarmed by Napoleon's escape from Elba, but their son was to die, not at the hands of the French, but of typhoid in Berlin.

Social attitudes to soldiering in the eighteenth century

Sir William's hopes were all pinned upon his son. Apart from his wife and sister, (who made only infrequent appearances) he never mentioned his relations in his diary; they in turn regarded him as selfish and unfeeling. Like many respectable people of his day, although he was happy to cheer on the armed forces and live secure in their defence of his country (not to mention making a fortune from his military contracts) he did not want to get any closer than that to the rude soldiery. Cockburn's recollection that the sight of uniforms was an alien one in Edinburgh until war broke out with France in 1793 is very telling.[41] There was a curious ambivalence to British attitudes to soldiering; the public revelled in its glories but found it somewhat distasteful, and had a rather poor opinion of the morals of those who embarked on a military career (Maria Fettes' brother managed to accrue £1450 in pay and investments in the admittedly mercenary John Company in Bengal and Madras). A large standing army, especially one created by conscription – the nation in arms, as the French were later to see it – was impossible in Britain. The nation of shopkeepers (and Fettes was a prince in such a realm) saw such bodies as instruments of tyranny, and ruinously expensive ones at that. Two Stuart monarchs had lost their thrones for trying to create them. This meant that the regular Army and Navy were, in effect, professional mercenary bodies, although the corruption involved in becoming an officer and the frequent use of press-gangs to recruit the rank and file makes both terms dubious. Although undoubtedly courageous and particularly skilled with firearms, they often enjoyed a low status. Many joined for negative reasons; landless peasants, unemployed urban workers, petty criminals and assorted rebels from the 'Celtic Fringes' of Scotland and Ireland were all trying to escape a singularly uncongenial reality in civilian life. As Lawrence James points out, they often ended up doing this twice – once by getting drunk and then by sobering up on board a ship or stuck in an army camp. Recruiting-sergeants were paid handsomely for their prey – certainly more than the actual men got, for the prize per recruit was £5 whilst the unlucky new soldier himself got only £2 18s, much of which would have to be ploughed back into his uniform purchase.[42] Once signed up, the best option was fatalistically to accept one's fate, and try to become a loyal member of a small, somewhat eccentric, yet remarkably successful war machine. When military success was achieved, or indeed when there was simply pay and a spot of leave, the British fighting man applied his considerable stamina to a frenzied assault on gambling dens, ale-houses and brothels. The army had a dark side; the upper limit for beatings was set at a thousand lashes in 1807, dropping to fifty over the next half-century, which reflects the brutal reality of service life and a mentality which saw victory as the fruit of savage discipline. One eighteenth century officer, Lt-Col Blackader of the 26th Foot, referred to his men as 'mercenary fawning, lewd dissipated creatures, the dregs and scum of mankind.'[43]

Although he was part of a social class which intermarried with the military gentry, embraced the regrettable utility of force in order to expand markets, and undoubtedly profited from their success, Fettes did not seek a life in uniform for himself or his son. When offered a coronetcy in the Scots Greys ('a good sober corps commanded by General David Dundas') for 16-year-old William the younger, he turned it down, commenting in his diary, 'I declined as I did not wish my son should be a soldier and he had made no particular choice of profession.'[44] He must have been pleased when the boy became a lawyer. It is not as if being an officer represented a giant moral leap from the bawdy, violent world of the private's mess. Indeed, the officer ranks of the British services, except perhaps the Artillery which was regarded with suspicion as the home of upstart technocrats, cannot be said to have been filled with men who, like Fettes, might have been expected to use their minds profitably for advancement in the civilian world. Blind courage was the key requirement for officers, and, whilst undoubtedly more literate than their men, they were not expected to be vastly more intelligent. Some generals, such as Sir Charles Napier, even worried that more sophisticated equipment which would allow them to kill at a greater distance would remove a fighting spirit which required close-quarter action with bayonets, officers leading by example and slashing madly at the enemy. Having bought their commissions (a habit William III, in his pedantic Dutch Calvinist fashion, had attempted unsuccessfully to stamp out) officers were expected to conduct themselves as gentlemen.[45] Duelling was common – an activity regarded by the bourgeoisie with horrified fascination as a relic from an earlier, more primitive age, but also as something excitingly, and roguishly, aristocratic. Cockburn recalled that the death of Sir George Ramsay at Musselburgh in 1790 at the hands of Lt Macrae 'made us all shudder at the idea of duelling.'[46] In peacetime, and in proximity to marriageable ladies of the Jane Austen type, they might lead Jane Austen lives, but away from home they often shared the same objectives as their men, specifically finding saleable loot, plentiful alcohol and willing whores. Anthony Clayton, whilst admiring the courage of the Georgian officer class, nonetheless refers to 'absenteeism and endless 'bumpers on' drunkenness, and the neglect of any professional training or education.'[47] Corelli Barnett describes the officer as 'a corrupt tradesman or a rich playboy instead of a salaried state servant'[48] – altogether more *Vanity Fair* than *Sense and Sensibility*.

'French troops plundering and firing a village in Germany' – a print of 1818 which justified the wars against Napoleon.

This is not, of course, anything like the whole story. As Barnett himself shows, this disreputable band of cut-throats were extraordinarily successful in battle when able to close with the enemy, which they did for most of the eighteenth century. William Fettes was in his first year at the High School, under the tutelage of a Mr John Gilchrist, when Britain won a remarkable series of victories around the world. He would have joined in the national jubilation when General Wolfe's men climbed the Heights of Abraham and took Quebec. The steady resolve of British redcoats at Minden in Germany, holding their ground and blazing away with muskets, held off repeated French cavalry charges and entered the national psyche. The French navy had hoped to send its Toulon fleet out of the Mediterranean to mount an invasion of Britain; it was destroyed off Portugal. Admiral Hawke then pursued the Brest fleet into a gale at Quiberon Bay and annihilated it. The following year, British control of India and Canada were confirmed, and the Marquis of Granby, losing his wig in a successful cavalry charge at Warburg, gave birth to the phrase 'going for them bald-headed.' When Fettes was at the height of his powers, the British soldier and sailor were winning engagements around the world, demonstrating bold seamanship at Trafalgar, ruthless efficiency at Copenhagen, courage and grit on the Iberian peninsula, and of course achieving final triumph at Waterloo. Clayton concludes that the British Army in the Napoleonic Wars demonstrated the 'paradox of the privileged easy-living gentleman displaying unexpected courage and skill in battle coupled with an appreciation that being an officer was more than just a job.'[49]

Fettes, Scotland and Victory

The Scottish professional soldier's contribution to the eventual British victory over France in 1815, and each small success in the build-up to it, was celebrated with bonfires and the obligatory heavy drinking, such as Sir Walter Scott's party for the Abbotsford workmen after Salamanca in 1812. The people were – albeit briefly – aware of the courage and suffering of their army and were willing to overlook the defeats and indiscipline which had marked the fighting in the 1790s. This was very much a British campaign, despite the tendency of both Englishmen and foreigners to refer to the victorious power simply as 'England'; just as London had been anxious to bring the Scots on board with the imperial project in the aftermath of the '45, so too the Irish had to feel loved after the '98. A Scots song after the battle of Vittoria in 1813 celebrated this:

> The English rose was ne'er sae red
> The shamrock waved where glory led
> And the Scottish thistle waved its head
> And smiled upon Vittoria.[50]

A key factor in the rehabilitation of the highland warrior tradition was the success of Scottish regiments, clad in kilts, in combat against the French. Indifferent or hostile to the highland tradition before the turn of the century, lowland burghers like Fettes began to find that victory, from Egypt in 1801 to Waterloo in 1815, 'seemed almost to require the presence

17

of the valorous highlander.'[51] Through the course of the nineteenth century all of the Scots regiments would acquire national symbols in a mammoth exercise in cultural rebranding. No longer regarded as culturally retarded or threatening, there was now something noble and romantic about the highlander. This was accentuated as the century wore on; 'notions of highland heroism stood among the few positive features to emerge from such conflicts as the Crimean war and the Indian mutiny, campaigns that otherwise seemed to reflect equivocally on British military and administrative organisation.'[52] Edinburgh soon sprouted a host of impressive memorials to them and their lowland comrades, to the chief of which, on Calton Hill, Sir William subscribed (what he thought of the failure to complete it we do not know). As Devine points out, many Highlanders in the British army were partly coerced into joining up, or were simply fleeing the dire poverty of the north-west, and would subsequently suffer the agonies of the notorious clearances.[53] The treatment of the Highlanders can be seen as especially hypocritical in that by this time the tartan craze, which lifted off with George IV's bizarre 1822 visit, was in full swing. Sir William was one of those admitted to the Royal Presence, and his niece Georgina sent a delighted account of the great event to her brother, who was guarding Napoleon on St. Helena:

His Majesty has gone away with a good impression of us; they say nothing gave him a greater pleasure than seeing the perfect order that prevailed. He said that he had always understood that we were a proud nation, and we had reason to be as we seem to be a nation of gentlemen. In Ireland they say if he was quite as well received, but the appearance of the common people was very different, someone wanting a shoe, others a bit of their coat and so on, but in Edinbr. the people were remarkably well dressed.[54]

This great scene of order had been painstakingly organised by Sir Walter Scott, who, like the bulk of his countrymen – especially the bourgeois, Presbyterian, lowland establishment – was keen to impress upon the crown the loyalty and respectability of a Scotland which had moved a long way from the riotous past, but still had a rich culture. *The Scottish Gael,* a compendious book on all the various traditions and myths of tartanry was published in 1831 by James Logan, who had not let the smashing of his skull by a 17lb hammer at a Highland games and its replacement with a four-inch steel plate dent his enthusiasm for all things Caledonian.[55] It is hard to avoid the conclusion that it would not have appealed to Fettes, and it did little to help those real 'Celts' being evicted in the north. We can only imagine what Fettes would have thought of an Edinburgh public school's war memorial featuring someone wearing what, as Macaulay put it, 'before the Union was considered by nine Scotchmen out of ten as the dress of a thief.'

Mrs Fettes' extended family noted Sir William's comfortable place in this world; one letter of 1822 from a visitor to his sister, Mrs Bruce, who lived with him in Charlotte Square, described the house as 'comfort and elegance… completely joined.' Lady Fettes proudly took the visitor to see a 'fine aqueduct bridge' of eight arches which connected Edinburgh's canal to Glasgow.[56] This trip cannot have been easy for the delicate Maria, who was so nervous of travel that she was known to require coachmen to use an extra set of reins when tackling steep hills. The altogether more robust Sir William, a family letter noted in 1827, 'in high health and buoyant spirits, is now purchasing estates at a great rate – one in Fife, one in Ayrshire, & Red Castle in Inverness-shire.'[57] These cost him around £200,000 (over eight million today) but were worth even more than his earlier – and in the eyes of upper-class contemporaries more vulgar – adventures in trade. His relatives, however, felt that he did not shower them with as much of his benison as they considered their due. Because the 'ever to be regretted' young William had left small sums to his favourite cousins, Sir William evidently felt that he was under no obligation to subsidise his wife's vast family. His sister-in-law wrote irritably in 1827 that 'there is not the smallest chance of Sir William giving either her [his niece Charlotte, who often acted as a companion to Lady Fettes] or any member of the family any solid proof of his friendship.'[58] Even when he took her for rides in his carriage, which he did frequently, these seem to have been the means for him to get to town, where he would abandon the women to play billiards in the New Club.

Early nineteenth century Scotland saw a revival of radical activity: the 'Radical War' of 1820 saw a huge strike in Glasgow, with perhaps 60,000 workers taking part, and an attempt to seize cannon from an ironworks which ended with the 'Battle of Bonnymuir' against cavalry. The middle classes flocked to join volunteer units against domestic revolution. Although there were uprisings elsewhere in what was now the United Kingdom, and all of the revolutionaries met with defeat, in Scotland 'the radical challenge in 1820 was much more serious than anything the government had to face in England in those troubled years'[59] and it has lingered in socialist folk memory. The army was to reappear on the streets of Scotland in Sir William's lifetime, this time to stamp on the Reform agitation of the early 1830s. These political and economic crises cannot have given the old man completely unalloyed pleasure in his well-heeled retirement.

Sir William Fettes does not always come across well to historians. In 1806 he listed in his notebook 45 people to whom he could look for assistance, yet his references to those who looked to him for help were rare and irritable, and his wife's family's letters, published in the thirties, are full of criticism of his tight-fistedness. However, his work on Edinburgh council was (admittedly by his own estimation) 'satisfactory to ALL, particularly to the Poor' and his development of his country estates was instrumental in 'uplifting the condition of the people'[60] (whilst, hardly coincidentally, increasing the land's value). He had a great deal of property around the Moray Firth, and improved this through drainage, road-building and improvements to the housing stock; at Kessock, he set up a steamship ferry to replace the erratic old rowing boat service. This cost a fortune and yielded no profits, as few could afford to use it, but in the spirit of benevolence, or perhaps misplaced optimism and a rare failure of business judgment, he subsidised it for several years all the same before replacing it with large sailing boats, big enough for his passengers to put their carts on.[61] He also imitated his Ayrshire neighbour Mr McAdam in applying a revolutionary new road surface to his estates there. He was known to be a friend of the poor, and Miss Clementina Stirling Grahame, a society lady known for the then-popular custom of 'mystification' – that is, impersonating someone else, usually someone destitute or aged – got half a crown out of him in 1826 by pretending to be the impoverished daughter of an old friend of his, abandoned with five children by a wastrel soldier husband who had run away with another woman. Sir William seems to have understood that women were easy prey for the charms of a uniform. 'I am sorry for you, and grieved to see Sandy Reid's daughter come to this,' he said, 'but you must be sensible, that for a person in your situation, your present dress is rather too showy and extravagant.'[62] Thus speaks the authentic voice of the successful Scots businessman. Miss Grahame was quick-thinking enough to claim that she had borrowed her bonnet and shawl from a lady's housekeeper because 'gentle servants are no' civil to poor folk when they come illdressed.' Sir William gave her half a crown to be going on with and promised to try to find her children places at the Hospitals, then Edinburgh's main source of free education. At this point Miss Grahame's hidden friends erupted with laughter. It is not known what Fettes' reaction was to this curious example of early nineteenth century 'Candid Camera' style humour.

Sir William Fettes' tomb in the Canongate Kirkyard

Fettes died in 1836, before the Victorian age of balance was signalled by the 18-year-old last of the Hanoverians promising to be good; in the few last years of his life he would have read the news of wars in Poland, Portugal and Texas. So enthusiastic were many middle-class Scots about proving their national valour that in the decades after Fettes' death they sent volunteer detachments to fight for liberty in such wars. The respectable war profiteer left money to a range of relatives, business partners and servants, and to a school which would take his name to the farthest corners of the world.

Fettes Peak in New Zealand, photographed by Andrew Murray on a school expedition; it was named in honour of Sir William

NOTES

[1] Quoted in H.R. Pyatt (ed.) *Fifty Years of Fettes* (Edinburgh, Constable, 1931) p. 3

[2] Dr Samuel Johnson, *A Journey to the Western Isles of Scotland* (London, 1775) p. 402

[3] William Robertson, *A View of the Progress of Society in Europe from the Subversion of the Roman Empire to the Beginning of the Sixteenth* Century (Edinburgh, 1769) Section I, Parts vi–x

[4] Quoted in E. McCamley & W. Dunbar (eds) *Belfast Royal Academy* (Belfast, 2010) p. 15

[5] W.C.A. Ross, *The Royal High School* (Edinburgh, Oliver & Boyd, 1934) p. 47

[6] Quoted in Robert Philp, *A Keen Wind Blows* (London, James & James, 1998) op. cit., p. 7

[7] Henry, Lord Cockburn, *Memorials of His Time* (Edinburgh, Black, 1856) p. 71

[8] Mary Cosh, *Edinburgh: the Golden Age* (Edinburgh, Birlinn, 2003) p. 312

[9] Marguerite Wood, 'The Notebook of Sir William Fettes, Bart.', *Book of the Old Edinburgh Club*, 1953

[10] Cockburn, p. 10

[11] *Fettesian*, March 1881

[12] William Robertson, *A History of Scotland* (London, 1759) p. 322

[13] Ursula Low, *Fifty Years with John Company: from the letters of General Sir John Low of Clatto, Fife 1822-1858* (London, John Murray, 1936) p. 4

[14] Quoted in Low, p. 5

[15] Robert Burns, *Poems, Chiefly In The Scottish Dialect* (London, 1787) p. xxiv

[16] James Grant, *Old and New Edinburgh*, (Cassell, Edinburgh, 1886) Vol III, p.173

[17] T.M. Devine, *The Scottish Nation 1700-2000* (London, Penguin, 1999) p. 203

[18] See A. T. Q. Stewart, *Belfast Royal Academy: The First Century 1785-1885* (Belfast, 1985) Ch. 2

[19] Gertrude Himmelfarb, *The Roads To Modernity* (New York, Random House, 2004), p.96

[20] T.M. Devine, *Scotland's Empire* (London, Penguin, 2007), p. 196

[21] Ibid., p. 200

[22] Quoted in Michael Burleigh, *Earthly Powers* (London, Harper Perennial, 2006) p.81

[23] Ibid., p. 66

[24] J.D. Mackie, *a History of Scotland* (London, Penguin, 1964) p. 317

[25] Cockburn, p. 81

[26] From his entry in Chambers' *Biographical Dictionary of Eminent Scotsmen* (Edinburgh, Blackie, 1856)

[27] Cockburn, p. 71

[28] Devine (1999) p. 215

[29] Ibid., p. 71

[30] Ibid., p. 193

[31] Alexia Lindsay et al., *William Fettes* (Edinburgh, Fettes College, 1996) p. 9

[32] Quoted in Low, p. 7

[33] Grant, p.173

[34] Cosh, p. 312

[35] Lindsay, p. 11

[36] Paul Kennedy, *The Rise and Fall of the Great Powers* (Fontana, London 1989) p. 172

[37] Quoted in Lindsay, p. 16

[38] See Lindsay, p. 13

[39] Quoted in Wood

[40] Quoted in Lindsay, p.11

[41] Cockburn, p. 71

[42] Lawrence James, *Warrior Race – a History of the British at War* (London, Little, Brown, 2001) p.234

[43] Quoted in R.E. Scouller, *The Armies of Queen Anne* (Oxford, OUP, 1966) p. 235

[44] William Fettes, diary entry, 29 November 1804

[45] Corelli Barnett, *Britain And Her Army* (London, Weidenfeld & Nicholson, 2000) p. 137

[46] Cockburn, p. 8

[47] Anthony Clayton, *The British Officer* (Pearson, London, 2006) p. 66

[48] Barnett, p. 139

[49] Clayton, p. 90

[50] Quoted in James, p. 279

[51] S. Allen & A. Carswell, *The Thin Red Line: War, Empire & Visions of Scotland* (Edinburgh, NMS, 2004) p. 21

[52] Ibid., p. 23

[53] Devine, 1999, Ch. 13 Pt. 2

[54] Quoted in Low, p. 15

[55] See Eric Hobsbawm & Terence Ranger (eds), *The Invention Of Tradition* (Cambridge University Press, 1983) Ch. 2 for a detailed account of the development of this phenomenon

[56] Quoted in Low, pp. 21-2

[57] Quoted in Low, p. 35

[58] Quoted in Low, p. 54

[59] Devine, 1999, p. 229

[60] Norman Macleod, *Fettes College Register* 6th Edition, (Edinburgh, Constable, 1932) p. v

[61] Ibid.

[62] Clementina Stirling Grahame, *Mystifications* (Edinburgh, Constable, 1865) pp. 61-2

Chapter Two

'Greek civilization has made us what we are'

Victorian Fettes and Empire

The early years of the school

The trustees of Sir William Fettes' will invested it wisely; the funds available had swollen from the original £166,000 to almost half a million pounds – well over £34 million today. This enabled them to build the most grandiose product of the imagination of Sir David Bryce, an architect whose style had become steadily more Gothic (some said eccentric) through the years; he had even been black-balled from the Architectural Institute of Scotland by the classicist William Playfair. Playfair, who had been the original choice to design the school, had died and, rather than get another of the Greek temples which housed Edinburgh schools, the boys of Fettes would study in a hybrid of Scottish baronial fortress, French Loire chateau, and Rosslyn Chapel . Sir David's vast confection might lack the austere good taste of the New Town, but it is an unmissable feature of the Edinburgh skyline. It built was on a hilltop in largely empty land at Comely Bank (one of Sir William's estates) and so was easily visible from the castle, grandstanding proudly on the skyline. Its vast windows, the despair of bursars faced with heating bills, were characteristic of Victorian schools and had their own purpose. As the wind blasted through the school, wrote Clem Cotterill, one of the first masters, it 'serves but to brace and harden them; to clear their brains and sweeten their tempers; to purify not only their blood, but surely to help, in so far as we can be helped by such agencies, to purify also their hearts.'[1]

The first pupils – 51 boarders, the eldest aged 14 – arrived in 1870 to find Fettes still under construction. 'Ladders and shavings were common in the corridors, and the smell of paint and varnish blended curiously with our strange weird feeling,' wrote one of the 'patriarchs' as these very first 'new men' were to be called.[2]

A Victorian glass-plate photograph of the school in its early years, before pollution blackened the sandstone

Certain other features of the school were also far from ready; only one of the boarding-houses where the fee-payers were to live was complete, and the great Fettes institution of responsible and mature prefects (young officers in the making) was postponed for half a term when six of the candidates for this office were caught smoking. It was an inauspicious beginning to a tradition based on the first Headmaster's belief that a school 'cannot be governed otherwise than by Prefects.' One early pupil wrote to his mother that his study was a 'dirty little hole' but that he was otherwise content; himself from Carlisle, he was amused by the way one of his new friends from Whitehaven in Cumbria said 'yis' and 'naw'.[3]

The uniform was rather more drab than today's chocolate and magenta striped peacockery, consisting of a drab grey suit, a white shirt with Eton collar issued each Saturday night; although it was supposed to last the week, H. Crichton-Miller recalled that 'its pristine glory had generally departed by the Sunday evening.'[4]

The system of ablutions, he wrote, was 'archaic' – each boy had a flat tin bath in which he was to clean himself in cold water each day (although this particular piece of Victorian grit has largely passed into history, there are still parts of Fettes where hot taps are welded shut). Despite its apparently grim conditions, the school was both academically successful and, by the standards of the time, remarkably cheap. By the 1880s it had grown to 173 pupils, 108 from Scotland, 63 from England, one Irish and one from Italy; its days as an international school were still a long way off.[5]

It was advertised in the *Scotsman* in 1872 as being in Comely Bank 'near Edinburgh'; the entrance fee was ten guineas, tuition in 'Classics, Mathematics, Modern Languages, Natural Sciences, Singing and Gymnastics' cost £25 and boarding – which everyone was expected to do – cost £60.[6]

£85 per annum was relatively cheap, certainly for the reasonably comfortable type of clergyman, doctor or solicitor; according to the National Archives, £85 then is less than £4,000 in modern money, so it is hardly surprising that so many fathers saw the school as a cheap investment.[7]

The first masters and pupils of Fettes College

The village schoolmaster and less well-benificed minister might still find places for their sons through the plentiful scholarships, whose recipients were known as foundationers.

The character of the first Head of School (a post more recently labelled Head Boy when it became a joint role alongside a Head Girl) gives an insight into what the Victorian Fettes staff valued. William John Lee was 'of good stock', the son of the Church of Scotland minister and ecclesiastical historian Dr William Lee and grandson of Dr John Lee, Moderator of the Kirk and Principal of St Andrews and Edinburgh universities.[8]

A sound student of the classics, Lee won a scholarship to Cambridge and went into the law, devoting himself in retirement to the Kirk and, during the First World War, the Red Cross, in which capacity he was awarded the OBE. A 'quiet, courteous, scholarly boy', Lee was not an especially gifted athlete, but was 'universally liked' and in his prefectorial role displayed 'judgment and impartiality.' When Lee left Fettes, Headmaster Dr Potts told him 'Your career here has been most honourable' – the highest compliment he could give. Potts' successor, the Rev Heard, was of like mind: 'he expected everyone to be on their honour with him as he was with them, a trait which made a great impression on the boyish mind.'[9]

The late Victorian British Army

The military landscape at the time of the school's opening more than thirty years after Sir William's death was much more recognizably modern than the one which the founder saw. For several decades, Britain had continued to fight a succession of small imperial wars which were fought largely by the same kind of people, in the same sort of uniforms, as had been seen at Waterloo. Indeed, the high command of the armed forces in the Horse Guards still contained a quotient of elderly men who had served with Wellington and remained loyal to the British traditions of unswerving discipline and cold steel which had, they pointed out to such critics as they deigned to notice, defeated their traditional enemies on numerous occasions. This was to prove slightly embarrassing when ageing generals such as Raglan, commanding in the Crimea, absent-mindedly referred to the enemy as 'the French' even though the latter were now Britain's allies. The Crimean War, which students of European history know primarily as the occasion for the emancipation of Russia's unfortunate serfs, is largely remembered in Britain for two debacles which exposed significant shortcomings. The charge of the Light Brigade at Balaclava was a supreme example of suicidal folly, and persistent rumours attributed it to the poor judgment of Lords Cardigan and Lucan, whose personal animosities hindered communication. The fame of Florence Nightingale and Mary Seacole as nurses reflected poorly on an army which had need of such (initially unwelcome) volunteers to sort out the chaos and misery behind the lines. Sergeant Adam, the Fettes physical education instructor, recalled the 'simply awful' hardships. 'No less than eighty men out of my battalion were carried off by cholera,' he told an interviewer for the school magazine on his retirement in 1911, 'then 1000 of us were packed like pigs onto the troopship *Kangaroo*, though there wasn't room for 500 on her.'[10]

Although clearly proud of the army's military successes, such as when the 'thin red line' of Scots halted the Russian cavalry at Balaclava, and at Inkerman when 8,000 British soldiers defeated 40,000 Russians, Adam's recollections of the poor food and absence of winter clothing make depressing reading. A much more literate public, supplied with mass-market newspapers and photographs of the fighting and its aftermath by train, were made aware of, and angry about, the suffering of the troops in a way that had not been the case in earlier wars. 'Never before,' James suggests, 'had a war so infiltrated popular culture'[11]; this was true in terms of music-hall patriotism, genuine interest in the campaign's progress and concern for the troops. 'For the first time in history,' comments Barnett, 'the nation knew what its soldiers were going through, and cared. General progress had made the traditional horrors of war unacceptable.'[12]

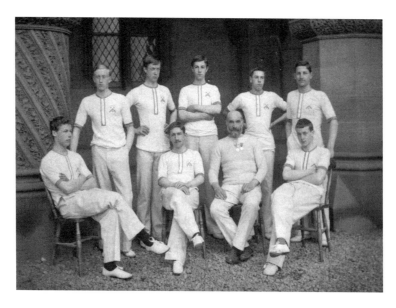

'The Sarge' Adam, wearing his Crimean War medals,
with the 1894 gymnastics team

Other changes were affecting the army. Shortly after the Crimean War, Indian sepoys sent shock-waves through the imperial system by mutinying. The terrible potato famine of the late 1840s wiped out much of the lower peasantry of the west of Ireland who had formed a huge proportion of the army's recruits; Irish soldiers went from 42.2 per cent of the total in 1830 to 27.9 per cent in 1870,[13] though they were still over- (and the Scots under-) represented as a proportion of the UK's population. It had also created a substantial class of extremely angry Irish Catholic emigrants in the USA (and indeed Scotland), some of whom set up the Irish Republican Brotherhood or Fenians, the direct ancestor of the IRA. As the products of Fettes and the other public schools sailed obediently round the world setting the empire's bounds wider still and wider, Ireland lurched from crisis to crisis, its increasingly polarized population threatening civil war on several occasions. One of Fettes' Irish pupils described the situation in his area for the school magazine:

Our home was so damaged by dynamite that we cannot live there. The 'Leaguers' [agrarian radicals] are not satisfied yet, and I don't think they ever will be. So to protect us we were supplied with nine policemen…I am beginning to think we require more guards for this house than you have for Edinburgh Castle. They have not shot many people recently, because that is generally reported in the English papers, so they only boycott them or slit their ears. They do not boycott us, because landlords can always get their provisions sent from London; the people who they generally boycott are farmers honest enough to pay their rents.[14]

The shortfall in Irish recruiting was hard to make up in mainland Britain; the Highland clearances, the urbanisation of England and lowland Scotland, and increasing mechanisation meant that the supply of sturdy, deferential peasant lads was also decreasing. The British people were increasingly literate and politically engaged, with the vote being extended first to the urban middle class and then to the 'aristocracy of labour', the aspirant skilled workers. The industrial proletariat was not an ideal substitute for the peasantry, since if workers were remotely good at their jobs they stood only to lose income by joining the forces, and in any case their membership of trades unions was looked on by the military authorities as training in attitudes of insubordination and communism. Nor was the vast lower middle class – the artisans, shopkeepers, and clerks who formed the bedrock of Victorian respectability and who were the backbone of Germany's superb army – especially interested. However, the public had at least lost the residual hostility to the army which dated back to the Revolutionary era of the seventeenth century, when it was seen as the armed with of a potentially coercive crown; with their string of victories, Victoria's warriors had brought glory on the nation, which eulogized them in music-hall culture and could be moved to protest at the poor conditions which Britain's heroes were forced to endure. In Bond's words, however, 'they were sometimes willing to pay for war but not to risk their own lives.'[15]

At times of prosperity, this left only the lumpenproletariat, which Karl Marx frankly described as the 'social scum, that passively rotting mass' to act as what he called 'bribed tool of reactionary intrigue.'[16] That is, the poorest of the poor, the desperate and the dodgy characters, and not the healthiest of the dodgy characters at that, were the most likely to join the army, 'the only welfare service provided by the British state for the rescue of such unfortunates.'[17]

This might have suited the amoral Hanoverians, but the Victorians, drinking deeply from a potent cocktail of religious improvement and Darwinian selection, were not going to be satisfied with it. The Boys' Brigade and the Scouting Movement were only two of the many worthy attempts made by the officer class of the day to bring discipline, health and morality to the nation's children, but it was still the case as late as 1900 that 'standards of physical fitness, intelligence and education could not be high'[18] so long as the poor were a large part of the army's rank and file.

Gradually, reforms were introduced, chiefly associated with Gladstone's gifted Secretary of State for War, Edward Cardwell, though some had begun in the 1850s as a result of the Crimean scandal. John Beith, a Fettes pupil and master better known as the writer and military propagandist Ian Hay, saw Cardwell as the father of the modern army he so admired and which he and his fellow Fettesians would serve with such loyalty; before Cardwell, he wrote, 'chaos reigned supreme', and it was 'signal proof of the man's greatness' that he achieved his ambitious twin goals of professionalizing the Army and putting it under rational, homogenous, democratic control.[19]

He changed the terms of service from 21 years to three, with nine in the reserve, on the European model, and gave permanent homes to regiments in the hope that this would create organic bonds of local pride between soldiers and society. He transferred control of county militias from the lords–lieutenant to central government and brought the Horse Guards under clearer political control. Most importantly, in 1871 his Army Regulations Bill abolished the purchase of commissions, so that 'the officers must belong to the Army, and not the Army to the officers'[20] – an important reform which would allow middle-class Fettesians to get on, but which was vigorously opposed by traditionalists. In much of this, Cardwell was guided by the German model which had been so frighteningly impressive in the defeat of France in 1870-1. The Old Fettesian who entered the army in the late nineteenth century was joining a force which was undoubtedly more popular in terms of public esteem than it had been before, even if huge sections of the public were still unwilling to take their jingoistic support so far as to actually join it, and one which was groping its way towards greater professionalism. The first ever issue of the *Fettesian* magazine recorded that Hutchinson, Lenox-Conyngham and Swinton were at Sandhurst, whilst Cook had already passed out and gained a staff-appointment in India.[21]

The author of an early letter from Sandhurst to Fettes, who signed himself 'κώπη', hoped 'lots more Fettesians will come here as the times go on', but did point to a key reason why, despite the abolition of purchasing commissions, the officer ranks remained closed to people of working-class origins:

Pay consists of 3s. per diem (one never sees it), and one's outlay for the same period is 3s. 11d. [for food and laundry]… For the year that one is here one pays £125 in two sums of £62, 10s., one at the beginning of each term, and also at the beginning one pays £25 for uniform and £5 contingent…[22]

The average wage for a skilled worker was £62 per annum, which ensured that no such people would disturb the respectable atmosphere of the officers' mess. This would not have been considered in any way odd to the Victorian mind; everything, it was reasoned, needed to be paid for, and a chap who couldn't pay his way had no right to want to be an officer. In any case, as previously noted, most skilled workers simply didn't want to join. Fettesians, by contrast, most certainly did. Virtually every issue of the school magazine from its inception a few years after the place opened its doors had some reference to old boys who entered Sandhurst or Woolwich, and others who were on active service. This announcement will stand for all the others:

The following have appeared in recent Gazettes:- The Suffolk Regiment – Lieut. F.P. Hutchinson (O.F.) 1ˢᵗ Batn., a probationer, officiating squadron-officer, 19ᵗʰ Bengal N.I., is about to be admitted to the Staff Corps, with effect from August 5, 1880. The Gordon Highlanders – Gent. Cadet R.S. Hunter-Blair (O.F.) from Sandhurst, to be Lieutenant. The Sherwood Foresters – Gent. Cadet T.G. Gordon-Cumming from the R.M.C., to be Lieutenant. Both commissions dated October 22, 1881.[23]

The same number also carried news of Lieutenants James Hope and Walter Cook, who had been decorated, J. Rutherford-Clark, W.D. Sellar and D.A. M'Leod, who had entered Sandhurst, and R.S. Hunter-Blair and L.S. Gordon-Cumming, who had passed out of it. The sheer tide of such information forced the *Fettesian* to start printing formal Army Lists from March 1882, when 17 names appeared in full-time service – a remarkable total for a school of less than a hundred boys which had only been open for ten years. Within ten years there would be over 60, plus three surgeons and five retired soldiers. Many of the names are familiar ones from the school's annals; Allen, Bax, Carruthers, Douglas, Grant, Henderson, Lenox-Conyngham, Macleod, Riddell and Scott, to name but a few.[24]

One letter from Sandhurst exhorted potential officers to get into the right frame of mind if they wished to become soldiers of the Queen:

Let me advise future candidates to develop as much honest muscle as they can (a great necessary now-a-days), combined with all the other requisites of a soldier, to be summed up in a few short words – the feelings of an officer and a gentleman.[25]

'A Recruit' wrote to the school in 1878 to describe the actual process of training:

For an hour we are doomed to sit and listen to the attempts of a professor to impress upon our imaginations the different peculiarities of the missiles used for smooth-bore and rifled ordnance, etc… we have exercised our arms, we have done our best to develop our chests, and the next part of the setting-up process is dedicated to the acquirement of that erect and soldier-like bearing, the beloved of every colonel in its acquisition, the abhorred of every recruit… From 10.25 until 2 there is little variation – tactics and fortifications, fortifications and tactics… Little time is given for relaxation; half-an-hour to scramble through some luncheon, and the bugle once more rings out its summons, and we have to tumble out and parade until three, unless it happens to be a gymnastic day…[26]

This would of course have been meat and drink to the Fettesian, for whom regimented, institutionalised life, not to mention constant exercise, were absolutely normal. Indeed, it was not merely the discipline and intellectual skills of the public school which made its products such ideal officers, but the obsession with good conduct.

The Fettes curriculum: Latin, Greek and Games

Victorian progressives had a much more elaborate conception of the gentleman than the Georgians; they believed in a chivalrous code of behaviour which included temperance, marital fidelity, educational rigour, social duty and religious observation – some of which the average army officer in William Fettes' youth would have dismissed as the eccentricities of Methodists or similar 'enthusiasts'. The improvement of schools, hospitals, prisons and every other institution the high-minded Victorians found wanting, went hand in hand with army reform.[27]

George Eliot was one of many intellectuals with a vision encompassing all of society: 'identifying the absence of teaching as a factor in the growth of what she referred to as "the criminal class", she urged trade union members to send their children to school "so as not to go on breeding a moral pestilence among us."'[28]

Fettes College was built on the model of Rugby School and, therefore, aimed squarely at the middle class; this was controversial, since Sir William's will clearly stipulated that his money should be used for a free school for the unlucky ('young people whose parents have either died without leaving sufficient funds…or who, from innocent misfortune during their lives, are unable to give suitable education'), rather than the mix of scholarship boys (foundationers) and fee-payers which it became. Unfortunately for those Edinburgh citizens who objected, and there were many, including MPs, ready to criticize the 'Sardanapalian luxury' of Fettes (a cultural reference, obscure even then, to an Assyrian king who lived as 'an effeminate debauchee, sunk in luxury and sloth' – hardly the life of a Fettesian of any era) the traditional Scottish free school was in decline and English public schools were on the way up. At Rugby, Dr Arnold had reformed both conditions and curriculum to create a modern educational institution aimed at moulding Christian gentlemen, for Christian boys, he famously commented, one could scarcely hope to make. C.L.R. James, the great Trinidadian Marxist writer, summarised the great man's goal as the creation of 'a body of men in the upper classes who would resist the crimes of Toryism and the greed and vulgarity of industrialists on the one hand, and the socialistic claims of the oppressed but uneducated masses on the other.'[29]

Arnold's pupils would be self-disciplined, self-reliant, able 'to govern themselves so as to be able to govern men.' Fettes' first headmaster, Dr Potts, 'a man of high principle, of enlarged and progressive views'[30] was formerly the sixth form master at Rugby and a passionate devotee of the Arnoldian vision. All of the Victorian educational reforms were designed to build a nation fit to lead the greatest empire the world had ever seen, and the improvements in the public schools were meant to train a group of young men who would, in turn, lead that chosen nation. As Mangan puts it in his study of public schools and imperialism, Victorian schoolmasters saw empire-building as a 'moral endeavour' they were 'the repositories of effective moral education.'[31]

The military application of Victorian teachers' muscular Christianity was all too apparent. If the public schools were changing in order to produce a more intellectually, physically and morally healthy alumnus than the gentleman thug of yesteryear, so too the army was, sometimes reluctantly, modernizing. Indeed, it can be argued that much of what we know of the British army today dates from the late Victorian era, whether its full-dress uniforms, regimental structure or obsession with all forms of sport (rather than just gambling and hunting, as was the case in earlier times).[32]

Fettesians, whether in the armed forces or the Indian Civil Service (another great repository for these dutiful young men) could bond with people of widely differing backgrounds thanks to their thorough grounding in the many things a chap could do with a ball. They had, after all, not merely helped develop rugby in Scotland but were also sufficiently keen on association football to take on the mighty Hearts, who duly thrashed them 8-2 in 1878.[33]

A writer to the school from Sandhurst in October 1879 certainly saw the sporting side of life as a major attraction of an army career:

The life suits anyone who is at all manly, and consequently would suit most of the rising generation, shall I say? Of amusements there is no lack: football and cricket in their respective seasons, tennis… The Staff College hounds, and sundry packs of beagles, are always on hand if one wants a run.[34]

Niall Ferguson comments that 'what made public school products capable of heroism on the Empire's behalf was not what they leaned in the classroom, but what they learned on the games field.'[35]

Fettes' first official football match took place a week after the school opened and involved every pupil healthy enough to play, and several masters, fighting it out for possession of a round ball in a very long game with over 50 people on the pitch at any one time. Although Eton and Harrow promoted association football, whose format was more or less agreed by 1870, Arnoldian Fettes was bound to play what became known as rugby, but the final codification of this game had to wait a little longer. An 1874 photograph shows the 1st XX lounging indifferently in long trousers, but by 1876 we have 15 knickerbocker-clad toughs posing with the degree of menace appropriate to the British rugby player.

The 1873-4 1st XX and 1875-6 1st XV

The *Fettesian* of the late nineteenth century devoted the majority of its pages to detailed accounts of team games, with the 1st XIs and XVs given honoured place as the school's heroes. These reports reflect a world in which key values of team spirit, tactical thought and physical speed were taught via both rugby and association football, with cricket imparting the virtues of patience and calm. A *Fettesian* article spoofed a lecture on comparative mythology in the New Zealand Academy in 5000 AD.[36]

This was based on the conceit that Fettes was an invaluable archaeological resource because the site had preserved many 'traces of the savage mind peculiar to that barbaric age' following the great Edinburgh earthquake of 1900. The most important, if inexplicable, aspect of the Fettes cultus involved an outdoor ritual: 'Fettesians were wont to repair to a field, on which the lines were marked out, which I shall describe afterwards, and there, attired in strange costumes, they struggled over a ball of oval shape.' Unlike other totemic activity, the ball was 'rudely kicked about' so perhaps this was a form of amusement rather than ritual, taking place between two 'sides' – a term which was linked to the Latin for 'to sit', 'for it appears that one fellow would not infrequently embrace another round his neck, and the two combatants would then sit down in the mud together.' The possibility that the ball was considered divine – hence Fettesians prostrating themselves before it, and the taboo status of the referee and his decisions – was also considered. So too was the idea that the four quarters of the field corresponded to the seasons, and the striped colours of the players' costume corresponded to the rays of the sun as they fought for possession of the round, brown earth symbolized by the ball. Sporting metaphors and ideals were common in the military recollections of former Fettesians. George Dillon of the 26th Punjab Infantry, desperately keen to lead his men against a 'refractory tribe of wild hillmen, who thought fit to molest us', but on tenterhooks in case he was told to stay behind and look after the post, said 'my feelings were something like the day when Pon [Stewart Posonby, the founding captain of the school football team, and later a distinguished clergyman] told me I should have my cap if I played well.'[37] A letter from D. Watt in Jambatai Kotai describes being hit by a bullet which had already passed through a comrade's brain as 'just like a tremendous "hack" at football. It made me feel a bit queer.'[38]

Vernon Hesketh-Prichard, whose exploration, novels and professional cricketing made his probably the most famous Old Fettesian of the late nineteenth and early twentieth centuries, ran a sniping school during the First World War and evaluated his pupils' skills in similar terms: 'when one is playing a very close game, in which no points can be given away, between skilled antagonists as we were doing in sniping, one sometimes wished for a little less wooden- headed 'bravery' so-called and a little more finesse.'[39]

Whilst still a pupil at Fettes, Hesketh-Prichard himself had turned down the chance to play for Scotland against South Africa, on the grounds that his school need him for a match against Loretto, and that was where his loyalty must lie. Although not an especially gifted footballer or cricketer, Sir John Simon, to the end of his life, displayed irritation if Monday's *Times* did not carry reports of Fettesian sporting engagements.[40]

Robert Bruce Lockhart, in pre-war Moscow, was invited to chase a larger ball with a local team, the Morozovtsi, set up by a British industrialist 'as an antidote to vodka drinking and political agitation', which had become champions of the Moscow League.[41]

Lockhart had, in fact, been mixed up with his brother, a gifted sportsman at Cambridge, and was in any case more of a rugger than soccer man, but, like all Fettesians, 'always ripe for adventure', he accepted. In any case, 'five years in the worship of athleticism' at Fettes had prepared him for anything. Football mythology has it that when the Charnocks initially punted a ball in the direction of the Russian public they fled, believing it was one of the spherical bombs favoured by anarchists, but they soon got the hang of things. Lockhart's experiences led him to a conclusion not dissimilar to that of the British politicians who considered sending a cricket team to revolutionary France: 'If it had been adopted in other mills, the effect on the character of the Russian working-men might have been far-reaching.' Whilst the notion that more sport might have averted the communist bloodbath of the twentieth century is historically debatable, Lockhart's sporting prowess undoubtedly stood him in good stead in his role as a diplomat. At one point, he was attempting to persuade a police inspector not to prosecute two British naval officers who had been arrested for shoplifting, and having little success, until the inspector's son arrived. Like many young Russians, the lad was an ardent enthusiast for football, and greatly admired Lockhart's prowess on the pitch. An amicable solution was duly achieved.[42]

For the less athletic, however, this obsession could make schooldays a nightmare; one asportual OF calling himself 'Litterae Inhumaniores' wrote in 1906 that:

A Balliol scholarship will hardly compensate for an entire indifference to games. It is exhausting to have to go through school life like one on a secret errand. How often as I passed the haven of the sixth-form library did I taste the bitterness of Balzac's cry, 'Sans genie, je suis flambé!' I hope I wasn't a prig, I know that I was unhappy.[43]

However, to use a popular Fettes expression, he 'grun and bore it' as part of the necessary warp and weft of school life. This manly stoicism was only half of the story for the Victorians. Not just playing, but also watching, games could be shared across classes to weld the nation together and create a sense of common endeavour, as Eric Hobsbawm has written in his study of nationalism:

What has made sport so uniquely effective a medium for inculcating national feelings, at all events for males, is the ease with which even the least political or public individuals can identify with the nation as symbolized by young persons excelling at what practically every man wants, or at one time in life has wanted, to be good at. The imagined community of millions seems more real as a team of eleven named people.[44]

Friendly rivalry in an age of increasing nationalism could be displayed on the hallowed turf, and Hobsbawm considers it probably no accident that the rugby Triple Crown and football's British Home Championship have their origins in the 1880s, when there was a surge in patriotic consciousness expressed through a Celtic revival and demands for Home Rule – it certainly let the Austrians and Hungarians, in not wholly dissimilar circumstances, blow off some steam.[45] It also helped unify the Empire, transcending racial divisions, especially in cricket; as Ferguson puts it, 'the English habit of losing to colonial teams would help knit Greater Britain together.'[46]

C.L.R. James, despite, or because of, his Marxist political leanings, saw cricket in particular as imparting the Puritan values of restraint, honesty, teamwork, patience and skill born of incessant practice, and thus as one of the pillars of what the Empire's supporters saw as its moral justification. He completely rejected Trotsky's dictum that the workers were deflected from politics by sport, and presumably also the notion that it was a mechanism of social control and eugenic development. Although there were of course earnest public-school alumni, active in the codification and organisation of games, who had great visions of sport's moral potential for the masses (and also some sinister fascist types who had more cynical objectives) the workers were quite happy to adapt it to their own requirements. Philip Waller has pointed out in his study of the Victorian town that 'their health was not improved by chain-smoking and standing in damp weather; their character not enhanced by submergence in a crowd, shouting themselves hoarse and provoking their favourites beyond the extremities of fair play.'[47]

Baden-Powell, indeed, specifically identified the mere watching of, as opposed to participation in, sporting events (along with loafing, smoking, socialism and masturbation) as one of the prime sources of British decadence which his Scouting movement was intended to curtail. Cecil Reddie, a progressive Fettes master who arrived at the school in 1885, had even broader doubts about games:

There is considerable analogy between the cram of athletics and the cram of 'classics.' The boys are tied down, with little regard to individual tastes, to playing the same few games. And these — mainly Cricket and Football — are highly elaborate and artificial... It is further unwise that boys should be constantly herded together, as, for instance, on the cricket or football field, to watch gladiatorial shows till their conversation is narrowed down to mere athletic 'shop.' They should have a wider horizon than the walls of the playing-fields.[48]

Fettes had no such doubts about the efficacy of games or classics, and Reddie soon departed to set up his own school at Abbotsholme.

Because of their own obsession with games, foreigners' attitudes to sport always interested Fettesians. W.K. M'Clure, an Old Fettesian reporting on Italy's conquest of Libya in 1912, appreciated that his readers might find it strange that Italian troops, in moments of boredom, built elaborate sandcastles: 'British soldiers, in similar circumstances, would have organised cricket or football matches; but the Italian is not a player of outdoor games.'[49]

A great admirer of the Italians, he hastened to point out that this in no way meant they were inferior fighting men who were letting the European side down, pointing out that whilst the Arabs may indeed have thought the soldiers' activities odd, 'some of our most popular amusements may have excited similar feelings in Oriental minds.' Hesketh-Prichard, by contrast, was as delighted by the games prowess of his elite sniper pupils as by their other skills ('we always had a really first-class centre forward, left wing and half-back upon the premises'[50]). The arrival of Portuguese troops in France did not, in the view of most military historians, do much to tip the military balance, but they added to the strength of the snipers' football team, much to Hesketh-Prichard's delight.

At Rugby, Arnold himself was solely concerned with intellectual development, and seems to have had an almost Platonic notion that the function of schooling was to train a bunch of philosopher-kings rather than muddied oafs or flannelled fools. His successors, Potts included, preferred the development of all-round character – flannelled philosophers, perhaps. John Yeo, one of Potts' most popular housemasters, was undoubtedly a man in this mould. Whilst he 'really liked fielding cover-point on a raw day or going for a run in a blizzard' he was also 'a genius at expounding mathematical problems.'[51]

Historians have debated where the balance lay between intellect and sporting heroism. J.A. Mangan's work focuses heavily on the emphasis in Victorian public schools, and thus the Empire, on manly (that is, sporting) character – physical and moral fortitude – rather than academic learning, whereas Clive Dewey suggests that despite their desire to be seen as muddied oafs at the goal, empire-builders were actually quite bright. Some teachers veered very much more in one way than in another. Hely Hutchinson Almond, Headmaster of Fettes' neighbour Loretto, although himself an intellectual, and totally committed to 'the training of the governing class', aimed primarily at strength of will and body rather than cleverness. 'I would rather have a school of dull boys than of clever ones,' he once wrote to a parent.[52]

Physical fitness would be welded to *espirit de corps* and self-sacrifice so that his Christian soldiers would go throughout the Empire 'spreading the contagion of their vigour.'[53] In flagrant opposition to the thinking of most reformers, Almond wanted *less* academic study for future warriors at Sandhurst rather than more – football and hunting would be far better training for young officers, imparting as they did teamwork, instinct, healthiness and endurance. At Fettes, he had a keen disciple in Clem Cotterill, Housemaster of Glencorse, uncle of Rupert Brooke, and friend of Dr Potts. Almond's biographer quoted with approval Cotterill's book *Suggested Reforms in Public Schools*, where he described the wonders wrought by the hour's daily exercise he imposed on his boys.[54]

Cotterill was all for character:

Cleverness – what an aim! Good God, what an aim! Cleverness neither makes nor keeps man or nation. Let it not be thought that it ever can. For a while it may succeed, but only for a while. But self-sacrifice – this it is that makes and preserves men and nations, yes, and fills them with joy – only this. Big brains, and big biceps – yes, both are well enough. But courage and kindness, gentle manliness, and self-sacrifice – this is what we want.[55]

Cotterill's gentle manliness went to the extent of taking his coat off and getting involved in punch-ups; an argument with a referee during a match between Fettes and 'Scott's School' (possibly the Academy, who believed that they alone knew how games should be played in Scotland) over a punted goal turned 'sanguinary' in 1871, and Cotterill joined in. He once famously told his pupils that 'there will be a voluntary run tomorrow afternoon for this house, and if any boy does not go I will flog him within an inch of his life.'[56]

Although Potts was a good friend of Cotterill, he did not share his distrust of brains. The Headmaster was a Classicist in the more traditional sense. When Potts died, the governors did consider Cotterill – who saw himself as the natural successor – but then considered his opinions on abolishing competitive examinations and his poor discipline in lessons, and opted for the more academic Rev Dr Heard.[57]

There was much about Fettes which conforms to the neo-Spartan image of the character-building Victorian public school, which, like Yeo,

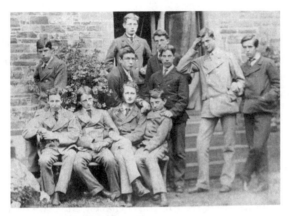

Clem Cotterill with some of the boys of Glencorse House

'epitomised the virtue of enduring hardness', However, also like Yeo, it was always more than this, celebrating and developing the mind as much as the body. Unlike Almond, Fettes masters did want a school of clever boys, and the intellectual training was to be through the Classics. H.W. Auden, a Fettes master who went on to lead Upper Canada College, wrote of his personal heroes in 1906:

The genius of the people, with its instinct for beauty, its versatility, its keen sense of proportion, raised them to such a high degree of civilization, that in art, philosophy, literature, and all the higher spheres of thought, their influence on the world has surpassed that of any other nation. Greek literature is the fountainhead of all western literature; the influence of Rome is only intermediate. Our tastes, our ideas, all the hidden motives of modern thought, and art, all the moulds of our expression of thought in speech are in the main of Greek origin; we are intellectually the direct descendants of the ancient Greeks. Greek civilization has made us what we are in thought and feeling. The fact, too, that the Greek language more than any other possesses flexibility, delicate precision, and the capability of expressing fine shades of meaning, has caused it to become the international language of scientific thought. Any knowledge that we can gain of the Greeks, their genius, and their language makes intellectual life easier.[58]

Robert Philp, who taught at Fettes from the 1960s and later wrote the school's official history, explains a practical rationale behind the masters' classical obsession:

…the Classical training was something of a gospel, taught in the conviction that the future character of their charges depended on their teaching. Even the business of grammar and syntax maybe had its bearing on later life. As he battled through the jungle of gerunds or the mass of Oratio Obliqua, *the Fettesian might be showing the very fibre that would fit him to administer a colony or sit on the Bench. The training was general, befitting the future of a wide and varied empire.*[59]

When the boys wrote about the Empire (which was often) they tended to use allusions which connected it to the civilization of the classical heroes. This poem appeared in the *Fettesian* in 1904, following the Coronation Durbar in Delhi:

The Western came, with Industry and Law;
Fought, seized and Ind for his dominion took;
And ninety years and nine revolving saw
Her troublous land a peaceful ruler brook.[60]

These attitudes lasted well into the twentieth century. When he was 89, OF Alyster Jackson explained to a modern audience how the British thought in his inter-war schooldays:

I felt very proud to be a Briton and took it for granted that we were a superior race; I suppose the Romans must have felt the same in their time. I was an international snob, without realising it.[61]

The manly sense of duty which characterised the Spartan or Roman Republican was summed up by Dr Potts' dying words, read out to the

Fettes' classical culture extended, like that of its contemporaries, to envisioning the founder in a toga; its first Headmaster, Dr Potts, was one of the great classical scholars of his day

pupils by Alfred Hamilton Grant in the school chapel an hour after his death in 1889:

I wish to offer to all the boys at Fettes College, particularly to those who have been there any time, my grateful acknowledgement of their loyalty, affection and generous appreciation of me. I wish, as a dying man, to record that loving-kindness and mercy have followed me all the days of my life; that faith in God is the sole firm stay in mortal life; that all other ideas than Christ are illusory; and that duty is the one and sole thing worth living for.

Hamilton Grant, the Head of School (most senior prefect), went on to become a prominent member of the Indian Civil Service, Chief Commissioner of the North-West Frontier and negotiator of the 1919 Treaty with Afghanistan. The pupils were well aware that for Potts, the ideal of duty was not mere rhetoric or humbug. In 1895, one of the patriarchs wrote to the school from India and described his feelings about the death of the Headmaster:

Many of us had been for four, five, or six years in his form, and had renewed and deepened, in the closer intercourse of after years, the ties of reverence and affection so formed... As I glance up from this page, I catch my old Headmaster's eye, looking at me from a very speaking likeness which I am fortunate enough to possess and which stands always on my writing table. I find a solace in that constant companionship.[62]

This kind of hero-worship is uncommon today, but it was as important to the Victorian Fettes pupil as it was to the citizen of Sparta or the Roman Republic. Not only the Headmaster, but other charismatic members of staff and, even more frequently, sporting heroes of the sixth form such as Charles Fleming, Vernon Hesketh Prichard and David Bedell-Sivright were admired to the point of idolatry by the lads. When Fleming died in 1948, an OF wrote from Canada that 'the finest flowers of the Fettesian garden are the scholar athletes' and hymned the 'magnificent physique' of this native of Kintyre who captained the Oxford XV (the first OF to do so), played for Scotland and then devoted his life to education. This admiration reflected a pattern in wider society which celebrated, for instance, General Gordon and W.G. Grace. When, between the wars, Mr Pyatt of the English department put together a book of Fettes reminiscences, he found that so many OFs had quoted Genesis VI.5 ('There were giants in the earth in those days') that he inserted an index entry: 'Giants, prevalence of.'

Fettes and Empire

The Empire which this patriarch, and countless others, served is not one of the most fashionable institutions to defend these days, enthusiastically though some have tried. Criticisms have been many and various; to name but a few, it can be argued that at certain points it ruthlessly exploited its subject peoples, imposing alien economic and cultural values on them and leaving a post-colonial political legacy in its successor states which more or less guaranteed that many fell into corrupt authoritarianism. The slave trade of the eighteenth century and famines of the nineteenth undoubtedly killed millions. It has also been argued that it was not particularly good for the British themselves, leaving, even unto the third generation, an entirely unwarranted sense of superiority over others and a false sense of commercial complacency and inability to face reality. It also slaughtered exotic animals without a qualm; modern readers would surely feel a thrill of horror on reading the retirement notice in *The Englishman* for Old Fettesian imperialist John Arbuthnot, 'an unerring shot' in India: 'none but himself can say how many tiger, elephant and rhino have fallen to his rifle'.[63]

No-one, not even Niall Ferguson, allegedly the court historian of the right (who subtitled his book on the Empire 'how Britain invented the modern world') today avoids the darker side of Victoria's global colossus. Indeed, he refers to the swarming of the British across the globe as a 'white plague' in the eyes of the nations they penetrated. A group of schoolboy poets ('T, etc.') in the *Fettesian* of March 1899, could, in their verses entitled *Adventurers*, illustrate how idealistic patriotism blended with national acquisitiveness and Social Darwinism in the imperial mission:

> For her we wandered, and for her we died,
> And to her we brought our trophies red;
> For her we bargained, fought and strove and tried,
> That unto her our honour might be wed.
>
> By land we lost our lives amid the snows
> That lie above the sunny Indian plains;
> Backwards we rolled the war-might of our foes,
> Or left our bones to rot 'neath Burma's rains.
>
> We brought her merchandise, we brought her gold,
> Our chosen strength we sold to work her will.
> By war, red war, the lands we won we'll hold
> Through storm or fair, through good report or ill.
>
> We are her power, hers hold we in our hand;
> So shall it be until the end of all.
> With hand on sword we guard our native land,
> And gladly die, if once we hear her call. [64]

The fact that this poem was on the first page of the *Fettesian* speaks volumes for the opinions of the time. Fettes' neighbour Edinburgh Academy was even more blunt about its alumni's world. The fourth verse of the school song, first sung in 1896, ran:

Hi complexi sunt honorem
Pacis imponentes morem,
Indulgentes hi virtuti
Signa Martis sunt secuti.[65]

This was 'cribbed' by former Academy pupil Dr Walter Blaikie, a publisher and historian, as:

Some cut quite respected figures,
Dealing law to conquered niggers;
Some, whose cry for glory's louder,
Yield themselves as food for powder.*

Yet, as Ferguson points out, the Empire was not simply a picture of consistent Anglo-Saxon international thievery. Whilst the eighteenth century British Empire had been an 'amoral' grab for land, power and slaves, the Victorians ' dreamt not just of ruling the world, but of redeeming it.'[66]

Most people did not see it the Empire as evil at the time. It is clear from the pages of nineteenth century copies of the *Fettesian* that the schoolboys on the hill at Comely Bank certainly didn't. They proudly served the imperium in the British Army, the Indian Army, the Indian Civil Service, the British Civil Service, the Volunteers and assorted colonial militias. They were doctors, schoolmasters, administrators, merchants, planters, soldiers and missionaries. Empire meant adventure, and Fettesians undoubtedly caught the fever of excitement when one of their number, D.M. Watt of the King's Own Scottish Borderers, was pictured in the *Daily Graphic* fighting off three Pathans in the Malakand Pass single-handed.[67]

The journalist Henry Hamilton Fyfe, one of his contemporaries, later recalled that as a boy, Watt (who ended up a highly-decorated Brigadier-General, having fought more or less everywhere the British Army went) was discussing with some other pupils what they would become. One was to be a lawyer, another was destined for medicine, a third for a family business, and so on. Watt kept silence until all the rest had spoken, then said solemnly, 'Ah'm goin to be a ma-an'. 'He kept his

---

* This is not, obviously, the Academy's preferred translation today

word,' commented Hamilton Fyfe.[68]

It has even been suggested that some of the rhetoric employed by the OF Tony Blair as Prime Minister was coloured by imperial allusion. His 2001 Labour conference speech, for instance, was full of Victorian high-mindedness:

So I believe this is a fight for freedom. And I want to make it a fight for justice too. Justice not only to punish the guilty. But justice to bring those same values of democracy and freedom to people round the world.

And I mean: freedom, not only in the narrow sense of personal liberty but in the broader sense of each individual having the economic and social freedom to develop their potential to the full. That is what community means, founded on the equal worth of all.

The starving, the wretched, the dispossessed, the ignorant, those living in want and squalor from the deserts of Northern Africa to the slums of Gaza, to the mountain ranges of Afghanistan: they too are our cause.

Blair's successor, speaking in Dar es Salaam, said that Britain should not apologise for the Empire but instead 'should talk, and rightly so, about British values that are enduring, because they stand for some of the greatest ideas in history: tolerance, liberty, civic duty, that grew in Britain and influenced the rest of the world.' Scots were major players in the Empire on this basis, and genuinely saw themselves as playing a constructive role in shaping a better world through its structures, though of course commercial opportunities were also important. By way of example, the little churchyard of the Fife village of Elie, near Mr Brown's childhood home and with memorials to local OFs killed in the Great War, is mute testament to Victorian Scotland's imperial engagement with, according to its weather-beaten tombstones, Tasmania, New South Wales, South Africa, Ontario, Bombay, Bengal, Benares and Penang. For Fettesians and other educated Britons, one of the most important and prestigious forms of imperialism was the work of the Indian Civil Service, a small elite of about a thousand highly-trained professionals who ruled over three hundred million Indians. Clive Dewey summarises the position of the Civilians, as its officials were known:

They collected the revenue, allocated rights in land, relieved famines, improved agriculture, built public works, suppressed revolts, drafted laws, investigated crimes, judged lawsuits, inspected municipalities, schools, hospitals cooperatives – the list is endless. The long lines of petitioners, choking their verandahs and waiting patiently outside their tents, paid tribute to their power.[69]

Whilst it should be borne in mind that the Civilians were not entirely alone in their work – they had a significant number of local clerks to help them, the so-called 'brown sahibs' who would later aspire to rule India themselves – there is still something extraordinary about this tough and high-minded caste. Patriarch Alan Duff, for instance, Deputy Commissioner at Jubbulpore, died in 1897 of 'brain fever brought on by overwork' during the terrible famine of that year. He was, 'though half-unconscious, constantly planning relief works, or forming schemes to save his district from want.'[70]

Although the British handling of the disaster has been severely criticised[71], this popular and able man, not to mention his wife who died two months later as a result of the disease which ravaged the land in the famine's wake, genuinely believed he was there to help. So too did another former pupil, John Campbell Arbuthnot, who in that same year was Deputy Commissioner at Shillong, which was devastated by one of the most dramatic recorded earthquakes in Indian history. 'Mr. Arbuthnot, who, with his wife and children, had a very narrow escape, greatly distinguished himself by the prompt and vigorous measures he took to combat the terrible effects of the earthquake.'[72]

His valete in *The Englishman* described events:

Houses and offices came tumbling about the ears of great and small, and if any one under such circumstances lost his presence of mind it was surely excusable, but not so the D.C. He was out day and night working to rescue the dead and injured from the fallen ruins, and organising shelter and food for the survivors amid the torrents of rain and repeated severe shocks of earthquake which continued after the great catastrophe.[73]

One of the earliest pupils of the school, Arbuthnot went on to become the longest-serving member of the ICS, retiring in 1914 at the age of 56, having learned Persian, Kassia, Garo and Miri and gained an encyclopaedic knowledge of the tribes of Assam and the Frontier. W.E. Wait, an OF based in Ceylon, wrote to the school to describe how, in June 1903, he and two local policemen had to try to deal with a riot against Roman Catholics by Buddhist agitators; rather than risk deaths, he 'tried a bit of bluff' by pointing unloaded rifles at the mob sacking the parsonage, and was relieved to see the troublemakers bolt. He then cycled round the city ensuring the safety of the nuns and organising local headmen to keep their people quiet.[74]

Morris notes that in the prestigious Indian Civil Service examinations 'it was rare to find two entries in one year from the same school'[75] but Fettes provided an extraordinary number, each issue of the magazine reporting on their successes in it; one issue, for instance, reported that W. Grindlay, A. Duff (presumably the great Duff of Jubbulpore) and W. Morison had come in the top twenty of the Indian Civil Service examinations, and would shortly be posted to Bengal, the Punjab and Bombay, respectively.[76] Lockhart recalled that the coach for the Indian Civil Service examination recommended fathers who wanted their sons to pursue this career should send them to Fettes – 'the education there is the best that I know of.'[77]

As Clive Dewey has explained in his study of the ICS, it was an extraordinarily intellectual organization – despite its members' desire to be seen as rugged men of action, the academic ability they possessed was second to none. To get in and get on, successful Civilians needed to amass, analyse and interpret vast quantities of data and create from it concrete proposals; they had to suggest possible solutions to complex problems, weighing up various options; they needed to refine and explain policy.[78]

A Fettes education, which emphasized rigour, literary and linguistic analysis, capacious memory skills and dexterity in advancing an argument, was an ideal background for this; no-one seems to have needed to attend the London crammers such as Wren's after leaving Comely Bank (or, if they did, they never admitted it). In 1908 there were enough Indian Army, ICS and other Fettesians at Pachmarhi alone (and not only that, but for them to have been contemporaries in Carrington House) for there to be an OF polo team; it reached the finals of the local tournament.[79]

Not everyone could hack it, of course; Douglas Gordon Schulze, one of the many rugby internationals produced by the school at the turn of the century and, on graduation from Merton College, Oxford, destined for a career as a colonial school inspector, arrived in Rangoon on 7 June 1908 and resigned on the 25th – not even an interview with the Lieutenant Governor could change his mind, and by early July he was on the boat home, happy to reimburse the £47 6s. travelling expenses.[80]

He prudently changed his surname to Miller in the xenophobic days of 1914, by which time he had become Rector of Kelvinside Academy in Glasgow; he was subsequently Headmaster of Aberdeen and then Manchester Grammar Schools. The great Charlie Fleming, another OF international who returned to Fettes as a schoolmaster (interestingly, remembered as the only member of staff in the 1890s with a strong Scots accent) went out to Sudan in 1900 but, as an 'incurable northerner' he 'found the tropical heat of the Sudan so constantly irksome that he resigned.'[81]

Race and the Victorian Fettesian

With such cheery self-assurance forming the background to their global dominance, some of the opinions which the nineteenth century correspondents to the *Fettesian* express about the locals are undoubtedly a little jarring to modern ears: 'a despicable race they are, lazy, cruel, but withal good-tempered enough as far as grinning at you goes when you chaff them… in habits and sanitation they are simply filthy,' to quote, for instance, OF George Dillon, writing about the Burmese whilst on campaign with the Indian Army.[82]

People at that time spoke of foreigners in a way which would not be normal now. It has to be understood, however, that it was normal then, and indeed was considered both scientific and logical. Darwin had taught that species evolve, (an idea which in economic, political and biological senses had been discussed in Scotland since the eighteenth century) but which other Victorians took much further, turning it into what Ferguson calls the 'scientific snake-oil known as "eugenics".'[83]

It did not look like snake-oil at the time; surely, the Victorians reasoned, if the races evolved at different rates (as Darwin thought they had) then presumably the British, who, in the words of Old Fettesian W.C. Sellar in *1066 and All That*, were 'top nation', must have evolved faster than other people. The Old Fettesian who wrote from Waziristan in 1895 about the practices of the local people, including the relative prices of compensation depending on the sizes of their wounds, was simply interested in them.[84]

In any case, much of the amateur anthropology of these young imperialists was appreciative of the qualities of the other peoples among whom they worked, as Walter Cook's 1895 letter to the *Fettesian* from Afghanistan shows:

...let us have a glance at them as they swing along beside us. They are chiefly Sikhs and Pathans. The Sikhs, tall, straight, strong men with well-cut regular features; rather thin in the shank, but very Westons* to walk, for they have little superfluous flesh and plenty of hard muscle... their moustachios curled and brushed upwards give a fierce expression to their faces, while their tout ensemble is eminently soldier-like. The Pathans show rather larger bone than the Sikhs, and are perhaps on the whole bigger men. Many of them have fair hair and blue eyes, which go well with their high and somewhat Scottish features; in fact they remind one not a little of our own highlanders at home. Inured to all kinds of hardship among their wild and almost inaccessible mountains and well accustomed to face danger in the prosecution of their numerous blood-feuds, they enlist in our ranks, savages it may be, but with little to learn as light infantry soldiers.[85]

Dillon, too, intensely admired the Sikhs: 'no English troops with full accoutrements carrying rifle and forty rounds of ammunition could have marched 82 miles in three days in intense heat as my Sikhs and I did.'[86]

He was also deeply impressed with the way his Afridis refused to take cover whilst he himself was in the open. Another Old Fettesian, Major Arthur Barnes, wrote an account of his service with the now-forgotten Chinese Regiment, raised in the British leased territory of Wei-Hai-Wei and used to suppress the Boxer rebellion. He was not just hoping to describe what had happened, but to give a positive picture of the 'loyal' Chinese (and those of his regiment in particular) at a time when they were being held up as treacherous and cruel. 'No one who has served on the same side as Chinese, as we did, will ever allow it to be said, as it is so often by the ignorant, that they are cowards.'[87]

He pointed out that in the capture of Tientsin the Chinese Regiment were the only British unit to enter the city with the predominantly Japanese assault. He attributed the success of his troops to fairly traditional methods:

I can only give my own opinion, which is, that the behaviour of the men was due simply and solely to the steady drill all the recruits had, and have, to undergo. I am well aware that this same steady drill is regarded in some circles as old-fashioned and out-of-date, but without it, I am sure, no regiment of Chinese will

---

* A reference to Edward Payson Weston, the then world-famous American walking enthusiast, who once walked from Philadelphia to New York in 24 hours – a distance of over 100 miles

51

ever succeed, whatever may be the case with other organisations more or less similar.[88]

Africa was seen as another important field in which dutiful young men from the best schools might spread the benefits of British civilization, and it is here that some Victorian opinions are especially disturbing to the modern reader. If Asians, who self-evidently had a wealth of ancient civilization behind them, and who had met Europeans on militarily equal terms until the mid-nineteenth century, could benefit from British tutelage, the black man virtually required it. Vernon Hesketh-Prichard, exploring Haiti ('first of the Negro republics') was impressed with the country people's honesty and generosity – 'never once would my hosts, however poor they might be, allow me to pay for my entertainment'[89] – but put this down to the simplicity of their lives and necessity to work for themselves. 'I have accepted the hospitality of his roof and lived with him,' wrote the explorer cheerfully of the black peasant, 'and, apart from his natural laziness and his inclination towards snake-worship, have found him a simple and unobtrusive being.'[90]

The town-dwellers he found corrupt, tyrannical and pretentious ('there is no doubt, even while criticizing in the friendliest spirit, that the Haitian Negro is too French – he is apt to overdo it') with a political class drawn from army officers, cartoonishly garbed in fancy uniforms, and in thrall to the sinister cult of voodoo. In *Where Black Rules White*, his detailed study of the country, he described some of its less attractive features:

The so-called wild people of the interior are utterly maligned. You may chance, as I did, to run up against some priest-dominated Vaudoux [voodoo] worshipper who will try to poison you by means of some obscure and potent drug. You may witness orgies and sacrifices, if you can contrive to be present and are willing to take the risk. They go on all the year round, although with greater license at certain periods. If you offend the authorities in any out-of-the-way place, yours may not be a very enviable fate, for when the negro finds a white man in his power the result, as far as the white man is concerned, becomes precisely what the negro's whim may make it.[91]

His assessment of the economic potential of the black man was not optimistic, for he had

...no sense of morality in our meaning of the term. Wives are to the negro a source of wealth. They work for him, while he, with constitutional and ineradicable laziness, sits in the shade of his largest hut, and smokes a pipe with a red clay bowl all day long. Meantime his women and young children work... I say advisedly the young children, for directly the young buck becomes of an age to understand the dignity of his sex, he joins his father in lolling away the days, and works no more thenceforward for ever.[92]

It ought to be said that one of the aspects of backwardness once associated with Scotland was precisely this tendency of men, believing any role other than that of warrior to be beneath them, to sit around doing nothing whilst their wives and mothers did all the work. Dr Johnson noted with approval on his tour of the Hebrides in 1773 that clan chiefs were finally trying to get these people to do something useful,[93] and also had strong views on the laziness, superstition, lack of hygiene and general moral turpitude of the Highlanders he encountered. The British, in their imperial pride, had either forgotten what their ancestors had been like, or assumed that the United Kingdom's apparently rapid ascent from primitive squalor to industrial wealth was due to some sort of superior quality which other people lacked. Hesketh-Prichard concluded his detailed examination of Haiti by addressing directly the question which lay at the heart of British (and French, Portuguese and Belgian) justification for governing large swathes of Africa:

Can the negro rule himself? ... We had not long ago the savage rule of President Salomon, a notorious sectary of snake worship, beneath whose iron hand the country groaned for years, and public executions, assassinations, and robbery were the order of the day. And at the present time? Today in Hayti we come to the real crux of the question. At the end of a hundred years of trial how does the Black man govern himself? What progress has he made? Absolutely none. When he undertakes the task of government, he does so, not with the intent of promoting the public weal, but for the sake of filling his own pocket... Today, and as matters stand, he certainly cannot rule himself.*[94]

What was a young Fettesian of that era to think when he read this, as so many undoubtedly did? This was no bar-room racialist bigot but an

---

* Haitians remember this statesman rather differently, as a reformer who attempted to expand education and introduce a postal system.

intelligent and courageous observer (not to mention a highly successful professional cricketer who scored over 7,500 runs for Hampshire and the MCC, so presumably a trustworthy sort of chap) who had thoroughly explored a black nation, recognized the qualities of its people, and reached what he believed was a balanced conclusion. It is worth saying that Hesketh-Prichard was perfectly well aware of the inadequacies of his own people, writing in another of his books that:

The attitude of the young Britisher abroad towards the rest of the world in general is at once a source of great national strength and of serious national weakness. First, as we know, he is a poor linguist, who prefers to go on speaking his own language, and, when not understood, attempting to enforce comprehension by the very simple expedient of shouting louder… By his attitude in this matter — an attitude dictated partly by a too common lack of the linguistic faculty and partly by a certain rooted conviction that a man who cannot speak English is a man of 'lesser breed' — the Britisher has to a certain extent forced English upon a very unwilling world.[95]

A hundred years later, whilst Hesketh-Prichard's views on black people are no longer common currency except among a small lunatic fringe, much of his assessment of the British still rings true. At the time, his readers felt it was the duty of the white man to steer his black brother towards the path of righteousness. Lord Lugard, who was to administer much of West Africa in the first half of the twentieth century, summed up the reasons why Africa particularly needed former pupils of Fettes and similar institutions. As the heirs to '2,000 years of Christian ethics', they had learned a strong, if sometimes unwritten, ethical code:

Among primitive people this ethical code has to a large extent to be created by the force of example, and hence the necessity, at least in the early stages, of a strong British staff of the right type, who in the daily social intercourse and in the play-fields will impress on the boys what the school expects of its members: self-respect devoid of vanity, truthfulness, courage, good manners, self-control and honesty – because these qualities are the necessary essentials which make a gentleman.[96]

Lugard was referring specifically to the type of person he wanted in mission schools to educate the natives, but in fact the general attitude among the Victorians was that all Africans were, essentially, children, whilst all the British in Africa – whether administrators, soldiers, farmers, missionaries, or traders – were their schoolmasters. As one historian of Empire, R.H. Heussler, put it:

The Briton was an underpaid schoolmaster in an over-populated school. He lived in the house and took a full part in its life, without ever crossing the line. He knew the boys well and liked them and sympathized with their problems. His discipline was unyielding and fair, and it was as constant as sun and rain.[97]

The Old Fettesian who went out to India saw himself much as he would have seen his schoolmasters; a mixture of teacher and policeman, as well as judge, priest and all-round fixer, helping the people of his district just as the boys of his house had once been helped towards adulthood by its tutors. Two letters from old boys, both serving the Empire, were received in 1895 which explicitly mentioned this as their ideal.[98]

Writing of the Second World War, Lt Kenneth McCallum spoke thus of his paternalistic relationship with his men in King George's Own Bengal Sappers & Miners:

My men had adapted marvelously to the many different tasks required of them as front line sappers. I had their entire respect and unquestioning obedience. In return I loved them the way a father loves his children, and 65 fighting fit young men is a large family. I didn't need to ask a man his regimental number or trade rating or size in boots – I knew.[99]

Sir Frederick Terry Rowlatt, who came from an imperial dynasty (he was taken as a child of four to see the opening of the Suez Canal) was at Fettes from 1880 to 1885, but returned to Egypt as soon as he could. Appointed by Lord Cromer to run the new National Bank there in 1906, he remained a director until 1947 and 'gave his heart to the country of his adoption'. He once said that 'I shall always come back to Egypt even if I have to be carried up the gangway.'[100]

He seems to have been universally beloved, and was as comfortable in the company of Egyptians as in that of the British – something which most certainly could not be said for all of his generation. It was probably fortunate that his death in 1950 prevented him from seeing the Suez debacle.

Academic interest in 'exotic' peoples was also apparent; Hector Maclean was keen to find out whether or not there was any truth in the story of Greek settlement on the North-West Frontier, and after his death his father donated to the school some archaeological finds which indicated some Hellenistic artistic influence. Various military historians have commented on how the army was both less jingoistic and less racialist than the Victorian public; as George Orwell pointed out, the attitudes ascribed by Kipling to imperial troops were not as hypocritical as those back home (Barnett blames the distance between the British and the Indians on 'stern memsahibs, stiffly corsetted with Victorian morality and etiquette and resentful of the voluptuous competition of sari-ed brown bodies'[101] – a notion with which at least one OF, as we shall see, would have agreed). The Old Fettesians were typical young men of their era and background in their attitudes to the foreigners they met; they had, as Mangan puts it, a 'narrow and decent ambition'[102] which could have been a lot worse. The British were less genocidal and cruel, for instance, than either the Germans or Belgians, and sometimes intervened to stop bad behaviour towards 'natives' – most famously by abandoning slavery and then forcing everyone else to do so. Major Barnes, stationed in China with the international forces, was disgusted at the behaviour of other Europeans in the looting which followed the Boxers' defeat:

I have seen officers, of foreign troops, be it well understood, wrangling with soldiers of their own and of other armies over articles that possibly neither wanted. No doubt foreigners say this sort of thing went on in our force; but I am proud to think that such could never have been the case, for our discipline was, on all points, far away above that of our Allies as a whole.[103]

Serious incidents emerged when Japanese soldiers began abusing the populace, the Germans shot an old man at random, and the locals begged Barnes for protection because they were afraid to harvest their crops because they were afraid of the Russians. Barnes wrote that, 'It was a very liberal education — as indeed was the whole campaign — on the ways of various nationalities who may not always be on our side.'[104]

By the time he died in the late thirties, Barnes would indeed have seen his country fight the Germans, Austro-Hungarians and Russians, and be on its way to fighting the Italians and Japanese. Of the international forces in China in 1900, only the Americans had not fought Britain at some point, which would not have surprised Barnes: 'The Americans were, as was the case all through this queer war, our great friends, and for all that politicians may say and papers write, I am convinced that the campaign has done more than fifty old treaties to bring the two nations together.' Of course, the British were the natural leaders, inspiring those who fought for them against their own races with such confidence that the gospel of British benevolence was spread by word of mouth. On one occasion, the international forces had to borrow some junks to sail up-river to relieve Peking, and the Chinese Regiment proved ideal ambassadors for this task:

Our men, after a little, inspired the villagers and others with great confidence, so much so that large numbers naturally preferred to take service willingly with us and be certain of pay, rations, and good treatment (points on all of which our men were well able to reassure them), to continuing their present riparian existence with no certainty of any of these good things, and the constant risk of visits, the reverse of friendly, from other less well-disposed 'foreign devils.' Naturally, all our crews were not entirely volunteers, some requiring a little more or less gentle persuasion to get them to join our glad throng, and to remain once they had come, but the majority were quite glad of the chance.[105]

Fettes and the Public Service Ethos

Many Britons did feel that they offered something better for the unlucky inhabitants of foreign parts – better than what was on offer from local despots, and better than what might come from alternative imperial conquerors. On this basis, Fettes was confidently to continue supplying the human material for all aspects of the Empire for decades to come. Four of the forty-five non-English officials of the Sudan Political Service – an administrative body explicitly modelled on the ICS – were OFs (though an astonishing fifteen had attended the Edinburgh Academy).[106]

The sporting accomplishments and sound schooling which the Victorians saw as central to the future imperialist's training meant that the nickname applied to the Sudan was just as apposite for much of the rest of British Africa – 'the land where blacks were ruled by blues.' Their confidence can be seen in microcosm through the work of Henry William Auden, the Fettes master who became Principal of Upper Canada College in 1902. Faced with the threats of American influence and vague stirrings of separate identity, Auden blithely promoted Empire Loyalism and the superiority of the British race and way of life to young Canadians through publications such as *Simple Rules of Health and Courtesy for Those at School* (1911) and, of course, sport. He wanted more immigration into the colonies, announcing after a trip round the Canadian west that American settlers, who knew the soil, might be most ideally suited if they could be persuaded to stay, followed by the Scandinavians, the Doukhobors (a Russian pacifist sect) Galicians (Ukrainians, Poles and Jews from Eastern Europe) and Englishmen – who he found a little disappointing. Best of all, of course, was the 'Scotchman'.[107]

Fettes was keen to produce men who would live up to this ideal. It was in the twenties that, as the *Fettesian* put it, having taken a heavy toll on the younger generation during the Great War, death laid his hand on the bulk of the founding pupils, better known as the patriarchs, and other Victorian OFs. Their obituaries were, in many cases, descriptions of lifetimes of service. Dr Arthur Latham died in 1923, having been one of the most eminent experts in the fields of tuberculosis; his death was followed a few months afterwards by that of the Rev Dr Bruce M'Ewen, who in addition to parish work in Haddington and London, and a lectureship in Apologetics at Edinburgh, served as a machine-gun officer in the Great War, was invalided home but returned to rise to the rank of major and was mentioned in dispatches, and became Minister of First Charge of Aberdeen Cathedral. The following year, Major-General Adam, whose name, appropriately, was first in the school register in 1870, died in Inverness. Although an undistinguished scholar, he had been one of the finest bowlers the school cricket team had ever had, and went on to serve with the 40th Foot (later the 1st Battalion, South Lancashire Regiment) with whom he saw action on the North-West Frontier and in South Africa. He had been known for his deep concern with his men's welfare, and had taken the salute at the Jubilee celebrations in 1920. Indeed, he had done so when the Corps was founded in 1908, little knowing that his only son, who led the parade that day, would be killed ten years later at Arras.

The ultimate service was to apply one's talent and energy in the inhospitable climates and among the peculiar peoples of the Empire. One who did was William Thomson; younger brother of a Fettesian who served with distinction in the Indian Army on the North-West Frontier and won the DSO and Croix de Guerre in the First World War, he was District Officer of Bornu, Nigeria, until his death in the sinking of the SS *Umgeni* in 1917. The *Fettesian* quoted the obituary which appeared in a local newspaper:

By nature a student, and lover of literature and music, a man of culture and refinement, he added thereto that practical common sense, power of initiative, understanding of the native races, and love of sports and adventure which are supposed to distinguish the average administrator in our African Crown Colonies. In that distant land by the Tchad his conversation, the books he would lend, the charm of his character, all helped keep us up to the mark. His tact and knowledge of French made cooperation with our friends and present allies always an easy matter, whilst his enthusiasm for the true progress of the people and his command of both the Kanuri and Hausa languages turned the Maiduguri polo grounds into the finest possible school for the future rulers of the province. There three times a week during nine months of the year the sons of the emir and his chiefs learned to 'play the game' on equal terms with the Europeans. By these players especially he will be sadly missed, as well as by all who came into contact with the charm of his personality, and the Nigerian Service is sadly the poorer by his death.[108]

This was what the Victorian Fettesian was made of.

NOTES

[1] Quoted in Philp, p. i

[2] Quoted in *Fettesian Centenary Supplement*, 1970

[3] Ibid.

[4] Ibid.

[5] *Fettesian*, July 1969

[6] Quoted in Ibid., Spring 1973

[7] See http://www.nationalarchives.gov.uk/currency/

[8] *Fettesian*, December 1932

[9] Macleod, p. xxii

[10] Ibid., March 1911

[11] James, p. 389

[12] Barnett, p. 285

[13] Quoted in James, p. 391

[14] *Fettesian,* November 1887

[15] Bond, p. 26

[16] Karl Marx & Frederick Engels, *the Communist Manifesto* (London, 1848) pt. 1

[17] Barnett, p. 313

[18] Ibid

[19] Hay (1950) p. 18

[20] Ibid., p. 25

[21] *Fettesian,* April 1878

[22] Ibid

[23] Ibid., November 1881

[24] Ibid., June 1891

[25] Ibid., October 1879

[26] Ibid., October 1878

[27] Philp, p. 3

[28] Angelique Richardson, *Love and Eugenics in the Late Nineteenth Century* (Oxford, OUP, 2003) p. 17

[29] C.L.R. James, *Beyond a Boundary* (London, Hutchinson, 1963) pp. 213-4

[30] Dr Kennedy, Cambridge Professor of Greek, testimonial for Dr Potts, quoted in Philp, p. 12

[31] J.A. Mangan, *The Games Ethic and Imperialism* (London, Frank Cass, 1998) p. 18

[32] Barnett, p. 314

[33] *Fettesian*, October 1878

[34] Ibid., October 1879

[35] Niall Ferguson, *Empire: how Britain made the modern world* (London, Allen Lane, 2003), p. 260

[36] *Fettesian*, December 1895

[37] Ibid., November 1887

[38] Ibid., July 1895

[39] Vernon Hesketh-Prichard, *Sniping in France* (London, Hutchinson, 1920) p. 102

[40] *Fettesian*, April 1954

[41] Robert Bruce Lockhart, *Memoirs of a British Agent* (London, Putnam, 1932) p. 67

[42] Ibid., p. 84

[43] *Fettesian*, November 1906

[44] Eric Hobsbawm, *Nations and Nationalism since 1780* (Cambridge, 1990) p. 143

[45] Ibid., p. 142

[46] Ferguson, p. 261

[47] P.J. Waller, *Town, City & Nation* (Oxford, OUP, 1983) p. 103

[48] Cecil Reddie, *Abbotsholme* (London, Allen, 1900) p. 23

[49] W.K. M'Clure, *Italy in North Africa* (London, Constable, 1913) p. 242

[50] Hesketh-Prichard (1920) p. 82

[51] Macleod, p. xxiii

[52] R.J. Mackenzie, *Almond of Loretto* (London, Constable, 1905) p. 158

[53] Quoted in Mangan (1998) p. 25

[54] Mackenzie, p. 243

[55] Quoted in J.A. Mangan, *Athleticism in the Victorian & Edwardian Public School* (London, Routledge, 2000) p. 110

[56] Quoted in *Fettesian Centenary Supplement*, 1970

[57] Philp, p. 15

[58] Henry William Auden, *A Minimum of Greek* (Toronto, Morang & Co., 1906), p. 1

[59] Philp, p. 16

[60] *Fettesian*, July 1904

[61] Alyster Jackson, (Unpublished) Memoirs, Henderson Archive

[62] *Fettesian*, November 1895

[63] *The Englishman*, 30 March 1914

[64] *Fettesian*, March 1899

[65] Quoted in Magnus Magnusson, *The Clacken and the Slate* (London, Collins, 1974) p. 242

[66] Ferguson, p. 113

[67] *Daily Graphic*, 30 April 1895

[68] Henry Hamilton Fyfe in H.R. Pyatt (ed.) *Fifty Years of Fettes* (Edinburgh, Constable, 1931) p. 107

[69] Clive Dewey, *Anglo-Indian Attitudes: the Mind of the Indian Civil Service* (London, Hambledon, 1993) p. 3

[70] *Fettesian*, March 1897

[71] See, for instance, Mike Davis, *Late Victorian Holocausts* (London, Verso, 2000)

[72] *Black and White: A Weekly Illustrated Record and Review* (London) 22 January 1898

[73] *The Englishman* magazine, March 30 1914

[74] W.E. Wait, letter to school from Aduradhapura, 16 June 1903

[75] Morris, p. 187

[76] *Fettesian*, June 1891

[77] Robert Bruce Lockhart, *My Scottish Youth*, (London, Putnam, 1937) p. 260

[78] Dewey, p. 6

[79] *Fettesian*, July 1908

[80] Clive Whitehead, *Colonial Education* (London, I.B. Taurus, 2003) p. 14

[81] *Fettesian*, July 1948

[82] *Fettesian*, November 1887

[83] Ferguson, p. 264

[84] *Fettesian*, November 1895

[85] Ibid., July 1878

[86] Ibid., November 1887

[87] A.A.S. Barnes, *On Active Service with the Chinese Regiment* (London, Grant Richards, 1902) p. 86

[88] Barnes, p. xiv

[89] Vernon Hesketh-Prichard, 'Haiti: Life in the First of the Negro Republics' in J.A. Hammerton (Ed.) *Peoples of All Nations* (London, Educational Book Co., 1920) p. 2559

[90] Vernon Hesketh-Prichard, *Where Black Rules White* (New York, Charles Scribner, 1900) p. 242

[91] Hesketh-Prichard (1900) p. 233

[92] Ibid., p. 249

[93] James Boswell, *Journal of a Tour to the Hebrides with Samuel Johnson, LL.D* (New York, Viking Press, 1936, first published 1775) p. 192

[94] Hesketh-Prichard (1900), pp. 281-4

[95] Vernon Hesketh-Prichard, *Through the Heart of Patagonia* (New York, Appleton, 1902) p. 298

[96] Quoted in Mangan (1998) p. 111

[97] R.H. Heussler, quoted in ibid., p. 112

[98] *Fettesian*, November 1895

[99] Kenneth McCallum, *A Sapper's Story* (Memoir, Henderson Archive)

[100] *Fettesian*, April 1950

[101] Barnett, p. 278

[102] Mangan (1998) p. 18

[103] Barnes, p. 95

[104] Barnes, p. 195

[105] Barnes, p. 105

[106] Mangan (1998) p. 83

[107] H.W. Auden, 'Immigration of the West' *Daily Herald* (Calgary) 28 September 1903

[108] Quoted in *Fettesian*, March 1918

Chapter Three

'Fettes has not been behindhand in doing her best for the Empire'

Adventures Overseas, 1870–1905

The First Casualty

On 22 January 1879, James Adrian Blaikie, an Old Fettesian from Aberdeen, was killed fighting the Zulus at Isandlwana, in what is now the KwaZulu-Natal province of South Africa. After various incidents which increased tensions between the Zulu nation and the neighbouring white territories, Lord Chelmsford advanced into Zululand to teach King Cetshwayo a lesson. Unfortunately, a series of errors led the ill-defended British camp at Islandlwana to be attacked and destroyed by a mass assault. Reading between the lines of his 'In Memoriam' notice in the *Fettesian*, it is clear that Blaikie had not been enormously successful as a pupil. He is described as 'a strong, roving, kind-hearted boy, not much in love with the discipline and regular work of a public school, but with an honest desire to do well'[1] (though a South African publication said 'he was long remembered for his remarkable intelligence'[2]). The faintly freebooting style of the Natal Carbineers (Volunteers) and the 'independence and freedom of an open-air colonial life' must have suited him well; when he set out with his unit, 'contrary to his usual habit, he spoke very seriously of the risk he knew he was running.'[3]

In his last letter, he asked his sister to tell his mother that he was reading his Bible. The importance of such messages to parents in an age when youth was in perpetual danger of being cut short but when most Britons were united in the hope of a better world to come cannot be overestimated. Victorian *Fettesians* carried more reports of untimely ends from illnesses and accidental injuries, which now might be treatable, as they did of old boys killed in battle; a diphtheria epidemic in 1883 carried off a pupil, Duncan Campbell, and the Headmaster's wife and youngest son, and required the boys to be evacuated to Windermere for a term until the school buildings could be decontaminated. The chapel's

St Cecilia Window commemorates the music-loving and loyal Mrs Potts. Of Blaikie:

Little is known of his end. Muirhead, the only carbineer who escaped, reported that he died nobly, cool and steady, and encouraging the men to the end. He and Lieutenant Scott [the unit's commander] were together; they both kept their heads throughout, though some of their comrades fainted. We may judge of the horrors of the field, when we are told that the greatest comfort his friends had was that he had two gunshot wounds, so that he would probably be dead before the Zulus came to close quarters.[4]

The line about the comfort of his friends is a reference to the belief that the Zulus tortured and mutilated prisoners; although they did indeed 'desecrate' the dead – believing that the soul was released through disemboweling, and that a dead enemy's jawbone made an effective lucky charm – Saul David believes that this did not extend to tormenting people who were still alive, however much those at the time (especially the horrified comrades who had to retrieve the distorted bodies) thought it did.[5]

The Natal Carbineers had, in fact, made a heroic last stand with Lt-Col Anthony Durnford, a senior officer they apparently disliked because he had accused them of cowardice after an incident at Bushman's River Pass earlier in the campaign. David notes of the Carbineers that 'they were all excellent horsemen and crack shots, and could easily have escaped as a group, yet incredibly they chose a hero's death.' Zulu witnesses recalled that they kept firing until all their ammunition was gone, then 'formed a line, shoulder to shoulder, and back to back, and fought with their knives.'[6] A war correspondent who accompanied a patrol to the battlefield recorded that the Natal Carbineers were found dead around Dornford, 'riddled by assegai stabs'.[7]

Blaikie's body was identified by a relative from the size of his head (which was rather large) and he would later be buried in his own grave, made of Scots granite. The *Fettesian* obituary's reference to Blaikie's widowed mother's hopes for her son, whose 'premature and awful death must have brought a peculiarly bitter sense of desolation' is one of the most stiffly touching elements in a generally robust publication. It clearly affected the school, which he had only just left (he was nineteen when he died) and there was soon a proposal that a memorial be erected. What is striking is that the rather prescient pupil making this suggestion in the

Fettesian was perfectly well aware that Blaikie was most definitely not going to be the last to be killed in action:

Might we not erect a marble tablet in the College, on which to be engraved the names of Blaikie and those Fettesians whose fate it may be to die a soldier's death?…We hold up before the School the names of those who have won honours at the University. Surely those who die like Blaikie are worthy of a small space on our walls.[8]

India and the Frontier

Plenty of opportunities were going to come the way of Fettesians to die like Blaikie; despite the frequent possibilities for violent ends in India and Afghanistan, and the huge numbers posted there, most survived – just – the Second Afghan War and the various police duties in East Asia. India had been more or less subdued by the time Fettes was opened, but the North-West Frontier with Afghanistan was a running sore for a host of reasons. The tribes of the region were aggressive, occasionally prone to becoming over-excited by some new Islamic prophet, and relaxed about raiding the lands of Indian farmers they despised. Afghanistan was also a potential route for the Tsar into India, and Russian invasion was a constant fear of the Victorians. At least a dozen OFs served with distinction on the Frontier, and others were involved in administration, medicine or education there. The third issue of the school magazine carried a detailed account from 'Piffer' (the nickname for soldiers of the Punjab Frontier Force) of a day's march:

We are obliged to march early in order to avoid the noonday heat; so the 'Révaillé' sounds at 2.30 am [the officer cadets at Sandhurst, incidentally, had groused good-naturedly at having to get up at 7.00] *and in a few minutes every one is up and awake, the camp echoing with a medley of sounds, camels groaning, as only camels can, mules braying, and men chattering as they strike their tents, for Jack Sepoy is a tremendous fellow to talk even at 3 o'clock in the morning… so 'quick march ' off we go, tramp tramp to the skirl of the bagpipes; for, O incredulous Scot, the gallant – Punjab Infantry does boast of bagpipes and stalwart pipers too, albeit they may be a shade darker than their Teutonic brethren, Dougal and Donald of the 42nd! We step along merrily, for the morning is sharp and cold, although the sun will be hot enough in an hour or two, and the men soon settle down into their long swinging step which, although less regular than British marching, yet takes them along at about four miles per hour. But now the morning star has risen and soon the rising sun gilds the snow-clad peaks of the lower Himalayas, some hundred miles to our right, while to our left the morning mist rises ghost-like from the broad Indus. The air grows sharper just as the sun tops the horizon, but the men step out more freely, now they can see where to tread…*[9]

The romance and enthusiasm of this is unlikely to have been lost on the young readers back at Fettes, even though in retrospect it is possible wryly to note that British soldiers, including several OFs, are still enjoying beautiful views of the North-West Frontier over a century later. The following year 'Piffer' wrote from the Khyber Pass, where he was taking part in an attack on the fortress of Ali Musjid:

In the grey dawn, as our men are eagerly scanning the long defile which now lies at their feet, a body of the enemy's cavalry, some 200 strong, appears round a corner of the Pass, in retreat from Ali Musjid. A couple of shots brings them to a halt, and their leader motions them to retire where an intervening rock gives safe cover from our fire. They have only two courses open to them to follow, one is to at once surrender, the other to run the gauntlet of our fire up the Pass. Their leader, brave fellow that he is, prefers the latter. Dashing forward, he fires his pistol, and at the signal the whole troop put spurs to their horses and gallop madly up the Pass. A sharp fire is poured into them, and many a good horse and bold rider falls struggling on the fast reddening stones…[10]

'Piffer' was probably the pseudonym of Walter Cook, one of seven 'patriarchs' to join the army. He was later reported to have 'greatly distinguished himself in the defence of the Shutargardan position'; he was wounded but 'thanks to a stoutish rib, the ball fell out again' as his letter put it.[11]

The modesty to which the *Fettesian* editor referred was no idle compliment; he had in fact been recommended for the Victoria Cross. The enemy positions were well entrenched on a rocky ridge, the approach to which was 'difficult and almost precipitous, affording scarcely any cover'; they could only be taken in a coordinated attack from two sides, which, in the days before radio, was much harder to achieve. Cook, on the right of the hill, ran 200 yards to the 21st Punjabis on the left, under heavy fire, to organize this, and, when his senior officer was hit, also went to get help, despite even heavier fire. Cook could have ordered one of his men to take a note to the Punjabis or to the dooly-wallahs (stretcher-bearers), but felt it would be better if he could explain the situation in person. He was severely wounded at Kabul on 11 December 1879. Walter's older brother John, was fatally wounded there the following day; he had missed out on a Fettes education but won the VC in 1878.[12]

Walter described the battle, and John's fate, in a letter:

John led the advance with two companies of our Regiment and we soon came under the enemy's fire, which occasioned a few casualties among the men. We got about half-way up the hill, but the enemy's fire became so galling that it was found impossible with our small numbers to get any further, and it was determined that we should take shelter under some rocks and await reinforcements from cantonments. Whilst lying under these rocks your brother observed large bodies of the enemy coming up to a spur to help those already on top of the conical hill, and he went back about fifty yards to inform Colonel Money of the 3rd Sikhs, who was in command of us, of what he had seen. No one could show the smallest part of his body from behind the rocks without having several bullets fired at him; and in going back to Colonel Money a heavy fire was kept up on John, but he escaped untouched. In returning, however, he had to run the same gauntlet, and just as he reached the rock under which we were lying, a bullet struck him, passing through the bone of the left leg just below the knee…

John was pluckily optimistic about his fate, reckoning that if his leg was amputated he could still do a desk job in the Pay Department and shoot snipe, but the operation killed him. On being told that this was likely, he simply said 'Dulce et decorum est pro Patria mori', which Walter saw as the normal observation of a soldier. His career was followed by admiring OFs; a letter from a friend in Calcutta in 1881 said Cook was on Roberts' march to Kandahar, when he had his horse shot from under him, and was subsequently stationed in a small frontier station in the Punjab[13]; by 1887 he was taking command of a force of police in what was then called Burmah.[14] This kingdom on the borders of British India had steadily expanded and become a threat, so the Empire struck back, first weakening and eventually swallowing it. It was from Burma that the jovial George Dillon sent his first dispatch in 1886, apologizing in advance that it would savour of what his 'compositions used to be at Fettes, baldness.'[15]

Like Cook, he was unduly modest. Unlike Cook, he did not have the slightest interest in making the 'queer little place' in which he found himself sound remotely impressive:

You at home in luxury do not know what 'rain' means out here; if you want to find out, get a man to turn a garden pump on you for six hours or so without cessation, and even then you don't approach it. Our journey here was not very pleasant – 1000 miles by rail to Calcutta, 1000 miles by sea thence to Rangoon, and another 1000 miles by river up the Irrawaddy to here. I suppose I ought to write volumes on the subject of the ever-varying scenery coming up the river, but, as a matter of fact, the scenery on either bank was just about as tame as you could see; nothing wild about it at all... I thought India had taught me what a mosquito was, but to see mosquitos as large as snipe and in coveys you must come to Burmah. Any man under twelve stone is lifted from his bed and mangled without the slightest difficulty. I have made a vow to despise the midge of England when I have the luck to meet him.[16]

Dillon had been sent to the area 'with instructions to kill and slay' the gangs of murderous dacoits (robbers) which supposedly infested it. He ended up marching around over 'fiendish country', covering 37 miles in 48 hours, but ended up only arresting a few 'gentlemen'. A subsequent experience of battle when his company and another tried to seize some mountain stockades led to some rueful observations:

That it was pretty hot work you may gather from the fact that, out of six officers under fire, three were wounded (two severely) as well as nine men. The sensation of being 'under fire' is very funny, and not as pleasant as it might be; these fellows creep up pretty close in the jungle and let fly with a muzzle-loader crammed with slugs as big as your fist, and which make a hole you could put your head in.[17]

In a subsequent report, he described the emotions of battle – 'I had a sort of funny feeling in the pit of my stomach until I caught sight of one of them, and then one hadn't time to bother much; besides, I got a wee bit bloodthirsty.'[18]

Most of the Fettesians regarded this sort of thing as a price worth paying occasionally for what Dillon called 'a rather jolly posting' but there were still other, more permanent risks. Chief among these was disease. In November 1898, for instance, Archibald Hepburne-Michelson in Singapore and Edward Boyle in Malta were recorded as having died young; typhoid or enteric fever were the usual culprits. Dillon himself survived four campaigns and was awarded both medals and clasps, was mentioned in dispatches three times and was awarded the C.B. in 1903, but died of illness at sea in 1906.

War returned to the North-West Frontier in the 1890s – it was never far away – and the *Fettesian* carried many letters from former pupils there. An OF wrote from the Frontier at the request of the Headmaster to describe what was happening there as the British attempted to fight the fiery Mahsud Waziris.

Month after month stories of looted caravans, burnt villages, women and children carried off, were brought to the authorities; the marauders were chased, but with little effect, as they escaped across the frontier, and policy demanded that we should not cross this frontier, as the Amir of Kabul was very apt to take umbrage at any infringement of his territory under any circumstances. The Waziris, however, neither acknowledged the Amir nor the British, so that, with very few exceptions, the marauders escaped without punishment.

Last year, however, the Amir consented that his frontier should be demarcated, and pillars built to define exactly the limits of Afghanistan and the limit up to which the British could penetrate without trespassing. The malihs or small chieftains of the Waziris were called together to meet the British commissioner, and agreed to assist the escort of the British officer told off to carry out the demarcation between their country and Afghanistan. In the autumn of 1894 the British party started, marching into Waziristan accompanied by a strong escort of troops to meet the Afghan representatives. For a time all went well; the Waziris gave no trouble, assisted in procuring supplies for the force, for which they were paid, and appeared to be on the most friendly terms.

On the 4th November, however, the British camp was rushed just before daybreak by 2000 or 3000 Waziris, who got into the camp and killed a certain number of men, followers, and animals. The countryside was in a blaze, the mullahs or priests preaching religious war on the so-called invaders of their territory, signal fires on every mountaintop calling all the young men to arms, and matters looked very serious.[19]

The author, who felt that the British had been 'too long-suffering' in the face of Waziri marauding in the past, had been 'hoping, without any hope' that he would be asked to join the punitive force which was drawn up to overrun Waziristan and teach the 'young bloods' to behave. He was delighted to receive a telegram appointing him Deputy-Assistant Adjutant-General to the 3rd Brigade, and made a three-day train journey and 80-mile trip in a cart from his base at Quetta in Baluchistan to Bannu, where he was immediately set to work organizing the fitting out of the force with fifteen days' rations for 2,500 fighting men, plus their followers, 1,800 camels and 1,000 mules. Horses were of little use in the high mountains, so they marched for 12 to 14 miles a day, spending Christmas Eve bivouacking at 8,000 feet without tents, sending out flying columns to punish offending villages by seizing their cattle and destroying their defences. The Waziris were related to the Pathans, who the author commanded and admired, so he was able to gain a little insight into their way of life:

The tribe it is estimated at about 12,000 fighting men, principally armed with swords and matchlocks, though of late a good many rifles have found their way into the country. They make their own swords, and beautiful weapons some of them are (we came across numberless smelting places on the hills, which abound with iron). They are all thieves, and proud of being so, and personally brave.

Men and women alike are addicted to tobacco chewing, but none drink intoxicating drinks. Their food consists mainly of wheat, Indian corn, rice, and barley, which they grow themselves. Hospitality is a prime virtue amongst them and the life of a guest is safe so long as he is within the precincts of the village. There are no doctors or physicians, the usual and only treatment of a practical nature being to roll the patient in a sheepskin for twelve hours; but they mostly rely on charms and incantations…

They are very ignorant, and as a sure result very fanatical, trusting themselves entirely to their priest. Every village and every homestead a strong stone tower into which they retire when attacked. This goes far to show the pleasant terms on which they live with each other.[20]

An Old Fettesian sent a cutting from the *Daily Graphic* to the school which described his contemporary Donald Watt's work at Malakand:

At eleven o'clock the main attack was made on Malakand by the Scottish Borderers and Gordon Highlanders. The enemy disputed every inch of ground, but after four hours' fighting the position was carried by the two regiments with great gallantry. Second Lieutenant Watt, of the Kings' Own Scottish Borderers, was the first to reach the summit. Thinking his men were close behind him and he rushed at a 'sangar', out of which three of the enemy came to meet him. These he promptly shot with his revolver, upon which more of the tribesmen came out. Lieutenant Watt, finding himself alone, turned back to his men, who at that moment came over the crest. The sangar was then carried by storm.[21]

'Fettes leads the way in India as well as in Scotland,' crowed the former pupil, 'may she ever do so!' A letter from Watt, published a few months later, pointed out that much of the really important work at the battle had been done by Sergeant Ewan from Marnoch, Banffshire, who expertly deployed the Maxim machine-gun and 'killed any amount' of tribesmen, making the advance possible. Watt wanted to get to the top before the Borderers did (despite the *Graphic* report's claim, he was in fact an officer in the Gordons) and was pleased that the KOSB afterwards said that they could not have advanced without Ewan's help. Of his own exploits, he was rather matter-of-fact:

To the left the way was easy, but we could not advance owing to the heavy fire of the enemy; to the right it was like going up a rope, pulling yourself up by means of grass tufts and cracks in the rocks. Whoever started first would be up first. As I was afraid of the K.O.S.B.s getting up first I started off, telling the nearest men to follow. At the top there was a tree, and I got under cover of this and had a look round. There was a house about 4yds. or so from it, and I saw several 'nigs,' but presently they all disappeared. Then I went towards the house, shouting to the men to come up. They had been too beat to follow me. My shouting at once brought three 'nigs' from the other side of the house. I killed two and wounded the third with my revolver, and then went and looked down both sides of the spur, but not a soul was coming up, so I went back and found five or six of the enemy, and any amount behind them making for me. So I let fly at them with my revolver. Then I had another look, and seeing more coming up I sat and slid down the hill back to the 'sungar.' I went down the exposed side, as the other was too steep to get down quickly without going to the bottom of the hill. On the way, my sword fell out of the sheath and run into my leg; it went in the front of my thigh and came out just where the leg joins the body, making two holes about 4in. apart. It got caught in a bush and so was pulled out; I picked it up and got into the 'sungar.' The enemy had been firing and chucking stones at me, so I got the first men I met in the 'sungar' to come to the left corner of it and answer their fire. The first was a corporal in the K.O.S.B., and just as he was going to aim he fell dead down the hill, and I got at the same moment the most awful smack on the left shoulder. A bullet had cut the shoulder strap, scored the leather strap of my revolver case, and cut my coat behind the shoulder. It made me jump a bit.[22]

Watt recovered from his injuries and rose to the rank of Brigadier-General. Another OF, Major Norie of the 1st Battalion, 2nd Gurkha Rifles, was so badly injured by a dum-dum bullet in the Bara Valley that his arm had to be amputated. Norie would become a distinguished intelligence officer and author of many significant military reports on Asia. On 17 August 1897, Hector Lachlan Stewart MacLean of the Corps of Guides was killed trying, 'under a very heavy and close fire', to save a wounded comrade from enemy swordsmen at Nawa Kili, Upper Swat.[23]

Winston Churchill, in *The Story of the Malakand Field Force*, described Maclean's earlier 'wonderful escape', when 'a bullet entered his mouth and passed through his cheek without injuring the bone in any way.' At the time of Maclean's death, he wrote that:

It was also officially announced, that Lieutenant Maclean would have received (the Victoria Cross), had he not been killed. There are many, especially on the frontier, where he was known as a fine soldier and a good sportsman, who think that the accident of death should not have been allowed to interfere with the reward of valour.[24]

Maclean did eventually win a rather belated Victoria Cross when Edward VII decided posthumously to honour those whose bravery would have earned them decorations had they survived. MacLean is buried in the Guides Cemetery, Mardan, Pakistan, near another Guides VC winner, Godfrey Meynell, killed during the Mohmand Campaign in 1935. Maclean's supreme sacrifice made a great impact on the boys. The magazine carried a glowing tribute from a former Head of School, Hamilton Grant of the Indian Civil Service, who informed the readers that Maclean 'was one of the most popular men in one of the most popular regiments in India, and was renowned as one of the finest polo-players in the Punjab.'[25] (The unfortunate G.L.H. Milne, MA, MD, who died less spectacularly of an unpleasant illness in South Africa, received less attention – a mere three lines compared to Maclean's two and a half pages). Grant also sent the school a poem in honour of his friend:

Hold fast your tears: it is not meet to weep.
Tears are the meed of deaths that, incomplete,
Cut down the flower, ere yet the hue doth peep
From out the velvet bulb's sheath. Tears are meet
For shipwreck'd lives, and deaths that bring an end
To barren hopes, to want, disease, to shame.
So hold your tears. For he, MacLean, your friend,

Died not as frost-nipp'd bud, an empty name,
Nor yet in hopes unfruitful; want, disease,
Or shame had never sullied the fair page
Of that brave, vigorous life. From tears then cease.
E'en the wild foe to wonder turn'd from rage,
As, self-forgetful, on to Death he hurl'd –
True to his corps, a Guide to all the world.[26]

Life, Death and Fun in the Empire

Not all Old Fettesians in the Empire were in harm's way through combat. Accidents claimed many: patriarch Henry Holmes Gallie accidentally shot himself whilst looking for a tiger in the middle of the night on a tea plantation in Upper Assam on 26 October 1882,[27] whilst Lt A.S. Stephen slipped on the steps of his bungalow in Ranjapur and broke his spine. He doggedly dragged himself onto a horse and rode thirty miles, but had to be taken back home to die. Two fellow Old Fettesians, serving with the 5th Punjab Cavalry, were among the pallbearers.[28]

Of course, such tragic accidents were not confined to the Empire – Scottish landowning OF Duguid Rae Milne, out shooting with his older brother, snagged his gun's trigger whilst climbing over a barbed-wire fence and was killed instantly.[29]

It was not all hard work. A 'griff' (junior officer) in India wrote to the school describing the sport which could be enjoyed on leave, including 'the king of sports – pigsticking':

The first pig broke near our party, and, after giving it sufficient law, we gave chase. My pony dashed off, and we were soon close behind the boar, who, of course, then changed his course. I, however, didn't – or rather couldn't – and when I managed to stop my beast the pig was its death throes. Shortly afterwards another broke out at the same place, and the same performance was gone through. As we charged wildly on I saw a herd of water buffaloes loom large in the distance, and, though I had no say in the matter, thought that my mare could not be such a fool as not to avoid them. However, she didn't, and we cannoned into one with a crash which nearly made us part company. This rather steadied down my wild steed, and I managed to turn her in the direction of the others, who were closely following the pig, and then let her rip. As we came up to them at an angle the pig saw us and turned in to take us sideways. I put down my spear, onto which piggy ran, and then I went on. When we again joined the party the bore was laid out at the feet of the others, and I was informed it was mine. I trust I bore the unexpected honour with becoming modesty.[30]

It has to be admitted also that not all of the Fettesians in Asia were brave or high-minded warriors. A letter from Ceylon in 1879 was fairly frank about the tea-planter's life in the highlands:

The coolies have to turn out every morning at six o'clock to muster, wet or dry, and so have the 'Sinna Dorés' or 'young sirs'; the 'Peria Dorés' or 'big sirs' staying in their bungalows or in their beds according to their inclinations, and only coming out when they want to do or say something particular, or occasionally to catch a coolie sleeping in a drain when he ought to be at work cutting it, or perhaps to catch the Sinna Dorés playing pranks, instead of looking after the coolies. The Europeans of course enjoy this cool weather and snap their fingers at the rain; but it is altogether a different matter with the coolies. Thinly clad in cotton cloth, which gets immediately wet, they look the very pictures of misery, and although the estate provides them with 'Cambulies', a sort of thin blanket which they wear over their heads and shoulders, their shivering forms and loud complaints as they work away all show how much they feel the change in the weather. The other day a Kanganie, in the cast-off suit of some bygone Sinna Doré, with the rain pouring in small cataracts from his nose and chin, asked me if in the country I came from I had plenty of wind and rain, that I did not seem to care for it here. I told him we had plenty of it and to spare and, and tried to explain ice and snow to him; but either his skull was too thick or my Tamil was too bad, for somehow or other he could not take it in.[31]

The author was also breezily matter-of-fact about working practices on the plantations:

A Kanganie is a sort of a head man who has a few coolies under him, and is told off to drive a lot in such and such a work, the which he accomplishes by means of a stout stick, and he is no mean hand in wielding it, and loud are the howls and execrations one hears sometimes, attesting both to their power of arm, volubility of tongue, and fertility of imagination. At any rate the Kangani gets 'nailed' by the Sinna Doré if anything is wrong in his work so he has to adopt the maxim of 'spare the rod and spoil the child.'

That he did not feel any need to keep quiet about such matters speaks volumes for the assumptions of the time. Like many OFs abroad, the author was keen to encourage his successors to come out and give this opportunity a try:

Planting is a rough life, and was one must means be no carpet-knight to succeed well in it. But although it has its fatigues, and to a beginner they are somewhat formidable, yet the life is active, and plenty of fun can be got from it…

Another glimpse of the Empire's less glamorous aspects was provided by Robert Bruce Lockhart, who, before his days as a diplomat, made an unsuccessful attempt to increase the family fortune in the Far East. Unlike some other OFs, he did not flinch from describing the sordid underside of colonial life. In the thirties, he remembered Madame Blanche's 'frail army of white women recruited by the professional pimps from the poorest population of Central and Eastern Europe, and drifting farther East as their charms declined, via Bucharest, Athens and Cairo, until they reached the Ultima Thule of their profession in Singapore.'[32]

No British girls, of course – the authorities did not allow this on political grounds, lest the dignity of the imperium be called into question by 'a Malay princeling or Chinese towkay' hoping to satisfy 'an exotic and perhaps politically perverted desire for the embraces of the forbidden white women.' The bulk of the prostitutes were bought from poor Japanese families by local 'contractors' who brought them to Malaya to service the thousands of Chinese coolies in the mines; until a girl had worked off her purchase price, 'she was to all intents a slave, and, more often than not, unless some European planter bought her out in order to minister to his loneliness, her thraldom lasted for the rest of her earthly existence.' Although Lockhart wrote that 'this traffic in human souls had roused in me feelings of resentment both against the Japanese and against the existing social order' and that 'in my moods of reflection I had been disgusted by this cruel and senseless wastage of human life,' he admitted to lapses on his own part; his antics with other young Britons were certainly not the sort of thing Fettes wished to encourage among its alumni. After football matches he had taken part in 'jollifications' with other young expatriates which involved copious drinking, boisterous horseplay, ribald songs and visits to brothels. Alternatively, he had 'driven down the street furtively, with the hood of the ricksha up, afraid lest any pair of eyes behind the shuttered windows were witnesses to the white man's secret shame and not daring to emerge until one had ascertained if Rose or Madeline or Wanda were free.'

Lockhart wrote this description of Singapore's seedy delights and hidden horrors in 1936, by which time the drive of the imperialists for improvement had largely eradicated the vice trade, or at least its most obvious and pernicious manifestations, and provided – predictably – a vast array of sports facilities in which young Britons might work off their excess energy in a healthier fashion. In 1906, however, Lockhart saw the challenge of going 'up-country' as the way to break free from the expatriate cycle of business, sport and drunken debauchery, and was sent to open up a new plantation in an inhospitable area with an unenviable death-rate from malaria: 'I had to make something out of nothing, an estate out of jungle, to build a house for myself, to make roads and drains where none existed.'[33]

He was able to gain the respect of the locals by shooting a cobra which had made its home in the local well with a single, and rather lucky, bullet to the head. This gave the locals the impression that he always carried a revolver and was a crack shot, so he was not molested by troublemakers. Nonetheless, his midnight rides through ten miles of jungle, most of which was uninhabited, on his bicycle were a special kind of thrill. After six months living apart from other Britons, and a whole year apart from white women, the 23-year-old Lockhart noted that 'steeped in an unhealthy romanticism, I was ripe for temptation', which came in the form of Amai, the dazzlingly beautiful ward of the local sultan. Despite being warned by his Malay headman that 'the crow does not mate with the bird of paradise' and by the Irish colonial police commissioner that since native women all looked the same anyway he ought to go for others more easily attainable and less dangerous, Bruce Lockhart arranged secret meetings with Amai, who moved into his bungalow. This caused a scandal in Malay society; whilst the British may have believed themselves to be superior, so far as the local aristocracy was concerned this was a mere tradesman who had made off with a princess. An Anglophile footballing prince tried to talk Lockhart round over stengahs, but he stood his ground, claiming that he was ready to convert to 'Mohammedanism' if necessary. Malay friends and staff melted away and Lockhart developed malaria; when his uncle heard of it, he sent a car and bundled the enfeebled romantic into it, then onto a ship, where he gradually recovered his health whilst pining for his beloved and writing bad poetry.

Will Ogilvie, by contrast, was known for his good poetry. After leaving Fettes in 1888, he worked initially on his family's land at Kelso, but spent twelve years roaming around the Australian bush as a stockman and horse-breaker. He was friend of the flamboyant Australian horseman 'Breaker' Morant, executed for killing prisoners in the Boer War, who he described as 'full of romance and void of fears', a cavalier who should have been in the service of King Charles. Ogilvie's flair for poetry had been noticed at Fettes, where he won a prize for it, but his passion for the wonders of the outback made him beloved in Australia; his entry in the *Australian Dictionary of Biography* eulogises the way that 'his rhythmic lines seem to keep time to the beat of horse-hooves, the crack of the stockwhip and the clink of snaffle-bars.'[34]

In 1893 Ogilvie wrote a poem for the *Fettesian* which encapsulates both the excitement of Empire and the love of the old school which inspired so many of the former pupils in the nineteenth century (not to mention the pervasive influence of Longfellow's 'Hiawatha'). It was written on the back of a copy of the school magazine as Ogilvie sat at the foot of a gum tree:

I am writing from Australia,
From the land of gold and gum trees,
Writing to my younger brothers
In the land of fight and fives-balls,
In the land where snowy fives-balls
Leap way above the side walls
To the thieving roofs, and stay there.

Here we hunt the brown opossum
From his home among the treetops,
In the moonlight from the treetops
Drop him with the double barrel;
Take his skin as prize and trophy,
Weave it into rugs for winter
For our friends in far-off Scotland.
Here we mount our steed at morning,
In the golden South-land morning,
Gallop out among the ranges,
Follow from the rocky ranges
Where the kangaroo, the brusher,

Leads the chase across the hollows,
Spur the good horse up beside him,
Stun him with the stirrup-iron –
Make his skin a wrap for winter…

So we toil or take our pleasure
In the Sun-land, in Australia,
In the very great Australia;
But we sometimes grow aweary,
And our hearts are sore within us
For the good old days in Scotland,
For the merry days at Fettes.
And we sometimes hear in sleeping
All the Fettes bells at morning:
First bell – second bell – at morning,
And we sometimes hear the last bell –
Very cruel was the last bell –
And we hear at times the cheering
Coming from the crowded touch lines,
When we battle with Loretto,
With the scarlet of Loretto,
When the feet are thundering goalwards
Like the roar of battle squadrons
In a dribble of the forwards.
And we sometimes see in dreaming
All the corridors of Fettes
Thronged with many laughing fellows
Rushing to their different classrooms
When the bell is nearly stopping.
And we wake, and are not happy,
For those merry days are over,
All the fun and laugh is over.
Is it strange we love our masters,
Love our tutors and form-masters?
And our merry, merry comrades –
Is it strange that we should love them?

Golden through the gum tree branches
In its splendour glows the sunset,

And I canter slowly homewards –
No! I am not late for lockup –
But my heart is sad for Fettes.[35]

Despite the absence of armed enemies in these corners of the Empire, danger still lurked; the school learned in 1895 that Fred Marshall, a popular member of the 1889 1st XV, had died far from home. 'A boy of splendid physique', although 'intellectually he did not take a high place' he had studied at a colonial college to prepare for life as a 'sturdy squatter' in New Zealand:

His death was sad, and characteristic of the boy. Seized with illness some distance out in the bush when almost alone, he started to ride home. As he rode on over the rough track he found himself getting weaker, till it last he could ride no longer. But he gamely struggled on on foot, and literally crawling the last few miles of the way, he got home just in time to die.[36]

A 'Letter from Buenos Ayres' in 1880 described the joys of ranching in Britain's 'informal empire', those countries over which the mother-country enjoyed considerable economic influence without the inconvenience of having to garrison or administer them:

My duty was to catch the lambs and hold them for the others to cut them [dock their tails]. *If any one desires real hard exercise I can recommend this. You set your mind on a certain lamb and say, 'I will catch that lamb.' You stalk the little beast most carefully, and just when you're going to lay hold of its tail it doubles round, and you find it twenty feet off at the other end of the pen.*[37]

A not insignificant number of Fettesians lived in Argentina, returning to Europe to fight in British uniforms in 1914 and 1939. Naturally, they enjoyed observing the local eccentricities:

We are now living in a state of fear of revolution, and all day long you may see the police being drilled. They look like a number of very small boys playing at soldiers, as they attempt to march in step to the music of a trumpet, which sounds as if the trumpeter had taken his first lesson the day before. He keeps up one continued note, and when he is tired the note is taken up and continued by another.

Politics in this country is the all-absorbing interest and study of the natives. Little boys in the train talk politics over their paper cigarettes, and as every man hopes to gain something when his party comes into power, self-interest enters considerably into the patriotism of which they are never tired of talking, although I believe there are hardly a dozen men in the country who possess it in its proper sense.[38]

War in Africa

Despite the physical and moral dangers of all the many global postings Victorian Fettesians might experience, it was Africa, especially the North-East and South, that was to see their largest deployment, and a significant number killed. In December 1882 the *Fettesian* carried an extremely long account of service in Egypt with the Gordon Highlanders, who were attempting to defeat Arabi Pasha's anti-European uprising and safeguard the Suez Canal. An anonymous old boy described the boredom, insufferable heat, confusion and occasional excitement of middle eastern warfare in a way that would surely be familiar to those who served there under Montgomery or those who would come later in Iraq and Kuwait. His accommodation, for instance, was 'fairly comfortable, except for mosquitoes, which were terrible: the place had been a good deal knocked about by the shells of the fleet, and there was one hole particularly noticeable in the wall of our sleeping-room, about nine feet across.'[39]

The reach of modern technology, so crucial to British success, was also apparent; when the 40-pounder gun battery opened up, the narrator couldn't really see the effect, except that lots of people were running about, 'so I fancy they must have been rather alarmed.' When he himself advanced (after 'a capital lunch') he and his men were grateful for the soft sand, which meant the enemy's shells buried themselves in the ground without harming anyone. It was a source of genuine pride to him that 'the kilts have never been anywhere but well to the front', though he did recognize their impracticality in the desert heat when 'one poor chap fell down dead on the spot from sun-stroke.' He gave an excellent account of the Battle of Tel-el-Kebir in September 1882:

It was four o'clock when an order was issued that parade was to take place at five, in 'fighting order', 70 rounds of ammunition carried, and water-bottles filled with tea... tents were to be struck at 6.15, packed and taken with such baggage as we possessed to the nearest point of the railway: the Brigade to fall in at 7 on the desert beyond the railway, and make a night march on Tel-el-Kebir: the enemy's position would be approached to within 200 yards, when the whole line would break into a cheer, the pipes commence playing, and the enemy's earthworks were to be taken at a rush...

What really impressed this unnamed warrior (from the context, it must be Lt R. S. Hunter-Blair, the only Old Fettesian in the Gordon Highlanders to serve at Tel-el-Kebir, though not the only one at the battle as Capt G. R. Cavaye also fought there with the Camerons) was that this plan was followed to the letter – and actually worked. Given that military cliché has it that elaborate planning never survives contact with the enemy, this is pretty impressive. The British troops advanced across the desert in perfect silence, wondering if, in the pitch darkness, they had 'mistaken their way':

About a quarter to five, I noticed the ground seemed to be gradually rising as we advanced. A minute or two later three or four shots fired apparently about four hundred yards to our front in rapid succession, removed all doubts as to our whereabouts: without halting, the order was given to fix bayonets: they were hardly on, when a shell screaming high over our heads seemed to give the enemy the signal to open fire. A long line of parapet in front of us, not more than 150 yards from us, burst into a perfect blaze of fire, which was kept up steadily till we were into them. The incessant roar of rifles, the thunder of artillery, the explosions of shells, the swish and ping of bullets over our heads, all combined to make the most fearful uproar imaginable, and of course hearing any word of command or bugle was out of the question. But none was needed, a deafening cheer, a thousand times more exciting than any words could ever have been, was raised along the whole line; one rush of seventy yards or so brought us to the trenches, and the ditch and slope to the parapet were gained. The enemy stood well so far, keeping up an incessant though wildly-directed fire; but as our men poured over the parapet, using the bayonet freely, it became more than they could stand, and a general stampede took place to the second line. All this time no shot had been fired by us, and not until the second line of entrenchments was taken, was any shot fired at the now retreating enemy. It was at this time when those opposite us had been driven back that we suffered most. Very few had fallen while charging up the glacis; everything nearly went over our heads, but after the charge and when we were more or less mixed up with the men of other regiments inside the work, we observed a heavy fire being directed on us from a large redoubt some

400 yards to our left, which had not been captured. For about ten minutes this went on, and here and there men were being knocked over, while an endeavour was made to get them into some sort of formation. Very soon this redoubt was taken, and a general advance was made through the position towards where the camp lay. There was no more opposition. The whole country before us seemed covered with men, hurrying off as hard as their legs would carry them: while our horse artillery, which had come into action splendidly some minutes before, poured shrapnel into them, and further away on the right, the Bengal Lancers were galloping up in pursuit.

The attack on the trenches at Tel-el-Kebir

Arabi Pasha surrendered, thus ending the war, shortly after this, and Hunter-Blair remarked that, although his current posting, Ghezrieh Camp near Cairo, was 'a most unpleasantly dusty spot', on the bright side 'there seems to be fair shooting to be got' and he concluded with the hope that 'an occupation of a few months ought to pass pleasantly enough.' Hunter-Blair, along with other Fettesians such as Captains M'Leod and Cavaye and Lieutenants Brack-Boyd-Wilson, Findlay and Sellar, was later to serve in the Nile Campaign of 1884-5 and in the Sudan in 1885-6; many were decorated for their efforts. At Fettes, the defeat in 1886 of the Islamic forces which killed the national hero

General Gordon was hymned in such a way as to merge the optimistic vision of a peaceful, industrious Empire with a rather more bloodthirsty craving for revenge:

> Thou standest where the rushing waters meet,
> Thy white walls shining in the tropic sun,
> And heavy lie thy shadows on the sand
> That reaches out around thee; in the east
> Are seen the distance skyward-towering heights.
> Thou art at peace at last; the bloody wars
> So often waged amidst thy dreary wastes
> Are past for aye; thou shalt not see again
> The tide of battle surge around thy gates;
> The glitter of the sun strikes not today
> The barbarous speare and roughly-shapen shield.
> But in thy streets is heard the busy hum
> Of those who barter up and down the world.
> Yet 'midst of these scenes of peace, there lies a spot,
> Beneath the palm-trees by the river's brink,
> Which we do gaze on with a misty eye,
> For there he died, a soldier undismayed;
> Died like a hero – desolate – alone.
> 'Remember Gordon' do these rivers cry?
> Yea, we remember; for the goal is won,
> The vengeance is complete, for which we looked
> So many years. And now hicks Pasha's host,
> Metemmeh's raid with murder foul and black,
> At last revenged. And though we were too late
> To save our hero – only two short days –
> The name of Gordon is not lost as yet;
> The greatest Christian general of the age
> Shall be remembered by all British hearts
> With love and pride; and if he died alone,
> Yet Death hath placed her laurels on his brow.
> Khartoum and Gordon – Oh, thou cruel Soudan,
> What misery thy hell-born hosts have given,
> What shame have put upon the British Arms –
> But vengeance is complete, so may his shade
> At last find rest from struggle, toil, and war! [40]

Short notes added to the school's Army List mentioned everyone who had seen combat,[41] though none was to send such remarkably detailed news of his activities as Hunter-Blair had done. Charles Findlay, 'an athletic fellow, popular at the school'[42] was later to die fighting the Dervishes at the Battle of Atbara in Kitchener's final conquest of the Sudan. A bestselling history of the campaign recorded his death:

…he had been married but a month or two before, and the widowed bride was not eighteen. He was a man of a singularly simple, sincere, and winning nature, and the whole force lamented his loss. Probably his great height – for he stood near 6 feet 6 inches – had attracted attack besides his daring: he was one of the first, some said the first, to get over the stockade, and had killed two of the enemy with his sword before he dropped.[43]

The victors celebrate after the Battle of Atbara, as shown in the Graphic

The *Fettesian* was pleased to record that Queen Victoria had taken a personal interest in Findlay's widow, giving her child – unborn at the time of Atbara – a baptismal gift and offering to stand as godmother.[44]

Another officer who fought at Atbara, 'frank, fearless and kind-hearted' Duncan 'Daddy' M'Leod, came to visit his old school after the campaign; 'he was as keen to talk over old times as he was reluctant to talk about himself or the events which led to his early promotion.'[45]

Remembered with equal affection by schoolmates and soldiers for 'his kindly disposition, as much as for his pluck and manliness', M'Leod was to die, not in war, but in the notorious Thirsk railway crash of 1892. A signaller, distraught over the death of his child the previous day but forced to work despite his lack of sleep, accidentally routed the London to Edinburgh express into the path of a goods train, killing M'Leod and nine others. A subsequent court case established the contributory negligence of the railway company, which was presumably of little comfort to the relatives of the casualties but did at least establish a precedent for the future. A poem about M'Leod was quoted in the *Fettesian* Christmas number in 1892:

> *He braved the battle's roar;*
> *He stood the foe before;*
> *He nobly fault and bled.*
> *In sultry eastern climes*
> *Death passed him many times,*
> *Yet never touched his head.*

> *At soldier good and true!*
> *Whene'er the bugle blew,*
> *MacLeod was at his post.*
> *Pluck was his guiding star,*
> *He'd fain have died in war,*
> *Facing a hostile host.*

> *It was not thus to be;*
> *This was not Fate's decree;*
> *Fate willed another death.*
> *A train speeds through the gloom;*
> *A dash! - a crash! - his doom!*
> *He's drawn his latest breath.*[46]

Written by 'H.E.G.', (not an Old Fettesian, it seems) this originally appeared in the *Weekly Scotsman*, an indication of how popular M'leod was in Scottish society. (By a tragic coincidence, another OF, Lt Eric Salvesen, was one of over 200 Royal Scots killed in the Gretna train disaster of 22 May 1915.) Other imperial announcements in that issue of the *Fettesian* included the death from typhoid at Poona on 15 August of Lt Henry Simson, 'an exceedingly smart officer' who had been a member of the school cricket XI. A.G.H. Carruthers, serving in China, had 'evidently lost none of his old skill and cunning' on the pitch, helping Shanghai defeat Hong Kong in the interport cricket match – an event overshadowed by tragedy when the returning Hong Kong players were lost with the SS *Bokhara*, which sank in a typhoon. On 14 November at Rangoon, Carruthers' brother Robert, an officer in the Bengal Lancers seconded to the Burmese Military Police, married Miss Florence Wintle; he would later captain the Military Police polo team and the Rangoon, all-Burma and Police cricket teams against a visiting side from Ceylon, and was an accomplished practitioner of the equestrian art of tent-pegging, winning championships in Rangoon and Mandalay. On December 12, Lt Cecil Mitchell-Innes, stationed in Pachmari, became a proud father (he later became Chief Constable of Lincolnshire). Imperial life was undoubtedly crowded for OFs.

Fettesians sent their alma mater tales of life, both military and civilian, elsewhere in Africa; Alexander Miller Graham wrote from Mashonaland describing the progress of the British expedition there, which was intended to overawe the locals in the name of the Queen and add to her dominions. He was full of excitement at their progress through the 'splendid high country', and how rumours that an impi of Lobengula, King of the Matabele, was abroad led to the formation of a laager of well-armed wagons.[47]

A subsequent letter on the 'Matabele Difficulty', however, had a more harsh tone; he explained that the British South Africa Company had been forced to take action against some of Lobengula's men after they 'actually had the audacity to pursue Mashonas into Fort Victoria, killing some of them in the main street. Of course this was too much for the whites, and they promptly turned out and shot some thirty of the marauders.'[48]

Lobengula was, unsurprisingly, incensed at this, and Graham's letter concluded that peace in the region would depend on driving the irritable monarch across the Zambezi; 'many good men will be killed before that is accomplished.' Lobengula was defeated, partly through the use of Maxim guns, in the First Matabele War. An 'account of an Old Fettesian's adventures', taken from a South African newspaper, appeared in the *Fettesian* in March 1894. It described how Graham, 'a hearty and well-connected Edinburgh lad', was seeing a lot of the 'adventurous side of South African life.' After service in the Pioneer Corps in Mashonaland, he was put in charge of the Labour and Transport Department of the British South Africa Company. The bulk of the report, however, was taken up with an account of a hunting expedition:

They spent three weeks at Zumbo, shooting plenty of hippos, and having some good days with the buffalo in the fly; but it was on their return journey that their greatest luck befell them. They came across six white rhinos. Eyre shot a mother, while Coryndon and Graham shot a babe. Next morning they also caught another little one alive. They tried very hard to keep it in life with a view of bringing a £500 curio into Salisbury. They had no milk, however, and the interesting animal would not take the grass they tried to feed with. Although they tried to lead it on their journey back to Mashonaland, and did their best for it, they only kept it alive for seven days. The mother was stuffed and sent to the Chicago Exhibition, where she created a big sensation. Mr. Graham also shot an enormous lioness one night at eight feet distance with a Martini-Henry bullet, whilst under his trading wagon. He carries one of the big teeth on his watch-chain as a trophy. Mr. Graham is a man we shall hear more of.[49]

Sadly, this was all too true. Graham, who became the Native Commissioner at Inyati in Matabeleland, was one of a group of whites besieged and subsequently massacred in the native uprising of 1896.[50]

The *Scotsman* said that he had 'met a soldier's death' with his colleagues; 'they might probably have saved themselves by seeking refuge in Bulawayo, but they no doubt scorned to desert the district which was placed in their charge.'[51]

Jim Normand, another Old Fettesian, was one of the settlers who helped suppress the natives. This uprising was partly encouraged by tales among the tribesmen of a mystical, messianic leader, and was the inspiration for Buchan's *Prester John*. Similarly, N.A. Wilson, 'a great favourite with all who knew him at home or abroad', was to die in a mutiny by Sudanese mercenary soldiers in Uganda the following year.[52]

The Sudanese had initially rebelled out of discontent about pay, but seem to have developed ideas of creating an Islamic state in Uganda. Along with a Major Thruston, Wilson was 'treacherously' seized by supposedly loyal troops and imprisoned in Lubwa's Fort. After a fierce firefight with the remaining Europeans and Sikhs, some of the mutineers were on the brink of surrender, but the officers, Bilal, Mabruk and Rehan, decided to stiffen their resolve by executing the British prisoners.

Thruston apparently said contemptuously, 'If you are going to shoot me, do so at once, but I warn you that many of my countrymen will come up, and that you will have cause to regret it.' He and Wilson were promptly shot, as was another British soldier called Scott who had attempted to escape. This ensured that there would be no turning back by soldiers who were having second thoughts about their rebellion, which was eventually crushed by a British expedition, one of whose officers was another Old Fettesian, Capt W.M. Southey of the 27th Bombay Infantry. Wilson was buried with the others in the churchyard of the Church Missionary Society on Namirembe Hill in Kampala.[53]

The assault on Lubwa's Fort, Uganda, as depicted in With MacDonald in Africa

In West Africa, several Old Fettesians ran similar risks as the Empire's bounds went wider yet. In 1900, 24 British officers and 700 locally-recruited troops entered Northern Nigeria, warned by Sultan Attahiru that he would 'never agree with you... Between us and you there are no dealings, except as between Moslems and Unbelievers – War.' The British imposed client rulers and, faced with a charge by thousands of Africans, machine-gunned them to traditional effect. They then held a grand ceremony at which the populace was assured that their customs and religion would be respected so long as they obeyed the laws of Queen Victoria. Old Fettesian Featherston Cargill, who had been in Africa since

1895 and taken part in a variety of expeditions attempting to impose the imperial order, became the British Resident at Kano. Unfortunately, British actions had simply inflamed religious and patriotic feeling, and with Attihiru still at large Cargill wrote to his superiors in a panic warning of a jihad.[54]

Matters became worse when another local leader announced that he was the new Mahdi, leading a holy war against the infidels. A small British force suffered an embarrassing reverse at Burmi before their superior firepower finally crushed the revolt; the decapitated heads of the defeated leaders were photographed for the edification of other would-be opponents of the spread of civilisation. Radical Islam, and of course resentment at the British occupation, remained a problem for administrators for decades. Cargill attempted to reorganise Kano, replacing assorted Islamic forms of taxation with a uniform poll tax and imposing a system whereby an Emir was the sole native authority and his chiefs were regional representatives. He attempted to bring Sharia law into line with British legal norms and to dissuade the local nobility to dismantle their elaborate institutions of slavery, befriending a number of ex-slaves. Although he was awarded the CMG in 1905, his incessant reforms irritated both his bosses in London and the local aristocracy, as well as introducing unwanted instability into the lives of the peasantry with his attempts at economic innovation. He retired to Britain as early as 1909, and is not widely regarded by historians as a success – a recent study of early British colonial policy in Northern Nigeria was bluntly titled *Cargill's Mistakes*.

The British Army was becoming more expert in fighting Africans and its losses in battle, especially with the introduction of the machine-gun, were comparatively small. African resistance and rebellion, bloody and terrifying for civilians caught up in it though it was, ultimately failed within a year or so, crushed with the swift ferocity the Army had learned through the centuries. For Fettes, the casualties seem to have reached double figures just before the beginning of the Boer War, and the suggestion that a memorial be set up was finally acted upon. The 'Memorial Brass' was announced in the *Fettesian* in November 1898. It was to be erected in the school chapel to honour those 'killed while in the Imperial Service' – Blaikie of Isandlhlwana, Findlay of Atbara, MacLean of the North-West Frontier, Graham of Matabeleland, and Wilson of Uganda – though not the dozen or more victims of accident or disease ('The decision as to whether a name is to be inscribed or not, to be vested in the Headmaster, without appeal'). Subscriptions of up to ten shillings were invited, the cost being estimated at £30. C.J.N. Fleming, the treasurer of the appeal, was an OF and Scottish rugby international who returned to the school as a master.[55]

Other names would be added – sooner, and in greater numbers, than anticipated, for the Boer War was about to break out.

The Anglo-Boer War

Not all Fettesians went out into the world with formal training, jobs in the family firm or estate, academia or military service ahead of them; some really did head off into the Empire in the hope of making a fortune from scratch, and for this sort of adventurer South Africa was, quite literally, a gold-mine. An anonymous OF wrote to the school in 1896 to describe how he had turned up in Johannesburg to 'try my luck.' He was taken on by J. Hubert Davies, an electrical engineering firm servicing the mines, as a workman on £4 per week, with the promise of promotion after a month if he proved he was 'worth anything'. £4, he wrote, was quite low in comparison with the £7 earned by foremen and skilled technicians, but he could easily live on it, spending about £10 in a month on his living expenses and trying to save as much as possible. On pay-day, the first Saturday of the month, every man in the place went 'into town on the spree' and thought nothing of spending £10 in an evening; other surplus cash was spent in stock exchange dabbling. He had some useful advice for his successors:

There is no doubt that this is a splendid place for any fellow who has had a mechanical training, and is prepared to start low down and work hard. It certainly is hard work, but I think one is certain to get on by sticking to it… There are an enormous number who come here with a gentleman's education and expect to drop at once into a good job. But they soon find their mistake. I must own that I had thoughts of finding a better job than I have present, but I soon found that it was necessary to start the bottom, and am now not at all sorry for it.[56]

Lurking behind this vision of streets paved with gold were simmering tensions which would erupt into the Boer War. In contrast with the wars against black Africans, generally less well-equipped than the British, the South African or Boer War was not settled quickly. Defeating them was a huge enterprise; the school magazine published specific lists of old boys serving there, running to around 80 names in total, a remarkable number for a school which had only reached a population of 200 in 1890. Tensions with the Dutch-speaking Boers or Afrikaners had been building for some time; there had been a brief and, for Britain, embarrassing war in 1880-1. In 1888, 'J.G.B.S.' wrote to the school to report that the King of Swaziland cracked open the champagne 'after ascertaining we were not Dutch' and that in the mining town of Barberton there had been 'a very fair prospect of an anti-Dutch riot'.[57]

Serious fighting finally broke out in 1899, but both British and Boers had been spoiling for a fight for several years in squabbles over mineral rights, the independence of the Afrikaner Republics and the grievances of English-speaking 'Uitlanders' in Dutch-speaking territory. There were several provocative incidents, most notoriously the raid by the Matabeleland Administrator Dr Jameson in 1895-6, in which two old Fettesians, 'Pat' Normand and Sydney Bowden, participated.[58]

Normand, who had been prevented by a knee injury from joining the British Army, had gone to South Africa in the hope of becoming a gold-miner, and walked 300 miles from Mafeking to Bulawayo, where his brother Jim worked. Joining the Matabele Mounted Police, he was recruited by the British South Africa Chartered Company as a Corporal in 'C' Company for the raid, but was captured along with his comrades. Unable to pay the fines required by the Boers for their release, Normand and Bowden were deported back to Britain.[59]

Ironically, it was probably the denuding of the area of troops by the raid that permitted the uprising which killed the unfortunate Graham (whom Jameson had personally appointed) to spread out of control. After several years of agitation, the affronted Boers issued an ultimatum for British forces to back off in the autumn of 1899. This was greeted with hoots of derision in the British press, as the army, which had seen the trouble brewing, already had thousands of troops and much modern equipment either in or en route to South Africa in readiness to crush these strange Old Testament figures. Fettesians were there from the outset, and within a few months of the outbreak of war the school was receiving the doleful news that several had already been killed, names to be added to Blaikie, Findlay, Maclean, Graham and Wilson on the memorial.[60]

As one of the most recent histories of the war argues, the British officers who sailed south in 1899 were supremely confident in the reforms and experience of the army that 'if ever a war looked as if it was going to be over by Christmas, it was this one.' [61]

The senior military commentator Henry Spenser Wilkinson proudly announced that 'the Army was never in better condition either as regards the zeal and skill of its officers from the highest to the lowest, the training and discipline of the men, or the organisation of all the branches of the service.'[62]

The British also genuinely believed that they were in the right, and that this was a war of principle for fair governance in South Africa, something which only they could bring. This message had been trumpeted in the loyal dominions of Canada, Australia and New Zealand, and they supplied volunteers to add to those flocking to the colours at home. The British were armed with modern weapons and had developed sophisticated supply techniques. Unfortunately for them, the Boers had been busy making preparations too, stocking up with modern weapons of their own including French artillery and German rifles. They made use of their knowledge of the countryside and avoided taking part in too many pitched battles, where the superior British numbers would count against them. General Kitchener expressed the general disapproval felt by the high command for the new enemy's tactics in a letter, complaining that 'the Boers are not like the Sudanese who stood up to a fair fight. They are always running away on their little ponies.'[63]

The Boers were presumably aware that the Sudanese at Omdurman had been massacred by machine-guns and were not inclined to share this experience of 'fair fight.' Although less disciplined than the British, they showed great initiative in exploiting their enemy's weaknesses, and were aided by foreign volunteers from Holland, Germany, France, Ireland, America and Russia, most of whom had professional military experience – in the case of the Irish, often with the British Army. This was not going to be over by Christmas.

A letter to his father from Pat Normand, serving with the Imperial Light Horse – a force which had been organised in a mere three weeks, so thick on the ground were suitable troopers in the southern Africa of the day – gave some indication of how difficult the war was going to be. He made light of his wound received at Elandslaagte, and dismissed the heavy casualty list from the battle by saying that 'although it appears heavy, still we taught the Boers a good lesson, and showed them that British soldiers could face any hail of bullets.'[64]

His concluding thought was that 'if there is a big engagement, I expect it will finish the war… the soldiers are all in excellent spirits, and I am sure they will give the Boers a good licking.' As the rest of his letter shows, he must have been aware that this could be interpreted as rather optimistic, given the facts, which as he admitted were that a quarter of his unit were dead or wounded, that the Boers had fought to the end, having to be bayoneted by the Gordons and Manchesters (regiments he was too modest to admit that his colonial rough-riders rescued from defeat) and that, in the meantime, the British had been forced to evacuate Dundee. At the same battle, another Old Fettesian, Capt Matthew Meiklejohn, 'received three bullets through his upper right arm, one through his right forearm, one through the left thigh, two through his helmet, a wound in the neck, one of his fingers blown away, and his sword and his scabbard were shot to pieces.'[65]

A few months later, the *Fettesian* began with an article headed 'Our First Victoria Cross':

Just as we are going to press we learn from the London Gazette *that the Queen has been pleased to confer the decoration of the Victoria Cross for conspicuous bravery in South Africa on Captain Matthew Fontaine Murray Meiklejohn, Gordon Highlanders. Captain Meiklejohn was recommended for rallying the men after losing their leaders and wavering, and leading them against the enemy's position, where he fell desperately wounded in four places, at the battle of Elandslaagte last October. Subsequently he had his right arm amputated. We may well be proud of Captain Meiklejohn, who has been the first Old Fettesian to gain the Victoria Cross, and we hope he will be but the first of many who will gain this distinction, and whose names will ever be held in high honour at Fettes.*[66]

The aftermath of the Battle of Elandslaagte, at which Capt Matthew Meiklejohn
won the first Fettes VC

That month's rhyming editorial was optimistic:

> *The war in the Transvaal is nearing its close,*
> *Where Roberts and Powell have settled our foes,*
> *So there's almost no news to report from the front,*
> *Where the A.M.B. bravely is bearing the brunt,*
> *Save that several O.Fs have been winning a name*
> *By rising a step on the ladder of fame.*
> *But though in the Transvaal the war's nearly done,*
> *In China we feel sure it has only begun;*
> *Still, several O.Fs have already gone out,*
> *And we hope they will soon put the Boxers to rout.*[67]

The 1900 'Vive-la' shared this optimism, reflecting the (premature) hopes of imminent victory which followed the relief of Mafeking:

> *In Mafeking's honour we scored a whole holiday,*
> *And shared their relief from hard work by a jolly day:*
> *And we quite hoped another would come for Pretoria,*
> *But only shared there in the* Honor et Gloria.
>
> *With our cheers let us all make the old Gym. resound*
> *For O.Fs who are fighting on Krueger-Steyn ground;*
> *And now that things there are beginning to shake down,*
> *May they help the New Company 'Kart'Oom to Cape Town.'*[68]

It is worth noting that sporting heroes occupied a much larger section of the 'Vive-la' than military victory – David 'Darkie' Bedell-Sivright, who was to be one of the greatest Scottish sportsmen of the age, was mentioned three times for his 'footer' exploits for Fettes, Scotland and his university. Elandslaagte had been a hard victory for the British, and it was followed by several humiliations known as 'Black Week' in December 1899. First, General Gatacre was defeated at Stormberg, partly through his over-ambitious idea of repeating the Tel-el-Kebir night march over much more complex and hilly terrain. Then Lord Methuen attempted to march to Kimberley, taking the entrenched Boer positions on Magersfontein Kop with the same method, adding the more traditional elements of an artillery bombardment followed by a Highlander charge. Unfortunately, the Boers were not on the Kop, but at the bottom of it in trenches, and the shelling only wounded three of them, so the dawn probing by the Highlanders was met with furious resistance which inflicted heavy casualties and forced the British to retreat. The British suffered almost a thousand casualties, the Boers less than a third of that, and the leading units of the Highland Brigade lost 60 per cent of their officers.[69]

These included two Old Fettesians, J. Rutherford Clark of the Seaforth Highlanders, an experienced officer who had been with the regiment since 1882, and W.B. King of the Argyll and Sutherland Highlanders, who had not seen active service before. D.B. Moñypenny of the Seaforths survived Magersfontein only to die as a result of wounds received at Paardeberg in February the following year. He had been a keen sportsman, 'one of the finest all-round athletes ever produced by the School', winning the prized Challenge Clock for running, captaining various teams and, just after leaving the school in 1898, playing rugby for Scotland. He was, therefore, known to most of the boys still at the school, and the *Fettesian* spoke of him as 'one of the very best.'[70]

It subsequently carried a poem, 'To D.B.M.' which encapsulates the attitudes of the time:

> *And art thou sped, light-hearted comrade, thou*
> *Our schoolboy hero one brief year ago?*
> *Thy country craved thy strength, and thou didst go*
> *To fight her battle, should thine hour allow.*
> *Already hadst thou seen stern fights enow:*
> *We marveled at thy prowess, thews, and speed;*
> *Thou wast not as thy fellows, and the meed*
> *Of larger worth seemed destined for thy brow.*
> *Thou hast not failed us: in the roll of fame*
> *Among the elect there is nor first nor last;*
> *Who nobly does, does best in small or great:*
> *And when the final call to duty came,*
> *And thy young life was on the waters cast,*
> *Well didst thou strive, we know, and take thy fate.*[71]

Slightly more cheerful news came with the Relief of Ladysmith, during which Normand was again wounded whilst standing up to point out enemy positions to his Commanding Officer. He was to win the DSO twice (the second was cancelled on the grounds that it could only be

95

won once) and receive three mentions in despatches. His home country would honour him by making him a Burgess and Freeman of the Burgh of Dysart. At Fettes, when the news about Ladysmith came through, the Headmaster granted a half-holiday and the boys made merry; the money for medals at the school sports went to sponsor a Fettes bed in a front-line hospital. Young patriots bombarded the school magazine with poetry so jingoistic even the *Daily Mail* might have been alarmed. Several sub-Kipling efforts appeared, such as this one, entitled 'Tommy on the War':

> *We have lately called on Steyn*
> *In his home in Bloemfontein:*
> *But he'd gone, vamoosed, with all his wrongs to Reitz;*
> *For he'd bolted like a bullet,*
> *With a biltong in his gullet,*
> *And his heart a-flopping down among his lights.*[72]

This appeared on the same page as a letter from an actual soldier who described life on board one of the troopships – where there were seven Fettesians, all from the same house, Glencorse – in tones so measured as to render the experience rather boring. It mostly revolved around the meticulous arrangements for looking after the horses. It was followed by another, even worse, poem about naval guns and, 25 pages later, a brief announcement to the effect that David Rew had been killed in action. Further information came through later from one of the other Fettesians in his unit, the 23rd Imperial Yeomanry; the Boers had attacked them at dawn, and when Rew's Colt machine-gun jammed he was killed trying to fix it. Another Fettesian in this engagement, C.B.C. Storey, 'was splattered all over the face with bits of lead… how his sight has been spared to him is nothing short of a miracle.' The British got their heavier weapons working and the Boers 'funked it and fled, leaving seventeen dead' – something of a Pyrrhic victory since 'I was appalled to find that we had lost twenty-five killed and four wounded.'[73]

These details appeared in an edition of the magazine with reports of two more Imperial Yeomanry Old Fettesians dead in South Africa: George Frederick Shaw ('a promising football player') and 'Ben' Grieg, remembered as 'singularly massive and powerful'. G.L. Greene of the Madras Survey Department, it was announced, had also died of cholera in India. In November 1900 the *Fettesian* editorialized, with cautious flippancy:

...it is extremely gratifying to find that Fettes has not been behindhand in doing her best for the Empire. Not only is the School well represented in the regular army, but when the call came, many O.Fs volunteered. This enthusiasm extends to present Fettesians as well; for when some 'gentlemen in khaki' dined in hall before starting for the front, the cheering and singing were enthusiastic and inspiriting. These gentlemen showed themselves true not only to their country, but to the traditions of the School as well – by asking for a half-holiday... Our masters, too, are keen patriots. Some, however, are not so keen on the War, for they find that the Army Class and accordingly their work have increased alarmingly.[74]

As the last deaths were reported to the school, it was noted with pride that Lt William Thomson of the Royal Munster Fusiliers, a keen cricketer, had been mentioned in Lord Kitchener's final despatches.

Remembering and Forgetting

In December 1900, the school magazine announced that work was to commence on the memorial, and named those who were to appear on it. By this stage, Lt Douglas Oliver of the 2nd Battalion, Norfolk Regiment, had died at Myistroom on 27 August 1900, of wounds received in action two days previously. Four months later came the news that another old boy was dead; Bernard Armstrong Hebeler, killed at Hartebeestfontein on 18 February 1901. He had sailed to South Africa at his own expense, and had been 'conspicuous for his gallant behaviour', carrying a wounded comrade to safety under fire and carrying on fighting, despite a leg wound, until he was shot through the head. His Captain wrote that 'there was no better or braver soldier in the whole regiment' and a fellow-trooper added that he 'met his death, where he always was, right in the very front.'[75]

A small plaque, depicting one soldier cradling another, was put up in the school, but as it did not have a name on it a workman put it in storage during refurbishment and it has only just been rediscovered.

Hebeler's would be the final name on the memorial, but it can reasonably be argued that at least four others ought to be on it (had there been room on it, which there is not). G.G. Smith, of the Natal Volunteer Ambulance Corps, was killed at Spion Kop trying to bring water to the wounded, 'struck by a shell and literally smashed to pieces.'[76]

Oddly, despite a letter to the school saying that his commanding officer believed he deserved the VC, he does not appear on the war memorial in the chapel. Nor does George Coulson, who 'died of malarial fever contracted in service in South Africa'[77]

nor Claude Auldjo Jamieson, whose his horse, shot by the Boers, fell on him; badly injured, he returned to Scotland to die in September 1902.[78]

Neil James MacVean, a teacher and field sports enthusiast, had joined the Imperial Yeomanry and died on Christmas Day 1902 in Pretoria of enteric fever, probably the same illness that carried off another OF, George Shaw, whilst William Smith died of typhoid at Kimberley at around the same time: the war had fanned epidemics among the troops – not to mention amongst Boers civilians in the concentration camps. The memorial also fails to mention others who were dying elsewhere in the Empire. Just after the Boer War, Bengal Lancers John Nairne, Durrant Steuart and John Lindesay Stewart died of enteric fever in various parts of India, as did the gallant Lt William Thomson. Accident continued to carry off Fettesians in South Africa and elsewhere; Alfred Valentine Pulford was struck by lightning at Pietermaritzburg in January 1904, and on Christmas Day 1907, Capt Hugh Stanton Craig drowned, with his wife Nell, in a boating accident near Maraisburg.[79]

Capt George Rothney Lamb of the Royal Artillery was killed by a fall from his horse on Salisbury Plain. It may be that, since that illness could carry off boys in the school itself – Guy Hamilton Ziegler, aged sixteen, and John Kerr Anderson, aged eighteen, died within a week of each other in 1898 – it may not have 'counted' to the Victorians as anything other than an occupational hazard of life itself. That is not to say that the school was blasé about it. In 1887 Fettes had been quick to expel a boy from the West Indies who was believed to have leprosy; when he sued for breach of contract, the judge, whilst accepting that leprosy might not be contagious, found in the school's favour, noting that the existence of such a disease in the midst of a community of boys 'was calculated to create such terror as to impair the usefulness of the institution.'[80]

That former Fettes pupils should be found fighting wars at the beginning of the twentieth century and also of the twenty-first is probably unsurprising. That the political and cultural ramifications of these wars should have such a great deal in common is perhaps a little less so. The Anglo-Boer War, as it now tends to be called, has a number of extraordinary resonances for today's observer.[81]

98

The memorial to Bernard Hebeler, and a notice from the Victorian school which suggests that death did not only lurk on the battlefield

It split opinion violently; broadly speaking, the right, including Tory government ministers and MPs, plus the rowdiest newspapers such as the *Daily Mail*, and the jingoistic parts of all social classes, was in favour of it. Their aggressive nationalism was rather too much even for that ardent imperialist Rudyard Kipling, who sneered at members of the public 'killing Kruger with your mouth', something the (luckily anonymous) *Fettesian* poets were all to keen to do. There was a distasteful sense that in this quarter, any criticism of the war was tantamount to national betrayal – one certainly gets it from one of the schoolboy bards who fulminated against Lord Bryce, one of the most gifted statesmen of his generation, for daring to suggest a compromise. The left, that is, part of the Liberal Party and the socialism movement, was less gung-ho, and was assailed as 'pro-Boer' by jingoists, although in fact they were also keen to see Britain win so long as victory was cleanly won and magnanimously imposed. One such was one of the first Old Fettesians to become a Member of Parliament, John Deans Hope, who was elected to Westminster in 1900 to represent West Fife. Hope's membership of various radical committees is what has identified him to historians as a 'pro-Boer' – he made no speeches in the House in almost a quarter of a century and asked only nine questions, so cannot be said to have made a great impact for the cause. Irish nationalists, by contrast, openly rejoiced at England's failures and many went to fight for the Boers. Britain's European neighbours, who had so slavishly paid obeisance at Queen Victoria's Diamond Jubilee in 1897 – *Le Figaro* going so far as to say that Britain had surpassed

Rome[82] – were uniformly hostile, and, as previously noted, supplied the Boers with weapons and volunteers. In distant Haiti, where Vernon Hesketh-Prichard was exploring at the time of the war, the Francophone press summoned up the spirit of one of Britain's old foes:

Napoleon, risen from his tomb at the Invalides, addresses his old soldiers: The English, the eternal enemy who conquered you — for in conquering me she conquered you — the English of Trafalgar and of Waterloo, recoil before the energy of a little people of Africa. The mercenaries of the Old Queen draw back, and are broken; the officers fall to save the honour of the flag that these mercenaries have not the heart to defend; Albion fights no longer… Albion dies… [83]

Admittedly, the Haitians were not desperately familiar with the exact circumstances of the war; one of their (many) generals hoped the Boers would win because 'Boers were negroes persecuted by the British.' Major Barnes, serving in China with the international forces fighting the Boxer rebellion, was irritated by a German's views on the subject:

As we had halted at the same time we got into conversation with one of the officers, who spoke perfect English, and in due time asked him if there was any news. His answer was startling:
    'Yes; the Boers have retaken Pretoria.'
    This struck me as being a somewhat needless falsehood, so I went one better;
    'Oh, is that all? We have later news than that. The Chinese have retaken Peking.' [84]

As the war progressed with pointless British losses and evidence of atrocities against civilians, more criticisms emerged at home, of which the soldiers in the field were undoubtedly aware. They cannot have avoided the feeling that there were elements at home who did not actually want them to win, although this was unfair. Those sympathetic to the troops, by contrast, lambasted the government for not supplying them well enough. Whatever the faults of the Boers – a form of racialism more virulent than anything the British could devise being one – both their tenacity in fighting and their real suffering in the concentration camps were trumpeted by the world's press. Even members of the government had their doubts, Arthur Balfour noting to the cabinet that were he a Boer he would be reluctant to accept what the British had to offer.[85]

    The widespread view that it was not a war of principle or for civilisation, but for what lay under the earth, and thus being fought on behalf of greedy capitalists, further undermined the cause.

Another issue was the alleged faults of the British Army itself. The sheer scale of the numbers involved, of course, made it all the more likely that the public would take notice; whereas 30,000 men had gone to the Crimea and 16,000 to Egypt, 448,000 troops went to South Africa in a campaign which cost £230 million and almost 22,000 British and imperial dead.[86]

On only two occasions since the Crimean War – at Isandhlwana and the lesser-known battle of Maiwand in Afghanistan, neither of which was really typical – had British Army lost over a hundred men in a single engagement. This was happening all too frequently in South Africa, and an irritated officer wrote that the British 'did not know that bloodshed was a usual consequence of the armed collision of combatants. Hence, the outbreak of hysteria with which they received the news of our casualties.'[87]

Journalists stirred the pot further, also much to the fury of the professionals. Leo Amery's *Times History of the War in South Africa*, published in a succession of enormous volumes between 1900 and 1909, claimed that the Army was 'nothing more or less than a gigantic Dotheboys Hall.'[88]

Although harsh, judgments like these were both common and widely believed, led to public demands for further reform. These were often mixed with the faintly sinister eugenic notions of the period, especially the issue that the great British race might be in decline in its industrial cities; 'the Darwinian idea that development might move in a direction that could be conceived as backward – that humans might reel back to their primordial ancestors – posed a terrifying threat to the Victorian narrative of progress.'[89]

Hence the creation of such august bodies as the Inter-departmental Committee on Physical Deterioration in 1903, special attention being paid to Glasgow, where some of the most shockingly underfed and enfeebled recruits had emerged.

By the time the South African war finally ended in the middle of 1902, the Fettesians were no longer Victorians. They marked the old lady's passing with the cancellation of both lessons and games and an 'interminably long and depressing' memorial service in chapel. Lockhart remembered that he 'wandered aimlessly about the corridors and prep room munching biscuits and afraid to raise my voice, not so much from respect for the dead monarch as from fear lest a prefect would reprove me for making a noise.'[90]

He doubted the wisdom of enforcing the solemnity of death on small boys, who tended to be bored by it, and where their emotions were affected 'the reaction is generally mawkish and unhealthy.' This good sense tended to be the norm for the following century at Fettes, where mourning was, by and large, kept to a minimum, even after the admission of girls. An Old Fettesian, J.M. Smith of the Royal Marines Light Infantry, took part in the funeral as his regiment's colour-bearer.[91] Although it is not apparent from the *Fettesians* of the period – schoolboys not being, as a rule, privy to the discussions of a closed circle of politicians and generals – the military world was about to change again. As Corelli Barnett put it, the Boer War 'shattered the Victorian complacency of the British ruling classes, if not of British public opinion' because 'it had demonstrated the feebleness of the land forces of the British Empire before a gloating world'.[92]

War against the Boxers

This was not how it seemed to the victorious Major Barnes, based in the colony of Wei-Hai-Wei. This had been leased by the British because the Russians (and later the Japanese) had possession of nearby Port Arthur, and the United Kingdom could not afford to be left out of the informal control of China which both Europeans and Japanese considered their right and duty. Whilst there, Barnes helped lead a locally-recruited regiment against their own countrymen in the nationalist rebellions of 1900. The Boxer Rising, as it is generally known, was a violent protest against the foreign financial institutions and Christian missions which had been penetrating the Empire for decades. Seizing Peking, and declaring the Dowager Empress their figurehead leader, they besieged the legation quarter and launched attacks on foreigners and local Christians throughout North China. The British, Americans, Russians and Japanese, with support from France, Germany, Italy and Austria-Hungary, retook Peking with great slaughter and, as we have seen, looting. The official account of the punitive campaign was also written by an Old Fettesian, Frontier veteran Maj E.W.M. Norie, but Barnes's jocular account is much more entertaining. He was breezily indifferent to why he was fighting – 'Who or what was responsible I do not consider it within my province to inquire, or even to conjecture' – but was proud to note that one of his comrades had struck 'the first blow of a long series which China has since been dealt, to show her that the Western barbarian has come to stay.'[93]

Barnes's brutal candour about neither knowing nor caring why the rebellion broke out, and about the crude motives for the international effort to crush it, need to be set against his genuine feelings of horror at the 'appalling' atrocities committed by the Boxers.

Corpses there were, naturally, in large numbers, most of them in fairly advanced states of decomposition, and covered with flies. In one place we came upon an entire family, from all appearances, huddled together and almost hidden by a perfect canopy of flies. Most of them, children of tender years, had received wounds of a nature such as to put all hopes of recovery out of the question, even had the victim been a strong man, and out of which the mother, herself badly hit, was striving, in vain, to keep the swarms of noxious flies. It was a sad and gruesome sight, but there were worse, the mention even of which can serve no useful end.[94]

He did, incidentally, admit that this particular area 'had been exposed to our fire on the one hand, and the depredations of the Boxers on the other', so it is not impossible that these were the victims of British artillery – the account is not entirely clear, but it seems more likely that he was referring to enemy atrocities. He was impressed by the power of artillery – which was to be the biggest killer on the Western Front a few years later – noting on one occasion when a British shell hit a Chinese magazine:

The explosion that followed was one of the most lovely, and, at the same time, the most extraordinary, sights I have ever seen. A huge pillar of snowy whiteness rose slowly and majestically into the air, and when its summit was five or six hundred feet above the earth, it slowly opened out like a vast sunshade, and after hanging in the air for ten minutes or so, slowly dissolved. I have since seen summer clouds of similar appearance, but never anything to surpass this death-dealing cloud for the beauty of its pure whiteness.[95]

Like Old Fettesians a century later in Afghanistan and Iraq, after the fighting Barnes found himself responsible for law and order in part of the conquered territory; although not specifically trained for the task, the British officer was supposed to use his common sense and ideals of fair play and act as mayor and policeman when the previous (and often unworthy) holders of these posts had fled:

I found a good deal of employment in the early part of the day, owing to the large number of merchants, mostly outside the wall, who came or sent to complain of

Major Arthur Barnes (photographed whilst still a lieutenant) and some of his Chinese troops

looters. I went out with a party on several occasions, and was the means of inflicting summary punishment on a lot of palpable scoundrels who seemed to be not behaving nicely. All these merchants wanted British protection, and as this seemed to be a free issue, consisting merely of a notice to that effect in English and French, and as the petitioners were, to all appearance, quite peaceful and law-abiding, most of them got their wish.[96]

Barnes saw the defeat of the Boxers in global terms:

Without doubt the teeming millions of China were watching, with eager eyes, for the outcome of this rude arbitrament of war, either to rise in their strength and expel the 'foreign devil' once and for all, or to lie low, perhaps, for another opportunity. Nor must we forget the anxiety of Europe, either merely commercially, or for the safety of friends, not only in Peking and Tientsin, but all over China. The issue was, of a truth, far more momentous than can be gauged by the blood that was shed to bring it about.[97]

People who witnessed such a victory for the power of Western, and especially British, arms over such a vast country could hardly be expected to believe that the nation's power was waning. Fettes would continue to send its brightest and best to serve the Empire, and it is time now to look at the school itself to see what the boys themselves felt in those decades before 1914.

NOTES

[1] *Fettesian*, April 1879

[2] J. Forsyth Ingram, *The Story of an African City* (Maritzburg, Coetzer, 1898) p. 141

[3] *Fettesian*, April 1879

[4] Ibid.

[5] Saul David, *Zulu: the Heroism & Tragedy of the Zulu War of 1879* (London, Viking, 2004) p. 151. Professor David gave an excellent talk about imperial warfare to the Fettes Historical Society in 2007.

[6] Zulu warrior Mehlokazulu, quoted in ibid.

[7] Archibald Forbes, *Daily News*, quoted in ibid.

[8] *Fettesian*, July 1879

[9] Ibid., July 1878

[10] Ibid., April 1879

[11] Ibid., March 1880

[12] See the Second Anglo-Afghan War Database Project, – a treasure-trove of information about this largely-forgotten conflict

[13] Letter to the *Fettesian*, April 1881

[14] Ibid., February 1887

[15] Letter to ibid., April 1886

[16] Ibid.

[17] Ibid.

[18] *Fettesian*, November 1887

[19] *Fettesian*, November 1895

[20] Ibid.

[21] Quoted in *Fettesian*, June 1896

[22] Ibid., July 1896

[23] Ibid, March 1907, and citation, *London Gazette*, 9 November 1897

[24] Winston Churchill, *The Story of the Malakand Field Force*, (London, 1897) p.81

[25] *Fettesian*, November 1897

[26] Ibid.

[27] Ibid., December 1882

[28] Ibid., March 1899

[29] Ibid., November 1895

[30] Ibid., July 1896

[31] Ibid., December 1879

[32] Lockhart, (1936) p. 108

[33] Lockhart (1932) p. 13

[34] Clement Semmler, 'Ogilvie, William Henry (Will) (1869 - 1963)', *Australian Dictionary of Biography*, Volume 11, (Melbourne, MUP, 1988) pp 70-71.

[35] *Fettesian*, July 1893

[36] Ibid., March 1895

[37] Ibid., July 1880

[38] Ibid.

[39] Ibid., December 1882

[40] Ibid., April 1899

[41] See, for instance, ibid., June 1892

[42] Ibid., June 1898

[43] G.W. Steevens, *With Kitchener to Khartum* (New York, Dodd, Mead & Co., 1911) p. 154

[44] *Fettesian*, December 1898

[45] Ibid., November 1892

[46] Ibid., December 1892

[47] Ibid., December 1890

[48] Ibid., November 1893

[49] Ibid., March 1894

[50] Howard Hensman, *A History Of Rhodesia* (Edinburgh, Blackwood, 1900) p. 83

[51] Quoted in the *Fettesian,* April 1896

[52] Ibid., December 1897

[53] See H.H. Austin, *With MacDonald in Africa* (London, Edward Arnold, 1903) pp. 42-9

[54] See Richard Gott, 'Death of a Sultan', *Guardian*, 3 November 2006

[55] *Fettesian*, November 1898

[56] Ibid., March 1896

[57] Ibid., June 1888

[58] Ibid., March 1896

[59] C. Normand, *Normand Conquests*, (Family History) p. 140

[60] *Fettesian*, November 1898

[61] Denis Judd & Keith Surridge, *the Boer War* (Palgrave Macmillan, New York, 2003) p. 55

[62] Henry Spenser Wilkinson, *Lessons of the War, being comments from week to week to the Relief of Ladysmith* (London, Constable, 1900), p. 3

[63] Quoted in Barnett, p. 340

[64] P.H. Normand, letter from Ladysmith, 27 October 1899, published *Scotsman* 21 November 1899

[65] *Fettesian*, December 1899

[66] Ibid., July 1900

[67] Ibid., July 1890

[68] Ibid., July 1890

[69] Judd & Surridge, p. 124

[70] *Fettesian*, March 1900

[71] Ibid., April 1900

[72] Ibid., June 1900

[73] Letter from G.F. Maxwell, printed in ibid., November 1900

[74] Ibid., December 1900

[75] Ibid., June 1901

[76] Ibid., April 1902

[77] Ibid., June 1901

[78] Ibid., November 1902

[79] Ibid., March 1908

[80] See Rod Edmond, *Leprosy and Empire* (Cambridge, CUP, 2006) pp. 86-9

[81] For an excellent overview of this issue, see Judd & Surridge, pp. 1-14

[82] Quoted in Morris, p. 28

[83] Hesketh-Prichard (1900) p. 229

[84] Barnes, pp. 169–70

[85] See Judd & Surridge, p. 46

[86] Ian FW Beckett, *The South African War And The Late Victorian Army* (Conference Paper, Australian Army History Unit Conference, 1999) p. 2

[87] FN Maude, *Notes on the Evolution of Infantry Tactics* (London, Wm. Clowes and Sons, 1905), p. 134.

[88] Leo Amery (ed.), *The Times History of the War in South Africa*, Vol. II (London, Sampson Low, Marston, 1900–9), p. 40.

[89] Richardson, p. 42

[90] Lockhart (1936) p. 299

[91] *Fettesian*, March 1901

[92] Barnett, p. 353

[93] Barnes, pp. 1–2

[94] Ibid., p. 88

[95] Ibid., p. 36

[96] Ibid., p. 99

[97] Ibid., p. 82

Chapter Four

'A good beginning for a permanent tradition'

The Boys of Fettes and the Study of War, 1870–1914

Current Affairs

There is no doubt that Fettes tried to do its best to keep boys informed about the great events of the world around them. Speakers with magic lantern slide-projectors, such as Captain Reade, who spoke to the boys about the joys of the Royal Navy in November 1895, were regular and popular additions to the curriculum. A month later, Professor Prothero spoke on Imperial Federation, then a hotly-debated topic as the increasing wealth of, and Britain's dependence on, the white dominions became more apparent:

Great Britain must therefore either sever herself completely from her Colonies, or else allow them a share in controlling the foreign policy of the Empire, and also in bearing the burden of maintaining the forces necessary to defend its coasts and commerce. If we choose the latter course we may effect it by admitting a minister from each of our great Colonies into our Cabinet for foreign affairs. If, on the contrary, we separate ourselves from our Colonies or allow them to separate from us, we shall be isolated in time of war, and liable in a moment to be starved out; so Great Britain will soon become a second- or third-class power. The lecturer closed with a passionate appeal to our patriotism, and the great future which lies before the Anglo-Saxon race, if they only combine and seize their opportunities now.[1]

A lecture to the pupils in February 1896 by a Mr H.V. Peatling was somewhat chaotic due to a missing magic lantern, but the message was clear. The Boers were singularly ungrateful, having allowed the British to defeat the Zulus for them and then declared independence. With 'considerable feeling' Mr. Peatling made clear his sympathies with Dr. Jameson and the Uitlanders, and ended with 'an appeal to our patriotism, to which all responded most heartily.'[2]

In the field of ecology, in 1899 a Mr F.T. Bullen gave a talk to the school on 'Whales and Whale-Fishing', a detailed explanation of this now-unfashionable pursuit in which he had taken part as a crewman on an American whaler. The lecturer was very popular, 'electrifying his audience by an imitation of the weird cry which signifies that the man in the crow's nest has cited a while, and graphically describing the successive operations of pursuit, capture, and bringing his carcass to the ship' not to mention 'describing the animal's death struggles.' In addition, 'he touched upon the great courage of whales, particularly of a cow-whale, which did not move while the blows of her captors were being rained upon her, since she feared to betray the presence of her calf beneath her sheltering fin.'[3]

This was all very well, but it was not quite military enough for the real enthusiasts. In the early days of Fettes, those boys who were impatient to go to war and whose aggression was not vented on the sports fields expressed themselves unofficially through the improvisation of firearms out of pieces of piping, the most impressive being William Oliver's 'twelve-inch Woolwich Infant' with which he 'used to bombard people from his study window as they were coming up from Glencorse.' In the 1870s, recalled the celebrated journalist George Campbell, 'the smell of gunpowder was strong in classrooms and passages.'[4]

The obituary of Neil MacVean, who died of fever just after the Boer War, mentioned that 'many O.F.s will remember how his face was pitted with blue marks – the result of incautiously looking down the barrel of a loaded gun.'[5]

This was obviously no substitute, fun though it was, for a more formal structure. The very first issue of the *Fettesian* carried 'an appeal to the martial spirits of Fettes' in the shape of a letter asking for a cadet corps. 'Ενθουσισμός' – the classical enthusiasms of the school extended to the very nicknames boys chose for themselves – said that he recognised there was the risk of enthusiasm dying out, but it would be worth a try, and would at any rate do something about the slouching for which the boys were constantly being told off.[6]

The cadet movement had begun in 1860, partly influenced by the Cardwell reforms, the Crimean shock, and fears of invasion by Napoleon III (which also gave Britain coastal forts known as 'Palmerston's follies'). The first independent cadet unit is regarded as having been established by social reformer Octavia Hill in Southwark, ('the making of many a lad', as she put it) and various schools soon tried to set up their own bodies. Glenalmond, after all, already had a corps, and Merchiston, the High School and the Academy (which had experimented with a drilling class in 1859) would all get one before Fettes. Requests for a cadet corps were almost a hardy perennial in the pages of the school magazine, and became even more frequent around the time of the Boer War; a correspondent at the time wrote that every one of the sons of Fettes would like to help in the national effort, but often they were rejected as Volunteers because they knew nothing of drill or the use of arms. This was somewhat disingenuous, as the Volunteers were full of OFs whose unmilitary schooling had presumably not been held against them. The writer promises that masters will not 'bear the drudgery and burden of the whole affair', doubtless because plenty of masters had said that this would be precisely what would happen.[7]

The school finally responded with an authorised statement in the magazine. The masters were, they said, worried about a decline of enthusiasm after initial interest – something which several of the pleading correspondents had indeed recognised as a potential problem – adding that this sort of thing had to be taken seriously, for 'he is no true friend to his country who plays at being a soldier'. There was also an admirable awareness on the masters' part that there was already a lot of compulsory activity at the school, so attempting to evade the problem of fluctuating interest by making everyone join might be unpopular. They also pointed out that Fettes, after some controversy over the terms of its existence, the founder's will implying something rather different from the school as it actually was, was being left alone on the condition that it was giving the best possible academic education. Anything which interfered with this might drive down attainment and attract unwanted attention. They were, in any case, waiting to see what the government would do once the South African War was over.[8]

Fettes concentrated, in the late nineteenth and early twentieth centuries, on turning out enthusiastic and conscientious young men. One OF recalled that the two cardinal virtues of the school at the time were 'heartiness' and 'respectability', and its most terrible sin 'advertising'.[9]

Bruce Lockhart recalled that at Fettes, 'for all the school's reputation for 'rugger', brawn, except in a few rare instances, was never cultivated at the expense of brain, and I know no school to which Kipling's stricture of 'muddied oafs' applied less.'[10]

A glimpse of this can be seen in the school's fascination with the activities of scientists such as OF Alan Campbell Swinton, who, whilst a schoolboy in 1879, read a description of the telephone (invented in 1877) and promptly built one to link Glencorse and Moredun Houses (he was equally promptly told to dismantle it and get back to his Latin).[11]

This attitude of intellectual curiosity and determination to do one's best was something which the government hoped to make universal throughout the system, rather than being confined to a small number of respectable Scots whose role models were their housemasters. In addition to honing their skills on the pitch and in the classroom, the boys of Fettes had been arguing about all aspects of military, foreign and other policy for years. The first school magazine reported a debate on whether or not war was necessitated by British interests, and conscription itself was discussed in October 1878. Rowlatt (a keen debater who went on to become a distinguished judge), proposing that 'compulsory military service is desirable in England' (a distressingly frequent verbal slip to which Fettesians were all too prone at this time), argued that 'at present, it was the worst men who enlisted' and that if conscription was introduced people would get used to it as part of the natural course of things. He was supported by Hornsby, who pointed to the increasing global and treaty commitments of the country, and noted the strength of the German army – the first vaguely hostile reference to the Germans in the *Fettesian*. They were vigorously opposed by Bowden, who argued that 'the riff-raff of our large towns made splendid soldiers' and that both socialism and starving families would result from national service (he later became a vicar in New Zealand). Grindlay pointed out that the whole point of compulsory service was that it was compulsory, and would therefore apply to the tender plants of Fettes as well as to the aforesaid riff-raff. The motion was defeated, as it was again in 1882 and 1886, just as it was in cabinet, but the arguments remained in circulation for decades – interestingly, long before the National Service League made this a major issue of public debate in the aftermath of the Boer War.[12]

Fettesians had a remarkable interest in these great affairs of the nation, and some of the Victorian debates were masterpieces of detail. A year after the conscription debate, and as a number of old boys were fighting there, the motion was 'that the present war with Afghanistan is unjustifiable.' It was proposed by Mr Johnson, one of the masters, who explained that it was Britain's somewhat fickle treatment of Afghanistan's

Amir, Shere Ali, which had forced him into the arms of Russia (late Victorian wars were generally, Saul David argues, fought 'to prevent other European powers from muscling into territories that Britain regarded as strategically vital' rather than for any trade advantage – Afghanistan hardly being a cornucopia of wealth for the City[13]). Mr Johnson's opponents argued patriotically – but with obvious depth of research – that whilst Mr Gladstone's government had indeed been 'blind and timid' (Fettesians tended to be, unsurprisingly, enthusiastic partisans for Mr Disraeli and Lord Salisbury), the present government was trying to rectify this, in view of the threat to India and the threat from Russia. The motion was defeated 11-3.[14]

Later that same year, the Society debated the fate of Sir Louis Cavagnari, the British Ambassador to Afghanistan, who on 3 September had been murdered along with dozens of his staff and soldiers, triggering the Second Afghan War, in which a number of Fettesians served. On 24 October 1879 the motion was 'That her Majesty's Government is not responsible for the murder of Sir L. Cavagnari and the embassy.' This was amended to substitute the words 'to blame' for 'responsible'.[15]

Liberal motions were generally defeated, though in fairness not without their opponents, as in the case of the Ireland debate of October 1880 or women's suffrage in February 1881, having to make sophisticated cases. Modern Fettesians might disagree with young Fischer's point that 'women are impulsive and excitable, wanting in the judicial faculty, and both mentally and physically unfit for a part in political life.' With a certain music-hall timing, he added 'take Miss Parnell...' – a reference to the rabidly nationalist sister of the Home Rule leader Charles Stewart Parnell, who was privately embarrassed by her – and was rewarded with cries of 'No! No!'[16]

Other Victorian debates included a critique of the Short Service system, part of Cardwell's reforms, and one on the retention of flogging in the forces – a debate which was 'singularly devoid of interest', though the motion was passed, possibly on the grounds that if they were going to get beaten, it was some comfort to Fettesians to know that adults were too.[17]

The army's increasing concern to recruit the best possible officers led, by the early twentieth century, to the establishment of the commissions for graduates scheme, whereby a young man could simultaneously study for a degree and undertake basic training through a university's volunteer company and its military lecturer. Capt Johnstone, formerly of the Royal Engineers, was Edinburgh University's military lecturer, and he wrote several times to the school in order to advertise the scheme through the *Fettesian*.[18]

Pressure groups such as the Navy League also tried to drum up support for stepping up expenditure on capital ships, and bombarded the *Fettesian* (and indeed any other publications aimed at the nation's youth) with long and, frankly, tedious letters on the topic of maritime supremacy.[19]

Interest in military matters was kept high by such apparently trivial events as the departure of the Czech art master, Mr A.F. Bohuslav-Kroupa, author of one of the most memorable school reports in educational history: 'He is a horrid little boy. I hate him.'[20]

This may well have been because 'B-K' famously 'exerted not the slightest control over his classes' which accordingly degenerated into a 'bear-garden'; in the school's centenary book of reminiscences, Sir John Spencer Muirhead recalled shamefacedly that 'it is chastening to contemplate what torments generations of Fettesians inflicted on a charming old gentleman.'[21]

Ineffectual he may have been as a schoolmaster, but 'B-K' had a remarkably exciting pedigree; his valete in the *Fettesian* said there was 'certainly no master, probably few men in the kingdom, who had led a life of more stirring adventure: always in every crisis taking the weaker side, always defeated, and keeping to the last the unbroken, high-souled, chivalrous spirit.'[22]

He had studied art in Paris, lived as an Indian in America, explored the line for the Canadian Pacific Railway, invested in a mine which would have made him a fortune had it not caught fire, made his way across central America where he was robbed by brigands, worked in a bar (which he 'had to vacate suddenly as an irate American, for whom he had mixed the wrong cocktail, was looking for him with a shooting-iron'), sold fruit and drove a mule which powered a public cistern, before catching 'Yellow-Jack' fever and having to treat himself on a quarantine ship in Havana harbour. His military experience began in the war between Russia and Poland, which was struggling to regain its independence: 'with this war Mr Kroupa had no natural or special concern, but it was a war between a strong side and a weak one, and to a nature as chivalrous as his that was enough – he *must* go and help the weaker side.' He also fought as an Austrian officer against Prussia at

Sadowa, and was lucky to escape with his life; the boys believed that his oddly-shaped head was the result of having been had been scalped by an enemy sabre. Kroupka's departure was marked by an 'all-nighter' by the teaching staff of a kind sadly less common today; apparently the retiree was the last man standing, still singing into the dawn. It is not known how well he got on with 'Froggy' Goldschmidt, the Head of Modern Languages, of 'Prussian birth and Hebrew origin', who was called up to fight in the Franco-Prussian War whilst still teaching at Loretto. Fettes, with its (relatively) intellectual and international outlook must have been a relief to Goldschmidt; Loretto's headmaster, Hely Hutchinson Almond, loathed foreigners, telling his wife that 'there is scarcely a sanely living man in the lot, so far as I can hear from those who have been abroad' (which he never had) and when challenged by a language teacher on a point of honour retorted 'you take me for a German.'[23]

Prussian methods were clearly more effective than Bohemian ones – Goldschmidt would hurl the property of 'careless or stupid' Fettesians out the window.

Fettes and the Edwardian military world

The war in South Africa should not have taken, so far as the optimists were concerned, more than a few months, but had dragged on for three years, and to some extent had been won by the 'methods of barbarism' which split British society – the use of concentration camps, Kitchener's scorched-earth policy, and the ill-treatment of civilians.[24]

The British defeats had shocked a public, which, whilst used to the occasional noble martyr to eulogise – Gordon of Khartoum, the subject of a prize-winning Fettes poem, and the reason all those OFs were tramping round the Sudan in the 1890s, being a particular favourite – they did not expect such regular and major setbacks. A Royal Commission into the war, published in 1903, indicted 'almost every aspect of the army and its organisation, from Wolseley, the Commander-in-Chief, down to the private soldier.'[25]

Transport, supply, planning, training and manpower – both quality and quantity – were criticised. The private soldier was all too often unfit and ill-educated – which came as no news to the army, which knew perfectly well that in its present state it was not something a fit and educated manual worker would choose to join. This led to a lack of resourcefulness on the battlefield, but the training too was at fault, for the iron discipline of the old close-order tactics which worked well in the eighteenth century, when other Europeans used it, and also against disorganised tribesmen, was of little use against guerrilla warriors like the Boers. If anything, it just gave them easier targets. The officers, too, were criticised; despite the Cardwell reforms a quarter of a century earlier, there was still a large number of officers 'from a leisured class to whom professionalism too often appeared as vulgar careerism.'[26] Knowledge and skill were less important than money and style in the most prestigious regiments; the Akers-Douglas Committee investigating officer training was told that 'keenness is out of fashion... it is not the correct form.'[27] Barnett notes that 'in the cavalry, where living expenses were highest, professional standards were said by the Report to be lowest.'[28]

It was found in South Africa that the army was aided enormously by the experience of local settlers (like Fettes' unlucky Blaikie and the more successful Normands) who knew the countryside and had acquired fieldcraft skills both from the natives they fought and those they recruited, and who formed 'rough-riding' volunteer units in the Imperial Yeomanry – 'accustomed to horses and wide open spaces, enterprising and intelligent'[29] – they were infinitely better than the allegedly pampered darlings of the regular cavalry regiments. Interestingly, Fettesians seem to have been unwilling or unable to spare the cash to join the latter, but they were heavily represented in the former. There were by 1900 at least half a dozen former Fettes pupils serving in various colonial mounted units, and twice as many again in the British volunteer yeomanry.[30]

It was the infantry, however, which those who joined the Army most often entered, and this was undoubtedly becoming much more professional in outlook and bourgeois in composition as the nineteenth century wore on. This is not to say that there were no Fettesians of gentle birth – there was a sprinkling of titles, and an even larger number of impressive pedigrees, in the army lists. Nonetheless, the Fettesians who wrote home about their army experiences all demonstrate the 'keenness' which the Committee was told to be bad form and certainly seem to have been striving towards some sort of professionalism.

Fettesians were also, as previously noted, found in considerable numbers in India. The Indian Army was in some ways the antithesis of the British, because its British-born officers were mostly recruited (like William Fettes' in-laws) from the upper middle class. Professional soldiering was a job to them. They were, accordingly, slightly looked down upon by the fancier regiments of the British Army. This did not stop them from surrounding themselves with an aura of aristocratic splendour whenever possible. Old Fettesian Capt A.I.R. Glasfurd published *Rifle and Romance in the Indian Jungle* in 1905. This enthusiastic hymn of love to the joys of big-game hunting was a thrilling read for the pupils, and must have inspired at least some to emulate the Captain's adventures:

In the distance a glow of little fires shows some of our men occupied with their evening meal, and a murmur of voices behind the camp discloses others, who are engaged in rubbing wood-ashes into a certain broad peg-stretched skin.

Yes! It has been a lucky day, and the first tiger is already bagged. Happy thought that prompted the placing of an extra 'stop' at the very spot which he should choose to break out of the beat, and a fatal pause that which he made, right under our tree! A shy, game-killing beast of the denser jungles, what long, weary ways his tracks had led us that hot day, until we ' ringed' him, at home, so far from his ' kill' of the previous night!

And so he is slain over again. Anticipation, realisation, fond recollection; threefold charm of these forest scenes; pleasures that will be ours long after the jungle knows us no more!

The white sheets look invitingly cool in the moonlight; and the cheroot can be finished there.

'Call me at five o'clock, Abdul!'

How delicious to stretch one's pleasantly fatigued limbs on the smooth linen, and gaze up at the thought-bringing stars, while dreams of the morrow's sport trail gentle sleep in their train. So the East doth call to us who are her foster-children.[31]

Captain Glasfurd would have met plenty of his school contemporaries when not pursuing India's wildlife. In 1907, the *Fettesian* printed another Army List. It showed 56 OFs on active service with the Indian Army – 14 in the cavalry, 34 in the infantry and four medics. All, of course, were officers. A further 114 were (or had been when they died) in the British Army, and 47 of these had been decorated, mostly for service in South Africa. Of these, 20 were in the cavalry, and only three of these were regular officers in prestigious regular regiments – Maj J.W. Ferguson, 20th Hussars, Lt G. Macleod, 16th (The Queen's) Lancers and Lt W. Duguid-M'Combie, 2nd Dragoons (Royal Scots Greys) who contributed to a regimental history in the 1920s and lived until 1970, when he was 96, and had outlived most of his contemporaries, their regiments, and the Empire they served. The band of the Scots Greys marched up the drive his estate at Easter Skene, Aberdeenshire, to mark his ninetieth birthday. The other horsemen were mostly non-commissioned or, in a few cases like that of P.L.A. Gabbett, held honorary rank; the vast majority were members of the Imperial Yeomanry, though H.E.C. Anderson served five years in the ranks of the 20th Hussars, retiring in 1905. He rejoined the Army and became an officer in the 9th Leicesters when the First World War broke out. By contrast, all 54 of the Old Fettesians serving with infantry regiments were officers, over half of whom were in Scottish regiments.

Captain A.I.R. Glasfurd and a contemporary image of Imperial Militia troops

There were also 25 OFs in various artillery regiments, eight engineers, five doctors and two in the Army Service Corps, and there were three Royal Marines. 15 OFs were in the Reserves, 12 in the Militia, 20 in the Volunteers (most of whom did not hold commissions) and 11 were retired – a grand total of 241. Of the regulars, 61 had seen active service in South Africa, 22 on or near the North-West Frontier, ten in various parts of East Africa, and others in Burma, China, Tibet, and Aden.

The service records of some of the career soldiers were remarkable. Maj E.W.M. Norie of the Middlesex Regiment, first commissioned in 1883, served in Burma in 1887-9 and on the Chin-

Lushai expedition of 1889-90, was a signaller with the Malakand Field Force in 1897 (the punitive expedition on the North-West Frontier immortalised by Winston Churchill), worked extensively in military intelligence, took part in, and wrote the report on, the crushing of the Boxer Rebellion in China, was an adviser to the Egyptian Army, and Aide-de-Camp to George V. His brothers also had stirring careers; Charles served on the North-West Frontier (where he lost an arm), in the Boer War and on the Salonica Campaign of 1916, whilst Frank was assistant commander of the Apa Tanang expedition to the North-East Frontier and won the DSO in France in the Great War, later becoming a spiritual healer.*

One more unusual record at Fettes is for Kenneth D. Robinson, who was appended to the military list as having fought in Theodore Roosevelt's 'Rough Riders' in the Spanish-American War in Cuba. Such an exotic connection will have been impressive enough for the boys, but those who read Roosevelt's own account of the war would have been delighted to learn that he caught they eye of the future president:

Kenneth Robinson, a gallant young trooper, though himself severely (I supposed at the time mortally) wounded, was noteworthy for the way in which he tended those among the wounded who were even more helpless, and the cheery courage with which he kept up their spirits.[32]

Robinson, a wealthy real estate agent who lived on Broadway, was one of several wealthy New Yorkers to join in the ranks – he was a friend of William Tiffany, son of the jeweller, the noted equestrian Craig Wadsworth, and Reginald Ronalds, son of Sir Arthur Sullivan's mistress Fanny, young men of substance and style who 'grasped the opportunity to join Roosevelt's regiment and desert the ballroom for the malarial fields of Cuba.'[33]

28 Fettesians were recorded as having died in Her Majesty's Service, 17 through disease or accident, nine in combat and two in native uprisings; seven had been severely wounded, losing limbs and eyes.[34]

---

* Another OF in this line of work was Arthur Findlay, who became a leading light in spiritualist circles and left his home, Stansted Hall, to become the national College for the Advancement of Psychic Science, which it still is.

A field hospital in the Sudan in 1898: Old Fettesians' mortality rates from injury and disease were as high as those from combat

These former pupils were pioneers of a kind, scholarship boys or products of the middle-middle-class who could afford the £85 per annum charged by the new school, almost entirely recruited from mainland Britain, but now scattered to the four winds and enjoying great success. In 1895, one of the Patriarchs wrote from his Indian bungalow that, despite a gap of only 20 years since he had left the school, he felt 'chilled and expelled' by the knowledge that he didn't know anyone at the school, a fact harshly brought home to him when he had experienced 'feelings of isolation and estrangement' at a Fettes-Loretto match: 'no doubt it is a wholesome lesson for us to learn that our memory quickly dies; but it is individually unpleasant when we encounter for the first time a generation which knows not Joseph.' However, he took comfort from the fact that Fettes, through its pupils might not think of their predecessors on a daily basis, did at least publish the Fettesian and *Register* which enabled him to find out what his contemporaries of 5 October 1870 had got up to:

Alas! They are thinning ranks. Of the 52, eight are dead and four more cannot be traced. On the other hand, eighteen are married, so that there is ample promise of a future crop of sons of patriarchs to replace at school their fathers who have passed away. What an interest there is in seeing into what kind of man has grown to the boy who we knew so well and have so completely lost sight of! So poor old Chimpanzee was killed by the bursting of a boiler, was he? Well, some of us can remember how often he blew himself up, with less serious results, in his study. I recall him as of gigantic size, and I suppose he really was big for his age. I think of the awe with which a circle of very small boys heard him declare at the end of his last term at school that if his master kept him back for his 'lines', he would knock him down and walk to his home in Edinburgh. I have no doubt he was kept back – he always was – the poor Chimpanzee had no memory; but his exit was quite peaceful and law-abiding. As I write I suddenly recall his mysterious power of wagging his ears, which he delighted to display. All the other names I see printed in the sad italics call up many memories which I have neither time nor space to record. Turning to the living, it is strange to see how widely scattered over the earth we have become. Assam, Ceylon, Burma, India, Spain, Australia, Gibraltar, Haiti, Java, Canada, Mashonaland, Basutoland – what a list it is! We may well say, 'Quae regio in terris nostri non plena laboris?' [What region of the earth is not full of our calamities?] *Soldiers and civilians, priests and physicians, lawyers and bankers, engineers and farmers, in how many capacities are we earning our bread and trying, let us hope, to do an honest day's work in the world!*[35]

He was notably impressed to see how many of his surviving contemporaries had become ministers of religion: 'so "Kiff" is an archdeacon! ... And "Albe" is a missionary, for the like of which career we marked him out at a very early stage.' The most prominent clergyman, Stewart 'Pon' Ponsonby, he remembered as a wonderful influence on the early school, 'always, and in all things, exercised to forward whatsoever things are noble, and true, and pure, and of good report, and to repress their opposites.' An article on a later *Register* analysed the careers of the 1,613 pupils who had passed through the school's doors since they opened. Of these, 195, well over a tenth, had since died – an indication of Victorian mortality rates, even as they affected the middle and upper classes; the oldest surviving OF at this time was in his early fifties – and 54 could not be traced.[36]

The average boy entered Fettes at about thirteen or fourteen and spent four years there, though one managed ten years, leaving when he was 21. About a third of the boys went to university – 184 to Cambridge, 143 to Edinburgh, 132 to Oxford, 76 to other 'Scotch universities' (mostly Glasgow) and 35 to other universities, half of which were in England or Ireland. Almost half of those going to Oxford, and a third of those going to Cambridge, were on scholarships, though former pupils going anywhere else seem to have relied on their own resources. In terms of careers, the single largest group (267, or 15.804 per cent) went into business, followed by the regular 'profession of arms' (180, or 11.184 per cent, of whom about a third were in India), land (144, or 8.923 per cent), law (132, or 8.175 per cent) and engineering (102, or 6.321 per cent). There were also 92 doctors, 84 bankers and accountants, 55 clergymen (two-thirds of them in the Church of England, a reflection of Fettes' refusal to be pigeonholed as a purely Scottish school), 49 civil servants, 48 teachers (mostly in schools rather than universities) and 40 assorted writers, artists and musicians. Within these groups, 95 were farmers or planters abroad (apart from a few in Argentina, always on 'British soil'), 41 worked as Indian or colonial civil servants, 20 were Indian or colonial police, and ten were engineers for the Public Works Department in the Empire. Outside the armed services, then, 166 – around an eighth - were involved with the Empire, a slight majority for profit, but at least 71 in some form of public service.

The military clock, whether the school knew it or not, was ticking. The Russo-Japanese War of 1904 was noted in the school magazine because of several Fettes connections and because of its impressive modernity. Lt-Col William Grant Macpherson, one of the most prominent 'patriarchs' and a distinguished member of the Royal Army Medical Corps, was attached to the Japanese forces in Machuria and was awarded the Order of the Sacred Treasure for his work there; he would later be a British Delegate Plenipotentiary at the Geneva Convention of 1906, write the official history of the RAMC in the Great War and end his career as that Corps' Colonel Commandant. OF Lt Smith, who had represented the Royal Marines at the old queen's funeral, was serving with a squadron in the Pacific and visited Port Arthur, which the Japanese – then Britain's glorious allies for their part in humiliating the loathed Russians – had taken from the Tsar. He found the Japanese 'most polite and friendly', and on seeing the extent of their military achievement, commented that when their soldiers saluted the British officers, 'it ought to have been us who took our hats off to them.'[37]

The battlefield at Port Arthur offered an insight into what was to come – the fortified hillside had cost 10,000 Japanese and 5,000 Russian casualties, and the Japanese Navy had fired 20,000 tons of metal at it, whilst trenches, saps, tunnels and counter-mines, not to mention savage hand-to-hand fighting for every inch of ground, had characterised the fighting. The idea of the Japanese as Britain's allies must have seemed bitterly ironic to the Old Fettesians who fought in that most cruel of wars in the Far East in 1941-5.

Attitudes to Germany

The Japanese were not the only future enemies to get a good press at Fettes. The Germans were regarded reasonably affectionately, at least until they expressed sympathy towards the Boers in 1899-1902. One of the 'Patriarchs' – the first boys to join the school – recalled that during the Franco-Prussian conflict of 1870-1, raging just as Fettes opened, 'we were keen partisans, and it is odd to recall that about five were 'German' to one 'French' – I suppose from a wish to be on the winning side.'[38]

In 1882 it was the French who inspired one of the many 'war scares', when a plethora of thrillers depicted Britain's closest neighbours as invading via the channel tunnel, then widely believed to be on the point of construction, disguised as tourists and waiters. At that point, the Germans were, by contrast, harmless, engagingly different but not unpleasantly exotic like certain other nations. W.B. Adam, whose engaging memoirs of life at Fettes and in the Royal Navy are one of the delights of the school archive, recalled one of the servants overhearing two Germans deep in conversation, and commenting 'Ain't it wonderful how them two fellahs can understand each other, talkin' like that?'[39]

A number of enthusiastic Fettesian musicians attended the Deutsche Sängerbund Fest at Hamburg in the summer of 1882, and wrote very affectionately of it. They were undoubtedly impressed by the 'quiet, sober Germans' in the Bourse, the excellence of the arrangements for the song festival, the incredible quality of the music, and the fact that 'people were there to listen – not to be seen or talk'.[40]

A further trip to the Wagner Festival in Bayreuth in 1889 also gained a glowing review:

It is impossible to give anything like a true description of what is indescribable even to oneself. One is completely carried away; one's own personality and all the petty egoism of the outside world is utterly forgotten. It is like a new kind of life, where music is the medium by which the emotions are expressed, a medium far more subtle and expressive than mere words.[41]

The Germans would doubtless have been impressed with this boundless enthusiasm – here was at least one Briton who understands the romantic intellectual soul! Another OF, however, wrote from Marburg University in 1890 that the German student, whilst as hard-working as his British equivalent, 'may be best described as a beer-drinking and fighting animal.' He gave a faintly bemused account of the duelling which undergraduates see as their most important sport, a weirdly ritualised activity in which members of two clubs would slope off to a rural pub and then, clad in leather aprons and 'iron spectacles', proceed to 'rain in blows at each other's head and face, the only objects of attack, with what seems to the spectator terrible violence.' The correspondent regards this as 'a form of vanity which we cannot understand' and concludes that football is undoubtedly preferable.[42]

What is now called a 'duvet', was seen at that time as a bizarre Teutonic eccentricity, and a characteristically awful poem entitled 'Made in Germanye' refers to the 'bulbous bagge' under which no true Briton could be expected to get a decent night's sleep.[43]

These are, however, generally affectionate references. Cecil Reddie, the progressive Fettes master who went on to set up his own school at Abbotsholme, positively idolized the Germans and wrote copiously about how the British public school could benefit from their educational ideas, emphasizing practical learning and cooperation rather than abstract classics and pointless competition.[44] In 1906, H. W. Auden, the former sixth form master at Fettes who became Principal of Upper Canada College, could write that 'where Germany leads educationally, we may usually follow with advantage.'[45] The *Fettesian* was even proud to report in 1908 that Kaiser Wilhelm II had conferred the Order of the Red Eagle (Second Class) on Lt-Col R.S.F. Henderson, a distinguished military medic who had been an early pupil at Fettes in 1873.[46]

A German does, admittedly, appear as the comedy villain, Count Donnerwetter-Ueberunterhinterberg, played by Mr Rhoades (later a supply organiser on the Western Front) in the masters' theatricals of Christmas 1910, which says as much about the teachers as it does about the pupils. The review of this performance – 'we should have liked to hear him repeat his magnificent name a little more frequently' – was written by R.H. Gordon, later to distinguish himself as a skilled wartime pilot.[47]

As late as July 1914, there were friendly encounters with the future enemies of civilisation. William Neve Monteith, an OF of 1890s vintage, was sailing on the SS *Manila* off Norway when he was invited on board a German battleship:

We were shown over the ship, we were treated with the utmost courtesy and consideration, we were shown how the big guns were handled and the idea of pointing them at British ships was treated as a jest: 'It's what they were made for, no doubt,' was in effect what the Germans said, 'but they will never be used for that.' [48]

The most negative view of the Germans written by an Old Fettesian in this period came from Barnes's account, written in 1901-2, of the international effort to crush the Boxer Uprising. He was deeply unimpressed by an attempt by the Germans and Russians to capture the Pietsang forts without waiting for British help, a 'miserable fiasco' which cost the arrogant continentals dozens of casualties (the Italians, who refused to advance without the British, were spared – the 'one bright feature' of the affair).[49]

Although, to be fair, the relative ease of communication made slights from them more obvious than those from the Japanese, who arguably behaved with the greatest brutality, Barnes was more disapproving of the Germans than any of the other nations:

…we found all the officers of that nation who passed through — and they were not a few — always very friendly. As far as I can ascertain, however, there was something in the air of Peking and its environs that made them somewhat arrogant and not very friendly either to us or to the Americans. Perhaps… they imagined that they were the only pebbles on the beach, and acted in accordance with that idea. This seems to have been the case, more especially in the later days, when, possibly, they had learned all they could from us, and thought they could then afford to be rude. [50]

Barnes also quoted with obvious approval a newspaper report which compared the relative utility of the British and German approaches to warfare and the leadership of foreign troops:

The difference between the English and German soldier is not spiritual, but national… The individuality, capacity for initiative and independence of the Englishman have made him supreme in the world; the German, who readily

submits to authority, and lacks self-reliance, has been forced to play a lesser part...
how is it that Germans so signally fail to rule foreign peoples? Their Chinese
regiment, raised in Shan-tung, went over in a body to their own people at the first
opportunity; the Chinese regiment raised in Wei-hai-wei has proved its devotion
to its British officers over and over again. That our system of education is defective
may be admitted; that the sense of duty is more highly developed in Germans
than in ourselves must be denied. By their works ye shall know them.[51]

Even the most dedicated patriot might have been aware that the Germans
signally failed to rule foreign peoples not because of any failures on their
part but because the British and French had largely beaten them to it.
This report, incidentally, came from *The Broad Arrow: A Paper for the
Services,* which was published by the government and presumably reflected
at least some of the opinions of the British high command. The First
World War would soon demonstrate conclusively that the German
soldier had, in fact, vast reserves of independence and initiative – more so
than many Britons.

Fettes' Social Darwinists and the Invasion Scare

One intellectual theme which ran through the late nineteenth and early
twentieth centuries is that of the desirability, on Darwinian grounds, of war
in general and a titanic struggle between the nations in particular. It has
even been argued that this contributed to the outbreak of war in 1914, a
whole generation of young men having been indoctrinated with ideas of
the desirability of struggle, and their leaders convinced of racial survival
depending on the destruction of the country's rivals. These ideas were
reflected in art, philosophy, literature and even psychology. At a more
particular level, the British popular press of the early twentieth century was
awash with scare-stories about possible German invasion, France having
been enthusiastically embraced by Edward VII and his Liberal ministers.
There were now plenty of novels from the likes of William le Queux with
titles such as *When William Came: A Story of London under the Hohenzollerns,
Spies of the Kaiser* and *The Enemy in our Midst* which hypothesised about a
Teutonic takeover. The *Daily Mail* even advertised such material by sending
men dressed as German soldiers to march around London. There is some
evidence that a degree of notice was taken in the school of all of these
influences. The *Fettesian* editorial for February 1886 was entitled 'Is the
Human Race Degenerating?' a discussion of the views of the then
prominent philosopher Herbert Spencer.[52]

'The idea that the destructive effects of war were beneficial, that war cleansed and renewed society,' Hew Strachan observes, 'was one familiar to Social Darwinists. Both they and the younger generation of intellectuals were ready to welcome war as driving out decadence.'[53]

This was certainly an idea familiar to the Fettes College Debating Society. The debaters addressed the issue of war's benefits to mankind as early as 1879, with Bowden – clearly an enthusiast for Darwinist thought – arguing that 'war was a great a beneficial purifying instrument when nations become corrupt, as in the case of Rome and Carthage. It was like the physician's knife which caused momentary pain but brought lasting benefits.' Against this, Lupton suggested that war was no more natural than disease, and, since it arose from 'the indulgence of the passions, we may say that it is not a necessity for the human race.' Lupton could have been a contemporary of the young Fettes' intellectual friends in the eighteenth century; 'as enlightenment spreads nations will cease to hate and make war on each other.' 'Ignorance of another country and its inhabitants' he says later, 'is often a cause of hatred of them… as knowledge spreads and intercourse increases, friendliness will spread too and wars will cease.'[54]

What is especially striking about these snapshots of late Victorian thought at the school is that the boys rejected the notion of Darwinian struggle; the editorial argued (influenced, it explained, by an article in the July 1885 issue of the German magazine *Nord und Süd*) that the human race was not degenerating, but becoming bigger, stronger, healthier and longer-lived than before. Similarly, Bowden's motion lost by eleven votes to three.

Such arguments continued up to the start of the war in 1914. A sardonic letter from Oxford in 1908 commented that the members of the University Officers' Training Corps 'hope to be efficient officers by the time of the German invasion – or Mr le Queux's next novel on the subject.'[55]

This tends to support, tiny cases though these are, Niall Ferguson's view that there was as much anti-militarism around as there was militarism, and the notion that the intellectual climate of Europe from around 1870 'prepared men so well for war that they actually yearned for it'[56]

is not entirely true for any class, not even the educated 'hearties' of the public schools who might have been expected to absorb uncritically the more aggressive rhetoric of the period. It was not, then, some great miasma of aggressive thought beyond the control of the statesmen which started the war, but the active decision of politicians who genuinely thought it a good idea at the time.

The creation of the Officers' Training Corps

Fettes' young ironsides were clearly excited by the army reforms which followed the Boer War, as they pointed towards some sort of role for the youthful volunteer as well as what the government optimistically hoped would be a more professional adult soldier. St John Broderick, the Tory War Minister, wanted to build up the army in terms of both size and equipment. For instance, the 'Long Lee' having been found unwieldy in South Africa, a more practical version was ordered, the .303 SMLE, less than four feet long, weighing less than nine pounds and with a ten-round magazine. Versions of this fine weapon would be used by Fettes cadets up to the present day (the No 8 .22) whilst the descendants of the Indian soldiers and policemen trained by Victorian OFs can be seen using them against Maoist and Islamist troublemakers. The Esher Committee reconstructed the army's 'brain' to ensure better organisation, and when the Tory government was ejected in the Liberal landslide of 1905, the extraordinarily gifted Scot R.B. Haldane, an alumnus of Fettes' rivals the Edinburgh Academy, took up the baton of reform. More than any of his predecessors, he had a vision, which the Fettes boys would have recognised, of the 'nation in arms':

...not a nation organized for jingo swagger; not a nation that desires fighting for fighting's sake; not a nation that holds a war lightly; but a nation that realizes the terrible nature of war, because its manhood knows what war means; a nation which is averse to strike the unless the blow to be called for in self-defence or in vindicating the cause of justice and righteousness.[57]

Working closely with his fellow-countryman, a professionally-minded young general called Douglas Haig, he set about creating a detailed training programme and a flexible, fully-equipped expeditionary force which could be sent overseas at short notice. He also reorganised the chaotic system of amateur county militias and volunteer units into the Territorial Army – a quarter of a million strong by 1910, and nicknamed (with some irony) the 'terrors'. He recognised that conscription, as demanded by Lord Roberts and the National Service League, was politically impossible in Britain and did not pursue it.[58]

Linked to the creation of the Territorials was the idea of cadets at schools and universities to create a group of young men who would be ready to step in should the military need arise. Haldane envisaged that this would create, over a period of eight years, a body of several thousand potential officers, trained cheaply – the cost of the OTCs was around £150,000 per annum – and, in addition, ensuring that the student would render 'that service which the nation was entitled to expect from its manhood.' The scheme offered a capitation fee of £1 per efficient cadet, with £10 for each one who gained a certificate and joined up, either as a regular or Territorial officer. The elaborate Scots uniform of the time cost around £3 each, and parents could contribute to this if they desired. Haldane faced criticism from both the left, who were simultaneously concerned about the militarization of education and reliance on the public schools, and the right, who accepted that things had to change but were not sure how.[59]

Nonetheless, committed to the OTC as a central (and cheap) plank in the building of 'the nation in arms', bringing the army and the public (or at least middle-class boys) together, Haldane toured the country in the late 1900s, encouraging and promoting his creation – to the extent that, after opening yet another OTC at Reading in 1909, he wrote that 'it is a great bore to do those things, but they have to be done.' Haldane's vision for his cadets was clear; without the unBritish, illiberal and expensive expedient of mass conscription:

…it is not too much to expect that, in the event of the supreme national emergency, feelings of patriotism would, as has always been the case in the past, induce a certain number of gentlemen to come forward and take commissions… many of whom would have had the advantage of the improved training given in the Officers' Training Corps.[60]

Hew Strachan has perceptively commented that 'popular enthusiasm played no part in causing the First World War. And yet without a popular willingness to go to war the world war could not have taken place.'[61]

Fettes reflected that willingness when, at long last, it embarked upon the military training for which so many boys had yearned for so long. Shooting began as a school sport five years after the Boer War ended, with a creation of a miniature rifle range in the gymnasium, a fact recorded in the 1907 'Vive-la' song commemorating the year's events:

We've a deadly machine which would please Mr Haldane
Set up in this Gym – but it's carefully walled-in.[62]

The technical marvels of the range – its concrete floor, glass roof, rails for retrieving targets and bullet-catchers – were lovingly described in the *Fettesian* to an admiring readership.[63] A rifle club was formed and a shooting team went to Bisley for the first time in 1908, possibly inspired by the fact that this was the year of the first London Olympics, when Britain won 147 medals, three times as many as the USA, which came second. Boys being boys, there was to be a lengthy correspondence in the pages of the *Fettesian* about shooting colours, which initially consisted of a hat-band – 'of remarkably little use to anyone: for who is going to wear a straw hat in the winter term?'[64]

Subsequent letters complained about the 'grotesque and unintelligible hieroglyphic' on the hat-bands, and another simply damned the fact that 'so manly a sport should be represented by so effeminate a token'. The (eventually) improved colours aside, shooting alone was not quite good enough for the true enthusiasts, and so, following Lord Roberts' 'appeal to youth' and incentives from the government, in November 1908 Fettes established an Officers' Training Corps, with Mr T.B. Franklin as Officer Commanding and Mr J.H. Beith (better known as the author Ian Hay, 'a gentle but firm disciplinarian, who was immensely popular'[65]) as Company Officer; neither 'spared themselves, nor those under them, in promoting efficiency'. The *Fettesian* announced the new body's creation with pride in November 1908:

Fettes is at last in possession of a Cadet Corps, and, on the principle that one volunteer is worth ten pressed men, it is highly satisfactory to note that no compulsion of any kind was required to fill the ranks to overflowing.

Our establishment is to consist of a Company of one hundred. No less than 137 volunteers came forward in response to the Headmaster's appeal – practically all the eligible members of the School, in fact – with the result that many excellent candidates had to be rejected. However, a 'reserve squad' has been formed, which, though 'off the strength', will serve as a very valuable feeding-force to the Company as vacancies occur.

Parades have been proceeding briskly since the beginning of October, and already squad drill has been sufficiently mastered to make it possible to form a Company. There has also been some simple skirmishing, and many embryo warriors have received their first lesson in the art of taking cover – in the Fettes pond...[66]

The Corps was divided into four house sections, and devoted itself to drill once a week until it had 'lost the appearance of a football crowd which had suddenly found itself in unaccustomed groups.'[67]

By the end of its first few months, an unidentified reporter could note that, although 'a somewhat trying time', it had been 'an excellent term's work, characterised all through by a keenness which augurs well for the efficiency of the company next term.'[68]

In the absence of uniforms and significant numbers of rifles, much of the early cadet activity revolved around square-bashing, which 'though very necessary, is hardly exciting' and the 'lack of rifles, ammunition and uniforms gives the impression that it is not quite the real thing.' The existence of the 1907 Fettes Shooting VIII, and inter-house competitions, however, gave the new cadets something to aim for. College, the scholarship boys in the main building, won the first Efficiency Cup in 1908 with 90 points out of a possibly 110 (Carrington got 83, Glencorse 77 and Moredun with Kimmerghame 75). Uniforms and weapons arrived early in 1909, on the pattern of Scottish regiments of the time with khaki tunics, Glengarry caps and kilts. The first Senior Cadet Officer was Norman Macleod Adam, and the hunting version of the Macleod tartan was accordingly adopted for the cadets' kilts. Training became steadily more intense with lectures on tactics, attack and defence schemes and a full dress parade in February 1909.

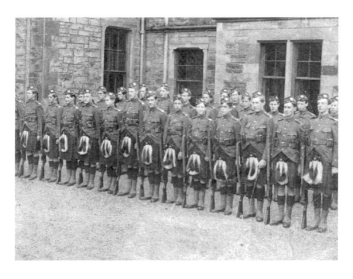

The Glencorse cadets in their uniforms, 1909

130

Lord Rosebery allowed them to use Dalmeny Park for exercises, and in the spring of that academic year they were in a position to hold a field-day on Corstorphine Hill against Edinburgh Academy; they seized the enemy's position through the clever use of a holding attack on the left flank and then a real one on the right. Unfortunately, the subsequent attempt to fight a rearguard action as they retreated downhill cost Fettes many 'casualties'. The umpires decided 'that our first attack was carefully screened, well delivered and entirely successful' but the retreat demonstrated 'slowness of retiring, and lack of covering fire.'[69]

This reckless bravery and unwillingness to retreat had already characterised those OFs who had perished in combat, and would be readily apparent in the coming years. The *Fettesian*, however, was boundlessly enthusiastic, editorialising at the end of the OTC's first year that it 'had been taken up in the right spirit and thoroughly mastered'; the Headmaster's Founder's Day speech not only praised the teachers who led it but addressed 'the importance of putting the country in the right state of mind as well as the right state of body.'[70]

Founder's Day also featured the innovation of a cadet march past and bugle call, and the 'Vive-la' had an unprecedented two verses on the corps:

> *Of late we have startled the tax-payer frugal*
> *By the rattle of arms and the blare of the bugle,*
> *And the mothers of Stockbridge have trembled with dread*
> *At the sound of our volleys – though minus the lead.*
>
> *For to add to his 'terrors' a flavour that's Spartan*
> *Mr Haldane has dressed us in khaki and tartan,*
> *And he'll surely be cheered in the midst of his trouble*
> *To see Mr Franklin come up at the double.*

The first year of the Fettes cadets finished on something of an anti-climax, for owing to an outbreak of measles the boys could not attend a summer camp. However, by the following March, they were taking part in an elaborate exercise at West Calder alongside the Edinburgh University OTC (including, excitingly, their artillery and machine-gun) against the Academy and George Watson's College. Although impressed by their enemies' bravery – they 'retired with a disregard for personal danger which would have been very admirable had we been supplied with ball-cartridge, but in actual warfare they would have been wiped out' – the Fettesians were still delighted when Mr Franklin led a charge which forced the enemy back 'in utmost disorder' leaving Dalmahoy Hill 'covered in a gesticulating crowd of Watsonians, still indignant at the rough usage they had received'. The umpire, 'mystified by the widely divergent reports of the rival officers, refused to give any decision' but this did nothing to spoil 'an instructive and enjoyable day'.[71]

That summer, Pte Tommy Stout put up an appropriately robust show at Bisley in appalling weather; also a successful rugby player, he was to die at Gallipoli in 1915, rescuing a superior officer. Mr Franklin gained useful insights by spending part of his 1909 holidays conducting military research, with Wellington College at Christmas and at Easter shadowing the army's preparations against a possible invasion of Dunbar. Finding the exercise director's car, containing a picnic with several bottles of beer, he and a colleague helped themselves in true soldierly scavenger fashion. 'No mention was made of the theft,' he remembered on his retirement, 'but that evening, when our papers were returned, we found written across our solutions in red pencil – "this scheme shows signs of alcoholic confusion." Field glasses are evidently useful like on occasion for other than military purposes.'[72]

The original Officers' Training Corps, 1909: John (Ian Hay) Beith, the first adjutant, is holding a sword in the foreground.

The school's early concern about cadet activities interfering with school study was not, apparently, without foundation, for in 1910 a warning had to be issued that reading and revision for the important 'Certificate A' examination (essential for advancement) had to be done out of school hours. This was taken extremely seriously by the boys who sat it – more proof, if it were needed, of the Fettes determination to 'get things right' – the March 1913 *Fettesian* carried both a review of a useful revision guide to this exam (written by Captain Franklin himself) and a poem, 'Dulce et Decorum est pro Patria Mori':

I saw a youth at break of day,
Who toiled with pick and shovel.
He dug a trench three feet each way,
And straight within did grovel.
But out he sprang with look of pain,
'By Jove! I quite forgot the drain.'
'Why do you thus? Pray tell me, pray!'
'I'm working hard for Certificate A.'[73]

In 1914 an incentive system was introduced as for boys to make greater efforts; seven points were needed to get a special silver badge, and could be gained for efficiency (one point), Certificate A Oral (two points), Certificate A Written (three points), shooting (one point), winning a competition (one point) or attending camp (two points). The first summer camp attended by the Fettes cadets was in late July 1910 at Blair Atholl, 'a vast field of mud, covered with what looked like a crop of large dingy-white mushrooms' in which, despite being prepared 'for all kinds of hardships' the boys slept 'in pools of water and shockingly bad tempers.'[74]

Awoken at 5.30 'by a confused sound which might have been anything from the expiring effort of a domestic cock to the plaintive trumpeting of a dyspeptic elephant' but was in fact a bugler with a sore throat, they embarked on a programme of marching which was cut short by a torrential downpour. The next day's field exercise might have been a military success, 'but it could hardly be described as enjoyable'; 'lying flat on your stomach in wet heather, and feeling the moisture gradually penetrate your uniform till it reaches your shivering skin, is certainly a novel sensation, but it is not a pleasant one.' The authorities decided to strike camp and on the Sunday the boys returned to Edinburgh, where they marched from Haymarket station to the school, 'a strange spectacle', for since their uniforms were too wet to wear they had on a strange assortment of pyjamas and rugby socks beneath their greatcoats and glengarries. 'We look back on camp as on a bad dream' concluded the *Fettesian* reporter. Subsequent camps were rather more successful; Barry in 1911 was sunny and allowed for both drill and realistic exercises, though the reporter noted with envy that other schools had bands. This was soon to be rectified with the creation of a pipe band in 1912; it took fourth place at the camp competition that year, despite the fact that its existence had been 'a mystery' throughout the camp (no-one having seen it). Admittedly, there were only five schools at the camp that (again, very wet) year, but it must have been a great comfort to Fettes that on their first outing they had beaten one of them. Needless to say, schoolboy perversity ensured that no sooner had the pipe band they so desired been established than 'scathing sarcasms and invidious innuendoes' were levelled at the musicians.[75]

Nonetheless, it was to attract considerable attention at church parades and other public events, though it did not acquire the status it now enjoys until much later. By the 1913 camp, it had been given £100 by Old Fettesians to support the purchase of uniforms and instruments, and came third in the competition, being singled out for praise by an officer for both appearance and efficiency.[76]

Memories of the period, nonetheless, vary considerably. George Gillen was enthusiastic about his time as a cadet; some years later, he recalled the battle on Corstorphine Hill in 1909 'where the new Corps fought with great élan and some skill', although 'a laudable attempt to give greater fire effect by the insertion of BB shot in blank cartridges was not, however, looked on with favour.'[77]

The nature of the cadets' activities can be seen from his memories of a combined field day at Dumyat Hill on June 15 of that year:

The Corps entrained at Waverley, after marching down to the strains of J.M. MacDonald's pipes, and put in a full day's work under more or less service conditions. It does not seem to have suffered from the unaccustomed strain of carrying rifles and full cartridge belts (and full haversacks) for many hours, as it attacked uphill in the afternoon with an impetuosity which called forth loud (but scarcely admiring) protests from the umpires.

He remembered with some pride that at their first formal inspection, a mere ten months after the unit was established, the Inspecting Officer considered the results of the training reflected 'great credit on all concerned' and that 11 per cent of his contemporaries joined the army. The *Fettes College Register* provides other insights; by way of a sample, 46 out of 53 of the class of 1905, who were the among the first to join the OTC, joined the armed forces either immediately on leaving school or, more commonly, on the outbreak of war (by contrast, nine out of the 35 boys of 1878 saw some sort of service, six of them as professional soldiers just after leaving school). Of these, 25 joined the infantry (mostly in Scots regiments), and seven the Artillery; small numbers joined the Engineers, the Royal Navy, the Royal Army Service Corps, and the RAF; two went into the Indian Army, one as a cavalryman. Nine were killed. Of the boys from that period who did not serve, most had died of illness or accident before they could join up. Fifteen OFs of the 1906 cohort were killed, and the same number for 1907, with another dying in peacetime as a result of his wounds. All but three of the 1910 class also served, and 19 died.

Not all of the boys were so fascinated by cadet life. Alfred le Maitre's near-contemporary, Sir A. Murray Stephen, said the OTC 'was accepted without great enthusiasm at first and was regarded as an amusing novelty.'[78]

So far as he was concerned, there was 'a naturally sloppy look of a half-grown boy fitted out in a stock-sized Army kilt and hung around with unaccustomed trappings'; 'I can remember the overloaded feeling of everything being a size too big for my immature frame.' His recollections of cadet life were of a Royal Inspection in Windsor Great Park when, after a twelve-hour train journey, they were drawn up with a strong summer sun beating down on them, and 'one after another the smaller boys pitched forward, until we were faced another way.' Mr Franklin recalled afterwards that:

We were to be inspected almost last, and men were fainting right and left in the other schools. As yet none of us had fallen out, but at last a man in the front rank swayed… disgrace imminent… But his near rank man with admirable presence of mind and callousness, jabbed his bayonet point into the back of the man's knee and drew blood. The swaying stopped.[79]

The Windsor event was the first official public appearance of the OTC as a body, 20,000 strong, from schools and universities across Britain, and the *Fettesian* covered it enthusiastically, noting that the 'swinging sporrans and flashing accoutrements' of the Scottish contingents were popular both with spectators and royals, and that the martyrs to heatstroke had not fallen in vain, because it meant everyone was allowed to sit down. The King's highly complimentary message to Minister for War Haldane was reported with pride:

It points with no uncertain hand to the existence of that 'individual efficiency' by which nowadays we rightly set so much store, and which is only achieved by unfaltering keenness, unquestioning obedience to discipline, and cheerful compliance with what are very often tiresome and monotonous conditions. In that great camp we are proud to state that Fettes and Loretto were especially singled out for praise in this respect. That is a good beginning for a permanent tradition.[80]

Loretto, incidentally, had its own eccentric tradition; in keeping with the strictures about rational dress of its great headmaster Hely Almond, its corps wore open-necked shirts and slouch hats. They thus escaped, legend has it, the suffering of the Fettes cadets in the blazing sun. For all the delight that the Corps took in the admiring comments of captains and kings, undoubtedly the praise which meant most to the boys was from 'the Sarge'. Like many schools, Fettes employed a succession of former army sergeants to teach physical education, and the longest-serving and best-loved of these was P. Adam, formerly of the Scots Guards. In 1911 he gave an interview to the *Fettesian* in which he described his experiences in the Crimea, where he had fought at Alma, Balaclava, Inkerman and Sebastopol, and told the boys that the cadets were 'doing jolly well. Sometimes when I see you start out for a field day I just wish that I could go along with you: but my old bones are getting stiff with rheumatism'[81]

Another great role model for the boys was Old Fettesian Major Mieklejohn, VC, who was also a great enthusiast for the cadet movement. Before the Great War, Meiklejohn visited the school, where this 'modest and inspiring hero' made a great impression. Although he was not very eloquent and made no mention of his valiant actions at Elandslaagte, he spoke of doing one's job, and the kind of public service that a school like Fettes could and did perform on the young. The young Robert Bruce Lockhart left the assembly 'with a new determination in my heart to do my own job better than I had done it before.'[82]

This good resolution lasted all of twenty-four hours. Meiklejohn lasted only a little longer. In 1913 he was at a parade in Hyde Park when his horse bolted, straight for some women and children; he tried steering it away, which was difficult owing to his having lost an arm, and he was impaled on a fence at Rotten Row; 'in this last desperate act of gallantry both mare and rider were killed.'[83]

The school was distraught. A fund was set up to establish a memorial to him (now in the school chapel) and to educate his three children. The *Fettesian* obituary concluded:

Sad as is the premature removal of so distinguished a Fettesian, and deeply as we sympathise with his bereaved relations, we cannot but feel pride in the courage and heroism that marked his life no less than his death. His example cannot fail to inspire not only those among us who are going to be soldiers, but all who aspire to do good work in the world and show themselves brave men.[84]

The approach of War

What is rather surprising about the *Fettesians* of the immediate pre-war period is the relative absence, in comparison with those of the Victorian and Edwardian eras, of significant interest in current affairs. The 1909-12 *Fettesians* represent a kind of pre-war peak of topical debates and references. A satirical interpretation of the *Daily Express* editorial 'Tariff Reform means goals for all' had supposed quotes from other sources about how our national games would be 'more in accordance with modern civilisation' if each side could choose its 'own time and manner for kicking goals'.[85]

There were also letters from worthy bodies and individuals exhorting the boys to join, for instance, the Agenda Club (which hoped to involve school- and university-leavers in a kind of voluntary service among the disadvantaged) the Red Cross and, of course, Lord Roberts, who wrote a blanket letter to schoolboys in 1912:

You have had great advantages as British public schoolboys, and as British citizens you will have even greater privileges. What do you mean to give your country in return? It is in the power of every one of you to give personal service, that is, deliberately to work for your nation as well as for yourself; but personal service means some sacrifice of self, the giving up of some leisure and of some amusement. At the present time your personal service is needed to persuade your fellow-countrymen of the great necessity there is for every able-bodied man being trained to defend his country in time of need.[86]

The Debating Society was, as always, the first port of call for the boy who, in addition to training to fight for his country, wanted to discuss how it worked. A 1909 debate on Lloyd George's 'People's Budget' was marred by J.M. Benson's 'personal attacks upon the character and antecedents of the Budget, and he had to be called to order' (this debate was followed up by a poem in which manful attempts were made to find rhymes with 'Budget' – 'grudge it' and 'judge it' were achieved).[87]

In 1910, there were some truly excellent debates on the House of Lords – then at the centre of a constitutional scandal for their attempts to meddle in the celebrated Budget – and Tariff Reform. The following year, the Debating Society covered Ireland; Gordon, future pilot of renown, proposed that Home Rule 'compatible with the supremacy of the British Parliament, be granted to Ireland' and R.A. Hendy, later to be killed in the post-war 'troubles' there, was in the chair. The motion, before 'a strongly prejudiced audience' lost by four to 25. The Society does seem to have become a bit rickety at this point; after some ill-tempered and poor-quality debates in the winter of that, J.A.G. Leask, later to win the MC in France, wrote in his report for the *Fettesian* that it 'has had a somewhat precarious existence for some time, but it is to be feared that this crowning disgrace will prove its death-blow.'[88]

There was one final flaring of discussion of the great events of the day in the spring of 1912, when a passionate and often clever debate took place on the trustworthiness of the government, followed up by a witty bout between two of the masters on the subject of tipping, but thereafter the debaters' consideration of great events disappears from the pages of the *Fettesian* – but then, as Leask noted regretfully in the final report, 'what can one say of a Society whose Secretary appears late, and in bedroom slippers?' This is not, of course, to say that with the collapse of the Debating Society the boys completely lost all interest in the world beyond the iron railings. It is true, for instance, that they followed enthusiastically the career of John Simon, probably the most politically successful OF until Tony Blair, as he progressed through the Liberal ranks and occupied posts such as representative of the Board of Trade in the *Titanic* Inquiry. Still, it would be hard to tell, looking at copies of the school magazine for 1913, that the Balkans were wracked by war and the civil peace of the United Kingdom was threatened by anarcho-syndicalist agitation in Wales, the Suffragette campaign (which saw Fettes' upper classroom set on fire) and, most disturbingly, Ireland's split into two armed camps which were ready to fight over Home Rule (though the *Fettesian* did record that one OF and brother of a Fettes master, William Lenox-Conyngham, was following up his Boer War career with service in the Ulster Volunteer Force). The 'Vive-la' for that year jocularly referred to the Balkan wars in the context of games:

> *The XI, we feared, would be made to play Turkey*
> *To Academy's Servia and the Bulgars of Merchi*

That, however, was about the limit of coverage. A letter from an OF in the army, sent to the school in November of that year, concerned not great world events but the trials and tribulations of introducing association football to the Indian Army. Apparently Sikhs did not take very well to it because of their turbans ('a circumstance which naturally is not conducive to accurate heading') and preferred hockey, for which they had 'a fine natural eye', but the Gurkha was an excellent soccer-player, although 'arms were freely used for forbidden purposes, usually with more skill than the player exhibited with his foot.'[89]

Less cheerfully, there was a sad, perfunctory death notice for the unfortunate Charles Ralph Warwick, who had left the school a mere five years previously and died in the sinking of the *Empress of Ireland* in the St Lawrence, which with over a thousand fatalities was almost as great a disaster as the *Titanic* two years earlier.

The *Fettesian* was pleased to note that another OF, W.K. M'Clure, had written a highly-praised account of Italy's war in North Africa. M'Clure's book is a fascinating insight into the thinking of military-minded imperialists in the years immediately preceding the Great War. Italy had angered most of her neighbours by seizing what is now Libya from the crumbling Ottoman Empire, and, like the British in South Africa, attracted international condemnation. M'Clure, an early 'embedded' journalist with the Italian forces, robustly scorned the rest of the world's 'hypocrisy and forgetfulness.'[90]

Believing that the Italians must play a part in the civilising mission of all white men, he defended the use of force as necessary when dealing with less developed peoples – 'in order to win an Arab by words it seems essential to demonstrate that behind the will to persuade lies the power to compel.'[91]

M'Clure painted a savage picture of the 'Mussulman' way of war whilst brushing aside any talk by 'atrocitymongers' of excesses by the Italians. Coming upon a 'ghastly scene' at El Hanni, where the mutilated bodies of fifty tortured Bersaglieri had been dumped, the Italian soldiers impressed M'Clure with their 'controlled and dignified behaviour.'[92] Any reprisals taken by the Italians were 'fully justified' and 'errors and excesses, however regrettable and blamable, were not unnatural or altogether unpardonable.'[93] Arab violence, by contrast, consisted of 'unprintable obscenities', 'hideous scenes of cruelty and mutilation, outrages committed upon the dead and wounded while the battle was still raging.' Like the British, the Italians were bringing the advantages of modern medicine to the dark continent, and M'Clure paid tribute to their doctors' efforts in stamping out cholera and malaria. The methods might have been severe – 'the streets were liberally sprayed with disinfectants, with the result that the manifold odours of Turkish Tripoli were soon submerged in the all-conquering smell of carbolic' – but so far as he was concerned this was a small price to pay for the advantages of civilisation. An even more exciting glimpse of modernity came from above, for this was the first war in which air power was heavily and successfully deployed, and the Italian airships and aeroplanes left M'Clure 'firmly convinced of the practical value of aviation' Although he was most thrilled by flights of 140 miles, then a great feat, he believed that reconnaissance and mapping were the most likely uses of aviation. Bombing, the war's key innovation, 'does not appear to have been attended with any great measure of success, and it is not unlikely that the possibilities of early development in this direction have been exaggerated.'[94]

Did the keen militarists at Fettes take on board the lessons of this war? We cannot be sure, because the school's copy of *Italy in North Africa* was erroneously placed in the travel section of the library, where it remained for several decades.

The *Fettesians* for that last summer of peace in 1914 mention Henry Hamilton Fyfe's new book on the Ulster crisis, and there was a comment that the turnout of OFs at Founder's Day was lower than in the past because the frequency of 'camps and training corps' were keeping the undergraduate officer cadets away. The man from the War Office who inspected the cadets on 8 July was impressed by the 'efficient and well-turned out' pipe band, the keen officers, useful signallers and good marching, but also noticed that 'a good many cadets wanted their hair cut' and that during the exercise 'there was a good deal of laughing and talking' which 'rather spoiled the whole thing.'[95]

By this stage the Archduke Franz Ferdinand, heir to the throne of Austria-Hungary, had been dead for a week, murdered by Serbian nationalists, and his close friend Kaiser Wilhelm of Germany had given a 'blank cheque' to Vienna to punish Belgrade. That said, there had been trouble in the Balkans before, and 'for the previous decade Serbia had been regarded as a thorough-going nuisance, a nest of violent barbarians whose megalomania would sooner or later meet the punishment it deserved.'[96]

Sir Alfred le Maitre remembered that, whilst the murder of the Archduke Franz Ferdinand in 1914 was undoubtedly noticed, 'on the whole, like most healthy people, we didn't worry very much. The possibility of a war had never been very far away from us, and most of these political businesses got smoothed over one way or the other.'[97]

The teachers, however, sensed something in the air. Adam recalled a sad little remark by his housemaster, in that last term of peace, to one of the war's many innocent victims:

...during the last week of term the serenity of its passage was disturbed by the touch of a cold shadow. On the Sunday night, when leaving K. P.'s room, the boy immediately in front of me – the youngest in the house and son of the naturalized German consul at Sunderland – paused in saying good-night, and K. P. remarked that it looked as if we would be at war with Germany in a few days. Within a fortnight Ahlers' father had been arrested for 'communicating with the enemy' and had been condemned to be shot. Later he was reprieved, but his family suffered great privations.[98]

Ahlers' father had, in fact, been arranging for his countrymen to return home when war was declared, in the sure knowledge that they would be called to the German colours, and the case attracted the attention of both the *New York Times* and the House of Lords. The last day of term proceeded as normal with prizegiving in the gym; Adam won his for Middle School Maths. Looking back many years later, he recalled that:

The Cloud gathering on the European horizon and did not cast its shadow over the end-of-term festivities, and that night there was the 'House Pop' in the tea-room at Glencorse, with several O.F.s down to join us, a good 'groise' (i.e. feast) and a sing-song.

But after the Cloud came the Storm. Within a week war had been declared and the Old Order had vanished. Of those present that night, who were subsequently old enough to see active service, one-fifth had been killed before the signing of the Armistice. The school generation immediately before that of my first term suffered still worse with a toll as high as one-third. Gone were thoughts of careers in the professions, in the civil services, in business, or in the management of family estates; to those leaving school there was now only one sequel – War, on the land, on the sea, or in the air.[99]

NOTES

1 *Fettesian*, December 1895
2 Ibid., March 1896
3 Ibid., March 1899
4 G.F. Campbell in Pyatt, p. 35
5 *Fettesian*, July 1903
6 Ibid., April 1878
7 Ibid., March 1900
8 Ibid., April 1900
9 John Spencer Muirhead in Pyatt, p. 190
10 Lockhart (1936) p. 310
11 Philp, p. 24
12 *Fettesian*, October 1878
13 Saul David, *Victoria's Wars* (London, Viking, 2006) p. 417
14 *Fettesian*, April 1879
15 Ibid., December 1879
16 Ibid., April 1881
17 Ibid.
18 See, for instance, Ibid., March 1905
19 Ibid., March 1904
20 Philp, p. 44
21 Muirhead in Pyatt, p. 187
22 *Fettesian*, November 1905
23 Quoted in Mackenzie, p. 146
24 See Judd & Surridge, Ch. 12
25 Barnett, p. 341
26 Ibid., p. 344
27 Akers-Douglas Committee Report, quoted in Ibid., p. 344
28 Ibid., p. 344
29 Ibid., p. 347
30 *Fettesian*, March 1900
31 A.I.R. Glasfurd, *Rifle and Romance in the Indian Jungle,* (London, John Lane, 1905) p. 4
32 Theodore Roosevelt, *The Rough Riders* (New York, Collier, 1899) p. 177
33 *New York Times*, 25 August 1898
34 *Fettesian*, November 1907
35 Ibid., November 1895
36 Ibid., July 1909
37 Ibid., December 1905
38 J.W. Parsons, in Pyatt, p. 17
39 W.B. Adam, *Naval Interlude* (MS, Fettes Archive, 1934-52)
40 *Fettesian*, December 1882
41 Ibid., November 1889
42 Ibid., April 1890

43 Ibid., December 1903

44 See Reddie, Ch. 1

45 Auden, p. iv

46 *Fettesian*, April 1908

47 Ibid., March 1911

48 Quoted in Elie Parish Church Guild, *Rev. W.N. Monteith* (booklet, 2008)

49 Barnes, p. 164

50 Ibid., p. 169

51 Quoted in ibid., p. 208

52 *Fettesian*, February 1886

53 Hew Strachan, *The Outbreak of the First World War* (Oxford, OUP, 2004) p. 177

54 *Fettesian*, April 1879

55 Ibid., December 1908

56 See Niall Ferguson, *The Pity of War* (London, Penguin, 1998) Ch.1

57 Quoted in Edward Spiers, *Haldane – Army Reformer* (Edinburgh, University Press, 1980) p. 190

58 For a detailed account of the army reforms of 1902-14, see Spiers

59 See Spiers, Ch. 7

60 Haldane, speech to Parliament, 13 May 1912, quoted in Spiers, p.141

61 Strachan, p. 206

62 *Fettesian*, July 1907

63 Ibid., November 1907

64 Ibid., December 1910

65 Lockhart (1936) p. 291

66 *Fettesian*, November 1908

67 Sir George van B. Gillen in Pyatt, p. 194

68 *Fettesian*, December 1908

69 Ibid., June 1909

70 Ibid., July 1909

71 Ibid., April 1910

72 Ibid., April 1921

73 Ibid., March 1913

74 Ibid., November 1910

75 Ibid., December 1912

76 Ibid., November 1913

77 G. van B. Gillan in Pyatt, p. 194

78 Sir A. Murray Stephen in Pyatt, p. 195

79 *Fettesian*, June 1921

80 Ibid., June 1911

81 Ibid., March 1911

82 Lockhart (1936), p. 301

83 Ibid., p. 302

84 *Fettesian*, July 1913

85 Ibid., March 1911

86 Ibid., July 1912

87 Ibid., November 1909

88 Ibid., November 1911

[89] Ibid., November 1913
[90] M'Clure, p. 2
[91] Ibid., p. 270
[92] Ibid., p. 236
[93] Ibid., p. 76
[94] Ibid., p. 261
[95] *Fettesian*, July 1914
[96] Edward Crankshaw, *The Fall of the House of Hapsburg* (Longman, London, 1963) p. 377
[97] Sir Alfred S. le Maitre in Pyatt, p. 214
[98] Adam, p. 38
[99] Ibid., p. 39

Chapter Five

'Business as Usual'

Life at Fettes in the First World War

First Reactions

I remember well the day before we left for Camp hearing T.B. Franklin, who commanded the Corps, saying 'It looks like war within a week.' Whether it was the alliteration or something in the air, I don't know, but I kept that in my head all day, and on the morrow it ran to the tune the band played as we marched off to Camp. In Camp the excitement died down for a day or two…On the third day of Camp, however, things changed. The general order for mobilisation had gone out, for we awoke in the morning to find that the Commanding Officer and the Adjutant had gone off to their regiments, and Camp was to be struck without delay.[1]

So Alfred le Maitre remembered the outbreak of hostilities when contributing to a book of OF reminiscences published in 1931. At the time he contributed one of the popular sub-Kipling 'mockney' poems to the school magazine, beginning with 'Left, right, left, right, the 'orficer 'e roars' and exploring the attitude of the cheery prole to route-marching ('some'ow we rather likes it'). Also in the first *Fettesian* of the war was the product of the collective mind of the middle school, a high-minded indictment of the enemy, which, whilst unlikely to win any prizes, does at least scan, most of the time, and serve as an illustration of how people genuinely, and in the view of many historians accurately, saw the whole point of the war as being a moral crusade against the rape of Belgium. It is entitled, probably much to the editor's despair, 'The German advance on Paris – and the retreat that followed.'

On swept the threat'ning masses! On they rolled!
And writhed, and rolled, and crept their way along;
Nor heeded they the cries that rent the air.
For all the earth lay bathed in tears, and told

Its sorrow to the stars, who stopped their song,
And everything was brought low that was fair.

Upburst the whole of nature! Wreathed in wrath.
And every tree, and stream, and star, and cloud,
Almighty shook! In one great anger blent.
The mood waxed pale and deadly in her path,
And vengeance in her awful cry was loud –
But only loathsome things this time were rent!

And still the threatened *masses roll along,*
But now they reap the harvest of their wrong.[2]

Another, anonymous poem expresses the general hatred of the Kaiser, which was, like the middle school's contribution, expressed in terms of the vengeance of nature, which would 'sweep thee from thy hated throne.' If these sentiments are typical, and most of the evidence suggests that they are, the British saw themselves as fighting an aggressive bully who, despite his pretensions to *kultur*, was attempting to take over Europe. This enemy's war crimes, exaggerated though they may have been by the often hysterical propaganda of such paragons of journalistic subtlety as the *Daily Mail* and *Daily Mirror* (both of which partly owed their racy style to an OF, Henry Hamilton Fyfe, who became, ironically, one of the most frank and honest reporters of the war) really were brutal, though in fairness the greatest savagery of the war was meted out by Austria-Hungary, whose forces left a swathe of civilian corpses as they pushed into Serbia, and Ottoman Turkey, whose massacre of the Armenians represents the first great genocide of the century. So far as the British were concerned, Corrigan writes, 'Germany had fomented this war; Germany had struck the first blow; Germany had violated neutral countries that were no threat to her.'[3]

The deluge of patriotic poetry which constituted approximately forty per cent of the *Fettesian's* cultural content during the war years (the remainder was about equally split between sporting and academic themes) undoubtedly confirms Mackie's view that the conflict 'brought out the latent belligerency, and emphasised the capacity for self-righteousness which had always been part of Liberal Scotland's personality.'[4]

Lest it be thought that somehow the mixture of jauntiness and patriotism might have diminished as the casualty lists grew, this poem appeared in the aftermath of Passchendaele and a full year after the school had seen dozens of former pupils, some still in their teens, wiped out at the Somme:

One Private Arthur Snookson of the Tooting Volunteers
Was a man to be relied upon, and active for his years;
Quite martial was his bearing when in uniform arrayed,
And you wouldn't catch him tripping, forming fours upon parade.
But he had a little weakness that was bound to make him fret:
He could not catch the spirit of the service bayonet.
When confronted by the dummies that do duty for the Hun,
He felt the perspiration down khaki copy collar run;
And, instead of giving brother Boche the cold steel in the neck,
He succeeded in inflicting but a feeble little peck.
'Now, bustle up,' the sergeant said, 'your hair ain't out of curl;
Go for 'im − don't be too perlite, as if it was your gurl!'
But all in vain, though hard he tried, no better could he get;
He could not catch the spirit of the service bayonet.
In time it came to worry him, it got upon his mind,
And he took to having nightmares of the most distressing kind.
One night, as in a waking dream, he took from off the wall
An ancient Turkish weapon he had hanging in the hall,
And, softly opening the door, he crept out to the park,
When the straw and canvas Boches were a-hanging in the dark.
Then with his scimitar he fell to wiping off old scores,
Till of those hatred effigies he was soon was forming fours;
And when the squad turned out next day, they found to their despair
There wasn't left of Brother Boche enough to stop a chair.[5]

Religion and the War

In their patriotic fervour the boys were supported by the clergy. Fettes, like virtually all public schools, was an explicitly Christian institution and the Victorian imperialists liked to imagine that they had been acting as God's Chosen as they rampaged about the globe, so it was inevitable that the Lord of Hosts would make an appearance when war was declared. Episcopalian pupils at Fettes heard Canon Terry of St John's in the West End (now, ironically, a strongly activist congregation which supports a variety of pacifist causes) fulminating against the Germans.[6]

The established church went one further; Lauchlan MacLean Watt, minister of the local parish church of St Stephen's, became a chaplain with the British Expeditionary Force and sent the Fettes boys a 'message from the front' in May 1916 whose emotive intensity is still breathtaking almost a century later:

This war is, above all, a war of sacrifice; and the people at home must recognise that, and act upon it. The men out here are willing and resolute — facing, and ready to face, what men have never hitherto had to encounter, in all the history of human experience. If the war be lost — which God forbid! — it will not be through the fault of these brave fellows, but through the intermittent forgetfulness of those who are at home.

Let all who love their country, and esteem the ancient story of our people, and value the heritage our fathers bequeathed to us cease not, day or night, to stir the sluggards to a full awakening. Every thought, every energy, every gift should be concentrated on the means of securing victory... For the immensity of the thing is far beyond our mental grasp, in its fullness; and the issue of it will affect ages far beyond the limit of our present endeavour. Therefore we are called to a true martyrdom, a witness-bearing unto death, lest all that makes earth sweet, and human life worth living, be for ever swept out of the world.[7]

Although a later generation of clergymen, including the Principal Roman Catholic Chaplain of the British Army in the 1990s, Mgr Stephen Louden, was to recoil from such talk as chillingly blasphemous,[8] at the time rhetoric suggesting a Manichaean struggle between Good and Evil was quite normal. At least one OF found it repellent; the highly-decorated Christian socialist Maitland Hardyman poured scorn on the clergy's role in a poem, published posthumously after the war:

See on the wall in fiery letters writ:
How shows the nation in this hour of stress?
Our prelates at reprisal meetings sit,
Our prophets pander to the halfpenny press.

Our poets — well, we have none; and our priests
A double income drain from Church and State.
The foe is at the gate; the city feasts —
With fur and feathers at the usual rate.[9]

In fairness to the churches, the frequency of their intemperate language was also accompanied by a readiness to live up to it in practice, and a genuine compassion towards the troops. In this sense, Watt appears to have been a thoroughly decent man, who was missed by the boys when he joined the Highland Division. He was to contribute several poems to the *Fettesian* in the course of the war, each one urging a virtually religious awe of the dead and wounded to whom he was ministering, and wrote a rousing memoir of his service. An avid listener to Calliope's prompts, Watt was, noted Adam, known in pre-war days for the way that 'few sermons closed without some excursion into verse – generally of his own composition' and he also played the bagpipes in the pulpit.[10]

One OF, James Brough, who had been a teacher before taking holy orders, was one of fifteen old boys to serve as a chaplain and was mentioned in despatches for his bravery in France; he had the immense poor fortune to die of pneumonia on the very day of the armistice.[11]

Another, the Hon Walter Chetwynd, who was in his fifties at the time, was awarded the OBE for rescuing the workers in a shell factory after an explosion despite being severely wounded himself; he never fully recovered from his injuries and died shortly after the war.[12]

OF James MacBean Ross, writing of his experiences as a medical officer in the Royal Naval Division just before the war ended, considered the chaplain's role vital:

A few words whispered in a severely wounded man's ear by his priest are almost magical in effect. An ineffable change appears on his face, he thinks no more of his wounds, death has now no terrors for him, and he passes into the great hereafter content and uncomplaining, at peace with all the world and fit to meet his Maker.[13]

Churchmen did not merely preach about war or act as regimental chaplains; some took part as combat troops. The Rev William Neve Monteith, one-time guest on a German battleship, was minister of Elie parish church. He had no doubt that Britain should be involved in the conflict, and reminded his congregation, in a sermon preached on 9 August 1914, of the words of the prophetess Deborah to the people of Meroz, who maintained their neutrality when Israel was being oppressed by Sisera's 900 chariots of iron:

Curse ye Meroz, said the angel of the Lord, curse ye bitterly the inhabitants thereof; because they came not to the help of the Lord, to the help of the Lord against the mighty. That is what would have been said of us in many a country of Europe, if we had stood aside and contented ourselves with looking on.[14]

Monteith had firm views as to what were and were not the right things to do. He condemned those 'cowards of Londoners' pictured in the newspapers, flag-waving mobs 'behaving as though we had just won some great victory instead of having just entered what promises to be the fiercest, most ghastly struggle that anyone alive has ever seen.' Those who panic-bought food and hoarded were 'criminally wrong-minded'; 'such conduct merely forces up the price of food artificially, and makes it even harder for the poor... it is not fair, it is not playing the game.' Given these views, he was depressed to discover that he was expected to encourage others to enlist whilst he stayed safely at home, becoming, in effect, precisely the kind of cleric Hardyman loathed. He decided to enlist, and, aware of the controversy this caused in sections of the parish, preached a final sermon on the subject on 4 September 1914. He would not have joined up, urged others to do so or even cared about the result had this merely been a war of conquest for the extension of the British Empire, he told them – if it were, 'it would have been well for us to be trampled into dust.' But this was a war about 'sacred treaty rights' and fighting for 'justice against iniquity' to prove that might was not always right:

I have never asked you to do anything which I was not prepared at least to try to do myself, and please got I never will. Shall your brethren go to war and shall ye sit here [Numbers XXXII. 6, the text for the sermon]? *Was I to remain comfortably and at ease at home while other men fought this great battle for me? Emphatically no: I could not look upon it as my duty to remain at home.*[15]

He closed the sermon with the words which every Fettesian sings at the end of term: 'God be with you till we meet again'. Joining in the ranks of the Fife and Forfar Yeomanry, he had risen to the rank of Lieutenant when he was killed in September 1915, leading his men into the attack at the Battle of Loos, 'shot instantaneously about 20 yards from the German parapet.' His Company Commander, Capt Brand wrote, 'we held the trench for about 12 hours but were ordered to retire and I am sorry we were unable to bring back his body.'[16]

William Monteith had just been married and his wife gave birth to their son that Hogmanay; his brother John survived him by five days. A career soldier who had both served in South Africa and been an enthusiastic big game hunter there (shooting four lions in a single day), he was killed by a sniper, again at Loos. He had only just recovered from a leg wound; his wife gave birth to a child a few hours after his death.[17]

A brother officer wrote 'Personally I feel Jock's loss very much; he was a gallant, loyal soldier, and helped me very much in the task of taking over the command of an entirely new battalion... I had always set down Jock as the Commanding Officer of one battalion of the Regiment, and I fear he will be very hard to replace.' The youngest Monteith, Hugh, won the DSO and OBE, serving with the RAMC, and survived the war to serve in the colonies. (Another Old Fettesian appears on the war memorial at Elie; one of William's parishioners, Ord Adams, who joined up straight from school, was killed at Ypres in 1916, aged 19.)*

The Rev Dr Bruce McEwen, (whose nephew, George Preston, would follow him to Fettes and become a housemaster there) was minister of St Machar's Cathedral in Aberdeen, and also served as a soldier rather than as a chaplain, despite being nearly 40 when war broke out. A Major in the Royal Signals, he was machine-gunned whilst riding a motorcycle and, although he returned to the ministry after the war, never fully recovered from his injuries and died in 1923.

The Zeppelin

The rather ferocious image of the Germans whipped up before and during the war meant that one of the most general expectations among the British public in 1914 was of air raids. Indeed, not just the British public, for Alfred le Maitre recalled later that at the cadet camp at Barry that year, which took place in the fevered atmosphere of the July Crisis, the German manager of the military canteen 'insisted that at any moment "our aeroplanes" would come and blow Barry sky-high.'[18]

He was simply confirming fears which had been haunting the British public for some time. Indeed, as early as 1909 (just after the publication of H.G. Wells' *The War in the Air*, which predicted the obliteration of cities by airships) there had been a panic as far away as New Zealand. German advances in this field ensured that articles with titles such as 'The Black

---

* By an odd coincidence, both Elie and the neighbouring parish of Upper Largo now have former Fettesian Chaplains as their ministers, the Revds Brian McDowell (the author's father) and John Murdoch.

Shadow of the Airship' and 'Germany: Lord of the Air' had a wide readership. It was believed that when war came, fleets of giant German airships would drop hundreds of tons of bombs on a defenceless British population. Such mass Zeppelin cruises did not happen, nor could they have since at the outbreak of war the Germans had the grand total of 26 rigid airships, of which only seven were of types which might reasonably have been expected to reach the United Kingdom on a good day, carrying some sort of offensive material. However, the actual technical capabilities of Imperial Germany were neither here nor there, either to its own public or that of the British Commonwealth, given the profusion of war scares and 'faction' novels in the years leading up to 1914. The school magazine noted that Fettes was not tardy in taking precautions against the Lord of the Air, and early in the war a blackout regime similar to that of the second war was instituted:

> ...it is at night that it is most impressed upon us, when all the windows are hermetically sealed with shutters and curtains. During prep. we manfully endure it, but no sooner does the 'half-hour' go than we rush forth and go from study to study in vain attempting to get a breath of air. Some studies resemble a hot-house, others a Turkish bath, and yet others are reminiscent of a zoo.[19]
>
> Altogether there are many who would prefer the risk of extermination by a bomb dropped by a Zeppelin, to nightly suffocation in their studies.[20]

Because of the proximity of the Rosyth dockyards, the Admiralty did make some preparations for Zeppelin attack, but their concern was mainly about an assault from the Baltic by sea. The various islands along the Fife and Lothian coasts were turned into 'stone frigates' whose crumbling concrete gun emplacements may be seen to this day. Torpedo boats, searchlights, Q-boats (armed trawlers disguised as innocent fishing smacks), hydrophones, anti-aircraft ('archie') and anti-ship guns were all part of the area's defences. The boys of College house, looking north towards the Forth from their dormitories high in the main building, noted this activity, and one wrote an anonymous poem about it, entitled 'The eyes of night':

> You yellow shafts, how weird the light
> With which you pierce the black of night!
> For now you cross, and now you part,
> Unceasing to and fro you dart.

Now through the clouds you carve your lanes,
Is case perchance some hostile 'planes
Creep past concealed, or gliding hosts,
Of Zeppelins attack our coasts.

And now you scan the stormy deep,
For oft, while men are bathed in sleep,
With dread torpedo comes unseen,
Beneath the waves, the submarine.[21]

The last point was prescient, for although the Zeppelin and its airborne successors were responsible for what social scientists refer to as 'moral panics' before, during and after the Great War, it was the U-Boat which caused more damage in the Edinburgh area (and indeed elsewhere) during the conflict. During the American Civil War, the CSS *Hunley* had demonstrated the both the potential of the submarine, when she sank the USS *Housatonic* using a bomb on a spike, and its perils, when she herself went permanently to the bottom almost immediately after doing so. The first ship ever to be sunk by a submarine-fired torpedo was HMS *Pathfinder*, which blew up when hit by Otto Hersing's U–21 in the Forth on 5 September 1914, losing 259 of her 268 crew. The torpedo hit the magazine and the ship exploded in a cloud of smoke clearly visible from the shore. The government, aware of the existing panic about Zeppelins, decided not to add another fear to the public's list of worries and claimed *Pathfinder* had accidentally hit a mine, presumably on the grounds that it was healthier to believe that the armed forces might be sufficiently incompetent to kill one another than that they were in any danger from the Germans.[22]

Fettesians did not get to encounter a real air raid until the night of 2 April 1916, when naval Zeppelins L14 and L22 attacked Edinburgh in the only moderately successful visit they made to Scotland. The Germans claimed that:

Explosives and incendiary bombs were thrown with very good success on Edinburgh and Leith, dock establishments on the Firth of Forth, and at Newcastle, and important shipbuilding works, furnaces and factories on the Tyne River. There were numerous fires and violent explosions.[23]

The British government dismissed the German claims with classic understatement as 'imaginative inexactitude'[24] and it is true that in comparison with the suffering inflicted on London the destruction was limited. The Germans certainly left undamaged what is generally assumed to have been their intended target, the massed transport fleet and naval squadrons in the Forth. This may have been because of the anti-aircraft fire which the ships sent up, or more prosaically because airborne navigation was in its infancy. Zeppelins were rather hard to steer with any degree of accuracy – two of the original four raiders failed to make it to Edinburgh at all. The fact that their bombs were about the size of flour-bags and were dropped by hand out of the airship window was, likewise, less than conducive to pin-point strikes on the Allied war machine. Whatever the reason, the first building to be hit was a bonded warehouse in Leith which erupted, one eyewitness recalled, 'like Vesuvius', illuminating the whole city at a cost of £44,000 worth of whisky – some of it not destroyed but looted by opportunistic sailors. Either by accident or design, Kapitänleutnant Böcker (who knew the area from his time as an officer of the Hamburg-Amerika Line), then headed at 11.50 pm towards the Castle Rock, dropping bombs on Lauriston Place, Marchmont Crescent, Lothian Road and the Grassmarket, where four people who had emerged from the White Hart to see the spectacle were injured, one fatally. Like many people in the city, the boys of Fettes had by now acquired a somewhat blasé attitude towards the 'Zepps', which may or may not have been an improvement on the earlier paranoia. W.C. Sellar, later to make his name as a schoolmaster and co-author of *1066 And All That*, was a boy in Schoolhouse at the time, and recalled that the raid shook them out of their new-found complacency:

A certain boy who was awake, and whom I shall call 'X', put his head out of the skylight in his cubicle and listened, and looked far into the distance; then he returned, as it were, to to earth, uttering the one word 'Zeppelins' to a dreamy and incredulous audience. 'X' had the reputation of being a 'Cutester' – that Fettesian expression which covers such a multitude of strange characteristics; one felt that 'X' knew too much and was too sure of his opinions, and so his idea of Zeppelins was sleepily derided. But not for long: as usual, the 'Cutester' was right, and ten minutes later we were all huddled together, (some of us severely frightened) along the ground-floor passages. The bombs which dropped in the Grassmarket and on the Castle rock sounded to our inexperienced ears desperately close; like Queen Victoria, 'we were not amused'.[25]

Adam remembered the raid with a little more sangfroid:

About twelve o'clock that night we were roused with the warning that Zeppelins were reported as having crossed the coast. Looking out we could see searchlights from Rosyth and from the mobile units in Edinburgh wheeling and crossing in the sky. We were called down to K.P.'s room where there was still a fire and soon could hear the rattle of naval antiaircraft guns. The airships passed over Leith, where bombs were dropped, crossed almost overhead, and finally reached Edinburgh, where they distributed their bombs in a triangle round the castle. Little material damage was done, but about eight people were killed. Next, heading towards Rosyth, but finding the reception too hot, the airships made off as quickly as possible for home. So the holidays came around again...[26]

The raid did no damage to the buildings of Fettes, but at George Watson's College the west wing was sufficiently badly hit for an early start to the Easter holidays, which was greatly relished by the pupils. The *Fettesian* contained an appreciative reminiscence of the 'souvenirs' left by the Germans. The raid had, however, cost thirteen lives, including two children, one a baby in a crib. The rather limited defences of the city of Edinburgh – the one o'clock gun firing blank rounds and a very lightly-armed Avro 504K training aeroplane from East Fortune, whose lonely sortie failed to make contact with either airship and led solely to injury on the part of its pilot who crashed on landing – caused a scandal. It was irrelevant to Edinburgh residents that the cost to Germany of building airships was five hundred per cent of the cost to Britain of the damage their raids caused. Indeed, they cannot have known this. Edinburgh's pain was presumably exacerbated by the fact that the damaged buildings had not been insured against air raids. Characteristically, as Sellar records, one Fettesian sixth former was moved to record 'the drowsy but vehement language used by a fierce youth when awakened at dead of night by his Housemaster' in vivid Latin hexameters. 'Unfortunately, the verses have perished, and so, to speak the sad truth, has their author along with many who received their trifling baptism of fire in the draughty Fettes corridors.'[27]

When Mr C.H. Tremlett left the school in 1916 to become Headmaster of the King's School at Bruton in Somerset, the *Fettesian* expressed the wry hope that the Tremletts' 'freedom from the Edinburgh east winds and the Zeppelin menace' would compensate them for all that they missed at Fettes. However, the Germans did not raid the city again (until the next war, at any rate), leaving a despairing school poet to demand whether, in the absence of further attacks, he might write about the anniversary of the only one the school had seen.[28]

L14 and L20 made a fruitless trip to Aberdeenshire in May, when the former bombed fishing boats in the Tay under the impression that they were warships in the Forth, missing all of them, whilst L20 drifted over the Highlands and ended up in the sea off Norway.[29] Edinburgh's defences (anti-aircraft guns arrived shortly after the raid) remained on alert; Robert Hardie, who joined the school in the last year of the war, recalled 'the chilly pencils of the searchlights wheeling through the sky [which] spoke of a strange world of mystery and fear.'[30]

The increasing impact of war

One of the reasons why the 1914-18 war has been so deeply etched into the British psyche is the extent to which it involved the civilian population – their mobilisation, their exposure to attack, and their sharing (though never to the degree of the soldiery, nor that of continental non-combatants) in privation and material hardship. There had of course been shortages in previous wars, as Sir William Fettes had noticed during the struggle against Napoleon, but they had largely affected the poor, not the middle or upper classes, nor even, much of the time, the skilled artisan. The better-off were affected only by the increase in taxation (which actually led to riots by angry members of the middle class), but for many, including Sir William himself, this was offset by the opportunities for profitable employment. This modern war was completely different, with the hand of the state reaching not only into the manufacturing and service industries, but also into what the British public had historically defended as its traditional liberties as a nation of free individuals. The state interfered with where they could go, what they could do for work or leisure, what they might read or even say, and dictated the contents of their larders. Whatever was happening outside the great iron railings because of the war, however, Fettes' historian notes that 'at first the clockwork routine of the school day kept it at arm's length.'[31]

The gloomy casualty lists and belligerent poems apart, the school magazine remained much the same as it had in peacetime, devoting as much attention to recording the minutiae of sporting fixtures as ever it had. The first school magazine of the war years contained the editorial observation 'At Fettes we are affected so little by the war, that it is almost possible at times to forget that there is a war going on at all.'[32]

Given that the magazine had a heavier barrage of jingoistic poems than usual, this was surely an exaggeration. In all, the first wartime *Fettesian* devoted nineteen of its 31 pages to what might be described as military matters, but, of these, ten were army lists and accounts of cadet activities. It is also worth saying that much of the eight pages devoted to sport were in closer type than the rest and that there was probably more written about the match against Glasgow University (which, in fairness, Fettes won 17-0), than on any given military issue. The Christmas 1914 number was back to its usual content, with well over half the magazine devoted to the traditional highly detailed accounts of the heroics of the hallowed turf. The reminiscences of old boys also support the notion that, at least in the early stages of the war, life trundled on as best it could. Sellar, for instance, doubted

…whether the average boy thought much less about his school work or school games because his father or brother was at the front; after all, no-one can live in a continual state of emotional excitement, and the regular time-table of school life is the most effective sedative in the world… one was caned no less severely for being low in the weekly Form order just because there 'happened to be a war on.'[33]

Other aspects of school life ploughed on; the singing in chapel, such an important feature of Fettes culture, was as lusty as ever, whilst Mr Cumberlege's Shakespeare Society, 'Johnnie' Coast's Chess Club and the encouragement of boys to apply for university scholarships continued as before. The robust athleticism which characterised pre-war Fettes was also a key part of the wartime experience, with Alfred le Maitre showing huge promise on the running track as well as shining in the classroom, if not in poetry lessons. E.H.P. Mallinson and C. Macnab (who had, in a glorious moment in one of the last matches of the glorious peacetime summer of 1914, nonchalantly caught a ball which was whizzing towards the Headmaster's daughter) excelled at cricket, whilst the rugby team featured W.G.B. Mackenzie and J.P. Maclay, later Cambridge blues, and, in the latter case, an MP. The 'Belows' – inter-house competitions – continued with the brutal enthusiasm which still makes them the despair both of Western General Hospital and of the games staff, who now, as then, cling to the naïve belief that sporting efforts should be directed outwards in order to achieve glory at the expense of other schools. Sellar was at his most lyrical in these recollections:

House Belows were to a great extent wallowings in slush, and, like battles in the Great War, they belong to that romantic order of events which it is more glorious to look back upon than it was actually pleasant to engage in. There were some who revelled in the fray, while to others the game was less enjoyable than the hot bath which followed it. (Hot baths were rather rare events: normally, one per boy per fortnight, until one became a prefect). If there was an unnecessarily brutal spirit pervading these games, it is fair to add that the brutality was more evident amongst the spectators, and in the threats preceding the game, than in the actual playing of it. There were radiant moments in House Belows, as in all hard games of rugger – moments many must look back upon as amongst the proudest in their recollections… When there were no referees the games were apt to develop into a 'rabble' – but this did not often happen.[34]

The war did intrude into sport, in that sixth formers, who were at the peak of their game, tended to disappear in the middle of the season when called up, and soccer disappeared in order to make room for more cadet activities. The war interfered with games in other ways – Adam remembered vividly that 'rugger was sometimes made unpleasant by the presence of choking fumes of nitrogen peroxide let loose by a munitions factory in Craigleith and one's attention was at other times diverted from the game by the antics of aeroplanes from Turnhouse Aerodrome practising the "falling-leaf" or the "spinning nose-dive."'[35]

War also gave a splendid new set of similies for use in describing the more vigorous matches – the most brutal, of course, being House Belows:

Take all the horrors that torture the tympanum,
Barrage and drum-fire, and whiz-bangs and crumps,
All the worst noises you know – without skimpin' em,
Mine detonation and bombing of dumps…

Take all these noises I've mentioned, and jumble them,
Adding each other that anyone knows,
Into each ear indiscriminate tumble them,
That's what it sounds like at our House Belows.[36]

Matches were played against visiting servicemen, including South African troops and naval crews, and the *Fettesian* provided a helpful glossary of terms to help the uninitiated decipher the detailed reports which appeared in its pages:

> *Shone in the open – slunk every scrum.*
> *Passed most unselfishly – too much of a funk to run himself.*
> *Conspicuous out of touch – could not hide behind anyone else.*
> *Captained the team well – secured the offices of the referee.*
> *The game was pleasant and well-contested – we won.*
> *Play was rough and disagreeable – we lost.*
> *The referee was conspicuously impartial – gave everything in our favour.*[37]

Phil Macpherson, another OF who contributed to the 1931 book of school memories, confirms much of Sellar's recollection about the continued dominance of music and sport – but then, as a keen athlete who later represented Scotland, he probably would. Although for him 'memories of prowess in games' were the warmest, like Sellar he was not sorry to see the end of one particular Fettes sport, 'dorm-rugger', which was banned in 1917 – not because of the war, but simply because, although initially winked at by some Housemasters, it was too savage and injury-prone an activity to continue in a civilised school. Describing this 'exercise in robust ferocity', Macpherson said that although the ostensible purpose of the game was to score tries by smashing oneself and the 'borrowed' small boy's sponge-bag which served as the ball into the wall (conversions were effected by kicking the 'ball' out the window), in reality 'one of the principles of the match was to teach the new men a respect for their superiors'.[38]

'Remembering the fury with which the game was played,' recalled Sellar, 'I cannot think why we were not all killed. The strong loved the game, but weaker brethren regarded it with awe and played it only because they dared not decline.' Macpherson's house spread the rumour – in order to undermine the morale of other houses in the run-up to Belows – that the reason the game was banned was because his friends were 'making matchwood' of their dorms.

Running like the lettering in a stick of rock through all accounts of what most certainly did change at Fettes in wartime is the theme of shortages. Some of these were very welcome – the absence of starch meant permission for soft collars, and raised hopes that the top hat, 'our ancient and inveterate enemy' but a compulsory feature of school dress when

Rugby taught boys vital lessons in manly fortitude and continued throughout the war: of this 1st XV photographed a year before war broke out, a third were killed and a third wounded

going 'up-town' or to church, might also be abolished. Since the younger non-teaching staff had joined the masters in France, there was a shortage of people to ring the bell for lessons, or at any rate a shortage of people healthy enough to ring it punctually and long enough to have an effect, resulting in an epidemic of lateness for lessons. Coal shortages were also painful, as a poem in the autumn of 1918 showed:

> *Mr. Joseph Inthemire*
> *Can no longer have a fire.*
> *Now the Coal Control controls,*
> *Stopping his supply of coals.*
> *He has used up all his wood;*
> *Absolutely all he could*
> *Find about the garden lying,*
> *Whether growing, dead, or dying –*
> *Every bit he could acquire,*
> *This he cast upon the fire.*
>
> *Now all day you see him hacking,*
> *With a rage entirely lacking*
> *All precision mathematic,*
> *Uncontrolled and demonatic*

At his banisters and stairs,
Sideboards, tables, bureaux, chairs:
Like a ravenous old vulture,
Like a Hun enforcing 'Kultur',
Every sense of shame he lacks,
All things fall before his axe.[39]

But it was food which bulked so large in memory – or rather didn't, as quantities went down steadily in the course of the war. And rightly so; the government was well aware that the masses refused to believe that the better-off were sharing their hardships. Public schoolboys, therefore, did not merely experience rationing, but were photographed digging allotments to prove that they were doing their bit to feed themselves. Selwyn Lloyd recalled that his housemaster spent a lot of time digging in the kitchen garden, clad in a 'threadbare shirt with no collar and an old handkerchief round his neck, accompanied by an aged and bad-tempered dog.'[40]

'Cheese is scarce,' commented the *Fettesian* in March 1918, 'people don't dream as they used to after a College supper.' The next issue noted 'daily more severe' restrictions on food, with more and more meatless days, though these supplemented by the potatoes the boys grew themselves. Beer at lunch was halted as part of the general drive to conserve cereals and sugar, which was encouraged by the powerful temperance lobby. Although the national issue was held to be the danger and social consequences of munitions workers getting drunk (alcohol, Lloyd George announced, was a greater enemy than Germany) Fettes beer was widely believed to have no intoxicating content at all. Both the government's Food Controller and the school's Steward, George Scott, were blamed for all this. Hardie remembered that:

One was – had need to be – hungry in those days. Of all the war phenomena, that which touched us closest 'where we lived' was the food shortage… No doubt our grousings and our rancours were grossly unjust, but George Scott was not a popular figure in those days.[41]

Scott did his best, of course, and Sellar, writing in retrospect from the other side of the adult-pupil divide, said that 'a great deal of praise and gratitude' was due to him. Nonetheless, Sellar remembered the scarcity of bread (a Fettes staple), the expense of jam, the shortage of milk, and a general theme of 'dull and simple' food, made worse by the Headmaster's placing a nearby dairy, which sold chocolate and buns, out of bounds. Macpherson recalled the difficulty, as a fag, of trying to toast thinly-cut bread for one's prefect, and the worry that the lack of sugar would lead to fainting fits. The housemaster of Glencorse, K.P. Wilson, was robust in his approach to diet; Adam recalls having met a lady entrusted with the care of female students in an English university who had asked this noted educationalist what to do about problem eaters. Wilson's reply 'was that he would take a plate of porridge in one hand and a cane in the other and say "Choose."'[42]

A poem in the Christmas 1917 *Fettesian* commented wryly on the food situation:

Father Christmas, great immortal,
Ruddy-cheeked and holly-dressed,
When this year you cross my portal
I've a few things to suggest.

Haply you have heard a rumour
Through the clouds of war up-rolled
Of the woes of the consumer,
Sorrows of the food-controlled.

Think not this year of investing
In expensive games and toys;
They're no longer interesting
To our daughters and our boys:

But, with loving foresight gifted,
When you hover o'er a bed
Drop a bag of 'lump' or 'sifted'
In each tiny sock instead:

Or in case of older folk a
Gift appropriate will be
Half a pound of fragrant Mocha
Or of Mazawattee tea.

Or if stockings over-roomy

Put your kindness to the test,
Any garden-stuff will do me –
P'rhaps potatoes would be best.[43]

By the time the war was nearing its close, even the editor of the *Fettesian* – who generally followed a 'business as usual' line and did not mention the war – looked forward to peace because it would see a return to material comforts:

With pen and ink I must compose a screed
Which future editors perchance may read.
While I do sit in study cold and chill
Be-coated and be- mufflered (for no fire
Graces my little grate), the icy draught
From 'neath the door blows o'er my freezing limbs,
And bitter breezes play around my neck.
But coal is not the only rationed thing.
We need our cards and coupons still for meat,
For sugar, and for fat; but 'spite of this
Another thing is to be rationed – jam.
What can I do 'mid these vicissitudes?
What's to be done? I look unto the day
When peace shall reign again upon the land
(And certes that blessed day seems near at hand).
But think of peace! We hardly realise
All that it means, all it will bring to us.
Controllers will not hold us in their hands;
We will have fires here, there, and everywhere,
Each in his study will be warm, serene.
No food cards need be used. What a joy it will be
To lord it over grocers, not to cringe
Begging a piece of cheese; or tiny chop
From Mr. Bones the butcher. Ah! What dreams!
And ere long they may be realised.
Since Germany now seems to think of peace
Not on her own terms. Her fine dreams of power
Have fallen about her like a host of cards.
No doubt we will have early school again
On winter mornings drear après la guerre;

But what of that? 'Tis but a small detail.
And now to matters personal we turn.
To thee, our noble captain, Cunningham,
We wish you luck in every coming match,
Especially against our rival schools...[44]

Founder's Day, of course, had to be suspended for the duration of the war, prompting sad reflection; after several years without it, an anonymous pupil wrote:

The match was set, we bowled and caught,
On summer grass the sun was gay;
Then like a shadow came the thought –
This should have been our Founder's Day.

Now should have been that happy tryst
Of sundered hands from far away,
That interchange of heart unpriced,
Rebirth of friendship hale and grey.

But though afar on sea and land
Many unloved one bides away,
United still in heart we stand,
Fettesian brothers, we and they.

And when the world hath rid its wrong
By help of those for whom we pray,
And Evil faints and Good is strong,
We will yet hold our Founder's Day.[45]

The boys were, of course, equally well aware of the mounting casualty lists, which were not, and could not have been, hidden from them. The memorial service of 1915 does not seem to have been repeated, but there were plenty of other tangible reminders of the missing – every few months at the back of the school magazine, for instance, with major battles producing particularly horrendous casualty lists. That for the Somme in 1916 was actually longer than the space taken up by accounts of the games fixtures. Indeed, Adam remembered the summer of 1916 as a turning-point:

Memories of this summer include a sodden game of cricket and wet afternoon at the beginning of June when the even more damping and depressing first news of the battle of Jutland was received... During this term a change of attitude towards the war gradually became noticeable in the school. The parades of the OTC and training in the use of rifles and bayonets had merely accustomed us to the handling of arms, but another aspect of warfare became evident after the first week in July. The first month saw the first large-scale offensive conducted by the civilian army at the Battle of the Somme, and by now many boys of the school had brothers as serving at the front. (Alfred [his brother] had left for France by this time.) In the first few days of this battle nine recent members of the school were killed, and from then onwards, as a matter of course, the morning papers were opened first at the page showing the casualty lists. Conscription had not yet been introduced, but every member of the school joined up on leaving without apparently and giving the matter much thought. It was not until many years later that I discovered that this was not the universal outlook throughout the country.[46]

And yet the relentless turnover of small boys which characterises schools, and the relentless fixation on the here and now which characterises small boys, meant that, for Robert Hardie, entering Fettes in 1917, 'the casualty lists were hardly more significant than cricket reports.'[47]

The people on them had been gone for some years and were unknown to the new cohorts of pupils entering the school every autumn, and in a world devoted to concepts such as manliness and pluck it is unlikely that they were going to be overtaken by morbidly dwelling on misery. In this they were helped by the former pupils in khaki. Alfred le Maitre, writing admittedly of the beginning of the war (he left in 1915) had this to say:

Every now and then someone would disappear, gazetted Second Lieutenant, and our O.F. visitors were no longer men on vac. from the 'Varsity, but men on leave from the war. I think that the bearing of our visitors, especially those from the front, was the most encouraging thing that came the way of those of us who were not yet due to follow. Newspaper reports and casualty lists were terrible and inspiring things, but the casual indifference of men a year or two older than oneself braced everyone up. I don't think I remember anyone coming back to Fettes on leave from France with any story of how beastly it was, and so the idea of our joining up when our turn arrived became as normal as the idea of going into business or up to the 'Varsity. I expect it was the same in every school in the country.[48]

Le Maitre undoubtedly took these encouraging visits to heart; he joined the Black Watch in 1915 and won the MC for conspicuous gallantry whilst leading a raid. He was fired upon whilst breaching the enemy wire, but was first into the enemy trench where he killed two Germans and captured another. He was, however, so severely injured whilst taking his prisoner back to the British lines that he was invalided home; a promising athlete in his schooldays, he had to leave the army, later becoming a prominent civil servant. The Headmaster recalled after the war that 'the rush to join the army, which began at the very commencement of the war, never thinned or slackened for the whole four and a half bitter years.'[49]

By 1916, the government had introduced conscription – an issue over which the Old Fettesian and classical liberal John Simon, who had had his doubts about the war in the first place, resigned his post as Home Secretary – and the school magazine carried an announcement from the commander of the OTC that cadets who obtained recommendations from him would be eligible to enter one of the Schools of Instruction for officers. If they did not, they would be classified as Group One under the Military Service Act, which meant they would enter the ranks.[50]

Optimistic and reassuring news did still come from those who were undergoing the process; late in the war, The *Fettesian* carried a letter from an anonymous old boy who was training with the Artillery 'somewhere in England.' It has the same mixture of jovial insouciance, good-natured grousing and honest patriotism visible in such writing before the war; although he comments that the kit rarely fits, orderly officers are irritatingly pernickety about playing football indoors, and the work is hard, he is upbeat:

... a jollier lot of fellows you couldn't find anywhere. All are keen on their work. All want to get through and help others get through. They get plenty of work during parade and plenty of work 'after school hours.' Their life is not a bed of roses, but it is the kind that makes good officers.[51]

Nonetheless, Macpherson, describing this part of the war, describes a 'careless fatalism' pervading the school; 'every one was swept into the

Army. The choice of a next step was possibly limited to the selection of the service or unit to enter.'[52]

Thoughts turned to the perpetuation of one's memory; Adam was one of many who built his own sepulchre, a hollowed-out part of study wall or desk in which would be placed a piece of paper with his details of occupancy. Known as 'graves', these macabre little hollows were then carefully sealed over; sadly, the turnover of furniture necessary in a school full of energetic teenage boys meant that they can no longer be found at Fettes. Popular older pupils due to leave and join up might also receive artistic commemoration from the younger lads. Adam was 'dragged with great gusto by a small boy of thirteen to see his handiwork in my old study, where he had carved my name deep in the table at which I had sat for nearly three years.'[53]

He did not recall the point of departure with any great misery, though:

With a cheery fatalism we all took it as a matter of course that the war would last indefinitely and that, at any rate, before long that we would be killed. It did not depress us in the least, and to those who looked forward to this career in the Service as keenly as I did, the separation from so many friends and from such a pleasant life had its compensations in the outlook for the future. Besides, I had that promised appointment to keep with the German Fleet.[54]

The Corps in wartime

The OTC was, obviously, of greatly increased importance now that war had arrived. Adam recalled that cadet activities were now 'regarded as being of sufficient consequence to interfere on occasions with the almost religious ritual of rugger games'[55] and lesser sports disappeared altogether. Tuesday and Thursday soccer was abandoned and replaced by military training, with a special Officers' Class on Fridays and a further session on Saturdays. Sellar felt – possibly with a schoolmaster's hindsight – that all this added to the strain on both Housemasters and boys; 'a boy who in normal times would have been working for a scholarship and doing extra Classics had to do extra Corps work instead, and, knowing that he was leaving school quite soon, he was inclined to lose interest in Latin and Greek composition.'[56]

Strain notwithstanding, Mr H.R. Pyatt, the Housemaster of Carrington, who was a rather more sensitive soul than the usual run of Fettes staff (he heretically declared rugby 'a game for louts and bullies' and cricket 'a waste of time') did his bit for the cause by writing poetry extolling the Corps' virtues:

Left, right! Left, Right!
All of them keen to join in the fight;
Not very big, but as keen as can be,
Kaiser, look out for them over the sea.[57]

Real life was rather less lyrical; as a report in the spring of 1916 noted, it had generally rained or snowed all term. Looking on the bright side, this had meant considerable progress in Morse Code, which would mean a lot of signallers when the cadets left school ('whether they like it or not', the author commented).[58]

The boys were deeply frustrated by the introduction of a new form of drill half-way through the war, which, accompanied as it was by the introduction of the Daylight Saving Bill, drew the ire of the *Fettesian* editor, and a piece of rather fine nonsense verse:

Right Dress! Upon the final 'ss' you leap with all your strength
(A foot in height the jump should be, and half a pace in length),
Then shuffle slowly backward till you stand behind your head,
Salute the marker, wake yourself and then jump out of bed.[59]

Lessons learned on the battlefield were also being filtered down to the cadets; the importance of clear commands and of responding intelligently to them, for instance, and training in the use of Lewis light machine-guns and what the Russians were later to call 'pocket artillery' – the hand grenade. Bloodthirstiness was occasionally inculcated by the 'sarge' during bayonet practice – an activity no longer indulged in by cadets but then considered necessary for the successful attack. 'Samson Agonistes', a schoolboy poet in 1918, described the relevant technique:

If he says 'I'm a Boche!' lest you're thought to be lazy,
You leap at him hard just as if you were crazy.[60]

Much of the training delivered by the older masters, who stepped in for the younger teachers who were now at the front, but initially had to be 'kindly but firmly drilled with the rest of us' until they could, like the mild-mannered Mr. Cumberlege, who also ran the Shakespeare Society, attain such a level of expertise that they could ask devastatingly pointed questions of officers who came from Edinburgh Castle to lecture the school.[61]

They made considerable progress, and when Deputy Chief of the Imperial General Staff Major-General R.D. Whigham (an old boy) inspected them in the summer of 1916 – a few days before the opening of the Somme offensive which would claim dozens of Fettesians – they were delighted to be complimented on the quality of their drill, leadership and overall performance. The General reminded the cadets of the key qualities of an officer – discipline, resolution, loyalty and unselfishness, and said he was confident that these values characterised the modern schoolboy.[62]

He was no armchair brass-hat; a veteran of Atbara, Khartoum and Paardeberg, in October 1914 he had been in conference with the rest of the 2nd Division staff at Hooge Chateau, near Ypres, where the Germans came close to making the breakthrough they craved. A German spotter plane flew over and, shortly afterwards, a salvo of accurate shells landed on or beside the building, killing or seriously wounding everyone except Whigham.[63]

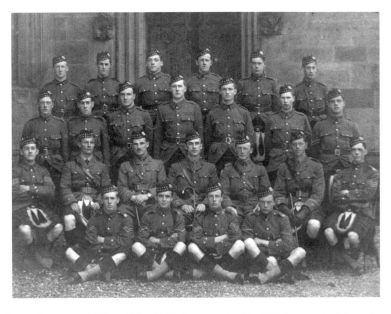

The Officers and NCOs of the OTC photographed in 1916: several of these boys would be killed within months of leaving school

Discipline and resolution may well have been in shorter supply than the General would have liked, as the endless drill clearly irritated enough boys for occasional notices about its importance to appear in the school magazine that autumn. The staff may well have been put out by the disastrous (from their perspective) summer 1916 field day, when, if the facetious report in the *Fettesian* is to be believed, the boys managed to lose their officer and spent the day dozing in the sun and eating sweets – an introduction to the traditional army 'skive' if ever there was one. Adam certainly enjoyed it. The chance to take a dip in the Forth and watch the destroyers heading out to the North Sea made a welcome change from exercises characterised by 'the usual general air of confusion on the part of the combatants and officiousness on the part of the officials.'[64]

A rather po-faced account of the subsequent field day suggested that greater realism would be added to proceedings if, instead of sitting around eating sandwiches whilst waiting for the action to start, the cadets were to get picks and shovels and start digging trenches.[65]

For some, simply taking part in standard training on the playing fields was realistic enough:

Corps days that dwell in the mind were bitterly cold, when gloveless hands froze on to icy butts and a chill wind played round bare throats, while the N.C.O. in charge, begloved and swathed in a Bigside scarf, and, if a real 'blood', covered in parts by an extremely tattered blazer (the bigger the blood the more disreputable the blazer), strode heatedly up and down in front of a chittering squad.[66]

Adam recalled an exercise when a platoon, making good progress in a night attack on the school, suddenly found itself silhouetted on the crest of a hill by the searchlights from Rosyth and therefore, in theory, open to massacre by the defending unit in the great stone fortress of the main building. He also remembered a certain problem unique to Scottish cadets:

Striding along the streets in kilt and military tunic we were soldiers for the nonce, but the most gratifying thought was that we could travel half fare on the Glasgow trams. We soon realized, however, that to ride with delicacy on the top of the tram while wearing a kilt presented problems totally unknown in the rough and tumble of school life, where the act of throwing ourselves on the ground while attacking in open order across the playing fields on a windy day meant the exposure of a row of bare bottoms to the indifferent gaze of the few onlookers.[67]

What the boys would really have liked was a tank, for these supposedly war-winning pieces of technology made their first appearance in the later stages of the Somme campaign and immediately inspired some truly horrible schoolboy poetry:

When I stand above their trench
Then the boldest Germans blench
As I rake with deadly aim their serried rank:
And their useless bullets spit,
But I mind them not a whit,
For I'm ever yours, the Armoured British Tank! [68]

Given that they were not going to get any tanks (which were not, in any case, invincible – OF Miles Atkinson, who had been training before the war to become a doctor, was killed when the tank he was navigating was hit by enemy fire) there is little wonder that they got rather bored with it all. Adam was, in any case, more interested in ships; he plastered the walls of his study with silhouettes of the fleet and graphs showing the losses of the submarine campaign. This indifference seeped upwards; 'no incident of particular interest has happened' was the terse report of cadet activities in April 1917. There were, however, a few sparks of interest that year, for the pipe band was re-started and they were able to go to camp again, both pleasures having been denied them for much of the war. The band was, apparently, very good despite having had two years without practice – Adam remembered with affection turning in after a strenuous day to the sound of 'Hey, Johnnie Cope, are ye waukin' yet?' – and 93 boys went to the camp at Barry. Only two, Sergeants Cox and Young, had been on the last camp back in 1914. A subsequent field day at Gullane saw the cadets trying to see off an amphibious landing by Loretto, Watson's and Heriot's schools (in the absence of amphibious vessels, it was decided to assume that the enemy had somehow got ashore already and would be dealt with on land). Because of the high turnover of boys joining the armed forces and the eagerness of the forces to have those with such experience and skills as corps life gave them (often, after 1916, calling them up in the middle of term), the Fettes contingent, was, by 1918, having real difficulty in keeping stable numbers of NCOs. The Corps did, nonetheless, give the boys at least some inkling of what was in store for them, both in terms of hard slogging and appreciation of the small delights of the Soldiers' Home (later the NAAFI) after a hard day at camp:

> *Did you carry a leaden rifle that chafed your shoulder away,*
> *On a dusty road all morning, and cleaned it the rest of the day?*
> *If you did, then you will remember, wherever you chance to roam,*
> *How pleasant you found the rest at the longed-for Soldiers' Home.*
>
> *Did you go to the evening concert, or sample the honest fare?*
> *(Better you'll not discover, though you seek it everywhere.)*
> *If you did, then you'll always remember, wherever you chance to roam,*
> *To honour what most deserves it, the work of the Soldiers' Home.*[69]

Fettesians were determined to contribute to the war effort in other ways. In 1915, for instance, the Fettesian-Lorettonian Club donated a motor-ambulance to the Red Cross, and concerts were given for the entertainment of convalescing troops in the nearby Soldiers' Home. Others, such as Adam, helped out in the holidays on an individual basis as members of the Scouts or Boys' Brigade; he cycled 20 to 30 miles a day as a despatch-rider to a Dublin barracks and was used for bandage practice by would-be VAD nurses.

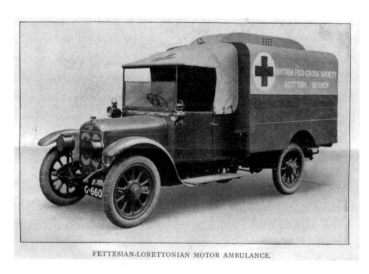

FETTESIAN-LORETTONIAN MOTOR AMBULANCE.

The Fettesian-Lorettonian motor ambulance

173

Probably the most notable aspect of Fettesian support for the national struggle was the surrender of large parts of the summer holiday to working in inhospitable conditions at Lumber Camps. The idea was that they boys would denude highland hillsides of trees, which would then be sawn up and used as props for mines in Britain and trenches in Flanders. The first of these camps was held at Pitlochry in the summer of 1916. The preceding summer term had been characterised by appalling weather, which flooded the pitches, giving the school a 'watery complexion', and combined with an outbreak of Roseola to inflict disaster on the inter-house cricket leagues. The *Fettesian* editorial at the beginning of the holidays said that 'good weather is absolutely essential to the success of the Lumber Camp, which, amid the hills and woods of Pitlochry, ought to prove very enjoyable.'[70]

The weather was indeed favourable, though this was initially a problem as some boys found conditions stifling. Others took some time to realise that 'an axe will chip a leg as easily as a tree', and Sellar recalled being devoured by horse-flies but in general the vigorous outdoor life appealed to the boys, who lived under canvas, washed in the River Tummel, and climbed fifty minutes up hill each day in order to work all day chopping down trees, fortified only by a two-inch thick sandwich for lunch. Evenings were spent cycling, walking or visiting the bright lights of Pitlochry; a football match against the Scottish Horse was an attraction 'too expensive to be repeated' as it left several boys injured and unable to work. Having chopped down at least four thousand trees for the war effort, and sacrificed most of their holiday to do so, the Fettes boys were – probably rightly – rather proud of themselves. Nonetheless, they came up against two great British traditions which rather took the shine off their achievement. 'It is characteristic of a country that prides itself on "muddling through" that we were only fully armed the last fortnight,' commented the *Fettesian*, noting the inadequacy of the loose-headed axes with which they were supplied.[71]

This 'muddling through' has been a consistent theme of the British approach to politics in general and war in particular, and one vigorously criticised by historians. No doubt when this anonymous writer went into adult life he continued to be frustrated by it, but at least he had been forewarned. The second feature of our public discourse which the boys encountered was the spiteful carping of the press; it was claimed in the pages of the *Scotsman* that they had merely been enjoying a holiday at public expense. What manner of holiday requires the participant to carry out back-breaking work in the mountains was not specified, but the criticism undoubtedly stung since the *Fettesian* felt obliged to comment on it, and Sellar still remembered it fifteen years later. The public might well have been further outraged, as they are today by tales of drugs, alcohol and YouTube, by the knowledge that those boys whose parents had given permission were allowed to smoke (this was, Adam noted, allowed at the end of term anyway, when boys waiting for cabs, from the ages of twelve to eighteen, potter about the garden with cigarettes). The weary pupils were reassured by a letter from a former masterer serving in France who told them that 'I am glad to hear you have been cutting pit props; we live on them out here; they support all our trenches and dug-outs.'[72]

Bolstered by this, in 1917, they looked forward to doing their bit on Inch Cailloch, an island in Loch Lomond planted during the Peninsular War to provide the Royal Navy with timber for its ships, 'which should be even better than Pitlochry', the *Fettesian* opined optimistically, adding a musical appeal:

> *Ye canna hae yer coal when the coal-pits are shut,*
> *Gin there's pit props enou' I' the Highlands;*
> *Sae, come a' ye braw lads there's wood tae be cut*
> *I' the bonniest of a' Scottish Islands.*
>
> *I'll tak' the oak tree, an' ye'll tak' the beech,*
> *An' wi' tents we will a' mak' our home on't:*
> *There's a muckle lot o'work there for a' an' for each,*
> *On the bonnie bonnie isle o'Loch Lomond.*[73]

Unfortunately, after a blissful first few days, constant rain allowed a tally of only a thousand trees, 'sadly short of what it might have been.' The following year, the boys were to be dispersed onto various farms for their summer work, but this proved impracticable, not least because of the impact of Spanish Influenza.

The Masters and the War

Apart from the former pupils who fought and died, the greatest impact of the war was probably on the staff common room. As Sellar recalled, the departure of the younger masters to fight led to both a shortage of people who could teach and some lowering of the overall standard of work. All the cadet officers, naturally, were called up as soon as the war started, and were followed by men like 27-year-old (he was known to the more aged staff as 'the Babe') Alec Ashcroft, who was mentioned three times in dispatches and won the DSO as well as the Order of the Crown of Italy. Sellar remembered him as 'a young and enthusiastic Master whose head was prematurely turning bald'; the sixth form got him a cigarette-case as a leaving present when he left to join up, and his house gathered in the darkness to cheer him off as his cab headed out the East Fettes drive. Ian Hay, the popular cadet officer, not only served with distinction, winning the MC, but continued to write his comic novels. *The First Hundred Thousand* appeared in 1916, and is a thinly-fictionalised account of the training and deployment of Kitchener's 'New Armies'. Hay initially published the book as a series of anonymous essays in *Blackwood's Magazine*; he may have feared trouble from on high as he did not shrink from describing the muddle, waste, pain, fear and discomfort of war, despite a general tone of levity. It is very clearly written from the perspective of the officers, and is boundlessly affectionate towards the men, but it is hard to avoid the conclusion that writing about adult, working-class males in exactly the same schoolmasterish way he did about his pupils in *The Lighter Side Of School Life* does not always endear Hay to some modern readers. It was loyally well-received at Fettes, of course, for he loved the place and its people, and was well-loved in return, not least because, as le Maitre recalled, his fertile and crowded mind could easily be distracted from the lesson in hand and onto more amusing topics. These gifts were subsequently put to good use by those on high, who sent him to explain the British cause to the Americans, with, apparently, some success. Music master Thomas Fielden was wounded twice and eventually invalided home, whilst Morris Meredith Williams, the art master, put his talents to good use in the Intelligence Corps, working with camouflage. In this he was joined by Edward Wadsworth, an Old Fettesian artist who played a leading role in the Vorticist movement, probably the only genuinely worthwhile artistic development of twentieth century Britain – he appears on the left of W.M. Roberts' painting of the group at the Restaurant de la Tour Eiffel, keeping company with the likes of Ezra Pound and Wyndham Lewis. Wadsworth's dazzle camouflage, which disrupted the outlines of ships to hinder the work of U-boats, gave wartime vessels a distinctive appearance and saved many lives; his painting of his handywork, *Dazzle-ships in Drydock in Liverpool*, is one of the great images of the conflict. Not all the teachers, of course, were in a position to fight, and Sellar reflected after the war that:

It was, of course, the Masters who really suffered. Many whose lot was cast at home in those years endured emotions of which they can never speak; and none had more to bear in this sphere than the Housemasters who were faithful to their workaday jobs. It is perhaps sufficient to say that out of the nine House Prefects (an unusually large number) in College in the summer of 1914, six were subsequently killed on the battlefields and one badly crippled...[74]

Their housemaster, A. W. Hudson, was 'obsessed with the idea that he was a shirker and left Fettes in 1916 to become an ambulance driver on the Italian front.'[75] Known for 'the vigour of his batting at the nets and the persistence with which he instructed us as to the order of French pronouns preceding the verb', Hudson was a popular figure, and Sellar recalled that he knew of more than one boy who wept uncontrollably when this kind, fair-minded and anguished schoolmaster gave his farewell speech. Hudson exorcised his demons; he served with distinction in the British Red Cross and was decorated twice by the Italian government, but he did not return to teaching and became a painter after the war. K. P. Wilson, Housemaster of Glencorse, was, according to the future Foreign Secretary and later Chancellor, Selwyn Lloyd, who entered Fettes in 1918, 'numbed by the deaths.'[76]

Such cases illustrate the torment suffered by so many of the Fettes staff; Mr John Mackay Thompson, 'to his intense disappointment, declared unfit for war service' therefore had the 'grim and unenviable work of tabulating casualties and keeping the *Fettes War Register* up to date.'[77] The extraordinary pain suffered by this remarkable man is palpable from the original version of that book. In December 1914, the school published *Fettesians Serving*, a printed ledger with plenty of space for more names to be inserted, and he added updates throughout the war in a precise hand, with decorations in red ink, new recruits 'not all in exact alphabetical order, but nearly so', and, of course, 'names of killed underlined, in red or black.'[78] He had underlined half of the original list of serving former pupils beginning with 'A' by the time the war ended, often adding tiny details about where they had served and how they had been killed.

NAME.	HOUSE AND DATE OF ENTRY.	RANK AND REGIMENT, ETC.	NOTES.
Allender, G. F.	M 1881	Lt.-Col.(T.F. Res.) 5th Bn. King's (Liverpool Regt.)	D.A.Q.M.G., H.Q. Stq., Western Command.
Anderson, Alex. R.	M 1898	Lovat's Scouts	a Lieut. 3rd H.L.I.
Anderson, C. H.	M 1902	Lieut. 1st Bn. H.L.I.	Serving with I.C. in ... Egypt
Anderson, E. K.	M 1910	2nd Lieut. 5th Bn. H.L.I. (T.)	O.T.C. p. Capt.
Anderson, W. H.	M 1895	Capt. 2nd Glasgow (Service) Bn. H.L.I.	Lieut.-Col.
Anderson, A. W.	C 1898	2nd Lieut. 4th Bn. Border Regt. (T.)	
Anderson, Matthew	C 1900	Lieut. 9th Bn. H.L.I. (T.)	Capt. Killed in France.
Anson, G. F. W.	C 1895	Capt. Indian Army	Temp. Maj.
Arrol, A. T.	G 1896	Capt. 9th Bn. A. & S. Highrs. (T.)	Wd., France; rep. 18.5.15
Ashcroft, A. H.	Fettes Master	2nd Lieut. 10th (Service) Bn. Worcestershire Regt.	Temp. Capt. South Staffs. Regt.
Auld, J. H.	M 1909	Midshipman R.N.R.	O.T.C.
Aymer, A. L.	S 1903	R.A.M.C. No. 3 Ambul. Train	Lieut.
Baird, B. H.	M 1891	Capt. 1st Bn. H.L.I.	
Baker, C. T.	M 1908	Capt. 5th Bn. Bedfordshire Regt. (T.)	O.T.C.
Barclay, J. W.	G 1892	2nd Lieut. 9th Bn. H.L.I. (T.)	Capt. & Adj.
Barclay, P. C. R.	S 1885	Maj. 122nd Rajputana Infantry, Indian Army	Temp. Lt.-Col.
Barnes, A. A. S.	S 1881	Maj. 1st Bn. Wiltshire Regt.	

The Fettesians Serving *book: underlinings represent a former pupil's death*

Non-academic staff also served, and one of them, Pioneer-Sergeant Peter Grant, who had been an instructor in the school workshop and son of William Grant, a former gardener at Fettes, was killed on 24 March 1918 – the same day as his brother. Despite the constant grind of bad news, Mr Pyatt, the English master, could contribute a grimly rousing verse to the *Fettesian* in 1918, urging a last push 'unto the end' which was in the same spirit of the poetry of 1914:

> As he who thirsting toiled – so fables tell –
> Up the grim slope to roll the pitiless stone
> That thrust him backward heedless of his groan,
> Towering above him in the murk of Hell;
> So have we, fainting, seen above us swell
> The hideous bulk of sin-engendered war,
> And thrust against its spite with striving sore,
> Oft backward borne, where none should rise that fell.

178

And now, at last, we seem to near the verge,
Steadfast though fainting — eyes with anguish sealed —
And fluttering hearts that scarce have skill to hope.
A loosening hold the monster seems to yield:
Be ours the strength the last few spans to urge,
And send it shrieking down the further slope.[79]

It was, of course, on the Headmaster, Dr Heard, that all of this fell most heavily. 66 years old when the war started, he had talked of retirement, but felt it his duty to stay on. As the war progressed, he was worn down by the relentless stream of names of lost boys; as le Maitre recalled, 'to most of us the killed were men of two or three years older, and that is a big difference, but the Head was of all generations, and his friends were in every list.'[80] The fact that no less than six Heads of School – the boy with whom the Headmaster must work most closely – were among the dead was a source of particular pain. Visibly exhausted, this once-brilliant scholar's sermons in chapel were dreaded by the boys – 'dreadfully boring', as Selwyn Lloyd wrote to his mother.[81] That said, he retained his sense of humour to the last, and when not too tired he could speak clearly and amusingly, once reading out a 'Greek Dictation' to be copied down by some over-sleeping sixth formers (who had enjoyed themselves too much at the previous night's Shakespeare Society) which turned out to be a comic account of their misadventures. Adam wrote of 'the Gussy':

The feeling of aloofness, natural to his position, did not prevent his strong sense of humour showing up on occasions; even when in the middle of rather a dull sermon which he was preaching in chapel he saw in school's air of somnolence the target for a shaft of wit. Coming to a suitable passage he chose his moment and, raising his voice, shouted 'awake, thou that sleepest' and passed on, with a strong effort to control a smile, at the effect produced on the school.[82]

'He was, potentially at least, a Great Man,' Sellar concluded, and Macpherson, although he had only seen Dr. Heard towards the end of his career, concurred. 'There can be no doubt' he wrote, 'that this self-sacrifice shortened his life' – for the Headmaster was to die less than two years into his retirement in 1919.

The Rev Dr W.A. Heard, who led the school through the First World War

After the war, Ian Hay wondered what it must have been like when the school was 'pervaded to its innermost recesses by the realisation of the fact that each boy within its walls will, upon reaching the earliest limits of man's estate, transfer himself automatically to the heart of the roaring furnace overseas.'[83]

More prosaically, Sellar asked 'was life at Fettes enjoyable?' Not for younger boys. Fettes was a dark and dismal house of pain in which virtually institutionalised bullying made the life of the 'new man' deeply unpleasant. This is partly to be expected. As the school's official history records, 'The fatalism of seniors who knew that to leave school was to go to likely death in the trenches produced a harshness that made this the unhappiest period in the school's history.'[84]

The more squalid type of homosexuality occasionally cropped up in nakedly exploitative relationships between senior and junior boys in the last years of the war. This was ruthlessly stamped out by the new headmaster, Dr Ashcroft, much to the approval of the young Selwyn Lloyd, whose good looks had attracted the unwelcome attentions of some senior boys; they knew him as 'Jezebel' from his initials 'J.S.B.', but unlike the Biblical monarch he had right on his side and the pederasts were expelled.[85]

Yet Sellar, possibly with the nostalgic love of school which makes people become teachers in the first place, was sanguine when he remembered the place a decade later. 'Nearly all boys,' he decided, 'were at least contented most of the time and were positively happy a great deal of the time.'[86]

This especially applied as one got older, and the unhappiness of the 'new man' receded, until one reached the top, where 'the life of the prefect was the life of a god.' He accepted that Fettesians, for all the hardships, still had a better life than most of the unlucky inhabitants of Europe at the time, and did not feel that there were any marked or surprising changes to the life of the school:

The truth is that under cover of the simple motto 'Business as Usual,' Fettes, like every other institution in the country, maintained its determination to 'carry on' with as little display of emotional excitement as possible.

There is, in the aesthetic realm, an atmosphere about a School which is made by its natural surroundings and which wars cannot alter; it belongs for ever to all who are sensitive enough to perceive it. War did not modify the west winds that beat relentlessly on our dormitory skylights, nor dim the blaze of hawthorn and laburnum along the Green Walk in June; among the shadows, the blackbirds and greenfinches went about their business.[87]

NOTES

[1] Le Maitre in Pyatt, p. 128

[2] *Fettesian*, November 1914

[3] Gordon Corrigan, *Mud, Blood and Poppycock* (London, Cassell, 2004) p. 38

[4] Mackie, p. 357

[5] *Fettesian*, June 1918

[6] Sellar in Pyatt, p. 241

[7] Quoted in *Fettesian*, June 1916

[8] Stephen H. Louden, *Chaplains in Conflict* (Avon Books, London, 1996) p. 58

[9] Maitland Hardyman, *A Challenge* (London, Allen & Unwin, 1919) p. 30

[10] Adam, p. 45

[11] *Fettesian*, December 1918

[12] Ibid., April 1919

[13] G. Sparrow & J.N.MacB. Ross, *On Four Fronts with the Royal Naval Division* (London, Hodder & Stoughton, 1918) p. 257

[14] Quoted in Elie Guild, p. 6

[15] Ibid., p. 10

[16] Ibid., p. 18

[17] *Glasgow University Magazine*, Memorial Number, December 1915

[18] Le Maitre in Pyatt, p. 128

[19] Any contemporary teacher or prefect on duty would note that the latter condition was by no means merely confined to wartime.

[20] *Fettesian*, November 1914

[21] Ibid., December 1914

[22] R. Morris, *Aboard HMS May Island* (Save the Wemyss Ancient Caves Society, 2006) 2004

[23] Official German statement to neutrals, 3 April 1916 as reported in *New York Times*, 4 April 1916

[24] Quoted in *New York Times*, 4 April 1916

[25] W.C. Sellar in Pyatt, pp. 229-30

[26] Adam

[27] W.C. Sellar in Pyatt, p. 230

[28] *Fettesian,* April 1917

[29] Thomas Fegan, *The Baby Killers: German Air Raids on Britain in the First World War* (Barnesley, Pen & Sword, 2002) p. 180

[30] R.S. Hardie in Pyatt, p. 253

[31] Philp, op. cit., p. 48

[32] *Fettesian*, November 1914

[33] W.C. Sellar in Pyatt, p. 224. Sellar was, of course, writing in an age before girls went to Fettes, and therefore could not have imagined that one day the school would see that a large chunk of its clientele could indeed live in such a state.

[34] Ibid., p. 236

[35] Adam, p. 59

[36] *Fettesian*, November 1917

[37] Ibid., April 1916

[38] G.P.S. Macpherson in Pyatt, p. 250

[39] *Fettesian*, November 1918

[40] Quoted in D.R. Thorpe, *Selwyn Lloyd*, (Jonathan Cape, London, 1989), p. 16

[41] Hardie in Pyatt, p. 254

[42] Adam, p.27

[43] *Fettesian*, December 1917

[44] Ibid., November 1918

[45] Ibid., July 1918

[46] Adam, p. 57

[47] R.S. Hardie in Pyatt, p. 253

[48] Le Maitre in ibid., p. 216

[49] Rev. Dr. W.A. Heard, Founder's Day Speech, 1919

[50] *Fettesian,* March 1916

[51] Ibid., March 1918

[52] Macpherson in Pyatt., p. 243

[53] Adam, p. 71

[54] Ibid., p. 72

[55] Ibid., p. 40

[56] Sellar in Pyatt, p. 231

[57] *Fettesian,* April 1916

[58] Ibid.

[59] Ibid., June 1916

[60] Ibid., March 1918

[61] Sellar in Pyatt, p. 232

[62] *Fettesian*, July 1916

[63] Sir J.E. Edmonds, *Military Operations, France & Belgium 1914* (London, Macmillan, 1937) p. 324

[64] Adam, p. 60

[65] *Fettesian*, March 1917

[66] Macpherson in Pyatt, p. 246

[67] Adam, p. 65

[68] *Fettesian*, December 1916

[69] Ibid., November 1917

[70] Ibid., July 1916

[71] Ibid., November 1916

[72] Ibid.

[73] Ibid., July 1917

[74] Sellar in Pyatt, p. 225

[75] Philp, p. 49

[76] Quoted in D.R. Thorpe, p. 17

[77] Sellar in Pyatt, p. 220

[78] J.M. Thompson, *Fettesians Serving*, (Edinburgh, 1914), handwritten notes

[79] *Fettesian*, November 1918

[80] Le Maitre in Pyatt, p. 215

[81] Quoted in Philp, p. 49

[82] Adam, p. 70

[83] Hay in Pyatt, p. 270
[84] Philp, p.49
[85] Thorpe, p. 17
[86] Sellar in Pyatt, p. 238
[87] Ibid., pp. 241–2

Chapter Six

'Such men cannot die'

Fettesians on the Western Front, 1914–18

The Outbreak of War

Because of the school's enthusiasm for all things military, by November 1914 331 OFs were already serving (250 of whom were either already in the forces or were recalled from reserve on the outbreak of war) and five had been killed; John Erskine Young, the first to die, fell in the retreat from Mons on 24 August.[1]

The *Fettesian*, listing the 331 names with pride, had editorialised that 'this war gives to all, both at home and in the Colonies, an opportunity of showing what the much-talked-of loyalty and patriotism of the British Empire is worth,' and the school certainly put its money where its mouth was. Writing after the war, Ian Hay, the former schoolmaster known to the boys as 'Jock' Beith, wrote that in 1914 there were considerably less than 2,000 Fettesians around the world, the oldest entering his sixties; 1,090 joined up and a quarter of them died, with another quarter wounded.[2] This proportion certainly compares favourably with J.M. Winter's estimates for the great English public schools, with one in five being the usual ratio, and one in six for Irish schools.[3] The death toll of boys who left school just before the war's outbreak, at thirty per cent, was similar to that of Oxford and Cambridge Universities, and suggests that there is indeed some truth in the notion of a 'lost generation'. As Jay Winter put it, war losses 'were unevenly distributed within the British population in a way that was unfavourable to the well-to-do and the highly educated.[4]

By the Christmas of 1914, the *Fettesian* was reporting the death of Lt Alan Dickson, who had left Fettes in 1911 to study at Merton College, Oxford; joining up as a university candidate, he was quickly gazetted on 4 August and killed at Ypres on 14 November; his body was never recovered and he is commemorated on the Menin Gate memorial to the missing. He was one of the first of the eager recruits of 1914 to be killed – most of the school's other casualties at this time being professional soldiers like D.S.R. Macpherson, son of Surgeon-General Sir William Macpherson, who had entered Sandhurst in 1908, and John Tullis, who had served in the Boer War. Another casualty of 1914, Lewis Robertson, had joined the Cameron Highlanders in 1903 but was best known as a rugby international – 'one of the finest football forwards of his time' – capped nine times for Scotland, and one of 45 members of London Scottish, three-quarters of the club's players, to be killed.[5]

A further 23 OFs had been injured, and five were missing. It was also, however, possible to focus on more positive developments; fatalities were not inevitable (after all, three-quarters of Fettesians who served did survive) and the *Fettesian* Christmas 1914 number recorded, alongside its bad news, that Archibald Williamson was still alive, having been interned in Holland along with almost 1,500 other members of the Royal Naval Division who had been forced across the border after the fall of Antwerp. Eight OFs had been mentioned in dispatches and Capt Herbert Stewart won the DSO for single-handedly eliminating two German machine-guns which were enfilading his trench. The French decorated Captains William Marshall of the Gordon Highlanders and James Hope of the HLI with the Legion d'Honneur for their gallantry in the first weeks of war. Lt Kenneth Mackenzie's heroism in plunging into the harbour at Leith to rescue a Cpl Forsyth, who had fallen in, received press attention, and he was awarded the Royal Humane Society's Medal. Where details were available, the *Fettesian* would sometimes print the story of how an old boy had met his fate. Capt Malcolm Bell of the 54th Sikhs was killed in France on 21 December 1914. His commanding officer wrote:

We have been hotly engaged with the Germans the last few days. I had sent Captain Bell to hold a certain trench of very considerable importance. He apparently was unable to get a good enough view of the Germans position from the trench itself, and got up outside; he was shot in the head and died immediately.[6]

Decorated Boer war veteran Edmond Peel Thompson died on Christmas Eve 1914. His sergeant major wrote that, despite being hit, Thompson had refused to be taken to a hospital until his injured men had been evacuated: 'he lay outside his trench all day wounded, and still issued orders to his men till he died from exposure.' Right from the start, then, the wider Fettes family was experiencing the full impact of the First World War. Given the school's intimate connection with the armed forces, which even before the war had extended to sporting fixtures with Royal Navy ships docked in Leith and Rosyth and visiting army units, this is hardly surprising.

A lucky escape

It later emerged that an OF had been holidaying in Germany that summer as Europe slid towards war; Frederick Wallace, later to be wounded serving with the 4th Scottish Rifles, had arrived in Cologne on Friday, 31 July, with his father. By this point, shooting had already started in the Balkans as Austria-Hungary, determined to punish Serbia for the murder of the heir to her throne, began bombarding Belgrade on the 28th and Russia, the self-appointed protector of Slavdom, mobilised her troops, including those on the German border, on the 30th. Britain's Foreign Secretary, the fly-fishing Sir Edward Grey, had warned Berlin that the United Kingdom would not stand aside if the war spread. Unfortunately, just as Germany's politicians took this on board and urged Austro-Hungarian restraint, the German military leaders were ramping up the tension with demands that their allies prepare to fight Russia as well. On the Rhineland, Wallace and his father saw 'soldiers in grey uniforms and spiked helmets', machine-guns and searchlights being hoisted onto Cologne cathedral, and German civilians 'buzzing themselves into the frenzy of war.'[7]

The rumour-mill fed this buzz; the Russians wanted war, Japan was ready in turn to attack Russia, and French spies were everywhere. In the town of Caub (Kaub am Rhein), suspicious locals watched their every move. Initially 'we put it down to pastoral simplicity' but an angry mob soon gathered and they were hustled along to the Rathaus, accused of being French spies. Although they managed to escape, the knowledge that two Frenchmen had been arrested for painting the local scenery meant that Wallace prudently dropped his three dozen photographic plates into the Rhine, lest they be the cause of his incarceration in 'some dank cell during the War Lord's pleasure.'

The Fettesian experience of recruitment

Although OFs often joined in the ranks, promotion was rapid for the young man of good education, especially if, like the Fettesian, he had

187

been a cadet at school; had he passed Certificate A and received his commanding officer's recommendation, he could go straight to Sandhurst. By way of comparison, at Fettes, which had a cadet corps, only fifteen of the 250 war dead did not hold a commission, whereas around half of the names on the war memorial of another classically-based Scottish baronial-style school, the Belfast Royal Academy, which did not (the government being unaccountably reluctant to put even more weapons into the hands of people in Ireland at that time), are those of privates or NCOs. Lacking a cadet CO's recommendation, their progress through the ranks was slower, regardless of their proficiency in Latin or games. The army which these men had joined was bigger, more professional and better equipped than any in the nation's recent past. It should, one recent historian observed, 'be judged, with the wisdom of history, as one of the most remarkable institutions in the long history of the British Isles.'[8]

The Staff College, filled by tough competitive examinations, took its responsibilities in training leaders very seriously; 'the course inculcated an ethos of duty and service, the subjects taught being more practical, broader and less mechanistic in presentation…staff rides set exercises involving not only the issue of orders but complex logistics and medical problems.'[9]

Despite what has been claimed by those who want to damn the officers, or at least the generals, of the British Army in 1914 as mindless 'donkeys', at least some of the lessons of recent wars were taken on board. Lord Kitchener, who was appointed Secretary of State for War, had as much experience of war as any British officer, and more than most, having served with distinction in the various African campaigns; he recognised right from that start of the war that it would last for years and that Britain needed to prepare accordingly. At the Staff College, Sir Henry Wilson encouraged the study of hypothetical wars in Belgium and France, and General Robertson, famous (or notorious) as one of Douglas Haig's closest allies, rather usefully introduced the study of retreat. A quarter of a million strong, the British Army of 1914 had 32 cavalry regiments, 154 infantry battalions, over 60 assorted brigades of horse, field, mountain and heavy artillery, 62 companies of Royal Engineers, 75 companies of the Army Service Corps (20 of which were mechanised) 35 companies of the Royal Army Medical Corps and 13 companies of vets. Admirable though this was, it ought to be admitted that since the main continental armies had at least three million men apiece, it was understandable that the Kaiser should allegedly refer to it as a 'contemptible little army.' One of its historians, Captain Cyril Falls, later commented ruefully that '*Armées d'élite* would be invincible if wars were fought without casualties. Things being what they are, *armées d'élite* are unlikely to remain so for long.'[10]

Most Fettesians, whether they were pupils or old boys, did not see the British Army as a vast collection of clueless incompetents, and were equally unlikely to see the war, as many people seem to in the twenty-first century, merely as a meaningless slaughter for no rational goals. On the contrary, the war had a very obvious point – national self-preservation and honouring British commitments to allies. After the Second World War, Ian Hay looked back on what went wrong in the First and led to both a grim stalemate and catastrophic losses. He defended the BEF of 1914 as 'beyond, or almost beyond, criticism'; it had learned in South Africa the value of mobility, marksmanship and the intelligent use of cover, and since supply, transport and medical services had been modernised.[11]

He did admit that the British were not as strong in machine-guns as they should have been, 'for we had entirely failed to foresee the destructive effect upon closely massed troops of this particular weapon' and had only two Maxim or Vickers guns per infantry battalion. Machine-guns and artillery maintained the stalemated trench-line extending from the North Sea to the Alps: 'strategic warfare had come to a standstill, for you cannot outflank an opponent who has no flank, and who, if you do achieve a breakthrough at any point, merely retires to an even stronger position slightly to the rear.' The one consolation in this was that the Germans' elaborately-worked-out design for the conquest of Europe had been brought to a standstill. In the twenties, he tried to explain to a later generation of Fettes pupils that the unglamorous hobbit warfare which ensued was not generally understood at the time:

Our one fear before we went out had been lest the war should be over before we got into it. In short, disillusionment had not yet arrived. The latter part of the war, with its hope deferred, its intensified discomforts, its air raids at home, and submarines at sea; its industrial unrest; and lastly, its remorseless and ever-increasing casualty lists, was a very different business for the resolute but weary people who took part in it. But in 1915 war was still a thrill.[12]

Hay was not the only one; James Ness MacBean Ross, a medical officer with the Royal Naval Division, co-authored a book before the war was even over in which he observed:

How many of us at the outbreak of war joined up quickly lest it should come to an end before we had a chance of participating in it? Bets were freely exchanged, even amongst Service men, that all would be over by Christmas 1914, and here it is in its fifth year, having outlived so many of these gallant optimists.[13]

By the time he wrote this, Ross been severely wounded (he was eventually invalided out of the service), had lost many friends – Old Fettesians in the RND suffered terribly at Gallipoli – and his sister, the pioneering Dr Elizabeth Ness MacBean Ross, dead of typhus on her 37th birthday whilst caring for Serbian wounded in the Kragujevac hospital.[14]

Given this optimism and excitement, it was not surprising that soon after the outbreak of war, the *Fettesian* carried a number of articles submitted by some of the many who joined up in the ranks, describing their training in gently self-deprecating terms:

'The objective,' said the Sergeant, 'for present purposes is the gap in the hedge, to the right of the gate. The range at present is 400.' Not a word, mind you, about advancing by sections or anything of this sort, simply the objective. Like one of the true bulldog breed, I set my face towards the goal, opened my bolt, put up my safety catch, extracted the magazine, and waited. They made me undo everything I had done, but I knew what was coming and scorned their petty jealousy. At last the signal came to advance, and relentlessly, with eyes fixed on the ground, rifles at the what-d'you-call-it, we advanced at the double. I was just getting my second wind, and catching up my comrades, when they stopped and threw themselves down for a breather. I was sorely tempted to follow with their example but staggered along with the word of encouragement (encouragement? –ed.) from my section commander. Soon I was overtaken by ten or twelve others, who in turn threw themselves down. But I was made of sterner stuff. 'So much for the sprinters,' thought I, and pushed along for all I was worth. I am an athlete, be it understood; I have had my place in quarter mile heats; I have swum my two lengths; but never did I exert myself as I did that day. I cleared the below railings like a bird – the kind that hits the top rail but two and blacks its eye with its rifle. Finally I reached my goal and flung myself down exhausted. Behind me, and to the left and right, stretch the long line of my competitors, evidently taking a last breather before the final sprint. When at length they arrived – a dead heat of

about 60 — I approached my platoon sergeant, held out my hand, and with a frank smile said, 'Dulce et decorum est' — the rest I couldn't remember; I knew it was something about 'Up Guards and at 'em,' but couldn't get it exactly. The Sergeant looked at me long and steadily; then with a wail of emotion he replied, 'Of all of the absolute, unutterable, unprintables —- '[15]

The magazine also published an anonymous 'diary of a recruit' which encapsulated — though again with a certain wryness of tone — the feelings of the heady days of 1914:

September1st.

10:00 — get up.

11.00 — breakfast.

11.30 — designed to enlist, being sure that my presence is required at the front.

13:00 — lunch.

2.20 — arrived at recruiting office.

2.20–2.30 — answered numerous questions with regard to age, etc.. (should have thought they would have jumped at the chance of a man like me without asking questions; but still.)

2.30– 2.45 — medically examined, or rather punched and pinched all over.

3 — full private in Kitchener's New Army.

3–3.30 — inspect my future comrades from afar.

3.30–5.30 — drill. Sergeant instructor quite unnecessarily abusive.

5.30 — quite exhausted and confused. (which is my right hand?)

5.45 — Tea. Quite uneatable. Not quite sure that I was meant for a soldier.

6.30–8.30 — extra drill. Why the Sergeant chose me for extra drill I can't think. Must be jealous of my soldierly appearance. Sergeant even more abusive. (Have I a right hand?) Quite sure I am wasted as a soldier.

8.30–9 — again inspect my F.C.s from afar.

9 — supper. Managed to swallow a little.

9.30 — apparently have to sleep on the floor with two brown horse-cloths called blankets. Twenty people in one small room!

9.45 — try to find a vacant place.

10 — all lights suddenly extinguished. Seems a feeble kind of joke to play. In desperation lie down somewhere. Seem to have alighted on an earthquake.

10-10.5 — horrible language from same, accompanied by most ungentlemanly violence against my person.

10.10 — think I am still alive. Can't possibly go to sleep like this.

September 2nd

6.00 – rudely awakened by someone. Most have slept a little after all.

6.30 – seemingly have to arrange blankets etc. in a heap.

6.40 – got mine done at any rate. How difficult some fools seem to find it.

6.45 – Sergeant seems annoyed. Since my things aren't arranged at all. Suppose I'll have to do this again to satisfy him.

6.50 – not quite so easy as I thought, but have got it done at last.

652 – Wrong again! Sure the Sergeant has a spite against me.

6.59 – thank goodness! Right at last.

7 – parade with rifles.

7.15 – disgusting exhibition of temper by man on my right. It is true that I dropped my rifle on his toe; but mistakes will happen, as I pointed out to him. Seems quite murderous. Shall have to be careful in future.

7.45 – never thought a rifle was so heavy before.

7.50 – let my rifle slip by mistake and seem to have hit the man on my left on the head. But I apologized and there was no need to call me all those names.

8 – breakfast at last. Feel I could eat anything.

8.20 – much more comfortable. Food seems to be better today. Find some of the men not so bad.

9 – parade.

12 noon – dinner. Exhausted.

12.30–2.00 – rest and smoke. Find a lot of the men very decent fellows.

2– 5.30 – route march. Distinctly noticed several people admiring my smart appearance.

5.30 – tea. Everything greatly improved since yesterday.

6.30 – free to do what I like. Make a lot of friends. Agree with them that this is all first-rate fun, also that we shall be able to finish off any number of Uhlans in a few weeks' time.

9 – excellent supper.

9.30–10 – prepare my bed, etc.

10 – roll myself up. Seems much more comfortable tonight.

10.5 – asleep.

September 20th – feel very fit; can't imagine how I found the work hard or confusing, or my comrades unpleasant.

October 15th – promoted to lance-corporal. Always said I was meant for a soldier.[16]

As previously noted, the British Army of 1914 did its best to apply scientific thinking to its training and practice. This could bewilder even the best-educated new recruit:

A few days ago they put me against a wall and asked me how to far away was an object on the other side of the field. By way of helping us they compared a golf drive to 200 yds. This was rather an eye-opener, but, like a Briton, I grun and bore it. I rather think we had ten seconds in which to judge it and write it down. A flash of inspiration make me liken it to hole at home, which I can usually compass in fifteen. Allowing ten full shots and five putts, varying from 10 yds. to 3 in., I put down 2000yds. 15ft. 7ins. I raised, they tell me, the average of my section by about 200 yds., a colossal achievement. My section commander and platoon sergeant explained the situation afterwards. They might have had more consideration, because it wasn't my fault if my golf-drive unit had been deliberately misled by my platoon commander.[17]

Once a Fettesian had made his meteoric but hardly unexpected rise from the ranks to the officers' mess, he had a new world to get used to, of his own responsibilities, of unspoken codes and unchallengeable hierarchies. Ross commented on a bewildering learning curve for the junior officer – the modern military obsession with initials, which led to a bewildering 'alphabet soup':

A highly placed official at Whitehall gives the traveller hasty instructions to report to the R.T.O. at Charing Cross, the M.L.O. at Folkestone, his opposite number at Boulogne, the D.A.D.R.T. at St. Pol, and suggests that the M.F.O. may be persuaded to arrange about the baggage. On reaching his destination a M.F.P. directs him to D.H.Q. and he interviews the G.S.O.I., who details a runner to take him to the A.A. and Q.M.G. From there he is sent to the D.A.Q.M.G., who tells him he should not have reported to ' Q ' branch at all, but to the A.D.M.S. With infinite difficulty he locates the habitation of this dignitary, only to find he is not at home.[18]

Still, as Hay observed, the young subaltern generally mastered it somehow, and again the public school background was useful, since the 'new boy' experience was more or less identical – 'the same natural shyness, the same reverence for people who afterwards turn out to be of no consequence whatsoever, and the same fear of transgressing the Laws of the Medes and Persians – regimental traditions and conventions – which alter not.'[19]

An artillery cadet, writing to Fettes later in the war, combined cheerful cynicism about the rougher side of army life ('should your boots be too large it is permissible to wear three or four pairs of socks; if too small, the correct procedure is to amputate the toes'[20]) with stern patriotism ('no branch of the army can boast of finer traditions, and they know it's up to them to keep them unsullied.') Hay also noted one of the temporary discomforts of the more medically sophisticated modern army, being vaccinated by the medical officer ('an unsentimental man of coarse mental fibre,') against the likely diseases of the front, including the enteric fever which had carried off so many Victorian OFs: 'It is no joke handling a rifle when your left arm is swelled to the full compass of your sleeve; and the personal contact of your neighbour in the ranks is sheer agony.'[21]

In retrospect (writing after the Second World War) Hay accepted that the process of gearing the hundreds of thousands of eager recruits in 1914 was 'a hard schooling' – especially since most recruits 'enlisted under the firm conviction that they would be provided forthwith with uniform, rifle and ammunition and dispatched overseas to shoot Germans' – and then had to put up with eight months of 'foot-slogging, floor-scrubbing, trench-digging and make-believe warfare with dummy weapons'.[22]

As the months of training wore on, a certain ennui creeping in; indeed, the thrill presumably made the waiting more tedious than it already was. Hay's first military book originally appeared as a series of anonymous, very thinly fictionalized, and generally jocular, bulletins in *Blackwood's Magazine* and retained this tone when it was collated into *The First Hundred Thousand*.

The new British citizen-soldier, Hay observed, no longer got drunk out of habit (unlike the old soaks of yesteryear) but because of one of the various irritants of service life. When a man drank heavily, it was 'because there were no potatoes at dinner, or because there has been a leak in the roof of his hut for a week and no one is attending to it, or because his wife is not receiving her separation allowance.' The level of drinking at a given time was 'a most reliable and invaluable barometer of the regimental atmosphere' and the officers were not unsympathetic to the men's frustration. For all his cheery patriotism, Hay could be scathing about the 'Department of Practical Jokes' which seemed to run 'Olympus', the Army bureaucracy, and this is probably why, despite changing attitudes to the social assumptions in his work, it has remained both in print and a treasure-trove of army lore for military historians and serving officers.

This sympathy did not mean discipline was allowed to slide, as Daniel Vawdrey, a young officer who would later be a much-loved Fettes master, wrote to his parents:

I had to go on a tiresome 'penalty' route march. A foolish man in my platoon got drunk yesterday, so the whole platoon had to go for a route march the same evening from 4.30 to 8.30, and I had to take them – very trying both for me and the rest of the platoon. However, it was quite cool. We had a long rest at the village four miles away, and while, for the sake of justice, the prisoner was kept under close guard, the rest were allowed the usual drink at the inn! [23]

The Road to the Front

In a letter to his parents on Good Friday 1915, Vawdrey described the process of getting to France, as experienced by millions of British personnel throughout the war:

This finds me safely at the base of the 2ⁿᵈ Division at Harfleur, five miles out from Havre. We came across from Southampton on 'the Brighton', the boat that took me across ten years ago! We were escorted by two long lean torpedo boat destroyers, one on either side, but our crossing was uneventful, and we arrived early this AM at the harbour, and here (5 miles inland) at 12. There is a capital officers' mess, and the men are very comfortable in tents; beautiful weather, but fairly dusty. My 80 men behaved very well, but were in high spirits all the way out. There are plenty of Services here at different places – civil and military – two early Celebrations every weekday, and three on Sunday, so I hope to go on Sunday (Easter Day). What a life it is, and what an Easter! It is jolly being in France, and I am already talking as much French as I can to French Tommies, and manage quite well, with a little help from a dictionary occasionally. There is plenty to remind you of England round the base camps: English civilian workers, motor-lorries, and English faces everywhere. I have got a square eight-foot canvas hut to myself in camp. There is a full programme of work to do at the base here every day. Everything does look so strange, and is full of interest. Children swarmed around me and my men all through half from crying 'biscuittes' (wanting the men's rations to eat). I emptied my haversack among them. Please tell everyone who will write to me and wants a letter back to enclose an addressed envelope (but not stamped). Envelopes will be very scarce out here. Havre was a most busy place this a.m., rivaling Southampton, teeming with military lorries and accessories. [24]

Vawdrey's letters brimmed with optimism and constantly looked on the bright side. He was very impressed with the system of provisioning, writing on 7 April 1915:

I wandered through the huge A.S.C. stores this AM and saw great stacks of honey, dates, figs, vaseline, oranges, cheese, corned beef, etc., for the troops, also solid heaps of tobacco and cigarette crates about 100ft. x 40ft. x 10ft. high.[25]

Several days later, he wrote home to describe another marvel:

I was at the A.S.C. baking stores, where the men threw loaves into sacks (100 per sack) and loaded up the trains for the front. They handled all the bread consumed in one day by about half the army, 150,000 loaves. I worked myself with them, and probably handled two or three thousand loaves myself.[26]

He was keen to get to the front line, writing on 26 April:

'Off at last!' *We were all called up at 8 p.m. last night, and almost the whole camp is clearing out for the front. I am taking all my 'whole' men, about 75 out of 100, and we start at noon today. This is* the real thing at last, *thank goodness!* [27]

Part of the journey to the front was by train, as he wrote two days later:

We started from Harfleur, about 4,000 of us, marched three miles, and entrained in two trains. Our train had about 2,000 men. I contributed 75 Worcestershires, including three capital sergeants. Everyone was very merry. The men were eight to a carriage, or else in cattle trucks with their legs out of the door. We crawled slowly along the coast, and after 24 hours arrived here at noon yesterday.[28]

The railway system to the front had become very well organised, if not desperately comfortable, as Hay observed in one of the best-known parts of *The First Hundred Thousand*:

Most of us, in our travels abroad, have observed the closed trucks which are employed upon French railways, and which bear the legend –
    Hommes: 40
    Chevaux: 8
    Doubtless we have wondered, idly enough, what it must feel like to be one of the forty hommes. Well, now we know. [29]

Soldiers were billeted behind the lines either in huge tented cities or in borrowed farms and chateaux. This was not luxurious either; but, as Hay remarked, for both officers and men sleeping on straw after a hard day's marching was not a feat of great difficulty.

Into Battle

Ross was one of the first Old Fettesians to see combat; the Royal Naval Division was deployed to Antwerp in an ill-fated attempt to save the city. By the time the RND arrived, it was too late:

All night long a hail of shells passed over our heads into doomed Antwerp. Fires soon broke out in the city and, as the water supply had been cut off, no attempt could be made to subdue them. A bombardment of increasing intensity was also opened on all the trenches, gun positions, and roads, making our position far from enviable... The evacuation of wounded was an exceedingly difficult problem, as there were no certain means of transport to Antwerp and no place of safety on arriving there..[30]

Ross left an unforgettable description of the horrors suffered by the civilian population during the retreat from Antwerp. It was, of course, something which was replicated across Belgium and Northern France, in Eastern Poland and Serbia, as the enemy forces crashed forwards.

Most of the refugees in their hasty flight forgot to provide themselves with provisions, and many, worn out by fatigue and lack of food, were unable to continue the journey. Expectant mothers gave birth to premature children and the aged died of exposure. The confusion was indescribable and the noise deafening, as the weary, starving, homeless, hopeless Belgians shuffled along, the cries of the women and children drowned by the hum of motors, the rattle of carts, the clattering of hoofs, the groans of the wounded, the alternate pleading and cursing of the men, and the roar of guns in the near distance.[31]

Horrors of war such as this were real enough, but British journalists, characteristically, sought to go always a little further, and their atrocity propaganda has been criticised for its mendacity and xenophobia. Hay, whose accounts of army life in *The First Hundred Thousand* were based on real incidents, with only the characters fictionalized, seems to have fallen for one of the most pernicious myths of the war:

197

Outside this farm stands a tall tree. Not many months ago a party of Uhlans arrived here, bringing with them a wounded British prisoner. They crucified him to that self-same tree, and stood round him till he died. He was a long time dying. Some of us had not heard of Uhlans before. These have now noted the name, for future reference — and action.[32]

This story had appeared in *The Times* in May 1915 and quickly entered the realm of folk myth (the author heard it from the pulpit as a child in the seventies). The victim is generally described as a Canadian sergeant (according to British historian Iain Overton, who gives the story some credence than most, Harry Band of the Central Ontario Regiment) and debate has raged over its veracity ever since.[33]

Hay himself does not seem to have been ulcerated by hatred for the Germans, and was later to concede that 'Whatever we may think of the Bosche as a gentleman… there is no denying his bravery as a soldier or his skill in co-ordinating an attack.' However, the men who saw scenes of terrified refugees and burning towns – which had not been witnessed in Western Europe in their lifetimes – could hardly have felt that this was anything other than a righteous crusade against barbarism. The children were particular objects of pity for British troops, and quickly learned to exploit this, as Vawdrey told his parents:

This is a very healthy place, and the camp is on the slope of a hill, facing another hill on which, about 500 years ago, the English beat the French at the battle of Harfleur. Now the French look upon 'perfidious Albion' as their saviour, and the children buzz round the Tommies asking for souvenirs and admiring their equipment and rifles![34]

Hay, as befitted a pre-war author of comic novels, was incapable of dwelling on horror and suffering (he would have thought it bad form to do so). Posted to a small town near the front, he described bombardment to his readers with a mixture of compassion, drama and surreal levity:

You who live at home in ease have no conception of what it is like to live in a town which is under intermittent shell fire. I say this advisedly. You have no conception whatsoever. We get no rest. There is a distant boom, followed by a crash overhead. Cries are heard — the cries of women and children. They are running frantically — running to observe the explosion, and if possible pick up a piece of the shell as a souvenir. Sometimes there are not enough souvenirs to go round, and then the clamour increases.

Hay's keenness to play down the dangers of warfare ('there is always the cellar to retire to if things get really serious') a tendency which has led some to see him as a misleading propagandist, was in fact almost universal and, in any case, the Tommies (and, in Fettes' case, Jocks) of the Great War did not spend all (or even most) of their time in harm's way. Vawdrey described the system to his family:

Tomorrow the battalion goes into the trenches – we march about four miles, thence through one and a half miles of communication trenches to our position at C-- on the very south of the British line. We're all getting pads for our mouths. I'm feeling very fit. The real adventure begins to-morrow about 4 p.m. To-day I got up early and went to a very nice Holy Communion on the stage at the theatre at B—, which has become the English church by now on Sundays. The Bishop of Khartoum took the Service, a dear old man, who afterwards at 11.30 preached a rousing sermon to the whole battalion which just filled the theatre. He told them to look on God as their Father, as the One who thought of and pitied them, in the trenches and out of them. The men seemed to like it. W— and I are going to an evening service in the theatre again, so I shall have had three Services to-day, quite like home! The little French children are very sweet; they murmur 'Officier Anglais' under their breath to each other and, and then salute. When you offer your hand they all make a grand at it, and are much honoured! It is quite decently safe down at C—, where we go to-morrow, good deep trenches, 200 yds. from the Germans. Two days we shall be in the firing line, two days in the reserve line, and then four days in billets well to the rear, that is the normal sequence.[35]

Further behind the lines, although there was irritation at some of the more obnoxious drill-sergeants in camp (which briefly blew up into the Etaples Mutiny of 1917), relaxation was available, and life could be quite pleasant, as Hesketh-Prichard recalled after the war:

We were welcomed with open arms. White wine which started the war at 90 centimes was 1.50 a bottle. Eggs, fruit, and everything else were cheap … I have often marvelled how little friction there really was between us and the French. If a French Army were quartered in England in the same way that we were quartered in France, I do not for a moment believe that our people would show towards them the same kindness and consideration which we received from the French.[36]

Ross, writing after the hard life of Gallipoli and Passchendaele, was also nostalgic for the moments of peace and hospitality behind the lines:

Who does not recall with pleasure the charming though anaemic vender of boots in Bethune; the dainty little lady who sold us identity discs in the jeweller's shop at Bruay; the delightful Blanche who looked after our wants in the estaminet at Hersin, and poured forth into our astonished ears wondrous tales of the doings of her fiancé at Verdun; or the jovial, hospitable priest of Bully Grenay who stuck to his post in spite of the shelling.[37]

Where their needs could not be supplied by the locals or the army, the modern postal service and proximity of the mother country meant that soldiers could get packages from home. Arthur Lloyd, the son of an Irish clergyman, wrote from the Somme on 22 October 1916:

Before I forget, I wish you would send me half a dozen Gillette razor blades please: that is a small packet – should be very easy to send in a letter. Also I would be glad if you would send me the Weekly Scotsman *every week. We never know anything about the War or anything else that is going on and the* Weekly Scotsman *gives a synopsis of the week's doings and also the Fettes rugby matches.*[38]

From his consideration to his family to his ignorance of the war and his interest in ordinary life back home, this is a fascinating insight into the mind of the soldier in the trenches. Every major battle or campaign, including many now forgotten by popular folk memory, saw young Old Fettesians taking part, of whom more than one generally ended up dead or injured. At the battle of Neuve Chapelle, for instance, fought 'essentially to prove to the French that their ally was not standing idle'[39] at least five OFs were killed, including W.A. Maclean, a former accountant for Nobel's Explosives Company, H.M. Mactier, aged 48, who had survived innumerable colonial adventures since first joining the army a quarter of a century earlier, and Robert Paterson, 21 years old, whose colonel recalled that 'instead of collecting reports, he went forward, taking no-one with him, saying that he thought it too dangerous for his men. He was never seen again.'[40]

Although valuable lessons were learned from the battle – particularly 'that the biggest constraint on the conduct of land war was the lack of real-time communications' which had meant that success (in this case a village captured in less than an hour) could be blighted when misinformed artillery shelled their own side.[41]

No fewer than 40 OFs were killed in France between the outbreak of war and the onset of the Somme campaign in the summer of 1916, many of them seasoned veterans who the army could ill-afford to lose.

Two Fettesian casualties of 1915-16: Lt Robert Paterson, RHA, and Cpl James Stewart, RE. Neither has a known grave.

By this stage the trench system had become highly developed. At the beginning of the war, it had been haphazard at best. Ross was horrified by the Heath-Robinson affairs hurriedly erected at Antwerp:

My impression of these trenches, the first I had ever seen, was distinctly discouraging. They were shallow and broad, and instead of being dug in, were mainly built up. Where the fire-step should have been were primitive dug-outs which afforded neither comfort nor safety. In front of the trenches was an elaborate system of electrified barbed wire on which our searchlights played incessantly. Roofing over us was an artificial network of branches and foliage— a mode of camouflage, it struck me at the time, on a par with the ostrich who buries his head in the sand and hopes to pass as a palm-tree. Battalion Headquarters was a small unpretentious stone erection which might possibly have kept out a summer shower, but was totally unfitted to withstand even the lightest artillery. There was no sign of any support or reserve lines.[42]

At this stage, there was still a war of movement, but this was gradually worn down into stalemate. 'For the first few months after the war broke out,' Hay wrote, confusion reigned supreme; Belgium and the north of France were one huge jumbled battlefield, rather like a public park on a Saturday afternoon — one of those parks where promiscuous football is permitted.'[43]

No-one could be sure whether a given village was occupied by friend or foe, and 'if you dimly discerned troops marching side by side with you in the dawning, it was by no means certain that they would prove to be your friends.' The trench system 'put all that right... everybody has been carefully sorted out — human beings on one side, Germans on the other.' This meant that by the middle of 1915, at any rate in the chalky lands of Northern France, and in decent weather and given time and skill to construct something more durable, trench accommodation was rather better than it had been in 1914. Hay was pleasantly surprised by the efforts made by the Welsh unit which preceded his to make their stretch of the line – a 'thoroughfare' of 'little toy houses' – more habitable, with doors and painted wooden walls decorated with elegant extracts from the *Sketch* and *La Vie Parisienne*. Again, Hay was perhaps over-egging matters for the purposes of reassurance, but there is no doubt that on quiet sections of the line, and in good weather, such accommodation was no figment of a propagandist's imagination but a very real possibility. Vawdrey, always at pains to tell his parents how safe he was, wrote home at about the same time that 'Our cellar is quite cosy and there is even a piano in it, brought down from above out of the wreckage there; we play on it at night, only half a mile from the Huns!'[44]

'Wipers'

Although the most famous campaign, so far as modern British popular culture is concerned, is the Somme, Ypres was better known to the public until the BBC's landmark documentary of 1966; its possession as a little peninsula of Allied territory in a sea of Germans symbolised Britain's commitment to Belgium. Hay wrote that it looked as if 'a party of lunatics had been let loose on the city with coal-hammers'. Photographs of the city after two years of war show an alien world of jagged ruins on a moonscape, but Hay, like many other British officers, was proud of its defiant survival, the result of 'the obstinacy of a dull and unready nation which merely keeps faith and stands by its friends.'[45]

The first report from the trenches at Ypres to appear in the *Fettesian* came two years into the War. It was written by Richard Moncreiff of the 9th Royal Scots, whose brother Norman was to die of wounds later that year and who would himself succumb to injuries after the war ended (the school's fives court was donated by their mother as a memorial). He had fought at the Second Battle of Ypres, which had taken place a full year earlier; he had not been able to write earlier because he had not had the time, but having been badly injured in a collision with an 'excitable Frenchman' and sent home 'for seven months' holiday' he had by this point had more than enough of enforced leisure. [46]

Second Ypres is known to posterity because the Allies had experienced the first gas attack on the Western Front. Moncreiff's men had been resting at Vlameringhe when they were interrupted by a flood of rumours, refugees 'carrying with them such of their household gods as they could get away' and casualties 'apparently suffering from some extraordinary disease' – the first victims of the chlorine gas. The Royal Scots headed for the city under bombardment: 'although the Hun, with his usual persistence, shelled us all morning, we escaped unscathed. We spent our time at Potijze in little one man dug-outs like graves.' Moncreiff described with a complete absence of passion how his troops tramped or burrowed about Hill 60 and Hooge for a month, often missing 'Fritz' except for being shelled. He was nearly killed when a bullet hit his walking-stick early in the battle, but one of his key complaints was not having been able to remove his clothes for thirty-two days. (Vawdrey had a similar experience in France, writing home that 'To-night, *for the first time since March 28th when I left home,* I shall sleep between sheets, which will be a great luxury!'[47]) The same issue of the *Fettesian* carried an account of life in the Flanders dug-outs of the Royal Field Artillery, which light-heartedly described the rather boring day which was often spent by soldiers not engaged in combat:

Another favourite method of occupying our spare time is to watch aeroplanes being shelled. Writing letters and reading help us to pass the weary hours till the mail comes up about 7.30 pm. People have been known, driven to desperation by boredom, to clean the breech, but that is a last resort.

We are always ready to be called into action, which usually happens at meal times or when we are shaving, or at night time, just when we are dozing off to sleep. German working parties are quite the most inconsiderate people I have ever had any dealings with.[48]

The final school magazine of the 1917-18 academic year carried a poem by W.S. Wingate Gray, MC, about Kemmel Tower, one of the landmarks of the battered topography of the Ypres Salient. He had written it in 1915 but had only just got round to sending it in, presumably because he had better things to do.:

Kemmel Tower on Kemmel Mountain (give the order, fire the gun) –
Thee the German shells have battered
All thy fairest slopes are spattered
With the shrapnel of the Hun.

There's the Wytchaete ridge o'er yonder,
There the German big guns' lair,
Belching forth their smoke and thunder,
Tainting all thy perfect air.

Thou, the highest hill in Flanders,
Crowning o'er the pleasant plain,
Where the sluggish Yser wanders
Through the fields of ripening grain –

Thou the scene of hard-fought battles,
Struggles both by day and night,
Thou canst tell of deaths of heroes,
Bring their glorious deeds to light.[49]

The Ypres Salient was doggedly held by the British throughout the war, and despite attempts to break it, a stalemate, punctuated by bouts of blood-letting, remained in place along this section of the Western Front. Many Fettesians served, and thirty were killed, in Belgium; around half have no known grave. Alan Buchanan was helping get a machine-gun into position in a captured German trench at Hooge, when he was killed instantaneously by a shell. Former prefect and cricket captain Archibald Moir was killed on 25 April 1915; Andrew King was gassed on the same day; poisoned, he continued working, but was mortally wounded by shrapnel whilst helping some other casualties on the 28th.[50]

Trench Warfare in France
After the battles of 1914-15, the British sector of the front in France

was slightly quieter. Although direct confrontations between between the ground troops were on a small scale, sudden death was always possible because of the ritual of the 'artillery duel' in which gunners behind each set of lines would open fire. The artillery was regarded as a nuisance by them men in the trenches; Hay felt that it was 'as if two big boys, having declared a vendetta, were to assuage their hatred and satisfy their honour by going out every afternoon and throwing stones at one another's little brothers.' [51] Vawdrey explained the soldiers' dislike to his parents:

Last night a huge gun rumbled up on a traction engine, or rather, in bits, on several traction engines (equal to the Queen Elizabeth's *guns, but hush!). As soon as it begins pooping we shall have no peace, as the Huns will reply. The attitude of infantry to artillery is 'for heaven's sake don't start pooping off, as the Huns are sure to reply, and* we *shall be the victims, not* you!' [52]

He did, however, make light of his own brush with death under artillery fire, and also sought to reassure his family about the other horror-weapon of the war:

We were heavily shelled, but the Boche shells bark worse than they bite. All we five company officers were behind one traverse (20ft. long) when a heavy 4.5in. shell came slap at the breastwork, after hundreds had missed, just where we were, and brought the breastwork on top of this. We all got up laughing, and smothered with earth and sticks, absolutely none the worse. We have all got respirators, so that is quite all right, and they have not used gas down here. We also have sprays to spray hyposulphate on the gas, and make it harmless. [53]

Preserved trenches at Sanctuary Wood, photographed by Allan Forbes on Fettes pilgrimage, 2009

Ross, as a front-line medical officer, gave a hypothetical example of how he and his colleagues dealt with a mortar-fire casualty from during 'quiet times' in the trenches. As with Hay, Vawdrey and the anonymous OFs who wrote to the school, he was trying to give reassurance, but there is no doubt that the system he described for dealing with the wounded was a great leap forward from the medical support available to soldiers of the previous century:

The stretcher-bearers of his company are quickly on the scene. They apply a first field dressing, and, as he is unable to walk, carry him on a stretcher to the regimental aid post, a dug-out which is as close as possible to, and equidistant from, all four companies. The battalion medical officer's main duty is how to get this man back with the least possible pain, and, if there is not a rush of cases, to dress the wound in such a way that it need not be touched until the patient is put on the operating-table of the casualty clearing station. All serious cases are given morphia; severe bleeding is arrested by tourniquets, and splints are applied to broken limbs. Shock is treated by the application of warmth—blankets and hot drinks, with sandbags round the legs. The patient is then carried back by stretcher to the advanced dressing station of the field ambulance. This is usually about two miles behind the line, and is the nearest possible point to the line to which a motor ambulance can be brought. He continues his journey by car to the main dressing station of the field ambulance, which is usually about five miles behind the trenches. If it be a serious case and the man comfortable, he is at once sent on to the casualty clearing station by motor ambulance; if it be a slight case and there be sufficient accommodation, he is redressed and kept in the main dressing station. The casualty clearing station is, as a rule, seven to ten miles behind the firing line. It is equipped as a modern peace-time hospital. Here all serious operations are performed, and as soon as the patient is convalescent, he is despatched by hospital train to the base, from where he is sent over by hospital ship to England.[54]

Vernon Hesketh-Prichard, the veteran explorer, noted the games of psychological warfare, 'typical of the careless and grim humour with which the Scottish regiments were at times apt to regard the Hun', played in the stalemated trench system by a battalion of Seaforth Highlanders with access to an artificial grouse-beater or 'stop':

One night some adventurous and humorous spirit crawled out and placed the 'stop' about sixty yards from the German parapet, and then set it going. The Germans at once leaped to the conclusion that the tick-tick-tick was the voice of some infernal machine, which would, in due time, explode and demolish them. They threw bombs, and fired flares, and officers and men spent a most haggard and horrible night, while opposite them the Scotsmen were laughing sardonically in their trenches.[55]

Not all such pranks were carried out; another battalion had 'the brilliant idea of preparing a notice board on which was printed in large letters and German: "Bitter Fighting in Berlin" and then, in smaller type, some apocryphal information.' The idea was to shoot any Germans who raised their heads above the parapet in an attempt to read the smaller lettering with their field-glasses. This plan not actually put into practice, since, as someone realised, it would inevitably have led to a heavy bombardment of the trenches in which the notice was shown. Another form of trench warfare during quiet periods was to dig tunnels beneath the German lines, fill them with explosives, which would then be set off. Vawdrey's first day in the trenches was a rapid initiation into this tactic:

Our company (A) was helping all day yesterday at the three mines we are laying, a most uncanny job! The German first lines are only 70yds. away. They were mining too, and there was fearful excitement as to who would make good first. The entrances to the mines are just like pit-heads, and go down 20ft., and then the tunnels begin. My platoon fetched and carried for the miners, and hauled up sacks of earth and worked the water and air pumps. At 4.45 a.m. I had just stood my platoon to arms as is always done at dawn, and was watching the early morning bombardment from our reserve trenches when a terrible explosion took place, and we saw sheets of smoke and earth in front of our first line rising into the air. The Germans had won the race, but being much worse miners than us had, as usual, been well out in their reckoning, the explosion taking place well in front of our first line. We had only six slight casualties, and no damage to our trench. They have shot their bolt and failed, but our mine is still intact, and will, I hope, blow them up later on. We shall feel safer in the front line to-night now that their mine is exploded.[56]

This in turn created a new opportunity for mischief:

On the night of May 5th my commander told me to start a sap toward the crater of the mine which had exploded, and send out six men to hold it during the night to prevent the Germans reaching it and dropping bombs on us from it. I volunteered to go out with them, as it was an exciting job. We crawled along the new sap for 10yds., and then for 20yds.more we had to crawl in the open, halfway between the German lines and ours only 70yds.apart! Luckily it was a dark night and no moon, but flares were constantly being sent up by both sides, and then we had to lie like logs and pretend we were lumps of earth or cabbages, or anything but living foes of the Huns! They did not spot us. It was an exciting adventure for my first night in the firing line to walk about right under the Huns' noses, only 30yds.or so away.[57]

One of the few surviving mine craters on the Western Front at La Boissee, photographed by Allan Forbes on Fettes pilgrimage, 2008

In a letter to the *Fettesian* later in the War, 'Hootch' – a nickname with so many possible origins that it has not been possible to trace the individual behind it – described the ritual of the two-hour 'tour of duty' experienced by a subaltern in a front-line trench at 2.55 AM in France. Boredom and routine were the most frequent features:

The subaltern walked along the line, visiting the posts. The night was quiet, and only disturbed by the occasional whistle and crash of a shell, the rattle of machine-guns, and the splutter of a Verey light. On such occasions one feels very much alone. At each post to the subaltern got onto the fire step, where the two sentries over the post were standing, and looked out over No-Man's-Land. No-Man's-Land is a wilderness of weeds, pitted with shell holes. Our own wire be seen against the sky, and whenever a Verey light goes up the enemy wire appears. The sentries have to watch this wilderness for any sign of movement, which is remarkably difficult to spot. Patrols go out every night, right up to the enemy wire, and in many cases never have a shot fired at them. The time gradually dragged on, till at length the relieving officer arrived, and the subaltern who had been on duty departed hastily, accelerated by the news that the mail had arrived. When he reached the dug-out he found the sorting of the mail still in progress. Then he settled down to write a report on his tour of duty. The chief difficulty of making these reports is to find material to pad them with. In consequence their veracity is not above suspicion. At last the report was finished, letters read, and the subaltern once again lay down for a short hour's sleep before going on duty again.[58]

It was, in fact, often very dull:

What one really wants most out here, I think, is the light literature – anything to take one's mind off the war. Otherwise one thinks of nothing else! Any light books or magazines on natural history, art, fishing, etc., would keep me and my brother officers' minds off the war.[59]

Hay, 'Hootch' and Vawdrey left out – as virtually all private and public correspondence did – one of the most pervasive and notorious aspects of trench life, but Ross, as a medical officer, felt it was his duty to enlighten his readers:

Lice are always found where men are crowded together. They are not, as is popularly believed, the result of uncleanliness, but they always flourish best in dirty surroundings. Going round the trenches on a fine day, it is customary to see every man who is off duty stripped to the waist, hunting in his shirt for these noxious insects, and viciously torturing them to death between his finger-nails.

To be bombarded heavily by hostile artillery is bad, to contract lice is worse, but a combination of the two is the very acme of discomfort and enough to make even a phlegmatic Scotsman seriously contemplate suicide.

They get into one's clothing, and wander all over the body, causing intense promenade as the polite French say. Sleep is impossible. The unfortunate victim lies awake scratching every portion of his anatomy until he is finally a mass of bleeding excoriations. In addition, it must be remembered that typhus fever, relapsing fever, and trench fever are all carried from man to man by lice.

On one occasion I was credibly informed that a certain platoon commander of my acquaintance caught forty-two on his trousers alone in the space of one short hour, and that his company commander had been even more successful in his researches.

This is, I know, an unsavoury subject, but it is one of paramount importance to those affected. That such a condition exists is hardly realised and never talked of by those at home, but it is one which is deserving of the greatest sympathy.[60]

With boredom, lice, intermittent shelling and, above all, the fact that they were not achieving anything, it is little wonder that both sides made sporadic attempts to break the stalemate. Vawdrey wrote home just after the Battle of Festubert in May 1915:

As usual the Germans mass their troops always against us; perhaps it is a compliment to Tommy Atkins, but he does not seem to appreciate it! They were ready for us, and, as the papers tell you, our show was not a success. Of course we helped the French indirectly a great deal by taking away German troops from opposite them, but that was all…

My platoon had to carry heavy bridges to put across a ditch defending the second Hun trench, after we had taken the first trench. As luck would have it, some of our men were seen or heard crawling over our parapet to the ditch in front, from which they were to start rushing across; the Huns took alarm, and two minutes before the appointed hour of attack – 11 p.m. – they poured in a terrible storm of machine gun and rifle fire, before which no troops could stand. None of our men reached the front German line, and those that were not hit had to return. We had 250 casualties out of 800 fighting men, and were lucky not to lose more. Fortunately we had only a few officers hit – one killed. Poor Scott (my old school-fellow) died of wounds next day, and four were slightly wounded. The Huns were ready for us, and had about eight machine-guns sweeping our parapet and the ground in front. I was not supposed to leave our parapet ill the front Hun line was taken, but in that fearful storm of bullets and confusion one could not tell what was happening, and I was so afraid of failing our men in front that I gave the order, and we began lugging the bridges out of a hole in our breast-works. Why we were not hit Heaven knows, though f course it was dark and they could not aim well. I got some of my platoon a quarter of the way, but had to go back myself for each bridge… Then I saw it was hopeless as the remains of the front line were returning, so I drew my men back, and fortunately we had no one hit in our platoon.

They took us back to our old billets half a mile next day, but instead of resting us they put us back in our second line of breast-works, where the Germans rained shells on to us, and the battalion lost another hundred men, just sitting there all day. In the middle of the next night (16th), about 2 a.m., the longed-for relief came and the 2nd Worcesters came out into billets three miles back, 450 men out of 800. Of course only about 150 of our casualties are dead or badly wounded, but we have had the most nerve-wracking time, no proper rest, and not a night with boots and putties off for nine days. To add to this, while I was sitting reading my letters in our ruined billet the evening after our attack, a big shrapnel shell came right at the wall of the room, and blew part of the wall on top of me, breaking the legs of my chair; it luckily only bruised my shoulder slightly, but it was rather nasty shock coming so soon after my previous night's performance! [61]

Despite his experiences at Festubert, Vawdrey felt he had yet to do his bit, and wrote home in frustration on June 15:

I have been at the front two months next Monday, and have not yet seen a Hun close to, nor has anyone in the battalion! Such is life here – all of the strain and privation, and none of the sporting, exciting side. For the latter we shall have to wait till we actually get into a Hun trench. [62]

Like many OFs, Hay fought at the subsequent Battle of Loos in September 1915, which he described as 'the battle of the slag-heaps' because of its setting in the industrial grime of Northern France. He described Loos as 'one of the biggest and longest battles in the history of the world' and was convinced tat the time that he had taken part in an epic feat of arms. Another OF at Loos was Lt Desmond Fitzgerald Underwood of the 5th Battalion, the Lincolnshire Regiment, which attacked the notorious Hohenzollern Redoubt on 13 October, the last day of the offensive. The Lincolnshires did manage to take some German positions, but, as with the Ulster regiments at the Schwaben Redoubt on the Somme a year later, this left them exposed to enfilading fire, as the official history records:

The wire in front of the Redoubt was well cut, and the Battalion swept over the W. and E. faces with few casualties but on advancing over the open ground in front of the Fosse trench came under such heavy rifle and machine gun fire from the front and from both flanks, that the lines melted away, and further advance became impossible; although numerous isolated parties maintained themselves in shell holes at various points until dusk, the line as a whole was compelled to retire to the E face of the Hohenzollern Redoubt, which was consolidated for defence. The 1/4th Leicestershire Regiment on our right were in the same situation, exposed to very heavy frontal and enfilade rifle and machine gun fire, as the Brigade on our right was unable to advance owing to uncut wire, and the German position at Mad Point on our left was a nest of machine guns which our artillery were unable to silence. All ranks behaved most gallantly, but the very heavy casualties in Officers and N.C.O.s deprived the men of leadership, just at the time it was most needed, with the result that a certain amount of crowding took place, causing additional casualties. [63]

All but one of the 5th Battalion's 23 officers were killed or injured; the sole survivor led the retreat, and the unit had to be completely recreated. Although Underwood was transferred to the quieter life of the Nigeria Regiment, the experience shattered him; his son writes:

I have no doubt that he never recovered from the Hohenzollern attack, with subsequent deep depression and alcoholism. Despite these problems he was a delightful man with an Irish sense of humour, and a great father.[64]

Underwood's later career was damaged by the effects of the fighting; Churchill advised him to jump before he was pushed from an Admiralty post in the Second World War, though afterwards he spent what time he could serving the community as a councillor. Loos, although now forgotten by British popular culture, did come close to success, not least because of Haig and Trenchard's innovative use of aircraft for tactical bombing and target identification. Many were convinced that had the initial British breakthrough been supported by fresh troops to relieve the exhausted and depleted 'Jocks', and more artillery ammunition been available to eliminate the flanking fire from clearly located machine-guns, a breakthrough might have been achieved. Hay was certainly optimistic – and had the honesty to allow his predictions of autumn 1915 to stay in later editions of *The First Hundred Thousand* despite his having been proved terribly wrong: 'It [the Front line] still surges backwards and forwards over the same stricken mile of ground; and the end is not yet. But the Hun is being steadily beaten to earth.'[65]

It would, however, be years before a final breakthrough.

Slaughter at the Somme

The end of term *Fettesian* of July 1916, which printed a poem, entirely in Greek, dedicated to the late Lord Kitchener, went to press just as early reports were coming in of the attempt to break the stalemate at the Somme. This was to be a major test of the New Armies, ('K1' because they were the first wave of volunteers to answer Kitchener's call). The Somme campaign did not, on the face of it, end this stalemate, as the Allies gained relatively little territory, but it did maul the professional German army and keep it boxed in for a while. It is for its casualties that the Somme campaign is best known to the British today. The first day of the assault came too late for any sort of literary reference in the summer number of the *Fettesian* – none, in fact, ever appeared – but the magazine

212

was published in time to announce eight fatalities of 1 July. Ian Scott, a Second Lieutenant in the King's Own Scottish Borderers, had won scholarships both to Fettes and Edinburgh University; he was killed in the suicidal attack on Y Ravine at Beaumont-Hamel, aged 19, and is buried in Knightsbridge Cemetery, named for the old trench used as a mass grave. The Highland Light Infantry, a popular destination for Fettesians, was especially hard hit in those early days on the Somme; Lt Edward Gallie and Capt Robert Cassels, both formerly of the 1st XV, were also killed on 1 July and are buried at Lonsdale. Lt Archibald Smith-Maxwell, another keen rugby player in the HLI, died on the same day and is buried at Serre Road No. 2 Cemetery. Lt William Philip Rettie, Capt William Tullis and 2/Lt H.G. Walker, the latter a member of the school shooting team who had represented Yorkshire at rugby and risen through the ranks to become an officer and instructor, were also killed on the first day, but their bodies were never recovered so they are commemorated on the Thiepval Memorial to the Missing. The most senior OF officer to die on the first day of the Somme was Lt Col Arthur Dickson, who had worked his way up from the rank of Trooper in the Boer War and was 42 years old. Capt Robert Pringle, a gifted scholar who won the Governors' Prize for Greek Prose in 1911, lies in Colincamps. Two more later died of wounds; another HLI officer, Lt Alexander Begg, MC, who had been the first colour-sergeant of the Fettes cadets, on July 10, and Lt Robert Reid of the Royal Engineers on July 13. It was later reported that Telford Spence, serving as a private in the HLI, had also been killed on July 1, hit by shellfire whilst taking possession of a German trench.

Two of the 40 Fettesians lost at the Somme: Capt John MacDonald, Cameronians, killed at High Wood on 20 July, and Lt Edward MacIldowie, Highland Light Infantry, killed in the attack at Lesboeufs on 1 November. Neither has a known grave

The campaign continued – not without success – for several months, claiming the lives of several more OFs: Mathew Anderson, a gifted runner; Thomas Barton, who had flown at Gallipoli but chose to return to the trenches; Edgar Boase, a 47-year-old manufacturer who had run for Parliament in Dundee; William Cassels; George Chree, who had earlier won the MC for 'conspicuous gallantry under shell-fire'; Horsburgh Gibson; Robert Jenkins; William Lindsay; Edward MacIldowie; John MacDonald; schoolmaster Arnold Mackay who was, like Alastair Mackinnon (1914 winner of the Greek Prose Prize) and Robert Scott, a gifted classical scholar, and another son of the manse; James Mackay; Norman Martin, DSO; Norman Moncreiff; Patrick Monteith; Richard Ross, MC, who had been in the first teams for hockey, rugby, cricket and fives; Alan Shewan; Reginald Smith; Houston Wallace, and James Wyper, who gave up a shipbroking career in Chile to serve. There were casualties from the dominion units which won fame at the Somme too – Cecil Clift of the Newfoundland Regiment and Hector Macleod, killed in the South Africans' epic battle at Delville Wood. As well as Scott, six more 19-year-olds who had just left the school were killed on the Somme: George Boyd, George Davidson, a former prefect; Alexander MacCormick, killed leading his men on a moonlight attack on German trenches, dying on the enemy parapet; keen sportsman William Macfarlane; Alexander Shaw and David Simpson. Sandy Lindsay, who after the war would join the Fettes staff, had a lucky escape on 30 July as he left a dug-out occupied by B Company, 16th Royal Scots; just as he left, it was struck by an explosive incendiary, killing four men outright and entombing two more ten feet underground in burning wreckage. One of the trapped men was on the verge of shooting himself to escape being burned alive when he heard Lindsay's voice; the men were rescued but one later died. So many officers and senior NCOs had been killed in that first month of July that Lindsay, although still 19, was promoted to CSM.[66]

So many old Fettesians were killed in the campaign that the obituaries occupied a quarter of the school magazine at the autumn half-term, the only time in the magazine's history that any single subject took up more pages than the sports reports.[67]

Although the *Fettesian* never carried any accounts of the battle, Ian Hay, who by this point had won a Military Cross, wrote a fictionalised version in *All in it: K(1) Carries On*, the follow-up to *The First Hundred Thousand*. He described the concerns of the troops before the offensive:

The Boche's dug-outs here are thirty feet deep. When crumped by our artillery he withdraws his infantry and leaves his machine-gunners behind, safe underground. Then, when our guns lift and the attack comes over, his machine-gunners appear on the surface, hoist their guns after them with a sort of tackle arrangement, and get to work on a prearranged band of fire. The infantry can't do them in until No Man's Land is crossed, and — well, they don't all get across, that's all! [68]

This was, of course, the problem; for all Hesketh-Prichard's scepticism about concrete fortifications ('many Germans no doubt saved their lives by going down their deep dug-outs and into their concrete pill-boxes, but many more, as is common knowledge, when our men came over, stayed down too long and were bombed to death'[69]) the Allied troops were cut down in their thousands by enfilading rifle fire, distant artillery and, notoriously, surviving machine-guns. One of Hay's most endearing characters, Angus (a good-natured, rugby-playing son of the manse who might have been the sort of boy Hay had studied with and later taught at Fettes) is killed trying to capture one. Given such unmitigated slaughter, it is often hard to see any kind of justification for it. Hay, writing in the immediate aftermath, nonetheless felt that the Somme campaign had been worth the losses, since 'the Hun threw in his hand' and withdrew to the Hindenburg Line, and 'some thousand square miles of the soil of France had been restored once and for all to their rightful owners.'[70]

It was hardly surprising that Fettes' losses were so considerable; officers were much more likely to be killed than private soldiers for the simple reason that they were required to lead by example, and from the front. The fact that 3,274 Sandhurst graduates were killed in the war, 5,131 having been commissioned between 1914 and 1918, is telling. 'In attack,' Anthony Clayton writes, 'platoon commanders, armed only with a revolver, would lead at the head of their platoons, closely supported by bombers to throw grenades into enemy trenches and bayonet men to complete the "'clearing up'".' [71]

Company and battalion commanders – that is to say, captains, majors and lieutenant-colonels – were generally also to be seen leading from the front. Ian Hay, writing after the First World War, explained what had happened:

Thanks to the timely foundation of the Officers' Training Corps in 1908, our

Public Schools were able, in 1914, to supply to those raw levies, the New Armies, thousands of capable young officers, who at least understood the rudiments of military routine, and could drill a company. Very few of these young officers are alive now; but they saved the British Empire, for the simple reason that they were both ready and willing at a time when all were willing and few were ready.[72]

Wherever possible, the school magazine celebrated the decorations won by its former pupils. It had plenty of opportunities to do so; OFs amassed a glittering array of medals, including two VCs, 55 DSOs and 135 MCs. They were mentioned in despatches 424 times. Many medals were also awarded by Britain's allies – in addition to 14 Legions d'Honneur and 13 Croix de Guerre from France, honours were presented by the USA, Japan, Belgium, Italy, Romania, Serbia, Greece and Egypt.[73]

As a proportion of medals awarded per head of volunteers, this is remarkably high. One DSO was won by 2/Lt Norman Martin in the autumn of 1915 for an extraordinary act of bravery during a bombing raid on a German trench. Three parties of bombers having been either killed or wounded, 'Martin then commenced throwing bombs himself, after which he expended all the rounds in his revolver, and continued to fire with a rifle. It was largely due to his coolness and courage that the barricade was held till more bombers had been obtained.'[74] For so young and junior a soldier (Martin was 18 years old at the time) to get the DSO was unusual – it was generally reserved for Lieutenant-Colonels. Martin was killed in the Somme campaign.

Medals were awarded for gallantry off the field of battle, too; Lt W.B. Mitchell, who had, coincidentally, won the Bannerman Rescue Prize whilst at school, gained an MBE aged 20 for throwing himself on top of one of his men to save him from a hand-grenade which the latter had inexpertly thrown in such a way that it bounced back. Mitchell had left school at 17 to join up; despite his injuries from this act of heroism, he captained the Glasgow University rugby XV after the war.

Sniping
One former pupil who was, considered, at 37, rather a very Old Fettesian, too much so to fight, was Vernon Hesketh-Prichard. He fought hard to get to the front, and was decorated for his efforts in a field which is still regarded as his special contribution to British military development. A noteworthy feature of the *Fettesian* 1914-18 casualty lists was the number

A night raid on the Western Front, as depicted in Old Fettesian Vernon Hesketh-Prichard's Sniping in France

of officers killed by snipers; Hay's thinly-fictionalised account of 'K1' mentions a German known, from his habit of hiding in trees, as 'Zacchaeus', but since he never managed to kill the officers he sought he was considered to be of a 'persevering, rather than vindictive, disposition.'[75]

Few others were so accommodating, and many officers, including several Fettesians, fell victim to well-aimed shots from skilled riflemen. Hesketh-Prichard described the grim reality of German tactics:

From the ruined house or the field of decaying roots, sometimes resting their rifles on the bodies of the dead, they sent forth a plague of head-wounds into the British lines. Their marks were small, but when they hit they usually killed their man, and the hardiest soldier turned sick when he saw the effect of the pointed German bullet, which was apt to keyhole so that the little hole in the forehead where it entered often became a huge tear, the size of a man's fist, on the other side of the stricken man's head.[76]

During lulls in the fighting, a single German sniper could kill thirty men in a steady psychological water-torture which eroded morale even more quickly than it depleted numbers of men, especially trained officers and sergeants. Hesketh-Prichard was later able to reveal why the higher ranks were so quickly picked off in battle; a captured German sniper revealed that officers' riding-breeches, worn even by the infantry, made their legs look different from those of the privates, even though they wore the same helmets on the front line.[77]

Hesketh-Prichard became so committed to sniper training that he took a cut in rank and went without pay for several months in order to get his school (where, in the absence of specialised targets, soldiers shot at copies of the *Daily Mail* [78]) off the ground. His services were not universally popular; despite the proven success of somewhat eccentric British units in the wars in India and South Africa, many considered such methods unsporting. The novelist Mrs Humphrey Ward, visiting the sniper school, said that she 'thought sniping the terrible and ruthless killing of men with weapons of precision one of the most dreadful sides of the war'; Hesketh-Prichard informed her that it actually saved British lives, and, converted, Mrs Ward wrote a very complimentary account of her visit. One General nonetheless told him 'You are not here officially, you know, and any Germans you may have killed, or caused to be killed, are, of course, only unofficially dead.'[79]

Hesketh-Prichard wrote about his experiences just after the war, and gave many examples of where scientific fieldcraft and observations skills had paid off. At Beaumont-Hamel on the Somme, for instance, a sniper known as 'Ernst' (they seem always to have been given individual nicknames) was proving especially troublesome. Hesketh-Prichard spent several days assessing the lie of the land and assessing possible spots from which Ernst might be shooting. The easiest, but not safest, way to do this was to be shot at:

The first shot had cut the top of the parapet just beside my head, and I noticed that several shots had been fired which had also cut the top of the sandbags. Behind the line of these shots was a group of trees, and as they stood on slightly higher ground I crawled to them, and at once saw something of great interest. In the bole of one of the trees a number of bullets had lodged, all within a small circle. Crouching at the base of the tree, and with my head covered with an old sandbag, I raised it until 1 could see over the parapet fifty yards in front, and found at once that the line of these shots, and those which had struck the tree behind my head, were very nearly the same, and must have been fired from an area of No Man's Land, behind which it looked as if dead ground existed on the enemy's side, and probably from a large bush which formed the most salient feature of that view. I then went back to the trenches, and warned all sentries to keep a good look-out on this bush and the vicinity. Very soon one of them reported movement in the bush. With my glass I could see a periscope about three feet above the ground in the bush, which was very thick. Being certain, as the periscope was raised so high, and as it had only just been elevated, that it was held in human hands, I collected half a dozen riflemen and my batman, and giving them the range, and the centre of the bush as a target, ordered them to open fire. On the volley the periscope flew backwards and the activities of Ernst ceased forthwith.[80]

His private army of Lovat Scouts – a 200-strong unit of Scots gamekeepers, operating in modern sniper-spotter pairs to 'bag a Boche', in 'HP's' favourite phrase, was extremely effective.[81]

Where the German sniper of 1915 was killing thirty British soldiers, by 1918 Hesketh-Prichard's top marksmen had 'bags' of a hundred; as one Fettesian schoolmaster admiringly commented, 'Saul hath slain his thousands, and David his ten thousands.' The sniper-scouts' training was reminiscent of what would later be required of elite special forces; they:

…were first-class shots, knew every detail of the course, and could pass an examination equal to any officer. At the physical training and ju-jitsu, which they had almost every day, they were really young terrors. In fact, I remember a commercial joy-rider who was visiting the school, and whom I was showing round, on seeing two of the boys doing ju-jitsu, saying with infinite tact: ''Ere, where do you live when you are at 'ome ? I'll keep clear o' your street on a dark night.'[82]

Not everyone who asked was chosen; a young volunteer seemed a ideal recruit because he had worked for Daniel Fraser, the Edinburgh gunsmith. Unfortunately, 'the staff who unearthed this applicant did not continue to congratulate themselves on having produced exactly the article wanted, when, through a letter to Messrs. Fraser, it transpired that, though it was quite true that the man had been employed by them, the position that he had held in the firm was that of errand boy, and that his knowledge of telescopic sights was consequently not one which they felt they could confidently recommend.'[83]

Vawdrey played his part in helping the snipers, writing home about an expedition to organise a hide for one of the marksmen:

Here we are again, holding the line. It is very quiet. The Huns are disposed to live and let live, and I expect they have by no means as many men available as they would like… Last night I went out on a venturesome patrol with Sergeant Shepherd and another man. Our object was to try and find one of our own sniper's posts which had not been used lately, and to explore the No-man's-land of corn and poppies. We were also told that the general was looking for a Hun alive or dead, so as to identify the troops opposed to us. It is most creepy work crawling through long corn never knowing when you were going to come across quite a large Hun patrol. We three kept very close and advanced slowly, listening for Hun voices or coughing. We emerged into the open cornfield from the listening post, and went about 200 – 250 yds. further. The night was dark, and every large poppy looked like a Hun's head! Not a sound or sign of an enemy patrol, so we returned and half way back came across the sniper's post, a shallow lair, dug in about 3ft., with sandbags for head cover. In the dark we could not tell what it was, so with bayonets presented at it, we hoarsely summoned it to surrender. It refused to reply, I leapt into it with a revolver in one hand and a bomb in the other, only to find it empty, save for a half a tin of jam! [84]

Hesketh-Prichard did not long outlive the war, succumbing to the effects of a gas attack and old malarial infections less than four years later. Vawdrey came through more or less unscathed, and became a popular, and rather eccentric, master at Fettes.

Tragedy and triumph

1917 saw British successes; Arthur Lloyd, who had emigrated to Canada before the war and enlisted in the 52nd Canadian Regiment, received a field commission at the heroic seizure of Vimy Ridge as three-quarters of the officers in his battalion had been killed or wounded[85]; another Canadian OF at Vimy, Fortescue Duguid, would later help design the maple leaf flag. Ross described the complexities of preparation for such a modern 'push'.

The preparations for an attack involve the whole-hearted co-operation of every branch of the Service, and its success largely depends upon the smooth co-ordination between each of these branches. The artillery arrange a barrage timetable and an adequate supply of ammunition; the trench mortars and machine-guns conform to this timetable, and in addition are prepared to move forward as required; the engineers lay mines, and at the psychological moment explode them; the Army Service Corps provide the necessary food and the battalion transports take it up to the new positions as soon as circumstances will allow; the medical services select suitable aid posts, and clear the battlefield of wounded; the pioneer battalions are in readiness to push roads forward in the back areas and to dig trenches during the consolidation of the objectives; and lastly, the infantry have to understand what is expected of them, and at 'zero' commence their advance.[86]

As Medical Officer, he took into battle the latest and most potent kit of the day – 'hypodermic syringe, a bottle of morphia solution, two water bottles — one full of brandy, the other of water — a haversack containing shell dressings, tourniquets, and a few instruments, and an abundant supply of cigarettes.' He went on to describe how the first day of a big push played out:

Dawn is just breaking and a thick mist envelops everything. The companies are all on their jumping-off trenches waiting for 'zero' time to arrive. Officers are standing, watch in hand, ready for the fateful minute, non-commissioned officers are encouraging their platoons and giving final directions, and the men — from their cheery appearance it might well be thought they were going for a picnic, and indeed such is the term many of them apply to such an affair as the present. The commanding officer, adjutant, and medical officer are in a trench a short distance behind. 'Zero' time arrives. Bang - bang — bang - bang - bang — bang - bang, go the field guns; Crrr-ump — crrr-ump go the howitzers; shrapnel bursts overhead and machine-gun bullets whizz past.

Hell seems to be let loose on the countryside.

The artillery have formed a barrage, under cover of which the infantry advance on the enemy trenches. The barrage slowly creeps forward; our men unconcernedly follow it. Up go the Boches' S.O.S. rockets until the scene resembles a Crystal Palace Brock's Benefit Night. The enemy artillery quickly reply to the frantic signals of their infantry, and their barrage opens. Many of our men fall — some dead, others wounded. The remainder push on and are in the Huns' front line directly our barrage has passed over it. Then bombing of dug-outs and hand-to-hand fighting ensues. Many of our men fall, but few of them before doing all — or even more than all — that is expected of them.

The scene in 'No Man's Land' is indescribable. The ground is a mass of shell craters and almost impassable. The cries of the maimed and dying mingle strangely with the shriek of our own shells overhead and the explosions of hostile shells around us...

Large batches of prisoners are now beginning to come across 'No Man's Land.' These are at once commandeered to carry wounded back. Most of them appear only too willing to do so; those who object are quickly shown the error of their ways…

The battalion has now reached its final objective, and the medical personnel, having collected all wounded, joins it in the new line which is being dug. Suddenly the enemy open a furious barrage. Large numbers are seen congregating in front of us. They are advancing to counter-attack and drive us out of our new positions. Our artillery liaison officer quickly telephones back to his batteries. We open fire with machine-guns, Lewis guns, and rifles, and await events. There are a few minutes of suspense and then our deadly artillery barrage opens. The advancing line is seen to be greatly thinned, it wavers, and the remainder then ignominiously take to their heels. Our barrage lifts slightly and catches that remainder. The night is spent in consolidating the new line and repelling further counter-attacks.[87]

This, at any rate, was what was meant to happen. In the 1917 battles, the Fettes death toll mounted, with at least 20 killed at Arras and Cambrai, including L/Cpl Bertie Barton, one of the few non-commissioned OF fatalities, Capt Thomas Beaumont, and Medical Officer Capt James Black. At Roeux, five miles east of Arras, the school gained a third Victoria Cross winner in April 1917 when Lt Donald Mackintosh of the 3rd Seaforth Highlanders captured an enemy position despite being mortally wounded. The *Scotsman* carried a lengthy interview with his sergeant which the school magazine reverently reprinted:

It was the strangest sight you ever saw. A doubly-wounded man, with the nervous twitching of his face telling the agony he was enduring, toiling painfully along and encouraging his men as he went. The little band kept on their way, and rushed the position, from which they drove out about ten times their own number of the enemy. It was in the moment of success that Lt. Mackintosh fell. He tried to get up again and go with the men into the trench from which they had driven the enemy, but he was then too weak from loss of blood to do so. We could see he was in great pain. He would not hear of any of us assisting him until he saw the position was safe, and whenever we suggested aiding him he ordered us away… He was one of the bravest. The men would have followed him anywhere at any time. He was always thinking of the men, and did all he could to make things easy for them.[88]

Mackintosh's citation stated that 'the gallantry and devotion to duty of this officer were beyond all praise.' His portrait now hangs in the Upper, the largest classroom at Fettes. Although Arras and Messines saw impressive Allied successes, the collapse of Russia into revolution and France's disastrous Nivelle Offensive and army mutiny ensured that the stalemate continued. 1917 is now best-remembered in British popular culture for Passchendaele – the muddy attritional bloodbath also known as the Third Battle of Ypres. Launched in the hope of breakthrough in Flanders to hit the German U-boat pens on the Belgian coast and, as with the Somme, relieving pressure on the French, it was soon bogged down by the heaviest rain for thirty years which rendered men, mules, lorries and tanks immobile in a sea of mud, made worse by shelling which shattered the water table. Fettes lost several former pupils, though not as many as in other battles: Lt John Watson of the Machine Gun Corps, hit by shellfire at Sanctuary Wood on 22 August, Capt Peter Alexander, wounded in France in 1915 and awarded the MC, killed on 12 October and buried at Tyne Cot (one of only 30 per cent of those buried there to be identified) and Capt John Halliburton Mitchell, dead from wounds on 26 October, and buried at Mendinghem. Two others have no known grave, 19-year-old 2/Lt. J. Murray, who had only just arrived at the front on leaving school, and Lt George Watson. Their names are among 33,783 British missing from Passchendaele recorded on the Tyne Cot Memorial, along with two 'college men-servants' as they were described in the *Fettesian*, Privates Alexander Mackie and William Wilson and L/Cpl. John Mumberson. Ross gave a brief account of the battle as he experienced it on 26 October:

The Royal Marines, Howe, and Anson Battalions, gallantly plodded through the waist-deep mud under a withering machine-gun and rifle fire, along the banks of the Paddebeek, down the slopes of the Wallemolen spur in the direction of Goudberg and Passchendaele. From countless pill-boxes and redoubts bullets rained like hail on our dauntless men, but many of these strongholds were captured at the point of the bayonet or by bombing attacks. My further recollections of this gallant fight are somewhat mixed, as, owing to circumstances over which I had no control, on the afternoon of October 26th I found myself being conveyed back to field ambulance.[89]

Ross was very modest; at Passchendaele he severely wounded and gassed (he was, indeed, injured three times in the course of the war, which affected him physically for the rest of his life) and won the MC and Croix de Guerre with Palms, but this was the only allusion he made to the fact in the book (Hay was equally modest; indeed, no OF described how he won a medal in the entire history of the school magazine). By the time Ross was hit, the campaign had been going badly for weeks if not months, but (admittedly writing before the war ended and presumably unwilling to let the side down) he could still rationalise what now looks like suicidal folly:

About this time the collapse of Russia quite negatived any hope of the British advancing from Passchendaele against the German line of communication with Ostend and Zeebrugge, but it was essential to continue the attack in order to contain a large number of enemy troops in this region, which otherwise might be sent to Italy to press home the unexpected defeats sustained by General Cadorna's forces.[90]

The second Fettes VC of the War represents an even greater tragedy. In the Fettes Roll of Honour there are a dozen instances of two brothers being killed; in the case of the Ross family, three. The Andersons, however, lost all four of their sons, the eldest, William, known to the family as Bertie, being the last to die. From a family of Glasgow accountants, they were unlikely heroes, just decent, golf-loving, hard-working Scots; Fettes' official history records that they were fairly undistinguished on the playing fields and in two cases 'so frail they were nicknamed "Crocky"'.[91]

Frail or not, Charlie was killed in a German counter-attack at Festubert in 1914, on his ninth day of active service, and his body never found. Ronnie had written to his mother 'If I get killed, don't say "So like Ron's careless way"'; a tall man, he 'failed to notice that where he was standing the parapet of the trench dipped, leaving him visible to enemy snipers'[92] and was killed in December 1915. Teddie, the youngest, crashed during a training flight over England in a Sopwith Camel in March 1918. Nora Anderson got to bury one of her sons close to home; Teddie lies in New Kilpatrick churchyard in Bearsden. A week later, Bertie fell. He died in the aftermath of the offensives by the Germans in 1918, intended to deliver a knockout blow to the Anglo-French forces in the west in the interval between the Russian withdrawal from the war and the arrival of American troops. This was an extremely dangerous time for the British Army; 1918 saw the Germans putting into practice the lessons they had leaned in the previous four years, with combined use of tear gas and phosgene to knock out Allied artillery, shorter bombardments to stun and surprise, and stormtroopers – fanatical shock troops armed with the new sub-machine-guns and other portable weapons, moving quickly into the British lines under cover of fog and generated smoke. The school was to lose a further thirty former pupils as the Germans smashed into the British positions, some gained at tremendous cost at the Somme and Passchendaele. Adam, the eager recruit of the Royal Navy, believed that this was the Senior Service's great opportunity:

The retreat of the Fifth Army had started on March 21 and had continued for several weeks; Alfred [his brother] had been in the middle of it, at the spot where the enemy advanced 40 miles near St. Quentin, but against this apparent setback there was the great event of St. George's Day, when a force under the command of Rear-Admiral Roger Keyes stormed the mole at Zeebrugge and sank three blockships in the Bruges canal – a feat since regarded as the finest naval raid in history. The German army had struck and failed to break through completely; it looked as if the next move might lie with her high seas fleet. So we marched around the parade grounds, tied our knots in places, bent on our signal hoists, and manoeuvred our ships in miniature, hoping that when the final fleet action came we would be in it.[93]

There were 38, 512 British casualties on 21 March alone, and by that summer, the Reich dominated more territory than it had at any previous point in the war. It was close to Paris and had taken the Baltic provinces of Russia as well as the Ukraine, and its allies were advancing in the Caucasus and in Italy. Several Fettesians won the MC for their desperate rearguard actions that March; Lt W.I. Nicholson kept his battery firing until all the ammunition was expended, then, under heavy bombardment, organised the guns' removal, and Lt W.E. Warden of the RFC flew both reconnaissance and 'strafing' sorties over the advancing German columns.[94]

Others were lost. Capt Ian Mackenzie, MC, winner of scholarships to Fettes and Oxford, former head of school and 'one of the most promising classical scholars the School has ever produced', was killed instantly on the morning of the German attack of 21 March when he was cut down by machine-gun fire[95]; 19-year-old Alastair Davis and 20-year-old John Prentice, both members of the class of 1912, had only recently arrived at the front when they were killed within a few days of each other in April. So severe was the German onslaught that the British command structure broke down for a week, and in mid-April, in response to the second thrust through Flanders, Haig, the overall British commander, issued his 'backs to the wall' Order of the Day, appealing to the often demoralised British troops who faced the very real possibility of defeat. On 25 March, Bertie Anderson's 12th HLI were holding, after two nights' rail journey and a seventeen-mile route march, a defensive line between Hardecourt and the Somme. An accountant and father of two, he was remembered by his contemporary C.A. Lely as a 'quiet-spoken lad' who at bedtime in the tiny top dormitory in Moredun would simply say 'Dix' – the school code for temporary silence – and proceed to say his prayers.[96]

The 36-year-old last of the Andersons rounded up whatever troops he could – 'clerks, cooks, servants and signallers' and counter-attacked, swagger-stick in one hand, revolver in the other. 'He was cheering me on, his face wreathed in smiles at the way the counter-attack was progressing,' wrote a comrade to Bertie's widow, 'His last words to me were, "Carry on with those on the left, Cox", and the last I saw was the swing of his stick going on.'[97]

Bertie's VC citation detailed his extraordinary courage under heavy fire:

The enemy attacked on the right of the battalion frontage and succeeded in penetrating the wood held by our men…Grasping the seriousness of the situation, Colonel Anderson made his way across the open in full view of the enemy now holding the wood on the right, and… personally led the counter-attack and drove the enemy from the wood, capturing twelve machine guns and seventy prisoners, and restoring the original line. His conduct in leading the charge was quite fearless and his most splendid example was the means of rallying and inspiring the men during the most critical hour.

Later on the same day, in another position, the enemy had penetrated to within three hundred yards of the village and were holding a timber yard in force. Colonel Anderson reorganised his men after they had been driven in and brought them forward to a position of readiness for a counterattack. He led the attack in person and throughout showed the utmost disregard for his own safety. The counter-attack drove the enemy from his position, but resulted in this very gallant officer losing his life. He died fighting within the enemy's lines, setting a magnificent example to all who were privileged to serve under him.[98]

Mrs Anderson had a further agony; telegraphing the War Office to confirm a rumour that her last son was dead, she was told on 3 April that 'No report of any recent casualty to Lt Col Anderson of HLI received.' The cruel hope was doused when Gertie, Bertie's wife, received a telegram two days later. The *Fettesian* carried – along with seven obituaries for the school's fallen in the opening phase of the offensive – a fulsome tribute from General Foch, the Allied Generalissimo, who in a speech to the 15th and 51st Scottish Divisions used Anderson as the supreme exemplar of 'Spartan devotion to duty', a concept which will have impressed the young classical scholars. Recalling that 'the gallant Scots have always had a warm place in my heart and the heart of every Frenchman' he claimed that when the 'Boche' had to fight the Highlanders they asked for more guns and more reserves because they knew how hard they fought. Having been told repeatedly of the Colonel's sacrifice by men of the HLI, Foch with 'tears in his eyes' spoke at length about him:

Throwing himself into the fight with the lion-hearted courage so characteristic of his race, he inspired his men with his own determination and his own will to conquer... Your brave Colonel was killed in the terrible fighting. Such men cannot die. He lives today in your hearts and in the hearts of all men who revere heroism... If I wished to call for supreme sacrifice from Highland troops, I could find no better preface to my call than to ask you in the name of Col. Anderson.[99]

Both Glasgow Cathedral and the Military Chapel at Sandhurst commemorate the brothers with plaques, Bertie Anderson's VC is now in the Imperial War Museum, and in 1948 his old room-mate Lely could still write, at the end of his account of the Fettes of his Victorian youth, that 'invariably my thoughts return to that first meeting at Moredun with that great soul W.H. Anderson, with his simple faith – an example and inspiration for all time to past and present Fettesians.'[100] Robin Scott-Elliott, Bertie's great-grandson, has recently (2007) written a moving account of the family's destruction.[101]

It is generally assumed that the model for the fallen highlander on the school's war memorial is a hybrid of Donald Mackintosh (who was clean-shaven, as is the statue) and Bertie Anderson, who used the phrase 'carry on.'

The school's portrait of Donald Mackintosh, VC, and a wreath placed by pupils on the grave of Bertie Anderson, VC

The Road to Victory

In retrospect the German successes of 1918 – crucial to Hitler's later claim that his country was undefeated in battle and was stabbed in the back by the usual conspiracy of selfish liberal capitalists and treacherous leftists (all, of course, freemasons operating under Jewish control) – can be seen as illusory. The stormtroopers, poorly backed up by their increasingly ramshackle supply trains, overreached themselves and frequently, on finding well-stocked British supply dumps, sat down to gorge; the British Army also rose to the challenge, whilst the German Navy did not. The German offensives, for all their initial success and for all the consternation they caused, ultimately failed. Although the Germans had a great opportunity in the spring to severely damage the British forces, they failed to focus on the weakest part of the Allied system – a vast and taut global communication network. The BEF learned from its mistakes and commenced a vigorous counter-attack in the summer.

Unusually, the July 1918 issue of the magazine carried no obituaries. The last *Fettesian* of the war, published in the month of the Armistice, carried sixteen, for the months of success were almost as bloody as the years of stalemate – indeed, it was not until this last phase of the fighting that the British killed proportionately more Germans than the Germans killed British. The Fettes dead including Lt Kenneth Mackenzie, famed for rescuing a comrade from drowning at Leith in 1914, Capt Ian Nairn, who had survived Gallipoli and Palestine and won the MC but was killed on 3 September, and 19-year-old 2/Lt James Tombazis, cut down whilst leading the attack on 8 October. It also carried a rather jolly story from an un-named OF in which he described how the requirement to identify oneself in wartime (it being insufficient to reply 'me' to 'who goes there?') had eliminated the British male's self-conscious tendency to 'stutter and stammer and look perfectly imbecile before he can bring himself to say his own name.'[102]

The indefatigable Chaplain Lauchlan MacLean Watt contributed another of his poems to the magazine, this time in praise of the battalion runner, 'the bravest boy out here' who he felt was being ignored in the press in favour of 'the fellow that leads the charge.' The most famous battalion runner of the war was, of course, a Cpl. Hitler of the List Regiment in the German Army, though presumably he was not the sort of Christian soldier the good Reverend had in mind. By this stage the British Army was no longer the small professional body of 1914, nor even the big volunteer force of 'Pals' battalions which fought at the Somme in 1916, but a vast conscript machine, somehow moving forward and constantly upwards on a perpetual tactical and technological learning curve. Lewis Guns, gas, trench mortars, the 106 fuse, tanks, radio and ground-attack aeroplanes were not new but they were being used more efficiently and in greater numbers – from four Lewis Guns per battalion in 1916 to 30 in 1918, along with smaller and better supported fighting units. The tank, by this point, was one of the great symbols of British success. Hay described this novelty as it first appeared in 1916:

From the depths of the wood opposite came a crackling, crunching sound, as of some prehistoric beast forcing its way through tropical undergrowth. And then, suddenly, out from the thinning edge there loomed a monster — a monstrosity. It did not glide, it did not walk. It wallowed. It lurched, with now and then a laborious heave of its shoulders. It fumbled its way over a low bank matted with scrub. It crossed a ditch, by the simple expedient of rolling the ditch out flat, and waddled forward... Then it stopped. A magic opening appeared in its stomach, from which emerged, grinning, a British subaltern and his grimy associates.[103]

At least one grimy British subaltern in a tank was an OF; trainee doctor Miles Atkinson, only son of the mayor of Leamington, had joined the Motor Machine Gun Section as a private and was commissioned into the new Tank Corps. He was killed at Cambrai 'when the tank he was navigating came under fire of a German field battery at point-blank range.'[104]

In many ways the British success of the 'hundred days' was a remarkable victory; the remorseless, 'bite-and-hold' roll-back of the enemy advance, a concerted effort by the Allies, now including America but with the leading role played by the troops of the British Empire, hammered Germany into surrender. Haig, with the effervescent emotion for which the Scot is famed, noted in his diary that 'The Armistice came into force at 11am' when the war ended, and British troops often simply noted the strange, unwonted silence. Nonetheless, here was a momentous event – the defeat of one of the most efficient and remarkable military machines in the world. The popular conception of the Great War is such that this victory is has been largely erased from folk memory, much to the irritation of many military historians; Gary Sheffield, indeed, entitled one recent publication *Forgotten Victory*. He noted that in 1998 his colleague Professor Sir Michael Howard wrote to *The Times* suggesting that the 80th anniversary of the Hundred Days, 'the greatest series of victories in British military history', should be marked with the same 'wall-to wall media coverage' that occurred on 1 July 1996, the 80th anniversary of the beginning of the Somme offensive, which was universally portrayed as a disaster. Needless to say, no such commemoration took place.[105]

It was not always thus. Writing half-way between the two world wars, Ian Hay came to the conclusion that Fettesians had been more or less everywhere between 1914 and 1918, but were especially well-represented on the Western Front, a fact of which he was extremely proud. He kept bumping into former pupils at the front; when the 9th and 15th Divisions, Scotland's sections of the Kitchener New Armies in which most OFs served, were concentrated around the La Bassée area for the battle of Loos, the *place* of Bethune 'might have been Princes Street on the morning of an International.'[106]

He wrote with palpable pride of the huge collection of medal citations, which between them covered well over half of those served. Twelve OFs served with the cavalry, 66 with the Royal Army Medical

Corps or ambulance units (the oldest of them, Surgeon-General Sir W.G. Macpherson, a 'patriarch' of 1870, losing his only son in 1914), 130 with the Artillery, 35 as engineers and twenty with the Royal Army Service Corps or in some form of motor transport. The rest, the vast majority, were to be found in the infantry; 75 with Indian and around 100 with English regiments, plus at least 30 with Canadian, Newfoundland and ANZAC forces. 340, naturally, were with the Scottish regiments, 68 in the Argyll and Sutherland Highlanders and 56 with the HLI – with the exception of the Scots Guards, which had only seven, all Scots regiments had at least a score of OFs. For all the pride, however, Hay could not help noting the casualties; eleven sets of brothers, for instance, among the 246 dead, and the virtual annihilation of the original band of Fettes Regulars. How many of the boys posing stiffly for his 1909 photograph of the OTC had dreamed, he wondered, that in ten years' time their names would be on a memorial near where they were standing?

NOTES

[1] *Fettesian*, November 1914

[2] Hay (1923) p. xiv

[3] J.M. Winter, *The Great War and the British People* (London, Macmillan, 1986) , p. 98

[4] Ibid., p. 98-9

[5] *Fettesian*, December 1914

[6] Ibid., March 1915

[7] Ibid., December 1914

[8] Clayton, p. 161

[9] Ibid., p. 154

[10] Cyril Falls, *The First World War* (London, Longman, 1967), p. 16

[11] Hay (1950) pp. 52-3

[12] Hay in Pyatt, p. 266

[13] Sparrow & Ross, p. 2

[14] 'Ceremony in Serbia to honour forgotten heroine of war', *Press & Journal*, 23 January 2009

[15] *Fettesian*, November 1914

[16] Ibid., November 1914

[17] Ibid.

[18] Sparrow & Ross, p. 254

[19] Ian Hay, *The First Hundred Thousand* (London, Blackwood, 1915), p. 37

[20] *Fettesian*, March 1918

[21] Hay (1915) p. 16

[22] Hay (1950) p. 51

[23] Vawdrey letters, 13 June 1915 (Fettes Archive)

[24] Ibid., 2 April 1915

[25] Ibid., 7 April 1915

[26] Ibid., 11 April 1915

[27] Ibid., 26 April 1915

[28] Ibid., 28 April 1915

[29] Hay (1915) p. 193

[30] Ibid., p. 22

[31] Ibid., p. 23

[32] Ibid., p. 199

[33] See Arthur Ponsonby, *Falsehood in Wartime* (London, Allen & Unwin, 1928) p. 91

[34] Vawdrey, 18 April 1915

[35] Ibid., 2 May 1915

[36] Hesketh-Prichard (1920) p. 92

[37] Sparrow & Ross, p. 146

[38] Many thanks to Barrie Lloyd who passed on this excerpt by email, 12 December 2008

[39] Barnett, p. 382

[40] *Fettesian*, April 1915

[41] Strachan (2003) p. 171

42 Sparrow & Ross, p. 21

43 Hay (1915) p. 227

44 Vawdrey, 5 May 1915

45 Ian Hay, *All in it: K(1) Carries On* (New York, Houghton Mifflin, 1917) pp. 16-17

46 *Fettesian*, June 1916

47 Vawdrey, 30 May 1915

48 *Fettesian*, June 1916

49 Ibid., July 1918

50 Ibid., June 1915

51 Hay (1915) p. 202

52 Vawdrey, 3 June 1915

53 Ibid., 11 May 1915

54 Sparrow & Ross, pp. 156-7

55 Hesketh-Prichard (1920) p. 47

56 Vawdrey, 5 May 1915

57 Ibid., 9 May 1915

58 *Fettesian*, April 1917

59 Vawdrey, 15 May 1915

60 Sparrow & Ross, pp. 232-4

61 Vawdrey, 19 May 1915

62 Ibid., 15 June 1915

63 T.E. Sandall, *A History of the 5th Batt. Lincolnshire Regt.* (Oxford, Blackwell, 1923) p. 49

64 Email to the author, 12 August 2010

65 Hay (1915) p. 340-1

66 Jack Alexander, *McCrae's Battalion* (Edinburgh, Mainstream, 2003) pp. 186-7

67 *Fettesian*, November 1916

68 Hay (1917) p. 192

69 Hesketh-Prichard, (1920) p. 140

70 Hay (1917) p. 226

71 Clayton, p. 164

72 Ibid., p. 164

73 A. Lawrie & J. Mackay Thompson, *Old Fettesians who served in His Majesty's Forces at home and abroad during the Great War* (Edinburgh, 1920) p.ii

74 Citation, December 7 1915, quoted in *Fettesian*, December 1915

75 Hay (1915) p. 181

76 Hesketh-Prichard, (1920) p. 28

77 *Fettesian*, July 1919

78 Hesketh-Prichard, (1920) p. 12

79 Ibid., p. 17

80 Ibid., p. 51

81 A. Dougan, *Through the Crosshairs* (New York, Carroll & Graf, 2006) p.174

82 Ibid., p. 82

83 Ibid., p. 59

84 Vawdrey, 17 June 1915

85 Email from his son, Barrie Lloyd, 12 December 2009

86 Sparrow & Ross, p. 190

87 Ibid., pp. 195-9

[88] *Scotsman*, 11 June 1917, quoted in *Fettesian*, July 1917
[89] Sparrow & Ross, p. 214
[90] Ibid., p. 211
[91] Philp, p. 48
[92] *Scotland on Sunday*, 11 November 2007
[93] Adam, p. 71
[94] *Fettesian*, July 1918
[95] Ibid., June 1918
[96] Ibid., April 1948
[97] Robin Scott-Elliott, 'Band of Brothers', *Independent*, 6 November 2008
[98] VC Citation, *London Gazette*, 30 April 1918
[99] *Fettesian*, June 1918
[100] Ibid., April 1948
[101] Robin Scott-Elliott, *The Way Home* (Leicester, Troubador, 2007)
[102] *Fettesian*, November 1918
[103] Hay (1917) p. 194
[104] *Fettesian*, December 1917
[105] Sheffield, p. 5
[106] Hay in Pyatt, p. 265

Chapter Seven

'We call ourselves the Final Crusaders'

Other Forces, Other Fronts

The aviators

The vast majority of Great War Fettesians served on the Western Front, and it is there that the majority – around three-quarters – of casualties were sustained. Of these casualties, the great majority were junior officers in Scottish infantry regiments. However, Fettesians followed the flag wherever it went and served in other branches of the armed forces. After the Somme, with 48 killed, the campaign which cost the largest numbers of OF dead was in the Dardanelles, where 21 lost their lives. Another 17 died in the Middle East – Fettes lost more former pupils in the heat and dust of Mesopotamia than in the mud of Passchendaele. Although Fettes was not a maritime school – the Royal Navy's habit of recruiting boys at 14 did not fit well with education to 18 – Hay estimated that some seventy former pupils served in the Senior Service in some capacity, and 55 in or attached to the Royal Flying Corps.

Although the Royal Navy was the Senior Service, thanks to 'Biggles' the newest arm of the British forces in the Great War is the one which most often catches the imaginations of today's young. The First World War was not decided by aircraft, but it did see their imaginative use; not yet as effective as they would be in the Falklands, for instance, or in 1944, but useful nonetheless. The most notable of the airborne Fettesians were Frank and Harold Barnwell, who had built Scotland's first aeroplane (according to some sources, as early as 1900) and, sadly after the Wrights' success in America, Scotland's first aeroplane which could actually fly. Scotland's first powered flight, on 28 July 1909 ('in the dark ages' as a 1920 issue of the *Fettesian* put it) involved a biplane with two propellers making a series of hops of 80-100 yards with Harold at the controls. Although the flimsy aircraft often crashed, they always repaired it and Harold, frequently injured, 'modestly ascribed the worst smashes to errors in judgment in steering.'[1]

The school magazine had followed their pre-war careers, when Frank addressed the Glasgow University Engineering Society in 1910 on the subject of the five aeroplanes he and his brother had made, when Harold won the £50 Scottish Aeronautical Society prize in 1911, and when they had taken part in the *Daily Mail* Aerial Derby in the spring of 1914. Frank Barnwell's book, *Aeroplane Design*, published in 1916, was one of the most influential works on the subject ever written; a recent article in the American Institute of Aeronautics and Astronautics in-house journal claimed that 'what we think of as the continued and sometimes spectacular advancements made in airplane design since then have, in reality, been due mainly to the application of new and advanced technology hung on the framework of Barnwell's original design philosophy.'[2]

Frank Barnwell was the creator of a host of aircraft, including the 'Barnwell Bullet', the Bristol Scout and the Bristol F2B, the famous 'Brisfit' which took part in the first RAF offensive as an independent air force and served until 1932. He succeeded the Romanian engineering genius Henri Coandă as *Chef Technique*, or chief designer, at the British and Colonial Aeroplane Company (better known as Bristol); they valued him so highly that they refused to allow him to fly, probably wisely since he was so badly injured in an accident that he had to be invalided home from France. Harold Barnwell worked for Vickers, where he designed on his own initiative the Barnwell Bullet, a tubby, sleek little fighter which was developed into the Vickers FB19 (not, it should be said, as popular a plane as those designed by his brother – the pilot's view was not as good as in other types and its engine was underpowered). Harold suffered the fate of many Fettesian pilots – he crashed a Vickers FB 26 Vampire night fighter at Joyce Green whilst testing its handling in a spin. A memorial has been erected at Causewayhead in Stirling, site of the original Barnwell factory, in honour of this great Scottish pioneering family, and Frank is also commemorated at the Smithsonian Air and Space Museum in Washington, DC.

Knowledge of tragedies such as Harold Barnwell's could not take away from the thrill of flight, even with the added perils of frequently superior German fighters and 'Archie', as flak was then called. One of Fettes' first pilots, Teddie Anderson, wrote excitedly of his operations over the Somme:

It is most awfully interesting work and I would not have missed it for anything.

We have to fly low and pick up signals from the infantry by lamp etc and drop messages at Corps Headquarters giving whatever information we have obtained as regards Huns, their artillery etc.

I was up about two hours after the attack, by which time the Hun lines were in our hands and the attack on the village of M_____n was beginning. I saw the attack and capture of the village which was of course intensely interesting. We were down at about 1500ft most of the day and were not troubled by Archie at all, but were rather badly strafed by Hun Machine Guns, and our machine had to be sent away as unfit as there were so many holes in it. The GOC of the corps for which we were working was very pleased with the work the squadron did and wrote a very nice letter to our CO.

The attack is still going strong, the French doing splendidly, and our two Corps on their left getting on slowly but steadily. Further north the Huns are putting up a better resistance.

Yesterday I had the satisfaction of knocking out a Hun battery. I saw it firing from a wood and came down quite low. Looking through glasses I saw the three guns and about 20 men standing round. So I flew off and sent down by wireless the position of the battery to the Corp Heavy Artillery and about 20 minutes later had the satisfaction of seeing it blown up by a direct hit!! [3]

He also enjoyed 'balloon-busting' in his fighter:

I see in today's paper it says in the official communique 'We destroyed five of the enemy's kite balloons yesterday' so I suppose I am at liberty to tell you about it, having taken part in the destruction. In my letter to Dad I think I told you I had been practising dropping a new kind of bomb for destroying balloons. Well Jack Coats and I each carrying 48 of these and accompanied by another type of machine carrying a species of rocket, set off to strafe a Hun Kite balloon, commonly called a 'Sausage'. These are captive balloons which are sent up from a good way behind the trenches to watch the result of their batteries fire and to try to see the enemy guns firing. A little balloon at the back keeps it steady and facing into the wind, and the observers sit in a little basket underneath.

The aeroplane with the rockets was to attack first, then I was to drop my bombs and then Jack Coats drop his.

This was to happen to all the 'Sausages' on the line at the same moment so that they would not have time to pull them down after seeing another come down. We started off for our balloon which was about five miles behind the German lines at the appointed time. When we approached the balloon, Archie got very busy and the air was simply thick with them bursting all round. Then the machine with the rockets which was much faster than we were, dashed away ahead, down to the level of the balloon, while we had to remain about 3,000 feet above it (i.e. about 7,000 off the ground) to give our bombs time to get well lighted. He fired his rockets and hit the balloon just as I was going to drop my bombs because I thought he had fired and missed. The balloon just disappeared leaving a ball of flame with a trail of black smoke behind as it dashed to earth. I was not going to return with all my bombs so I dropped them on the Huns who rushed out to the remains of the 'Sausage' and Jack did the same with his!!!

Poor defenceless sausage!! It was a huge golden affair, and disappeared utterly!!

The Archies attended us on our homeward journey and were fairly good shots too. I enjoyed it all immensely, and felt so 'bucked' that I sang lustily most of the way home!! When I looked over the machine on landing, I found six little Archie holes in the wings so they were quite near.[4]

One of the most successful OF pilots was son of the manse Lt Archibald Miller of 29 Sqn, who shot down six Albatros D.IIIs in a French-built Nieuport 17. This was no mean feat, since the Albatros had been the scourge of the Western Front, accounting for many Allied aircraft in the 'Bloody April' of 1917, and the Nieuport, although maneuverable, was slower, less powerful and had only one machine-gun where the Albatros had two. Miller's six kills made him an 'ace', but the RFC at the time did not recognize this system. Lt William Warden was awarded the Military Cross in 1918:

When on a low flying patrol he attacked seven hostile scouts, one of which he succeeded in sending crashing to earth. Previous to this he had attacked and sends down out of control another hostile scout. He has also brought back accurate and valuable information regarding hostile movements, and has flown at very low altitudes in order to engage enemy troops, guns and transport. His skill, determination, and courage have been most marked.[5]

He emigrated to Argentina but returned to the colours in 1939, serving as a Pilot Officer in the RAF. Away from the Western Front, Captain Thomas Hinshelwood – like the Barnwells, a distinguished pre-war aviation pioneer – led his sea patrol squadron on photographic and long-distance bombing raids 'with great ability and judgment' for which he was awarded the Distinguished Flying Cross.[6]

'The high standard of efficiency achieved by his squadron,' reported

Flight magazine, 'is almost entirely due to his personal influence.' He also served in Iraq, as did another DFC winner, Captain J.H. Storey, whose remarkably far-flung service included Italy, the Balkans and West Africa. Squadron Commander Robert Gordon of the RNAS was in command of the Air Squadron supporting British operations in German East Africa, where a cat-and-mouse game was played with enemy ships and colonial troops in the Rufiji Delta. The first aircraft sent out – award-winning Sopwith Seaplanes – had a disconcerting tendency to fall apart in the glue-melting, wood-warping tropical heat, whilst their replacements, Shorts 'Folders', stayed together but were unable to climb high or fast, making bomb runs dangerous, if not suicidal. American Curtiss flying-boats, borrowed from civilians, were also unsuccessful. Nonetheless, Gordon's fliers were vital to the task of defeating the German cruiser *Königsberg*, which had become a threat to British shipping. Their position was helped enormously by the arrival for four French land-based aeroplanes, two Caudrons and two Henri Farmans, the latter specially adapted to tropical conditions; an airfield at Mafia was expanded and Gordon ensured that both his men (who had previously been felled by heatstroke) and machines were protected from the elements. Because the *Königsberg* was out of the British line of sight in the mangrove swamps, Gordon, aloft for hours at a time in a Farman, gave gunnery instructions to HMS *Mersey* and *Severn* via a primitive and unreliable wireless set; the Germans, lacking aircraft, employed a daring officer sitting in a tub in the mud. The *Königsberg* was eventually sunk, though her guns were removed by enterprising troops and used as land weapons. This is generally regarded as one of the earliest examples of what would later be known as 'combined ops' with air power integrated into the work of other arms. Gordon's recommendation for the DSO noted that he 'was indefatigable in his work, and ran great risks in spotting and reconnoitring'; he later enjoyed a distinguished career in the RAF.

Death in action was statistically just as likely for pilots in the Royal Flying Corps as for their comrades down below in the trenches – on top of at least three killed in accidents and one who died of disease contracted on the Gallipoli campaign, twelve Old Fettesians died in action and another twelve were injured, often severely. The British generally viewed observation as the most important function of aircraft; unfortunately, the kind of stable reconnaissance platform ideal for this work was easy prey for the aggressive Fokker monoplanes which appeared in 1915. Capt W.C. Adamson and his observer, Lt Braddyll, were on artillery patrol over the German lines at Mount Sorrel in September 1915. Their FE2, with a 'pusher' engine and gunner in the nose, was one of the few British aircraft of the time that could dish out some punishment to the Fokker, and Adamson and Braddyll distinguished themselves by 'vanquishing three enemy aeroplanes'[7] but were shot down by anti-aircraft fire. Adamson was killed instantly, but Braddyll was taken prisoner. He later succumbed to his wounds and the two are buried close to one another at Harlebeke cemetery. Lt Charles Field, originally from Ontario, stood no chance; flying a BE2, a slow and steady machine which became known as 'Fokker Fodder', he was shot down and killed over the German lines in January 1916.

George MacDonald Watt, originally from Inverness, was an old (at 27) Burma teak hand who 'packed his duds' and returned home to fight. On 17 March 1917 he and his observer, Sgt Earnest Howlett – an experienced soldier who had distinguished himself on the ground before joining the RFC – had been conducting dangerous low-level (2,500 feet) observation for the British artillery over the German-held village of Farbus for several hours when they encountered the dreaded Red Baron, Manfred von Richthofen. A post-war biography of von Richthofen, who had already shot down a British aircraft after breakfast that day, described their fate:

They were so close to the front lines that English Tommies witnessed the fight at five o'clock, when Richthofen swooped down upon then and raised his day's toll of lives from two to four. Watt tried to shake Richthofen off by throwing the old B.E. into sharp curves, which also gave Howlett the opportunity to rip out streams of lead toward their faster adversary every time he approached within range.

Then the Tommies saw the tragedy. At a height of 1,000 feet, the hard-pressed B.E., suffering from the strain of the curves and dives into which Watt was throwing her, collapsed in midair.[8]

The BE2 – which was, as the author of this account hinted, obsolete by this point and little match for the Red Baron's much faster Halberstadt – crashed in no-man's land and was promptly riddled with bullets from the German trenches. British soldiers crawled out after nightfall and retrieved the bodies of Watt and Howlett, later burying them together at Bruay; their BE2 was Richthofen's 28th aircraft downed. Watt had been at the front for exactly two months when he was shot down. E.R. Whyte was one of the crew of naval airship C27, shot down in flames by German seaplanes over the North Sea in 1917. Even fighter pilots were not immortal; Miller fell to the guns of Hans Ritter von Adam on 13 July 1917 (the victor survived only a few more months) and A.R. Adam, another Nieuport pilot, was killed at the same time. Another five OFs were shot down and survived only to be taken prisoner.

The Dardanelles and Salonica

Air power could not decide the Western Front, and nor, it seemed, would anything else. Because of the frustrating stalemate there, Winston Churchill became enthusiastic about an alternative strategy directed against Ottoman Turkey. It was hoped that the seizure of Constantinople would knock the Turks out of the war, relive the pressure on Serbia and open a warm-water route to Russia for the war supplies the Russian armies so desperately needed. In the long term, it might even leech German troops away from France. It failed to do any of these things – but, as Ross, the OF medic in the Royal Naval Division, recalled, it seemed like a good idea at the time:

The campaign had been opened with a breezy confidence that Constantinople would soon fall, and only nine months later we were forced to evacuate our small foothold, leaving behind so many gallant dead; and somehow it seemed a great price to pay for what in the end proved to be worthless…

I well remember a conference of officers on board the transport a few days before the landing. We were shown maps of Gallipoli with the fortifications marked on them, and were told the general scheme of the attack. One sentence stands out clearly in my memory. 'Our outposts will be on Achi Baba at dawn of the second day.' It certainly seemed quite simple on paper, and how little we thought, as we listened, that the very ship in which we then were would return to Alexandria in a few days laden with wounded, and that we should never even get within a mile of Achi Baba! [9]

The Allies landed on 25 April 1915, and were not always opposed – Lt T.A.G. Miller of the 1st Battalion King's Own Scottish Borderers (brother of the air ace and a noted rugby player) was able to land at Y Beach unmolested, as Ross explained:

This narrow landing-place, situated due west of Krithia, lies at the foot of steep scrub-covered cliffs. So inaccessible did it appear that no attack was expected, and the Plymouth Battalion Royal Marines, along with the King's Own Scottish Borderers, were able to scale the cliffs with little opposition. A further advance was, however, impossible, and being unable to get in touch with the Fusiliers on their right, in face of repeated counter-attacks by an enemy frequently reinforced, they were compelled merely to dig them-selves in on the summit of the cliffs. Not only were they outnumbered, but the configuration of the ground favoured the enemy in such a way that our ships' guns could not be brought to bear on him.[10]

The few Turks to appear were beaten off, but uncertainty about communications and command allowed panic to set in and the Allied troops were evacuated from Y Beach the following day. By this point, the Allies had suffered their first casualties, including Miller, who seems to have been killed in the enemy's dawn counter-attack on 26 April. As on the Western Front, a stalemate gradually developed with trenches and all their attendant discomforts:

In the fire trenches there was much of interest — sniping through loopholes or with a periscope rifle, and firing hand-grenades from prehistoric-looking catapults, said to have come from Carnage's; but however the scene might vary, always the same intense heat, overpowering smells, and ubiquitous flies. How those flies pervaded everything! Food became black with them immediately it was uncovered. They swarmed around the unburied dead and infested the habitations of the living. They spoilt the temper of the healthy and added greatly to the sufferings of the wounded and sick. No wonder men ate little. Unopened bully beef tins were stuffed in the parapet for want of a better use — meat for the asking, and yet few had any desire to touch it. Tins of jam in plenty, but none cared to sample them, except perhaps the Turks, to whom we slung them over in our catapults. Tickler's artillery, named after a firm of jam makers, soon became famous. It consisted of 'plum and apple' tins, emptied of their legitimate contents and filled with high explosive, odd lumps of metal, and a detonator.[11]

Just as the first day of the Somme campaign produced a harvest of dead, so too did individual pushes at Gallipoli. On 4 June, the Allies launched the Third Battle of Krithia in the hope of making a tentative breakthrough from the trench system which had developed over the previous six weeks. Although the Royal Naval and 42nd Divisions gained their objectives, the attackers on each side of them were beaten back, and they were caught by enfilade fire; the Collingwood Battalion almost annihilated. Ross wrote that the first batches of wounded were quite cheerful, believing they had succeeded, but as the day wore on 'the spirit of optimism gave place to one of shattered hopes, and they had no knowledge of victory to help them bear the pain of their wounds, the intolerable flies and the sickly smell of blood in those dirty, stuffy aid posts, most of which were no more than an unoccupied portion of trench.'[12]

On that day, Ross's fellow-OFs Sub-Lt J.W. Hart of the ill-fated Collingwood Battalion of the RND, Lt L.G. Liebenthal, Cameron Highlanders, Royal Marine Major S.J. Sparling, 33, and Gurkha Capt Gerald Turner were all killed. Turner, 'one of the best cricketers Fettes ever had,'[13] had already lost, earlier in the Gallipoli campaign, his old classmate from the 1899 intake, preparatory schoolmaster Bernard Herford, who in turn had lost his brother Geoffrey in the sinking of HMS *Monmouth* the previous year. A pulpit was installed at their father's church in Leith in their memory. Although, like Y Beach, there were those who argued that had the Allies pressed on they would have had greater success (Ross certainly thought this a possibility) the assault was called off after 4,500 British casualties and a Turkish counter-attack. 'It was evident, Ross wrote, 'that all hope of a speedy termination to the campaign was ended, at any rate, for the time being, and that siege warfare must now be inevitable.'

On 28 June, at the Battle of Gully Ravine, the British again had some successes but without artillery support – always in short supply in the Dardanelles – were similarly unable to press home any advantages. Old Fettesians in the Cameronians were especially hard-hit that day: Lieutenants H. McCowan and Tommy Stout and Captains Eric Templeton Young and R.C.B. Macindoe fell, along with Lt R. Moncrieff Galloway of the Royal Scots. Tommy Stout, a gifted rugby player, was killed after only two weeks in the Dardanelles in the act of rescuing his superior officer, who was lying wounded in a communications trench exposed to heavy bombardment. The Battalion Medical Officer wrote to his parents that 'it will be some little comfort to you to know that he met his death while bravely assisting a comrade. He died a true British soldier.'[14]

Young, who had been a Scottish flanker in the Calcutta Cup match of 1914 (one of six members of the squad to be killed) was recorded by the Commonwealth War Graves Commission as being killed on this day in France, and his name was on the Le Touret Memorial in the Pas de

Calais until 2008, when the Cameronian Museum succeeded in relocating him to the Helles Memorial. At least half of the Old Fettesian casualties of the Dardanelles are on memorials rather than marked graves; most bodies were unidentifiable by the time the CWGC got round to reorganising the cemeteries after the war, thanks to inaccessibility, climate and artillery. 27,000 names appear on memorials to the missing of Gallipoli.

Two Fettesian casualties of the Dardanelles: David Bedell-Sivright, rugby international, and Bernard Herford.

Gallipoli is known in popular culture for the role played there by the Australian and New Zealand Army Corps (ANZAC). For Australians and New Zealanders, ANZAC Cove has become a shrine and 25 April a sacred date. To this day, Australian teachers at Fettes lead an ANZAC Day service in chapel each year, and Neville Clark, the former Housemaster of Glencorse who himself served with distinction in the Australian Army in Vietnam, recently gave the school's Historical Society a detailed account of the battle. Maitland Hardyman, whose brother Malcolm served alongside the ANZACs in the Middle East, contributed a rather desolate little poem to the *Fettesian* entitled 'Australia's Prayer':

JEHOVAH, Lord of all Gethsemanes,
Of thorn-crowned Truth and broken purposes,
Our stricken motherhood, our tortured brain,
Shrill with the piercing cry, 'Is it in vain?'

No dream of conquest, no mad lust for power,
Found us at England's side in danger's hour,
The Bays of Suvla and of Anzac prove
The strong example of that Greater Love.

Gladly we gave the noblest of our youth
To fight for England and, we thought, for Truth;
Now we are weaker, numbed with constant pain —
Is it in vain, Lord God, is it in vain?

Out of the rending silence God replied:
'You ask the triumph I My Son denied.
Have faith, poor soul. Is not all history
Triumphant failure, empty victory?' [15]

Cecil Gray-Buchanan, a Glaswegian OF who became a sheep-farmer in Queensland, enlisted as a trooper in the Australian Horse and is buried in Shrapnel Valley Cemetery, near Lone Pine Plateau. Not that the Australians – epic though their experience was – were the only Allied troops there, as the *Fettesian* obituaries demonstrated. Edward Weatherill, an Irish OF, enlisted in the 'Football' Company of the Royal Dublin Fusiliers, and was promoted to sergeant of their machine-gun section before becoming an officer.[16]

The official history of the 10th (Irish) Division describes the circumstances of 2/Lt. Weatherill's death on 16 August, which could stand for the frustrations experienced by Allied troops throughout the campaign:

Since advance was impossible, the troops were compelled to remain on their position, exposed to a perpetual fire of grenades, to which they had no means of replying. The sun rose higher in the sky and reached the zenith and still the bombing went on without intermission, and the men of the 10th Division continued to suffer and endure. The faces of dead comrades, lying at their sides, stiffened and grew rigid, and the flies gathered in clouds to feast on their blood, while from the ridge in front came the groans of the wounded, whom it was impossible to succour. The men lying behind the crest knew that at any moment a similar fate might come to any of them, and they might fall a shattered corpse, or be carried back moaning, but still they held on. The unceasing noise of the bursting grenades, the smell of death, the sight of suffering, wore their nerves to tatters, but worst of all was the feeling that they were helpless, unable to strike a blow to ward off death and revenge their comrades.[17]

Weatherill and his brother–officers did their best in the savage conditions, but in doing so exposed themselves to greater danger:

Everywhere the few remaining officers moved about among their men, calming the over-eager, encouraging the weary, giving an example of calmness and leadership, of which the land that bore them may well be proud. In doing this they made themselves a mark for the inevitable snipers, who by now had ensconced themselves in coigns of vantage on the crest of the ridge, and many died there.

Edward Weatherill was hit by one such sniper. Thanks to the prevailing conditions which made it impossible to recover the bodies of the fallen, he has no known grave. Described by his colleagues as 'a boy who had made himself conspicuous in a very gallant battalion for courage', he had been an officer for five months when he was killed. Ross's account of Gallipoli is the most detailed by an Old Fettesian that we have, but Ayrshire-born James Innes Miller of the Royal Field Artillery, who was wounded there but survived (with enough of a taste for the exotic to become a civil servant in Malaya after the war), wrote back to the school to describe his experience with a poem, 'Suvla Memories':

I remember, I remember,
The ships astride the bay,
The 'planes that soared the cloudless blue,
Horses, guns, gunners, none so true,
The flies benighting day.

The matchless morn in splendour born,
Thje wealth of evening sun,
Setting in mystic majesty
Behind the isles of Greece. And aye
Some hero's day was done.

The holy wells, the unholy smells,
The mule-track round the shore,
The teams that tramped it night by night,
Jingling along by faith, not sight;
The graves of men no more.

Where sappers fagged and snipers bagged,
Sulajik, F.O.P..
The whistling orchestra o'erhead
Of shrieking shell and lashing lead
In martial harmony.

Till in a scrap, where things near hap,
A murderous missile sang,
'I know thee. Thou art mine. My breath
Will waft thee to the shores of Death –
Whizz – BANG!
Thither all Allah's foes must wend.'

And here my Suvla Memories end.[18]

Frederic Littleboy, an English OF in the year below Miller, is buried at
Suvla after having died of wounds there. As with previous generations of
OFs sent to fight in hotter climes, those in the Dardanelles suffered
terribly from illness with the onset of summer. As a medical officer, Ross
fought in the front line against the diseases which began to proliferate in
June:

Chief amongst these were typhoid, paratyphoid, dysentery, enteritis, jaundice,
malaria, and that obscure condition known in the Army as P.U.O. (pyrexia of
uncertain origin). The 'Gallipoli Gallop' was a term largely used by the men and
covered any complaint of which the words are suggestive or symptomatic. The
amount of sickness was so great that the Division, in spite of numerous
reinforcements which continually arrived, would soon have become non-existent if
every sick man had been evacuated to hospital. Hence all who could carry on at all
were kept with their battalions, and treated by the battalion medical officers. The
men, with a very fine esprit de corps, appreciated the adverse conditions under
which we laboured and made light of their complaints.[19]

One of the most famous figures of the time to perish at Gallipoli was
David 'Darkie' Bedell-Sivright, a promising doctor and one of the most
famous Scots sportsmen of his generation. He had been capped 22 times
for Scotland, led the Lions to Australia and New Zealand in 1904, and
was Scottish amateur heavyweight boxing champion. Whilst at Fettes he

had hidden a bottle of ink in the fireplace of the eccentric Mr Kroupa to see what would happen, and was gratified to see that it exploded, covering the room with ink and glass. A giant of a man, Bedell-Sivright is supposed to have laid down in front of a tram on Princes Street for an hour, unmolested by terrified police, wrestled a carthorse, and drunk heavily before matches, sometimes arriving late and stomping up and town the touchline, muttering dire threats to the opposition, as he waited to be sent on: 'When I go on to that field I only see the ball,' he once said, 'and should someone be in the road, that is his own lookout.'[20]

He was lost to septicaemia following an insect bite and buried at sea, and is remembered today on the Commonwealth War Graves Commission's booklet about sportsmen killed in war. He was one of six OF Scottish rugby internationals to die in the war (the Scotland side suffered the greatest losses of all the home nations, with 30 casualties to England's 27, Wales's 11 and Ireland's 9). It will be recalled that to die from an infected insect bite in the Eastern Mediterranean was also the fate of Rupert Brooke (whose father had taught at Fettes and married Clem Cotterill's sister); two other OFs later died of illness contracted on this campaign. William Park, an RNAS airman based on HMS *Ark Royal,* who won the DSC as 'one of the most valuable spotting officers' at Gallipoli, died of malaria after his return from the Mediterranean, as did T. Yorston Stout of the RNVR. Disillusioned with the Dardanelles project, the Allies withdrew early in 1916 in a masterful evacuation which turned out to be the only real success of the whole campaign. Ross – admittedly writing in 1918 and not wanting to let the side down – was philosophical:

Though a failure, it will pass down to posterity as an exhibition of the most superb heroism and bravery on the part of all ranks. In the historic landing the Royal Naval Division played a prominent part, and, from that day, until the evacuation, were conspicuous by their bravery…

The Evacuation, though such a triumph of organisation and so brilliantly successful, was a sad blow to all.[21]

Old Fettesians were also to be found in Greece and the Middle East. Ross and several others were sent to Salonica with the intention of trying to help the Serbs from being overrun by Austria-Hungary and Bulgaria. This gave Ross the opportunity to provide local colour by describing the Greeks amongst whom the British were based both going to and coming from Gallipoli. His animal-loving instincts were roused by the common sight of 'a small pony carrying not only a stout peasant and his buxom spouse, but also in addition an enormous sack of grain.' That said, he was no sentimentalist. 'A mule can negotiate the steepest track with a characteristic sang-froid, often craning his neck over the brink of a precipice to gather some tempting shrub with a confidence which is scarcely shared by his rider'[22] he wrote of the chief form of transport in the rugged Balkan terrain. The Salonica campaign was not a great success; spending much of their time frustrated and with limited mobility, the British were even defeated by the Bulgarians at Lake Doiran in April 1917. An OF, Capt. Walter Purves of the East Lancashires, was killed then; Charles Patten had died of wounds in October 1916. The Bulgarians were not finally pushed back until just before the war ended.

The Middle East
One of the only records in the *Fettesian*, the Gallipoli poems apart, of OFs serving outwith the Western Front came from the Middle East. An anonymous officer who sent an article entitled 'My Friend the Camel.' He was very impressed both with the animal and with the British soldiers' ability to adapt to these exotic beasts:

The affection that the genus T. Atkins has for animals is proverbial, and this is displayed in his dealings with the camel. A company of the battalion that happens to be garrisoning Khartoum is formed into a British Camel Corps. In a surprisingly short space of time – surprising to those who do not know the camel – Thomas is on the best of terms with his new mount, though the camel may have been nothing more than a zoological curiosity to him only a few weeks before. As the British mounted man is ordered to 'make much of his horse' (i.e. pat and stroke it) when he dismounts, so the British cavalry make much of their camels, and they respond at once.[23]

Needless to say, as a Fettesian the author was keen to address the sporting possibilities of his new friend:

The term stalking-horse is, in my experience, a misnomer. It is difficult to train a pony to act in a sensible way when close to game. But the camel requires no training; presumably he understands. I have often managed to work close up to a gazelle, right in the open where there was no cover, by walking alongside my camel, and keeping him carefully between me and the victim; finally taking my shot under his neck or between his legs, for no camel is fool enough to be gun shy.

Aware that not everyone would regard this as entirely sportsmanlike, he added that 'when meat is badly wanted, and the nature of the ground precludes an unaided stalk, it is more 'sporting' to call in the aid of a camel than to risk a long shot with all its possibilities of wounding without bagging.' Needless to say, these postings took their traditional toll, and a number of OFs died of disease or as a result of untreatable accidents there. A detailed first-hand account of Middle East fighting was given to Fettes by the daughter of OF Lt A.M. Fawcett, who had run away from school to join up when war was declared and wrote much of the War Diary of the 2nd Battery Royal Field Artillery. His post-war account, typed up from notes onto now- yellowing foolscap, is frank about the combat conditions prevailing in the harsh environment of the Ottoman Empire. The entry for April 22 1916 reads:

Since March 1st to this date rations for man and animals have consistently been both bad and insufficient; animal rations frequently only 4 lbs., some days none at all; men's rations, the bare bully beef and biscuit, frequently only half rations of that; tea, jam, sugar, cheese or bacon only very occasionally, milk and vegetables never. In addition fighting of some sort was practically continuous, moving and digging new positions almost continual, generally without any protection from the cold of the March nights or the heat of the April days, and with no possibility of change of clothing. Great additional work in unloading such rations as there were from the boats often many miles from the Battery positions, digging banks to keep the floods back to preserve dry ground to fight on, and every imaginable form of fatigue. In addition bad sanitary conditions and continual bivouacking on old battlefields produced such unimaginable swarms of flies as to make eating between sunrise and sunset almost impossible.

All this affected very adversely the health of the troops. Strength of Battery in March was 175 and despite drafts dwindled to 120 in July. A large percentage of those admitted to hospital died as a result of the lack of invalid diet.[24]

Writing after the war (with, it appears, the full consent of his immediate superiors) meant that Fawcett was free to comment acerbically on the eccentricities of the high command; General Maude's arrival gained the confidence of the troops because they had been disillusioned by his predecessor Gorringe, but he himself caused a great deal of 'fedupness' with a blizzard of optimistic communiqués.[25]

Wounded whilst acting as Forward Observer on operations on the Tigris in February 1917, Fawcett described the chaos of river crossing under fire:

...a lot of the rowers were hit, and many boats spun round in the current and drifted off down stream. The empty boats of the first party got entangled with these, and it was impossible to tell, in the bad light, whether our infantry had made good or no. I think that the worst part of this show was having to sit in a boat and be shot at with no means of retaliation. I never thought we had a chance of succeeding, and I am sure the infantry didn't, either.[26]

Yet succeed they did:

Good targets kept appearing and the Battery did some telling shooting. At 2.30 after an artillery barrage about 200 Turks on the opposite side of the river from the Battery surrendered. They could have made matters very unpleasant had they been in any mind to do so. At 4.30 the Sappers had completed the bridge and the cavalry crossed that evening. The Battery was shooting till dusk, when it was withdrawn, but on the following day crossed by the bridge at about 3 pm. The Turks had made some sort of resistance, probably to safeguard their people at Sunnaiyat who were in retreat, during the morning, and the Battery fired 1400 rounds before they received the order to cross. Bivouacked on the left bank of the river that night. Now commenced the pursuit to Baghdad...

Unfortunately, the cavalry was unable to make good on its advantage, and it was to be another three weeks before Baghdad was taken. Although sometimes cynical (especially about the cavalry), Fawcett reserved his real ire for those in authority who appeared to have forgotten about the Middle East campaigns – or interfered with them unnecessarily. He noted with irritation in the entry for 3 February 1917 that officers of the battery were so poorly equipped that they had been forced to hire their own tents from the Indian government (to whom the 2nd RFA officially reported), 'a relic of ancient campaigns in the days of the East India Company'[27]; when control was transferred to the War Office, they took too much interest and sent out irritating orders. After five months of hard fighting in the first half of 1917, culminating in a 'wide and sweeping movement against the Arabs in which a lot of cattle and sheep were captured and several Arab villages destroyed' in the 'almost unbearable' summer heat, the top brass decreed a period of training. Fawcett could never 'understand why, in the war, the first care of a busy staff was ever to devise drills, schemes and plans of training for troops who only wanted good food and to be left alone.'[28]

For all Fawcett's gripes, he was proud of what his Battery achieved and did not, at least on paper, question the whole point of an enterprise which sent him to endure such suffering in the desert. Likewise, one of the best letters to appear in the *Fettesian* also came from the Middle East. Lt Wolfenden's report from liberated Jerusalem, which appeared in the war's last spring, was a mixture of ironic detachment, melancholic disillusionment and faint hope, entitled 'The Final Crusade':

We call ourselves the Final Crusaders with just that touch of conceit which tries to cover up the stern practicalities of war in the garb of romance. We feel that our achievement, whether it be (in the technical sense) of strategic value or not, has the larger sense of an uplifting power reilluming the cause for which we fight.

The symbol of it all to my mind was Christmas Eve 1917, when a truly historic private garbed in shorts stood sentinel over the Manger in the Church of the Nativity, Bethlehem, to keep the warring sects preaching their various forms of Christian love from joining in something other than fraternal embraces.

For hundreds of years before this, Christian peace had been kept by a Turkish soldier – and be it said in fairness, well kept.[29]

Of the fighting, he said little, partly because the key engagement of this campaign had been at Gaza, where the most ferocious artillery bombardment of the war outside Europe, co-ordinated from the air, and followed by a charge of thousands of Imperial cavalrymen, had, on the third attempt (an OF, Lt Col Harold Thompson, was killed on the second) forced the Turco-German forces north of Jerusalem, which was thus taken bloodlessly. 'Jerusalem', Wolfenden observed, 'was captured at Gaza when shell and bomb in combined unceasing shriek broke the enemy *moral*.' The young officer, brought up on the Bible like all of his generation, was rather disappointed with the holy city – 'more romantic from outside the city walls or from the air than from within', where it was full of 'squalor and misery' – but he finished his tale with a little elegy for Jerusalem which offered an (as yet unfulfilled) optimism:

Still, Jerusalem has that perennial quality which distinguishes great cities; she can arise phoenix-like from the dead ashes of her past, and re-mantle the glories of the place which nature has given her and no squalor can ever destroy in the lesser but dignified splendours of man.

It was a day of re-birth to Jerusalem when we entered it, and so long as the faith of our island and of Europe centres around One whose sorrows were chiefly borne among those historic hills, the pride of Christian man will be to make the Holy City worthier of its unique past.

Fawcett was slightly less romantic about the heritage of the Middle East. Writing of the assault on Kut in December 1916, he commented that 'it seems strange nowadays' that General Townshend had assured the Turks that he would not 'molest' their minarets, 'bearing in mind that in this flat country minarets are such wonderful O.P.s.'[30]

Their commander was eventually persuaded that houses near this one were havens for snipers who were making life a misery for British troops, and permission was given to fire on the area. 'I think every battery within reach opened, and whether the snipers were intimidated it is hard to tell, but it is certain that Kut minaret came down with a bang in the first few rounds.' Capt. R.P. Dunn-Pattison, an OF military historian best known for his book *Napoleon's Marshals*, might have given a different view, but he was killed before reaching Kut. Fawcett was also immune to the ancient charms of Baghdad, 'a most disappointing place' with 'dirty and odoriferous' bazaars and a populace pock-marked with boils.[31]

He was rather more impressed with King Darius' carvings on the side of the mountain at Bisitun in Persia, partly because of their magnificence but also because of the river in which they were able to bathe. Unfortunately, some locals caught and killed the battery dog, Fritz, who had been with the men since he was adopted in France in 1914, and accompanied them everywhere, always on foot, barking at the dust kicked up by enemy gunfire. 'A rotten ending to be caught and done in by a lot of dirty Persians.'[32]

A keen jockey who won many races after the war, Fawcett was nonplussed to find that the Persians regarded a British racecourse with contempt; their idea of a proper race was 124 miles, with the added thrill that whoever beat the Shah's horse faced instant death, for some reason of faith and heritage. The Shah himself was in no position, at this point, to administer such sporting justice; considered pro-German, he had been arrested by another Old Fettesian, 'Jock' MacDonald of the Camerons, who saved the imperial family from execution by over-zealous Anglophiles.[33]

MacDonald, like Fawcett, also worked with Russians in the region, and was awarded the Order of St. Stanislav; his apparently modest claim that it was merely 'for a record consumption of vodka' would have struck contemporaries as perfectly possible, since he was a tough, shinty-playing, Gaelic-speaking laird of the old school. Like many who served in the Middle East, he became dangerously ill, but discharged himself from hospital as soon as he could walk, pausing only to let an even more tough-minded medical orderly stamp 'cancelled' on his death certificate. He made a full recovery and he served in Burma in the Second World War. In total, around forty OFs served in the Middle East and 17 were killed, mostly in the fighting around Jerusalem or in Mesopotamia. Eight are buried or commemorated in the Commonwealth cemeteries in Iraq, and OFs serving in Operation Telic recently visited the graves. When the War actually ended, A.M. Fawcett was 'not much stirred, as we were thoroughly fed up with Persia by this time.'[34]

Having marched all the way there, they now had to march back again.

The Easter Rising

One pupil got close to the firing line of another conflict with unholy overtones during the Easter holidays of 1916, when radical Irish nationalists led by Patrick Pearse staged a rebellion which they hoped would be a 'stab in the back' for Britain. W.B. Adam was in Dublin when rebellion broke out on Good Friday and left a fascinating record of it:

In my diary written at the time, the entry for Monday, the 24th of April, 1916 reads, 'put the felt on potting-shed roof' and then, apparently as an afterthought, 'riots began'. Such was the momentary impression, for the association of Irishmen and riots was sufficiently natural to call for little comment. There was, however, a greater air of tension the following morning and father announced that he would take a stroll into town. No doubt he felt that it was his duty as a county magistrate to restore law and order, but in actual fact both he and I were consumed with curiosity to see for ourselves what was afoot…

Nothing out of the ordinary happened until we reached College Green and were passing in front of Trinity College when a burst of rifle fire broke out from the roof, the bullets singing around our heads. The few people in the streets bolted for cover, but there appeared to be little danger unless the enemy decided to reply from the houses in Dame Street in which they had barricaded themselves. Further on towards the centre of the city the fighting appeared to be more continuous, the main area of hostilities being the western side of Sackville Street. After watching the scene for a while I decided to go back home for lunch, but father stopped in town till the afternoon and at one time helped to carry off the few of the wounded.

From out at Holywood next day we could hear the sounds of the rifle fire in the city rising and falling. The battle was now pitched in dead earnest, for here was no pate-breaking riot, but Armed Rebellion stalking abroad or entrenched behind barricades in the streets or in captured buildings. Troops hastily dispatched from England were arriving at that day at Kingstown and, cycling down by a circuitous route, I saw some of the companies landed. One of the regiments suffered severe casualties by being ambushed...

During the next two days of the noise of battle increased and by Friday night the tide had reached its highest. From the flat roof of our house we could, in the daylight, see the whole of Dublin, and now, with night turned into day, the scene was so brilliantly illuminated that all the landmarks were clearly visible and the outline of the city was silhouetted against a red glare. For the whole of one side of Sackville Street was burning furiously, with the flames reaching far above the tallest buildings great to pursue... the silence of the night was obliterated by the almost continuous rattle of rifle fire and the staccato stutter of machine-guns.[35]

As a protestant and an enthusiast for the Royal Navy, Adam's fascination with the rebellion was tinged with an awareness of its possible personal impact on himself and his family. Although the Irish Republicans claimed (as they still do) to guarantee civil and religious liberty for all and to cherish all the children of the nation equally, the Rising's personnel was almost entirely Catholic. Moreover, the poetry of its leader, Pearse, was imbued with a surreal Roman mysticism, with talk of blood sacrifices and Christ-like redemption of the enslaved nation. In fairness, equally barmy hymns to slaughter were being dashed off by plenty of British patriots at the time – not least the pupils of Fettes College, Edinburgh – but a protestant in Ireland at the time was probably in no mood to indulge in comparative textual analysis. The majority of Fettes' Irish pupils came from the kind of well-off families whose integration with the rest of the United Kingdom extended to educating their children on what was often called 'the mainland'; they included the McGillycuddys of the Reeks, one of whom was killed in the First and one in the Second World Wars. Thomas Eyre and Charles Erskine Barton, two sons of the Anglo-Irish protestant ascendancy (their father owned the vast Glendalough House estate in Wicklow) who came to Fettes in 1897,

255

became officers in the Royal Irish Rifles. Adam's family certainly worried:

Normal communications were naturally interrupted and by the end of the week there was a shortage of certain food supplies. I have a vision of cycling out into the country and returning with a precious cargo of a dozen eggs somewhat a precariously conveyed in a paper bag. By the Sunday we had become sufficiently accustomed to the idea of rebellion to give our minds to the reception and propagation of rumours, and of these there were many. Perhaps there was some truth in the belief that several of the larger houses in the neighborhood or marked down for occupation by the rebels. It was certainly the case that a few days previously we had had a queer visitor at the door 'feeling faint' and asking for water, who took the opportunity of exploring the hall, the lounge and the smoking-room when left for a moment to himself. Later our gate was found to be marked with a strange sign which was repeated on the house and the end of the road – a position which commanded one of the main entries from our district to the city. This house also received an unconventional caller about the same time…

I also had a vague idea of placing a Union Jack on a flagstaff on the roof but as a gesture this appeared, on second thoughts, to be merely asking for trouble.[36]

The rebellion delayed, perhaps unsurprisingly, Adam's return to school for the summer term, but, as is the way of schoolboys, he soon forgot about it, and his next diary entry recorded only that he 'Arrived Edinburgh 11.25 – went run with Reid and Bairnsfather.' Ian Hay, whose literary talents had led to his recruitment to the cause of propaganda aimed at the United States, lost his usual easygoing jocularity when it came to explaining the Easter Rising. Although he could cheerfully accept the perils of German snipers and even crack jokes about shelling, he was roused to almost unreasoning fury by the Republicans:

In order to put their amiable intention into effect, the Sinn Feiners proceeded, on Easter Monday of 1916, to deal the British peoples, including some three hundred thousand of their own compatriots serving on the Western Front, a stab in the back in the shape of that grim medley of tragedy and farce, the Dublin 'revolution.' The farce was supplied by Germany, which deposited upon the western shores of Ireland, from a submarine, a degenerate criminal lunatic named Casement, who had already failed egregiously in a monstrous effort to seduce the Irish prisoners in the German prison camps from allegiance to their cause.

Casement was promptly arrested by the local village policeman, and his share in the matter ended. But in Dublin there was no lack of tragedy. The forces of the 'revolution' struck the first blow for Freedom by an indiscriminate massacre of such British soldiers as happened to be strolling about the streets, unarmed, in their 'walking out' dress. The killing was then extended to a large number of innocent civilians, not all of the male sex; and the apostles of Freedom then settled down, with the able assistance of the slum population, to the unrestrained looting of the shops and houses of Dublin.[37]

This was rather unfair – the looting was often carried out by the wives of loyal Irishmen who were serving the crown overseas, whilst the rebels' devout and somewhat conservative Catholicism seems to have restrained them from crimes against property or women. A small number of rebel leaders were tried and shot by firing-squad; unnecessarily brusque, perhaps, but an infinitely more restrained punishment than would have been inflicted by the Central Powers for similar behaviour in their bailiwicks, as the Serbs, Armenians and Belgians would doubtless attest. However, the exemplary Catholic deaths of the rebel leaders, and what was seen as John Bull going back to his old cruelty, inflamed local sentiment; Sinn Fein encouraged a mawkish notion of martyrdom and victimhood. Support for the ultra-nationalist movement grew; the Bartons' brother Robert, who had not had the advantage of a Fettes education but had been sent instead to Rugby, seems to have shared this sympathy, for in 1916 he resigned his army commission and became a passionate republican. He was arrested by the authorities but escaped, became a Sinn Fein MP, signed the Anglo-Irish Treaty of 1921 and then renounced it (he was a friend of Erskine Childers, the great spy novelist turned Irish nationalist, whose career followed a similar trajectory until brought to an abrupt halt by one of Michael Collins' firing squads). Thomas Barton was killed at the Somme and Charles died as the result of gassing in the 1918 German offensive; Robert lived to be 94 and enjoyed considerable prosperity in the Republic whose cause he had embraced.

The Senior Service

Adam was one of the relatively small number of Fettesians that served in the Royal Navy during the Great War; anyone destined for the Senior Service entered it long before a normal school had finished with him, at around the age of fourteen. The popular image of the Navy, encapsulated in young Adam's pictures on his study wall, was of great Dreadnaught

This memorial to the Easter Rising of 1916 combines both pagan and Catholic imagery to venerate nationalist rebels; Fettesians of the time had a rather different view of them

battleships policing the world for the freedom of the seas, and, if necessary, taking on the German High Seas Fleet for the ultimate showdown between Britain and the upstart militarists of Berlin. For many of the fifty or so Old Fettesians afloat between 1914 and 1918, the war was much less glamorous. Some are listed in *Fettesians Who Served* as having, like L.J.L. Walker, been in 'home waters' or having been, like Ninian Ballantyne Stewart, employed in minesweeping duties along the coast. Norman Neill served on HMY *Adventuress*, a commandeered steam yacht with a gun hurriedly bolted to her foredeck, which spent the war pottering around Dublin Bay in the forlorn hope that German U-boats would turn up to support an Irish nationalist rising. John Neill McNeill was attached to HMS *Egmont*, a hulk at Malta, whilst J.D. Hawkins uneventfully ploughed the North Sea in the trawler *Rugby*. These were not, of course, pointless or even danger-free tasks – the fate of the *Pathfinder* showed how dangerous home waters could be – but they can hardly have been the hoped-for careers of the more ambitious young men on board.

There were some OFs, however, who served on board the great beasts of the sea, two who went down with them, and others who were fortunate not to do so. Geoffrey Herford, a clergyman's son from Edinburgh who had joined the Royal Marines Light Infantry on leaving school in 1900, was one of the 678 men to go down on HMS *Monmouth* when she was crippled by *Gneisenau* and finished off by *Nürnberg* at the Battle of Coronel on 1 November 1914. Although Coronel was swiftly avenged off the Falkland Islands, it was an embarrassing failure for the British. Several Old Fettesians took part in, and survived, the Battle of Dogger Bank in 1915, when the Royal Navy engaged a German squadron at range and chased them back to port, sinking the *Blücher*. Naval Engineer Francis H. Lyon, a Victorian OF of naval background and a career sailor, was with the Harwich Squadron in the battle, whilst Keith Macleod Lawder, Paymaster on HMS *Lion* and another career sailor, saw his ship badly damaged and hauled back to Rosyth for emergency repairs. The greatest confrontation between the rival fleets, however, was the frustratingly indecisive Battle of Jutland, known to Germans as *Der Tag* (The Day) which saw around a dozen OFs, mostly junior officers, taking part. Some, admittedly, were at a distance; Archibald Rettie, on HMS *Cochrane*, did not see a shot fired from his ship, whilst J.M. Casement, one of the few OFs of his era to command a ship, was in charge of the scout cruiser HMS *Blanche*, which was kept to the rear because of her relatively weak seagoing capacity. Others were closer to the action; Sub. Lt. John Vital Brian de la Motte, on board HMS *Warspite*, ended up going round in circles after his ship was hit 14 times, whilst Eric Read, on *Marlborough*, was lucky to survive when his was torpedoed. John Steggall, an instructor on HMS *Invincible*, was less fortunate; he was one of over a thousand sailors to perish with his ship when shells from *Lützow* and *Derfflinger* blew her apart after detonating the midships magazines. Adam, who joined up after the Jutland debacle, was the only naval OF to leave a detailed account of his adventures from start to finish. His first posting was to HMS *Victory VI* – which was not quite what he expected:

As we trooped off to see our quarters we passed into the main body of the Crystal Palace – that vast and draughty conservatory which was used as a forcing house for young officers and ratings of the RNVR, and for ratings of the RNAS. Here, stranded on top of Sydenham Hill, lay HMS Victory VI, *built uniquely of steel and glass, and lying in a berth conveniently immune from submarine attack. The area immediately outside the central part of the building was no longer a mere terrace — it was the Quarterdeck, with its flagstaff carrying a white ensign on a yard-arm and a commodore's pennant at the peak. There was no mistaking that this was one of His Majesty's ships, for 'liberty-men' paraded each evening for leave ashore, and the whole place hummed with nautical phraseology. It was a queer game, this playing at sailors, but it served its purpose of taking the chill of the plunge into one of the permanent naval establishments which had to be made before appointment to a sea-going ship.*

Victory VI's naval appurtenances extended even to the sleeping arrangements:

To the new snotty [midshipman] *on his first night the two rows of hammocks looked innocent enough; only when he tried to enter his own did he realize that a thousand devils lay there to torment him. At first it would merely capsize and let him down gently on the side from which he had made the attack; but the monotony of this action soon bred recklessness, and then action became more violent. Sudden upheavals of the hammock caused the attacker to take part in a series of involuntary gyratory movements which eventually landed him on the deck on the opposite side from that on which he started — a bewildering and undignified exhibition of gymnastics which was both exhausting and painful. Then suddenly, and for no known reason, the resistance would cease and the hammock permit him to enter with disconcerting ease. Later on, in the early hours, it would take on a list and let his blankets slide overboard.*[38]

Adam had high hopes of seeing action when he arrived for his training in the spring of 1918. The German offensive and the retreat of the British Fifth Army had started in March and had continued for several weeks (Alfred had been in the middle of it, at the spot where the enemy advanced 40 miles near St. Quentin), but against this apparent setback the Navy could look to Rear-Admiral Roger Keyes' successful attack on Zeebrugge, which sank three blockships in the Bruges Canal. The German army had struck and failed to break through completely; so, Adam hoped, 'it looked as if the next move might lie with her High Seas Fleet.' The new sailors marched around the parade grounds, tied knots and splices, learned signalling and manoeuvred ships in miniature, 'hoping that when the final fleet action was fought we would be in it.' This thought was obviously in the mind of one of the training officers, who showed his kindly disposition when he said that 'he would make things as easy as possible for us as we would be at sea in a few weeks and, for all he knew, be killed before the month was out.'

Adam's first ship was a patrol-boat used for convoy escort duties in British home waters. The P-boat was a lightly-constructed, shallow-draft craft of about 570 tons displacement, armed with a 4-inch gun mounted on the low fo'c'stle and a 2-pdr Pom-Pom amidships, with 20 to 30 depth-charges as the vital weapon for fighting submarines. With the Channel crowded with merchant shipping, the P-boats based at Portsmouth had little rest, and spent the greater part of their time on patrol duties, or escorting ships from Spithead to Havre, or from the Needles to Cherbourg. For traffic passing up or down channel the Portsmouth escort linked up with the Dover Patrol in the east and the Devenport escort in the west. The life had its advantages, but the threats were always out there:

In the early afternoon we dropped another depth charge for experimental purposes but, but this time we waited until we were close to a shoal of fish. The force of the explosion killed a large number and we lowered one of the ship's boats and picked up over a hundred. Just after hoisting the boat inboard an SOS came through from a ship which had been torpedoed.

She was just visible on the horizon and proved to be a tanker of about 2,500 tons – the Royal Sceptre. *Few types of ships can be more difficult to sink than an empty oil tanker, and our first duty on arrival at the scene was to persuade her Lascar crew, who were already in the boats, to return to their ship. By this time other P-boats had appeared, and, our captain being the senior officer present, we ordered the torpedoed ship to proceed under escort to Portsmouth where she arrived without further mishap. But the day's havoc was not complete, for another SOS came through at five o'clock from a merchant ship which had been torpedoed at a spot six or eight miles away. Here there was a sadder story to tell, for the torpedo had done its work properly and the* Shirala *of Glasgow – a ship of 3,400 tons – lay motionless with her back broken. When we arrived the officers and crew were going about their duties quite calmly and swung the boats outboard to be ready for the time when it would be necessary to abandon ship. There seemed little doubt that the submarine had made her escape it once, but we towed our search gear for the three hours up and down in the hope that we might trace her on the sea bottom...*

Before we had finished our little turn the torpedoed ship had sunk, the seas first covering her upper deck amidships, leaving the bow and stern clear and tip tilted slightly towards each other; but as time went on these two settled down and finally slipped slightly out of sight… one more unescorted ship had gone to the bottom.[39]

The 'snotties' eagerly discussed possible postings with an enthusiasm which makes clear that in the summer of 1918 the idea of the war being over by Christmas had finally disappeared:

A few wished to serve with the Grand Fleet where there was the possibility of being in a fleet action, but against this there was the monotony of the life; the long days in harbour at Scapa Flow, or the dreary sweeps southwards in company with the battle squadrons. It seemed an endless job, this is screening of big ships in all weathers. Under blue skies, or when heavy seas ran through the Pentland Firth, the G. F. destroyer flotillas had to be there; and in the winter, when the northerly gales beat against Cape Wrath and Rattray Head, spray froze and hung down in long icicles from the mastheads. No, the G. F. flotillas did not appeal to me.

Adam was eventually posted to Immingham, near Grimsby, where he joined HMS *Vehement*, part of the 20th Flotilla of minelaying destroyers tasked with keeping enemy ships away from British waters and with disrupting the Heligoland Bight. The key offensive objective was that 'the activity of the enemy's ships was to be restricted inside their own waters as well as outside', hemming ships into port and making the passage of U-boats more difficult. Only fast, shallow-draft ships could be expected to carry out the task effectively. Although relatively unglamorous, the work was both vital and dangerous (as Adam observed, 'we could hardly expect that they would let the flotilla go about its destructive work unhampered') and the First Lord had referred to the 20th Flotilla as a 'corps d'elite' – which the sailors rendered as 'corpse delighty'. Because the destroyers had had their rear-facing guns removed to make way for the mines, the crews were acutely conscious that if pursued they could not fire back, and this made for lively arguments. The monotony of life in port pursuing tedious administrative tasks was also wearing; Adam described the four o'clock tea being 'served in an atmosphere of unrelieved gloom.' The chief excitement was the possibility of a U-boat attack – though sightings might well be 'an illusion in the overheated brain of *Vehement's* snotty.' Disaster struck the flotilla, however, on the night of 1 August. At eleven minutes to midnight the crew of *Sandfly* saw 'a sheet of orange-red flame leaping upwards from one of the ships close ahead of us.' On the grounds that this had been caused by a

German mine, the flotilla stopped engines, everyone 'wondering who had been struck and pitying the poor blokes on board and also those whose voices could be faintly heard crying from the sea into which they had been cast by the force of the explosion.' It subsequently emerged that *Vehement* had yawed slightly into the path of the mine; her young captain, battered and bruised, recovered consciousness in the sea some distance away, where he inflated a lifejacket and saved a crew member whom he supported until a boat picked him up a quarter of a mile from his ship. Taken to *Vanoc*, it was reported that 'he promptly tried to go up onto the bridge under the impression that he was back on his own ship.' The No.1 was flung by the explosion right over the high foremost funnel and landed head-first on the upper deck, fatally injuring his skull. The junior Sub. had been heading aft to collect a cup of cocoa before taking up his duties on the bridge for the middle watch, and this saved his life. It is worth quoting in full Adam's experience of what happened next:

Knowing almost for certain that we were in the midst of a minefield we wondered uneasily whether it was to be our turn next to touch a fatal horn, hoping that if the explosion came it would be below us on the bridge rather than beneath our cargo of 40 mines and four depth charges carried aft. But it was better not to let the imagination wander to explore the dark waters below, where the mines strained upwards on their mooring wires and swayed gently as the hull of a ship slid by; or straight over to Vehement *where the whole of the foc's'tle was torn off, the mess decks a shambles, and the bodies of stokers lay on the upper deck parboiled in the blast of steam which had blown up with them from the shattered boiler-rooms.*

Shortly after midnight, about twenty minutes after the explosion had occurred, I was standing on the starboard side of the bridge looking towards Vehement, *where oil from her damaged fuel tanks had ignited on the surface of the sea, forming a beacon which advertised our presence in enemy waters only too well. From time to time flashes occurred on board as cartridges or shells from the disrupted magazine burned or exploded. Then the second disaster occurred – a great burst of flame and shower of wreckage rising from the sea about four cables off our starboard quarter, with a picture in the centre of a small destroyer, her forepart almost demolished; a couple of seconds later came a dull thud, like the beat of a distant drum. We knew, from that momentary glimpse, and from her position, that it was* Ariel, *the last ship in our line. Poor old* Ariel, *she had been the first British destroyer to sink a submarine in the war and now she had served her last commission. In that exclusion, which had detonated her forward magazine and burst her boilers, there had perished her Captain, No. 1, Sub., Sub. RNVR, and 31 men. As last ship of the line she had had her depth charges set to 'Fire', but the keys locking the firing mechanism were on the bridge and consequently unavailable for the purpose of setting them to 'Safe' and thus avoiding a violent explosion when the ship sank. The end came at three minutes past one when, by the light of the blazing wreckage on* Vehement, *the remains of* Ariel *were seen to settle down and sink. A moment later a heavy underwater explosion shook the remaining ships of the flotilla as her depth charges exploded.*

Unpleasant as it was on the bridge, where we could see each stage of the tragedy as it unfolded, the strain on those whose duties kept them below must have been far more severe. In the engine rooms and stoke-holes there were long silences with engines stopped, punctuated by the three underwater shocks each of which gave increasing course cause for speculation on the final fate of the flotilla. In one ship, only a few minutes after Ariel *had struck, a sound was heard that caused her crew to hold their breath – a hollow scraping on the side of their ship, starting near the bow and grinding slowly aft; then silence, as the mine swung clear of the stern without exploding. Grim as those moments were there were others of light relief, as when a stokehole hatch on* Abdiel *was flung open and a grimy head appeared. Surveying the scene of* Vehement's *fiery beacon lighting the wreck of* Ariel *he addressed his mate below with the words 'Blimey Bill, you'd almost think it was the fifth of November!'*

As the moments wore on there was little for us to do on the bridge of Sandfly *other than watch the dim shapes of destroyers as they stood motionless on the dark sea, reflecting faintly on their grey hulls the glow of the fires on* Vehement. *Then a bright shaft of light appeared towards the east, but before we could see in it a sign of some further misfortune the beam broadened and rode clear of the horizon in the shape of the moon, a few days advanced in her last quarter. The silver rod of light she cast across the sea followed us throughout the rest of the night and possibly saved us a little later from a fate similar to that of* Vehement *and* Ariel. *We were then close enough to add to* Vanoc *to give her a hail and inquire whether her captain knew what our next move was to be. A laconic reply informed us that was likely to be upwards unless we went to stern pretty quickly as there was a floating mine just visible in the moon's track only a few yards from our bows.*[40]

The flotilla's small boats attempted to rescue survivors from the mined ships and *Telemachus* attempted to take *Vehement* on tow. After two o'clock a 'hesitant and wavering' passage out of the minefield began, taking over an hour, and the flotilla was still inside German waters as dawn broke, picking up wireless signals which indicated that enemy ships were hunting for them. *Vehement*, the ship on which Adam had spent his first destroyer service, was released from her tow-line and subjected to gunfire from *Telemachus* and *Vanquisher*. This failed to sink her quickly, so, at 0410 a depth charge was deployed:

Vehement began to move, her stern rising slowly until her full length seemed to rest on her submerged and shattered bows. Thus she remained for a moment, and then with gathering speed slid slowly downwards. With three-quarters of her length below the surface her stern much have struck the sea bed for her last movement was to roll over on her side, showing for a moment her after deck with the mainmast carrying her ensign. Then the sea closed over her in a cap of white foam.

The flotilla returned to port under grey skies at 0500. Later that day, Admiral Sir David Beatty, Commander-in-Chief of the Grand Fleet, and Admiral Sir Rosslyn Wemyss, First Sea Lord, sent signals of sympathy to the survivors. The latter noted that the fact that this was the first time such losses had been incurred in six months of dangerous and difficult work was 'a testimony to the excellent seamanship and navigation displayed.' A few mornings later, 'the public read a bald announcement as they cracked their breakfast eggs' stating simply that two destroyers had been sunk by mines with the loss of five officers and 92 ratings. Adam subsequently had a rather disturbing experience – one which was not, in the circumstances of the war, entirely uncommon. The No.1 of HMS *Leander*, the Immingham depot ship, hailed him with the words 'Hi, Snotty, what are you doing alive?' It turned out that Adam's transfer to *Sandfly* had never reached official ears, and because he was not on the list of survivors from *Vehement* it was assumed that he was among the 48 lost at the time of the explosion. This news clearly circulated around the fleet for when a new snotty arrived on *Sandfly* some weeks later he produced a letter from a comrade at Scapa Flow which started 'Have you heard Adam has been lost in *Vehement*?' and went on to the tune of 'the good 'uns die young.' At least Adam was in a position to put things right; Alfred Sutherland of the 5th Seaforths, one of the 37 Old Fettesians of the class of 1903 to serve, was reported as one of eight from that year to be killed. His survival was not noted until the early thirties, when the survey conducted for the *Fettes College Register* found that he was alive and well and working in the Finance Department of Shanghai Municipal Council. By this stage his name had appeared in bold type in the *Fettesians Who Served* book and indeed on the school war memorial, where it remains to this day. As nine men in the Seaforths called A. Sutherland were killed in the war, it must be assumed that he was misidentified with one of these, though the confusion seems odd since they were all privates or junior NCOs, and the three who were in the 5th Battalion were all too young to have been the Fettes Sutherland, who was 23 when war broke out.

Adam spent the rest of the war on HMS *Venturer*, another minelaying destroyer, and found that autumn weather presented as much of a challenge as enemy ships and mines:

In the darkness of our bridge I could just make out the line of our foremast as it swept in a great arc over a sky studded with stars and racing clouds. Down below in the wardroom there was no chance of a rest, with chairs adrift and sliding to and fro, and with the sound of the mines as they bumped and strained noisily overhead. Our course lay a little east of south and dawn saw us within sight of the island of the Texel. The scene might have been a seascape by Van Ruisdael – steep seas in the foreground with a hailstorm driving towards the coast and a patch of brighter light on the island showing quiet farmsteads and the moving sails of windmills. We laid our minefield so that it just reached Dutch territorial waters and then set course for home. An underwater detonation shortly afterwards led us to hope, in our innocence, that we had accounted for a U-boat, but we had no confirmation of this.[41]

Ironically, *Venturer* was to play a part in the sinking of a submarine – unfortunately, it was British. On the morning of 6 October, Adam's nineteenth birthday, *Venturer* was in harbour, tied up with *Vanquisher*, when a C-class submarine leaving the lock-gates lost its power and was swept by a five-knot ebb tide into the two destroyers and promptly sank. After some leave in which he visited Fettes, Adam was 'christened' – fully accepted into the fraternity of the Navy in a comic ritual in which the snotty was required to kneel blindfolded before a 'throne' in the wardroom and sing 'Onward, Christian Soldiers' to the tune of a popular song on the gramophone – a concept subsequently adopted by the radio comedy programme *I'm Sorry I Haven't A Clue*. A soup-plate was then dropped on Adam's head with the mystical words 'I am a miserable wonk' and the rest of the evening was given over to merriment. By this stage in the war Germany's army was in full retreat and her civilian population demoralized by blockade. The Royal Navy believed that the Germans might attempt to destroy it at the eleventh hour, and indeed Admiral von Scheer planned a two-pronged attack on the Flanders coast and the Thames, with mines and U-boats to cripple the Grand Fleet as it swept southwards to intercept. This was expected to take place in late October, and on the 24th Adam, and thousands of others, received 'most urgent' messages to put to sea. By the 28th – when the British had expected a major confrontation – it became clear that 'we were waiting for an enemy that never came' and the flotilla headed for home 'with the usual sense of disappointment.' In fact, when the Kaiserliches Marine had received its orders to set sail on the 24th, its sailors began to desert, and by the 29th were in open revolt, sabotaging their ships and refusing to set sail on what was obviously a suicide mission. Oddly, von Scheer and the rebellious sailors had similar intentions; he hoped that a successful attack would, by demonstrating Germany's strength and determination, ensure that the Allies gave fair peace terms, whereas the mutineers believed that with the war already lost and peace feelers being made, they ought to keep London happy by minimizing the risk of further casualties. In Adam's flotilla, however, hopes remained high that some kind of confrontation might come:

On returning to base we find that the tension had not yet relaxed and, with the minimum of delay for oiling and loading mines, we set out on our next operation. There was still a feeling of confidence that we might meet the enemy, as we knew that our big ships continued to patrol the seas to the north and east of Holland. That evening in my cabin I entered in my diary the pious and fervent hope that a hitherto unenterprising enemy might see fit to come out at last and 'try a slap at us', as the monotony of life in a destroyer with 'no Huns, no mines (except the one that just missed us yesterday), no torpedoes and no bombs' was quite intolerable. But the night wore on undisturbed and all next day the skyline remained unbroken till we sighted the English coast at sunset.[42]

It was 31 October, and, unbeknownst to Adam and indeed most of the rest of the Royal Navy, this was to be their last minelaying operation. Early November saw the admirals lose almost all control over the fleet and shipyards, where left-wing activists and workers joined the sailors in demanding peace and bread. On 11 November, Adam, who had been working on the wardroom wine accounts and arranging ship's games, was accosted by the No.1 and told firmly that he was to stop fighting. A 'rather hilarious and unconventional' parade was arranged, though Adam still felt that 'amid all the rejoicings there was a sense of disappointment in having finished the war without a fleet action.'

Reporting the War

Today's popular attitudes to the First World War – idealistic young soldiers sent to experience unimaginable horror, with the truth suppressed at every turn – can often obscure how people thought of it at the time. Of course, it is true that there was censorship. The Old Fettesian journalist Hamilton Fyfe railed against what he saw as the rank idiocy of the government censors which prevented him from telling the truth about what was happening:

Censors work in the dark. They are supposed to prevent information leaking out which might be useful to the enemy. But how do they know what he will find useful? A censor, therefore, is sure to cut out more than is necessary, simply as a precaution. He is sure to exaggerate the enemy's ignorance. I wanted once to say that an allied army had been obliged to retire some distance. This was not permitted. I said, 'But that can't tell the Germans anything. They know how far they have advanced.' 'Are you sure of that?' inquired my censor, with a cunning glance from under his bushy eyebrows. 'Perhaps they may not.' What an exquisitely comic idea — the Germans waiting for the English newspapers to tell them how much ground they had gained! [43]

The press was not universally popular with the troops, however, and Vernon Hesketh-Prichard certainly had his doubts about some reporters who visited his sniping school, who wrote 'a large and glaring article' about one of his new inventions despite being told to keep it secret. On the whole, however, he dismissed soldiers' cynicism as 'a rather stupid pose adopted by the younger officers, who usually copy some downright senior'[44] and found censors just as bewildering as his Fettes contemporary Hamilton Fyfe. Mrs Humphrey Ward's account of her visit to the sniper school impressed him, but when it appeared in print he found that it had been heavily, and apparently randomly, censored:

Why they had cut it out no one could ever tell. We had at that time a good number of snipers' robes of painted canvas at the school. The Germans had somewhat similar robes and both sides knew that the other was using them; but the British Censorship would never allow any mention of these robes. You might mention something really important, some new invention, or the effect of some new bullet, or any other matter which would be of real assistance to the Germans, but these robes were the one thing which seemed to interest the Press Censorship. Speaking as an Officer-in-charge of a very technical branch of work, I can only say that the Censorship was at times just like an ostrich hiding its head in the sand.

Ian Hay, as we have seen, generally produced up-beat accounts of service in the trenches. Yet this was not for propagandistic purposes; as he observed, everyone did it. Censorship was unnecessary except in the rare case when someone gave away important facts. Men at the front, in his experience, had both an 'obvious desire to allay anxiety' and a disapproval of boasting, lying or complaining. They censored themselves, confining their subject matter to 'tender inquiries after bairns and weans' and 'assurances to anxious wives and mothers that the dangers of modern warfare are merely nominal.'[45]

Hay's own writing, of course, is a good example of this being taken to a much higher level, though it is noticeable that, in his later work as the war wore on, a degree of bitterness crept in – not about conditions at the front, with which most soldiers would generally put up, but with those at home who did not play their part, especially strikers. Ross had similar experiences with the Royal Naval Division – men who were rather embarrassed by emotion and undemonstrative by inclination did not want to cause their wives distress – 'why should he trouble her with his fears, which are probably only the figment of an over-active imagination — has she not sufficient worries without his adding to them?'[46]

The letters home of Daniel Vawdrey, with their perky references to enjoyable Holy Communions and friendly bishops, are examples of how one young officer tried to reassure his parents. The desire to avoid causing pain was poignantly illustrated in the case of Teddie Anderson, who survived aerial combat over the trenches, but ran out of luck whilst testing a Sopwith Camel in England in March 1918. 'That he enjoyed life to the last moment and that complete and instantaneous unconsciousness must have made death painless may be a small consolation,' wrote Teddie's Commanding Officer to Mrs. Anderson, 'We can ill spare Officers of the type of your son in the Air Force.' A somewhat contradictory letter came from the matron of the Winchester hospital to which he was taken after the crash:

He was in a very bad way when he arrived with us, yet to the very end he was an officer and thinking of others even in his state and at such a tender age. He came in on the 16th and passed peacefully away the following day.

I was with your boy nearly all the time and talked to him. In a sense he was conscious, but not entirely so. You see he had morphia to save him from the pain. His mind was full of his work, and I am sure he thought he was in a 'plane.

He did not realise how bad he was. But he was very thirsty, and was so grateful for drinks, and always thanked us, and said how sorry he was to be 'such a jolly nuisance.' Towards the end he was quiet under the influence of morphia, and felt no pain at all. Dr Dingley said he would have felt very little and he slowly slipped away to a better place.[47]

This inability to get the story straight must have caused agonies of suspicion in Mrs. Anderson's mind. As for what was sent to the school, the OFs at the front were much more restrained than their predecessors had been in Victoria's wars, partly because secrecy mattered more in a large war with a technologically advanced enemy than it did in the scrub of Africa. It is also hard to find a great deal which is introspective or sensitive in letters from the front, a fact which jars with the modern post-Diana sensibility of dwelling on the emotions, and indeed the contemporary schoolboy's diet of 'endless bloody poetry' about the Great War, as *Blackadder* put it. This was partly a product of the age and its rather greater emotional continence, and the fact that it would have been considered distastefully morbid at best and treasonable at worst to dwell on the horrors of war. Most letters from Old Fettesians concentrated on the lighter side of training or other aspects of barrack life: in 1915, a former pupil serving in an English regiment wrote about the result of his attempt to introduce his 'fellow Tommies' to the joys of Scots cuisine, in particular the white mealy pudding, which was so disliked that 'I was marched off in under a strong that guard to the wet canteen where I had to stand whiskies-and-sodas all round to prevent a serious diminution of the battalion strength.'[48]

Ross – who, as we have seen, was remarkably frank about such horrors as lice – insisted that most of the time, the British soldier's morale was not that bad:

How curious it seems that these cheery, high-spirited fellows, sitting in the local estaminets, each with his glass of innocuous 'vinne blank,' puffing perseveringly at the inevitable Woodbine, and making amorous advances to the delightful French girls, were only yesterday face to face with a very imminent death, and have by their reckless devotion to duty added a fresh lustre to the traditions of their already famous Division! [49]

He also had first-hand experience of the stoicism and devotion to duty which the War brought out in officers and men alike:

An officer came into my aid post one night with a man of his platoon who was suffering from a fractured leg. After the somewhat lengthy operation of immobilising the fracture between a rifle and a pick handle, I was somewhat surprised when the officer apologetically asked me to look at his eye, as he had got ' a bit of mud or something in it.' On examination it was obvious that his sight in that eye was irretrievably lost. He walked down to the field ambulance behind the stretcher bearing the man, encouraging him to stand the pain, and making light of his own much more serious injury.

A company sergeant-major had his arm blown off at the shoulder, but seeing his company commander approaching, drew himself up smartly to attention, apologised for ' being no more good,' and then collapsed in a heap on the ground.

Such incidents as these could be multiplied indefinitely, but they would only go to show the courage, endurance, unconscious humour and unfailing optimism of the soldier when confronted by the unutterable tragedy, suffering, and horror of a great war. [50]

One OF who began to entertain serious doubts, and whose writings were only published after the war, was Maitland Hardyman. His career reads like that of an Owen or Sassoon – remarkably brave but increasingly blighted by his contempt for the mindless nationalism prevailing at home and concern that the war was not, after all, being fought for the noblest of motives. He wrote poetry which resembles that of his more famous contemporaries, but was killed before he could apply his belief in social justice to the post-war world. [51]

'On Leave', written in February 1915, expressed his early qualms about the war, which at that time he was able to put aside:

Is this, then, youth's fulfillment? Mothers all,
It was for this ye bore us: Duty's call,

Poor bleeding Belgium's honour, Austria's Duke!
The Jingo's claptrap is his own rebuke.

Get thee behind me, Satan. Well I know
That through self-sacrifice the soul must grow.
And that this testing time, this struggle sore,
Shall leave old England stronger than before.

Having already won the MC after 'displaying great bravery in the organizing the clearance of wounded from a medical aid post near an ammunition dump, which had been set on fire by a shell' he went on to win the DSO in 1918. His citation was quoted with approval in the last wartime edition of the *Fettesian* (which also recorded his death):

After the enemy had penetrated the line in three places he went forward through a heavy barrage to the forward posts, rallied the garrison, and encouraged them by his coldness and absolute disregard of personal danger to successfully repel repeated enemy extending over two days and three nights. Thanks to his gallant leadership and endurance, the position which was of great tactical importance was maintained.[52]

Like other officers who could have got out of further combat (including another OF, Lt Joseph MacLellan, invalided home with shell-shock in 1916, but returned to France and was killed in 1918), he went back to the front to be with his men, despite the option of a safer posting as Adjutant to a battalion of Somersets. He killed outright by a shell on 24 August 1918, at the age of 23 and as the youngest Lt-Col in the forces, fighting, in the words of the epitaph he wanted (but did not actually get) 'for abstract principles in a cause which he did not believe in.' Although contemptuous of the role played by the clergy in whipping up war fever at home, he did have a religious sense of what was being played out in Flanders:

Lord Jesus of the trenches,
Calm 'midst of the bursting shell,
We met with Thee in Flanders,
We walked with Thee in hell;
O'er Duty's blood-soaked tillage
We strewed our glorious youth;
Yes, we indeed have known Thee,
For us the Cross of Truth.[53]

Lt Col John Hay Maitland Hardyman, DSC, MC, twice mentioned in dispatches, poet and doubter, and his one volume of verses

Reflecting on loss, and what it was all for, was not confined to poets. Ross, invalided home after Passchendaele, described the experience of describing a man's death to his fiancée:

> *In the lounge of the Savoy all was laughter and merriment — the only sign of war a few figures in khaki or blue and gold. Sitting in my comfortable chair, I wondered when she would come, and ran over in my mind for the hundredth time how I could describe to her the manner of his death. It was only last week that we were walking along that shallow bit of trench when a German sniper got him in the chest. Such an everyday affair. I'd seen it happen hundreds of times before, but somehow or other it seemed different when it was one's best pal who was lying in the mud slowly bleeding to death, and our vaunted medical science could do nothing to save him. We carried him back to my aid post and there he died, his last thoughts and his last words all of her. Next day we buried him, sticking in the ground a flimsy wooden cross with his name rudely scrawled upon it. Just another officer killed. It makes no difference to the war. The guns still thunder as usual and all is outwardly the same, but I have lost my best pal, and the girl I'm waiting for has a blank in her life which can never be filled.*[54]

Even this most loyal of officers could display a hint of anger when he thought of the reaction of those who did not know the casualty:

Weeks later his name appears in the casualty list. Do you, my readers, as you sit at your comfortable breakfast-table, casually glancing through this list of killed, realise the pathos which is attached to every name? Remember sometimes that each one of these knew that he was probably going to his death, but went cheerfully, so that you might continue your placid existence untroubled by the awful tragedy of war in England.

Hopes for the Future

Both Ross and Hay, however, believed that the War might bring some good. It is striking to note what they believed during the War itself – writing which came out of endless discussion in billets and behind-the-lines estaminets. Hay – whose comic novels would undoubtedly fall foul of modern gender politics – had his wounded officers extolling the praises of the British women now working as bus-conductors, window-cleaners, and munitions girls (who 'deliberately sacrificed their good looks for the duration of the war.'[55]) He went on to say that 'those of us who come out of it are going to find this old island of ours a wonderfully changed place to live in.' The reason for this was the change in attitudes which the comradeship of the trenches had wrought:

You can't call your employer a tyrant and an extortioner after he has shared his rations with you and never spared himself over your welfare and comfort through weary months of trench-warfare; neither, when you have experienced a working-man's courage and cheerfulness and reliability in the day of battle, can you turn round and call him a loafer and an agitator in time of peace – can you?

Ross believed that broad-mindedness would result in another sense:

The war has undoubtedly broadened the Briton's outlook on life. His patriotism is no longer the old Jingo patriotism of former days, but is a real and personal thing, entailing hardships and sacrifices hitherto undreamt of, and often even death – the supreme sacrifice of all.

Tragically, the relationship between social classes degenerated between the wars, and the British, whilst undoubtedly less jingoistic than before, lost little of their xenophobia. A few years after the War, Hay was philosophical, if no longer optimistic, when he wrote about Fettes' losses:

We who are left will remember them always. Oddly enough, we shall not

274

remember them as young soldiers going into battle in the full pride of their manhood; but as schoolboys – schoolboys of twelve, fifteen, eighteen – schoolboys in magenta and brown – schoolboys playing in House Belows with us, or panting manfully with us to the third milestone on a wet October afternoon, or joining with us in a study area rag afterwards…

Too many of them died before their time, on the edge of manhood. 108 of them were under 25 years of age. Still, let us not forget that they saved their country. I say this in no conventional sense: it happens to be literally true.

The Great War was largely a war of Second Lieutenants… in the confused, unending, indeterminate turmoil of the Great War, the real – sometimes the only – dependable fighting unit was the platoon. There are sixteen platoons to a battalion, and most of those platoons were officered, fathered, and inspired by boys barely out of 'teens.

Some day, when we have outlived our present attitude of mild apology for having participated in the war at all, we shall realize and recognize what we owe to the Officers' Training Corps. When the storm burst in 1914 – when everybody was willing to do something but no one was quite ready to do anything – that Corps provided hundreds of young officers both ready and willing to undertake the training of our new, leaderless armies. They did not know much, but they knew enough to lick a platoon into shape and subsequently to lead it wherever duty called. That is the justification for the long lists of Second Lieutenants which you may behold upon a hundred school war memorials today. Let us not altogether regret the sacrifice they made, or call it a vain one. Would they have done so? [56]

Shortly before his death, Hay looked back on the First World War with slightly less sangfroid, comparing the tactics of the time unfavourably with those of the Second. In a *Fettesian* article in 1948, he explained that the machine-gun drove the armies underground into a series of lines 'which could not be outflanked and which no system of assault could piece. Consequently thousands of lives were squandered on either side, in desperate mass attacks'.[57]

He could still argue that failures and losses on the Western Front were 'not due to callousness or lack of thoughtful planning on the part of our high command' but were imposed by the conditions of the time. One aside, however, leaps out at the modern reader as Hay explains what is now called the learning curve of the British Army, during which so many thousands were killed. 'Plainly,' he admits bleakly, 'this was sheer murder.'[58]

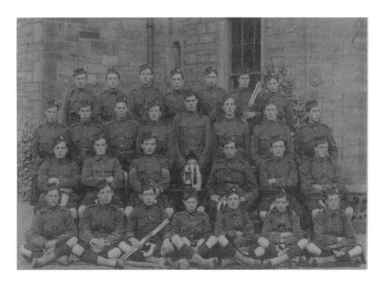

The Moredun House section of the Fettes OTC just before the outbreak of war. A third of these boys would be killed in the war and a third wounded. Five would receive decorations, and two be mentioned in dispatches. In the third row are Donald Mackintosh (second from left) and Teddie Anderson (fourth from left)

NOTES

[1] Obituary, *Flight*, 30 August 1917

[2] J.D. Anderson, Jr., in *AIAA Journal*, December 2006

[3] T. Anderson, letter to parents, 4 August 1916; thanks to Robin Scott-Elliott

[4] Ibid., 26 June 1916

[5] *Fettesian*, July 1918

[6] *Flight*, 26 September 1918

[7] *Fettes Roll of Honour*, p. 2

[8] Floyd Gibbons, *The Red Knight of Germany* (New York, Doubleday, 1927) pp. 144-5

[9] Sparrow & Ross, pp. 117-121

[10] Ibid., pp. 58-9

[11] Ibid., p. 78

[12] Ibid., p. 79

[13] *Fettesian*, June 1915

[14] Quoted in *Glasgow University Roll of Honour*

[15] *Fettesian*, March 1916

[16] Ibid., November 1915

[17] Bryan Cooper, *The Tenth (Irish) Division in Gallipoli* (London, Jenkins, 1918) p. 174

[18] *Fettesian*, July 1916

[19] Sparrow & Ross, p. 81

[20] David Walmsley, 'Bedell-Sivright pulls no punches', *Daily Telegraph*, 30 June 2005

[21] Sparrow & Ross, pp. 116-7

[22] Ibid., p. 40

[23] *Fettesian*, November 1917

[24] A.M. Fawcett (ed.), *War Diary of 2nd Batt. RFA*, MS, 1929 (?) p. 26

[25] Ibid., p. 28

[26] Ibid., p. 34

[27] Ibid., p. 31

[28] Ibid., p. 37

[29] *Fettesian*, April 1918

[30] Fawcett, p. 29

[31] Ibid., p. 35

[32] Ibid., p. 43

[33] Obituary, *Fettesian*, 1980

[34] Fawcett, p. 44

[35] Adam, p. 51

[36] Ibid., p. 54

[37] Ian Hay, *The Oppressed English*, (New York, Doubleday, Page & Co., 1917) pp. 68-9

[38] Adam, p. 73

[39] Ibid., p. 87

[40] Ibid., p. 98

[41] Ibid., p. 104

[42] Ibid., p. 126

[43] Henry Hamilton Fyfe, 'My Censors' in *War Illustrated*, 22 December 1917 (at WW1 internet archive 21 July 2009)

[44] Hesketh-Prichard (1920) p. 85

[45] Hay (1915) p. 221

[46] Sparrow & Ross, pp. 219-20

[47] Matron H Appleton, letter to Mrs N Anderson, March 1916; thanks to Robin Scott-Elliott

[48] *Fettesian*, March 1915

[49] Sparrow & Ross, p. 222

[50] Ibid., pp. 225-6

[51] Hardyman, pp. 4-5

[52] *Fettesian*, November 1918

[53] Hardyman, p. 20

[54] Sparrow & Ross, pp. 255-6

[55] Hay (1917) pp. 233-4

[56] Hay, in Pyatt,, p. 271

[57] *Fettesian*, July 1948

[58] Hay (1950) p. 59

Chapter Eight

'The same in service, strength and loyalty'

Fettes in the Aftermath of War

Peace comes to school

We have passed through a half-term which has been the most eventful for several, perhaps for many years. In the first place, it has witnessed the signing of the Armistice, but this wished-for event has been delayed for so long that of Fettesians who knew Fettes in pre-war days only four are still among us. The coming of Peace has not made much difference to our daily life as yet; but to the older members of the community it has made the greatest difference, because many who would have left at the end of this term or next owing to the war are now able to wait till the end of summer or longer. Unfortunately, owing to the continued food scarcity, the School was unable to exercise its jaws in any celebration befitting the occasion, but it certainly exercised its lungs to the full.[1]

The other great events which the editor of the *Fettesian* put into second and third place were the restoration of the chimes on the College clock (a topic which had filled his postbag for some time) and the 1st XV's thrilling matches against the Academy and Merchiston. They didn't even beat Merchiston, but apparently it was still a more noteworthy event than, say, the Battle of Cambrai. It was also not entirely true that life would now return to normal for older boys who would have been expected to join up; the same issue of the school magazine carries a note from the OTC announcing that until the 'happy event' of demobilisation they had orders to carry on with the same amount of training as before, and that boys aged 18 and over on 11 November were expected to 'hold themselves in readiness to be called on if required.'[2]

The boys – like everyone else – were not in the best of health, having been stricken by the Spanish Influenza epidemic which scourged the world at the war's end. An anonymous poet produced some fine doggerel on the subject:

In good Queen Bess's golden day
The Armada came in grand array;
But now it's not the 'Spanish fleet',
'Tis 'Spanish 'flu' we have to greet…

It stops our matches, stops our leaves,
And many other things bequeathes;
And so we curse this wretched 'flu,
Which leaves us nothing nice to do.[3]

In the summer term, the flu had already led to the bizarre spectacle of boys staggering from the sick-house to the crease in a heroic cricket match against Loretto, which Fettes won thanks to the sheer grit of its wheezing players. Hardie, convalescing in November, remembered the din of celebration breaking out, and a fellow-patient blurting out 'My God! Peace!' Macpherson was able to join the throng at the front of the school 'to send cheer after ringing cheer into the frosty air.'[4] Although he welcomed the post-war revival of Sports and Founder's Days, he was less overjoyed to see the return of the stiff collar as a 'symbol of peace'.

The weeks after the end of the war saw a number of excitements for the boys. On 21 November, the King visited Edinburgh, and, thanks to some of Mr Pyatt's contacts, the school was able to get a space at Waverley Station to welcome the royal visitor, who asked that they be given a holiday. In the unlikely event that Fettes had been harbouring republican radicals, this – along with the cancellation of prep that night – will doubtless have reconciled them to the monarchy. The boys were rather less impressed by a newspaper report of the day which did not refer to their blazers as brown and magenta:

For when it described how we made the air ring
With cheer upon cheer for our Sovereign and King,
It informed us that we (of the paper 'tis slack)
Were apparelled in blazers of purple and black.[5]

Somehow the boys managed to live with this, and three days later, following a kind offer by Admiral Startin, the senior naval officer at Granton, were taken to see the German fleet, which was required by the terms of the Armistice to sail to the Royal Navy base at Scapa Flow in

Orkney. Although most went on the large and (relatively) 'palatial' minesweeper HMS *Glen Usk* and whaler *Zedwhale*, some were lucky enough to travel on the *Jessie Tait*, a converted Fraserburgh trawler euphemistically described as 'no pleasure boat' by a Fettes reporter. Determined to look on the bright side, he said that it helped the pupils understand what life must have been like for those serving on such uncomfortable and cramped vessels. The *Jessie Tait*'s key advantage, however, was that her small size enabled the lads to get close to the German cruisers – 'dark, sinister-looking vessels, badly in need of paint.' Hardie remembered the trip – possibly due to his health, since a flu victim can hardly have enjoyed the turbulent waters of the Forth in November – as 'a rather horrible performance'. The anonymous chronicler of 1918, however, was delighted:

The German battleships next took up our attention, the Markgraf, *the* Kaiserin, *the* Grosser Kurfurst, *the* Friedrich der Grosse, *the* Bayern, *the* König Albert, *ships of which we might have read, but which we had hardly hoped to see. Here was the fleet which had at last been tempted from its well-protected harbours, not to a battle, but to surrender. Like the light cruisers, the German battleships were badly in need of paint, and rust was appearing at many places on their sides, showing that it was not mere journalistic talk when newspapers described the German fleet as rusting in the Kiel Canal. However, they were truly great and powerful ships.*

We had a good opportunity of seeing the German sailors, as the Jessie Tait *was able to go very close to the battleships. The Huns seemed very happy and contented – crowds of them lined up along the decks to watch us pass, but there was no demonstration on either side. On board one ship a concertina and some other instrument were being played; on another, a Boche showed his gymnastic skill by doing long and short arm balances on the parallel bars.*[6]

It is hardly amazing that the 'Huns' were contented, since it was precisely because the German sailors at Kiel had refused to fight in 1918 that the Kaiser's regime had collapsed. These were not embittered Teutonic nationalists who wanted to carry on fighting – at any rate, not in 1918, when the punitive terms of the Treaty of Versailles were several months away. Or it may just be that they had seen the RAF Avro 504K which crashed into the Forth whilst shadowing the enemy fleet and were amused. Either way, C.L. Potts was not impressed with them; their ships were 'disgustingly dirty', he wrote to his parents, 'they were rusty all over' whilst the sailors' lack of discipline was 'very remarkable. The crews were all wandering about on the quarter deck and were doing absolutely what they liked.'[7]

Old Fettesian Midshipman William Adam, on board HMS *Venturous*, saw the scene from his destroyer on the morning of 21 November. A sailor had come to the wardroom with the words 'Message from the Captain, Sir – Enemy in Sight'; Adam felt that 'the words had an odd ring about them, and conjured up the prospect of a long-awaited meeting, but we gave little thought to this as we hurriedly finished or left our breakfasts and went up top.'[8]

His memoir melodically listed the German ships as they sailed past – the battlecruisers *Seydlitz, Moltke, Hindenburg, Derfflinger* and *Von der Tann*, then the battleships *Friedrich der Grösse, König Albrecht, Kaiser, Kaiserin, Prinzregent Luitpold, Kronprinz Wilhelm, Grosser Kurfürst, Bayern* and *Markgraf*, then the light cruisers *Emden, Frankfurt, Brummer, Bremse, Köln* and *Dresden*. They were followed by 49 destroyers. He naturally thrilled to the sight of the British fleet as *Venturous* waited off May Island, spotting the *Courageous*, which he had illicitly sketched as a schoolboy, the aircraft carrier *Furious* with her flat flight deck and dazzle camouflage (made famous by his fellow Old Fettesian, Edward Wadsworth) and the tripod masts of the Secomd Battle Cruiser Squadron. Anchoring off Granton, *Venturous* passed by the combined fleets near Inchkeith, and Adam witnessed the Germans, on the order of the British Commander-in-Chief, hauling their ensigns down at sunset for the last time. The British crews then settled down to an evening of toasts, rowdy games and 'a good deal of laughter which grew noisier as the evening wore on and more childish in proportion to the seniority of the officers joining in.' Adam reflected that it would have been nice to visit Fettes, but no shore leave was granted:

The determination which I had expressed while at Fettes to be present when the British and German fleets meant for the next time after Jutland had been realized, though not in the way I had hoped and it would have been good to let my friends know that I had been at the final meeting. It had been an historic day, but few of us felt much satisfaction at seeing a once-proud fleet submit to the humiliation of surrender.

Adam tried to put the losses inflicted on his comrades in the context of the damage they had done to the enemy: 'the exact number of enemy ships forced by the flotilla to keep company with *Vehement* and *Ariel* on the bed of the North Sea is unknown, but it must represent a fair-sized fleet.' He was to spend the two months after the arrival of the German fleet in the Forth on paperwork, rugger, walking in the Lincolnshire countryside and the occasional ceremonial parade, for which he was disappointed not to receive a sword. Demobilised on 27 January 1919, he explored London for a few weeks, and in March went up to Cambridge for the first time, and was somewhat taken aback when a lecturer addressed the undergraduates as 'gentlemen' – 'for a year I had been a dogsbody and now, apparently, I was a gentleman.' Adam's notes, as they had done in his Fettes days, turned into doodles of destroyers, each of a different type with varying funnels and superstructures, and with high bow-waves showing that they were moving at speed.

The window curtains had known been drawn and illustrations showing the structure of minerals appeared on the screen. What odd names the minerals had – diorite and periodite and dolerite and syenite – like tribes in the Old Testament. Through a chink in the curtain I could catch a glimpse of the court outside, where the birds sang and the sun shone and banks of white cumulus drifted across a blue sky, while over the recumbent heads in the darkened room the lecture's voiced droned drearily and the flotilla spent on towards its unknown destination. Looking at the line of urgent ships I was reminded not so much of the major events of those few months I had spent at sea, as of the routine which I would experience no longer – of leaning on the bridge rail in the middle watch with eyes fixed on the green glow of the wake of the next ahead, of the flicker of summer lightning as it lit up the rim of the horizon, of the Aurora waving its red streamers in the northern sky, and of grey dawn breaking over the North Sea.

The minute hand of the clock on the wall crept round to the hour, the lecturer ceased his discourse, the curtains were drawn, the sleepers awoke, and the assembly dissolved and vanished. As a crumpled the paper in front of me and tossed the idle sketch into the basket I knew that the naval interlude was ended. For a year I had tried to be a sailor, but the end at the end was still raw and inexperienced. Had I had another year at sea I might have known better how well suited I was to the life, but things had changed and from now on I must try to become a scientist and forget the smell and sound of the sea and the harsh hoot of a destroyer's siren...

Edinburgh was to play its own little part in ensuring that the Germans signed the Versailles Treaty; the Scottish-built R34, one of Britain's most advanced airships and a thrilling sight since, being over 600 feet long, it was the size of a Dreadnought, was dispatched from East Fortune on armed patrol along the coast as a reminder of who had won. Hardie remembered it gleaming in the sun over the city en route to its duties, and its name was a popular pseudonym for anonymous contributors to the *Fettesian*. Hamilton Fyfe, reporting from Paris for *The War Illustrated* (a favourite with the boys which continued publication after the end of hostilities), had seen both justice and hope in the negotiations, for it was in the Hall of Mirrors that Germany had humiliated France several decades before:

I like to think of all this because it gives me greater faith in God's justice; because it tells me that, though wrong may endure for a while, right cometh in the end; because all that Bismarck wickedly plotted and cemented together with blood and tears has been brought to naught…

The only hope for a future saner and more peaceful than the past is a settlement to which all shall subscribe, not perhaps willingly but with the feeling that, though some have had to suffer, and though many hopes have been disappointed, there has been a square deal, with nothing tricky or underhand to leave bitterness behind.[9]

This was, of course, not what happened, but it was a reasonable wish. Bruce Lockhart could discern problems in Britain. The election of 1918 means different things to different people; for feminists, it was the first in which women could vote, whilst for Irish Republicans, it was the only island-wide vote in which Sinn Fein secured a majority and is still referred to as justification for their campaign. However, its global significance is that it returned David Lloyd George on a highly questionable ticket of 'squeezing the lemon until the pips squeaked' – as Lockhart saw it, a 'surrender to the hysteria of victory'[10] which led to what he considered an unduly harsh peace treaty with Germany, full of 'flagrant injustices.' Such, at any rate, the Germans claimed, and British sympathy for their arguments in the thirties would divide the western camp in the face of Hitler's revived nationalism.

Ashcroft's reforms
The boys at Fettes, of course, could not know this in 1919. Peace for them meant a relaxation of some of the wartime austerity, especially when Alec Ashcroft, the popular pre-war Classics teacher turned decorated Major in the 7th South Staffordshires (whose regimental

history he wrote just before rejoining Fettes), replaced the exhausted Heard in 1919. Although Heard was undoubtedly respected, Ashcroft was a breath of fresh air. A keen sportsman who had broken a jaw playing rugby at Cambridge, he had written for *Granta*, which referred to his 'boyish enthusiasm', and, less happily, lost three of his five brothers in the war (he served at Gallipoli, the Somme and Ypres). A former master of the time summarised his virtues to an Old Fettesian gathering in London: 'second in command of a battalion, a DSO, a Rugby Blue and International, and a classical scholar – surely every qualification that should commend him to schoolboys.'[11] he had presumably seen enough discomfort to last him a lifetime, and accordingly improved the school food and installed a central heating system, which, if its belligerent clanking still sounds like a knight in armour having an argument with an ironmongery shop, did at least warm the school, on good days, for almost a century. One of the reactionary school poets missed the old days:

We always used to sit before a fire blazing hot
But that was in the days gone by
We never thought of radiators, radiating not
But that was in the days gone by.[12]

Nothing Ashcroft installed, however, could have made the winter of 1919 any less bitter; 'it is not pleasant to get up and find your cold bath a solid mass of ice, even if it affords an excuse for not having that bath.'[13] The plumbers' strike of 1920 prevented the boys from moving into the reopened Kimmerghame House, so they had to live in the sick-house.[14] Coal strikes also made for a certain absence of creature comforts, but warmth was certainly generated by the certain freedom of expression, not to mention friendlier atmosphere, which Ashcroft encouraged. In the words of the 1921 'Vive-la':

In spite of the coal strike we started in May
And are here, going strong still, to greet you today:
And a shortage of fuel's not able to cool
The warmth of the greeting of staff and of school.[15]

Macpherson recalled 'a sound spirit of anti-Philistinism and anti-traditionalism' in the Sunday night discussions, where 'those who had during the war little interest in party politics were stung by the taunts or arguments of friends to adopt views.'[16]

The tradition of inviting lecturers to talk to the boys on various subjects was revived, one such being an address by Mr Barclay Baron of the Cavendish Society on social service – 'helping those who have not had the chances in life that we have had' – with an emphasis not on what one could do *for* someone, in the patronage-oriented Victorian way, but *with* him.[17]

Talks on Toc H, the famous Poperinghe soldiers' home, mountaineering and other improving topics were also enjoyed. Ashcroft was generous with encouragement and help for the intellectually curious, even giving up holiday time for the boys, and he did his best to stamp out the brutality which could so easy blight the lives of younger pupils. Although Ashcroft's successor Donald Crichton-Miller, himself an inter-war 'new man' at Fettes, may have been exaggerating when he wrote in 1986 that 'a new civilisation began'[18], shouting for fags was abolished in 1920, and Hardie recalled that the 'barbarous existence' he survived in 1917 was transformed; 'life, as a whole, became brighter and freer.'[19]

Selwyn Lloyd's biographer, himself an OF, comments that if he had survived the thuggery of Fettes in 1918, Aneurin Bevan in full cry over Suez in 1956 was manageable. Lloyd flourished under Ashcroft as a prefect, an actor (he was a 'riotously successful' Bottom in the 1923 *Midsummer Night's Dream*), a cadet Sergeant-Major and editor of the *Fettesian*.[20]

Lloyd had no desire to inflict the cruelties visited upon him and other boys (including Michael Tippett, whose parents actually withdrew him from the school) and was a key ally of the Headmaster in this process. So too were the sporting Scott brothers, who, despite their robust athleticism (J.M. Scott later became an accomplished Polar explorer) were 'alike in their gentleness towards the poor and oppressed' and believed that 'the fag was not a serf'.[21]

Ashcroft was joined at Fettes by a number of other former soldiers: W.J. Lodge, who had joined the Royal Scots in the ranks and risen to Lieutenant-Colonel, Major Newman of the Worcestershire Regiment and the Rev J.F. Spink, formerly chaplain to the 39th Divisional Artillery, all entered the staffroom in 1920, and were later joined by Captains H.J. Dixon, MC, and D. Ll. Vawdrey, the prolific letter-writer of the trenches. 'Jerry' Lodge, at 6'7" one of the most imposing figures of the common room, was remembered with great fondness by Alexia Lindsay, the school's archivist. As a little girl growing up on the campus, daughter of the Clerk of Works, she was not aware that the teacher's kindness derived from the fact that her father had served with Lodge's brother, who had died in the war. Cuthbert Lodge and Sandy Lindsay had both been in the 16th Battalion of the Royal Scots, better known as 'McCrae's' and famous for having eleven players from Heart of Midlothian – then Scotland's best football team – in its ranks. Not everyone was favoured with Lodge's gentler side, and he seemed to agree with the line quoted by Cecil Reddie, the Victorian Fettes master, that 'the parent is the schoolmaster's enemy.'[22] A pushy mother who told him that her beloved offspring's study in Carrington 'wasn't fit for pigs to live in' was informed that whilst it might not be fit for pigs it was certainly good enough for her son.[23] In a termly report, he told another mother that her child was like a barnacle, because 'he clings resolutely to the bottom of the class.' These men were revered by the boys (or at least the brighter of them) as imaginative, entertaining and intelligent figures, and could command absolute loyalty as well as encouraging academic success.

What is rather striking about the Fettesians of the immediate post-war era is a sense of excitement about the future, doubtless encouraged by the dynamic young head, his enthusiastic staff common room, and the new technology ushered in by the war. The school magazine was full of predictions about the thrilling new way of life just around the corner:

In twenty years no-one will deign
To go in trains or cars,
We'll travel then by aeroplane
And go for lunch on Mars.

Then aeroplanes will be the rage
And earthly engines done,
And in a fireproof Handley-Page
We'll travel to the sun...

'The school will play the Eskimo'
Is given out in hall;
To Greenland then we all will go
To see them play football.[24]

'Utopianus', writing during one of the coal strikes when getting out of bed required, he said, 'more courage than had any of the heroes of Homer', had more domestic, if equally impractical, dreams – of miniature tube trains running through heated corridors to the form-rooms, and a warm grandstand from which to watch rugger matches.[25]

Other prophets were more cynical. A description of 'Freewill College' in the year 2000[26] featured lessons about 'kinematography, pyrotechnics, aeronautics, dancing and deportment' taught by 'Adjudicators' ('to avoid even the appearance of authority') who would allow the boys to vote on what the right answers were. Typists and valets would save the boys' labour, whilst modern languages (including, broad-mindedly, German) would be 'acquired rapidly and colloquially by means of a system of waiters' from every land, and the Chaplain would encourage this promiscuous mix of tongues by reading, every Sunday, the story of the Tower of Babel. The modern teacher, in an age of coursework and performance targets, might recognise the prediction that the 'Adjudicator' would be 'remaining all day at his desk in case a boy should drop in casually to ask for instruction' – not to mention the prediction in the contemporary magazine of Collyer's School in Sussex that in the 'sensible and enlightened' educational system of 1990 'the masters are punished if the form is ignorant.'[27]

Remembrance

All were acutely conscious of the great shadow cast over them by the experience of the war. Less than a year after it had broken out, on 27 June 1915 (the day before the anniversary of Franz Ferdinand's murder) the school had held a memorial service for her dead. The choir sang anthems by Elvey ('The Souls of the Righteous are in the Hands of God') and Stainer ('What are these that are arrayed in White Robes') and the names of the dead printed on the Order of Service.[28] These ranged from Midshipman James Hamilton Auld, who died aged 20 after only two months' service when the armed merchant cruiser HMS *Clan MacNaughton* mysteriously sank off the coast of Ireland[29], to John Erskine Young, killed whilst serving in the Royal Scots Fusiliers only a few weeks after war broke out. There are 40 names in total, and another nine are listed as missing – one of whom, Capt Donald Alistair MacGregor, was later reported as a wounded prisoner of war. He died in Germany and is buried, with 708 others, in Hamburg Cemetery. The other missing were all later confirmed as dead. Understandably, this exercise was not repeated. It was clear that some sort of permanent memorial was going to be in order, and Dr. Heard set up a committee for the purpose. The uptake was astonishing, with £14,117 and four shillings pledged by December 1917. Sums ranged from £1,000 from, among others, the Campbells and Curries, to assorted clerics and serving officers giving a pound each. More money was raised by the sale of a portrait of the headmaster, and advertisements were placed in newspapers in Britain and India. The donations were invested in National War Bonds at five per cent interest.[30]

Not only would there be a fine monument to act as a daily reminder to the boys of their fallen brethren, but also a system of bursaries and scholarships for the education of the sons of those who had served, especially the fallen. Sir John Simon, who himself pledged £500, saw this as part of a great tradition:

In the Hundred Years' War, after the battle of Agincourt, there was founded in Oxford a great Society by the benevolence and generosity of the men of that day, which was expressly declared to be established to keep in memory the names of the faithful who had died at the battle of Agincourt. He would like to feel that in the measure of their powers they were doing something similar for their own School.[31]

Word soon got out about the great project; Captain W.R. Wilson, who had been mentioned in despatches for his service in France and Italy, wrote to the Committee in January 1919 asking for assistance for his son to go to the school. This was granted, though the boy did not live to see the benefits of his Fettes education, being killed in an accident in 1930 at the age of 24. The speeches and poetry of Fettes in those years were full of eulogy for the old boys who had fought. Dr. Heard, in his valedictory address to the boys on Founder's Day 1919, began his speech by reminding them (or at least the two remaining pupils who would have been there) that the presiding governor at the last such event in 1914, Col Clark, had been killed in action a few months later.

…he would never forget until his dying day the courage and fortitude with which Fettesians had marched to their place on the battle-fields in every corner of the world. No less than six heads of School had fallen in rapid succession in the trenches of Flanders, all of them young men of great promise, scholars of their Colleges in Oxford and Cambridge. As an epitaph upon those who died, he knew none better than that of Simonides, engraved upon the tomb of Leonidas

and his 300 Lacedæmonians who fell at Thermopylæ –
ὦ ξείν᾽ ἀγγέλλειν Λακεδαιμονίοις, ὅτι τῇδε
κείμεθα τοῖς κείνων ῥήμασι πειθόμενοι [32]
(Tell the Spartans that here we lie, obedient to their commands.)

Birnie Rhind, the celebrated Glaswegian sculptor responsible for the Scots Greys, KOSB and Black Watch monuments in the centre of Edinburgh, was commissioned to create the school memorial. As the final product was not yet ready, a model of it was placed outside the front door of the school, so that on Jubilee Day, 9 October 1920, (Fettes' fiftieth anniversary) the OTC could perform a silent march past, bayonets fixed. Pyatt subsequently wrote verses on the occasion.

> *Time hath not spoiled the great and manly mould:*
> *Thus ever linked may past and present be,*
> *The same in service, strength and loyalty.*[33]

The OTC marches past the temporary War Memorial in 1920

The decision was made that the memorial would look best at the side of the school, so the model was duly moved, in the course of which the crane dropped and broke it. The completed monument was finally unveiled on 15 October 1921, at a service attended by so many relatives of the fallen that there was room for a only a few pupils in the chapel.

Former pupil Maj-Gen Sir William 'Tiger Mac' Macpherson, Colonel-General of the Royal Army Medical Corps, unveiled the memorial and addressed the school, saying the 246 names cast in bronze beneath the fallen Highland officer were a record of heroism of which the school ought to be proud. His speech was characteristic of the times:

In this Memorial you hold their memory and the memory of their gallant deeds in trust, and when you go out into the world go with the determination that you too will uphold the principles for which they gave their lives.

Duty and sacrifice are the foundations upon which the patriotism, justice and freedom, the birthright of every citizen of our great empire are firmly and everlastingly fixed. Carry these principles into your lives and so keep the spirit of those who sacrificed theirs for them a living presence amongst you. There may be clouds on your horizon and dark days in front of you, but do not forget that it was their indomitable spirit of duty and sacrifice that dispelled the clouds in the days of greatest darkness.

You probably all know that beautiful sonnet to the dead by Rupert Brooke, who himself gave his life during the war and who, though not a Fettesian, was the son of a Fettes master. Words in it come irresistibly to my mind at this moment –

'And those who would have been,

Their sons they gave, their immortality.'

I feel it is you, Fettesians of today and of tomorrow and for ages to come, that will take the place of those sons who would have been, and that if your conduct in life is inspired by all that this monument signifies, the Dead can live forever!

They cry to you, their message to you is – to 'Carry On!' [34]

Wreaths were then placed at the base of the monument, as they have been each year since, and the cadets marched past and presented arms for the last post. It was noted afterwards that an additional wreath, with ribbons in the school colours, had been laid with the inscription 'In grateful remembrance of many gallant gentlemen.' It had been placed by the sister of a Fettesian who lost both of her own sons in the war. [35]

Some years after the war, an additional memorial was added in the shape of the fives courts, built in memory of her sons at the expense of the Hon Mrs Moncrieff. Norman Moncrieff had died of wounds at Courcelette in 1916, and his brother Francis never fully recovered from the war and died ten years after the Armistice. [36]

In addition to their own monument, Fettes boys could take pride in

General Macpherson at the unveiling of the Fettes War Memorial

the knowledge that the drawings of Scots soldiers by their Art master, Morris Williams, formed the basis for the frieze in the National War Memorial to the nation's 100,000 fallen in Edinburgh Castle. His painting, 'A Sentry at Calonne' was also praised by the reviewer of the Royal Academy's Exhibition of War Pictures in 1919, as 'an intensely moving witness to the endurance and the great temper of the England of our days'[37] – a comment quoted with relish in the *Fettesian*. In this, and in the bold phrase 'Carry On' beneath the bronze highlander at the end of their East Drive, they were at one with a country which was marking a national experience in a way which stressed continuity with an inspiring and heroic history. When Macpherson himself died, a contingent from Fettes attended a service in St. Giles' High Kirk for the unveiling of a plaque in his memory.

The fractious peace
Those former Fettesians still in khaki immediately after the war, unless committed to a service career, were happy enough to be demobilised,

like the O.F. who described the bewildering bureaucracy involved to the *Fettesian*, offering a handy hint to others in the same boat:

Here it may as well be said that to say that you are a university candidate is the surest way of getting out. Get your college boss to write to your Commanding Officer, asking for leave to take up your studies (?). This is a great secret, and is given gratis and for nothing. If you are inclined to be honest, tell the truth, and say you are a hanger-on, or gather whelks on the shore at low tide. You must now wait for an uncertain period of time, taking great care to question the Demobilisation Officer as to the probable date of your release at least once a day. The more you do this, the quicker you will get away. He will vote you a beastly nuisance, and will do his best to get you off his hands.[38]

Of course, the Old Fettesian had a profitable, or at least interesting, life to get away to. Some harboured hopes of a new beginning for Britain from the ashes of war; Ian Hay had written in 1917 of how the comradeship forged by army service would rejuvenate society:

That Army will consist of men who have spent three years in getting rid of mutual misapprehensions and assimilating one another's point of view — men who went out to the war ignorant and intolerant and insular, and are coming back wise to all the things that really matter. They will flood this old country, and they will make short work of the agitator, and the alarmist, and the profiteer, and all the nasty creatures that merely make a noise instead of doing something...[39]

Unfortunately, all too many working-class Scots returned to poverty, and outwith Fettes, the post-war Scottish landscape was often bleak. Alec Ashcroft may have learned a number of valuable lessons in the trenches, but power remained in the hands of men who had seen nothing of them; the sclerotic industrial system remained in place, as did the unpleasant sectarianism reintroduced to the country as a result of Catholic Irish immigration. The social tensions of the Edwardian period erupted in post-war cities, especially Glasgow, where the strikes, demonstrations and rent boycotts of January 1919 were interpreted by the panicky authorities as evidence of a Bolshevik rising in the making. Twelve thousand troops poured into Clydeside, supported by tanks and machine-guns. Soldiers would be deployed on British streets again, in the General Strike of 1926 and in Belfast in the 1930s. The Fettes cadets even lost their rifles for a while, the government wanting to keep its hands on every available weapon during the coal strike. As in William Fettes' time, the holders of property in Scotland rallied round the state in fear of the revolutionary masses, but this time the latter had the vote on their side and used it to send fiery MPs to Westminster, where they sang covenanting Psalms in honour of the nation's radical heritage. This did not impress the Protestant clergy, who urged the faithful to cleave unto the Conservative and Unionist Party as the only bulwark against atheistic Marxism. The Catholic priests, stung by the naked sectarianism around them (aimed specifically at Irish immigrants rather than, for instance, surviving Roman pockets in the Western Isles) supported Labour in droves. Whilst the modern observer might wearily conclude that only in Scotland could the Irish Catholic be seen as some sort of communist, it is worth saying that the term 'Bolshevism' was promiscuously used at the time to mean more or less any threat to the placid running of the Empire. It was, if one believed the press, everywhere. Accordingly, Scottish Liberalism, one of the great political forces of the previous century, went into decline.[40]

The *Fettesian's* first post-war edition suggested that at least one of the staff already had some inkling of the uncertainty in the air within Scotland itself:

> *O, let us hope that Peace may truly be,*
> *A real peace, and may not civil strife*
> *Usurp the foeman's place and in a sea*
> *Of troubles dire engulf the nation's life.*[41]

Lloyd George's slogan 'a land fit for heroes' remained just that, as the Scots discovered that wartime camaraderie and shared effort might not extend into the grey and depressing peace. Some efforts were made; one OF, J. Currie, was on a committee to award training scholarships to wounded soldiers who wanted commercial training, and another, Lt-Col Theodore Morison, tried to organise a scheme whereby serving troops could develop the skills they needed to resume their pre-war careers. At a personal level, Ashcroft, like many officers, shared Hay's paternalistic concern for his men. After his death, the school was contacted by a Sedbergh man who explained that his grandfather, Ashcroft's wounded batman, had been given a home in Beeston at a peppercorn rent and looked after all his life; the middle name Ashcroft was bestowed on each succeeding generation of the family in honour of this example of Fettesian loyalty. Such acts of kindness were not, of course, universal, nor could they have been when by 1918 40 per cent of officers were coming from the ranks and could not afford to take care of their men, no matter how much they wished so to do. Their desire to do their best by one another was still one of the features of the wartime officers so often forgotten by contemporary popular culture. Loyalty was rarely extended, in either direction, between the returning officers and those workers in reserved occupations who had not been to the front and were now engaged in industrial action; one angry OF, describing the destruction wreaked by the Germans in the territories they occupied, commented bitterly in a letter home that 'this is the kind of war that none of our people at home have had. Those Clyde strikers need some of it.'[42]

A demobbed former pupil served in the National Defence Force created by the government to maintain order and keep industry running during the strikes of 1921. Led by Territorials, the ranks included workers, apprentices and a number of middle-class ex-officers. They guarded coal pits, arsenals, power stations and airfields, and protected the voluntary labour which was preventing the mines from flooding. Reminders of wartime experiences were omnipresent, from the incessant off-duty football to the YMCA catering for their creature comforts. This camaraderie was in the face of what they believed was an extremist threat as real as the Germans had been:

As everyone knows, Glasgow and the whole Clydeside is a regular hotbed of Sinn Feinism and communism, and these gentry did their best (a) to obtain rifles in the case of the former and (b) to spread discontent and lies among the troops with, however, but small success.[43]

This writer was saddened to notice that more than four-fifths of his former comrades in the Defence Force returned to unemployment when the adventure was over, though he failed, on paper at least, to make any connection between this fact and the unrest he had been recruited to quell. One indication of the difficulties of the time was the career of Drum-Major West, who instructed the Fettes pipe band in the 1930s and 1940s. A talented musician and instructor, who was later to judge competitions of the Scottish pipe Band Association, he had served with distinction in the war, winning the DCM and leaving the Army as a Quartermaster and Lieutenant; despite this, for years he was janitor at London Street School.[44]

Had he lived, Maitland Hardyman would have been more

sympathetic to the strikers; he was on the Council of the Union of Democratic Control and a friend of Labour leader Ramsay MacDonald. General Whigham, inspecting the Fettes cadets in June 1921, attempted to combine a passion for order with a degree of understanding:

…he spoke of the necessity of maintaining the O.T.C.s and Territorial regiments not merely in order to be prepared in the event of another war, but also as an antidote to the spirit of Bolshevism. Nothing, he said, was more calculated to combat the spirit of unrest than the discipline instilled in such bodies as the O.T.C.s, Boy Scouts and Cadet Corps started in State-aided schools… Another point he urged was to keep free from 'aloofness'. All classes should systematically endeavour to grasp the points of view of others and sympathetically balance the bad and the good in the policy and the claims of all.[45]

As in Sir William Fettes' time, when the sunrays of liberty – however fantastical – beamed from France, so too the discontented of 1918 had a vision of a possible alternative world. And as in Sir William's day, this was not regarded with approval by the Scots bourgeoisie – and, in fairness, Bolshevism (even if its genuine adherents in Glasgow were few in number) really was a terrible and a cruel force. Professor Wilden-Hart of Oxford, a former intelligence agent, came to tell the boys about it in March 1921. His lecture rehearsed the then-popular view that the Russian Bolsheviks and German nationalists were in cahoots to dominate Europe. He also described (not inaccurately) the very real ambitions of the German High Command in the war and eulogised the traditional role of Poland as the rampart of western civilisation ('staving off the inroads of savage hordes from the east'), a role which it was the 'bounden duty' of the Allies to restore, with Lithuania and Estonia, though not, oddly, Latvia, as her helpmeets.[46]

Several OFs had seen the Bolsheviks at first hand and were quick to let people know just what was out there. Robert Bruce Lockhart admired the liberals who took over the Russian empire after the collapse of Tsarism in February 1917, but was painfully aware that their government could not survive the brutal class divisions, economic chaos and pressures of war which handed the initiative to Lenin.[47]

His breezy reminiscences of his time in Russia, during which he was held by the Bolshevik secret police in the notorious Lubyanka prison for his alleged role in the attempted assassination of Lenin, are still in print. He met Lenin, Trotsky and many other revolutionary leaders, and saw them, as did Hamilton Fyfe, as a mixture of pragmatists and idealists, admittedly of a fairly ruthless type. Although some actually fought in the ill-fated Allied intervention (such as Engineer-Commander F.H. Lyon, of HMS *Attentive*, who won the DSO for his actions in keeping the ships and motor-launches armed and ready for operations against the Bolsheviks on the River Dwina, and future Fettes master Lt-Col D.A.G. Bannerman) those who left the most on paper were non-combatants. E. H. Wilcox, a contemporary of Maclean VC in the Fettes class of 1885 and later Petrograd correspondent of the *Daily Telegraph*, wrote extensively on the subject, and unlike Professor Wilden-Hart realised that Lenin had been using the Germans, rather than the other way round:

Bolshevism has drawn to itself every kind of folly and rascality, because its doctrines are alluring to empty minds and its tactics are profitable to rogues. But the real danger of the thing lies in 'the one just man.' To him, Bolshevism is a religion, for which he is prepared to die himself and to make others die in thousands, in hundreds of thousands, if need be. It is his sincere and self-sacrificing fanaticism which gives Bolshevism its firmest grip on the masses and holds them in the belief that all the blood and tears, that so far have been its most noticeable results, will some day be redeemed by the Millennium...[48]

Among other OF Russophiles, neither Robert Bruce Lockhart nor Hamilton Fyfe believed that Britain's intervention to crush communism in Russia would succeed. Lockhart escaped from Russia by the skin of his teeth and was engaged in frustrating discussions about his experiences. Government ministers accepted that his view that intervening against Bolshevism relying 'merely on White Russian bayonets and Allied money' was futile, but were stuck in their ways, whilst at left-wing meetings he was often barracked by communists, led by a 'burly curate' and proceedings degenerated into brawls.[49]

When he patiently explained that the White armies had a 'foolish political programme' and accordingly had no chance of consolidating any territorial gains they might make, he was ignored by Winston Churchill, who, Lockhart noted gloomily, 'saw himself riding into Moscow on a White Russian horse.' The belief of many in the west that intervention would lead to the recouping of investments in Tsarist Russia added a sordidly mercenary quality to proceedings. As Hamilton Fyfe, who agreed with Lockhart that the Bolsheviks were the nearest thing Russia had to effective government, put it:

Russia owes me fifteen thousand roubles, or did owe me until I wrote that sum off as a bad debt. God forbid that men's lives should be lost for the advantage of my bank account! [50]

This division in interpretation of Soviet communism, whether Lenin and his successors were ideologically-fired millenarian psychotics or hard-headed realists trying to manage events and bring order to a chaotic country, persists among academics to this day, and is studied by Fettes pupils who take modern history. The pupils at the time had a simpler view, one which chimed with the prevailing notion amongst the Scots bourgeoisie. When two (presumably irritating) junior boys, outraged that no-one was taking any notice of their interesting suggestions for making life at the school better, wrote to its magazine to complain in print, they signed themselves 'Lenin and Trotsky.'[51]

Although the red scare of the post-war era proved a damp squib, the violence in Ireland was real enough. The 1918 general election saw Sinn Fein, with its demand for an Irish Republic, wipe out the Irish Parliamentary Party, and its policy of limited Home Rule, now so discredited (at least amongst Irish Catholics) by its Imperial loyalty. The failure of the British government to recognise this seismic shift in Irish demands launched a war in John Bull's other island. Knox Cunningham, later an Ulster Unionist MP, recalled that one of his early bouts of homesickness was 'traced to the sound of firing on the rifle range, which recalled home and the sound of shooting in Belfast.'[52]

The 'Vive-La' of 1922 had a topical reference to the 'troubles':

International sports at Belfast saw the Scots
Thanks to Ponsford's fine running win most of the pots;
He got off the mark with the speed of a train
For he knew that the starter belonged to Sinn Fein. [53]

It need hardly be said that few in the school saw much of Yeats' terrible beauty in the activities of the IRA; the 'Shinners' deserved to be blotted out and rased by their rebellion from the Book of Life, and a number of Fettesians served in Ireland against them. Indeed, Adam recalled that, at the time of the rebellion in 1916, he had not been the last pupil to return to school late, for others wanted to get stuck in immediately:

...there were two fire-eating brothers still left in Belfast. At the side of the first shot in the south they had girded up their loins for the battle and had since been so busy joining local volunteers, shouting defiance in the direction of Dublin and being demobilized again, that they had not been able to keep the usual appointment at the beginning of term.[54]

Although Ulster loyalists like this were both loud and enthusiastic during the 1916-22 period in seeking to prosecute the war against the 'dirty rebels', it is a regrettable fact that a large amount of the actual fighting in Belfast consisted of sectarian pogroms as Catholic civilians were evicted from the city, creating one of the biggest forced migrations in the English-speaking world in the twentieth century. Although many of those who carried out the atrocities were had fought in Flanders and had a lack of empathetic feeling for those they considered 'disloyal', it is hard to have any more sympathy for their brutal purges than for the sectarian assassinations carried out by Michael Collins' IRA in the south. As in the last decades of the century, the British Army was deployed with the simultaneous tasks of trying to keep order and hunt for gunmen. Lt Ronald Hendy of the Royal Warwickshire Regiment, scholarship boy, 1st XV rugby player, prefect and grandson of the great Dr Potts, survived the trenches and the ill-fated Russia expedition only to be killed in Ireland in 1922. He was

...one of three officers who were murdered in April 1922. For nearly two years the bodies lay in a pit near the place of the crime. The rude grave was discovered early in December 1923, and the remains were brought to Aldershot and buried with full military honours on December 14. Three holders of the Victoria Cross took part in the ceremony.[55]

The burials were filmed for Pathé News and screened all over the country. The details of the shootings, however, were more murky. In 1921, a truce was signed which allowed the Irish Free State autonomy so long as it respected Northern Ireland's right to separate status and accepted George V as titular head of state. This resulted in violence from de Valera's hard-line anti-treatyites who refused to compromise. Since the new Irish Free State forces were dealing with this, the British army was slowly withdrawing from its bases in Ireland. Hendy was one of four British soldiers – three officers and their driver – who were arrested by West Cork republicans, held at Macroom Castle for several days, and finally shot. Whilst Hendy and his comrades were being interrogated, ten local protestants were murdered on the grounds that they might be informers (as previously noted, Roman Catholics were subject to similar attacks in Northern Ireland). Recent evidence suggests that Hendy, who was Bernard Montgomery's intelligence officer, might have been spared had he not been in the company of a Lt Dove, who was notoriously brutal with IRA suspects.[56]

The killings extended to the dog the officers had brought with them, and controversy has raged for years about what actually happened, particularly with regard to the protestant civilians – modern Irish liberals have condemned what they see as an embarrassing bout of sectarian murder, but traditional nationalists continue to regard such tactics as fair game and see any criticism of the 'good old' IRA as tantamount to disagreeing with Irish independence. Some even go so far as to suggest that British intelligence shot all these people themselves as part of a 'dirty tricks' campaign.[57]

The IRA at Macroom Castle: some of these men may have been involved in the killing of Old Fettesian Ronald Hendy or the sectarian massacre which took place at the same time

Bitterness over the Irish war would linger for decades. Moir Mackenzie was one of Robert Bruce Lockhart's contemporaries in the vigorous pre-war Fettesian rugby teams, where he scored two tries against Scotland as a schoolboy in January 1905 before joining the legendary K.G. MacLeod in the national side; they were the youngest players in a team which included six OFs in the autumn of that year when Scotland played the All Blacks for the first time. His sporting background, like that of his contemporary Bruce Lockhart, was to prove invaluable when, as

Empire Director of the Federation of British Industry in the thirties and forties, he had to deal with that prickliest and most reluctant of Commonwealth leaders, Irish Taoiseach Eamonn de Valera. Luckily, their shared love of rugby ensured that the meeting went swimmingly, with 'Dev' commenting in respect of his last match for Blackrock that, just as in politics, 'Just as you think you're about to score, someone trips you up.' Since hard-line Catholic-nationalists considered rugby a 'foreign game', it was vaguely hoped that stories like this would endear the premier to Mackenzie's contacts in the disgruntled and dwindling Protestant community of Dublin. At a meeting of former Irish internationals at Trinity College, reality was brought home when a famous full-back boomed 'By God, Moir, if we'd ever guessed that the blighter would turn out the way he has, he'd never have left the field alive.'[58]

Mackenzie was to find his work in America and Canada infinitely easier.

Fettes' soldiers in the twenties

Fettes in the 1920s was, as ever, a robust and challenging, though potentially rewarding, environment for the young men who filled its houses. Alan Harvey came from a Scottish family based for over a century in India to join Kimmerghame and entered a world of classics and sport which had changed little for decades.

When I left prep school it seems that I was scholarship material. My scholastic record was dismal from then on. I spent two years in the Upper Fourth and never got further than the Upper Fifth (Freddie Macdonald). Nobody ever seemed to wonder why - except me. The theory was that I had not developed physically until I reached Fettes and my brain had developed well. Fettes (cold baths/showers and rugby) started to develop me physically, and my brain reacted and ceased to develop. I did pass the entrance exam to Cambridge but failed the school leaving certificate exams and at Cambridge I was very ordinary... Perhaps I can't blame Fettes, but my recollections are that the teaching was extremely poor. All teachers were highly qualified in their subjects, but couldn't teach - especially the Sciences. All I learned was H^2O and H^2SO4 and how the Forth Bridge was maintained and painted![59]

Some examples of questionable teaching methods included one mathematics master's habit of poking with a compass those who got things wrong, and Mr Havergal's ruthless weeding-out of potential choristers by deciding within seconds of their renditions of 'Three Blind Mice' whether or not they were good enough to train. Havergal was, despite or because of this Darwinian approach, a very successful music teacher, who, as Alyster Jackson, another twenties OF, put it, 'achieved the well-nigh impossible task of making music acceptable, instead of cissy, in hitherto dinosaur Fettes.'[60]

The quality of the choir and orchestra long remained in the memories of twenties Fettesians, even if they were cast out from performing. Alan Harvey was the last Fettesian to remember the old Kimmerghame, 'about six 3-storied residential properties with holes knocked in the interior walls to give interconnection', outside the walls of the school and decidedly inferior to the other houses. During the twenties, the new Kimmerghame was built, on the same pattern as the Victorian Moredun, Carrington and Glencorse, but lacking their gothic frills and decidedly more spacious – 'worth waiting for'. Alyster Jackson was in Glencorse, where each night there was a 'somewhat fearsome but traditional ceremony before lights out.' Each boy had to run and catch a bar, about five feet from the ground, and loop his feet and body over it – a trial for the 'less athletic, or very small, who could not do it, try as they might, and despite quite painful stick encouragement from the two seniors in charge.' Jackson's more positive memories included Dulcie Cook, the beautiful daughter of the Kimmerghame housemaster and, as the only girl on campus, responsible for the first flutterings in many Fettesian hearts, Mr Yarroll's carpentry lessons, in which he made a table, and, like many of that era, the English lessons of Mr Pyatt, the talented, unorthodox housemaster who disliked sport. Although as patriotic a wartime teacher as could be found, he shared the enlightened enthusiasms of Sir William's day – and indeed of America's President Wilson in 1918 – that a new world order might be created in which war would cease. The June 1919 *Fettesian* carried one of his more optimistic poems, summoning the survivors to Founder's Day:

> *Once more our joyous signal flies,*
> *Once more they flock from near and far,*
> *The Light of Peace within their eyes –*
> *For they have dug the grave of War.*[61]

Harry Pyatt, as any colleagues who knew his views on rugger would soon have opined, might be a great housemaster, and a published poet, but was of course quite wrong about certain major issues. The Great War might have been buried, some would argue temporarily, but there were plenty of other conflicts in rude, indeed downright offensive, health. The Armistice did not mean an end to Fettesians in the firing line, even though it did mean some changes in the scale of operations. The British are often blamed for blindness in military affairs between the wars, allowing a situation to develop in which the fascist powers could later inflate both their strength and their ambitions, but this was not the fault of the soldiers themselves. Those who remained in uniform or who joined up afterwards – and the *Fettesian* records a steady trickle of these – were kept busy in the untidy inter-war years. The politicians, and the public who voted for them, may not have wanted a large force for continental operations, but they were quite happy with the small professional Army doing its job as imperial gendarme with reasonable efficiency. Even if Europe was staggering from one crisis to another, with the early twenties seeing the rise of fascism and communism, the British could with reason argue that they had other things to worry about. Britain could not realistically expect to be invaded from, or need to mount a major assault on, continental Europe, and so from 1919 to 1933 the Ten Year Rule (devised, ironically, by Winston Churchill) was in force, basing military planning on the quite legitimate assumption that war with a major power was unlikely to take place for at least a decade. The 'Geddes Axe' swung into action after December 1921, and cuts to defence spending were made each year for the next decade – again, understandably, for the economy was hardly sparkling at the time. The Royal Navy, although attenuated, was still key to both national defence and maintaining imperial sea lanes, whilst the RAF's funding rested on the notion that it could deter aggressors – a revival of the fantasy of terror-bombing; the infantry and tanks experienced only sluggish support.[62]

The RAF was assiduous in attempting to recruit Fettesians; Wing Commander S. Grant Dalton lectured on the subject to the school in November 1921, urging the boys to join the air force 'without hesitation':

If one had a steady nerve, there was not the slightest danger in flying, barring extraordinary accidents. After briefly tracing the history of flying, he proceeded to show by means of lantern slides the use of aircraft in photography, bomb-dropping, etc. Among his slides were the last two photographs taken of the R38 before its disaster...[63]

The R38 had crashed off Hull earlier that year with the loss of 44 lives, and the boys' beloved R34, pride of East Fortune, had survived a record-breaking transatlantic crossing only to bounce off a mountain in heavy fog, limp back to base to incur more damage in a gale, and end up being dissected for scrap. Despite such glamour and poor financial support, it was the soldier, and in particular the infantryman, who was key to the bulk of British military activity in the fifteen years after the end of the First World War – with Fettes College providing a respectable number of the young officers who had the greatest responsibility for the day-to-day patrolling, policing and skirmishing which this involved. The numbers slowed down, of course – whereas only one of the thirty-odd boys who came to the school in 1911 did not serve in some capacity (and twelve were killed in the war) only two of those who came in 1917 became regular soldiers on leaving, though five joined the Territorials. Six of the immediate post-war intake joined the Army, though another eight (out of a total of 48) went to work in the colonies, James Maurice Scott making a name for himself as a Polar explorer and Everest mountaineer.[64]

In some ways, the experience of the Fettesian who joined up in the 1920s was not so very different from that of his Edwardian predecessor. A good 90 per cent of his fellow-students at Sandhurst would have been the products of public schools, and they remained as enthusiastically wedded to sport as the key to a manly, healthy existence (one OF, for instance, William Green of the Black Watch, won the Army Golf Championship in 1921). Robust military exercises with firearms and trench-digging were accompanied by lessons on imperial history and geography, ceremonial drill and, since these young men would be expected to set the highest possible social tone, 'instruction on writing cheques, answering invitations and the importance of engraved rather than printed visiting cards.'[65]

More sophisticated leadership training, however, was not generally carried out until the officer was with his regiment, and, moreover, had risen to the rank of captain. The Fettesian record suggests rather mixed success in achieving this level, and many young officers dropped out after only a few years' peacetime service. And who could blame them, when more exciting and lucrative endeavours, such as silver fox farming in Canada – subject of a lengthy article in the *Fettesian* in 1929 – awaited in civilian life?

Charles Jenkins was one of a comparatively small number of Fettesians to join the Royal Navy between the wars, becoming a cadet in 1919 just as naval recruitment was slashed by nine-tenths. After the Second World War, he wrote a memoir, *Days of a Dogsbody*, which remains, along with Ross's book on the RND in the First World War, one of the most delightful, if sadly forgotten, accounts of a service career. Jenkins enjoyed his training, which was intensely practical – no one could accuse the RN, which required officer cadets to spend time carrying out all the duties of ordinary seamen, including scrubbing decks and coaling, of pursuing a leisured, gentlemen's club approach. Coaling competitions were held between separate holds manned by officer cadets, marines and actual stokers, all shoveling furiously to get the contents of a lighter into bags and on board ship, at the end of which sixty blackened cadets would scramble to use a dozen small hip-baths of cold water.[66]

He was rather less impressed with the fact that the navy still seemed to work on the assumption that its 'snotties' were the small boys of 13 who had once been a core element of its recruitment; although his ship called at exotic ports across the Mediterranean and along the Norwegian coast, 'our lives were circumscribed, and a few short hours for games were all we got.' Although he had a 'grand life' on board, with 'cheerful companionship and laughter', he felt that recruits of his era lost 'those most essential attributes of an officer, *savoir faire* and knowledge of the world.' Not for the first or last time, the armed services were replicating both the good and bad aspects of schooldays at the chilly gothic institution on Comely Bank. To be fair, he did have an eye-opening experience in pre-Franco Barcelona, when the city gave the entire British fleet free seats (and champagne for the officers) at a theatrical performance called *Zigzag*, which turned out to feature a great deal of female undress, with an entirely nude leading lady. The British admiral gave a gracious speech of thanks, at the end of which he was enthusiastically kissed, to the delight of the assembled sailors, by the lead performer – which, after a moment's hesitation, he gallantly returned. Jenkins' duties in the twenties included minesweeping – possibly retrieving some of the mines so assiduously laid by Adam during the war – and conducting experiments in naval aviation which involved firing a small aeroplane from the six-inch gun turret of HMS *Caledon*. He thoroughly enjoyed life afloat, which, in the albeit reduced peacetime Royal Navy, could involve, for the lucky, all manner of entertaining amateur theatricals (with a disproportionate amount of transvestitism and comedy foreigners) sport and drinking. A slightly more respectable report of a naval cruise was sent to Fettes by the devoutly Christian Maj James MacNair-Smith of the Royal Marines, a veteran of the Great War who was attached to the World Tour Special Service Squadron. These six ships (including HMS *Hood* and *Repulse*) set out in 1923 and made their way around the world, calling at Sierra Leone, Cape Town, Durban, Zanzibar, Dar-es-Salaam, Mombasa, Trincomalee, Penang, Port Swettenham, Singapore, all of the principal Australian and New Zealand ports, Fiji, Honolulu, British Columbia and San Francisco before dividing into South American and West Indian routes. MacNair-Smith, who took the opportunity in Buenos Aires to drink a toast to the old school with several OFs working there, estimated that he had sailed 45,000 miles.[67]

Those pupils interested in careers in Latin America would have been inspired by a subsequent letter in the *Fettesian* describing how German-run 'hydroplanes' (seaplanes) were opening up the interior of this 'very rich, comparatively young' country.[68] Most who did emigrate to Latin America, however, continued to go to Argentina.

The Empire in the 1920s

MacNair-Smith wrote that 'we have had a wonderful reception everywhere, and the very strong ties and affection that exist between the Dominions and the Mother Country have been most remarkable.' Fettesians were, of course, still serving the Empire on terra firma, both as soldiers and administrators, and their experience was not always so positive. The British had been fighting in Baluchistan, a troubled section of the Afghan frontier, for years; it is not impossible that those in that area who killed OFs 2/Lt Alexander Bell Duncan of the 28th Indian Light Cavalry in 1916 and Capt. Francis Charteris Davidson of the South Waziristan Militia in 1917 were not aware that they were taking part in the First World War (though there were bizarre rumours that a German army had been seen in Afghanistan and six 'rippelins' were hovering over the Punjab[69]). George Cunningham, of the Indian Civil Service, went to the Frontier during this period to be assistant to the local Chief Commissioner, Sir George Roos-Keppel, and recorded that incursions by the Mohmands led to a great deal of fighting:

They were met with aeroplanes, field guns, howitzers, armoured cars and retired much dazed to their hills. We watched the fight from Subhankhwar Post. The whole front from Michni to Abazai had been shut in by a barbed wire line with a live wire in front. We saw the first boy caught on it, 'a black charred mass' like Phaeton.[70]

It is an indication of how turbulent the area had been that their report for the last year of the War read 'In a world at war it is curious and pleasing that the North West Frontier has no history in 1918-19'. War flared up again in 1919 with an Afghan invasion of India which Sir Alfred Hamilton Grant, another Fettesian in the I.C.S., described as 'the most meaningless, crazy and unnecessary war in history'. It was Grant, as Roos-Keppel's successor, who negotiated a Treaty with Afghanistan in 1919, by which point the situation had been complicated by the danger of communist infiltration and increased nationalism among the Indian middle class. Cunningham did not approve of the concessions granted by the British to the nationalists during this period, writing in his diary that 'the cry for Reform has come only from the clever lawyer class and this surrender to their clamour is in a way a betrayal of the contented agricultural masses to the Lawyer-Politician.'[71]

Cunningham believed that a firm but fair administration of justice, allowing law-abiding subjects to go about their lives in peace, was what most Indians wanted, and, on his appointment to the Sub-Division of Hangu in Kohat District on the Frontier in 1920, that is what he tried to impose. One of his old assistants wrote an admiring biography of Cunningham in 1968 and described the regime:

On one occasion some of his colleagues were said to have run a book on how many years' imprisonment he would in the aggregate impose during two particularly busy days in Court. The figure in fact exceeded one hundred years. But the culprits in such cases were desperadoes of the most vicious type, and their fate was more than deserved. The vast majority of the population were cheerful and simple, and undoubtedly had a great liking as well as respect for Cunningham. This is not a matter of speculation or of sentimentalising of a period long past. The fact was that any man who committed injustice on the Frontier very soon knew all about it. He risked losing his life to a bullet from ambush if he failed to distinguish between justice and oppression. The crowds of men, women and children who surrounded Cunningham, either at his house or round his camp fires when he was on tour, were either the helpless coming for help or friends coming to see a friend.[72]

In his subsequent posting as the Political Agent in the troubled region of

North Waziristan, he organised the building of roads from Wana to Jandola, from Jandola to Tank, from Tank to Bannu, Bannu to Razmak, Razmak to Wana, and Wana to Bannu. This integrated the area and made administration a little easier in the previously inaccessible mountains. In his spare time he played football and hockey, and on a trip back to Britain to see his elderly father reached the third round of the Amateur Golf Championship. Elsewhere, OFs put down troublesome locals with the latest technology; this report from East Africa of a former pupil's exploits made for thrilling news at the school:

The plan of campaign was that an independent air force, self-contained in all respects, under the command of Group-Captain Gordon, was to attack the Mullah, his followers and his stock, and to disperse them. In the event of these independent operations proving successful, the rounding-up of the Dervishes would be undertaken by the ground troops with the cooperation of the Air Force.

As was anticipated, the aerial attack demoralised and effectively broke up the Dervish forces so that, apart from the physical difficulties involved, the troops had a comparatively easy task. Although the Mullah himself escaped capture, he is without power or possessions, and Dervishism as a cause in Somaliland is declared to be at an end.[73]

Group-Captain Gordon, who had joined up in 1900 as a Royal Marine, transferred to the Royal Naval Air Service in 1911 and then become an officer in the infant RAF, had served in, or more accurately over, the North Sea, German East Africa, Mesopotamia and Russia, was awarded the CMG and DSO for his efforts. This campaign proved to those who believed in air power that it was truly the weapon of the future; the banditry of the 'Mad Mullah' had been a festering sore in the side of the Somali administration since the beginning of the century, and millions of pounds and many lives had been lost in attempts to force him from his mountain fastness. Thanks to Gordon, 'for £77,000 and three weeks' action there had been resolved a situation which had looked unanswerable on a small scale. Somaliland was to enjoy undisturbed peace until World War II brought the Italians.'[74]

Fettesians would also spend the inter-war years dealing with trouble elsewhere in the empire – Egypt, Palestine, Cyprus, Burma, India, Afghanistan and Iraq. Tennant M'Neill was killed rallying troops and police against neo-Mahdist insurgents, followers of a millenarian sect who saw the British-backed administration as the Antichrist and wanted to hasten the second coming, in the Darfur region of Sudan[75]. An OF on peacekeeping duties in the new Mandate of Palestine wrote back to describe the life at Surafend, 'a pretty desolate spot'; 'the chief part of the population consists of Jews and Arabs, who need only the slightest excuse to start killing each other.'[76]

As with his predecessors who had upheld dominion over palm and pine, however, the bulk of his report consisted of descriptions of sport – hard-baked earth making golf difficult, taking the troops bathing wearing only sun-helmets, and an old classmate, Wingate Gray, breaking his collar-bone in a racing accident. In 1931, the *Fettesian* quoted with great approval a reference to an OF in a book which had just appeared about the Scottish missionary Alexander Paterson, who had devoted his life to the Holy Land. It is worth quoting at length because it illustrates some of the attitudes which underlay the imperial administration in the twenties:

It was a red-letter day for Palestine when J.H. Scott came from Egypt to the position of Judge of Appeal under the British Administration in Jerusalem. It was a position of extraordinary difficulty, but during his term of office he did more than any single man to impress the common people with a sense of British judicial fairness. Through experience gained in the Egyptian courts he had a thorough knowledge of oriental ways and clear insight into oriental character, of the better elements in which he had a genuine appreciation. His high forensic ability, legal acumen, utter integrity, fearlessness and unflagging industry soon made his name a household word in Palestine for inevitable and unquestioned justice...

Scott had to administer the Turkish Code in a country of the three conflicting faiths, of irreconcilable interests; a large part of it lawless; where the parties and witnesses in every suit were nearly all incorrigible perjurers: and this in a period of turmoil, unsettlement and discontent. His day of labour ran on an average from twelve to sixteen hours.

It was characteristic of this strong and outspoken man, moved by a keen sense of the fitness of things, to make a vigorous and successful claim that Christians, except in cases of necessity, should be free from official duties on Sundays. We are universally recognised, especially in the religious East, as a Christian power. Of Christianity, Sunday is the outward calendrical symbol. Failure to insist on its proper observance while paying homage, out of mistaken deference, to the Mohammedan Friday, as in Egypt, only provokes a reaction of contempt upon ourselves: first, for religious indifference, and, second, for political weakness. As a display of tolerance it is lost upon an essentially intolerant East, which interprets it either as weakness or pusillanimity.[77]

After a controversial case in which he made a politically unpopular decision against rioting 'Jewish braves', Scott resigned. Worn out by overwork, and never fully recovered from the malaria he had contracted as a soldier in the Boer War, he died of enteric at Cairo in 1925. Indeed, disease was still the chief enemy of the Briton (it had carried off 18 of the Great War fatalities). In 1920, George Craigie Prophit, 22-year-old Lieutenant in the I/39 Garwhal Rifles, India died of cerebro-spinal fever at the military hospital, Mosul, whilst on active service with his regiment. The school magazine printed the letters sent by his senior officers to his mother:

From Major-General T. Fraser –
We buried your boy yesterday on a clear sunny afternoon, very typical of his own bright straight personality. I know he is deeply mourned by everyone who knew him here. He was exceedingly popular and took a leading part in all our sports and games.
From his commanding officer –
A subaltern when he dies is entitled to a gun carriage and artillery drivers to lead the horses of the team but for your son the gun teams were ridden by officers; this special mark of esteem was thought of and arranged by the officers of the 44th Battery R.F.A.
Every officer in Mosul went to the funeral, and the men of the regiment lined the route and formed the escort whilst the Northumberland Fusiliers sent their band.[78]

It should be said that the mortality of young men was not confined to the stifling corners of the Empire; Alan Harvey was one of three pupils confined to the school sanatorium with nephritis in the late twenties; one of the others, Smith of Glencorse, died. Not all of the imperial OFs were soldiers – there were many administrators and teachers, one of whom was the poet Norman Cameron, who sailed for Nigeria in 1929 to take up a post as an education officer. A friend of Robert Graves and Dylan Thomas, he was instinctively a man of the left, and was not desperately keen on the more conventional colonial types he met on the boat. 'I thought that it was meeting too many people that I loved or liked that was dissipating my slight energy in London,' he wrote to the

American writer Laura Riding, 'I certainly haven't met anybody lovable or likeable on this ship so I hope for good results.'[79]

On arrival in Lagos, he quickly acquired the services of a capable cook and a tough steward, as well as a pleasant house, and appreciated that there were undoubted attractions in the colonial life – 'a middle-class paradise.' However, what Lockhart found occasionally endearing in Malaya evidently terrified Cameron. A girl from whom he bought some bananas made a gesture which he supposed was 'a sort of technical blessing'; answering 'bless you' he returned home and was deeply alarmed when she followed him and 'started to make a sexual demonstration.' 'I daren't smile at any African girls any more,' he wrote gloomily. He found his colleagues dispiriting; they failed to understand that picture-books with robins and other British images were unlikely to be effective teaching aids for African children who had never seen such things, and, even worse, as 'new boy' he was expected to organise the Empire Day celebrations, 'a really beastly job': 'sports, football matches, a huge procession of fourteen thousand children, and about ten enormous excursions to cocoa-works and things, and every bloody detail left to me.' The heat and tedium took its toll. 'I'm not at all young, sweet and carefree now; but old and sinister and at times wondering where the hell I am.' He escaped on leave to join Graves in Majorca and eventually resigned in 1931. Ian Williamson's experience was altogether more enjoyable; arriving in Java in the late twenties, he was taking a bath in his hotel when the telephone rang; Gourlay Macindoe, a fellow OF, had been looking at the shipping lists, saw someone who was travelling from Scotland, and immediately fed him and got him into several sports and social clubs. It was only later that Macindoe discovered that they had been at the same school and the same house a few years apart, which enhanced Williamson's status further.[80]

The *Fettesian* of June 1926 carried a long article about Kenya, 'one of Britain's youngest and most promising colonies', then over two weeks away on the ships of the Union Castle Line. Fettes pupils in that grim year of the General Strike must have been enchanted at the thought of a land where there was 'some of the finest big-game shooting in the world' and where 'grapes, pears, peaches, bananas, oranges, figs, pineapples, and the more tropical fruits such as paw-paws, mango and guava are to be had nearly all the year round.'[81]

The author, a 26-year-old who had swapped Windygates in Fife for

311

The 1913 1st XI: most of those who survived the First World War went on to work in the empire as soldiers or farmers

the life of a coffee planter, rhapsodised over the scenery and climate before going on to describe daily life. He warned that between 8.00 and 4.00 each day Europeans had to wear helmets or double felt hats because of the sun's rays (then a common belief) but that a 'well-regulated' plantation got going just after sunrise at 6.00, with the manager ensuring that he saw the natives off to work. The natives themselves 'are still very uncivilised and wear little or no clothing' but 'when one gets to know them, they are not in the least repulsive creatures; in fact, many of them are of an extremely pleasant disposition, they are rather like children and should be treated as such.' Although the manager himself did no manual labour, 'the superintendence of the natives is very trying, and means very long hours' teaching others how to do things – a task which also required the learning of Swahili. Like OFs in more established colonies, he was very glad to put himself at the disposal of anyone who wanted to make a life for himself in Kenya.

Of the 150 or so Fettesians entering the school in the 1922-26 period (who were in their early twenties when the *Register* was compiled) only a dozen were recorded as being in professional military service – virtually all in the Indian Army (one of whom, J.E. Lean, died of disease at Calcutta in 1931), the Engineers, Artillery or RAF. Nonetheless, there was a steady trickle, and many issues of the *Fettesian* in the later twenties carried news of appointments to the forces or, as was of course traditional, the colonial services. As always, there were the letters from Old Fettesians, describing the exciting world which awaited those who entered the service of the King-Emperor. One such, Allan Macdonald, based in Kandy, Ceylon, numbered among the OFs on the island two 'ancients' – pre-war pupils – who were 'sahibs high up in the Civil Service', one of whom was believed to 'live most of his days in a tent in the jungle on a diet of quinine'. Some of the 'moderns' were keeping up the school tradition of playing rugger in wholly unsuitable climes; D.B.H. Scott was the only disgruntled figure, having expected to be posted to India (which was in the grip of nationalist agitation at the time) and thus equipped himself with 'a perfect armoury of rifles, six-shooters and ammunition', but ended up required to 'cook the accounts of the P. & O. Line'. 'He goes about with a rather puzzled look, as if wondering whom he is supposed to shoot among streets full of one-man hansom things (rickshaws!)'.[82]

Fettesians in Europe

Before the First World War, both military and civilian Fettesians who went abroad generally served the crown or their pockets in British colonies or in parts of the 'informal empire' such as Argentina. Apart from a few eccentric aesthetes who went to German music festivals, there seems to have been little exploration of continental Europe. However, some of the Fettesians who joined or remained in the armed forces after the war found themselves in the novel position, for British troops, of garrisoning parts of Europe to enforce the peace treaties or help protect the recovering nations. One OF, engaged in post-war reconstruction in Romania, described himself as 'sort of chief of a tribe', organising the rebuilding of a village bridge, and dispensing 'law and aspirin and quinine'. The Romanians, 'a most charming people', whose country had been brutally sacked by the Germans and Austria-Hungary after they sided with the British (a point often forgotten by those who dwell on the supposed iniquities of the post-war Versailles settlement) were generous in their Anglophilia. All the British officers had been invited to tea with Queen Marie (quite appropriately, as she was the daughter of Alfred, Duke of Edinburgh) and will doubtless have been flattered to hear the story that Romanian dogs barked at German but not British soldiers – 'it must have been in the smell'.[83]

'Viator', also writing home in 1919, was part of the British force which occupied Cologne as part of the Armistice arrangements, was understandably less keen on his hosts; the opera house was 'fine in a vulgar sort of way' and the 9 pm curfew meant that 'many a portly Boche has been seen hurrying home with fear on his pudgy countenance'.[84]

Hamilton Fyfe witnessed and rejoiced at the liberation of Alsace and Lorraine from the Germans, sharing this understandable, though fortunately temporary, dislike of a nation with which Britain had been engaged in a fierce struggle for so long:

If the Prussians had not been the dismally stupid race that they always have been they would have seen that they could only make the people of Alsace forget they had been annexed by treating them, with exceptional mildness… Just and friendly treatment would have won them. Instead, they had the Prussian jackboot applied to them — with the natural result.[85]

By 1923, Lockhart was depressed to see that the French, in their zone of occupation, were exercising a ruthless and rigid control over the Germans, storing up precisely the resentment that Prussia had created in Alsace and Lorraine. In order to rub salt into the wound, they garrisoned the Ruhr with Senegalese troops, and although Lockhart accepted that they behaved with 'admirable restraint' (despite claims by the Germans of atrocities) nonetheless, 'their presence in a European country and the powers given to them over a white race depressed me and filled me with foreboding.'[86] He was impressed by the British, however, who happily fraternised with the poverty-stricken Germans, and were, indeed, in advance of public opinion at home.[87]

Lockhart found this out the hard way; when he had the temerity to raise the subject, the secretary of his London club discreetly took him aside and suggested that in future he confine such opinions to the privacy of his own flat; 'some of the old colonels had complained about my disgusting pro-Germanism.'

Fed up with talking to British politicians who did not want to listen to his advice about Russia, and having been inspired whilst at school by the literally Bohemian art master Mr Kroupka, Lockhart accepted with alacrity the post of Commercial Secretary at the new British legation in Prague, where he received mail addressed to 'Prague, Czechoslavia; Prague, Yugoslavia; Prague, Czechoslovenia; Prague, Vienna, and even; The Prague, Poland' – an indication of the depths of British ignorance about 'abroad.'[88]

His experiences are worth noting because he was the first OF to write in any detail about Europe, and the hardships and eccentricities he witnessed in the twenties still have certain resonances today. Although the actual military campaigns of the Great War had been on the edges of the continent, he found Central Europe shattered by revolution, giant lurches in national boundaries, ethnic conflict and economic collapse. Travelling by military train to his new post, at the frontier of the truncated Austria he was discomfited to see 'starved faces' at broken window-panes, heat and light coming from candle-stumps. Both the aristocracy of Austria and their cousins, the German-speaking nobility of Bohemia, loathed the new dispensation and refused to co-operate with it. 'Aristocrats by divine right, they had all the mental laziness of the Russian nobility without a tenth of the talent,' Lockhart snorted, with all the contempt of the industrious Scot for those whose 'effort to help themselves was confined to sighs for the departed glory of the Hapsburgs and to cheap sneers at their new masters.'[89]

Hungary, the sister kingdom, was equally degraded, her territories shorn even more brutally than Austria's and her aristocracy – although Lockhart found them more virile and attractive than their neighbours – just as reactionary. The Serbs, meanwhile, impressed Lockhart because 'a nation, which in the head of a Belgrade summer, can breakfast off slivowitz, is not to be despised' even if their national assembly, the Skupština, 'was more like a monkey-house than a parliament.'[90] The Serbs were 'jolly buccaneers with the priceless quality of guts' and their defects 'merely the infantile diseases of a healthy, virile child'; unfortunately, they lacked the tact to deal with the Croats, the second-largest ethnic group in the new Yugoslavia, and Lockhart appreciated that it was only Croat fear of Italy and Hungary that made them remotely loyal to King Aleksandar. Relations grew so bad that, during one of Lockhart's visits to Yugoslavia in 1928, a Montenegrin MP produced a gun in the Skupština and proceeded to shoot the Croat front-benchers. The Croats seethed, overcame their suspicions of Italy and Hungary, discovered fascism, and, when the time came in 1941, took genocidal revenge. Lockhart was prepared to like everyone he met, but his favourites were the Czechs, to whom, like the Victorian Fettesian and his Sikh troops, he paid the ultimate compliment:

Like the Scot, the Czech is thrifty, hard-working and ambitious... Once one has plumbed his depth, one finds sterling qualities of grit and courage. He has a fine physique, is one of the best gymnasts in the world, and has a passionate love of the hills and streams of his country. Beneath his practical material exterior he has a soul for poetry. His love and understanding of music are inborn… [91]

Lockhart had a ringside seat alongside politicians and top businessmen as a new Europe dragged itself into being. As well as the high politics, he enjoyed a rich social life, dining with the intelligentsia and drinking hard in the nightclubs of Europe's capitals in what he described as a 'post-war carnival… a wave of extravagance and self-indulgence.' In such an atmosphere, a creed like communism which demanded 'self-sacrifice and self-denial' was unlikely to make any headway. His main concern was for the state of his liver and the poor prospects for promotion occasioned by his hardened hedonism, but 'fortunately for my physical welfare and for the salvation of my immortal soul' he spent his weekends shooting and fishing in the countryside.

The rise of pacifism? The Corps carries on

A posthumous publication of the work of the questioning, doubting soldier-poet Lt-Col Maitland Hardyman, DSO and MC, entitled *A Challenge: Poems*, got a mention in the *Fettesian*. Although the editor saw his as one of the most remarkable of the careers cut short by the war[92], his poetry got considerably less attention from the boys than the prose of another OF, the swashbuckling Major Hesketh-Prichard, also DSO and MC, on sniping. The lessons of Hesketh-Prichard's experience, and others, were being incorporated into the training of the OTC, which (to the irritation of the fags who had to Brasso the buttons on the older boys' uniforms) continued in only mildly abbreviated form. The absence of rifles meant that the shooting team became 'erratic' – 'from the fair sprinkling of misses, one would not have been surprised to see some peaceful sheep, pasturing quietly on the Pentlands, drop dead in their tracks'[93] – but on the whole the officers and boys did their best. After all, as Ian Hay noted in an address to the Old Fettesian Dinner in London in 1921, the OTC had provided leaders when they were most needed, making the British Army better than its American counterpart, where 'officers and men were democratically on an equal footing of absolute ignorance.'[94]

The government obviously agreed. Like other schools, Fettes received a letter of thanks from the War Office expressing thanks for the OTC contribution in filling the commissioned ranks of the forces, and was given a captured German trench mortar as a war souvenir (these were later reclaimed by the state for scrap purposes when war returned in 1939). The OTC was more interested in resuming the joyous punch-ups with the Academy, Merchiston and Loretto which were dignified by the title of 'field days'. After one of these, in March 1921, they marched from the Pentlands to the transport terminus at Gorgie and commandeered trams back to Comely Bank, 'to the concern of the drivers and the undisguised disgust of people waiting along the line.'[95]

The Edinburgh citizen, for whom in William Fettes' day uniforms in the streets were an uncomfortable novelty, was by now wearily accustomed to this sort of thing, though for this military *droit de seigneur* to be exercised by schoolboys clearly rankled. Still, at least it was safer than the Armistice Day route-march of 1919, when, led by the band and sporting their latest kit, the Corps attempted to parade along roads covered in solid sheets of ice, with unsurprising casualties.[96]

On 29 July 1920, the worthy burghers of Edinburgh were 'aroused from their breakfasts by the warlike sound of the pipes' and 'the business of banks and institutes was held up for a time' on George Street, as the boys marched off to camp for the annual exercise in sleeping on straw in tents, crawling around with rifles and getting dirty, which needless to say they adored.[97] (Lest this be taken as a sign of the innately militaristic robustness of Fettesians, it should be noted that they had equally enjoyed the previous year's camp, which had considerably less army content but was miraculously sited between a golf course and a beach[98]). Signalling, whose importance had been amply demonstrated by the war, remained a popular cadet activity for the ambitious and, it was hinted, the pedantic or bossy:

> *I am the signalmaster staunch,*
> *Pillar of the Signal Service.*
> *At scarlet tabs I do not blanch,*
> *So wonderful my nerve is.*
> *Their messages I scrutinise,*
> *Reject them by the score, oh!*
> *That most emphatic, automatic, autocratic,*
> *Signalmaster of the Corps, oh!* [99]

For the less technically-minded, Sergeant-Major Giles, formerly Middle-Weight Champion of the Gloucesters and subsequently of the St. Helena

Garrison (the latter possibly not the hardest battle of his career) coached boxing. For half an hour a week, around 40 lads turned up for the new Corps Boxing Club, which later affiliated to the Scottish United Amateur Boxing Association and held a contest in April 1921. 'There was not a great deal of science' noted the cadets' sports reporter, 'but what was lacking in this department was made up by the tremendous keenness and good feeling in every round.'[100]

Although it was robustly defended by its supporters ('how can a pupil with a boxing temperament be discovered until he has taken some hard knocks?') less pugilistic Fettesians expressed doubts about this kind of activity, particularly given the amount of blood spattered around. Henry Giles' favourite term of encouragement to the sloppy boxer or scruffy cadet was to describe him as 'a sack of shit tied up loose' may well have been visited upon such faint-hearts.

Fettesians at OTC camp in 1920

Despite Fettes' continuing addiction to the arts of war, since 1922, when Lloyd George was forced out of office after a rash attempt to commit British troops at Chanak to fight the Turks in support of Greece, it had been apparent that neither the British public nor its elected representatives were keen on war. Gary Sheffield sees the dam as finally bursting in the years between the General Strike and the outbreak of the Great Depression, with the publication of Siegfried Sassoon's *Memoirs of a Fox-hunting Man*, Robert Graves' *Goodbye to All That* and Richard Aldington's *Death of a Hero*. In addition to literature, film and theatre (R.C. Sherriff's

Journey's End appeared at the same time) the conduct and impact of the war were discussed by military thinkers such as Fuller and Liddell Hart, neither of whom had many good words to say for the military leaders of 1914-18.[101] Pacifist groups, from Hardyman's Union of Democratic Control to Dick Sheppard's Peace Pledge Union, were now as noisy as the aggressive militarists such as the National Service League had been in Edwardian England.[102]

Many people at every level of society were repulsed by war; the establishment, whose sons had been such a disproportionate element of the casualties, the liberal middle class with its pious hopes of redemption through the League of Nations, and the proletariat, promised and denied homes for heroes and increasingly convinced that they had been cannon-fodder for Wall Street. Labour politicians even toyed with abandoning Remembrance Sunday in 1930, though this was a step too far. As Gary Sheffield and other revisionists have pointed out, *Journey's End* was not intended as an anti-war play, the overwhelming majority of veterans were proud of their service, and most people remained sturdily patriotic.[103]

One of the first school trips organized by Fettes was to Ypres in 1925, and the report is an interesting insight into what was already being called a 'pilgrimage in all seriousness'. Large structures such as the Menin Gate were still under construction, but the boys did get to see the unveiling of an un-named memorial (probably that of the 18th Division), and were disappointed by the 'not very imposing gathering', not to mention the rather variable turn-out of some of the cadets they met. What struck them most of all was 'the newness of every building in the town and on the landscape' and the 'sinister' fact of the smallness of the area: 'a cricket field would cover Hill 60, Sanctuary Wood and Zouave Wood – three of our most costly battlefields.'[104]

These were, they wrote, not being returned to cultivation, and were still piled high, seven years on, with the debris of war cleared from the British cemeteries ('beyond praise'). Sanctuary Wood, with its muddy preserved trenches, shell-holes and rusting barbed wire, remains a point of pilgrimage for school visits to Flanders today, much to the despair of health and safety officers, but the boys' speculation (common at the time) that the Ypres Cloth Hall would be left in its ruined state as a memorial proved unfounded. Although respectful (and noting that the Germans buried British dead with great ceremony and proper headstones, a fate

Tommies who died in their own lines were denied) there was none of the mawkish sentimentality or pacifist analysis one can see in such reports from more or less every school in Britain in the latter decades of the twentieth century. A subsequent poem about Ypres by junior master (and war veteran) W.C. Sellar was melancholy but dignified:

> *The leaves are gathered to your gates*
> *That once our trees in splendour wore,*
> *And Earth shall know their pride no more.*
>
> *Those laurels green, too soon the Fates*
> *Shall heap on Time's dead mouldering store*
> *With bays of cities crowned of yore.*
> *The leaves are gathered to your gates*
> *That once our trees in splendour wore.*
>
> *What sheen yet girds your wrack awaits*
> *The mist that rolls from that far shore*
> *Where ghost to wistful ghost relates*
> *Dim tales of Troy and Agincourt.*
> *The leaves are gathered to your gates*
> *That once our trees in splendour wore,*
> *And Earth shall know their pride no more.*[105]

Visiting generals at the Fettes OTC naturally 'still addressed the school, silent and perspiring in inspection order, on the assumption that Britannia ruled the waves and policed the Frontier.'[106]

Former pupils' memories of the period are, nonethelessss militarily focused than those of the pre-1918 era – indeed, Ian Harvey's autobiography doesn't mention the Corps at all – but the drilling and shooting did continued as normal. Alyster Jackson, whose father had gone down with the *Lusitania* in 1915, had, on Selwyn Lloyd's recommendation, applied for a Foundation Scholarship ('for boys of Scottish descent whose parents, through no fault of their own, could not afford the fees') and entered Fettes in 1925. For him, the OTC was just another element of the rigid caste system kept different years apart. His day started (as his successors' still do) at 7.00 with a bell ordering the boys from their beds, followed by another one shortly afterwards which really meant it and was the signal for a cold shower (an institution which has not survived). As a fag, his military training was quite simple and he did not even have a uniform until his second year, but the most onerous duties revolved around cleaning the prefects' kit. This was extremely elaborate, despite the war having demonstrated once and for all that bright colours and shiny buttons were fatally tempting targets for machine-gunners. As another inter-war Fettesian recalled:

We wore army boots, diced (diamond patterned) kilt stockings, kept up by cloth garters, not elastic but wound round the leg and tucked in, and ornamented with red flashes. Over the ankles and covering the boot top were puttees, also wound round and fastened with a tape which continued the winding round and tucking in. A full adult size kilt (my first) and sporran were topped by a khaki kilt jacket with brass buttons and a webbing belt with a brass buckle and more brass buckles to fit shoulder straps when a pack was carried, and other accoutrements such as ammunition pouches, a water bottle and so on. Our personal weapon was the Short Magazine Lee Enfield and a bayonet whose scabbard was also attached to the belt. With all the gear hanging round it there was not much chance of the kilt being blown upwards by the wind, which was just as well because by army tradition nothing was worn under it.[107]

I.A.H. Moore, who entered the school in 1928, saw the cadets as 'a grim duty – cold knees, icy rifle butts and frenzied polishing – that fell far short of qualifying us for war.'[108]

G. Morrison, who joined the school shortly after him, was more positive but equally unconvinced of the OTC's military value, remembering camp as 'a holiday rather than a serious military exercise.'[109]

Reports from the *Fettesian* in this period bore this out to a certain extent; there was certainly a much less warlike attitude to these immersions in army life and a greater emphasis on the fun and games. The Scottish weather, as always, did its best to add to the fun. The 133 cadets who went to camp in 1923 were virtually flooded out, and a tank officer almost drowned by a sudden thunderstorm. Camp in 1929 saw an uncomfortable combination of rain, insects, thistles and sunburn. 'However,' noted the reporter, who was clearly aware of the realities of warfare, 'we charged and advanced over the ground so bravely and so visibly that we doubt if a single man would have come home alive.' The high point for him was undoubtedly the fact that the camp was held at Elie, also known as 'Fettes-on-Sea' for its connections with the school, and a great favourite for its sandy beach, golf course and cafés.[110]

The following year's camp, also at Elie, featured jazz music, though the orchestrally-trained Fettesian players gave the impression that they had come from the Usher Hall and were probably not really getting into the swing of things. As in 1929, a suicidally optimistic attack (with the novelty of spotter aeroplanes from RAF Leuchars) won the admiring comment from a visiting officer that in 1916 'several of the contestants would have been awarded VCs, but he would not like to say how many would have been alive to receive them.'[111]

Camp was not without its real dangers, as Alyster Jackson discovered when he was nearly killed by a train whilst he and some friends were trying to explore a railway tunnel. The 1926 camp at Blair-Atholl was also seen as a great success – because of the superior food, excellent golf at Invertilt, soccer and jazz, though admittedly 'we engaged in the usual unpopular, but, we suppose, necessary manoeuvres.'[112]

The pipe band at camp in the mid-twenties: on the far right is Charles Gray, later adjutant of Skinner's Horse and champion pig-sticker

Other activities seem to have been equally varying in how far they demonstrated the boys' professionalism. Field Day in March 1923 saw the Academy and Fettes (the 'Picts') escorting 'a valuable convoy consisting of Scottish works of art' to Musselburgh, and defending it against the 'Scots' of Merchiston and Loretto, who 'made up in courage what they lacked in intelligence, a fact which they proceeded to demonstrate. Thus was the stage set for a veritable Comedy of Errors.'[113]

Unable to find the enemy after marching for several hours, the Moredun section (houses were still the basis of cadet activity at Fettes) opened up with 'well-directed volleys' of blank rounds at another force, which they 'annihilated'. Unfortunately it turned out to be their allies from Academy. The Carrington and Glencorse sections 'vanished away' whilst Kimmerghame simply 'lay in a field', with the result that 'headquarters arrived to find a scene of hopeless confusion.' The reporter nonetheless concluded that it had been 'a thoroughly successful day.' A repetition of the exercise the following term was written up by 'Billiken' (later famous as the poet Norman Cameron), who was sufficiently unmilitary to have been summoned before the camp commandant for attending breakfast parade 'tastefully' clad in gym shoes; his chief recollection was of how the heartiness of the laughter on the day varied according to the size and strength of each person who fell into a bog.[114]

The OTC was inspected in June 1924, and although discipline and drill were good, two platoons were 'indifferently' turned out and the signalling, once Fettes' pride and joy, was merely 'satisfactory'. As for the shooting, Fettes came 51st out of 66 schools at Bisley that year.[115]

In fairness, the War Office Inspection of 1926 was rather more complimentary, though presumably the army was worried about the boys' 'inadequate' knowledge of the workings of their rifles. 'Brigadier Gerard', writing about a summer's parade under 'a tropical sun' recorded only that 13 boys had to be carried from the field with heatstroke, including himself ('the ground rose up suddenly; I struck it smartly with my face').[116]

His pre-war ancestors would have added at least some military details, but only the use of the words 'parade' and 'rifle' tell us this was a cadet event. Otherwise, it just reads like a bizarre act of mass punishment from a wartime Japanese prison camp. The other extreme of weather, perhaps unsurprisingly, hit the platoon competition of February 1929 hard – the *Fettesian* for that term notes that a tactical exercise was abandoned after one attempt, by Kimmerghame, who got extra marks for their valiant attempt to conduct manoeuvres in the snow.[117]

An account of the 'Lachrymosities of a Lance-Corporal' in the same issue describes how its author lost his stripe after an afternoon of unmitigated chaos, made worse by 'a Lewis gunner making a noise like a dentist's drill behind my back', was relieved only by one of his men's inventive addition of a pencil to a blank round to bag a rabbit for prefects' tea. 'I have just sent my contribution to the League of Nations,' notes 'Juggins', 'I have always approved of disarmament.' A cadet could still have great, if mixed, feelings of pride when called upon for ceremonial duties, as Alyster Jackson recalled; when the Duke and Duchess of York (later King George VI and Queen Elizabeth) visited Edinburgh,

…Fettes, along with other school OTCs, supplied contingents to line the High Street as crowd control. We were spaced out singly, some ten paces apart, with our backs to the control cord. As the royal couple in their carriage came down the High Street, and the crowd surged forward, our line was almost broken, and probably would have been if we had not been reinforced by a few heavyweight policemen. However, the crowd was in good humour. We had to put up with many witty remarks about what was under our kilts – some attempts were even made to lift them up and have a look.[118]

Another great moment for the Fettes cadets, or at least the pipe band, came when in the mid-twenties they were used as models for the pipers and drummers on the Scottish American War Memorial on Princes St. Charles Douglas Gray, later adjutant of the famous Skinner's Horse, recalled being marched repeatedly round Charlotte Square so that the sculptor, Robert Tait Mackenzie, could get his sketches right. The final work is a remarkable and elegant tribute to the transformation of Scots of all backgrounds into the legendary fighters of the war; as the farmers, fishermen and clerks cease to be shuffling civilians and march along with determined pride, they are led by a band whose pipers may have the faces of moustachioed old sweats but whose drummers are unquestionably young lads.

Part of the Scottish American War Memorial, apparently modelled on the Fettes pipe band

Genuine military feelings filled the hearts of cadets, Morrison recalled, only when there was an inter-house competition, as that was the primary focus of loyalty (indeed, the OC was required to point out that the OTC was 'essentially a *School* organisation and not a mere collection of individual House units.'[119]) Even then, however, true enthusiasm for warfare was limited. When Ian Thomson was killed near Ypres in the Second World War, a contemporary's obituary notice for him says much about attitudes to these events in the 1920s:

I believe he was the only boy at Fettes in my day – or anyone else's – who really enjoyed the Corps Competition. On Corps days he became almost fanatical, and he must easily have been the smartest and most efficient soldier among us. His fervour could be quite embarrassing for the less enthusiastic like myself, whose feebly polished buttons and rather dusty boots called forth a torrent of ridicule and denunciation.[120]

Thomson was not entirely unique. Harold 'Pete' Pyman was another who enjoyed being a cadet, as well he might since he became CSM in 1926 – he later said that in his three years as a member of the Cambridge OTC he 'did not learn much more militarily than the Fettes Corps had already taught me.'[121]

He later became a general, and many other 1920s Fettesians were distinguished in a variety of martial fields. Alan Harvey, who was to win an MC in Italy, wrote in the *Old Fettesian Newsletter* in 2005 that 'when I joined the Army as a Fusilier (private) in the Royal Fusiliers, I found the OTC training of immense value and even at Sandhurst where I went for officer training.'[122]

He added that whilst he heartily recommended it, he expected it had been dropped from the curriculum – 'Not so' commented the *Newsletter* editor proudly. As with the obsession with rugger which permeates every single issue of the *Fettesian* from its first appearance to the present day, Ian Thomson's rarity value was probably due less to a pacifist social climate and more to the fact that boys are naturally interested more in their own daily trials than in readying themselves for the adult world. 'My time at school covered the period of the great economic slump, the fall of the second Labour Government and the rise to power of Hitler,' Moore ruefully admitted, 'but these events passed most of us by.' This was not true of everyone, of course. Quite apart from anything else, certain events could hardly escape notice. Day-to-day learning was affected during the General Strike of 1926 as younger masters volunteered to keep services going by driving buses and trains or acting as part-time policemen. Alyster Jackson remembered that during the strike the heating packed up, and he was so cold 'that I piled every possible thing - dressing gown, clothes, towel, Corps kilt and tunic, even the khaki webbing - on to my bed to try to keep warm.'[123]

Charles Jenkins, who had already done some work during the 1921 coal strike, making use of his shovelling skills, remembered 1926 for partly selfish reasons:

We had a very good time in Cadiz and the other places, but every one on the ship gave me the impression of living for the next Baltic cruise. Many were the tales I heard of Copenhagen, of Reval [Tallinn] of all-night parties where one felt no weariness, of the hospitality and friendship of the Danes and Esthonians, of the beauty of the women to be met, and of how our little squadron had all these things without interference from greater fleets.

And then instead came the General Strike. Instead of the intoxication of dance-bands came the strain of guard duties, for the gay throngs of hospitality came the solitude of lonely rounds inspecting sentry posts, for the soft whisperings of beautiful women came the occasional brick-bat of a sullen crowd. In other words, we missed our Baltic cruise and had to work.[124]

Jenkins' work was to protect the dockyard at Avonmouth against 'rioting and sabotage' and ensure the safe workings of the pumping house, unloading banana-boats, and touring sentry pickets, a 28-mile round trip which he initially performed on foot until an asthmatic lorry was provided – a vehicle so ancient that it carried only candle-lanterns and whose sailor-driver dared not switch off the engine in case it never started again and so worked on a backlash principle to avoid driving over the dock's edge . The Royal Navy retained a sense of humour throughout the sad episode; asked by a visiting government 'big-wig' if he had 'sufficient men to deal with the winches', Jenkins' captain replied that he had about 400 men to deal with the wenches. When visiting Bristol off-duty, he wandered into a crowd which was listening to a fiery orator, who shouted 'And let me tell the captain of the *Caledon* that the first round he fires from his guns into the streets of Bristol will start such a conflagration in the West of England as will never die down.' 'Hear, hear,' shouted the worthy officer, who was rather surprised to hear that his rather small cruiser could have lobbed a shell that far. There were government ministers, including Winston Churchill, whose belief that the General Strike represented the advance of Bolshevism led them to advocate aggressively churlish responses to the workers' understandable demands, but the guns were never used. Jenkins was having a day off playing golf when the gunnery officer semaphored the news that the strike was over; this was so unexpected that Jenkins asked him to repeat the message. Fettesians at the time believed that one of their alumni was responsible for the strike's sudden end, and there is some evidence for this. Sir John Simon, whose radicalism had declined somewhat since his wartime resignation over conscription (a recent Liberal Democrat parliamentary candidate who addressed the Fettes Political Society was shown Sir John's bust on the mantelpiece of the school's Callover Hall, and said rather sniffily that he was no longer considered 'one of us') delivered a ferocious speech against the General Strike from the Liberal back-benches on 6 May. Since it was not against an individual employer, it was not covered by the protective legislation he had helped pass in 1906. On the contrary, it was a strike against the state, against the people, and was therefore an insurrection – which made each trade union leader who participated liable to damages 'to the utmost farthing of his personal possessions.' As Roy Jenkins wrote in 1998, the power and authority of this statement, coming as it did from one of Britain's greatest legal experts, who was, moreover, 'one of a limited number of oracles of the nation', helped break the strike, for most British trades unionists were not revolutionaries and wanted neither the stigma nor the financial penalties associated with such a label.[125]

At the time, Fettes celebrated the intervention with a verse in the 'Vive-La':

> *There's another K.C. that I feel I must rhyme on,*
> *For the General Strike was outgeneralled by Simon;*
> *And thus you've been able to come for your Luncheon,*
> *And the Staff to hand over their armlet and truncheon.*[126]

Fettes pupils and the world

Despite some OFs' claims of woeful ignorance, there were plenty of current affairs lectures, and enough interested observers of world events to see the *Spectator* and *New Statesman* being stolen from the Fettes library on a regular basis; one aggrieved reader suggested that chaining them to the table would 'prevent the frisky little creatures from straying.'[127]

Awareness of the Bolshevik threat was ever-present; a short story in the *Fettesian* in 1924 told the tale of Walter Davies, originally a gentleman but now working for the British Soviet to spread 'black lies' and 'bring his native land to ruin.' Davies' eyes are opened when a Russian communist incites some English workers to 'preach the gospel of the bayonet and the bomb' and 'wreck the instruments of capitalistic tyranny' in the bloodthirstiest of terms. He turns on the sinister foreigner and shows the swarthy brute a bunch of fives. For his pains, he is thrown into a black, polluted river, but escapes, physically and morally.

The *Fettes Register* for 1933 recorded that some boys of the 1924 intake (those who would have left at the time when the anti-war feeling was really working up a head of steam) had been members of University OTCs or, if based down south, joined the London Scottish Territorials, but there were few full-time soldiers amongst them. 'Pete' Pyman (who went to Fettes in 1920) was by that point working hard in the Royal Tank Corps. That the army differed from the navy in its approach to training can be seen in views of some of his brother-officers at Pinehurst; they did not share his enthusiasm for the army, finding any sort of duties a crashing bore. Pyman christened them the 'reluctant debutantes' and was grateful for the expertise of the NCOs, many of whom later gained commissions.[128]

The London Scottish, it should be said, encouraged Fettesians to join, as a letter from their Medical Officer in 1930 illustrates, with its enthusiastic descriptions of 'what a wonderful show it is', what with all the sports, reel-dancing, and a canteen which 'is the friendliest club-room in London.' At least ten OFs had joined recently – 'but we still want more… anyone who doesn't join of his own free will is crazy.'[129]

It was in another letter in 1930 that we have one of the earliest references to fascism in the school magazine. J.S. Fisher, writing from Sicily, dismissed talk of banditry thus: 'Now there are no brigands in Sicily. Mussolini has cleaned them out; they have migrated to Chicago, and beaten their knives into machine guns.'[130]

That stalwart band of current affairs enthusiasts, the revived Debating Society, which Ashcroft encouraged, tackled many of the issues of the day with considerable gusto. Their knowledge of global events was assisted by the wireless, which despite its name revealed its existence in the form of wires festooning the school tower and chimneys – once the school authorities had overcome their suspicion of this potentially subversive medium. Alyster Jackson initially had to keep his crystal set a secret from the masters, but, as with today's innovative pupils who can find ways round the school's internet security, he was much in demand from his colleagues 'when there was a rugger international or if Hibs were playing Hearts.' 'Jerry' Lodge, the former Royal Scots officer turned housemaster, did much to make radio respectable. He set up a wireless station in an old dormitory under the College roof, where boys could 'listen in' to whatever they liked; 'all that is necessary is to push in a plug or two, turn a few dials, ring up the Exchange – as you were, that is the method for the telephone – and then a varied programme is ready for them.'[131]

The fact that other listeners' efforts to tune in made a 'jolly noise, reminiscent of a beaten puppy' did not detract from the excitement of hearing news of the cabinet, the stock exchange or the London Hippodrome. Scottish nationalism was one topic mischievously discussed – although organisationally its modern form is considered to date from 1927 and the formation of the Glasgow University Scottish Nationalist Association, since 1919 the *Fettesian* had been carrying letters demanding that, as a Scots school, Fettes ought to fly the Saltire. This exciting raw nerve was enthusiastically prodded by the Ulster loyalist Knox Cunningham, who argued that Glasgow, fifty per cent of whose inhabitants were drunk on Saturday nights, was a disgrace to civilisation, and the only reason Scottish education was any good was because English masters, out of love, taught in its schools.[132]

J.R. Cuthbert, whose father lived in Belize, responded with all the ferocity of the expatriate, suggesting that an Irishman could hardly call anyone else a savage: 'Cunningham had very little ground to stand on, and when 12½ stone was in that predicament it was disastrous.' I.F.H. Boyd added with cavalier disregard for chronology that St Patrick, a Scot, took Christianity to Ireland, and, when he left the country, Sinn Fein developed. It was also pointed out that Cunningham could hardly know what it was like on Scottish streets at night when in Ireland you could be arrested for going out after midnight. Scotland's merits were debated again in 1930, with witty sallies from Mr Pyatt and various other masters who argued that the bagpipes were invented by an Irishman, who for a joke (which they still hadn't got) told the Scots they were a musical instrument. Against this, it was argued that there should be a Memorial to the Flying Scotsman, since the country had lost more good men travelling south on that technological wonder of the age than she had in the war.[133]

A sign of how the world had changed was the debate on whether Americans should stay at home – proposed by Donald Crichton-Miller, who was later to be Headmaster of Fettes – and full of references to chewing-gum, obnoxious tourists and slang, which were countered by comments on democracy, sporting prowess and the contrast between British snobbery and the well-meaning Americans. America cropped up repeatedly in the popular culture of the school, with poetry which referred to gangsters, jazz, cinema and the other delights coming across the Atlantic; by contrast, one of the only references to Germany in the 1920s was when, in a debate on whether or not a boy might keep his study in as dishevelled a state as he chose, enthusiasts for hygiene were condemned for their 'Prussianism'. A later debate covered the idea of a Channel Tunnel, and a rather twenty-first century fear of hordes of European immigrants on one-way tickets (from Germany, Scandinavia and Poland) was voiced by J. M. M'Neill, one of the masters. Unlike their forefathers, who debated the issue in 1882, the 1920s Fettesians rejected a Channel Tunnel. In October 1929, the Society debated whether 'in the event of another European war, we shall all be conscientious objectors.' Sadly, those who pursue an insight into the serious growth of pacifism among educated Britons through the minutes of the F.C.D.S. are likely to be disappointed. This debate was not of the importance of the notorious Oxford Union motion on the same topic, nor was it conducted with the same level of seriousness. Seconding the motion, W.E. Catto:

...asked the house to look at him and decide whether he was man or worm. The decision was obvious. He then blamed the stress of the war for having produced his horrible bodily state... Modern war was the even more useless than in primitive times; then at least the warriors were cannibals, but the modern soldier only got bully beef! [134]

The mood of the meeting was unfavourable to such subtleties of argument, and there was an interesting flash of the old Social Darwinism which had creepily popped up in pre-war discussions. J.M. Kenion rose to say that 'he had, as requested, looked at the hon. seconder of the motion, and he was more than ever convinced that destructive war was the only means of preserving their own standards of the race.' A.G. Baird 'whose mincing manner and daintiness of diction assorted ill with the terrible contents of his speech', said that our civilization was a mere varnish over the uncontrollable desires for slaughter and carnage.' J.H.T.

Maxwell weighed judicially the pros and cons of the situation; war wasted money, 'but it led to beneficial inventions and clearances of superfluous population.' Alongside these rather disturbing, vaguely fascist points, were the usual diatribes against 'conchies' as 'merely unpatriotic shirkers whose objectionable consciences prevent them from facing danger or helping their fellow countrymen in the power of need.' A.W. Wainman valiantly refuted the claim 'that a conscientious objector, a man of strong moral courage, could be in any sense a coward or shirker. War was contrary to all precepts both of religion and of common sense.' He lost by 13 votes to 32. It is probably worth saying that Catto, so ashamed of his feeble failure to live up to the virility of the race, served with distinction in Burma in the following war, and was wounded twice; the robust J.M. Kenion was killed in 1944, fighting for the Gothic Line in Italy.

Fettes' social conscience

For the first time, Fettesians of the 1920s could become involved in public-spirited duties. Although their magazine could blithely dismiss the General Strike of 1926 as a passing fad which had come and gone with little effect – on the school, at any rate – there were plenty of masters and boys well aware of the dire conditions endured by the Scottish poor and determined, in the spirit of muscular Christianity and social duty, to do something about them. In March 1923 the Headmasters of Fettes and Loretto announced that they intended to set up a Poor Boys' Club in Edinburgh with 'social and moral' aims, and appealed to former pupils for financial and practical assistance. By November of that year they could announce that they had found premises at 24b St Giles St, near David Bryce's Roman-Baroque Bank of Scotland, and equipped it with a gymnasium, a reading-room, and ping-pong and billiard tables. They appealed to past and present pupils to send in such boxing-gloves, chess sets, books and other delights, and appointed two old soldiers to run it – W. 'Nunky' Hewetson Brown, formerly of the RAMC, and Sergeant-Major Oliver, late of the Argyll and Sutherland Highlanders.[135]

In 1924, a report in the *Fettesian* described a visit to the club in glowing terms, taking in its myriad of entertainments and comforts, with boys energetically pursuing all kinds of sports and gymnastics, reading or just enjoying a hot bath – such a popular activity that a time limit of five minutes per person had to be imposed, with bathers forcibly ejected towards a cold spray, 'the popularity of which varied considerably.' Given that the public schoolboys of Fettes rarely experienced hot water, the joy of this novelty for children of Edinburgh's slum districts can only be imagined. Later that year, they held the first of their summer camps, taking 44 boys to Kilconquhar, Fife (now one of the parishes of a former Fettes chaplain); after a Sunday morning church service, conducted by a minister camping nearby and commandeered for the purpose, they threw themselves into sports and exploring – no dour Sabbatarianism here – and spent a healthy week enjoying country life whose only flaw, according to the boys, was its brevity. In its small way, the club provided a valuable resource for at least some boys who otherwise could never have afforded the amusements it offered. An anonymous writer of 1925 (possibly Ashcroft himself), reporting on the longer summer camp of that year, saw the club through the eyes of Old Testament prophets, 'rebellion in the name of the Kingdom of God':

From the scent of new-mown hay to the sweat of one-roomed houses makes rebels of us all. Boys who have seen mountains rightly refuse to be content with blind alleys. Lads who have found life for a fortnight in doing everything can be counted upon to realise that no work means death, and youth will fight rather than die. Men who have seen heaven will inevitably create hell if heaven's gate is really barred.

By starting boys' clubs we do not solve a single problem; we only precipitate the need for solving problems that are old, and thereby lay on ourselves (gladly let us hope) the further responsibility of personally taking part in their solution…

Just to take the boys to camp and to build them baths and to stop there would not be worth while at all; on the contrary, it would be a red-hot mockery. But such was never your purpose. You have made a glorious start – sixty splendid rebels!

Will you help to make it a hundred next year? Will you come in the winter time and the summer time to learn and teach this new rebellion, whose weapons are so much stronger than swords? [136]

The Fet-Lor Club was never to be a Godly revolution, but it did do some good, and it certainly provided an outlet for Old Fettesians who hoped to live up to Dr Potts' ideals of duty. Maj Dick Moncrieff, a devout Christian and Fettes' first thirty-third degree freemason, took his commitment to charity and fraternity very seriously, and was one of the OF stalwarts of the Fet-Lor. In addition to mucking in at the club and its

A Fet-Lor Club member enjoying the seaside

camps for some thirty years, he discreetly helped its members by paying bills and in one case buying a lorry for a young man with an entrepreneurial streak.[137] It was only when he died in 1966 that Fet-Lor 'graduates' came forward to speak of this generosity, the full extent of which is unlikely ever to be known.

Retrospect

Reflecting on the twenties, Robert Bruce Lockhart 'felt a sense of futility and shame', and wondered if the 'Mussolinis and the biologists' who said that war was an inevitable fact of human nature had been right.[138]

Yet his successors at Fettes, relieved of the apprehension of impending or ongoing war, and in relative ignorance of the boiling hatreds of Europe and the strengths of its Mussolinis, took part in military training fairly good-humouredly, but in the belief that it was just another part of school life rather than readiness for inevitable war. Their experiences were certainly more pleasant than those of the wartime generation, whose sufferings were passing into distant folk-memory. John Guest, a rather aesthetic boy, looked back wistfully in his wartime journal of 1943 on his time at the school in the second half of the twenties.

The long green stretches of playing fields, the grass avenues through the woods, the chapel – Sunday evening service and walks in the summer sunset up the hill behind to see Edinburgh melt into grey smoke and flashing windows and the colours drift off the mountains beyond; the quiet of my study, literally a refuge, where I lost myself in the Georgian poets and thrilled to the disturbing voices of a few new ones, and sweated over my own verses; and so many other things – football matches, the noisy dusty classrooms that smelled of ink and sweat, roll calls, concerts in the gym with the stage a bower of begonias and greenery; cricket matches where one made gliders of leaves and lay on rugs under the trees, only occasionally looking up when a master or a prefect passed, to glance at the scoreboard or see the little white figures from whom came the delayed sound, pock, of a ball being hit; and, perhaps most of all, summer O.T.C. camps in the Highlands, heather, pine-trees and salmon leaps; or by the sea, cliffs, rock pools and my most loved wildflowers…[139]

When he revisited the place in 1941, his first reaction was the common response of the adult going back to his old school – fear of breaking the rules, then realisation that this no longer mattered. He arrived during Sunday chapel and waited for the service to finish, listening to 'the solid massed sound of the voices with the trebles soaring in a descant and the rich brilliance of the organ shaking the sunlit windows.' He returned to Carrington to see his housemaster and matron. 'She just looked up without surprise, laid down her knitting and said: "Hello, Guest, and how are you?" – that, after all those years, as though I had just walked in to ask for a dab of iodine!' He felt, as he wandered about his old haunts on that sunny autumn afternoon – when the school is at its most beautiful – 'a hardly definable sadness, as though I had mislaid something valuable and didn't know how to replace it.'[140]

For Guest, the Fettes of the twenties had been in most ways a happy place, and, like so many others faced with the terrible world which came later, he missed it.

NOTES

[1] *Fettesian,* December 1918
[2] Ibid.
[3] Ibid.
[4] Hardie & Macpherson in Pyatt, p. 255 & 246
[5] *Fettesian,* December 1918
[6] Ibid.
[7] C.L. Potts, letter, 24 November 1918, quoted in *Fettesian Centenary Supplement,* 1970
[8] Adam, p. 145
[9] H. Hamilton Fyfe, *The War Illustrated,* 18 January 1919
[10] Robert Bruce Lockhart, *Retreat from Glory* (London, Putnam, 1934) p. 19
[11] *Fettesian,* June 1921
[12] Ibid., November 1921
[13] Ibid., December 1919
[14] Ibid., June 1920
[15] Ibid., July 1921
[16] Macpherson in Pyatt, p. 248
[17] *Fettesian,* March 1921
[18] Ibid., 1986
[19] Hardie in Pyatt, p. 256
[20] Thorpe, p. 20
[21] *Fettesian,* 1986
[22] Reddie, p. 61
[23] Philp, p. 60
[24] *Fettesian,* April 1919
[25] Ibid., November 1920
[26] Ibid., December 1920
[27] Quoted in D.B.McDowell, *A Brief History of Collyer's* (Horsham, 2002)
[28] *Fettesian,* July 1915
[29] This is how the *Fettesian* reported his loss at the time. Hay later said that the ship had struck a mine off the Hebrides.
[30] Minutes of Meeting of War Memorial Executive Committee, 7 November 1917 (School Archive)
[31] Minutes of Meeting of Old Fettesians, 21 January 1918 (School Archive)
[32] Rev. Dr. W.A. Heard, Founder's Day Speech, 1919 (School Archive)
[33] *Fettesian,* November 1920
[34] Quoted in ibid., November 1921
[35] Ibid., December 1921
[36] Ibid., June 1929
[37] Ibid., November 1919
[38] Ibid., July 1919
[39] Hay (1917) p. 285
[40] See Devine (1999) Ch. 14

[41] *Fettesian*, December 1918

[42] Ibid., March 1919

[43] Ibid., November 1921

[44] Ibid., December 1947

[45] Ibid., July 1921

[46] Ibid., April 1921

[47] Lockhart (1931) p. 165

[48] E.H. Wilcox, *Russia's Ruin* (New York, Scribner, 1919) p. 249

[49] Lockhart (1934) p. 23

[50] *The War Illustrated*, 8 February 1918

[51] *Fettesian*, July 1920

[52] Sir S. Knox Cunningham in H.F. MacDonald (ed.) *A Hundred Years of Fettes* (Edinburgh, Constable, 1970), p. 176

[53] *Fettesian*, July 1922

[54] Adam, p. 56

[55] *Fettesian*, March 1924

[56] I am grateful to Dr John M. Regan of the University of Dundee, who has made a special study of the Bandon Valley killings, for clarifying this school mystery.

[57] See, for instance, Jack Lane, *Sean Moylan — was he a rebel?* (Cork, Aubane Historical Society, 2010) p. 20

[58] Robert Bruce Lockhart, *Friends, Foes & Foreigners* (London, Putnam, 1957) p. 16

[59] *OFNL*, November 2005

[60] Alyster Jackson, (Unpublished) Memoirs, Henderson Archive

[61] *Fettesian*, June 1919

[62] Bond, p. 146

[63] *Fettesian*, December 1921

[64] Lawrie, *Fettes College Register (5th Ed.)*

[65] Clayton, p. 197

[66] C.A. Jenkins, *Days of a Dogsbody* (London, Harrap, 1946) p. 17

[67] *Fettesian*, November 1924

[68] Ibid., April 1926

[69] Norval Mitchell, *Sir George Cunningham* (Edinburgh, Blackwood, 1968) pp. 27-8

[70] Quoted in ibid., p. 33

[71] Ibid., p. 37

[72] Ibid., p. 40

[73] *Fettesian*, December 1920

[74] J.D.R. Rawlings, *The History of the Royal Air Force*, (London, Temple Press, 1984) p. 33

[75] See Gabriel Warburg, *Islam, Sectarianism and Politics in Sudan since the Mahdiyya* (London, Hurst, 2003) p.88

[76] *Fettesian*, June 1921

[77] W. Ewing, *Paterson of Hebron* (1931) quoted in *Fettesian*, June 1931

[78] Ibid., December 1920

[79] Quoted in Warren Hope, *Norman Cameron: his Life, Work & Letters* (London, Greenwich Exchange, 2000) p. 48

[80] *Fettesian*, July 1967

[81] Ibid., June 1926

[82] Ibid., December 1930

[83] Ibid., March 1919
[84] Ibid., April 1919
[85] *The War Illustrated*, 30 November 1918
[86] Lockhart (1934) p. 216
[87] Ibid., p. 218
[88] Ibid., p. 56
[89] Ibid., p. 59
[90] Ibid., p. 280
[91] Ibid., p. 62
[92] *Fettesian*, December 1919
[93] Ibid., July 1921
[94] Ibid., June 1921
[95] Ibid., April 1921
[96] Ibid., November 1919
[97] Ibid., November 1920
[98] Ibid., November 1919
[99] Ibid., June 1920
[100] Ibid., June 1921
[101] Sheffield, p. 8
[102] Paul Kennedy, *The Realities Behind Diplomacy* (London, Fontana, 1981) p. 241
[103] Sheffield, p. 10
[104] Ibid., December 1925
[105] Ibid., July 1926
[106] G. Morrison in MacDonald, p. 196
[107] Murray Hunter, (Unpublished) Memoirs, Henderson Archive
[108] I.A.H. Moore in MacDonald, p. 193
[109] G. Morrison in MacDonald, p. 196
[110] *Fettesian*, November 1929
[111] Ibid., November 1930
[112] Ibid., November 1926
[113] Ibid., April 1923
[114] Ibid., June 1923
[115] Ibid., July 1924
[116] Ibid., June 1925
[117] Ibid., April 1929
[118] A. Jackson, (Unpublished) Memoirs, Henderson Archive
[119] *Fettesian,* November 1926
[120] Ibid., November 1941
[121] Pyman, p. 17
[122] *OFNL* Nov. 2005
[123] Ibid., July 2000
[124] Jenkins, p. 64
[125] Roy Jenkins, *The Chancellors* (London, Macmillan, 1998) p. 379
[126] *Fettesian,* July 1926
[127] Ibid., March 1923
[128] Pyman, p. 18
[129] *Fettesian*, December 1930

[130] Ibid., February 1930
[131] Ibid., November 1923
[132] Ibid.
[133] Ibid., February 1930
[134] Ibid., November 1929
[135] Ibid., November 1923
[136] Ibid., November 1925
[137] Ibid., July 1966
[138] Lockhart (1934) p. 367
[139] John Guest, *Broken Images – a Journal* (London, Longman, 1949) p.134
[140] Guest, pp. 61–3

Chapter Nine

'Your friends looked at you oddly if you weren't in the TA'

The Road to the Second World War

The Kraken wakes

In 1934, the *Fettesian* carried a review of Robert Bruce Lockhart's *Retreat from Glory* which noted that the book ended 'on a note of warning and depression.'[1]

In the book, Lockhart described a meeting in 1929 with Gustav Stresemann, the most prominent of inter-war Germany's democratic leaders, who declared bitterly that he could have carried the German people with him and with democracy had the British made more concessions and not continually sided with the French in a vindictive position – a problem which had exercised Lockhart since the early twenties. 'Nothing remains now except brute force,' he concluded, 'The future is in the hands of the new generation.'[2]

Just after meeting the dying statesman, Lockhart lunched with a friend at Wannsee, outside Berlin. As he was drinking tea, he was disturbed by the sound of marching feet. Down the road came a band of young men dressed in brown shirts, whose 'physique compared very favourably with that of British youth.' His friend explained that they were National Socialists – 'young fools' who no-one took seriously. Lockhart was not so sure.

Despite this unhappy premonition of what Auden called a 'low dishonest decade', many Fettesians thoroughly enjoyed the 1930s. Popular folk-memory of Scotland in that era is split; one version focuses on the grim conditions on the Clyde, devastated by unemployment and presided over by bewildered, cowardly politicians who spent their time crawling feebly before Hitler and Mussolini. At the other extreme is a vague idea, based on television mini-series and the works of P.G. Wodehouse, that people in the thirties were glamorous sybarites, flitting from party to party in evening-dress and Rolls-Royces, smoking cigarettes in long holders and desperately trying to catch the eye of the Prince of Wales.

For bourgeois intellectuals, reared on the works of Orwell, it was a decade of Manichean struggle against fascism, epitomised by Pollitt's suggestion to Spender that the most useful thing he could do for his cause was 'go to Spain and get killed – we need a Byron in the movement.' Yet it was still an age when, despite the attention-grabbing views of left- or right-wing activists, most people celebrated Armistice Day with religious reverence; Alyster Jackson recalled how all London could come to a silent standstill for two minutes every 11 November, the population rigidly at attention, hats off, cigarettes extinguished, trains halted.[3]

How much of this was understood by Fettesians cannot be proved. Doubtless the 'Fet-Lor' Club did expose the more public-spirited boys to life's brutal realities, though it did comment plaintively that it wasn't getting as many visitors from the school as it used to.[4]

One can be sure that the more adventurous sixth-formers must have pined for a world of dinner-jackets, cocktails and androgynous females, but they were a minority. 'There must be many Fettesians of those years whose knowledge of Edinburgh and its people is nearly nil'[5] Morrison wrote, whilst one of his successors was to comment that the school was 'too introspective… the red railings surrounding the grounds did more than delimit permitted territory; they shut out the surrounding world.'[6]

Also in a minority were those boys who applied their minds to the sinister, increasingly militaristic, geopolitics of the decade. Most boys were – as is normal – primarily interested in the day-to-day distractions of house rivalries revolving largely around sport, which, as Ian Harvey noted, 'had all the trappings of a religion… cultural activities were not frowned upon but they were the province of the few.'[7]

A number were also interested in learning things. 'Later generations might visualise the thirties at Fettes as a period of unrelieved fear and gloom,' recalled Morrison, 'But what memory recalls is a series of quiet years which may indeed have borne a close resemblance to that other halcyon period forever lost – the years before 1914.'[8]

A poem in 1935 summed up the apolitical hedonism to which those in the thirties who could afford it, and indeed countless millions who couldn't, aspired:

How I love this modern music, how I revel in the yells

Of syncopating niggers, and the notes of saxophones.
I adore the clash of cymbals, and I love discordant bells,
I simply rave about the trumpet's muted groans.
I'm modern, I'm jazzy, I'm blah,
I'm the epitome of everything that's bad,
I'm irreligious, flighty, and completely void of brain,
But I'm a perfect gentleman, a sahib, sir, and a cad.

I neglect the Ten Commandments and I'm always telling lies,
I break with great abandon all the laws of School and Man,
I laugh at all the patriots, and their sentimental prize,
I devour all the books which have a ban.
I'm sordid, I'm horrid, I'm rude,
I'm claimed by all my masters as a fool.
I never do my work and I'm aesthetically void,
But I'm the perfect product of the British Public School.[9]

The less superficially cynical 'A cry of youth' appeared in the *Fettesian* of November 1937:

I'm a member of the younger generation;
I'm told I should be knocking at the door,
But that's a very stupid occupation,
And what should I be knocking at it for?

When Spain's a seething mass of tribulation,
While Japan and China struggle on the floor,
When Mussolini wants a better nation,
Why do we poor devils hammer on the door?

There are better things to do than all this knocking,
At a door that isn't really there at all.
Why, every European nation's rocking,
And every ruling party's going to fall.

Why has the modern world got indigestion?
Who's furnishing the Polish corridor?
Can Mr Eden solve the Eastern question?
Or is there going to be another war?

341

No, we haven't got much time for modern history;
We're much too busy knocking at the door.
I suppose they'll hear us soon, but it's a mystery
Why they haven't heard us hammering before.[10]

The Corps prepares for war

In this age of uncertainty, the OTC did try to carry on with the military tradition, not always with great efficiency, on the grounds, as an inspecting officer told them, that 'The type of man who had gone through a public school, who had taken orders from others and given orders, who had spent two hours a week in arduous drilling voluntarily, that was the man who was most likely to serve his country best in the time of need.'[11] A 1931 report on an inter-house tactical exercise noted that 'there was a tendency to be over-cautious when the enemy was still at a distance' but it is probably stretching a point to see this as proof of latent pacifism.[12]

The 1933 Efficiency Cup inspection by some officers and NCOs of the Argyll and Sutherland Highlanders was generally positive but noted that the right markers were a bit slow and that not all platoons remembered the importance of clean hands. Part of the competition was the Tactical Scheme, an exercise in decision-making and analysis based around a scenario which was described in detail:

The enemy are expected to effect a landing at Granton on March 6 or 7.
Your battalion has been ordered to provide the outposts for the Brigade which is billeting today in Edinburgh.
Frontage from Craigleith Hospital to Botanical Gardens inclusive.
Your company is the left forward company, with a frontage from Craigleith Hospital to Fettes College Main Building.
Your platoon is the right forward platoon, with a frontage from Crewe Road exclusive to Fettes College (the left forward platoon is responsible for the Crewe Road.)
1.   Platoon Commander: give the approximate dispositions for your four sections.
2.   L.G. Section Commander: (a) lead your section to its post, and indicate the positions to be occupied by each of your six men. (b) A shell bursts near the post and wounds the Section Commander; ask any one in the section what he thinks should be done.
3.   Rifle Section Commander: (a) Explain how you would draw up a Range

Card, and give a Fire Order. (b) Ask two of the section what they would expect to be told if they were put on sentry duty at night.[13]

General Whigham, addressing the boys on Founder's Day that year, seems to have been concerned about the climate prevailing in the country which was unfavourable to any manifestation of the martial spirit: 'Many people were ignorant of the exact position in which the OTC stood; it was essential for the emergency defence of the country; there was nothing aggressive or militarist about it.'[14] Two days later he returned to this theme in more detail as he inspected the cadets:

He complimented the Corps on its all-round efficiency, and he said he was thoroughly satisfied with all he had seen. He went on to say that he intended to show as shortly as he could how the O.T.C. could be reconciled with Disarmament. Disarmament had first been tackled in the Navies, but now it had also been put into effect in the Armies by the decisions reached at Geneva a year ago. These decisions, though deprecating a large standing army, recognised the fact that, for the present, countries must have a means of mobilising a national army if the need should arise. The means in Britain was the Territorial Army and the O.T.C. It was, of course, extremely unlikely that there would be war in the near future: nevertheless a government would not be doing its duty to its people if they neglected their protection. Moreover, Britain was well within her allotted limits both in her Regular Army and in her Territorial Army. People who wrote to papers about armies and O.T.C.s did not know what their real object was: there was nothing militarist about the O.T.C.; it was only a means of safeguarding the country. The General went on to speak of the Regular Army, and pointed out that it was essentially a police force rather for preserving peace than for breaking it.[15]

The description of the inspection in the summer number of the *Fettesian* was followed by an account of a lecture given to the Certificate A candidates on artillery support for infantry and the following poem by 'Christopher Robin':

> *'Arma Virumque Cano'*
> *Dedication.*
> *To the countless Generals, Colonels and Majors whom the War Office has sent to tell us that the O.T.C. is the only way to stop War, War-Mindedness, and everything to do with War.*

Corps!
Corps!
Sweating, bickering, incompetent Corps!
How I adore
Corps!
I love to be cursed,
To be sworn at, to run till I burst;
It's a wonderful treat
To march past in the heat
With my bayonet fixed
And my shoulder ricksed;
I delight to attend
Parades without end,
To learn, and still less,
To get my hands, my clothes, my mind in a mess,
To pull through my rifle,
Wear tunics that stifle,
To be casually told when I've toiled,
And boiled
In the grass and the fleas
To 'Stand at Ease,
Stand Easy,'
To get myself greasy,
Smell oil
And broil
In the sun,
Double on at a run
Just the same
Again
And again,
To attack in the rain,
Get a cold, do the same
Once again.
'Ugh!' It makes me sick.[16]

The General did not take exception to this, but to what he considered the *Fettesian* reporter's inaccurate account of his speech. In a lengthy letter of August 1933, he not only corrected the mistakes but also added more points. What he had actually said, apparently, was that 'even in sober

344

and respectable journals' there was editorial disparagement of the part Britain had played in the process of disarmament. In fairness to the General, he had a point – the press, especially on the left, constantly vilified Britain's position whilst turning a blind eye to the iniquity of other powers. The Royal Navy's tonnage had been slashed by 47 per cent whereas that of fascist Italy, Britain's rival for control of the Mediterranean, had been cut by only 20 per cent. The Regular Army had lost 29,000 men. As with the era of pre-1914 peace, this arguably made the role of the Corps in forming a pool of trained manpower for future emergencies all the more necessary. Unlike the years before the Great War, however, there was a pacifist mood abroad which despised any manifestation of military activity – and which was in turn despised by Hitler and Mussolini, who saw war as the expression of the Darwinian process and became convinced that liberal capitalism was so decadent that it could easily be crushed. 'Christopher Robin' would not have been allowed to express his subversive, bolshie opinions in an Italian or German school magazine. Nor would an Italian or German school have welcomed Mr A. Wilson, who gave a lecture on the League of Nations and disarmament. He drew attention to the profligate waste of money on weapons in which he (unlike General Whigham) believed Britain to be indulging – it would take a man working trade union hours two hundred years to throw this expenditure away at a shilling a second, a somewhat odd image but one which mightily impressed the boys.[17]

Even OFs were occasionally moved to write in opposition to cadet activity, with a letter from 'A.M.M.' in June 1933 claiming that they were 'the greatest deterrent to Disarmament and World Peace that remain unopposed' and that the values they taught were undermined by the fact that they were fundamentally a compulsory form of military service for schoolboys.[18]

In 1935, the *Fettesian* carried a spoof article purporting to come from its July 1980 edition, 'on Fettes College Joining the League for Total Disarmament':

OBITUARY
At Fettes College, on 1ˢᵗ July 1980, O.T. Corps. Funeral Private. No mourning by request.
It is with great grief that we note the passing of that loyal citizen and honoured servant of the School, O.T. Corps…
O.T. Corps was one of those who helped foster and maintain that ever-happy

spirit of inter-house competition. He also fostered in us the spirit and desire to wear our national dress; of firm character, Corps was always adamant; never would he let us have the better of an argument, and he taught us that what is must be, and that we must always face life with a stiff upper lip and quell those muttered curses behind the strong barrier of our teeth. When we sat in dark classrooms, shivering at the hail and wet outside, the thought of a pleasant afternoon with Corps acted as an immediate tonic…[19]

An 'Over-worked' pupil wrote in 1937 that whilst he would like to absolve himself from charges of being '(a) a pacifist or (b) merely a lazy shirker', he really did think that the Leavers' Examinations were rather more urgent than inter-house Corps competitions, which took up rather more than the couple of sessions per week officially allocated. The housekeeping for the competition was onerous, as Murray Hunter recalled in 2002:

For this each platoon had to perform all the drills they had learnt, and all uniform and gear was minutely inspected. Boots, brass buttons and brass belt fittings had to be mirror-bright, and rifles 'bright clean and slightly oiled.' The trickiest area was the legs. Stockings had to be exactly symmetrical with the front central line of the diced pattern perfectly centred on the shin. The tops of the stockings had to be folded over at exactly the correct height, two fingers-widths below the small bone that can be felt on the outside of the leg about a hands-width below the knee. The garters were hidden under the fold, but the flashes attached to them had to cut exactly the middle of the next diamond out from the centre. The puttees were difficult because their length took about three turns round the leg, which had to be started so that the finish brought the base of the triangular endpiece exactly in line with the front central line. Any deviations lost marks for the platoon.[20]

Meanwhile, the messages given by the Army to the cadets were, unsurprisingly, often based on the lessons of the Great War. One military lecturer told the Certificate A candidates that for all its merits, artillery must remain an auxiliary weapon; 'the chief weapon in attack in the bayonet, and in defence the machine-gun'.[21]

Morrison noted that it was at OTC camp 'that the black cloud of disaster loomed most heavily on the little world of school, as the fresh wind of the Fifeshire coast rustled the flaps of the marquee where, in the stuffy, canvas-smelling shade, a bemedalled officer in tartan trews pointed with his cane to the latest infantry weapon – the new Czech Bren gun.'[22]

That said, in the mid-thirties, it was easy for the shadow to disappear 'after a sunlit afternoon spent swimming by the seaweed-encrusted rocks, followed by fish and chips from the village shop (and cigarettes for the bold)...' In February 1937 an OF, Lt D.A. Duke, gave a demonstration of the Bren, including both the wrong and right ways of going into action. The following month, he arranged for thirty cadets to visit Glencorse Barracks – owing to the SMT bus strike, they had to use transport 'begged, borrowed or stolen from the Caledonian Motor Traction Company.' This was an interesting exploration of the minutiae of the soldier's life, from incessant drill and physical jerks to the apparently amazing efficiency of the stores, which had issued each of the Royal Scots reservists recently dispatched to Palestine with complete kit ('from rifles to socks to razor blades') in twenty minutes. Military exercises ensued in the form of a vigorous snowball fight with the troops. A Sergeant gloomily informed the boys that, although recruits 'seem to enjoy themselves on the whole, once they get in the Army... it is terribly difficult to get them to join even when they are "down and out" with no prospect of getting jobs.'[23]

The traditional British notion that there was something faintly disreputable about soldiering had clearly returned. Ian Hay, the OF schoolmaster turned novelist turned soldier turned propagandist, was appointed War Office Director of Public Relations in 1938 with a brief to reverse this depressing trend. Nonetheless, even by 1937 *Fettesians* were recording a rise in Army promotions for OFs, eleven being noted with pride in the June edition. One, Harcourt McWilliam, came to visit and display his full uniform, including sword. In July of that year, a Fettes contingent paraded before George VI at the Edinburgh Royal Review. 'The King was wearing Admiral's uniform with the green riband of the Thistle, the Queen (in pale blue) was bowing very charmingly – at least six members of the Contingent claim the honour of a personal smile – and the Princesses looked interested and very pretty in pink.'[24]

After a march-past by all the regular and reserve military units of the city, Fettes, behind the Academy, took their turn to salute the King – 'definitely a great moment!' – and were overjoyed to see him return the compliment, 'the Queen still smiling, and the little Princesses apparently still interested in soldiers.' Of such encounters are schoolboy memories made. The brush with disaster – one of the pipers' sporrans had 'broken its strap by sheer malice' and had been 'held in place by sheer will-power alone until the Saluting Point was safely passed' – made it all the more exciting. The band piped them back to school, marching along Princes Street to the West End and along Queensferry Road to Comely Bank 'taking no notice whatever of policemen or traffic lights.' The 1937 camp at Elie was 'both efficient and enjoyable' though the new motorised platoon organisation did require more creativity to work than the old bayonet charges against trenches:

…we were followed by bicycles representing platoon trucks. It is to be feared, however, that this representation was not wholly convincing, for on the training areas too much has to be imagined, and to visualise from a humble bicycle a truck loaded with Bren Guns, ammunition, entrenching tools, et hoc genus omne, *is difficult for an amateur Company Commander.*[25]

In general, John Younie remembered, the Corps carried on unchanged in the six years before war broke out, but it was 'perfectly sound training for an infantry officer – the true heroes of war.'[26]

Fettes, the Empire and the World

There is a characteristic reference to the Corps in the *Fettesian* Christmas number to the war scare of 1937, when, as the editorial put it, 'Mussolini and Goering are getting together to discuss their next bombshell'. Apparently, because of the daily spit-and-polish round of button-cleaning on the old-style uniforms, 'everyone wanted war; in war-time you get the buttons painted black.'[27]

What, then, did the 1930s Fettesians know of the outside world? The school magazine carries rather fewer of the articles about military derring-do in the Empire which had been so popular in the Victorian era. 'It was an inescapable fact,' commented D.J. Grant, who was at Fettes from 1935 to 1940 and later became Chairman of Darlington Chemicals, 'That despite an unceasing flow of talent and endeavour the frequency of Rugger Blues and International Caps had fallen to a level previously unknown. Might this not presage a similar decline in the representation of Fettes on the Viceroy's Council and also in other seats of responsibility and authority?'[28]

There were some imperial notes. A letter from Calcutta in 1931 listed no fewer than two dozen non-military OFs living in India, a mixture of businessmen, administrators, teachers and policemen who had a good golf team.[29]

The anonymous author of the letter concluded with a traditional

Fettes imperial invitation: 'Life in the East is very pleasant, and there is always plenty of exercise to be had – cricket, tennis, golf, soccer, hockey, and during the rains a short season of rugger.' One can only guess at what lay behind references to a rarely-seen chap who 'is said to live in more than oriental splendour' and another's assurances about 'false rumours circulated to rob him of his stainless reputation.' In 1932, another eight or so OFs were at various locations in Malaya, and three took part in the Burma Golf Championship, one of whom, J.L. Esplen, won it. However, increasing numbers of Fettesians were looking across the Atlantic. In March 1932 no less than twenty OFs were listed in various occupations (mostly farming but with a few accountants and engineers) in 'the Argentine.'[30]

A lecture that October by a diplomat from the British embassy in Buenos Aires persuaded they boys that this 'great South American Republic' was well worth seeing. The November 1932 Fettesian carried a lengthy article by the Anglo-Canadian Education Committee urging British boys to apply to university in Canada, 'the Dominion which is most likely to make the earliest recovery from the present world depression.'[31]

It listed a host of advantages to this choice and summarised them as follows:

1. *Smaller outlay before qualification.*
2. *Greater opportunities for partial self-support by vacation work.*
3. *Greater incentive to work owing to the competitive atmosphere.*
4. *Greater freedom of living conditions.*
5. *Greater opportunities after graduation in the rapidly developing industries and commerce of the country.*
6. *Experience of new-world methods and ideas.*

Although the committee emphasised that this course should be embarked upon only by 'a boy with the right temperamental qualities of adaptability and unpretentiousness' it is extraordinary how up-to-date such advice still is.

This did not mean that attitudes were becoming especially progressive. In November 1934, an OF wrote from Peshawar, where he was serving with the 2nd HLI, to say that the first thing one did on arriving in one's post was to collect a 'wog' who would then find 'tents, camp-food cook, food and a stretch of river' where one can go fishing.[32]

'Considering that it is entirely wog run' he continues with breezy indifference to the *Fettesian* editor's squeamishness ('is it really a "wog"?' he inserts, 'My dictionary fails me') 'I must say Kashmir in the city of Srinagar is very up to date.' Such arrogance was not confined to the younger generation. Sailing east in 1935, Lockhart was delighted to see that the Dutch crew had chalked up the result of the England-Wales match. This turned out to have been the doing of a fellow-passenger, an OF in his sixties called Hewan, who had complained to the director of the steamship company, who had telephoned Britain for the result. Bruce Lockhart felt this was typical of Dutch politeness, but wondered how an English captain would have said, the previous year, to a foreigner who had demanded the result of the Italy-Czechoslovakia World Cup game.[33]

But then, as he noted, sport was a 'ruling passion' for Fettesians, and *civis Britannicus sum* had the status of a world passport. The 'Vive-la' for 1934 noted an India-based OF's success:

> *In India the trophy most prized, so they say,*
> *Is the cup called the Kadir, this year won by Gray:*
> *In this pig-sticking contest the Army's elite*
> *Had to bow to our subaltern's wonderful feat.*[34]

This was Lt (later Col) Charles Gray of Skinner's Horse, who had been drum-major of the pipe band at Fettes and subsequently joined the Indian Army. During the Second World War, he wrote about the wonderful feat and the article was republished sixty years later by the Old Fettesians 'partly because of its inherent interest and partly because of its reminder of a long vanished world.' Gray was riding Granite, as he called the flecked grey gelding from Australia he had borrowed for the purpose from regimental trumpeter Hardwari Singh:

When I competed there was a record entry of 120 horses on the card - almost all being Cavalry Officers from British and Indian regiments, together with several Gunners. Riders drew for places in heats of four, taking their turns on the line - left, central and right, each with an Umpire carrying a red flag. There were about 300 beaters on foot and, behind them, some 20 elephants used as moving grandstands for spectators - the whole scene sweeping across the riverine terrain in an area where many wild pig had been driven in from the surrounding country during the previous week.

As a rideable boar got up, the nearest Umpire followed with his heat and shouting, 'Do you all see him? NOW RIDE,' dropped his flag and away they galloped - competing for first spear, the winner to show blood on his spear-point to the Umpire, putting him into the next round. Heat followed heat over the next three days until the final was reached - in my year by three riders. Granite was in his element and, with his greyhound qualities and speed, he took me into the final.

A large boar soon got up in the final run, breaking back through the line of the beaters and elephants, with Roscoe [Harvey, of the 10th Royal Hussars] *and me in flat-out pursuit. Our target came back to us rather quickly and we both reached for him together in one dual swooping lunge. My spearpoint hit the boar's quarter, turning him so that Roscoe's thrust hit the ground - bad luck for him. We both stopped, dismounted and Roscoe sportingly wrung my hand while the Umpire, Mr. Lobb Parr, signalled with his flag to the line of elephants 'Granite wins.' It was a great moment for me, only made possible by my marvellous horse – for he had won the Kadir Cup – on that memorable day. He was then 15 and I was 24.*[35]

Sir George Cunningham, one of the Edwardians, became Governor of the North-West Frontier Province in 1937, at roughly the same time that W.H. Beaton, on service in Singapore, was accidentally killed; Major Arbuthnott won the DSO for conspicuous gallantry in Palestine (where Arab-Jewish tension had been an issue for over a decade) in 1938. Nonetheless, there was a marked decline in the number of tales from either administrators or soldiers in the tropics. The *Fettesian* carried the obituaries of the old guard, but relatively little information came from their successors. Indeed, one retiring OF, W.D.C.L. Purves, wrote rather peevishly when he retired from the Sudan Political Service in 1938 that he was going to settle in Africa, but 'I only wish more of our kith and kin would realise how much more you get for your money there than in these islands. They are crying out for more settlers…'[36]

A poem appeared from India, supposedly written by three colonels, in 1937 decrying the fact that Fettes could not produce what it had in Victoria's day:

I spent my adolescence
At a school that was the essence
Of manly virtue, honour and esteem,
And I'm horrified to hear,

As I did the other year,
That it can't turn out a single polo team.

Give us polo!
We're not solo
When we want our school to have a polo team.[37]

At another climatic extreme but around the same time, Patrick Ashley Cooper became Governor of the Hudson's Bay Company, and carried out a tour of its Canadian outposts on the *Nascopie*, looking at the fur-trading posts, presenting gifts to the Inuit and reviewing social conditions. Despite this and other proofs of the benevolence which the British liked to believe underpinned their Imperial Mission, by this stage there was a great deal of nationalism among their subject peoples. This was not least because, in order to run such a vast enterprise, a layer of non-white businessmen, administrators, journalists, teachers, lawyers and doctors had come into being, and they didn't like being referred to as 'wogs.' Nationalist pressures were undoubtedly being felt by the author of the 1931 letter; amongst the jollity, several OFs were trying to cope with real problems. W.D.R. Prentice (a member of the Bengal Legislative Council) had been given responsibility for 'confining political agitators in prison for indefinite periods of time' and had a 'bag' running 'well into the thousands.' Policeman R.G. Watling was 'one of those to whom credit must be given that India is not in a far worse state than it is today.' K.F. Jenkins of the Ceylon police, however, had no concerns about politics: 'he finds that native servants are an ideal continuation of the fagging system, and has now quite forgotten how to lace up his own shoes.' To be fair, Jenkins was not just lazing around at the Police Bungalow in Ratnabura, where he was second-in-command – he was teaching rugby football to the natives, starting with sevens but hoping to move up to full-scale games. Although Pyman, for one, kept his head down with regard to these political matters (he had more than enough to keep himself busy elsewhere, he said) within a generation, there would be hardly any OFs running large slices of India or Africa; within two generations, there would be none at all.

Robert Bruce Lockhart, revisiting his old Malayan haunts in 1935, sensed decline in the air. Life now was very comfortable for the expatriates, which he believed might sap the rugged manliness which had won the Empire in the first place. They preferred the comforts of town to showing the flag up-country, and 'form attractions with young women of their own class at a far earlier age in life than they used to do' and pen-pushing accountants meant that they devoted themselves to business in the heat of the day, then wasted the productive cool of the early evening drinking 'pahit' (spirits and bitters), a habit which he believed was 'mainly responsible for that absence of intellectual interests which is a defective feature of British colonial life.'[38]

The younger generation was also in danger of letting the side down sartorially; once, they had been immaculately clad in white suits, but by the thirties 'the European's undress uniform, seen almost invariably on the golf course and occasionally even in Raffles, is the shortest of shorts, a sleeveless shirt, and white stockings or socks...'[39]

This was not a good idea if the white man was to maintain prestige in an Oriental city, but the women were even worse, since 'the Oriental's respect for the white man's woman decreases in inverse proportion to the amount of her body she exposes', the 'alluring semi-nudity of a film houri duplicated in the strangely scant attire of fashionable tourists passing through Singapore' was leading Britain's imperial subjects to believe that 'the white man is not what he was.'[40]

Women were also sitting around in idleness, playing bridge and tennis, gardening (which he admitted did at least make the place look smarter) and, worst of all, sharpening class divisions by insisting on 'a replica of the same social life that exists in Britain... a disturbing and undesirable feature.' He rather pined for the old days when the planters could live pleasantly productive lives, could flout social conventions as they pleased, and 'there were no white women to interfere with the prevailing code of pleasure.'[41]

For old times' sake, he revisited Malay Street in Singapore, and found the licensed brothels gone; although accepting that it was a cleaner and healthier city than in his day, he worried about British servicemen. They either caught diseases from unregulated women or engaged in risky adulterous affairs. On the whole, however, although the white man's prestige in the East had 'declined in startling fashion', the armed forces' presence in Malaya, developing impressive defences against a possible Japanese attack, had done much to recover the 'former glamour.'[42]

He was impressed that the younger British males, who despite the corrosive effects of their shabby dress and the presence of white women were keeping fit through rugger and joining the local volunteer forces. He also found the new Malay Regiment 'impressive and slightly terrifying' and was confident that the new defences were impregnable. This rare optimism in his inter-war output turned out to be rather more misplaced than the gloomy prognostications of his writing about Europe.

These Fettes cadets photographed in the thirties look as if they are about to be shipped to the colonies, but are simply relaxing at a seaside camp in Scotland; their sun-helmets would soon disappear from western tropical dress forever

Fettesians' peacetime adventures overseas still provided significant casualty lists for the school magazine thanks to the old enemies of accident and disease. In 1931, for example, Lt David Simpson, a strapping player for the school XV and later the army, died of pneumonia whilst serving with the KOSB.[43] A few months later, Lt Ian Ferguson, PT Supervisor to the Egyptian Command, succumbed to the same illness in Cairo. Charles Leresche, formerly of the Royal Navy, latterly of the Indian Railways, died in an accident whilst inspecting the Hungarian State Iron and Steel Works at Miskoloc that summer, and A.W. Rose of the West African Medical Service was lucky to survive an infection acquired from a rabid dog on which he was conducting a post-mortem in Lagos. Grizzled veteran Maj Robert Ritchie, OBE, who had served with the RAMC in Egypt, Flanders and Italy during the Great War and thereafter on the North-West Frontier, was killed by heat stroke in Shanghai in the summer of 1932.

There were many pieces in the *Fettesian* about exploring, for J.M. Scott, an associate of the celebrated adventurer Gino Watkins (whose posthumous biography he wrote) often sent articles or books about his travels to entertain the boys of his old school. In 1933, for instance, we find him climbing Everest, an attempt which the Tibetans believed doomed to failure and which their Grand Lama initially forbade – partly because he believed it impossible, partly because the mountain gods had been angered by the Mallory-Irvine expedition of 1924.[44]

Scott's book *The Land that God gave Cain* – an account of the Gino Watkins expedition to Labrador – got a rave review from the *Fettesian Literary Supplement* (he also wrote novels, one of which, *Sea Wyf and Biscuit*, was turned into a film starring Richard Burton and Joan Collins). Over the Christmas of 1934, G.C.N. Johnson attempted to be the first person to scale Mount Fettes in New Zealand, named after the school's founder by a nineteenth-century surveyor, Charles Douglas, who had been the great man's nephew. After many adventures he and his comrades, clad, like the school's first mountaineering expedition in the 1920s, in tweed jackets, reached the top, where they buried a school hat-band in a biscuit-tin and, in defiance of the blanketing fog, enjoyed a hearty lunch and a smoke.[45]

Subsequent experiences as they made the first crossing of the Sierra Range of a twelve-hour blizzard and being trapped foodless and frostbitten in a mountain hut for two days did not, he wrote, give them half as much satisfaction as that first ascent of Mount Fettes. Alexander Glen, whilst still an undergraduate, led a variety of expeditions to the Polar regions, an achievement which would be remembered by the authorities when war came. Not all the OF adventurers were successful. In November 1931, the Hamilton brothers attempted to break the England-Australia air record, but crashed their Puss Moth in fog in Austria.[46] One of the brothers tried again the following year but crashed again in fog, this time in Italy.

Highly impressed, the 'Vive-la' for that year hymned the work of some of these intrepid figures:

> *Glen again to the Arctic as leader will go,*
> *To snap-shot the walrus and sleep in the snow;*
> *While Governor Cooper, who Hudson's Bay rules,*
> *Is Keeper of Seals, and inspects the Whales' Schools.*[47]

Alexander Glen's Spitzbergen expedition of 1933, from his book Young Men in the Arctic, *and a Fettes climbing party on Mont Blanc a few years earlier (note kilt)*

Technology continued to fascinate. The *Fettesian* quoted an article in *Motor Sport* about K.W.B. Sanderson, one of the wartime OFs whose racing achievements were singularly impressive:

Like many others, 'K.W.B.' graduated from motor cycles, and between 1917 and 1922 he was a conspicuous performer in the leading events on a variety of machines, ranging from a 2½ h.p. Enfield to an 8 h.p. Brough Superior and side-car. His first car was a 13.9 h.p. Scripps Booth, and has been succeeded by an A.C., Ariel, Rhode, Riley, Alvis and Singer. To date he has won no fewer that 36 'golds' and first-class awards, 17 cups and special awards, 5 silver medals and one bronze... [48]

As impressive as the victories, surely, is the almost musical list of British manufacturing companies now tragically lost to history. Aviation, needless to say, remained of great interest. Another of the future-predicting poems appeared in 1933 with a thoroughly indulgent vision of tomorrow:

Now in Hall they give you absolutely anything you like,
And the least of us has got his private racing motor bike.
And the Corps is now a Flying Corps (Please notice the recruits
From the dizzy empyrean dropping down by parachutes.) [49]

In 1932, the school hosted a lecture by Oliver Simmonds, MP, one of the most 'air-minded' politicians of the era (hardly surprisingly, since he had worked with Reginald Mitchell) on Flying. He offered the appealing vision of airship flights from London to Paris for £6 6s (£210 today) where passengers 'floating off' could look down on 'that miserable cork in which some few antiquated people still risk their lives'.[50]

There were occasionally opportunities for 'air-minded' boys to take wing; several went flying from Turnhouse, aeroplanes from Leuchars increasingly featured as part of summer camp experience, and a minority of OFs joined the RAF. To give one year as an example, in 1934 K.D. Stanion and A.O.D. Cox successfully passed out of Cranwell as Pilot Officers, and Wing Commander J.C. Russell, DSO, took over 502 (Ulster) Squadron at Aldergrove. B.M. Watt joined de Havilland as an engineer and pilot. Equally, the sharpness of death stabbed OF fliers in this era; a notice in the April 1933 *Fettesian* tells of the death of Robert Brandon Young, whose Westland Wapiti had crashed at Ambala in India on 16 March. Frank Barnwell of the Bristol Aeroplane Company was killed when a light aircraft of his own design crashed on 2 August 1938. His obituary in the *Times* claimed that 'the reputation of the Bristol machine was largely due to his genius in aircraft construction'[51] – just as his F2B fighter had been the first aircraft used by the RAF on its formation in 1918, so his Blenheim bomber would be the first to be used on offensive operations in 1939, and all three of his sons would be killed in the course of the war. Mr Eric Preston, an OF living in Weybridge, had a narrow escape in November 1933 when an aeroplane disintegrated in mid-air above his house; its fuel tank dropped into his garden and exploded, creating a fifty foot wide sea of flame.[52]

Nonetheless, the boys hugely enjoyed the Empire Air Day at Turnhouse in May 1939, thrilling to the Skua dive-bombers, the Gloster Gladiator air battle with Avro Ansons, and the high-speed passes by a Spitfire. Perhaps the greatest thrill was when Richard Humble, a former pupil who had been living in South Africa, zoomed low over the playing fields to drop a message to his old housemaster, Harry Pyatt, having made a special diversion to do so on the last leg of a flight from Cape Town.

The involvement of senior OFs in the great issues of the day helped generate interest in current affairs. W.G. Normand and Douglas Jamieson were Lord Advocate and Solicitor General for Scotland respectively, but the most prominent politician was Sir John Simon, who was Foreign Secretary and heavily involved throughout the thirties in attempting to secure peace. Simon remained in close contact with the school, which he clearly saw as having given him, through its classical education, all the skills needed by a busy Foreign Secretary. In 1934, the *Fettesian* reprinted a new translation of a fragment of Menander which someone at the Foreign Office felt was relevant to the era of (admittedly unsuccessful) collective security and disarmament:

> *Now if each would prepare, as his personal care,*
> *To punish the evil that men did,*
> *And would boldly declare he was ready to share*
> *In the sanctions for those that offended,*
> *Then the wicked would know*
> *They were watched – and go slow –*
> *And aggression would soon be exceedingly rare*
> *Or would even be utterly ended.*[53]

'It is perhaps sufficient to say that it is attributed to a later Simonides' remarked the editor dryly. The unfortunately-worded 1936 'Vive-la' had a rather less sophisticated assessment of Sir John's efforts:

> *At Geneva John Simon has forged many links,*
> *Uniting in friendship Slavs, Slovenes and Chinks* [54]

Simon has not been treated especially well by history; the 'Chinks' certainly had no reason to be fond of him since, as one of the first great appeasers, he favoured a policy of concessions to the Japanese as they rampaged across Manchuria. In 2008, Fettesian fifth-formers taking GCSE History found a David Low cartoon in their paper depicting their distinguished forebear prostrate and applying 'face-saving kit' to a female personification of the League of Nations over whom a jackbooted Japanese soldier was trampling. Roy Jenkins has written that Simon's address to the League of Nations in Geneva urging appeasement of the Japanese was 'probably the most self-damaging speech of his life' though he conceded that this might have been the result of a legal training which required him to pursue his brief – in this case, the Prime Minister's vague idea that there were faults on both sides – with unnecessary rigour.[55]

He infuriated the Air Ministry with an idea about banning military aeroplanes, and managed only an ineffectual protest to Hitler in 1935 over Goering's recreation of the Luftwaffe. In that same year he told a delegation protesting against an England-Germany fixture at White Hart Lane that he 'wanted to uphold England's tradition of keeping sport and politics separate.'[56]

The fact that Sir John was guided by a very real desire to avoid war and to save money in an era of international depression did not cut a great deal of ice with the authors of *Guilty Men*, which named him as one of those responsible for the debacle of 1940. His somewhat forbidding personality did not help; even his brother-appeaser Neville Chamberlain commented that 'I am always trying to like him, and believing I shall succeed when something crops up to put me off' whilst Harold Nicolson described him as 'a toad and a worm'. His contemporaries at Fettes, according to Lockhart, remembered him as 'more of a master's pet than a rugby football stalwart' and his wicket-keeping was poor; 'in manhood the brilliant scholarship is forgotten or taken for granted, but the sins against the Sport God are remembered against us by our schoolboy contemporaries until death.'[57]

Nonetheless, when Simon died in 1954, Fettes genuinely mourned the loss of 'its most distinguished and one of its most loyal sons.'[58] There were many tributes to his legal skills and the quite extraordinary generosity which he showed to others in private. It was agreed that his reputation for 'coldness and contempt for the errors and failures of lesser men' was unfair. Simon was a shy man, emotionally shattered by his first wife's death, and felt uncomfortable with superficial 'friendly goodwill'. A.P. Herbert wrote of him:

Here lies a statesman, cruelly maligned:
Men missed his merit, dazzled by his mind.
He had a heart as well, which few believe;
But then, he did not wear it on his sleeve.

So far as the school was concerned, 'as Attorney-General, Home Secretary and Lord Chancellor, three great offices concerned with the administration of justice, his eminence has never been disputed.' His role as an appeasing Foreign Secretary and Chancellor of the Exchequer was not mentioned, never mind criticised. Fettes thus showed more decency than the rest of British society, which appeared to have forgotten that the policy of appeasement, whose spokesmen were now reviled, had at one time been almost universally popular.

The school's impressive bust of Sir John Simon

Not all prominent former pupils were appeasers; Group-Captain Lachlan Loudon Maclean, a veteran of the Royal Flying Corps and subsequently British Air Representative to the League of Nations, was outraged by German rearmament and briefed Churchill for speeches on Britain's 'frightening unreadiness'.[59] He did not mince words, lambasting the British government's 'wholesale deception and deceit' and 'defeatist policy'. Resigning in 1939 in a flurry of angry newspaper articles, some of which were suppressed, he was recalled before war broke out and commanded bombing and training groups.

The boys did not merely experience the outside world vicariously through reports about adventure, politics or warfare; they also went on little trips to look at it, such as a visit in October 1934 to the Newbattle Colliery, a seriously eye-opening encounter with the cramped and dirty reality of working conditions for a huge number of contemporary Scots. The following month they went to Granton Gasworks and the

Brown Bros. Engineering Factory, which was making the steering gear of the *Queen Mary*. At a more political level, Alec Ashcroft continued with his mission to educate them about it through the medium of outside speakers. These included talks on the League of Nations and its efforts to promote peace (November 1934), European problems in the aftermath of King Aleksandar of Yugoslavia's assassination (February 1935), the work of the Royal National Deep Sea Mission (November 1935), the Anglo-Egyptian Sudan (February 1937), the Japanese invasion of China and the role of the Navy in Imperial Defence (both in February 1938). In February 1934, Professor Arthur Newell of Boston gave a detailed talk about America, explaining the nature of the Wall Street Crash and its impact, and how President Roosevelt, of whom he was clearly an admirer, was trying to clean up the mess. He spoke with feeling about the need for Anglo-American friendship, not based on any 'possibly mythical community of "Anglo-Saxon" blood' but on something deeper, what Lord Bryce called 'intellectual and moral influence'.[60]

This was clearly something of a jibe at those who believed in racial spirit, a common faith at the time even in Britain. Were Fettesians conscious of the obdurate pride and steadfast hate being preached in Europe at this time? Ian Harvey, noting that he had gone up to Oxford when Hitler became German Chancellor, commented 'not that there was any great significance in that'; however, there is considerable evidence that a reasonable number of pupils were aware of fascism even at this stage. John Younie remembers that 'we were not politically conscious, but we knew of Hitler's rearmament and military parades – and his ambitions… war was just something that was likely to happen some day.' The school magazine in the thirties is littered with editorial allusions to them and poetry – invariably disapproving – appears in the new *Literary Supplement*. In April 1933, with Hitler's jackboots only just through the door of the Reichkanzlei, the *Fettesian* editor remarked 'we beg to congratulate President Roosevelt on his appointment, and Herr Hitler on appointing himself.'[61]

The same issue carried a poem beneath a swastika deriding the National Socialist obsession with Jews (who had been subjected to one of their earliest travails on the first of that month with the shop boycott) and their apparent easy identification by the nose, which apparently looked like the number six:

THE 'NĀSIS'
(with apologies to Herr Hitler)

At Fettes we have noses
Of every size and shape.
They vary as the roses,
From pink to crimson-lake.

Another poem, entitled 'Heil!' appeared that winter:

A.   O have you been to Germany, and what did you see there?
B.   I saw a short fat tubby man, with long lean stringy hair.
A little black moustache he had: in large loud soap-box tones
He poured forth streams of bilge and tripe, dished up with howls and groans.[62]

Britain's home-grown 'Imperial Autarch' as Sir Oswald Mosley once styled himself, was the subject of a blistering attack by 'Y.A.H.' who wrote 'An Epistle to a Grand Panjandrum' in the mid-thirties:

Strong iron arm! Firm iron will!
Cast-iron skull with little in it!
Restrain your flow of bilge and swill,
Or pour some reason in to thin it,
No need to shout, for we aren't deaf:
Thump not the tub; reel in your lingo,
From fear, O (self-styled) great B.F.
You'll wake that sleeping bulldog, Jingo.

We know the troubles Jingo brings,
By Jingo, I should think we do, sir,
So speculative peer of kings,
Ver' sorry, but you'll be the loser.
So pack your traps, and leave the stage
Quick time, dynamic, forceful hero;
And take your head – to cool your rage –
And shove it in a bucket.[63]

Given that the bulldog Jingo had been a favourite pet of Fettesian versifiers for the first half-century of the school's existence, this is a remarkable shift in thinking. The fascist movements of Italy, Germany and, for some reason, Ireland, took a kicking from R.B.T.'s poem 'Shirts' in February 1934:

Black shirts of Italy from distant Florence,
Standing at attention in Mussolini-town,
With their hearts full of Fascism,
Child-production, discipline,
Corporate dictatorship and physical renown.

Brown shirts of Germany from beer-soaked Munich,
Marching round the Reichstag with the Hohenzollern heirs,
With a vanguard of Steelhelmets,
Swastikas and Stormtroopers,
Jungfolk, Schutzstaffel, and Reich 'Commissionaires.'

Blue shirts from the country of the 'wearing o' the green'
Hidden under overcoats in every Irish street,
With a veto from de Valera,
And sarcasm from Bernard Shaw,
Hostility from everywhere and daily Dail defeat.[64]

It is worth noting that, whilst George Bernard Shaw did indeed condemn the Irish Blueshirts, these fascists did receive the support of W.B. Yeats, a poet whose Celtic meanderings clearly interested the more aesthetic boys. The most prominent of these was George Campbell Hay, later a leading light of the Scottish nationalist literary renaissance. Writing as 'Ciotach', some of his earliest published verses appeared in the *Fettesian* in 1934:

For Eastward here the sea
Is dark, and dead, and grey:
And I wish that I could be
In Innse Gall today.[65]

A minister's son from Tarbert, by Loch Fyne on the West Coast, he despised Fettes as 'a little piece of "Forever England"' and used English as

363

little as possible in his writing, learning Gaelic and Lallans to write in a more authentically Scots fashion. At least one reviewer considered that he deserved to be ranked with the other literary patriots who gathered in Milne's Bar, including Hugh MacDairmid and Sorley Maclean. Even more nationalist than the others, and self-taught in Gaelic, he spoke disparagingly of Fettes' Unionist character – one draft from 1960 spoke of 'seasons spent at school in Edinburgh, speaking Latin and being whipped like dogs.'[66]

It was certainly true that thirties Fettes was not especially welcoming to pupils with his views. The Debating Society's motion 'this house approves of Scottish Nationalism' featured many references to Wendy Wood, one of the founders of the modern independence movement, who earlier that year had removed the Union Flag from Stirling Castle and replaced it with the Lion Rampant. It is hard to avoid the impression that the topic was not being taken seriously, and the motion was roundly defeated by 15 votes to 67 in October 1932.[67]

One of his contemporaries did question this version of the poet's boyhood; Robert Rankin, Hay's closest friend, believed that the rigorous classical curriculum was a joy to the young poet, who could correctly translate any word from the Greek dictionary opened at random. Apart from fagging when they were junior boys, Rankin believed that 'we had quite a lot of freedom, and the company was in the main congenial.'[68]

We cannot be sure, but Hay is a possible candidate for the authorship of a *Fettesian* article about leprechauns which for sheer depth of sentimental Celtic guff takes some beating.[69] Sir William's corpse, not to mention those of his contemporaries Adam Smith and David Hume, must have been revolving hard enough in the grave to power Edinburgh for a fortnight. In place of Enlightenment rationalism, in place even of the bluff and manly patriotism of the Victorian Fettes man, was an account of how the Englishman can never understand the Irishman, or at least the 'pure unspoilt Celt', because he has lost his belief in fairies. Luckily, the same 1934 *Literary Supplement* did carry a corrective in the shape of a satirical account of Scottish Nationalists trying to recruit a gamekeeper in the Highlands, in which Hay redeemed himself with a pleasing degree of self-mockery. (This is fortunate, since, as his *Fettesian* obituarist recalled, if anyone else had mocked him they would have found that 'it was wise to keep well clear of him when he had a bayonet in his hand.'[70]) Hay was undoubtedly a poet of genius and his 'Bizerta' is widely considered one of the best Scottish war poems of the twentieth century; however, by his own admission, he did produce some pretty eccentric material in the service of the cause.

Less flamboyantly engaged with great issues was the Fettes Debating Society. Just over half of its meetings in the thirties had a political focus (the others were on issues such as the superiority of dustmen over actresses, or the undesirability of bloodsports) discussed communism in 1937 with some visitors from the University of New Brunswick in Canada. 'Communism' proposed J.B. Fitzpatrick, 'provided a meaning for life and an ideal to strive for'; he was supported by J.B. Rutherford's economic statistics which proved, he said, that the 'Communists had confounded their critics by their industry.' One of the visitors pointed out that since the British Empire was built not on economy but on cricket, and the British were not interested in politics but sport, communism was a non-starter. This 'heated bicker' was put to the vote, and a mere 24 members seem to have been convinced that communism was a good idea, whilst 82 thought otherwise. That year also saw a debate on the motion that 'Germany is the country most to be feared by Great Britain.' By this stage, it should be noted, Hitler had been vigorously and openly rearming for several years and had remilitarised the Rhineland, which the Versailles Treaty required German troops to stay out of in order to provide France with a buffer zone. Morrison recalled that the first transmission he heard on the private wireless sets of the school was news of this event.[71]

The proposers of the motion, G.A. Turner and J.B. Fitzpatrick, pointed out this terrific pace of rearmament and Hitler's greed for territory. Against them were range a host of counter-arguments – Germany had been unjustly treated at Versailles, said J.B. Gibson, and if fairly treated 'would be one of the very foremost in the cause of universal peace'.[72] R.E. McCraken argued that Germany was less of a threat than Soviet Communism. It was also argued that the German people were our relatives and that we had nothing to fear from them, as anyone who visited the place would know. The motion lost by ten votes to 17, a reflection of the public climate at the time.

'Fettes was not quite untouched by those political issues of the thirties which stirred so deeply not only the universities but also many sixth forms,' D.J. Grant recalled later, although, in wry comment on Edinburgh's most famous internationally-minded teacher, he did add that 'If any Fettesians came under the influence of Miss Jean Brodie in her prime they certainly kept it quiet.'[73]

That is not to say that everyone connected with the school was immune from the thrilling appeal of the stiff right arm. OF Sir Cecil Hanbury, an enthusiastic gardener and Tory MP for North Dorset, was a friend of Thomas Hardy. He was also a friend of right-wing extremism. When Italy invaded Abyssinia he did not join in the universal chorus of execration at this unprovoked act of fascist aggression against a defenceless country, but sent £100 to the Italian Red Cross as a token of sympathy 'with Fascist Italy and her magnificent soldiers.' He used his position in Parliament to oppose the 'iniquitous' sanctions imposed by the League of Nations, and complained of the 'barbarous system used by the Abyssinians against the heroic Italian soldiers.'[74]

His wife was believed to be the first Englishwoman to enrol in the Fascist Party, and Mussolini made him a Grand Officer of the Order of the Crown in recognition of his contribution to Italian life at Ventimiglia, where his magnificent gardens, La Mortola, can still be seen. The *Fettesian* politely reprinted an obituary and made no other comment. Fascism was, of course, primarily a young man's creed, and it would have been surprising if none of the boys had shared Sir Cecil's interest. Alyster Jackson, working in London after leaving Fettes and a keen member of the London Scottish, gravitated from being a 'chucker-out' at Conservative events (the rugby-playing type being much in demand for this role) to performing a similar task for Sir Oswald Mosley's New Party. He freely admitted that he knew little about fascism but was impressed by the leader – 'an exceptional speaker and an intelligent man.'[75]

Jackson never wore a black shirt himself, which was just as well, since they were eventually banned by Sir John Simon in the 1936 Public Order Act, one of the few occasions, said the cynics, when the distinguished OF stood up to fascism. Jackson was later involved in a huge fight between communists and fascists at the Bull Ring in Birmingham in the autumn of 1931, during which he rescued Sir Oswald's expensive camel-hair coat. His employer, however, was unimpressed and ordered him to stay away from politics of this kind, which he did. Iain Macleod, later a famously liberal Tory Colonial Secretary, represented the New Party in a Fettes debate in October 1931, 'because he believed that youth was the only thing to save the country.'[76]

He came third, with 23 votes, after the Conservative (45 votes), National Government (25 votes); curiously, Mr Woodhead, one of the masters, gained a respectable 16 votes on the prohibitionist ticket – he argued that with two-thirds of the price of a bottle of whisky going to the government instead of to the workers, it was time to assess the nation's priorities ('a splendid speech,' noted the secretary, I.D. Harvey, himself a Tory MP after the war, 'but one whose theme was unpopular with a Scottish audience.') Woodhead did better than the Communist, A.W. Newsom, who offered special exemption for those (four in total) who voted for him 'when the Russian Wave of Blood flooded the land and the tyrants were destroyed.' The Liberal, W.E. Catto, begged the House to remember all Lloyd George had done for the country in the war – could they imagine Fettes run by the Germans? He gained a solitary vote. (Macleod showed a characteristic mixture of progressive idealism and traditional Tory pragmatism when he defended the exploits of Amy Johnson in another debate in 1931, in which he pointed out 'the importance lent to British goods through her achievement.'[77])

Fettesians were not without first-hand experience of the dictatorships. Plenty of former pupils saw Germany on business, including Alyster Jackson, who witnessed a gang of Brownshirts come into a café in Lübeck:

They took one of the large tables, sat down and began talking and noisily throwing their weight about. Where there had been happy conversations going on at all the other tables, it suddenly became hushed. It was, I suppose, a foreboding of what was to come.[78]

Sandy Glen, indeed, saw a group of Jews forced to clean the pavement by Nazis in 1935, but, as he put it himself, 'chickened out' of helping them, as to do so would have led to a beating. [79] Rhoderick Macleod, brother of Iain, lived in Germany in the thirties as an apprentice textile designer. He learned several important lessons there: 'how much booze I could drink without falling over, how to cope with teenage and older girls and, most importantly, not to try and interfere in affairs that I could not alter, such as German politics.'[80]

Norman Cameron, who was bitterly anti-Nazi – 'The Germans are filthy beasts… they boast of having orgasms when they drop bombs on wretched defenceless people' – had in-laws in the Reich. On a visit in 1937, he was furious to discover that their house had been searched for books of which the Party disapproved and that a Jewish friend had been forced to put metal grilles on her windows and could not trust her own servants. He was later arrested by stormtroopers and interrogated at length for spying, on the grounds that he had taken photographs of German tanks – which were on display at the Nuremberg rally.[81]

In August 1935, a party of fifteen Fettesians went with Mr Hoare, the German master, to Heidelberg, and had a splendid time. Douglas Rae remembers it as being very peaceful; they swam in the River Neckar and rowed boats, doing very little work, and he saw neither preparations for war nor indeed many Germans, since the university was on vacation.[82]

Labour Camps (not, incidentally, concentration camps, which discouraged visitors, but job-creation schemes in which people from all walks of life came together for public works programmes) were an obligatory stop on any tour of Germany, and seem to have been the one piece of Party Time the Fettesians experienced. The one they saw was described at the time by 'J.M.F.D.' in the *Fettesian* as 'the *tour de force* of the whole show':

These Labour Camps are a visible example of the Modern German Philosophy – to get as far back as possible to the simple things of life, and away from the super-civilisation of today. They eat, sleep and work under the simplest conditions – aristocrat side by side with labourer – and I am convinced that they leave the Camps a lot healthier, mentally as well as physically, than they enter them… after saluting the whole guards presented spades we took our leave, and drove home very impressed and confirmed Nazis.[83]

The reality of these camps was that they were an exercise in forcibly reducing the unemployment statistics, and neither aristocrat nor labourer was necessarily bursting with National Socialist zeal to get into them, but since all trade unions had been forcibly merged into the Workers' Front they had little choice.

Despite Nazism's brutalities, this was a time when many people were willing to believe that liberal capitalism was failing (evidence for this being all too obvious) and that alternatives to it were highly attractive and desirable. Alyster Jackson had, in the late twenties and early thirties, been casting around for new ideas, even going so far as to sleep in a haystack whilst inspired by George Borrow's *The Wind on the Heath*. Others went in the opposite direction. Having supported the loyalists in the Spanish Civil War, Murray Hunter joined ('like all freshers') the Cambridge University Socialist Club (CUSC) in 1939 and 'was able to get some impressive Russian posters.' This Popular Front was shaken by the Soviet invasion of Finland that same year, and CUSC split into rival Labour and

Communist factions. A loyal member of Cambridge Presbyterian Church and Officer Training Corps, Hunter naturally sided with Labour against the Marxists. James MacGibbon, who left Fettes to go into publishing, joined the Communist Party with his wife in 1936 because of the abandonment, by the political mainstream, of the Spanish republican government to the tender mercies of Franco. In addition to his campaigning, he helped to run a home for Basque orphans, and was later arrested for writing 'Save the Czechs' graffiti in London after the Munich conference. J.G.D. Hooper, an OF engaged in the export trade, sent the *Fettesian* a long and detailed report on the USSR after he visited Leningrad on business in 1932. It is probably safe to say that few pupils will have been converted to communism from Hooper's description of it.

On landing, the first thing that strikes one is the apparent happiness and friendliness and healthy appearance of the people – at least, of the peasants. Eastern fatalism must be the cause, as semi-starvation and ragged clothes are hardly conducive to happiness, except in the most ascetic of philosophers! They rarely ask any one on the ships for food, but they have no hesitation in keeping up a constant demand for English cigarettes – they are very heavy smokers, and when their ration of cigarettes is exhausted, smoke brown paper or anything else they can lay hands on, with every appearance of enjoyment.

Their chief ambition is to buy old clothes from seamen, and they pay fabulous prices for garments only fit for the dust-heap. I must confess to having sold two ancient pairs of socks for 7 roubles a pair – that is, at the present absurd rate of exchange, £1 a pair...

The labour conditions are fairly good in Leningrad – there is no slave labour, and the work is carried on in eight-hour shifts, with constant intervals for gossip and cigarettes, which no foreman with even the most imaginative of language can interrupt. I did see one of the winch girls work for twenty-four hours on end, but it was a rare occurrence. Conditions in other parts of the country, are, I understand, different – in Archangel, for instance, slave labour and indiscriminate shooting are the order of the day, if reports are true.

The workers are paid with ration tickets, which entitle them to a bare minimum of food (chiefly black bread and herrings – which they very often eat raw, head, tail, and all!), a most inadequate supply of clothes, a certain number of cigarettes, and entrance to various places of amusement...

Quite naturally they have no incentive to work, and are very slow.[84]

Leaving the docks to inspect the former glories of imperial St Petersburg,

Hooper found that the basic essentials of life were hard to find, and came to a rather damning conclusion:

The people walking about in the streets of the city are not quite so badly dressed as those at the docks, but all are shabby, and one rarely sees a man dressed as well as the poorest of English shop assistants... There is a complete absence of all luxuries, and soap, silk stockings, and scent are dreams of paradise to a Russian girl. One sees the men and women bathing in the Neva and in the harbour, rubbing mud and sand over their bodies in an effort to get clean. Nudism is practised in Russia, not as a cult, but as the natural thing to do.

The only people who have a fairly reasonable standard of living are all those who are directly employed by the Soviet, including soldiers, and the sailors in the Sovtorgflot ships (the Russian merchant fleet). There seems to be a complete disregard for their idealistic ambitions of Equality.

Hooper apologised for the rather negative impression given in his report, admitting that it was 'the more drab aspects of the country that meet the eye, and redeeming features remain hidden beneath their respective bushels.' Some improvements were appearing (this was the era of the five-year-plan) such as artisans' flats in the latest German style, parks and football pitches. He did not get the impression that the Russians had enthusiastically embraced communism. The ordinary peasant would say, in response to half-humorous enquiries, 'communist ni dobra' (no good) and 'capitalist dobra.' They did seem to have a 'very great respect for Stalin' though Hooper wondered if this might have been 'because discretion is the better part of valour.' Hooper decided that the ordinary Russian was 'probably no better off than he was under the Czarist regime and expects a pretty wretched time as a matter of course.' Such reports had little effect on the communist believers in the West.

The last year of peace

With war approaching, the Corps also held its first field day for over a decade on 1st June 1938, with a relatively competent exercise being carried out at Castlelaw in the Pentlands, disturbed mainly by 'a somewhat militant black bull.' There was no cadet camp in the summer of that year, owing to an outbreak of mumps, but the War Office did demand a set programme for cadet training, leading to a scaling-down of the inter-house competitions (as previously noted, the only bit most people cared about) and instead training everyone for Certificate A and thereafter for 'semi-specialised course in Intelligence, Signalling or Machine-Gun.'[85] September 1938 saw almost hysterical fear of war over Hitler's claim that he would seize the Sudetenland by force; when Chamberlain simply let him have it on the gentlemanly grounds that if we all behaved like

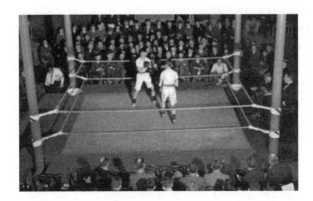

Boxing competitions were, for some, the most important training for the imminent encounter with the Germans

rational chaps the Führer would calm down, there was near-universal rejoicing, orchestrated, according to Roy Jenkins, by Sir John Simon, the 'cheerleader' for appeasement, who led the cabinet out to the aerodrome to bid the Prime Minister Godspeed: 'it was he who on Chamberlain's return poured such Cabinet unction on his head as to play a major part in turning the highly arguable "low case" for Munich into the unsustainable and discreditable "high case"...'[86]

That is, appeasement might be tactically understandable, but making a pacifist religion out of it was disastrous. Hitler's seizure of Prague in March 1939 wrecked the cult of Chamberlain, and with it the reputation of his high priest Simon. Did the pupils understand what was going on? If Simon didn't, they could hardly be expected to. Reminiscences vary. A.J. Mackenzie Stuart, a pupil in 1938, remembered decades later that:

...we were scarcely aware of the tensions mounting in Europe. The Munich Settlement was accepted at face value if it was considered at all, and the hastily dug trenches in front of College were its only reminder. The trial 'blackout' of Edinburgh was the intimation of things to come. I remember lying awake in 'C' dormitory in Carrington watching the lights go out over Comely Bank and the

rows of houses rising to where the Castle stood poised on the skyline. To none of us did it occur that three-quarters of our time at Fettes was to be spent in conditions of shuttered windows and dim lights. Other and more important things occupied us that year.[87]

These more important things included the Headmaster's honorary degree from St Andrew's, a rare approved visit to the cinema, claret cup dispensed on Founder's Day and, thrillingly, 'a very temporary armistice from regulation' which permitted an inter-dormitory water fight. By contrast, Sir Tommy Macpherson's memoirs suggest a very real fascination with world affairs among Fettes pupils; either way, post-Munich disillusionment set in very quickly across the country. A sense of shame seems to have infected most of the British. Labour, not for the last time, exercised a sharp u-turn on policy and became belligerent. Up to this point, they had managed to convince themselves that it was simultaneously possible to oppose fascism and to disarm unilaterally. At least one Fettes poet spotted, as Orwell had, the humour of such a position:

> *There's a Peace Group at the bottom of my garden,*
> *Whose resolutions sweetly bloom in May;*
> *And they feel their duty is to be on guard in*
> *Case the situation goes astray.*
>
> *Once a week they hold a very secret meeting,*
> *To tell the Army just where it gets off,*
> *And in the intervals of biscuit eating*
> *At other creeds intelligently scoff.*[88]

Now the mainstream left could see, as could those Tories like Eden and Macmillan who started to gravitate towards Churchill, that Hitler was not a gentleman. In November 1938, the Nazis unleashed Kristallnacht, the most public act of mass terror against the Jews seen in peacetime Europe for centuries. Even right-wing British peers such as Lord Redesdale (father of those perpetual entertainers the Mitford sisters) were appalled and ceased to give the Germans the benefit of any doubts they had previously entertained, though his daughters Unity and Diana remained enthusiastic fascists.[89]

Goebbels claimed that reports of Kristallnacht were being whipped up by the 'Masonic world press.' In early 1939, however, Germany's occupation of Czech-speaking Bohemia did not require a Judaeo-Masonic conspiracy to identify a breach of 'self-determination', and OFs flooded into the Territorial Army. Ten TA commissions and fifteen promotions in the Regular Army were recorded, and ten members of the London Scottish pictured, in the November 1938 *Fettesian*. One of the London Scottish, Douglas Rae, remembered that most of his friends were in it, and 'we used to meet at their headquarters in Buckingham Gate at weekends and drink much beer.'[90] His brother Stanley was in the Honourable Artillery Company, again with most of his friends. Dick Normand recalled that although he and his contemporaries initially became Territorials as part of a way of life, and also to be able to get three weeks a year out of the office in an era when holidays were hard to come by, things became more serious in 1938-9. 'It was the done thing,' he said, 'your friends looked at you oddly if you weren't in the TA.'[91] In the 'Dandy Ninth' (the Territorial battalion of the Royal Scots) were at least ten OFs, one of whom, Lt Walter Rose, was subsequently killed in the defence of Hong Kong. Normand saw it as his duty to recruit as many people as possible in this time of trial, and when the battalion received its first Bren Carrier he drove it up and down Princes St. explaining what it was. He was especially keen to recruit mechanics, and a visit to the Ford garage (the Carrier had a Ford V8 engine) netted ten – which ensured that his unit never had a vehicle unserviceable for more than half an hour.

George Campbell Hay was, perhaps unsurprisingly, one of the only Old Fettesians to remain immune from patriotic volunteering – even the Communist MacGibbon was prepared to ignore the Molotov-Ribbentrop Pact and enlist. Having left Fettes for Oxford, Hay became an extremely active Scottish Nationalist, with views which sometimes sounded like 'a homegrown Caledonian fascism', and looked forward to seeing England punished. If Germany won, 'there will be starvation – in England. It will be an interesting thing for Ireland to watch...'[92] One poem, 'Is Coma Leam Cogadh no Sith' ('War or Peace, I Care Not') looked on the coming war with cynical contempt for the establishment, and expected to see the streets littered with war-wounded beggars. He himself was unwilling to fight save in the defence of Scotland, should Germany drop parachutists; he would not defend England – 'the word itself is a purgative to me to be spat out, just as it is to the Indians, the Arabs, the Egyptians...'[93]

His was a fairly lonely voice. Copies of the *Fettesian* for the first half of 1939 represent, in microcosm, a Britain wearily but doggedly getting ready to tell the Germans that enough was enough. Mr Fabian Ware's epidiascope lecture on feeling in art encompassed Picasso's *Guernica* (unsurprisingly, for this master, the son of the founder of the Imperial War Graves Commission, was regarded by most pupils as an enthusiastic communist); three pages of the March edition of the magazine covered military appointments; the inter-house Corps competition was to be abolished to make way for intensified training; an OF wrote from Baghdad to assure the folks at home that despite their bad press, the Iraqis were great friends of Britain in times of crisis; Mr Donald Grant's lecture in February explained that Germany, Italy and Japan were seeking expansion at all costs; Commander Moncrieff came to give a recruiting talk for Royal Naval engineers; the OTC would be taking part in an exercise with regular troops in the Pentlands in May. Such a dominance of the magazine by one exterior theme had not been seen for a quarter of a century. In June, the OTC inspection saw the boys demonstrating their skills with Bren guns on tripod mounts for close air defence and with the Boy's anti-tank rifle, on loan from the Royal Scots, and carrying out intelligence work at Davidson's Mains. Camp was cancelled again, not because of mumps but because the government was using every last military training area and instructor to ready the adult population for war, which duly broke out, like the previous one, during the summer holidays.

Charles Gray, still out in India, saw his cavalry regiment readied for war. In this case, it meant mechanisation, and farewell to Granite.

By then Granite was an old gentleman of 20 and, with the uncertainty of the War, I decided he would have to end his life in Bannu. The fateful day came and our Veterinary Surgeon had agreed to put him down by an injection, as I did not want to see him shot. When we both arrived at the chosen place, I was astonished to be met by a small crowd of regimental syces (grooms) and some of the other Trumpeters, led by Hardwari Singh. They had dug a large grave and had surrounded it with flowers. Hardwari hung a garland of marigolds round Granite's neck, and when the effect of the injection started, the old horse just lay down and 'went to sleep.' Many, including Hardwari and myself, were in tears over the passing of our beloved horse.[94]

Allan Herriot, who had just left Fettes and was working in Sweden, hurried back to Britain to join up:

I knew what Germany had done in Europe and something of what was happening in Germany vis-a-vis the Jews, Brown Shirts & Hitler Youth. I was utterly clear that Germany could not be allowed to rule the U.K. and had to be fought and beaten.[95]

NOTES

[1] *Fettesian*, November 1934

[2] Lockhart (1934) p. 363

[3] Alyster Jackson, (Unpublished) Memoir, Henderson Archive

[4] *Fettesian*, November 1937

[5] G. Morrison in MacDonald, p. 198

[6] A.J. Mackenzie Stuart in ibid., p. 210

[7] Ian Harvey, *To fall like Lucifer* (London, Sidgwick & Jackson, 1971) p. 22

[8] G. Morrison in MacDonald, p. 196

[9] *Fettesian*, March 1935

[10] Ibid., November 1937

[11] Ibid., July 1932

[12] Ibid., April 1931

[13] Ibid., April 1933

[14] Ibid., July 1933

[15] Ibid.

[16] Ibid.

[17] Ibid., December 1933

[18] Ibid., June 1933

[19] Ibid., July 1935

[20] Murray Hunter, (Unpublished) Memoir, Henderson Archive

[21] *Fettesian*, November 1934

[22] G. Morrison in MacDonald, p. 196

[23] *Fettesian*, March 1937

[24] Ibid., July 1937

[25] Ibid., November 1937

[26] J. Younie, letter to the author, 31 August 2008

[27] *Fettesian* December 1937

[28] A.J. Mackenzie Stuart in MacDonald, p. 209

[29] *Fettesian,* June 1931

[30] Ibid., March 1932

[31] Ibid., November 1932

[32] Ibid., November 1934

[33] Lockhart (1936) p. 28

[34] *Fettesian,* July 1934

[35] Col. Charles Gray, 'Granite – the Story of a Great Australian Horse' *OFNL* January 2001

[36] *Fettesian*, June 1938

[37] Ibid., December 1937

[38] Lockhart (1936) p. 85

[39] Ibid., p. 99

[40] Ibid., p. 117

[41] Ibid., p. 199

42 Ibid., p. 98
43 *Fettesian*, March 1931
44 Ibid., March 1934
45 Ibid., June 1935
46 Ibid., November 1931
47 Ibid., July 1935
48 Quoted in ibid., November 1934
49 Ibid., March 1933
50 *Fettesian*, April 1932
51 *Times*, 3 August 1938
52 *Daily Mirror*, 24 November 1933
53 *Times*, 29 January 1936
54 *Fettesian*, July 1936
55 Jenkins, p. 383
56 I am extremely grateful to Jonathan Irons for this insight into Sir John's views
57 Lockhart (1936) p. 28
58 *Fettesian*, April 1954
59 Obituary, *Fettesian*, 1981
60 Ibid., March 1934
61 Ibid., April 1933
62 *Fettesian Literary Supplement*, December 1933
63 Ibid., June 1934
64 Ibid., February 1934
65 Ibid., June 1934
66 Quoted in Michael Byrne (ed.) *Collected Poems and Songs of George Campbell Hay* (Edinburgh, University Press, 2003) p. 449
67 *Fettesian*, November 1932
68 Quoted in ibid., p. 450
69 Ibid.
70 *Fettesian*, 1984
71 G. Morrison in MacDonald, p. 199
72 *Fettesian*, June 1937
73 D.J. Grant in MacDonald, p. 202
74 Quoted in *Times* Obituary, 11 June 1937
75 Alyster Jackson, (Unpublished) Memoir, Henderson Archive
76 *Fettesian*, November 1931
77 *Fettesian*, March 1931
78 Alyster Jackson, (Unpublished) Memoir, Henderson Archive
79 Sir Alexander Glen, *Target Danube* (Lewes, Book Guild, 2002) p. 62
80 Rhoderick Macleod, (Unpublished) Memoir, Henderson Archive
81 See Hope, pp. 113-5
82 Stephen Douglas Rae, letter to the author, October 2008
83 *Fettesian*, November 1935
84 *Fettesian*, November 1932
85 Ibid., April 1938
86 Jenkins, p. 386
87 D.J. Grant in MacDonald, p. 202

[88] *Fettesian*, April 1938

[89] I am grateful to Mr. Andrew Collins, the noted journalist and broadcaster, for providing clarification on this point.

[90] Rae.

[91] In conversation with the author, October 2008

[92] Quoted in Byrne (ed.) p. 465

[93] Quoted in Byrne (ed.) p.569

[94] Gray

[95] In e-mail to the author, July 2008

Chapter Ten

'Vastly greater keenness and efficiency'

The School in the Second World War

The Germans come to Fettes

Although the school had taken some time to catch on to the realities of the Kaiser's war in 1914, the boys were singularly thrilled when Hitler's announced itself very quickly. On the afternoon of 16th October 1939, they were playing in the House Belows rugby tournament when anti-aircraft fire was heard from the direction of the Forth. Jack Mackenzie Stuart, later a prominent judge but at the time a 14-year-old schoolboy, wrote excitedly to his mother:

...at 2.30pm. while changing boots for House Belows, a plane was observed very high up – so high indeed that it was assumed to be a British one – (at this moment no-one had been informed of the reconnaissance flights in the morning). after Belows had been in progress for two or three minutes firing – both machine gun & antiaircraft fire started after 7 minutes. During which the firing was very heavy, and we could see the planes & puffs of smoke from the bursting shells. The sergeant raced up & yelled that we were to go to our shelters – at that moment there were some almighty bangs. (the wireless account said 'popping noises' & presumably this was right over Fettes as shrapnel (not much) was picked up outside Glencorse. We stayed in our shelters some time and the firing ceased – we were then told that the game would begin again at 3.30.[1]

The decision to resume their games, in the view of American pupil Bingham Kirk, 'typified the British public school spirit.'[2]

Mr G.C. Beamish was refereeing that day, and also acting as 'Air Recognition Officer' – which was odd, mused former pupil John Humphries, as he was so short-sighted that he wore pebble glasses.[3] Humphries spotted another aeroplane, marked 'with a big black cross', and, reared on Biggles, thought he ought to say something.

'Excuse me, Sir,' said Humphries, 'I think we have enemy aircraft overhead.'

'Nonsense, boy,' came the reply, 'the alarm hasn't gone, scrum down.'

They did, but now came the sound of machine-gun fire. Humphries popped his head up from the back row.

'They do sound hostile, sir.'

'Goodness me,' replied Beamish, 'Boys, stand under the trees until it is all over.'[4]

Jack Mackenzie Stuart described what happened over the game he was taking part in:

The ball had emerged from the loose scrum and one of the centres kicked ahead to the east. The forwards followed up making for the opposing full back who stood facing west ready to gather the ball. Suddenly his expression changed to one of complete astonishment and the ball sailed unnoticed over his shoulder. The whole game stopped and with a tremendous roar a German bomber swept low across the field with smoke pouring from one of its engines.[5]

Kenneth Hall, a 'new man', remembered the events with vivid clarity almost seventy years later:

I was one of a number of smallish boys playing rugby on the playing fields at Fettes College, Edinburgh – only a few minutes' flying time from the Forth Bridge and Rosyth Naval Dockyard. There was distant gunfire and puffs of cotton wool in the clear blue sky; but no air raid warning; ack-ack practice we said and carried on with our game. Wrong! Minutes later there was the unmistakable rat-a-tat of a machine gun and a Heinkel bomber appeared over the trees with two Hurricanes sitting on its tail. Perhaps fortunately for us, the RAF pilots held off and all three planes flew off in the direction of the Pentlands.[6]

'Everyone stopped to look,' said Hamish Liddell, 'though my recollection is that one of the players was not going to let the war get in the way of rugby and picked up the ball and scored!'[7]

The German bomber, although damaged, seems to have made it home. Willie Geddes, who was playing fives that day, remembers seeing 'the tail-gunner slumped down in the rear of the 'plane.'[8]

The British fighters were in fact Spitfires, and official accounts of the raid insist that the German bomber was a Junkers 88. With the Air

Training Corps not yet in existence, perhaps we can forgive this lapse in aircraft recognition skills. Wilfred Lodge, housemaster of Carrington and Great War veteran, commented afterwards that 'I'm sure we all thoroughly enjoyed our first air raid and indeed, apart from the thought that a couple of miles away some poor chaps were being done in, it was jolly good fun.' He went on to express appreciation for the German pilot – 'He had a machine gun, and if he had not been a decent Christian he could have wiped out Fettes House Belows.' Jack Mackenzie Stuart recalled this as 'an unexpectedly sympathetic old comradely attitude to the German aircrew: normally his references to the German nation were in language which today would have earned him instant dismissal by any politically correct Headmaster.' It was, of course, not any kindness on the part of the German airmen (several of whom were killed, and buried with military honours by the RAF) which had saved the place, but, according to school mythology, the efforts of George Denholm, an Old Fettesian who was flying one of the British fighters and, as the official Fettes history puts it, 'courteously stopped firing over the playing fields.' After the war, the Fettesian referred to another OF, Wing-Commander A.M. Grant, as 'one of the pilots who took part in the first air battle over Britain in 1939 – when the planes passed lover over Fettes when the House Belows were in progress' and it may be that this is where the Denholm story originated.[9]

A German Junkers 88 of the type which flew low over the school in 1939

Elsewhere, Alexia Lindsay, daughter of the school's Clerk of Works, was playing with her sister and waved at the aeroplanes, thinking they were all British. A German pilot who survived the raid later recorded that 'the Scottish peasants, clearly disaffected, waved sympathetically at us.'[10]

The *Fettesian* recorded these events as an exciting experience which left the boys quite unconvinced of the horrors of war; 'however,' it noted, 'we realise that air raids are not always of such a spectacular nature and already the sirens have shown us what a bore as well as what an excitement they can be.'[11]

Indeed, rather like the First World War, Fettes saw actual violence quite rarely during 1939-45, as Kenneth Hall remembered rather ruefully; 'many air raid warnings and nights in the air raid shelter followed – mainly when Glasgow, Clydeside and Belfast were copping it – but disappointingly for us we didn't again have anything as exciting as that first air raid of the war.' Hall was literally correct – this was the very first air raid on the United Kingdom by the Luftwaffe, and also the first in which the Spitfire saw action, the first British air victories being a Dornier 18 flying-boat downed by Skuas on 26 September. 602 (Glasgow) and 603 (Edinburgh) Squadrons, based at Turnhouse, did indeed repel the enemy attack, with Denholm leading 603's Yellow Section (he later won the DFC).[12]

The day was unsatisfactory from all sides; the Germans had failed to sink any ships in the Forth, though they did kill sixteen sailors on HMS *Mohawk* (the only civilian fatality was a dog which had to be put down after being hit by a splinter), and lost two aircraft, whilst 603 Squadron alone had fired 16,000 rounds and downed only one enemy. Edinburgh had been sprayed promiscuously with stray bullets, bomb shrapnel, pieces of falling debris and the detritus of anti-aircraft fire. The Lord Provost's house had been spattered with British bullets, and, like his predecessor during the Zeppelin raid, he was deeply unimpressed with the city's preparation for air raids. In a letter to his parents, Jack Mackenzie Stuart put it into perspective:

Well, congratulate me on a most exciting experience, playing in (a) the only House Below ever played under fire, (b) seeing a real live air-raid, (c) (MUCH THE MOST IMPORTANT), beating Glencorse 24-0.[13]

Ultimately, Edinburgh escaped German bombing lightly in comparison with other Scottish cities, with the Blitz of 1941 hitting Clydebank and

Greenock heavily, and Frazerburgh becoming known as 'Hellfire Corner'; 2,298 Scots were killed in air raids, but only a couple of dozen in Edinburgh, as German planes in that part of the country inevitably focused on Rosyth and shipping in the Forth. Over 60,000 people were killed by bombing in the United Kingdom as a whole, around half in the London area, mostly in the 1941 Blitz, before Germany turned east to fight the Soviet Union. Bombs over the U.K. claimed the lives of two OFs, R.B. Lawrie (who was too ill to serve but became involved in ARP work) and Flying Officer William Airey. Two further OFs were injured: Captain James Kirkness, who survived the evacuation from Dunkirk only to be wounded in the ferocious bombing of Belfast in 1941, which claimed almost a thousand lives in a single night, and Lt Col John Pearse, in one of the late raids on London in 1944. The Rev W.R. Sanderson was ARP Warden of his parish, and was somewhat distressed to return from duty only to find that his own house was among those hit. When Hamish Liddell left Fettes to go up to Oxford, he became a member of the Balliol College fire brigade, which consisted of a Coventry Climax Pump and a Morris 12 as a towing vehicle, plus a number of undergraduates led by one who, in the vacation, had fought fires in the London Blitz. 'This gave one,' he remembered fondly, 'an intimate knowledge of the college roofs and unauthorised ways of getting into college after midnight.'[14]

John Guest, serving in an anti-aircraft battery in Sevenoaks, had less happy thoughts when the sound of air-raid warnings and aircraft engines filled the night sky: 'I imagined nightmare figures in Wellsian garments, strange helmets and goggles, floating silently down clutching machine guns.' Luckily, his officer completely lost his head, running about waving a revolver wildly hunting for the machine-gunner, whispering orders as loudly as he could, and this provided 'a splendid diversion'. Since the machine-gunner (who couldn't in any case be found) was the only person with any ammunition, there was not a great deal his section could have done.[15]

Although actual air raids on Edinburgh were to prove infrequent, their potential for havoc cast a huge shadow over the school, which was lucky not to lose any of the pupils who lived in bigger cities – John Humphries recalls that 'I spent my holidays in London in a basement with my mother suffering the nightly onslaught of the Luftwaffe'[16] and that the family rabbit was killed by shrapnel. Writing after the war, Lord Normand, who had been Chairman of the Governors, explained the confused situation, which was rather reminiscent of the wild speculation prevailing before the Great War:

At that time there was no clear idea of the nature of air attack which was to be apprehended. There were vague suppositions in high quarters that there would be on the outbreak of war violent attacks on the great cities and that Edinburgh would be on the list of targets. Estimates of the probable air-raid casualties in the first weeks of war were very imprecise, and as it turned out wildly exaggerated [The Ministry of Health actually predicted 600,000 dead and 1,200,000 injured]. *It was well for Fettes that it had in Dr Ashcroft a Headmaster whose courage and leadership had been proved on the battlefields of the First Great War. He had on his staff men who had passed through the same ordeal with equal distinction. Parents had every reason to be confident that all possible steps would be taken for their sons' safety and that there would be no panic if an attack came.*[17]

Perhaps, but, as Mr MacDonald, the Moredun Housemaster who later wrote an essay on the wartime school, anxious mothers did not apparently retain this confidence after the excitement of that first air raid; 'the boys who wrote and thanked their parents for sending them to a school "where you can see the air-battles" perhaps had more than a little to do with the fall in numbers.'[18] Parents were, after all, being urged by the government to evacuate their offspring to the countryside, though Jeffrey notes that only two-fifths of Edinburgh children left the city, many of whom returned fairly quickly, partly because of the absence of anywhere comfortable to put them.[19]

Fettesians, of course, sometimes went further afield; Bingham Kirk's parents, for instance, put him on a ship back to America in 1940, and in the nature of the school there were plenty of Commonwealth connections where children could be billeted. Jack Mackenzie Stuart wrote rather mournfully of the situation in 1940:

Very many people are leaving Fettes for South America, South Africa and Canada. Some have gone, some are departing shortly, others leaving at the end of term. It's rather sad to see one's friends go; however it is only to be expected.

Carrington has closed down a small dorm of 3 beds, and I am now in one of the Big Dorms, this is definite step up the social scale. It is not so matey however and one misses the small dorm.[20]

For Fettesians in general, however, bombing was just a nuisance. On more than one occasion, when the sirens sounded, the spectators at a rugby match would have to retire to the shelters, leaving the players to carry on unwatched. 'A regular chore' A.R.H. Cumming remembers, 'was applying screens made of opaque material on a wooden frame to the windows each evening, and removing them each morning.'[21]

These blackout arrangements could be a terror for fags, who were responsible for ensuring that regulations were strictly applied to their allotted windows and, in houses with more authoritarian prefects, could be severely punished for failing to do so. Neither the chapel nor the concert hall could be satisfactorily blacked out, so could only be used in daylight, forcing plays to be put on in the cramped old music room. The national paranoia about the blackout was apparent from the start, with a crotchety headline in the *Edinburgh Evening News* on 5 September 1939: 'Last warning to citizens – "black-out" most unsatisfactory.'[22]

Several weeks later the *Scotsman* informed its readers that smoking a cigarette at night could bring the Germans flocking from miles around, and all manner of agonies were suffered by the authorities as they tried to reconcile one wartime necessity with another. The nation needed food, so greenhouses were necessary, but then again they were visible for miles around. Might they, someone on Falkirk Council suggested, be covered in black paper? Presumably someone with a greater understanding of photosynthesis explained the difficulty with this proposal, and Scotland's greenhouses glinted merrily throughout the war. The Edinburgh blackout was, in many ways, more trouble than it was worth; given how rarely the Luftwaffe actually visited the city, it is almost certain that far more injuries, and not a few deaths, were inflicted through accidental collisions in the dark than through the efforts of Hitler's fascist hordes. There were constant battles between the police, the local authorities and the Edinburgh Safety First Council over the level of light required in order for the city to function during the long hours of winter gloom. Although the pilots from Turnhouse reported as late as October 1940 – the onset of the Blitz – that 'during the hours of darkness, Princes Street looked like Wembley Stadium'[23] it is hard to avoid the conclusion that none of this mattered much. The Firth of Forth is a very distinctive feature and the Germans had mapped most of the United Kingdom before the outbreak of war in any case. Nonetheless, at Fettes, the whole school day was pushed back, resulting in the welcome abolition of 'early school' at 7.30; breakfast was moved to 8.15, and chapel to 9.10, with shortened lessons to keep as many as possible within the few hours of daylight in the grim Scots winter. Founder's Day, of course, had to go; massive concentrations of people travelling great distances and consuming vast amounts of food were neither encouraged nor physically feasible in wartime.

Mackenzie Stuart noted that the air-raid threat gave Wilfred Lodge an excellent opportunity to apply his creative scientific mind to an alarm system, whose 'spider-like collection of wires', as Willie Geddes recalls, ran from the library windows to each of the houses. D.J. Grant, who helped Lodge install the system, remembered that the Headmaster 'expressed sincere and rather surprised envy at Lodge's superior qualification for meeting the technical problems of modern war'[24] – a generous observation, for Ashcroft distrusted scientists in general and occasionally fell out with Lodge so badly that they would communicate only by letter. Lodge's experiments sometimes suggest a reasonable basis for the Headmaster's distrust; Ian Mackenzie, who came to Fettes later in the war, remembered one in which a ballistic test with a real rifle almost ended tragically when the bullet narrowly missed a passer-by, and another in which a classful of boys linked hands with a huge battery and were given a massive electric shock. Lodge's response was to stroke his beard and muse, 'Mmm; I could have killed you all there.' Of Lodge, Mackenzie Stuart remembered that 'His conversation was always a delight, his vocabulary highly coloured, his comments on boys penetrating and on his colleagues scathing'; schoolboys like that sort of thing, though headmasters and teacher training establishments despair of it. The elaborate Carrington early warning system Lodge devised spread through his house. A bell rang by his bedside, alerting him to raids, whereupon he would signal each dormitory, whose own bells would ring until a senior boy, satisfied that everyone was out of bed, switched it off. Responsibility for sounding the overall school alarm rested with a rotated picket group of eight or ten boys who slept in the Library, from where they had a fine view over the city and could brew cocoa and produce an unofficial magazine called *Gargoyle* (whose erratic proofs bore witness to its production in darkness). 'Neud' wrote a poem about picket duty for the Christmas 1939 number of the school magazine:

> *The wind is whistling cheerlessly round the clear-cut frigid stone*
> *Chilling our swathed-up bodies to the minutest bone.*
> *The snores of heavy sleepers rise discordant from the floor,*

Annding to the discomfiture that chills us to the core.
I pull my coat on tighter, but still the draughts seep through,
I rise and walk about a bit for lack of else to do.
I look at scores and scores of books and wonder which is best,
And scramble over unseen things, disturbing those at rest.
At last I pick a volume which I hope I have not read,
And stumble over bodies crumpled up like frozen dead.
I read the first few pages, but my eyes begin to close,
I shut the book, and stretch myself, and then begin to doze,
Sleep drifts in slowly, slowly; pictures begin to form,
Of a world serene and happy, forgetful of the storm.
'Wake up!' my dream is shattered; my partner looks aghast,
'To think you had the nerve to sleep – it might have been your last.'
I think I hear a siren – no! it must have been the gale,
Whistling through the leafless trees in the dawn so cold and pale.
We watch the clock go forward with a motion deadly slow,
Until at last our hours are up and back to sleep we go
To dream of warmer things in lands where the sun is shining bright;
Where people do not know of wars, nor of picketing at night.[25]

Geddes remembers that he 'obtained some pleasure in getting everyone out of bed.' J.B.A. Smyth was 'a bit shaken when Stuart Mackay produced a bottle of sherry.' As a prefect, it was his duty to take the bottle away, but there was a war on, and they would all be leaving soon, so 'we all had a tot.' The picket system was abandoned when it was demonstrated that the town air raid sirens were sufficiently irritating to need no additional help.

Firewatching, however, remained necessary. In the early stages of the war, whilst there was still fuel to burn, this had a different meaning at Fettes. Charles Herzberg noted the school's eccentricity in this respect:

When there was an air raid, the boys, or 'men', as all boys at Fettes were called, went into the air raid shelters which had been dug into the bank at the front of the school, but two senior boys were kept at the Houses to 'fire watch.' Unlike the usual interpretation that fire watching was to guard the buildings against fire bombs, our fire watching was mainly concerned that the many open fireplaces in the Houses and Housemasters' houses did not get out of control! [26]

Fettes' Old Library, with its view over Edinburgh, was the base for its ARP volunteers

Robin Donald was one pupil who appreciated this task – he recalls that it meant one didn't have to go to the shelters. When coal was severely rationed later in the war, the school became 'a community of hewers of wood' where anxious individuals were either 'walking about in aimless fashion searching for any stray twig' or 'manhandling outsize lumps of timber to places where they could be disintegrated to more proper proportions by axe or saw.'[27]

The *Fettesian* editor wondered how many studies had lost precious wood fittings to the fires. At Christmas 1942, Mr Pyatt contributed a poem from his retirement:

I'd love to be firewatching,
And should not like to shirk
For any selfish reason
Such patriotic work.

But I'm economising
With austerity that's Scotch
And huddled in a dressing gown
I have no fire to watch.[28]

That said, the air raid shelters designed on 'the advice of a man sent down from Whitehall' were pretty uncomfortable; 'as we were to find out,' Mackenzie Stuart recalled, 'it was quite clear that the Man from the Ministry had at that stage never spent a night in a contrivance of his own devising.' He noted that the roll-call in the shelters sometimes showed that someone had managed to sleep through all the alarms. Their creation after the Munich Crisis was at least partly carried out by the boys themselves; Bingham Kirk remembered that 'the shelters were completed in record time; all the students assisted in their construction by hauling away tons of dirt and debris.'[29]

Although there were occasional gripes about the invariably inappropriate temperature, the *Fettesian* noted that it was rare for a house to forget to bring a gramophone along to the shelter. Some pupils, including S.W. Park, would don top hat and tails in a show of defiant eccentricity as they headed for the shelters. At the Christmas of 1940, it could be observed that 'shelter life seems to have a far from depressing effect on members of the School... some of the chosen few are lucky enough to have electric light.'[30]

Jack Mackenzie Stuart was slightly less blasé in a letter home:

Do not be surprised if this is not a coherent or intelligent letter as I spent 2 hours from 12-2 last night in the A. Raid shelters. I had just fallen into a lovely sleep when I heard the sirens go and a second later the bell in our dorm. I put on my things and was one of the first 3 or 4 in the shelters, all was quiet. After we had been in for an hour or so, during which there had been muffled sounds of gunfire and aeroplane engines, the first explosion came and more and more every where, growing louder as a plan passed low, 2000 feet above the town.

The gun fire was terrific for about one minute and seemed right over our heads. It was rather frightening, I must confess.

One of our masters, a special constable came and gave us a description. The German plane was being hard pressed and from the light of tracer bullets we seemed to be filling it with lead. The sky was lit up with A.A. shells and flaming onions.

Then at the dismal [h]our of 2.a.m. the all clear went.[31]

Overall, despite worries about the new Ferranti factory at Crewe Toll (which from 1943 was producing top-secret gyroscopic gunsights for aircraft) and the 'indifferent blackout' at Western General Hospital, Fettes was in this aspect of wartime life much more fortunate than other schools; Petworth School lost its headmaster, an assistant mistress and 29 boys when it was destroyed in an air-raid of September 1942, and a single bomb killed six teachers and 37 pupils at Sandhurst Road School in London in 1943. Hamish Liddell recalls:

Fortunately we didn't have to go to the shelters too often as they were cold and damp and the worst occasion was the Clydebank raid when there was a constant procession of planes going there and back throughout the night accompanied by very loud gun fire from a heavy anti-aircraft battery somewhere on Fettes Row and we spent a cold and sleepless night. The only other raids I remember were a single bomb being dropped near Edinburgh Academy while we were doing prep (no siren on this occasion) and when a bond store somewhere behind Donaldson's Hospital was set on fire. Again, no siren and we could see the fire from our dormitory window. The story we subsequently heard from Joe, our Houseman, was that the whisky was running in the street and people were out with containers getting as much as they could but it is doubtful the raw spirit would do them much good! The other story was that the firefighters were getting drunk on the fumes and had to be relieved every 20 minutes![32]

There were those who mourned the Germans' obstinate refusal to appear on a more frequent basis. Willie Geddes certainly had good reason to:

The Germans raided on Thursdays which exactly coincided with our weekly Latin test with Mr. Hoare, who could be rather fierce. If the Germans failed to appear, all those of us who had done no prep were badly let down and got stick. If the boy near the window saw the balloons going up, then we knew that we were spared.[33]

Air raids over Edinburgh declined markedly after 1941, though a military presence remained at Fettes in the form of HMS *Vernon*, which used Kimmerghame House (along with other requisitioned school buildings at Roedean) 'for secret purposes' until 1946. Kimmerghame's usual occupants were transferred to Glencorse in what the *Fettesian* called a 'peaceful Anschluss', though some boys got into the habit of sneaking down to Kimmerghame's normally idle sandbagged gun pit to sunbathe. They might have been less sanguine about doing so had they realised that the naval teams were engaged in dismantling German mines in order to develop counter-measures, a task which cost the lives of several

The air-raid shelters at the front of the school

Vernon engineers, though not, apparently, at the Kimmerghame site. The Fettes section of HMS *Vernon* seems to have been primarily concerned with developing methods of triggering magnetic mines by acoustic and water pressure, and was staffed by a number of prominent scientists.[34]

The Corps goes to war

The Corps, of course, loomed large in school activities during the war, and whilst an absence of skilled instructors as the younger masters, including the popular 'Dick' Evers, went off to fight, did curtail some activities, new ones were introduced – it was, recalls Humphries, a serious business in wartime. There were difficulties in getting away to train elsewhere, though the shooting team, deprived of its usual range and indeed of the annual Bisley championships, did at least find a temporary home with the East of Scotland Club at Dreghorn. Sam Park recalled that the Corps was almost compulsory in those days and can only remember one individual being excused, a boy who went on to be a minister.[35] The Basic Marching Drill, M.C. Lyons thought, 'would probably have been recognised with approval by veterans of the Crimea.'[36] Weapons Drill began with .303 Lee Enfields which were then replaced for most purposes by Canadian Ross rifles and American Springfields, which A.R.H. Cumming remembers as being more accurate; there was also occasional light machine gun training with the Bren. Mackenzie Stuart recalled that there was a new 'emphasis on individual fitness and agility', with the 'strange innovations' of assault courses and forced marches. Certificate A ceased to contain written exams and became entirely practical and physical. The Physical Efficiency standards included a five-mile walk, one-mile run, high jump, long jump and rope-climbing, and other tests included map-reading and patrolling. The school retained, despite only one hour a week being set aside specifically for PT, an excellent track record in this. The boys were also taught bayonet technique on dummies made of straw. A.R.H. Cumming still remembers the instructions: 'Stab the enemy to a depth of six inches maximum, any deeper and you will pierce the enemy spine and perhaps be unable to withdraw the bayonet.' It is the unarmed combat that sticks in John Humphries' mind – the idea being that the German paratroopers they expected daily might be immobilised by such techniques as the 'Japanese stranglehold' – a move at which this particular Old Fettesian is still expert. Unfortunately, the boys became at little over-enthusiastic about unarmed combat and took to practising them on one another, so the experiment was halted. As with the use of bayonets, the cadets were then exposed to equipment which today's safety-conscious parent might consider dangerous in the extreme. The boys became expert on 'down-crawl-observer-fire!' with hand grenades. 'I can well remember Sgt.-Major Giles' "Don't throw the fucking thing, it's not a fucking cricket ball!"' says Humphries, 'We were shown how to handle sticky grenades. With these the boy was expected to crawl up to a German tank and stick the grenade on the tracks.' He notes that none of this was the slightest bit of use to him in his actual service career on the bridge of a destroyer, which is just as well since the sticky bomb (or No. 74 ST Grenade as it was officially known) was inherently more dangerous to its users than to the enemy, partly because it was more likely to stick to clothing than to tanks.

The Corps uniforms to which this soon-abandoned device was likely to stick changed considerably. The old Corps tunics, with their multiple brass buttons and traditional, complex webbing, were abandoned, unmourned by the fags who had been responsible for looking after them – Cumming recalls that it was 'the part I hated most' about Corps life. The kilt, too, became less frequently worn; as Mr Sale, the OC, noted in 1942, 'if German clothing is inadequate for a Russian winter, so is the Fettes kilt for snow-covered ground, and most of our parades have had to creep indoors.'[37]

It seems to have finally gone in 1943; Robin Donald remembers that he 'next wore a kilt when I was part of a small group chosen to attend the Usher Hall to see Field Marshall Earl Alexander, Admiral Lord Cunningham and Air Marshal Lord Portal receive the Freedom of the City of Edinburgh in 1946.'[38] After a temporary issue of denim overalls, the uniform was standard issue Battledress and the kilt.

With the outbreak of War the annual School Camps were cancelled, not to be resumed until 1942, but there were still opportunities to get out and about, cycling to Castlelaw Ranges, for instance, for weapon demonstrations and conducting exciting, if rather difficult, night exercises. Practical training was also available. 'I vaguely remember a Mechanical section,' says Robin Donald, 'with cadets tinkering with an old car', whilst NCOs could go on courses in the holidays, such as the one for signalers at Catterick in the Christmas of 1942. Sam Park remembered that the senior cadet NCOs also used to give up a week of their holidays to help instruct 70-odd pupils at some of the other Edinburgh schools which also had Contingents but did not have enough officers or NCOs capable of doing so. Among the pupil instructors were J.D. Cowie, who taught the use of the Bren gun, and Alastair MacLaren, who explained map-reading and fieldcraft. Mr Sale recorded proudly that 'very favourable comments were made on the instructional powers of the Fettes NCOs. Indeed, more than one OF, in response to appeals to information for this book, has paid tribute to the incomparable value, in later war service, of the map-reading he learned as a cadet at Fettes – 'I was much better at it,' remembers Freddie Scott, 'than many senior regular officers.'[39]

During a major exercise, No. 1 Platoon 'managed to cover some 22–23 miles in the course of the day without any loss of personnel.' This was no mean feat, according to M.C. Lyons, who recalled with embarrassment another, more ambitious affair in which two-thirds of the force sent to a 'private battle' by the Forth Bridge failed to find it on time. The cadet training imparted by the Corps was also useful in terms of morale. John Humphries, in the Royal Navy in September 1943 just after leaving the school, wrote a poem entitled 'JTC' (the OTC having been renamed as the rather more democratic Junior Training Corps):

We played at soldiers! The long afternoon
Of battle drill and a rifle drill is done
Our mock encounters worried out and won
Behind these hours there lies the thought that soon
A sterner enemy will bar our way

Shall we remember, as we face the Hun
The hours we pondered in polemic play?

I think we will and, if the lessons taught
Be hidden in some recess of the mind
We shall remember, yes, and smiling
Find new confidence. Most certainly we ought.
For thoughts of these dear fields and thoughts of home
Will give that strength which cannot be defined
But helps us face a multitude alone.[40]

Defenders of the Realm

In addition to new forms of training, other changes befell the Corps. The 'more elderly' boys, as Geddes puts it, formed a unit of the Local Defence Volunteers (later known as the Home Guard), which involved their being allowed to keep bicycles for a mobile patrol to be called upon should the need arise. It never did, and the school's magnificent Callover Hall was transformed into a bike-shed for the sole purpose, cynics claimed, of enabling the sixth form to go on Sunday outings. The LDV was formed as the Germans successfully rolled back the supposedly mighty French Army, and the British Expeditionary Force headed for Dunkirk. Jack Mackenzie Stuart remembered 'the Prime Minister's historic broadcasts and the realization that a German invasion was not only a possibility but was hourly expected.' Fettes had responded immediately to the call for volunteers; two sergeants came down to the school on Mondays to teach the Home Guard bayonet-fighting, and, as part of 'Moffat Mobile Force' along with the boys from Merchiston, they took part in an exercise in May 1941 as a rehearsal for what was euphemistically described as their Emergency Role, which was in fact the last-ditch defence of the North Esk in the event of a German invasion. This did not, of course happen, but, one sublime occasion in 1940, the warning sounded and within a quarter of an hour 'thirty-odd fighting Fettesians have been changed into uniform and armed and ammunitioned'. The rest, having no specific tasks to do, immediately went to sleep.[41]

The following February, they took part in a reconnaissance exercise:

Snow was falling – mercifully; as it either completely covered, or at least disguised, some of them worst excrescences on the landscape. A slag heap is almost a thing of beauty when it has been covered with a delicately woven mantle of snow. The rank and file, on push-bikes, ploughed along roads which were coated with a mixture of slush and snow packed tight, and glared with jealous eyes at the two despatch riders on motor-cycles who periodically passed moving at high speed. For a wonder, both motor-cycles were still in running order when the force returned to Fettes, a record in the annals of the Home Guard. After a pleasant morning of careful and accurate reconnaissance, the force adjourned to a barn to eat the delicious picnic lunch provided by the College and to thank their stars that they had brought their own additional supplies with them.[42]

One of the fortunate elite was Willie Geddes, whose father had bought a James motor bicycle for seven pounds; he rather enjoyed the exercises but accepts that it was pretty wearisome for everyone else. Fettesians were also expected to turn out in extremes of heat – at a grand military parade at Holyrood on a scorching summer afternoon, the sun progressively knocked out so many of them that eventually Geddes stood alone. Not in the least fazed, the Queen's conducting officer simply pointed at him and said, 'and this is Fettes.' Another task of the Fettes Home Guard, Major J.B.A. Smyth recalls, was cycling into the Pentland hills with their rifles to search for downed German aircrew[43] whilst Ian Stewart remembers drawing up a detailed map 'for the perimeter defence of Dalkieth.'[44]

David Fairweather took part in the weekend patrols:

The Home Guard unit, on Sundays, cycled from school (rifles slung over shoulders but not loaded) along Ferry Road to Leith, and then followed the main road along the coast to Portobello, Joppa and Musselburgh. Here we turned right, and followed the river up to the point where the railway to London crossed it, together with a parallel bridge whose tracks turned right to Smeaton Junction... At the time, there were numerous coal-mines active on those lines. The railway to Smeaton, slightly on an embankment, was to be the location we would defend against hordes of Germans.[45]

Luckily for the boys, their services were never required, and the Home Guard as a whole was stood down in 1944. That is not to say that invasion was not a very real threat in the 1940-1 period, and Ian Harvey, for one, was not optimistic about Britain's chances, noting that after he completed a tour of the south coast defences he and a colleague decided that their best option was to down several large whiskies and keep a

395

loaded revolver by one's bed; 'once they had established a firm bridge-head I reckon that Hitler's tanks would have got to London faster than the *Brighton Belle*.'[46]

Had invasion come, Fettes would not have escaped the attentions of the invaders. SS Sturmbannführer Walter Schellenberg prepared a detailed handbook for future German occupiers, the *Informationsheft Grossbritannien*, in 1940. A section of this is devoted to the role of public schools:

It is here that the future English [sic] gentleman is educated, the gentleman who has never thought about philosophical issues, who has hardly any knowledge of foreign culture and thinks of Germany as the embodiment of evil, but accepts British power as inviolable. The entire system's purpose is to train those of strong willpower and boundless energy, who consider spiritual issues a waste of time, but know man's nature and understand how to rule. These are educated people who in conscienceless manner represent English ideals and see the meaning of their lives in the promotion of the interests of the English ruling class.[47]

The irony of a National Socialist criticising someone else's anti-intellectualism, indifference to other cultures and obsession with willpower and energy was presumably lost on the notoriously humourless readership of this publication. As the alma mater of Sir John Simon, who was by this point Lord Chancellor under Churchill, Fettes got a mention alongside Eton, Harrow and the rest. Schellenberg's master, Reinhard Heydrich, spelled out exactly what schools could expect under Nazi occupation in the context of his post as Reichsprotektor in Prague. It was, he said, essential first to 'pounce upon the Czech teachers' who were a 'training corps for opposition.' Once they (and the universities) had been 'smashed', children could be educated – largely through the medium of sports – into healthy, Germanized enthusiasts for the New Order, uncontaminated by the subversive patriotic influences of parents or schoolmasters.[48]

Terezin concentration camp, and indeed the firing squad, awaited such Czech teachers and students who failed to co-operate. If this was the fate of the generally orderly Czechs – the hopelessness of whose position had been cruelly brought home to them in 1938 – what would have become of the (then) boisterously patriotic British educational system? It is an interesting insight into the Nazis' priorities that Schellenberg devoted more of his book to the sinister roles of the public schools and Boy Scouts ('a disguised instrument of power for British cultural propaganda, and an excellent source of information for the British Intelligence Service') than he did to either the British Army or the Tory Party. But then there was more on freemasonry ('a pivotal element of English Imperialism') than the economy, and more on the Jews ('Cromwell recognised the similarity of the English scheme for world domination and the Jewish version') than the government. The Home Guard did not, of course, know that the Germans had such detailed information about such everyday Scots pursuits as the apron and the woggle, but they did insist that Fettes should keep its sturdy, pointed Victorian railings as a line of defence against the fascist advance, thus saving them from the generally pointless fate of countless other metal objects taken away allegedly to be made into Spitfires but actually dumped in the Forth.

The Boys in Blue

A more lasting change to the Fettes war machine was the acquisition of a sibling in the form of the Air Training Corps, 'suspected at first as a shirkers' refuge' whose PT consisted, according to one sly *Fettesian* editorial by an army cadet, of playing ring o' roses.[49]

It soon proved its worth for delivering basic aviation skills to future fliers. The growth of the ATC in wartime was meteoric, and reflected the obsession with the air which had characterised not only the inter-war period, but also much British strategic thinking in wartime and the subsequent myths of popular culture. Founded in 1938 as the Air Defence Cadet Corps, it was chartered by Royal Warrant in 1941 as the ATC more than four hundred units were in existence by the spring of that year. Led by Mr Beamish, 511 Flight, as the Fettes unit was called, conducted training both in the school, where Mr Goldie-Scot taught navigation, signalling and Morse Code, and at RAF Turnhouse. Here there were activities to make the present-day air cadet green with envy, with regular flights in DH Tiger Moths and Miles Magisters ('most of us have now had valuable instruction, while some are already showing signs of becoming competent pilots', the Flight report noted proudly in July 1941[50]) use of the Link Trainer and cine-camera gun, and what must surely have been a very uncomfortable exercise in the gas chamber. The lessons were not always very effective – aiming to emulate the 'commandos' of the JTC in 1942, the ATC set forth to march five miles in an hour, and returned two hours later claiming to have done a round trip via Rosyth and the Pentlands 'having mistaken the sun for the Pole Star and steering a course without allowing for wind resistance; so much for our future navigators.'[51]

Not everyone thought solely in terms of how he might best serve King and Country when he joined the ATC, as this Gilbertian poem by 'Patience' in the *Fettesian* demonstrates:

When I first put this uniform on
I said, as I looked in the glass,
'It's one in a million
That any civilian
My figure and form will surpass.
But the R.A.F. boys have a charm
That no personal blemish can harm,
So when dressed up in blue
I'll be rivalled by few
As I stroll with a dame on each arm.'
The fact that I counted upon
When I first put this uniform on!

I said, when I first put it on
'It is plain it to the veriest dunce
That every beauty
Will feel it her duty
To yield to its glamour at once.'
But Ellen and Lisbeth and Nan
Saw the chromium buttons, and ran
'They're cinema lackeys
Or lift boy's from Mackie's
And we'd hoped for an R.A.F. man.'
Which I never counted upon
When I first put this uniform on.[52]

In 1941 and 1942, the ATC enjoyed its first camps 'on an aerodrome somewhere in Scotland' (David Fairweather remembers this as being Lossiemouth) and began the pattern of section visits familiar to air cadets to this day. Their favourite activity was undoubtedly doing duty in the Duty Pilot's Pill-Box, 'the nerve-centre of all comings and goings on the 'drome' where they could enjoy the 'thrill of reporting the planes over the telephone, and watching them land and take off.' Although the RAF undoubtedly taught the boys a great deal about wireless communications, station defence, machine-guns and meteorology, it is hard to avoid the conclusion that they also took the opportunity to make good use of the lads as free labour, cleaning Hurricanes and Spitfires ('which is one of the best ways of becoming familiar with the planes', the loyal reporter, Charles Denis McWilliam, later a clergyman, put it) and digging trenches. They also enjoyed flights in a Magister, a Rapide and, in David Fairweather's lucky case, a Beaufighter, one of the most capable aeroplanes of the era; he still remembers how the whole aircraft slowed down when the Polish pilot tested the massive ten-gun armament by firing it into the sea.[53]

The boys also heard an inspirational talk from Lord Trenchard, the RAF's founder. It was a splendid experience overall, McWilliam noted, 'but not until we have all passed on to the RAF or FAA will the full benefits obtained at this camp become apparent.'[54]

Food, Morale and Morality

Opinions like this one seem to reflect a generally positive feeling towards cadet life during the war, which most boys saw as useful and important; Mr Sale, writing the JTC report for December 1941, commented that although one could never quite tell what boys were thinking, the war seemed to have brought 'vastly greater keenness and efficiency' to the Corps. Sam Park's brother Sandy – a popular, unselfish and enterprising 1st XV back-row forward and head of house at Kimmerghame – died on active service in Bombay in 1942, and he felt that this 'may have made him throw himself into it with an extra vigour than most. He even ran Up-Town one afternoon and tried to join the RAF.' Sam finally joined the Army through the normal channels on leaving school, becoming a Lieutenant in the Camerons, still a frequent destination for OFs despite the great attraction of the blue uniform. 'The vast majority,' he recalled, 'felt it was what they had been being prepared for by being in the Corps and it was just their duty.' Willie Geddes, who freely admits to having been 'a dismal performer' (except when Mr Sale switched him on to history), went to the recruiting office on George Street as soon as his age permitted. A man who failed the eyesight test just as Geddes passed it told him that in peacetime he had been a trawler lookout. Bingham Kirk was undoubtedly impressed by the wartime Fettesians, though with an interesting caveat:

I came to admire many facets of British character – steadfastness, courage and traditions. However, as a people they also had flaws. Their arrogance might have been their worst shortcoming. On many occasions people whom I had just met would think they were complimenting me by saying that I was 'not at all like an American.' Similarly, I seldom heard complimentary remarks about people of other countries.[55]

Then again, one can hardly be surprised at the emergence of nationalism in wartime. A nation which regards others as superior to itself is unlikely to be in a mental position to win. The strength of purpose and relative unity of the wartime school may partly have been due to the low numbers – only 166 boys at one point – and Lyons believed that, whatever people's likes or dislikes, this enabled everyone to know everyone else and create a strong feeling of cohesion. Mr MacDonald attributed to other factors the fact that conditions were definitely better than during the First World War, when boys were aware of how likely it was that they would be killed shortly after leaving school, and this made them impatient of school discipline and, in some cases, less than kind to their younger brethren:

Nothing of the kind it seems to have happened in the Second War: it is certain that nothing of the kind happened at Fettes. Everyone knew that things were being managed better this time, and that no one would be sent into action until he was properly trained, and until he had a real chance of doing what he was sent to do. The effect of this was that everyone went on with his job, undistracted by rebellious thoughts; nor had anyone time for the engendering a frivolous attitude. Life was real and earnest, and Dr. Ashcroft gave us a magnificent lead.[56]

A pressing issue for many boys, however, was food. Even compared with the Great War, Britain was regulated and militarized to a degree scarcely imaginable today. Always a rather robust environment, Fettes could be rather uncomfortable in the war as food and fuel were rationed, making the halcyon days of the 1930s an era of myth spoken of fondly by the older boys. Lyons left a detailed account in *A Hundred Years of Fettes*:

Food is a standard schoolboy preoccupation, but few generations of Fettesians can have thought about it with quite such wholehearted concern as we did. As the War went on and rationing grew stricter, the kitchen staff did wonders with what they had. It is bitterly unfair to brood about their failures but Tuesday's College stew and Monday's watery mince did serve to cast a gloom over the start of the week. In our first year chocolate was unrationed and the tuck shop still had a fairly flourishing trade. Later, though, this came almost to a standstill and the chocolate ration was served out, I think once a month, by house prefects. One of the highlights of the eating day was the evening brew. Fried bread was the standby if there was anything in which to fry it and it could be washed down by cocoa if there was any milk. Eggs could be got in their anaemic powdered form, while some hardy spirits imported gulls' eggs and claimed to enjoy them. Certainly one of the most powerful inducements to study was provided by Mr. Richardson, who kept hens and would sometimes offer to the lower forms a real egg as a price for learning French irregular verbs. Then, when the brew was finished, we could retire to dream of that other great Fettes delicacy, the breakfast roll. So accustomed did we get to wartime food that when at the end of the war the first bananas appeared at lunch just before the House Below rugger finals, word was passed around to one team not to eat them until the game was over as it would make them sick.[57]

David Fairweather remembers that the caterers did wonders with the rations, though this did not prevent those serving it from putting a grim face on things. 'My table was waited on by a houseman from Carrington who, when asked what was for pudding, would give a gap-toothed leer and say "spunk, and Chinamen's balls" (political correctness was unheard of).'[58] He also remembers the Headmaster's dry Latin gag on the *benedictus, benedictat* grace when it was announced that, although ration reductions meant that only potatoes and soup were available, it would be possible to have second helpings, hence *benedicto, benedictate.* The *Fettesian* observed in 1941 that, with the shortage of jam, the school had formed three distinct classes; aristocrats with private stocks, an enterprising bourgeoisie who came up with new solutions such as meat paste, and a proletariat frugally surviving on rations alone.[59] 'I remember the sweet rationing scheme,' says Robin Donald, 'because as a House Prefect, I became the Chocolate King; I think we were limited to 6d per week and my task was to take orders from the members of College from the short list of products, and then distribute the goods.'[60]

Plenty of recent studies have suggested that, despite people's grumbles, the British ate more healthily in wartime than they have since, and David Arbuthnott summarizes the situation by saying that 'we were fed adequately, if monotonously, and remained in good health and strength'

– which is as much as can be hoped for. Ian Stewart is more cheerful still about the wartime diet – 'feeding at hall in Fettes, *after* rationing of food took effect (in 1941, I think) got rather better!'[61]

It might be worth noting that Mr Stewart left in June 1941. 'It was pretty Spartan in any case,' Alastair MacLaren remembers of Fettes in those days, 'and wartime restrictions merely made it yet more Spartan.'[62]

This did have a positive side; the top hat and tails, which the boys disliked, disappeared, and most of the wartime OFs who wrote to the school to supply their memories for this book recall this as one of the war's great blessings. The 'sober pomp and show' of the tails, and 'topper shining like th' Assyrian spear' were not, as Humphries noted at the time, in his first published poem, really suitable for the boyish rough and tumble of school life. The jug of milk, the 'detested tin tack', dust of the road to church and other contributors to 'smudge and smirch' soon reduced the elegant kit to shabby remnants. The *Fettesian*, noted, however, that relaxing the uniform regulations had led to some downright eccentric efforts in 'make do and mend' – although battered tweeds of various colours and levels of cleanliness were acceptable (as of course they still are in respectable Scots circles) the editor drew the line at the chap who appeared to have made himself trousers out of the green baize fabric of a billiard table.

One of the most notorious aspects of Edinburgh's wartime history seems to have passed unnoticed by the schoolboys, if their recollections and contemporary observations were anything to go by – though a distinguished Old Fettesian was very much aware of them. A cartoon in the Christmas 1941 *Scottish Field* depicts a crowded tea-room in which suave Polish officers, glamorous French sailors, burly Australians and debonair Canadians are successfully chatting up local girls whilst a doleful, lonely Royal Scots Fusilier plaintively asks a hostile waitress if he might have a cup of tea.[63]

Edinburgh was full of Britain's allies, and as Robert Bruce Lockhart, back in the city of his schooldays to be treated for crippling eczema, noted, 'drunkenness, rowdiness, and immorality were unbridled, and on Saturday nights an unescorted girl avoided Princes Street.'[64]

The Poles were not, apparently, rowdy, but relentlessly pursued the girls 'with the courtesy of old-world cavaliers, and their successes were many.' He tells the (not necessarily apocryphal) story of a Polish pilot who, on his first leave, found companionship in the shape of a platinum blonde; he wined and dined her with true Polish courtesy and, as he had no hotel, was delighted to accept her invitation to share her flat for the night. After the young lady, responding gallantly to his unwonted charm and politeness, had cooked him breakfast in the morning, she was alarmed when he kissed her hand and said goodbye. Revealing her true colours, she pulled him up with a husky cry, 'What about some dough, duckie?' The Pole looked bewildered. 'Cash,' said the good-time-girl, 'M-o-n-e-y. Money.' The Pole smiled gracefully, clicked his heels and bowed. 'I, Polish officer,' he said, 'I, man of honour. Polish officer never take money.'

Fettes' contact with our ally seems to have been through the Music Club, which was adorned several times by the presence of Polish émigrés such as Lt Marian Blaszczynski, who gave stirring piano recitals. Altogether more blatantly capitalist were the Americans, whose arrival in 1942 as 'the real disturbers of a once staid Edinburgh' was accompanied by their vast wealth; 'to girls who had never seen a ten-shilling note in their hands the pounds which the American soldiers distributed freely were an irresistible magnet.' Whether in chasing women of buying alcohol, the Americans, who thought nothing of buying up a pub's stock of whisky at the vastly inflated sum of five pounds a bottle (it was fifteen shillings in 1939), 'left nothing for the unfortunate Scottish soldiers who could not compete financially.' Bruce Lockhart did not entirely blame the Americans; dutifully traipsing round the Red Cross tour of the Castle, St Giles' and Holyrood, they had had a surfeit of culture and sought entertainment on the streets. From his hospital bed, Bruce Lockhart could see the queue of young girls for the venereal disease out-patient clinic, and, although not easily shocked, concluded that wartime Edinburgh had opened his eyes; not only was 'the process of demoralisation' rapid, but the city, indeed the country, seemed to be losing its identity, becoming centralised by the English economy and state, 'losing its individuality and its virtues' – becoming provincialised.

The Headmaster, if he was worried about the erosion of the Scots virtues on Princes St, was well able to channel the energies of his boys in positive directions. Although the *Fettesian* was not quite so heavily inundated with jingoistic poetry as it had been in 1914-18 (partly because of the existence of *Gargoyle* as an outlet for young versifiers, as the editor admitted), the general feeling of robust patriotism still shone through, and Jack Mackenzie Stuart recalled that there was a real impatience to get on with life once they had bagged the relevant examination results and not to hang around school any longer than necessary, an attitude he believed began in wartime and has continued to the present day. Dr Ashcroft was moved to contribute the following poem, 'To One who is Under-Age for War Service' in November 1941:

> Grieve not, my son, that still thy days are spent
> In sheltered haunts: that not to thee as yet
> Has come the call for tears and toil and sweat,
> Or noble part in war's arbitrament;
> Who 'stands and waits,' his purpose straitly bent
> To face his lowly duties without fret,
> He will best serve when sterner tasks are set,
> His powers unnumb'd by selfish discontent.[65]

Dr Ashcroft, recalled DJ Grant, was a devoutly religious man, fond of the Prophets and the Book of Revelation, and reserving his greatest warmth 'for those who might become Pastors of their flocks.' John Humphries still remembers a sermon the Headmaster gave in December 1943 on Joel III.14 – 'Multitudes, multitudes in the valley of decision! For the day of the Lord is near in the valley of decision.' Explicit connections could be made which linked the struggle of the Old Testament – some commentators have seen Joel's Valley as that of Armageddon – and those of the twentieth century. The young Humphries was undoubtedly moved, and wrote a poem for the *Fettesian*:

> I see Jerusalem's ancient walls,
> The foe before the gate,
> While from the rampart Joel calls,
> 'On, Jews, the Lord is Great'…
>
> The Menin Gate at Ypres I see,
> And hear the watchman's cry.
> I hear the tramp of feet decree,
> That multitudes must die…
>
> I see the Libyan sandy waste,
> And hear the battle's roar;
> I see the few who bravely faced

The foe who numbered more.
Then in a silent interlude,
I feel that foe's derision,
And I long to join the Multitude
In the Valley of Decision.

Alec Ashcroft and Jerry Lodge

Fettes does its bit

Grant believed that he was disappointed in his desire to see the world remade, but the pages of the *Fettesian* during the war illustrate that it was not for want of trying on his part. In order to keep those too young to fight occupied, other forms of war work also took place; Park remembered volunteers being recruited to help clear ground at Drem, just outside Edinburgh, for the new airfield. Sandy Johnstone, who was later to command 602 Squadron in the Battle of Britain, was stationed there at the time, and wrote in his diary that his CO, known as 'Batchy', had 'managed to talk the headmaster into sending his boys to Drem for a day, arguing that a spell in the fresh air would do them more good than sitting in classrooms conjugating Latin verbs.'[66]

David Fairweather, who took part, was involved in building blast walls to protect the skilled mechanics working on aircraft in the event of low-level strafing by the Germans. So many boys volunteered that the school organised buses, where shelters were built from pit props and turf, 'probably adequate for machine gun fire at that stage of the war.'[67]

Ian Stewart and others felled trees on the Wemyss estate at Lingniddry to make space for a dummy aircraft dispersal, and were rewarded by lunch in the RAF Drem officers' mess and given a personal inspection of a Hurricane.[68]

John Younie was lucky enough to be taken up for an evening flight by the CO, who was adjusting the glide path indicator for night landing; this led him to choose flying as a career, and he went on to become a fighter pilot, winning the DFC. Impressed by the way the boys 'seemed happy to toil away with nothing more to look forward to than a couple of square meals in the airmen's dining hall,' the pilots were keen to reward as many Fettesians as possible with flights, as Johnstone recorded at the time:

Batchy decided they should be taken for a trip before returning to school, whereupon every multi-seater aircraft at Drem was mobilised to form a sort of aerial circus. The Tiger Moths and Harvard plus a gash Fairey Battle were pressed into service and the force augmented by a visiting Blenheim in which Batchy took the boys up four at a time. On one occasion I spotted this bomber flying inverted across the airfield at nought feet with four unfortunates on board who, incidentally, assured us they had thoroughly enjoyed the experience. Diplomacy must take a high place on the curriculum of Fettes College! [69]

Others 'dug for victory' in the new school allotments or on Lord Rosebery's Dalmeny Estate. 'We most earnestly urge them to dig with courage, cheerfulness and the rest, for we all know where that leads us,' commented the *Fettesian* drily, referring to the notoriously unpopular poster which implied that the public were required to do all the work for the government, who were presumably going to reap the rewards. Sixth-formers were recruited by the Civic Administration office in George St to prepare ration books prior to distribution. A National Savings Group was established under the tutelage of Mr Vawdrey, who got a little exasperated by 'those who buy stamps occasionally, only to cash them back in a moment of financial stringency'; they were 'throwing a little sand into the war-winning machinery'. 'Saving money is admittedly a dull job, but no more exciting alternative has yet been discovered whereby those who stay at home can help to win the war' he pointed out, though was pleased to note that by early 1943 the school had lent £1370, 5s. to the government.[70]

Later in the war a diverting alternative was indeed found in the shape of the Harvest Camps at the appropriately-named village of Ceres in Fife. The Headmaster and Mrs Ashcroft, Mr Sale and others gave up their holidays to organise and care for boys who were allocated to local farms to help bring in the abundant wheat for which the area is known, and also flax – Robin Donald notes that this was the only time he had ever seen a field of it. Not only the feeling of doing something energetic and useful – ten-hour shifts were not uncommon – but the engaging experience of all the teachers and boys mucking in together and socialising in the evenings over shove ha'penny and bagatelle, with the Headmaster doing the washing-up and his wife offering the second helpings which could mysteriously appear in the countryside, was very important. One boy later wrote:

The skin on my hands has not yet fully recovered from my month's harvesting in Fife, but just as my stay there has left its imprint on my hands, so it has left a more permanent imprint on my memory… Everyone, masters or boys, joined in to pool their experiences during their day's work: we heard of the six-foot sheaves, of rabbit catching, or unintelligible Italian prisoners and still less intelligible Fife gaffers, and, from those who fished in the evening, stories of two-ounce fish which had been caught and two-pound fish which had not.[71]

The lively local girls appear to have caused the Headmaster some embarrassment by arranging games of postman's knock, but on the whole the enterprise was a great success.

Culture and Politics

Dr Ashcroft ought also to have been heartened by the fact that the cultural life he encouraged continued, under albeit straitened circumstances, and many of the boys continued to take an enthusiastic interest in the outside world and to participate in cultural and intellectual activities (though one OF wondered if this was to take their minds off the absence of food). Film shows every other Saturday mixed Mickey Mouse cartoons with Ealing comedies, imperial melodramas and Ministry of Information films. The Literary and Dramatic Society held readings of contemporary and classic novels, and the Art Society held meetings on such worthy topics as 'Methods of Etching and Engraving' and the works of Van Gogh. Houses continued to put on plays, and whilst rehearsals were sometimes interrupted by sirens, by some extraordinary stroke of luck no performances were. One of the most successful of these was, appropriately, *Journey's End*, performed by Glencorse in 1943. Slightly less successful was a visit from some strolling players, as Liddell recalled:

…a travelling acting company was to give us a night of Shakespeare. It was dire and the acting appalling, and the applause at the end was modest, to put it mildly. The next day the Headmaster addressed the school and apologised to us for submitting us to such a poor production, and congratulated us on our receiving it so politely. There can't have been many occasions when a headmaster has apologised to his school! [72]

A dance band, the de Lambère Knights, swung merrily through many of the war years. The Debating Society tackled issues such as the Modern Woman's improvement on her predecessor – A.G.R. McFadyen, who believed matters had regressed, gave a heart-rending account of how an uncle's modest outlay of a few coins on fish and chips had 'received a greater reward from the unfair sex than had McFadyen himself, though his expenditure had been vast.'[73] The proposal that PT should replace team games in November 1943 was vigorously opposed by Mr Newman, who ignored the claim that rugger was barbaric and argued that the mass enthusiasm for PT was a 'dark conspiracy' for three reasons – 'it emanated from Germany, it destroyed individualism, and it didn't teach grit as well as games.'[74]

Intellectual stimulation continued to be supplied by lectures on such topics as 'Where stands the USA?' and France's role in the war (the speaker, Professor Matthieu of the Free French Cabinet, urged the boys to remember that 'when we do defeat the Boche, we must keep him down.'[75]) Straightforward military topics were also frequent. A member of the Parachute Regiment, for instance, came on a recruiting drive. 'After demonstrating all his battle equipment,' Robin Donald says, 'he climbed a tree on the West Drive and jumped from a height of 14 feet to show us how to land.' Despite everything, German works were still performed by the school orchestra, which performed Beethoven's 'Eroica' Symphony in December 1941 and a selection from Strauss the following year. The Music Club concert of November 1943 consisted of sonatas and songs by Mozart, Schumann and Schubert, which were brilliantly performed by Younie, Macdonell and Cowie, and were loudly applauded. The Library notes for that month mention the acquisition of books by Goethe and Schiller. Despite the vastly greater destruction they visited on the United Kingdom's population – not to mention that of Eastern Europe – the Germans were not, then, quite the same objects of hatred that they had been immediately before and during the Great War. Or not, at least, for the sensitive intellectual element. One gleeful poem, which it must be said is relatively untypical, rejoiced in the destruction of one German city by the RAF:

When the War is over
How we'll gorge once more!
Tasty soles from Dover,
Ham and eggs galore!

Herr von Sauerkrauter
Eggs may hope to cram,
But he'll be without a
Single bit of Hamm! [76]

In the early years of the war, victories over Italy in Africa were among the few causes for celebration, since Germany showed little inclination to give up Europe and despite the propaganda, the RAF's bombing raids on enemy cities were having little effect. One poem on the subject suggests a greater degree of sensitivity towards the enemy than that displayed by the boy who exulted in the destruction of Hamm:

'Twere sad if victories o'er our Roman foes
Were greatly marred by cheap and ugly jests
Which smirch their name and ours. Our honour rests
Not only with our soldiers, but with those
Who here at home their highest faith repose
In that fine magnanimity, which wrests
All scorn and hatred from the victors' breasts,
And gives the vanquished hope amid their woes.

Foolish they may have been, these sons of Rome,

Too easily by a braggart's vaunts misled:
But though the flower of Freedom droops its head,
Though Law and Justice flee their ancient home,
If we forgive her in her hour of stain
Rome's pristine virtues will shine forth again.[77]

The ability to distinguish between an enemy nation's culture and its leadership was rather more visible in the second war than the first – shades, perhaps, of 'Don't let's be beastly to the Germans.' That said, given the horror stories coming from the Far East, it is unsurprising that a school of the Empire like Fettes would be rather more viscerally hostile to the Japanese. John Humphries frankly admitted that they all hated the Japanese; when hostilities were over and the scale of the atrocities were known, he was serving in the Royal Navy and 'felt no remorse' as he stood in the ruins of Hiroshima. There are, however, few references in the wartime editions of the *Fettesian* to enemy war crimes. An exception, entitled 'Pogrom', appeared in November 1940:

Through the arches of the ages sound the footsteps of the Jew,
The wanderer whose face is lined and sad;
His eyes are looking backward at a fast receding view
Of a land of milk and honey that once happily he knew,
A home, Jehovah's favour which he had…

Avaunt, crucifix, which are the brand upon his face,
The curse of blood that lies upon his head!
Jehovah, let thy people, let thy chosen Hebrew race
Have some glimmering ray of pardon in their miserable case,
Revive, O God, their hope that long is dead.[78]

This appeared long before the Nazis engaged in the systematic extermination of the Jews, though they had of course enacted anti-semitic legislation in the 1930s and were undoubtedly already treating the Jews of Poland with greater brutality than was being meted out to the Christian Poles (though that was foul enough). Most boys, of course, were aware that the Nazis committed atrocities – that's what Nazis *did*, of course – but were concerned primarily with the performance of the national armed forces in which their relations and friends were serving. In 1940, remembered Hamish Liddell,

...the war began to impact on us and more so with the fall of France as many of us had relations serving in the Army. The general view in the school seemed to be that although it was a disaster we had got our soldiers back and we would be better on our own without France. Churchill became Prime Minister and the House always gathered in the common room to hear all his very rousing speeches.

Awareness of what was going on was encouraged by both the headmaster and his staff. 'Jerry' Lodge's efforts to explain matters to his boys in Carrington were greatly appreciated, as David Arbuthnott recalled:

He had served in the First War and so could speak with authority. There was a map of the world in the common room and from it we were kept up to date on the progress of the war. In the evening he would tell us of any important event and the news of those who had gone from Carrington. Dr Ashcroft was also excellent at telling us what was going on, especially in chapel when the casualties were reported.[79]

In College House, David Fairweather remembered, G.C. Beamish arranged for an extension from his wireless set to transmit Churchill's speeches and BBC news bulletins to the pupils. Mr Richardson's French class, Ian Stewart noted, read *le Figaro* and *le Monde* each week (including the 'stop press' item 'Rien de signaller' from the Maginot Line)

...until all hell broke loose in May 1940. I was in Dick Evers' form at that time, and a map on the wall showed each day the line of the German advance moving further and further into France. We were conscious of the anxiety surrounding those with fathers and elder brothers in the BEF.

Mackenzie Stuart recalled that although in the 'Phoney War' of 1939-40 they avidly read glossy magazines extolling the invincibility of Allied might, only to be shocked by Germany's seizure of the Low Countries. So excited did both the media and the public become over Dunkirk that on 4 June Churchill was obliged to explain that the situation was truly desperate, wars were not won by evacuations, and that 'what has happened in France and Belgium is a colossal military disaster.' As the joy over Dunkirk was soon replaced with paranoia about invasion, Fettesians seem to have kept their spirits up pretty well. The Battle of Britain was, of course, very exciting – 'we followed avidly the daily results of the air battles and the number of planes shot down,' recalls Hamish Liddell, 'figures subsequently shown to be exaggerated.' The loss of great ships such as the *Hood* and *Prince of Wales* was keenly felt, but David Arbuthnott remembered a general feeling of optimism:

Of course we were concerned about reverses in Russia, the Far East and North Africa but I think it may have been Jerry Lodge's upbeat briefings that kept us confident. Somehow, against all the evidence, we knew we would win. There was a framed quotation of Queen Victoria in the common room which said 'Please understand that there are no considerations of defeat in this house. They do not exist'. I imagine Jerry Lodge put it up.[80]

Robin Donald concurred:

Throughout the war we were fully aware of its progress, and immensely patriotic.
    I remember the delight of hearing about the victory at El Alamein. As we knew D-Day was imminent a member of the Signals Section kept us informed on one of the Corps wireless sets. The disaster of Arnhem was bemoaned, but we followed the war's progress until on VE day we had a holiday.[81]

Written information during the War was carefully controlled by the government (though, in fairness, historian John Keegan has said that the HMSO publications were 'models of objectivity' – 'whilst putting the best face on things, they tell no lies and admit a good deal of the truth'[82]) and the masters of Fettes were keen to do their bit to reinforce the need for security. The school's self-censorship extended to a bizarre article in November 1940 about the summer holiday war work carried out by about a dozen pupils and masters, which, whilst glorying in the fact that 'several important and highly distinguished persons' had been 'very greatly impressed by what had been accomplished by Fettesian voluntary labour', skilfully evades mentioning who they were, what the work was or where they did it.[83]

    Later on, a talk was given to the boys by Lt Pertwee (later the second Dr Who) of the RNVR on the subject of 'careless talk'– 'though punctuating his words with many very amusing anecdotes, he left his hearers, especially after the tale of the Murmansk convoy, in no doubt as to their responsibilities in the matter.'[84]

    This dark side of the war was what really brought home the dangers of the situation to the boys, at least one of whom saw at first hand the horrors of u-boat attacks. Ronnie Shaw was a passenger on the SS *Sarpedon* in a convoy which was attacked in the Bay of Biscay in late 1941:

We had to stay on deck with our life jackets on all night for five nights, watching other ships being torpedoed. You could see people in the sea; a woman was engulfed by flames which spread across the water to her. We couldn't do anything. There is nothing nice, pleasant or entertaining about war. [85]

Alastair MacLaren notes that, as a Foundationer – a pupil with a scholarship and thus expected to apply himself rigorously to the Classics – he was immersed in his studies, which 'left me with little time or inclination for much else, and I think it was the same for many others.' Yet reality could still intrude:

The war, fascist threats etc., were brought home to us abruptly, however, when Dr Ashcroft started to pin on his noticeboard outside his study door a manuscript roll of OFs who'd been killed. The list grew remorselessly, and when the names of boys you'd known to appeared on it, you realised jolly well that hellish things were going on. [86]

Robin Donald remembered specific examples of this:

It was particularly poignant to hear of the death of N. G. Millar, a Spitfire Pilot, as he had been Head of School, and of College [House] *in 1941 when I arrived. Later D.B. Lyall, an Infantry Officer, was killed and he had been a House Prefect in College in my first year.*

John Humphries summed up the feeling of loss in a poem unpublished at the time:

We kneel in silence and we think of you
Just one more name upon the honoured roll?
No, something far, far, dearer – one more soul
Who lived this life: who prayed within this pew,
Who loved all that we love; who daily grew
From boyhood's imperfection to Man's goal
Within these walls. A laughing boy whose whole
Existence seemed for pleasure. But you knew
What should be done and you have done your all.

Did Bigside seem to you an Olympian height?
And did the Upper charm your vision too?
And then when you obeyed your country's call
Perhaps you thought of Fettes. So tonight
We kneel in silence and we think of you.[87]

In a Founder's Day speech in 1982, when he was able to relate his subsequent naval experience to the Falklands conflict, Viscount Arbuthnott gave the modern pupils a sense of how heavy the losses had been for the intakes of the thirties. 'An average of eight out of the entry of 60 for each of those ten years were killed,' he said, 'and by 1945 we had all known those whose names were later to join those hundreds of others on the War Memorial.'[88]

The casualties of the Great War had fallen most heavily on the masters, some of whom had known all of those who joined up, and this war was no different. Dr. Ashcroft wrote a moving poem when an OF, Ronald Parker, was killed on a training flight at Cranwell in 1940:

I'll not forget that day of glad surprise
When you came back, dressed in your Air Force blue:
I'll not forget the gleam that lit your eyes,
Like that in Wendy's, when she cried 'I flew!'
I'll not forget that even then I knew
An ice-cold shadowy dread you did not share;
My heart was heavy with my fear for you,
But you knew nothing of my grounding care,
You who had quaffed the blithe brave spirit, the air.

That day 'twas mine to taste the richest joy
That can befall the teacher – to behold
The boy, the often wayward tiresome boy,
Grown self-reliant, happy, strong and bold.
That's joy remains e'en in the hour I'm told
Those icy fears were pregnant with the truth;
This dark sad hour is yet shot through with gold;
I shall remember, 'mid the grief and ruth,
The parting handshake, and the proud salute of youth.[89]

Not only did the school lose some of its finest pupils, but also a popular master, 'Dick' Evers, who John Humphries remembers as an inspirational English teacher, not least because of his encouragement for literary leanings among all that classicism. Just before he left to join up, he treated the boys to a musical evening on his banjo which included Percy French's 'Abdul Abulbul Amir and Ivan Skavinsky Skavar.' After service in Britain, 2/Lt Evers was posted to Algiers to become an instructor, where, MacDonald writes, 'He was not going to instruct men to risk their lives until he had seen some action himself. So he was sent up to the front, and on the way his jeep struck a mine.'[90]

His obituary in the *Fettesian* records a gifted, amusing and compassionate man with a fondness for Mars Bars; he was genuinely loved by colleagues and pupils alike, and the impact upon them all was severe. The fact that this had happened before, and that an earlier conflict was remembered every year in Corps parades around the war memorial, was not lost on Humphries. In January 1943, he was in his last year at the school and about to join the Royal Navy. Unable to sleep on a moonlit night, he lifted a section of the blackout from his window in College East, and looked down at the bronze highlander:

There's a misty moon tonight
Shining down upon these walls,
And it bathes in gentle light
The places where it falls.
They look fairer in the moonlight than they looked in light of day,
And the statue on the gravel seems no longer cold and grey.
It was pregnant with a new life and its 'carry on' is gay
In the memories and thoughts which it recalls.

Khaki figures stand around it,
There are dark blue by its side.
They seem to quite surround it
And they gaze on it with pride.
A captain tells a major 'I say sir, d'you know
They built this statue for us when we went in the last show
To remind them how we left them, and how they too must go –
Though I think it is a pity that we died...

There are footsteps on the gravel,
Footsteps brisk and fast,

Steps that briskly travel
The path were once they passed.
A silent figure in the moonlight, dressed in Air Force Blue,
Comes, solitary, walking along the way he knew.
The captain murmurs softly 'The first, sir, of the Few.'
And the major answers 'Would he were the last...' [91]

As victory came in sight, Fettesians allowed some of their much-vaunted military keenness and efficiency to slip in pursuit of earthier joys. Douglas MacGregor remembers one of the great escapades of 1944, when a trio of cadets led by Colin Guthrie (later a successful Glasgow lawyer) got fed up with shivering in the sleet of the Pentlands, where they were supposed to be acting as the enemy on an exercise. They used their Great War surplus P14 rifles to hold up a passing Post Office van, got themselves to the centre of Edinburgh, and went to the picture house on Prices St. Returning by tram to Comely Bank, they beat the search party back to school and greeted their bedraggled pursuers with the words 'You nearly found us a couple of times, but you just weren't looking hard enough.' MacGregor wonders if the silhouette of a spreadeagled body remains in one of the studies at Glencorse, since Guthrie decided to cap his desertion by lobbing a thunderflash into one.[92]

When Germany surrendered, the school had a holiday, and the boys allowed, for the first time, to wander off where they pleased without any sort of record being kept. The Carrington boys took themselves off to Waverley, and some, like Lyons, got a train to Stirling where they scrambled round the Wallace Monument and tested the generosity of shopkeepers willing to sell food off the ration. Later, a further holiday was granted, and a great bonfire lit on the playing fields. The defeat of Japan several months later coincided with the first full day of the new academic year, and the boys went 'up town' to see George VI take the salute in a victory parade on Princes St. They were wearing the 'uneasy compromise' between the morning dress of pre-war days and post-war informality, the grey flannel suit with soft felt hat. 'We looked', recalled new boy Ian Mackenzie, 'like an infestation of dwarf Chicago gangsters.'[93]

Mackenzie, overcome by heat and crowding, was sick into his hat. On reporting it to Mr Beamish, the housemaster – who had been at the school since the days of Dr Heard – raised his eyebrows and said 'You have had the courage to express exactly what I think about those hats.'

Meanwhile, Dr Ashcroft, realizing that there would be a scramble for new headmasters when the war ended, had ensured his succession to an OF, Donald Crichton-Millar, and prepared to hand over the reins to him. He had served the school faithfully for a quarter of a century, and done a remarkable job. Looking back in 2008, David Arbuthnott summed up the experience of the wartime school simply and appreciatively: 'My general memory was of a safe and sheltered environment where we were fostered by sensible and level-headed men.' Still grateful to Mr Evers, Lt John Humphries, RN, would, as his ship sailed into the unknown, murmur to himself lines from Macaulay's *Horatius*:

And how can man die better
Than facing fearful odds,
For the ashes of his fathers,
And the temples of his gods?

'That,' he said, 'was the spirit of the Fettes war generation.'

NOTES

[1] Jack Mackenzie Stuart, letter home, 19 October 1939 (thanks to his family for sending this)

[2] B. Kirk, *Industria*, May 2001

[3] In conversation with the author, December 2008

[4] J. Humphries, letter to the author, 23 September 2008

[5] A.J. Mackenzie Stuart in MacDonald, p. 212

[6] Kenneth Hall, *OFNL*, July 2005

[7] H. Liddell, letter to the author, 15 September 2008

[8] W. Geddes, letter to the author, 19 September 2008

[9] *Fettesian*, March 1949

[10] Quoted in Philp, p. 63

[11] *Fettesian*, November 1939

[12] Andrew Jeffrey, *This Present Emergency* (Mainstream, Edinburgh, 1992), Ch. 2

[13] Quoted in *OFNL*, July 1999

[14] Liddell, op. cit.

[15] Guest, p. 11

[16] John Humphries, *A Lifetime of Verse* (Bicester, Dogma, 2006), p. 2

[17] Lord Normand, *Fettes College Register 1870-1953* (Edinburgh, Constable, 1954) p. xviii

[18] MacDonald in MacDonald, p. 232

[19] Jeffrey, Ch. 1

[20] Jack Mackenzie Stuart, letter home, 26 June 1940

[21] Letter to the author, 4 August 2008

[22] Quoted in Ian Nimmo, *Scotland at War*, (Edinburgh, Scotsman Publications, 1989)

[23] Quoted in Jeffrey, p. 120

[24] Grant in MacDonald, p. 205

[25] *Fettesian*, December 1940

[26] Charles Herzberg, *OFNL,* July 2005

[27] *Fettesian*, February 1942

[28] *Fettesian*, December 1942

[29] Kirk

[30] *Fettesian*, December 1940

[31] Jack Mackenzie Stuart, letter home, 26 June 1940

[32] Liddell

[33] Geddes

[34] See, for instance, Prof. J. Jackson (obit.) at http://www.rse.org.uk/fellowship/obits/obits_alpha/jackson_john.pdf

[35] I am extremely grateful to Sandy Park who kindly talked to his father about the war years for this book.

[36] Lyons in MacDonald, p. 223

[37] *Fettesian*, February 1942

[38] Letter to the author, 9 August 2008

[39] Letter to the author, 7 August 2008

[40] Humphries, p. 9

[41] *Fettesian*, July 1940

[42] , February 1942

[43] Letter to the author, 4 August 2008

[44] Letter to the author, 16 August 2008

[45] Letter to the author, 7 August 2008

[46] Harvey, p. 39

[47] Walter Schellenberg, *Informationsheft GB* in *Invasion 1940* (Little, Brown, London, 2001) p. 26

[48] Callum MacDonald & Jan Kaplan, *Prague in the shadow of the swastika: A history of the German occupation* (Vienna, Facultas Verlags- und Buchhandels AG, 2001) p. 76

[49] *Fettesian*, July 1941

[50] Ibid., June 1942

[51] Ibid., December 1942

[52] Ibid., November 1941

[53] Letter to the author, 7 August 2008

[54] *Fettesian*, November 1941

[55] Kirk

[56] MacDonald in MacDonald, p. 233

[57] Lyons in MacDonald, p. 224

[58] Letter to the author, 7 August 2008

[59] *Fettesian*, June 1941

[60] Letter to the author, 9 August 2008

[61] Letter to the author, 7 August 2008

[62] Letter to the author, 4 August 2008

[63] See Allan & Carswell, p. 113

[64] Robert Bruce Lockhart, *Comes the Reckoning* (London, Putnam, 1947) p. 280

[65] *Fettesian*, December 1941

[66] Sandy Johnstone, *Spitfire into War* (London, Grafton, 1988) p. 130

[67] Letter to the author, 7 August 2008

[68] Letter to the author, 16 August 2008

[69] Johnstone, p. 130

[70] *Fettesian*, March 1943

[71] Ibid., December 1943

[72] Liddell

[73] *Fettesian*, March 1942

[74] Ibid., December 1943

[75] Ibid., July 1942

[76] Ibid., November 1940

[77] Ibid., February 1941

[78] Ibid., November 1940

[79] Letter to the author, 1 August 2008

[80] Letter to the author, 3 August 2008

[81] Letter to the author, 9 August 2008

[82] John Keegan, *The Battle for History* (London, Pimlico, 1997) p. 35

[83] *Fettesian*, November 1940

[84] Ibid., March 1944

[85] In conversation with the author, October 2008

[86] Letter to the author, 4 August 2008

[87] Humphries, p. 13

[88] *Fettesian*, December 1982

[89] Ibid., July 1940

[90] MacDonald in MacDonald, p. 230

[91] Humphries, p. 11

[92] In conversation with the author, October 2008

[93] Ian Mackenzie, *Brief Encounters: A Fettes Memoir* (privately published, 2002) p. 2

Chapter Eleven

'Terrific team spirit and the solidity of tradition'

Fettesians at the Front in the Blitzkrieg Era, 1939–41

Joining Up

Thanks to the protracted period of nervous inactivity known as the 'Phoney War', the pupils on the rugby pitch at school in 1939 saw combat long before most of their older brothers in the armed forces did. The military memories of surviving OFs in this period often revolve around training followed by regular shuntings from post to post without seeing a single German. Indeed, the first Fettesian to be killed in action between 1939 and 1945 died in one of the interminable imperial policing campaigns on the North-West Frontier rather than fighting the fascist menace. On 11 February 1940, Lt David Potts of the 1st Battalion, 16th Punjab Regiment, was shot by armed tribesmen near Bannu in what is now Pakistan, and subsequently buried in Karachi. He does not appear in the *Old Fettesians Who Served* book for the Second World War presumably because he was not killed, technically, killed in that war, though it does include a number of OFs who died in accidents in 1946-7. Writing the book's introduction in 1948, Dr Ashcroft noted that around a thousand Fettesians served in one capacity or another during the Second World War 'which is just about the full intake of the school over a period of twenty years.'[1]

As with the Great War, Fettesians not only joined up wholeheartedly but also distinguished themselves, with 170 decorations and 135 mentions in despatches. Likewise, the death toll was disproportionately high; although the casualty rate for the British armed forces was around five per cent in 1939-45 (much lower than in 1914-18) among Fettesians it was over eleven per cent.

Although the RAF, both before and after 1939, had an enormous hold on the public imagination, most British servicemen wore the khaki of the foot-soldier, albeit in a smaller overall proportion than in 1914. In

Back Row (left to right)—Pte. P. Rockwell, Pte. J. L. Watson, Pte. W. H. Watson.
Middle Row—Cpl. J. A. Scott, Pte. G. E. Crombie, 2nd Lt. A. J. Thomson, 2nd Lt. A. F. MacMurchy, Capt. G. P. S. Macpherson, 2nd Lt. S. D. Rae, C.S.M. J. C. Meiklejohn, Cpl. M. Scott.
Front Row—Pte. D. F. C. Fleming, Pte. J. A. Duncan, L.-Cpl. R. S. Ross, L.-Cpl. J. Henderson, Pte. J. T. H. Macaulay, Pte. A. S. Ross, Pte. P. M. Wood.

Old Fettesians in the London Scottish in 1939

November 1939, a hurriedly-drawn-up Fettes Army List recorded that 72 were serving with the infantry, mostly with Scots regiments, 38 in various artillery units, 17 in the RAF, 16 in the Royal Navy or RNVR (mostly the latter), 14 in the RAMC, a dozen in the Engineers or Signals, and ten in armoured or cavalry units, sundry others being Staff or RASC officers.[2]

As these bare statistics suggest, the British armed services which went to war in 1939 were much more technical beasts than those of 1914. The army had completed mechanisation by the outbreak of war, and its technical and support arms were much bigger than before. In the year between the Munich Crisis and the German invasion of Poland, feverish rearmament had seen the introduction of conscription – no agonised liberals this time – the doubling in size of the Territorial Army, and the crash production of a wide variety of military vehicles. This was, in part, the achievement of the arch-appeaser Sir John Simon. During the thirties he had been reluctant to interfere with an economy which was struggling back to its feet in order to prepare for a war which might, conceivably, be avoided; in any case, he well understood that the

British public has always been hypocritical on such issues, keen to demand low taxes and growth in employment but growing indignant when they discover that 'our boys' are under-equipped. Yet Simon's financial prudence and emergency measures once war became inevitable ensured that by the time of his final budget in 1940, the government could dispose of £2.7 billion, only half of which needed to be covered by borrowing. He engineered subtle tax rises and a quiet devaluation which prepared the British economy better for war than it had been when the country fought the Boers or the Kaiser. Nonetheless, when Chamberlain resigned, Simon – described by the leader of the majority Liberal faction, Archibald Sinclair, as 'the evil genius of British foreign policy' – was one of the 'guilty men' under whom opposition MPs refused to serve.[3]

Fettesians' letters throughout the War reflected a greater level of professionalism; R.J. Knight, an assistant master who joined the Gordon Highlanders, wrote from his Officer Cadet Training Unit in 1940 of the impressively rigorous preparations for war he was experiencing – 'marching, weapon-training, P.T., and, above all, cleaning!'[4]

Hamish Liddell's experience was pretty rigorous, as he recalled sixty-five years later:

...I was called up and went to the Pre-O.C.T.U. at Wrotham where we seemed to go up and down the escarpment regularly and ran everywhere rather than walked. After four months there I went to Mons Barracks in Aldershot which was really Sandhurst (which had been taken over by the Royal Tank Regiment). There we were chased around by Guards Sergeant-Majors and our time there was interrupted by a week in Snowdonia at a Battle School – needless to say it rained all the time.[5]

Kenneth McCallum, by contrast, vividly remembered having to put out the frequent fires to which the Yorkshire moors were vulnerable in the hot summers of the early forties. His brother, A.D.D. McCallum, a training instructor attached to the RASC, was impressed by the enthusiastic professionalism of those recruits who had emerged from the part-time structure: 'I find the Militia very quick and interested in their job; they even do voluntary parades under NCOs in their spare time.' His key frustration was the absence of sports kit which limited games to the odd informal game of football, a tragic waste when one of the other instructors was former England scrum-half Jack Ellis.[*]

After the War's early setbacks, the amount of physical training and games was increased to a fever pitch. 'Some officers,' Clayton notes drily of the new emphasis on fitness and professionalism, 'found this uncomfortable.' Fettesians quite clearly did not. By 1940, the armed forces were calling people up in ever greater numbers, dropping the age of entry into the army from 19 to 18, a move which allowed keen school-leavers to do their bit. One such was Freddie Scott, who had left Fettes in 1939, aged 17, and was working for British American Tobacco in Surrey. As soon as he reached 18 in June 1940:

… I went to the nearest recruiting office in Kingston on Thames. Asked what I wanted to join I said 'Anything' (i.e. Army, Navy, or Air Force) and so I became Private Scott in the 70th Battalion in the East Surrey Regiment and I was sent to Rochester in Kent. I telephoned my father to let him know and his response was 'Why didn't you join the Gunners? I could have helped you.' I didn't tell him that was the last thing I wanted… The officers and senior N.C.O.s tended to be old (over 40!) and slightly disabled. The privates who eventually got promoted to junior N.C.O.s were all under 20 years old and mainly, like me, 18.[6]

Like many OFs, he wanted to do his bit starting in the ranks, into which men of every possible background were being thrown. Willie Geddes, housed in accommodation at Bovingdon which had been condemned in the twenties but did not seem unreasonable to the lads of 1940, was in a largely working-class unit; those public schoolboys who failed to 'muck in' or sounded affected were mocked by those of less gentle birth. The social mixing had unexpected benefits, as Freddie Scott recalled:

Of the 30 odd people in my platoon only one other had been to public school and spoke 'proper.' He had, when I arrived, already been nicknamed the 'Dook.' This meant that I got away without being ridiculed for being posh. The others were mainly from London and many had been given the option by the court of joining the Army or going to a young offenders' prison known as Borstal. Because of this I deemed it wise to get an expensive padlock for my locker. Then one day I lost the

---

[*] Ellis was a member of the England team which beat Scotland 9-6 at Murrayfield in 1939. Although his career was effectively halted by the war, he was the oldest surviving rugby international player at the time of his death in 2007

key. It was one of those that you have to lock manually and, I thought, pretty strong. I was sitting on my bed no doubt looking miserable and pondering what to do when a certain Private Dexter asked me what was the matter. I told him and he immediately said 'no problem.' Out of his pocket he produced a dart stuck into a cork to prevent him damaging himself. He took the dart and flicked open my expensive padlock with no difficulty... I was fascinated and asked Dexter to give me a lesson which he did and a few days later I was quite proficient at lock picking. I still am.

Unfortunately, Dexter had not explained how to close a lock once picked, so when the young Scott demonstrated his skills to his father – a Brigadier in the Royal Artillery – on a coin-operated gas meter in the Spa Hotel Tunbridge Wells, he was embarrassed to discover that, having poured shillings onto the floor, he was unable to refasten the padlock. An unimpressed Brigadier Scott was forced to explain the situation to an even less impressed hotel manager, and was probably relieved when his offspring was interviewed for officer training. Three senior officers questioned him in a fashion that would be downright illegal today:

> The leader said, 'Right young man – what school did you go to?'
> 'Fettes, Sir.'
> 'What games did you play?'
> '1st XI Hockey, 2nd XV Rugby, 4th XI Cricket, Sir.'
> 'Do you hunt?'
> 'Yes, sir, my father was a Master of Hounds.'
> 'Right, off you go to Sandhurst.'

Although this might seem odd, to say the least, in defence of this system it should be said that several years of compulsory cadettery at Fettes was an invaluable background for a young man in the armed forces and it would have been a waste of the whole project, as envisioned in 1908, not to make use of it. Ronnie Guild, later one of the stalwarts of the post-war Fettes staff common room and Corps, explained:

> It was very obvious who could march, and who would therefore be an ideal section commander – an unpaid Lance-Corporal and the first step on the ladder to promotion. We could also read and write, and that was by no means automatic in those days, since the government told the young offenders in the borstals that they could get off their sentences if they joined up. There was a fair sprinkling of these

chaps in my unit. So once one reached the right age, one could be selected for officer training, once the paperwork caught up.[7]

He remembered it as a three-step process; house prefect to private soldier and then, since he was in the Indian Army, leading men from six different ethnic groups. The products of boarding schools, in Geddes' view, had a number of other advantages:

As a bunch we settled in easier than the others; we had all been boarders whereas the others had never been away from home. The discipline seemed to us to be quite acceptable, but to the others it was strange and hard to get used to.[8]

It was still a culture shock for a sensitive character like John Guest: 'I am undergoing a land-change into something coarse and strange,' he wrote of his days in the ranks, noting later that in his 'gestapo-like' interview for promotion 'the sort of answers expected are those that a keen, healthy young officer would normally give, and the consequent strain on one's inventive faculties is acute.'[9]

Even Freddie Scott, who looked back with some pride on his wartime service, referred to the process of teaching young men how to kill as 'legalised vandalism.' In his case, his officer interview was a false start since he was not yet 19, so he was returned to his unit and spent some time defending various airfields, including Shoreham, from which Lysanders took British agents into occupied Europe. Here there was a very convenient pub, popular with Wrens stationed at Lancing, near the strongpoint his section was intended to defend; pleasant though this was, he was relieved to get on with serious officer training, and pleased to discover just how much he already knew from his days in the Corps. However, he was not to see any actual combat until D-Day in June 1944; similarly, Alan Harvey, who joined up in 1940, spent years pottering about in England on various (doubtless useful) training courses, and finally saw the enemy west of Monte Cassino during the Italian Campaign.

Some OFs went to great lengths to do their bit. Alyster Jackson was in the Dutch East Indies, and flew to Australia (where the *Sydney Herald* took his photograph as he came off the aeroplane and captioned it 'Patriotic Brits come to join the Army') then sailed to Vancouver via Fiji and Hawaii. He then travelled somewhat circuitously to Montreal ('I wanted to see a little more of the world') taking in San Francisco, where the locals found the British accent captivating and a trainee nurse he had befriended showed him round. 'I suppose in these days it would have led to our going to bed together, but it did not in those days', he wrote, decades later, 'Anyway, it was enjoyable for me.' He eventually reached Britain in the autumn of 1940, having set out in July, and joined the Royal Artillery. The McCallum brothers came from Argentina, among 2,200 to do so; Kenneth later remembered the circuitous route from Buenos Aires via Iceland, when he manned a 1914-vintage Hotchkiss as air defence for the bridge. During the four-week journey, the volunteers were given refresher lessons in PT and drill by a Marine Royal sergeant.[10]

His training in the Royal Engineers was completed in the summer of 1942, whereupon he was shipped to India, learning Urdu on the way as he was to join King George V's Own Bengal Sappers & Miners. There he had to get used to the multilingual, multi-ethnic, highly professional Indian Army and its ways, such as circulating air through rooms by means of a phanka, a cloth frame on the ceiling linked by pulley to the toe of a phanka wallah who lay on his back pulling it to and fro all day. After a lengthy familiarisation, he was shipped to Iraq and thence to Palestine and later Syria, where he wrote that the driving sand was 'a signal of nature's contempt for man and his machinations.'[11]

George Campbell Hay, by contrast, took to the hills rather than serve in an 'imperialist' war; he was captured by a plain-clothes policeman at Arrochar and given ten days in Sauchton Gaol. He enlisted in the RAOC to stop the authorities from tailing his mother; and was pleased to discover that 'you meet a lot of political bad boys in the Ordnance.' 'It's startlingly like life in a boarding school,' he wrote later, 'except it isn't so bad.'[12] His ferocious nationalism meant that he only mixed socially on his own terms:

The Caledonians and South Britons mix no better than oil and water...The most noticeable characteristic about the English is how docile they are, and it's not a docility with after-thoughts and reservations. But most of my compatriots, God be thankit, haven't the faintest trace of the spirit of subordination and they are incredibly outspoken for poor bloody privates.[13]

For all his reluctance, Hay found that he took to Ordnance work quite well, successfully running an Oxy-Acetylene depot in North Africa single-handed until he was replaced by a sergeant with five staff – 'this glorious career will take some explaining' he commented. Career paths through the armed forces could be as complex as the journeys to and from Britain. J.M.A. Lumsden had a remarkable career; in December 1940 he wrote to Mr MacDonald:

I am now a private in the Pioneer Corps. When I registered last December I was put in Grade III by the doctors because of my eyes, and heard no more till a month ago when I was told to report here. Fortunately they are not turning us all into navvies, and they are giving us infantry training, so my five years in the O.T.C. are being turned to good account. I am hoping eventually to get a commission, but at present it is very difficult for any one not in Grade I to do so.[14]

Thirsting for valour and excitement, Lumsden did not stay a Pioneer private for long; as Clayton notes, the shortage of officers was sometimes so acute in the War that Canadians were sometimes loaned to British units. By 1941 Lumsden was writing again to announce that he had managed to convince the medics that his eyesight was good and thus get a transfer to the Artillery; he was on leave, helping his father, another OF, to teach at Uppingham School in Rutland; at his OCTU he had come across no less than seven Fettesians. By 1942 he was a Temporary Major in the Mediterranean Expeditionary Force, ending the war Mentioned in Despatches and Adjutant to the 24th Field Regiment, Royal Artillery. Allan Herriot had an even more varied career. When called up, he was classified C3 because needed he spectacles – 'most depressing' – and became a Clerk Class 3 in the Royal Army Pay Corps. Luckily, his application to serve as an officer in the Indian Army was granted, so he spent three months getting to Bombay with transhipments in Durban and Suez and a further three months training at Bangalore before being posted to the 7th Gurkha Rifles Regiment, 5,000 feet up in the Himalayas. In December 1942 he sailed to Suez and found himself in Reinforcement Camp 8 beside Mena pyramids. Herriot then joined his regiment's 2nd Battalion, which was training for mountain warfare in the Lebanon and started skiing, whereupon the Battalion was sent to Bitter Lakes to train for seaborne invasion. He saw his first action in January 1944 with the 4th Indian Division at Cassino, and spent the rest of that year fighting up Italy as far as San Marino, and was promoted twice. After service in Greece, Herriot returned to India, this time by air in three days; he expected to be sent to invade Malaya, but the atom bomb made that unnecessary, and he was demobilised as a Captain.[15]

One of the relatively few naval Fettesians was John Humphries. He had been a signaller in the Corps but when his papers arrived he was offered the chance to clear mines or join the Royal Navy. 'We've never had anyone in the Navy, dear, and they are the Senior Service,' his mother said, 'Heaven knows why they want you.'

Reality bites

Mr Milman, another schoolmaster turned officer in the RASC, had the time of his life during the 'Phoney War' of early 1940; once the initial frenzy of preparing the logistic structure in France was over, there was plenty of free time to play rugby against other British units and local French teams. He wrote enthusiastically to his old colleagues and pupils about life on the placid Western Front:

The main local teams are very good, and unbeaten so far this season, though we have succeeded in drawing with them. Their star player, an international, has a large black beard and whiskers (which we try to pull at every opportunity) but that does not prevent him from being a first-class player.[16]

He also rather enjoyed the concert parties. Morale during what some wags called the 'Bore War' seems to have been fairly high, reflected by the popularity of 'We'll be hanging out our washing on the Siegfried Line' amongst both troops and civilians. Although Mackenzie Stuart later ruefully saw the song as 'ill-starred', there were grounds for optimism. After all, the Army had been modernised and was working together with the French, whose armed forces were (officially at least) highly impressive – against 93 German divisions with 2,700 tanks were 93 French, 22 Belgian, ten British, nine Dutch, and three Polish and Czech divisions, with twice the German strength in tanks and artillery pieces and a similar number of aircraft. Additionally, the French had the impregnable Maginot Line defending the border. Even if there were none of the fantasies of 1914 about it all being over by Christmas, there was a media consensus, noted by the Old Fettesians who were at school in the war years, that the British forces were on course for an inevitable victory.

The reality was rather different; the outnumbered Germans used modern technology more efficiently than the Allies and pushed them back to the coast. General Sir Harold 'Pete' Pyman, one of the most distinguished OFs of the war, later said 'I would at that time rather have fought from a German tank than a British one.'[17]

Early British tank training, as he experienced it in Delhi, required the ramming of enemy vehicles rather than their destruction by shelling from a distance – 'most gallant', he conceded, but pointless. OF Lt W. Dudley Logan of the Fife and Forfar Yeomanry was killed in France on 27 May 1940; a letter from another OF, Maj A.O. Hutchinson of the same regiment, paid tribute to this unruffled, kindly and much-loved officer, still missed by his men, killed instantly when an enemy shot went right through the cupola of his tank.[18]

Willie Geddes, who was to fight in Italy, was scathing about the way this appalling state of affairs continued for so much of the war. Noting that British morale was excellent, thanks to 'terrific team spirit and the solidity of tradition', he added:

We did, however, have strong feelings that our equipment was always inferior to that of the Germans. We were in tanks and they could shoot us up from half a mile before we could shoot at them; our shots largely bounced off, but theirs came in and our tanks frequently blew up. British tanks were always out of date and undergunned as soon as they came out. Until almost the end, our infantry were similarly poorly-equipped. Our lorries and transport had two-wheel drive and continually got stuck in mud. Everything the Germans had seemed to work, and their discipline was superb, even to the end. We did the blame the government for all these inadequacies; until Churchill and Montgomery came along it was felt that the army was still clinging to the habits and methods of previous wars.[19]

Rather than repeat the Schlieffen Plan's arcing attack through Belgium prior to wheeling round on Paris, for which the British and French had prepared, the Germans punched through the Ardennes Forest into the vulnerable Allied flanks, then hammered through to the coast to encircle 35 divisions, including most of the British Expeditionary Force. Holland, Belgium and Luxembourg fell quickly to the fast-moving German forces. By 14 May, the first Old Fettesian to be killed in action, Lt A.S. Raeburn of the Gordon Highlanders, was hit whilst leading a dangerous night patrol on France's eastern border where the second wave of German attacks came in a reprise of the 1870–1 campaign at Sedan. Raeburn's commanding officer wrote bleakly to the school:

We all loved him, and were all cast down. His men loved him too, and would follow him anywhere – and they did. I loved the charm of his nature, his love of birds and green things.[20]

Lt G. Rae Duncan of the 2nd Oxford and Bucks Light Infantry was killed on 21 May, the same day as 2/Lt. Robert Gallie, who fell covering the retreat on the Scheldt in Belgium. Although ultimately this allowed a huge number of Allied soldiers to escape to Dunkirk and thence to England, by this point the British government was calling for Sunday 26 May to be a National Day of Prayer for the 'troops in peril in Flanders'. The following Tuesday, Lt Ian Scott Thomson, the 'fanatical' Corps NCO turned career soldier, was killed leading Bren Carriers in a rearguard action on the Ypres-Comines Canal; a comrade wrote of him that he was 'doing magnificent work under heavy fire… he was so loved by his men.'[21]

He is buried, like many OFs of the Great War, in one of the many Commonwealth War Graves Commission cemeteries near Ypres. On Wednesday 29, another OF, Capt Robert Craig of the Royal Artillery, fell on the road to Dunkirk. These young men – part of a small band of professional soldiers, not unlike the 1914 BEF, were sacrificed to cover a humiliating retreat to the coast. Iain Macleod, digging a trench as part of a roadblock to obstruct the German advance at Neufchatel, found a skull from the First World War. He wrote a poem about it, part of which reads:

And these dead things seemed to sneer
'Ye are here, ye men of war,
Digging trenches – digging graves
Dying where we died before:
We were here:
Long ago, long ago.'[22]

The roadblock was incomplete when a German armoured vehicle crashed into it, sending a log into Macleod's leg and badly injuring him. With an almost pulverised thigh strapped up with a bayonet as a splint, he was evacuated by destroyer from St Nazaire. On the day Craig died, the Belgians capitulated; there was a very real risk that, isolated as it was, the BEF might do the same. The 'miracle of Dunkirk' was, therefore, very welcome news for the British government, not only for what it achieved in terms of the rescue of valuable troops (including Milman, among other Fettesians) but also for its astonishing effect on public morale. An OF, Harry Moncrieff of the RASC, spent a week on the beaches at Dunkirk, where he found a constructive way of making his trucks unserviceable by using them to make breakwaters so that troops could be more easily evacuated. He finally got back to England on one of the last ships to leave.[23]

John Guest, on guard duty in Sevenoaks, could hear the sounds of battle as the tragic heroism played itself out. He wrote in his journal that 'all through the night we can hear the guns on the other side of the Channel – a terrible continuous dull thumping and muttering, sad and evil.'[24]

Even more Old Fettesians were to be lost in the aftermath of Dunkirk than in the initial Battle of France, for the 51st Highland Division, fighting on with the French 10th Army, were finally forced to surrender to Rommel's 7th ('Ghost') Panzer Division at St Valery on 12 June. The autumn 1940 issue of the school magazine reported that nine, all members of Scots regiments, were prisoners of war (though on the bright side, two – G.L.F. Finlay and A. Irvine Robertson – were initially feared killed, so the news was a relief). Despite the public's frequently rosy view of the situation, those serving in the armed forces would undoubtedly have seen the first few years of the War as truly desperate times. Hewan Dewar, a Fettesian of 1920s vintage, was working in a hospital in Jerusalem in 1940, and recalled his feelings sixty-five years later:

…we listened to the BBC telling us of the Fall of France. The Cabinet in London had to listen to the Foreign Secretary advising that Mussolini should be approached to find if he could secure better surrender terms for Britain from Hitler. In our Kaiser's Hospice we had to put up with one of our consultant colleagues, who was equally defeatist. The rest had their own thoughts. Being single and remembering that a number of Polish officers had already managed to make their way through the Balkans to enlist in the British Forces in Palestine and Egypt, I decided that, if Britain surrendered, I would try to make my way to Canada. Then the BBC broadcast that wonderful and unmistakable voice which told us: 'We shall fight on.'[25]

Almost everywhere, with the exception of the rebuffing of the Luftwaffe in the Battle of Britain and the defeat of Italy in East Africa, Britain was in retreat. In Norway, despite mauling the Kriegsmarine, the Royal Navy proved incapable of seizing the country in the face of modern airborne tactics as the Germans deployed paratroopers and bombers, neither of which the Allies had at their disposal. This campaign's few redeeming features were indirect and visible only with hindsight, in the sense that one can see now that taking and holding Norway used up so many German ships and soldiers that it made a successful invasion of Britain unlikely. Norway was such a debacle that it brought down Neville Chamberlain and led to his replacement by Winston Churchill – ironically, the actual architect of the campaign, but undoubtedly the right man for the premiership.

The aviators

Many years after the war, Alyster Jackson wrote that he felt that getting killed was 'a probability, rather than a possibility.' Having grown up in an age where everyone knew someone who had not come home from the Somme or Ypres, and aware that wars could go on for 30 or 100 years, and that 'the arms manufacturers had been busy developing much more deadly means of destroying the enemy than were known in the 1914-18 war,' Jackson believed 'one's chances of survival were not good.'[26]

Fettes, as previously noted, gave proportionately more of its young men in World War Two than British society as a whole. However, the school's fatality statistics reached positively Somme-like proportions – just under a quarter – among the 142 OFs who served in the Royal Air Force or its Commonwealth equivalents. 34 of the school's 118 war dead were in the RAF, with at least another three killed serving in the FAA and one soldier, Capt N.V.M. Adams, was a glider pilot who died at Arnhem. Aviation's massively enhanced place in national defence, and, even more importantly, national attack in the absence of viable land campaigns, put aircrew into the firing line throughout the conflict. One of the school's first combat casualties was in Norway. P/O Michael Craig-Adams of 263 Sqn was part of the first wave of pilots sent there, flying Gladiator biplanes from frozen Lake Lesjaskog, where he suffered the indignity of a crash through engine failure. The squadron was withdrawn to Britain to recuperate, during which time Craig-Adams visited the school. He expected to be sent back to Norway, he said, 'because I'm one of the few people who knows where it is.'[27]

He did return, and on 22 May 1940 he fell after engaging an enemy formation, and then running out of ammunition; a comrade wrote to the school that 'we think he glided into a German machine to bring it down with him.'[28] Crashing into Høgfjell, Craig-Adams was killed and is buried in Narvik.

Høgfjell in Norway, photographed by Kjell Sørensen; OF Michael Craig-Adams, the school's most northerly casualty, crashed just below the central peak in 1940

Local people later erected a memorial to him in the village of Salangen, and the wreckage of his Gladiator, N5719, has been recovered and is being rebuilt to flying condition by Retro Track and Air of Gloucestershire.[29]

The German pilot, August Riehle, is still unsure of what exactly brought his aircraft down; still hale and hearty at the time of writing, he himself demonstrated exemplary courage by flying with an injured arm and desperately trying to get his stricken plane back to base after it was badly damaged. It was possible, he told his son, that the Heinkel was crippled by splintered rock flying up from the walls of the fjords (the 'Tommies' were firing at these in order to double the shrapnel effect) or even by a bomb dropped by his colleague von Bothmer, who was attacking the British ships in the fjord from a mere 200 feet. As it was, despite the best efforts of the crew to help the injured pilot keep it airborne, the Heinkel ploughed into a creek, losing both its wings. If Craig-Adams did sacrifice himself in a suicidal ramming attack, it was probably unnecessary as the enemy aircraft was already doomed. August Riehle recovered consciousness to see 'a man without head standing on his shoulders' – this was his observer, who had been thrown clear of the aircraft and ended up embedded in a mud hole. The Germans, all of whom were in considerable pain, armed themselves with the cockpit machine gun and emergency rations of Schokakola, then set off, as RAF escapers were wont to do, for neutral Sweden. 'After four days and still approximately ten kilometres off the Swedish border we came to a small house. Nobody was there and the only thing to eat was a block of old goat cheese that looked and tasted like a bar of soap.' It was in these uninspiring circumstances that they were captured; Riehle spent the rest of the war as a prisoner in Scotland and Canada.[30] (An OF was lucky to escape death in the far north in a war which didn't happen; J.M. Scott, the Polar explorer, was a platoon sergeant in the Scots Guards and was part of a shipload of British troops intended to give succour to Finland, which was attacked by the USSR, but the British government realised that taking on two giant dictatorships at one go would be too much even for the Empire, and his ship stayed in the Clyde.[31]) Another Fettes Gladiator pilot was Sgt I.R. Currie, who died during the defence of Malta in 1941. Appallingly, of the 38 or so deaths among Fettes' wartime aviators at least 16, and possibly as many as 20, were the result of accidents; several of the soldiers on the war memorial were also killed in air crashes. This was not wholly surprising, if the letter to Mr Macdonald from J.D. Ireland, training in Canada, is anything to go by:

...I had a rather nasty crash six weeks ago while at elementary school, owing to my engine failing. I made a very bad forced landing, into a haystack of all things, and smashed the port wing into little bits. I wasn't hurt at all, however, and as I was only six miles from the aerodrome all I suffered was a long walk back.[32]

A.R.H. Cumming was in training when he saw an Albemarle glider-towing aircraft nose-dive into the ground 'in a huge gust of fire and with a noise like a bomb.'[33]

The first recorded death of the war among Fettes alumni was, indeed, an RAF officer killed in an accident; P/O Patrick Fraser of 92 Sqn crashed on 12 December 1939 whilst flying a Blenheim, Frank Barnwell's last design. Allan Britton, who had served alongside Craig-Adams with 263 Sqn in Norway, died exactly a year after Fraser when his Westland Whirlwind (which he had warned his superiors was a death trap) crashed into Sand Bay off Somerset.[34] Both he and the Whirlwind are probably still down there. Britten had been a distinguished classicist, winner of scholarships both to Fettes and to Cambridge, where he had gained a double first. Ashcroft wrote a brief poem in his memory:

Not like the daring Icarus of old
Did you in proud ambition ride the skies:
Your country's hour of danger made you bold,
And nobler far your youthful sacrifice.[35]

Two of the Millar brothers were killed in crashes, as was Sub-Lt C. J. Scott-Moncrieff, whose obituary by Mr Beamish, his old housemaster, gives some sense of the tragic waste this young man's death represents. A sensitive and artistic young man 'impatient with the discipline and the Philistine side of Public School life'[36], he had won awards for his writing and might have looked forward to a distinguished literary career. Ironically, 'his horror of the cruelty of war caused him to join a small group of sincere pacifists, but the outbreak of hostilities shattered his ideals and he at once joined the Fleet Air Arm.' Scott-Moncrieff lies a few plots away from another naval OF who died during training in Trinidad, Leading Airman T.H. Morrison, at the Port-of-Spain Military Cemetery. G.A.B. Johnston, who had commanded 502 (Ulster) Sqn and been mentioned in despatches, was a more experienced pilot. However, exactly four years after Craig-Adams was killed in Gladiator N5719, he died trying to land in a crosswind at Gibraltar in Gladiator N5717, an aircraft so obsolete and starved of spares that it could rarely achieve the two meteorological flights a day required of it. This was a problem in every theatre. 'From 1942-1946 one was constantly aware that spares were insufficient,' remembered Ian Stewart, 'Even as late as 1945/46 while I was with 209 (Flying Boat) Squadron in S.E. Asia we had to go from base to base to obtain the most basic components.'[37]

Not all the mishaps which befell RAF Fettesians were aviation-related. Douglas Wilson survived the Battle of Britain and was promoted to Wing Commander with administrative duties in Ceylon. It was in this capacity that he was seriously injured in an accident – sleepwalking out of a top floor window. He had to spend months encased in a plaster jacket, into which was moulded a special depression which he claimed was an ashtray but 'everyone could see that it exactly fitted a tumbler.' His 'coming-out' party on release from the plaster was, apparently, talked of for months in Colombo with great respect.[38]

The RAF tried valiantly to make a valuable contribution to the prosecution of the war's early stages through offensive bombing, in which a number of OFs took part. Vernon Stanion had travelled from China, where his parents lived, to Kimmerghame House, but unlike most expatriates, who went by sea, he made the journey overland through Siberia, never an easy route but in 1923 one which meant negotiating a land recovering from a vicious civil war and in the process of consolidating a dictatorship.[39]

It must have been an interesting experience for an unaccompanied lad in his teens. He abandoned his job with Imperial Chemicals in Tsingtao when war broke out to become an RAF officer. He served with 83 Sqn, which flew the Handley Page Hampden medium bomber, known, because of its boxy shape and cramped interior, as the 'flying suitcase.' From behind it resembled the German Dornier, with which it shared a long, thin, twin-ruddered tail, a feature which led to 602 (Glasgow) Sqn attacking and downing two Hampdens over the Forth in 1939. The Hampden squadron subsequently 'bombed' Turnhouse with lavatory paper. Stanion won the DFC for his courage on one of the early raids on occupied Europe:

On the night of the 17th April 1940, this officer was observer of an aircraft which reconnoitred northern Denmark, during which operation large concentrations of enemy aircraft were observed at Aalborg aerodrome. On the night of 20th April he was observer of an aircraft which carried out a two-run attack on Aalborg aerodrome under adverse weather conditions and in spite of intense opposition from the ground. A fire was started in one of the aerodrome buildings as a result of the second attack. He has displayed outstanding keenness and determination as Gunnery Leader and has set an excellent example to all other Air Gunners in his squadron.[40]

Shortly afterwards, he was fortunate to survive when the plane he was crewing, piloted by Jamie Pitcairn-Hill (the son of an OF Scottish international turned Presbyterian minister) ran out of fuel after a nine-hour flight to Berlin and back, and was forced to ditch in the sea.[41] Stanion died in a road accident in 1942 whilst training on Lancasters.

The British bombing in the early stage of the War was, of course, fairly ineffective – not only inaccurate and hampered by bizarre 'political correctness' such as the idea that crews should avoid hitting private property, but also pointlessly dangerous. The Vickers Wellington and Bristol Blenheim were the best aircraft available, with others such as the Fairey Battle being shot out of the sky at every turn, but the Blenheim was too small to inflict serious damage. One of the bombers' few early successes was the destruction of the barge fleet assembled in France for a possible German invasion of England, though this has never received a lot of attention. Rather more visibly successful was the RAF's role in one of the few Allied victories in the early part of the War, the Battle of Britain. Fettesians were prominent among the 'few' which fought off the Luftwaffe in 1940, one of them, Sgt David Frier, being wounded four times and eventually invalided out. Sqn-Ldr 'Uncle' George Denholm's 603 (Edinburgh) Sqn distinguished itself, downing 54 enemy aircraft in six months, 14 of them on one day, 31 August. On 23 November, Denholm's squadron became one of the few RAF units to shoot down Italian aircraft on one of the Regia Aeronautica's rare sorties over Britain. The Italian Fiat CR42 was undoubtedly one of the best biplane fighters of all time, and could easily outmaneuvre a Spitfire. The Spitfire, however, was much faster and carried twice as many guns. Denholm described the carnage for a wartime history of the RAF:

The Italians looked quite toy-like in their brightly-coloured camouflage, and I remember thinking that it seemed almost a shame to shoot down such pretty machines. I must have been wrong, for the pilot who saw six going down at the same time said afterwards that it was a glorious sight. But I must say this about the Eye-ties: they showed fight in a way the Germans have never done with our squadron.[42]

Denholm chased one Fiat half-way across the Channel, but had to let it limp home as his own engine started to splutter. His final tally in 1940 was three definite, one unconfirmed and three probable kills, three definite and one probable shared kills, and six damaged[43]; he later won the DFC. The success was undoubtedly due to Denholm's tactic of getting his planes to a decent altitude before heading towards the enemy position as given by the controllers, for going straight to the enemy's bearing, climbing en route, too often led to being 'bounced' by Messerschmitts. Despite his skills and experience, he still had to bale out twice from damaged aircraft. He survived, but many others did not, and it was his duty to write to their parents or widows. Tam Dalyell recalled that, as a teenager, he once asked of Denholm what he did when friends failed to return from a mission, and was curtly informed that 'We accepted it, and got on with the job.'[44]

To remind his squadron that they were named for Scotland's capital,

A Chinese image of British troops in action against the Boxers. Several Old Fettesians took part in this highly successful operation.

The memorial on Edinburgh's North Bridge to the men of the King's Own Scottish Borderers lost in the imperial campaigns of 1878-1902. The Sculptor, Birnie Rhind, would later create Fettes' own memorial.

The trenches of the Great War: a painting by Fettes art master Meredith Williams,
who also contributed to the decoration of the Scottish National War Memorial

Poznan British Cemetery, Poland: two Old Fettesians are buried here, one the victim
of the Gestapo executions following the Great Escape

Old Fettesian veterans on Remembrance Day, 2009

The school gathers for the two minutes' silence.

Cadets on exercise at Fallingbostel in Germany.

Adventurous activities at camp in Cultybraggan in the 1990s.

The Fettes shooting team at Bisley in 2006. This has been an important event in the school calendar for a century.

Cadets at annual camp, surrounded by twenty-first century hardware, a world away from the kilts and brasso of 1908.

The service at St George's Church, Ypres, as Fettes unveils a plaque to its fallen in the centenary year of the OTC.

Fettes pipers join in the last post at the Menin Gate in 2008.

The most glamorous aspect of Fettes life is undoubtedly the pipe band, seen here at Edinburgh Castle in 2008.

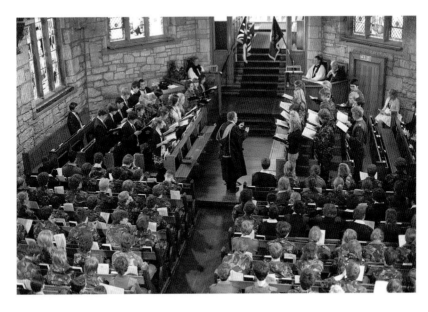

The 150th anniversary of the creation of the cadet movement is marked by a service in the school chapel in 2010.

Well over a century since the first letters to Fettes described war service against the Afghans, former pupils are fighting the Taliban. This deceptively peaceful view is from the turret of Oliver Blake's Warrior AFV.

Oliver Blake in a moment of relaxation in Afghanistan.

he served Drambuie every night in the mess after dinner – for which, as a well-turned-out flier himself, he insisted they dress formally rather than just wheel up looking 'operational.' For some years the Battle of Britain Memorial Flight's oldest Spitfire flew in Denholm's colours as XT-D and the replica Spitfire at Edinburgh Airport still wears them; today's Fettes pupils can feel a twinge of pride as they pass the giant plastic model en route to jetting off on holiday.*

Africa and the Mediterranean

The Battle of Britain apart, one of the only other Allied successes in these early way years was in East Africa, where the Italians were gradually forced out of Abyssinia and Somaliland. Here the British faced a determined enemy, the Italian Savoia Division (parts of which continued with a guerrilla war in the Somali mountains even after Italy changed sides in 1943) and at least one OF, Kenneth Milne, fell fighting them at Keren in 1941. A friend, J.W.S. Hamilton, wrote that 'he led the remnants of his platoon right up to the top of Sanchal Hill – almost into the town – before he was killed in the first and unsuccessful assault.'[45]

Hamilton had known Milne for years, being in many of the same classes and teams at Fettes, studying together at St. Andrews and training in the same OCTU at Dunbar. When Hamilton was wounded, Milne had visited him in hospital, 'with a surprised grin as he had been told I had kicked the bucket at Barrani' (Patrick, first of three of the four Nimmo brothers to be killed, had indeed died there). C.R.D. Gray, of Skinner's Horse, wrote to Mr Pyatt to describe his own brush with death in Eritrea:

Judged by what some other people got, my wound was nothing, and was the result of my own foolishness. I was going up one of the Keren mountains, and stopped to wipe the sweat off my forehead. Just as I had my 'tin' hat in my hand, a mortar bomb landed beside me, and a piece went into the top of my head, but thanks to a very thick skull (as you well know, sir!) I only suffered a bad cut and a headache.[46]

Although the fighting was hard, nature was a permanent enemy. D.S.D.

---

* Aviation buffs will be distressed to note that the Turnhouse Spitfire is a later model than that actually used by Denholm in 1940.

McWilliam, convalescing in hospital, made it clear which he found most trying:

Back in February we had the Ginka show, with one or two battles, notably at Bulo Erillo, and a lot of travelling over very bumpy and dusty roads… we got the lorries embedded in a perfect mass of thorns, where you literally couldn't take more than one step in any direction without tearing clothes and skin. But I think the worst aspect of the whole campaign was the heat. Whenever I had a spare moment I used to crawl under a lorry and sleep where the only shade was, and where at least one got a through current of air.[47]

The African and Mediterranean theatres absorbed huge numbers of Fettesians in the early forties – Hamilton, who later won the MC, estimated that 'there must be OFs out here in their scores' – and many remain there. The technical superiority, increasing numbers and greater professionalism of the Commonwealth troops did eventually put the Italians on the defensive in East Africa, much to the irritation of those who were looking for adventure. Capt J.B. Robertson, writing from East Africa where he was serving with the 2nd Nyasaland Battalion of the King's African Rifles, grumbled that:

…I am sorry I came out here now. What looked like a promising little campaign in September '40 is just about over now, leaving back-waters where East African and Imperial officers are marooned with little hope of getting out. I hoped when I came out to get into a first line battalion of the K.A.R., but there were no vacancies, and somehow I found myself in Movement Control, with little but climatic conditions to contend with… A blistering sandy gale blew all morning, and all afternoon and night the air stood still in an overpowering heat.[48]

Two years later, he was still marooned, hoped that a posting to Ceylon 'will be a step towards the Japs' though he was depressed to note that there were those who 'having said a boisterous goodbye to the Italians' wanted to 'sit back and watch the war being won from the grandstand.'[49]

To the northwest, matters were complicated in 1941 by the arrival of the Germans. Hitler had never had much interest in either Africa or the Mediterranean, but since Mussolini was clearly in difficulties the Wehrmacht was dispatched, officially to beef up the exhausted Italians (who, Alexander Knox Gallie recalled, were becoming prone to 'over-anxious surrender' – they 'marched across into our lines in thousands, like a regulated crowd exodus from a rugby international'[50]) and preferably secure access to oil as well. In February 1941 the Afrika Korps arrived in Libya, and in April the Germans entered Yugoslavia and Greece. The brief euphoria of January was swept away, as indeed were the Allied defences. 1941's 'second Blitzkrieg' in the Mediterranean saw the British thrown out of Greece and Crete, then pushed back in North Africa. As in the Fall of France a year earlier, the British found themselves improvising furiously as they retreated to the relative safety of Egypt and the Palestine Mandate. Some of their escapes were remarkable. Capt R.I. Macrae, an OF serving in the Veterinary Corps, wrote to his father (an OF Great War veteran) after the Germans' ferociously quick seizure of Greece:

I never expected to live to write this note, but anyway here I am still alive and well. I got back from Greece yesterday, and this last month seems to have lasted a lifetime. I was on a ship which was blown to pieces by dive bombers and I managed somehow to swim ashore, about 1½ miles, I think. Then I found myself with absolutely nothing in the world except a pair of sodden wet slacks, a shirt and a revolver. To make matters worse I was on the wrong side of the line – Jerries all over the place. I had a pretty thin time creeping about the mountains with no shoes and no clothes. I joined up with a few others later and we got badly shot up by aircraft at intervals, but some of us were lucky enough to get through to one of the beaches just in time to be picked up by the Navy...[51]

A poignant letter from Lt D.W. Souter, serving on HMS *Witch*, informed the school that his younger brother Ian had been missing since his ship, HMS *Hereward*, was attacked by dive-bombers during the fall of Crete.

He was last seen swimming in the water and may have reached Crete eight miles away. He may still be carrying on in the mountains of Crete with the British Marines and other forces. Alternatively, he may have got in a boat and reached one of the Greek islands, and we may not hear anything further till the end of the war.[52]

Ian was never found. Despite its proximity to Rosyth and Leith, Fettes remained obstinately wedded to the Army, adventurous souls being more inclined towards flying, but 132 OFs did serve in the Royal Navy, RNVR, FAA or Marines, and 15 were killed. Another sailor in the Mediterranean was A.J. Allsebrook, who, according to a letter of naval gossip printed in December 1941, had enjoyed himself tremendously on destroyers and rather missed them now that he was on a battleship. He had, in fact, hoped to be a pilot, but colour-blindness held him back. The vessel to which he had been reluctantly posted was the 31,000-ton HMS *Barham*, where he met another Fettesian, Lt Ronald Watson. On 25 November 1941, torpedoes from Hans-Dietrich von Tiesenhausen's U-331 hit the *Barham,* which blew up in a matter of minutes, killing 862 of her crew. She was the biggest British naval vessel to be sunk by a submarine; shortly afterwards, Italian frogmen put her sister ships *Queen Elizabeth* and *Valiant* out of action in harbour at Alexandria. Not wanting to let either the enemy (whose intercepted communications showed no awareness of the situation) or the public know that they were three battleships down, the government hushed up the news for two months. It was the *Barham* case which drew attention to the medium Helen Duncan; almost immediately after its loss, she claimed to have been told by a sailor wearing the ship's hatband that he had been killed when it sank. Mrs Duncan was eventually prosecuted for witchcraft in a case which added a layer of absurdity to a great naval tragedy. Souter, Allsebrook and Watson, along with Wireless Mechanic Hugh Jones, who also died in the Mediterranean, and 19-year-old Ordinary Seaman Norman Hudson, lost when HMS *Firedrake* was torpedoed in the Atlantic in 1942, represent the bulk of the school's naval fatalities, but another sailor won the highest award achieved by an OF in World War Two. On 14 March 1940, a bomb accidentally went off on board the aircraft carrier HMS *Eagle*, killing thirteen and injuring others. Sub-Lieutenant Alexander Mitchell Hodge, RNVR, won the George Cross for his bravery:

The bomb-room was in darkness, full of heat and fumes, and smoke rising to the main deck suggested fire below. Sub-Lieutenant Hodge had no knowledge of the behaviour of bombs in great heat or violent movement. When the explosion occurred he at once left the main deck and went into the bomb-room. He examined this and was able to rescue and send up several badly injured men. . He found one of the wounded men crushed under two very heavy bombs, which could not be moved single-handed. Obtaining help, he dragged the wounded man clear, and sent him up.

Sub-Lieutenant Hodge did not go on deck until he had satisfied himself that no one was left alive below. Throughout he showed outstanding courage, enterprise and resource, without any thought for himself. He saved all the lives he could though, for all he knew, further fatal explosions might have occurred at any moment.[53]

'Sandy' Hodge served all over the world with the Royal Navy, and later became Chairman of Standard Life. He wrote breezily to Mr Newman a year after his exploit, which he modestly refrained from mentioning, concentrating largely on old school gossip:

Our chief engineer, Comdr. (E) E. Read (S. 1912) on special occasions wears a 1ˢᵗ XI blazer which is nowadays somewhat tight round the middle. At Singapore I met Pat Kirkwood (K. 1925), who is in the I.M.S. and is attached to an Indian regiment. He has a magnificent army-type moustache which looks as though it might have been cultivated in Poona...[54]

This modesty continued throughout his life; when invited to address the pupils of Fettes on Founder's Day, four decades after his exploits, he said nothing of himself and instead spoke about admirals, including Andrew Cunningham and Raymond Spruance, under whom he had served and whose dedication he admired. He left the Fettesians of 1981 in no doubt about how serious the Mediterranean defeats of 1941 had been:

The German attack on Crete... lasted six days and they were among the longest, most nerve racking, harrowing and saddening in Cunningham's experience. It left his fleet in ruins and his surviving officers and men utterly exhausted. It would have broken the spirit of most commanders. That Cunningham lived through those days of unremitting crisis with courage undimmed and with outward serenity was because he had already braced himself for the shock.[55]

This was, of course, in 1981, and to an audience for whom forties gossip would have been of limited interest. At the time many letters revolved, like Hodge's, almost entirely around how nice it had been to bump into other OFs, and of course this would have had the invaluable function of spreading the word (though this was, all too often, out of date by the time the *Fettesian* was distributed) of who was still alive. Hodge could not, of course, say more other than that 'at the start of the Italian business we were sent to the Med.; our present whereabouts is of course secret.' The letters home from OFs at this time are often unrevealing, partly because of the need for security – the mail was sometimes censored three times, first by the author, worried lest he incriminate himself, then occasionally by the authorities (officers were usually exempt from this) and finally by the masters at Fettes, who were anxious not to get the school into trouble or hamper the war effort in any way. As in the Great War, serving personnel were also reluctant to give any hint of being downcast or even uncomfortable, so the *Fettesian* was sent remorselessly upbeat letters. Macrae managed to put a jovial gloss on his deeply frightening and painful experience:

I am absolutely destitute but curiously enough remarkably fit, and by some miracle I still have a whole skin, apart from hands rather burnt by an explosion and full of small splinters of metal, and my feet were in ribbons... Those of us who survived are all in good heart and ready to start again.

Medical Officer Lindsay Lamb, who managed to escape from the German seizure of Crete, albeit after 'a strenuous time', wrote with classic British understatement that 'it was an interesting experience, but not one I should like to repeat in a hurry.'[56] (His obituary in 2003 noted that the interesting experience left him so dishevelled that he was refused admission to the officers' mess in Alexandria for being improperly dressed.) Even David Souter's letter about his missing brother concluded on a cheerful note:

We get a great kick out of life and play golf wherever we go. Also I manage to see my wife for a week about once a month when we are at our base. I do enjoy reading the Fetts *and appreciate the Headmaster's letters very much.*

On one of his last encounters with his brother, Ian congratulated him on the birth of his son – who he did not see until he was two and a half years old, so being able to be with his family was a real luxury. Serving on a Motor Torpedo Boat defending the Malta convoys (in which capacity he made many friends by rescuing a cargo of whisky from a sinking vessel) David Souter's life was a hard one. The charming Mediterranean diet beloved of tourists had been replaced by 'bully beef and baked beans for breakfast, the reverse for lunch and the two mixed together (pot luck) for supper'[57] and on a later posting he found himself on HMS *Windsor*, which was so infested with cockroaches that a butter-lined tumbler was black with them after a few hours. This was not a glamorous war.

Humiliation in the Far East

On the other side of the world, another Blitzkrieg, this time by Japan, swept down on Britain's imperial possessions. Anthony Chenevix-Trench, later to be Headmaster of Fettes but at the time a Captain in the 4th (Hazara) Mountain Battery, Frontier Force, was unquestioningly loyal to his Indian troops but had his doubts about the white population of Malaya. 'A more money-grubbing, unpatriotic set I have never seen,' he wrote, 'when you think that there is no income tax, and though we are fighting for our lives, the war fund of this, the wealthiest area in the Empire, is $3,200,000, or just £400,000, it gives you an idea of the unspeakable meanness of these dollar millionaires, of whom there are all too many here.'[58]

Although this might have been unduly harsh, it was true that, contrasted with the Europeans, the Japanese did indeed have a ruthless and efficient army which punched into Northern Malaya just before the attack on Pearl Harbor. British aircraft were swept from the sky with an iron broom and the *Prince of Wales* and *Repulse*, the Royal Navy's prize capital ships, sent to the bottom on 10 December. Although Chenevix-Trench's battery and other Indian units succeeded in halting the Japanese landings near Kuala Lumpur, the evaporating food supply and collapse of morale from effective bombing meant that defeat was not far off. Robert Hardie, the hungry schoolboy of the First World War, was now a doctor in Singapore. He left a depressing description of developments on 11 February, when Singapore was 'clearly doomed', with disorganised mobs of undisciplined men wandering about in a city everyone now knew had no organised northern defences.

So weak was the defence that I believe that not only was the main Japanese landing quickly established, but even the feint landing at another point met with practically no opposition and established itself without difficulty. Some self-respecting units continued to fight well, but it was evident that in general morale was low, and Wavell's last blistering order two or three days before capitulation made painful reading.[59]

OF Major Ian Graham was a member of General Wavell's Southwest Pacific Staff and the officer to whom the Supreme Commander dictated the order that 'it will be disgraceful if we yield our boasted fortress of Singapore' and rather than surrender, 'commanders and senior officers must lead their troops and if necessary die with them.' The Staff itself had to be evacuated, and this was not without difficulty, as Graham's son, himself an OF of post-war vintage, described his father's experiences in an obituary for the school:

In the days before the Allied Singapore garrison surrendered, Wavell had been operating out of a temporary headquarters in Java at Lembang. Graham accompanied Wavell on a final 48 hour trip to assess the possibilities of holding back the advancing Japanese. The mission nearly ended in disaster. Graham was loading at midnight the last sensitive documents from Government House at a pier to be ferried to a waiting Catalina flying boat, when he heard a loud cry from Wavell. Fearing that Wavell had been attacked by looters or Japanese commandos in a raid on the harbour, he rushed with another officer to the landward end of the jetty. There he discovered the supreme commander had fallen almost six feet, and was lying blood-covered amidst a tangled mess of barbed wire. With great difficulty Wavell was subsequently brought aboard the Catalina. Nursing Wavell with iodine and doses of whisky, a nervous Graham waited with the Catalina crew for the harbour to clear of small craft while flames from the burning naval depot oil tanks lit the sky, making the aircraft an easy target for Japanese air raids. [60]

Graham's aircraft took off for Batavia in Java in the knowledge that Britain was about to suffer one of its greatest military reverses, and arguably to witness the beginning of the end of the Empire – the loss of Malaya and the great fortress of Singapore. When Singapore fell on 15 February 1942, Graham was sent to reconnoitre an escape route on the south coast of Java. However, the idea was abandoned when Wavell was ordered back to India and Graham was left as part of an emergency staff group ordered to hold off an imminent Japanese assault. Their hasty defences were never tested as the Dutch civil authorities surrendered. Like Chenevix-Trench and Hardie, Ian Graham was to spend the rest of the war in that most unenvied of situations, a 'guest of the Emperor.' Other Fettesians made the supreme sacrifice in the fighting. Brigadier William Aird Smith died, probably from drowning, trying to escape the fall of Singapore, but his fate was not ascertained until well after the war, and he has no place on the school memorial. Walter Rose, one of Dick Normand's contemporaries in the Edinburgh Territorials, was killed in the defence of Hong Kong on 11 December 1941; William Thomson went down with HMS *Hermes*, the aircraft carrier intended to redress the balance after the loss of *Repulse*, when she was sunk by Japanese dive-bombers south of Ceylon in April 1942.

War in the Desert

The humiliation in the Far East made it all the more important that some kind of success be achieved in the Mediterranean basin. E.G. Richards, a minister's son from Inverbervie destined for a career in forestry, describes the scene of the key battles well:

For those who have lived only in Europe it is difficult to imagine the special importance of the road that leads from Alexandria to Tunis. The first of thousand miles' stretch from Alexandria to Tripoli must hold a special nostalgia for every man who ever served in the 8th Army. Mile after mile of black ribbon stretching across wastes of Western Desert, scene of advance, retreat and advance again. The lone vehicle cruising hour after hour in the blazing sun at speeds of 50 to 60 miles an hour. The long convoy calling steadily forwards at twenty miles an hour. No side roads, no trees, no road verges, few permanent habitations, and those often several hours' journey apart.[61]

Insects were another curse to add to the heat. Alexander Knox Gallie remembered that 'your mug of tea would be half full of flies before you could drink it; a slice of bread and jam would be stripped of jam as you watched.'[62] Everywhere was sand, 'a suffocating cloud', as Murray Hunter recalled, clogging the engines of jeeps, the tracks of tanks and everything that lived.[63] John Guest, meanwhile, recorded the local colour with the same mild censoriousness of his Victorian forebears, writing that 'Morality doesn't enter into it – stealing and scrounging are just their livelihood.'[64]

As in East Africa, nature was as vicious an enemy as other soldiers; although he loved the extraordinary variety of flora in the more temperate regions ('a hot-house at Kew') and the tortoises 'with their mild, modest expressions', Guest was deeply distressed by the discovery of a mixed nest of hundreds of snakes and scorpions, unearthed in a gun-pit. His men enthusiastically set the scorpions fighting one another and chopped the snakes' heads off, watching fascinated as the bodies still writhed even hours after decapitation. Alexander Knox Gallie's 'Jocks' had an even darker form of amusement; well aware that the local Arabs, 'an unattractive mob', were becoming wayward, they would add petrol to the latrine pit. When the 'wogs', as the Jocks invariably called their hosts, gathered for a communal lavatory stop, chat and smoke on cigarettes purloined from the British stores, it was only a matter of time before a discarded fag end produced 'spectacular results, a great joy for the spectating Jocks – many flying white robes.'[65]

Although this grim humour, perhaps inevitable in the circumstances, reflected the men's tough outlook on life, there were moments of pathos; Gallie had to deal (during a period of great discomfort and suspense living in slit-trenches near the Mareth Line) with a Private Robinson who was convinced his wife was being unfaithful to him. Within days of their reassuring chat, a bundle of letters arrived for Robinson – who was subsequently killed by a mine.

Fettesian casualties mounted in the effort to push back the Axis in the Mediterranean. Flt/Lt Norman MacQueen had worked his way up from the ranks and took part in the defence of Malta as a Spitfire pilot. He was known for his chivalrous behaviour; after shooting down a German pilot, he visited the man in hospital. Overall, he is estimated to have shot down as many as seven enemy aircraft, raising him to ace status, and he was awarded the DFC on 1 May 1942. Three days later, he was attacking some Messerschmitts over Malta in his Spitfire when he was himself hit by tracer fire from a German fighter and killed. Lt-Col P.R.H. Skrine, DSO, who had left school at seventeen to join up in the First World War, was killed leading his Battalion of the Rajputana Rifles during the attempt to relieve Tobruk in 1941. The December 1942 *Fettesian* records the deaths of three former pupils in North Africa – the diminutive but determined Michael Day, who had enlisted as a private and gained a commission after the Battle of France, William Lockerby, who took a two-year course in gunnery in five weeks, and Bill Doughty, who just before the retreat to El Alamein turned down a staff promotion because 'I came out here to fight.' Another four were reported killed there by the time the next issue came out. El Alamein was described by Churchill as 'the end of the beginning', and it undoubtedly contributed a great deal to Allied morale, even if the Soviet Union, whose troops were dying by the million, continued to regard North Africa as an irrelevant sideshow. One Fettesian who played an important role in the battle was (then) Brigadier 'Pete' Pyman, CSM of the Fettes Corps in 1926, who, according to a newspaper report gleefully quoted by the school, was responsible for tactics which were both 'most brilliantly conceived' and 'largely responsible for the successful issue of the campaign which led up to Alamein.'[66]

He was, by his own admission, somewhat obsessed with the issue of tank gunnery and the need to hit the enemy from a distance before moving the infantry forward. He had been involved in the planning of

Operation Crusader, which relieved Tobruk and eventually forced Rommel back. This was part of the British 'learning curve' in which, rather as they had in 1914-18, the planners found by trial and error the best ways to deploy tanks and artillery. Montgomery's arrival made planning even more of a meticulous affair, and Pyman's memoirs are full of praise for this. From gunnery practice to disguising tanks with frames to make them look like harmless lorries, and from ensuring complete inter-service co-operation with the RAF to clearing paths through the minefields, Montgomery's 'clear, concise and confident' approach to preparation ensured that the officers who served him were able to do battle with confidence. Pyman admitted that, in retrospect, the 8th Army had the ultimate advantage because they were able to replenish themselves, whereas German and Italian supply ships were regularly sent to the bottom by RAF torpedo-bombers or the Navy's destroyers and submarines. Of course, this did not make the battle any easier for those fighting it at the time. One such was E.G. Richards, whose minesweeping teams were charged with breaching a 300 yard deep enemy minefield in the Munassib Depression in the teeth of withering fire from the tough Italian Folgore (Lightning) Division:

...as brave an enemy as the experienced, battle-hardened Green Howards had encountered. For us sappers it was our first experience of a set-piece battle, walking in with leading infantry under an advancing smoke an high explosive barrage from our own 25 pounders and disarming and lifting anti-personnel S mines and anti-tank mines under mortar and small arms fire, including from snipers well dug into deep trenches covered with black camouflage material in the hill above...[67]

Richards and the sappers succeeded in laying out a path of electric torch lights on metal posts which enabled the attacking Allied troops to advance in a massive column – a dangerous task which nearly cost another Fettesian minesweeper, Graeme Ferguson, his life at Walcheren later in the war. Rommel packed every man he could onto transport and retreated to his original lines, but only after a terrific fight in which decorations were hard won. C.W.K. Potts, an ordained clergyman and apparently a 'reincarnation' (when unshaven) of his grandfather the Headmaster, had resigned his post as padre and the honorary commission which went with it when his CO refused to let him take part in a commando raid on Syria.[68]

Enlisting in the ranks as an ordinary soldier, he gained promotion quickly and was a Lieutenant when he won the MC at Alamein for single-handedly blowing up a tank whilst on foot and armed only with a revolver and some explosives; realising that the Bren carrier which had been covering him had been hit by a mortar round and its crew wounded, he then ran through 700 yards of increasing fire to get help. Later, he rescued men from a burning vehicle, and was nicknamed 'the fighting parson'.[69]

Another Fettesian at Alamein was Murray Hunter, an artillery officer in charge of a group of six-pounder anti-tank guns. His unit had advanced under cover of darkness, replacing dummy Maskelyne vehicles and digging in on the rear slope of a small rise:

…the expected tanks appeared over the crest. We could distinguish both German and Italian, about 50 in all. They shot up our vehicles but apparently had not yet seen us, so we held our fire until they were well over the crest, about 400 yards away. Then the 6 pounders started on the German tanks which were the more dangerous. The small arms compelled their crews to close down their turrets and drivers' visors, which meant they were firing relatively blind and we didn't suffer many hits. The .5 inch anti-tank rifles took care of the Italian tanks, whose armour was little better than a Bren gun carrier's. The German tanks that had not been hit hid in the smoke from their burning colleagues and tried a little serious gunnery while the Italians gallantly renewed the charge. By this time the fog of battle was a serious handicap for them at a few feet above ground level while we could still see underneath it. We were not counting at the time, but were able to claim 17 kills, and they must have decided enough was enough… we saw some very fancy fast reversing.[70]

Not everything Hunter witnessed was so successful; many of the new American-built Shermans 'brewed up' rather quickly because of their high octane fuel, housed in thin-walled tanks, and the even newer Churchills were fired upon by their own side, since no-one recognised them. The Germans went into retreat – 'they had helped themselves to all the Italians' vehicles and hastened west on the road,' Hunter noted, with a touch of indignation, whilst the Italians, 'marching westward in good order' were overtaken by the British advance. Hunter went down with jaundice.

The Allies continued to push west, with increasing success, but Algeria and Tunisia were not going to be easily won. Murray Hunter was back in action and a lucky escape whilst fighting the Italians near the Tunisian border:

My face was covered in blood, but I could feel no real wound. When we could eventually stop we saw that a bullet must have hit the helmet exactly on the rim and bounced upward, made a large hole, and bounced again up to the sky, having peppered the area in front of my left ear with tiny fragments of bullet and helmet, producing a dramatic amount of blood and quite a headache but no more.

Despite such experiences, and the heat and flies, there was still much to enjoy. Guest was enchanted by the wonders of North African botany, thrilled by proximity to Carthage and grateful for whatever comforts a lucky billet could bring. Murray Hunter enjoyed the Viennese pastries and orchestral concerts whilst on leave in Jerusalem, where he could also count on a warm welcome at St Andrew's Scots Church. Even the crotchety Hay was enchanted by much of what he saw, refracting it through his usual tartan spectacles:

Africa is admirable, and there is a general air of life and a tolerance in small details (probably due to poverty) which are lacking in industrialised N.W. Europe. There is none of the ugliness which is the rule by the Clyde or the Tyne; there is more of natural good manners and less of convention and there are also some very bizarre smells to be dodged here and there…

I would always want to come back and see the dockers, old white beards mounted on donkeys, serious country folk in striped hooded burnouses, fat pale shopkeepers in tarbushes and pantaloons, ragged beggars screeching in chorus…[71]

However, even as the Axis forces were 'rolled up', the mines which McCallum and Richards so assiduously hunted were still a terrible threat (and still are, with thousands having been sown all over North Africa) as he saw when his friend Eddie's Bren carrier hit one on the edge of the Sahara:

When the smoke cleared we could see the carrier upside down, but at first no sign of the crew, and the carrier began to burn. We all stopped and with my crew I walked over, looking out for mines. When we reached the carrier we could see Eddie lying half way out with the carrier's side pinning him down across the chest. He was alive, but the small fire which we had seen, though apparently only a small petrol leak, was licking round him. We put it out with sand and then the fire extinguisher from my carrier. Some of the other carriers started to approach to help but I warned them to stop, except for the Sergeant's which was to come in very carefully having checked for mines in the way in order to use a towing rope to pull the damaged carrier right way up and let us get the crew out. The radio operator, a Lewis boy called Morrison, stayed in the carrier and was looking over the side when to our horror a small mine which had not been detected went off just under him, wounding him fatally.[72]

Eddie and Morrison both died; the Colonel issued a rum ration to the platoon and stood the men down for the rest of the day. Hunter had to write to Morrison's parents; he told them that their son was a good soldier, well-liked, killed whilst performing a rescue in a minefield, but he felt inadequate in his powers of expression. It was his first 'next of kin' letter, but would not be the last. The next day he and his men were under fire again, pinned down by German machine-guns in a rocky pass. He managed to spray the Germans' vehicle laager with machine-gun fire but was forced to abandon and destroy a carrier in retreating when they replied with mortars. His own luck ran out when he was scouting for a group of Tiger tanks, the monstrous and allegedly indestructible member of a Nazi armoured menagerie which included the Panther, Elefant and Puma. Having crawled forward to a suitable observation point and found six of them, he called down British fire from 25-pounder guns but was wounded when the Tigers fired back:

The shell landed a few yards away, straight ahead so that the tin hat took most of the shock, but I also felt a mighty bang on my left elbow and some minor impacts elsewhere, on my shoulder and right thigh… My carrier crew took me down to the RAP [Regimental Aid Post] for my arm was bleeding quite a bit and was in rather an odd shape. The MO decided he couldn't deal with it and organised my evacuation. The Padre gave me a cigarette and a cup of the proverbial hot sweet tea. Within minutes, sedated with opium, I was on my way to the Division's field hospital.

Hunter made a full recovery, though a 1994 x-ray prior to a hip operation revealed that one of the shell splinters was still there, 'nestling quietly by the lower end of the thigh bone.' At Oran, he found himself in the care of the Americans, whose luxurious facilities were the stuff of dreams for any British soldier: eggs, bacon, huge mugs of coffee, pancakes, salads, a cinema (where he was particularly impressed with Disney's *Fantasia*) and a USAAF room-mate whose friends flew in whisky from Tunis. To crown the experience, he received a newspaper cutting from home informing the people of Kircaldy that he had been awarded the Military Cross, a fact of which he had been previously unaware. The much slicker approach to war associated with America's entry to it, incidentally, did not stop some of the frustrations of the type earlier experienced by Robertson from recurring. Hamish Liddell remembered a long journey and intensive training which appeared to have little ultimate point:

I was commissioned into the Black Watch and after three months seconded to the King's African Rifles and set sail for East Africa. We were the first troop convoy through the Mediterranean after the successful North African campaign. We set off from Glasgow in the Cameronia *from the KG V Dock which meant sailing down the Clyde – quite interesting in a big liner. Apart from one suspected U-boat attack near Gibraltar and a big one day storm when the water was breaking over the boat deck and our escorting corvettes were standing on their heads it was an uneventful journey. Shortly after our arrival a 6-week course learning Swahili I was posted to a battalion in Abyssinia which was reached by a fortnightly vehicle convoy through the Northern Frontier District of Kenya and Somaliland – a 1500 mile journey by road... On arrival at a fort (very reminiscent of the Foreign Legion) in Lugh Ferandi in Abyssinia I was told that the battalion was going back to Nairobi the next day so I went all the way back!* [73]

NOTES

[1] A.H. Ashcroft in H.G. Newman, *Old Fettesians who served in H.M. Forces during the War 1939-45* (Edinburgh, Fettes 1948) p. 5

[2] *Fettesian*, November 1939

[3] Jenkins, p. 389

[4] *Fettesian*, March 1940

[5] Hamish Liddell, letter to the author, 15 September 2008

[6] F. B. Scott, *Freddie Scott's Anecdotal Account of How He Helped To Win The Second World War 1939–1946* (family notes, 2004)

[7] In conversation with the author

[8] Letter to the author, 19 September 2008

[9] Guest, pp. 5 & 23

[10] Kenneth McCallum, (Unpublished) Memoir, Henderson Archive

[11] Ibid.

[12] Quoted in Byrne, p. 471

[13] Quoted in Helen McCorry, *The Thistle at War* (Edinburgh, NMS, 1997) p. 15

[14] *Fettesian*, December 1940

[15] E-mail to author, July 2008

[16] *Fettesian*, March 1940

[17] Pyman, p. 33-4

[18] Ibid., February 1941

[19] Letter to the author, 19 September 2008

[20] *Fettesian*, June 1940

[21] Ibid., November 1941

[22] Quoted in Fisher, p. 45

[23] Obituary in *OFNL*, July 2002

[24] Guest, p. 7

[25] Hewan Dewar, 'A Visit to Petra in 1940', *OFNL*, July 2005

[26] Jackson

[27] Quoted in MacDonald, p. 229

[28] *Fettesian*, June 1940

[29] For information about O.F. casualties in Norway, I am indebted to the research of Kjall Storensen whose website details the crashed aircraft of that country.

[30] August Riehle, *Opas Absturz*, 25 July 2008. I am grateful to his son, Hans Riehle, for this.

[31] *Fettesian*, 1986

[32] Ibid., July 1943

[33] Cumming

[34] MacDonald in MacDonald, p. 231

[35] *Fettesian*, February 1941

[36] Ibid., March 1942

[37] Stewart

[38] *Fettesian*, December 1943

[39] Ibid., March 1943

[40] *London Gazette*, 31 May 1940

[41] Mark Postlethwaite, *Hampden Squadrons in Focus* (London, Red Kite, 2003)

[42] Quoted in Norman MacMillan, *The Royal Air Force in the Second World War*, Vol. II (London, Harrap, 1944) p. 292

[43] Alfred Price, *Spitfire Mark I/II Aces* (London, Osprey, 1996) p. 94

[44] Tam Dalyell, obituary for George Denholm, *The Independent*, 27 June 1997

[45] *Fettesian*, November 1941

[46] Ibid., December 1941

[47] Ibid., November 1941

[48] Ibid., February 1942

[49] Ibid., March 1944

[50] Alexander Knox Gallie, (Unpublished) Memoir, Henderson Archive

[51] R.I. Macrae, letter, 17 May 1941, quoted in *Fettesian*, July 1941

[52] Ibid., November 1941

[53] *London Gazette*, 2 August 1940

[54] Quoted in *Fettesian*, November 1941

[55] Ibid., November 1981

[56] Ibid., July 1941

[57] David Soutar, (Unpublished) Memoir, Henderson Archive

[58] Quoted in Mark Peel, *The Land of Lost Content* (Durham, Pentland, 1996) p. 46

[59] Robert Hardie, *The Burma-Siam Railway* (London, IWM, 1983) p. 18

[60] Obituary for Ian Graham, *OFNL*, January 2004

[61] E.G. Richards, letter to the author, August 2008

[62] Gallie

[63] Hunter

[64] Guest, p. 104

[65] Gallie

[66] *Sunday Express*, 4 April 1945

[67] Richards

[68] *Fettesian*, December 1944

[69] Ibid., February 1943

[70] Hunter

[71] Quoted in Byrne, p. 474

[72] Hunter

[73] Letter to the author, 15 September 2008

Chapter Twelve

'It was like an absurdly magnificent film'

Fettesians as Liberators, 1942-45

Italy

The gradual squeezing of the Axis out of North Africa was followed in 1943 by the invasion of Italy, which Churchill hoped – as he had with Gallipoli in the First World War – might mortally wound the enemy in his 'underbelly' – to which an unwise general appended the adjective 'soft.' Many senior British officers and politicians harboured hopes that the northern Balkans could be entered from Italy, enabling an attack through the Ljubljana Gap to reach Vienna before the Russians did. Even if not a decisive blow, Churchill, with his usual eye to history, hoped it might still be a 'running sore' – constantly draining enemy attention, men and materiel – just as Spain had been for Napoleon. None of these hopes came to fruition, partly because history had moved on and the Germans were able to resupply their troops by rail and air whilst the Allies were still trekking through the Mediterranean. Churchill had become a prisoner of his own hopes, and of the policies of the Americans, whose vision of victory was rather different, and in so doing doomed thousands of British troops to enduring a lengthy slog through Italy rather than delivering a fast knockout blow. Many of the Fettesians who had joined up just after the outbreak of war saw their first action in Italy after years of training or fruitless deployments; many are still there.

Sicily was the Allies' first port of call. Enemy aircraft operating from the island had represented a running sore of their own during the Mediterranean campaigns and the success of the amphibious assault on Morocco and Algeria had provided a template for the rapid conquest of territory. First ashore were new special forces units, the Combined Operations Assault Pilotage Parties ('Copps'), whose role was to gather information about landing beaches without detection, frequently under the noses of the enemy. Ronnie Williamson, a Fettesian from Shetland, was one of the commandos who carried out this task from February

1943, swimming around the in-shore waters to check defences.[1]

The actual assault, Operation Husky, took place on 9-10 July 1943, and with 2,590 ships and half a million personnel represented one of the western allies' most elaborate operations, covering more landing zones and using more divisions, at least initially, than D-Day. Gordon Roberts, one of the Scots Diaspora in Latin America whose childhood had been somewhat traumatised by an uprising of Patagonian sheep-breeders, was one of several OFs who took part in the invasions by means of the relatively new assault gliders. These were supposed to land behind enemy lines in Syracuse, but 'the planes towing them, presumably alarmed by anti-aircraft fire coming from the coast, released the gliders too soon and they landed on water in the dark.'[2]

Fortunately, he and his comrades seem to have been close enough to British ships to be rescued; he went on to take part in the D-Day landings. E.G. Richards, whose minesweepers had cleared the way at El Alamein, provided a detailed account of the shipborne landings. His unit was to land near Avola, a fishing village between Syracuse and Cap Passero:

Our first sight of the island was against a brilliant red sunset made more dramatic by the outline of Mount Etna with its volcano towering above the surrounding countryside. No-one on the ship will forget the mixture of awe and foreboding which this mighty wonder of nature created in us. Then, as darkness fell, the checking of kit; the parade for a last meal aboard; the mustering at our boat stations; the final instructions brought us back to reality. In the early hours of 10th July, we clambered into the assault craft as they hung from the davits of the liner on which we had sailed. They were flimsy peace-time American pleasure-boats slightly modified for naval use and powered by V-12 high-octane petrol engines. Each man – whatever his rank – carried nearly 1 cwt of stores on his back in a Yukon pack.[3]

It was a momentous event; Alyster Jackson, serving with the Royal Artillery, said that the landscape would be forever burned upon his memory (though when he went back there for a family holiday in 1963, he did not recognise any of it).[4]

Progress to the beaches was not without difficulty. Richards' boat was damaged when it bounced off the side of the ship, then its stern tackle became entangled, threatening to tip all the men into the sea. Fortunately, the Bosun was armed with an axe for precisely this eventuality and managed to free them, and they powered towards the shore. At this point good old-fashioned British stubborn indifference to reality intervened and the R.N. officer in charge wanted to sail for the wrong beach. Richards, who had studied the RAF photo-reconnaissance material, identified the right one, and, after some time, managed to persuade him to head in the correct direction. By this point, the rough seas had scattered much of the flotilla, and to make matters worse the Italians began shelling them. Luckily, HMS *Carlisle* managed, after only two ranging shots, to destroy the enemy artillery piece covering Richards' target beach. The Merchant Navy captain of the 'mother ship', rather than drop the remaining troops miles off the coast, hoisted his anchor and sailed for the shoreline. He subsequently sent fresh rolls and marmalade to Richards' busy engineers, who had been clearing the enemy mines and laying metal tracks to enable lorries to advance into the interior. Richards was later promoted, and his successor with the sappers was killed, possibly as a result of inexperience, lifting mines from a dried-up 'torrente', a river-bed in which the retreating enemy had sown large numbers of different devices to hinder the Allied advance. At another landing point, A.J.M. Morrison 'met with very little opposition, one of our first objectives containing four Wops, one Wopess and some turkeys, the latter very much alive.'[5]

His letter to the *Fettesian* adds that the BBC's enthusiastic descriptions of how well things were going were quite accurate, and that he had never seen soldiers in such high spirits. Sicily fell after a month, and Richards found himself assisting the British Local Government Officer in restoring services such as electricity, water and sewerage, as well as helping farmers whose land had been sown with mines. John Guest saw the necessity for this role further north:

I have only two more items of news for you and then I must stop. Many of the women here carry shallow round baskets on their heads about a yard in diameter. These are usually piled high with washing, bread, vegetables, etc… This morning just as I was returning to Troop H.Q. from moving one of the guns, I heard a terrific explosion on the hill above us. Black smoke rose from the trees and above it, one of these baskets, level and neatly piled with something, going up and up into the air with the slow motion of a film. When it had reached a height of about 200ft. it started to come down, still without upsetting and finally disappeared into the treetops again. It seems that one of these women had decided to take shortcuts to her house across the fields: she had trodden on a mine, and there was nothing worth mentioning left of her. The other thing concerns me more nearly. I lost my only pair of woolly gloves the other day...[6]

As with the activities of the Victorian OFs and those in Europe in 1919, the work of Richards and countless others like him tends to contradict the idea that the British Army has only recently developed a humanitarian, social support role under the sinister aegis of political correctness. Of course, this role was easier to perform in an environment where the local people were fed up with the old regime and accepted that their own armed forces were defeated. Although a lamentable lack of co-ordination between the American and British invaders allowed an Axis Dunkirk as 100,000 enemy soldiers escaped to the mainland to fight another day, Italy was almost finished. A few elite divisions apart, the Italian army offered little resistance when the Allies landed in the 'toe' of their country in September. The early autumn saw rapid advances as the Germans pulled back to more easily defensible positions near Rome, in some cases, as in Naples, being thrown out by the locals. J.M.A. Lumsden, finally posted to where something was happening, wrote to the *Fettesian*:

You will have heard about the reception we got from the Italians. It isn't a bit exaggerated. I was lucky enough to be in Naples within the first hour of our reaching it, and it was an unforgettable experience. It really made four years of war seem concretely worthwhile. Of course the treatment which the Italians are getting from the Germans simply beggars description for its brutality. The pro-ally sentiment seems to be genuine enough and mercurial as they are, I simply cannot understand how they stuck Mussolini for so long.[7]

Although he recognised that 'the Fascists reduced their countrymen to misery,' Norman Cameron was less sympathetic. When an Italian complained that since the Allied invasion there had been no flour, Cameron retorted 'The Greeks have had no flour since you went there.'[8]

The government in Rome adroitly sacked the Duce and changed sides; Guest, accompanying German prisoners on a train, was disgusted to see Italians at level-crossings making shooting and throat-cutting gestures. 'The Italians are brave,' said one of the Germans, quietly.[9]

In fairness, many Italians were brave – unfortunately for the British, a lot of these remained with the Germans clinging on in the northern Italy, a headache for the Allies until 1945. Both tough German units such as the Fallschirmjäger (paratroopers) Panzer Grenadiers and SS, and hardcore Italian fascists such as the ferocious 'Vendetta' Division (who so impressed their normally dismissive allies that they were given Waffen-SS status – the Nazis' idea of the ultimate compliment) ensured that any notion of a 'soft underbelly' was swiftly dispelled. Lt-Col Alan Johnstone of the RASC had met few other OFs until he found himself diving into a slit trench at Monte Cassino, where the Fallschirmjäger, occupying the hilltop monastery, were proving nightmarishly difficult to evict. Much to his surprise, taking cover in the same trench was Capt H.M. McNeill of the Argyll and Sutherland Highlanders. They had been at Fettes together during the First World War and had not seen one another since. Kenneth McCallum wrote home and described the conditions the Allies encountered as they advanced through the scorched earth the enemy had left behind:

The first thing you notice is the Destruction in towns and villages. Destruction, which appalled us when the Germans raided London and Coventry, Bristol and Glasgow, but which is insignificant compared to this country. The second thing you notice is Hunger… the older folk just stand and watch as our convoys rumble through their shattered towns and the kiddies hold out their tiny hands begging for 'biscotti', for the Germans have taken everything. Needless to say, the Germans have blown every bridge and culvert, embankment and defile, that was ever worth blowing…

This front has been static since December when our men captured this sorry little town which is now a deserted shambles inhabited only by a few hawks and a solitary cat… We are busily engaged preparing the road for heavier traffic, though just now only jeeps and light armoured vehicles are allowed to use it as it is under full observation of Jerry in two places. The disabled tanks with their attendant graves, both ours and theirs, the trees barren and, in most cases, blown off half way up the trunk, the fields pockmarked with craters of all sizes, and the buildings just a shambles.[10]

This desolate spot was still shelled by the Germans, especially when they discovered the sappers' repair work. McCallum had a few lucky escapes, such as the time when a haystack took the splinters from a shell which landed ten yards from him; 'the shrill whine rose to a colossal crescendo and everything went blank for a few seconds – everybody was amazed when I picked myself up, dusted off the straw, and walked away, and so was I.' He concluded by saying that 'it is all jolly good fun and I have no doubt that, by the time you receive this, you too will be in the thick of it, enjoying every moment.' For the benefit of later generations, he explained that when he said 'fun' he meant they were soldiers doing the job, albeit a dangerous one, for which they had volunteered and had been well trained, and were doing their duty.[11]

It was truly a sapper's war, with bridge-building, road mending and mine clearance – and often enemy clearance too, for on more than one occasion McCallum found that the Germans had left men behind, or artillery trained on, the blown bridges he needed to repair. Even an expert like him could trip a mine – luckily for him, he did so with enough force to knock off its bakelite fuse, saving everyone in a hundred yard radius from its effects. Although the work of an engineer was generally considered unflashy, it was McCallum who had one of the most glamorous experiences of any of the Fettesians in wartime. Near the village of Calbenzano, he was carrying out some reconnaissance work when he was approached by two civilians, one of whom offered him a cigarette, which when unrolled contained a message:

My two peasants will tell you about our sad plight. They are truthful. Also they will give you information as to the hills and who is there. M.A.B.B.

M.A.B.B., it turned out, was Maria Adelaide Borghese, Contessa Bastoggi. She had been detained by the Germans in her magnificent home, the Castello Valenzano. Rather than take the peasants, with whom he had been communicating in his Argentine Spanish, back to HQ for interrogation, it made sense to find the Countess herself, since she obviously spoke English. 'Take me to her,' said McCallum. Under cover of hedgerows and vineyards, they reached the castle's outer ramparts. The Divisional newspaper *Diagonals* later printed an account of the raid:

McCallum, with a small party of Sappers, crossed the River Arno and soon appeared below her castle, which overlooked the ground across which the Countess was to be conducted in broad daylight. The Germans had turned the castle into an observation post and defended it with four machine guns. Before the Boche could know what was happening the Countess had slipped out of the house, under cover of her orchard trees, and was well on her way escorted by McCallum. Carrying her across the river in his arms, the gallant Lieutenant saw her safe to Brigade HQ. The grateful Countess declared that her ambition was to see her castle used as

Brigade HQ where she could act as housewife to the Brigade Staff and provide all the comforts of home, etc.[12]

Much to his embarrassment, McCallum was saddled with the soubriquet 'the Gallant Lieutenant' – clearly applied by the Countess when she was being 'chatted up' at Brigade HQ – but forgot to write an article for the *Daily Telegraph* about his exploit when they asked him. 'We were not glory seekers,' he said, 'It had all been in a day's work.'

Alan Harvey, serving with the Reconnaissance Corps, had not especially enjoyed his time in Africa – he had been given legal duties and his job was 'to defend soldiers who were misbehaving in times of idleness' – but finally saw action at Cassino. Shortly afterwards, he was in command of a patrol of two light reconnaissance cars near Strada. The leading car became ditched, and at the same time both cars were fired on and set alight.

Ordering the two crews to bail out and take up the fire position in the ditch near the ditched car, Lt. Harvey, noticing a German hiding in a slit trench five yards away, went forward and killed him with his revolver. Noticing two more Germans firing from a position near a haystack about forty yards distant, Lt. Harvey crawled forward under cover from his patrol's fire and knocked them out with a grenade. At this stage Lt. Harvey saw yet another German position manned by two men in a slit trench and again crawled forward and put the position out of action with a phosphorus bomb.[13]

For extricating his men without a casualty and for exceptional courage under fire, Harvey was awarded the Military Cross. His willingness to expose himself to danger rather than risk the lives of others was further illustrated when, ordered to check out a large orchard for Germans and booby-traps prior to a planned advance, he went in alone and found himself being mortared, and had to beat a hasty retreat as bombs rained down around him. 'The mortar pursued me as I zigzagged and sometimes zagzigged – anyway, he didn't get me,' he recalled with a nonchalance characteristic of the wartime generation, 'It was like a game with about a dozen bombs.'[14]

The dangers of the war in Italy were constant; on one brutal occasion, he found three sergeants dead in the church where they had taken shelter from the sun. A German barrage had descended whist Harvey was away: 'they were sitting in their chairs with their brains splashed on the walls; the force of the blast had sucked out the backs of their heads.' Harvey also encountered some of Germany's latest technology; a salvo from a Nebelwerfer multi-barrelled rocket-launcher caught him in the open, and on another occasion a Panzerfaust (German bazooka) hit his scout car, but luckily glanced off the sloping armour and failed to explode. He seems to have been extraordinarily lucky; on one of the various 'find the enemy' expeditions, he and his men stopped in a peach orchard only to have their dining disturbed by an enormous explosion up the road – the Germans had cratered it with high explosive. 'Perhaps the peaches saved our lives,' he mused. His only serious injury, in fact, was sustained in Greece, when a distracted ambulance driver accidentally veered his vehicle into Harvey's jeep, which came off the road, hospitalising him for a fortnight. Ian Findlay was also fortunate; finding two men paralysed in a trench, he discovered that a shell had whistled past them, grazing one on the shoulder, and buried itself in a neat hole, three inches across, in the earth. Curious as to its ballistic properties, Findlay acquired a three foot long stick and inserted it into the hole.

'Please be careful, Sir, you might set it off,' suggested one of the soldiers.

'If it didn't go off thumping into your trench,' Findlay replied, 'It's unlikely to go off if I tickle its bottom with a stick.'

As it was, the shell was unreachable, and the nearest his men came to disaster was when three American fighters 'which had somehow or other got north and south of the smoke screen mixed up' strafed them at low level. 'Looking back,' he wrote in 2001, 'I acknowledge that I had a very, very lucky war.'[15]

Kenneth McCallum's luck also persisted; near the Gothic Line, he was chatting in camp with a friend who had just popped round for a beer to mark his twenty-third birthday when an enemy salvo ripped into the tents and stores, setting alight a haystack which promptly toppled onto an explosive store, setting off 300 detonators. They struggled through the fumes to rescue the flaming boxes to safety and succeeded – 'just!' On Christmas Eve, 1944, he was en route to rescue some tanks trapped in a forward position on soft ground when German 88mm guns opened fire.

The sapper next to me in the trench took a shell splinter in his forehead which came out through the back of his head; I could only watch while for all of two minutes his heart went on pumping blood through the hole in his forehead. I also remember watching the snow kicked up by the shells as they hit the ground all around us. Eventually, the enemy fire slackened and ceased. They had achieved their object: they had stopped us from reaching the tanks.[16]

Sadly, other Fettesians serving in Italy missed out on such near-misses and other good fortune; James Stuart-Menteth, a Lieutenant in the Scots Guards, lost both legs at Anzio, where Michael Scott, described by his commanding officer as 'a most brave and gallant man', and James Leckie, a former *Fettesian* editor turned schoolmaster, were both killed. Dr A.P.R. Borrowman was awarded the MBE for his medical services at the Anzio beach-head, but did not long outlive the war. George Holmes Gallie, scion of a Fettesian dynasty, was killed crossing the Garigliano in January 1944, whilst Richard McGillycuddy and Colin Dick died at Coriano Ridge, the latter a former Head of House in Glencorse who was killed when a shell landed in his weapon pit. Paddy Buchan, 'a first class troop leader' was hit by a shell near Rimini on 10 September. The Germans in Italy held on for as long as their comrades in the fatherland; one of the last OFs to be killed was William Grant Waugh, who fell on 21 April 1945 (when the Ruhr had been taken and the Russians were massing outside Berlin) and is buried at Ravenna. Ian McCallum was attached to Popski's Private Army, the maverick special forces unit commanded by the eccentric but effective Vladimir Peniakoff; he had just taken over command of B patrol when his jeep was hit by a panzerfaust at Lake Commachio in one of the last actions of the war in Italy on 23 April 1945, a week before Hitler's suicide. His sapper brother spent 2 May celebrating the surrender of German forces in Italy, and received the news of Ian's death three weeks later. He drove to the village of Connachile and found the blackened remains of Ian's jeep and beret; Bianca, a village girl with a brother in the partisans, had laid flowers on the grave. Later, he erected a white cross made by his men, and enjoyed the hospitality of Ian's unit, including the legendary Popski himself and two Yugoslav partisan twins, Rita and Utsha, with whom he went swimming.

Montgomery allegedly said that he was never quite sure what the strategic purpose of the Italian Campaign really was; in fairness, like the Somme, it cost the Germans half a million casualties and allowed for successes elsewhere, and the men who fought there bitterly resented the appellation 'D-Day Dodgers' by those who thought they were having an easy time in 'sunny Italy.' Conditions had been bad enough in June 1944 when McCallum wrote home; when winter came, mud clogged all movement and conditions resembled Ypres in 1917.

Dodecanese Interlude

One of the more unusual operations undertaken by an OF in the Mediterranean at this time took place in the Dodecanese, just off the Turkish coast. Following the Italian surrender, Churchill's arguably unhealthy interest in the Balkans was revived and his long-cherished project to bring Turkey into the war – with forty divisions, enviable positioning with regard to German positions in Yugoslavia, and warm-water access to Russia at her disposal – dug out of mothballs. The Americans were doubtful but the British charged ahead into disaster. Major Alan Smyth and his battalion of 4/13th Frontier Force Rifles (Wilde's) sailed from Cyprus in commandeered Italian steamers for the island of Castel Rosso, the easternmost island, sixty miles from Rhodes – onto which the Germans were holding firmly.

The island is rocky and crisscrossed with goat tracks. The harbour lies facing Turkey and is sheltered by a cliff some 900ft. high. Apart from the houses in the harbour area, there is only one building and that was painted brilliant white which made a wonderful aiming mark for Jerry bombers coming from Rhodes. This was battalion H.Q.; it was almost on the cliff edge and was bombed about four times per week. On one occasion when the bombers had gone I walked across to the light A.A. gun crew and leaned on the wall; while doing so I noticed that there was a 500lb. bomb lying just the other side. When the R.N. patrolled in the area they would pull into the bay on the Turkish coast; the first time I saw them there they were bombed and a cruiser was badly hit with a lot of casualties. The Turkish guns, however, opened fire and drove [the Germans] away.[17]

Major Smyth is very quick to point out that this expedition did not feature the improbable Hollywood derring-do depicted in *The Guns of Navarone*, and his mission undoubtedly seems to have had its bucolic episodes, albeit interrupted by war:

I went with our 2 I/C to have a swim on the other side of the bay but on arrival there the ominous sound of bombers came to our ears so we decided to wait and took cover in slit trenches. Two R.A.F. N.C.O.s came along and we stopped to advise that they had better wait a little, but they just said that they would go on

465

and did so. About six bombs promptly fell higher up the cliff and brought down a cascade of rock and stones. The two airmen were lying on the track about 50 feet from us. One was wearing unbroken glasses but was dead, the other was alive but a heavy rock had bounced on his knee breaking the cap and removing the skin. I then discovered blood running down my own arm but no pain – wounded in action! The M.O. cleaned it up and put on a piece of sticking plaster. We decided not to have a swim.

One of Smyth's odder duties was supplying fuel to the neutral Turks – to whom the British gave all sorts of assistance, including the loan of engineers to build roads – using landing craft which sailed at night. One evening, he was enjoying a cigarette when the Jemadar, the Viceroy's Commission Indian platoon commander, came to say that the boat was almost loaded but one oil-drum was stuck to the bottom of the ramp. On further investigation, it turned out that its progress was being impeded by an unexploded 500lb bomb. The landing craft, needless to say, promptly departed. Despite its (admittedly theoretical) merits, the Dodecanese operation was abandoned by the British after a vigorous German counter-attack and the capture of thousands of Allied prisoners – some of whom were tragically killed by their own side when ships carrying them to the mainland were sunk by Royal Navy submarines. Smyth's men were evacuated from Castel Rosso, leaving one platoon of about 30 to await further orders. However, the Germans do not seem to have bothered retaking it, confining themselves to grabbing bigger islands such as Kos and Leros (the actual inspiration for *The Guns of Navarone*; Castel Rosso was the setting for the Italian film *Mediterraneo*) and Smyth's remaining men remained in possession of it. In 1947, Britain handed it over to the Greeks, who call it Megisti. Back in Cyprus, Smyth was enjoying a drink with an RAF officer who casually mentioned that there was a useful emergency landing ground on Castel Rosso. The pilot was deeply shaken when Smyth told him that his unit had sown mines in the area to prevent the Germans dropping paratroopers there. Luckily, as Intelligence Officer, Smyth was able to furnish a map of the strip with the position of the mines indicated, and thus saved some pilots from unnecessarily bumpy landings. Elsewhere in the Aegean, Nick Hammond and another British officer came upon a Greek village – 'a burnt-out shell' full of dead children, women and old men. 'This,' said the young officer, 'is what we are fighting to prevent here and at home.' When they talked of home, Hammond discovered that his new friend was another Old Fettesian, Jock Hamilton.[18]

The RAF in the years of victory

Unlike the Great War, when virtually all OFs served as officers, many remained in the ranks throughout 1939-45, often voluntarily. Neil Irvine of the RAOC is one ranker who still gets irritated at cinema portrayals of glamorous, infallible, unflappable officers; he is proud to have remained in the ranks throughout his service career. Most of those without commissions, however, were in the RAF. Twelve per cent of the OF casualties in the air force, and around seven per cent of those who served, were non-commissioned. Brian Watt wrote to the school in January 1942 to tell them that he was working as ground crew in the RAF – 'I expect I am the first Fettesian on record to become a Fitter N.C.O.' He found his métier with 517 (Meteorological) Sqn., which he served as a Sergeant. His contemporary F.E.T. Dann actually refused a commission twice, though finally succumbed. J.R. Campbell became 'something in the City' on leaving Fettes in 1940, and was immediately exposed to the German air raids. Accordingly, he joined the Royal Air Force in order to strike back. One of the most enthusiastic cricketers the school had ever produced, he enjoyed his time training in North Wales because it coincided with the arrival in Britain of the three hundred or so West Indians who joined the RAF in 1941 – 'One or two had actually played for the West Indies at home, and all, I think, for their islands,' he wrote excitedly to his housemaster in early 1942, 'Needless to say, we were unbeaten.' The glamorous role of the fighter pilot, however, was not to be his:

I flew, and enjoyed it, but could not land safely enough... I suppose I'm one of those chaps that just can't land. So that was that; I had to do something, so decided to become a gunner. For ten weeks I've been banging away at towed targets in order to become an efficient 'tail-end Charlie.' The course is most interesting and I've enjoyed myself much more than I expected. One needs to fire four m.g.s at the same time at something to understand what a feeling of power one has. Of course there has been no opposition so far, but I feel confident that when it does come along I shall be able to give as much as I can take.[19]

It was as a rear gunner that Sgt Campbell served, both a dangerous job since German night-fighters would aim for the 'tail-end Charlie' to render a British bomber defenceless, and an uncomfortable one since the minus 40 degree air at high altitude whistled through the turret, freezing flesh to metal. Campbell was killed on a raid later that year and is buried in the British military cemetery at Rheinberg in Westphalia. The bomber offensive of 1942-5 is undoubtedly the most controversial aspect of the Allied war effort in Europe. Max Hastings has written of the purpose of Bomber Command as 'the progressive, systematic destruction of the urban areas of the Reich, city block by city block, factory by factory, until the enemy became a nation of troglodytes, scratching in the ruins.'[20]

Although the bombing campaign has been criticized, it did crack the Germans' transportation network to the west, making it harder to reinforce their troops in France after D-Day, kept 10,000 anti-aircraft guns and half a million men away from the battlefronts, blazing away expensively at aeroplanes they rarely hit (16,000 shells were fired for every bomber shot down) and denied both fighters and fuel to soldiers on the front line.[21]

Allied bombing was pursued in order to bring the war to an end, by young men who were being shot at and a huge number of whom were killed – 55,000 in total, more than all the British officers lost in the Great War. Around a tenth of Fettes' wartime casualties lost their lives in the bombing campaign. P/O Ronald Rutherford Morison ('so quiet, and yet so keen and so enthusiastic, and with the heart of a lion', as the CO of 149 Sqn. put it, 'no matter how hot the spot, he would always sail through, and never deviated from his purpose, which was to bomb the target he had been given'[22]) lies with the rest of the crew of his Wellington, the only Britons in the village cemetery of St. Sever-Calvados near Bayeux. J.P. Muirhead DFC of 12 Sqn., one of the first Pathfinders, is likewise buried with his Wellington crew in a communal cemetery on the Ile de Re off the Biscay coast (Alastair Stewart, another Pathfinder, was killed when his Lancaster blew up over England in 1945). F/O Peter Wood was killed over Holland on 12 April 1944 when the Lancaster he was navigating was shot down.

Sgt Ian Cameron had written to the school in January 1943 to say that after training as a navigator he had been turned into a bomb-aimer with little notice, but he phlegmatically noted that it would be useful to be able to take over someone else's job. He noted that there were several 'all-rounders' in his crew, who were 'all very young and all sergeants; the pilot, an old Etonian, is just 21 and is the oldest of us.'[23]

Two Old Fettesian fliers: Bing Kirk with his USAAF Mustang, and Pathfinder Alastair Stewart

He had been on Wellingtons, and was hoping to be transferred to 'lighter crates' like Bostons, but expected that he would end up on the 'four engine stuff'. He was, and was shot down in the Lancaster he was navigating to Hamburg in 1943, and his body washed ashore on a Frisian island 'in a direct line from his base to the target'[24]. Like 'Bill' Esplen of 214 Sqn. and Hugh Mackenzie Scott of 207 Sqn., both killed on raids on Berlin, he is buried in Germany. Cameron had almost been killed before even getting to fight, for the ship taking him back from training in Canada was torpedoed. His obituary in the *Fettesian* noted that:

It was typical of him that he had allowed his parents to remain under the impression that he was still training, when he had in fact been out on no fewer than 17 operational sorties, including some to North Italy. How many of us could have refrained from telling our families about adventures like these? These quiet and humble people, who say nothing, but go on doing their duty, are the very salt of the earth.[25]

Jim Winterschladen also flew bombers, in his case the Liberators of 53 Squadron which flew out of Reykjavik, searching out u-boats and protecting shipping routes as part of Coastal Command (John Humphries, often seasick on the Arctic convoys to Russia, was one of the beneficiaries of this work).[26]

J.D.R. Shaw was protecting Britain from enemy raids in a Mosquito;

this task was made difficult by British searchlights which illuminated his aircraft rather than the Focke-Wulf he was chasing, but in the end he caught it with his four 20mm cannon and the German plane exploded, leaving Shaw's covered in soot.[27]

Other OFs in the RAF were tasked with the kind of low-level attacks which, as the Allies gained air superiority, demoralised the Germans. John Younie, whose entry in 'Characters of the 1st XV' in a 1940 *Fettesian* had described him as 'useful in attack',[28] flew Mustangs over Yugoslavia in support of Tito's partisans:

A typical day would start with a noisy airman ('erk') coming into my tent with a mug of tea about 05:00 to remind me that it was 'press tits' for take-off at 06:00 in order to be over Yugoslav coast before the enemy could park and camouflage their double hull barges or Siebel ferries. Then we would go up to the Austrian border to look for a train to strafe before going home to a cigarette and a delicious breakfast of fried eggs (bought with cigarettes or soap) and soya link sausage more than three hours after take-off.[29]

Younie, like all the military OFs, is remarkably modest about these operations (asked for details, he reluctantly supplied information but commented that 'it smacks of line-shooting to me') but both his own experiences, and those of other OFs, point to the considerable risks run. Several were lost on missions like this: both James Hardie Brown, DSO, DFC, in a rocket-firing Hurricane IV, and Patrick Mar Clark, going in at mast height against the Italians in a Blenheim V, were killed in low-level anti-ship operations. The Commonwealth War Graves Commission, incidentally, has two James Hardie Browns on file, the other being an infantry captain and MC winner killed in 1918; also an OF, he was the father of the pilot, who had never known him. On 23 February 1945, Younie was asked to check out the claim by a Beaufighter squadron that they had sunk a ship in harbour at Fiume. Because of the poor light, and despite the fact that he had only flown this particular Mustang for the first time the previous day, he went into a shallow dive – hitting 505 mph, a good 60 mph faster than the aircraft would normally go and well on the way to the sound barrier – and flew along the dockside to see the ship lying on its side, totally submerged. His number two, however, was hit in the radiator, and had to bale out; Younie circled round until relief came. 'I enjoyed my breakfast that day,' he recalls, and presumably he also did when he hit a train a month later and saw 'a long line of flashes of different colours and shock waves in the mist' – it had been packed with ammunition. He was lucky to avoid the fate of many other Fettesians engaged in low-level strafing; about two weeks before the end of the war he was covering convoys of retreating Germans when a bullet entered the cockpit and splattered on the armour behind him. 'Wee bits of metal somehow got through my clothing and under my skin,' he says, 'The MO said, "They'll do you no harm. We'll just leave them there." He was right.' Had the worst come to the worst and the plane crashed, Younie, like his colleagues, carried a revolver, not to shoot Germans with but to give to the partisans as a thank-you present for their hospitality. Another Fettesian Mustang pilot was Bing Kirk, who had joined the American forces in 1942 and flew reconnaissance missions in the F-6 variant. His particular role, 'tac recon', was to liase by radio with artillery and help it to find, and zero in on, possible targets. By the time he reached the front, however, he was too late to see action, and enjoyed testing his aircraft's agility in stunt flying with other pilots.

Non-combatants in the War Effort

Other Fettesians served in different ways. Richard Humble, who had flown over the school in 1932 to drop a message to Harry Pyatt, ran a munitions factory in Dartington:

He eventually employed 20,000 people, most of them women. He was very concerned that his 'girls' should be well fed, knowing that that was one of the keys to morale, so he employed a top London chef to take charge of the catering. When the factory was established he summoned the shop stewards and said 'In this factory we are not going to have any bloody nonsense about strikes' and they didn't.[30]

The Rev W.R. Sanderson, a Church of Scotland minister, ran a Church Hut for soldiers at Rouen before the fall of France, whilst the Rev Duncan McGillivray, Chaplain of St. Andrew's Hostel in Jerusalem, organised similar facilities, including mobile canteens, in the Middle East, and was honoured for his work. Away from the firing-line, seven OFs were working in one capacity or another for the Ministry of War Transport. The oldest was Sir William Currie, a surviving Victorian and Chairman of P & O, who brought a knowledge of liners to the job, whilst others included Joe Maclay of the Glasgow shipbuilding family, who as an MP liaised between government and Admiralty, and travelled to Russia to organise the convoys on which several OFs were sailing to supply the Soviet forces. John Humphries did not meet him; when his ship docked in the frozen north, the only Briton there was a hopelessly drunk officer and it was too dark and cold to fraternise with the locals; his crew were hugely cheered by the sight of a lorryload of fresh cabbages, but these were promptly removed, and a visit to the local cinema ended with the Royal Navy being sent home in disgrace for smoking in a wooden building. Desmond Goodbody's health prevented him from fighting, so he got a job in aircraft construction, whilst J. Martin helped design landing craft. A. W. Newsom, invalided out of the RAF, taught English in neutral Turkey. He observed that 'Ankara must be the most cosmopolitan place in the world at present, and it's strange to sit next to Japs and Italians in restaurants, and to go to a swastika-covered exhibition of German architecture complete with a vast metal bust of the Führer looking thoroughly intuitive.'[31] John Smart, an actor and producer, rose to the rank of Captain and worked with ENSA in North Africa and Italy.[32] R. F. Keith was in the Revenue Department of the Government of the Sind, and was nearly killed by severe malaria 'which he caught when out in the Sind desert fighting the locusts.'[33]

D-Day

Thanks to Hollywood's best efforts, with *The Longest Day* and *Saving Private Ryan*, D-Day is etched onto the western mind as the pivotal point in the Second World War; the Russians have a vague notion that the Anglo-Americans may have sent a few chaps ashore somewhere. Stalin, his usual paranoia having returned following a bizarre lapse into good faith regarding Hitler's 1939 promise not to attack the Soviet Union, had been badgering Churchill for years about a Second Front, and insisted that Italy, like North Africa, did not count. Since the Allied advance there was painfully slow, and certainly showed little sign of getting anywhere near Germany, he may have had a point. The Allied commanders, especially Montgomery, were haunted by a collective folk-memory from the First World War of what could go wrong if attacks were badly planned and inadequately supported. Operation Jubilee, the disastrous Dieppe raid of 1942, cost over 3,000 men, over half those committed to it; the West was not keen to repeat either this or the severe mauling it had received in the aftermath of the Anzio landings in Italy. Accordingly, the Allies were not going to set foot in Normandy until they were good and ready, and preparations extended to the research of the tides and sands of every beach from the Bay of Biscay to Holland. Several Fettesians were involved in the planning of the operation, most prominently 'Pete' Pyman, whose memoirs record that he would have been broken-hearted had he not been used in North-West Europe; Montgomery told him that he didn't want to waste Pyman's talents in training and made him Chief of Staff of 30 Corps, which was designated for assault.[34]

Although he almost blotted his copy-book by protesting about the appointment of Lord Lewes (later the Marquess of Abergavenny) to the Headquarters Staff – 'We'll have no flipping peer from the Life Guards here' – he worked well with his extended 'family' of officers and men in the meticulous planning of the campaign, which was rehearsed in Cambridge. Meanwhile, Montgomery was fighting battles with the American generals about precise dispositions, which have been recorded by some historians as proof of major flaws in the Allied approach. Pyman would have none of this, and in his memoirs he assessed his leader and friend in glowing terms as 'the perfect British Officer, without peer… woe betide the man who tries to belittle the achievements on the battlefield of our Monty.'[35]

Lower down the Allied chain of command, Selwyn Lloyd was wondering what his next appointment would be. He was a natural pessimist and wrote to his mother that he expected 'at any moment to be relegated to some haven of rest like the Hebrides.'[36] It was not to be; already GSO1 at Headquarters Second Army, he was made Deputy Chief of Staff by Montgomery in February 1944. He spent frantic weeks of preparation on the south coast of England and was one of the representatives of Second Army, along with General Miles Dempsey, whom he revered, at the service of dedication of the great armada on 4 June. Iain Macleod, later to join Lloyd in government, was supplementing his income as a staff officer with the 50th Northumbrian Division (in which role he found out about Overlord's objectives by accident when he found a map receipt for Normandy – rather than the expected Pas de Calais – in a file, which he discreetly burned) with playing poker and bridge for high stakes at Crockford's; he always recouped his expenses and made between £20 and £50.[37] (A keen gambler, Macleod once fired a shot through, and then battered down, the door of a superior officer who refused to play cards with him after a night of heavy drinking. After passing out on the floor, Macleod demanded an apology the next day for his superior's anti-sociability.) Dick Normand was nowhere near all this frantic activity. He was an unwitting participant in Operation Fortitude, which sought to convince the Germans that the widely-expected invasion would come somewhere other than Normandy. This was to be achieved by the creation of the US First Army Group in East Anglia, a fictitious assembly of dummy tanks supposedly aimed at the Pas de Calais (Fortitude South) and Britain's Fourth Army, vigorously and publicly training for mountain warfare in Scotland, apparently getting ready to invade Scandinavia (Fortitude North). Normand, serving with the 52nd Infantry Division, recalls that, as one of the few genuine units in Scotland at the time, they tried to be seen throughout Aberdeenshire, the idea being that they would embark from Greenock for Norway. They were even inspected by King Haakon and given scripts for wireless communications – which they were told were in order to test the equipment – whilst in Nissen huts at East Fortune the German transmissions were monitored to see if the enemy was taking the bait. By this stage, the Germans were unlikely to be able to send many reconnaissance flights over Scotland, so the British relied on spies – some of whom were their own double-agents – to do the job for them. It seems to have had some effect; only Rommel, of all Hitler's generals, was convinced that the Allies would come to Normandy, and Hitler remained committed to defending Norway from the red herring of an Allied assault until at least the winter of 1944.[38]

On 5 June, Normand and the rest of the 52nd Division had their radios impounded and were given leave with orders to clear out of Aberdeenshire, the better to convince the rumour-mill that they were indeed en route for Scandinavia. He booked into a hotel in the Borders and, as he put it later, 'spent D-Day in the arms of my wife.' Neil Irvine, closer to the action but not deployed until later, found himself in a village near Aldershot in a region swarming with army units and military vehicles, each of which would have its crew bivouacking nearby. When the great day came, he was on a course, and remembers his instructor saying, as aircraft galore trundled overhead at 100 feet, 'the invasion has started!'[39]

One of E.G. Richards' old Desert Rat corporals, Bill Balfour, recorded some reminiscences for him in 2002, and chuckled at the tale of how the bored sappers, waiting for D-Day, amused themselves by setting booby-traps for American soldiers, several of which had explosive igniters and caused a Board of Inquiry when a jumpy GI responded to the loud report by emptying the magazine of his carbine into the darkness. He was less amused when the sappers were sent to put out a summer fire in the grounds of Lord Mountbatten's country seat. 'Mountbatten never even offered us a drink,' he said, indignant in a retirement home nearly sixty years later, 'We should have let the place burn.'[40]

Lord Mountbatten also made a less than brilliant impression on OF Lindsay Gordon, who won an MC but lost an arm in the war. Always enthusiastic about new gadgets which might provide short-cuts to victory, Mountbatten arranged for Winston Churchill to come and see a display of the tanks named in the Prime Minister's honour towing sledges full of troops from the Durhams. Unfortunately, as Gordon recalled, the Durhams had recently been recruited from the local borstal: 'When I looked out of the turret, I saw that they had scarpered.' Gordon and the other tanks crew had to trundle past Churchill dragging what were, in effect, empty boxes behind them – 'it must have looked ridiculous.'[41]

Those who actually invaded Europe on 6 June had a rather less pleasant experience than Normand; although Pyman remembered it as 'an exciting day', he also felt profoundly seasick as he stood on the bridge of HMS *Beagle* on the way to the landings, and only a powerful and mysterious pill provided by a sailor saved him from having to use the bucket next to his Corps Commander. He was further disconcerted by the task of getting from a ship to a small landing craft, 'bouncing around like a pea on a drum.' Royal Artillery Major I.H.K. Rae, one of four serving brothers, three of whom won MCs (the fourth, captured in 1940, was unable to complete the set) also took medicinal precautions:

The embarkation took place at Newhaven, and I never saw men in better heart. When the operation was postponed 24 hours, there was great disappointment; and when it was finally decided upon, one would have thought from the singing they were all going on block leave. The Battalion was embarked on three LCIs, and when these light top heavy craft began to roll on the choppy seas, singing ceased and many were thoroughly sick. I pinned my faith to Hyocine Tablets, and remained fit the whole time, finding myself almost the only officer able to serve out the maps which were unsealed on the afternoon of 5 June. About 90% of the craft inspected those maps with more interest than they ever showed before or since; it was the first time they knew for certain where the landing was to take place.[42]

More sombrely, Selwyn Lloyd had altered his will to stipulate that £120

– the total awarded to him as a scholarship from Fettes to Cambridge – be returned to the school for similar help to someone else. His letter to his parents to be opened in the event of his death, which of course they never read, is worth quoting in full, as it must stand for many of the Fettesians who appreciated the advantages they had had in life and were willing, through military service, to give something back, and indeed to make the ultimate sacrifice:

If and when you read this, I shall be dead or missing. You will already have had the shock of receiving the telegram and will be much upset. The purpose of this letter is to tell you how I feel about it myself, into the hope that it will alter your view and be a measure of comfort to you.

I do not want you to grieve for me; in fact my last request is that you should not do so. I feel that there is really nothing tragic about what has happened. I am not trying to be melodramatic when I say that it is a proud moment for me.

I have had an extremely happy life, thanks largely to both of you. It has been interesting and, I think, not unsuccessful – the Leas, Fettes, Magdalene, the Union, Macclesfield, the Council, the Northern Circuit and now the Army. I have had many friends and received much kindness, and throughout have felt myself protected by your love and care.

After all that I can think of nothing more fitting than to die in the service of one's country and for the generations to come. When you think of the kind of various kinds of death that can come to one – accident, disease, etc. – possibly leaving one disillusioned with life and discontented with oneself, having lost faith in one's fellows, and possibly even in God, you must admit how much better and finer it is to die in some sort of higher service, when still in the prime of life and still believing in it all.

If you say how sad it is when you think of what I might have done or become, my answer is that I have finished on a high note. If I had survived, who can tell what dark places full of unhappiness and doubt might have had to be traversed.

If you say how sad it is to be separated from me, in fact that separation is likely to be much shorter than otherwise it might have been. I have no doubt at all that this life is a preparation for another life and in that belief I know that we shall meet again soon. I do believe in a just God and the immortality of the human soul and so I ask you to be of good cheer and not to grieve about what has happened to me. It is only an incident in something far bigger.[43]

Iain Macleod also had premonitions of death, but, as his biographer notes, having been convinced before 6 June that he would be killed, on surviving it he felt, with an equal lack of logic, that he would see out the war. Twenty years after the events, in an article for the *Spectator*, he wrote that 'It was as though every ship that had ever been launched was there and as if every plane that had ever been built was there.'[44]

He wrote to his parents immediately afterwards that 'the invasion forces seemed to be smashing at the beach defenses and countless squadrons droned in after one another to bomb. The enemy batteries blazed back but did very little damage.'[45]

Then, like so many others, Macleod heard the instruction over the ship's Tannoy – 'Assault parties, man your craft' – and scrambled down the net into the Landing Craft (Troops). In a moment of martial ardour, he attempted to load his revolver, but found that his ammunition pouches had, in a strange echo of Shaw's *Arms and the Man*, been filled with boiled sweets by a batman who knew more about war than he did. Thus prepared, he stepped into waist-deep water just off the beach, and waded ashore to find the aftermath of the successful assault, and found both shambles and order, dead, wounded, prisoners, wrecked vehicles, and the obligatory tea. 'It was like an absurdly magnificent film by Cecil B. de Mille,' he wrote, 'It was like war.'

One of those in a still-functioning ship was Lt David Soutar, transferred from MTBs to the destroyer HMS *Montrose*, a veteran of the Russian Civil War, escorting the troop carriers across the Channel. After a fortnight of going backwards and forwards *Montrose* was hit by another ship in thick fog, and Soutar spent the rest of the war as No.1 of the landing craft working up base at HMS *Artella*. Freddie Scott, meanwhile, arrived in France by air, in a Horsa glider towed by an Albemarle:

All was quiet and I started a sing song to keep my platoon occupied. It was only partially successful as it was difficult to tell what was going through the minds of the men. I think like me they were anxious to get on with it. Crossing the channel it was wonderful to see the armada of ships beneath us and the mass of other tugs and gliders alongside...We cast off just before the French coast and I could see a number of gliders already on the ground. I could also soon see our objective. This was the offices and two large tanks of a small petrol depot on the Western bank of the Caen canal and some ¼ mile north of the bridges which D company had so recently captured. The Germans had erected poles all over our landing zone (Rommel's Asparagus) but in true Teutonic fashion they were in straight lines and so our pilots went into land between the rows in such a way that the poles removed our wings but this helped to slow us up and caused no damage to the body of the glider. Having pointed out our objective to the pilots they put us safely down only some 200 yards away from it – Perfect! So quickly we were at our objective which was deserted! [46]

The Germans, he guessed, had probably gone to the coast to try to repel the seaborne invaders. The only one he saw was a corpse which he found whilst on patrol. It was only after a couple of days that he had a serious encounter with the enemy, in the intimidating shape of armoured vehicles. Unfortunately, the man with the anti-tank PIAT was in a ditch on one side of the road, whilst the man with its ammunition was on the other. Scott and his men retreated to the trenches they had dug earlier and summoned artillery support – the German tanks having inconsiderately stopped a hundred yards away, just out of the PIAT's range. Eventually, the Germans were driven off, leaving half a dozen tanks and armoured cars. 'Our opponents, we later found out, were the notorious 21st Panzer Division and the 1st SS Division, so we were pretty pleased with ourselves.'

Freddie Scott photographed at the time of D-Day

Later on, Neil Irvine arrived in France when the Mulberry Harbours – floating temporary docks designed to facilitate unloading at captured beachheads – had been installed. To reach his target Mulberry, he (and indeed the countless thousands of other soldiers doing the same thing) had to cross over three other boats on a gangway made out of two planks. 'If you fall in,' advised a naval Petty Officer, 'run like hell when you touch the bottom.' The Mulberries themselves rose and fell with the waves; 'land,' recalls Irvine, 'seemed miles away' and when they finally got there the soldiers had to get in step and march up the road, watched by curious locals who seemed to have nothing better to do. Finding themselves halted by a field in which German prisoners were corralled – 'the SS in smart black uniforms and the Wehrmacht in grey and looking dejected' – they tried to outdo the captured enemy in a singing competition. This was never easy since the German army had always had a culture of singing, on which the Nazis built with classics such as the 'Horst Wessel' song and the curiously Teutonic mix of nationalistic propaganda and sentimental mush written by, among others, Norbert Schulze. Irvine noticed that an accordion had struck up 'Lili Marlene', the Afrika Korps song written by Schulze which was also popular with the British – Vera Lynn recorded a very good version – so his unit hummed along to it. The Germans applauded them, and someone called 'Danke,' followed by 'Guten Nacht,' to which the only appropriate response was 'Goodnight, Jerry.' Sadly, on this evening Irvine lost the kitten he had liberated from his boat; 'I hoped it could miaow in French,' he mused.[47]

As Pyman had hoped, the invasion was a superb display of tri-service co-operation. Bomber Command had pounded the German supply lines whilst smaller ground-attack planes and light bombers had harassed front-line positions in a crushing update of the Nazi Blitzkrieg tactics of 1940. 'Uncle' George Denholm was one of several OFs overhead strafing enemy positions with cannon and rockets before and after D-Day. Cliff Cooper, who was lucky to avoid execution after the Great Escape, was captured when his Typhoon took a direct hit whilst 'beating up' a train in Holland. The Navy, meanwhile, served both as taxi and artillery. This enabled the infantry, in Macleod's words, to go 'up the beaches under fire as if they were doing an exercise on Ilkley Moor.' Freddie Scott had reason to be grateful to the senior service:

In addition to the artillery support upon which we could call we also got help from the Royal Navy in the shape of, we were told, H.M.S. Warspite which must have been at sea some 8-10 miles away and yet landed, accurately, enormous shells in Escoville. Unlike the anticipated noise of an artillery shell the Warspite's roared as they passed over us and could be clearly seen. How we got this assistance I do not know.[48]

That is not to say that this was a bloodless victory; other Old Fettesians lost their lives, including David Smith, 'a great example to us all by his courage and cheerfulness', in the words of his CO.[49], and R.M.M. Tindall, a former member of the Shooting VIII and MC winner. Sub-Lt Colin Backhouse, a former Kimmerghame house prefect and captain of the Shooting VIII, 'a singularly clean-cut, straightforward boy whose cheerfulness was infectious and whose integrity of purpose was an inspiration', was lost in a commando action off the coast.

Lt Douglas Goodbody, who had been a sergeant in Greece, was commissioned in time for the landings but was badly wounded at Vire; his brother was able to report to the school that his 'foot and arm are both recovering and can be used to some extent.'[50] Malcolm McCallum's left jaw was shattered by a mortar bomb, for which he was treated by pioneering plastic surgeons Harold Gillies and John McIndoe, both subsequently knighted for such work. Lt Bobby Anderson of the Gordons was injured by booby-trap near Caen which left the lower half of his body paralysed, though he could 'get about with some assistance'. 'By a curious coincidence,' wrote K.D.H. Cattenach to the *Fettesian*, 'I was taking over Bobby's platoon when he was injured.'[51] Lt I.F.S. Greenaway, MC, received a crippling wound just after D-Day, but later wrote to the Pyatts that 'if I had not the stick you would not know I had an artificial leg.'[52]

Hospitalised near Bayeux for a recurrent health problem around the time of the breakout from the Falaise pocket, Neil Irvine was washing (he had hoped for a shower and was given a small basin and towel) when he noticed a man lying on a table under a Union flag with only his feet showing.

'Don't worry about him,' someone said, 'He's beyond worrying.'

The 'Dead March' was played every so often on the tannoy.[53]

Irvine, as previously noted, is one of many OFs who is dismissive of the glamorous Hollywood portrayal of the war, partly because as a foot-soldier in the RAOC he tended to see the deeply unglamorous practical side. As they climbed onto a Sherman tank on which they had been detailed to work, Neil Irvine's mate said, 'Jock, you stand with your feet on the seat and keep a good lookout for Jerry aircraft.' 'Then what do I do?' he asked. As his mate slid into the driver's seat, he shouted 'duck.' They then enjoyed speeding across a base field in the tank. The problem with this sort of thing was that it gave people the impression that one could drive, which Irvine could not. A few days later, he was sitting in the passenger seat of an ambulance which was part of a fleet due to be taken to a forward position when an angry officer ordered him to get out and drive another one. Protests about his absence of qualifications were unavailing.

'Left foot on that pedal,' barked the officer, after Irvine was bundled behind the steering wheel of the next vehicle, 'push down hard on the floor... right foot on that pedal... now, start the engine... now, easy, raise your left foot... easy, EASY I said!' The officer thumped the dashboard in frustration and the engine went dead. The officer was then left rubbing his shoulder after an attempt to move forward in first gear. Eventually, however, Irvine set off as 'tail end Charlie' of a convoy heading east past fields with lurid notices declaring 'Achtung! Minen.' He was enjoying himself immensely when he realised that the gap was growing between his and the other ambulances. As his machine ground to a halt, he noticed that the fuel gauge was at 'E'.

'What was I to do now?' he writes, 'Nothing in sight – just wait where you are and try to look intelligent, and hope that a Jerry plane doesn't use this vehicle as target practice.'[54]

He had been sitting there for some time, and had eaten all his sandwiches and drunk all his water, when a sergeant appeared in a jeep.

'It stopped,' said Irvine.

'I can see that,' said the sergeant, 'You're out of petrol and you have driven in first gear!'

Refilling the tank from a jerrycan, the sergeant ordered Irvine to follow him, and they eventually arrived at the forward field park, where the other mechanics cheered lustily and raised their mugs in a mock salute.[55]

An OF who could drive was Lt-Col Herbert Waddell of the Glaswegian rugby dynasty. Commanding a tank regiment which saw action at Caen and the Seine, he wrote home cheerfully that 'I now have more battles to my credit than international caps'[56] (he had 15 of these). His Churchill Crocodile tanks were an effective weapon against enemy fortifications – specially adapted with a flamethrower replacing the hull machine-gun, they towed six-ton trailers of fuel which provided eighty one-second bursts. An excited journalist described Waddell's tanks in action in Normandy:

Astride a roadway the attack went in – one troop of tanks on each site of the road, each troop followed by a platoon of the infantry, one section keeping close up to the armour. Suddenly through the half-light enormous flames roared out and licked fiercely at the hedgerows and forward undergrowth of the woods. Bushes and saplings were wrapped in fire. In that fiery, crackling inferno no man could live. From this awesome threat of being consumed the Germans turned and ran, presenting their backs as targets for the bullets of the Scottish infantry. Some stayed, and were burned. And the position was taken without loss to the attackers. Subsequent interrogation of prisoners left no shred of doubt in the minds of the questioners as to the devastating and utterly demoralizing effect of this flood of liquid from our Crocodile flame-throwers.[57]

Years earlier, whilst Waddell had been studying in France, he went down with peritonitis. The French nuns charged with his care treated this by putting him in a bath full of ice, an experience which came as close to killing him as anything the Germans managed to do. During the campaign in France, he found himself at the same nunnery in which he had been frozen years earlier, and popped in to have a bath for old times' sake. Freddie Scott, meanwhile, was patrolling at St Come:

The relatively small fields were bounded by hedges with a ditch on both sides and I soon realised that the Germans expected our patrols to use these ditches. It was therefore much safer at night to crawl across the middle of the fields where the grass not being eaten by cows etc grew very long. In fact early on I had a nasty experience in a ditch. I was convinced that someone was coming towards me and so fired straight ahead down the ditch. Thinking my fire was being returned I dived through the hedge into the ditch on the other side. In my haste I dropped my Sten gun and so when all went quiet I crawled back to retrieve it. What had happened was that I had shot a cow coming toward me and the rebounding traces of my bullets kidded me that my fire was being returned. At the time I told no one!

Advancing towards the Reich

By September 1944, the Allies had retaken most of France and Belgium; Scott recalled with fondness the welcome of 'hugs, kisses and cider.' Pyman's comment 'off we scampered to Paris, Brussels and Antwerp' provides an inkling as to how quickly – in comparison with many other campaigns – the advance had proceeded, especially once the Falaise Gap was dealt with. At one point, Selwyn Lloyd covered 250 miles in one week, as the Allies swept in days across the lands of northern France and Belgium over which their fathers had fought for five stalemated years. Just before Christmas 1944, great perturbation was caused by the Germans' sudden counter-attack in the Ardennes. On Christmas Eve, Maj A. Lyle Barr of the 91st Anti-tank Regiment, Royal Artillery was commanding his battery on the field of Waterloo (the second and latest British officer so to do). In the general 'flap' a staff officer roared up in a jeep. 'Major Barr, the brigadier wants to be assured that you've sited your guns in the right place.'

'Well, sir,' replied Barr, whose MC citation referred to his 'infectious sense of humour', 'I've placed them exactly where the great Duke did – I didn't think I could improve on that.'

'Harrumph,' said the staff officer, and drove off.[58]

When Maj Barr's son was driving exploring the Ardennes, long after the war, he found a Sherman tank with a small memorial commemorating the achievement of an American unit in gloriously crossing the Meuse in the autumn of 1944. What it didn't say, and he didn't know at the time, was that his father's battery was rushed there on Christmas Day 1944 to prevent the Germans repeating the exploit in a westerly direction.[59]

The British involvement in the Ardennes battles is often forgotten today, but whilst it is generally remembered that this offensive was a last, desperate gamble by the Germans, this does not mean that the Allies had an easy time. Like the Germans in the 1918 Spring Offensives, one problem was that the Allies were advancing faster than their supplies could keep up; indeed, having scampered to Antwerp on 4 September, the British armour ran out of fuel and allowed the German 15th Army – over 100,000 men – to carry out another Dunkirk-style evacuation over the Scheldt into Holland. This led to debates about how best to defeat the Germans – a quick thrust to Berlin, which would have the advantage of beating the Soviet Union to the prize, or a broad, more slowly-moving front. There was also the issue of simply heading east through France or going north and liberating Holland. Pyman wrote that Montgomery would have preferred simply to smash eastwards as quickly as possible; 'militarily, I agreed, and still do,' he wrote in his memoirs, 'he always knew exactly what his soldiers could do.'[60]

However, the political decision was made to send the British Second Army to Hamburg through Holland, and a plan was accordingly devised which involved flying three airborne divisions (35,000 men) to strategic Dutch towns, where they would capture the bridges and allow the tanks which would be following them on land to enter Germany with ease.

Both Pyman and Lloyd were heavily involved in the planning stage; it was Lloyd's greatest responsibility thus far in the war, but he knew Pyman from his Fettes days and this reassured him. The potential for disaster was, however, immense. 'The knowledge that any mistake you make may cost men's lives is burdensome,' mused Lloyd, 'Also, we are fighting some very complicated battles; however, a price must be paid, I suppose, for making military history.'[61]

In his memoirs, written in 1971, Pyman outlined precisely what could go wrong, including the issue of a single road being used for 60 miles, limited off-road access, and the coordination of anti-aircraft weapons, bridging vehicles and gliders within a single communications system.[62]

With so much to go wrong, it is hardly surprising that it did. Operation Market Garden began on Sunday, 17 September, 1944; debate still rages over whether or not it could – given the right support – have ended the war by Christmas of that year. Pyman went to his grave with this belief, insisting in his memoirs that the Germans had picked up intelligence of the airdrop from alcohol-loosened tongues in London – 'public bars can be very dangerous places.' The Germans did indeed get the plans, but only after the British landed. Alistair Horne has argued that the problem with Arnhem was that it was literally 'a bridge too far' – three days' drive from the tanks – and Wesel, further south, would have been a better bet. Whether it was feasible or not, mistakes were made. Lloyd found the whole thing a logistical nightmare, writing to Pyman later that having the transport aircraft operating and controlled from England and the tactical support fighter-bombers run from Belgium was a dangerous problem – he recalled being radioed with requests for an air attack on German ground targets and having to tell him that the skies had to be kept clear for flights from the UK. Additionally, not enough transport aircraft were available to take all of the paratroopers and gliders to Holland in one go – it took three lifts, thus spoiling the element of surprise which is the sole strength of an airborne operation. Only half of the 1st Airborne arrived in Arnhem – or rather eight miles from the town – on the first day of the operation. Capt Eric Mackay, who had left Fettes in 1940, was serving with the 1st Parachute Squadron, Royal Engineers, was so worried about this issue of distance that he briefed his men to double the amount of ammunition they were carrying and also to learn escape and evasion techniques.[63]

In addition to this problem, two German tank divisions were resting, unnoticed by Allied reconnaissance, in the vicinity. As Mackay observed after the war, the joyous reception the Dutch civilians gave the paras when they landed both slowed the advance and alerted the panzers to their presence. His repeated feelings of bad omen were amply justified.

As Mackay had feared, the casualties were appalling. Norman Adams, an OF from Boroughmuir who had left the Royal Artillery to train as a glider pilot and was almost killed in Sicily, was lost along with his troop-carrying Horsa on 18 September. Three days later, Lt 'Jimmy' Hunter was killed. The son of Liberal MP Joseph Hunter, he was Officer Commanding, 13 Platoon (D Company), 7th Battalion The King's Own Scottish Borderers, and fell leading his men at Oosterbeek, where he is buried. 'Fate cannot harm us,' says the inscription on his gravestone, 'for we on honey dew have fed and drunk the milk of paradise.' Mackay reached the first bridge, near Oosterbeek, only to see it blown by the Germans, and then he found that a second had been dismantled; 'typical,' he thought, 'of the whole cocked-up operation.'[64]

After fighting on the march for several hours, he and his men reached the main bridge at Arnhem, a high-arched girder construction which Montgomery had optimistically hoped would be the pivot of the operation. Mackay and his parachute engineers seized a school by the northern ramp of the bridge, from where they supported those trying to take out nearby German pillboxes and then rush the bridge itself. Thanks to the Germans having been alerted, the latter proved impossible. Panzer Grenadiers rushed to the south side of the bridge and prevented any further advance. The following morning, a troop of German armoured cars rushed the north end of the bridge; lacking anti-tank guns, Mackay and the other paras could only hope to pick off drivers with lucky shots or PIATs; 'I just watched helplessly,' he said later. Yet the German counter-attack was slowed, and eventually stopped, leaving the bridge clogged with damaged vehicles. Having acquired the plans for Market Garden, the Luftwaffe hoped to play its part, since it now knew when the British supply planes were supposed to arrive. Fortunately for the RAF, but unluckily for their colleagues in Arnhem, Britain was fog-bound; the reinforcements and ammunition were denied to the troops, but the Messerschmitts were denied their turkey-shoot. The paras in Arnhem were now trapped, but continued to fight. Mackay's men had only two useable rooms in a building which was being steadily shot apart by panzerfausts and fried by flamethrowers. The entire southwest corner of the school had been blown away. So confident had the Germans become that at one point they simply surrounded it and waited. Spotting a group of them simply standing around on the grass outside – presumably confident that they had won because the British had stopped firing – Mackay led his men quietly to the windows and, with the paras' battle-cry 'Whoah, Mohammed' (invented in the Western Desert) they opened fire with Stens, Brens and grenades, wiping out dozens of the enemy. After fighting off three attacks in two hours, they left four times their number in enemy dead. This could not last; by the time the Germans brought up their Tigers, Mackay and his men had been awake for 48 hours, fuelled by Benzedrine and little else. The Tigers punched four-foot holes in the walls from a safe distance before retiring to get more ammunition. Mackay told his superiors that his position was unlikely to last another night. He was told that no help could come. As he later wrote:

We were alone. All the houses on the eastern side had been burned down except for the one to the south which was held by the Germans… The men were exhausted and filthy and I was sick to my stomach every time I looked at them. Haggard, with bloodshot and red-rimmed eyes, almost everyone had some sort of dirty field-dressing and blood was everywhere. On each landing, blood had formed in pools and ran in small rivulets down the stairs.[65]

On 23 September, Lt-Col Charles Mackenzie, who had been a Corps NCO at Fettes and was now General Urquhart's Chief of Staff, conferred with his commander in the shattered Hartenstein Hotel as the Germans fired shell after shell at the beleaguered British troops. Urquhart's 'Red Devils' were now 'merely a collection of individuals hanging on' and Mackenzie was to cross the Rhine in a rubber dinghy to make contact between the Airborne Division and the British Second Division, and appraise them of this fact. Under fire from the Germans, Mackenzie and the chief engineer, Lt-Col Myers, made it across the river and rode a bicycle to the headquarters of the Polish Paratroopers. He impressed upon General Horrocks the need for immediate support for the beleaguered men at Arnhem, but failed to get many men across since the amphibious DUKWs became bogged down and all that remained was a handful of two-man inflatable dinghies. On the way to Nijmegen his armoured car was hit by a shell from a and he was forced to take cover in a turnip field as the Germans searched for him. When they lost interest he made his way towards the surviving British armoured cars, which opened fire on him, fortunately without effect. At General Browning's headquarters, dead tired, frozen stiff, and with chattering teeth, Mackenzie and Myers seemed to their hosts 'putty coloured like men who had come through a Somme winter.' Mackenzie explained at length the dire situation on the other bank of the river and stressed the urgency of action, but as he returned to Urquhart, he was struck by the ambivalence of his reception. On the one hand, there was sympathy for the isolated paras and faint hopes that a support operation might be mounted, but on the other a realisation that a crossing was bound to fail. 'Which was better?' he asked himself, 'Tell him that in my opinion there wasn't a chance in hell of anyone getting over? Or that help was on the way?'[66]

For the purposes of morale, he decided on the latter, but was not surprised when he and his surviving men were evacuated 48 hours later. L-Cpl William Gilchrist, a former sergeant in the Fettes Corps, was one of those who failed to get out; wounded in the fighting, he was taken prisoner. Of the 10,005 men who landed at Arnhem, only 2,163 got out, with the remainder either dead or imprisoned. Every year, on the anniversary of the arrival of the British and Polish paratroopers who tried to liberate their grandparents, Dutch schoolchildren lay flowers on the graves of the dead in Oosterbeek Commonwealth Military Cemetery.

As the British continued to fight their way through Holland, where John Cowie found the Dutch 'always welcoming and kind'[67], and into the Reich, more Fettesians were added to the Roll of Honour. Lt Adrian Kidston of the Royal Artillery had won the belt for best cadet at his OCTU, where he was the only candidate to get an A, was killed instantly in the attack on Flushing on 1 November 1944 when acting as Forward Observation Officer for his battery. Dr Joe Swanson was killed in the Netherlands in February 1945 when his field hospital was hit. One of his comrades from the 1st XV of the thirties wrote an appreciation for the *Fettesian*:

The writer of this notice was visiting recently in a hospital a severely wounded Fettesian, who told him that a gunner, occupying the next bed to him in a hospital in the south, was loud in the praises of the M.O. who had attended him in the front line, saying that his skill, bravery, and devotion to duty were the talk of the whole division. It transpired that this M.O. was none other than Joe Swanson, a contemporary of this wounded Fettesian, and a member of the same house.[68]

Maj Bruce Rae, who had joined the Gordon Highlanders in 1940 to avenge the defeat of that regiment by Rommel in 1940 (when his brother Ian was captured) was the last of twenty rifle company officers in his battalion. He had already been wounded in North Africa when he was shot twice in the chest and once in the jaw whilst leading an attack on a country house near Boxtel, and was lucky to survive. Maj Arthur John Thomson, one of the first Fettesians (apart from POWs) to enter Germany, had always been irritated at being held back from combat postings. He was commanding A Company of the 1st Gordons when he was killed in February 1945 by a sniper in Goch, and is among three thousand British casualties buried at Rheinberg. The crossing of the Rhine was made physically possible by the work of men like E.G. Richards, who had made his way from North Africa to Italy and then to the Western Front; he and his engineers built new bridges to create crossing points where the retreating Germans had blown up the old ones. He remembers it as 'a time notable for cold discomfort, long hours in biting raw cold, handling cold steel, working in icy wet mud.' At Rees, in March, he and his colleagues waited in a sumptuously-appointed caravan, 'the pride and joy of our workshops' which had been created by the skill of the unit's craftsmen and the ingenuity of the officer responsible for scrounging. They were to follow in a meticulously-organised flotilla of bridging vehicles after the artillery had softened the enemy defences and the assault troops had stormed the town. By nightfall the far side of the river had been taken and sappers and pioneers began their work of running ferry services and erecting floating bridges. Rees fell after two days' house-to-house fighting and the British surged forward into Germany. One of those doing the surging was Major Dick Normand, who was with the infantry supporting the 7th Armoured Division. On 17 April, his company was tasked with cutting off the Germans' line of retreat from Soltau, moving through darkened streets infested by enemy snipers and anti-tank teams. He won the MC for keeping the advance moving 'with complete disregard for his own safety', moving from platoon to platoon to direct operations, deploying flamethrowers when the Germans held up progress, and personally leading the assault when it resumed.[69]

Over two hundred enemy soldiers were captured and the operation was a great success; 'Dick even had the time to stop and loot a shop,' wrote his wife Audrey, 'picking out some very nice underwear for himself and stuffing them into the front of his battledress jacket – and then continuing with the battle.'

At about the same time, Selwyn Lloyd, now a Brigadier, accompanied General Dempsey to Belsen. It was an experience which would haunt him for the rest of his life; although there were 10,000 unburied corpses, he did not recall a smell because they were just skin and bone, with nothing to putrify. [70]

Lloyd only referred to Belsen once. 'I saw the conditions there, the huts with the dead, the dying and those just living,' he said in a Parliamentary debate in 1960, 'That was a sight and experience I shall never forget to the end of my life.' Freddie Scott remembers that subsequently 'British troops were kept well clear of it – it being felt that if we saw the state of those imprisoned there by the Germans we might vent our wrath on our own German prisoners and even perhaps the civilians.' Major Lyle Barr was second-in-command to Lt-Col Taylor in taking over the administration of Belsen, in the early stages when the camp was first relieved. Of this, his son says, 'he would never speak, though happy to talk facetiously of other aspects of 'total war', which in some ways he clearly found fulfilling.' Near Hanover, one of John Cowie's men 'contrary to my instructions, went to spend a penny in one of the nearby woods' and came back green-faced and distressed. He had found human hands protruding from the soil; 'we had discovered an execution site of some thirty Jews.' The local mayor shot himself.[71]

Pyman wrote in his memoirs that humanitarian considerations slowed down the pursuit of the enemy, but the British could hardly 'bypass Belsen and like disgraces.' He did not, however, allow the actions of the Nazis to colour his view of the Germans as a whole, or even their ordinary soldiers; 'they were a hard and harsh enemy,' he reflected, 'but not a despicable one.' He was present when General Dempsey took the surrender of Hamburg on 3 May. George Denholm, who was always aware that he had been fortunate to survive, ended the war as a Group Captain and Station Commander of RAF North Weald, and, partly thanks to his Scandinavian business connections, was one of the Allied officers who received the surrender of the German forces in Norway.

For most OF, however, the end of hostilities in Europe were at less exalted levels, and more prosaic. Neil Irvine was stationed in Belgium when, on 8 May, a local civilian burst into his quarters with a crate of beer.

'Bonjour, M'sieur,' he shouted, as he reached for a bottle, opened it and poured the contents into a large glass as he babbled away, 'Monsieur, c'est un grand jour. La guerre est fini et les Boches caput!'

Irvine's friends were not at home, so he was alone with the garrulous Walloon as he consumed several bottles of Stella Artois on an empty stomach. He tottered unsteadily to lunch and then fell asleep in the grass outside the tent, only to be woken up for tea by his mates who held a celebratory sing-song with the rest of the beer.[72]

Freddie Scott was among those front-line troops who celebrated with the Soviets:

At a place called Bad Kleinew, a spa and railway junction at the northern end of the Schwerin Sea (a large inland lake) we met our Russian allies arriving the other way and from whom many of our prisoners had been running away, fearing most of all how they might be treated by the Russians.

I took one small party to make contact with the Russians. Communication was very difficult as neither of us spoke the other language and any Germans that we had picked up was of little value – 'Hander Hoch' 'Hands up' and 'Bliebenze in Keller' – 'Stay in the cellar' were not a lot of use – my German spelling is probably wrong too! However, we got along pretty well with sign language. The Russians suggested we shared a drink to which we naturally agreed. A Russian girl soldier of whom there seemed to be quite a few produced some vodka and when she was asked to get some food (blotting paper!) she conjured up eggs, squares of white pork fat, and black bread. We toasted Stalin, Churchill, Roosevelt, Montgomery, Rokossovsky (their commander) and so on. This in neat slugs of vodka. The Russians cracked the raw eggs straight into their mouths following up with the cubes of pork fat and a hunk of bread. Neither I nor my colleagues could compete and we soon withdrew drunk and very fragile.

On VE night, the 8th May, both sides made a fine display we firing Very (signal) lights etc and the Russians using live mortar shells etc. Also in the railway yard there were a number of tanker wagons containing aviation fuel which the Russians found a good alternative to vodka.[73]

Selwyn Lloyd was to have one more eerie experience in the aftermath of the ceasefire when he had to identify the master of the concentration camps, Heinrich Himmler, who had fallen into British hands. Harold Pyman had an understanding with General Dempsey that he would not disturb him after supper, but felt that the Nazi warlord's capture was of sufficient import to risk the commander's disapproval. The General received the news with little apparent interest. 'Good,' he said, 'Good night.' Shortly afterwards, the news came through that Himmler had committed suicide – whilst undergoing a medical examination he took a cyanide pill – and Pyman had to telephone Headquarters again. 'What is the matter with you tonight, Chief of Staff?' barked Dempsey. Pyman told him that Himmler was dead. 'Good. Good night,' Dempsey said again, and put down the phone.[74]

Once awake the following day, Dempsey sent Lloyd to investigate. The gramophone in the mess was playing 'My Blue Heaven', which was promptly renamed 'My Blue Himmler.' Lloyd found the late and thoroughly unlamented S.S. leader lying on the bare floor of a requisitioned villa.

'Is that Himmler?' he asked. A corporal put his big army boot under the head and lifted it up. Rigor mortis had not yet set in and all the double chins fell into place, so Selwyn realised it was in fact him. Then the corporal took his boot away and the head fell back with a dull thud on the floor, a sound that Selwyn said stayed with him for the rest of his life. There goes a man, he later recalled, who was responsible for the deaths of millions and millions of people.[75]

War in the East

The war in the Far East was of a different order to that in Europe and North Africa, fought against an even more fanatical enemy and receiving much less coverage in the domestic press. Like Fawcett in Mesopotamia in the Great War, James Finlayson and his comrades shared 'the general feeling that the 14th Army was rather ignored at home.' Statistically, Fettesians were relatively speaking less likely to serve against the Japanese, though a respectable number did and more would have joined them had not the nuclear attacks on Hiroshima and Nagasaki shortened the war. A.N.A. Waddell was a District Officer of the Colonial Office in the Solomon Islands, and managed to evacuate 'his' civilians with some difficulty. Finding himself a District Officer without a district, he reinvented himself as Private Waddell, and spent fifteen hazardous months behind enemy lines radioing details of Japanese movements to Allied HQ, for which he was decorated (in another classic example of modesty, he played down both the duration and difficulty of his activities in his letter to the *Fettesian*, and did not mention his medals at all). Although hauled out of the Army, he managed to get himself into the Australian Navy Reserve, in which capacity he witnessed the Battle of Guadalcanal from an American destroyer:

So far the Japs have had a frightful hiding. They were taken completely by surprise when the attack was launched at dawn on August 7 in the two Tulagi-Guadalcanal area. The staff work of the Americans was perfect, and the Japs were being pounded by waves of dive-bombers and naval guns before they knew we were anywhere near. They fought desperately on land, using snipers and concealed machine-gun nests but the American marines and the commandos of the U.S. forces wiped them out. The Japs then tried an aerial blitz, but only scored one hit; their bombers were simply blown out of the sky, and out of 27 in the attack none got home. They attacked by sea on the night of August 8 and 9, a wet, depressing night, but they were again routed. It's not so bad being bombed by day, but one feels very puny on a destroyer on a wet night in the middle of a cruiser battle, and I wasn't at all sorry when the Japs were driven off. So far all their counter-attacks have failed, and the first and second rounds have gone to us. I'm sorry I can't give a detailed account for censorship reasons – but it was a wonderful show, and the Americans are grand fighters, by sea, land and air.[76]

After the war he served for five years as a Principal Assistant Secretary in North Borneo before being sent to the Gambia as Colonial Secretary, then to Sierra Leone, of which he became ultimately Deputy Governor; he was subsequently knighted. From 1960 to 1963 he was the last Governor of Sarawak.[77]

Some other Fettesians in Asia also witnessed the triumphs of American technology witnessed by Waddell. Ronnie Guild, later of the staff common room, was impressed by the 'Flying Tigers', flying over the Himalayas in support of the Chinese, but wryly noted the shocking effect on more straight-laced members of the Raj of these 'guys who did not even wear their caps straight, lolling around with dames and with sergeants ordering booze that needed a British Brigadier's pay.'[78]

'Sandy' Hodge saw a different side to these boisterous capitalists; he was on the bridge with Admiral Spruance at the great clash of the US and Japanese navies at Okinawa, and was impressed by the American's dedication:

To see him on the bridge of his flagship apparently unconcerned, one would not have realised the stress to which he was exposed nor that he'd lost his [original] flagship, two carriers and many other ships all put out of action by crashing Kamikazes. But, shortly after hostilities ended, when I was standing talking to him in the wardroom of KG5 in Tokyo Bay – and I have never forgotten this – it took him both hands to get his coffee cup to his mouth. He was completely drained; to achieve success he had given all he'd got, a case of total involvement.[79]

Others were hard at work in the jungles of Burma, where a protracted but ultimately successful British campaign was conducted in conditions which made the trenches of the Great War seem positively luxurious. James Finlayson described his route to the Far East:

In 1944 we were issued with pith helmets and tropical kit and left Greenock by P. and O. troopship for India. The six week voyage was uneventful apart from a U-boat scare in the Bay of Biscay and we spent part of each day being taught Urdu (as things turned out, Hausa would have been more relevant). On arrival at Bombay our pith helmets were replaced by bush hats and we found ourselves assigned to 81 West African Division which had just completed its second campaign along the Kaladan River in the Arakan in North Burma. After a few weeks I developed amoebic dysentery and spent time in hospital in Dacca before rejoining my unit which had moved to a camp some 150 miles West of Madras, there to prepare for a seaborne invasion of Malaya. This included 'waterproofing' vehicles so that they could be driven through 3-4 feet deep water during landing. I remember testing a jeep so modified, driving it with only my head above the surface.[80]

Casualties were high in the war against the Japanese, but disease was less of a threat to these soldiers as it had been to their Victorian grandfathers; so far as we know, only one Fettesian, Sandy Park, succumbed to illness, whilst in Bombay. Sergeant-Major Robert Gordon Downie never made it to Burma – his East African Artillery battalion was on aboard a ship torpedoed en route to Ceylon. Most of the rest were killed in combat; John Miller is buried at Imphal, as is Maj 'Geordie' Nimmo, one of four brothers of whom only the eldest survived. Capt Alastair McKellar died the same year and is buried at Taukkyan. At the Battle of Kohima, OF Colin Hunter's 'D' Company of the 1st Bn. Cameron Highlanders famously wore tennis shoes for a successful night attack on the Japanese. A small hill which they captured on the north side of the village became known as Hunter's Hill. The Headmaster's son proved a chip off the old block, and was decorated after an ambush:

Captain Ashcroft was in command of a reconnaissance patrol and succeeded, owing to his inspiring leadership and determination, in locating the enemy and forcing them to disclose their positions. At the same time, he ambushed an enemy platoon, a Japanese officer and ten Japanese being killed and several others wounded in the action. His coolness and presence of mind, says the citation, was an inspiration to all ranks under his command. He himself was under was often under heavy enemy fire, of which he was completely regardless.[81]

A Fettesian pilot in Asia, David Dick, flying first of all reconnaissance Mosquitos and later P-47 Thunderbolts in close air support, survived the war only to come within a whisker of being killed whilst testing a Gloster Javelin in 1955.[82]

The majority of Fettesians in Asia, however, did not actually see combat against the Japanese. Many of those who contacted the school could comment, like James Finlayson, that their many preparations 'proved unnecessary with the dropping of the atom bombs.' Sir Robert Saunders was called up in 1943 and was sent to the Highland Fieldcraft Training Centre at Poolewe in Wester Ross under Lord Rowallan, who later became Chief Scout. He later recalled the CO's welcoming words:

I hear people saying they are here because they failed a WOSB. This is completely wrong. You are all young and short of experience and your various WOSBs have felt you would benefit from further training before going forward to OCTU... The Directing Staff's instructions are that if you are going to make a mistake and fall into shallow water and learn a lesson, they will let you do so. But if you are going to fall 200 feet onto shallow rock with no possibility of learning a lesson then they will restrain you.[83]

The training included 'a marvellous 3-day scheme on Skye' and climbing 3,200 feet up Slioch; ideal preparation had the British Army been called upon (as it expected might be possible) to liberate Norway, but Saunders was eventually posted to Bangalore, where he found unexpected luxuries in the form of local bearers to bring tea and rounding hills on exercise to find tables laid for lunch – not privileges encountered at the OCTUs at Dunbar or Barnard Castle. John Cowie was another who was trained in Scotland for Japan, following General Laycock's announcement that 'I am in charge of the invasion of Japan which is going to be horrible; I need officers blooded in battle but not sick of it.' Despite several weeks at Auchnacarry, he did not invade Japan.[84]

Ronnie Guild, comfortable but rather bored ('being as a result of my youthful pledges a total abstainer and all that') at Secunderabad, where he blotted his copy-book by suggesting to the Divisional Commander that he cut down on the use of his personal staff car in the name of fuel economy, took part in a practice landing from the Polish ship *Piłsudski* at Ratnagiri. Unfortunately, his landing craft became stuck half-way down the side of its mother ship, just below the galley outflows at precisely the moment the cook decided to pull the plug on the swill tub. His most searing experience, 'which remains as vivid as though it were yesterday,' was when he was sent to Calcutta to take part in the relief of the Bengal famine:

There is a ritual about the approach to any big Indian railway station. Several miles outside the train will stop at a junction of tracks and here the beggars will gather. (They probably live there). An unending wailing, moaning and weeping draw all but the most hardened traveller to the open carriage window. There are the lepers with their seeping fly-covered sores, the emaciated babies hanging at their emaciated mothers' breasts, the blind old men and the terrible cripples. Some travellers close the windows, some throw coins before the train crawls forward through the depressing shanty outskirts. At Calcutta this meant Howrah Station, Howrah Bridge and the Hooghly River, horrible follow-ups with their heat and stickiness and smell... the orders were brevity itself: 'The problem is famine, aggravated by Calcutta merchants hoarding. There is your area. There are your sepoys, your traucks and your grain. Now get cracking.' I had about a platoon to help distribute grain across an area half as large as East Lothian.[85]

Stationed in one of the government's network of Dak bungalows 'which had to serve as an island of vigour and good order in a sea of starving depression and hopelessness', Guild and his troops conducted a daily round of food deliveries to their villages. Along with the grain, Dr Cameron, the battalion medic, administered cholera jabs and malaria tablets, and the Muslim sepoys helped Hindu youngsters build a sports pits. For all its faults, Guild notes, 'the Raj could do this'. After leave in the Himalayas, he was posted to the traditional destination of so many of Victoria's men, the Afghan frontier, for training on the Vickers machine-gun, and finally to Burma, where his enthusiastic gunners opened fire on strange lights in the darkness only to discover that they were traditional frog hunters and had killed an innocent villager. Guild was about to set forth to clear the hills of Japanese with a new unit of Shan tribesmen, previously well-armed and handsomely paid by the Americans, now rather less so by the British. 'For a while, I must confess, the whole thing scared me silly,' he writes, 'Then, suddenly, came the big bombs and the Japanese surrender.'[86]

It was over.

Mr. MacDonald, writing from the Fettes perspective, summed up the wartime experience thus:

The six years of war are a period of her history in which Fettes may take a pride that is congruous with the much greater pride she will always take in those of her sons who fought in this war, and especially in those who fell.[87]

E.G. Richards, the sapper officer, had more personal thoughts. The summer of 1945, for him, meant the completion of a semi-permanent bridge over the Rhine, and a reflection on the work of his unglamorous but vital regiment:

As the tape was ceremonially cut by a sapper I thought of lying on the sands of Gazala, of Dougie bleeding to death at Alamein, his back torn open by a bomb, of Sapper Hudson lying white and cold on a Bren carrier at Munassib, of Surtees and Dodds who lifted one mine too many, of many others killed and maimed. And I looked around to see how many faces I would recognise as having sailed from England in 1941.

The few that were left had survived not a war of rifle and bayonet, not the heat of the infantry charge, but the war of the sapper, carrying out his peculiar and skilled task, often in heavy fire, of removing delicate mine mechanisms, levelling a bridge site with spirit level, bulldozing craters in a road, erecting an observation tower, manning a canvas boat filled with infantry, welding the intricate steelwork of a half-destroyed bridge, removing booby traps; work not requiring the sudden upsurge of spectacular bravery but the gritty courage to carry out the slow skills of the craftsman in the discomfort and danger of the front line of war.[88]

Richards' fellow-sapper Kenneth McCallum was studying Judges VII – Gideon's selection of warriors on the basis of their drinking with an alert posture – in a Bible class many years after the war. Asked 'as an army man' why this was important, he found himself explaining the need for vigilance in warfare, and then recounting some of his experiences. Afterwards, his wife Diana commented that this was the first time in forty years that he had ever said anything about his time in the army. He realised that he had indeed 'unknowingly kept silent on what I had been through.' He took Diana to Italy, visiting the castle at Valenzano and the village of Coccanile where his brother was killed, and forming friendships with the residents of both. He reflected in his retirement:

As one who survived the war, I still feel a deep sense of humility to those who gave their lives including Diana's only brother, Peter, a year younger than myself, a Beaufighter pilot of Coastal Command in the RAF. We were not a generation of ideologists; we lived in momentous times and it fell upon us to perform our duty as we saw fit. It was a long, hard war, but I do not regret the experience. We learnt the true value of companionship, the true appreciation of the qualities of others, which is perhaps what I value most from my experiences. Diana says that I should never have left the army. I think she's right.[89]

NOTES

[1] Revd. Colin Sinclair, funeral address for Ronnie Williamson, quoted in *OFNL*, July 2002

[2] Gordon Reay Roberts Obituary, *OFNL*, January 2006

[3] Richards

[4] Obituary, *OFNL*, July 2005

[5] *Fettesian*, December 1943

[6] Guest, p. 159

[7] *Fettesian*, December 1943

[8] Quoted in Hope, p. 144

[9] Guest, p. 218

[10] Quoted in McCallum

[11] Ibid.

[12] Quoted in ibid.

[13] MC citation, quoted in *Fettesian*, March 1945

[14] Letter to the author

[15] Ian Findlay, Autobiographical Notes (Henderson Archive)

[16] McCallum

[17] Maj. J.B.A. Smyth, letter to the author, October 2008

[18] *Fettesian*, July 1965

[19] Ibid., February 1942

[20] Max Hastings, *Bomber Command: The Myth and Reality of the Strategic Bombing Offensive* (New York, Dial Press, 1979), p. 139

[21] See Williamson Murray, 'Did Strategic Bombing Work?' in Robert Cowley (ed.) *No End Save Victory*, (New York, Putnam, 2001)

[22] *Fettesian*, July 1941

[23] Ibid., February 1943

[24] MacDonald in MacDonald, p. 231

[25] *Fettesian*, March 1944

[26] Obituary, *OFNL*, June 2004

[27] *Fettesian*, July 1956

[28] Ibid., April 1940

[29] J. Younie, letter to the author, 20 September 2008

[30] *Fettesian*, 1983

[31] Ibid., December 1943

[32] Obituary, *OFNL*, January 2004

[33] *Fettesian*, December 1944

[34] Pyman, p. 65

[35] Ibid., p. 68

[36] Quoted in Thorpe, p. 81

[37] See Fisher, pp. 50-1

[38] See M. Young & R. Stamp, *Trojan Horses* (London, Bodley Head, 1989) p. 234

[39] N.C. Irvine, letter to the author, 8 November 2008

[40] Bill Balfour, 2002 taped reminiscences for EG Richards, Henderson Archive

[41] In conversation with the author, 14 November 2010

[42] I.H.K. Rae M.C., contribution to Henderson Archive

[43] Quoted in Thorpe, p. 83

[44] Quoted in Fisher, p. 52

[45] Ibid.

[46] Scott

[47] Irvine

[48] Scott

[49] *Fettesian*, Dec. 1944

[50] Ibid.

[51] Ibid., March 1945

[52] Ibid., July 1945

[53] Irvine

[54] Ibid.

[55] Ibid.

[56] *Fettesian*, December 1944

[57] *The War Illustrated*, 29 September 1944

[58] Email to the author, 13 August 2010

[59] Email to the author, 13 August 2010

[60] Pyman, p. 75

[61] Quoted in Throrpe, p. 88

[62] Pyman, p. 75

[63] Cornelius Ryan, *A Bridge Too Far* (London, Hamish Hamilton, 1974) p. 160

[64] Quoted in ibid., p. 250

[65] Quoted in ibid., p. 394

[66] Quoted in ibid., p. 483

[67] John Cowie, Recollections (Henderson Archive)

[68] *Fettesian*, July 1945

[69] Normand Family History, p. 180

[70] Thorpe, p. 92

[71] Cowie

[72] Irvine

[73] Scott

[74] Pyman, p. 82

[75] Thorpe, p. 93

[76] *Fettesian*, February 1943

[77] Obituary, *OFNL*, February 2000

[78] Ronnie Guild, *Own Tales* (Edinburgh, 2008), p. 51

[79] *Fettesian*, November 1981

[80] Letter to the author, August 2008

[81] *Fettesian*, July 1945

[82] Obituary, *Daily Telegraph*, 14 August 1999

[83] Sir Robert Saunders, letter to the author, October 2008

[84] Cowie

[85] Guild, pp. 46-7

[86] Ibid., p. 74

[87] MacDonald in MacDonald, p. 233

[88] Richards

[89] McCallum

Chapter Thirteen

'The best of a bad job'

Fettesians as Prisoners of War

Treatment

> *In the recent unpleasantness Hitler effected*
> *O.Fs have done what of O.Fs was expected.*
> *You will hardly expect us to name them all here;*
> *But for Prisoners of War we've a special warm cheer.*

So ran the 'Vive-la' for 1945. The masters and boys, amongst their other wartime duties, did their best to keep in touch with captured brethren, with varying success for this was not always easy; they couldn't have been named in the song for there were over sixty of them. The Second World War saw huge numbers of British prisoners taken in all theatres, almost 150,000 by the Germans and Italians and 50,000 by the Japanese, kept in widely diverging degrees of confinement and hardship. Their story, says Charles Rollings, author of a recent history of the POW experience, has become a kind of 'postwar cultural icon, a symbol of the will to survive against the odds and of defiance against tyranny and arbitrary rules.'[1]

There was, however, no one prisoner of war experience; many did not survive, and those who did were subjected to comparative leniency by some guards and genocidal cruelty by others. Fettesians seem to have seen virtually everything the war had to offer except a Soviet Gulag. Luckiest, in one sense, were those held by the Germans in Europe, where there was at least some sort of infrastructure through which communications could be sent and, as one OF recalled, 'a comparatively acceptable standard of living'. Technically, under the Geneva Conventions, prisoners were to be treated humanely, not engaged in war work, fed as well as depot troops of the army which captured them and allowed free association to worship and entertain themselves. They were even supposed to be paid for labour performed in captivity – as the Axis POWs the

Fettes boys encountered harvesting in Fife were – and the money thus earned could be used to buy luxuries. The British, French, and Americans were generally fairly well-treated by the Italians and Germans, but a decent quality of POW life was not guaranteed. OF John McGlashan, who spent nearly four years in the hands of the Nazis, comments:

Thanks to the Geneva Convention we were treated correctly most of the time by the regular German forces (but not by the Gestapo, the S.S. and the Hitler Youth). That this was not due to any fancy idea of German military honour is shown by the fact that, since the U.S.S.R. had not signed the Convention, the Germans treated Russian P.O.W.s, and the Russians treated German P.O.W.s, as sub-human.[2]

Indeed, to be a Soviet POW in the hands of the Germans was to be subjected to such brutality for racial and political reasons that there was less than a fifty-fifty chance of surviving the experience – 3.3 million of the 5.7 million prisoners taken by the Axis powers on the Ostfront perished. Stalin's German captives counted themselves lucky if they were able to return home in the 1950s. British captives were often held in camps with Russian compounds and could see at first hand just how differently even the respectable Wehrmacht 'Landser' (who after the war blamed the SS for each and every atrocity) treated communist prisoners. Hitler regarded special forces, partisans and other irregular fighters as terrorists, whether or not they were communists; captured in Salonika, commando Jock Hamilton was 'beaten and maltreated' to the point where he feared execution, despite having been wounded.[3]

The Italians were chaotic, moving prisoners haphazardly around as their front lines retreated and, like the Germans, sometimes putting them in the hands of brutally enthusiastic fascists. Conditions in Italian POW camps varied from the indulgently lax to the squalid and terrifying. POWs in Europe, McGlashan notes, were at the mercy of three overriding and variable determinants: the Geneva Convention (which fanatical guards might ignore), the availability of Red Cross food parcels, and the progress of the war. He comments that 'it was noticeable that after Stalingrad the Germans were not quite so sure as before that they were going to win and their attitude to POWs subtly changed for the better.'

The most dreadful experiences, of course, were at the hands of the Japanese, whose attitude towards any captives was not dissimilar to that of the Germans towards the Russians. The Japanese saw their prisoners both as racial inferiors and as cowards for having allowed themselves to be captured in the first place. It has even been argued that had General Percival known what awaited his men at the hands of the Armies of Nippon, he would not have surrendered Singapore with such unseemly haste. Used as forced labour in the jungles of the Far East, Allied prisoners had little or no contact with their families for years, and a third failed to return home.

Prisoners before 1939

There had been Fettesian prisoners before, of course. Pat Normand and Sydney Bowden, captured in the Jameson raid against the Boers in Victoria's reign, were probably the first. They were held at Doornkop on the Natal/Transvaal border and given the choice of being deported or paying a fine which they could not afford; eventually, they were sent back to Britain on the *Harlech Castle* but returned to fight in the subsequent war. In a fine display of irony, Normand later became Governor of the Fort Prison in Johannesburg, originally built by Kruger to defend the city against the likes of him. In 1906 he was the unwitting host of Mahatma Gandhi, jailed for protesting against registration cards for Indians. (Pat's son, R.J. 'Dick' Normand, was born in the prison in 1912 – 'because my mother happened to be there at the time.') Bowden was later a Sub-Inspector of the Cape Police. In the First World War, Captain Oliver Moodie was captured on 25 September 1915, and, after a year's hospital treatment, held at Friedberg in Hessen, from where he wrote to the school magazine in December 1916:

This camp is not nearly so large as the last one I was at (Guetersloh). There are two buildings – one for Russian and French officers, the other for French and English – along two sides of an oblong, with a gymnasium at the other end, opposite the English house. There is a sort of football ground in the centre, along of the side of which there is the cook house, and on the open side there are small gardens, kept by the prisoners, but of course they are very depressed-looking at this time of year. Interspersed with the gardens there are various aviaries, and a rabbit-hutches, with all sorts of animals and birds, sparrows, blackbirds, pigeons, guinea pigs, squirrels etc.

There are six officers in this room besides myself – all of us came from Constance having been rejected by the Swiss commissioners. It is quite a decent-sized room, in which we have installed a large range, on which we do all our cooking, taking it in terms to be the cook, and as we do all our own meals the cook is quite busy. There is also a captain Usher here, who was at Merchiston at the same time that I was at Fettes, and from whom I am learning the pipes. There is also a fellow Brown, who was at Fettes with me.[4]

Moodie was fortunate both to receive decent treatment – James's verdict is that 'at their rare best, German prisoner of war camps were spartan'[5] – and to outlive the war. So too did eleven others in enemy hands, including Lt Charles Cooke-Taylor, captured by the Bulgarians whilst serving with the Red Cross in Serbia, Capt J.D. Currie and 'Caesar' the College porter. Sub-Lt Archibald Williamson was interned in Holland at the start of the war and found the process of repatriation in 1918 painfully slow; he later commented that being 'first in, last out' might be good for a cricketer, but wasn't much fun in wartime. Others did not survive captivity, often because they were captured just after being severely wounded; Capt Donald MacGregor died in hospital at Hanover in 1915, whilst 2/Lt. James Couper, badly wounded when taken prisoner in the German Spring Offensive of 1918, died shortly afterwards. Another OF, Sergeant George Russell Drysdale, died in Turkish hands in 1917; death from disease was very common in the Middle East. Drysdale is buried in the Baghdad CWGC cemetery. Lt-Col William Farmar, also captured by the Turks, did survive, possibly because his higher rank and age (he was 46 when he was captured at Kut in 1916) gave him better treatment. Great War Old Fettesians were to be found on the other side of the wire as well. Lovell Newton acted as an interpreter, and the great athlete K.G. Macleod was OC of the German camp on the island of Raasay in the Hebrides. Here the mining company William Baird illegally used German prisoners to dig for iron-ore, in contravention of the Geneva Conventions (Macleod was presumably overridden by the Ministry of Munitions, as it is hard to imagine that he was happy about the arrangement). A protest over wage differentials by imported Scots mainland workers led to the additional issue of the Germans being used as strike-breakers, bringing the sorry tale to light and eliciting embarrassed denials by the government. Although themselves on such limited rations as could be brought by sea, many of the devoutly Free Presbyterian locals felt so sorry for the prisoners that they smuggled food into the camp using the same trouser-bag technique immortalized by British POW films such as *The Great Escape*. They also put up a memorial to Kagerer and Sosinka, two prisoners killed in mining accidents.[6]

In the Second World War, Alec Purves, a Victorian OF and rugby international serving with the London Scottish, also served as a camp officer, supervising Germans and Italians in the Highlands.[7]

Most Fettesians in POW camps, however, were on the wrong side of the wire.

Capture

During the Second World War, the school gained information about Old Fettesians taken prisoner in a slow trickle; first a man would be reported missing and possibly wounded, and only later would clear information come through; all this was, of course, filtered through families and friends first. By the winter of 1940, the front lines in Europe had largely stabilized, though hardly in Britain's favour, and clearer information could come through. So many OFs had been rounded up in the BEF's defeat that on 9 November 1940, a Fettesian-Lorettonian 'Dinner' (the correspondent's inverted commas) was held at Oflag VII C/H. J.A. Tweedie contacted the school to say that he had been joined at this (one hopes morale-boosting) event by C.N. Cairns, J.R. Cameron, D. Cunningham, W.F. Dundas, G.L. F. Finlay, C.D.M. Hutchins, J. Inglis, H.C.R. Laslett, J.D. Mackenzie, N. MacKinnon, J. Macleod, J.M. Moir, D.P.B. Prosser, S.D. Rae and G.F. Raeburn – over a dozen men in one camp. Douglas Rae, Signals Officer to the 1st Battalion of the Gordon Highlanders, had been marched from France, where he was captured, through Belgium to the Rhine:

We carried a few of our possessions – I carried some books – but later we became exhausted and let them drop. The German guards with rifles wouldn't let us pick them up, though afterwards they send a truck and gathered them up and returned them to us. In the French and Belgian towns people in the streets watched us pass in silence, and some brought us hot soup and poured it into our tin mugs. When we reached the Rhine we were put on boats which took us into Germany down to near a town called Laufen, near Nuremberg, where we were locked up in an ancient castle.

In such circumstances, Rae remembers, 'the German guards were strict, but if you didn't step out of line they weren't too bad – though you had to be careful.' One of his colleagues, an artist, put his head out of a window whilst painting, and was shot and killed by a suspicious guard below. Another of the reunion diners, Raeburn, later got into trouble with the Gestapo, who insisted on his being shackled – seen by prisoners as the most irksome punishment, and one apparently carried out with reluctance by the camp commandant and guards, who were 'humane and considerate about it… they hated it as much as the prisoners and wished it would stop.' Once restored to favour, he was able to perform in a production of 'The Tempest' and go bird-watching.[8]

His endeavours in the study of birds and butterflies were of sufficient scientific worth to merit repeated mentions in *The Field*, and for one of his fellow-prisoners to remark that 'to a non-entomologist he would seem to live in a fantastic world where painted ladies flutter round with red admirals.' The compiler of the Fettes Diary for July 1942 notes that Hutchins and Mackinnon are still together at Oflag IX /H, 'all fit but very bored, and very appreciative of letters' – though the problem remains 'that what satisfies the censors will not interest one's correspondent.'[9]

Hutchins clearly got a number of letters as a result and wrote back to express his appreciation. By March 1943, with the theatres of war now spread far beyond the remit of the BEF, the *Fettesian* was printing names and addresses of additional prisoners; six held by the Italians, three by the Japanese and seven by the Germans. Reunions were now being held in Italy, with P.W. Allsebrook writing to say that seven of them are in the same camp and greatly appreciate news from the school.[10]

As with the dinner in Germany in 1940, it was possible to have representatives of each house at Fettes imprisoned in the same place, as at Chieti in 1942 where there were enough Scots, apparently, to set up a Masonic Lodge. From elsewhere in Italy, Tommy Macpherson wrote to his father to reassure him that all was well, despite his being transferred to Camp No 5, which was situated on top of a thousand-foot-high rock, the better to supervise troublemakers who had previously attempted to escape. Macpherson apparently kept himself busy as the camp translator, explaining Italian news to the others, though the rugby balls sent by the Red Cross, whilst they 'felt very nice when we chucked them about in the mess-room' were of little use owing to the Italians' refusal to provide exercise space. He was touched by his Fettes Christmas card:

…at the foot were all the familiar signatures of the masters whom I knew, with those of the four heads of houses and the captain of football. All four heads of houses were in my charge in the Colts rugger and hockey long ago. Eheu fugaces…[11]

Camp 5 might fairly be described as 'Mussolini's Colditz' – the prisoners were housed in a mountaintop castle which was believed to be escape-proof. The one man who managed to get away in Macpherson's time was picked up near the Swiss border.[12]

At the same time, his brother Archie was writing home cheerfully of 10,000 German and Italian prisoners a day being driven past his post in Tunisia. Their father was delighted since Archie could post almonds and nuts home, a welcome addition to the wartime rations in Britain. After one battle against the Italians, Lt-Col Charles Gray met a prisoner of great significance to the average Fettes pupil:

I met one English-speaking N.C.O. who said he had had an ice-cream and cake-shop in Comely Bank for eighteen years, and when on a visit to his father in Italy had been press-ganged into the Army. When I told him I had been at Fettes he nearly fell on my neck! [13]

The successor to this POW's enterprise, Franco's Italian pizzeria and chip shop, remains a firm favourite with Fettesians to this day, much to the disapproval of health-conscious elements of the academic staff. The choleric Scottish nationalist George Campbell Hay found his linguistic skills put to use supervising Italian prisoners, but did not wholly enjoy his encounter with the vanquished foe, who he found had 'the servile characteristics of crawling to their superiors and bullying those to whom they calculate it is safe to do so'; he had to 'pull them up quite frequently for buggering Arabs about.'[14]

In addition to British soldiers scooped up in North Africa and Malaya, there were increasing numbers of airmen being captured on bombing sorties over Germany or Italy; John McGlashan, aged only 19 and on his tenth operation as skipper of a Wellington, was returning from a raid on Berlin when he was shot down over Düsseldorf on 7 November 1941. In total, around 11,000 Bomber Command aircrew ended up as POWs, though he is the only OF pilot listed as such in the 1948 record – which is, presumably, why unlike the army officers in Italy he never met any classmates. Another large group of prisoners, including OF L/Cpl William Gilchrist, was captured after the failure of the airborne assault on Arnhem in 1944. The 1943 Christmas card was received by at least 19 OFs in Germany, a welcome reminder of home and loyalty. In addition to cards from masters and boys, the prisoners received parcels of cigarettes from the Old Fettesian Association. Douglas Rae remembers that parcels from home were very welcome, especially clothing for men were captured in the kit they stood up in and naturally needed replacements. The most useful parcels, however, contained pieces of a radio, which was gradually assembled and hidden by one of Rae's fellow-prisoners inside a football. This enabled the POWs to follow the course of the war. Not everyone was so lucky; John McGlashan received nothing from the school, despite the fact that his fellow joint head of house in Carrington, David Grant, was in his squadron. Grant telephoned 'Jerry' Lodge to let him know that McGlashan had been posted as missing, and whilst the Housemaster wrote to McGlashan's father to commiserate, the prisoner himself heard nothing from the school during his long incarceration. Despite receiving no letters from Fettes, McGlashan remembers that 'the vast majority of POWs maintained their morale and tried to make the best of a bad job.'[15]

Given the length of their captivity – and prisoners could have no idea whatsoever when it might end – many tried to put their enforced absence from regular employment to good use developing new skills or trying to entertain one another. The presence of people from all over the world in the Allied forces meant that there was a great pool of talent in many of the camps. Douglas Rae recalls that the Highland Division prisoners did a lot of Scottish dancing, and learned its Maori equivalent from captured New Zealanders. Prisoners were also able, at least if held in the more tolerant German camps, to study for some British examinations. I. Weston-Smith was one OF who took his Bar exam in Roman Law this way; having been captured in Italy whilst serving with the Scots Guards, he decided to put his vast amounts of free time in Oflag VII B/7 to good use.[16]

Likewise, Douglas Rae was allowed to study for his banking exams, the papers being sent from London, and he passed with honours. Formal education like this could be made difficult by the Germans' habit of moving prisoners around. John McGlashhan spent time at Stalag VIIIb (Lamsdorf), Stalag Luft III (Sagan), Stalag Luft VI (Heydekrug) and Stalag 357 (Fallingbostel); nonetheless, 'in that time I taught Latin and Greek, learnt Spanish and Portuguese, organised rugger and basketball games (when we were fit enough to do so) and became a pretty good bridge player.'[17]

For all the comforts that might be provided, however, for all the ornithology and exam-cramming, being a 'Kriegie' was not an experience to be relished by healthy young men. Naturally, if they were depressed, they did not write to their families or their school to say so; they would neither be allowed to nor wish to, for this would only hurt the loyal hearts at home. When the 2nd South African Division's staff was captured with the fall of Tobruk in 1942, R.G. McKerron, an OF Law Professor at Witwatersrand who was serving in a legal capacity, was taken prisoner. A message home pluckily declared that he was 'disappointed, but not down-hearted.'[18]

A colleague of Major Ian Graham, a professional soldier from an old army family (his father had run the Indian Army Medical Service) observed that captivity was actually worse for the career warrior than for the civilian called to the colours: 'In Britain's hour of need their skills and experiences were being wasted. Others, they knew, would be making their names in the various theatres of war around the world.'[19]

A poem in the *Fettesian* in 1941 was entitled 'From a Prison Camp in Germany', but we have no idea if this was accurate. Would it have got past a censor? It pours forth classical imagery so enthusiastically that the female civilians employed by German POW camps might have suspected it of being some sort of coded message. It has something of the style of Dr Ashcroft or Mr. Pyatt, but one never knows:

> *Full half these weary hours of prison life*
> *Have passed enveloped in a mist of dreams;*
> *My mind, so deeply wounded in the strife,*
> *Has found repose in Lethe's healing streams,*
> *Though first, embittered with my hapless fate,*
> *I cared not whether life itself was mine.*
> *I swiftly overcame that shameful state,*
> *And dreaming, stored up all that was yet fine;*
> *As once Odysseus, on Calypso's Isle,*
> *Yearned seven long years to see his native land;*
> *So, gazing on the mountain tops awhile,*
> *I seem to see those other mountains stand,*
> *Where stormy skies will change again to blue*
> *In heavenly peace where all my dreams come true.*[20]

Escaping

It was natural that some would try to escape. This was difficult, and depended as much on the neighbouring terrain and its inhabitants as it did on outwitting the guards. German and Italian camps were often officered – perhaps unsurprisingly – by schoolmasters recalled to the colours (more than one camp commandant was a former head), whilst the ordinary guards were frequently recruited from the local peasantry and therefore cunning, innately suspicious of foreigners, and knowledgeable about the surrounding area. There was also the problem of acquiring the endless paperwork required to prove one's identity in these totalitarian societies. At least a Briton running around Germany and occupied Poland could, if he kept his mouth shut, pass as a local, but it was a long way to the sea or to neutral frontiers. Italy had greater potential, with its long coastline, but of 600 prisoners who tried to escape between 1940 and 1943, only two made it back home, and another four holed up in the Vatican. Italian guards, at least in Tommy Macpherson's experience, were even more tiresome than the Germans when it came to keeping tabs on prisoners. Quite apart from anything else, blending in with the local population was hard for the more fair-haired British fugitives, and even in disguise their general demeanour was hardly Latin. Things changed after the Armistice of 3 September 1943 when, in the words of one cynical historian, 'suddenly hundreds of friendly peasants appeared, having been "anti-fascist" and "pro-allied" all along.'[21]

Many British prisoners, however, were in the north, still held by the Germans and the fascist hardcore, and could not afford to take the risk of trusting them. After being recaptured in the Italian Social Republic, Tommy Macpherson found that many local people and even a policeman said in private that if only they'd know he was around, they would have sheltered him from the Germans. That, however, 'was not the impression we had set out with' since at a time of turmoil many Italians would have been only too happy to curry favour with the Germans by handing them over.[22]

Disregarding the orders of the Allied high command to stay in the camps (Montgomery did not want thousands of POWs charging about adding to the confusion already reigning on a battlefront which was not going as well as Churchill had hoped) 5,000 escaped to Switzerland and 12,000 went south to join the advancing Allies. Those who stayed put (including, with reluctance and only after he had tried to hide, Tommy Macpherson) were shoved onto trains and taken to Germany.

Escape from Japanese camps was hardest because of jungle conditions and also because of the total impossibility of pretending to be locals; Hardie recalled that when not working the prisoners could wander about with a degree of freedom, since their guards knew perfectly well they would be unable to get far. Sir Richard Sharp knew only too well what would happen to would-be escapers when caught by the Japanese:

Recaptured, they were beaten up, and put in prison... they were brought out, their hands tied, and were blind-folded. The Senior Officers from each area in Changi were paraded as spectators. Protests were unavailing. Sikh riflemen, who had joined the Indian National Army, were lined up with their rifles. They were ordered by the Japanese to shoot the four white prisoners under the eyes of white officers – a pleasing symbol of the coming of the Greater East – and were disconcerted. Their aim upset, one volley rang out, then another, and then sporadic shots, till all four lay stretched in the sand before them. The moral was complete.[23]

When sent to work on the Burma railroad, he found that it was necessary to counsel men not to escape and indeed to report them when they did:

'Four fusiliers are going to make a break for it.' It's impossible – tell them not to be silly. It was no good, they made their break. Swinton managed to give them a good 12 hours start, and that, in the absence of communications, was enough for the mere getaway. We reported it to Kokubo, who sent his guards scurrying here and there, uselessly, gave us a cup of tea and biscuits, grinned amiably, bowed politely, and, 'We shall have to shoot them; and if they are not caught, we shall have to shoot the commander of their Battalion.' They managed to get 100 miles away, but were then caught, brought back to Chungkai and shot.

Despite all the risks, a number of OFs did escape, mostly from the Germans, and often by taking advantage of some prevailing confusion. Maj Colin Hunter was captured at St. Valery-en-Caux during the fall of France, but escaped through Spain in August 1940 to fight in Burma; Maj Alexander Irvine-Robertson, a Company Commander in the Argyll and Sutherland Highlanders, who was wounded and captured at Franlieu during the fall of France, escaped at Lille once the Germans had operated on him. He was one of those helped to safety by the 'Tartan Pimpernel', the Rev Donald Caskie, a Church of Scotland minister who ran an escape route out of Marseilles.[24]

With the fall of Italy came more successful bids for freedom; Peter Allsebrook, along with D.D. Mitchell and D.S. Carmichael, jumped from a train shuttling POWs between Pescara and Rome. At one point, they ended up working in a German garrison, disguised as Italian workmen; Allsebrook even worked as personal servant to the CO. When the Germans pulled out, the officer's last words were 'If only all Italians were as efficient as you, we wouldn't be losing this bloody war.'[25] They then lived for months behind enemy lines until the New Zealand forces caught up with them, and sent a jaunty message home from No 2 Allied Ex-POW Repatriation Centre in July 1944, asking for a special toast to the Kiwis on Founder's Day.[26]

Tommy Macpherson tried several times to escape during the transfer from Italian to German captivity, first at the station (where a sporting German officer wished him better luck next time but an irritated sergeant, who had had to chase after him up a hill, literally kicked him onto the train) and again at the Austrian transit camp at Spittal. After a long and arduous trek through the mountains, he was recaptured at Chiusaforte. The Germans then shunted him around their country until he ended up at Stalag 20A at Toruń in Poland, which he was astonished to find was a remarkably well-supplied and liberal regime compared to the discomforts and constant surveillance of the Italian camp at Gavi. Thanks to the good offices of two 'natural spivs' among his fellow-prisoners who had gained useful positions working in the camp rabbit farm, close to the wire, he got out and was picked up by a Pole called Joe Yotkovski, 'king of the local black market'. Yotkovski's lorry whisked Macpherson and his fellow-escapers well away from the camp, first to Bydgoszcz, where they rested, and then to Gdansk, where they made their way by train and bus to the port of Gdynia – a distance of over 100 miles. There they stayed with a family of Poles before stowing away on a Swedish ship. As he boarded it, he found himself illuminated by the quay lights, so nonchalantly produced some sandwiches and proceeded to eat them, giving the impression that he was going about his legitimate business. The ruse worked and he sailed to Sweden (hidden in a pile of coal dust for much of the time) from where he was able to return to Britain.*

---

* Sir Tommy's recently published memoir, *Behind Enemy Lines*, gives full details of this and his many other adventures.

Some Old Fettesians were extraordinarily slippery. 'Pete' Pyman managed the feat of escaping after one day. He was among several high-ranking British officers in General Messervy's command vehicle when it was overtaken by a German battle group in the Western Desert. They continued fighting until all of their cars were on fire in order to give them time to burn the War Diaries and remove their badges of rank. Nonetheless, a German medical officer began to stare intently at the general. Their conversation ran as follows:

'You look like an old man to be serving in the desert.'

'I am no longer a boy, but I am a good fatigue man.'

'You must be older than I am, and I am 35.'

'Yes, yes, just a year or two older.'

The general was, in fact, closer to 50, but fighting nearby interrupted the conversation. Pyman himself nearly gave the game away by calling the general by his rank, but fortunately no Germans heard. After dark and under cover of a British attack, the captives ran off and hid for three hours, then walked for sixteen miles until a Scottish challenge told them they were safe.[27]

Capt Eric Mackay was captured at Arnhem with the only three of his fellow Royal Engineers who could still walk after the fighting for the schoolhouse on the north bank of the river. He had valiantly resisted capture on several occasions; a German approaching his beleaguered position with a grimy white flag, shouting 'surrender' was told 'Get the hell out of here. We're taking no prisoners.' Mackay's men supported him, yelling, 'Bugger off! Go back and fight it out, you bastard!'[28]

Only when he was down to a dozen men capable of walking, each of whom was down to his last clip of ammunition, and a Tiger tank was pouring shell after shell into his position, did Mackay attempt to escape. He had hoped to take the wounded with him, but a mortar added to their number so he reluctantly advised those not able to move quickly to surrender. He and the remaining five engineers made a run for it. Coming face to face with a pair of tanks with over fifty soldiers, the six paratroopers opened fire with their Brens and scythed down a large number of the enemy; 'the Germans just dropped like half-filled sacks of grain,' he said later. Two of his own men were hit in the return of fire, one fatally. The remnant then attempted to make their way to safety individually. Unfortunately, Mackay was found by the Germans whilst resting under a rose bush. Although he pretended to be dead, the

Germans poked him in the buttocks with a bayonet. Furious, Mackay leapt to his feet and asked what the hell they meant by stabbing a British officer. He drew his pistol but, on realising that it was empty, lobbed it behind a wall so they couldn't have it as a souvenir. They did take his watch and his father's silver flask, however. Still determined to keep going, Mackay went round other captured paratroopers in a building the Germans were using as a prison and reminded them of their duty to escape. Taken for interrogation, he informed the Germans that, since they had clearly lost, he was quite prepared to take their surrender. The unconvinced Germans bundled him onto a lorry with the rest of the prisoners. Nothing daunted, Mackay jumped off at the first opportunity, having previously arranged with the others that they should crowd round the guard and prevent him from using his rifle. He dropped to the ground within three feet of a sentry, with whom he promptly started fighting. The sentry's colleagues beat him unconscious. [29]

Within 24 hours, however, he and three comrades had escaped and, along with fellow-escapee Lt Dennis Simpson, Mackay later received the MBE. The citation reads:

Captain Mackay and Lieutenant Simpson were captured on 20th September 1944 after fighting for three days at Arnhem. When they were sent to a transit camp at Emmerich (Germany) the following day, they were not searched; Captain Mackay was thus able to retain a hacksaw blade and a map. Under his instruction two N.C.O.s filed through the bars in the cookhouse and through this aperture the party, accompanied by Lieutenant Simpson, escaped the same evening. Walking through the town they gained the open fields and proceeded west to cross the frontier into Holland near Elten. The Rhine was reached near Tolkamer. After keeping the river under observation throughout the day, they stole food and a small boat; in this they travelled down the Rhine to Nijmegen, where they encountered British troops.

He was one of 35 Britons decorated by the Americans for their efforts, and later joined MI9, the branch of British intelligence concerned with escape and evasion.

One OF even managed to escape from the Japanese, at least for a while. The obituary of David Cassels Brown recorded that, having been 'despatched to distant shores to seek his fortune', he was working as a shipping clerk in the Philippines when the Japanese invaded:

David also evaded capture for one day only but after four months in prison he and a small group of inmates escaped. For an astonishing two years he managed to hide in the jungle until he was recaptured in late 1943. He spent the rest of the war in Santo Tomas concentration camp and was relieved by the American forces in 1945.[30]

Others, of course, were less successful. Lurgan man J.M.H. Johnson wrote a cheerful letter home in 1944 to say that his third attempt to escape had ended after a few days of freedom. Ian Weston Smith worked on the longest tunnel in any camp; its engineer had worked for the London Underground and was determined to get it right, so much so that it was still incomplete when the war ended. K.A. Waugh was captured in Libya in 1941, escaped from a train in Italy in 1943, and was then recaptured north of Cassino in 1944. They were fortunate; Lt Denys Alabaster, captured after the fall of Crete, escaped from Salonika into Yugoslavia, and survived for several months before running into a Bulgarian patrol.[31]

He is buried in Belgrade.

The Great Escapers

One of the most remarkable stories of Fettesian escapology, albeit one with a tragic ending, is that of Alistair Gunn, who took part in the Great Escape of 1944. The son of a Perthshire doctor, Gunn joined Carrington in 1933, and distinguished himself by robust performances in House Matches, where on one occasion his 'good kicking' drove back Kimmerghame and contributed to a 20-0 victory.[32]

A member of the 1st XV for 1936-7, he was also a reasonably successful cricketer, with 'Characters of the 1st XI' in the summer 1936 *Fettesian* noting that he was 'a medium paced bowler who can swing and turn the ball quite well' although 'as a batsman he usually comes off when most needed (as he did in the Merchiston match), but can scarcely be relied upon.' This (thankfully anonymous) collation of faint praise concluded that he was 'a safe field.'[33]

A Pilot Officer in the RAF from 1941, when he was mentioned in dispatches, Gunn was notable for two events; his capture and his escape. The pilot of a photo-reconnaissance Spitfire, he was on a lonely flight over enemy-occupied Norway on 5th March 1942 when he was 'bounced' by Leutnant Heinz Knocke in a Messerschmitt Bf109E, named after his wife Lilo. Gunn's posting to No 1 PRU at Wick was a tribute to his skill

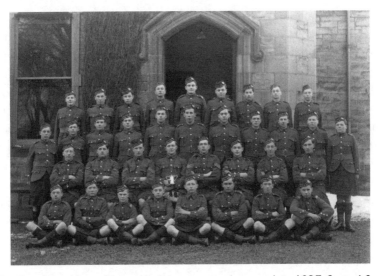

The Carrington House Platoon looks appropriately staunch in 1937. Second from left in the first seated row is A.D.M. Gunn, whose tough demeanour may give some clue as to his future career

as a pilot, and as the Battle of Britain amply demonstrated, the Spitfire was more than capable of gunning down its German rival, but this depended entirely on its having guns in the first place. The PR Mk IV version did not, something Knocke realised when he saw the intruder's methodical flight patterns, a sure sign of aerial photography. After the war, he wrote his memoirs (published in English as *I flew for the Führer*), in which he paid homage to his enemy's skill:

I open my throttle wide and check my guns as I swoop down upon him. In a few seconds I am right on his tail. Fire!
My tracers vanish into his fuselage. And now he begins to twist and turn like a mad thing. Must not let him escape. Keep firing with everything I have.
He goes into a dive, then straightens out again. He begins trailing smoke, which gradually become denser. I fire yet again…[34]

Knocke's engine began to malfunction, so it was his wingman who finally defeated Gunn. As the burning Spitfire hurtled in flames towards the snow, Knocke found himself shouting 'Bale out, lad, bale out!' because his opponent was, after all, 'human too; a soldier, too, and a pilot with the same love of the sky and clouds that I feel.' He felt 'pure joy' when the parachute opened and Gunn drifted slowly to earth.[35]

It was a strangely honourable little moment in a conflict made a thousand times more sinister and protracted by Knocke's associates' war crimes. That night, the German pilots, delighted at having got their first kill without having actually killed anyone (though, as an RAF veteran of the Battle of Britain told Fettes history students recently, this was not generally something which actually bothered most fliers) opened a bottle of brandy in the mess to celebrate. They were soon joined by Gunn himself, brought along by the soldiers who had captured him in a Fieseler Storch reconnaissance aircraft fitted with skis, and he joined them for a drink before being led off to a prisoner-of-war camp. Unaware that he had survived, the *Fettesian* noted anxiously in March 1942 that he was reported missing; fortunately, the next issue could report that he was now a POW.

The wreckage of Gunn's Spitfire can still be seen in Norway

In the camp, he met up with Clifford Cooper, a child of Empire whose widow recalled that after going to Fettes in 1930 he never saw the family home in Darjeeling again.[36] After distinguishing himself at Fettes as a boxer and record-setting swimmer, Cooper trained as a chiropractor in America. He had been shot down in a Typhoon in 1943 whilst strafing enemy convoys in Holland. Cooper was also an experienced pilot, with over 70 fighter sorties to his name as well as a spell as a flying instructor. In baling out from their disabled aircraft – in

Cooper's case, at a mere 500 feet, close to the minimum needed for survival – they became members of the 'Caterpillar Club'.

'Sufficient is known in Auchterarder of Flt. Lt. Gunn's character both as a boy and a young man to realise that his was just the type which, sooner or later, would rail against the irksomeness of capitivity,' a Perthshire journalist noted at the time.[37] Gunn's will to evade pursuers did indeed extend into his internment in the famous Stalag Luft III airmen's prison camp at Sagan in Silesia (then part of eastern Germany, now western Poland) for he was a participant in the famous Great Escape of 1944. Immortalised by Paul Brickhill's 1950 book and the subsequent film, this event has entered British popular culture as a glorious episode in the history of British ingenuity, courage and defiance of authority. Originally begun in January 1943 under the leadership of South African pilot Roger Bushell, the escape tunnels – 'Tom', 'Dick' and 'Harry', took more than a year to complete. The tunnelling, in which Gunn was very active, was truly elaborate, with electric lighting and intricate plans for the disposal of sand and soil, and with all truly elaborate enterprises it suffered numerous setbacks, from collapsing shafts to discovery by the Germans. Clifford Cooper was in the Dean and Dawson Group (named after the travel agency), which was responsible for creating the forged documents. These required no less than 99 different copies of rubber stamps made from boot heels, uniforms and other accessories necessary for the escapees to succeed. It was as laborious a process as the tunnelling; Cooper was part of a team of fifty forgers and 'stooges' (watchmen) working three to five hours a day for a year to create a detailed fictional documentary life for each man.[38]

However, by the spring of 1944 the prisoners were ready to make their escape, and Alistair Gunn was one of the 76 who fanned out into the forests of Silesia on the night of 24-25 March. Unfortunately, the tunnels did not extend as far as the tree line outside the camp and the plan to get over a hundred men out had to be abandoned; 'Cliff,' his widow wrote, 'was standing at the end of Hut 5 and was the next man to go when shots were heard.' Hearing those shots saved his life.

The main options available to the escaped aircrew were heading north to the Baltic in the hope of reaching neutral Sweden, to make their way south-west towards Switzerland, or to go south-east to the Balkans. Sympathetic Poles near Sagan might help – at near-terminal risk to their lives – but the further west the escapees went, the more purely German the population would become, and 'terror-fliers', as Goebbels had dubbed the RAF, were unlikely to get a lot of support from the people they had been bombing. Hitler flew into a rage on hearing of the breakout and ordered a ruthless crackdown on British POWs; Goering, not normally a man known for his sentimentality but nonetheless himself a former pilot, allegedly talked his increasingly insane leader down from his initial decision to execute every last one of them, and more besides. A figure of fifty seems to have been settled on, and the Gestapo got to work, rounding up and shooting the fugitives as they found them. Gunn was one of those murdered in this way; captured at Görlitz, he was last seen alive on 6 April. Brickhill records that on that day, he and five other escapees were shot by Obersekretär Lux of the Gestapo in the concentration camp at Breslau, now Wrocław. The official line that they were all shot whilst trying to escape fooled no-one as 49 sets of ashes from the camp crematoria turned up at Stalag Luft III. The *Fettesian* noted, with understandable suspicion, 'No official explanation has so far been sent from Germany, and the whole affair is still a mystery.'[39]

Historical opinion on the Great Escape remains as divided as that of the few survivors; interviewed for Tim Carroll's book on the subject in 2004, Tony Bethell quoted Roger Bushell's desire to 'harass, confuse and confound the enemy' – that, he said, is 'exactly what we did.' [40] Hugh Falkus, on the other hand, told Charles Rollings that 'it made no sense and there was no glory in it. It was a miserable affair.'[41] The Germans had already been on edge because of the bombing, and many camps adopted stricter regimes; British military leaders sent secret messages to senior captive officers to discourage further escape attempts.

The Fettesian Prisoner in Canada

One of the strangest and saddest stories of wartime captivity was that of Charles Herzberg. His father had been an officer in the German Army in the Great War and subsequently helped organise the right-wing Freikorps, who fought communists on the streets of Germany in the chaotic years between 1918 and 1923. However, his Jewish background meant that this impeccably patriotic record cut no ice with the Nazis, so he organised his family's escape to Britain, where on the recommendation of a Scots friend in the Foreign Office he sent his sons to Fettes in 1940. 'At first we had some difficulty to understand some of the Scottish accents, as well as the schoolboy slang developed by all schools,' Charles remembered later, but found aspects of the strange new regime useful:

Boxing (Army Rules) was compulsory and stood me in good stead in my life, as did the tough regime and the potentially good food, badly cooked! Incidentally, bullying was not known in our time at Fettes. I think that boxing had something to do with this.[42]

A few months after his sixteenth birthday, Herzberg was on a Corps exercise when he was told to report immediately to his Housemaster's study. This was to be the start of a dreadful and prolonged nightmare, in many ways worse than that suffered by most of the British OFs in German hands. In the study was the Headmaster, accompanied by 'two gentlemen in trench coats.'

I was told that as I was over 16 and lived in a fortress area, which Edinburgh had become, I was to be interned as an enemy alien. The policemen thought that I would be out within a few days. When I was interned, I was first taken to Donaldson's Hospital, which had been turned into a prison camp. From there several of us prisoners were taken to the Old Scotland Yard in London, which was grim, and from there to Lingfield Racecourse in Surrey.

After some time living with several other young internees in a horsebox, nicknamed the Empire State Building, he was ordered to pack, and, with around two thousand others – a mixture of POWs, exiles, Jews, Italian restaurateurs, downed aircrew and just plain unlucky people born in the wrong place at the wrong time – shipped from Liverpool in the MS *Windsor Castle* to Canada. It was at this time that the SS *Arandora Star*, also carrying German and Italian internees, was sunk by a U-boat with the loss of hundreds of lives. Charles Herzberg's family – who were still at liberty in Britain – lost track of him and came to believe that he had been among the dead, a belief which persisted for months because of the incredibly slow progress of his Red Cross letters home. As it was, he survived the cramped voyage without mishap, using his Fettes Sunday suit as a pillow as four captured riflemen played cards above him. Arriving at Quebec, they were moved westwards to Red Rock at the northern end of the Great Lakes. Here, an abandoned timber camp was being turned into a prison under the ferocious discipline of 'a particularly nasty Canadian sergeant major with a long rhino whip.' An old Imperial German Navy officer, Commodore Scharf, was the prisoners' leader and organised them on maritime lines. Although the food – Canadian Army rations – was surprisingly good, conditions in general and the typical prisoner's feeling of loss and isolation led to what they called 'barbed wire psychosis.' It was a harsh life, especially in winter:

The huts were H shaped with the ablutions in the centre. The walls were only planks of wood, covered in roofing felt. The nail heads holding the felt onto the timber protruded into the huts. At the very low temperatures (40C minus was usual) the humidity from the prisoners' breath froze on these nails, which made them look like rivets in a battle ship...

I did some outside work lumbering. We cut down large fir trees, and eight men had to carry these out of the woods on our shoulders. If one or more dropped the tree without the others doing the same, the tree trunk would whip and smash the unfortunate person's shoulder. To protect our feet at those low temperatures we wore first ladies' silk stockings, then army issue socks, then a layer of newspapers and then army issue felt boots. But after eight hours the cold struck through. One had to wear a scarf or roll neck sweater over one's mouth as one's nose froze up and breathing cold air through the mouth hurt the front teeth!

When the German government learned that members of the master race were being kept in such misery, Hitler furiously ordered that the Canadian conditions – down to 15-inch windows as the sole source of daylight for 14 people and jam-tins as night lavatories – be replicated for 400 British POWs imprisoned in the Polish fortress of Toruń (which was Tommy Macpherson's last billet before his escape). [43]

This was quite a common German tactic – whenever they heard that their people were being treated in a particular way to which they objected, the camp authorities would impose it on prisoners of the nation responsible. When the Americans put some prisoners in handcuffs, the Germans running Rae's camp did likewise to some men there; luckily, 'we found that we could open them with a sardine tin key, so I took the place of one of them for a while.' In fairness, the Canadians did try to improve things and it is a kind of testimony to the relative decency of the British prison regime that so many Germans and Italians elected to stay at the end of the war – 25,000 Germans, Herzberg included, in the U.K. alone. Like British prisoners, the Germans tried to divert themselves from their conditions. One made a violin from old boxes, using only a dinner knife and broken pieces of glass, whilst one of the von Richthofens, a cousin of the Red Baron, wrote his memoirs on rolls of lavatory paper. Herzberg himself learned how to make bottle ships and belts out of old cigarette carton wrappings and leather from old boots. They acquired news from an illegal radio and papers smuggled in as wrappers on food. Still, plenty were desperate to escape, though on at least three occasions attempts to do so were punished by death; other prisoners went mad. One of these thought he was a dog and started biting other people, so Herzberg was given the responsibility of knocking him unconscious; 'I first wound a towel round my hand to do as little damage as possible, but when I hit him he had his tongue between his teeth. Sadly he ended up a horrible mess.' Given the incredibly diverse nature of the German internees, it would have been surprising had social harmony prevailed all the time. On one occasion, Herzberg had to fight a 'duel' with a Hungarian German prisoner, the objective being to disable the loser without doing the kind of permanent damage which could lead to a spell in the 'Cooler' which was boiling hot in summer and freezing in winter. The absence of Queensbury Rules meant that different tactics were called for, and Herzberg had some ideal back-up:

My team was headed up by an enormous German sailor who had sailed before the mast and was a real bruiser. He and my other friends decided that some psychological warfare was also indicated. So I was put through a tough routine in full view of everyone. On the day of the duel a tight ring of prisoners was formed to prevent the guards from seeing what was going on. At the start, my opponent, who was taller than me and had long arms managed to hit the side of my head. But once he uncovered his side I landed the intended liver hook. He collapsed immediately and I was declared the winner.

The British had not differentiated between hostile enemy aliens and those who had been born in Italy or Germany but were opposed to their regimes; this is still a point of bitterness amongst the many Scots-Italians who lost relatives on the *Arandora Star*. The British authorities either did not know or did not care about the official position of Jews in Germany, and often interned them with card-carrying National Socialists. The prisoners' doctor at Red Rock was a German Jew, and Herzberg recalls that he was 'beaten up by some Nazi thugs who boasted that they were Gestapo men.' Fortunately, Herzberg's escape from internment was as sudden and unexpected as his introduction to it:

Without warning, one day I was taken by two armed Canadian orderlies to the

British commandant, a full colonel, whom we had never seen before. He said to me, '144101, you do not look like U Boat crew. Where were you taken?' I said: 'From the playing fields of Fettes!' He jumped up, held out his hand and said 'I am Wellington!' I was then told that I was to go home.

What had happened was that one of his father's friends spoke to the London Director of the Canadian Pacific Shipping Line, who did not believe that Herzberg had been on the *Arandora Star* and circulated his name and details to all his agents. By chance one of these, based in the Great Lakes, showed the signal to a guard at Red Rock. Although he was now free, the situation had not been transformed into one of instant comfort. The journey back to civilisation was as rugged as the deportation from it:

I found myself amongst a column of prisoners being moved at night. It was bitterly cold. We marched in columns of three with a Canadian Rifleman or a soldier with a portable search light on the outside. The station was an old railway coach. We spent twenty minutes in the coach and forty outside in order not to freeze to death. After many hours the prison train arrived and we were taken to a town in Quebec. The camp was a horrible old railway roundhouse with hundreds of bunks covered with old blankets to keep out the drafts. I spent some time there laying pipes in the frozen ground. Pipes were laid six foot down to avoid freezing up in winter! It was more like mining than digging. After some time eight young prisoners due for return home were taken from the camp and sent under armed escort to Montreal.

After another Atlantic crossing, Herzberg was arrived at Gourock and was promptly re-arrested; nobody had notified the British Authorities that he and the other young Germans were coming. 'When we told a sentry who we were, he was so angry that he threw his rifle against the wall!' Luckily, reason prevailed and, after a night train journey to Penrith and a lift on a newspaper lorry, Herzberg arrived at home at Keswick:

I still had my Fettes best suit and stiff collar. As I walked towards my home, I suddenly saw my father driving our car, coming in the opposite direction. He went white, as he did not know that I was alive and he thought he saw my ghost! I was told to hide whilst he broke the news to my mother. I then wrote to Dr Ashcroft, who sent a four page handwritten letter in reply. The gist was: 'We want you back; come as soon as possible!'

Herzberg rejoined the school, the cadets, and British life, eventually being coached for Cambridge where he entered Sidney Sussex. His brother Hans became Head of House in Glencorse and CSM in the Corps.

Prisoners in the Far East

In the Far East, a considerable number of OFs – at least 18 – became prisoners of the Japanese and some did not survive the experience. Most were captured when Singapore and Malaya fell at the outset of the enemy offensive, so spent over three years in captivity. Sir Richard Sharp recorded his experience of capture for the school archives:

The 'Stay where you are' order came with the 'Cease fire', and till the morning of the 17th we stayed where we were, dully awaiting sentence. Then 'Pack your kits, move to Changi'. Newcomers, we looked at the map, and found Changi in the N.E. corner of the Island. We were now on the west side of town. 'March'. In to the town, through the streets, deserted by natives as by Japanese, draped mournfully with the desolate tram cables, here and there and overturned tram car, past the sullen-faced houses, at which there already hung the miserable insurance of a Jap flag, red blot upon a white field, and out on to Serangoon road. Fork right, down Tampines road, straight and smooth across the swamps and through the trees. And from here to the road's end there was nothing but troops, troops and more troops, marching to captivity. In step, out of step, columns, heaving, swaying, khaki as far as the eye can see. Where have all these sprung from? How were we defeated, and these still fit? And past them all, lorries career by, in defiance of Jap orders, carrying stores, provisions and anything they can think will come in handy.[44]

Captured Fettesians ranged from seasoned veterans such as Brig R.G. Moir to the part-time soldiers of the Singapore Straits Volunteer Force such as Cpl Alan Mackenzie, a rubber planter remembered as 'a cheerful and enthusiastic member of Glencorse' who died in the camps.[45] So did Stephen Johnston, 'a slight, fair-haired boy with an attractive manner', and 'fundamentally one of the most honest men I have ever had the privilege of knowing' as a contemporary put it.[46]

They were, as previously noted, much more isolated from home than those held in Europe. C.J.N. Fleming, a Victorian OF whose son J.C. Fleming was interned in Shantung Province, told the school in December 1944 that he got hardly any information and that the last communication was a Red Cross Message in June 1943. A rare letter from came from Maj G.B. Sanderson, who wrote to his brother from Japan in 1944:

Hope that you are all well. I am in best of health though three stone less. Meals consist of rice and vegetable stew. Nippon soldiers very kindly presented 700 of us one day with two ducks. A great treat. Have had two lots of Red Cross parcels. Hoping for a third. No letters so far. Complete silence. Surroundings comfortable. Our time is well employed. My heart is back in Scotland mid the sights and sounds of home.

Please give my kind regards to all.
Oh! for bacon and eggs.[47]

One of the most detailed accounts of life as a prisoner of Japan comes from Dr Robert Hardie. Captured when Singapore fell, he spent three and a half years in various camps trying to do his best to keep his fellow-prisoners alive with limited supplies of medicine in tropical conditions and under the lash of an often sadistic captor. Writing on tiny scraps of paper, he managed to keep a diary of his experiences, and indeed to make delicate drawings of the local flora, which fascinated him, and the Imperial War Museum published it after his death. Hardie had a meticulous eye for detail and left highly exact descriptions of Japanese camps and the life therein. Like Sanderson, Hardie's contact with home was rare. The British prisoners were given postcards to fill in whenever they moved from one camp to another, but these took some time to reach home and post coming the other way was similarly slow. In January 1944, he received three letters – sent in July 1942, November 1942, and January 1943. A comrade told him that he was lucky – in another camp where he had been held, the Japanese burned the letters of the sick as punishment for their weakness. They were also inclined to plunder the Red Cross parcels which occasionally arrived; some of Hardie's Dutch fellow-prisoners were issued with supplies of American medicine, whereupon each Japanese soldier took 500 tablets of M&B 693 antibiotic and 200 anti-malarial atebrin pills, whilst the commandant seized all the lint and had it made into three pairs of pyjamas and a set of curtains.[48]

The Japanese counted life, at least that of their enemies, as cheap. At Chungkai, they banned all prisoner recreational activities for the funeral of one of their men who had been knifed in a pub brawl; Hardie noted bitterly that they hadn't stopped playing tennis when 15 or 16 bodies a day were being carried past them from the makeshift camp hospital to the cemetery. Bodies would later be burned, as Sharp noted, making the parallel with Nazi concentration camps almost complete:

Shallow latrines at Prai, with maggots seething, boiling, crawling here, there, everywhere. Trainloads of men with the 'trots' excreting on the grassy verge of a trim railway station – any railway station. Public? What did the public matter in the face of necessity? …Cookhouse swarming with flies. Hospital, bamboo and attap, beds on raised bamboo slats, place flooded, water up to bed level, floors swimming in excrement from flooded latrines. And the patients? They either get better or die. Life is as simple as that… The dead were burnt now, outside the camp, in the jungle, and a small, friendless service held over their ashes, confined for their short eternity in a bamboo casket. Lonely, without comfort of human kindness, five to a shallow grave – where was the labour to dig any customly honoured grave in that earth which so soon after we had passed would show no traces of our eternity – seeming transience? When we came by that way again, not many months thereafter, there was naught that we could recognise.

As a doctor, Hardie reflected on the contrast between his poorly-equipped, insanitary camp hospital and the provision for the sick back in Scotland: 'I have thought with longing of the luxury of minor illnesses at home – cool clean sheets, cool drinks – all the comforts so strikingly absent here where bedding is always damp, dirty and smells of sweat, and the food primitive and monotonous.'[49]

In 1943, he and his comrades were marched up-river to Takanun, where they were given an inadequate number of tents and ordered to clear the jungle for the railway (a project, incidentally, once considered by the British imperial authorities but abandoned as not merely impracticable but dangerous. The Japanese were not so squeamish). A cholera epidemic soon broke out, with dysentery following close behind. 'If it were not that we have gradually become accustomed to the human misery and emaciation in these camps, one's blood would be curdled daily by the sight of the human wreckage lying in helpless exhaustion and starvation in the huts.'[50]

When tented camps were abandoned, the sick were left behind in the monsoon rains to die. Sometimes he was lucky – the camp at Chungkai, where he spent most of the remainder of the war, had a canteen where more elaborate rations, including fudge made from coconut and ginger, were available, and there was a hospital laboratory with some modern equipment. Like all the other camps, however, the accommodation was 'hot, crowded and infested with bugs', and the laboratory hut collapsed in the monsoon rains. The Japanese were highly suspicious of the British troops' attempts to amuse one another, banning a stage show with the nonsense title of *Thai Diddle Diddle*; Hardie's theory was that they had looked up the word 'diddle' in a dictionary and, learning that it meant 'cheat', 'suspected some subtle criticism of the Co-Prosperity Sphere. It is astonishing how tortuous the Japanese are in some ways, and how gullible in others.'[51]

Overall, however, the (relatively) civilized camp was such an improvement on Takanun that he was relieved to get there. Likewise, Tony Chenevix-Trench learned to appreciate Changi Gaol in Singapore after the horrors of the Burma Railway; like the captives in Germany, he used the time to learn languages and grow fruit and vegetables. Sharp believed the relatively better opportunities at Changi were the result of work by the General Officer Commanding, Major General M. Beckwith Smith, who did his best to maintain discipline and morale:

A Secondary School and a University were opened, and encouragement given to all who wanted to attend. Libraries popped up all over the place. The concert party that had started through the keenness of few entertainers was given every encouragement. 'The New Windmill Theatre' was opened for stage shows, and the play 'Dover Road' set the ball rolling on 'Becky's' birthday. He'd go round the hospital, encouraging the sick, seeing that they were not neglected by either the Hospital or their own units; take a look in at the University, listen to the lectures that were being given, and on his way past St George's Church, have a word with the padre about the services. Watch any games that were being played, and sometimes play himself – one of the pitches for hockey or soccer, St George's Church and the main lecture rooms of the University all lay cheek by jowl. When he paid an official visit to a unit, it was usually not so much of a bugbear as most General Inspections are to the troops themselves, for though they still had a bit of polishing up to do, the inspection was always in the early morning, before breakfast, and he'd stay to see what sort of food they were getting. So, of course, the Q.M. had to dig into whatever reserves he held, to put up a good show. And that the troops loved, naturally. Due to him it was recognised that the morale and discipline within the Division were better than elsewhere.

Although there were moments of levity and leniency – the occasional concert party was permitted, and some Japanese interpreters showed real kindness, brutality was apparent throughout Japanese captivity, especially 'up-country', away from any prying eyes. There, it became an accepted fact of everyday life, though for a long time Sharp tried to maintain his dignity and sanity by denying this:

As the men came hurrying out of the tents – to a Jap, a thing had to be done, had to be done hurriedly, – he laid into them, left, right, left, right, great swinging blows, and was the more pleased that these tents were in the officers' lines. Then he chanced with one blow to fell a man to his knees, and his anger evaporated, satisfied, so that the play was over. The novelty of beatings up had not at that stage worn off, and I well remember the passion of cold rage that seethed within me, and the feeling of helpless degradation, at a mere cuff. But here too we were to change, and by and by, a beating became part of the day's work. Avoid it, of course, if you could: but if you couldn't, well get it over and done with. Better that way than the tortured waiting for something to happen that the Jap liked, cat-like, to inflict.

Although he was spared the sight of the real extremes of sadism (unlike Chenevix-Trench who was 'interrogated' by the Kempetai, the Japanese Gestapo, and saw a fellow-prisoner crucified to a tree with bayonets) a recurrent theme in Hardie's diaries is the cruel treatment of the sick. Regarding them as shirkers, the Japanese forced them to work until, resembling the famous images of concentration camp victims, who they closely resembled – 'mere skeletons, gaunt, fleshless and despairing' – they died. Sharp witnessed a particularly brutal Japanese engineering officer's reaction to seeing large numbers of sick prisoners:

Kidiama shouted 'What the hell! Is that why we're not getting enough workers?' (or words to that effect!), and ordered all the sick on parade. Frantic palaver, because the numbers did not tally with the figures. Then the Japs raged up and down the lines of sick, beat three out of four, because they said, they were fit to work, and just being idle: stormed at Swinton, the British Commander, and the doctors, beat them all up for allowing such things, and left the camp.

In the summer of 1943, the Japanese (claiming that conditions would be better than in Singapore) hauled 'F' and 'H' Forces – parties of some 7,000 British and Australian POWs taken from Changi Gaol – northward to work on the railway. Chenevix-Trench, who was in 'H' Force, trying to work in a swamp near the River Kwai at Hintok, worked from 5.30

a.m. to 9.30 p.m., seven days a week, for six months, without a day off.[52]

He survived, but almost half of the other POWs did not. In November 1943, Hardie noted the fate of 'F' Force, marched 200 miles along jungle tracks by the Japanese, who beat an officer who had the temerity to produce a document drawn up by one of their own doctors testifying that some of the men were too sick to go on. Fed less than a pint of watery stew and rice per day, 'treated very savagely' by the engineers, the sick were taken out to the line to work on stretchers and forced to break stones for ballast. Cholera, beriberi, ulcers, diptheria, malaria and dysentery were rife, but 'practically no medical supplies were issued.'[53]

Life stretched on miserably, but clinging to hope was all the prisoners had. Hardie had an 'extraordinarily vivid dream that I was walking about the lawns round the ruined cathedral at Dunkeld', and hoped he would see the flowerbeds of the little Scottish town again, 'perhaps before very long.' It was August 1942; a secret radio set kept the prisoners informed of Allied advances, such as the attack on New Guinea, but it was to be three miserable years before they, or rather those of them who survived, were released. On 31 December 1943, he wrote, 'This is the last day of 1943, a year to be said goodbye to without regret, holding as it did nothing beyond captivity and depression, weary waiting, and above all the sight of immeasurable human misery, suffering and death.'[54]

Hardie did his best to be stoical; stricken by fever in July 1944 he wrote 'many men have had far worse and longer illnesses, so I should not complain.'

Major Ian Seymour Graham, who had accompanied Major-General Playfair to surrender near Batavia wearing his Seaforth Highlander's bonnet and carrying his crumoch, was equally determined to stick things out and do his duty. Transported with some 1600 American, Australian, British and Dutch POWs in the open hold of an iron ore carrier on a harrowing five-week journey to Japan during which many died, he was sent to work in a coal mine and then moved to Zentsuji, a slave labour camp on Shikoku Island. Sir John Fletcher-Cooke, one of his fellow inmates, described Graham as 'the finest type of British army officer', whose 'sole concern was for others…He would and did give away the shirt off his back if he felt someone had a greater need of it than himself.'[55]

War did not, however, always bring the best out of people in this way.

Sharp reflected that British morale was at a very low ebb, leading to failures which otherwise would have been unacceptable:

We had lost a part of our self-respect with the capitulation. The feeling that British Arms had failed again, the disappointment, all the reaction to the surrender, possibly deep down, the feeling of disgrace, brought about a break down of discipline and a collapse of morale. Men, who had let down themselves, their officers and their regiment, felt themselves let down, and were contrarily self-assertive. Hunger added wings to a self-discipline already in flight, and thieving of money and of food, became wide spread. Disobedience was common, and mutiny not unknown.

Hardie's diaries refer to a 'Major W' who refused to help the other prisoners with even the most essential sanitary chores, and to a sergeant cook caught selling rations to the locals. 'It is almost incredible that people should behave so when their comrades are short of food,' Hardie wrote, 'but this captivity has revealed that the veneer of decent behaviour is very thin indeed in all ranks.' His own extraordinary fair-mindedness extended both to those Japanese who behaved decently and to the Chinese, Asian, Thai, Malay and Burmese populations who, he recognised, were suffering even more terribly than he was. Despite their claims to be liberating these peoples from white colonialism into an Asiatic New Order, the Dai Toa Kaigi, the Japanese treated local civilians much as the Germans did the Russian peasantry, as sub-human, and therefore expendable, beasts of burden. Sharp saw the first 'coolies' arrive at his camp:

Tamils, Malays, Chinese, a jumble of miserable humanity, journeying with their goods upon their heads, upon their shoulders, oftentimes with their wives and their small children, going they knew not where at the command of the dominant race, whom they did not like, but dared not defy. Defy their masters, and they were starved into submission. Be submissive, and they were driven like cattle to work, cursed, beaten, cudgelled, and in the end, were tumbled into the common pit that was dug for them. It was small wonder they lived without hope, and hopelessly laid themselves down to die. 'Master,' said one, 'May I come into your tent, so that I may die?' Out of every four that went up the river, only one came back.

Referring to the Chinese at the camp at Nikki, Hardie reported that 'so many were sick that the Japanese one day invaded their camp in force and flogged the sick out with bamboos.' Whilst in the unremitting squalor of disease-ridden Takanun, he met a bombardier from another camp who had been forced to bury Tamil and Chinese cholera cases before they were actually dead; elsewhere they were killed off with hammers. The Japanese, terrified of catching the disease themselves, got the British POWs to do their dirty work, ordering them to the task at gunpoint and hosing them down afterwards; eventually the British 'steadfastly refused to do any more.' He reflected that the prisoners of war, in spite of all the cruelty visited upon them, were 'being treated with comparative consideration.'[56]

Liberation

As the tide of the war turned, hope came for prisoners, whether in Europe or the Far East, in the form of air raids. By 1942, the RAF's campaign heavily to assault the German heartland was under way, and a letter from Hutchins, who had started school at Fettes in 1911, ends on a thrilled note:

We heard our own aircraft for the first time the other night. Do you remember the Zepp raid over Edinburgh? What excitement, and what child's play compared to these days! Perfect weather just now – everyone black from sunbathing. Love to old friends. [57]

McGlashan remembers that 'the faces of our German guards told their own story of the probability of defeat as they watched up to a thousand Flying Fortresses in massed formations in broad daylight sail majestically over their heads and the ground shook below their feet.'[58]

Unfortunately, bombing also disrupted the supply of food, which was an obsession for all prisoners. The German food was profoundly uninspiring at the best of times, and whilst prisoners in Italy at least had the chance to barter with politically apathetic peasants and get fresh fruit unimaginable to their families in Britain, in both countries there was always a fluctuating amount of anything to eat. Hence John McGlashan and his comrades were, as Rollings puts it, 'charity cases' dependent on the Red Cross parcels which were supposed to be supplementary luxuries but were actually vital necessities. McGlashan remembers that Red Cross parcels were 'a life-saving addition to the basic German rations, and gave us the energy to take part in physical exercise.' Douglas Rae came up with a cunning plan:

We were pretty hungry in the camp so I had the idea of writing to the Pope to ask for a food parcel. It duly arrived with tins of condensed milk – a great luxury. One of my fellow officers was rather indignant as I wasn't even a Catholic, as he was, but a Scottish Presbyterian! [59]

Unfortunately, the Allied harbingers of liberation in the sky disrupted the railway system so that from late 1944 the parcels dried up and many prisoners lost several stones in weight. After the war, incidentally, Germany and Italy 'made astronomical claims for POW food and accommodation, expecting to be fully reimbursed.'[60]

One tragic victim of the bombing was OF Capt William Steel, taken prisoner in 1941 and killed in an air raid less than a month before the war ended. Douglas Rae was lucky to escape a similar fate:

Towards the end of the war the Germans threatened to send us all to the south to be hostages, but the American General Patton moved his troops so quickly across Germany that they didn't have time. We were being taken from our camp to one further south, and soon after breakfast we started and were moving along fairly slowly in a column when some American planes fired on us, thinking we were German soldiers. Most of us ran like anything into the fields, but a few were killed. One casualty was a B.B.C. man who was a very good pianist – he had run a class for piano playing on the camp – but was shot in the hand.[61]

He was liberated in the spring of 1945; the guards abandoned the camp he was in and the Americans arrived. Battle continued to rage in the surrounding area, but Red Cross food parcels and, eventually, permission to go for walks in the countryside were a welcome relief. John McGlashan's experience when the war in Europe finally came to a close has entered into Fettes mythology:

On 25th April, 1945 I was at the back of a truck in a convoy carrying liberated P.O.W.s from Stalag 357 to a German airfield to be flown home. Our convoy, which had priority over vehicles travelling in the opposite direction, proceeded in fits and starts. A squadron of tanks moving up to the front pulled off the road to allow us to pass. My truck stopped opposite a tank with, to my astonishment, the head and shoulders of John Cowie (who had been my fag at Carrington five years previously) sticking out of the hatch. Our eyes met and immediately, without saying anything, he disappeared into his tank, and I presumed he had not

recognized me (which was not surprising). But he immediately reappeared with a
bottle of Scotch which he brought across to me. I forget what we said to each other,
but it was very brief as my truck moved off. There were fifty of us in that truck and
by the time we reached the airfield we were all gloriously drunk.

Fifty-five years later we met again by chance and he told me the sequel. The
next time the squadron stopped after our meeting John's sergeant-major asked
him, with every appearance of concern, whether he was feeling all right. When
John, somewhat irritated, said that of course he was all right and asked him why
he was asking such a silly question, the sergeant-major said 'Well, Sir, that's the
first time I've ever seen a Scotsman give away a bottle of whisky!'

Even at this late stage, disaster could still strike the liberated prisoners.
Rae was part of a group of ex-POWs being flown home from Moosburg
in Austria in Dakotas; the first plane was too full and crashed on the
runway. Luckily, he was on the second plane, which eventually made it to
England, where the route from the airfield to his army camp was lined
with children singing 'Welcome Home':

I was given a jacket and a ticket to Scotland. I got out of the train in Edinburgh
and ordered a Gordon kilt, because I had gone through the war wearing a London
Scottish kilt. Then a train to Dundee, where my mother met me, and we went to
father's office to shake hands.

Although McGlashan, Rae and their comrades in Europe were now
home, in the Far East the war dragged on for several more months until
nuclear weapons finally made their convincing point. Hardie had to treat
several men who were injured when an Allied aeroplane accidentally
bombed a prisoners' working party, leaving, he noted gloomily, 'the Nip
[guard] unscathed.' As in the case of Germans, those held by the Japanese
– never having been very well-fed in the first place – saw their rations
slashed in those last months of the war as transport links crumbled.
Chenevix-Trench later recalled that they were receiving less than 800
calories a day, a third of the necessary amount for healthy young men.
The Japanese also became more irritable, as Hardie noted on 17 April
1945:

Yesterday's theatre performance (simple songs and turns) was suddenly interrupted
by Turtleneck [Ishikura, the Japanese interpreter] *who strode up onto the stage*
in the middle of one of the early turns, slapped the surprised performers in the face

and said that there must be no turns, only orchestral music... Today orders have been issued that the theatre building is to be pulled down. The theory is I think that the Japs feel it is wrong for us to sing and be cheerful when Japan is in difficulties.[62]

At Santo Tomas in the Philippines, where David Brown was interned, the prisoners believed that the Japanese were deliberately starving them to death, and rumours circulated that there would be a massacre before they could be freed. In the end, American troops stormed the camp.[63]

Later, the Japanese set the prisoners in Hardie's camp to work beautifying their surroundings, including the creation of an elaborate curved bridge over a duckpond. By now, Hardie's hope was on the verge of running out: 'Sometimes we feel they are trying to get the place to look a bit better in case the war ends, and then we decide that that is only wishful thinking.' The week after the singing ban, the British Sergeant-Major was summoned to see the Japanese officers, and returned to tell the other prisoners that they would now come under their own discipline. There was a tremendous burst of cheering, and the national anthems of Britain, Holland and the United States were sung, followed by 'Abide with me.' 'It was almost impossible to grasp,' wrote Hardie, 'at such a moment surely one should feel some overwhelming emotion: one just felt rather numb, rather shaky and rather inclined to sob.' [64] Appropriately for a Fettesian, a Latin tag occurred to him: 'Sunt lacrimae rerum, et mentem mortalia tangent.' ('Human deeds have their tears and mortality touches the heart' – Virgil, *Aeneid*, I.462). Sharp's knowledge of the war's end came from a hospital party:

They marched or were carried to the railway line, and there while awaiting the train, observed the strangle behaviour of the Thais. For the Thais, standing at a distance, kept nodding their heads eagerly up and down, and grinning widely. Then a certain Nai Pong, well-known to our people for the good he had done to all the camps on the river, cycled up the road, smiled at those he knew, and said 'Peace to-day'. The camp, already alive with rumours, now seethed with them. Betting and speculation went on, on all sides. That evening we sat and talked on the parade ground. And no 'lights out' was blown. Then from the first hut we heard three cheers; and from the second and so on right down the line, like an echo caught in a vista of mirrors. Then there arose the strains of 'God Save the King', slow and dignifiedly beautiful, rising out of the dark night on a thousand voices. There followed the Star Spangled Banner and the Wilhelmus. We were free.

The end of the war meant that the Japanese finally gave the prisoners access to the Red Cross supplies they had denied them for three and a half years; money, drugs, food and clothing. More food was dropped from Dakotas. As the sick were brought in from the up-country camps, Hardie noted that to see them was to revive one's animosity against the Japanese, which had sunk quite low 'seeing them so submissive and orderly and now harmless.' In Singapore, Chenevix-Trench noted with some irony that the British actually had to save the Japanese:

The arrival of our troops in Singapore was the most moving thing; after three and a half and years of incredible oppression under the Japanese whips and scorpions the population was crazy with joy and showed it. The main difficulty was to protect the Japs, blow them. Starvation, death and hatred are all the Japs had left from their Dai Toa.[65]

Although the July 1945 *Fettesian* was able to record the liberation of the European POWs, it was not until the Christmas term that news of the Far Eastern prisoners trickled through. G.D.McK. Sutherland, who had been held in Malaya, was 'lying low for a bit, simply enjoying being clean and quiet.' [66]

He had been imprisoned with D.A. Duke and Richard Sharp, 'great-hearted people' who were also on their way home. John Humphries, serving with the RNVR, was crewing one of the ships which was taking liberated prisoners home, and was wearing his old Fives zephyr for games when someone asked him if he had been at Fettes. It was G.B. Sanderson, who was looking fairly fit 'in spite of being in pretty rigorous captivity.' (By an extraordinary coincidence, Sanderson later found himself dancing with a girl in London who turned out to be Humphries' sister.) Houston Scott, it was reported, 'looks well if somewhat shaky.' Given these men's experiences, it would hardly have been surprising had it been otherwise. Chenevix-Trench managed to meet up with his brother Godfrey, who was serving on HMS *Cleopatra* in the Malacca Straits, and they had a lengthy talk on board the ship, where Tony received his first decent bath for years. Godfrey told their parents that he found his brother, despite his ordeal, 'just the same Tony as ever' – other prisoners were less fortunate, having 'suffered a psychological blow which makes them listless and almost unaware of their changing circumstances.'

Some writers claim that the boarding-school experience equipped men for captivity, a concept reinforced by the popularity of post-war books and films about prisoners depicting them as mischievous chaps always seeking new ways to outwit camp commandants who resemble authoritarian headmasters (which some had indeed been), albeit with access to infinitely more severe forms of punishment. There is a little truth in this; instinctive British libertarianism is not wholly mythical, and making jokes about and playing pranks upon one's captors was a not unnatural response to imprisonment, though it was rather less in evidence among those held by the Japanese, whose sense of humour was limited to the infliction of pain. There are not many jokes in Hardie's diaries. Overall, it was not an experience one would wish on anyone, and surviving, and keeping up morale, were the priorities; perhaps the robust life at Fettes and similar institutions did prepare men to a certain extent. 'To go from any public school into the RAF and then into a prison camp,' comments John McGlashan, 'was essentially to exchange one authoritarian organisation for another' [67] – a sentiment echoed by several other OF POWs. Sir Tommy Macpherson, looking back on his days in the grim fortress-prison of Gavi, wrote that 'I am sure the experience of no heating at Fettes stood me in good stead, because at Gavi I was not that uncomfortable, while the complaints from English, New Zealand and South African officers were fortissimo, and I think they suffered considerably.'[68]

Hector Braine, another Fettesian doctor incarcerated by the Japanese,

...rarely spoke about his four years in Changi, apart from remarking wryly that his experience of Fettes had been good training for survival in the camp. He occupied himself by studying languages, for which he had always had a marked aptitude, learning Chinese and Russian, but by the time of his release his weight had almost halved, from over 12 stone to below 7 stone.[69]

Brian Brown, the only Fettes FEPOW to make contact with the school regarding this book, was reserved about his experiences, writing 'My military career is not very noteworthy'. Having been called up as a Belisha Boy in 1939, he served with the Royal Signals at Prestatyn before going to OCTU at Aldershot. Posted to Malaya in 1941, he was taken prisoner at the fall of Singapore, taken to Siam, forced to work on the railway from Chungkai to Krian Krai, separated from his men. He ended up in Nakom Nayuk, north-east of Bankok, from where he was liberated on 15 August 1945, and was brought home in the first ship from Rangoon. 'Finally demobbed April '46, still a Subaltern,' he wrote, 'No promotion in POW Camp.'[70]

Most British POWs survived the war, and most of these went on to enjoy their peacetime lives. Many resumed interrupted educations – John McGlashan, for instance, went to Oxford and, despite the privations of the latter part of the war, won a rugby blue. Noting the natural ability of the body to recuperate, he recalls that he weighed eight stone when released from prison but 'by the following December I was 11½ stone and fitter than I have ever been, or ever will be... of the 30 players in that Varsity match there were five other ex-POWs besides myself.'[71]

He later followed a traditional Fettesian path to join the Diplomatic Service, and was stationed in Baghdad, Tripoli and Madrid. The intrepid Tommy Macpherson also enjoyed sporting success, representing Britain at the World Student Olympics in Paris in 1947. William Gilchrist, the Airborne Lance-Corporal captured at Arnhem, ran Punch's Hotel in Doncaster, where it must be assumed he demonstrated greater hospitality than was shown to him in the war years. Robert Hardie stayed in the Far East as a General Practitioner and then returned to Scotland where he helped run the nascent National Health Service. His widow, writing an introduction to the published version of his diaries in 1983, said that she was often asked how captivity had affected him:

The impression that is left with me is that he was a very easy person to live with since for him nothing could ever be as bad as the experiences he had endured. He was tolerant, understanding and kind, but prepared to stick up for what he thought was right. There was also something special about his friends who had been fellow prisoners. They knew each other so well and knew what each had overcome and I think this led to lasting friendships... despite or because of his experiences in Siam he was able to enjoy life to the full.[72]

Nonetheless, whatever their peacetime careers some – especially those held by the Japanese – were scarred by their time in the camps. Chenevix-Trench's career as a headmaster was, it has been argued, blighted by it; because of what he endured, he refused to give the school's Remembrance Day sermon – 'I can't do it,' he told the chaplain, George Buchanan-Smith, 'because a colleague of mine was crucified.' Both physically and psychologically, 'the past returned with a vengeance, its bitter memories an eerie curse upon the present.'[73]

He died on the eve of his retirement from Fettes, aged barely sixty, his health wrecked by the after-effects of dysentery and malaria. Ian Graham's final camp was around a hundred miles from Nagasaki, and he witnessed the mushroom cloud from the second atomic bomb. 'It was never clear whether the Americans knew of the location of their camp,' his son says; 'three weeks later he saw the devastating effects of the blast when taken through Nagasaki.' He was one of the last POWs to be repatriated and spent three years recovering his health, which had, like Chenevix-Trench's, been wrecked by the camps. Many FEPOWs have never forgiven the Japanese; Chenevix-Trench's Senior British Officer at Hintok, Lt-Col Edward 'Weary' Dunlop, summarized this view in the 1940s when he described them as a 'Disgusting, deplorable, hateful troop of men-apes.'[74] John Humphries, seeing the ruins of Hiroshima, was convinced that the Japanese had deserved it. As late as the 60th anniversary of VJ-Day, there were still veterans who, as a spokesman put it, 'have an implacable hatred of anything Japanese.'[75]

The British government did not help matters; unlike the American and Commonwealth administrations, which were lavish in their generosity towards returned prisoners, it had continued to tax them despite their clearly having been non-resident for years, and actually docked a third of the back pay owed to captured officers to repay the Germans, Italians and Japanese for their hospitality (clearly deciding that this might be seen as bad taste, but unwilling to return it, the taxman then pocketed the money). Those used for forced labour received no recompense until a token payment from Tokyo in the 1950s, which was not accompanied by a substantial apology (Japan having reinvented itself as a victim in the war, owing to the nuclear attacks; this remains the official line in school textbooks). 'The British [prisoners],' notes Rollings with disgust, 'were well and truly shafted.'[76]

Those who died in Japanese captivity tended to be buried in inaccessible stretches of jungle and are commemorated on memorials, such as that in Singapore on which Corporal Mackenzie's name can be found. Not all were bitter; John Naiff, who taught science at the school after the war, had been cruelly tortured by the Japanese in Burma, bearing burn marks on his feet until his death in 1991, but retained a love for the Burmese and after his death his ashes were scattered there.[77]

Alastair Gunn's grave in Poznan Garrison Cemetery, with poppies from Fettes

Alastair Gunn now lies, along with 48 other victims of the cruelty and spite which followed the Great Escape, in the Old Garrison Cemetery in Pozna , on the southern edge of the old citadel. His ashes are buried in row 8D; beside him are a New Zealander, a Pole, an Australian, a Greek, a Canadian and an Englishman, symbols in death of the multinational nature of the escape (of the 50 airmen executed, 21 were British, 16 came from the Commonwealth and 13 were Europeans) and indeed of the struggle against fascism. Parts of his Spitfire can still be found at Bøverdalen in Norway. Another OF lies nearby; Lt John Ronald Cameron, Argyll and Sutherland Highlanders, Writer to the Signet and participant in the prisoners' Christmas dinner of 1940, died of peritonitis in captivity in 1941 and is buried in row 4D. Gunn's parents had his grave inscribed with the words 'May he rest in peace and awake with joy to the Resurrection.' Clifford Cooper survived the war and had a successful career in the RAF, serving with distinction as commander of 33 Squadron against the communists in Malaya before his retirement in 1963. His obituary recorded that he never forgot the friends who were murdered in 1944. Alastair Gunn and John Cameron have a lot of company in Poznań. Next to the Commonwealth War Graves Commission's section of the cemetery is a monumental Polish memorial and graveyard for the men of Poznań killed both by the Nazis and, after 1945, by the Communists – for the country Britain went to war to save ended up with an even longer tyranny than Hitler's. Beside that is the vast Soviet cemetery, guarded by four elderly cannon and with a huge obelisk surveying it all from the old ramparts. A message from Stalin remains at its foot, but the great red star which once glittered on the top was ripped off by the Poles (partly because it was rumoured to contain real rubies) as soon as the hated socialist system collapsed. Next to that are the white headstones of the Polish troops who fought in 1918-20 to liberate the region from the Prussians who had dominated it since the Partitions of the eighteenth century. Within the grounds of the old citadel is a war museum in which elderly tanks and aeroplanes rust peacefully, and where the photographs of hundreds of Poles executed there by the Gestapo in 1939-44 look down from the walls. The rest of the citadel is a park, where red squirrels dart about among the brutalist Soviet-era monuments. When the author went there to lay poppies, the quiet was disturbed by the shriek of a jet engine. Overhead was one of Poland's new American-designed F-16 fighters, symbol of the NATO membership which the people ardently hope and believe will prevent the horrors of their twentieth-century history from recurring. It seemed appropriate somehow.

NOTES

[1] Charles Rollings, *Prisoners of War* (London, Ebury, 2007) p. 8

[2] Letter to the author, 6 August 2008

[3] Nick Hammond, *Venture into Greece* (London, William Kimber, 1983) p. 156

[4] *Fettesian*, April 1917

[5] James, p. 497

[6] Torcuil Crichton, 'Fragments of a war history forgot', *Sunday Herald*, 7 November 2007

[7] *Fettesian*, July 1940

[8] Ibid., March 1943

[9] Ibid., July 1942

[10] Ibid., March 1943

[11] Ibid., July 1943

[12] Sir Tommy Macpherson & Richard Bath, *Behind Enemy Lines* (Edinburgh, Mainstream 2010) p. 78

[13] *Fettesian*, December 1941

[14] Quoted in Byrne, p. 475

[15] Letter to the author, 4 September 2008

[16] *Fettesian*, July 1944

[17] Letter to the author, 6 August 2008

[18] *Fettesian*, July 1944

[19] Obituary for Ian Graham, *OFNL*, July 2004

[20] *Fettesian*, June 1941

[21] Rollings, p. 272

[22] Macpherson & Bath, p. 95

[23] Sir Richard Sharp, *Jap-happy: a memoir of captivity*, Henderson Archive

[24] *Fettesian*, 1990

[25] Quoted in Philp, p. 64

[26] *Fettesian*, July 1944

[27] Pyman, p 43

[28] Quoted in Ryan, p. 362

[29] Ryan, pp. 424-6

[30] David Cassels Brown Obituary, *OFNL*, July 1999

[31] *Fettesian*, December 1944

[32] Ibid., April 1936

[33] Ibid., July 1936

[34] Heinz Knocke, *I Flew for the Führer* (London, Cassell ed., 2003), pp. 66-8

[35] Ibid.

[36] Mrs. Theodora Cooper, obituary for C.C.F. Cooper, D.F.C. in *OFNL*, 2005

[37] Quoted in *Fettesian*, July 1944

[38] Paul Brickhill, *The Great Escape* (London, Cassell ed., 2000), p. 117

[39] Quoted in *Fettesian*, July 1944

[40] Quoted in Tim Carroll, *The Great Escape from Stalag Luft III* (Edinburgh, Mainstream, 2004) p. 3

[41] Quoted in Rollings, p. 270

[42] Herzberg

[43] Rollings, p. 294

[44] Sir Richard Sharp

[45] *Fettesian*, March 1946

[46] Ibid.

[47] *Fettesian*, July 1944

[48] Hardie, p. 149

[49] Hardie, p. 34

[50] Hardie, p. 101

[51] Hardie, p. 141

[52] Peel, p. 54

[53] Hardie, p. 124

[54] Hardie, p. 131

[55] Ian Graham, Obituary, *OFNL*, January 2004

[56] Hardie, p. 109

[57] *Fettesian*, December 1942

[58] Letter to the author, 6 August 2008

[59] S.D. Rae, letter to the author, 17 September 2008

[60] Rollings, p. 137

[61] Ibid.

[62] Hardie, p. 167

[63] Frances B. Cogan, *Captured: The Japanese Internment of American Civilians in the Philippines, 1941-1945* (Atlanta, University of Georgia Press, 2000) p. 268

[64] Hardie, p. 176

[65] Quoted in Peel, p. 61

[66] *Fettesian*, December 1945

[67] Letter to the author, 4 September 2008

[68] Macpherson & Bath, p. 78

[69] Dr Hector Braine Obituary, *OFNL*, February 2002

[70] Email to the author, 4 August 2008

[71] Letter to the author, 4 September 2008

[72] Elspeth Hardie in Hardie, p. 12

[73] Peel, p. 66

[74] Quoted in Ferguson (2003), p. 345

[75] David Wilson, quoted in *Asian Political News*, 8 August 2005

[76] Rollings, p. 365

[77] *Fettesian*, 1991

Chapter Fourteen

'The Professional Assassin'

Fettes and Bondage

The most famous Old Fettesian

Sir John Simon, Iain Macleod and Edward Wadsworth are all very well, and indeed so is Tony Blair, but, when it comes to international recognition, the most famous Fettesian of all time does not actually exist. He is not, despite the present-day obsession with another quintessentially British fictional hero who attends a richly gargoyled and turreted Gothic educational institution, Harry Potter.[1]

Fettes' hero is a man who strikes fear into the heart of Britain's enemies wherever he goes, and can secretly execute Her Majesty's designs, despite every barman in the world knowing what he drinks and the fact that he somewhat pretentiously insists that the ingredients are shaken rather than stirred, Cdr James Bond, OF. One of the lighter items of Fettesiana is an enlarged photograph of the 'obituary' notice of special agent 007. It hangs in the Headmaster's study for all, especially visiting parents, to see that Bond finished his schooling at Fettes after leaving Eton. He would have attended Fettes just before, and possibly at the very beginning of, the Second World War – Fleming claimed he was born in 1924, and entered the armed forces in 1941. A variety of theories exist about the connection, but one which persists on the internet can be dismissed straight away. According to Wikipedia:

While Fleming never claimed there was any other source for the name of Bond than , an American ornithologist, there was a real life James Bond who did attend Fettes. He was a frogman with the Special Boat Service, much as the fictional character Bond has a naval background.[2]

There was no Old Fettesian called James Bond who could have attended the school in the years in question; the *Fettes College Register 1870-1953* jumps from Bonar to Booth.[3]

There was, however, at least one Fettesian frogman in a clandestine organisation, Ronnie Williamson of the Combined Operations Pilotage Parties which made covert surveys of the enemy coasts prior to the invasions of Italy and France. The task of the Coppists, as they were known, was to be dropped by submarine some miles off a hostile coast, paddle in silently in canoes under cover of darkness, establish the nature of tides, hazards, and even types of soil and sand, then return to base, weighed down by bags of shale samples, to prepare charts to help smooth the arrival of invading forces. Only around 250 men ever served in these tiny elite units, whose first mission's codename, Party Inhuman, says a lot about them. Williamson and his comrades needed to be superbly fit, completely familiar with a then-dazzling array of modern kit (infra-red homing gear, underwater writing tablets, beech gradient reels and much more), and observant to a preternatural degree. During the Sicily reconnaissance, in which Williamson participated, five out of the fifteen Coppists deployed were killed and five captured. Two are believed to have committed suicide to avoid capture. In the dark nights of January 1944, Williamson was deployed to France, a difficult job, as military historian William Seymour notes:

The nearer to the shore the worse the weather became; steep waves impelled by the ever-strengthening wind reared over gunwhale height, and several of the party including both soldiers succumbed to the paralysing effects of violent seasickness. Nothing was going right: rain poured down, visibility was poor, incompetent seamanship by raw borrowed crews resulted in one anchor and sounding pole being lost overboard, the two swimmers were in no shape for their ordeal, and Clogstoun-Willmott [the commander] seriously thought of heading back... only the great importance of the mission kept him going.[4]

'Seafaring, adventure and endurance would be in their blood,' noted Seymour of these extraordinary men. So secretive were the 'Copps' that their very existence was not acknowledged until an American journalist accidentally uncovered them in 1959; Ronnie Williamson's role was only made known to the majority of OFs at his funeral in 2002 – his entry in *Old Fettesians who Served* simply says 'RNVR', a very modest piece of understatement about someone who in fact 'volunteered for the commandos when little more than a boy.'[5]

Then again, Bond's fictitious *Who's Who* entry gives just as little away.

Writing in the *Sunday Times* on the question of who was the real James Bond, Sir Alexander Glen said:

When Bond was killed [in *You Only Live Twice*] *I wrote the obituary. Fleming knew I had been at Fettes and asked me to fill in that bit of Bond's life after the slight hiccup that had led him to leave Eton at rather an early age. We did this over lunch at the Savoy…*[6]

According to Glen's contribution, Bond went to Fettes after being expelled from Eton for 'some alleged trouble with one of the boys' maids.' Some of the basic skills for a life of international intrigue were honed at his father's old school:

Here the atmosphere was somewhat Calvinistic, and both academic and athletic standards were rigorous. Nevertheless, though inclined to be solitary by nature, he established some firm friendships among the traditionally famous athletic circles, at the school. By the time he left, at the early age of seventeen, he had twice fought for the school as a light-weight and had, in addition, founded the first serious judo class at a British public school.[7]

Judo only began at Fettes in 1966 (when the *Fettesian* noted that the school was finally taking up James Bond's suggestion), but boxing, as we have seen, was an important part of the inter-war toughening-up process. Fettes was also a good choice of school for a hero who would undoubtedly be classy, but not effete. A recent Bond biographer, Henry Chancellor, explains that 'Fettes, being Scottish, stood outside the snobbery associated with the major English public schools, yet it said just enough about wealth and a good sporty background to vouchsafe Bond's entry to the club.'[8]

Apart from Glen, Fettes has another direct and proven link with the government-issue Cold War killer in the shape of Sean Connery, who as a young man delivered milk to the school and enjoyed the sporting opportunities offered by the Fet-Lor Club before becoming an actor.[9]

However, given the persistent debates on the issue, it is worth identifying some of the names that have been bandied about Fettes as inspirations for Bond. Adventurers, special forces heroes and shadowy intelligence operatives have not been in short supply in the school's history.

The cricketing giant

A kind of proto-Bond amongst the ranks of Old Fettesians was a product of the Victorian school. Vernon 'Hex' Hesketh-Prichard, 'a golden-haired, grey-eyed giant of six feet four inches'[10], died just after the First World War, and a review of Eric Parker's biography appeared in the school magazine in 1924, listing some of this swashbuckling hero's adventures. When only a few years out of school, he had been the first white man to explore the interior of Haiti: 'he went absolutely alone, not knowing the language or customs, through an unknown land, the people of which bore the [undeserved] reputation of being murderous cannibals.'[11]

When warned about the difficulties, 'Hex' apparently announced that his height would do the trick of impressing the natives, and survived unscathed to write up his experiences in *Where Black rules White*. Other travels included an expedition, funded by the *Daily Express*, to Patagonia to find the giant sloth or mylodon, a wild-goose chase since, despite the excited speculations of some fin-de-siecle zoologists, this elephant-sized beast had been extinct for 12,500 years. Unsure of what weapons to take, a fellow-adventurer advised him to 'take a dozen cricket balls and bowl at the brute'. (Hesketh-Prichard was a skilled cricketer who played professionally for Hampshire, London County and the MCC; his early talent led to an offer to play for Scotland against South Africa, but Fettes had a match with Loretto and school loyalty came first.) Hesketh-Prichard did not find a giant sloth, though he admitted that it was always

Hesketh-Prichard (extreme right) as a member of the 1894 1st XI

possible that one might be hiding somewhere. This expedition apparently inspired his friend Sir Arthur Conan Doyle to write *The Lost World*. His most ambitious exploration was through 'trackless Labrador', which won him the praise of President Roosevelt. This was a particularly impressive feat since a previous explorer had died of starvation in the inhospitable, barren landscape.

During the First World War, his sniping school 'inflicted enormous casualties on the enemy' and he developed a series of Bond-like gadgets to aid in the detection of German snipers. One was a papier-mache head on a pole which could be made more lifelike, and attract more attention, by the addition of a cigarette, smoked by a man in the trench below through a rubber tube; when hit, this was lowered and the position of the German deduced from the angle between the bullet's entry and exit holes; he could thus be dealt with by a British sniper.

One of Hesketh-Prichard's ingenious contraptions for 'Boche-bagging'

On another occasion, he created an elaborate 'hide' by reproducing a corpse:

> ...a huge dead, yellow-bearded Prussian lay, on a point of vantage, staring at the sky. He was photographed and copied, and from the hollow shell, clothed in his uniform, another observer fulfilled his duty. A dead horse likewise was replaced and used.

Hesketh-Prichard became known as 'the Professional Assassin'; no less an authority than Kipling wrote to congratulate him on his book *Sniping in France*, which the poet said 'beats most novels and detective tales.'[12]

An enterprising editor of the *Fettesian*, possibly Selwyn Lloyd, came up with the wheeze of getting another retired officer to replace the editorial (writing which was a permanent chore) or otherwise pad out an issue with a detailed book review, an exercise repeated when the Major died in 1922. This noted several lessons of the war, such as the way in which the users of each technological innovation in turn – the Lewis gunners, the bombers and so on – all imagined that they alone had the key to success. But it was the snipers who quietly honed their skills, and Hesketh-Prichard's book had a variety of ideas for how these might be incorporated into the post-war training of patriotic British boys.[13]

He also wrote fiction prolifically, creating a psychic detective called Flaxman Low, a Hispanic Robin Hood, Don Q. (who later appeared in a Douglas Fairbanks Zorro film) and a crime-fighting Canadian backwoodsman, November Joe. A keen naturalist, he successfully fought against seal-clubbing and the use of exotic bird-feathers in women's hats. One of Hex's sons, Michael, attended Fettes, and became an Intelligence officer, but it was the younger, Alfgar, an Old Etonian, who proved the biggest chip off the old block. Taught how to bowl by his father, he passed these cricketing skills on to Czech special agents who used them to attack Reinhard Heydrich, the Nazi Reichsprotektor of Bohemia, with grenades. The Hesketh-Prichard mentality was summed up in his conclusion to his memoir and manual, *Sniping in France*:

> When we took German prisoners, they were very often in a state of pitiable fright, for they had been absolutely fed by their officers with stories of the most circumstantial nature of the habitual brutality of the British to their prisoners; and yet it was a fine sight to see a German prisoner, obviously afraid to his very bones, and yet absolutely determined to give away nothing. One really laboured under an almost incontrollable impulse to go and shake such a man by the hand. After

all, courage of the lonely sort is surely the most glorious thing that we can hope to witness, and whether it is displayed upon our side or upon the other, one feels the better for having witnessed it.[14]

To the author's mind, 'Hex' is one of the towering figures of the age, but, although he was a friend of John Buchan (who helped support the sniping school)[15] and served with Sir Arthur Conan Doyle's son, there is no evidence that Ian Fleming knew of him.

The Plotter

Fleming certainly did know Robert Bruce Lockhart, who was in Russia for most of the revolutionary period. Given his career, it is perhaps ironic that Lockhart's football team, Morozovtsi/OKS Moscow, renamed Dynamo Moscow in 1923, was taken over by the secret police after the Bolshevik Revolution and has been associated with them up to the present day. As a diplomat in Moscow during the First World War, he witnessed at first hand the collapse of the Tsarist regime in February 1917, which he blamed on a 'system of unparalleled inefficiency and corruption' with which the people became profoundly fed up. Although he was busily fighting the British corner, trying to keep the new Russian republic fighting alongside Britain, Bruce Lockhart was sent home after 'I had made myself talked about' by becoming involved with a lady who was not his wife – not his first indiscretion with the opposite sex and an aspect of his character which some have argued makes him a possible candidate for a proto-Bond.

Whilst on his enforced leave, Lockhart discovered that Lenin had seized power in the October Revolution, displacing the pro-western liberals of the Provisional Government. Although he had spent most of his time with the bourgeoisie, he was aware of the Russian far left and got to know it much better; it consisted, he later wrote, of 'men who worked eighteen hours a day and who were obviously inspired by the same spirit of self-sacrifice and abnegation of worldly pleasure which animated the Puritans and the early Jesuits.' Such a force, in the circumstances, he recognised as both powerful and attractive; accordingly, he found the blimpish bigotry of the London politicians and generals difficult to take. Most people in London seemed to believe, no matter what Lockhart told them, that 'the Lenin régime could not last more than a few weeks' or that Lenin and Trotsky were German staff officers in disguise or at least servile agents of German policy.' In January 1918 he was sent back to Russia on the not unreasonable grounds that he knew better than most what was going on there. His 'Great Adventure', as he called it, was to try to develop a working relationship with a new regime which had already signalled its character by acts of brutality. Whilst making his way to Russia through Scandinavia, Bruce Lockhart learned that two old friends, liberal ex-ministers of the brief Kerensky government, had been murdered in their beds. This was an ominous warning of the kind of treatment he might expect if things went badly. The Bolsheviks were already negotiating with the Germans at Brest-Litovsk, which Lockhart had predicted but which the Allies feared because it would release more troops for the Kaiser to use in Flanders. However, 'while German militarism and British capitalism were equally hateful to the Bolsheviks, German militarism was for the moment the greater danger' and Bruce Lockhart hoped to persuade Lenin that London's support could be useful. There was still confusion as to what exactly was going on and indeed what exactly the great powers actually wanted. This was illustrated for Lockhart one evening in Moscow, when Raymond Robins, the head of the American Red Cross Mission, described Trotsky as 'the greatest Jew since Christ', denounced Allied hopes in the Russian bourgeoisie, then read John McCrae's poem 'In Flanders Fields' and announced that Germany had to be defeated. Accusation and counter-accusation, often based on forged documents, flew around in an atmosphere of paranoia. Lockhart was, to some extent, able to soothe Trotsky by appealing to his vanity, but Lenin was a different matter; with his 'boundless self-confidence and conscious superiority… Lenin was impersonal and almost inhuman.' The Bolshevik leader was willing to use Allied support against the Germans, but did not trust the Allies to provide it, given their 'reactionary' tendencies. The severity of Germany's peace terms caused outrage, and the Germans were now pressing heavily on the Allies in France, but Bruce Lockhart, still on reasonable terms with the Bolsheviks, found that his political masters (and those of the other Western agents) were keen to work with assorted 'White' generals rather than the actual Russian government. Some military co-operation was achieved, but rival British agents provided other perspectives and repeated rumours which alarmed London (the Bolsheviks supposedly having armed thousands of German prisoners, for instance). 'In this game of protest and counter-protest' he wrote ruefully, 'I was a sadly battered shuttlecock between the battledores of the two Governments.' In London, right-wing MPs were furious that 'the British Government maintained an official representative with a government of cut-throats who boasted of their determination to destroy civilisation' whilst the left 'charged the British Government with the folly of not maintaining an accredited representative in Moscow in order to protect British interests and to assist the Bolsheviks in their struggle with German militarism'.

The chief joy in his confused life was his mistress, the glamorous Baroness Moura Budberg. Relations with the Bolsheviks steadily worsened and the calls by British military figures – some based in Northern Russia officially to help the new regime – for 'intervention' grew louder, especially once the Czech Legion, which was directly linked to France, started fighting its way across the country. When the British began landing troops at Archangel, Lockhart, who had maintained contact with his old bourgeois friends, was immediately under suspicion, and rumours began to circulate that he was plotting a counter-revolution with the aid of his associate Sidney Reilly, who had been trying to do a deal with the Latvian riflemen who formed a kind of Bolshevik Praetorian Guard. Fanny Kaplan's assassination attempt on Lenin was blamed on them, and Lockhart was arrested by the secret police. He destroyed possibly incriminating evidence by using his diary as lavatory paper, but his position was fragile, and he was eventually released to discover that Cromie, a British diplomat in Petrograd, had been killed when the Bolsheviks stormed the embassy, and the press was carrying lurid details of a 'Lockhart Plot' to murder Lenin and Trotsky, shrieking for vengeance. Lockhart went back to the Lubianka to plead for Moura Budberg's release and was rearrested. From his cell he saw people being taken out for execution as the Bolsheviks applied the 'red terror' to actual, potential or imagined enemies. His transfer to the Kremlin alarmed him even more, since no previous prisoner had left it alive, but he did at least have the relief of knowing that Moura had been released (there are various theories as to why: one is that she offered certain favours to the chief guard, another that she denied all knowledge of our hero's political activities, allegedly saying 'All I can talk about is Lockhart's sexual prowess. I don't know anything else.'[16]) His guards believed that he was soon to be shot, but he was eventually exchanged for Litvinov, who had been arrested in London. Before his release, Jakob Peters, the senior secret police official who had been his gaoler, said to Lockhart that since capitalism was doomed anyway, he might as well stay in Russia, where the Party could find plenty for him to do. Peters himself, described by Moura as being like Count Dracula, would be a victim of the terror system he created, executed by Stalin in 1938.

Part of the Kremlin, where Robert Bruce Lockhart was imprisoned

Lockhart returned to Britain just as news of the final collapse of the Central Powers came through. Lockhart insisted that he was playing a purely diplomatic role in Russia, His memoir's, and his, title, of *British Agent* had no overtones of espionage (a frankly disingenuous notion since he must have been aware that the thousands of readers who made it an instant bestseller can hardly have been aware of the difference); when he witnessed the Communist purge of the Anarchists in April 1918 he did so at the invitation of Dzerzhinsky, the head of the secret police. His memoirs implied that if anyone was spying and subverting the revolution, it was Reilly rather than himself: the 'Ace of Spies' had decided to use his imagination and organize a coup without any instructions from the official British representative. In 1934, Hollywood made a spy film starring Leslie Howard and Kay Francis, *British Agent*, loosely based on the story of Moura and Lockhart; although a 'blockbuster' in its day, Lockhart was deeply embarrassed by the liberties it took with history, for instance, portraying 'his' character haranguing the Prime Minister.

During the Second World War he was Director General of the Political Warfare Executive, which produced propaganda to be broadcast to or dropped on continental Europe. Although 'Bomber' Harris allegedly believed that leaflets only solved the enemy's toilet paper problem, the evidence suggests that British propaganda was increasingly absorbed (mentally) by the Germans as the war turned against them. George

Orwell is supposed to have used the propaganda broadcasting system as the model for his Ministry of Truth in *1984*. When the PWE disbanded in Bush House on 31 August 1945, it took Sir Robert, as he now was, an hour and a half to shake hands with the 600 staff who came to bid him farewell. Lockhart has enjoyed some posthumous notoriety because of his Bond connections. When Garry O'Connor was transferred from Hibernian to Lokomotiv Moscow a century after Lockhart played for Morozov, the Scottish media made a great deal of the connection. *Ace of Spies*, written by Lockhart's son Robin, which focused primarily on Reilly, was turned into a mini-series in 1983 in which the Robert Bruce Lockhart character was played by the great Scots actor Ian Charleson, best known for his role as Eric Liddell in *Chariots of Fire*. The silver cigar-box which Reilly gave to Lockhart as a memento of their escapades, along with some of his medals, can be seen today in the International Spy Museum in Washington, DC. Moura subsequently formed attachments to Maxim Gorky and H.G. Wells, and lived in Estonia before fleeing to Britain when it was taken over by the Soviets; she worked as a scriptwriter and occasionally advised MI5, but is today most famous as Mr Nick Clegg's great-great-aunt. Apparently she told the future Deputy Prime Minister, when he was a small child, that he mumbled too much.[17]

The Clegg connection revived the idea of Bruce Lockhart as a model for Bond (for instance, in the *Guardian*[18]) and as this book went to press, Lockhart was being accused by Professor Robert Service of having been committed (despite his evasions in *British Agent*) to overthrowing Lenin. Professor Service, a noted expert on Russian history, argued that certain documents suggest that Reilly was not, in fact, acting off his own bat but that he and Lockhart, presumably under orders from London, really were trying to overthrow communism. With Reilly dead, Lockhart, and to an even greater extent their masters, denied this, because Britain 'has a policy for its intelligence services that is openly averse to subverting foreign governments or assassinating foreign political leaders... the British have always been clean.'[19] This, as Service argues and Lockhart, Reilly and Bond surely knew, was not the case.

One Old Fettesian did succumb to Soviet blandishments; James MacGibbon, the engaging left-wing publisher, apparently confessed on his deathbed in 2000 to having passed military secrets to the Soviets during the Second World War.[20] Like all communists, he was a strong supporter of the creation of a second front in Western Europe to take pressure of the USSR, and believed that Churchill was not being completely frank with Stalin. Accordingly, he used his post in the War Office to get information about German troop movements and send it to Moscow. The rather gentlemanly vetting procedures of British intelligence at the time, which allowed even big fish like Kim Philby to slip through the net, ensured that he got away with it. Conservative writer David Pryce-Jones blogged that the 'treachery' of this 'standard fashionable lefty' was 'a failure of morals and intellect affecting a significant part of the elite.'[21]

To be fair, however, MacGibbon did not (unlike Philby) continue to spy for the Russians when the war ended. His son wrote in the *London Review of Books* that helping an ally who was bearing the brunt of the war effort was hardly a major crime, and in any case MacGibbon had already disobeyed the Party line by joining the army before Barbarossa (good communists believing, against all the evidence, that there was nothing to choose between Hitler and Churchill).[22]

Mountain Glen

Sir Alexander 'Sandy' Glen has been claimed as another Bond candidate. He got started on his career whilst one of Harry Pyatt's bright lads in Carrington House at Fettes in the 1920s:

Short-sighted as I was, rugger was of limited appeal, as I tended to find myself playing for the other side. But there was an ambition which surpassed everything else, to own a .32 Browning automatic pistol.

If you wait in life, opportunity does come, retribution too. Opportunity came with an invitation from the kindly Mr Beamish to join him and three others in his bull-nosed Morris Cowley to Albania in summer 1927. 'Yes, please, Sir,' and I was away up town, top hat, morning coat, umbrella de rigeur, to Martin's the gunsmith.

Mr Martin, in frock coat, received me. 'This will do you nicely, Mr Glen. But we will require a firearms certificate and I will accompany you to the Police.' The Police seemed most accommodating; they also addressed me as Mr.

Hunkydory, it seemed. Two weeks later, the Loretto match it was, two large constables appeared by the Pavilion. They wished to speak to Master Glen and his Housemaster. Henry Pyatt was found, in his charming way: 'Oh yes, I am sure Glen told me all about this, can't quite recall when, but I am sure he did, nice, dependable boy.'

Still seemed OK until at the ominous hour of 9 pm I was summoned to Henry Pyatt's study. 'I quite understand, Glen; you want to shoot Beamish.'

'No, Sir, certainly not, Sir.'

'Not shoot Mr Beamish? Your judgment must be very faulty. I am going to beat you for bad judgment,' and he did. No pistol, no Albania and thereafter always a curious look from Beamish, who seemed to avoid me.[23]

After leaving Fettes, Glen several Oxford University Arctic Expeditions, but is best known for an unofficial trip he made to Spitsbergen in August 1934, on which he was accompanied by Evelyn Waugh. Glen had suggested the trip to Hugh Lygon, one of the aristocrats Waugh so assiduously worshipped, and the author asked to come too 'on what he imagined would be high jinks in the snow.'[24]

An encounter with an unborn whale, lying on the quayside at Tromsø by its 'semi-existing' mother, which was being flensed by Norwegian sailors, was a rather shocking start to the trip, but the discovery of a hitherto unknown nesting-place of the ivory gull was more pleasing. They spent three days in a rickety sealing boat in rough seas, drinking a local liquor called, ominously, 60%, before arriving at Spitzbergen to trudge about the grey perpetual daylight of the tundra pulling a sledge (they had, incorrectly as it turned out, been advised that dogs were of little use on the island). Waugh described it to Tom Driberg as 'a fiasco very narrowly retrieved from disaster.' Glen, who wrote that Waugh 'proved himself an irrefutable prophet by constantly forecasting the worst,' did not see it in that light, though he did admit that it was quite heavy going. Waugh tried to prove his superiority by making 'sophisticated' conversation about a social world Glen could not have known, but the younger man simply roared with appreciative laughter.[25]

Glen himself noted that the 'conversation ran mainly on food and people' and that Waugh decided his next holiday would be in the Dordogne, accompanied by a valet-chauffeur. When Waugh fell into a fast-flowing river, he saw this as proof of Glen's inadequacies, shouting 'If I hadn't joined the Church of Rome, I could never have survived your appalling incompetence.' From Glen's point of view, the 'great disaster' of the river incident (which was simple bad luck) was that they had lost their hats. This exposed them to the attacks of terns, which were much more dangerous than polar bears and dived to peck their heads and every opportunity. Ration bowls worn as helmets were more trouble than they were worth, as the pinging seemed only to encourage other birds to join the attack. Waugh provided more amusement for Glen by his refusal to look on skis 'as anything but despicable athletic implements'[26] but in general the trip was a success.

In 1935-6 Glen led a ten-man team to North-East Land in the Arctic, which carried out a great deal of scientific research; their work on how radio waves were affected by atmospheric layers ionised by ultraviolet sunrays at high latitudes was later used in the development of radar. Glen loved these wild and inhospitable places, and his leadership and expertise ensured that one Polar historian describes this as 'one of the most successful expeditions of the interwar period.'[27]

Unlike most undergraduate expeditions of this kind, the Glen expedition wintered in the Arctic; they set off from Norway in July 1935 and did return until August the following year, a remarkable feat of endurance which included bear attacks, blizzards and accidents on the sea ice. Glen spent four months manning Northern Station, an exposed site on top of an ice dome from which he conducted glaciological and meteorological surveys, as well as analysing the movements of pack ice. It was, he said later, possible to enjoy below the ice comfort comparable to Henley in June even if it was minus forty outside, though returning to the real world was disconcerting. Young men whose lives were focused on tasks such as making an oven out of moraine boulders were required to address 'complicating factors as politics, international disputes, fascism, assassinations.'[28]

However, Glen's work in the Arctic was not as inconsequential as all that. His account of the expeditions, written before the war, could not include their sequel, which he put into his last book, published in his retirement. Part of his research in the Arctic was intended to gather data of use to the development of radar, and when Glen casually mentioned to his supervisor, Professor Appleton, that their camp had been visited by two Germans who wanted to see their maps, he was taken to see the Assistant Director of Naval Intelligence.'[29]

'With visions of a life in the tower of London', Glen made his first acquaintance with what is now called the 'intelligence community'. When war came he was transferred from his meteorological duties with the RNVR by Admiral Godfrey of Naval Intelligence to act as Assistant Naval Attaché in Belgrade.

'Thank you, sir,' said Glen, racking his brains for some recognition of Balkan geography, 'I am very interested in... mm... Rumania, sir!'

'Well, that ought to stand you in good stead in Yugoslavia,' replied the Admiral, through whom Glen got to know Ian Fleming. In 1940, he was inserted into the British Embassy in Belgrade. The newly arrived young Scot was initially unaware of the ethnic complexities beneath the surface of society, and touched by the high opinion the people had for what was, since the fall of France, the most important ally for pro-western elements in the Balkans. Glen was particularly moved by 'the continuing regard for all that the Scots and English nursing missions had done in the 1917 typhus epidemic'[30] but alarmed to find that the British intelligence files on the Danube basin mostly dated to the years immediately after the First World War. Local affection for the British was based on more than nostalgia; the Serbs feared both Italian and Hungarian territorial designs on their country, especially since many Croats had turned towards fascism and might act as a fifth column. British policy in Yugoslavia in 1940 was twofold: to help and maintain Yugoslav neutrality and to encourage Yugoslavia against sliding into any association with the Axis powers' whilst covertly undertaking covert operations against the Axis' on Yugoslav territory. Much the same policy was being followed in oil-rich Romania. Yugoslavia 'opened horizons of life and emotion very different from anything I had ever known before' in more ways than one. Glen 'fell violently in love with a Yugoslav girl' and his description of her in his memoirs is that of a Bond heroine:

Tall, very Slavonic and with Byzantine looks, Zorica looked the immaculate product of a Paris salon. This hid a willingness to embark on the most hazardous enterprise with a total disregard of danger or hardship. With command of almost every European language, she also had the gift of being at home immediately with those of any and every background or nationality.[31]

Sir Sandy was rather different from the ruthless womaniser of Fleming's imagination, and did not look the part either. His friend Sir Fitzroy Maclean, doyen of the Balkans adventurers, said of him that 'nothing could have been more deceptive than his mild, even slightly owlish appearance, as he peered at you benignly from behind a large pair of round spectacles.'[32]

The future Lady Zorica Glen's first comment on seeing him was, apparently, 'Who is that little Englishman with the unpressed trousers?'[33]

'Englishman, indeed!' snorted the man in question, who subsequently enjoyed ribbing her about her ancestors' involvement in the bloodier aspects of Serb politics. Sir Sandy, in his genial and unassuming memoirs, described himself as 'thoroughly cowardly'[34] and offered a colleague as the real role model for Bond: 'Michael Mason's fit was good enough, better than any other.'[35]

Mason, known at the time as David Field, was sabotaging German supplies coming from neighbouring Romania, and rumours abounded in Belgrade 'of a Superman character who, in a schoolboy way, was quite inspiring.' Once he threw two German agents off a speeding train in the middle of the night, and was subsequently telephoned by their 'truculent' boss who told him in detail how he would be tortured to death. When he blew up a German boat and three survivors staggered ashore; he shot one, clubbed another to death with his pistol, and strangled the third.[36] Sadly for Fettes, Mason was an Old Etonian.

Glen was highly impressed when, after Prince Paul reluctantly signed Yugoslavia up to a formal alliance with Germany and Italy, pro-British officers mounted a coup in March 1941; it was 'foolhardy' in its blatant disregard of reality, but also brave, both of which he saw as quintessentially Serb characteristics. It brought upon Yugoslavia *Unternehmen Strafgericht* – Codename Punishment, the Führer's aptly-named response to those who defied him. Belgrade was bombed and Axis troops poured into the country. Their explosives hidden in a swimming-pool, Sandy and Zorica Glen escaped Belgrade taking with them several prominent Serbs and British diplomat Hugh Seton-Watson, who insisted, despite the German carpet-bombing, on making sure he had his best trousers and a copy of *War and Peace*. Attempting to get to the coast in a legation Packard, they skidded in the mountains near Sarajevo and found themselves perched on a cliff-edge. Glen found a Bosnian peasant with an ox and asked for help. 'How strange,' said the peasant in English, 'I have been living in Manchester and have just come home.'

It was on this journey that Glen became fully aware of just how vicious the local hatreds were when he saw Croatian soldiers cut the throats of Serb officers. At the coast, the strange rules of diplomatic immunity were brought into play, helped by the fact that this area was occupied by more easy-going Italians who allowed a British submarine and flying-boat to take away the highest-profile refugees. Glen, Zorica and around a hundred others were evacuated by the Italians to Spain.

Back in London, Glen's tolerance for cold weather and Polar knowledge was put to His Majesty's Service with a posting to the Arctic island of Spitzbergen. Seen as strategically vital both for its mineral deposits and as a vantage point for the Arctic Convoys, Spitzbergen would also be a piece of moral authority for the Norwegian government-in-exile if it could be recaptured. In 1941, he made a detailed reconnaissance of the island which did not achieve a great deal, and another in 1942 which was intended to secure it for the Allies. The man who told him about this mission was Ian Fleming, the Personal Assistant to the Director of Naval Intelligence; Glen had come to appreciate 'the remarkable skill with which he combined his responsibilities to DNI whilst keeping a light but encouraging rein over the more unorthodox members of the Division.'[37]

Unfortunately, the Germans got wind of their presence and four Focke-Wulfs came roaring out of the midnight sun just as the party landed. Both of the ships were sunk, killing 17 of the 70 men on the expedition, and all of the food was lost. Fortunately, Glen remembered where there were food stores, including a farmful of frozen pigs, Russian tea and German brandy. They cannibalised machine-guns from an immobile Junkers 88 and used them to ward off German attacks for several weeks whilst supplies came in by flying-boat. After about a month, several Royal Navy destroyers arrived, and Spitzbergen had been secured, both against possible use by the Germans as an airfield from which to attack the Arctic convoys and as a defiant symbol of Norwegian independence.

Having left the Balkans in a hurry in 1941 during Operation Punishment, Glen returned in 1943. He was initially inserted by sea into Albania, where he spent some time based in a cave spying on enemy installations in the company of Anthony Quayle, a retinue of Italian prisoners, and thousands of fleas and scorpions. When the Italians changed sides, Glen and other British officers liaising with the partisans would arrive at their bases and politely commandeer weapons and supplies; unfortunately, the Germans stepped in, granted Albania independence, and thus guaranteed that the Albanians would be too busy quarrelling with one another to threaten them. Glen's real interest was in going back to Yugoslavia, which had been carved up between the Axis powers and a viciously sectarian Croat regime in Zagreb, but which he believed would always resist occupation. The British hoped to co-ordinate the mining of the Danube, liaise with the resistance, and ultimately make contact with the advancing Soviets. In contrast to the great success of the Special Operations Executive in the west, SOE Cairo were less efficient, and were none too happy about this interloper from Naval Intelligence on their turf. Weeks of telegraphic exchanges followed, but eventually, on 28 June 1944, Glen and a radio operator, Sergeant

Turner, were dropped into Yugoslavia from a Polish Halifax, which would soon be shot down whilst attempting to relieve the Warsaw Uprising. The warm embraces of the partisans, and shots of raki, were 'a welcome far preferable to the chilly customs today at Heathrow or Gatwick and, of course, no Customs or Immigration!' After the war, when on the board of BEA, Glen compared the 'slight technical delays' of airlines with the slick promptness of the RAF's delivery service. The agents were taken to a warm and comfortable, indeed chintzy, cottage, given proper beds and fed well, enjoying the protection of the male and female partisans. (Another OF in Yugoslavia, David Whyte of the Raiding Support Regiment, was very impressed by this aspect of Balkan warfare. 'The girls who were freedom fighters in Yugoslavia were very beautiful,' he recalled, 'When one of my friends had his way with one of them, he told me that he had given her a bar of soap and a hand grenade!'[38]) Glen realised that such comfort and good relationships meant that he was 'incredibly lucky'. When, through accident, enemy action or, most frequently, political misunderstanding, anything went wrong, comfort was the first casualty. When one of Glen's colleagues incurred the wrath of the Cetnik leader Mihailovic, he was forced to spend a lonely, freezing winter in the mountains, living on nettle soup. The murderous faction-fighting of the region was one of the biggest problems for the Allies; they had initially supported Mihailovic's Cetniks, who had been the first resistance movement, but, as he compromised his position following German reprisals, western support gradually moved towards Tito's communist partisans, despite the fact that these had not taken part in the conflict until after Operation Barbarossa. As well as these major resistance groups, and the occupation armies they were fighting against, there were Serb collaborators (Ljotic and Nedic auxiliaries), ethnic Germans (organised into SA units), Hungarians and Italians, Albanians in Italian uniforms, Bosnians and Croats in the German uniform of the 13th Mountain Division, and, the worst of all in Glen's estimation, the vicious, genocidal Ustachi, Croatian fascists dedicated to 'purifying' the region by killing non-Catholics, especially Serbs. 'No one knows how many were murdered,' Glen wrote later, 'It might have been 250,000; it could well have been 750,000.'[39]

He believed that it was as much the actions of the Ustache as the Italo-German invasion that triggered the serious upsurge in communist resistance in the autumn of 1941; young Serbian men and women, with no homes or families to return to, joined the partisans along with Croats,

Slovenes and Bosnian Muslims who were sickened by the excesses. Glen also noted that 'it is significant how much importance the Party placed in a young person's ability to stand up to torture' and considered the communists 'almost Calvinistic' in their outlook.

The partisans could be brutal too; Djilas, who Glen admired, wrote in his war memoirs that his unit massacred an entire Italian regiment after they surrendered, and threw their bodies into the river. Djilas and the other partisan officers shared a 'malicious joy at the thought of Italian officers on the bridges and embankments of Mostar stricken with horror at the sight of the Nerveta choked with the corpses of their soldiers.'[40]

Despite the savage background, Glen found life with the partisans 'surprisingly relaxed' during the summer months, with little sign of the enemy in any of his guises. After a pig ate his glasses, Glen stumbled about for several days until a replacement pair arrived, dropped by parachute from a bomber − much to the disgust of the partisans, who had been hoping for something more exciting. The first contact with the Russians raised more problems. One partisan complained to Glen that the Soviets did not appreciate their efforts − 'they treat us like dogs… they're worse than you are!' whilst a Russian officer said that rather than work with these 'tin-pot amateurs' he would prefer to be in combat.[41]

When he first met a Russian, however, Glen embraced him, tears streaming down cheeks, overwhelmed at the thought that, for the first time, the Eastern and Western fronts had met up. He was fortunate, since he and the partisans he was with had almost run the Russians over in a stolen motorbike combination. Glen admired the Soviets' toughness, efficiency and, in the case of two female secret police officers, beauty ('if it was going to be the Lubianka, then I wouldn't mind if it was they who took me there!'). A Soviet general, seeing the British party off to Sofia, plied them with wine and vodka for several hours. When the vodka ran out, he ordered his aides to bring a substitute in the form of petrol, which was promptly drunk. The aides promptly keeled over, much to the general's embarrassment. He apologised and begged Glen not to judge the Red Army by these mere wartime soldiers − 'not professionals like you or me.' On another occasion, when the RAF accidentally killed a Russian general, Glen was told by furious commanders that he was required to attend the funeral, marching behind the coffin for five miles to the outer Sofia railhead. A more chilling insight into the Soviet mentality came in a discussion with a secret police colonel about the dangers in exposing their troops to the capitalist quality of life visible in the countries Russia was liberating.

'Certainly there are dangers,' he said, 'and we are prepared for them. There are several categories. Most of the men will simply pass through, loot, rape, enjoy and forget. Then there are those who may be influenced; they will go to re-educational units, two, three or five years should suffice. Then the third category, those who draw conclusions. They will not see the Soviet Union again! [42]

Glen believed that communist control of Yugoslavia was inevitable after 1944, though he was pleased to see that after the war Tito pursued a more independent line and, as dictatorships went, was 'benevolent in some respects'. Glen went on to have a varied career in shipping, travel and tourism, in which his experiences sometimes came in handy. When one of his employees was arrested for currency smuggling in Greece in the early seventies, Glen, who had arrived as a character witness, told the court that he was once guilty of smuggling into Greece. After an ominous pause, the judge asked him to explain. 'Machine guns and ammunition into Crete in 1942' Glen replied, and was immediately mobbed by effusive security policemen, one of whom whispered that he still had a Bren gun. The employee went free. [43]

Today, the Glens are remembered at Fettes for the comprehensive library in the art department which they left to the school.

Major Eggs

Elsewhere in the Balkans, more Old Fettesians were busy creating havoc for the fascist occupiers. Nick Hammond, a Cambridge don whose studies in Greek history had led him to embark on long walking tours and archaeological of the region before the war, was being put to good use by the War Office. His fluent Greek and smattering of Albanian provided ready-made expertise; he was sent by the Special Operations Executive to Athens in March 1941 to train Greeks to resist a future fascist occupying force. As in Yugoslavia and Romania, the situation was complicated by the fact that part of the ruling class was pro-German, whilst the communists, who he recognised as 'the tougher characters', were standing aloof from what they saw as an imperialist war between rival capitalists. Unfortunately, Britain's natural allies, the liberal Venizelists, were few in number, but Hitler's decision to invade the Balkans (from which he had hitherto stood aloof, allowing Mussolini a free hand which the latter dealt spectacularly badly) drew more potential resisters to the cause. The Germans' superior tactics outflanked the Greeks on the Albanian front, where they had held off the Italians with ease, and the Wehrmacht advanced on Athens, forcing Hammond to stash his equipment just as Glen had done in Yugoslavia and join the British retreat to Crete and then Egypt. Going via Cairo to Haifa, he trained groups of Greeks and Jews (including Moshe Dayan) in the use of explosives (he was known to the Greeks as Captain Vamvakopyrites, Guncotton), before being parachuted back into Greece in February 1943 to lead and co-ordinate guerrilla activities. Like Glen's agents in Yugoslavia, these included the use of limpet mines and the destruction of any facilities which might be of use to the Italians or Germans.

Once he had collected his Greek commandos, he made contact with ELAS, the left-wing Andartes (resistance fighters), 'dim, ragged figures' who were fascinated by the new arrivals with their new kit and, in Hammond's case, faceful of frozen blood and deep scratches. As one said later, it was a queer-looking Englishman who had dropped to them from Heaven. The living conditions in Greece were rather less luxurious than that which Glen had arrived to – tents in the frozen mountains and a monotonous diet on lentils or beans. Where accommodation was available in huts, they were often infested with lice or fleas. However, the Greeks shared with the Serbs a brutal clarity of vision regarding their occupiers. One 'thin, gentle-looking man of wide interests' had joined the Andartes after seeing children starving in the streets as a result of the Axis invasion, and blamed both the occupiers and Greek collaborationists; he was the group's executioner, and took great pride in beheading traitors. Although 'clearly unbalanced in this one respect' he was a cultured man, and good company. The other fighters were mostly local peasants whose motives were mixed: 'partly patriotism, part love of adventure, part vainglory as would-be heroes; and it was also a way of being fed.' Their activities in Thessaly were, partly because of their limited equipment and numbers, largely limited to 'pin-pricking Italian morale'. As in Yugoslavia, a bigger game was afoot; it soon became apparent that ELAS, although nominally inclusive, were communist in their sympathies (Yanni, one of Hammond's Athenian colleagues, was able to identify the jargon). This raised a problem; whilst the British and the Greek government-in-exile regarded the struggle as a continuation of the invasion begun by Italy in 1940 and accelerated by Germany in 1941, ELAS, and their possible masters in Moscow, might have other ideas:

In those days we did not think of Russia as a gallant ally; for the memory of her pact with Germany, her bombing of Helsinki and her partitioning of Poland and the Baltic states was too vivid in our minds. The Spanish Civil War, too, had taught us the lesson that any communist party in touch with Moscow was out to seize power and then conform with Russia's policy. The days when the Russian system of communism had been regarded as a paradise of egalitarian liberty had passed along since... In short ELAS could not serve two masters. If its loyalty was to Russia, the sooner we became aware of it the better.[44]

ELAS' continued attempts to get as much money as possible to fund questionable activities, their ruthless treatment of prisoners – they executed a 'harmless' German engineer and his wife when it became inconvenient to keep them alive – and their sectarian attitude towards other resistance groups cast a shadow over Hammond's attempts to do something useful, such as derailing trains. ELAS, for their part, were disconcerted that the British 'Major Eggs' (from Hammond's Fettes nickname) was not a dapper figure in full dress uniform but a scruffy figure who dressed (and smelled) like a peasant and, more annoyingly, spoke demotic Greek and insisted that he wanted to work with any resistance organisations.[45]

Hammond attempted to create village committees independent of ELAS, made up of those who had held authority before the invasion – the headman, the priest and the schoolmaster – in order to ensure that the British aid money and medical supplies were going to the right people. ELAS appointed their own village 'responsible', often the roughest inhabitant, whose job it was to get supplies by whatever means of persuasion he felt most appropriate. Hammond attempted to look on the bright side, and hoped that as the organisation expanded, the real communist element – always a minority – would be diluted. Ethnic tensions were also a problem; the Italians told the Bulgarian-speakers that the Greeks, being nationalists, would burn down their villages, and encouraged them to take up arms in Komitaj bands. Although Hammond persuaded some of them that it was the Italians, being invaders, who were most likely to do this, ELAS initially embarrassed him by doing so. However, in response to Stalin's policy of creating a Macedonian people's republic of Greeks, Serbs, Albanians and Bulgars, ELAS started recruiting the latter. They also acquired Russian former prisoners, who refused to take part in ELAS attacks on rival organisations, insisting that they only wanted to fight Germans. Like Glen, Hammond was drawn into the Russians' drinking habits, but he lacked the Scotsman's appetite for vodka and passed out in the midst of a 'tea-party' with some Soviet liaison officers. He eventually resigned his position because of his worries about the dangers posed by ELAS, which were proved correct when they attempted a coup following the German withdrawal. Allan Herriot, serving with the regular forces, later led his Battalion to western Greece, but they had to be evacuated by sea when the ELAS rebellion started. Returning to Patras, he recalled, 'ultimately we beat up ELAS there and were transferred peacefully to Salonica. We saw no further action.'[46]

The Greek civil war was to continue into the late forties; Britain's financial difficulties meant that the Attlee government had to ask the Americans to take over the job of crushing the communists, thus drawing the USA fully into the Cold War. Hammond's ability to blend in with the locals with his perfect peasant Greek was almost exposed twice; once when a little old lady tried to engage him in conversation about the best way of making the local cheese, and once when a little girl on a bus, having spoken to him at length, told her mother that 'he is different' – because he was the only man on the bus with blue eyes. His OF colleague in Greece, Jock Hamilton, made no attempt to blend in and strode about in a kilt; he was later wounded and captured, beaten and threatened with execution, but eventually 'pardoned' and sent to a prison camp in Germany. Hammond rose to the rank of Lieutenant-Colonel and winning a DSO, two mentions in dispatches and the Greek Order of the Phoenix.[47]

Turnbull of the Baltic

Further north, the Nazi dawn assault on Scandinavia woke up Ronald Turnbull, an Old Fettesian who was ostensibly the press attaché to the British Embassy in Copenhagen but in reality was providing intelligence on attitudes in neutral countries. Turnbull and the other diplomats were evacuated in a sealed train to London, where he married his fiancée, the daughter of the Brazilian ambassador. Recruited to SOE, he initially helped analyse the reports coming from occupied Denmark, where the Nazis, as elsewhere in 'Aryan' Western Europe, were less heavy-handed than they were in the Slavic East. Having established that there were enough people likely to for a resistance organisation, and was sent back to Scandinavia in December to set up an SOE station in Stockholm.[48]

Thanks to the fascist stranglehold on most of Europe, he and his now-pregnant wife had to take an extraordinarily circuitous route.

Sailing on 15 December to Cape Town, they then took a flying-boat to Cairo, crossed the Suez Canal in a rowing-boat, and made their way through Palestine and Asia Minor to Istanbul by car and train. From there they sailed on 6 March to Odessa via Bulgaria, went by train to the British embassy in Moscow, and then flew to Sweden, finally arriving on 12 March. Because the Germans had been initially relatively liberal in their treatment of the Danes – to the extent of allowing their parliament to operate and some army units to remain in existence – it took some time to set up a viable resistance organisation, but eventually one came into being, helped by the post-Barbarossa crackdown on communists and Hitler's furious reaction to King Christian's offhand response to the Nazis' fulsome birthday tributes.

Turnbull's role was to act as the only channel of communication between Denmark and London, and also to ensure that home-grown Danish resistance fighters acted in concert with the trained agents who were sent in by parachute. This often required the massaging of egos and balancing the demands of hot-headed patriots for action with the warnings of the cautious about the danger of reprisals (a good 6,000 Danes ended up in concentration camps, of whom a tenth died, and hundreds were executed). He arranged supplies of arms and ammunition to the increasingly large resistance forces, and in August 1943 a wave of strikes, sabotage and unrest swept the country, with the result that the mask of Nazi politeness was removed and Denmark placed under the same system of open repression suffered by other nations. This only had the effect of increasing resistance, and Turnbull's intelligence network became one of the most efficient in Europe. He was able to provide London with details of the first flying bomb, which had been fired from Peenemunde and landed without exploding on the Danish island of Bornholm. It was also Turnbull who persuaded the Nobel Prize-winning Danish physicist Niels Bohr to escape from Denmark to Stockholm and work on the atomic bomb, putting the scientist on a Mosquito fighter-bomber for London in September 1943. Other tasks included applying pressure to Danish businessmen who were cooperating with the Nazi war effort, letting them know that any short-term profits would not be worth post-war bankruptcy or worse. Some rapidly developed links with the resistance. He was also instrumental in persuading Montgomery of the necessity of getting British troops into Denmark as soon as possible in 1945. The British had initially imagined that, having run the country themselves until 1943, the Danes could simply disarm the Germans and reorganise the place on their own, and only intended to occupy Denmark five weeks after the German surrender. Turnbull was acutely aware of the necessity of showing the people that they were not an afterthought – a British victory parade months after the German surrender would be a public relations disaster – and his advice was listened to, ensuring post-war Anglo-Danish friendship. One historian of SOE has described the Scandinavian operations as a model of their kind.[49]

After the war, the US government conferred the Medal of Freedom on Turnbull, who by this point was living in Brazil, where he was secretary of the local branch of the Old Fettesian Association. The citation was for 'exceptionally meritorious achievement which aided the United States in the prosecution of the war' and praised 'his unusual tact, considerable experience, sound judgment and keen sense of imagination and resourcefulness.'[50]

Turnbull was also awarded the OBE and a Danish knighthood, and died in 2004, believing to the last that a road accident immediately after the war, which killed his first wife, had been some sort of revenge attack set up by surviving Nazis.

Commandos

As well as the paratroopers of Arnhem and the various agents, OFs took part in what the school generically referred to as 'commando actions.' Stewart Black and George Pyman, much-loved brother of the Brigadier, took part in Operation Ironclad, the invasion of Madagascar. This was the first amphibious assault by Commonwealth forces, and saw them up against a strange combination of Vichy French troops and Japanese submariners. Black and Pyman, who had been at the school together in the early twenties, when their 'high sense of duty' was noted, were killed on the first day of the attack, 6 May 1942, and are buried near one another in Diego Suarez, where their graves were visited recently by former Fettes housemaster George Preston. 'Pete' Pyman found it sadly ironic that his brother, an ardent Francophile, had been killed fighting the French.

At least two OFs took part in the St Nazaire Raid of March 1942. Capt Donald Roy of the Liverpool Scottish was an important participant in the daring and successful cross-channel commando raid on the huge docks at St Nazaire, seen as a threat to Britain because they were Germany's only possible Atlantic battleship base. Operation Chariot now reads like an insane work of fiction: an old destroyer, HMS *Campbeltown*, was to be deliberately rammed into the docks and blown up, whilst commandos, some of whom would be on the ship and others on fast attack boats, would swarm through the port facilities destroying them with explosives. A tough eccentric known as 'the Laird', Roy allegedly insisted that his men in 2 Commando wear kilts in the raid; they were on *Campbeltown* as she sped into the dock at 19 knots and hit it with such force that her bow crumpled thirty feet. Many commandos had been killed or injured as the Germans sprayed the ship with machine-gun fire, but over a hundred still made it ashore. Roy's task was to clear Germans from the targets and hold off reinforcements, allowing other troops to get on with blowing up winding gear, pumping equipment and other vital installations. Although they were able to wipe out German resistance on the pumping house, Roy and his men came under sustained fire from anti-aircraft guns on the submarine basin nearby; these multiple 20mm cannon inflicted many casualties, but such was the ferocity of the commandos' response that the Germans scuttled one of their defence boats, fearing that it would otherwise be captured. Once as much damage as possible had been inflicted, some commandos tried to escape on the fast patrol boats whilst others, including Roy, tried to fight their way through the streets in order to join up with the French resistance.

Unfortunately, he was captured and spent the rest of the War as a POW along with 213 others; 169 commandos and sailors had been killed, and few made it back to Britain as the Germans fought the escaping fast boats. Another Old Fettesian, R.J.G. Burtinshaw, a tall, monocled demolition officer, 'full of enthusiasm for his work in the commandos'[51] when he visited the school in 1941, was one of those killed whilst trying to blow the northern caisson with underwater charges. Legend has it that he hummed 'There'll always be an England' as he and his men, armed only with pistols, charged a German unit which was attacking the troops who were laying the explosives; the Germans withdrew, but not before Burtinshaw had been mortally wounded. He died on the dock. The following day, as curious Germans clambered over the *Campbeltown*, her three tons of explosives finally detonated, taking hundreds of enemy personnel with them. Five VCs were won by participants on the raid; Donald Roy was awarded the DSO and remained a lifelong supporter of the St Nazaire Society, an eccentric figure who, in his son's words, 'marched up the middle of the road, handlebar moustache, Deer Stalker and Inverness Cape flowing.' The St Nazaire Raid, with its heroism, sacrifice, ingenuity and valuable tactical effects, was seen by military historian John Laffin (who was always quick to criticize failure – one of his books is entitled *British Butchers and Bunglers of World War One*) as 'the greatest raid of all'.[52]

The Lunatic Scotsman

Undoubtedly the best-known of Fettes' special operatives today is Sir Tommy Macpherson, the successful escaper. On leaving Fettes in 1939, he initially joined the Cameron Highlanders, but transferred to 11 (Scottish) Commando in 1940 and was trained in the highlands under Lord Lovat to, as Churchill put it, 'develop a reign of terror down the enemy coast'. He had not been a keen cadet at Fettes – he disliked the spit-and-polish routine and preferred piping – but, like many modern Fettesians who joined the services, he was addicted to outdoor pursuits, and spent part of his childhood tramping through the rugged landscape of the Macpherson country in the Cairngorms. He took part in a variety of operations in 1941, against the Vichy French in Lebanon and the Germans in Crete, before joining Operation Flipper, the attempt to kill Rommel and disrupt Italo-German command structures prior to the North African offensive of November 1941. The mission was a total failure, and 30 of the 32 of the commandos were killed or captured, the rescue submarines being unable to pick them up. Macpherson and several others attempted to walk to Tobruk, despite having neither maps nor supplies, and were eventually captured by the Italians and sent to the 'naughty boys' prison camp in the fortress at Gavi in Piedmont (though not before he had killed a guard dog with his commando knife and tried to hold up his captors whilst 'demonstrating' the use of a British pistol).

After repeated attempts to escape, first from the Italians and then from the Germans, he finally made it to Sweden in October 1943, returning home exactly two years to the day since his capture. Having established himself as an ingenious young man and having used his time in captivity to develop his language skills, he was selected for the Jedburgh teams. Created by SOE and the American Office of Strategic Services, these three-man units were dropped into France to organise the French resistance and help make the D-Day landings a success. Macpherson was parachuted from a Halifax into the Massif Central in June 1944 with a Frenchman (in fact, the pretender to the throne) and a British radio operator. Macpherson, eager to establish the British presence, wore a kilt, with the result that the local resistance thought that a French officer had arrived 'with his wife.' The Massif Central contained the tough 2nd SS Panzers (Das Reich – the most combat-decorated SS division) who had to be kept away from Normandy for as long as possible. Hardened by service on the Eastern Front (where they captured enough Soviet T34 tanks to equip an entire battalion) and experienced in anti-partisan operations, the men of Das Reich were not known for taking prisoners, though they were undoubtedly enthusiastic in taking reprisals. Although the Germans initially had a 'lighter touch' with Western Europeans than with Russian communists, the greater daring of resistance fighters led to their removing the gloves, and Das Reich became best known to history for the Oradour massacre, when they killed over 600 French civilians in retaliation for local raids.

With that in mind, Macpherson had to give the impression that he was in command of much greater forces than was actually the case before the Germans put their characteristically brutal screws down. Within a short time, he organised the motley local teenagers and brigands into a serious nuisance, destroying communications and killing German soldiers – in one case by rigging a level-crossing barrier so that it decapitated an officer and his driver. In order to give the impression that the British were there in force and that they were the new masters, Macpherson wore his military battledress with kilt and traversed the countryside in a hijacked police Citroen with a Union Jack and a cross of Lorraine flying from the bonnet. Daily sabotage included the demolition of bridges and pylons, with a spectacular operation on Bastille Day sending eight lines of the latter toppling over. Railway lines were also blown up to prevent the Germans sending troops north. When he in turn was ambushed by the Germans in Decazeville, Macpherson dashed to a nearby bridge, waited for the enemy armoured car to pass beneath it, and destroyed it with makeshift explosives.

As Das Reich trundled in their tanks and half-tracks up the road at Bretenoux, Macpherson and the resistance fighters attacked with booby-traps, holding up the column with fallen trees and hosing down the Germans with Sten guns as they tried to clear the obstruction. Although this led to reprisals – almost a hundred people were hanged in revenge – the effect was to galvanise the locals into believing in resistance success (no such operations having been mounted before) and making the Germans believe that south-eastern France was no longer the cosy posting it had once been. Das Reich had been sent there to regroup after a mauling by the Russians, and now that they found themselves harassed by apparently vast resistance forces they were unable to drive north to help their comrades in Normandy. Macpherson, 'that lunatic Scotsman who keeps blowing up bridges', had a 300,000 franc reward on his head, but decided to push his luck still further, partly because he was well aware that if the Germans realised how flimsy his forces really were, they would quickly defeat them. He and his colleagues tore through checkpoints in a 'borrowed' lorry and made their way to Pont d'Arcay, where he emerged in the full kilted menace of what the Germans had once called 'the ladies from hell' to inform the local Wehrmacht officers that he had 20,000 men at his disposal, artillery to hand, and an RAF bomber squadron ready to unleash untold misery if a surrender was not immediately forthcoming. Major-General Botho Henning Elster agreed the terms, which he later ratified with the Americans at Beaugency, and 23,000 German troops ceased fighting – though so frightened were they of the resistance that they were allowed to keep their weapons for self-defence; for this 'misguided humanity', the SS condemned him to death (though they were hardly in a position to carry it out) but today's German Wikipedia claims that he 'rettete somit viele Leben'[53] (thus saved many lives). From Macpherson's point of view, the most important thing was that the Normandy front was denied German reinforcements for two weeks, allowing the Allies more time to gain a foothold without the interference of the SS tanks.

He went on to serve in Italy, where he was involved in more shootouts – one with an Italian officer, who shot him at close range. Macpherson survived, but the Italian did not. Despite his wound, he was able to organise more disruption behind the Axis lines, and was, like Hammond and Glen, able to see at first hand the mutual hatred between different groups within the resistance.

After the war, he resumed his politics degree at Oxford and enjoyed a distinguished career in business, chairing the European Chamber of Commerce, and enjoyed some sporting success, beating Roger Bannister over half a mile playing for Oxford against the All Blacks. Today Britain's most highly-decorated veteran, with three MCs, three Croix de Guerre, the Legion D'Honneur, and both British and Papal knighthoods, he told a recent *Scotsman* interviewer that he was simply 'doing my job' and that he felt rather in the shadow of his older brother Phil, who captained the first Scottish Grand Slam team in 1925 – 'I suppose in feeling this frustration rather than achievement, I was conscious of the burden of my brother Phil's reputation upon me.'[54]

If any member of the Fettes wartime generation was being unduly modest, it was surely Sir Tommy.

Sir Tommy Macpherson (centre) at Fettes Founder's Day in 2001, with Chairman of Governors Lord Maclean and Headmaster Michael Spens

Special Operations in the Far East

Fettesians were also involved in special operations against the Japanese. Flt-Lt Jim Ponsford, who had been frustrated that, despite having flown 650 hours and on virtually every major type the RAF had – and quite a few American aircraft as well – he had 'never seen a Jerry' (partly because of his age, since he was in his forties) finally got to see action in Burma. He told the school that he couldn't talk about what he was doing, and for once this was not standard wartime paranoia, since he was in 357 Sqn, a little-known 'special duties' outfit which was formed to drop and support agents behind enemy lines. The work was even more dangerous than the normal run of jungle flying, since it had to take place at night, over remote areas and often at low level. On 14 March 1944, Ponsford was co-pilot of a Hudson transport aircraft which flew from Calcutta to drop supplies to agents from Force 136 – SOE's Asian branch – near Bhamo. In ferocious weather and at the limits of the aeroplane's range, they peered out into the darkness looking for the drop zone – a tiny clearing halfway up a mountain. On the second run, the Hudson hit a tree and cartwheeled into the jungle, killing four of those on board. Ponsford, a keen athlete in his schooldays, overlooked his own injuries to drag F/O Prosser, the navigator, out of the burning machine. The agents who had been expecting them rushed to the crash site and radioed for help. Such was the camaraderie among the special forces that the squadron medic, Dr Graham, volunteered to be air-dropped in to help the injured men, despite never having used a parachute before. Helped by a flight-sergeant, he jumped into the trees on the 15th, but was too late to save Ponsford. Prosser, however, was carried to safety.[55]

Major Bill Nimmo had learned Chinese en route to the Far East in the belief that he would be required to work with Chiang Kai-shek's nationalist forces, but when the Generalissimo changed his mind about having British help Nimmo volunteered for General Orde Wingate's Chindits. As Force Demolition Officer, Nimmo commanded many of the combined British and Kachin parties which operated on the Japanese line of communication between Bhamo and Myitkino, hampering the enemy by road cratering, bridge destruction, mining, booby trapping, and ambushing. The citation for his MC commended his leadership and personal example and his hard study of the Kachin language which enabled him to lead the guerrilla bands in the hills. After taking part in the second Chindit operation, which went in mostly by air in 1944, he qualified as a parachutist and then volunteered for the Operational Group of Force 136 which was harassing the Japanese who were retreating from the 14th Army and preventing them from regrouping and making counter-attacks.[56]

He lived to a ripe old age, but lost all three of his brothers in the War. Jimmy Nimmo, also a Major in Force 136, was dropped by parachute into the Burmese jungle in order to link up with Maj. Hugh Seagrim and the Karen resistance. Unfortunately, the Japanese used torture to extract information from the locals and both the British operatives and Karen fighters were eventually tracked down. Seagrim surrendered in order to protect the people of the village in which he was staying, and was later executed. Jimmy Nimmo was betrayed by a local headman who was terrified that his village would be subjected to the same burning, looting, torture and murder which had been inflicted on others. Nimmo, surrounded, came out fighting but was killed instantly. The Burmese operations, however, did represent a severe headache for the Japanese, and may have hastened their withdrawal.

Assessment

Since the War, other Fettesians have been involved in intelligence work, one of the most recent having operated out of Lisburn in counter-terrorism work against the IRA on the road to the Irish peace process. They have preferred to remain anonymous, for obvious reasons. James Bond is, of course, a fictional character and the best assessment of him is that he is the kind of person Ian Fleming would have liked to be, rather than a conscious representation of any living individual. However, Fettes produced a remarkable number of buccaneering adventurers, spies and raiders who risked, and often lost, their lives in secretive or unorthodox missions; several of them were friends of Ian Fleming. Fighting fascism, but with an eye on the dangers of communism, they were products of the same confused wartime landscape which produced Bond, but, unlike him, really did make a difference in the real world.

NOTES

[1] Tour buses occasionally trundle round the school, their drivers telling Japanese tourists that it was the inspiration for Hogwarts, and photo-shoots take place with young models dressed in vaguely occultic fashions or clutching owls and broomsticks. J.K. Rowling herself has never made an explicit connection between her hero and Fettes, and in any case, as thousands of irritated English teachers have pointed out, it hardly takes a genius to write that a school for wizards would look like a castle designed by a lunatic. Had Harry Potter attended a sixties-era comprehensive run by people obsessed with performance targets, that would have been an infinitely wittier leap of imagination.

[2] Wikipedia entry for real-life inspirations for James Bond: accessed on 3 November 2008

[3] *Fettes College Register 1870-1953* (Edinburgh, Constable, 1954) p. 441

[4] William Seymour, *British Special Forces* (London, Sidgwick & Jackson, 1985) p. 195

[5] Revd. Colin Sinclair, funeral address for Ronnie Williamson, quoted in *OFNL*, July 2002

[6] Quoted in *Fettesian*, September 1976

[7] Ian Fleming, *You Only Live Twice*, Ch. 21 (Obituary)

[8] Henry Chancellor, *James Bond: the man and his world* (London, John Murray, 2005) p. 60

[9] Linda Summerhayes, 'Sir Sean Connery's football, jammy pieces and that milk round', *Scotsman*, 21 August 2001

[10] John Sutherland, *the Stanford Companion to Victorian Fiction* (Stanford, SUP, 1989) p. 510

[11] Quoted in *Fettesian*, December 1924

[12] Ibid.

[13] Ibid., June 1920

[14] Hesketh-Prichard (1920) p. 206

[15] Ibid., p. 8

[16] Dimitri Collingridge, 'Aunt Moura, the frisky spy in Nick Clegg's closet', *Sunday Times*, 2 May 2010

[17] See Ben MacIntyre, 'Is there a bit of the baroness in Nick Clegg?' *Times*, 27 April 2010

[18] Luke Harding, Nick Clegg hailed as "Russian Aristocrat"', *Guardian*, 20 April 2010

[19] BBC News, 'Did Britain try to assassinate Lenin?' 19 March 2011

[20] Magnus Linklater, 'I spied for Stalin at War Office, Publisher Confessed', *The Times*, 30 October 2004

[21] David Pryce-Jones, blog at National Review Online () accessed 7 July 2011

[22] Hamish MacGibbon, 'Diary', *London Review of Books*, 16 June 2011

[23] Sir Alexander Glen, 'The Fettes of the Twenties', *OFNL*, January 2002

[24] Jane Mulvagh, 'Blueprint for Brideshead' in *Daily Telegraph*, 24 May 2008

[25] Obituary for Sir Alexander Glen, *Daily Telegraph*, 10 March 2004

[26] Glen (1935) p. 235

[27] William J. Mills, *Exploring Polar Frontiers* (Santa Barbara, ABC CLIO, 2003) p. 264

[28] Glen (1935) p. 257

[29] Glen (2002) pp. 3-4

[30] Glen (2002) p. 34

[31] Glen (2002) p. 44

[32] Fitzroy Maclean, *Eastern Approaches* (London, Jonathan Cape, 1949) p. 373

[33] Obituary for Sir Alexander Glen, *the Times*, 9 March 2004

[34] Alexander Glen, *Footholds against a Whirlwind* (London, Hutchinson, 1975) p. 65

[35] Glen (2002) p. 56

[36] Glen (2002) pp. 49-55

[37] Glen (1975) p. 91

[38] *OFNL*, July 2005

[39] Glen (1975) p. 127

[40] Quoted in Christopher Hitchens, *Prepared for the Worst* (London, Chatto & Windus, 1989) p. 211

[41] Glen (1975) p. 169

[42] Glen (2002) pp. 97-8

[43] Glen (1975) p. 215

[44] Hammond, p. 26

[45] Hammond, p. 39

[46] E-mail to author, July 2008

[47] Obituary, *OFNL*, July 2001

[48] Michael Turnbull, 'An Edinburgh real-life James Bond hero', *The Scotsman*, 22 November 2006

[49] Patrick Howarth, *Undercover* (London, Routledge, 1980) p. 231

[50] Quoted in *Fettesian*, March 1949

[51] *Fettesian*, July 1942

[52] John Laffin, *Raiders* (Stroud, Sutton, 1999) p. 106

[53] Wikipedia entry, Gen. Elster (http://de.wikipedia.org/wiki/Botho_Henning_Elster) accessed 22 August 2010

[54] Richard Bath, 'Tommy Macpherson, Britain's most decorated former soldier', *Scotsman*, 31 May 2009

[55] Robert Farquharson, *For Your Tomorrow* (London, Trafford, 2004) p. 259

[56] Obituary, *Herald*, 17 May 1997

Chapter Fifteen

'The one afternoon of the week that was bound to be free of rugby'

Fettes Enters the Cold War

A new regime

'Fettes was handed over in 1945 as a going concern,' J.N.H. Blelloch, a pupil from 1944 to 1949, wrote in 1970, 'small, like most things in the country a bit shabby, but in good heart and ready for whatever might be required of it.'[1]

He was later to become a senior civil servant in the Ministry of Defence, having been told by a contemporary that a job described by a visiting speaker as simply going to an office to push paper about sounded just right for him – or so, at any rate, he said in 1987 when, as Sir John, he addressed the school on Founder's Day.[2]

Like the rest of Britain, Fettes was to get something of a shock when peace came. Far from ushering in an era of peace and plenty, victory in 1945 was merely the half-way point in a decade of rationing, austerity, state control and military preparedness. In part this was a deliberate decision by the new Labour government to 'win the peace' through the same methods of centralized planning and public ownership which had won the war, but it was also because Britain was broke. Two World Wars, limited investment in industrial modernization, the demands of a debtor Empire and the expense of remaining at the international top table meant that the British were not to enjoy the pleasures of peace for some time. T.H. Beament, who came to Fettes from Canada, was astonished to see, as late as 1951, that rationing was still in place and London was still devastated by bombing. 'The post-war years were fairly drab, not only because of shortages and rationing, but the aftermath of the war had left people emotionally drained,' agrees his near-contemporary Christopher Normand. An anonymous air cadet's report of a trip to Germany wrote that although in parts of Hamburg 'only about one building in five is still defying the laws of gravity', its shop windows were crammed with an abundance of 'commodities that are never now seen in a British city.'[3]

In 1948, the *Vive-La* brought austerity into its second verse:

Though our ménage once more is a trifle austere
We extend a warm welcome to everyone here;
And we wonder if any have managed – with great skill –
To sidestep the petrol restrictions of Gaitskell.[4]

William Sharp remembers the simple, though in fairness nourishing food:

Butter was put out at the end of each table on a small plate and whoever got there first carefully divided it up into the appropriate number of sections with his knife. There was, of course, a rush to get there first for the privilege of being the divider. We always had porridge for breakfast and one of my favourite dishes was herrings in oatmeal. Porridge was also always available after prep in the evening in your house. For at least one year we didn't have breakfast until after we had done a session of prep in our houses. This was the idea of the headmaster, Donald Crichton-Millar, who was convinced that the best work was done during that period. Austerity affected the tuck shop, which was a wooden pavilion where the dining hall now sits. I remember it as being open only on certain days, I suspect three afternoons a week, and it mainly sold sticky buns, all sweets and chocolates being rationed. I have liked sticky buns ever since![5]

A symbol of the shortages at Fettes was the introduction in 1948 of the 'lumber jacket', also referred to as the 'borstal', which appalled traditionalists but which was to remain as school uniform for a decade and a half. Christopher Normand was the fifteenth member of his family to go to Fettes and he clearly recalls the new sartorial order:

The school uniform had changed somewhat since Dad's days at Fettes, when day wear was a morning coat. Due to clothes rationing, the weekday wear was now long grey flannel trousers or a kilt, a grey shirt (changed once a week), a 'house' tie (Glencorse had a light blue tie), and a grey corduroy 'battle-dress blouse' type of jacket – known as a 'lumber jacket'. The latter was a hideous utilitarian garment, but it did 'grow' with you, so I think I only needed 2 of these in my 4 years at Fettes. School caps were compulsory when off the school premises (one stood out like a sore thumb if one went "up town" into Edinburgh!)... On Sundays, we had white shirts, worn with the school tie, and a suit (or kilt & kilt jacket).

Sunday white shirts had attachable collars, so we were introduced to studs and cuff-links. My new uniform was a 'graduation to man-hood'.[6]

The new Headmaster, Donald Crichton-Miller – the first Old Fettesian, and the first non-classicist, to hold the post – was well aware of the painful economic climate, and was determined that the school 'expand or perish'. The boys who would wear the lumber jacket would henceforth be recruited from a much wider field; advertising through the British Council, Crichton-Miller sought pupils from Europe, Hong Kong, North America and Persia. He was not unduly worried at the thought that increased numbers might damage Fettes' reputation for academic excellence; this would, he announced at Founders' Day in 1946, be sustained, but there would also be 'special attention to the mediocre people.'[7]

The classical sixth, the school's former elite, was ejected from its home in the Upper – the vast classroom overlooking Edinburgh, where the brightest boys had learned Latin and Greek from the Headmaster whilst sitting around a great horseshoe desk – and science made compulsory. This required new facilities and indeed more space, for numbers were rising all the time; laboratories appeared, as did a horrific extension to the chapel which destroyed the Gothic line of Bryce's design by bolting a kind of shoebox onto it.

The practical world of Crichton-Miller's Fettes: boys wearing the 'borstal' corduroy battledress jacket learn woodwork.

Crichton-Miller's masters were often former military officers; the *Salvete* in the March 1946 *Fettesian,* for instance, included Majors Milman, McCallum and Ellis, and many more were to follow. Charles Besley, who had won the MC for capturing a Japanese machine-gun, could be relied upon to be undaunted by the task of constructing the Biology Department from scratch.[8]

Ian Sutcliffe, games master and Head of the Bachelor Common Room from 1946 to 1979, had served with an anti-aircraft battery of the Royal Artillery during the war and was consequently rather deaf.[9] This, his cheerful anti-intellectualism (when an art master said he had bought a Bechstein, Sutcliffe remarked 'Surely you've got enough paintings already?') and his heavy smoking, which provided him with the backs of cigarette packets on which he wrote all his notes, did not prevent him from becoming one of the school's most successful games teachers – an all-weather pitch is now named in his honour.

For all Crichton-Miller's terrifying modernizations, some Fettes traditions remained and were even enriched. This was partly because Crichton-Miller appears to have shared the contemporary paranoia that unoccupied children would inevitably get up to mischief. 'Societies multiplied' records the school's historian – reels, model railways (which set up shop in the air-raid shelter), debating, discussions, drama, bell-ringing and music. This was partly because of the terrible weather in the 1940s, which saw some of Britain's worst recorded winters. The *Fettesian* of April 1947 made the connection:

Certainly not within the memory of the present generation of Fettesians and probably not within that of many generations past has the weather been so obstinate as it has this term. Apart from a short spell during the first week, rugger has been out of the question. Finding suitable forms of exercise has been a major problem and P.T., basket ball, fencing, boxing, soccer and walking have all been employed to keep fit and relieve the drudgery of School runs. Needless to say, fives and squash courts have been in great demand and an Under 16 Fives competition has been held. Our gratitude must go to Mr. Sutcliffe and Sergeant-Major Taylor for their endless work in and around the Gym and also to Mr. Vawdrey who has done all the 'donkey-work' associated with skating... It may be due to the weather that the number of clubs and societies in the School must be almost the largest on record. New notice-boards seen outside Hall recently have proclaimed the activities of a Science Society, a History and Geography Society and a Wireless Club.[10]

In the autumn term of that year, the Wireless Club visited the Ferranti works, the Science Society went to McEwan's Brewery and Calton Hill Observatory, and the Shakespeare Society attended a production of *King Lear* at the King's Theatre. Although the Wireless Club has gone the way of that eponymous piece of technology, the others are still thriving in Fettes today. George Booth and Tommy Evans were especially active in promoting drama, with *The Bartered Bride* in 1948 and – for the first time in Britain since 1890 – Carl Maria von Weber's proto-Wagnerian *Der Freischutz* in 1950; demanding works by Ibsen, Eliot, Shaw and Chekov also appeared. The Film Society continued, and its members seem to have been especially impressed by *Brief Encounter*, one of the first films to 'discard the cheap formulas, the easy solutions, the saccharine sentimentality of the average American film.' 'Through rain-drenched squares, drab streets, soulless suburban railway stations, an illicit and unsought love stumbles between whispers and subterfuges to its inevitable end, the acceptance of the laws of God and Society,' commented the appreciative reviewer.[11]

The new Edinburgh Festival was visited by a curious locally-based pupil who aspired to 'combining Morningside suavity with Bohemian jauntiness' – much like the Festival itself. He recommended it to his peers, despite having caught flu from incessant queuing in the rain, but accepted that they were more likely to be tramping in France, bathing in the Cotswolds or being at home – a sign of what was considered exotic and exciting in the late forties.[12]

The Fet-Lor Club continued to do excellent work with the underprivileged, though one Fettesian was somewhat nonplussed in the early fifties to be asked 'do three or four of you ever get together and beat up the Headmaster?'[13]

Other pupils took part in the Scottish Industrial Sports Association camps, where public schoolboys mixed under canvas – on good terms, apparently – with apprentices of the same age but vastly different backgrounds. Rugby, of course, remained a constant theme, at least when the weather permitted, as the focal point for loyalties and, in an era in which intellectualism was becoming less important, in many ways the school's defining characteristic. Between the end of the First World War and the close of the 1940s, more Fettesians had won Oxford or Cambridge Blues than the alumni of any other school. Although this declined in the post-war era, and the days when Fettes supplied a third of a Scottish international side were definitely over, the school could still boast that as late as 1955 none of its current pupils had ever seen the 1st XV beaten. Barry Clegg, a pupil in the mid-fifties, is frank about the sport cult, which then included compulsory boxing:

No matter how you despised or feared this sport, without a doctor's assurance of physical incapacity it was impossible to avoid the annual boxing tournament in your first two years.

The school venerated sports, rugby especially, but also cricket and to a lesser extent field hockey. Six days a week throughout the school year, come rain or shine, sleet or snow, we were required to participate in some 'game' or other. When the weather was too bad for field games, we would be led on runs through the city streets. Once in the depths of winter we worked off our frustrations in an organized snowball fight! Oh, I shouldn't complain - I suppose it was this regimen and the cold showers every morning that made me the man I am today!

Members of school teams enjoyed a variety of privileges in this secluded and tradition-ridden society. There was a fancy sweater and scarf for the cricket players. The rugby team could wear white laces in their boots and walk across a certain lawn; the rest of us had black laces and went around the grass. At term's end, photographs were taken of the teams, so that proud mummies and daddies could see that their money was being well spent and their sons were receiving a proper education!

People who shone in none of these manly activities were known as weeds or drips or dregs.[14]

The boxing training was crude – 'lead with the left, follow with a right hook, protect the chest with the elbows' – and Clegg decided that his best option was to be defeated in the first round of the tournament, so as not to have to go on to the second. Unfortunately, once in the ring, this resolution did not survive his opponent's first punch, and he fought back so vigorously that he was declared the winner, and went on to fight a boy ironically known as 'Brain', one of the leading lights of the 'Bummery' (the 'slow stream' set); 'while boxing is clearly not a contest of intellect, the fact that Brain's arms reached almost to his knees, and that his imagination was untroubled by thoughts of pain, defeat or very much else stood greatly to his advantage.' Defeated after a 'plucky defence' Clegg's boxing was over for a while, but when it resumed his peripatetic music teacher was horrified to see that he had sustained a bad cut to the lip. This, he said, could ruin his horn-playing.

'A fat lot anyone here cares about my horn-playing career,' Clegg answered. 'We all have to box in the first two years.'

Unimpressed, the teacher said that he cared and was going to do something about it.

'But no-one can get out of boxing unless they're missing an arm or leg,' said Clegg, 'It's never been done – it's probably never even been tried.'

In those days I accepted the school's conventional wisdom almost without question, and while objecting to many of the prevailing traditions I gave little thought to the possibility of change. My teacher's imagination was not so limited, and luckily he had the determination to fight for his beliefs. To my delight he took up the challenge, carried my case to unheard-of lengths (involving even the Headmaster) and achieved the extraordinary novelty of having me excused from further fighting. This triumph far surpassed my feeble victories in the ring, and might be said to have raised the status of musical studies in general. We judged it one in the eye for the sports-crazy school, at any rate.

This – and the fact that Clegg was not now going to have to fight the fearsome Harbottle, who hoped to become a professional boxer – was an apparently rare victory for the unathletic. The glittering prizes and public acclaim were still largely the province of the sports elite:

For the artistically and academically successful there was no corresponding recognition; no privileges drew attention to their achievements, no photographs were taken. The musicians and the scholarship candidates had to find their reward in other ways, making do without popular acclaim - good training I suppose for later life.

Perhaps unsurprisingly, some pupils hated the place. Just how much so was revealed to the present generation in 2006, when sixth-formers Sarah Fleming and Rachel Hunter decided to try to contact the OFs who had carved or written their names on the fabric of the main building's central tower, which had long been known as a haven for smokers and other ne'er-do-wells. They were shocked to uncover a well of human misery; one pupil from the mid-fifties said bitterly that 'I don't think the school even noticed I was there.'[15]

Another clock-tower rebel of the same time emailed to say that the school had left him 'socially ill-equipped to meet girls, academically ill-equipped to study on my own, and with a bruised self-esteem' – although he also said that this was useful training for National Service. One happier pupil from that era said that he had developed a taste for climbing around in high places thanks to his experiences in the tower, so when he joined the Royal Navy he took to placing toilets and baths on the roof at Greenwich. However, he realised that anyone who wasn't keen on sport 'must have had a miserable time', a view echoed by one of the other graffiti artists who said that 'to leave your mark, ideally you had to be good at games: failing that, outstanding academically or a very strong/distinctive personality.' All agreed that the presence of girls would have made Fettes 'a much better place'.

Although that was a step too far for him, Crichton-Miller understood that the world was changing, and Fettes needed to modernize if it was to survive. Many members of the traditional public school classes feared Labour's victory as a kind of revolution which would sweep them away. OF Ian Harvey, later a Conservative MP, warned darkly of some kind of sinister red dictatorship:

There is a spirit of collectivism abroad which if it is allowed to pursue its logical course must destroy the foundations of democracy.

The Socialist victory of 1945 which was hailed by so many as an advance for the forces of democracy was in fact potentially their greatest set-back. I say potentially because I do not believe the Socialist Party has yet come face to face with the political crisis that is inherent in its present policy and make-up. There are many Socialists, and the Trade Unions contain the majority of them, who do not admit that what their party is aiming at is the establishment of a highly-centralised, closely controlled society dominated by officialdom of the most insolent and incompetent kind, and totally devoid of any regard for individual human rights. Nor in fact is it inevitable at this moment that the Socialist Party will be led to a conclusion which will make it impossible to draw a clear dividing-line between them and the Communist Party. There is, however, considerable danger that that is the course that they will be forced to follow if only to avoid a political volte-face and to keep themselves in power...

Today, we have Mr Attlee drably bedight in sheep's clothing with an Old Haileyburian tie, tomorrow – ? [16]

As Tom Devine points out, this view was not shared by the Scottish working class, who had got used to Secretary of State Johnston's strongly interventionist policies during the war, wanted a 'reforming government committed to the welfare state and management of the economy for the public good', and gave Scottish Labour 37 seats in 1945.[17]

The post-war Corps

Yet, for all the changes of policy and in attitudes, the post-war Labour government was determined to keep British up military strength and prestige as far as economic constraints permitted. Whilst they had long accepted that India would gain self-government, ministers needed the armed forces to police the rest of the Empire and defending Britain from the red menace. Fettes' traditions of square-bashing and musketry – now with the option of gaining aviation skills in the air section – were therefore to remain important.

From 1948, the 'Corps' became the Combined Cadet Force, a free-standing organization. Although it had been more democratically renamed the Junior Training Corps during the War, it was still part of the university-based Officers' Training Corps, the assumption being that the cadets based largely in public schools would naturally become officers eventually. Labour ministers naturally felt that this smacked unhealthily of class privilege, so the CCF was formed, turning the original 'Corps' plus its light blue brother the ATC into different sections of one body. Christopher Normand summarises how it worked in 1950:

The School Cadet Force was a compulsory activity, once a week, for all of us throughout our time, from the age of 14 – mainly because the prospect of National Service was inevitable when we left. Initially we were organised into House Platoons in the Army Section, until we passed 'Certificate A' (I cannot remember what prowess was needed, other than being able to march in step!). Each term we all went on a 'Field Day', which involved an outing to a training ground somewhere outside Edinburgh. I particularly remember one which took place in the Fife hills, not far from Aberdour, and this involved being transported in a convoy of busses to South Queensferry, crossing the River Forth on a ferry, to Fife, and driving up into the hills, where we were instructed in tactics and undertook a series of manoeuvres – my only memory of this is the lunch-time picnic! I have a photograph of the Glencorse Platoon, which states that we won the Inter-House Cup, but, today, I have not the remotest idea what we did to gain this conspicuous success! After passing 'Cert. A', we could choose to continue in the Army section, or to join the Naval or Air Force Section.[18]

The new Combined Cadet Force gathers outside the foundations of the new art and music building.

Fettes' new Royal Navy section enabled, at least in theory, the tri-service training which so enthused General Pyman to take place. Sadly, many OFs have less than glowing memories of this; Mickey Bain, for instance, remembers 'chiefly the cumbersome radio pack I had to carry on my back during training in the School grounds'[19] whilst Hamish Thomson says 'I'm afraid I found life in the cadet corps absolutely awful with needless parades in ridiculous uncomfortable outfits.'[20]

In this, he is backed up by T.H. Beament: 'the endless applications of Brasso to brass, boot polishing, uniform ironing, marching practice and inspections are the things we probably remember the most.' There was a point to this, of course, as many recognised, including Tim Daniels, whose experiences mirror those of the pre-war Fettesians who found life in uniform more bearable because they had got used to it at school. 'On joining the Army, the ability to Blanco your belt, to polish your Brasses, to 'bull' your boots and iron your uniform were tremendous assets, and put you one step ahead from the very beginning,' he recalls, 'The majority of my comrades had never spent a night away from home in their lives, let alone having to attend to such military disciplines.'[21]

However, those who joined in the late fifties, when National Service was no longer the inevitable destination of the male school-leaver, were less likely to see the positive side of it. Barry Clegg rather enjoyed the evening sessions, because he did not have to dress up, and learned (in the 'time-tested military technique of endless repetition') potentially useful map-reading skills, though he did sometimes find it difficult to prevent 'my mind from wandering down more peaceful avenues.' On one occasion, snapped out of a daydream by the question 'Why should you always shield your eyes when a flare goes up in a night operation, Clegg?' his reply 'Er, so that your eyes don't light up in the dark?' did not go down very well. However, he remembers the long afternoon sessions in full uniform with less fondness.

They began with a general inspection, for which we each spent hours in preparation. Trousers and battle jacket had to be ironed (the disastrous smell of burning battledress rises even now to my nostrils); belt and gaiters had to be treated with blanco to produce a khaki surface of transcendent perfection; boots were polished to a dazzling black, and brass badges and buckles shone in brilliant gold flashes. With all the attention given to appearance, one might be forgiven for thinking that battles were won or lost according to some remote theoretical index of sartorial splendour.

Anyone who thought he would get an easier ride by joining the newer sections of the Corps was in for a rude awakening. The Royal Navy contingent was no less demanding in its dress code, as R.M. Webster, who came to Fettes in the early 1950s, notes:

First there was the job of getting to know all the wrinkles about a sailor's uniform, which in those days still had unique items such as the sailor's cap (to be kept white), complete with cap tally to be tied in a smart tiddly bow; a collar with 3 white stripes which tied round your waist and had to be washed in cold salt water; a black silk worn round the neck, also tied with tapes in a tiddly bow; a white lanyard to be washed regularly to keep it clean; a jumper which could only go on over your head; and finally bell-bottom trousers with a flap instead of flies and which were ironed (with the help of soap on the creases) and kept tied in a concertina for easier storage on board ship. I must have looked convincing as a sailor, as on one occasion when I was passing through London in uniform I was asked in the street by a lady of the town whether I wanted a short time![22]

David Kilpatrick, who came to Fettes from Northern Ireland in 1956, was a slightly less enthusiastic sailor, admitting that 'The CCF was regarded by most in the same way as compulsory games were regarded by the less athletic.'[23]

Once he had 'fled' the rigours of the army section for the relative civilisation of the senior service, he worked out a 'skive' with some friends, who were asked to paint a whaler. 'As this was located near the tuckshop we took time out to make regular sorties to it, and, as it was a cushy task managed to spread it out over most of a term without arousing any suspicion… I owe Fettes a debt for ensuring that I was never tempted to enlist!' Others were rather more keen, however, and were even inspired on occasions. John Ferguson was destined for a medical education, but an experience at Fettes opened up an additional avenue for him:

Major Bill Dalziel of the Royal Signals, speaking in the Sixth Form Room about the Territorial Army, made a very vivid impression on me. He would have been known to many Fettesians at that time as he was a Director of Aitken and Niven, one of the two Fettes outfitters, and regularly came to the School. On this occasion however, he was immaculately attired in No2 Khaki uniform and gleaming Sam Browne belt. I immediately adopted him as my role model and aspired to become someone like him. Through the Signals Section I did meet him regularly and his unit provided support for us both during term time and at Annual Camp. When I left Fettes it was quite natural for me to join the 52nd (Lowland) Signal Regiment while at University rather than the Officer Training Corps. Shortly afterwards I was put up for a TA Commission and remained with Royal Signals throughout my University time, eventually reaching the rank of Captain.[24]

Although the training was hugely useful to those who would later join the armed services, Tib Beament had hoped that, as a Canadian, he would be exempt from having to join the CCF, since National Service was not in force in his homeland:

I remember thinking how lucky I was going to be to not have to do it, thus leaving me free time to pursue what really interested me, the rather diametrically opposed field of art. To my chagrin my parents in their wisdom decided that I should join anyway – no doubt thinking it would be good for me. I suppose it was, in its way, however, to my adolescent mind it seemed like nothing but more discipline, of which there was already a great quantity in our daily life. To a North American boy, the level of discipline was somewhat of a shock, and certainly in telling of it to others on this side of the Atlantic, I was often met with incredulity. I am not for a moment saying that in retrospect I consider it a 'bad thing' – a small digression illustrates: When taking a course for my M.A. in Art Education, I had a Dr. McPherson as professor and in the first class he asked us all to tell of our education. When I told him I had attended Fettes, he asked in a broad Scottish accent:

'And what did you learn at Fettes, Mr. Beament?'

My response, in an equally broad Scottish accent, was: 'Dr. McPherson, I learned how to survive.'[25]

Another post-war Canadian pupil, Norman Cameron, was instantly assumed by his fellow-pupils to be American, and then taken to task for not having made the USA join in World War II in 1939. Despite Fettes' strong imperial connections, he never saw any awareness of special contributions made to Britain's wars by Canadian troops, in either the First or Second World Wars.[26] That said, the CCF did have its compensations in the rugby-obsessed school, as Gar Yates notes:

For anyone who was neither very athletic nor particularly keen on mud, it had the great attraction of providing the one afternoon of the week that was bound to be free of rugby football. I certainly enjoyed rifle-shooting, and (to my surprise) also rather enjoyed camping with the C.C.F. Having been an N.C.O. in the C.C.F. was no doubt some recommendation when one was called up for National Service and found oneself a 'P.O.C.'[27]

Gar Yates' experience was not unique, for what seems to have stuck most in the minds of post-war Fettesians was – for good or ill – the revived annual camp. William Sharp has fond memories:

The best thing about corps was the annual camp in the summer holidays. Although I believe this was voluntary I went on every camp I could. We went to Dundonald near Troon and to Barry near Carnoustie as far as I remember. We enjoyed competitions with other schools especially with the pipe band (I was the big drummer for my sins). The only other events I remember were games of golf (where better!) and buying fish & chips in the local chippy![28]

As he cheerfully admits, 'I'm afraid I don't remember anything about the army side of things which we were there for.' Dr John Ferguson, by contrast, feels that he learned a great deal from the Fettes CCF experience:

I enjoyed my military training of drill, map-reading and shooting small and large bore rifles, and passed Cert B (basic training). I then decided to join the Signals Section which had just got a hut behind the Pavilion in the trees. There was a No 12 transmitter and an R207 receiver but there was a problem with getting a good aerial in the trees. I put up a tall vertical metal whip aerial which worked quite well and we were able to listen to 'radio hams' in Europe, but could not send to them. I tried to put up a wire aerial attached to a meteorological balloon, but filling the balloon with coal gas did not give enough lift. One night while trying to transmit to Europe we subsequently discovered that with an umpteenth harmonic we had blanked out the BBC1 television sound signal in the local area! [29]

Camp could be an adventure which even reluctant cadets enjoyed for its genuinely military moments or its fun extra-curricular side, or a valley of the shadow of death which was there to be tholed. Mickey Bain is in two minds: 'I remember an enjoyable though uncomfortable camping experience at Carnoustie, (sleeping on straw palliases) in company with other schools, complete with dangerous 'Thunderflashes' instead of hand-grenades.' The *Fettesian* reported with commendable frankness that sleeping under canvas was always to be preferred to huts because, although there was always the down side of 'that unique sensation of waking up at night with somebody else's feet pressed under one's nose' there was the 'spirit of novelty and camaraderie which such conditions engender.' More importantly, 'huts will always suffer from the fact that, without an extensive knowledge of engineering, it is impossible to let them down on top of the sleeping heads inside them!... Loretto tents fall with particular satisfaction on Loretto heads.'[30]

Although the life could be quite tough, the Corps could provide a sense of achievement, as in the case of Robert Anderson:

My greatest week in Fettes was at the Cultibraggan camp. I recall three of us being dumped from a truck in the wilds of West Perthshire and told to find our way to a map reference point. We waded the river Earn at least nine times, sometimes up to our waist; we were first to arrive at the designated map reference point and consequently won the first prize. [31]

Andrew Ker 'quite enjoyed the awfulness of it in a perverse sort of way'; being woken by 'Hey Johnnie Cope' on the pipes was fun, and at camp he learnt to navigate using Ordnance Survey maps and acquired a lifelong enthusiasm for hill walking.[32]

A weary cadet relaxes after a post-war exercise. Note heavy boots

Barry Clegg wrote a detailed account of his time at Cultybraggan in 1959:

Leaving the train at Oban, I was one of a hundred nervous and excited schoolboy soldiers clambering into canvas-topped army trucks. Inside mine, there was barely room to stand amongst the baggage, but the sunshine and countryside soon cheered us up. Something had cheered the driver too, judging by his erratic course along the small country road. Unexpectedly meeting a car on a bend, he swerved abruptly and the truck overturned onto a grassy verge. Lucky for me that it was grassy, because having been at one side of the truck I was now at the bottom. Only a thin piece of canvas separated me from the ground. Above me, a heap of people and kitbags writhed in confusion. Somebody had a bleeding nose. When at last I climbed out, once everyone else and the baggage was at the roadside, I was examined with concern by the Sergeant. He seemed to think that I had been badly injured; but it was soon discovered that the blood streaked over my face was from someone else's nose and I was in fact unharmed.

We marched along the road some distance with our kit until another truck arrived, and we were ordered aboard. By now beginning to suffer from shock, we squabbled for places at the back so we could easily hop out if necessary. As the truck started on its way, there was silence amongst the troops; hands gripped tightly the tailgate and roof frame.

Entering Cultybraggan the truck had to ford a shallow river: it swayed and bumped over the river-bed till every one of us felt sure it would overturn. What pathetic military material we must have seemed!

The young Clegg was a member of the signals section, partly because he was genuinely interested in electronics but also on the grounds that it had a reputation for being rather more easy-going than the other wings of the Corps. It did not, unfortunately, go easy at Cultybraggan:

After a couple of depressing days of drill, training and footslogging, a 'night exercise' was announced. What with the debilitating effects of an Army diet centred around baked beans, uncomfortable nights in a tiny tent, and boots a size too small, I was no longer in prime condition. We could have defeated any army in the world, went my theory, if we could only force them into boots like ours!

The walkie-talkie I had was of such bulk and weight that it might well have been designed by a hostile power acting on a version of this theory. With that on my back, a rifle over my shoulder, and the dreaded boots on my feet, I was weighed down with discomfort and dismay at the thought of the exercise ahead.

As I set off alone from Camp for the mock battle, I carried out routine tests on my equipment. The radio's performance was erratic, but for fear of being issued a heavier replacement I chose to carry on. Soon I left the road and headed uphill towards a point where I was supposed to rendezvous with some other troops. I had a map, a compass, and a small torch, but no comprehension of how I fitted into the scheme of things.

I sent a few exploratory messages into the ether to identify myself and contact other members of my unit. Through the crackling and spluttering in my earphones it was easy to imagine human voices, but I could never quite discern a meaningful sentence.

When daylight disappeared and I still hadn't found my unit, I began to feel uneasy. I paused to set the compass for a night march, so that by aligning the luminous markings I could keep my direction. Looking up again, I saw the silhouette of a head ducking out of sight behind a nearby rise.

'Ah, now I see you - I'll join you in a minute,' I transmitted hopefully, and started again up the hill.

Over the rise a sheep was nibbling grass, but no-one was in sight. Disheartened, I sat down and ate a sandwich, wondering how long I should wait before returning to Camp. If I got back too early I would simply be sent out again into the battle zone. It seemed best to relax and ease my aching feet.

After several days in those ill-fitting second-hand army boots I had developed a profound dislike for them; because of the unnecessary and inescapable distress they caused me they had become a symbol of all that was senseless in army life. It gave me great satisfaction to take them off and throw them at the sheep.

591

After half an hour of inaction, guilt and the gathering cold stirred me again. I rose and groped for my boots by torchlight. The sheep had staged a successful counter-attack, and I discovered too late the droppings in one boot.

It was rather difficult to move across country now, so I made my way carefully down to the road and started back towards Camp. So far I had heard and seen nothing of the expected battle. As I wondered whether everyone else was equally disoriented, two figures jumped from the shadows and grabbed me.

'We've caught someone,' they hissed in exaggerated stage whispers. A torch shone into my eyes. 'Oh, it's only Clegg - he's on our side isn't he?'

'Hey, he's got a radio,' a Corporal noticed.

'Yes, but it doesn't work.'

Feeling somewhat useless, he found that an urge to do something decisive began to replace a deep sense of futility, especially once the bustle of self-important people – mostly corporals with no more idea of what was going on than their confused cadets – rose to fever pitch in the deepening gloom.

As false alarms and fears of sudden capture became more frequent, a sense of excitement began to develop. Three times I dropped to the ground with my useless load at some supposed danger. Self control was breaking down: it was not known whether the enemy had been discovered, but everyone now wanted to let off the things that flashed and the things that banged.

Thus the long-awaited event began.

A flare was sent up. I dutifully shielded my eyes. No enemy could be seen - a detail which did not stop us from going ahead with our battle. Lying in the damp grass I expertly loaded my rifle with blank cartridges and fired into the darkness. The noise was terrific, but profoundly satisfying after the hours of indecision and creeping about in the dark. Flashes and smells so confused me that I could not tell whether anyone was returning fire.

Spurred by an attack of military ambition, I advanced to a new point of cover, doing the leopard-crawl to ensure that my behind would not be shot off. I was proud of this show of initiative and imagined cool-headedness, and hoped no-one would notice that I had left my radio behind in the bracken.

When all the ammunition was used up, a stunning silence replaced the din of battle. All at once I felt guilty and anxious, as though this irresponsible self-indulgence had done some serious harm. But soon the spell broke: I managed to find my set again and joined the others back on the road.

No sign of the earlier excitement remained. Tiredness possessed us, and little was said as we made our way back to Camp. Who cared now about advance posts, escape routes and the textbook precautions of night marching in hostile territory? Our only concern was to get into our tents and lie down.

Stretching out later in my sleeping-bag, I had an inexplicable feeling that the army had somehow brought me one step closer to manhood.

John Urquhart, whose father was Commandant of Sandhurst in his later years at Fettes, took the CCF a bit more seriously, and appreciated Ronnie Guild's enthusiasm, but his chief memory is of a telling incident. On an exercise in the late fifties he was on a map-reading exercise when some of his section had a crafty fag. It was not as if Urquhart had enjoyed the experience – he was promptly sick – but for reasons which 'I have always struggled to understand and about which I would still like to interview him, without coffee' the section corporal decided to report them. His housemaster, Basil Timbs, devised an imaginative punishment – Urquhart was to weed his garden every day, so that 'the parents will think I'm rich enough to have a gardener.' Urquhart, who followed his father into the Army, spent 20 years with the Gordon Highlanders and now published audio books of military history, still admires Timbs – 'I had had a rare and privileged insight into cynicism, humanity and humour, from a thoroughly good housemaster and sympathetic human being.' He never smoked another cigarette, though.

Tib Beament also acquired some potentially useful skills:

For some reason I ended up in the Commandos, which seems strange for someone who was not overly enthusiastic about the whole experience – why pick the toughest of units? I vividly remember our kayak training held in the unheated swimming pool during the depths of winter. These were lumbering heavy WWII collapsible two-man craft, which we, in full uniform, had to tip upside down, then extricate ourselves from underneath with all due speed – if nothing else to avoid fast approaching hypothermia. Although I have never had occasion to do so thus far in life, I suppose that knowing how to strip down and reassemble a Bren gun may yet come in handy.

A slightly more traditional military lesson was learned by Chris Parker in the late fifties:

We arrived in the grounds of Ardmaddy Castle near Seil Island in Argyll after an overnight march and exercise. We were lined up by the Black Watch Sergeant who proceeded to explain that we were invited to the Castle that evening.

'One step forward all those who would like to dance with the pretty girls tonight.'

I and a dozen other innocents stepped forward.

'So you shall, boys, so you shall - but first you can dig the latrines!'

And so I learned the regular's motto - never volunteer for anything.[33]

The role of an RSM in a cadet corps is – as in the real armed services – extremely important in running the unit, dispensing 'buttons, bootlaces, blanks, First Aid, justice, fleas in the ear and anything else that is required of him.'[34]

Sergeant-Major Giles, who in semi-retirement after 27 years' service operated the telephone exchange in the old Porter's Lodge, died in 1947, to genuine grief. A poem in the *Fettesian* mourned his passing:

To him who served us eight and twenty years
Let this our 'Last Post' tribute now be paid.
In camp at Elie, or on corps parade
Or on the shooting-range he had no peers
'Mongst Sergeant-Majors. And how oft the fears
Of boxing novices he would dispel
By whisp'ring some kind words before the bell,
The word that falls like balm on Faintheart's ears.
That spare, lean form no longer shall we see,
In spite of years athletic to the last;
No longer hear his voice or share his smiles
As he described some Fettes victory;
But as we talk together of the past
We'll lovingly remember Henry Giles.[35]

Thirty cadets provided a military escort at his funeral. Drum-Major Alexander West DCM, who instructed the band in drumming and bugling, also died in 1947, and was also sorely missed for his inspirational enthusiasm. His successor, RSM Taylor, kept up the fine tradition. Failure to live up to the Sergeant-Major's standards in martial matters would lead to him giving an inefficient cadet's eardrums 'a good scorching.' A favourite phrase was 'Swing those arms, or I'll rip 'em off and hit you wi' the sticky end.' In order to minimise the amount of marching to which he was subjected, Christopher Normand joined the Navy Section, which offered its own opportunities for excitement, as when the cadets joined a frigate on a trip to 'show the flag' in Germany:

We were allocated space amongst boy sailors, in a 'mess' well below decks, and had to learn to 'sling a hammock' in which we slept – some of us never did get the hang of climbing into or out of a hammock, with some fairly hilarious results. The weather in both directions across the North Sea was atrocious, so many were sea-sick. We did very little, as the crew regarded us as a ruddy nuisance, but we managed to keep ourselves occupied, somehow, including standing watches on the wings of the bridge of the ship, which was fun, if cold. Going through the Kiel Canal, the Captain of the accompanying Frigate managed to ram our ship, opening a large hole in the side. While tied up at Kiel, an excursion was arranged for us Cadets to visit Lübeck for the day, which turned out to be a major shambles as only a few of us managed to catch the returning bus, and the remainder got back, much the worse for wear, near dawn the next day. Thereafter we were in disgrace for the remainder of the trip.[36]

Robin Webster had the sea in his blood; one of his earliest memories is of being handed up, aged three, onto the coastal motor launch commanded by his father, who taught him how to tie knots blindfold. It was inevitable that he would join the Naval Section and thrive in it:

…there was the Naval Section hut, with a working model of a ship's foc'sle, complete with anchors and cables, splendid posters of ships and naval life, ranks and showing how damage control saved ships etc, and knot boards. We certainly had good instruction in the special language of the sea and the Navy, basic seamanship and later in parade training (never drill for a sailor). The officer in charge of the Naval Section was Lt. Peter Shepherd R.N.V.R., who had actually served in the Navy during the war. En route to summer training somewhere I can remember him taking a party of the Naval Section off a sleeper and into the King's Cross Hotel for breakfast and the horror of the Head Porter at seeing us in his hotel – 'Not sailors, Sir!' – before eventually allowing us in.
On field days we generally went down to the naval base H.M.S. Lochinvar at Port Edgar at South Queensferry and perhaps got to sea for the day in a minesweeper or Coastal Forces patrol boat, or else instruction from an R.N. Chief Petty Officer, learning the naval adage that 'Them that are keen get fell in previous'. It always seemed to be cold but sometimes we were allowed to borrow Coastal Forces white polo sweaters and our packed lunch from the Fettes Steward

*George Cooper (himself a former R.N. commissioned 'pusser') was supplemented
with good naval soup.*

Camps for the Naval Section were much more exciting for the enthusiast
than the Army equivalent – no shivering under canvas – though they
were still hard work:

*One took us to H.M.S. St Vincent, the boys' training establishment at Gosport
across Portsmouth Harbour. There we had such delights as early morning P.T. on
the parade ground, morning divisions governed by the beat of the big drum, naval
food and spit and polish. When we went sailing or pulling (rowing to the
landsman) we had to march up and down to the Harbour. We were under the
charge of a young National Service Sub-Lieutenant – an excellent role model, as
at that time our age group still faced the prospect of National Service; and our own
leader was Cadet Petty Officer Ranald Maclean. Another 'camp' was spending a
week in H.M.S. Russell, a Blackwood class anti-submarine frigate, at Portland
Harbour Naval Base in Dorset. That was even more naval as we actually lived on
board ship, slept in hammocks and had to help cleaning and painting the ship.
While the ship itself did not get to sea, I can remember a day at sea in a sister ship
(probably H.M.S. Murray). For some reason I can also remember one of our
number falling foul of one of the ship's officers for answering back to him.*

*The Navy section struggles at Granton harbour with one of its whalers, probably in
the late forties*

Shooting remained important; in 1947, Fettes defeated Rossall, Edinburgh Academy, Merchiston, Watson's and Wellingborough, drawing with Denstone and losing to Loretto and Glasgow Academy; the average score was 95 per cent. For those who were keen, the CCF offered the chance to learn more modern skills and take part in activities which would not have been possible even for public schoolboys a generation previously. Robert Anderson still remembers with affection, over half a century on, how when he was in the Air Section he was flown from Turnhouse to New Scone, a grass airstrip, in the rear seat of a Chipmunk. 'I wondered where the hell we were landing,' he says, 'absolutely wonderful.' Flying was not, at that time, restricted to the RAF cadets; Robin Webster was one of several from other sections who learned to fly in Tiger Moths. In 1951 Fettes acquired what it called the 'Eaton Primary Glider' – in fact the Eton or Grasshopper, which like many British cadet gliders was a copy of a pre-war Nazi design. Able to be dismantled, which itself was a task providing valuable team-work, it was launched from the sports pitches 'by means of an elastic rope, stretched by a team of cadets; a height of about fifty feet can be attained.'[37]

It was hoped that the glider would be a turning-point in the history of the air section, who were criticised for doing too much classroom work (and doubtless envied by shivering army cadets); it was also a signal honour, for it was the first such glider to come to Scotland, and the first in England had gone to Eton. RAF camps were appropriately civilised:

We found ourselves provided with many unexpected amenities, for the station [R.A.F. Cosford] is primarily a mechanical training centre and is well designed to accommodate 300 cadets, having N.A.A.F.I. canteens with excellent billiard tables, a first-class swimming-pool and a cinema with four different programmes per week, enormous gymnasia, a luxurious information room with seven daily papers, and a frequent train service to Wolverhampton... The barracks were admirably ventilated and quite waterproof. The R.A.F. provided well-sprung beds complete with blankets, mattresses and clean sheets. Personal hygiene was encouraged by a constant supply of hot water which could be enjoyed in either baths or sprays. Each hut had its own loudspeaker which faithfully woke us (sometimes) at eight o'clock and for the rest of the day poured forth a somewhat limited repertoire of popular numbers.[38]

This report in the Christmas 1949 *Fettesian* mentioned that the air cadets all got to fly and 'experienced the thrill of opening the throttle of a

Meteor up to 10,000 revs per minute'; they also got a free trip to see the air races at Birmingham ('jet aircraft flew at almost supersonic speeds') and were supplied with lorries which 'carried us any distance over 200 yards'. It is hard to avoid the suspicion that they were letting the army cadets know just how much easier life could be in light blue.

The school glider is launched from Young's field, presumably in the days before, as the Daily Mail *would say, health and safety went mad*

Cultural activities were also available; pipes and drums had been part of the Corps' identity since 1912, and reels were danced from the 1930s onwards. Fettes had never been a hotbed of Scots nationalism – there was a current affairs talk on it in 1948, and in 1950 the Debating Society voted in favour of the Covenant, but the pupils regarded as odd, indeed sour, the demolition of E ɪɪ R postboxes – but it appreciated as much as any other community the value of folk tradition. After the War, there were enough serious highland dancers to take weekly instruction from a Sergeant-Major in the Royal Scots. They demonstrated their skills at Founder's Day and Guest Nights (staff dinners) as well as competing against other schools. Christopher Normand, an enthusiastic member of the team, recalls with pride that they performed in the Usher Hall, Edinburgh and on the esplanade in front of the Castle.

The height (or nadir?) of my competitive highland dancing career occurred while I was dancing the sword dance at a competition, when I lost balance and kicked the sword — it shot across the stage and plunged between two of the judges, point first, narrowly missing them. [39]

It was still a useful skill; contacts with the opposite sex were increasing – though not to the extent that Fettes dramatic productions could dispense with dressing up the more fresh-faced lads for women's roles – and in 1948 the *Fettesian* could report that 'the even tenor of Fettes life has been mildly disturbed by invitations to two dances, at St George's and St Denis' girls' schools.'[40]

More professionally, Robert Anderson also took part in the kind of courses which were increasingly available to those who really wanted to develop their talents. Along with his friend Richard Ling, he went on a special course at the Royal Naval Barracks at Chatham to learn to use the bosun's call and become qualified Quartermasters (naval quartermasters steering the ship and manning the side) and so entitled to wear a bosun's call on a silver chain instead of a lanyard. This was prestigious stuff for a lad in his teens, for it was not easily awarded and is still remembered today with appreciation.

By the late fifties, the CCF had become truly elaborate in its activities; the RAF section had assorted pieces of real aeroplanes and the Navy proudly sailed in their whalers, *Marilyn* and *Brigitte*, named after the screen goddesses of the day. Exercises at camp often reflected Cold War thinking; whereas the OTC had emphasised traditional infantry skills for traditional battles in its first few decades, now the secret agent or resistance fighter was a frequent player in war games. The camp at Cultybraggan in Perthshire in 1958 featured Exercise 'Stretch', in which Fettes played the role of resistance operators attempting to subvert the designs of an 'occupying power.' They had a deep patrolling group, with an SAS instructor, moving across the hills to Glen Lyon, canoeists, ferrying craft in Royal Engineers assault boats, and six 'partisan' wireless teams. Not everything went according to plan; the canoeists found the Dochart too rocky and spent some of their journey on 'a kind naval lorry', the patrolling group were let down by the unreliable Seagull outboard motors of the assault boats, and the parachute flare fired by the two-inch mortar was 'little more than a candle' in the vast darkness of Loch Tay. Despite all this, a good time was had by all; other activities included a Royal Engineers course with a River Kwai theme in which a stone bridge was blown up and then replaced by a wooden one, and mountain rescue training with a Bristol Sycamore from RAF Leuchars.

A sign of changed times was that the cadets who were winched up into the helicopter had 'special telephonic permission from parents', something which would probably not have occurred to earlier generations of Fettes masters.[41]

In the 'mixed success' of field day in the same year, a tri-service exercise saw part of the Naval section exercising in a Motor Fishing Vessel on the Forth; 'her zigzag progress readily revealed the identity of the crew to members of the RAF section in a Chipmunk overhead.'

The CCF storms ashore in a combined-arms exercise on the Firth of Forth

Ronnie Guild remembers one exercise when a small team of 'Soviet spies' infiltrated Oban and were making their way through the grounds of a castle when they were intercepted by its owner, a retired admiral.

'Who are you lot?'

'We're secret agents, sir. From Fettes.'

'You *were*. Now you're going to escort my daughter to a ball in town. Her original partner can't make it.'

It is a sign both of the times and of their unquestioning obedience to orders from superior officers that the boys did as they were told, though this did mean that the other cadets were unable to find their quarry when they went spy-hunting. The Fettes CCF encountered Soviet spies for real in the late fifties when making their way to camp the long way round to the west coast in a Motor Fishing Vessel borrowed, along with a sailor in charge of laundry, from the Royal Navy. The Fleet Air Arm was at that time testing the new Buccaneer jet, and word was received that a Soviet spy ship had anchored ten yards outside British territorial waters directly under the flight path for the runway at Lossiemouth. The Fettes cadets made a beeline for the Russians and sailed round their ship in circles, waving enthusiastically. Ronnie Guild reflected later:

I often wondered if the Russians thought NATO had gone mad – sending a bunch of schoolboys dressed as sailors with a skipper in a kilt and a load of laundry. There was our wee outfit and the big Cold War business. God knows what report they sent back.[42]

Remembrance once more

Naturally, the *Fettesian* continued to report former pupils' military activities, and, as in 1919, the immediate post-war period meant sad announcements about those who would not be coming back:

The end of the war has brought to nothing the hopes, long cherished, that Calder Allan might still be in hiding somewhere in occupied territory. As a sergeant in the R.A.F., he and the rest of his crew had been last heard of after being forced down far out in the North Sea on their return from a raid; and it had always seemed just possible that they had drifted to the Dutch coast. But now we have to count him among those who have died very young but not without having achieved much in a short period of service.[43]

Reports like this continued well into the late forties, supplemented by news about the tragic loss of OFs who had survived the war only to be killed in accidents. The courageous Bruce Rae MC, who had served continuously with the Gordon Highlanders through Africa, Sicily and North-West Europe, fell from a faulty balcony in his barracks in Germany. Hamish Campbell was killed when his car hit a bullock-cart in the Far East, and J.R. Hannay in a motor accident in Wilhelmshaven. Stephen Dunnett, who had always wanted to be a Mosquito pilot, achieved his wish just before the war ended only to be killed when his aircraft crashed into the Malayan jungle some months afterwards. They would be added to the new war memorial.

On the fourth anniversary of VE Day, Sunday 8 May 1949, at 11 am

The extension to the War Memorial is unveiled in 1949

precisely, the Corps commenced a slow march up the East Drive to the tune of 'The Flowers of the Forest.' They wheeled round the War Memorial and took their places with the choir and orchestra, the masters, Old Fettesians and relatives of the fallen. The Headmaster read several sentences from the Bible:

But the souls of the righteous are in the hand of God, and there shall no torment touch them... And having been a little chastised, they shall be greatly rewarded: for God proved them, and found them worthy for himself.

Greater love hath no man than this, that a man lay down his life for his friends.

And I heard a voice from Heaven saying unto me, Write, Blessed are the dead which die in the Lord from henceforth: Yea, saith the Spirit, that they may rest from their labours; and their works do follow them.

The 23rd Psalm was sung to Crimond, a prayer was said, and Dr Ashcroft read out the names of the wartime casualties, whose names now appeared on tablets on the little balustrade around the fallen highlander commemorating the dead of 1914-18. 'While he read and the assembly stood in silence,' recorded the *Fettesian*, 'the sun came out and the dark clouds which had been hanging over Corstorphine momentarily disappeared.'[44]

As the tablets were unveiled by Great War veteran General Whigham and Herbert Waddell, President of the Old Fettesian Association and tank commander in Normandy, to the sound of the Last Post, three Spitfires roared overhead. After the Reveille, 'clear, confident and tuneful,' wreaths were laid by OF representatives of each service. Mr. Newman read from the Joshua XXIV: 'Behold, this stone shall be a witness unto us; for it hath heard all the words of the Lord which he spake unto us; it shall be therefore a witness unto you, lest ye deny your God.' 'O God our help in ages past' was sung, and John (Ian Hay) Beith addressed the congregation – 'it may not be out of place to mention here that the loud-speaker arrangements were excellent' beamed the *Fettesian*. The old warrior and writer, a pupil of the Victorian school and a master in Edward's reign, managed to encapsulate many of the strengths, doubts and hopes of the austere post-war world:

Twice in a generation the youth of our country have answered the call of duty; and on each occasion Fettes, a comparatively small school as numbers go, has made an outstanding – one might almost say an extravagant – contribution, as our Rolls of Honour testify. But extravagant or no, there are moments in a country's history where there is only one course open – to give with both hands, rather than hesitate and count the cost. That at any rate was the instinctive view taken by those whose memory we here honoured thirty years ago, and those whose memory we are here to honour this morning.

... They had complete faith in the ultimate victory of a righteous cause, and among themselves were a band of brothers. Their cheery confidence and camaraderie were the wonder of friend and foe alike. Here, then, seems to be the talisman for which we are all groping. Its name is Duty – the simple duty of living up to the tradition in which those men of ours lived and died, and of carrying out the trust that they have bequeathed to us. So let us see to it that we do not fail them, for they never failed us.[45]

At the evening service, held in the Gym because Chapel was out of action, Dr Ashcroft, whose presence along with other retired staff was greatly appreciated by the former pupils who had returned for the day, preached the sermon. His personal feelings for his old charges were palpable, and his humane philosophy clear:

We knew them; we watched the promise of their first terms here with eager interest; we feared for them in the callowness of their youth; for they were

603

vulnerable; we saw their mistakes, the mistakes of inexperience which rather endear them to us than made us doubtful of their potential worth. We rejoiced to observe their varying degrees of development, their growth in purposefulness, the gradual thrusting down of self as their sense of service to the community grew – and then when the grim call came, and they donned their khaki or their blue, they seemed at once to put on with it a new stature, a clearer vision, and an inward assurance of spirit, a radiant gladness which quite masked the fears that so tremendous an ordeal must have set up in their hearts. They were indeed lovely in their lives, and in their deaths most worthy of our gratitude and praise…

There is only one place in which we can with true fitness set up their memorial. It is in our hearts – it is by making them our examples. And that means that the one thing they so clearly saw, we must see clearly too; that the great enemy to the welfare of mankind has been throughout all history, and still is today, nothing else than man's own pride; his belief in his self-sufficiency; his arrogant claim to be himself the measure of all things.[46]

Fettesians abroad

Old Fettesians in the armed services immediately after the Axis surrenders fell into two broad categories; those called up for war service who now found themselves – often to their irritation – kept on into peacetime, and those who now left school and were scooped up by National Service. Jim Winterschladen was posted to Ceylon for trooping duties as a Liberator Captain. One of his last missions was to fly his Liberator from India to RAF Leuchars in Scotland, when he made a detour over the village of Great Ayton, where his parents then lived, flying low over their home in the hopes of waving to his mother. It startled many in the village, but unfortunately his mother was out playing bridge at the time and missed him. He was demobbed in August 1946 after logging 1,000 hours of flying time and, as he put it, 'living to tell the tale.'[47]

John Humphries was still on HMS *Glory*, which, having repatriated POWs, was sent to Australia in the hope that the natives would be sufficiently impressed to buy it. Unfortunately, as he recalls, its Seafires occasionally overshot the landing deck and ended up in the water, and *Glory* ended up in mothballs, to be reactivated for Korea and subsequently scrapped. Humphries ended up in the law. Ronnie Guild made the best of his enforced stay in the Far East. Finding that he had little to do, a friend arranged for him to borrow a train and recruited a Japanese crew to drive it. Guild travelled hundreds of miles through the Thai jungle on his own private train, living in a huge tank transporter fixed to a flatbed, armchair and thatched roof supplied gratis. His progress was finally halted by the slow progress being made in repairing bomb-damaged bridges, which forced him to retreat to Bangkok, where he watched the 'nasty drama' of Japanese army doctors being tried for the murder of injured Allied airmen.[48]

Not everyone had time to relax; officers were often expected to stay on and help demobilise their men, as Hamish Liddell discovered after VJ-Day:

After that it was a case of waiting for shipment back to East Africa but I got UK leave and flew to Bombay (my first flight) and after a few days boarded a Liberator where we were situated in the bomb bay. Engine trouble forced us to land at Oman where we stayed for a few days enabling us to visit souks and resist the blandishments of Arabs trying to sell us pearls. We then boarded the plane again and flew home via Lydda in Palestine (loading up with oranges which were impossible to get at home) and Tripoli, arriving in Cambridge where one's first impression was of lovely green grass smelling of rain – a welcome change from India. After two months at home I once more set sail from KGV Dock to Kenya, where we started demobbing Africans. My Class B release to go back to Oxford came through and I spent a week getting organised and having parties to find that I had missed my ship home. However by dint of hard talking I was flown to Cairo via Khartoum, then ship to Toulon via Malta, then rail through war torn France and after demob I was back at Oxford.[49]

For Bill Clark, with the Royal Air Force Regiment in Germany, post-war service had threats which were not always of a military nature:

The words of the officer in charge still remain clearly in my memory... 'Gentlemen, you are headed for a part of Germany where over 8 out of 10 women are afflicted with venereal disease. Don't ever forget there is nothing so overrated as sexual intercourse and underrated as a good stiff shit.'[50]

There were, of course, great opportunities for Germany's new masters. At the war's end Lyle Barr was at Kiel, having moved from his battery to be brigade GSO1, and stayed there for about a year:

Administration duties included coping with a red-tabbed busybody who one day told him that the General required a yacht (what used to be termed a 'windfall') and please to source one. Father passed the order down to his subordinate. A few

605

days later the brasshat was back. 'Well, have you found that yacht yet?'
'Yes, sir.'
'It'd better be a good one - the General is very particular.'
'It ought to be - it belonged to Hermann Goering!' [51]

Maj Barr's son still has some of Goering's Carinhall writing paper 'on which he (my father, not Goering!) had written to my mother.'

Bing Kirk, serving with the USAF, was billeted at the village of Bad Soden in Hesse, captured by three Americans in a jeep thus undamaged by war, unlike nearby Frankfurt which was in ruins. The population did not believe the films shown to them of Nazi atrocities, so removed were they from the reality of the previous decade. Like many others in ravaged post-war Germany, Kirk took advantage of the fact that cigarettes had become a kind of stable currency, and made $500 profit on ten cartons which he sold on the streets of Berlin – a useful addition to his salary, which he had previously augmented with the winnings from poker games. Having planned to study law after the war, he was made a legal officer with the US military European Air Transport Service (EATS), but his experiences showed him that 'justice was not always correct' and he decided not to make a career out of it. Much to his delight, Kirk was able to fly a P-51 from the nearby base and enjoyed exploring the region by air, but once went too far east and realized that the soldiers on the ground were Soviets. Even at this early stage, with the great powers still formally allied to one another (official American sources such as the Library of Congress date the Cold war as starting in 1947) it was obvious that relationships were not what they might be. John Humphries, who as a child had been warned by his mother to steer clear of the Russian consulate – 'everyone knew the communists stole children' – had seen at first hand how uneasy relations could be whilst serving on the Arctic convoys. The Russian pilot who led the British convoys through the Kola inlet developed a very friendly attitude towards his guests and promptly disappeared. By early 1945, other OFs were sensing just how flimsy Anglo-Soviet friendship had been. As his unit moved through Germany, John Cowie, supplier of whisky to POWs, was ordered to shoot to kill if necessary as the Russian advance on Magdeburg was preceded by a flood of refugees. Robert Saunders, too late to fight the Japanese in the Far East, was sent to take a platoon 'up country' north of Singapore to investigate a report of communist activity, his last action before being demobbed. Alan Harvey had crossed to Greece from Italy to prevent ELAS, the local communists, from taking over in the power vacuum following the German collapse. By May 1945 Churchill was asking the Joint Planning Staff for a war plan against the USSR – the appropriately-named 'Operation Unthinkable'. The following year, he denounced Stalin for having dropped an 'Iron Curtain' across Europe, and Ernest Bevin, Labour's pugnacious Foreign Secretary, was commenting that the Russians were 'just like the flamin' communists' he had fought in the trade unions. Tensions were becoming more and more open.

The *Fettesian* noted cheerfully in 1948 that 'tired though we may be of troubles and misunderstandings in international and domestic politics, it cannot be denied that an occasional crisis makes for much brighter Current Affairs.'[52]

Topics included the Nenni Telegram Affair (when Left-wing Labour MPs were persecuted by their leadership for supporting a far-left candidate in the Italian elections), the theory of communism, nationalisation, Palestine, the South African elections (which would lead to the triumph of apartheid) the Corps in the nuclear age – and, naturally, Berlin. The Berlin Airlift of 1948 saw the British and Americans manage to keep the western part of the city alive against Stalin's attempt to starve them out of it. It was an extraordinary moment in history, in which two nations which had, only a few years previously, been fighting alongside a third against a fourth, fed that fourth whilst the third's fighters angrily buzzed their transports. Two million tons of supplies were delivered, a quarter by the British, and the Soviet blackmail failed. Life at Bill Clark's base was hectic:

The planes were taking off and landing at very short intervals. Everything was timed to the last second. Along the runway were stationed five or six bulldozers. If an undercarriage collapsed on landing the crew had to stay in place and the dozers pushed them out of the way just in time for the next plane to land without breaking the timing. We had many Germans working for us who had been in service during the war. It was surprising that not one of them had faced either the British or the Americans. To a man all their experience in dogfights and panzer battles had been on the Eastern front.[53]

He appreciates the diplomacy of the German recruits, and, like most British people at the time, much enjoyed the bounteous provisions the Americans had to offer. Rhoddy Macleod was stunned to be given five cases of turkeys, each containing four birds, to feed his staff of nine for Christmas, and rather shocked to be told that 'it is just not worth the trouble for us to break bulk; if you don't want them, dump them.' Other aspects of American generosity were equally strange, as Clark records:

Each weekend there was a line-up of transport aircraft, each going to a different capital. You could pick Rome, Paris, Brussels, London, etc. On board you were likely to encounter a tubby American flight sergeant sitting on the auxiliary fuel tanks smoking a huge cigar and depositing the ash right onto the tank. Quite unnerving, but not worth declining the trips.

Bill Clark's base, RAF Fassberg in Lower Saxony, was so close to the Soviet zone that one of his colleagues estimated that if Stalin attacked the Russians would be twenty miles behind them by the time they had dug their live ammunition out of the armoury. On one occasion, the officer leading a convoy back from the American zone had his map upside down and they ended up in the Russian zone. 'Contrary to popular belief they were not seven feet tall and they did not have snow on their boots,' Bill notes, 'though they did wear furry caps with ear flaps.' Having served His Majesty faithfully in Germany, he not unreasonably felt that his contribution to the West's defence of liberty had been made. Unfortunately, when he moved to the United States, it transpired that Washington had other ideas, and he was drafted to serve in the Korean War. The American services did have their advantages – as a private he was paid around four times his RAF Pilot Officer's salary, not to mention better food and, in his Heavy Weapons Company, impressive equipment such as .5 cal. machine guns, 4.2 inch and 80mm mortars and recoilless rifles. Nonetheless, he was in no great hurry to sample the delights of the Demilitarised Zone. Salvation came in the unexpected form of an insect:

One afternoon my company commander detailed me to take a message to the Regimental Colonel. While in his office a huge bluebottle came through the window.
  'Catch that thing, trooper.'
  I grabbed his ruler and swatted the animal on the fly!
  'Jesus!' he said 'You have good hand-eye coordination. Are you a good shot?'

Bill had, in fact, captained the Fettes shooting team, and this saved him from this most grim Cold war posting, for he was instantly whisked by jeep to the shooting range, where he spent the next two years teaching others the joys of what the British still quaintly called musketry.[54]

D.A. Cameron also had to suffer national service abroad, in his case with the Regimento Grenaderos a Caballo General San Martin, a 'fancy toy-soldier outfit' guarding President Peron of Argentina, who was subject to occasional coup attempts. Cameron and his comrades were required to defend the presidential palace during one revolution but had no idea how to use weapons since most of their training was ceremonial, with swords and fifty-year old Mausers. Isolated on the roof of the building, they awaited bombing by the rebels but found that everything had gone quiet; peering over the parapet, they found the place deserted, evacuated by friend and foe alike.[55]

Phil Macpherson's post-war career was more pacific but was strategically vital; he directed the financial section of the Allied Control Commission in Vienna and was awarded the CBE for his work in reconstructing the Austrian economy.[56]

The Buenos Aires Old Fettesians in 1947: much to their annoyance, some were now elibible for Argentine national service

Not everyone's service abroad was so lucky; Christopher Johnson, a pilot with the Royal New Zealand Air Force Reserve who had ascended Mount Fettes in 1935, died in the same mountains in 1953 when the Harvard he was flying in a search for missing climbers was caught in a downdraft and crashed.[57]

Korea

The debaters, current affairs enthusiasts and members of the Wireless Club naturally watched the nation's groping in the track of the storm with interest. The British armed forces, including plenty of Old Fettesians, were involved in a host of international confrontations during the second half of the forties, in Berlin, Greece, Malaya, Indochina and elsewhere. However, it was the outbreak of war in Korea in 1950 which, as Gar Yates puts it, even a 'hermetically sealed' Fettes saw as 'the main international crisis of the time.' As Christopher Normand recalls:

Although this was geographically remote from us at school, the realisation of the renewed horrors of war soon came to us, as news filtered through of the death, in action, of several recent leavers. This was followed, later, by first hand accounts of those doing National Service, when they came to the school after returning from service there. The distinct possibility of having to go to Korea immediately after leaving school worried a great number of us, so it came as a huge relief when peace talks started in 1953! [58]

So far as we know, only one Fettesian was actually killed in Korea. Lt. David Haugh had in the mid-forties been one of the enterprising group which sloped off from a tedious Corps exercise to go to the cinema. An old friend wrote of him with real sorrow that he had been 'a gentle person to whom everyone wished well.'

His family was in the Army tradition and he went to Sandhurst. One who met him soon after he was commissioned has told me what a splendid young man he had become. There can be little doubt that his future as an officer would have been a bright one. It seems so often that War takes the best; and while we can be thankful that it has claimed no other Fettesians in Korea, it could not have struck a harder blow than by the untimely death of David Haugh. [59]

Haugh was killed on 8 May, 1953, as peace negotiations and prisoner exchanges were already well under way. He is, to date, the last OF to have been killed in combat serving in the British Army. Dr. Gordon Wylie, one of a relatively small number of surviving Fettes Korea veterans, was on a short-service commission with the Royal New Zealand Navy on board HMNZS *Rotoiti*, the former Royal Navy frigate HMS *Loch Katrine*. *Rotoiti* was on 'general duties' off Korea, which included anti-mine patrols, mine-laying, blocking North Korean naval attacks, support for land troops, occasional landing parties and, beyond the war, trying to prevent the piracy which remains a problem in that area. *Rotoiti* was on her way to Hong Kong when a distress signal was received from the merchant steamer SS *Hupeh*, which had been captured by pirates in the mouth of the Yangese Kiang. The pirates threatened to execute all on board if any attempt was made to recapture the *Hupeh*, so Rotoiti shadowed it until an agreement was made that the pirates would leave the ship unmolested. Dr Wylie recalled that with the pirates' own guns trained on the *Rotoiti*, this compromise was in the best interests of all concerned, and the *Hupeh* was eventually 'escorted in some triumph' to Hong Kong, where the officers were presented with silverware and the men with beer.[60]

When Able Seaman Peter Pryke developed acute appendicitis, Wylie performed an emergency appendectomy in the cramped quarters of the frigate, saving the man's life. The press picked up on the story, with Scots newspapers proudly announcing 'Sailor Saved by Glasgow Doctor'; the *London Evening News*, on its front page, reported that Pryke 'owes his life to the skill of a Glasgow doctor who operated under extreme difficulties in the New Zealand frigate *Rotoiti* off Korea.'[61]

A less fraught task was collecting Christmas trees from an island off the Korean peninsula; a skeleton was found with a bullet-hole in the skull, presumably the victim of an execution. Wylie kept the skull for some years until it disappeared 'at the same time as a (white) South African locum completed his term of employment'. The *Rotoiti* also took part in raids on the North Korean coast, either by landing men or supporting those landed from other ships. On one such raid near Chinnampo, the port which served Pyongyang, the *Rotoiti* shelled an enemy gun position before landing 15 sailors, who killed one enemy soldier in the act of throwing a grenade; two more were captured and handed over to the South Koreans (Wylie observed that 'there is little doubt that they would have been shot in due course'). One of Wylie's shipmates, Able Seaman Marchione, became the RNZN's only Korean War combat fatality on a subsequent raid on gun positions at Sogon-Li; Wylie was, however, able to deal successfully with the injured from a raid led by the cruiser HMS *Ceylon*, and was gratified to receive a telegram from the bigger ship's captain thanking him for his 'excellent work.' The *Rotoiti* was one of the most active New Zealand vessels in the Korean conflict, providing shore bombardment with its four-inch main armament in support of ground troops, to disrupt North Korean railways and artillery positions, and to prevent enemy attacks by sea. It was, as the RNZN's official history put it, 'hard and monotonous but essential work - denying the sea to the enemy while making use of it yourself', and, like his predecessors in two World Wars and successors in the later Cold War, Dr Gordon Wylie can be justly proud of his contribution as a medical man to the Allied effort.

The extent to which the Korean War affected British life is rarely appreciated today; in effect, it brought down the government. The Chancellor, Hugh Gaitskell, introduced prescription charges into the National Health Service, leading to the resignation of Nye Bevan, the champion of the Labour left. The badly split party went into the 1951 election without the confidence of the middle class, which was also profoundly irritated at the persistence of austerity and willing to give Churchill another chance. Their belief that he was better equipped to address international crises than the mild-mannered and increasingly exhausted Attlee also helped overturn Labour's majority, though it was not until 1955 that the Conservatives actually secured a plurality of the votes. The Soviet Union's possession of nuclear weapons and bases in East Germany also increased the nation's paranoia, as demonstrated by Christopher Normand's grandmother:

…my grandmother, Nar, was convinced that the Government would soon re-introduce the black-out (against the threat of bombing – presumably by the Russians, despite the fact that they were not involved in Korea). She had thrown out all her black material in 1945, but insisted that we should be prepared and proposed to attend an auction in Perth where she would obtain sufficient material to make curtains for every window. She was deposited at the door of the auction rooms, by Aunt Barbie, who returned several hours later to bring her home. Nar announced that there was no black-out material on offer (because no-one else was so prudent?), but that she had bought a Queen Anne dining table, as it was a pity not to use the money she had allocated! Forever after, the family dined off what we called 'Nar's blackout curtains'!

Paranoia was not confined to grandmothers. The possibility of nuclear bombardment was a worry after the explosion of the first Soviet atom bomb in 1949; General 'Pete' Pyman, who rose up the military ladder in the early years of the Cold War (eventually becoming NATO Commander in Chief Allied Forces North in 1961) delivered a shocking lecture to the Royal United Services Institute after the Korean armistice warning that the war-winning doctrines of armoured warfare used in Normandy and at Alamein were obsolete in the face of the bomb.[62]

Political paranoia also reigned in certain quarters. This was the era of McCarthyism in the United States, whilst in Eastern Europe the Soviets were rounding up anyone who they considered a threat – including thousands who had resisted the Nazis, on the grounds that doing so might have involved contamination by Western values or simply a little independence of mind. Britain was not untouched by this – indeed, some have argued that it was Churchill and Bevin who roused the Americans into taking a more robust international stance, rather then returning to the isolationism of the post-1919 period. The fact that the Communist Party of Great Britain numbered only around 50,000 members was neither here nor there; it aggressively justified promoting its ends by the same means as Stalin was using further east. 'Those who want to put the clock back are enemies of the people,' declared Willie Gallacher, the Scottish Communist MP, writing in 1949 of the fate of those who dissented in Poland and elsewhere, 'There can be no toleration for such.'[63]

Although, characteristically, the British never produced a McCarthy, there were vettings, especially of civil servants and teachers. Some boys at Fettes with an interest in world affairs and a sense of humour discovered that the authorities were prepared to take this educational surveillance from the staff-room into the form-room, as Christopher Normand discovered:

Two of my contemporaries began to correspond with the Russian Embassy, as a lark, and persuaded me to join in, which I did, having several posters of the Russian leaders sent to us, which we posted on our study walls. I soon tired of the rather obvious propaganda being sent, and dropped out, but the other two went on, encouraging the Russians to believe they had converts. This jape turned out to be rather more serious, later, as they were questioned, at length and in depth, by 'Security forces', and I seem to remember that both of them were refused commissions during National Service, as they were thought to have communist leanings![64]

In another sign of the times, the July 1954 *Fettesian* printed a prizewinning poem by 'J.S.B.D.' written in the aftermath of the US Castle Bravo H-bomb tests at Bikini Atoll. It was entitled 'High Noon' and reflects its time just as much as the Victorian jingo and thirties cynicism do:

Twelve minutes to noon...

The soft-lined landscape of Pacific isle
Is broken by the harshness of the steel,
The granite, the glass, and wiring of the high
Bare gauntness of this ferro-concrete pile,
In eerie disagreement with the sky.

A wide, blue, circle, the Pacific wheels
Unbroken to its pale horizon's edge…
But, high atop the building, on a ledge,
Men sit, and watch, and all creation feels
Their tenseness for the thing about to fledge
Into its hideous, harsh Nativity.

Two minutes to noon…

Within this stony nest of hidden power,
Power which demands so many million tombs,
Each grave-cool corridor, the sheercut tower,
Each red-hot room of scientists, assumes
Its true importance in this final hour…

Noon… Noon whose coming seems the end of all things.

New values oust the old which used to bind
Our narrowness and safety, here on earth,
And newer hopes assail the human mind,
Which gropes unseeing, overwhelmed and blind
When faced with this new monster's shattering birth.

It flings itself against the rock of time,
And, breaking ease of self-retiring life,
Thrusts through complacent selves a searing knife,
While the years before us crumble as we climb.

All this, we know: but rather than forget
The hateful power we hold, we struggle yet
To blast the future to its very core,
To banish Peace of Mind from Earthly shore,

Expecting rest or happiness no more...

Let no more such events deprive us of our love
Of Thee! Our only hope is in the Heavens above...
We mar the hallowed Earth which You once trod –
Kyrie, Eleison!... Have mercy on us, God!...[65]

Fettesians and the World

At least one Fettesian actually went to the USSR in the fifties; Ian
MacIntyre wrote of his summer trip with a party of public school boys,
led by Etonians, for the *Fettesian*.[66]

He was impressed with the post-war reconstruction of the beauties
of Leningrad and Riga, but noted of the latter that the people, who had
been forcibly incorporated into the USSR by the Molotov-Ribbentrop
Pact of 1939, were 'not very happy'. He was not very happy himself
when he was arrested; he was soon released when they realised he was
'nothing but a harmless Scotsman' and surmised that the locals had
spotted a stranger in a kilt and, never having seen one before, reported
him to the police. In Moscow, apart from the usual tourist round of the
circus, the VDKNh exhibition and the Kremlin, the boys enjoyed
cocktails with the British Ambassador and visited a Soviet school, where
they were impressed by the 'politeness and intelligence' of the pupils. The
highlight was the 'Gruesome Twosome', Lenin and Stalin, 'deep frozen'
in the Mausoleum in Red Square. Arriving in Minsk, they were treated
to a football match before travelling to Warsaw, whose people's liveliness
he contrasted with the Russians' 'drab servility', and thence to Berlin,
where he found the Western zone 'fabulous', unlike the grim East.
MacIntyre wrote that there was much the west could learn from the
USSR 'in the way of Sputniks and scientific development.' However,
although he concluded that he was very impressed by the 'friendliness
and helpfulness of the average Russian', he felt that the Soviets had more
to learn from the west 'when it comes to treating men as men and not as
machines' and doubted that 'any British worker would want to exchange
places with his Soviet counterpart.'

Many Fettesians of the forties and fifties admit to having not the
faintest idea of what was going on in the outside world; the front pages
of the newspapers in the houses' common rooms often remained
virginally pristine, and when television finally arrived, Gar Yates recalls, it
too was chiefly used to learn about sporting engagements. Christopher

Normand, by contrast, is certain that

...we at Fettes took a great deal of interest in the daily world news – we were all conscious that it would not be long before we would be involved in some way. The House Common Room had several daily newspapers and these were read avidly – not just the sporting pages.

The late 1940s saw the introduction of an actual Current Affairs period, in which suitably expert members of staff or outside speakers would give talks on Friday afternoons for both the upper and lower schools; according to the *Fettesian*, most pupils attended these. In the spring term of 1947, for instance, there was a talk on that post-war obsession, regional planning, by officials of the South East Scotland Commission, on Municipal Government by the Depute City Chamberlain of Edinburgh and on India by a Lt-Col Priestley of the Army Education Corps. Masters who spoke included Mr Newman on Parliament, Mr MacDonald on Democracy, Mr Goldie-Scot on Germany and, appropriately enough, Mr Jehu on transport.[67]

One of the most prominent visitors was the French General de Lattre de Tassigny, who addressed the pupils in French, a problem only arising when neither he nor his interpreters nor the pupils could work out how to translate 'physicist.'[68] He reminded the boys that they had a new loyalty to cultivate – that of a European citizen. Although the EEC was not yet in existence, the generation of British politicians which would ultimately take the UK into membership was just coming to the fore. Not all talks were successful; a *Fettesian* report in December 1947 grumbled that despite the staff and senior boys doing their best to instruct and entertain the lower school – including a Brains Trust and films on the Scottish woollen and iron industries – 'attempts at getting members of the 'audience' to offer intelligent comments are, however, disappointing.'[69]

In 1950, which saw a record six OFs in Parliament, the Debating Society held a hustings at which pupils spoke on behalf of the three major parties, plus a Communist. There does not appear to have been a Scottish Nationalist, though the Conservative, C.K. Irvine, did take a sideswipe at the Scottish Covenant movement which had collected over a million signatures demanding a separate parliament; 'the two countries had been successful together and would continue to work together.'[70] He also promised an 'even course' between Liberal 'rashness' (the policies of a party which, he said, was in any case 'no longer a force in British history') and the 'corrupt pockets in Socialist nationalisation.' The Conservatives, he promised, would bring freedom, but would keep the National Health Service. The 'rash' Liberal policies, expounded by P.I.D. Barty, included ending national service, wider use of proportional representation, curbs on government expenditure, and devolution – all of which were later 'borrowed' by one or more of the other parties. Labour's C.K. Moon dwelt on his party's achievements – full employment and the skilful exploitation of Marshall Aid, not to mention nationalisation. 'His picture of Socialist Britain was very rosy' noted the Society's chronicler, though it does not seem to have convinced the audience. The Conservatives, accused by Moon of being 'the party of the rich against the poor' and by Barty of being a 'plutocratic clique' romped home with 96 votes to the Liberals' 43 and Labour's embarrassing nine. This victory was repeated in subsequent mock elections. The Society kept abreast of developments in the world, debating in 1959 whether Britain should ban the hydrogen bomb and deploring what was then called the 'colour bar.'

In 1952, the school mourned the passing of George VI, which the *Fettesian* described as a 'great catastrophe.' 'There was no doubt about the sorrow which every member of the School felt at the death of the King,' wrote Mr. MacDonald, 'The outward symbols of mourning bore witness to a very genuine sense of personal loss experienced by everyone.'[71] Black ties were worn by both boys and masters, flags flew at half-mast and a memorial service was held on the day of the funeral.

There was something to celebrate in the rapid promotion of OFs to senior posts in the new Conservative government. Three progressive Fettesian Tories were especially noteworthy as the grim Labour forties faded and the fifties golden age of the Conservative Party dawned. Selwyn Lloyd, MP for Wirral, Iain Macleod, elected to represent Enfield West in 1950, and Ian Harvey, a public relations expert who entered Parliament alongside him for Harrow East, were all rising stars in the Churchill and Eden governments. The 'Vive-la' honoured their promotions:

> *Of their pair of Front Benchers Fettesians are proud,*
> *For they see Selwyn Lloyd sit by Iain Macleod;*
> *And while Lloyd tours the globe on Pacific adventures,*
> *Macleod will attend to our glasses and dentures.*[72]

CCF Officers and NCOs wearing black armbands to mark the death of George VI

Macleod had impressed Churchill with a robust attack on Labour Health Minister Nye Bevan, and was later to occupy his post. Although today he is often remembered as the Health Minister who, in 1954, chain-smoked through a press conference on the link between tobacco and lung cancer, he was committed to the NHS and did a great deal to humanise its bureaucracy. Lloyd, however, was somewhat nonplussed to be offered the post of Minister of State at the Foreign Office. When Churchill offered him the post, Lloyd later recalled, the conversation ran as follows:

Lloyd: But sir, there must be some mistake, I've never been to a foreign country, I don't speak any foreign languages, I don't even like foreigners.'
Churchill: 'Young man, these all seem to me to be positive advantages.'[73]

Lloyd was soon to find himself at disarmament talks in Paris (returning in relief from the hot hotels and rich food, 'longing for some badly cooked English cabbage'), visiting bombed-out Tokyo and discussing the peace terms in Korea. He soon gained a reputation for standing up to the Russians, who included Stalin's sinister show-trial prosecutor Vyshinsky, a man with 'cold and cruel eyes'. At United Nations talks in 1951, when Vyshinsky had made a ferocious 45-minute peroration, Lloyd offended him by quoting a Polish proverb to the effect that the cow which makes much noise yields little milk. He went on to turn Vyshinsky's phrase about 'countries marching to victory under the Communist banner' on its head by announcing that 'they are not going to march over us or our allies, and let us have no mistake or misunderstanding about that.'[74]

New Elizabethans?

Selwyn Lloyd had previously been Chairman of the Broadcasting Committee, and had – after investigation of how it worked in America – become the 'godfather' of commercial television in Britain, a decision which fitted in well with the more business-oriented Tory administration but one which he later found to be one of the great disappointments of his life.[75]

Like so much else at the time, however, television of any sort was seen as the great marvel of the age. Copies of the *Fettesian* throughout the fifties refer to it with the kind of bemused wonder that would later be applied to computers and the internet, and would report excitedly any time a former pupil appeared on it. Scotland's first television programme, featuring country dancing, was hosted by kilted OF Alastair MacIntyre on 14 March 1952, and was attended by 'a Glencorse boy named Baird, whose father was the inventor of television.'[76]

The magic box did not arrived at Fettes until the Coronation on 2 June the following year, when a large gathering of masters, ground staff, their families and those boys who lived in Edinburgh assembled round the school's only set. Four OFs were in the procession, and several cadets were lining the route, but none of the viewers recognised them. On Founder's Day that year, the music was appropriately New Elizabethan, with Walton and Vaughan Williams featuring prominently. Sir Robert Bruce Lockhart was Guest of the Day, and his message was rousingly optimistic and patriotic:

At the present time Great Britain was much admired abroad, partly for her achievements in war, and partly because she had conducted a revolution without bloodshed. If Europe were to be saved, it would be saved by the efforts of Great Britain.

But with the growing restriction of individual freedom there was a dearth of leadership, which was dangerous; for to stand still was to slip back. It was the new generation of public-school men who must provide leadership.[77]

He urged the boys to shun apathy and embrace adventure, adding that this was symbolised by that the new young Queen. They, he said, should respond to the appeal of the unknown, show curiosity, travel, enjoy the beauty and diversity of the world, and have no regrets. An adventurous spirit and a capacity for unselfish service; such was the quintessence of life. Whether or not the modern world still wished to be led by Britons in general and public school men in particular was not something which was widely discussed in 1953. On 15 June, several of the Navy section cadets attended the great Coronation Review of the Fleet at Spithead – 'a great and inspiring occasion' – with almost 200 ships of the Royal Navy, including battleships and aircraft carriers. 'The whole horizon was jagged with the superstructures of innumerable types of ships,' wrote the *Fettesian* reporter, who was impressed by the 'conservative magnificence' of the Royal Navy's imposing vessels. Although tired from the long round trip and the ceremonies in which they, along with thousands of other cadets, had participated, 'not one of us would have missed such a milestone in naval history.'[78]

Harvey's *Talk of Propaganda* was covered positively by the school, though the reviewer noted that 'to many of us the words "propaganda" and "advertising" are somewhat repellent.'[79] (This was characteristically Fettesian. A 1952 report quoted with horrified fascination an American magazine's reference to 'British-born Dave Olgilvy', the OF seen by many as the father of modern advertising, producing the 'sockiest copy' in the business. As late as 1959 there was a tone of mild discomfort at his 'diabolically clever' techniques. When he wrote that 'people who feel diffident about driving a Rolls-Royce can buy a Bentley' the Americans 'bought Rolls-Royces in droves.'[80] It was that word 'diffident' that threw down the gauntlet to the confident superpower. By a remarkable coincidence, Harvey had fagged for Ogilvy at school, and was recruited by him later; what the master of the dark arts thought of Harvey's early efforts, which included 'Trouble with your urine – try Cystopurin' is not recorded.[81]) The *Fettesian* noted with delight in 1953 that Harvey had impressed the *Evening Standard* as Britain's 'toughest MP' for taking a swim every day, all year round, in the Serpentine.[82]

When in 1957 he joined Lloyd in the Foreign Office, the 'Vive-La' celebrated with one of its ingeniously convoluted rhymes:

Her Majesty's Office of Foreign Affairs
Is a task Selwyn Lloyd with two deputies shares;

> *He has lately appointed another Fettesian –*
> *(As Harveys are common, remember that he's Ian).*[83]

Sadly, Harvey's promising career was cut short in 1958 when he was found in the bushes of St James's Park with a guardsman. Arrested for gross indecency, he was fined £5 for breaking park regulations (sportingly paying his associate's fine as well) and resigned from Parliament.[84]

By a strange coincidence, his successor as MP for Harrow East was also the subject of a sex scandal, though in his case it was a KGB frame-up. The *Fettesian's* interest in Harvey – a loyal old boy who had shown enormous promise – froze. His name would not be mentioned for over a decade. Iain Macleod, by contrast, was one of those instrumental in developing the policy platform on which young Irvine stood in the mock election; realising that the public did indeed see the Tories as a shower of hard-hearted plutocratic skinflints who had presided callously over the thirties depression, he and colleagues such as Enoch Powell and Rab Butler plundered Labour's most popular policies, describing them as One Nation Conservatism, whilst attacking the controls and rationing which the public disliked. This was to prove a winning electoral formula through the fifties, which many still remember as an era of great optimism and progress.

The cheerful confidence of these days would be severely shaken in the following years. Some have seen Suez as a turning-point, and it undoubtedly did worry a great many people. Dominic Sandbrook's remarkable history of post-war Britain, *Never Had It So Good*, however, suggests that cracks were beginning to appear before then, epitomised by Kingsley Amis' brilliantly cynical *Lucky Jim*, which appeared in 1954. Equally, Sandbrook convincingly demonstrates that most people – including Britain's allegedly rebellious youth – held broadly conservative attitudes through the fifties and well into the sixties. Two pieces in the *Fettesian* in 1955 encapsulate this paradox. In the summer of 1955, the Queen visited Fettes, allegedly to see if it would be a good place to send Prince Charles. It was characteristic of the era that the school's response was one of unashamed, delirious, patriotic excitement. The royal party arrived in a Rolls-Royce and was immediately treated to three cheers; 'That must have been heard at the castle,' commented the Duke of Edinburgh. The *Fettesian* reporter wrote with an adoration which is as unimaginable today as the hero-worship of the Victorians:

...all the things we shall never forget about this day: waiting, half nervously and half incredulously, for them to arrive; and then suddenly a figure in white with a touch of blue, and there she was, the Queen, a few feet away watching us, listening, smiling. How attractive, how beautifully dressed, what wonderful poise – majesty and simplicity both. And the Duke's bubbling humour: 'Can you play the cello in a kilt?' 'You masters will have to do better than this after tea.' And he wears a double-breasted waistcoat and no turn-ups to his trousers, and takes two lumps of sugar in his tea! She asked me how long I had been here; she said 'No thank you' to me, when I offered her another sandwich. They both waved directly to me, as they left; they are just like ordinary people to talk to.[85]

Grant Mathew, as senior NCO of the CCF, was delighted to represent Fettes at the OTC's 50th anniversary parade in 1958, which was inspected by the Queen; he remains proud of the fact half a century later, and was especially pleased to get a letter specially commending him. Likewise, Fettesians are convinced that Prince Charles would have had a much better time at Comely Bank than up in the wilds of Moray.

The Queen visits Fettes, 1955 and Fettes (or at any rate Grant Mathew) visits the Queen, 1958

A poem in the *Fettesian* in the year of the royal visit, however, shows that at least one of the boys sensed how a place like Fettes could be seen in a changing world. In 'Points of View', 'DWHB' wrote:

Noble pile, within whose rugged walls
Friendships are born to live through war and peace;
Silent instructor, who direct the thoughts
Of those whose years you fill with humble pride;
Lofty protector, who to minds alike
In field and form-room give the power to think –
Your men, ambitious, grateful, confident,
Press on to make well-known your mighty name
And gain assurance from your fellowship.

Heap of vice, whose nauseating walls
In furtive corners shameful secrets hide;
Silent hypocrite, who warp the thoughts
Of those whose years you foul with base conceit;
Arrogant self-possessor, who alike
In field and form-room furnish narrow minds –
Your products, stereotyped, repressed, untried,
Despise their lower classes' harder way
And bribe success by uttering your name.[86]

Unlike the mildly cynical satires of earlier days, this was an astonishingly brutal statement about the school. It would be unimaginable in pre-war *Fettesians*. However, it was not a universal view. Alasdair Heron was relieved to escape both some of the more brutal aspects of the CCF (as a piper) and then National Service (when it was abolished) that 'most of us, if faced with a 1914 or 1939 situation, would have reacted as earlier generations of Fettesians did. It was our good fortune that we were not placed in such a position.'[87]

Anthony Jacobsen even sees the CCF as useful, having taught navigation skills before sat-navs became available, and giving schoolboys an awareness of service life.[88]

Britain had survived the dour socialist grimness of austerity with many of its old beliefs surprisingly intact, and indeed a renewed sense of vigour encapsulated by the Coronation and the ascent of Everest, but it would, in the late fifties, have to face up to decline. Fettesians, both as National Servicemen and as the last colonial administrators, would now witness Britain's great power status, which their forebears had done so much to build up, became one with Nineveh and Tyre.

NOTES

[1] MacDonald, p. 235

[2] *Fettesian*, 1987

[3] Ibid., July 1949

[4] Ibid., July 1948

[5] Email to the author, 30 January 2009

[6] Christopher Normand, *Memoirs* (draft)

[7] Quoted in Philp, p. 70

[8] *Fettesian*, April 1947

[9] Ibid., 1990

[10] Ibid., July 1953

[11] Ibid., December 1948

[12] Ibid.

[13] Ibid., July 1954

[14] Barry Clegg, notes provided for *OFNL*, July 2010

[15] *Fettesian*, 2006

[16] Ian Harvey, *Talk of Propaganda* (London, Falcon, 1947) p. 111

[17] Devine (2000) p. 555

[18] Normand

[19] Email to the author, 18 December 2008

[20] Email to the author, 19 December 2008

[21] Email to the author, 24 December 2008

[22] Email to the author, 18 December 2008

[23] Email to the author, 29 September 2009

[24] Ferguson

[25] Email to the author, 19 December 2008

[26] Email to the author, 1 November 2009

[27] Ibid.

[28] Email to the author, 30 January 2009

[29] Ferguson

[30] *Fettesian*, December 1949

[31] Email to the author, 19 December 2008

[32] Email to the author, 18 December 2008

[33] Email to the author, 13 August 2009

[34] *Fettesian*, December 1949

[35] Ibid., December 1947

[36] Normand

[37] *Fettesian*, December 1951

[38] Ibid., December 1949

[39] Normand

[40] *Fettesian*, April 1948

[41] Ibid., December 1958

[42] In conversation with the author, 9 November 2009

[43] *Fettesian*, July 1945
[44] Ibid., July 1949
[45] Ibid.
[46] Ibid.
[47] Obituary, *OFNL*, June 2004
[48] Guild, pp. 89-97
[49] Email to the author, 14 September 2008
[50] Email to the author, 22 December 2008
[51] E-mail to the author, 12 August 2010
[52] *Fettesian*, July 1948
[53] Ibid.
[54] Email to the author, 18 December 2008
[55] *Fettesian*, April 1956
[56] Ibid., 1981
[57] Ibid., April 1953
[58] Normand
[59] *Fettesian*, July 1953
[60] Dr. G.L.Wylie, letter to the author, 22 August 2010
[61] 'Doctor operates on Korea man in ship', *Evening News*, 18 August 1951
[62] *Fettesian*, Spring 1972
[63] Quoted in Kynaston, p. 343
[64] Normand
[65] *Fettesian*, July 1954
[66] Ibid., December 1958
[67] Ibid., April 1947
[68] Ibid., December 1949
[69] Ibid., December 1947
[70] Ibid., April 1950
[71] Ibid.
[72] Ibid., July 1952
[73] Thorpe, p. 153
[74] Ibid., p. 160
[75] Ibid., p. 143
[76] *Fettesian*, April 1952
[77] Ibid., July 1953
[78] Ibid.
[79] Ibid., December 1947
[80] Ibid., July 1959
[81] Harvey, p. 37
[82] *Fettesian*, July 1953
[83] Ibid., July 1957
[84] Stephen Jeffery-Poulter, *Peers, queers, and commons: the struggle for gay law reform from 1950 to the present* (London, Routledge, 1991) p. 40
[85] Quoted in *Fettesian Centenary Supplement*, 1970, p. 53
[86] *Fettesian*, April 1955
[87] Email to the author, 19 December 2008
[88] Email to the author, 26 December 2008

Chapter Sixteen

'Jammy Bastard!'

The National Service Generation

'You're in the Army now!'

Since it was abolished in 1962, National Service has had a mixed press, from those who see it as symptomatic of an authoritarian, collectivist post-war culture to those who feel it had its merits. By the first decade of the twenty-first century, concerns about a decline in youth morale and indeed morality meant that as 2008 drew to an unmourned close even the *Guardian* could carry a piece calling for the return of National Service, albeit in a less martial guise. David Cameron, then Leader of the Opposition and alumnus of the Fettes of England, had proposed precisely this in 2007, though there were concerns about whether or not it would be compulsory. No such quibbles existed in the post-war era, either about its compulsory nature or learning to shoot people, at any rate in the bulk of the Tory Party and indeed the majority of Labour's new mass ranks at Westminster. National Service, Bevin claimed, would 'democratise' the services, as well as guaranteeing a strategic reserve of trained men from all sections of society, not just the 'public-spirited public schoolboys' who had formed a disproportionate element of Britain's small forces before 1914 and 1939.[1]

The looming fact of Indian independence was also going to denude Britain of one of her largest pools of soldiers, and the white dominions, especially Australia, were no longer committed to the knee-jerk loyalty to the mother country which had sent so many to Gallipoli and Tobruk. Despite these arguments, some 72 Labour MPs voted against the National Service Bill in April 1947, along with the 13 Liberals; Churchill was apoplectic at the behaviour of these 'degenerate intellectuals.'[2]

Most MPs supported it, and so did the public, who shared Labour's assumption 'that Britain must continue to be a main player on the international stage'.[3]

The international stage was very large, including, in the late forties, the Berlin Blockade and the onset of the Malayan Campaign. The fifties brought Korea, the Mau Mau, Cyprus and Suez – which some believe to have been the beginning of the end for National Service because of the widespread disillusionment with the concept of Britain as a superpower.

The summons to His, and later Her, Majesty's Service came in the form of a plain brown envelope and a medical, which some sixteen per cent of teenagers managed to fail, either through genuine illness or ingenious contrivances such as Kenneth Tynan's scent-drenched campery. No Fettesian seems to have done this, and some were actually keen to do their bit, to the extent that when National Service ended people like Richard Ling were rather disappointed and found other ways to get involved with the services. For some, the initial impression was quite positive, as Robin Mallinson recalls:

Our first meal was lunch of roast lamb, roast potatoes, peas and mint sauce and was excellent but was greeted by grumbles from most of those round me. They had not suffered from Fettes food during and just after the war! [4]

Others, like Angus Macintosh, actually volunteered for short service commissions in order to increase the likelihood of doing something interesting and to have some choice of postings.[5]

Nonetheless, at a recent Fettes Commemoration dinner, when Ronnie Shaw mentioned that, as a Hong Kong resident, he only did one day's duty a week, his contemporary Douglas MacGregor jovially responded with the Army's standard response to the fortunate – 'you jammy bastard!'[6]

Many Fettesians who served in the fifties had a degree of choice about where they ended up. Some were influenced by their parents; Alan Waddell, son of the flamethrowing tank commander, was impressed by what his father told him about the Gunners – 'when you get up at five in the morning to go and attack the Germans you need to know the British Artillery are there' – and joined accordingly. Christopher Normand had wanted to join the Royal Navy, having enjoyed his time in that section at Fettes, but when his medical established that his eyesight was not good enough for the 'seaman's branch'; he could be taken in as a 'Purser' or clerk, but 'that prospect was too awful to consider, so I decided to bite the bullet and join the army.' This raised the question of which part:

Although my uncle Dick had had a distinguished war with the Royal Scots, and could have recommended me to that regiment, I was not keen on the idea of the infantry, as I did not relish marching all over the place! The Royal Signals appealed, mainly because at that time they recruited large numbers of sportsmen and won the Army Cups for almost every sport. So it was decided! [7]

John Jeff, however, actively sought the tough life:

I asked to join a Highland Regiment because two of my father's brothers had served as officers in the Black Watch and Highland Light Infantry respectively in the First World War, and also I wanted it to be as different and as hard an experience as possible. Having been at boarding schools since I was 4½ years old (packed off to a small school in Assam in 1943 when it was feared that the Japanese might reach Calcutta, where I had been born), N.S. held few fears for me – the institutional life, the institutional food, and Fettes C.C.F. were all, surely, a good preparation for this eager N.S. conscript?

Then the envelope with the Joining Instructions (Seaforth Highlanders?- never 'eard of 'em!), and Travel Warrant (Fort George? Must be somewhere near Inverness, that's where the ticket's to…) It was a similar feeling to my first train journey to Edinburgh as a Fettes 'new man', but now all I could take was a small suitcase, not a trunk and tuckbox. No Waverley Station taxi, but an Army '3-tonner' awaited the ill-assorted gaggle of scruffy, round-shouldered youth that wandered out of Inverness station. 'COME HERE, YOU LOT! You're in the Army now!' [8]

When he arrived at camp for the beginning of his training, the young Fettesian, like thousands of others, found himself thrown in with a host of strangers – some of whom were the 'delinquents' about whom the nation's elderly were so concerned. Jeff recalls some such, following the brutal regulation haircut, 'almost weeping to see their precious 'Teddy Boy' hair and 'DA' styling lying in heaps on the Barber Shop floor.'[9] (Some servicemen promptly started growing it again; the Provost Sergeant at Neil Macnaughtan's camp at Detmold famously bellowed at an Old Lorettonian corporal 'if you grow yer hair that long, you'll hae to tuck it in yer gaiters.') There was also the strange medical check, which no-one ever seemed to fail and at which no notes were ever taken, that involved dropping the trousers to cough.

Nothing to worry an O.F., used to communal nudity, cold showers, and draughts. But it was exactly as it has been portrayed in so many films, even down to each 'cough' along a line of scrawny, naked, male youths, all standing with eyes fixed firmly ahead, awaiting the dreaded cold hand. 'Flat feet? No? Good! Passed! – NEXT!' – all over.

The instructors made their presence felt in no uncertain terms. Robin Mallinson found himself 'banged up', albeit briefly, which was hardly an outcome desired by parents who had sent their sons to Fettes:

Most of each day seemed to be spent doing drill. I made a small mistake on one of our first parades, the squad was halted and I was doubled off the parade ground to the guard room where I was locked up in a small cell for a couple of hours. I still remember the only window was small and barred and ten feet off the ground– no chance of escape! It was, of course, a "pour encourage les autres" exercise but I did begin to wonder how long I was going to be incarcerated. We were not allowed out of the barracks for a week or two but gradually our fierce sergeant became quite human and soon we were drinking with him in the local pubs. It transpired that he had been wounded in North Africa and when we asked for details he said his platoon had been tasked with attacking a machine gun post. He went on, 'One of those la-di-da officers called on us to follow him in a charge but he was almost immediately hit so we retreated and I was shot in the backside.' If true it was a sad little cameo of the war in the desert.[10]

It was, initially at least, a bewildering and intimidating experience, but one which in retrospect Normand came, rather philosophically, to understand:

The Regular Army (the volunteers), however, regarded us as an appalling nuisance, as few of us were interested in anything other than surviving the allotted two years. With a constant stream of recruits flowing through the system, it followed that recruits should be trained as quickly as possible, so that the army could get back something in return from our remaining service period. There was also a hangover from much earlier years of army discipline, which believed that only by 'breaking in' a recruit could he be expected to obey orders without question and learn his duties. The basic training regime was expected, in six weeks, to turn a naïve recruit into a fighting machine, so there was no time to waste. There was a lot to pack into that period. The regime was harsh! I am sure that the system did break some spirits to the point of a mental or physical breakdown – there were suicides. However, most of us not only survived, but we also learned to be rather more resilient than we would otherwise have been... However, despite much warning, the unrelenting screaming (and the sheer bullying) of the N.C.O.s did get me down, and it was largely thanks to the 'esprit de corps' that was built up amongst our intake, that we kept our sanity and sense of humour.[11]

The Fettes background was useful for many because they been used to the Spartan life. As John Jeff notes, 'twelve years of Boarding School discipline, food, relationships, fagging, communal showers, rugby on Young's in sleet and gales' were an ideal training since they 'conditioned me perfectly to make light of the less pleasant aspects of Army life, and make the best of what was on offer.' The CCF – mostly run by people with real military experience and just as traditional in its outlook as the real army – also gave a genuinely useful grounding in military knowledge. For some this was absolutely vital, in that the school Corps taught them skills they did not learn in specialised units. Neil Macnaughtan was in the Royal Tank Regiment:

For some reason Regiment personnel were given no training in field craft or camouflage, both of which were part of CCF training at Fettes. This would have made tank crews vulnerable had they had to abandon tank.[12]

However, he found that the grind of looking after one's CCF uniform was an equally useful rehearsal for army life:

Kit issues on arrival was in a rudimentary state and much time was spent polishing boots and brasses to bring them up to standard. The brasses needed vigorous rubbing with cardboard soaked in Brasso. Pimples on the boots had to be burned off with a hot spoon or poker prior to polishing. Toes and heels of boots were polished almost to mirror perfection... Wearing boots was painful, particularly for those unaccustomed to wearing boots, until the boots softened up with use. Most of those who reported sick at this time did so because of blistered feet.

Even Fettes, however, was not as grim as conditions at Catterick in the winter of 1956, one of the coldest of the century:

Snow showers continued until early June. Even though the nissen huts were heated by a stove, webbing, which had been scrubbed and blancoed for parade the following day, became covered in hoar frost. The parade ground was frequently covered with snow and ice, and on occasions drilling had to be carried on in an

The Glencorse section of the CCF in 1952 prepare for National Service

empty nissen hut. Cold water pipes were frozen and washing and showering were practically impossible. In an attempt to alleviate this situation the temperature of the hot water boilers was racked up to the extent that the hot taps in the ablutions were painful to touch, emitted clouds of scalding water and super heated steam, and made shaving a painful experience. I came in time to associate the Army with experiences like this!

Angus Macintosh, having volunteered for the short service commission, was interviewed by his depot CO and learned that the possession of both parts of Certificate A excused him from six weeks' basic training. Following an assessment by senior NCOs, he was appointed a weapon training instructor after only ten days. As an acting corporal with the Highland Brigade's green and purple 'technicolour' armband, he found that new recruits avoided him because they wrongly thought the insignia was the badge of some kind of regimental policeman. Unfortunately, this armband later ensured that during his advanced training at Fort George he was given some of the most difficult jobs, though the enjoyment he derived from subsequent postings made up for this. Not everyone was so lucky, and John Jeff remembers two of those whose spirits were broken. One shot himself by leaning on his rifle and pushing down the trigger, making a hole below his collarbone and in the ceiling, the bullet ending up in the bottom of a tin wardrobe in the barrack-room above. Another managed to hang himself by his braces from a high-level lavatory cistern: 'not pleasant for those who had to cut him down, but a real tribute to the strength of army-issue clothing.'

The six-week training began with written intelligence tests, designed to identify potential officers – as various historians have noted, this often identified the former pupils of public and grammar schools, thus effectively reversing the socially integrationist role Labour ministers supposedly intended for conscription.[13]

Jeff believes that this was one of the reasons his 'posh' accent was not the object of ridicule in training with the tough 'Jocks', commenting that 'I can only suppose that it was assumed that I would soon be off to become an Officer, and might take revenge upon my return.' Few officers actually took revenge, a famous exception being the broadcaster Michael Parkinson, who was sadistically shorn bald on the orders of a Corporal Fotheringham; on promotion, Parkinson managed to find a single hair under his erstwhile tormentor's bed whilst inspecting his billet, and sent the unfortunate NCO doubling round the drill square.[14]

The fact of their education also made public schoolboys useful in barracks. 'A surprising number of my fellow soldiers were married, and/or had never been away from home before, or received 'Dear John' letters from their girlfriends (and sometimes their wives), or were unable to write,' says Jeff, 'On several occasions I was asked to write love letters for lads who couldn't 'do words', and some of the quite extraordinary dictation I received would make any O.F. blush!' Even after training, Neil Macnaughtan's unit held mandatory refresher courses in reading and writing for the 5-10% of recent intakes who 'did not possess an acceptable standard' in these areas. Despite such extremes of education and background, most recruits did muck in together, and Jeff attributes this to the regimental spirit:

The people I served with were superb, and we all had absolutely no *doubt that we were the very best Regiment in the British Army. Most people would do anything for anyone, there was no obvious resentment or bad feeling between people of differing backgrounds (and religions), off-duty there was a fair amount of fraternisation between 'other ranks' and officers (it was fairly normal to see officers and men together in the same bar in town), there was very little bullying, although one or two would 'throw their weight about' sometimes, and this wouldn't last for long as it would be sorted out very quickly behind the N.A.A.F.I. It was not unknown for the R.S.M. to 'deal' with a problem person somewhere quiet and dark, to save the bother of a formal 'charge'. I soon realised that I was part of a very special community. With the exception of all Lance Corporals and just one N.S. Subaltern ('Haw the hayll did they ivver gie yon laddie a bluddy pup?'), all our Officers and N.C.O.s were well respected, some even revered.*[15]

Working-class recruits were aware of the way things worked, though seem to have been relatively philosophical, as Christopher Normand recalls:

Sometime during the second evening at Catterick, I had realised that my watch had gone missing, so I asked the chap with the next bed if he had seen it. He had already told me that he had just been released from Borstal where he had been for some unspecified (minor) offence, and he was incensed that I could think he would steal from a 'mate' (as I had, apparently, become). Later that evening he disappeared for a while, returning with a black eye and a bloody nose, triumphantly clutching my watch – he had worked out who the 'thieving bastard' might be, and had fought the culprit for it! We were mates, after all! Later, when I was moving on, he said to me 'Well, I suppose the next time I see you, I'll have to salute you, you toff, but you're still my mate!' Sadly, I never saw him again! [16]

Whilst the results of the intelligence tests were being assessed, there then followed three weeks of high-volume square-bashing, in which 'the instructors really came into their own with their own brand of bullying', and kit inspections, in which their clothing was thrown out the window if it was not ironed, polished or blancoed to some NCO's satisfaction. This could be supplemented by dawn raids (known as 'gripping') on the men's billets by more senior recruits pretending to be NCOs and really wrecking the place; Normand, who had owned up to boxing at school and been press-ganged into doing so for his squadron, was let in on the secret and allowed to escape to breakfast, thus teaching him that volunteering was not always a bad idea. Neil Macnaughtan, en route to Catterick in 1956 for training, was told by an RAF sergeant that one should never refuse promotion, never lend money and never eat more than two cakes in the NAAFI. Further training, needless to say, revolved around physical fitness, in the form of long-distance runs, ten-mile marches and assault courses. Weapons training was also important; although Fettes' emphasis on shooting meant that marksmanship with a rifle came relatively easily, the Army presented a new challenge:

Hand grenades were terrifying! We began by hurling unprimed grenades, but eventually had to throw a live grenade on the range, in order to pass. It may sound simple to pull out the safety pin, keeping a grip on the grenade until 'bowling' it at the designated target! However, several otherwise quite well co-ordinated recruits managed to 'freeze' when holding a primed grenade, and the squad had to take evasive action a few times – once, the instructor had to hurl himself at a man, pluck the grenade out of his hand and throw it away, after the culprit removed the pin, released the lever, and froze! Whatever the dangers, I believe we all passed (and I do not remember any major accidents).[17]

Still fresh in John Jeff's mind are the long-distance slogs and the ways that recruits found to survive them:

…the final 20 mile Route March in full kit, finishing off along the shingle beach from Ardesier to Fort George, all determined to keep on singing (I learned some most *interesting versions of various songs) amid mutterings of 'wu'll shaw the bustud hisnae busted uz' – being sent off in pairs on a 48-hour Initiative Test around the Highlands with no money, being picked up after only an hour by a Brooke Bond delivery van who just happened to be delivering to* all *the Inns on our list (we had to bring back signed beermats from each one), and returning unseen that same evening to F.G. to receive a 'rocket' the next day for 'not showing the right sort of initiative.'*[18]

There were other ways in which the respectable young Fettes alumnus could find out about the real (or surreal) world of post-war British society and its defence policy. Mallinson again:

Recreation was limited to visiting pubs in Salisbury and finding out by trial and error how many pints you could take and noticing the effects of drink on others. The big fat barrack room bully became a teddy bear while another reversed the process. In vino veritas.

While at Larkhill we heard that volunteers were needed at Porton Down, which was not far away, to test cures for the common cold. This involved an easy life for a few weeks, no drilling and a small increase in pay. Tempting but not quite tempting enough. Years later it transpired that the tests were for something far more sinister and that there had been at least one fatality.

After the weeks of heavy slogging in denim overalls, the recruits were finally allowed to wear their finely creased battledress uniforms and given two days' leave. For Douglas MacGregor, serving at Fort George with one of the less popular services ('I was big and ugly, so I was in the Military Police') this meant the chance to spend 18/-6', which went a long way at the NAAFI – 'fifty cigarettes, the flicks and fish and chips.' Unfortunately for Christopher Normand, when he proudly entered Ma Scott's bar in Rose St on his return to Edinburgh, he was refused admission as a mere 'other rank', despite his having drunk there as an under-age Fettesian. It was only after he had passed 'Wosby' – the War Office Selection Board – that Ma Scott, who, apparently oblivious to the fact that Rose St was and is a red-light district, had pretensions to gentility – condescended to serve the freshly-minted officer. Officer training included more drill conducted by more terrifying NCOs, the difference being that one was now 'an 'orrible little man, *sir*' and that it was possible to see glimmers of humanity and something to admire in the Sergeant-Majors at this level than in the Corporals lower down. Training here was rather more detailed and, unsurprisingly, focused on leadership. This did not, despite what those who stayed in the ranks imagined, make it any easier, as Robin Mallinson discovered:

It was supposed to be fairly tough but the main test was to keep out of trouble. During a parade taken by Regimental Sergeant Major Brittain, who had the loudest voice in the British Army, we were told to shout numbers while performing some drill and the cadet behind me, in shouting, managed to spit on my neck. I stupidly turned round, was spotted by Brittain, doubled off the parade ground and, unbelievably, locked up in another cell. Again I was left for a couple of hours and thought I would be in trouble but Brittain had a sense of humour and, having frightened me and the others, took no further action. On another occasion I was in charge of the guard which was mounted each night and for which you had to be immaculately turned out. I only needed to shave every couple of days but to be quite sure I shaved for the second time that day before going on guard. Next morning I had to leave the guard room last to make sure everything was spick and span and be on normal parade at 8. I washed quickly but it was completely unnecessary to shave and I didn't. We were closely inspected as usual and the sergeant saw some small mark on my face and asked me if I had shaved that morning. I foolishly said I hadn't as I had shaved the previous evening. I was immediately put on a charge – 'conduct prejudicial to the maintenance of good order and discipline' – and in due course appeared before the major. He told me how serious the charge was and that even after D-Day the officers made sure that they shaved every day! I thought I would be chucked out – it was called 'Returned to Unit' (R.T.U.) – but fortunately the lieutenant directly in charge of me spoke up saying that up to that time I had showed some promise and I was given only 7 days confined to barracks. This involved reporting to the guard room no less than 5 times a day and being closely inspected each time. I thought if I had been 'more economical with the truth' and said I had shaved I would have avoided all the trouble.[19]

The physical training was also rather harsh, though by now politics had entered the equation:

Towards the end of the course we had an enjoyable change from Aldershot by going down to Okehampton for exercises on Dartmoor. For one night exercise we dug trenches and waited for the 'enemy's' attack. It was a moonlit night and some time after midnight one cadet got bad cramp, jumped out of the trench yelling with pain and giving away our position. He was 'Returned to Unit.' Back in Aldershot we had some forced marches or 'bashes' which involved jogging many miles with full pack and rifle. One bash was 10 miles and although the final one was shorter it included an assault course. It was believed that if you did not finish in the time allowed you failed the whole course and the directing staff usually drove you on without mercy. However, some weeks earlier two cadets had died on the bash and questions had been asked in the House of Commons so the staff were a little more lenient. The last obstacle on the assault course was a large construction made of scaffolding poles. Climbing up was fairly easy. In theory, you then stepped across the poles on top, which were a yard apart, and then climbed down the other side but in an exhausted state it wasn't that easy. One cadet 'froze' on top and two of us had to prise his fingers, one by one, off the pole which they gripping. This caused some delay but we were looked on sympathetically for a change and we all passed the test.

Once passed through the training process, Her Majesty had to find things for the thousands of National Servicemen to do. Some of these were profoundly tedious – Christopher Normand remembers painting coal white, albeit as a punishment designed to show if anyone had stolen this still-precious resource, which he managed to subvert by painting every last lump – but there were very real security issues even within the United Kingdom. The IRA, although a small organisation by its later standards, had decided in 1949 to renew its campaign of subversion, and spent the early fifties stealing weapons from Army barracks around the UK in readiness for an attack on Northern Ireland. National Servicemen, prior to postings elsewhere, were required to patrol Britain's extensive network of military depots, generally armed only with pickaxe handles, and see to it that no more weapons disappeared. It was not the most entertaining of tasks, though it may have been some comfort for the young soldiers to know that the IRA campaign fizzled out after the shootings of half a dozen policemen and the loss of eleven 'martyred' gunmen, who were essentially the victims of their own delusional politics but who now occupy the same place in Irish republicanism's pantheon of mawkish self-pity as the executed rebels of 1916.

Officers and Gentlemen

Gar Yates' experience as an officer in the Royal Army Service Corps ('You will, I imagine, have no correspondent whose contribution to the nation's security was slighter than mine') lacked international derring-do, but had its compensations:

I hadn't particularly wanted to be commissioned and tried to argue my way into one of the Russian-learning courses, but I clearly had enough of the right qualifications to be on automatic track for officer training. It would gave been sensible to send me to Germany but instead I served as second in command of a Supply Depot in Hounslow, messing with a Transport Company more or less on the edge of what was then called 'London Airport' (now Heathrow).[20]

It was enjoyable nonetheless; the Army taught him to drive and he was able to take advantage of the cultural life available in London, where the Royal Festival Hall was still quite new and a much-admired venue. By contrast, former air cadet Mike North went very far afield in an RAF service which was 'great fun from start to finish':

I was fortunate enough to be accepted for flying training, starting with three months at O.T.S. at Kirton-in-Lindsay in Lincolnshire. The trip to Canada was on the liner France - an unforgettable few days in the company of about 800 young American girls returning from their grand tour of Europe! Train from New York up to London, Ontario, and thereafter to Calgary, and up to Red Deer, Alberta, where we spent nine months doing basics on Harvards. Glorious weather, but bitterly cold - down to -47 degrees at one stage! There was the opportunity for ski-ing in Banff National Park, and a holiday roaming up the California coast. Then on to Portage la Prairie near Winnipeg, for jet training on T33 Silver Stars. This was even more fun than Harvards, and the Wings Parade came all too quickly. After a short survival course in the Rockies, back for a week in Ottawa,

637

and then back to the U.K. in the Chief of the Air Staff's Comet, which happened to be returning empty at the time.

Although, as a short service officer, he did not find himself actually putting his jet training to use, he did spend 'three very enjoyable months' as Officer Commanding the Mountain Rescue Section at RAF Valley in Anglesey. Tim Daniels, serving with the Royal Artillery, had rather less contact with high technology. He spent several months with the 47th Guided Weapons Regiment at Crookham Camp near Aldershot, but never got to see the guided weapon in question, although his Commanding Officer, Col Cordingley, did go to White Sands to see it in action. It was the American Corporal rocket, a now-forgotten weapon which the Conservative administration hoped would be the cornerstone of Britain's defence in the missile age. Some members of the Royal Artillery section of the CCF actually went to see the Corporal in action at the missile range in the Hebrides in 1965. Possibly fired up by childhood memories – Corgi and Dinky had made working models of the Corporal – they got up at six for the train to Glasgow and a flight to Benbecula followed by rattling journeys by army lorry to South Uist to see the great device. Promised 'the noise of half a dozen Boeing 707s in flight', as it turned out the missile did not work, so after 'a surprisingly original salad for such an out of the way place' they were shown the computer room and flown home, 'disappointed that we did not see the missile fired, but otherwise pleased.'[21]

Corporal's purchase, incidentally, led to the establishment of Britain's claim to Rockall, from where Harold Macmillan feared the Soviets might listen in to secret radio traffic on the Hebridean ranges. As it turned out, they simply sailed to St Kilda instead, and the Corporal, which had an accuracy ratio of 46 per cent, about the same as the Dinky version, was quietly shelved in the late sixties.[22]

George Preston, flying Hastings transport aircraft, also came close to Britain's nuclear arsenal. In journeys which lasted seven days, the Hastings would move a strange ticking cargo (whose identity was never revealed but which was put under armed guard whenever the aircraft touched down) from Britain to Woomera rocket range in Australia.[23]

Tim Daniels went on to Mons OCTS 'for 16 of the most arduous weeks of my life'; he was subsequently posted to 'comparative ease and comfort in the RA's Training Regiment at Oswestry.' Another OF Gunner was William Sharp:

Before passing out we could give our preference for a posting either to the Far East (that almost certainly meant Korea), the Middle East (the Canal Zone in Egypt), Germany or Home. In deference to my mother I gave a preference for Home or Germany and I was posted to The Royal Artillery Trials Establishment at Ty Croes, Anglesey. I then endured the most boring 18 months of my life! The purpose of the Establishment was to experiment with ack-ack guns and rockets automatically controlled by radar. This may sound exciting but in fact all the experimental work was carried out by regular army boffins and the only function of the national service subalterns was to administer and look after the other ranks, who did the donkey work in the camp, of whom there must have been about 100 or so. The only local habitation was the village of Rhosneigr where you were more likely to hear Welsh spoken than English. During this time there occurred the only occasion on which I have attended a church service when I was the only person there apart from the clergyman!

Sharp had a few excitements, but they were few and far between and, as with so much of the National Service experience, tinged with the darker side of life:

The only upside was frequent week-end leaves, but going home to Newcastle involved a train journey changing at Crewe, Manchester, and York, and I have vivid memories of standing for long periods on deserted station platforms during the night. I did manage to play some rugby which involved travelling to Eaton Hall near Chester to play for Western Command, and during the summer we played local teams at cricket.

Camp personnel were part of an emergency rescue unit for climbers in trouble on the Snowdon range of mountains and on one sad occasion we found that the climbers were dead and we had to recover their bodies. There were either two or three of them and even now I can picture the scene as it naturally made a great impression on me. I think it is the only time I have seen a dead body apart from relatives.

Life as an officer was not cheap – another of the reasons why few working-class National Servicemen and indeed less plutocratic OFs gained, or even sought, promotion. Christopher Normand, posted to Cyprus, was painfully aware of the financial burden:

When we were commissioned, our rate of pay rose from 4/- per day (before stoppages) to 11/- per day – almost a fortune! Arriving in Cyprus, I now had a "local overseas allowance of a further 2/- a day! – riches! However, our initial outgoings, at the time of being commissioned, were hefty. We had to buy our Service Dress hat (£15), a Sam Browne leather belt, 'officer quality' green shirts and khaki ties, and a choice of Service Dress or No. 1 Dress ('Blues') uniform (about £40, tailor-made). We also had to buy a black steel trunk (my old school trunk was not 'regulation'). Therefore the prospect of having to buy more uniform, after arriving in Cyprus, was daunting, especially as young officers were not allowed to run up debts and we could not arrange an overdraft with our bank.

Normand had, on his second day at Mons Officer Cadet School at Aldershot, been summoned to see the Commandant, an old friend of his mother's and of ancient Highland lineage. The Commandant felt that he ought to join a 'decent' regiment like his own 13th/18th Hussars, rather than a rather tedious outfit like the Signals. Expense was a very good reason why Normand did not do so, for a cavalry regiment was more or less impossible in the absence of a substantial private income. Certainly, John Jeff didn't fancy it. 'I succeeded in failing it without making it too obvious, as I had been coached on exactly what to expect,' he writes of 'Wosby', 'I knew that it would cost my parents at least £1,000 (a lot of money in 1957) to kit me out as an Highland Regiment officer, and I knew they couldn't afford this and I certainly didn't want to be an officer in any other Regiment but the Seaforths.'[24]

Cold Warriors

A large number of National Servicemen, and of course Regulars, found themselves on the Cold War's front line in Germany. It is often forgotten that there was a genuinely-held belief, when Kim il Sung's Red Hordes invaded South Korea, that this could be a prelude to a push west by the Soviets, across the inner German frontier. Alan Donald had got his commission and was serving with the Second Regiment of the Royal Horse Artillery (L 'Nery' Battery) in the summer of 1949. From Ranby Camp in Nottinghamshire the whole regiment went to Germany to serve with the Seventh Armoured Brigade of the 7th Armoured Division (the Desert Rats):

Our barracks were at Hildesheim near Hanover in a former Luftwaffe camp- so infinitely superior compared with the wooden huts at Ranby in the U.K.! The only excitement came in June 1950 when the North Koreans invaded South Korea. As a contingency, we prepared for war with the forces of the Warsaw Pact. All tanks geared up, S.P. guns with full limbers of ammunition, and two days rations ready for parade at 6am the next day. Our Brigade's H.Q. was at Celle, only a few miles west of the East German border. It shakes one up to realise that National Service could mean dying for your country. Happily the Soviets did not invade NATO space! [25]

Many OFs in Germany served under General Sir Harold Pyman, who commanded the 11th Armoured Division and later 1 British Corps. As an old warrior, one of the first issues he had to address was personal and historical. 'I was soon faced with the problem of deciding what my attitude towards the Germans should be,' he reflected in 1971, 'Having fought against them through the desert and North-West Europe, and having seen Belsen, I found it hard to be normal with them.'[26]

He grew out of this attitude through the example of General Sir Richard Gale at Army Group Headquarters, who had fought to a standstill in 1918 and taken part in the D-Day Landings; if this man could forgive, so could he – 'continued enmity would have been sad and senseless.' As it turned out, relations with the Germans were generally good except when their agricultural land was chewed up by Sir Harold's beloved tanks. 'Farmers were no doubt compensated for any damage done,' says Neil Macnaughtan, hopefully. Like other OFs, he found the Detmold Luftwaffe facilities in which the Royal Tank Regiment was based 'far superior' to Catterick, partly because it had miraculously escaped the wartime attentions of the RAF (unlike the nearby Arminius Monument, known as 'Herman the German', which was repeatedly strafed). Equipped with Centurion tanks and Daimler scout cars, augmented with Auster spotter planes, Detmold was patrolled by German guards wearing Afrika Korps-style caps; other Germans worked in the cookhouse and offices, and displaced persons cleaned the tanks. Macnaughtan met some mechanics who had served on the Russian Front, and saw on a visit to West Berlin how the city still bore the scars of war and how the Soviets were not above using the conflict for their own purposes. At Helmstedt on the inner German frontier they hung a portrait of West German Chancellor Dr Adenauer next to one of his predecessor Herr Hitler. The Russians were not the only offenders; John Jeff noticed that since 'the HLI had been sent in to 'clear' Munster at the end of the war and had done their job, it was said, with great "enthusiasm", we Seaforths weren't at all popular with the locals!'

A more permanent problem which Pyman identified with the role of the British Army in Germany was that the advent of atomic weapons – and, by the late fifties, these included tactical rockets and free-fall bombs (Britain's plan to bury in the North German Plain a series of Blue Peacock nuclear landmines, kept warm through the winter by chickens, was not followed through) – made previous thinking obsolete. One bomb, Pyman noted, could now finish off a D-Day-type operation in an instant. Concentrated groups of British troops in Germany would likewise be sitting ducks as soon as any conflict went nuclear, and even if it remained conventional 'our operational task was just within our capabilities for a limited time' because of the sheer scale of Soviet forces. David Whigham Ferguson, serving with the Royal Scots Fusiliers in Berlin, remembers that 'We were told that we had enough ammunition for 24 hours as it was felt we would not survive past that time.' The Soviets, irritated by this Allied enclave in East Germany, did try to provoke incidents which they hoped would lead to the collapse of West Berlin, but the lessons of the Airlift had been learned and nothing came of them. Nonetheless, Pyman's men in Hanover and Westphalia were trained for responding to a Blitzkrieg across the inner German frontier, as John Jeff recalls:

We were there in Germany as the Cold War was hotting up, not too far away from the Russians, and we never knew if, one day soon, we would be at war, so firearms and tactical training was taken seriously. We had a couple of alarms in the night, when we were woken in the early hours, with two hours to pack up the Battalion (everything) and leave to we-knew-not-where, not knowing whether or not this was the 'real thing' - it concentrated the mind, and we were all, naturally, most relieved that these turned out to be army test manoeuvres, as we knew we were outnumbered by 'Ivan' not too far away .

Under the regulations of the post-war treaties, the Soviets were allowed to monitor BAOR movements in West Germany; this was one of the few times Neil Macnaughtan saw one in the area Britain was charged with defending against communism. Although they were not supposed to visit the training areas, one intrepid Russian officer did so and found his Volkswagen 'trapped between two British tanks.' He was escorted off the premises and his incursion reported. British soldiers were doing the same thing in the eastern zone, so it was not a serious problem. There were, as previously noted, more substantial scares. In 1956, during the crushing of the Budapest uprising, Macnaughtan writes, 'it was rumoured that American and British troops would go to the rescue of the Hungarian freedom fighters'; the Hungarians seem to have believed this too, and continued fighting in that forlorn hope until tens of thousands were killed. Had NATO intervened, Neil Macnaughtan might have been in the front line; 7RTR were at Suez, but his 3RTR were in Germany and might, in theory, have entrained south-east to liberate Mitteleuropa. As it was, the Americans pulled their troops away from the Austrian border so as to reassure the Russians that they would not start World War Three over Hungary.

The following year, Macnaughtan and thousands of other national servicemen took part in major manoeuvres. A tactical exchange of nuclear weapons was by now regarded as the normal run of proceedings should war break out, and the troops were briefed on the details of atomic warfare:

...in particular radiation sickness and flesh burns. On one exercise experiments were conducted digging trenches to protect from atomic blast and, despite the summer heat, balaclava helmets and gloves were worn to add reality to the exercise. At one of the BAOR manoeuvres an atomic explosion was simulated using explosives and petrol, which produced a convincing mushroom cloud. Infantry then mounted an assault towards the mushroom cloud.[27]

During such exercises, the armoured vehicles kept in touch by radios which could be somewhat temperamental, suffering interference from solar flares and other radios, often hundreds of miles away; Macnaughtan's Recce Troop Sergeant, a decorated Irish veteran of the Second World War, could be hard to contact on exercise because he kept his set tuned in to Radio Luxembourg. Although tanks were audible from a distance when they travelled on roads, the RAF's jets, which joined in with the bigger exercises, were so fast that no warning was given of their approach. It was on exercises that the national serviceman in Germany was most at risk; several were killed whilst sleeping under tanks which settled into the ground during the night, and crews were subsequently warned against the practice. Realism was sometimes taken even further. Macnaughtan's commanding officer, Colonel Holden, went to the atomic testing grounds in Australia and was in a Centurion tank when a small nuclear device was detonated about 1,000 yards away. On another occasion, an unmanned Centurion was placed only 500 yards from a bomb; incredibly, it was driven away, still working, and served with the Australian forces in Vietnam. The Centurions were among post-war Britain's greatest exports; at least one OF, Struan Wiley, served in them during his National Service. Mancaughtan's regiment practiced firing their main guns on a range at Fallingbostel/Hohne, aiming at a mock-up tank on rails over 1,000 yards or an old German tank at 2,000. Their mixture of armour-piercing discarding sabot and high explosive shells was delivered to sidings near the former concentration camp at Belsen. American personnel unloading their shells with a fork-lift were surprised to see the British laboriously unpacking theirs one by one; this was because the American shells were made of expendable alloys, whereas the British were brass and expensive. Macnaughtan once saw a Conqueror tank, a giant beast with seven-inch armour, on a firing point on the ranges, but the Centurion crews were not allowed to see inside it 'because of the sensitive nature of the equipment.' The Conqueror was quietly retired after ten years' service, with less than two hundred built, whereas many of the 4,500 Centurions still soldier on.

Life in Germany did not entirely consist of preparations for war. Tony Gilroy's experience in Germany would have struck a chord with the Victorian OFs who so enjoyed the games at Sandhurst and in India:

This was still in the cold war period so our time was very much spent on training for a Russian invasion. This involved some very large scale exercises involving the forces of N.A.T.O. and was very exciting at the time even though no physical fighting was going on. Army life was hard but very enjoyable with sport playing quite a part in recreation time. Several of us used to play for the regiment on a Saturday and then play another game of rugby on the Sunday for a local German team who were always short of players. The army taught me to sail, ski, ride a motorbike and manage people. All skills I have used in later life.[28]

At Neil Macnaughtan's camp at Detmold, facilities included a running track, swimming pool, squash courts and shooting range; golf could be played down the road at Bad Lipspringe and various sports teams were fielded. John Jeff shone in Army sports:

While in Germany, I played Cricket for a representative Army side as well as the Battalion, though I had only reached the 4th XI and Farmers' XIs at Fettes. 'Paper Chases' and Cross-Country runs at Fettes stood me in good stead in the winning team in the inter-Company cross-country competion. From Glencorse House Hockey 'Belows' I progressed to playing on tarmac drill-squares in Germany, and my speed and fitness from boxing and cross-country allowed me to play inside-left in the Battalion side alongside Sgt. Greenhalgh, a former Scottish International, and after several matches I found myself teamed up with him in a representative Army side; to this day, the scars on my knees testify to the hardness of German tarmac! [29]

Winter sports had a serious purpose for those posted to Austria, which like Germany had been divided into Allied zones of occupation. Angus Macintosh, stationed in the East Tyrol, 'enjoyed three superb winters where a number of us became proficient skiers towards our role as mountain troops in any subsequent conflict.' Most of this was the cross-country langlauf form of skiing with full kit – a lesson learned from several wartime campaigns – but the more enthusiastic and efficient also enjoyed hurtling downhill at speed. Geoff Wilkinson, who had enjoyed tinkering with the school's Austin Seven, was posted to the REME Workshop in Berlin in 1957, where he had a valuable role as Junior Workshop Officer. Berlin's controversial 'island' status in East Germany meant that the workshop, which comprised 15 Army personnel and 400 German civilians, 'was responsible for the repair of all Army equipment from Tanks to Meat Slicers.'[30]

A good shot – he could even put in a good performance with the notoriously unreliable Sten in local competitions – Wilkinson also had his own driver and a stylish Mercedes 170Vs (bought for £40). 'Life was very interesting and pleasant,' he writes, 'as I met my future wife who came out from the UK to visit her parents who were stationed in Berlin with the RASC.' For him, National Service was almost like a gap year prior to a career as a naval architect, though he does note that others might have 'more realistic' experiences.

Life could indeed be tough, as John Jeff attested when giving a picture of the overall experience:

…rum in our sweet tea on 'exercises' (yuk!) – wet clothing hung to dry on trees in a German forest, heavy overnight frost, men trying to stand up in sleeping-bags while attempting to thaw/dry their clothes at the camp fire, then shaving in freezing water in a mess-tin, and eating breakfast off the unwashed tin – choking in the dust, on top of or behind a tank, wondering if I'd ever get clean again –

Geoff Wilkinson and Mercedes

being so tired that I fell asleep on top of our platoon's rifles on the floor of a truck – my first experience of death, when two Seaforths, having stolen a 'Champ' to go into Munster on a snowy evening, missed the main gate of our barracks on their return, and wrote-off the vehicle and themselves all along the avenue of trees outside - getting drunk myself, for the first time, on NAAFI wine (cheaper than the beer!) – marching onto parade with the 1st Battalion in full 'Number Ones', every kilt swinging in time to 'Scotland The Brave'.

The Firing Line

Still, despite all the confrontations and hardness of life, most notably in the late forties and again in 1958-61 in Berlin, the National Servicemen in Germany and Austria never saw a shot fired in anger. T.P. Durie, one of the wartime Fettesians, was awarded the George Medal in 1951 when he rescued a sergeant from electrocution at considerable risk to his own life. In Cyprus, however, there was a shooting war when a determined effort was made by nationalists to pursue Enosis – union with Greece – much to the disapproval of the Turkish minority and British administration. Cyprus had technically been a crown colony since the twenties but it had always been understood by the Greek population that it would join the motherland, whereas the British favoured autonomy without such incorporation, partly because they preferred the Turks. There were so many Fettesian National Servicemen in Cyprus that nine were able to celebrate a Founder's Day dinner in 1956. Christopher Normand generally found his own posting there very pleasant – it was sunny, food was good and cheap, and mess life was boisterous and amusing – but the EOKA guerrillas, who struck for the first time in 1955, were more than a nuisance. In 1956, for instance, they succeeded in blowing up a Skyways Hermes airliner at Nicosia airport, and were to kill a total of 156 British soldiers and policemen. British service personnel were required to carry arms at all times, and many made the effort to acquire extra weapons – usually, as in Normand's case, 'liberated' wartime German Lugers or Italian Berettas procured through 'non-regulation' channels. Although a number of the older officers had some experience with handguns, the younger generation, often with pistols in shoulder holsters worn under their jackets whilst in mufti, had to be trained in a hurry. 'We were like cowboys,' Normand recalls, 'worse, we were like a bunch of schoolboys with toys!' The reality of the situation was brought home forcibly at the St. Andrew's Night Ball, which his expatriate parents, committee members of the Cyprus Caledonian Society, had helped organise:

At 11.10 p.m., while we were dancing a waltz, all the lights in the hotel went out, but the band continued to play. Suddenly, I was struck on the ankle – a glancing blow, but painful nonetheless – and I heard a heavy object bounce twice on the floor. 'Bomb!' I yelled and we all dived to the floor. About a second later there was an explosion, a very bright flash, then silence. Even the band stopped. Then there was pandemonium! A paratroop officer thought he had seen someone leave through a window and dived out after him (landing 10 feet below!). Several others rushed to every exit to try to secure the place, and, almost immediately the lights came back on. It was obvious that a few people had been injured as there was a lot of blood around, but no-one was killed – which was a miracle.

In the ensuing tussle, all the Cypriot waiters were seized, Normand père threw an intrusive photographer's camera out the window, and a stout-hearted matron tried to restore perspective by climbing onto a table to sing 'Rule, Britannia'. Normand fils found the bomb which had bounced off his ankle; a Mills grenade, it had ended up near to the spot where his mother was sitting and, fortunately, failed to explode. Despite this experience, the senior Normands continued to live in Cyprus, and their son was able to alleviate the hardships of winter life by moving in with them – not an option available to most National Servicemen. Although her son's habit of cleaning his revolver in the drawing room and hiding ammunition beneath the sofa in the absence of a proper safe caused Mrs. Normand some distress, she did enjoy the bargain prices of the NAAFI. Cyprus was one of the most rumbustious NS postings, but others had the potential to turn nasty. Roger Christian, serving with 1st Batt. the Worcestershire Regiment from mid-1956, had spent some time in the by-now familiar surroundings of Sennelager Plain in West Germany. A more exotic posting, however, was to come, when at Christmas that year the Battalion was posted to the West Indies, sailing via Las Palmas to Trinidad, Jamaica and finally to Belize, British Honduras. Still a crown colony, British Honduras was periodically menaced by its large neighbour Guatemala, which claimed all or some of the territory and whose right-wing authoritarian governments would use the issue to distract attention from their own incompetence – a tactic repeated some years later in Buenos Aires. Christian 'spent the remaining nine months of his National Service on garrison duties and doing manoeuvres on the Guatemalan Border in the interior to dissuade them of their aspirations to take over.'[31]

British troops are still there, but, partly thanks to their presence, the Guatemalans have never invaded in force. Robin Mallinson also served in an exotic posting, the former Italian colony of Eritrea, which had become a United Nations mandate prior to its self-government and (temporary) absorption into Ethiopia. Given his previous record, there was something almost inevitable about his experiences en route:

At last I received orders to embark on the troopship Empire Ken *in Southampton by 4 p.m. on a certain day. I arrived about 2 p.m., gave my name to someone on boarding and found my cabin where there was a captain settling in. He told me the ship was not sailing until 4.30 the next afternoon. I told him I had an uncle and aunt who lived a few miles from Southampton and I wondered if it would be all right to go and see them and be back by noon the next day. He thought it a good idea and I stupidly attributed too much authority to him and walked off the ship. When I returned the next day I was immediately apprehended and taken before the colonel commanding the troops on board. Apparently there had been a hue and cry for me, I had been posted AWOL (Absent Without Leave) and my name had been notified to the War Office (no less). There was mention of serious consequences but instead I was told I would be Orderly Officer for much of the voyage to Port Said. This meant being on duty for 24 hours and making various inspections including going round the ship three times during the night. My inspections took me down to the bilges where defaulters who needed locking up were held. The cells were terrible, right over the propellers, some with little or no flat area and Dickensian in every way. I was a bad sailor for the first few days at sea but thought I could not possibly duck out of my duties so kept going despite sickness. Years later I met someone who recognised me and we discovered that we had met on the* Empire Ken. *He then said 'Of course, you were the chap with the green face who followed the colonel round on his morning inspections.' I enjoyed my days when I was not Orderly Officer and discovered a drink called John Collins. I liked it so much I was called John Collins before the trip was over!*

As a former seat of Italian colonial governance, Eritrea's capital was a pleasant enough posting, apart from the roaming bandits in the hills:

Asmara was peaceful with a good climate and the food with the Italian influence was very acceptable, especially as it included steaks which, of course, we did not get in the U.K. at that time. The local brandy was very cheap and not so good and I was put off brandy for ever. I managed to get around the country, which was largely dry scrubland, doing small welfare jobs, one of which involved visiting Massawa where there was a welfare yacht – a pleasant diversion.

On the *Empire Ken,* Mallinson had met a senior artilleryman who had been looking for keen recruits for his new unit in Kenya, and, as the only gunner officer in Eritrea, Robin Mallinson soon moved south to a new world. Although the 303rd East African Artillery Regiment was equipped with 25 pounder field guns and 3.7 inch anti-aircraft guns, and for firing practice would drive north to the Northern Frontier District for the kind of unrestricted blasting of which some gunners could only dream, it was the sheer joy which remained with him:

Nanyuki was a great place to be for a National Service soldier. There was plenty of sport throughout the year – hockey, cricket, golf, tennis, riding – and all round you there was wild game and even more in the N.F.D. Going on exercises there was not very different to going on safari but there were no tourists and few restrictions on shooting. We would shoot sand-grouse before breakfast, have them for breakfast, do training and firing, rest in the heat of the day, and in the evening go shooting guinea-fowl or just looking for game. The animals were magnificent-elephant, lion, oryx, giraffe, boar, hyena, rhino, zebra etc. and many different kinds of gazelle. Within a few weeks of arriving I was taking photos of a herd of elephants with my 5/- (25p) box camera. I was behind a bush trying hard to keep the camera steady with the elephants only about 30 yards away…

Another opportunity we had was to go on expeditions up Mount Kenya, which had permanent snow. You had to be a real climber to reach the summit, unlike Kilimanjaro, and it had only been climbed for the first time shortly before the war. We, in our army boots and with no proper equipment got to a lower peak of 16,000 feet and once two of us circumnavigated the mountain, starting in the dark and getting back to camp by moonlight.

Another feature of the landscape was the Rift Valley which had some magnificent vistas. There were places where there were vertical drops of thousands of feet and no tourists (or indeed anyone else) for many miles. Not all Fettesians had such inspiring experiences of exotic climes during their National Service. Charlie Lang served in another jungle, fighting communists in Malaya. Like the Victorians and the Forgotten Army of Burma, he was plagued by the local climate and fauna as much as by the guerrillas in the jungle. 'The mosquitoes were appalling,' he writes, 'They were huge and could bite through every part of our uniforms apart from our jungle boots and by morning my right eye was almost closed.'[32] As an experiment he folded a blanket, only to see a particularly enthusiastic mosquito penetrate two thicknesses. These were only the beginning of Mother Nature's Asiatic horrors:

Apart from the mosquitoes there were leeches which would gather round the waist and ankles, and on the back of the neck. They seemed to be everywhere, even in my dreams! They could be removed by prodding them with a lighted cigarette. Sometimes on returning to camp I poured some blood out of my boots where the leeches had become squashed. We often slept in hammocks, and cigarettes were also useful for stopping ants coming down the hammock ropes. They would not cross a barrier of soggy tobacco. The army supplied each man with 50 free cigarettes in a waterproof tin each week, and if working in the swamp, a tot of rum. There were jack ants 2" long which were harmless (we were told that they were good to eat), red ants ¾" long which were fierce, ants with large jaws which cut the skin, centipedes 6" long which had a nasty bite, enormous spiders which hung between the trees in the plantations, and the occasional scorpion. Once I walked through a hatching of white butterflies. They were so numerous that one couldn't see the ground, like a white out in the snow. While on patrol we were not allowed to use soap as the smell of it on the swamp might give away our position, and since many patrols lasted several days you can imagine what we smelt like by the time we returned to camp. The first shower was very enjoyable.

The conditions of jungle warfare were not merely uncomfortable; they could be fatal. On one patrol, a corporal felt unwell, complaining of a headache; by midnight he was dead. He had probably been bitten by mites from the rats in the local village, leading to scrub typhus and encephalitis. The soldiers' clothes were treated after washing, and the next person who felt ill was immediately evacuated by helicopter; fortunately, no one else died. Charlie Lang did, nonetheless, retain the OF's appreciation for nature's less unpleasant features, as well as for the qualities of the locals, most notably the Iban people, two of whom were seconded to his platoon to advise on jungle warfare:

The Ibans were from headhunting tribes in Borneo and were very proud of being in the British army. They liked their uniforms and their weapons and showed us many things including following and reading tracks in the jungle, and what to eat and what not to eat. They were quite superstitious. When we heard the blood-curdling screams of a howler monkey they told us it was the devil. We killed a monitor lizard 5ft long which they cooked and we ate. They also caught a large python which they prepared and ate. The Iban caught it by the tail and David Swinfen [Another OF] cut off its head. There were plenty of python steaks to go round but only the Ibans and the officers would eat it. The Ibans cut tasty bamboo shoots and wild lychees which were a bit sour and things like egg plants which we ate. I never saw a wild elephant but we sometimes saw their footprints and droppings and flattened areas where they had gathered. There were mouse deer, tortoises, monkeys in the trees, colourful birds and wild pigs which were told were very fast and dangerous. A pangolin (large scaly anteater about the size of a very large badger) walked into one of my ambushes and climbed onto a low branch in fear of the dog. Its scales glistened in the moonlight and it looked mysterious. I tapped its scales and it hissed at me. We held the dog back and the pangolin lumbered away into the darkness.

Again, as with previous generations of Fettesians, tropical military life had its compensations:

The officers' mess at C Company was a happy little community. I shared a grass house or 'basha' with David Swinfen. Major Colin Stoner was Company Commander with a captain, Bill Davidson as second in command, three 2nd Lieutenant platoon commanders and two intelligence officers who were captains.

The beds were fitted with mosquito nets which was very necessary. Abdul, a Malay, was cook and barman and Lal, a Tamil, was 'dhobi walla' (laundry) who sometimes cooked us a very hot curry and watched as we ate it. We wore only towels for this meal. There was a pineapple bush outside our basha which produced pineapples, but we were too slow and someone always pinched them. Because of humid heat and lack of sleep, operations were exhausting and during the spells in camp we relaxed by playing games, listening to records, reading and I continued my correspondence course which I had started while in the Suez Canal Zone. We also played Badminton and basketball and there were film shows in the camp.

On 15th December one of the intelligence officers, Andrew Myrtle and I went to a Malay festive occasion to socialize. After speeches in Malay, we ate a curry and walked round absorbing the atmosphere. Some of the young men appeared to be in a trance, dancing round on hobby horses, probably high on something. Someone produced a guitar and a microphone and I sang a cowboy song with the whole crowd clapping in time, followed by rapturous applause. We socialized with the local rubber planters who were very hospitable and liked having us around. One elderly planter called Puckeridge and his wife were particularly entertaining. Sometimes we heard gunfire from their direction and when we phoned to find out if they had been attacked, his wife would say that it was only 'Old Puck' giving a fire power display.[33]

As for the terrorists, they were progressively isolated in the jungle as Sir Gerald Templar's twin-pronged plan of clearing 'squares' of territory and 'hearts and minds' operations were put into effect. Whilst the rain forest had retained much of its traditional unpleasantness, there was now modern technology unknown to the Victorian soldier which could make military operations more efficient. Lang recalls with gratitude the new inventions; helicopters, which could drop men into primary jungle, where lightweight saws could be used to cut through the foliage to allow access. The 'Wickham Trolley', an armoured car named for an assassinated Governor, ran on the railway lines and had a machine gun mounted on the top, though the presence of mosquitoes by the track was a perpetual irritant. The serious work still had to be done by men wading through swamps carrying 70 pounds of kit, watched by a comrade covering them with a rifle in case of crocodiles.

Actual contact with the enemy was infrequent, and when it happened the training and equipment of the British soldiers did not guarantee success:

A patrol from another platoon following a track, found a small, temporary CT camp and killed two CTs but not before one of them had shot and killed the Iban who had discarded his carbine and had attacked them with his machete. The subaltern involved was awarded the MC. We sometimes found camps that had been hastily abandoned leaving food or bits of clothing and tools. We ambushed some pig sties for three days because the special branch thought the CTs might fancy some pork, ambushed paths to durian trees (durians smell of tom cats but taste all right and are very nourishing) and arrested curfew breakers.

The soldiers in Germany did not have such extreme conditions, but still had their challenges to face. Having evaded becoming an officer, John Jeff did get his stripes as an NCO, which put him, as occasional Battalion Duty Sergeant, in a position of being the first line of discipline against the more high-spirited soldiers:

The worst part of this duty involved clearing the NAAFI at closing time (terrifying job, especially on Thursday (pay-day) or Friday nights trying to remove very drunken Scotsmen who were quite happy where they were, thank you - surprisingly, no-one ever 'put one on me' or gave me a 'Glasgow Hello', although there was a lot of 'see you, Jimmy', which a mixture of humour and firmness usually managed to sort out.

The only time I had any real trouble with a fellow Seaforth was on exercise on a very cold night on a German heath; we were all in slit-trenches awaiting an attack on a clear moonlight night (how the eye plays tricks!) and I had finished, utterly frozen, my 2-hour 'stag' on sentry duty and woke up the lad sharing the other (covered) part of the trench to tell him it was his turn - he told me to 'go away' in his brightest Glaswegian, and, when I insisted, he drew his bayonet on me, and he meant it! I invited him to get on with it, but reminded him of the consequences, and told him if he removed the knifepoint, by now pressing on my waistband, I would 'forget' about it and not put him on a 'charge' - he saw my point of view, but it took a very long minute! A large proportion of our lads were from the tougher and less pleasant parts Glasgow, and many of those had been 'in trouble' before being called-up, so it is a great tribute to the spirit in the Regiment that things so seldom turned really nasty like this.[34]

Society had, in many respects, changed, and truculence amongst the troops was by no means uncommon. Even during the Second World War, the recalcitrant George Campbell Hay had been delighted to hear an Aberdonian ask a 'nagging' NCO, 'Did anyone ever hit ye afore, sergeant?'[35]

John Rankin, newly-promoted in the Black Watch and conducting operations against the Mau Mau in Kenya, had to deal with a troublesome old sweat called Fisher who was reluctant to accept orders from a 'Pepsi-cola drinking bastard from St Andrew's.' Placing the insubordinate soldier under close arrest, he was faced with the problem that the only accommodation in which to put Fisher was a tent.

One cannot ultimately confine a man in a tent if he does not wish to be confined there and Fisher did not wish to be so confined, nor did I seriously contemplate mounting a guard over him – he was the strongest man in the platoon and would obviously resist such a move with force – indeed he assured me that 'he would shoot his way out of this!' The unpalatable option was to summon an escort from Coy HQ and simply ignore Fisher until its arrival. As luck would have it, wireless communication had broken down and Fisher and I would have to endure each other's company for several more hours! On the following morning he refused to parade, but by this time I felt that he had lost any sympathy he may have had with the platoon – 'authority deserts a dying king' – and they realised that Fisher had far over-stepped the mark and was for it.[36]

Several months later, Rankin was dining with his Brigadier, who casually mentioned that his very good batman, Fisher of the Black Watch, had been 'badly handled' by a junior officer. The junior officer thought, but did not say, that he had felt in imminent danger of being badly handled by Fisher. On another occasion, a barrack-room lawyer called Keenan set himself up as platoon spokesman with a series of grievances. Rankin called all the men together and announced that, since they always heard from Keenan, it would be a nice change to have a contribution from one of the fighting men ('a rather unkind reference to Keenan's employment as platoon storeman'). There was silence so Rankin made some conciliatory remarks and left, hearing as he did so Keenan 'cursing the platoon as spineless idiots'. After this incident, oddly enough, the two got on quite well; 'I dared to think that I had earned his grudging respect for having ca'ed the feet from under him!'

Returning to Civvy Street

The majority of Fettes alumni who joined up in the late forties and through the fifties did their compulsory two years and left. When their service came to an end, several, including Christopher Normand, were offered the chance to stay on, but he was keen to go to university and, accordingly, set sail from Cyprus on the troopship *Dunera* on 24 August 1956. The journey was enlivened by the presence of a high-spirited colonel's daughter who was being sent home in disgrace having been found under a lorry and, more to the point, under its driver. The young subalterns were kept as busy as possible but with over two thousand servicemen on the ship there was not enough for everyone to be given a job and Normand's last significant military role consisted of playing records over the ship's radio – ably assisted by the colonel's daughter. John Jeff was 'de-mobbed' at Mill Hill Barracks in London at the end of February 1959, which he found a complete, and frustrating, waste of time. He would have loved to return to Fort George for one last time. Apart from reporting in twice every day, he was left to his own devices:

I had been promoted to Sergeant for a final week's Exercise with tanks on Luneburg Heath before leaving Germany, (to tempt me to stay on- I never even got to use the Sergeants' Mess!), so noone at Millhill knew what to do with me; I went home and collected my motorcycle so that I could travel home every day without too much expense. On demob., non-commissioned National Servicemen were all recorded as Privates, since any NS rank was never made 'Substantive'. I very nearly signed-on as a Regular - I would have kept my rank, and Sergeant's pay was very good compared to the salary I could expect to return to in 'civvy street', especially with all meals, clothes, and housing provided, but parental pressure persuaded me to be demobbed.

The process of standing around bored was always part of service life in one way or another. Nonetheless, all of those who contacted the school with information for this book felt that it had at least some good points, and many thoroughly enjoyed themselves, whether they gained commissions or remained in the ranks. Their reflections are interesting, and subtly varied. Robin Mallinson remembers the enjoyable parts of his experience in the late forties:

Within a few weeks I was enjoying the very different environment of being one of many thousand impecunious undergraduates at Oxford and feeling that this was the real world and the past two years had been a strange experience. Initially one had been rushed about, shouted at and bored at times but always there was something new coming up and always there were amusing companions. Being commissioned and going to Kenya made the whole experience memorable. My memories of Kenya are the animals, birds, deserts and mountains and the camaraderie of the mess. It is difficult to remember much about the soldiering. If I had spent the two years in some unattractive location in the U.K. I would probably have felt that it was a waste of time.

Christopher Normand, although he enjoyed many aspects of National Service, is frank about how many people viewed it:

Some of us did, actually, learn a trade or a skill that stood them in good stead in their civilian working lives. For most of us, though, it was a two-year period when, academically and financially, we just stood still, and many still think that it was two years wasted. Nonetheless, for most of us it was unavoidable. Having endured years of boarding school, I was better prepared than many for much of army life!

Neil Macnaughtan, who 'met servicemen from all walks of society' and 'struck up strong bonds of friendship' initially felt disorientated when he was demobbed after his two years' service.

Although service in the Army could often seem irksome, particularly for those in the ranks (in my case military service resulted in two years' loss of professional experience which I never really made up) it was something I would not have missed and it brought me into contact with many interesting people. And one felt physically very fit. Indeed I haven't felt like that since demob in early 1958!

John Weston Smith was one of those who felt he had genuinely learned the kinds of useful skills Normand talked about:

National Service, in the Royal Signals in the UK, was a memorable and formative episode for me. It was a continuation of my education after Fettes, with some 9 months' rigorous training and then putting into practice what I had been taught. In addition to basic soldiering, Signals officers had of course to master a range of technical matters, covering telephones, teleprinters and wireless etc., as well as management skills, which later proved invaluable for me in business life, especially when the computer age arrived. My training also gave me confidence at a young age to exercise leadership in my job, and it made me grow up.

John Jeff, meanwhile, was saddened by what happened to the Seaforths:

I never regretted a single moment of those two years. Perhaps I was lucky? I had assumed that National Service would be boring, which is why I chose to 'do it the hard way'…Naturally, I do regret that the Seaforths are no more, having been amalgamated and, later, absorbed into The Highlanders. I wonder how they teach Regimental History now? Had we seen action, we would have gone, proudly and primarily, as Seaforths, not as Scots, or Highlanders, or soldiers of the Queen. I'm so glad that I had the chance to be part of that special 'something'.

Gar Yates, too, found the experience valuable, and wrote:

It's not enough for me to say that on the whole I enjoyed my time very much, that I learnt to drive while on officer training, that, and so on. For anyone who was going to stay in academia thereafter it was a taste of slices not just of life (actually Fettes was not at all a bad preparation for it) but also of practical responsibility that would not have come any other way; I grew up a lot, and I think most of my contemporaries would say the same. It was an expensive burden on the exchequer, but when it came to an end in the early 1960s it left a gap; I find it hard to believe that society would have been so 'broken', to use Mr Cameron's term, had it survived.

NOTES

[1] Tom Hickman, The Call-up: A History of National Service (London, Headline, 2004) p. xiv

[2] Quoted in ibid., p. xvi

[3] Kynaston, p. 369

[4] Email to the author, 29 January 2010

[5] Letter to the author, 19th November 2009

[6] The annual Fettes reunion and opportunity for OFs to revisit their old houses and wonder if education has gone downhill since their day.

[7] Normand

[8] Jeff

[9] Ibid.

[10] Mallinson

[11] Normand

[12] Neil Macnaughtan, letter to the author, 21 January 2010

[13] See, for instance, Kynaston, p. 372

[14] Hickman, p. 19

[15] Jeff

[16] Normand

[17] Ibid.

[18] Jeff

[19] Mallinson

[20] Email to the author, 18 December 2008

[21] Fettesian, July 1965

[22] Paul Brown, 'British Warhead was a Dud', Guardian, 6 September 2003

[23] In conversation with the author, July 2010

[24] Jeff

[25] Email to the author, 26 December 2008

[26] Pyman, p. 119

[27] Macnaughtan

[28] Email to the author, 21 December 2008

[29] Jeff

[30] Email to the author, 10 January 2009

[31] Email to the author, 3 January 2009

[32] Lang

[33] Ibid.

[34] Jeff

[35] Quoted in Helen McCrory, The Thistle at War (National Museums of Scotland, Edinburgh, 1997) p. 16

[36] John Rankin, A Subaltern's Diary: Kenya 1954-5 (1990) p. 6

Chapter Seventeen

'It was fun while it lasted'

The Retreat from Empire

Premonitions

In the thirties, Robert Bruce Lockhart warned his British readers about the iron wheel of history, which would, one day, leave their empire in the dust – though he did accept that this might seem like a lack of faith equivalent to treason.[1]

As he travelled around the Far East, Lockhart was made aware of the rising educated classes of the imperial territories, politely but steadily developing nationalist and, in some cases, communist ideas: in Malaya, he saw a leaflet in several languages which urged the oppressed masses of all races to 'rise with one accord.' 'How long could Europe keep these Asiatic races, now fertile with new ideas and new ambitions, under subjection?' he wondered. The illogicality of his own position – seeing nationalism as a virtue in Europe but not outside it – was something of which he was painfully aware, but he could not bring himself to accept that British withdrawal would be wholly beneficial to the colonies. Britain had, after all, brought economic progress and a measure of order, clamping down on piracy and internecine warfare. Into any vacuum left by decolonisation might come communism or fascism. An obstinate Dutchman told him that the natives would be ready for independence in three hundred years; a British expert said twenty-five. When war came, as OF Malaya veteran Charlie Lang recalls, seeds were indeed sown of future trouble:

The situation in Malaya had originally developed during the Second World War. In 1942 the British in Singapore concentrated their defences against a Japanese attack from the sea, wrongly believing that an attack from inland through the jungle was impossible. They enlisted the support of the locals and trained them in jungle warfare to fight against the Japanese, and once the war was over these same people became a very effective force, controlled by the Communists, to drive the British out of Malaya.[2]

'Fettes was a school of the Empire, where lots of boys were encouraged to go out as administrators, soldiers or merchants,' recalls one OF, adding (he is a Londoner), 'Of course, that may have been because Scotland was such a bloody awful place and people wanted to get away from it.' He and his contemporaries were to see this state of affairs evaporate within two decades. John Darwin[3] has identified the seismic change in the world order occasioned by the Second World War as one of the most important reasons for the collapse of colonialism. It gave the USA and USSR the predominant global position once occupied by the British, changed the priorities of the public at home, and saw the white man humiliated by the Japanese. Additionally, the British abandoned their previous policy of leaving native populations alone as much as possible, and interfered with their lives to a much greater extent, for instance through both unwonted and unwanted heavy taxation, thus creating discontent among peoples who had previously tolerated imperialism. These peoples often became willing disciples for the new class of nationalist agitators, previously a bunch of bourgeois intellectuals – 'brown sahibs' – who had not previously been as popular as post-independence propaganda claimed. In the longer term, Britain was increasingly focused on its Atlantic position, both economically and strategically, and then developed an interest in Europe.

This was not, however, immediately obvious in 1945. Because of the collapse of France and Holland in 1940, the British found themselves in charge of even more colonial territories than they had held in 1939. These were seething with nationalism and the overstretched imperial forces were in the odd position of using both Indian and surrendered Japanese troops to keep order. Vietnam and Indonesia were held for their respective colonial masters by a Britain which was negotiating in Delhi for independence. Other colonies were considered as yet unripe for self-government. Post-war Fettesians, therefore, were to be involved in both decolonisation and attempts to keep the Empire together.

Forties withdrawals: Palestine and India

One of the earliest accounts we have from a Fettesian serving in the retreating Empire is from Freddie Scott, who had served with the airborne forces in Europe, and in 1946 was one of those trying to keep the peace between two heavily-armed groups with God on their side. In the then British Mandate of Palestine, Arab and Jewish nationalists were fighting each other, and the Crown Forces, over rival definitions of self-determination. Of these, the Zionists were, if the more recently-arrived, by far the better motivated (hardly surprisingly) and, thanks to wartime military service, often better trained. They were, therefore, the most irritating to the exasperated British soldiery:

Many 'terrorists' had been tried by the courts and sentenced to a term of imprisonment. However, then were very adept at then escaping. The prison authorities called in the Army to advise them how to make the prisons more difficult to escape from. At the time we were billeted between Jerusalem and Bethlehem and I was allotted Bethlehem prison on which to give my advice. It was only when I got to the prison that I discovered it was a female prison. Being shown round by the Governor (a lady) I was very embarrassed to be the subject of wolf whistles from the far from unattractive prisoners. However, I gave my advice – mainly the use of a lot of barbed wire on walls etc – and I learned that there were no subsequent escapes at least while I was still there, some 3 or 4 months before I was demobilised.[4]

Scott's memories of the Jewish groups are not favourable, and with atrocities such as the bombing of the King David Hotel staining the Zionist record this is perfectly understandable. Earlier Fettesians posted to the region had been sympathetic – A.R.T. Jackson, who had been at Sir Oswald Mosley's rallies in the thirties and was posted to Jerusalem during the war, remembered that 'even at that time, when the Jews were only beginning their State of Israel, it was remarkable to see what they had achieved out of really fairly barren country.'[5]

At that time, it was the Arabs who were seen as the troublemakers. Some things, however, hadn't changed. Like Lt Wolfenden, patrolling the Holy Land during the First World War, Scott was profoundly unimpressed by the behaviour of the competing Christian factions. In the Church of the Nativity:

I may have the specific sect wrong but the situation in the Church was something like this – the Catholics 'owned' the floor, the Greek Orthodox the walls, the Russian Orthodox the windows, the Protestants the ceiling and roof. So if the ceiling needed a repair the Protestants would have to lay a carpet so that they didn't walk on the Catholic floor, get a special pad from the Greek Orthodox to put on their ladder so that they could lean it against the wall etc!

This kind of thing could get out of hand, and one of the tasks of the

British Army – which was already busy enough trying to cope with attacks by the Stern Gang – was to try to keep order at the Church of the Holy Sepulchre, which like the Church of the Nativity was split between a plethora of bitterly hostile brothers in Christ, some of whom made quite extravagant claims of divine favour:

Every Easter the Patriarch of the Greek Orthodox church came to the church bearing an unlit candle which was 'miraculously' lit by a flame shooting out of the rock. In 1946 this ceremony at which the congregation lit their candles from that of the Patriarch had not happened since 1939 because of the war. In consequence an enormous number of pilgrims were expected and the British Governor was very concerned for the safety of the Patriarch who was small (about 5'2") old (±80) and frail. The Oxford and Bucks were detailed to look after him and I was in charge of things. Selecting our Rugby fifteen we formed a scrum round the old man and prevented him from being squashed. The crowd was enormous and when we got him up to the wall the 'miraculous' flame appeared and amid screams and yells the congregation of pilgrims lit their own candles and so on. I saw the priest with the 'Bunsen burner' creating the flame! However, I have always maintained that it would be unfair to tell this to any of the pilgrims, many of whom had saved all their lives to afford the journey.

Bemused Jewish policemen now have the responsibility for keeping order in such holy places, and, so far as the OFs who served there are concerned, good luck to them. Much to Scott's distress, his coveted red beret, which so intimidated the Germans, was stolen from a Jerusalem restaurant, but he lived to tell the tale, so this seems to have been the worst thing the various Zionist groups – who eventually achieved independence in 1948 – inflicted on him.

One of Freddie Scott's more pleasant duties in Palestine: providing a guard of honour for the Emir of Transjordan

Writing in 1971, Sir Harold Pyman, who also served in Palestine, took a long, if coloured, view. Whilst he said that he did not know which side was right, he went on to suggest that he had a pretty good idea:

I do think that the average Englishman tends to think of the Arabs through Lawrence's pre-1917 eyes and gets a too glamorous image of them. He forgets their laziness and shiftiness. And he thinks too lightly of the Jews, forgetting their industry and pertinacity, and forgetting, if he ever knew, the promises made by Balfour and others on behalf of England about their future home. He allows too the prejudice of centuries to colour their image and forgets too readily the shameful way the Jews were treated in Europe before and during World War II.[6]

Acutely aware of the treatment of the Jews was Rhoderick Macleod, whose ship home from Africa had dropped off a number of refugees, interned for the duration of the war in Mauritius, at Haifa. After the war he found himself Area Intelligence Officer Bremen, which involved liaising with the Americans, organising local security, and using the captured files of the local Gestapo to hunt for Nazis. Since the Soviet Liaison Mission was actively spying on the British, his role included counter-espionage. He was rather shocked to discover that the attractive lady friend of his American opposite number was on a secret wanted list of SS personnel. 'So what?' said the American, 'If she's in bed with me she ain't up to any mischief I can't handle.'[7]

Palestine, however, was officially a League of Nations Mandate rather than a prized imperial possession, and it had no oil; the British got out with great relief in 1947, handing the problem over to the League's successor, the UN, and whatever local Darwinian forces could triumph. India was different; countless Fettesians had been trained to work there and it was vital for imperial defence and trade. Yet it was the first to go; its large and sophisticated nationalist movement had been in action for years, and had a number of supporters in the Labour Party. Indian Army officers took it for granted that self-government was going to come after a war in which they had played their part; their country was already administered to a great extent by its own people (nine in ten judges, for instance). The problem was not so much whether India should govern itself, but how, since Jinnah's Muslim League was insistent that it would not be dominated by the Hindu Congress Party. In this intractable situation, two of the best-known imperial Fettesians played important roles. Experienced and dedicated figures ('few British civilians knew the Frontier more intimately' said the *Times of India* of Sir George Cunningham[8]) they nonetheless did not always possess that impartiality towards the different religions of the subcontinent in which Fettesians serving in the Indian Army had taken such pride. Like Lord Birkenhead, who, according to a disapproving Paul Johnson, 'saw the Muslims as the Ulstermen, the Hindus as the Irish Nationalists'[9] they had very strong preferences. Their actions in the years immediately following the Second World War remain bones of contention for politicians in the region even today. Sir George Cunningham, former Governor of the North-West Province and known as 'Pussy' whilst at school because of his cat-like quickness on the pitch, was the Guest of Honour at Founder's Day in 1946. In his speech, he made an allusion to how things were changing when he told the school that the young Pathan with whom he had to deal was not so very different from the British schoolboy – except perhaps for 'a greater capacity for bookwork.'[10]

He had seen the rise of Muslim nationalism in his fiefdom during the war, and was not unsympathetic, regarding it as better for Britain than the Hindu Congress Party, which occasionally showed interest in the Japanese and which he regarded as 'subversive'. 'Our Muslim Leaguers are still staunch and helping us with in doing the right sort of propaganda,' he wrote in 1942, noting later that, whilst the war lasted at any rate, 'the people are happier under the present form of government.'[11]

When Sir George died in December 1963, Iskander Mirza, the first president of Pakistan, wrote that 'I never came across a greater gentleman, nor a more brilliant administrator. He was an example to all the officers of the Indian Political Service.' Auchinleck told him, following Cunningham's subtle and successful handling of the INC's civil disobedience campaign of 1942, that Sir George was worth two army corps, since the North-West Frontier Province, traditionally a powder-keg, could now be used as a place of recuperation for troops exhausted by the malarial jungles of Burma.[12]

In 1945, whilst recognising that the Muslim League had been suitably loyal, Cunningham felt that their demand for independence was neither efficiently promulgated nor universally popular; even amongst educated Muslims ('hardly a large number') there was 'no enthusiasm among that class for Pakistan in its stark separatist form.'[13] The millions of inhabitants of the Frontier regions continued to vote on local issues, he believed, but that did not mean that they would view with enthusiasm incorporation into a Congress-run India.

Sir George Cunningham (centre, seated) with No 1 Squadron, Indian Air Force

Sir Francis Mudie, who left Fettes in 1908, was also known for his 'pro-Muslim sympathies' and it has been claimed that it was he who made it clear to Jinnah that Pakistan was definitely an option for which he should hold out, leading him to reject the Wavell Plan for parity with Congress in a united India.[14] He believed that the Muslims were not taken sufficiently seriously, and worked behind the scenes to redress the balance, as he saw it, between Jinnah and the wealthy, vociferous Hindus. Like many of the more devoted imperial administrators, they had developed a mutual fondness for their charges, as the 1946 'Vive-la' noted:

> *Sir George I next welcome from far Hindustan,*
> *Where he ruled, and was loved by th'unruly Pathan:*
> *A well-trusted leader he always has been*
> *Since the days when he captained the Fettes Fifteen.*[15]

Sir George was indeed genuinely appreciated, and when Pakistan became independent in 1947 he was invited back, aged 59, to serve a third term as Governor of the North-West Frontier; Sir Francis Mudie also served as Governor of West Punjab. The border regions were it in chaos as the local Muslims went on the warpath; in his diary Sir George wrote that he had received offers from almost every tribe to go and kill Sikhs in the Punjab: 'I think I would only have to hold up my little finger to get a lashkar of 40,000 to 50,000.'[16]

Mudie estimated that 60,000 people were killed in intercommunal violence in his region,[17] and that a further half a million Muslims died as a result of hardship or sectarian murder trying to enter Pakistan.[18]

He later wrote that he had to 'ignore any report of a riot unless it alleged that there were at least a thousand dead. If there were, I asked for a further report, but I cannot remember any case in which I was able to do anything.'[19]

Cunningham did his best to hold the new state together, dismissing local Congress politicians on Jinnah's suggestion and held jirgas (assemblies) at which the tribal elders promised to be as loyal to the new Pakistani state as they had been to the British Empire – thus fixing the controversial Durand Line as the still-disputed border with Afghanistan. Recent (admittedly Indian) studies have concluded that he must have known that the Pathans (referred to today as the Pakhtun) and Pakistani Army had been getting ready to invade the princely state of Kashmir, which hoped to remain independent, but apart from dropping hints to General Auchinleck Cunningham seems to have allowed them – in cahoots with sympathetic British officers – to get on with it, possibly because of his 'bonds of mutual appreciation.'[20]

He was also conscious of the need for Britain to remain on friendly terms with a buffer-state against the USSR in a revived 'great game'. The first India-Pakistan war followed. Sir George returned to Scotland with the good wishes of Pakistan; a clock tower in Peshawar still bears his name. Despite his apparently unhelpful attitude towards the new country, No 1 Squadron of the Indian Air Force still uses the crest which he presented in 1941.

Mr Crichton-Miller visited India and Pakistan at the end of 1950 and found a number of OFs still working there, such as A. Gidley Baird of Burma Oil, C.A.K. Wilson, Surveyor-General of Pakistan, and G. Cook of the National Bank of India. There were also plenty of relatives and friends, including Air-Vice-Marshal Atcherley, who had been in charge of RAF Drem when parties of Fettesians had dug slit-trenches there; he was now Commander-in-Chief of the Royal Pakistan Air Force. Many of the fellow-headmasters Crichton-Miller met as he popped into local schools were admirers of some Fettesian or other who had taught there in imperial days. OFs continued to meet up in India for several years after independence; in 1951, 17 of them could be found to have a dinner in Calcutta. N.S. Swan, working for the Assam Oil

Company, found himself in demand as a football referee, though bemused by the way that the local teams invariably lodged an appeal when they lost. These numbers would decline as the years went by ('gone are the days when the OFs and OLs sat down thirty strong to an annual dinner' wrote one of the half-dozen left in 1966, just before his own retirement[21]) and the local educated classes grew, but the gradual nature of the change seems to have ensured that the shock of a post-imperial hangover did not hit Fettesians too hard; as any Scot will attest, the best way of avoiding a hangover is to carry on drinking.

Soldiering On

Palestine, India and Pakistan, along with Burma and Sri Lanka, were gone. Some Old Fettesians interpreted this as a long-term message; Robin Mallinson, serving in Kenya with the East African Artillery in 1949 and entranced by the place, 'caught himself on':

Life was so enjoyable (Africa was casting its spell!) that I thought of joining the Colonial Service and had an interview in Nairobi. I was correctly advised that I should go to university first and I think I would have done that anyhow as I was very conscious that the British had left India only two years earlier and that the decline and fall of the Empire could well accelerate.[22]

Nonetheless, the rest of the colonies were not expected to join the Indians in heading for independence. Indeed, Attlee's government attempted to make money out of them through the East African Groundnut Scheme, which was intended simultaneously to bring modernity to Tanganyika and provide Britain with much-needed vegetable oil. Sir William Currie, Old Fettesian shipping magnate and pillar of the 1920s Raj, was Guest of Honour at Founder's Day in 1948, and cited the scheme as an example of as an example of team-work and guts – precisely the qualities needed for any successful endeavour.[23]

Sadly, thanks to a combination of poor soil, unbulldozable terrain and killer bees, it swallowed £49 million before being abandoned. Fettesians did not let this put them off Africa, however, and copies of the school magazine in the post-war era still contain reports from old boys making careers for themselves there. In December 1947, there was news of four living in Rhodesia, one of whom was finding the food a welcome change from austerity Britain – 'if I sent a menu card, everyone at Fettes would want to emigrate.'[24]

D.C. Rounthwaite was 'enjoying looking after 80,000 pagans in the Bornu Province of Nigeria', appreciating especially their especially potent beer. The following spring, news came from J.R. Cleland about OFs in Mombasa, one of whom was Secretary of the local Chamber of Commerce, and J.M. Alexander was running a mission at Embangweni in Nyasaland. P.V.M. Quiggin wrote with an update from Mombasa in 1951; he was senior past Master in the local Masonic Lodge (always a valuable meeting-place for Scots) whilst A.R. MacDonald was Colonial Secretary in Sierra Leone, C.W.K. Potts was in Uganda and J.A. Gillies in Tanganyika. Life could still be hard – thanks to 'phenomenal rains' communications had been brought to a standstill, but they were there for the duration, so far as they knew.[25]

Indeed, in 1951, P.W. Allsebrook wrote from Southern Rhodesia to say that he hoped to form an OF Society, and encouraged the boys to think about emigrating:

I wish there were more OFs out here. It is a remarkable country, and is expanding very fast. The opportunities for young people are extremely good, if they are prepared to come out here and work hard, and not expect all the luxuries of Europe. The standards and cost of living are very high (said to be the second highest cost of living in the world). The people are delightful, and of course anyone from Britain is most welcome. One lives extremely well here, with several servants, and a car is essential… I find my own job extremely interesting. We chiefly do industrial finance, and administration of companies.[26]

There were also letters in the spring of 1951 from other 'Rhodies' including chrome mine manager I.N. Stewart. G.McG. Thom wrote from Northern Rhodesia in 1952; he was one of only two white men in his district, which was the size of Wales and 400 miles from the nearest railway. D.S.D. McWilliam was in the Gold Coast Department of Cocoa Rehabilitation, trying to save this vital crop from the Swollen Shoot disease. Kenneth Cattenach was a colonial administrator in Enugu, Eastern Nigeria, and E.M. Catto had mastered the Yomba language, passing his exam in it first time – no mean feat for someone described as tone deaf. Three were administering North Borneo in 1951, though A.N.A. Waddell, who had been a junior administrator there before becoming an unofficial commando during the war, had been promoted and was Colonial Secretary in the Gambia. Hong Kong naturally had 'quite a nucleus' and OFs were still well-represented in parts of the informal Empire such as Argentina, where a dinner was held in 1947, and Persia, where at least three were working for the Anglo-Iranian Oil Company in 1951, and some pupils were being recruited, most famously Fereydoon Batmanghelidj, later a noted doctor and father of social entrepreneur Camila Batmanghelidjh. As with their Victorian forebears, Fettesians continued to do their bit for sporting prowess; the summer 1953 *Fettesian* reported that Atholl Blair was single-handedly reviving rugby in Ontario (where it had been in 'a shocking state of decay'), Dr W.L.N.L. Ross was on the committee of the Uganda Boxing Association, and Donald Ring of the Tanganyika Police was playing rugby for the Dar-es-Salaam XV.[27]

He found that the extreme hardness of the ground took a lot of getting used to: fifty years later, the Irish peacekeeping troops in Chad would be ordered not to play rugby for precisely this reason, because they had to be flown home after the unsurprising injuries sustained.[28]

A wry letter from N.R.L. Brown in 1955 implored Fettesians to come and visit him in the Belgian Congo and begged to be reinstated as OF Secretary for the colony, his name and important post having disappeared from the Fettesian lists:

It must be admitted that during my three-year tenure of office I have been singularly unsuccessful in helping OFs as a body, but if no OF dinner has yet been held in the Congo, it is because I have a horror of drinking alone. I now see that in order to regain my coveted former position I must induce some OFs to venture here. Surely the spirit of adventure is not dead at Fettes? If there be some who have been deterred from the prospect of life in the Congo by malicious and ill-informed gossip, let me reassure them.

1. The Congo is no longer the White Man's Grave. The Belgian Administration has become very broad-minded and anyone may now be buried here.

2. The Belgians show an intelligent interest in Scotland and Scottish affairs. This, admittedly, is generally manifested by concern as to why they are not always able to obtain their bottle of whisky daily.

3. A temperature of 100° and a relative humidity of 97% is not unpleasant if you remember those March winds whipping across Bigside.

4. Mosquitoes occasionally succumb to DDT.[29]

For all that, relatively few of the younger generation were going abroad in the post-war period; of those who left school around the end of the Second World War, for instance, only around half a dozen, according to the Fettes Register, were in colonial service or trade in 1953. By contrast, at least twelve of the 1916 intake had been or still were imperial administrators, merchants or planters, chiefly in India and Malaya.[30]

Put another way, in 1932 a dozen Fettesians aged around thirty were working in or indeed for the Empire; in 1953 there were four of similar age. Most of those who were writing home in 1951, except, interestingly, the Rhodesians, were of pre-war vintage; only one of the sixteen OFs mentioned in April 1950 was of the latest generation, most being from the twenties intakes and two even earlier. A 1954 list of Old Fettesians in the Far East and Africa (mostly businessmen in the former and colonial officials in the latter) ran to an impressive 55 names, but only eight had attended the school after 1940.

There are some obvious explanations for this. Obviously, the Empire was smaller with the loss of India, and the ICS and Indian Army, once major recruiters, were no longer possible destinations for young Scots on the make. National Service was now a compulsory, and university a more likely, fate of school-leavers in the 1940s. A young man was unlikely to find himself in the tropics aged twenty-one unless posted to some sweaty troublespot by the Army whilst on National Service. However, even taking that into account, the decline in Fettesian imperial enthusiasm was remarkable. References to the Empire disappeared entirely from the school magazine except in the letters of OFs; what did appear were the new interests of a post-war generation which was interested in Europe and the United Nations. In September 1951, Mr Newman, the veteran history master, brought a dozen boys to a meeting at the Usher Hall of the World Movement for World Federal Government and the Union of European Federalists. Newman had in fact arranged the meeting in his capacity as Chairman of the Edinburgh branch of the movement, and it was chaired by OF Niall MacPherson, Liberal Unionist MP for Dumfries and later Lord Drumalbyn.[31]

Ronnie Guild also encouraged engagement with modern progressive politics; despite, or because of, his wartime service with the Indian Army, he interpreted this in more immediate concentric circles which went from Edinburgh's underprivileged through Britain to Europe. Fettesians who wanted to make the world a better place would no longer start in the Far East.

Some OFs continued to serve the Empire until the very end. William Sharp applied to join what was then called the Overseas Civil Service during his last year at Oxford in 1956. The six young men (along with

Sharp, there was another OF, G.C.W. Donald) on the one-year course were the last intake to be recruited on a permanent pensionable basis, subsequent recruitment being on the basis of a contract for a certain number of years. Their training would have been at least partially familiar to the Victorians, and included instruction in colonial history, tropical agriculture and forestry, the geography of tropical Africa, economics, social anthropology, field engineering and surveying, social services in the colonies including social welfare, education, medical and health services, the judiciary, the police, labour and public relations, both English and Islamic law, local government (which included attachments to rural district and county councils) and, of course, a language, which in Sharp's case was Hausa.[32]

Both of the Fettesians and two others were assigned to Northern Nigeria; one of the remainder was posted to the Solomon Islands, and amused the others as he tried to learn Pidgin English. Sharp sailed for Nigeria from Liverpool in July 1957 on the SS *Accra*, leaving his wife of three months on the quayside to join him later. The voyage took two weeks, calling at Las Palmas, Freetown and Takoradi before docking in Lagos, and was followed by a 28 hour train journey to the Northern capital of Kaduna (where his sister was personal secretary to the Governor) and a flight in a small Dove aircraft to Maiduguri, the provincial capital of Bornu Province, and where he was stationed for his first 20 month tour. The hardships were similar to those of the old days, but at least modern science had some prophylactics against the killers of the Victorian era:

West Africa, known as the 'White Man's Grave', was considered to be a young man's region. To combat malaria we took Paludrine tablets every day. Unfortunately for our children, when they arrived, babies could not take Paludrine so they had to be given quinine. Try getting a baby to swallow something they do not like – even mixing it with something sweet didn't do the trick – eventually we had to hold their noses until it went down!

Apart from the heat, one of the most uncomfortable aspects of life was the plague of insects. At one time of the year there were earwigs everywhere. You always had to shake them out of your clothes every morning before getting dressed, and if you couldn't turn the key in a lock it was because it was jammed with earwigs. Then there were stink bugs, which gave off an awful smell if squashed, ants by the million and dung beetles which rolled bits of dung everywhere. The funniest sight was the ants on our living room floor after coming into contact with

alcohol from a miniature bottle of liqueur which had broken on the concrete floor.
They rolled around completely drunk, but were all dead in the morning.

Mosquitoes were, of course, the biggest curse, and to try to eradicate them our
bungalow, like all other buildings, was completely sprayed in DDT – the walls
were just running with it. In spite of today's ban on DDT we had no after-effects
that we were aware of.

The District Officer was required to do several tours of the region for which he was responsible. One of the purposes the tour was to inspect the local services which might include any or all of a primary school, market stalls, an abattoir (usually just a slab of concrete), a forestry nursery (neem trees from India), an agricultural project, a clinic, the water supply (a well) and to meet the village head and his council. At one point, Sharp had been in Nigeria about a year and had passed his language exams, so addressed a village council in his best Hausa; when he paused mid-way through the speech to ask if they understood, only to be told 'no, we don't speak English!' Naturally, an important function of the DO was the dispensing of British Justice:

This took the form of hearing 'complainants' every morning as one's first duty. As
I arrived at the office there would be a queue of such complainants, sometimes only
one or two but often six or eight of them. Being mostly illiterate they had good
memories and one would have to listen to a long history, sometimes going back
generations, of the reason for the complaint. This usually involved a dispute over
land boundaries, or the ownership of some animal or a complaint about tax or the
treatment received from some local civil servant, etc. Just listening to the complaint
was sometimes enough to satisfy the complainant, but otherwise it was a case of
contacting the appropriate department of the local authority or referring the matter
to the Alkali's (a Muslim judge) court. In Maiduguri I was also responsible for the
weekly inspection of the prison, which sometimes meant supervising the
administration of corporal punishment to which a prisoner had been sentenced.
This was usually six stokes of the cane on a bare bottom accompanied by cries of
anguish from the recipient. As an ex-public school boy this was a not unfamiliar
proceeding! The prison was really a toytown affair, where security was anything
but strict as illustrated by the fact that on one occasion a thief broke into the prison
and stole some of the prison clothing.

Sharp himself was burgled one night whilst sleeping outside his house on a stoop (a concrete platform) covered only in a mosquito net due to the heat with the door left open. The robber only took some clothes and was caught a few days later in the market because he was wearing a pair of the DO's shorts, but Mrs Sharp 'was more concerned that he might have come and looked at us in our nudity!' Whilst still in Maiduguri a senior civil servant had the bright idea that it would be cheaper to employ prisoners supervised by Distict Officers for small building projects rather than employing the Public Works Department. This led to Sharp being instructed to supervise the building of a school in a small town. Accompanied by his wife and new baby son (soon 'surrounded by a raucous crowd of inquisitive children and adults eager to see a white baby'), he took charge of twenty prisoners and two warders and tried to build a school. He was not terribly surprised when, a few weeks later, it was reported that the school had been blown down in a storm. 'What was surprising,' he writes in retrospect, 'was that, instead of blaming either me or my wife, it was confidently reported that the juju in the baobab tree beside the school was responsible!' This did not mean that he was immune to harm all the time, however:

I suppose the most serious event of our time in Nigeria was when I was speared by a fanatical Muslim (they are nothing new!) who had been taught, as they are still in some countries today, that he would go straight to heaven if he killed an infidel. The occasion was a Muslim festival in Sokoto when all the men of the town, together with the Sultan and all his retinue, had congregated at the prayer ground to pray to Allah. At such events it was the custom for the Sultan and his councillors to greet the Resident and the other District Officers at the end of the prayers whilst sitting opposite us in a long row of chairs. As the most junior officer I was sitting at the end of the row when a man came running out of the crowd waving a spear and from about six or eight feet away he threw it at me. By great good fortune it hit me in the midriff where it encountered the two thicknesses of cloth on the edge of my jacket (being a formal occasion I was wearing a suit) and two thicknesses of cloth at the top of my trousers and then a braces button, so that it only grazed my actual flesh and I don't even have a scar to show for it. In fact the dentist sitting behind me was more badly hurt on his leg when the man then thrust the spear at him. The Sultan was so upset that he cancelled the day's remaining celebrations; the offender, after being examined and declared sane, was charged with attempted murder and was sentenced to 10 years in prison; and I was compensated with a new suit! In view of the proximity of independence the whole episode was hushed up as it would have been bad for public relations, but I do have the evidence of the actual spear hanging in our dining room and his dagger, which was much sharper, hanging in my study. One good thing was that, just before the attack, I had had our son on my knee, but had put him down on the carpet to take a photograph. Had he still been on my knee I have no doubt the blow would have killed him.

Although OFs like William Sharp continued loyally and quietly to serve the Empire in Africa, those in Malaya received the most coverage in the school magazine, possibly because of their exciting adventures. Malaya was one of the most drawn-out imperial commitments; whereas in India the British simply tried to hold things together before their presumed departure, then left the locals to massacre one another, Malaya was going to be pacified before it got self-rule. A key difference was that Malaya's would-be masters were communists, generally of Chinese ethnicity, adding a Cold War component to the conflict; the Malays did not want to be ruled either by the far left or the Chinese. The emergency (it was referred to as such for insurance purposes on the insistence of the planters) was given added ferocity by the fact that the guerrillas had been trained and equipped as an anti-Japanese force by the British, and were efficient jungle warriors. Many Fettesians were involved in the fighting, initially career officers and then, as noted previously, national servicemen; one of the earliest reports came from Hugh Currie of the Coldstream Guards, who wrote in 1949 that 'the campaign against these fanatical communist bandits is not an easy or a pleasant one… their lines of supply are a very wide net and we can but cut them off slowly.'[33]

In 1951, A.J.R. Harrison of the Scots Guards wrote to confess that he had been unable to visit OFs at Klang – 'one has to have a good reason for cross-country journeys out here, as most roads are two-vehicle roads, and escorts for such duties have to be in some strength.'[34]

He had, however, met two other OFs, both military – Peter Moffatt in his own regiment and J.M. Franklin of the Artillery. Harrison was impressed by the Briggs Plan, an attempt to isolate the guerrillas from the population by moving half a million Chinese peasants into 'New Villages' out of their reach. This in theory meant that the British could operate at will in the countryside, but the practice was rather different; when he wrote, Harrison was sitting at the end of a telephone awaiting orders. 'We don't move unless they give us definite information,' he told the *Fettesian*, 'You never move at night near Malay Special Constables: they fire at fire-flies.' This worked the other way; national serviceman Charlie Lang's unit killed two policemen who had got lost and strayed into the wrong area. In October 1951, Kenneth Cooper took part in a bayonet charge on a guerrilla camp near Johore which left six enemy dead and gained him a mention in the *Scottish Daily Mail.*[36]

At the same time, J.F.W. Pearse, who had been at Fettes in 1917 and was now manager of a rubber estate, was involved in an ambush:

The first burst killed one of my five special constables and wounded my driver who, however, drove off at top speed. We drove around two corners through rubber, and then we were blocked by a military truck slewed across the road. Soldiers were scattered about, some firing, some still. Then the bandits opened up on us with Brens and Bazookas. They gave us everything they had. The din was terrific. We sat tight in the ditch until the first lull, and then got out into a ditch. Shooting went on for one and a half hours. It was awful. I crept up to the military truck, when I saw seven dead and several wounded.[37]

Pearse and a soldier managed to reverse a vehicle three-quarters of a mile in an attempt to get help, but it got stuck as it tried to turn. A terrorist popped out from behind a tree and joked 'You can turn here.' 'I gave him a burst from my automatic and he stopped being funny,' said Pearse, whose driver was mortally wounded and who had sustained a 'nick or two' himself. Malaya gained independence within the Commonwealth in 1957, becoming, with the addition of Borneo, Sarawak and Singapore, Malaysia in 1963. By then, Britain had experienced its greatest imperial shock. The Suez Crisis of 1956 split the country and helped topple a Prime Minister:

The British people had been brought to the edge of an abyss and had not liked what they had seen or they had sensed. The bitter divisions separating husband and wife, friend and friend, dinner partners and workmates were more characteristic of other, less happy lands.[38]

Decline and Fall I: Lloyd and Suez
In addition to dividing Britain, Suez froze the country's warm relationship with the United States and got the Soviets off the hook for the invasion of Hungary, alienated the Commonwealth and failed even to achieve its most basic objectives. It represents a symbolic turning-point in British decline; within ten years of the debacle, there would be little left of the Empire and attempts were being made to join the European Economic Community. The Egyptian leader, Colonel Nasser, believing that he had

been promised and subsequently denied western aid to build the Aswan Dam, nationalised the Suez Canal and equipped his armed forces with weaponry from Czechoslovakia and the USSR. Selwyn Lloyd, as Foreign Secretary, was charged with organizing the international operation about which his Prime Minister became almost fanatical. Sir Anthony Eden, to whom Lloyd gave the key Fettesian virtues of loyalty and diligence (some cruelly described him as 'His Master's Voice'), saw the Colonel as a new Hitler, an attitude exacerbated by the sacking of Glubb Pasha, British leader of the Jordanian armed forces, and other acts of Arab nationalism in the Middle East. The British government was keen to impose its will, not least because the Canal was an essential conduit for oil; according to Paul Johnson's *The Suez War*, written just after the crisis and published by an OF, the British feared a 30% rise of transport costs and an unachievable increase in the tanker fleet.[39]

A highly questionable course of action was decided upon, in which Lloyd played a pivotal and tragic role; 'by turns secret negotiator and public relations spokesman' his OF biographer D.R. Thorpe writes, 'totally unsuited to his honest inarticulacy.'[40]

Despite earnest negotiations with the Americans, who despite their dislike of Nasser and enthusiasm for intervention when they did it themselves, and himself referring in secret to 'the plan for which I do not care', Lloyd was despatched to Sèvres for secret discussions with the French and Israelis – neither of whom were traditional friends of the Foreign Office. A highly questionable plan was hatched: Britain and France would build up their forces in the Mediterranean, and Israel would invade Egypt in retaliation for the persistent fedayeen terrorist attacks on her borders. The Anglo-French forces would then intervene to 'separate' the two sides, retaking the canal as they happened to pass by. The plan was shrouded in secrecy as to build up the necessary forces was inevitably going to take an age, since the vast armada of landing craft created a decade previously had been largely sold off and doubts persisted as to whether or not the Fleet Air Arm's aeroplanes could take on the Egyptian MiGs. Officially, no-one was going to be invading anyone. Christopher Normand, coming to the end of his National Service on Cyprus, was well aware that what the government was claiming was not the whole truth:

It is now so long ago, that I am sure my signature of the Official Secrets Act cannot apply any more. What I remember differs wildly from the official story, even today. I know that French Paratroopers were on Cyprus for several weeks before the 'official' date – I saw them and their camp! I know, for a fact, that joint Anglo-French planning had certainly started in Nicosia by the beginning of August – not least because I saw French Generals there. In addition there was a huge amount of planning activity at Wolsey Barracks...[41]

The Israelis' Operation Kadesh began on 29 October with paratrooper and tank assaults on the Sinai Peninsula commanded by Moshe Dayan (who had received some of his wartime training from OF Nick Hammond) and Ariel Sharon. Lloyd sent an ultimatum to Nasser and the bombing began. By now there was huge disquiet in Britain; Anthony Nutting, one of Lloyd's junior ministers, resigned, and huge demonstrations were taking place in Trafalgar Square. The Americans were furious, as were plenty of British servicemen who might not have had principled views of the operation but were fed up with hanging around scruffy, overcrowded bases in Malta and Cyprus. Operations were made more difficult by equipment shortages. OF M.J. Mair was a troopship doctor with several years' experience and had just returned to Britain after years of travelling around when the call came to go to Suez:

So there we went, decanting our troops, many of whom were less than willing reservists, offshore into Landing Craft before retiring to Limassol for a couple of weeks when politics took over. We returned to Egypt to retrieve two and a half thousand men, a thousand more than the normal complement. Many brought intestinal afflictions on board so that the medical drug supplies were decimated. One Pioneer Corps Private presented with acute appendicitis and I was driven to perform in the middle of the Mediterranean what proved to be my last surgical operation, happily successful, since I subsequently specialised in anaesthetics.

America condemned the operation, as did some of the Commonwealth and, rather hypocritically, the Russians, who at the time were slaughtering thousands of Hungarians but who rightly calculated that the Third World, now emerging as a political force in its own right, would see Suez as the greater crime. Rumours persisted of Soviet 'rocket-bombing' of British and French cities if the operation continued. Labour leader Hugh Gaitskell broadcast to the nation on 4 November – despite Eden's attempts to muzzle the BBC – that the invasion had no law behind it, that Britain was isolated, that the Prime Minister must resign. The Americans applied financial pressure; petrol rationing, that symbol of post-war misery, was reintroduced, and Britain's gold and dollar reserves fell by £100 million. At Fettes, recalls Richard Thorpe – later to be the biographer of both Lloyd and Eden – the economy was a source of real worry, but the school knew where its loyalties lay:

The big fear was that petrol would be rationed and that Big Leave visits would be difficult on Sundays. My main memory is of 5th November 1956, when (housemaster) Charles Whittle arranged that an effigy of Gaitskell should be burned on the bonfire instead of Guy Fawkes. The mood as I recall was overwhelmingly hostile to Gaitskell, and Charles Whittle clearly thought him a traitor.[42]

This was true of much of the country; although popular folk-memory has it that everyone was against the operation from the start, huge numbers of British people accepted the view that their government was doing the right thing. Nonetheless, the barrage of hostility broke the always nervous Eden, whose health collapsed; Selwyn Lloyd loyally faced an angry House of Commons alone, trying to make the best of a bad job. He claimed that Nasser's 'plan for the aggrandisement of Egypt' and 'Soviet mischief making' had made war inevitable, and that Britain had achieved her objective of halting local hostilities and preventing 'the development of a general war throughout the whole Middle East and perhaps far beyond.' The UK would be delighted to go along with the UN resolution calling for withdrawal, since that had always been the plan. It had, all things considered, offered an opportunity to the United Nations for 'hope of wider settlement.'

The opposition benches sharpened their knives. 'We sympathise with the Rt Hon and learned gentleman in having to sound the bugle of advance to cover his retreat,' sneered Nye Bevan, adding 'I feel I would be a bully if I proceeded any further.' Hugh Gaitskell was incredulous at Lloyd's claim that Labour's arguments were 'on the lips of the enemies of this country'; 'does he mean that the United States is an enemy of this country?' Denis Healey said that the 'ridiculous and degrading apologia' would do nothing to disguise the fact that Britain had 'suffered its most serious diplomatic humiliation since Munich' and asked Lloyd if he would be putting his leader's name forward for the Nobel Peace Prize for the 'conclusive demonstration that aggression does not pay.' One Conservative MP, brushing aside Lloyd's denials that Suez had been a 'humiliation', asked if American permission would be required to bring

Eden back from Jamaica, and Jo Grimond called for the government to resign. It was the House at its most brutal and divided.[43]

Paul Johnson, angrily summing up the effects of the crisis a year later, summarised the 'bitter fruits' of that 'week of senseless folly' as 'a nation dishonoured, a government arraigned before the world as aggressors and conspirators, an economy in jeopardy, a Commonwealth divided, an alliance shattered.'[44]

On 8 January 1957 Lloyd told the cabinet that 'the time was now ripe for a fresh initiative towards a closer association between the United Kingdom and Europe'[45] and this was to be a policy he and his party would embrace more fully in the sixties. On Founder's Day at Fettes that summer, his cabinet colleague Iain Macleod told the boys that Britain was carrying out a policy of giving self-government and 'colonial administration was therefore a career to which fewer Fettesians could be expected to devote themselves, and none could ever expect a distinguished career like that of their Chairman, Sir George Cunningham.'[46]

The 'Vive-La' passed over the humiliation with an oblique reference:

The Vive-la looks round on the troubles of nations
But Fettes stands firm on its solid foundations;
While Arab and Jew fill the East with unrest,
The portals of Fettes stand wide for each guest.[47]

Decline and Fall II: Macleod and decolonisation

Selwyn Lloyd's obituaries in 1978 would, rather unkindly, refer to him as 'the man of Suez'[48]. Iain Macleod, by contrast, is remembered rather more positively as one of the prime movers in the dismantling of an African Empire which was more trouble than it was worth, in order, as he put it, to avoid 'a series of Dunkirks, of gallant, prolonged, bitter, rearguard actions.' That an intransigent policy would have created these was clear. In the same 1952 *Fettesian* which reported half a dozen colonial promotions, a letter from G. Aitken, a policeman in Nigeria, mentioned that he had been called out on Emergency Duty several times, on one occasion opening fire on an angry mob; he was later decorated for bravery. By 1953, the magazine was carrying reports from OFs who were hunting the Mau Mau terrorists in Kenya, though as with the wartime letters these often concentrated on contemporaries bumped into in the field rather than on enemy bumped off. After describing his pleasure at meeting up with Malcolm Ferguson, who had been two years below him in Schoolhouse, H.C.L. Tennant mentioned in passing that he had a led a patrol which captured an enemy hideout: 'three of them will Mau Mau no longer, and two for certain were quite badly wounded; the last one was winged, I think.'[49]

Although some dignified it as a sophisticated national liberation struggle, and indeed the most prominent pro-independence politician, Jomo Kenyatta, was locked up because of this, Mau Mau was essentially a revolt by angry members of the Kikuyu tribe, who had been denied ownership of the lands they had historically worked by a frequently decadent and virulently racialist gang of avaricious white settlers. Not all the Africans were unlucky natives innocent of the blood-curdling oaths of Mau Mau, and not all the whites were crypto-fascist snobs nostalgic for slavery, but enough people did fall into these categories to give the Kenya operations a sour taste even today – one recent history goes so far as to talk of 'Britain's Gulag'.

John Rankin, a subaltern with the Black Watch, had no doubt that, because of its cruelty, 'Mau Mau was an unmitigated evil for both blacks and whites and had to be destroyed, not only to make the lives of the inhabitants tolerable, but to make the government of the country tolerable after independence.' The problem was how to go about this. The Mau Mau operated at many levels, retreating into the fastness of the thick forests, hiding in the mountains or blending in with the population in order to conduct assassinations, often of employers, African Christians, or members of rival tribes (the latter categories were far more likely to die at the hands of the Mau Mau than were white settlers; as many Europeans died in traffic accidents as were killed by the terrorists – 32 in total – whilst thousands of Africans were murdered). The British employed a variety of methods, some of which were so brutal that they were condemned by both Enoch Powell and Barbara Castle. The RAF plastered Mount Kenya with obsolete bombs (which they charged to the Kenya government at the full rate) in an attempt to hit the Mau Mau. This, Rhoderick Macleod realised, 'only succeeded in killing game and thus providing fresh elephant and buffalo meat supplies for them.'[50]

Operation Anvil was slightly more successful, a swoop on 30,000 Kikuyu living in Nairobi who were removed to detention camps. Whilst it broke the back of Mau Mau operations in the capital, it also created the massive task of sifting the prisoners to identify the hard-core leaders as opposed to the rank and file, who 'did not constitute any great threat to security.' Macleod, who had both wartime experience of intelligence work and liberal instincts, was a specialist interrogator with his own staff of experienced Kikuyu loyalists and a secluded police station from which to work. As he recalled later,

My first task was to teach my new team the correct tried and proven methods for getting true information without resorting to physical violence. Physical violence is nearly always counter-productive in such situations… usually a prisoner is more likely to tell you what he thinks you want to hear rather than the truth, and that only wastes time in the long run.[51]

Sadly, not all interrogators were so sophisticated – hence the questions in Parliament. John Rankin and his Jocks were officially in Kenya, like the Army in Ulster later on, 'in aid of the civil power', and, whilst Macleod was impressed by distinguished and professional regiments such as the Black Watch, he was well aware of the dangers posed both to and by 'city-bred National Servicemen':

…the thick Kenya forests, particularly at night when normal forest noises are apt to become magnified, could result in terror for those whose natural habitat was an urban jungle. Indeed, one British Battalion ambushed and shot dead its own colonel simply through being jittery and 'trigger happy.'[52]

On one occasion, an army unit demanded that local forces were excluded from an isolated forest they intended to 'sweep' – presumably on the grounds that they would shoot any Africans they saw – and returned to report that there were no gangs in the area. When Macleod and his African policemen entered the same forest that night, 'we found over 30 terrorists who told us that they had spent the day up in trees watching the soldiers below.' An officer of the Northumberland Police ('a nice old boy who had made his reputation in solving run of the mill murders in Newcastle') astonished everyone when, on his first day on transfer to the Rift Valley, he tried to arrest for indecent exposure a batch of Masai warriors who were simply walking around in their traditional dress of a blanket thrown loosely over one shoulder. Another policeman, seconded to John Rankin's unit,

…was a complete waster and spoke openly and proudly of his police record (by this I mean from the inside looking out!) His only occupation, apart from

lounging about drinking beer, was to shoot baboons. This particular form of sadism almost led to his demise when a troop of baboons, enraged by the cries of a wounded comrade, surrounded him and began to hurl rocks at him. Had he been knocked out he would have been torn to pieces. In fact he made it back to his Land-Rover and escaped.[53]

The Mau Mau were still causing problems when Macmillan offered Macleod's politician brother the post of Secretary of State for the Colonies in October 1959 with the words 'Iain, I've got the worst job in the world for you.'[54]

By this point, there had already been some decolonisation, especially in Asia, and Macleod was well aware of the need to 'get a move on.' Although his predecessor, Alan Lennox Boyd, had hoped to see the African colonies self-governing in the seventies, Macleod believed that it was neither physically possible nor morally desirable to cling on by force; the horrible example of French Algeria was all too clear. Just before his appointment, the Hola Camp massacre in Kenya and the Devlin Report on Nyasaland had made Parliament uncomfortably aware that some colonies were considered 'police states.' In Nigeria, William Sharp was already making his bailiwick ready for independence, a process he found painful, though not because of any sentimental imperialism:

One aspect of this was trying to eradicate corruption which was almost a way of life for the locals. If you wanted anything, or if you wanted to influence anyone, then a financial 'dash' was the accepted way of achieving your objective. After I had been in Maiduguri for only four weeks my Senior District Officer sent me out on tour for three weeks to investigate the tax collecting in several villages where the suspicion was that not all of the tax collected was finding its way into the provincial treasury. As the wet season was only just over I had to go on horseback. In anticipation of this I had had a few riding lessons in Oxford, but horses and I didn't get on, and nothing could have prepared me for my experience during those three weeks which were probably the most eventful and traumatic of my entire life. We used different horses each day which was bad enough, but the real problem was that the local stirrups were too small for my large feet, so that a lot of the time I had to ride with my feet out of the stirrups which was most uncomfortable and resulted in my getting a boil on my backside! Due to the heat we would get up around three o`clock and ride until about 10 or 11 o'clock when we would arrive in the next village. Compensation for my discomfort was provided by seeing the sun rise each day which was one of the *most magnificent sights I have ever seen. The colours were just sensational.*

I was accompanied by my Government Messenger (who could translate for me) a representative of the Emir and several porters to carry my 'loads'. These included my camp bed, a collapsible chair and table, a tin bath and anything my cook-steward required such as pots and pans and some basic food ingredients. I stayed each night either in a 'rumfa' (a hut made of straw matting fixed to poles) which had been erected for me by the local village head, or in a 'rest house'. This was a brick built room without doors or windows, surrounded by a veranda in which one could set up one's camp bed, table, etc. On one occasion I had set up my bed and mosquito net on the veranda of one of these rest houses when I was awoken in the middle of the night by the sound of 'something' padding round my bed. When I went to switch on my torch the bulb blew and I was left in the dark with my imagination running wild!   I have never been so frightened in my life! To this day I do not know what sort of animal was investigating my presence but I suspect it was probably a hyena. Anyway, I survived, just!

Nigeria, like Ghana before it, had only a small settler population, so could be steered gently towards independence without anyone objecting. What made Iain Macleod's position difficult was that large white minorities existed in Kenya and the Rhodesias; these were decidedly unenthusiastic about black majority rule and, importantly, commanded support on the Tory back benches. Many believed that the improvements they had made to the land entitled them to perpetual governance thereof; some saw the Africans as latter-day Gibeonites, hewers of wood and drawers of water for the chosen people. They were outraged when Macleod (despite being a convinced abolitionist) refused to intervene for clemency for a white engineer who murdered his black houseboy and was subsequently hanged, but this was a vital 'test case' in the eyes of the Africans, proving the Colonial Secretary's sincere opposition to racialism.[55]

A British journalist, quoted in *Time* magazine, commented that 'It is a savage irony that future generations in Kenya will be able to point to 1960 as the year when the equality of the races was finally demonstrated, not by the granting of rights to Africans to farm on the White Highlands, or to become members of white clubs, but by the proposition that all men, regardless of colour, are equal on the end of a rope.'[56]

Rhoddy Macleod, a member of the liberal New Kenya Party, lost many friends when his fellow-whites realised that he supported self-government and would not use his influence to maintain a status quo unacceptable in London.[57]

Iain Macleod lifted the emergency powers and freed most of the detainees (though not yet Kenyatta) hosting his first colonial conference in January 1960. He did not reconcile the hard-line settlers (who flung thirty pieces of silver at the NKP delegates on their return to Nairobi) but managed to get the moderate whites and Africans to co-operate in a 'bridge' to independence which avoided the 'explosion' a lack of movement could have produced. The Kenya negotiations were held at Lancaster House, but many future meetings were held in Macleod's flat, with his wife Eve cooking for an apparently endless succession of African leaders and agreements hammered out in the dining room or kitchen. In an age when MPs are famous for the extravagance of their expenses, it is interesting to note that Macleod conducted these talks at his own expense, which unlike his more aristocratic predecessors he could ill afford, even cashing in a life insurance policy to defray costs.[58]

Macleod was later to develop cordial relations with Julius Nyerere of Tanzania and Hastings Banda of Malawi, and their peoples remembered him with affection. When he died in 1970, a schoolboy from Lilongwe wrote to the British High Commissioner expressing his sadness, and enclosing a 2s. 6d. postal order for Mrs Macleod.[59]

Many whites, however, never forgave him; Sir Roy Welensky, Prime Minister of the Federation of Rhodesia and Nyasaland, doubted if they had ever spoken the same language, and condemned his 'ignorance of Africa.' By the autumn of 1960 the whites had seen another colony become independent. William Sharp had helped organise the elections on the eve of Nigeria's accession to statehood:

All the D.O.s were Returning Officers and my constituency straddled the river so that I had to sail up and down it in order to visit the polling booths. Subsequently there was a legal action taken against the winner as the opposition claimed that he was not 21. Records of birth being noticeable by their absence it was difficult to prove one way or the other, but I believe it was finally settled by relating the birth to 'the year the elephants destroyed the crops!'

At the independence celebrations he 'had the pleasure of being in charge of letting off £100 worth of fireworks – a little boy's dream' and enjoyed the Durbar at Sokoto in honour of Princess Alexandra of Kent, 'a most memorable occasion with all the horsemen in their colourful regalia, including chain mail (supposedly from the crusades) and all the Emirs of the North in their grandeur with huge umbrellas being twirled above them by their servants.'[60]

Sir Abubakar Balewa, the first Prime Minister of Nigeria, spoke at the independence celebrations of Britain's colonial contribution 'first as masters, then as leaders, finally as partners and always as friends.' Macleod quoted this to the Conservative Party conference that year, well aware (partly, John Humphries recalls, because he took some flak at London OF meetings) that not all those attending were sympathetic to his measures:

I cannot promise you a popular colonial policy. There will be toil and sweat and tears; but I hope not blood and I hope not bitterness – although in the turmoil that is Africa today, of even that one cannot be certain. But this is the road we must walk and we can walk no other. The Socialists can scheme their schemes and the Liberals can dream their dreams, but we, at least, have work to do.[61]

In trying to settle the Northern Rhodesia question, both Kenneth Kaunda and Sir Roy Welensky complained about Macleod, which secretly pleased him since what he called 'parity of abuse' meant that he could hardly be seen as trying to sell out either side. Yet he was seen by the right in Britain, whose confidence had been restored by the Conservatives' rapid recovery from Suez and victory in the 1959 election, as doing precisely that. Lord Salisbury denounced Macleod bitterly as 'too clever by half, and having treated the colonists as opponents to be outwitted.[62]

The 'too clever by half' tag, which, as has been widely pointed out since, could be regarded as an insult only in the English-speaking world, clung to Macleod for the rest of his life. Macleod understood that he was out of step with the prejudices and assumptions of much of the Conservative Party, not just ideologically but socially and intellectually. Nonetheless, he forged ahead with his policy, convinced that it was right and determined to give Africa its democratic due regardless of the views of the white 'kith and kin'. He believed that an astute policy would avoid the violent horrors of decolonisation elsewhere; Britain should, he said, be quicker than the French in Algeria and slower than the Belgians in the Congo. Macmillan was later to move Macleod to the posts of Chancellor of the Duchy of Lancaster and Party Chairman – a promotion which famously prompted Lady Antonia Fraser to say that she would give all her Marks and Spencer shares just to see Lord Salisbury's face when he heard the news – but the decolonisation programme continued. By the time the Conservatives lost power in 1964, Kenya, Uganda, Tanzania (Tanganyika), Malawi (Nyasaland) and Zambia (Northern Rhodesia) had followed the West African colonies to independence. The whites of Southern Rhodesia clung to power for another decade and a half after declaring UDI in 1965, aided by South Africa and 'sanctions-busters' such as OF L.P. Normand (who was warned by MI5 to behave himself when he arrived in London).

The school's busts of Selwyn Lloyd and Iain Macleod

Fettesians in the post-colonial world

The climate of intellectual opinion at Fettes was by then unsympathetic to any form of imperialism, if the *Fettesian* is anything to go by. A poem about Lawrence of Arabia, for instance, contained the lines:

> *Stifling officialdom, full of 'Wogs?' and fishing,*
> *Suave diplomats and broken promises,*
> *An eternity away from the harsh crack of*
> *Desert life.*[63]

Rhodesian UDI was widely discussed at the school in the late sixties, guest speaker the Rev Efion Ndon, whose views may be guessed at, introduced the topic to the chaplain's group in 1965, whilst Michael

Clark Hutchinson, the 'reactionary' MP for South Edinburgh, talked to a Current Affairs meeting in 1966 from a different perspective.[64]

The African seems to have been better received than the right-wing MP; the latter's lecture, noted the *Fettesian* with a degree of disapproval, 'provoked many questions, but these were all answered with the adroitness and skill we expect from politicians.'[65]

The general feeling of those pupils interested in such matters seems to have been so strongly in favour of the Macleod line and so unsympathetic to the African whites that the Rev Ronald Selby Wright, the school's honorary chaplain, felt obliged to explain the Rhodesian case for the sake of balance. 'Without defending Mr Smith, he made us understand the reasons for UDI, and although he may not have converted anyone, he certainly provoked an atmosphere of fairer thought, which was his intention.'[66]

It is ironic, to some extent, that the most recent Fettesian to be lost in action was Robin Hughes, in the Rhodesian bush war. A lieutenant in the Selous Scouts, he was operating against ZANLA gunmen in Mtepatepa in 1973. His 'pseudo-terrorists' – African soldiers trained to infiltrate the enemy – were in the process of gaining the confidence of some villagers when real terrorists arrived. In the ensuing gunfight, Hughes attempted to give his comrades covering fire from a nearby cattle kraal but was himself shot. An obituary does not seem to have appeared for him in the *Fettesian*, but his name does feature on the brass plaque in chapel for post-war military casualties, near the Victorian bronze one whose first name is Adrian Blaikie, killed fighting black Africans almost a hundred years earlier. (During the 1979-80 transition from Rhodesia to Zimbabwe, the Deputy Commander of the Monitoring Force was another OF, Brig John Learmont.) Surviving Rhodesians understandably see the awfulness of Dr Mugabe's regime, and indeed the other sinister dictatorships which emerged after independence elsewhere in Africa, as proof that Iain Macleod's policy was flawed. Certainly, in an ideal world, the British should have encouraged the growth of a much larger indigenous bourgeoisie far earlier than they did, but Macleod did not find himself in an ideal world. Just before the end of his life, he was asked by a television interviewer whether, knowing how things had turned out: by this point some of the independent former colonies had already begun their slide towards darkness. Sir Abubakar Balewa was dead in a military coup, Nigeria shattered by the Biafran War, and there was scarcely a democracy from the Cape to Cairo. 'I could not have done anything else and stayed in politics,' Macleod replied, 'You must just take the consequences of the actions you believe to be right.'[67]

Politically, he paid a great price for this, and although Britain had no Congos or Algerias on its conscience, and the Commonwealth stayed together, there were plenty of horrors. Fettes retained a strong connection with Africa after independence through the Hope Waddell Training Institution at Calabar, the oldest school in eastern Nigeria, founded by Presbyterian Scots in the nineteenth century. In 1965, the Headmaster, post-war OF Colin MacDonald, wrote to describe the challenges and opportunities working there involved, and invited school leavers to consider spending what would now be called a gap year there. 'Bill' Aitken, the Fettes chaplain in the fifties, actually established his own school in Nigeria at Abakaliki, helping build it himself along with his teachers and pupils.[68] By 1967, the letters were taking on a more worried tone; the Biafran war had forced MacDonald to leave town, and he was getting reports of '2,000 Ibo civilians being murdered and thrown in the river, and of siege conditions with no water or food.'[69] The sixties ended with him talking to the boys in person, having been ejected from Nigeria altogether. MacDonald was not alone; the new Fettes Assistant Bursar in 1965, Major Winnington-Ingram, had taken over his family's farm in Kenya after retiring from the armed forces, but was required to hand it over for African settlement and returned to Britain.[70]

His arrival at the school coincided with that of Mr Z.A. Shah, a keen cricketer from West Pakistan, who taught science and seems to have been the first recruit to the staff from the New Commonwealth. After less than a century of Fettesians going out to educate the Punjab, the traffic was already being reversed.

The Sunset

Ian McKee was one of the last Fettesians to be posted 'out east' in the 1960s, where he enjoyed the luxuries of RAF Seletar in Singapore, built in the heyday of Empire as a flying boat station whose legacy was a de luxe slipway for the yacht club, the magnificent Short Sunderland having made its last RAF flight there in 1959. Indeed, Singapore was where many British aviation classics saw their final service – the Spitfire (1954), Mosquito (1955) and Beaufighter (1960) – but by McKee's time the base was largely flying unglamorous Scottish Aviation Twin Pioneers for jungle use and Andover medium transports, as well as the now-ubiquitous smattering of helicopters. In 1964, one of the only Fettes imperial cadet camp experiences was enjoyed by 'R.N. McK.', who had little to say about air base at Singapore as his main memory was of the lengthy flights there, and the excitement of swimming with 'a rather attractive WRAF sergeant' on the island of Gan.[71] One assumes he understood his readership. As a doctor, Ian McKee was occasionally posted up-country to remote airstrips, but spent much of his time in the fairly enjoyable surroundings of Seletar itself:

Conditions were quite luxurious except that we didn't have air-conditioning anywhere on the camp. It took a newcomer, easily identified by pale skin and nicknamed 'moonie', about 3 weeks to acclimatise. If we went into town to one of the up market restaurants, which were air-conditioned, we took warm clothing with us to put on before we entered. My main task was to look after the health of families of all three services – some of the wives couldn't cope with life overseas and mental illness was quite common.

The camp had shops, swimming pools, banks and all the facilities of a small town. The poet Pam Ayres was stationed in Seletar in my time and was the leading lady in a performance of 'Boeing Boeing' in the camp theatre. We doctors also had to look after the health of locally employed workers, many of whom had worked for the Japanese when they occupied Singapore. [72]

Because of the enervating effect of the climate it was possible to prescribe two weeks' recuperation in the cool Cameron Highlands of Malaysia, and McKee himself enjoyed this facility with his family, encouraged by authority to 'rest, play games and catch butterflies.' The army gave provided all the necessary equipment for the stay, even coming back to their bungalow after a week to change the croquet balls, as they might be dirty. When McKee came to Singapore it was 'in the throes of change'; there were over 600 British officers when he arrived, but when he left there were 46. Expatriate life continued among the civilians as well, though not always with its pre-war vim. The former pupils of Edinburgh schools had an annual dinner at the Singapore cricket club on the eve of the Calcutta Cup rugby match, and they ended the evening by sending a telegram to the Scottish team at Murrayfield or Twickenham. The president of the club had left the Royal High School in the twenties and only been back to the UK on two occasions, having been a guest of the Japanese during the war. Sadly, this meant that he tended to believe that his guests would be as fascinated by the entire contents of his old school's magazine as he was, and he insisted on reading out long extracts from it 'whilst the rest of us listened in various degrees of boredom.' Ian McKee doubts whether this particular colonial tradition still continues. Willie Ross, then a young soldier and later to become RSM of the Fettes Corps, was also stationed in Singapore and had rather earthier memories, as he told a school reporter in the nineties:

My favorite time was when we were stationed in Singapore – beautiful. I was a young, savvy, 26 years of age. I worked very hard. See the way I am now – the first six weeks I trained in Singapore I lost three and a half stone in weight, without being on a diet. Didn't stop drinking, just through sheer physical effort of training in the jungle – pure sweat. I thoroughly enjoyed it, though. In my free time – you don't really want to know about that, a lot of drink was involved – and a lot of nightclubs. Have you heard of Buggie Street? The thing about it is the most beautiful women there are all men. Of course at the time you don't know they're men, when you're chatting them up. Anyway, I got my nose broken, my jaw broken and I eventually got so bad they barred me.[73]

One of the official reasons for the continued British presence in the Far East was the possibility of a communist uprising; although, as McKee recalls, 'there was no trouble whilst I was out there', some Fettesians were involved in the protection of Malaysian Borneo from Indonesian attack in the mid-sixties.

From the 1960s onwards, the majority of Fettesians who went out to the dusty outposts of former colonies did so neither as soldiers nor administrators, but as participants in Voluntary Service Overseas. Lord Drumalbyn, the OF formerly known as Niall Macpherson and now a junior minister in the Home government, told the boys on Founder's Day in 1964 that people had three duties – not to be a burden on others, to serve their countries, and to work for the good of mankind. In the modern age, the latter was likely to be the most important, and especially so for his audience. 'If Britain is to play her full part in world affairs, more and more British people will spend some of their working lives, if not the whole of them, in the service of other peoples.'[74]

This service would be, of course, 'in ways acceptable to them as free and independent peoples' – no more khaki-clad housemasters – but this did not really need to be said, for the first cohorts of Fettesians were already returning from VSO, sometimes to tell rather hair-raising stories.

John King, an OF doing VSO at a school in Kenya, wrote to the school in 1963 to describe the local political situation. Believing that 'the battle against the settlers has been won' he saw the next problem as trying to find an accommodation between Kenyatta's KANU and their rivals KADU. Working at Maseno on the fault-line between two hostile tribes meant that 'for some days I had to teach with a mob rampaging near the school, forty houses in flames, riot police, tear gas and all the usual paraphernalia.' Whilst accepting that KANU ought to be in government, he was worried that their heavy-handed domination of the regions might lead to secession or civil war on the terrible model of Katanga.[75]

In 1967, the *Fettesian* carried a lengthy article by Duncan MacIntyre extolling the virtues of VSO, 'a unique chance to experience and appreciate the diversity of human nature and to see at first hand the great difference between 'the West' and the rest of the world.'[76]

He was frank about his own limitations – 'the pitiful quantity of good I did in Nigeria was swamped by the value of the experience Nigeria gave me' – but urged his successors to take the opportunity to do something for others. Many did, and twenty years later the magazine could still carry letters from former pupils doing voluntary work abroad, such as Charles Maclean, who worked in the Sudan, but the statistics do not suggest that many OFs were committing themselves to the good of mankind for the whole of their lives. In 1966, of the declared intentions of 75 school leavers, five wanted to be doctors, two vets, two firmly intended to join the armed forces, and one wanted to be a teacher. However, 15 were going into some kind of business, ten wanted to be accountants or actuaries, nine engineers, seven lawyers, four agriculturalists, three architects, journalists, artists and hotel managers, and a sprinkling of others – including an ecologist, one of the newer professions of the age.[77] (To be fair, some changed their minds whilst at university, but the overall trend was downwards.) By 1967, when Denis Healey announced the withdrawal of British personnel from the bases 'East of Suez' such as Singapore and Aden, there was no longer an Old Fettesian Secretary in India, for the three or four former pupils left in the country, mostly tea planters, were so widely scattered as to make meetings impossible.[78]

By contrast, another branch of the Association – one which had not even existed in Victorian times – was very cheerful about numbers: 'much of Fettes' brain power is still shifting to the United States of America.'[79] (This was, incidentally, despite various incidents such as the attempted mugging of Alasdair Macphail by 'two powerful black men' in the Harlem district of Chicago; 'I have only 60 cents in my pocket and I'll give you 30 of it,' he told his new acquaintances, who let him go.[80]) Sir Alexander Waddell, the hero of Sarawak, delivered a kind of imperial obituary to Fettes on Founder's Day that year:

His own life had been devoted to the service of the Empire, an ideal which was nowadays deprecated. It had been a hard, exciting life, spent mostly in rotten climates, but in the company of a fine body of men. He had been fortunate in witnessing the fascinating transformation of the old Empire based on dependence into a Commonwealth of independent countries. Sir Alexander deplored the present policy of withdrawal – whether it was withdrawal from East of Suez or South of Gibraltar. Such a policy could only lead to a West of Penzance mentality, the mentality of the turtle.[81]

Like Nick Hammond, another wartime adventurer who had delivered the address in 1965 and said that Fettesians 'have to give leadership to 600 million people whether in Cyprus or the Congo or Malaya in order that they may live at peace and in co-operation,'[82] Sandy Glen still saw the British in a special role, though not one of imperial domination. He wanted to keep the dream alive through VSO and as many contacts as possible with overseas schools, and to a considerable extent Fettes did do this, though like most British schools it did not do so in any sort of imperial or even Commonwealth spirit. By this point, forties Fettesian Robert Sanders (later Sir Robert) was a key figure in guiding Fiji towards independence, and like some of his predecessors, he was asked to stay on after this was achieved in 1970. One present-day Fijian diplomat recalled that Sir Robert encouraged high standards in new recruits to the civil service in the seventies (punctuality, discipline and no fashionable afro haircuts) a training which was invaluable for the realities of world politics.[83] Sir Robert spent many years there as Secretary to the Council of Ministers, but wisely left 'before I outstayed my welcome', and is still a popular figure in Fiji, delivering the eulogies when his old boss, former Prime Minister Ratu Sir Kamisese Kapaiwai Tuimacilai Mara, died in 2004.

The last word on the Empire should probably go Ian McKee, who by 2009 was, perhaps ironically, a Scottish Nationalist MSP:

It was strange being in Seletar as we knew we were at the end of Empire, the last to experience this lifestyle. When you sat at a mess dinner, in tropical mess kit, with seven officers guarding seven squadron standards all night and a Gurkha pipe band playing outside, it was almost like being in a play that you knew would finish soon and reality would come back. But it was fun while it lasted.

NOTES

[1] Bruce Lockhart (1936) p. 181

[2] Charlie Lang, letter to the author, 13 March 2009

[3] See, for instance, John Darwin, *Britain and Decolonisation* (London, Palgrave, 1988) Chs 1 & 2

[4] Scott

[5] Jackson

[6] Pyman, p. 101

[7] Macleod

[8] Quoted in *Fettesian*, December 1947

[9] Paul Johnson, *Modern Times* 2nd Ed., (London, Phoenix, 1999) p. 346

[10] *Fettesian*, July 1946

[11] Quoted in Ayesha Jalal, *The Sole Spokesman* (Cambridge, CUP, 1994) p. 115

[12] *Fettesian*, December 1963

[13] Quoted in ibid.

[14] D. N. Panigrahi, *India's partition: the story of imperialism in retreat* (London, Routledge, 2004) p. 266

[15] *Fettesian*, July 1946

[16] Quoted in Victoria Schofield, *Afghan frontier: feuding and fighting in Central Asia* (London, I.B. Tauris, 2003) p. 244

[17] Quoted in Gyanendra Pandey, *Remembering partition: violence, nationalism, and history in India* (Cambridge, CUP, 2001) p. 89

[18] Bharadwaj, Khwaja, & Mian, *The Big March: Migratory Flows after the Partition of India* (Harvard, John F. Kennedy School of Government, Working Paper Series ref. rwp08-029, 2008)

[19] Quoted in Alex von Tunzelmann, *Indian Summer: The Secret History of the End of an Empire* (London, Picador, 2008) p. 273

[20] Kuldip Singh Bajwa, *Jammu & Kashmir War 1947-1948* (New Delhi, Har-Anand, 2004) p. 85

[21] *Fettesian*, April 1966

[22] Mallinson

[23] *Fettesian*, July 1948

[24] Ibid., December 1947

[25] Ibid., July 1951

[26] Ibid., April 1951

[27] *Fettesian*, Vol. LXXV, Issue 3, July 1953, p. 177

[28] See BBC News, 'Irish Army finds Chad "too hard"', accessed 21 May 2009

[29] *Fettesian*, December 1955

[30] See *Fettes College Register* (1953 edn.)

[31] *Fettesian*, December 1951

[32] W.F. Sharp, email to the author, 23rd March 2009

[33] *Fettesian*, December 1949

[34] Ibid., April 1951

[36] Ibid., December 1951

[37] Ibid.

[38] Keith Kyle, *Suez: Britain's End of Empire in the Middle East* (London, I.B.Tauris, 2003) p. 3

[39] Paul Johnson, *The Suez War* (London, MacGibbon & Kee, 1957) p. 12

[40] Thorpe, p. 218

[41] Normand

[42] D.R.Thorpe, email to the author, 18 December 2008

[43] See *Hansard*,Vol. 561, 3 December 1956, pp. 878-95. Fettes College has all of Selwyn Lloyd's old copies.

[44] Johnson (1957) p. 142

[45] Thorpe, p. 258

[46] *Fettesian*, July 1957

[47] Ibid.

[48] Thorpe, p. 258

[49] *Fettesian*, July 1953

[50] Macleod, p. 23

[51] Ibid., p. 22

[52] Ibid., p. 23

[53] Rankin, p. 10

[54] Fisher, p. 141

[55] Ibid., p. 151

[56] 'White Man Hangs', *Time*, 29 August, 1960

[57] Fisher, p. 145

[58] Ibid., p. 149

[59] Ibid., p. 160

[60] Sharp

[61] Quoted in Fisher, p. 165

[62] Quoted in Edward Pearce, *The Lost Leaders* (London, Little, Brown, 1997) p. 286

[63] *Fettesian*, April 1964

[64] Tam Dalyell, Obituary for Michael Clark Hutchinson, *Independent*, 24 March 1993

[65] *Fettesian*, April 1966

[66] Ibid.

[67] Quoted in Fisher, p. 198

[68] *Fettesian*, July 1965

[69] Ibid., December 1967

[70] Ibid., December 1965

[71] Ibid., December 1964

[72] Dr Ian McKee MSP, email to the author, 20 April 2009

[73] *Fettesian,* 1999

[74] Ibid., April 1964

[75] Ibid., July 1963

[76] Ibid., December 1967

[77] Ibid., July 1966

[78] Ibid., July 1967

[79] Ibid., April 1967

[80] Ibid., April 1965

[81] Ibid., July 1967

[82] Ibid., July 1965

[83] Amelia Vunileba, 'The diplomat who could have been a champion', *Fiji Times*, 1 April 2007

Chapter Eighteen

'A fair amount of mischief to be had'

The Sixties Upheaval

'More secure than Colditz'

Monday 2 November 1960 was, as usual, a Corps day, and Richard Thorpe (later to be the biographer of several members of the government of the day) was the sergeant in charge of the signals section. He and his contemporaries were already excited by the news that theirs would be the first generation not to have to do National Service. That afternoon, however, Thorpe had another preoccupation. 'The verdict in the *Lady Chatterley* trial came through and the Signals had rigged up a connecting net to all units, and we broadcast the news that Lady C had 'won' when it came through,' he writes, 'Officers in the Corps could not understand what all the cheering was from all the huts.' The Headmaster declared shortly afterwards that any boy found with a copy would be beaten, but this was only the first of many challenges to an old order which Fettes had served so well.

Ian McIntosh, who led the school throughout the sixties, had taken over from Crichton-Miller in 1958 and was the first Scot to be Headmaster. With firsts from Aberdeen and Cambridge and a fierce Presbyterian work ethic, he had taught at Winchester, where he absorbed a belief in 'the pursuit of excellence for its own sake', and was Headmaster of George Watson's, where he taught pupils such as Malcolm Rifkind 'in the grand manner'. He would have been a worthy successor to Dr Potts in the late nineteenth century.[1]

He had more modern virtues, too; of a straight-laced pupil, he once commented that he felt like saying 'Here's £2. Go out and get drunk.' He was, in private, a witty and clever man, who wrote poetry, could play Scott Joplin and would turn a blind eye to boys who sloped off to watch Hearts-Hibs matches – partly on the grounds that he was himself a Cambridge Association Football Blue and thus a disappointment to those school 'bloods' who would rather have had a 'rugger-bugger' from

Wigan as their new head. Yet he was instinctively appalled by the cultural explosion that was taking place all around him. He once satirised his own position by telling the head of school that 'I'd like to hear everything you have to say before I say "no".'[2] One OF, Nick Ryden, later said that:

The school was probably more secure than Colditz in those days. It was about 50 years out of date and everyone was almost encouraged to do what they could to push the rules as far as they could. Outside the iron railings of Fettes, the world was changing, it was the Sixties, student were throwing stones and bricks in Paris and were walking around in chocolate and magenta uniforms, herded around like sheep and taught how to run the Empire. There was a fair amount of mischief to be had.[3]

Although, in fairness, Ryden exaggerates when he talks about the Empire – as we have seen, the school was perfectly well aware that it had gone – it was true that the McIntosh was deeply uncomfortable with change. The Edinburgh *Evening News* recently repeated a (possibly apocryphal) story that when he encountered a Fettesian with hair so fashionably long that he had been nicknamed Emily, he marched the lad straight round to the barber and watched as the precious locks were shorn. The boy was Tony Blair.[4]

Headmaster McIntosh with prefects in 1963, when even the Beatles were still wearing suits

697

Blair: the Years of Destiny

So much has been written, both inside and outside the school, about Blair's schooldays and their supposedly formative influence on him – in that the authoritarian traditionalism of Fettes provided pricks against which he would kick – that it seems invidious to focus, however briefly, on this one pupil as opposed to the many others who passed through the gates. More than one OF has pointed out, during the research for this book, that a one-sided picture of the school and its staff has been created because of the Blair focus. Yet Blair's experiences were not untypical of so many rebellious pupils' in that era, and in any case not to mention him is to ignore one of the most extraordinary figures in the late twentieth century and the influences of his youth. Like the fags of earlier generations, Blair had to fag for older boys, preparing CCF and games kit, polishing shoes and making toast. Although several older boys remembered Blair as an excellent maker of toast and not especially truculent, he bore a grudge for years about what he considered one prefect's unjustified beating for a petty misdemeanour.[5]

Blair was one of only two boys to choose to leave the traditional atmosphere of Kimmerghame for the new Arniston House, not least because of this kind of thing. In the more liberal atmosphere of Arniston, Eric Anderson famously remembered 'the grinning Blair face' appearing at his study door with some new idea for something which the school ought to change at once.[6]

One of Blair's objects of particular disapproval was the Corps, which he avoided like the plague after he had got the compulsory two years out of the way; his military connection with the school was to be three decades later. The contingent commander in the sixties, Leslie Barr, had two salient memories of the young Blair. The first was that Blair came to him asking to be transferred to a section where he could be working on something in a classroom; he objected to marching around in uniform being shouted at. The other was that, following one of the last OF Bisley dinners at the House of Commons, Iain Macleod said 'We shall not last here for ever, so, young Barr, when you get back to Fettes you tell the lads that there needs to be some more Fettesian Members of Parliament.' On his return, Barr discussed the matter with his lower sixth and fifth form mathematics classes, and one of the younger boys, one A.C.L. Blair, 'showed considerable interest.' 'The OF MPs and yours truly bear some responsibility for our present premier!' he wrote in 2003.[7]

Yet Blair's time at Fettes was hardly wasted, since he captained the school basketball team, played several leading roles in plays ('a very promising actor' as one reviewer put it[8]), and won a place at Oxford to read law. In an age when the school was becoming more open to the opposite sex – the first female speaker in chapel came in 1968, the same year that the Irish OFs broke with tradition and allowed their wives to attend their dinner – it was quite appropriate that Blair's first girlfriend should be the first 'Fettesienne', Amanda Mackenzie Stuart, who arrived in 1970. Some might argue that it was also entirely appropriate that he should be a founder member of a group called the 'Pseuds' which acted out contemporary drama – including the works of Harold Pinter, on whom Blair would be less keen as an adult.[9]

Teachers and contemporaries who had more sympathy for Blair recall someone bright and engaging, who, as English teacher David McMurray said, was 'someone who would make his mark in the world.' Blair was also described by former housemaster Bob Roberts (who caned him) as 'the most difficult boy I ever had to deal with.'[10]

John Rentoul, Blair's biographer, said that all the staff he interviewed for his book remembered the boy as 'a complete pain in the backside.' Public schools being what they are, teachers today occasionally encounter children parroting the views of parents to the effect that Blair was some sort of communist.

Blair's interest in politics was encouraged by the frequent visits to Fettes of former pupil Sir Knox Cunningham, the flamboyant Ulster Unionist MP for South Antrim (David Steel also spoke to the Chaplain's Group in 1969, but there is no record of the young Blair meeting him[11]). Sir Knox had spent the early sixties as Harold Macmillan's Parliamentary Private Secretary and the late sixties harassing Harold Wilson in a manner described by one historian as 'blimpish.'[12] As president of the Old Fettesians' Association, he opened the new boarding house, Arniston; faintly reminiscent of an inter-war fascist police station, it was known as 'Fort Knox'. Gordon Dowell remembers the scene:

I was part of the initial intake for Arniston in 1967 and was present when Sir Knox made an ebullient speech on the steps of the House, to open the establishment for business. I can remember him at the end, ripping off his tie and replacing it with an Arniston house tie, declaiming, 'that's the first time the Brigade of Guards has lowered its colours to a school.'[13]

The loyalist baronet's often rather eccentric opinions ranged from how people might get to the first floor of Aldergrove airport, and in what numbers[14], to the commercial opportunities of Radio Caroline and the undesirability of reform in Northern Ireland. Some remember him for genuine acts of kindness – Lindsay Keith, who omitted to tell Sir Knox that he was one of the few Roman Catholics at Fettes, is still grateful for 'an unforgettable tour of the H of P and other places there where the public don't get to see' – but he is best known today for his views. He seems to have enjoyed provoking the lads with what they considered outrageous opinions about issues of the day and on his frequent visits would go to the dorms for an argument. Cunningham, recalled Robert Philp, one of the Arniston resident tutors in Blair's time, 'used to come back rubbing his hands with glee, saying, "That's stirred things up a bit."'[15]

Although not yet party political in his outlook, Blair was a keen debater and enjoyed these verbal jousts. Sir Knox was not above encouraging the boys to challenge school rules with which they disagreed – advice he did not believe applied to the Roman Catholics of his constituency in Ulster. Blair's opinions may have been strengthened by a house trip to see Lindsay Anderson's *If...*, which portrays a schoolboy revolt; the headmaster was outraged, but Eric Anderson kept his job and Blair's contemporaries do not seem to have emulated Malcolm MacDowell's on-screen antics. Then again, as John Cormack, who was slightly older than the future Prime Minister and possibly slightly more typical of the average schoolboy of the era, comments, 'Most of us had absolutely no idea about that sort of thing. Anyway, it wasn't really like Colditz; most people just got on with things and lived in hope of meeting someone from the girls' schools.'[16]

Fettes and the World
There were plenty of exciting events in the sixties for Sir Knox to provoke Fettes' band of current affairs enthusiasts about. They could note, as in 1962, that 'world events have obtruded themselves upon us more than ever this term' – colonial unrest, war between would-be great powers in the Himalayas, difficulties with negotiating British entry into the Common Market and, above all, the Cuban Missile Crisis.[17]

Although the *Fettesian* mentioned it merely in passing as one of a range of events which had been discussed by school societies, there are plenty of former pupils who remember just how anxious the world was at the time. Charles McKean, for instance, remembers George Kennedy putting out the lights in his College East dormitory and saying 'Goodnight; I don't know whether we will be here tomorrow morning.'[18]

Another potential flashpoint was President Kennedy's assassination; Lindsay Keith recalls that the news came through when some of the boys were at an event in the Usher Hall, and David Sperry, the American exchange student whose presence did much to broaden their views, speculated that there might be a war.[19]

Alasdair Fox sums up his experience:

As post war babies we were of course only too conscious of the effects of the Second World War - my own father had, for example, been seriously wounded in North Africa. We had also lived through the Suez crisis and had therefore known both food rationing and later petrol rationing. The Bay of Pigs incident took place while we were at school and, when, shortly after lights out, the drone of an aeroplane was heard overhead we were convinced that it was the beginning of a nuclear attack, by Russia. I was a prefect when President Kennedy was assassinated. The cold war was at its height. We were well informed on such matters - although I remember that, having been invited through to the Housemaster's house to watch Sonny Liston demolish Floyd Patterson, the television was quickly turned off when the first item on the news consisted of pictures of Christine Keeler and Mandy Rice Davies, as the Profumo affair broke! We were also well aware that Iain Macleod, Selwyn Lloyd and Knox Cunningham held offices in the Macmillan Government and indeed Lord Drumalbyn was MP for Dumfriesshire, where I came from. Although the most recent ex-Prime Minister might not agree, this was the golden era for OFs in politics.[20]

In the autumn of 1964, the sixth form heard from the German Consul, Dr Theusner, on the problems of the recently-erected Berlin Wall, and had two animated discussions on South Africa with a representative of the Anti-Apartheid Group and a local Indian journalist; they also heard from three OFs who had just completed their VSO. However, it was admitted that by far the most popular and lively meeting was the one with Jock Stein, then manager of Hibernian and one of the only school speakers whose autograph was ever requested afterwards.[21]

The late sixties, unsurprisingly, featured talks on the Middle East (from a Mrs Weinberger), a heated debate on whether this house 'would support Czechoslovakia violently' and a number of talks and debates about Vietnam. In 1967, because 'one of the speakers was himself an

American due to go out to Vietnam fairly soon, the debate was a particularly fiery one'; interestingly, the motion, deploring American intervention was heavily defeated. Nicol Wilson, an OF who had emigrated to America, was drafted into the US army and found that thanks to the Fettes CCF, British drill was still ingrained in his memory – the skills were still useful, though, as he discovered when he was posted to Vietnam: 'Shape Shine Silhouette Surface Movement , or even more to the point, when crawling under fire - keep your bottom down if you don't want it shot off!'[22]

The *Fettesian* carried a number of poems on the subject, with titles like *A Soldier Thinks* and *The Cry For Peace*, and this one in 1969, simply entitled *War*:

His hand outstretched, the fingers clenched tight,
With war-scarred face, and eyes a bloody sight,
He lay. The blood dripped from his body down
And spread across the earth, which turned from brown
Into a sodden mass of gory hue.
All light by now had gone and slowly two
Dim stars appeared, as he, left there alone,
Thought dead by friends, deserted, gave a groan
And moved his aching torso to the left
To stay the constant flow of blood, bereft
Of which he knew he'd die. Then, thoughts of life
And tears with blood mixed in. Ah! Now the strife
With family, friends and even hated foes
Seemed useless. And for 'white trash' too there grows,
In his dying heart, a strange compassion,
Born of deadly fear faced oft in common.
He even liked to think on New York State,
Where in Black Harlem's ghettoes, by cruel fate
He had been placed, at birth, to suffer all
A man. But war had brought a dignity
To him, unknown before, respect and pity
And comradeship with white men. Thus he thought,
And pride swell'd in his soul to have there fought.
So happiness o'ercame his pain and fed
His mind. At dawn, still happy, he was dead.[23]

Whilst some (though not a Victorian Fettesian) might consider this a slightly eccentric interpretation of the Vietnam experience, it does suggest that those boys who wanted to know about the world had plenty of opportunities to do so. However, as several OFs of that vintage have commented, most schoolboys don't take much notice of those things, so estimates of how many people the school societies spoke for varies. Richard Davidson speaks for many when he says that 'Even those of us who were - or liked to think of ourselves as - politically aware, did not discuss foreign affairs much.'[24]

James Kirsop remembers that 'there was a thriving debating society when I was at Fettes – although I was not personally very active in it' adding that 'I think that a good proportion of my contemporaries (say 25%) was interested up to a point in politics and world affairs.'[25]

The changing intellectual climate and post-imperial, post-Cuba strategic situation led some schools, including Sir William's alma mater the Royal High School, to abolish their cadet corps. For Fettes, however, such a thing was unthinkable. The CCF was still believed to teach useful skills, and some at least of the 1960s generation recognised that, as Gordon Kirkwood explains:

...the experience of being in the CCF was helpful to me in later life. Perhaps just like the real army, I believe it helped form you as a person, made you better organised, helped you deal with people and allowed you to experience commanding (and taking responsibility for) others at a very early age.[26]

The camps and field days, increasingly imaginative, were enjoyed by many, although they increasingly incorporated non-military elements. The canoe section, for instance, might have some military aspects, and impressed a visiting colonel with their Eskimo rolls in 1969, but there was no martial component to their trip down the Tay or visit to Austria. As A.N. Sanderson recalled for the school's book of centenary memories:

...on one occasion as chief navigator I led our section off the open course across the Penicuik moors into a maze of woods and ravines; on another we had to lie for three-quarters of an hour in a tussocky field with five blanks apiece giving 'covering fire' for our Bren group as they attacked round the flank with thunderflashes and rattles. At the annual Camp there was a choice of activities, and I have satisfying memories of two summer Mountain Rescue camps spent

around Glencoe, and of another at Easter when armed with ice-axes, balaclavas, and snow-goggles, we scaled Bidean nam Bian.[27]

Ronnie Guild wrote enthusiastically of the adventure and fascination of the 1962 CCF camp near Loch Sween, and there was a detailed account by the canoe section of their adventures nearby, which included a night exercise in which the leading vessel capsized and its soggy crew squelched ashore into a hail of blank rounds. Map-reading was not, however, always well-taught, according to James Kirsop:

I remember a field day when I was about 15 years old (in maybe 1960), when I and two others (along with many other groups that were dropped off at different points) took part in an exercise that involved trying to navigate ourselves from a drop-off point to a designated point on a parallel main road which was about seven miles away across the Pentland Hills. Our group showed only limited ability to make proper use of the compass and maps that were given to us, and arrived on the main road at the opposite side about two miles from where we were supposed to have ended up. However, we did show initiative in hitching a lift so that we arrived at the designated destination point rather earlier than was expected, and ostensibly did better than the groups with whom we were competing. We felt quite proud of our achievement - although obviously we had done well only by cheating! [28]

(This sort of underhand activity was not always successful; Andrew Ayre remembers that a group in a later camp which tried the same thing were badly caught out. Having taken a two-mile detour to a railway station to get a train which would save them a 14 mile hike, they discovered that their ancient ex-army maps were printed before the station had closed.) The sailors, meanwhile, had their own opportunities for adventure; some stayed on HMS *Roebuck* at Plymouth, where they learned about squid bombs, naval manoevres, cleaning and submarine hunting. They won a regatta against cadets from other ships and, since the Queen was visiting, 'lined the decks while the ship steamed through the early morning mists past the craggy Devonshire coast directly astern of the Royal Yacht, jets and bombers flying past overhead and guns thundering a salute on the mainland.'[29]

Small parties could take part in naval cruises, such as those in 1966 on HMS *Tenby* and HMS *Agincourt* which went up to the Western Isles and featured opportunities to fire Bofors guns, explore the boiler room and learn about radar. Although there were aspects of its activities which were an irritant, especially the square-bashing, the CCF had become a much more civilised and enjoyable institution with opportunities even for the boys who had no military interests. Harry Reid, subsequently a prominent journalist and governor of the school, recalls that there was a discreet acknowledgment by the school that the range of opportunities available to the less militarily proficient boy ought to be as wide as possible. As a cadet who enjoyed the Royal Marines' Cliff Assault Troop summer training put it, 'I would strongly recommend this course to anyone who wants to learn how to climb without paying a lot of money for a mountain school.'[30]

Ronnie Guild, to this day something of a nonconformist, was not himself desperately worried whether or not his charges became professional soldiers, but recognised that the Cold War kept the armed services at a level of numbers and funding which enabled teenagers to use their equipment and expertise. He could be impressed by the unorthodox, such as one of his successors, Joe Hills, who overcame the recruits' inability to cook on primus stoves on inspection day by 'borrowing' food from the kitchen to present to honoured guest General Pyman, or use a herd of cows as camouflage.[31]

Abseiling quickly became a popular activity when introduced in the sixties

The worst experience during the sixties for Fettes in general, and the CCF in particular, was the death of James Heatley, a cadet killed in a road accident whilst returning from arduous training in the Nevis area in April 1963. A gifted scientist, debater and musician, his loss shook the school.[32]

When such tragedies occur in modern schools, their impact is all the more horrendous for their rarity, and in James Heatley's case the Headmaster so badly was so badly affected that he considered resigning. Nonetheless, given the vigour with which they have thrown themselves into such a wide range of hazardous activities, it is perhaps surprising that fatalities in the cadet movement have been, relatively speaking, so few. A report on the RAF section later in 1963 blithely mentioned that 'the glider, unfortunately, failed to survive' a recent outing, without apparently pausing to consider that the pupil pilot was presumably lucky to do so.[33] (An attempt later in the sixties to launch a visiting Admiral in the replacement glider was, despite determined efforts, unsuccessful, possibly to his relief.[34]) By the summer of that year, another camp was taking place in the idyllic surroundings of Loch Tarbert, for life went on:

The fishing was excellent and provided much pleasure, and mackerel for breakfast... The sight of a stag within a stone's throw of the assembled troops on the first morning stirred all hearts. Common seals made the loch their playground, terns, curlew, redshanks, greenshanks, oystercatchers and sandpipers were ever with us.[35]

This camp, like several others in the sixties, was 'combined ops' with members of the Naval Section putting in appearances on borrowed whaling-boats, leading the reporter to note that 'there was something of the "Hornblower" touch about the sight of a whaler under sail with armed men aboard under Naval command, fulfilling a traditional Naval role so of making a landing so as to come in on the rear of a shore position.' On another occasion, camp was enlivened by a Dunkirk-style evacuation from a beach at Kilfinan as Bren guns rattled blithely through driving rain. Camp was not always the smooth and purely educational event depicted by *Fettesian* reports. One 'Colour Sergeant Anonymous' recalls:

I will always remember the camp near Campbeltown. I was on the advanced party to set it up, staying in a local hall, sampling the local pubs and putting up tents and digging latrines - which was better at the beginning of the camp than having to fill them in at the end. The camp was interesting as each day we set out on some different challenge/adventure. My most lasting memory of the camp was from the night exercise, when I was leading a platoon to storm a farmhouse. I came round a corner and fell into a sheep-dip up to me neck as in the moonlight it was impossible to distinguish this from the concrete floor of the sheep pens. On the train home afterwards I stank to high heaven of the chemicals in the sheep dip, but I have never had any problem with Ticks since then!

Rob Douglas' camp memories of Otter Ferry in the mid-sixties begin with 'staying the night in some barracks at Gourock before marching through the streets to pick up the ferry at Greenock.'[36] Episodes which stuck in the mind included:

A night march where one of the number had a bottle of vodka which he worked his way through and at a particular point, he fell back off a river bank flat into the burn and lay there laughing away, his peals of laughter echoing through the otherwise silent night. Not surprisingly we were subsequently ambushed by the other team.

A local landowner being reassured by one of the officers that we would be careful not to disturb his game birds followed immediately by a volley of shots from one of the platoons in the vicinity.

One of the platoons setting up a road block on the local road and searching all the cars under the pretext of looking for, I think, an escaped prisoner, to the bemusement of some American tourists.

Watching the Polaris submarines passing close by our shore...

Alasdair Fox, like many cadets before and since, experimented with hitching lifts and using the time saved to smoke Senior Service. At a camp at Loch Sween, he and his friends tried to arrange a game of football with the local lads, but their arrangements were disrupted when, on the Sunday Church Parade, a 'rather fiery minister' preached a half-hour sermon on the sin of sabbath breaking and how 'we don't play games on Sundays'. The CCF could also make pupils feel useful; in 1964, the Royal Engineers Section, whose 'members are all now skilled in the use of the concrete-mixer and the wheel-barrow' build a road to the Corps stores.[37]

In keeping with the times, they also learned about mine-detecting and nuclear warfare. Even more excitingly, the Royal Armoured Corps Section could occasionally borrow Ferret scout cars from the Territorials, and the Royal Artillery Cadre trained on 40/70 anti-aircraft guns (though Ian Hamilton writes that the military's offer to take the boys away for the weekend to fire it 'was vetoed by the Headmaster who reckoned we were dangerous enough with 303s.'[38]) The RAF Section continued its gliding and ground-based instruction on the Link trainer, acquiring in 1965 an entire nose section from a de Havilland Vampire jet, 'which because of its enormous size and weight is at present lying in state in Flying Officer Herbert's section of the Masters' garages.'[39]

In that year, they attended camps at Wildenrath in Germany and Church Fenton in Yorkshire, where 'the highlight of our visit was an organised party which went to Rowntree's.' As before, the RAF section offered thrills unavailable to their grounded brethren, as Gordon Dowell recalls:

The RAF was a bit more civilised but I never took it very seriously either. It was good to go flying at Turnhouse in the two seaters, and to have a zero G experience while flying at a camp at RAF Oakington. We were taken up in a transport plane, I can't remember the brand, but we were completely unsecured in the back. The pilots put the plane through its paces above Cambridgeshire while their precious cargo rose, fell and generally slid about in the back. I don't think the current generation of risk managers would have been too impressed but we survived the experience and enjoyed it.

Ian Lowles had been told that the RAF section was the easiest option, with little drill more fun than camps at Cultybraggan or getting wet dinghy sailing in the freezing Forth. He found more positive advantages in the regular flying in Chipmunks at 12 AEF, then conveniently based at Turnhouse. 'The most memorable flight from was when one of the instructors was retiring,' he writes, 'and after a superb session of aerobatics over Loch Leven we were given permission to fly between the newly constructed Forth Bridge and the Rail Bridge at road height on our return to Turnhouse. How I wish I had had a camera.' He also soloed in a glider at the age of 16, singing 'We all live in a yellow submarine' as he did so. Always having wanted to be a doctor, he combined his vocation with the enthusiasm he had acquired through the cadets and spent 16 years as an RAF medic, serving at Binbrook, the fighter station, and on Cyprus. He is convinced that the air cadet experiences were invaluable for later life.[40]

Neil Jackson, as a piper, had to practice three evenings a week, but this relieved him of the weekly brassoing, blancoing and mudlarking. He was proud to represent the school and did not mind the occasional effort required to get the elaborate band uniform looking smart for such occasions. Pipers could still go to camp and he took the opportunity to visit Malta with the air cadets in 1968 for £1 a day. Although the mornings were spent in military pursuits, the afternoons were free for visits to the beach or exploring Valetta (where they were warned to avoid the street known as 'the Gut' because 'the ladies there were not our sort and it could get a bit rough'; needless to say, they went there to have a look). On a map-reading exercise on Gozo, Jackson's group used their initiative and took a bus, but this did not go down well with the authorities and led to a forced march across rough terrain.

The Civil Defence section, formed in the winter of 1963, learned about how – should the feared apocalypse descend – they might alleviate Edinburgh's distress. They were trained off-campus at the regional Civil Defence Headquarters, which featured a specially-built row of houses, stretching for about 75 yards, showing a gradation in the damage that would be sustained in a nuclear attack, from six to twenty miles. A report in the *Fettesian*, noting with pleasure that this training counted as Public Service for the Duke of Edinburgh's Award, explained how this was used:

At one end, a six mile blast zone is in total devastation where no living thing could survive. At the other, is a building with no doors or windows but where people could easily survive the blast, if they were removed quickly before the radiation became too intense. On Field Day we had two exercises. In the morning various members of the Section were buried in the most inaccessible places in the 'wrecked' building, while the others had to find and remove them. In the afternoon, under the popular guidance of Mr Armitage, a radio exercise was carried out, with some degree of success once a net discipline had been installed.[41]

Andrew Hunter remembers the Civil Defence section as a good way of avoiding long marches; it certainly 'beat going out to the ranges in the rain and shooting at targets.' Although it was 'good fun' he has his doubts as to how useful it was:

It was all played out that the epicentre was bad news but there would be survivors, number of missiles, possible targets etc., and some weird calculations as to a bomb dropping on X where should we start rescue operations for possible survivors! It was all upbeat, though the more astute Fettesians realised that the chances were slim… Very much blitz based and several of the instructors were ex blitz men.[42]

Fortunately, the Fettes Civil Defence section was never required to put their training into action, and was thus spared the horrific fate depicted in Watkins' film and indeed in 'The Bomb', a *Fettesian* poem of 1969:

> *I watched in awe*
> *As the ball of metal below suddenly burst*
> *Scattering ghastly death for miles around*
> *Devastating everything on the ground*
> *And the cloud it left*
> *The giant mushroom of red smoke*
> *Hung there – a trademark of destruction*
> *And I was helpless…*[43]

One footnote in history is provided by Dr John Ferguson, an Old Fettesian serving with the Royal Signals, who had a quite different role in the national arrangements for war on the home front – one which would be of significance later:

Regional Seats of Government were identified and there was concern about how these could communicate if the telephone system was not working. We were working with some of the early American and British microwave (UHF) equipment and realised that these could provide secure point to point communications which would be invaluable to the RSGs. I was given the 'Top Secret' task of trialling these communications and we discovered that we could put multi-channel equipment as well as voice and teleprinter onto these links. Most of us now use this technology every day with our mobile phones.[44]

Although Ronnie Guild still speaks fondly of Civil Defence, arguing that whether or not it would be of any use in an actual nuclear war which never came was of less importance than teaching schoolboys ways of being helpful to others in, say, natural disasters, it was quietly wound up in the era of détente. To some, it remained a 'skive' – rather like James Kirsop's ingenious membership of a section whose actual function was open to question:

I personally ended up in the CCF in a very 'cushy number'. I (a corporal) and a contemporary (T.A. Fraser, who I think was also a corporal) spent our last year in the CCF in a section that was designated as the 'Administration Unit'. It was our job to check on defaulters - people who had not shown up for their CCF duties. After having checked, noted down and reported the names of the defaulters, the two of us in the 'Administration Unit' spent our time playing around with models of battlefields along with a Fettes master called Bredin (Captain Bredin I think, in CCF parlance), using sawdust and other materials - coloured as necessary - to signify hills, rivers, valleys etc. The great thing was that we (the Administration Unit) didn't have to wear CCF uniform, which - because of the day of the CCF activity as related to the days when the laundry was carried out - meant that the CCF kit could never be laundered during any one school term.

Some remembered the CCF of the sixties as rather lax; NCOs might look the other way whilst alcohol was imbibed at camp, provided the officers and keen cadets were kept busy on some improving activity. R.H. Douglas felt that, in the early sixties it was 'never a particularly strenuous occupation' until Sergeant-Major MacAlpine, a man on a mission 'to create a military machine of the Fettes Corps' shook this up somewhat from the mid-sixties. 'Our unstrenuous occupation suddenly became an afternoon of hyper-military activity,' noted Douglas, 'much to the regret, not only of ourselves, but also I think of many of the masters.'[45] Gordon Dowell remembers one of the Sergeant-Major's eccentricities:

We called him 'the Bugger', more for his colourful language than any particular peccadillo. It happened that we discovered he was a farmer in real life. On one Field Day we were bussed to his farm and then directed to pick potatoes all day. Not quite the sort of Field we had in mind, but following this act of back breaking labour for those unaccustomed to it, he handed out 10 shilling notes to everyone on the way back to school. We only thought slightly the better of him for this act of charity but then we were probably pretty useless hoikers.

RSM MacAlpine, Lindsay Buchan writes, 'arrived in a Fiat Cinquecento every Wednesday and shouted at us a lot.' He used to preface his comments to the Corps in his slow Scottish drawl with 'With all duuuuuue respect to youuuuuu College boys ...' Nigel Herdman remembers another catchphrase: 'Don't smile at me boy, not even my wife smiles at me.' As Lindsay Clubb notes, however, 'underneath his often harsh exterior he had a heart of gold and was a thoroughly nice chap who did an awful lot for the school'; he is one of those who dislike the way that 'Blair's cronies' have tried to 're-write the memory of those days'.[46]

Tim Alston remembers that the officers wanting to promote him to sergeant as a leaving present, but were overruled by RSM MacAlpine, who did not want to devalue the grade. The RSM told Alston, who believed it was the right thing to do and admired the integrity of the decision, himself.[47]

RSM MacAlpine and one of his cadets, Lindsay Clubb

Although the reluctant recruits to the CCF have few positive memories of 'The Bugger' his methods paid off; by 1969 drill and turn-out was 'of the highest order' and there was a highly-trained cadre of NCOs. Shooting was also excellent, with high scores and trophies in Scottish and Northern Irish competitions, as well as Bisley, where Mark Haszlakiewicz and other OFs encouraged the pupils despite the inadequacy of their weapons, which unlike those of other schools had not been centre-bedded. Neil Fyfe was introduced to target shooting by the CCF and, as with many post-war Fettesians, found that he had discovered an interest which would last a lifetime. Notoriously, one of the Fettes shooters of this period accidentally killed a sheep at Dreghorn, and it was rumoured that the unfortunate animal later made it onto the school menu. As captain of shooting, he enjoyed the 'magical' trips to Bisley: 'the overnight sleeper train, breakfast at the Great Northern

Hotel at Kings Cross then traipsing through the underground and across Waterloo in kilts and battle dress tops with rifles over our shoulder and on to Brookwood station on Southern railway.' One of the highlights of those trips was dinner in one of the private dining rooms at the House of Commons, usually hosted by Knox Cunningham, 'a larger than life character' who Fyfe remembers shadow boxing with a cadet in one of the lobbies of Parliament. For the cadets to march around on public transport was then entirely normal; Colin Mitchell-Rose, who later joined the Royal Scots Greys as a regular, recalls going to camp:

I remember getting the train to Glasgow Queen Street, marching through Glasgow to Central Station and then catching another train to Greenock, where we stayed in a naval barracks before catching a McBraynes ferry the next morning 'doon the water' to Argyllshire where we had our week's camp with midges and rain – very difficult to keep our cigarettes dry.[48]

There remained the possibility of seriously tough exercises, such as the Army Outward Bound course of 1967:

At 7 o'clock every morning, to the sound of bells ringing, we leapt out of bed and ran half a mile down to the sea where we all ran shivering into the icy water. Most of the first week continued in this vein, with constant attention to the hazardous assault course, the 880 yards track and a rigorous series of circuit training. However, to offset this we had some more interesting training with canoes and some elementary rock-climbing and stretcher lowering... the climax of the course was a forty-five mile trek over the Welsh mountains, carrying all our equipment. For this we were allowed two and a half days, which meant walking from about 7 in the morning to 7 at night. On the second day we were met with a full force 9 gale (which they kindly assured us was the worst they witnessed in all their 140 courses) and apart from one case of exposure, one man impaled on a fence, and one who fell 40 ft. from the top of Calder Idris in mist, the entire course (about 80) completed the exercise![49]

For all the obvious pleasure derived from such activities – and in 1965 Lt-Col Barr could reflect with pride that 'keenness remains commendably high' – during the sixties it was increasingly possible to have adventures or learn about social duty without having to put on a uniform at all. Significant numbers of Fettesians who wrote in response to appeals for information for this book expressed the view that the period of compulsory CCF activity was a dark valley of square-bashing to be endured before entering the sunlit uplands of choice. Bob Bleakley recalls the grimmer aspects which he was relieved to escape:

Ill-fitting boots with nails poking through the inside of the soles, blanco to be applied to webbing belts and gaiters, brass to be polished, battledress to be pressed with a flat-iron heated on a gas ring…Field day – trying to traverse a field of swedes (neeps) but the wretched boots didn't fit between the neeps making progress difficult, and being told to determine the rate of flow of water in a river for which we used an orange but were told our sums were wrong when we came up with an answer… Taking the proficiency test and having to estimate the distance to a far-off object on a foggy day; couldn't see the object let alone guess how many cricket pitches away it was! [50]

One had to get the balance right, however, in passing the precious Certificate A proficiency test (considerably 'dumbed down' from its Edwardian officer-preparation origins) as Neil Sanders writes:

I should say about 10% treated it very seriously, about 10% as a joke and the rest with indifference so long as they could get out. That was the problem because you first had to pass Proficiency. Fail and you remained in till passing but do too well and you were NCO material and also had to remain! It was a nice balance to achieve. [51]

He ended up editing the *Fettesian*. Others adopted a more creative approach, as Lindsay Buchan recalls:

…a friend and I were heavily involved with the school theatrical dept and we argued that we spent a huge amount of our spare time on that so we should be allowed to do it on a Wednesday afternoon – amazingly this was agreed to and no-one ever saw us again on a Wednesday afternoon – I think we tidied the stage store and then ran out of things to do.

Lindsay Keith, however, found that one could be hauled back into uniform if one's housemaster, in his case Richard 'Spot' Cole-Hamilton, felt it would be better for one to do so:

Some creeps rose to be Under-officers but chaps like me looked for something more fulfilling and less strenuous, such as joining Edward Gage's Art Section. We did the mural in the Lower Dining Hall, great fun and a good job too. Much better than prancing round in the rain and nasty uniform. I rejoined reluctantly when made a prefect as Spot Cole-Hamilton said he thought it more appropriate to serve in the CCF than paint walls (he really meant being totally idle and was right about that, he was right about most things and we became good friends). CCF did get me a free trip to Sandhurst which was more great fun. Spot rumbled it straightaway as a 'jolly' but still let me go - he knew I'd already been eye and ear tested by the RAF and told I was technically blind and deaf, anything for a day out.[52]

It is worth noting that, despite his disapproval of those who took the CCF seriously, Keith joined the Territorial Army after leaving school, and found the thrill of firing large artillery-pieces on ranges from Wales to Germany 'hard to beat.'

The post-war CCF could often borrow some of the vast amount of equipment left over from the world war and national service eras, though this particular example appears to be suffering from another post-war British phenomenon

The Alternative Society

Although most pupils disliked the CCF simply because of the misery described by Bob Bleakley, for others, there were issues of conscience, and during the sixties a range of non-military activities emerged for them. Andrew Betts-Brown had become a Christian and developed strongly pacifist beliefs which meant he was not entirely comfortable with the CCF:

I think I took this pretty seriously and understood its purpose, though could not agree whole-heartedly! I did Certificate A part 1, but managed to 'opt out' therafter on grounds of conscience, and because the new Church of Scotland chaplain, George Buchanan-Smith, set up the alternative of Voluntary Outside Service in which I engaged with enthusiasm and enjoyment.[53]

James Allan, like Bob Bleakley, transferred to the Estates Group, also known as the 'Forestry Commission', although 'this did backfire a bit as it involved far more work than I had envisaged!'[54]

Bleakley didn't mind:

…we cut down, pruned and planted trees under the guidance of Major Ferguson, ex lecturer in forestry at Edinburgh University from whom I learned a great deal about tree culture. Camp with the Estates Group was at Inch Cailloch Nature Reserve (an island in Loch Lomond); this was led by Mr Alan Tothill and involved making steps with railway sleepers under the instruction of the Warden, Eddie Idle, who became Deputy Director of the Nature Conservancy Council - a seminal experience which introduced me to the concept of nature conservation as a career, and which ultimately became my career.

One option did not always keep its members; As Lindsay Buchan notes, the climbing section 'was fun except for the annual trip to Glencoe since it always rained and was always absolutely miserable.' The entire section was 'sacked' after everyone turned up at the Sanatorium with assorted ailments and no-one was available to go on the climbing trip. An especially popular alternative to the CCF was the Scout Troop, which (like most other sixties 'options', no longer exists); as Patric Colquhon puts it, the Scouts were 'much more relaxed and probably more useful in the sixties.' Chris Shennan writes:

I did not enjoy it [the CCF] *and at the first opportunity, I joined the Scouts. I forget the pretext of how I managed to escape - apart from simply enjoying one rather than the other. If I recall, Scouts and the CCF took place on Wednesday afternoon. We went skiing, sailing and on a long walk (30 miles) in the Cairngorms. All much more fun, to my mind, than marching back at school! Though the experience of sailing from clean Grantham passed the sewage outfall off Leith has put me permanently off sailing - from a fear of capsizing into the murky Firth waters!* [55]

Hugh Dunford also loathed the cadets:

CCF was a pain. No sooner had you chucked down your lunch than you sprinted down to house to change into the CCF gear only to sprint back up to main school dragging gaiters, jackets or whatever. Inevitably there would be something amiss which had to be polished, buffed or borrowed. Then to the parade ground for pin-point inspection by 'The Bugger' (Sergeant Major) followed by mindless drilling. Not my thing.[56]

He signed up for one of the most popular optional activities, Outside Service, and is still grateful for the lessons learned:

I escaped to the wonderful Outside Service which did useful and creative things like plays, singing, entertaining old folks, kids in care and the disabled. Run by 'Shorty' Philp − as true a gentleman as one could ever find − I think this unit offered me more than anything else in my time at Fettes. And that is not to denigrate my time there - it's just that caring, entertaining, overcoming shyness and feeling part of something is what it gave me.

Outside Service became a popular activity, with pupils painting, decorating and gardening for local pensioners, and pushing wheelchair-bound residents of the Cheshire Home to the cinema. Lord Drumalbyn, speaking on Founder's Day in 1964, especially valued this help, for whilst the welfare state could provide financial and medical assistance to the elderly, 'it cannot ease their growing loneliness and helplessness by acts of personal friendship.'[57]

Outside Service earned the appreciation of many others, from the elderly couple who wrote to the *Edinburgh Evening News* to express their gratitude to the 'polite and thoughtful' Fettesians to the local president of the Scottish OAPs' Association, who wrote to the chaplain to thank the boys for their 'wonderful job.'[58]

Awareness of the outside world and of ways in which the boys might help it indirectly undoubtedly grew in the sixties, when charitable appeals for aid to the third world became commonplace and well-supported. The Freedom from Hunger Campaign of 1963, for instance, raised £300 for Oxfam to help an Indian village − worth around £10,000 today when compared to average earnings. By 1964 this had increased to £420 and a special effort by Kimmerghame House brought it to nearly £800 – 'a noble effort' as the *Fettesian* rightly enthused.[59]

In the late sixties, Kimmerghame took to holding garden fêtes to raise money; the 1969 event featured woodlouse racing, a tug of war, distance record-setting by three hundred balloons (one reached Kendal), a prefects' Aunt Sally, six gallons of ice-cream, twelve gallons of Coca-Cola and three hundred hot-dogs. In that summer term, this one house raised £780 for the homeless, Shelter having become their charity of choice following the powerful play *Cathy Come Home*.[60]

Pupils who gamely went out with Oxfam collecting tins the day Hearts played Motherwell in October 1969 recorded a range of responses:

> '*Peter Cormack* (a rather thin Hibernian player) *would appreciate it.*'
> '*We need all our pennies to throw at the Motherwell players.*'
> '*Ah'm starvin' masel'.*'[61]

Fettesians were made aware of social change primarily through the efforts of the Chaplain, George Buchanan-Smith, who was, like Ronnie Guild and other post-war stalwarts of the common room, keen to get the boys interested in the outside world. In 1964, a speaker at the Chaplain's Study Group, one Dr Large, led 'a singularly frank inquiry into sex in all its aspects' and this experiment was repeated several times; in 1966 there was the first recorded talk on illegal drugs by a Dr Draper. 'Specific drugs – heroin, LSD – interested the group,' noted the *Fettesian*, 'and the facts which Dr Draper gave about them were very sobering.'[62]

The following year, the magazine printed its first drug-related poem, entitled *On a Growing Social Scare*:

> *The bite of metal:*
> *blood*
> *spurts*
> *trickles*
> *down the puckered arm*
> *A sigh*
> *a difference*
> *born out of a tube*
> *a difference*
> *for a fleeting moment*
> *exhilaration*
> *madness...*[63]

The Fet-Lor Club was still thriving; in the sixties it moved to prefabricated wooden buildings near the school which it still occupies, which made it easier for pupil helpers to attend. Like their inter-war forebears, some Fettesians showed a canny awareness about the unspoken function of the club vis-à-vis the young lads from Pilton and Drylaw estates who attended it. 'Perhaps it is as well,' noted one, 'that their energies are diverted into such innocent channels as learning the art of billiards.'[64]

This social conscience should not be interpreted as meaning that Fettesians were as one with their neighbours. One incident in the mid-sixties, David McCollum writes, 'was so extraordinary that I now sometimes wonder if it actually happened.' One summer evening the school was 'invaded' by a large group of teenagers from the nearby Pilton estates. The masters in charge of the CCF summoned their lads together and organised a military-style sweeping operation to repel the intrusion.

This we duly did and the mission was successfully accomplished, but not without some scuffles and unpleasantness, especially around the pond, greatly exaggerated afterwards no doubt by the more heroic among us. But it seemed at the time, and still does, to have been an extraordinary thing to do. There were some uncomfortable undertones in the imagery of the privileged sweeping the poor from our land.[65]

The energies of Fettesians also required diverting, and post-O- and A-level projects were established to keep the boys out of mischief between the end of public examinations and the beginning of the summer holidays. There was a mania for surveys and questionnaires, some of which are revealing; in 1968-9, they tracked the decline in Sabbatarianism, increased television use (though dissatisfaction with sex and violence), the increase in vandalism, attitudes to immigration and the new housing developments. Others were focused on the school itself; the average fifth former in 1964, for instance, read an average of 42 books per year, with the bulk preferring Ian Fleming, Hammond Innes and, for the traditionalists, John Buchan and Arthur Conan Doyle; a literary minority could still be found with Hardy or Bronte. At the same time, an exhaustive study was done of the boys in general and written up by the head. The average boy had 0.76 brothers and 0.9 sisters, was slightly more likely to be a Presbyterian than an Episcopalian, had a 50 per cent likelihood of coming from Scotland and 40 per cent of coming from elsewhere in mainland Britain.[66] Only a quarter had taken the eleven-plus, of whom a third had failed it, something which did not bother Nick Hammond, the 1965 Founder's Day Guest of Honour who airily told the boys that Fettes' inclusion of 'varying intellectual abilities' meant that 'we rise above class considerations.'[67]

Carrying On

For all of the changes in the society around them, British teenagers did not suddenly wake up in 1960 as rebels without a cause – not, at any rate, outside a few heavily-reported fashionable streets in London. The events described by Lindsay Buchan – an officer telling the entire assembled CCF that those who wanted to go to corps camp should take one step forward 'and not a single solitary person moving' – were relatively infrequent. Traditional attitudes remained, and not just amongst the masters. The Moredun Wild Life Society, for instance, regarded it as quite normal that their increasingly detailed understanding of the Scottish countryside's abundant fauna should find practical expression in shooting or catching it. The three nature films they watched in the spring of 1968 featured fly-tying for beginners, salmon-fishing and the safe handling of shotguns.[68] The school librarian reported in 1964 that one of the most popular books in his charge was an illustrated edition of Winston Churchill's rousingly patriotic *The Island Race*: 'it is impossible to go to the library at any time of day when some young man is not admiring this great work.'[69]

An article by fifth-former 'RMDY' in that summer's *Fettesian* reflected on the eccentricities of the Victorian editions of the magazine with a fluency and sensitivity at which teachers of modern pupils would marvel. Doubting that the alleged sixties 'intellectual revival' at Fettes was anything other than smooth talking by a bunch of 'shameless plagiarists' who in reality only read James Bond and Mike Hammer, he was extremely impressed by his nineteenth century forebears:

Historical events are re-born in that very ordinary and rather childish thing, the school magazine: the Irish troubles of 1885, the small and bloody wars along the Indian border, the Mashonaland expedition of 1891 and the Matabele wars, the Boer war, and even in retrospect the Crimea, are reported on in great detail, and the Fettesian of a few months later lists the medals won by O.F.

combatants. The home life of the Victorians is just as interesting...[70]

Eschewing contemporary intellectual fashions, he quoted a poem from 1899 containing the grim line 'by war, red war, the lands we won we'll hold'.[71]

'Patriotism, Jingoism, colonialism or whatever you want to call it,' he wrote, noting later on that anyone wanting to find out what became of the boys of this era need only look at the casualty lists in the 1914-18 *Fettesians*. He closed by remarking gloomily that the magazine of his own day did not seem to give such a sense of the place – 'our grandsons will find little of our Fettes in these pages' – and that if it had a literary flavour, it was sand. This was not entirely fair; whilst anyone with a taste for the kind of rollicking, rhyming, cheerfully nationalist verse favoured by the Victorians was bound to be disappointed, there was plenty in the magazine to demonstrate that some, at least, had a lively interest in the outside world. This is especially apparent in the space devoted to the death of Sir Winston Churchill in 1965 – more than any monarch received. Fettes cancelled lessons on the day of the former Prime Minister's funeral and held a memorial service in chapel followed by an hour-long 'concert' of his speeches, carefully edited onto tape by Mr Whittle, the Moredun housemaster; 'we had the chance to listen and to think: to remember and to wonder' noted the *Fettesian* reporter.[72]

Whittle and the sixth-form historians also put together a huge display to illustrate all the aspects of Churchill's life; copies of *Hansard*, seals of office, wartime memorabilia from the many conflicts with which he was involved, books, paintings and photographs. 'We can only say "Thank You, Thank You very much indeed,' concluded the report.

New and Old Statesmen
In the spring term of 1964, before the general election – after which no public schoolboy would become Prime Minister until 1997 – Fettes hosted speaker meetings by local party spokesmen (Arthur Woodburn MP for Labour and Sir Michael Fraser for the Conservatives) and distributed the pamphlets they provided amongst the sixth form 'with painstaking impartiality.'[73]

Despite the fact that the Liberals were re-emerging as a political force neither they nor the Scottish Nationalists provided a spokesman. The debaters decided that, were populist politician Mr Marples, John

Osborne, Dixon of Dock Green and Ringo Starr in a crashing balloon, they would save the Beatle.[74] Selwyn Lloyd, oddly enough, was accused of having the same priorities – a cartoon from the era has him doorstepping the Fab Four in order to recruit them for the cause of the unfashionable Conservative leader Sir Alec Douglas-Home.[75]

Home had replaced Macmillan, brought down by illness and a succession of scandals, following a highly questionable leadership contest. The brilliant, mercurial Iain Macleod refused to serve under him and lambasted the system for choosing Tory successors in a blistering *Spectator* article in January 1964. This exposure of the Old Etonian 'magic circle' was a reminder, as one of his biographers put it, that he was merely 'a GP's son attending a minor public school and a Cambridge college neither King's nor Trinity… a frightfully clever little *Hofjude*.'[76]

The *Hofjude* was unabashed, regarding 'the ability of the English upper class to conspire without noticing it' with the same contempt in which he held the other counter-productive prejudices of the Tory Party. Selwyn Lloyd, the perpetual loyalist, stayed on in in Whitehall. He had been one of the sacrificial lambs of Macmillan's panicky 'night of the long knives' when the Prime Minister peremptorily sacked a third of his ministers in the belief that this would make him look decisive and modern. Deeply hurt, Lloyd remained ready to serve, and was mystified by the rising tide of what would later become known as sleaze around the Conservatives. He is supposed to have enquired, with bemused innocence, how his colleague John Profumo could have found the time for his shenanigans with call-girls. His fellow OF in government, Sir Knox Cunningham, ought to have warned Macmillan (he was the Prime Minister's Parliamentary Private Secretary) about the brewing scandal, but whilst a much more worldly figure than Lloyd he seems to have missed the signals. The Conservatives went on to lose four out of the next five general elections. Name-checks in the 'Vive-la' apart, however, the *Fettesian* rarely mentioned such crucial developments. Vastly more exciting was the presence of Fettesians in popular culture, James Bond, the actor and writer Bill Corlett, and schoolmaster 'Ian Chesterton', the OF assistant of the BBC's eccentric time-traveller: 'Bill Russell fights Daleks to help Dr Who.'[77]

The sixties saw a breakdown in the Tory-Labour voting monolith, with a Liberal revival challenging the old guard's dominance – Ronnie Guild, indeed, stood as a candidate in 1964, and his picture, with poster-bedecked car and child helper, appeared in the *Fettesian*. In Scotland, nationalism emerged as an additional rival, with Winnie Ewing taking Hamilton in 1967 for the SNP. Although the *Fettesian* records considerable interest in international politics, neither the debaters nor the current affairs groups mentioned what was probably one of the most important moments in Scots politics for a generation. According to Mrs Ewing herself, 'a shiver went along the Scottish Labour benches looking for a spine to run up' but the junior section of the Edinburgh establishment being educated in Comely Bank was blithely unconcerned.

Post-Conscription Soldiering

The Cold War, after the near-apocalyptic standoff over Cuba in 1962, settled down into surly watchfulness in Europe and bitter proxy-wars elsewhere. One of the only 'war stories' of the mid-sixties was about one of the South American Cold War campaigns. It came from Keith Talbot, an OF living as a cattle rancher in Venezuela, whose farms and staff came under attack by Cuban-backed communist guerrillas. After he had spent a hard day inoculating 10,000 cattle, he was told that one farm had been robbed and burned to the ground, and later that a lorry had been hijacked and its crew murdered:

With all the vaccinating, people drowning and guerrilleros, we really are having a splendid time. All we need now is a Cockney prophet to come and tell us that the end of the world is at hand! And if he did, I'd be quite ready to believe him! [78]

In 1964, a sixth-former, 'D.B.S.' described a visit to the East Berlin, which, with its 'great rolling strands of barbed wire', gun-toting Soviet guards and people 'forbidden to wave' – not to mention the memorial cross to a 'freedom seeker' shot whilst trying to escape – left him profoundly dispirited, wondering 'What can I do?'[79] In 1967, Stuart Murray wrote to Mr Whittle to say that he had been visited by 'Bertie' Young, 'complete with broken nose – proof of shady escapades behind the Iron Curtain.'[80]

Sadly, this rather mysterious reference was never followed up. Those Fettesians who carried on joining the armed services despite the ending of National Service had little doubt about what to do, but they were, as previously noted, much fewer in number, and the magazine carried hardly any tales of military life. Even some of those who did join up were not always in the traditional mould of the dedicated young cadet

NCO who had determined on an infantry career at an early age. Ken Millar, who had joined the school a four foot ten, six stone, 'bespectacled midget' so scrawny he was nicknamed 'Belsen', acquired a taste for tramping over the hills on CCF exercises and somehow managed to keep up the interest.

After Fettes, where I was lucky enough to con the examiners into giving me A-levels of sufficient mediocrity to get into medicine at Glasgow, I joined the University OTC; my memory tells me that this was as a result of a letter I had received from that organisation, who had been informed by Fettes that I had been a member of the CCF – so Fettes continued to exert an unseen (and indeed unasked) influence over my life. I made much of my University OTC days (often to the detriment of my studies, as playing soldiers was much more fun than attending lectures or poring over books at the weekend), and progressed to the dizzy height of Senior Under Officer, which promotion I feel may have been more related to an exemplary attendance record than any military leadership prowess. As I still had many years to go before graduation, I had to move on and leave a space for the next chap to become SUO; this meant I either had to leave or attempt to take a commission. At this point it dawned on me that the Army were offering Cadetships for medical students. I applied (successfully – but the Army was very short of doctors at that time and my success had more to do with that shortage than with anything else, I fear) and was commissioned into the Royal Army Medical Corps in 1967.[81]

Just as he had found himself being trained by the same SAS officer who had conducted Fettes expeditions to Jura, now Millar was to find himself helping out with a Fettes 'Arduous Training' trip to the remote West coast of Scotland. 'Of course I was a bibulous medical student at that time so my recall for many events is a touch patchy,' he writes, 'Indeed, those masters who were involved may well remember my presence as more hindrance than assistance – but who can say.' A rare, and brief, report of service life came in 1967 when T.J. Dempster wrote to Mr Whittle to say that he had been posted to a small minesweeper in the Persian Gulf, and that the experience of handling 'House Bank' (the store for Fettes pupils' rationed pocket-money) was coming in handy.[82]

Army OFs might never see such exotic spots: Ian Couper, entered Sandhurst in 1961 and served with the Royal Army Service Corps and then, on rebadging, with the Royal Corps of Transport in West Germany, and later in England. After leaving the regular army, he became a

Territorial officer and served through the seventies and eighties in various capacities, ending up at the TA Staff College at Camberley. Ian McCoubrey, who served as a medical officer with the RAF between 1967 and 1997, writes:

Because of the history of the world as it was between 1967, when I was commissioned, and 1997, and also because of bad luck, I ended almost 30 years service without once having heard anything go bang in anger. I managed to scrounge one campaign medal, for service in Northern Ireland; but that was only for going for a week each year for five years to carry our medical boards for University Air Squadron applicants! [83]

Although the life for much of the armed services in the sixties revolved around the relative quiet of the North German Plain, there were still occasional flashpoints, especially the Indonesian confrontation over Borneo, when British service personnel were in the firing line, and where OFs were involved. One such was Capt Roddy MacDonald, a career sailor (later an admiral) who was Commander Naval Forces Borneo and who wrote the only substantial British report on conflict for the *Fettesian* in the sixties:

It is most interesting and fun too. I am responsible for preventing infiltrations by sea into Sabah, Sarawak and Brunei by Indonesians, whose ambition it is to add these countries to Soekarno's empire by either assault or subversion. The Commander Far East Fleet places under my operational command ships to patrol the coasts and support the Army. I also have ships from the Malaysian Navy, control RAF Maritime Patrol Aircraft and co-ordinate the Marine Police whose boats work with the Naval patrols. The smaller craft search out deltas of big rivers and lurk up mangrove swamps in close concert with the Army. There is also 848 Naval Squadron of Wessex helicopters from HMS Albion *deployed in support of the Army, in whom I take a great interest.* [84]

MacDonald enjoyed the variety and excitement of the work, which included dealing with local politicians and trying to stop the activities of both pirates ('a traditional occupation') and Filipino cigarette-smugglers; 'I don't think I have had such responsibility since I was Captain of Rugger at Fettes' he said. He described the extraordinary range of tasks and experiences he had had in the previous few days:

I flew over the jungle and sea in ten different types of aeroplane and helicopter; spent two nights on patrol in a frigate and a minesweeper, during which we boarded and searched a number of piratical craft, many under sail; flew to an Army forward position approachable only by helicopter, which lower themselves into unbelievably small holes in the jungle like a fat lady into her corsets; visited Ops involving an interesting walk through the jungle, not normally considered suitable for sailors... though sailors are definitely quicker up trees than Brigadiers; patrolled in a Shackleton LRMP aircraft over coral atolls, jagged reefs and the most beautiful sunlit sea with the North-East Monsoon clouds piling up all around the horizon; had an audience with the Sultan of Brunei in his elaborate Istana; attended a State Security Executive meeting as the Naval Adviser; inspected Naval and Military units in a steamy mangrove swamp by assault craft; and shot down the Kuching river crazily in a police hydrofoil in heavy rain, no visibility and a certain amount of anxiety.

The British were involved in protecting the area from Indonesian conquest for four years, and suffered around a hundred fatalities. MacDonald, who finished his naval career as a vice-admiral, was a veteran of the Second World War who had an unorthodox approach to the conflict, employing hearts-and-minds tactics to gain the allegiance of villagers; he is probably Fettes' most distinguished sailor, and his obituaries described the confrontation as his finest hour. Even when there was no actual fighting, there were still casualties, as Ian McKee, normally enjoying the good life as an RAF medic in Singapore, recalls:

Aircrew had to practice no matter what the weather, as the enemy wouldn't necessarily choose a good day to attack, and at one stage we were losing an average of one aircrew a month, 'flying into rock-studded clouds' as someone put it. We had a routine when an aircraft went missing – CO, squadron commander, doctor and padre would visit the families with as many words of condolence that we could muster. Then, when a fatal crash was confirmed, get the families back to UK on the next plane home and get on with life as before. No flags at half mast, no memorial service, nothing. If there was a dance due that evening it still went ahead.

Fettes' most recent fatality in the service of the crown was one such. Flying Officer Douglas Clavering, who had won the trophy for best first-year cadet whilst at Glasgow University Air squadron in 1961,[85] was killed when his Hunter fighter crashed into the sea on a low-level sortie south of Singapore in misty weather on 19 September 1964.[86]

R. deG. Hanson, a Surgeon Lieutenant from the post-war Fettes generation, was on HMS *Manxman* and Medical Officer to the Inshore Flotilla of the Far East Fleet. The death which stuck in his mind was neither by accident nor by enemy action, but when a Chinese crewman on the RFA *Gold Ranger* drank a bottle of whisky and stabbed a colleague to death during an exercise off Thailand. Police requirements meant that the body could not be buried at sea, but the Chinese cooks would not allow it in the freezer, lest the ghost get into the meat. Hanson and a fellow-officer sealed the corpse between two sheets of plastic with an iron and stitched it into a canvas bag before putting it in the cold vegetable store; apparently ghosts are purely carnivorous. Having been drunk, the murderer was judged by the Hong Kong authorities not to have guilty of murder; he was now responsible for the upkeep of the family he had bereaved.[87]

Although Britain did not get involved in Vietnam, nor the United States in Indonesia, the NATO allies did conduct joint exercises in the region, HMS *Manxman* cooperating closely with the USS *Epping Forest*, like her a fighting vessel from the Second World War adapted for mine-hunting ('poacher turned gamekeeper in her old age' as Hanson puts it). Putting in to the giant US base at Subic Bay in the Philippines offered the Royal Navy the opportunity to exercise its traditional sense of mischief:

Some of our divers thought it would be a good idea to swim across underwater and tie one of the buoys from a practice mine to her [Epping Forest's] *anchor cable with a bottle of whisky attached. This was done but come the dawn it was seen that their decks were patrolled by armed sentries to protect against such underwater attacks. The experiment was not repeated.*

Subic Bay was the key American naval installations operating in support of the war effort in Vietnam, and its security was tight; by contrast, Hanson recalls how he could arrange for Aldis signals from *Manxman* to summon him from the rooftop bar of Hong Kong's Mandarin Hotel, should he really be needed; on another occasion, a large local lady, pregnant daughter in tow, arrived on the gangplank and announced 'He said his name was Jack and he had a flash of lightning on his arm!' Fettes would later recruit an Australian Vietnam veteran, Neville Clark. The official account of one of his engagements reads:

On 6 August 1967, while taking part in Operation Ballarat in western Phuoc Tuy province, A company, 7RAR, encountered an enemy force and began to receive sustained small-arms and rocket-propelled-grenade fire. Forward observer Lieutenant Neville Clark directed artillery fire from the 106th Field Battery to within 50 metres of the Australian infantrymen, forcing the enemy to break off. The battery fired over 800 rounds in one hour, causing approximately 200 enemy casualties. Clark was awarded the Military Cross for his role in the fighting. Lieutenant Colonel Eric Smith, who commanded 7RAR, praised the battery's efforts, saying: 'they were quick; they were capable; and one felt confident in them.'[88]

Neville Clark became housemaster of Glencorse and OC of the CCF, and was one of the most respected members of the common room of his generation.

Revolution at last

If the early sixties were comparatively stable, Fettes undoubtedly took on board the sweeping change of the second half of the decade. The head occasionally allowed expressions of this to surface, as in a poem in the *Fettesian* in 1969:

Conformity, Conformity, there's nothing like Conformity,
There never was a word of such deceitful multiformity.
It always has a trick at hand, and one or two to spare;
At whatever time a thing takes place – Conformity is there!
They say that all annoying rules, in some most cunning way,
(For instance regulation dress, or chapel every day)
Are nothing more than offshoots from the world which all the time
Frustrates our nonconformity; this senseless pantomime.[89]

This was most spectacularly and unmissably apparent on Founder's Day. David Ogilvy, whose ascent of the advertising ladder gave fifties Fettesians a thrill of fascinated horror, was guest of honour in 1968 and delivered a brash, exciting and controversial speech of a kind never heard before at Fettes.[90]

He expressed his sympathy for Fettesians, having to endure the horrors of O- and A-levels, which he regarded as pointless fact-cramming, and urged the school to set up a continuous fund-raising programme to net £60,000 a year. A 'dud' pupil himself, he blithely informed the boys that there was no correlation between success at school and success in life. Just as they must hardly despise William Fettes the grocer, so they must not look down on advertisers. 'I dare to suggest that if Fettes produced more marketers and advertising men,' he continued, 'Britain's balance of payments would not be in such miserable shape.' He went on to extol the virtues of adventures, professionalism, and going to university in America. The climax of his speech, however, was not recorded in the *Fettesian*, probably because of the apoplexy it must have induced. Ogilvy reminded the boys that Sir William Fettes had endowed the school for the education of 'young people' and not boys alone, so it was high time girls were admitted. 'If the governors continue to ignore his wishes,' he announced from the rostrum to an ecstatic crowd of pupils and an increasingly horrified headmaster, 'I urge you boys to follow the example of your contemporaries – *riot!*' [91]

Ogilvy had lived up to the fears expressed a decade and a half previously (this did not stop the school later cadging several thousand pounds from him to buy a mini-bus, eliciting the reply 'you bastards!' and a cheque). Yet the following year, Sir Sandy Glen, explorer and special agent, urged the pupils to break out of the small box of Britain and embrace Europe; whilst he disapproved of revolt for its own sake, he must have raised eyebrows when he said:

I was in France last May and with little persuasion could have been on the barricades with the Sorbonne students. French education had stood still for centuries and badly needed the kick it got. [92]

As Fettes geared up for its centenary year, it might have avoided potential *If...* style revolts, but it was, like the western world in general, in a precarious cultural position. Classics and square-bashing, which had built the empire beloved of the earlier generations of Fettesians, were now almost as unpopular as the empire itself. The last issue of the *Fettesian* in 1969 carried letters which, whilst they might not have spoken for most boys of the time, did show that for some the dislike of tradition went further than resentment at discomfort and went to the heart of what Fettes held dear. One condemned 'the Rugger-playing neurosis which has affected Fettes for too long'; 'in an age of greater freedom, we as Fettesians are still forced to play Rugby Football by those who wish to break our bones and sacrifice our souls to the God of Tradition, unheeding of our cries.'[93] The other, signed simply 'A Pacifist,' was an assault on Remembrance Sunday:

Few people, when observing the two minutes' silence, and almost nobody does so voluntarily, think about the dead, and those who do, like the Fettesians inspired by the words 'To our glorious dead' and the soldiers dying with the words 'Carry On' on their lips, think of the heroics of war. In place of a husband with five young children dying ignominiously, in great pain, spewing up blood, not caring what good his death will do to the country, but wondering what will happen to his wife, comes a young hero, full of ideals and patriotic feelings, dies like a hero, painlessly, his last words being, 'Forward men! For King and Country!'

Far better than 'standing silent for two minutes round a statue of someone who never existed', wrote 'Pacifist', would be to show people footage of the horrors of war in Vietnam or Biafra. As Hugh Dunford puts it, with regard to the CCF, 'the Empire and National Service were long gone and for the majority at the tail end of the peace-loving sixties you wondered how they were still getting away with it.' Few, however, actually went as far as 'Pacifist'. He may have spoken for many people in the sixties, but was not really the voice of Fettes. Andy Murray does not remember the Fettes of the late sixties as a hotbed of radicalism:

You would have to go a long way to find such an ill-informed, complacent, right-wing bunch. There was never any in-depth political discussion of any kind. God knows how Tony Blair discovered Socialism, because there wasn't the slightest hint of it at Fettes when I was there.[94]

Neil Jackson is philosophical about the military life, and indeed the other tough aspects of Fettes life in the sixties:

I think it was like many things at that school, were they not to your liking: if you rebelled you got beaten or expelled; if you succumbed, you were just miserable. What you had to do was to find a way around it. The pipe band did that for me and gave me a skill which I have enjoyed ever since.

Everyone could, in fact, get something out of being a cadet, even if not quite in this way. David McCollum found the CCF 'hugely instructive.' It gave 'an insight into forces' culture and thinking' through marching, shooting and other military tasks, and also provided 'a fascinating experience of organisation and management.' Although keen and committed, those in responsibility often became 'self-important and quite pompous in their exercise of power' and competed against one another.[95] These were tendencies which he tried to avoid in his own professional career. Donald Jamieson saw the cadets as 'a pointless waste of time', to be 'endured rather than enjoyed.'[96]

Even he, however, benefited from the experience. Having been supplied with a stout pair of boots by the CCF, he decided to keep them when he left school (reckoning that the 35/- charge on the school bill was both good value and unlikely to be noticed by his father) and subsequently used them happily over the next 30-odd years for everything from climbing Munros to gardening.

NOTES

[1] See Philp, p. 81

[2] Quoted in Philp, p. 88

[3] Quoted in Sandra Dick, 'City Roots shaped Blair's rise to top,' *Edinburgh Evening News*, 27 June 2007

[4] Ibid.

[5] John Rentoul, Tony Blair, Prime Minister (London, Little, Brown, 2001) pp. 14 & 24

[6] Ibid., p. 17

[7] Leslie Barr, letter to the Headmaster, 28 June 2003 (school archive)

[8] *Fettesian*, April 1968

[9] Ibid., July 1969

[10] Quoted in *The Scotsman*, 23 July 2004

[11] *Fettesian*, April 1969

[12] Graham Walker, *A History of the Ulster Unionist Party*, (Manchester, MUP, 2004) p. 156

[13] Email to the author, 16 September 2009

[14] Kenneth Owen, *Flight International*, 31 March 1966

[15] Quoted in Rentoul, p. 18

[16] In conversation with the author, Cumberland Arms, Edinburgh, various occasions

[17] *Fettesian*, December 1962

[18] Email to the author, 18 December 2008

[19] Ibid.

[20] Email to the author, 16 September 2009

[21] *Fettesian*, December 1964

[22] Email to the author, 18 December 2008

[23] *Fettesian*, April 1969

[24] Email to the author, 16 September 2009

[25] Ibid.

[26] Email to the author, 17 September 2009

[27] A.N. Sanderson in MacDonald, p. 269

[28] Email to the author, 17 September 2009

[29] Ibid.

[30] *Fettesian*, December 1966

[31] Ibid., *Fettesian*, 1982

[32] Ibid., April 1963

[33] Ibid., July 1963

[34] Ibid., July 1969

[35] Ibid., December 1963

[36] Email to the author, 11 October 2009

[37] *Fettesian*, April 1964

[38] Email to the author, 27 September 2009

[39] Ibid., July 1965

[40] Email to the author, 16 September 2009

[41] Ibid., April 1964

[42] Email to the author, 18 September 2009

[43] *Fettesian*, December 1969

[44] Ferguson

[45] R.H. Douglas in MacDonald, p. 276

[46] Email to the author, 16 September 2009

[47] Email to the author, 14 September 2009

[48] Email to the author, 26 October 2009

[49] *Fettesian*, December 1967

[50] Email to the author, 16 September 2009

[51] Ibid.

[52] Ibid.

[53] Ibid.

[54] Ibid.

[55] Email to the author, 15 September 2009

[56] Email to the author, 16 September 2009

[57] *Fettesian*, July 1966

[58] Ibid., December 1963

[59] Ibid., July 1964

[60] Ibid., July 1969

[61] Ibid., December 1969

[62] Ibid., December 1966

[63] Ibid., July 1967

[64] Ibid.

[65] Email to the author, 21 September 2009

[66] *Fettesian*, December 1964

[67] Ibid., July 1965

[68] Ibid., April 1968

[69] Ibid., December 1964

[70] Ibid., July 1964

[71] See Ch. 2 for full poem

[72] *Fettesian*, April 1965

[73] Ibid., April 1964

[74] Ibid., April 1964

[75] Michael Cummings, *Daily Express*, 11 November 1963

[76] Pearce, p. 340

[77] Vive-la, 1965

[78] Ibid., April 1965

[79] Ibid., July 1964

[80] Ibid., July 1967

[81] Email to the author, 21 May 2009

[82] *Fettesian*, December 1967

[83] Email to the author, 18 December 2008

[84] Ibid., December 1965

[85] 'Protean Visitors', *Flight*, 27 April 1961, p. 575

[86] David J. Griffin, *Hawker Hunter 1951 to 2007*, (Raleigh, Lulu, 2006) p. 134

[87] R. deG. Hanson, letter to the author, 24 July 2007

[88] Unit History of 106th Field Battery at Australian National War Memorial Website

(http://www.awm.gov.au/units/unit_13931vietnam.asp) accessed 24 June 2011

[89] *Fettesian*, April 1969

[90] Ibid., July 1968

[91] Quoted in Philp, p. 92

[92] *Fettesian*, July 1969

[93] Ibid., December 1969

[94] Email to the author, 21 September 2009

[95] Email to the author, 21 September 2009

[96] Email to the author, 17 September 2009

Chapter Nineteen

'Our second century'

The Seventies

Activated Sludge and other attractions

The first issue of the *Fettesian* in the seventies opened with a photograph of Senior Under Officer Hugo Fraser, who had left the school a few years earlier, receiving the Queen's Medal at Sandhurst from Field-Marshal Lord Harding. The CCF notes, much briefer than in former years, recorded with pride that the Fettes OC and RSM had attended the Passing Out Parade at which this award for the highest-scoring officer cadet was awarded, and offered their congratulations. Appropriately, there was also a vigorous rebuttal by Mr MacDonald of the letter by 'Pacifist' which had appeared in the last issue of the magazine in 1969 ('He would certainly not have been allowed to do anything like this if the Nazis had won').[1]

The picture of Fraser appeared opposite one of the advertisements which had crept into the magazine in recent years, showing a smiling blonde withdrawing ten pounds from one of the new 24-hour cash dispensing machines of the Royal Bank of Scotland. Elsewhere, there was a review of the American novel *Myra Breckinridge* ('Is it possible, perhaps, that Gore Vidal used the kinky appeal of his book as a method of whipping up publicity?') and a report of a folk and blues night where Fettes pop group Activated Sludge clashed guitars with Merchiston's Iron Cross 'perhaps a little deafeningly and abruptly.'[2]

Other articles advised readers to see through the 'confidence trick of modern art' or to take up Russian O-Level ('one has the capability of being a Russian agent at one's fingertips'), the latter piece appearing a few pages after a cartoon, possibly left over from two years earlier, showing Czechoslovakia being eaten by the monstrous beasts of Germany and the USSR. A nationalist third-former piped up with a call to arms whose sentiments, if not its scansion, would have overjoyed George Campbell Hay:

Mackenzies, Macdonalds, Macphersons, must go,
And harass the English their terrible foe,
Drive them away over the border,
Drive them from Scotland in disorder.

Such cheeky disloyalty was not evident in the Fettes centenary celebrations in 1970. These included a visit from the Queen Mother, a ball, the floodlighting of the school and a rash of publications. One of these, the *Fettesian Centenary Supplement*, provided overviews of the life of the school through its first century. Drama, music, the Classics and, of course, sport were covered in a series of well-written essays. However, despite the fact that they had been vital parts of the school's identity since its inception, there was nothing about the military or about empire. In fairness, the CCF, embodiment of these aspects of Fettesianistry, was not yet a hundred years old, whereas rugby had been played from the first days. There was also, however, a reflection of the times in this omission; interest in things military had been in decline for some time, the empire was gone, and the relatively small number of Fettesians who were genuinely keen on joining the armed forces could expect to spend at least some time in the unremitting grimness of Northern Ireland, 'Britain's Vietnam'. The tone of references to conflict in popular culture – with the BBC's impressive documentary series about the Great War leading the way – was no longer proud, let alone triumphal, but sorrowful (though World War Two could still stir pride, as the popularity of the film of the Battle of Britain showed). The extraordinary *Fettes Masque* produced for the centenary – an epic telling of the school's story through more than two dozen little scenes, each a masterpiece of timing and style – did, however, mention the war. Many felt that the 1914-18 section of the *Masque* was the most powerful; a third-former expressed their views when he described it:

Boys were sitting in chapel. It was dark, lights flashed in the background. Doctor Heard, played by M.B. Macleod, stood on a rostrum, an eerie light shining on his face from a candle which was just in front of him. The Lacrimosa Chorus was played in the background as the names of the dead of the First War were read out. Three soldiers came on, and one died, at least pretended to be killed in slow motion which must have taken great practice. A truly superb scene.[3]

The *Times Educational Supplement*, which carried a report of an 'Ambitious Masque' found this scene 'impressive' and 'poignant.'[4]

The Second World War references included some (possibly welcome) comic relief with Mr Niven as a housemaster bombarded by memoranda and small boys, eventually tearing his hair out and throwing his vast array of emergency paperwork in the air. The Fettes imperialists of yore were sent up in a sketch in which Robert Winternitz addressed an African native in 'baby-talk' – as we have seen, not entirely a fair view of the earnest young men on the nineteenth century, but by 1970 a fairly standard one. Unchanged were the messages; the Rev Dr Ronald Selby Wright, at the William Fettes Memorial Service at the Canongate Kirk, spoke with pride of Fettes greatest alumni and frankness about the rest:

How great and how many are the men who have gone out from this School and influenced public life in one form or another: there is a Lord Chancellor and there a Lord Justice Clerk; there is a Chancellor of the Exchequer and there a Foreign Secretary; there goes a Cardinal and there a Moderator and there a distinguished Leader of the Armed Services... Before me here there may be, for all I know, a future Chancellor or Prime Minister or Field-Marshal or even an Archbishop; but you are the exceptions; most of us are called to play not a lesser role in life – to be good, honest, kindly people who do the best they can in the service of God and their fellow men.[5]

Founder's Day was turned into a weekend attended by 1,500 people, and incorporated the *Masque*, an exhibition, a Britten fanfare from the roof of the College, beating retreat augmented by Old Fettesians amongst the pipers, and a service in St Giles' Cathedral. The Headmaster addressed the parents and pupils with his customary dry wit:

Always be suspicious when a headmaster starts talking windy abstracts about 'a healthy, vigorous routine suited to the needs of Youth today, free from external pressures both material and academic, fitting young men to take their place in the new technological society, but as its masters, not its slaves.' Ten to one the heating system has gone wrong, the A-level results are down and there is another crisis in the Science department.[6]

The 'Vive-la' referred both to one of Ronnie 'Cocker' Guild's attempts to get into Parliament in that election year – the first in which 18-year-olds could vote – and to the educational issue which had dominated the previous decade:

Next Thursday's election decides if we've all
Never had it so good or not had it at all;
If our new teenage voters find hopes unfulfilled,
They can mortify Harold by voting for Guild.

The Vive-La now ends its Centenary song –
Selective, divisive and still going strong;
The next hundred years will confirm our intention
To see that the Vive-La defies comprehension.

Although Mr Guild failed to become an MP – his pupils' slogan 'Off your rocker? Vote for Cocker' can hardly have boosted his chances – the Conservatives were returned to power with Iain Macleod as Chancellor; Selwyn Lloyd later became Speaker. In the Fettes mock election, the Tories gained 150 votes; their nearest rivals were, characteristically of the times, the Youth Movement, led by Anderson, who 'generously presented his tuck-box to receive the ballot slips; the President, less generously, examined the said box for any traces of premature zeal on the part of Mr Anderson.' He won 44 votes, the Liberals 43, Labour 30 and the Scottish Nationalists 19.[7] Later in the year, there was a Royal Visit by the Queen Mother. Ruaridh Watters remembers her arrival:

I recall standing out on the playing fields behind the school one fine summer's day, the entire school standing in rows, dressed in CCF uniform waiting for the helicopter to deliver the 'Queen Mum' to visit Fettes as part of the centenary celebrations. We waited for over an hour in the blazing sunshine, and watched as at least a dozen boys (men!) fainted and had to be carried away on stretchers by the 'Red Cross Section' (which I guess would have been manned by the 'Outside Services' lot, run by Cocker Guild, as I never heard of or saw that particular group ever again). Finally a large red helicopter whirled over our heads and landed on what appeared to be the cricket square and out stepped Her Majesty with a beam and a wave.[8]

Following the grand military welcome, Her Majesty was presented with a bouquet of flowers by Amanda Mackenzie Stuart, the first female Fettes pupil, and opened the new Science Building. Much of the reporting of the day in the *Fettesian* had the same rather breathless qualities of the Queen's visit in 1955:

It's school tomorrow,
For that I don't care,
For the Queen Mum came today.[9]

The Queen Mother inspects the CCF in 1970

Commem, the great reunion celebration for Old Fettesians, was also especially lavish in the centenary year; Sir William's bust was re-mounted on a plinth of Carrara marble designed by Mr Gill, the Art Master and donated by OF W.H. Valentine (1910) and the school was floodlit, with elaborate fireworks. A great ball was organised in the Assembly Rooms, in part by 'Sir Knox Cunningham and his elusive team of devotees' in the Old Fettesian Association. It had been an extraordinary year of celebration and remembrance. Yet before it was out there were to be sad losses; Sir Robert Bruce Lockhart passed on, old and full of years, one of the last relics of the Victorian school who remembered the old Queen's death. More painful was the death of Iain Macleod, only just appointed to the job for which he had been born, who was struck down by appendicitis and killed by a heart attack aged 56. The *Fettesian* carried more than seven pages of obituaries for him; from the *Times*, from his fellow OF politicians Knox Cunningham and Michael Fraser, and from Mr MacDonald, who had taught him in the thirties. Hugo Fraser, the young Sandhurst cadet who had won the Queen's Medal earlier in the year, was killed in a car accident on the M1 just before rejoining the Gordon Highlanders in Germany. The tributes – like those for other young men whose deaths had been reported to the school from Victorian days – came from masters and senior officers. Recalling his Sandhurst career, his superiors noted that he had led a group of cadets through the North African desert, retracing the routes of the wartime LRDG, taken part in the Transatlantic Air Race and captained the judo team. 'He was neither a great natural games player nor a brilliant brain, though he had ample ability in both spheres,' wrote his College Commander, Brigadier Lithgow, 'the great success that came to him was not for what he did, but for the man he was.'[10]

Mr Whittle, Fraser's old housemaster, recalled how the young man, as Head of House, was invaluable in reassuring anxious mothers:

A brisk knock at the door, a pink and grinning face, a cheerful handshake, infectious enthusiasm, an obvious friendliness and unmistakeable kindliness, clean collar, shining shoes, impeccable manners, an engaging manner, gusts of laughter – I could see at once her fears disarmed by his transparent honesty and goodness!

His name lives on in a Fettes prize given by the Old Fettesians each year for service to the school community.

Attitudes to war in Fettes' second century

Ian McIntosh, who had steered the school through the sixties, stepped down in 1971. He wryly told the pupils at his last Founder's Day that 'in so far as the Headmaster is the man who is paid to say "no", members of the school probably feel that I have been only too conscientious in the pursuit of my duty.' 1971 also saw the last report on a pupil who was probably not top of Mr McIntosh's hit parade, Tony Blair, playing the tortured, whisky-sodden hero Stanhope in the war play *Journey's End* which his house, Arniston, put on as part of the annual round of house performances. The glowing review in the *Fettesian* observed that 'few events can have stimulated such a flood of writing as the First World War' and connected *Journey's End* with *Oh, What a Lovely War!* Sir Laurence Olivier, it was observed, had been in the original stage production of the former – playing Stanhope – and had just starred in the film version of the latter, playing a decidedly unsympathetic Sir John French. Arniston used songs from the musical in the interval, though these were the least subversive part of it, having been culled in general from the actual soldiers' repertoire of 1914. The review made some interesting points which illustrate how views of war had changed since *Journey's End* had first appeared in 1928:

It is easy to understand the appeal which this play had at a time when admiration for the heroism of those who had fought in the 'Great War' was only beginning to yield to disillusionment at the futility of it all. The current of veneration of those who went on 'sticking it, because they know it's the only thing a decent man can do' still runs strong, and as yet none of the participants presumes to ask what the war is for. War is seen to be thoroughly unpleasant, it is true. But although the immense strain on men is now frankly admitted – Stanhope, 'the finest officer in the battalion', who the men 'simply love', reveals that he would be quite unable to go into the front line without being doped up with whisky – in spite of this revelation that most heroism is Dutch courage, there is still a feeling that it was all worth while – if only to preserve that conservative and slightly romantic world of Edwardian England of which they speak so wistfully?

How does the play wear forty years on, when our attitudes to war in general have changed so much? The very impossibility of questioning war because it's not 'the decent thing to do' makes the play more of a personal tragedy in as situation where men have no choice. And it is chiefly the tragedy of Stanhope.[11]

By all accounts, Blair was magnificent, the *Fettesian* commenting that Arniston were fortunate to have him in the role. Whilst some teachers might have raised their eyebrows at the sight of the 'draft-dodging' and rule-bending Blair in a smart uniform, all who saw the performance were impressed. 'Blair brought out the febrile intensity of Stanhope,' continued the *Fettesian* review, 'wiring himself into his ever more circumscribed troglodyte world, speculating moodily on the worm that went down when it thought it was coming up.' Ably supported by other talented student actors, Blair made a real impression with this subtly-modernised (words like 'topping' were deleted) classic.

Tony Blair as Stanhope in Journey's End

The fact that it was consciously bracketed, both by those involved in it and those who watched it, with *Oh, What a Lovely War!* was telling, if, to many military historians, frustrating. The musical, which would also become a popular feature of school drama repertoires, was cordially loathed by some academics for its sixties attitudes and simplistic, class-driven, portrayal of the war in general and officers in particular. Freddy MacDonald's disapproval of schoolboy pacifism has already been noted, and plenty of other Fettes masters and Old Fettesians had enthusiastically maintained that the original interpretation of *Journey's End* was truest to their experience. The 1971 audience, however, was less traditionally-minded. 'My father was a military man, and had experience of both wars,' one commented, 'But after learning about Vietnam, I hadn't the slightest intention of following in his footsteps – no chance.'[12]

Poems about war in seventies *Fettesians* invariably had a pacifist bent, presumably as much due to the influences at university on younger members of staff as to any opinions of the pupils themselves. 'W.L.G.' contributed *Earth* in 1972:

The trench sits, cold, in fields of mud,
That once knew grass which greenly shone
Around the merry land, now gone.
Where are the cows who chewed the cud?

The land is bare, yet not so ripped,
As worn by fights, of future time,
Where, knarled by shells, by bullets nipped,
The earth will close the dead in grime.[13]

Even the junior pupils, whose grandfathers could be relied upon to produce rip-roaring jingoism at that age, were now writing material which would have found favour with the left-wing theatre workshops of the sixties:

Everything was still
Quiet
Everyone was paralysed
Quiet
Not a soldier was moving
Quiet

Then suddenly war started
Chaos
Bullets, flames, tanks, bombs, started moving
Chaos
Houses were burning down, bombs were exploding
Chaos
Many soldiers were killed in battle
Chaos
Blood spread on the ground —
Quiet.[14]

The Corps in the Chenevix-Trench years

These ideas were, it ought to be said, not widely discussed in the Corps, which continued to be a compulsory part of school life despite all the changes. McIntosh's successor, Tony Chenevix-Trench, was another classicist and another Englishman; like the great Alec Ashcroft, he had served his country in war. Here the similarity with his predecessors ended. Ashcroft had been decorated; Chenevix-Trench had been a prisoner of the Japanese, which left emotional and physical damage. Although accused by some Old Etonians and Salopians of undue enthusiasm for the cane (his greatest error, in fairness, was not beating boys *per se*, but beating boys who went on to write for *Private Eye*) he was in fact Fettes' most liberal head. He was less strict about uniform regulations than previous heads (team photographs of the period feature mullet haircuts of German proportions), and was reluctant to expel pupils, as one incident indicates. In 1973 an enterprising air cadet succeeded where the Luftwaffe failed in 1939 and bombed Fettes. This is almost as important a piece of Fettes folklore as the Germans' visit many years before, and has, accordingly, different versions — several names have been offered for the culprit, for instance. He had won a cadet flying scholarship which enabled him to go solo in the Chipmunk at Turnhouse, which was not yet the busy airport it became, and took the opportunity to zoom low over the playing fields and drop bags of flour on the sportsmen below. Chenevix-Trench spotted a first-class (if potentially fatal) prank when he saw one and confined himself to administering a caning because the lad had broken airspace regulations and sent air traffic control into a tailspin. The gradual addition of girls to the school through the seventies meant that Fettes became increasingly relaxed, and the CCF reflected this to a certain extent, though one young pupil's observations on 'those early Corps days' in the Fettesian suggest that powers of endurance were still required:

It's Wednesday, it's nearly ten past two… and you're going to be late for Corps! You scuttle and hobble along the ground like the Hunchback of Notre Dame, doing up the gaiter on your left foot. You fall in, breathless and tired and red.

It's roll-call – your name is called out. It's called out again, rather more volubly than the first time. It's called out once more – your name is bawled in your face. Rather astonished, you hastily come to the attention; but it so happens that a playful bit of boot-lace has crept out from inside your gaiter. It catches under your other foot, and in the middle of coming to the attention you stumble to the side and knock over the rest of your rank.

'An extra parade for fooling about!' says the rugged, well-groomed NCO. It's no use explaining… [15]

Sergeant-Major MacAlpine could still be a terrifying sight, as Allan Jardine, a new recruit to the pipe band, discovered when he went to pick up his kit:

'Flashes, two; spats, two; Glengarry, one; plaid, one….' He barked over the counter, as he glared down at me, and I could not help but be curious as to why he wore his tie over the top of his jersey. Secretly I was very excited about all this new gear, and couldn't wait to hump it all back to my dorm to try it on. It all weighed so much I had to get a friend to give me a hand. First on was the most handsome dark blue tunic, or 'doublet', and at once we could see a very severe problem indeed. The sleeves covered my hands, so how would I be able to play? My pal tried in vain to roll them up at the cuff, but the cloth was too thick. Holding the Hunting Stewart kilt against me confirmed our worst suspicions that that, also, was way too big. We just assumed the plaid would be dragging along the ground behind me, like a bridal train. The sleeves on my school blazer were also over my hands, but, as I had to keep on explaining to all the posh kids, that was for me 'to grow into', and anyway I could always remove it to write while in class.

A dilemma indeed. No way was I going back to The Bugger to complain his Store did not adequately cater for a wee 13 year old boy, who had made it into the big boys band. My friend unhelpfully suggested using scissors, or a knife perhaps, to trim everything down, even the sporran, but how silly would that look? [16]

The problem was solved by a secret night visit by Mr Jardine senior, who had the uniform altered – a keen piper himself, he would not have any son of his playing in a kilt which went over the knee like a woman's dress.

Young Allan Jardine in the elaborate uniform of the pipe band

The kit was only one of the eccentricities of the Corps in the seventies. One OF of the later seventies, Keith Miller, recalls it as somewhat ramshackle:

I would say that by my time the CCF was keeping up appearances (dress code etc.), but was viewed more as a chore than anything else by most of us. You couldn't really get out of it completely, but the sentence could be shortened if one had a good reason: mine was History of Art A level and going to galleries. I do recall that just before that, a friend of mine and I were demoted to 'Corps gardeners' - weeding the flagpole or some such, until Col. Hills just told us to leave, one Wednesday afternoon. So ended my military career.[17]

Despite attitudes like this, Raymond Maclean – who later joined the armed forces – felt that actual rebelliousness was fairly minimal. Rebels who disagreed with the CCF 'would refuse to Blanco their gaiters or march out of time or turn left on the "Right Turn" command... that was about the extent of the mutinous behaviour that I recall.'[18]

Attempts to 'skive' could backfire, as Robin Durham recalls. Having taken a bus to avoid a lengthy hike to a campsite, he and his section realized they had a problem:

I think the walk should have taken us about 3-4 hours, and it wasn't until we were hanging around the camp site that we realised staff would be turning up at some stage, long before we were meant to arrive, and would wonder how on earth we had made the walk in such astonishing time. So we all ended up hiding in a nearby hedge for the next 4 hours, watching as the staff arrived and started to set up tents, and waiting for the other CCF members to start arriving from the hill; only then were we able to sneak out of our cover and surreptitiously filter into the camp and try not to seem too fresh and out of place.

We agreed later that it would have been far more fun to have just gone on the walk! [19]

Jonathan Dunlop's experiences were typical of those of generations of small boys who tried to turn everything into a game:

The corp kit was itchy and my boots were excellent water absorbers but they also had the great benefit of being at least two sizes too big for me and thus made ideal skating/sliding boots. The Moredun path down from the basketball court was a regular slide track for myself and 'Wally' (Nigel Wardropper), upon MacAlpine s discharge, until my jump at the steps ended in an unforseen somersault, dislocated shoulder, severe concussion and stitches to the eyebrow which are still visible 30 years on! [20]

CCF Reports in the *Fettesian* became much briefer, sometimes not appearing at all. Instead of accounts of the various sections, which did still exist except where, as in the case of Civil Defence, they had withered on the vine, a solitary paragraph summarised the term's activity for the Corps as a whole. Piping and shooting got their own reports, as, occasionally, did the REME Section. It set out its chief aims in 1973 – 'to provide a basic knowledge of the internal combustion engine and the systems of a motor car' – but many joined in order to get the fringe benefit of driving 'vehicles of varying modernity' around the grounds. In the early seventies, the REME fleet consisted of a home-made go-kart (which, embarrassingly, buzzed around vigorously unless an adult – such as the Brigadier who visited in 1972 – got into it), a Morris 1000 ('of gentle character') and a 1931 Austin Seven, which unsurprisingly needed 'a fair amount of mechanical work' but which 'now chortles along merrily, much to the chagrin of the doubting Thomases and those who wanted to sell it for scrap.'[21]

The fact that the ancient vehicles broke down so often provided an incentive for the young combat engineers to learn the appropriate skills, since only if they could make the cards move could they go for the coveted

The REME Section's Austin Seven, photographed in 1974

spin. Jonathan Dunlop was a keen mechanic until an unfortunate accident:

We were told we could drive an old Morris Minor around school if ever we could get it going. The challenge had been set and with the aid of a Haynes manual or otherwise we were up and running in less than an hour. Field trials around Youngs went well until 'we' crashed into the Arniston gate at the rear of the pavilion, much to Housemaster s annoyance. I got 100% of the blame, which I thought was most unfair as I had only been on brakes and accelerator and others had been doing the gears and helping with the steering! I remember the subsequent inquest being particularly nerve racking as I thought expulsion might be on the cards.

Luckily, he was only expelled from the REME section.

'Chappie' Barr with the Kimmerghame Under-officers and NCOs in 1970; the uniform is still wartime battledress, but in many ways the cadets offered much more modern activities than this image suggests

747

The CCF was appreciated by its devotees for the cheap, fun adventures it offered. For very little money, the cadet movement offered schoolboys the chance to, for instance, drive armoured vehicles around in West Germany, as the Fettes cadets did in 1971; they also visited the Mohne Dam, the East German border and Belsen ('it is said that no birds are seen or heard within the bounds of the old concentration camp; this proved sinisterly true on our visit').[22]

Some experiences were truly spectacular and linger in fond memories decades later, even if they were born of a desire to seek the easy life. Chris Clayton, having 'calculated that I'd have less marching and more 'off-campus activity' if I joined the Navy section' got a lot out of the CCF of the early seventies, spending at least fifty per cent of his time either at Queensferry boatyard or at Rosyth. To those, like him, who were determined to get as much as they could out of the experience there was not only a host of exciting nautical activities but also the opportunity to gain a real 'understanding and appreciation of all things to do with the sea and boats.' Best of all were the opportunities to go on naval warships, usually at the beginning of the summer holidays. Not many took up these offers, but those who did could enjoy memorable 'cruises' lasting up to a week. The most memorable of these was a round Britain trip on HMS *Bristol*, a brand new guided missile destroyer captained by an OF Roddy Macdonald. The six cadets were given the normal tasks of naval ratings, best of which was to be lookout just next to the bridge and reporting directly to the officer in charge. 'Being port lookout for four hours in the middle of the night as we sailed through one of the busiest sea channels in the world (the English Channel) was an amazing experience.' The following year he sailed clockwise round Britain from Liverpool to Portsmouth on the assault ship HMS *Intrepid*, dropping anchor in Loch Scavaig off Skye and heading to shore on a landing craft for swimming, fishing, and diving for scallops. Clayton is one of many people who enjoyed the extraordinary opportunities afforded by the cadet movement (as it is now called, partly in honour of Octavia Hill) and, although he did not actually join up, his son (possibly inspired by these stories of life afloat) did, and spent some time being trained on HMS *Bristol*. Similarly, Nigel Herdman chose the RAF, which meant that after basic drill, 'we were taken away to classrooms to learn about aeroplane thrust and lift, which during the winter months was far more comfortable than outside Army pursuits.' The highlight for him was camp at RAF Kinloss, where the cadets mixed with regulars, toured the Nimrods and the control tower, and generally had a brilliant time. 'That event stays with me today 30 years on,' he writes, 'especially every time I take a holiday flight.'[23]

The Sub-aqua Section's 'very leisurely' camp in July 1973 at the Oban Divers' Centre was also much enjoyed, not least for the opportunity to explore the wreck of the *Breda*, sunk in Ardmucknish Bay during the war with a cargo of jeeps and aircraft. Like the mountaineering, canoeing and hillwalking which could be part of an interested cadet's experiences in the sixties, such activities could be the genesis of passions, in this case rather James Bond-like, which continued long into adulthood, Jonathan Dunlop, exiled from REME, notes:

I joined Sub Aqua with Tony Foley and loved the pool sessions and expeditions to go diving off St Abbs Head. I subsequently worked my way up within the ranks of the British Sub Aqua Club, ran a diving club for 3 years and have dived all over the world whenever the opportunity presents. I firmly believe the Fettes CCF gave me a great opportunity and initiated my lifetime's interest in shooting, fast cars and diving!

Other cadets went from sub-aqua to REME. Andrew Purves' first dive was 'into the blackness of Loch Lomond, the second into the brownness of the North Sea off St Abbs (this was followed by a few pints at the hotel on the headland, as I remember).' He 'converted' the Morris Minor by cutting off its roof (he is not sure why) and enjoyed racing 'bangers' along the old track at the back of the school, but for some reason seems to have escaped justice and went on to spend Wednesday afternoons in the library with girls.[24]

Ruaridh Watters invented the Skiing Section, drummed up a few recruits and took them to the Hillend Ski Centre every Wednesday afternoon, subsidised by the bursar to the tune of 50 pence per cadet. 'When the weather was inclement we would cancel the trip to Hillend and report to the St Vincent Pub at the bottom end of Frederick St and spend our 50 pence there instead. In those days that bought three pints (14p each) and a bag of crisps.' After getting rumbled, he too ended up in the REME section.

Although these were relatively small aspects of the CCF – in 1973, seven cadets went diving, and nine went to Malta – 58 lads could be found to go on that year's main annual camp, which incorporated Duke of Edinburgh qualifying expeditions, helicopter flights and a Royal Marines rock-climbing course at Ballater.

Adventurous training in 1973 – compare hair with 1963 prefects

Allan Jardine, employed as camp piper, found that his duties did not go down well with the other cadets:

If ever there was a more appalling and brutal way to be gently and delicately awakened from one's slumbers, this was it. I had made myself a target for an assorted range of make shift weapons to be found close to hand in a tent, such as boots, training shoes, mess tins, the odd golf ball and the other RAF shoe. I nearly fell into the ditch that served as the camp latrine to avoid a well aimed, wildly spinning, cricket bat.

The next morning I cautiously struck up a little further away from the snoring circle of tents, but they had pre-empted me, and some bastard took a shot at me with an air gun. Well, that was it. I stormed into the Officers' Tent, threw my pipes on the floor, and announced that I was having no more of this insulting and abusive treatment, not to say downright dangerous after this most recent turn of events. No one admitted to taking the shot, but I was replaced, along with my instrument, by a combination of a Corporal rattling a large saucepan with a heavy ladle; the idea being he could defend himself with the pan and hit back with the ladle.

One pupil, writing about the Adventurous Training at Glenisla ('a small, virtually uninhabited glen at the back of beyond') during one of the cold snaps of the late seventies, recalled conditions of real grimness in which the weather forced even Fettesian officers – whose appetite for adventure tended to surpass that of their cadets – to abort a number of expeditions:

Looking back, sitting in my study, it seems that the conditions we went through were nearly impossible. When I conjure up images of Adventurous (Arduous) Training, the image turns into a nightmare; huge great white lumps partially obscured by a howling gale and needles of ice slashing through the air. I can see the officers gleefully chasing us up the hills screaming 'Good game! Good game!' then pushing us upwards with the sharp end of an ice-axe. Apart from the failure to see any vultures it was a very successful week, and also enjoyable! [25]

The pipe band was a community within a community within a community. Founded in 1912 to lead the then OTC on parade, it developed a hard core of serious enthusiasts and recruited professional instructors, such as John 'Jock' Percival, of Edinburgh City Police Pipe Band. Scholarships would eventually be available for gifted young pipers, but the band would always be a mixture of enthusiasts from traditional Scots backgrounds and curious novices – who after World War Two were coming, like John de Chastelain, from all over the world – and it was remarkably successful. Allan Jardine remembers the camaraderie:

A Band of Brothers, so to speak. We were all in this together, stuck in the same boat of the Bagpipe. It was no longer just me against The World. Admittedly I was younger than everyone else, and the Pipe Major was even a School Prefect, one up from a House Prefect, so that was very scary. But somehow, in The Band, rank and age seniority ceased to matter, odd in a school where generally that sort of thing mattered a great deal. In fact I am sure my peers in the dorm must have been impressed, what with the new uniform and all, although they never let on. So from now on every Tuesday and Thursday evenings were spent sitting with our chanters at the desks in that musty old classroom, roughly in a circle, with Mr. Percival at the epicentre of all the whiney noise. My new friends were much better pipers than me, but the tunes were new to all of us, and over the last few years I had been used to much practice. Practice I did, because I wanted to be part of all this. I wanted to go 'over the top' with the rest of the lads.

Sure enough, he did go over the top, playing at the Castle with the massed pipe bands of the Scottish schools at the annual Beating Retreat ceremony, and was soon in demand for Burns suppers. Despite the rise of nationalism, Edinburgh in 1977 was still rather short of those who could play the people's instrument, or at any rate of those willing to pay for a professional to do so. Accordingly, the city's social clubs would contact its schools to get pipers on the cheap. 'Once our Pipe Major had bagged all the best ones, meaning the ones with the most free booze, the Pipe

Sergeant had the pick of the rest,' writes Pipe Corporal Jardine, 'and, as next in line, I was left with the Temperance Society of the Free Kirk Masonic Abstinence branch of Alcoholics Anonymous.' He soon regretted resenting this pecking order when his superiors sent him to a rugby club dinner where his giant hosts were already drunk. Their idea of a complimentary dram for the piper was rather larger than the civilised little quaichs used at Fettes.

I had not drunk whisky before, but at 15 I felt almost a man, so how hard would it be? This particular quaich was the size of a Great Dane's dog bowl, only deeper, and overflowing with the amber nectar. Well, I barely got the words of the toast out, in a very hoarse voice. 'Slange va ban Riach!' I gasped. That's not how it is written, but that is how it sounds. I struck up the Pipes, resolved to play 'Black Bear' and then went hell for leather back to the kitchen, as an unwelcome feeling started to well up in my stomach. The whisky, it would seem, did not like it down there and wanted out, and it wanted out now. The normally restrained clapping now speeded up in to a form of an applause, as I hurtled toward the sanctuary of the kitchen cold water tap. 'Black Bear' is a very fast tune to play, as per beats per minute, in its proper form, but I had no time for that. I remember being impressed with myself at the time, for not fluffing a single note, as I played the venerable March Past of the Argylls, at something approaching Warp speed.

Dashing into the kitchen for some cold water, Jardine soon felt unaccountably better, but was, nonetheless, circling a 'like battleship whose rudder has been blown off by a torpedo' and was driven by a kindly club member's wife back to Fettes, where some bemused junior boys had to drag him upstairs to his dormitory. He would later lead the band himself, playing at highland games and designing its crest, a variant on the school coat of arms featuring a piping lion and drumming stag.

The Monstrous Regiment does its bit
A very real novelty in the CCF of the seventies was the presence of girls, who were not initially required to join, unlike the conscripted boys, a privilege bitterly resented by some male pupils but secretly welcomed by masters who didn't want yet another problem to worry about. One of the first female cadets was Mary Mure, who joined in 1976:

We were equipped with uniforms from the boys' collection and I suspect joined to challenge the notion that girls wouldn't do such a thing at that time. I can remember the dreadful tones of 'I want to see the last man at the armoury' and us feeling that we could amble there as we were not men. I can remember being handed a rifle which seemed to weigh a ton and being asked 'would you like a crane, Mure, to lower you down?' ... the guilt continues as I fear we backed out when the going began to get a little tougher. Not a distinguished career in the CCF, I fear...[26]

It was to be several years before girls became cadets, and indeed pupils, on the same terms as boys. In the seventies, they tended to gravitate towards Outside Service, the school's contribution to the wider community as well as being a form of public duty for those who preferred to be out of uniform ('CCF refugees'). In 1971 the group helped refurbish a dilapidated church in the Gorbals; in a sign of the times, it was intended to become a 'combined recreation hall and discotheque.' Although hard work in bitter cold, the Fettesians cleared the church of inflammable material – plaster walls, rustily-nailed floorboards and the like – and saved £300 towards the final reconstruction of the building. 'While the majority of the CCF enjoyed the ephemeral delights of a ramble in the Pentlands, the Outside Service contributed greatly toward the realisation of a scheme which, it is hoped, will help to ease some of the social stress which a barren Hutchison's Town might experience,' noted the reporter.[27]

Other activities included the complete repainting of a blind widow's home in Pilton by the 'interior decorating branch' (1972), recitals by the 'entertainments group' to both an old people's and a remand home (1973), gardening and generally helping out at Mayfield House (a home for people with multiple sclerosis) and the Western General (1977). Angus Morrison, who came to Fettes in 1977, feels that pupils got as much out of Outside Service as those they helped:

Trips to Pilton were eye-opening. You soon appreciated that while life in Schoolhouse could be pretty austere, you were hugely privileged in many respects. Part of the reason for joining the Community Service was the fact that it was organised by GABS (the charismatic chaplain, George Buchanan-Smith) who was a very likeable and persuasive character. The other was probably the presence of girls - still something of a novelty in the late 70s.[28]

Large amounts of money continued to be raised for charity, including the popular scheme of sponsoring the education of schoolchildren abroad, such as one Adewole Adeleye of Nigeria, whose success was reported in 1972. Closer to home, however, the Fettesian-Lorettonian Club faced financial difficulties, which led to an appeal by its leader in the Spring 1973 *Fettesian* for more funds. Given the criticism of the welfare state which was beginning to grow in this era, it is interesting to note that the Fet-Lor considered its enemies to be not just social deprivation and inflation, but also the 'appalling apathy' of the authorities and their 'uncaring' officials. The Club, it was argued, offered a more personal form of contact and help than the anonymous, ineffective benevolence of the state. The appeal seems to have struck a chord, since the Fet-Lor continues to this day.

Soldiers of the Seventies

Although the numbers of Fettesians joining the services had, as we have seen, declined considerably, many still did. In the seventies it was still possible for strings to be pulled for a keen Fettesian to enter the armed forces. In the controversial account he co-authored with his youngest son, Robert Lawrence MC, of the Battle of Tumbledown and its aftermath, Wing Commander John Lawrence cheerfully admitted to phoning the army recruiting officer and dropping the names of Commanding Officers of regiments with which he had served at Sharjah in order to get Christopher, his eldest, a place at Sandhurst.[29]

In fairness, Christopher was clearly such a good candidate that, in a field of 60, he was one of only 21 young men selected for training. Although he was 'destined to be a general', Christopher Lawrence eventually left the army to become a stockbroker – 'to make some money.' Like many Fettesians, he did retain his military connections, in this case as a trooper in the Artists' Rifles, better known as the Territorial SAS. Motivations to join the armed forces varied, but the lure of excitement and sense of doing something important were not uncommon spurs to taking the Queen's Shilling. As with the two world wars, modern Fettes did not always send along the most obvious recruits. Robert Lawrence, who was to distinguish himself as a soldier and suffer severe wounds in the Falklands, was frank in his memoirs about the Fettes CCF in the seventies:

I hated the Army at Fettes. I joined the Naval Cadet Force at Fettes only because it seemed the biggest skive of the three. After doing that for the absolute minimum period, I joined the Royal Electrical and Mechanical Engineers because they had a go-kart and a couple of cars. Eventually, after doing a handbrake corner in a Morris 1000 on the school drive, spraying a master with gravel, I got kicked out of the Corps. The head of the Corps told me I should never go near any of the armed forces, because I was totally incapable of being disciplined.[30]

The Duke of Edinburgh's Award gave Lawrence a lifeline and a useful insight into the skills he would need as a soldier; tramping through the hills in the bitter cold, he would see bigger, fitter boys 'tear up along front and then collapse, whereas I would go along moaning and moaning – but never stop.' Once he joined the Scots Guards, this tendency was reinforced by the NCOs' habit of reminding him how good his brother Christopher had been – 'If your fucking brother could see you now, sir...' Lawrence later pondered his reasons for turning up at the recruiting depot in 1977 (and returning in 1978 because he had been too young the first time):

I saw my time in the Army as an opportunity to have a bit of a Boy's Own existence. The big thing that also appealed to me about it was that everything I did in the Army mattered. Every decision I made as a young man mattered. There are eighteen-year-olds running around in Northern Ireland, for instance, and if they make the wrong decision over something, someone else could get blown up tomorrow in Belfast or London. In a way, I think I also saw the Army as a transition period from school to the real world; I certainly wasn't ready for an office job.[31]

Army officer training in the seventies was, in certain respects, less gentlemanly than it had been a hundred years earlier when the first Fettes cadets wrote heartily from Sandhurst to describe a life not much different from that at a well-armed boarding school. This letter was written in 1879:

The Réveillé goes at 615, - and I may add produces little or no impression upon the slumbering 'generals of the future.' The bugle that produces a startling effect is the one at ten minutes to seven, which acts like an electric shock. Up we jump, tumble somehow into and out of our tubs, don the patrol jacket, which, as a former Fettesian here remarked, covers a multitude of sins (to wit, not infrequently, a robe de nuit), and tumble off to first study from seven to eight. Then breakfast bugle goes, when we fortify our inner man for a long day, out-air work or in-door as the case may be, then repair to the ante-room, and read the news, parade, riding, or gun-drill till ten, a few minutes' respite, and then work till two. Lunch, followed by an afternoon which one either has to one's self, or it is occupied by drill or gymnastics (if one is a junior), or by sword-exercise, or gun-drill or riding (if a senior)…

Mess comes at 7.30, and we sit down in our mess-uniform (a tunic worn open, and regulation waistcoat bordered with thin gold braid, and that very narrow red stripe down our invisible blue trousers, that seemed to be the one delight of the last Fettesian who was here) to our dinner. Thereafter, one plays billiards, or smokes and reads in the ante-room, or goes to the library, or goes and has a musical evening (if a friend possesses a piano), and so the hours go by till 11 p.m. (as we do not work in the evening), when the bugle signs a long G ('lights out'), and shortly thereafter Sandhurst, – well, Sandhurst if examined closely, – would be found napping.[32]

This genteel life was very much a thing of the past at Pirbright, where Robert Lawrence underwent the rigours of Brigade Squad, the eight week 'beasting' at which officer cadets were pushed to the limit:

During Brigade Squad, we had one weekend off in the middle. The rest of the time they had the right to bug us around twenty-four hours a day. It was classic Army stuff, weapons training, kit-cleaning, learning to march and drill. They could keep us up to 3 am in the morning and then suddenly say, 'Right. Bed. Thirty seconds!' And in thirty seconds we had to be in bed. Then at 5.30 am or 6 am the lance sergeants would come in, smashing the bed with sticks and screaming that we had to be straight up and out again…

They were beating the daylights out of us to see when we'd break. Twenty-six of us started and only about eight of us finally passed. Some guys cracked. I remember once, when we were running up a sand hill on a disused range, with packs on our backs, this chap suddenly collapsed; he lay there, saying, 'I want to die. Someone kill me. I can't bear this any more,' and I couldn't blame him at all.[33]

So in fear of their instructors were the recruits, Lawrence wrote, that it took something of a leap of the imagination to stop and consider that they would not actually inflict physical harm. At the end of the process, its survivors 'felt totally and utterly invincible… feeling fifteen foot tall' and Lawrence found Sandhurst proper 'a doddle' after the Guards Depot.

Although Northern Ireland and, of course, duties in Germany dominated the military scene of the 1970s, British troops continued to be deployed in small but important engagements around the world. In Oman, the now Brigadier and President of the Old Fettesian Association Ian Gardiner, then a junior Royal Marine officer, was to serve in a Cold War clash which, had it gone badly, might have destabilised the Gulf region and even dragged in the superpowers. As it was, he wrote later, 'a model counter-insurgency campaign brought about a rare, unambiguous and enduring victory over Communism.'[34]

Said, the profoundly reactionary Sultan of Oman, had attempted to keep his subjects in what Gardiner describes as a 'medieval time warp', and triggered a rebellion in Dhofar. The communists of South Yemen (formerly the British protectorate of Aden) jumped on this bandwagon with the People's Front for the Liberation of the Occupied Arab Gulf – not only a mouthful but an inaccurate one since Oman had never been occupied by the British Empire. PFLOAG hoped to win Oman's people, starting with the unruly Dhofaris, for Marxism, and to win its oil for the People's Democratic Republic of Yemen. In the turmoil, Said was overthrown by his son, Quaboos, a committed moderniser who had served with the Cameronians and had the support of Harold Wilson and Edward Heath. The British, who already had 'contract officers' – essentially mercenaries – in the region now sent greater levels of military assistance.

Like his Fettesian forebears, from the Victorian imperialists to the crotchety nationalist George Campbell Hay, Gardiner was interested to note similarities between the wild men of the Dhofar hills and the highlanders of Scotland. Tough, living by military service, clad in wraparound garments resembling the kilt, the Dhofaris were men of warrior beliefs. (Gardiner did also note that urban Omanis 'saw somewhere in every Dhofari an idle, wily and ungrateful thief' – not unlike the attitude of Sir William Fettes' generation towards their own highlanders.[35]) Gardiner's company medic, the *campowda*, to people in rural villages, helping treat eye and respiratory complaints; some people had scars which were the result of the traditional medical wisdom of treating pain with pain, such as red hot metal to cure a headache: 'I guess they didn't complain twice.'[36]

This was only one aspect of the harsh, primitive life to which the old sultan's reactionary medievalism had condemned his people. Roads were unpaved, illiteracy was rampant, electricity rare. Some stereotypes luckily proved to be untrue – the British were never offered sheep's eyes in the course of many communal meals, and when one was finally offered a goat's eye and politely refused, his host threw it away with the comment that they didn't like them either. When operating in the wilderness, accommodation was often 'reminiscent of Neolithic Skara Brae'.[37]

The enemy could be utterly ruthless, and this required tough measures on the part of the government. Gardiner once observed two Strikemaster attack jets taking off from Salalah; they were going to bomb the wreckage of an aircraft which had been shot down, both to ensure that nothing of value could be taken by the *adoo* and to be certain that the pilot was definitely dead and could not be captured and tortured. Although, like the Victorians, Gardiner was impressed with the landscape and people around him, he was under no illusions about the place, and wrote that if anyone was running the risk of hoping that romantic, unspoilt Arabia might be kept in aspic, he only needed to see the queue to see the medical officer. Being technically in the nation's service, British officers dressed as Omani soldiers, to the extent of growing luxuriant beards. Supported by two of the finest products of Britain's aviation industry – the Strikemaster and the Shorts Skyvan, a boxy transport aeroplane which could land on tiny, poorly-paved runways – the combined forces hunted for the *adoo* terrorists in the hot, dry mountains. The practical realities of fighting were learned the hard way, with firefights sometimes taking place when a government patrol stumbled into the *adoo*. Only in movies, Gardiner observed, did people know where to return fire; in real life it was rather more difficult. If they were lucky and could locate the enemy, and if their communications were working, the government troops could summon up supporting fire from mortars or howitzers, or air support from the Strikemasters.

Gardiner's unit always won, but there could be worrying moments. If the enemy had his own indirect fire, mortar shells could plunge into a position, creating a situation in which 'fear, utter confusion and blind desperation are waiting to overwhelm you, and only the best trained soldiers with the coolest NCOs and quickest thinking officers can turn such a situation round.' Brutal though the campaign was, it received little media attention, thanks to Northern Ireland and Vietnam. However, it was successful, dealing a heavy blow to communist ambitions in the region and providing the British military with a useful framework for counter-insurgency techniques. One recent Oxford University analysis of the campaign argued that 'it would be wise for political and military leaders to pay attention to lessons learned in Dhofar'[38] and Ian Gardiner remains proud of the work he and his comrades did in this forgotten war.

Although the number of OFs joining the forces had gone down, Ken Millar discovered that there were pockets of them to be found, perhaps unsurprisingly, in at least one Scottish infantry regiment:

I was posted in 1972 as Regimental Medical Officer to the Royal Scots – a veritable den of OFs! Not only was the Colonel of the Regiment an OF (a fairly fierce Major General Bill Campbell) but several officers were also from that Edinburgh stable. Chris Mitchinson, Peter McIntyre and Martin Gibson were all about in my first year or so; later they were joined by my younger brother, Hamish Millar, and by Kirk Gillies.[39]

Perhaps not so many as the days in 1916 when Ian Hay could see so many of his former pupils in uniform that a French village looked like Princes Street on the day of a rugby international, but certainly a sign that the sixties had not conquered all before them. A slow but steady trickle of Fettesians continued to keep the armed forces supplied in the seventies, and many enjoyed successful careers. One even became the public face of the army; the *Fettesian* reported in 1971 that Donald McGlashan, a young officer in the Greenjackets, had appeared in recruitment films and on posters.[40] There would have been even more Fettesian soldiers had Fergus Brownlee been less unlucky:

I was sent down to Sandhurst as a 15 year old with a friend in Moredun, also from a military family, to spend a few days absorbing army life. It all came to an abrupt end for me when the jeep lights came on and revealed the two of us on top of a red post box slightly the worse for a couple of pints of beer.[41]

Whereas previous generations of Fettesians in the Royal Scots had found themselves either shunted around the world on imperial duties or slogging through Belgium, Ken Millar's experience was of the new structures introduced for a multinational alliance, plus, of course, the obligatory tour of the dreary steeples:

I stayed with the Battalion for three and a half years, and visited Norway, Greece and Denmark with them as part of NATO's fire brigade formation, entitled (long-windedly and officially) as the Allied Command Europe Multinational Force (Land), or AMF(L) for short, but perhaps better designated as either 'Another Military F*** Up' or the 'Multi-coloured Swap Shop'! Then we moved on to Cyprus just in time to catch the Makarios Revival coup followed by *the Turkish invasion, which series of events rather put paid to our expectations of an idle couple of years in the Mediterranean sunshine. Returning to public duties in Edinburgh in 1975 would have seen the end of my tour with the Battalion, but when they were detailed for an operational tour in South Armagh it seemed silly to move on, so I extended until the end of that commitment in May 1976.*

Dr John Ferguson, who had been ordered into the Territorial RAMC in the late sixties, spent much of the seventies leading the Medical Subunit with Tayforth Universities OTC, where he had a good number of keen medical and dental officer cadets, some of whom went on to join the Regulars. In 1977 he became a Lieutenant-Colonel and Commanding Officer of 225 (Highland) Field Ambulance, where he soon identified a flaw in the deployment arrangements should war break out:

My unit had a mobilisation role in Germany. I discovered early on that the mobilisation plan would not work, as by the time we got ourselves to Germany our medical stores which were situated forward at Bielefeld, would have been overrun by the enemy. This prompted a major review which eventually resulted in all our mobilisation equipment and vehicles being moved back to Dundee. Suddenly, the GOC Scotland and Brigadier Highlands started talking about 'their' Field Ambulance as we were now able to deploy anywhere.[42]

A Fistful of Troubles
Northern Ireland was, for most British soldiers of the seventies, an inevitable and high-risk posting. The 'Vive-la' for 1969 had managed to combine the first tremors of the conflict with one of its most ambitious rhymes ever, a reference to a keen Old Fettesian marksman:

> *The rattle of gunshot in Ulster sounds grisly,*
> *But our shots were triumphant both there and at Bisley;*
> *A bullseye was scored at the same place this year which*
> *Reminds us the name was M.J. Haszlakiewicz.*

The shooting by Fettesians in Ulster (where the CCF had gone on camp in 1968) was of course in competition with Northern Ireland's schools; the other kind was rather bloodier and less friendly. The Roman Catholic minority of the province, primarily restive at second-class status rather than driven by ultra-nationalism, had emulated the Sorbonne undergraduates and taken to the streets in protest. Working-class

Protestants, fired by traditional animosities but also infuriated that what they saw as a bunch of trendy students enjoying higher education and government grants should claim to be oppressed, attacked them. They were supported by Ian Paisley's rural constituency, which genuinely believed that there was a popish plot to seize loyal Ulster and force her to join the Republic of Ireland. Sir Knox Cunningham MP, President of the Old Fettesian Association, appears wholeheartedly to have shared this prejudice. A depressingly large number of educated Ulster Protestants, who, like Sir Knox, ought to have known better, refused to see any logic in Catholic protests and reacted with the same inarticulate bigotry as the loyalists who were now rioting on the streets. Cunningham spent his last year in the House of Commons berating the government for not treating the Catholics with sufficient firmness. In 1969, he interrupted Norman St John Stevas to claim that there was no discrimination in Northern Ireland against Catholics, and later tried to refute as 'completely untrue' Gerry Fitt's argument that hard-line Glaswegian 'kick the pope' bands were deliberately provoking the population of Ballymurphy.[43]

Sir Knox deluged the unfortunate Roy Hattersley, Secretary of State for Defence, with increasingly odd questions about why the Union Jack did not appear on military recruitment adverts and whether Catholics in the Ulster Defence Regiment were being investigated for potential disloyalty.[44]

When the furious member for South Antrim urged vigorous arms searches on the Falls Road, Home Secretary James Callaghan wearily reminded him that he must not assume that the arms were only on one side. Sadly, Cunningham either did assume this, or, if he knew that the Protestants were armed troublemakers too, did not care about how blatantly inconsistent he was being. As a result, other MPs could safely ignore him. 'I do not want to indulge in any type of argument with the hon. and learned member for Antrim, South, for whom I do not have a high regard from the point of view of his political intelligence or otherwise,' said Gerry Fitt.[45]

Liberal leader Jeremy Thorpe also refused to debate with Cunningham, who asked if he was afraid to argue. Thorpe replied:

I am very much afraid of what the hon. and learned Gentleman has done and could still do by his voice being heard in Northern Ireland. There is one member to whom I would not give way, and it is the hon. and learned Gentleman. We do not need a poor man's Paisley in this house.[46]

Sir Knox was more of a rich man's Paisley, since unlike the bulk of the big man's followers he was well-off and well-educated, which only made matters worse. Even the headmaster was slightly perturbed by his old boys' leader's interests, nervously telling parents at Founder's Day in 1970 that 'you must realise that he is a member for S. Antrim and has had certain preoccupations with Mr Paisley and Miss [Bernadette] Devlin.'[47]

Rabble-rousing at home, connected with a variety of groups which were considering the use of force, and reduced to being Ian Paisley's mouthpiece at Westminster – it was a tragic conclusion to the career of an intelligent man. In the nineties his reputation would tumble further as his name was linked by imaginative journalists to a bizarre web including traditional favourites MI5 and the freemasons, but also, rather more oddly, the freakish paramilitary William McGrath and Soviet spy Anthony Blunt, whose biographer does not mention the President of the Old Fettesian Association anywhere in her exhaustive book.[48]

Reputable historians dismiss these claims; Sir Knox was, said one of his contemporaries, a man who, as an undergraduate, would 'box heavyweight for the university one day and the next give a lunch-party for some literary lion and walk through the streets of Cambridge in a black velvet suit and a wide sombrero.'[49] He had enjoyed the friendship of writers such as Forrest Reid and E.M. Forster,[50] and had loved, and been honoured by, the boys of his old school. After his retirement, he mischievously gave the school library a signed copy of Ian Harvey's autobiography *To Fall Like Lucifer*. (To its credit, and in a sign of just how much things had changed, the *Fettesian* carried a generally favourable review of this candid but bitchy apologia,[51] and later printed letters from Harvey, who was discreetly entrusted with the Iain Macleod donations, on points of school history – though his book did mysteriously migrate from the library to the archive.) The 'Vive-la' of 1972 mentioned one of Cunningham's achievements with a characteristically contrived rhyme:

And who would have guessed than Knox Cunningham was to
Be Provincial Grand Master Mason of Gloucester.[52]

He got a lengthy set of obituaries in the *Fettesian* when he died in 1976; Mr MacDonald, who had paid tribute to his former pupil Macleod in

1970, did the same for Cunningham – 'a splendid and devoted Fettesian, a public man of the highest standards, and a magnificent friend.'[53]

It has to be assumed that there was no Ulster-related irony intended in a CCF officer's remark that 'several generations of shooters will remember Sir Knox.' He was redeemed, as an OF from the twenties put it, by his sense of humour. This contemporary had last seen Sir Knox en route to an Orange march in Londonderry and accused him of being a murderer. Sir Knox 'grinned from ear to ear and called me a dirty rebel; we both laughed and remained good friends.' He had, the friend wrote, 'the Irishman's lack of logic' and 'never entirely grew up' – traits shared by so many otherwise intelligent politicians and activists in Northern Ireland that a lot of people never got to grow up at all.

By 1971 the *Fettesian* was carrying snippets of information about OFs serving in Ulster. One story carries a flavour of the times; Lt C.G.F. Mitchison, on patrol in the Grosvenor Road area with three soldiers, saw a crowd seizing a bus, forcing the passengers and crew off and clearly intending to take it to the Falls Road, where a company of Royal Scots was under attack by a nationalist mob. To seize buses, block roads with them and set them alight was a popular tactic of the period; over a thousand were destroyed and the practice was immortalised in a loyalist folk-song:

> ...and all around, the petrol-bombs are flying
> While burning buses light up all the town.[54]

Mitchison ran to the bus and evicted its unofficial driver, but by this point twenty rioters had got between him and the three other British soldiers. Although attacked by the mob, he stood his ground until help arrived – which, although it only took five minutes, must have seemed like an eternity to a young man surrounded by an angry crowd. He was subsequently awarded the Queen's Commendation for Gallantry. 'His action marked the turning point of the trouble in the Grosvenor Road,' the citation noted, 'The rioters lost the initiative and order was quickly restored.'[55]

Sadly, had order been restored fully in 1971, subsequent OFs would not have found themselves in Ulster until the twenty-first century, when Operation Banner, the official British military deployment in Ulster, was finally wound up. Neil 'Gurkha' Griffiths reflected on his experiences as a young soldier in 1976:

We all knew it was going to be a long campaign. There was too much despair and poverty for its victims not to be mobilised, especially against a background of warring tribes. Smuggling and extortion were easy, and practically impossible to eradicate, but it was the look in the kids' eyes that told us there would be no peace until at least another generation was born. We were not wrong.[56]

Like Mitchison, he experienced the problems of trying to deal with urban disorder. These often began with loyalist or republican marches, each one 'a territorial statement, a declaration and a threat', full of tension which would often, paradoxically, only be released when some actual fighting got going. At this point snatch squads would be sent in by the army.

Snatch squads of three men, only one armed, no berets, no watches, took up position. It was their job to lift the ringleaders without the telegenic violence which would make the Nine O'Clock News. The two unarmed soldiers did the lift, the third covering, as the target was whisked back to the Pig where he would be photographed with a Polaroid alongside the 'arresting soldier' - not normally the actual one, generally the platoon waster who wouldn't be missed if he had to spend a day in the Diplock Court.

It is axiomatic that when a crowd is subject to such squads, it must have somewhere to run. Charging a trapped mob leads to mayhem, and CS gas rarely hits the real rioters. All one is left with is passers-by - generally old folk whose tears make great TV. Practice made these procedures very smooth but there was no denying how wound up soldiers were on their first operation. Then there was the electrifying realisation that the crowd was terrified of you, and a hunter instinct took over as they fled.

Ian Gardiner learned to study details, especially the faces of the women in embattled communities, because they tended to take the strain while their menfolk were out creating havoc.[57] This would have been understood by his predecessors in the Burmese jungle, South Africa and North-West Germany. Other aspects of soldiering in Northern Ireland would have been familiar to soldiers in two world wars – 'the mind-numbing fatigue engendered by 20-hour shifts, the tetchiness and smells of close-quarter living and the discomfort of patrolling in the cold, dark and wet' – for outside the cities the army was tasked with patrolling the countryside in search of the paramilitaries' own patrols. These were known to visit local farmers in the dead of night looking for assistance, which might be granted voluntarily if they were the 'right' religion; alternatively, coercion might be applied. Either way, the security forces needed to know about it. The experience of the soldiers was frequently surreal, incorporating modern technology with touches of low comedy which might have come from the Great War, as Griffiths notes:

No-one wore army boots in the country; the prints would have been a giveaway, and we were choppered in, normally at night, to within a few miles of target. Naval helicopter pilots were preferred as they tended to fly without headlights - a substantial tactical advantage - but surprises could appear anywhere. No-one moved through a hole in a hedge without checking for booby-traps, and the Armagh thorns ensured we were yet more cautious. Nobody in their right mind touched a deserted vehicle, though there was a famous occasion when a car full of piglets was irresistible. The subsequent craze for pig-on-a-string mascots lasted only as long as it took young soldiers to realise the impracticality of keeping pigs in a Portakabin.

This Army Air Corps Sioux helicopter landing in the school quad in 1974 was a more frequent sight on observation duties over South Armagh and West Belfast

Almost as good as catching terrorists in the act was finding their weapons caches. On one occasion, Griffiths' unit found what looked like a keg of Guinness standing in a deserted country lane. Although fairly sure that it was harmless, kegs and milk-churns were often used as the casings for bombs; in any case, it was the bomb disposal officer's last day in Northern Ireland and he was going to have a little fun:

Having wrapped a length of Cordex (like white washing line but filled with explosive; it can cut a car in two) around the keg, we stood well back. Boom! The top was blown to kingdom come and a column of Guinness rose into the sky like a cartoon oil strike. We laughed until it hurt.

Not all Willie Ross's experiences were so funny, as he told the *Fettesian* years later. Violence could come from any quarter:

We were out and doing a patrol and we walked past this pub and a guy started shouting at us and suddenly the motorbike he was standing next to blew up and blew him to smithereens. Only the torso was left. What had happened was the boy had set a booby-trap that was meant to go off as we passed it but it went off when he passed it.

...The average Scottish soldier is highly trained but the difficulty with them is in peacetime when they're stuck in barracks. Nothing but drinking and fighting; most of it's blamed on boredom. Mind you, in my younger days I was involved in that as well. I've had 28 days in jail for street fighting with the locals and guys from other regiments. This man was using my face as target practice for bricks and so I knocked him out and threw him over a bridge.[58]

The pupils of Fettes had known little of the seething mutual dislike which lay behind the Ulster conflict and which had been building up for decades before the final eruption in the late sixties. Straw polls of Old Fettesians attending the school between 1960 and 1972 reveal almost total ignorance, frankly admitted to. This was, of course, more or less universal throughout British society. In the seventies, however, Northern Ireland was to crop up with some frequency in the poetry section of the *Fettesian*, and was probably the single most common theme of 'issue' verse. Five months after Bloody Sunday, for instance, 'A.M.G.' submitted *Ireland – A Ballad*:

The bells are tolling
The wheels are rolling
They are taking our dead away.
In this land so green,
There is strife unseen
And blood red is the light of day.[59]

A short story, *The Proposal*, appeared in 1976, touchingly describing a childhood romance rekindled during the Troubles but ending in an IRA assassination, and Angus Morrison remembers 'a General arriving at the school in some chauffer driven style to deliver a talk and warning us of the strong possibility that the Troubles in Northern Ireland might easily spread to Glasgow.' Although, as he confirms, 'Northern Ireland was the main issue of the day and you were very much aware of it', as early as the spring of 1972, there was an awareness of the average Briton's 'compassion fatigue' with regard to Ulster and other crises:

> Don't call me from my dreams
> And make me see
> The rule of hatred
> Across the Irish Sea.
> Don't tell me of the bodies
> Lying dying in the street,
> Of parents crying,
> Their children lying bleeding at their feet.
> Don't wake me! Tomorrow is Sunday
> And there's beef steak for a treat.
>
> Don't show me pictures
> Of the living dead
> That gather, swarming
> Waiting to be fed
> And helpless, fall
> With clutching bones
> And emaciated flesh
> As they struggle through the filth
> To die in Bangla Desh.[60]

Fettes, Scotland, Britain and the World

Although, thanks in part to the contemporary atmosphere of détente, the conflict for which Ferguson and others were prepared was probably less likely in the seventies than at any other point in the Cold War, they were regarded, both at the time and in successive decades, as years of failure. With industrial unrest, a stagnant economy and increasing urban radicalism, it was an era when Harold Wilson and Ted Heath were the nearest the country got to statesmen, and the supposed national consciences, Tony Benn and Enoch Powell, seem in retrospect to have been faintly eccentric. Some Old Fettesians were on the front line of the various rescue attempts launched to keep British industry afloat. Sandy Glen, for instance, was involved in the Export Council of the sixties (which he regarded as fairly successful), the attempt to save Upper Clyde Shipbuilders in 1971-2, the new British Tourist Authority (where, as chairman, he discovered that many English people were opposed to visitors coming to their counties) and with BEA (despite a fear of flying). Whilst negotiating at UCS, Glen was up against Jimmy Reid, then a communist and a true heir to the Red Clydesiders of the twenties. Reid told Glen to tell his political masters that he was not going to 'destroy this river' or 'execute Upper Clyde'. The normally mild-mannered Glen replied:

Don't forget I spent part of my life with a good Communist – Marshal Tito – and not a Stalinist either. We were not trying to destroy a country then; we werte trying to save one. And we're trying to save this river, not destroy it, either.[61]

Glen genuinely respected most of the trade unionists and businessmen with whom he worked in the post-war years, and he felt that there was hope for the future, but this was not universal. Although most people at Fettes had a decent enough time – the liberalisation of Chenevix-Trench having gone some way to remove more irksome restrictions – they undoubtedly shared some of the national sense of doom. In case the debaters and current affairs enthusiasts were not getting the message across, some of the guest speakers at Founder's Day used the opportunity offered by a joyous summer get-together to hammer home the message of national doom. In 1972, Chief Constable A.U.R. Scroggie spoke of 'a growing disregard for law and order'. 'Almost any kind of public demonstration or public dispute is liable to degenerate into disorder,' he warned, 'Some people seem to want to overthrow our present institutions in this country by violence, with no very clear idea of what they want to put in their place.'[62] The 'Vive-la' for that year indicates that the school knew perfectly well what he meant:

When the strike and the power cuts darkened the college
By bell, book and candle we still pursued knowledge.
If you hear we're abandoning afternoon school,
You'll know we're not slacking – just working to rule.

In 1974, the annual obsession with the weather which had gripped the planners of Founder's Day since Victorian times took second place to concerns about the fuel crisis; would there be enough petrol around for anyone to turn up? As it was, they did – though many confessed to having boots full of oildrums or jerrycans, 'like any East African Safari Rally'.[63]

In 1976, Richard Humble, the OF who had swooped over the playing fields between the wars to drop a note to his old housemaster, compared the 'strong, worthy and respected' Britain of his youth with the 'sorry business' of the contemporary nation – 'strike-ridden and up to the ears in debt.'[64]

'It is intolerable that it should continue,' he told the pupils, urging them to 'put this old country of ours back on its feet.' To be fair, his speech was best remembered at the time for the jokes. Other aspects of the collective seventies folk-memory crop up in the *Fettesian* and the observations of Old Fettesians. Abroad, Bruce Williamson, working on a kibbutz (another activity unimaginable to earlier alumni) found that his new home had bomb shelters should the Golan Heights become restive. J.F. Simonett, on VSO in Africa, was helped from the river-bed in Mozambique into which his lorry had crashed by Portuguese soldiers in an armoured car; they were fighting one of the last, lonely colonial wars in Africa.[65]

At home, Allan Jardine, the proud piper, remembers the impracticality of the band's impressive uniforms in the scorching summer and subsequent rains of 1976:

Believe me when I tell you, feeling the sweat dribbling down the inside of your thigh as you stride through 'The Barren Rocks Of Aden' wearing a kilt that feels like it is made out of an old duffel coat, and a tunic that was so heavy that it gradually bent its wire coat hanger, is not a pleasant experience.

It is even worse in the rain. The whole get up doubles in weight so that your knees ache, and everyone smells like a damp dog. I mean the plaid alone, flying out behind you like a long tartan hearthrug, absorbs water by the quart. But that's the Great Highland Bagpipe for you.

Despite the impracticalities of its dress, Scottish nationalism surged on the back of the discovery of North Sea oil, with eleven MPs elected as 'Scotland's political football team' in 1974. It took a battering when

Scotland's association football team was defeated in Argentina four years later. Fettes was now recruiting from a much wider net than the home nations and colonial expatriates, with Asian pupils increasingly common. It was perhaps not surprising that the *Fettesian* should carry a piece by a Canadian sixth-former arguing that nationalism be replaced by 'terrestrialism' and world citizenship.[66]

The Labour government attempted to buy off nationalist voters, and gain the support of the SNP at Westminster, with a Home Rule referendum, but this excited fewer passions at Fettes than it might have done. 'Some of the staff did their best to promote an interest in politics, notably Ronnie Guild,' remembers Angus Morrison, 'although I don't remember the Scottish Referendum stirring up as much interest as his efforts deserved.' The 'Vive-la' did, nonetheless, mention the issue in 1977:

> *Now everyone ends on the note 'Devolution'.*
> *It's a matter that doesn't require a solution.*
> *For the fact that the experts appear to forget is*
> *That Scotland will flourish – while Scotland has Fettes.*[67]

George Campbell Hay, who enjoyed a revival in the seventies, was unimpressed with the fact that the proposed body would lack the power even of a Swiss canton.[68] Most OFs, however, disapproved on unionist grounds.

Europe

Fettesians were encouraged throughout the seventies to look towards the Common Market rather than the defunct Empire for their careers and to fulfil the school's legendary demand for duty. In 1971, Sir Michael Fraser expounded on how ancient Britain had been settled by invaders from all over Europe, and had in return sent out missionaries in the Dark Ages, becoming subsequently France's 'Siamese twin.' 'Whatever the other arguments in which we indulge about whether it is a good or a bad thing to take our own part in the formation of a modern united Western Europe,' he urged any Powellites present, 'at least don't let us kid ourselves that we have at any point been an island entire unto ourselves and cut off from the mayne.'[69]

Lord Mackenzie Stewart, who as a boy watched the Junkers 88 fly over the playing fields and whose daughter was the first girl at Fettes, spoke in 1977 in his capacity as a judge of the European Court of Justice. He explained how important it was that Europe should be built on the rule of law, extolled the virtues of Luxembourg, and reminded the boys that for all that could be said for Scottish nationalism, Scottish internationalism was more important. Rather than hankering for the days of Empire when 'Scots were found in every boardroom from Gibraltar to Calcutta', they should bear in mind the role of Scots in France, Holland (where there was still a Presbyterian Kirk) and Prussia. There had only been ten Old Fettesians at a recent reunion in Brussels – he hoped to see numbers doubled soon, and exhorted the audience to learn languages.[70]

The Soviet Union remained, despite Nixon's détente, a threat. Chris Sutton remembers 'an attempt to get us concerned' in the late seventies, when 'some colonel from HQ Scotland' would give a presentation on the military situation. This featured 'a map of Europe with zillions of Russian tanks and rockets on the right hand side, and much less in the way of fighting power over in the West.'[71] Those Fettesians with the desire to see this sinister threat up close could go on a school trip to the USSR in 1974, which they undoubtedly enjoyed.[72]

The boys were very impressed with the Moscow metro, the Bolshoi performance in the Kremlin ('almost on a scale as lavish as the Tsars would have done it') and the cheap, speedy public transport, if not the gangs of 'bovver-boys' infesting it, attempting to swap badges of Lenin for chewing gum. They were also struck by the honesty of people who could, in theory, have reeled off free tickets from the dispensing machine on the trolley-bus, but invariably paid – 'it's for the good of the state!' It was a sign of the times that the student who reported the trip for the *Fettesian* wrote that 'alcohol is not cheap and drunkenness is discouraged even more by the threat of a cold shower and a shaved scalp' – not a warning which previous generations would have felt the need to mention. The visit also confirmed a few prejudices, and may have persuaded the boys that seventies Britain was not quite as bad as the alternative (which, by this stage in the nation's history, Arthur Scargill was already keen to offer). The stewardesses on the Aeroflot plane looked like 'rejects from the weightlifting event at the Olympics', clearing customs took an age and resulted in the confiscation of a subversive Snoopy book, offence was taken about being called English, and they got into a lengthy argument with some Soviet schoolchildren on the subject of religion.

The Fettes boys were struck by the omnipresence of images of Lenin, and offended by the controls over churches, and felt that the Russians seemed to worship Vladimir Illyich as a kind of god. They even made a point of going to one of the few churches legally functioning, and sat through an unintelligible two-hour Baptist service. It was an interesting, and impressive, indication of what some British teenagers felt the need to stand up for in the seventies. Some OFs, like Sandy Glen, likewise refused to be cowed into the prevailing gloom of the seventies:

Qualities in which we used to excel – compromise, conciliation, fairness – seem less evident. Have bloody-mindedness and the bully boy taken their place? I don't think so, for I am far from concluding that we are as yet inevitably headed for disaster. Quite simply I believe too strongly in the inward strength and adaptability of parliamentary democracy, particularly in Britain and northern Europe.[73]

He was, in many ways, to be proved right, and the doom-mongers of popular fiction (and indeed in the security services) who predicted a dictatorship by 1980 were wrong. For all that, it would be unwise to conclude from the efforts of the masters, the guests, the memoirs of OFs and the writings of the more worthy sixth-formers that Fettesians in the seventies were particularly aware of the world outside their own immediate 'childish things.' Walter Sellar, the Fettes master who wrote the classic of schoolboy howlers *1066 and all that*, would have recognised the results of a general knowledge exam set by Chenevix-Trench for the middle school in 1975. The *Fettesian* believed that some of the replies 'heavily underline the fact that the reading of the present generation is far different from that of their forebears' (though this is not borne out by the testimonies of pupils from previous decades who freely admitted to woeful ignorance of current affairs). Many of the answers were vintage Sellar, and reflect the comforting fact that plenty of people, especially the young, did not spend the seventies torturing themselves over oil wars, nationalism, terrorism or politics:

'Vichysoisse' might well be the wife of General Petain, even in a question on cookery, and 'a la carte' could mean food served on a trolley; but that 'bombe' should be Miss Devlin is carrying political realism too far. Would Mrs Thatcher be flattered to be thought the Old Lady of Threadneedle Street? If a frieze is an arctic landscape, and El Greco an urban gorilla (sic), Charles 1ˢᵗ on horseback could of course have been painted by Van Gout.[74]

NOTES

[1] *Fettesian*, Spring 1970

[2] Ibid.

[3] Ibid., Summer 1970

[4] Quoted in ibid.

[5] Quoted in ibid.

[6] Quoted in ibid.

[7] Ibid.

[8] Email to the author, 24 September 2009

[9] *Fettesian*, Autumn 1970

[10] Ibid.

[11] Ibid., Spring 1971

[12] Anonymous OF, in conversation with the author, 3 October 2009

[13] *Fettesian*, Spring 1972

[14] Ibid., September 1976

[15] Ibid., Summer 1977

[16] Allan Jardine, Unpublished MS, 2009

[17] Email to the author, 22 September 2009

[18] Email to the author, 26 September 2009

[19] Email to the author, 26 September 2009

[20] Email to the author, 27 September 2009

[21] *Fettesian*, Summer 1973

[22] Ibid., Spring 1972

[23] Email to the author, 15 September 2009

[24] Email to the author, 15 September 2009

[25] Ibid., Autumn 1978

[26] Email to the author, 16 September 2009

[27] *Fettesian*, Spring 1971

[28] Email to the author, 29 September 2009

[29] J. Lawrence & R. Lawrence, *When the fighting is over: Tumbledown* (London, 22 Books, 1987), pp. 3–5

[30] Ibid., p. 9

[31] Ibid., p. 10

[32] *Fettesian*, April 1878

[33] Lawrence & Lawrence, p. 11

[34] Ian Gardiner, *In the Service of the Sultan* (Barnsley, Pen & Sword, 2006) p. 1

[35] Ibid., p. 14

[36] Ibid., p. 41

[37] Ibid., p. 89

[38] Walter C. Ladwig III, 'Supporting Allies in Counter-insurgency – Britain and the Dhofar Rebellion', *Small Wars and Insurgencies*, March 2008   (http://users.ox.ac.uk/~mert 1769/Supporting%20Allies%20in%20COIN_wcl2.pdf, accessed 2 May 2011)

[39] Email to the author, 21 May 2009

[40] *Fettesian*, Spring 1971

[41] Email to the author, 2009

[42] Ferguson

[43] *Hansard*, Vol. 799, April 6-17 1970, p. 272

[44] Ibid., Vol. 801, May 4-29 1970, pp. 27 & 119

[45] Ibid., Vol. 799, April 6-17 1970, p. 276

[46] Ibid., p. 285

[47] *Fettesian*, Summer 1970

[48] See Miranda Carter, *Anthony Blunt: His Lives* (London, Pan, 2001)

[49] *Fettesian*, September 1977

[50] See Graham Walker, 'Belfast, Boys and Books: The Friendship Between Forrest Reid and Knox Cunningham', *Irish Review*, Issue 35, 2007. I am extremely grateful to Professor Walker for his thoughts on Sir Knox, which extended to a consultation in the Bow Bar.

[51] *Fettesian*, Summer 1971

[52] Ibid., Summer 1972

[53] Ibid., September 1977

[54] Author's dark and disturbing cultural memory

[55] *Fettesian*, Spring 1971

[56] Neil Griffiths, 'My Memories of a "Job Well Done"', *The Herald*, Glasgow, 28 July 2007

[57] Gardiner (2006) p. 40

[58] *Fettesian*, 1999

[59] Ibid., Summer 1972, Literary Insert

[60] Ibid., Spring 1972

[61] Glen, (1975) p. 234

[62] Ibid., Summer 1972

[63] Ibid., Summer 1974

[64] Ibid., September 1976

[65] Ibid., Summer 1971

[66] Ibid., Summer 1972

[67] Ibid., September 1977

[68] Byrne, p. 353

[69] Ibid., Summer 1971

[70] Ibid., September 1977

[71] Email to the author, 15 September 2009

[72] Ibid., Summer 1974

[73] Glen (1975) p. 258

[74] *Fettesian*, September 1975

Chapter Twenty

'I am very proud to be associated with such as they'

The Falklands Era

Fettes enters the Eighties

If military tradition had been corroded by the sixties and seventies' mentality of letting it all hang out, the eighties' obsession with pulling it all back in again and keeping it for yourself might appear to be little better. Despite many changes to the school and its surrounding society, however, the military traditions of the school continued; the CCF remained at the heart of extra-curricular activity, and pupils still joined the armed forces. If anything, numbers entering the services actually increased in the eighties in comparison with a decade earlier; of 103 pupils who left Fettes in the summer of 1980, ten intended to join up (mostly in the Army), and of 110 leavers in 1985, four were destined for Sandhurst and one each for the Royal Navy, Royal Marines and RAF, plus another for the police.[1]

Given that the leavers now included girls, who were not then encouraged to join the forces, this represents a very respectable percentage, greater than society as a whole. When Joe Hills stood down as CO of the school CCF in 1983, the *Fettesian* took the opportunity to remind its readers that 'during the past year, The Gordon Highlanders have owed their Commanding Officer, their Second-in-Command, and their Adjutant, to Fettes, while the Royal Scots have no fewer than nine Fettesians in the Officers' Mess, including the Commanding Officer.'[2]

These strong connections, and other developments in the 1980s, meant that the school and its former pupils would be more aware of the strategic changes in the world, and would be deeply affected by them. The domestic politics of that rambunctious decade were also reflected in the school. Increased patriotism of a pan-British nature, with an emphasis on the 'good war' of 1939-45 (a naval section report on a sailing trip in 1988 noted that the boys stocked up with *Commando* comic books, featuring wartime adventures)[3] and enthusiasm for the revival of a buccaneering type of capitalist individualism, appear in the school magazine and the memories of Old Fettesians, and would have made Mrs Thatcher proud.

Fettes had entered the Thatcher era with the tragic loss of Tony Chenevix-Trench, dead at the age of sixty only a few weeks after his last Founder's Day. He was replaced by Cameron Cochrane, another affable liberal who abolished the cane and made the school fully co-educational. The school's reputation was not what it was, and the Edinburgh dinner-party circuit buzzed with unhelpful and often inaccurate gossip put about by mothers with too much time on their hands and tigresses' levels of protectiveness towards their offspring, regardless of the latter's objective merit. Fettes' site twenty minutes' walk from the centre of Edinburgh was no longer seen as a virtue but as dangerous exposure to the drug fiends who supposedly haunted the city; boarding numbers halved in Cochrane's time. Mothers also exercised much more influence over choices of school and were demanding both more luxury in the accommodation offered and a greater say in day-to-day schooling. Cochrane's Fettes attempted to improve its image by tightening up on discipline, through the efforts of Australian Vietnam veteran Neville Clark, and selling land for development in order to fund refurbish the dormitories in a less Dickensian fashion, much to the bemusement of OF fathers who had found iron bedsteads and wooden floors perfectly adequate. A drive was also launched to reinvigorate the school's intellectual life, with a twin-track of A-levels and Scottish Highers in the sixth form to boost results by ensuring that the mixed-ability intake could study for examinations they were likely to pass.[4]

Cochrane himself was a man of wide extra-curricular interests, running (whilst still in charge of Fettes) the Commonwealth Village when Edinburgh hosted the Games.

The Regiment Conquers

The advent of full co-education was probably the biggest change to school life since the doors first opened, but it was both a rolling process and, as the recruitment statistics show, not a violent change to Fettes' relationship with the military. The presence of girls in the sixth form was still sufficiently odd in 1980 for them to merit a separate 'Fettesienne' report in the school magazine; it was noted that the Girls' Room had been redecorated with spice walls, cream woollen curtains, cushions, plants and posters.[5]

Readers who found this painfully stereotypical would have been relieved to see that girls, now subjected to compulsory sport, were throwing themselves into the acquisition of new skills, and forming teams which first took on Fettes staff and then played other girls' schools such as St George's. Trina Purves became the first Captain of Girls' Sport, and six others, including the actress Tilda Swinton, won Oxbridge places. The successes of the sixth-form girls did not mean that the feminine touch was universally welcomed when it subsequently came to the middle school. Jane McNeil put her experiences into verse in 1982:

> *All the boys looked horrified,*
> *When girls walked through the door,*
> *I could have cried – I nearly died,*
> *I couldn't stand much more.*

> *Why do they never speak to us?*
> *Have we done something wrong?*
> *Oh why on earth make such a fuss*
> *When girls join the Third Form?*[6]

Although separate reports on girls disappeared, when in 1983 Arniston put on an all-female house play, the political farce *Viva! Women's Lib* by Stuart Ready, the *Fettesian* reviewer could still announce that 'the inconceivable has happened, an all-women dramatic production at Fettes'.[7]

Arniston, Tony Blair's old house, had been the logical choice to be the first girls' boarding house in the early eighties. It was the newest building and, dating from the sixties, had no long and distinguished array of war heroes and eccentric masters, nor dynasties of old boys, associated with it; Arniston was also some distance from the other houses. The female takeover of Schoolhouse – the dormitories on the upper floors of the main building – was less enthusiastically received when it took place in 1984. Although the house's intellectual status as the residence of foundationers (scholarship boys) had disappeared decades earlier, it was still the historic centre of the school and home to boys who were very fond of it. They were deeply disgruntled at having to move out, especially since the school was taking the opportunity for some much-needed refurbishment. Dr Peter Coshan, the housemaster, guided the boys through the painful process, and the 1984 *Fettesian* put a brave face on it with a spot of (relatively) light-hearted joshing from one of the evicted men:

How will the girls cope with carrying hefty trunks up three floors of stairs? How will they dispose of the buckets of rubbish that accumulate every day? And to what extent − if at all − will the traditions of the oldest house in the school be maintained for posterity?...

It leaves us with regrets at seeing our old house ripped apart, and with some pique at the prospect of its being refurbished with every possible labour-saving device and luxury gadget... none of which will be available to the boys. So much for women's equality! [8]

A female riposte, printed on the same page, might have come from the then Prime Minister herself. Although its author was doubtless an excellent young woman, it had Mrs Thatcher's authentic notes of self-assured commitment to the iron wheel of progress, coupled with a certain indifference to those uprooted by the forces of change:

The boys seem to find the transformation and renovation of School House particularly distressing. They think it unfair that girls will have excellent surroundings and comfort there while they have to brave it out in their Spartan houses...

Some of the boys really are worried. They feel that their traditional superiority is being undermined by the increasing number of girls. They want to keep Fettes sitting in the Middle Ages, with no girls at all. School House was the first house of Fettes College when it opened and the fact that it is being taken over by girls symbolises to them the end of the ascendancy of boys at Fettes.

But introducing girls into the house shows that the school's policy is forward-looking and modern. It is catering to the demand for co-educational boarding schools. [9]

An unsurprising result of the full integration of girls was the explosion in hormones of both sexes. In the seventies, girls had been a relative rarity, confined to the sixth form and frequently the object of active dislike (for their exemption from many school requirements, including uniform) rather than lust. Now they were everywhere, and, once they had been forgiven for seizing lebensraum from Arniston and Schoolhouse (soon divided once more into Colleges East and West), their attentions were eagerly sought. Amanda Mair, later a teacher in the Fettes prep school but then an observant teenager, wrote an 'analysis of a Fettesian dude' in 1988, noting that coolness required being both sporty (affecting a limp to suggest stout service on the rugger pitch was a popular ploy) and stupid, with a string of missed preps and Saturday night detentions.[10] She does not seem to have been impressed with this, but enough girls were for new regulations to be introduced, as the 'Vive-la' noted in 1989:

> *Some popular practices needed correction.*
> *Alas! No more public displays of affection.*
> *No matter how loving and am'rous you feel,*
> *We don't allow kissing, however genteel.*[11]

Female integration extended to the CCF; whereas seventies Fettesiennes could easily evade military service by virtue of their age, younger girls were, from 1983, expected to 'get fell in' like other members of the fourth and fifth form. 'They have settled in extremely well and generally appear to be enjoying it,' reported CO Lt-Col Joe Hills.[12]

Summer camp at Warcop that year saw a dozen girls in the 52-strong Fettes contingent (the first co-educational one, and, perhaps not coincidentally, one of the largest for some years) and the first female officer, 2/Lt. Fiona Cochrane. Senior Under Officer P.R.B. Sutton, who reported on the camp for the *Fettesian*, was impressed by the girls' efforts, noting that on a day of demanding tests the largely female Section Two impressed a visiting brigadier with weapon handling and went on to beat not only the Fettes boys but sections from other schools and win the camp competition.[13]

By the following year, Sylvia Terris could write an upbeat account of adventurous training at Blair Atholl, which illustrated just how robust Fettes' new pupils could be.[14] There were certain difficulties – the boys trapped the girls into doing the washing-up, and, whilst abseiling, Sylvia 'despite all warnings, caught her hair in her figure-of-eight knot and dangled by it for a while from a cliff.' The victim had just had a haircut, 'and now had another, less stylish, one with a penknife.' The girls, like the boys, had to do their own 'self-reliance' expedition along Loch Ericht:

The expedition was certainly hard work. Our boots began to irritate and so did our wet, dirty clothes. But the tent didn't fall down! We developed a taste for hot Alpen in skimmed milk, and a great dislike for Star Bars. On returning to base camp, having hiked well over fourteen kilometres with heavy rucksacks, we felt we had achieved a great deal – especially since we were pioneers on the course. We deserved our good sleep that night… it was tough, but well worth the blisters and red noses.

Sylvia hoped that she and her team had set a standard for other girls to follow and encouraged more to follow in their footsteps – 'come on, girls, let's see more of you at the next camp, and let's show the boys that we are not only made for washing dishes!' The girls' feminine side was expressed elsewhere; Alexandra Layman, a keen shot, adopted a more nurturing approach to the shooting team than the RSM was used to, but got results. Indeed, girls often made better shots than boys. The 'Fettesienne' report for 1980, when girls were still 'rare birds' and had only just been required to do any sort of competitive sport, noted that Jenny Thomson, the best shot in the school VIII at Bisley, had been joined by Caroline Fortune and Trina Purves, 'neither of whom had held a gun before they came to Fettes.'[15]

Trina Noyes, as she now is, recalls that one of the most intimidating aspects of Bisley was having to salute officers, which she did not know how to do. Every time she saw one coming, she hid behind a tree. The experience cannot have been overly traumatic, since she still shoots today.[16] Enough female shots were found that year to defeat the all-male 2nd VIII, though as late as 1984 female air cadets were still going on separate camps, girls to RAF Locking and boys to RAF Abingdon.[17]

By 1985, however, the air cadets reported that in their night exercise at RAF Waddington 'certain girls proved to be very vicious'[18] and by 1987, the Royal Navy section was unselfconsciously referring to its cadets graduating as 'helmspersons' and the report for the Sub-Aqua section came, without fanfare, from a girl.[19]

The Corps in the last decade of Cold War
The life of the CCF in the eighties continued most of the patterns established in the sixties; 1981 saw considerable co-operation with local units such as 52 (Lowland) Territorials and the Edinburgh OTC, whose artillery section allowed exciting shoots at Otterburn with heavy weapons. Fifteen cadets visited the Royal Scots Dragoon Guards, a 'sabre' regiment on the Cold War's front line in Germany, where they were on 24-hour standby in Chieftain tanks. The 'excellent and interesting week' included learning about tank warfare, visiting the fortified East German

'Fettesiennes' to the fore in this CCF inspection in 1985

defences, and a trip to Belsen, where the absence of wildlife was attributed to 'excess acid used to disinfect the ground after its liberation' rather than any moral feelings among the local fauna.[20]

Summer camp was still a highlight, although the allegation in the *Fettesian* in 1981 that a captured adder was added to the soup at Lochgilphead suggests a level of excitement too far. As usual, the best part was the military exercise in which a terrorist organisation, led by Fergus Mhor and his 'Cuban adviser' John Broughton, was set on destroying the Crinan Canal and had to be 'annihilated' by Fettes' finest. Although flushed out of one of Dalriada's many impressive ruins, the terrorists counter-attacked through rain and darkness at two in the morning, blowing Cadet Edgar's tent sky-high with a thunderflash. That year's adventurous training, led by Mr Foot and Mr Reeves, involved abseiling, falling boulders and night navigation, with 'torch-flashes, shouts and ominous silences echoing through the woods.' (Mr Reeves, incidentally, was one of a number of masters who had no desire to wear khaki – he was somewhat disconcerted on arriving at Fettes to be vigorously saluted by cadets who had been ordered to practice military greetings on any adult that moved – but could happily take part in the essentially civilian outdoor pursuits which were added to the CCF's list of activities in the *Fettesian*.) More high-tech thrills were experienced in 1985 with Vietnam-style flights in a Lynx helicopter 'low over the paddy fields of Cumbria' with the doors open 'for realism'[21], though most of the time cadets were ferried around in three-ton lorries in which 'the disadvantage is that the exhaust fumes are blown into the back of the truck; the advantage is that one does not have to stop the truck in order to be sick.'[22]

These cadets at Lochgilphead in 1984 have finally exchanged the ancient and uncomfortable wartime battledress for modern camouflage, but are still equipped with the Lee-Enfield rifle of their forefathers

The naval cadets, whose 'cruise' in a rented sailing-boat up the west coast of Scotland became an annual event, could laugh off their own hardships ('force 9 gales, rain, mist and flat calms' which reinforced one officer's 'Presbyterian misgivings about sailing on the Sabbath') with the thought of the army cadets 'crawling about on boggy, midge infested hillsides.'[23] The 'magical beauty of a West Highland anchorage appreciated the more after a day's sailing and a full stomach', not to mention the genuine excitement and camaraderie of the crew, more than made up for a few soakings and difficult knots.

As before, there were high points for individual cadets, such as Pipe Major Alasdair Macleod piping senior NATO officers aboard HMS *Edinburgh* in Kiel in 1989, and sad losses, especially those of the piping and drumming instructors Ronald Ackroyd and Jock Ferguson, and RSM MacAlpine, whose death came as a shock to those who believed him to be indestructible. He was replaced by Willie Ross, a robust veteran of Northern Ireland who would see the Fettes CCF through to both its own centenary in 2008 and the 150th anniversary of the cadet movement in 2010.

Fettesians sailing off the west coast

The report which Andrew Murray, the contingent commander, produced on the CCF's 1986-7 season describes an organisation devoted to exciting activities, many of them subsidised by the Ministry of Defence. At Easter 1987, some cadets went on a cross-country ski expedition to Norway, across the Hardinger Vidda and the top of the Jokulen Glacier – 'this was such a success that we are encouraged to do it again.'[24]

In May, there was an inspection by Lt-Gen Sir Norman Arthur, who watched the naval section sailing at Granton and visited the army cadets by helicopter at Castle Law, and the pipe band beating retreat at the Castle Esplanade at which Ronald Selby Wright took the salute wearing his Moderator's tricorn hat. In the summer, the Army went to Warcop, the RAF to Stafford, and the Navy to the West Coast, where they covered over 230 nautical miles; the Sub-Aqua Section dived off Staffa, a small group under Lt Den Mather tackled demanding mountain passes in India, the shooting team scored highly at Bisley, winning the Brock Shield and Astor Cup, some sailors won the cadet section of the Royal Navy Scottish Bosun sailing championships, and individual officers and cadets took part in a host of other activities. There were plenty of good times in this impressive list of formal achievements; Sgt Alex Potter reflected fondly for the *Fettesian* on the march and shoot exercise at camp, and the NAAFI jukebox, and an 'enjoyable and enlightening week' of adventurous training. The relative informality of the era comes across in light-hearted reference to officers – Mr Murray's inability to erect beds and Mr Reeves' dreams of thick mists on the mountains – which would have been rare a few decades earlier. The Norwegian expeditions, codenamed in true CCF fashion 'Operation Glacier Blue', could lead to poetic reflections, such as Chris Eccles' in 1982– 'suddenly from the snow ahead emerged the sun, the colour of blood, heavy with the emptiness of northern wastes, fuller than wine, more precious than gold'[25] – or rather more prosaic ones, as inscribed by the 1989 group on a rock: 'we camped here, bloody cold.'[26]

Progress in the snow was made difficult by 45lb of CCF tinned compo rations in rucksacks (the weight of these ensured that crashing into snowbanks 'leaves a Desperate Dan outline a la *Beano*.'). Other adventures included, on 29 August 1986, a relay swim across the English Channel by four boys and two girls (Malcolm Sutherland, Victoria Wright, Alastair Thaw, Andrew Barnard, Sian Oxenham and Roy Leckie), who dodged tankers, fishing-boats and ferries and impressed their official observer – 'these Scots do maintain the stiff upper lip and certainly do rise to the occasion.'[27]

At another extreme, an expedition to Zanskar, the hidden mountain kingdom of India, required hardiness not just for the rugged trekking but also for local bureaucracy, military checkpoints, rivers so swollen by melting snow that pupils were kept awake by the 'bass thudding' of boulders clunking, high-altitude breathing that led tent-mates to wonder if their friends had died, crashes in jeeps and the local diet:

Elsa was a bit worried about hygiene to start with and when her boiled egg oozed green slime she didn't look convinced as we assured her she was unlucky. Unfortunately her second egg exploded with a loud band and she didn't eat anything for two days (except of course the two sorts of malaria pills, the Diamox, the Immodium and the multi-vitamins).[28]

The trip organiser, Lt Denholm Mather, noted with pride that the trip had cost £750 per head, a large sum at the time but less than half what it would have cost had he gone through official channels and booked something through the newly-fashionable adventure tourism companies; whether the cadets appreciated flying circuitous routes with Iraqi Airlines and spending eight hours in Baghdad airport during the Gulf War was another matter. The cadet who was impaled on an ice-axe in Ecuador probably felt that the toughening-up process and spirit of adventure had gone too far, though in fairness he appears to have fallen on it in a hotel.

For all these exotic adventures, much of Fettes Corps life was as it had always been, as Willy Inglis (later an officer in the Scots Guards) recalls:

I loathed it to start with: we had an incompetent, power crazy sergeant who had no concept of how to organise anything and used to make Wednesday afternoon's hell. He actually wasn't that bad once one got to know him, but power used to go to his head when he stood in front of our platoon. Wednesdays were spent doing endless drill and poorly planned lessons on the Mark IV Lee Enfield. After going to Corps Camp at Bellerby, near Catterick, I started to enjoy the CCF a bit more and decided to do the NCO cadre – we had a choice of staying in the CCF or doing something else on Wednesday afternoons, such as look after old grannies. My altruistic resolution was to make the Corps better than this power crazy sergeant had done; I have no idea if I succeeded, but I did make my way up to be joint head of the CCF with James Purves in 1985.[29]

Contingent Commander Neville Clark MC is escorted off the premises on his retirement in 1988

International Bright Young Things

In addition to becoming fully-co-educational, Fettes was acquiring more and more pupils from around the world, to the extent that it could, to a certain extent, develop pretensions to being an international school. In 1980, 71 new pupils had Scottish addresses, 19 were English, three came from Northern Ireland and 28 were from overseas; expats and foreigners made up around a fifth of the school's population as early as 1981, and this would grow steadily.[30]

Indeed, the decline in boarding by local teenagers meant that there were proportionately more from abroad 'living in'. In 1981 it announced that there were now 'Irish, Welsh, American, Argentinian, Finn, Norwegian, Swede, Swiss, Spaniard, Nigerian, Indian, Chinese, Malaysian, Australian and Canadian Fettesians.'[31] These pupils were frequently invited to give their points of view in the school magazine. Jenny Sauers, an American, described in 1988 what it was like to go from Shady Side Academy, Pittsburgh, to Fettes:

I was amazed to be told that I had been living in a glitzy, soulless culture in the last stages of moral and cultural decay for the last seventeen years. Somehow, I can't believe that everyone but me and my immediate family are staggering around in the money-oriented, fast-food infested state of ethical debauchery that was outlined by quite a few well-meaning people in Britain, including my cabbie to the airport. Suddenly, I was called upon to evaluate, and at times defend, my way of life.[32]

Jenny freely admitted that most Americans had not the slightest idea where Scotland was and regretted that they didn't care. She was also grateful, after an initial irritation with Britain's 'superficial social graces' – dress codes and cutlery, for instance – for the fact that Fettes had taught her to 'stand on my own two feet', becoming less insecure and dependent. The following year, there was an entire section on 'living abroad' with articles about Saudi Arabia, the Philippines and Malaysia. The latter two were enthusiastic and painted pictures of generally harmonious, lively societies, but the piece on Saudi Arabia, written by an expatriate doctor's daughter, had a darker edge, describing youthful burquaed brides, beggars, public corporal punishment and a more public approach to animal slaughter.[33]

Students from overseas made their presence felt in other ways; when the right-wing Tory MP Nicholas Fairbairn, widely seen as sympathetic to white South Africa, spoke to the Political Society in 1986, he reminded the audience that, after the British left their former colonies, 'one man one vote soon meant one man (a dictator) and no votes.'[34]

This led to an 'explosive' question time:

William Wanendeya took up issue with Mr Fairbairn over his failure to condemn the exploitation of the blacks in South Africa. Mr Fairbairn retorted by pointing out that in Wanendeya's own country of Uganda, black had exploited black through the millions of mass murders by Amin and Obote.

The Political Society was undoubtedly one of the glories of Fettes in the last decades of the twentieth century, and enabled hundreds of young people to learn more about the world than they could from lessons or newspapers. Mark Peel, the gifted and indefatigable head of the Politics Department, lured dozens of high-profile speakers to the school to address both the relatively small group of intellectuals taking the subject and a host of others who realised that this was an opportunity to meet important people. In the same year that Nicholas Fairbairn stirred things up, the Society heard from Alex Fletcher, Tory MP for Edinburgh Central, and John Smith, who would later lead the Labour Party. In 1985, Michael Ancram, James Naughtie, Margo Macdonald and Donald Dewar were among the speakers and in 1988 Lord James Douglas Hamilton, Alex Salmond and Menzies Campbell represented the Conservative, Nationalist and Liberal parties. The future First Minister of Scotland predicted that the country would be focused more on Europe, where important decisions were increasingly being made, though may have been on rockier ground when he concluded, with the old radicals, that 'in the future Scotland would be free or a desert.'[35]

The SNP was in the doldrums in the eighties, reviving only when the poll tax gave it a unifying platform against the wicked witch of the south. When Alex Fletcher lost his seat, the new incumbent, future Labour Chancellor and Old Lorettonian Alistair Darling, was invited to speak, and may have reinforced unionist prejudices by informing the pupils that, although devolution was necessary to maintain the fabric of the UK after a decade of Tory rule biased towards southern England, independence was impossible 'with only 2½ million taxpayers.'[36]

The only remotely 'nationalist' pieces in the *Fettesian* during the whole decade were George Campbell Hay's glowing obituary and a review of Lorimer's *New Testament in Scots* by pupil Rod Cameron, who was impressed with how the late OF had worked from the original Greek and recreated the 'pastoral atmosphere' of that text. Cameron, clearly a bright lad, spotted a witty nationalist reference to the Prince of Darkness in the story of the Temptation (Matt. IV): 'the Devil (sorry, the Deil) speaks English (spelt like Scots mispronounced) and his quotation from Ps. 91 follows the Authorised Version.'[37]

Cameron found it 'one of the sincerest and most genuine versions of God's Word that I know.' The accompanying verse in the 1984 'Vive-la' was blithely insouciant about the 'Hamely Tongue', which Cameron saw as a 'language in its own right':

Of Fettesian news there has been lots and lots,
Such as Lorimer writing the Gospel in Scots;
Instead of a High Priest we have a High-hiedyin,
And Judas Iscariot talking Glaswegian.[38]

Although nationalism was not a major issue at the school in the eighties, Alex Salmond's was not the only radical voice expressing opinions which differed from those of most Fettesians; Jimmy Reid, the fiery socialist, spoke on May Day 1985, decrying Mrs Thatcher's economic policies and arguing that the welfare state was the greatest British achievement of the twentieth century, a sign of a Christian and civilised society.[39]

A few months earlier, however, one of the academics who addressed the 'Polsoc', Dr Henry Drucker, suggested that Labour, which at that point had lost two elections in a row, was in dangerous decline and would need to compromise with other viewpoints if it was ever to regain power. The 'Vive-la' for that year contained the first reference to the Old Fettesian who would do precisely that to lead Labour back to Downing St:

The Treasury ministers have to take care,
When sniped at from Labour's front benches by Blair.[40]

Blair's success was still a long way away, and the school's interest was still largely focused on the right. In the late eighties, OF Richard Thorpe produced a biography of Selwyn Lloyd. Mr David Orchard of the History Department, reviewing the book, could still refer to Lloyd as 'the most successful Old Fettesian of the twentieth century.'[41]

On Founder's Day in 1982 the Headmaster – who was taking no chances on Mrs Thatcher's re-election and was deeply alarmed by Labour's threat to make the payment of fees for private education illegal within ten years[42] – introduced the Gilbertian 'Kinnock's Song' by Cameron Miller, which savaged the then shadow education secretary:

I want to see that everyone learns Socialism properly
And this is only possible inside a State monopoly:
All schools that I don't recognise will therefore be prohibited
And any Fettes Masters will be flogged or even gibbeted.

'We want to pass on to others the "sound and liberal education," the words used by the Fettes Trustees on Sir William's tomb in the Canongate Kirkyard,' said Cochrane, 'Politics must not divert us from our task.' He went on to introduce the Guest of the Day, Viscount Arbuthnott, an OF who had won the DSC for air operations against Japanese shipping in the Second World War and was, among other posts, President of the Scottish Land Owners' Association and Lord Lieutenant of Kincardineshire. He spoke enthusiastically about the importance of a world conservation strategy, including the need for recycling, but avoided party politics. The 'Vive-la' opened with the suggestion that, for all Kinnock's faults, others were not above reproach:

If you're feeling depressed, well, it's hardly surprising
When inflation is falling but school fees keep rising,
So please make the most of your welcome today, for
It's one of the few things you're not made to pay for.[43]

One of the delightful features of Fettes in the eighties was the rehabilitation of Ian Harvey. Having been cast into the wilderness by the regrettable incident in the bushes of a public park in the fifties, was gradually readmitted to the fold in the seventies, and was entrusted with the Iain Macleod funds and with creating the Selwyn Lloyd Memorial Politics Library, which included both the late Speaker's own books and donations from his contemporaries, including Harold Wilson and Margaret Thatcher. Harvey also contributed to the *Fettesian*, including a review of Robert Bruce Lockhart's diaries when they were published in 1982; it must have been with a certain bitter irony that he wrote of the diplomat that 'he was a man who, but for himself alone, could have taken to the heights.'[44]

When Ian Harvey died in 1987, generous tributes were paid, Lord Fraser, a fellow-politician, praising his 'vitality, individuality and wit – indeed, irrepressible high spirits.'[45] Harvey, in fact, received more column inches for his obituary than the rather more conventional Niall Macpherson, the National Liberal MP who discreetly and conscientiously served as a junior minister and was ennobled as Lord Drumalbyn, dying within a few months of his more rakish colleague. It was indicative of the times that 'AGS', one of Harvey's obituarists, felt he could write that 'in 1958, an indiscretion which today would scarcely have merited a headline caused him to resign.' The record of ministerial resignations in the following decades suggests that the writer had overestimated the tolerance of the British press in such matters. The *Fettesian* was on firmer ground with a satire entitled *The People's Rupert* in 1986, and opening with the lines:

> *As Rupert wakes he shouts 'Hurray!*
> *I'm truanting from school today.'* [46]

The same issue carried the lyrics of that year's 'Vive-la', which concluded with bleakly topical humour:

> *A warning so grim as to make your knees wobble*
> *Was last month's radiation escape from Chernobyl.*
> *But the fall out that you are awaiting, no doubt,*
> *Is the summons to lunch, and the order, 'Fall Out!'* [47]

The sixties arrive at last

The *Fettesian* magazine of the eighties is, in fact, the most obviously of its time of all its incarnations, right down to references to 'Rambo style' cadets, a moving short story about Tiananmen Square and a prediction of schoolboy life in 2084 with a sports stadium, vitamin pills and computer-aided learning created by an international teaching organisation. The thin pamphlet which had remained virtually unchanged between the eras of Benjamin Disraeli and Edward Heath gave way to a fatter, less frequent little book with a sans-serif typeface in the seventies, but in 1984 blossomed into a large A4 publication which gradually acquired increasing amounts of colour. In the eighties it was a riot of eccentricity. Much of this was visual, with illustrative cartoons: the picture by 'Sarah C.' accompanying the 1986 'Vive-la' – by then sung by the Head Boy and Head Girl – depicts the pair almost in the style of a Thompson Twins album cover, standing slightly apart and facing in different directions, as was the way of that less 'touchy-feely', more individualistic decade. Advertising occupied more than a dozen pages; in 1986, there were flamboyantly eighties appeals for pupils to sign up to banks (illustrated with space invaders) and a breathtakingly vulgar Porsche advert jostling for position with armed services recruitment and quaintly old-fashioned announcements by local school uniform suppliers and butchers. Editors such as Tony Reeves of the English department printed critical articles and opinions of a type which rarely graced its pages before or since. Some of these were obvious enough attacks on compulsory rugby in 1985: 'an old-fashioned form of macho-savagery' with a riposte denigrating 'sciving', a spelling error which may have confirmed the aesthete's prejudices. The following year a vibrant collage showed snippets from positive reports on the school overawed by a muscular, unshaven, spiky-haired thug and a pair of goalposts made up of the words 'rugby rugby rugby yawn not again rugby rugby…'

Others, however, were engagements with the national culture wars of the decade. A 1985 article savaged the cult of the 'Sloane Ranger': 'the Sloane who needs a flat after leaving school simply has to ask Daddy, and be fairly confident of getting a Mini and a stereo thrown in too.'[48]

'Perhaps I'm jealous because I don't qualify for the clique of the week,' snorted the author, 'but I sincerely do have better ways of spending a spare hour than achieving the Contrived Messy Look (nb hair must be long enough to run hand through in a distracted manner).' The enormous good fortune of the Sloanes, with their Rive Gauche soap and 'years off' as chalet-girls, was contrasted with the sufferings of 'the average Sharon' who needed to be pregnant to get a flat. It is hard to imagine a school magazine running something so cheerfully offensive today, but people in the eighties were expected to take offensive remarks on the chin, and, in any case, if Sloanes really were as dim as the authors believed, they were unlikely to have read the magazine. Class issues returned in 1987 with a satirical piece about that modern British obsession, the property market, in the form of adverts for pretentiously-described, madly overpriced parts of Fettes (the tiny athletics pavilion on Young's playing field, an 'unusual amalgam of modern architectural styles' whose 'walls display works of local literary greats' was offered at £743,000 – this was, after all, the era of the Knightsbridge broom cupboard).[49]

More serious comment came in a review of *The Good Schools Guide*, which was something of a daring innovation – so much so that many headmasters refused to speak to the (female) authors. The book 'comes from the same "stable" as the *Sloane Ranger Handbook* and is littered with references to Sloanes, accents, social classes and Rolls-Royces' with the result that it contained remarks such as 'nowadays far more locals has (sic) brought a suburban element in' and 'we detected some lower middle.' The reviewer found this truly hideous book's approach flawed – placing heavy emphasis on the personal charm of a headmaster (Cameron Cochrane, luckily for Fettes, 'looks a bit like Michael Caine') and displaying 'a fascination with the trappings of privilege and the minutiae of class distinction.'[50]

Although generally dismissive of this sort of nonsense, the reviewer (teacher Robert Philp, who would later write the school's official history) recognised that such publications were going to become more important. He accompanied the review with an article explaining the new GCSE examination, which would replace O Levels after 35 years, and gave it a cautious welcome, little realising that what he was describing in 1987 would, over the next two decades, snowball into permanent revolution in qualifications, the persistent interference in education of the parent-as-consumer, league tables and the constant driving of pupils to sit endless tests. This would erode the sense of fun in *Fettesians* of this era, which, in their rebelliousness, questioning and excitement, have something of a sixties feel – not the way the sixties actually were, of course, but how people think of them.

The Sloane and the Rugger-bugger: two cartoons from the increasingly liberal
Fettesian

The school chapel had long been a platform for challenging the pupils. In 1984, for instance, there were sermons from several ministers of tough inner-city parishes including Bill 'the Godfather' Christman, late of Easterhouse. David Weekes, chaplain through the eighties, continued the approach developed by George Buchanan-Smith of moral engagement with the real world, and began with the Fettesians themselves:

When he applied his faith to school life, his concern for justice came through. He hated unfairness and denounced mockery, unpleasant 'traditions' and the intolerance that spoils the harmony of a boarding community. At such times, the serenity of his Biblical addresses could change to a deep note of indignation.[51]

His constant efforts to get the school to think about public service featured dramatic measures such as locking himself and several pupils in a case on Princes St to publicise Amnesty International 'to startled passers-by.' He was also instrumental in forging links with disadvantaged local communities, including a Family Service Unit, where Fettesians helped small children with their homework. The *Fettesian* also increasingly hit readers with doses of real life. These were even franker about awkward social issues than the breezy accounts of public duty in the seventies. Reports came in 1985 from Lucy Bryson and Kirsty Macleod on Outside Service in Pilton, 'one of Edinburgh's deprived areas.' Lucy and her friend Sarah looked after two small girls, Jane and Gayle, who on one occasion responded to the 'cheery social-worker' suggestion of doing the washing-up with 'I'll batter ye.'[52]

Kirsty helped at Craigmure Primary School, which had a large number of underprivileged children, and reflected on what the point was – 'to encourage "community spirit"? To show them that we are not toffee-nosed after all?' – when it was obvious that 'in a few years many of these children will grow to resent their public-school counterparts.'[53]

She even worried that Fettes' efforts in this regard might 'pump more hate into them' because of a resentment of charity, but carried on anyway, since she believed in community spirit and, presumably, enjoyed working with children. One pupil described her pre-Fettes life at a North London comprehensive, a violent slice of multicultural Britain with 1400 pupils from forty-six different countries, taught by people with social consciences who were often bullied out of the classroom, and where those who wanted to learn were viciously mocked (the *Fettesian* editor added a nervous rider that this article reflected one person's experience and did not represent school policy towards comprehensives; he asked hopefully but vainly for a future report to redress the balance).[54]

Another article, by future housemistress Pippa Donald, explained the difficulties of teaching traveller children – 'one very intelligent boy of seventeen, a shrewd businessman who traded in anything and everything, was finding it embarrassing to be illiterate; he wanted to learn to read, so he could decipher invoices, and to write his name, so he could sign cheques.'[55]

A Fettesienne of less plutocratic origins described the everyday frustrations and humiliations of a part-time job, in her case, waitressing in a café in Elie, which most of her schoolmates saw as a holiday resort. Whereas in the past the school assumed that leavers would go to university, the family firm, the armed services or the Empire (and possibly a combination thereof) it now felt it necessary to offer serious careers advice. For those lacking the Sloanes' connections, school leavers were encouraged to think about careers in industry, especially the new fields of 'high-tech' – 'the prospect for engineers, which must include girls, has never been better' – and were reminded of the scale of unemployment.[56]

Pointing out that a good qualification from a polytechnic was better than a poor one from a university, the *Fettesian* urged parents and pupils alike 'not to spurn good vocational training.' As with other British schools, Fettes signed up to the craze for teenage wealth creation, with a young enterprise fashion show in 1989: 'the gains in experience made up for the losses in money,' noted Victoria Weekes, though ironically the pupils' business acronym, TYMAR, stood for 'take your money and run.'[57]

Soldiering On

Despite the wealth-creating opportunities for thrusting young individuals offered by Thatcher's Britain, many Fettesians, as previously noted, continued to join the armed forces, and many still ended up in Northern Ireland. Robert Lawrence, who did a tour there in the early eighties, described it as 'a very, very unpleasant place.' During a four-day leave from Belfast, he was shopping on the King's Road when a car backfired and he instinctively flung himself down in a shop doorway, to the consternation of passers-by – 'I reckoned I'd rather be seen as a bit stupid than be hit by a bullet.'[58]

However, if, like Raymond McLennan, a young officer in the Royal

Corps of Transport who had been in Arniston under Bob Orchard in the late seventies, a British soldier had Northern Irish connections, it was considered a bad idea to send him to Ulster. Local pressures might be brought to bear, and as the experience of Knox Cunningham and, decades earlier, the Lennox-Conynghams, had shown, it was possible for even the most respectable former military Fettesians to be lured in questionable directions. 'No wars for me, never a shot fired in anger,' admits McLennan, but he was still kept busy. So important was counter-terrorism to the British Army's role that J.V.G.P. Addison and F.R.C. Salvesen, two Fettes cadet NCOs who won places on the prestigious U.K. Land Forces Leadership Course in 1982, found themselves taking part in a 24-hour exercise against 'terrorists who pestering the local area.' This involved, like South Armagh, infiltration and exfiltration by helicopter and 'flares, thunderflashes, gunfire and "standard procedure" spiced with the smell of cordite.'[59]

The 1980s saw a re-intensification of the Cold War after the détente of the 1970s, with Mrs Thatcher's ferocious anti-communism shared with President Reagan. The decade's greater belligerence in this era saw a ratcheting up of nuclear rivalry; the Fettes sixth formers were 'forcibly reminded' of this in a visit by General Sir John Stanier, C-in-C UK Land Forces (on the day Mrs Thatcher announced the purchase of the Trident II missile system) when they were told 'from the horse's mouth' that the UK was playing chicken, and the USSR was playing spillikins.[60] Ken Millar, the OF army medic, played his own role in the curious, sinister world of nuclear warfare in the early eighties:

I served as the Staff MO at the Defence Nuclear, Biological and Chemical Centre in Winterbourne Gunner near Salisbury between 1979 and 1981 – a fairly arcane job concerned with protecting our soldiers, sailors and airmen against the effects of these unpleasant weapons, but one which had a lasting effect on me in a variety of ways – not the least of which, I suppose, is the fact that I have had my main domicile in Salisbury ever since.[61]

In the same year that they were told about Mrs Thatcher playing chicken with Trident, the CCF took part in 'Operation Dalriada II' at Lochgilphead, fighting off a 'Soviet infiltrating force with a tracker dog team (Capt. Murray and Susie!) and three brainwashed deserters from Highland Regiments, alias CUO Sutton, Pipe-Major Williamson-MacDougall and Sergeant Brew.'[62]

Hidden between a ridge and the 'Heights of Arniston', the fiendish Soviets refused to be destroyed by the CCF's first sweep, and harassed them by night in their camp at 'Schoolhouse Stockade.' Although one officer was 'shot' more than a dozen times, Fettes eventually defeated the red menace.

Francis Salvesen went on to join the Army and went up to Sandhurst, and published a light-hearted memoir of his training, *Journal of a Student at Arms*. This portrays a Sandhurst which was modern in a host of ways, from interviews designed to test recruits' understanding of world affairs, riot training for Belfast, and the use of helicopters, through to high-sprited social romps with young women bussed in from Norland nannies – not quite so savage as the training portrayed in Robert Lawrence's memoir, but very different from the laid-back monasticism of the Victorian officer cadets.[63]

Although the Anglo-American media, in films such as *Red Dawn* and *Threads*, sometimes portrayed the last phase of the Cold War in terms of nuclear attack on or invasion of the UK and USA, events played out, for the most part, in and above West Germany. Eighties Fettesians could be proud that the commander of 1st British Corps, BAOR, was Major General John Learmont. Raymond McLennan spent much of his career in Germany, where, the Cold War being restive, 'we would listen in to the Russians or East Germans telling us in English why we should defect to the East in their Lord Haw-Haw style propaganda.' Although there were tensions, most of his memories are of the lighter side of day-to-day military life, including the ingenious wheezes which soldiers have always dreamed up to make their lives easier:

The RCT never allowed officers to transport their own cars from the UK to Germany. You were supposed to arrange that with a civilian transport firm. But as a young Lieutenant on a meagre salary with high mess bills, this was not an option. I 'arranged' with the Sergeants' Mess that for a couple of crates of beer, they would organise the delivery for me. They did, but on the way there, the Colonel of the Regiment was showing the Brigadier our perfect transport formation from a motorway bridge (100m apart, lights on, flags all correct). The wind blew off the cover of car and the truck with noisily flapping canvas was easily spotted (without binoculars) going under the bridge, my mess kit hanging in the back and the registration number gave the game away and my identity with it. I was orderly officer for weeks and not allowed to use the car.

Ceremonial events such as Remembrance Day were also memorable, not least because a parade to the local church through the streets by hundreds of smart soldiers always ensured a good turnout of civilians. However, the modern uniform of combat jackets was, in McLennan's view, 'a bit dull, really,' so on his first parade as a Troop Commander, he mischievously paid tribute to the RCT's equine history by donning Number One dress: 'dark blue cap, dark blue Jacket, shiny Sam Browne Belt, tight dark blue jodhpurs with a white stripe down the legs, George boots and spurs'. To complete the effect, he borrowed a horse, which was kept hidden until the Sergeant-Major called out for the Troop Commanders to join in just before the 130-strong unit marched off:

As he shouted my name for the third time I made my entrance. Only a traffic light had a redder face than the Sgt Major; but as the Officer Commanding was laughing with the rest of the Squadron I knew I was all right. A quick change into Combats that were hanging in the back of the concealed horse-box soon brought the Sgt Major's blood pressure back to normal and we all marched off to church smiling.

McLennan did not emerge from the RCT entirely unscathed on the field of battle. As with all generations of British soldiers, practising for war could harbour danger for the unwary, as he discovered when taking a hill on an infantry exercise:

The hill was heavily defended by the Gurkhas and as we took the last machine gun post part of the drill was to move weapons out of reach of the dead and injured enemy. I grabbed the barrel of the GPMG to pull it away only to have my left hand stick to it as it was almost red-hot from firing. Cas-evaced out for a self-inflicted injury to hoots of laughter from the enemy meant I never made that mistake again. I still have the scars to prove it.

Mark Boyes remembered Germany as 'a fairly predictable lifestyle of large scale autumn exercises, adventure training, low level training, and then start the cycle all over again,' though he did add that 'I suppose I shouldn't complain too much as I got to spend most of each winter in Bavaria teaching soldiers to ski.'[64]

The Falklands
Although Northern Ireland and Germany were the inevitable postings

797

of a great many OFs during the eighties, it was the Falklands conflict that dominated public perceptions and the school's collective memory of the decade. At the time, the *Fettesian* gave a curiously jumbled account of former pupils' involvement:

…the two naval sons of George and Moira Stenhouse [the assistant bursar and his wife] *found themselves in the Task Force (Brian in the converted trawler* Cordella *and Ronald in the frigate* Active*), Allan Cameron's award-winning ride around Argentina was abruptly terminated after 250 miles and, very sadly, R.A.D. Lawrence (G74), a platoon commander in the Scots Guards, suffered severe head wounds in the fighting around Mount Tumbledown (Scottish newspapers reported the Queen's concern about Lieutenant Lawrence's progress, and it is heartening to learn that already he has made an almost complete recovery). The whole school is proud to learn that Lieutenant Lawrence's gallantry has since been recognised with the award of the Military Cross.*[65]

Pupils' memories of the time vary. Carl Longmore remembers that Fettes was certainly an environment where conflict and politics were discussed – especially because, at the time of the Falklands war, the second head boy was from Argentina. By contrast, Iain Miller recalls, the pupils followed what was going on in the Falklands, but the school did not go to any lengths to explain the war to them. Then again, the school did not bother telling the pupils why they had to be in the CCF. In those days 'not much about what went on at Fettes was explained terribly well.' The *Fettesian* reprinted Lawrence's MC citation – 'His actions were an outstanding example of leadership under fire and courage in the face of the enemy' – but as something of a rebellious youth in his schooldays, Lawrence found Fettes' interest in him somewhat ironic. Other OFs – and there were many more in the Falklands than the small list provided by the school magazine – found it rather unfair. But then, the war itself was an oddity, an 'ungentlemanly act' which appeared to come out of nowhere. Argentina had coveted the islands for generations, but, although the Thatcher government had an appetite for selling whatever family silver might conceivably pay for tax cuts, it accepted that they could not be handed over to a fascist regime in Buenos Aires which was both savagely cruel and manifestly incompetent. This perception of the Argentines meant that their seizure of the Falklands came as something of a shock. On 18 March 1982, OF Duncan Ferguson, Commander and Squadron Weapon Engineer of the Fourth Frigate Squadron, had been carrying out trials of a new computer programme on HMS *Arrow* and was relaxing in the wardroom of HMS *Rooke*, the Gibraltar shore establishment:

We read with some amusement that a bunch of scrap-metal merchants had landed on a remote island called South Georgia (which was apparently British) and had the cheek to raise the Argentinian flag. We didn't take the matter very seriously.

The full-scale invasion of the Falklands came two weeks later when he was on leave. Bidding farewell to his family at the windy dockyard gates, he set sail on HMS *Antelope* at 0600 on 5 April, cheered on only by dockside riggers. Although frantic preparations had been made to ready the ships for combat, 'to be honest, none of us considered war on the cards.' The first reality of action stations was when, having transferred to the tanker RFA *Olmeda*, he had to order the closing of the ship's bar, an essential, if unpopular, part of official war readiness. Royal Marines Oman veteran Ian Gardiner also had an unwelcome surprise:

At midday on Friday 2 April 1982, 45 Commando was due to go on Easter leave. At 5 o'clock that morning, I was informed by telephone that the Unit had been recalled. It was as well the Argentinians had not invaded the day before. Nobody would have believed it. It was a pretty peculiar feeling being called to war by telephone from one's bed. Time has not dimmed the memory of the sensation. The next half hour was spent scarting around in torchlight in the garden shed trying to get some kit together. I was in camp ready to go almost anywhere by 0600. The fuss was cooling somewhat. Nevertheless, it was with some awe that we read the FLASH signal ordering us to prepare for amphibious operations in the South Atlantic. [66]

Elsewhere, other OFs were involved in the frantic efforts to ready Britain's military technology for the South Atlantic. Rob Greaves had just left university for a job just up the road from Fettes at Ferranti, where, 'working with a 4-bit processor and using paper tape to program chips' he helped develop aircraft navigation systems. In the nature of Britain's Cold War defence commitments, these were designed to operate in Northern Europe, which presented the Ferranti teams with a problem:

The Navigation System was the 1980s equivalent of the modern car sat nav, except that the computer memory was very expensive and very small compared to current specs. As a result the maps were actually stored on film. The Navigation System depended on the Maps that had to be carefully produced on film which took the curvature of the Earth into account.

As you can imagine, when the Ministry of Defence instructed Ferranti to prepare the Sea Harriers to be able to operate around the Falkland Islands, engineers had to find out where the Falklands were. To make matters worse, there was a shortage of prepared maps ready to be filmed. Without these maps, the navigation system of the Harrier would have been severely limited. The Engineering Support that the MoD required gave the Harriers the ability to operate successfully around the Falklands, and this was all within a stone's throw of Fettes.

As the technologists worked unseen, the combat troops were embarked. Robert Lawrence of the Scots Guards made his way south on the *QE2* on 12 May. Experiencing, he later recalled, mixed emotions of apprehension and worry that by the time the Scots Guards got there the Marines would have finished the job and he would be stuck on garrison duty, he wrote a 'last letter home' to his parents – 'a bit like one of those 1940s Richard Todd movies.'[67]

He wondered if the advent of mass communication meant that soldiers now behaved the way they were expected to do based on the way they had seen people act in war movies. Ian Gardiner also reflected on the hours before 'contact':

It is not easy to describe one's feelings before one is committed to battle. Fear, certainly, plays a part but it is not fear of death itself. It is more a sadness for the grief that will follow one's death among one's family. As a company commander responsible for the lives of some 150 men, I felt pretty lonely in that hour when our preparations were complete and before we moved off, but I am prepared to bet that each individual felt just as lonely in his own way. I found that I didn't actually want anyone to speak to me. I spent my hour smoking a cigar and preparing myself to accept whatever disasters the night might bring – in a single word – praying. It was a mental exercise I would not care to have to repeat.

In addition to prayer, Gardiner, like most Falklands (and previous) Fettesians an officer, had the responsibility of preparing his men for battle, and described the process in an article for the Scotsman on the twenty-fifth anniversary of the war:

I set about explaining to my Marines that there was going to be a fight, and we were certainly going to win it. But they should be ready for the unexpected, and they should be ready to take casualties. I asked them to think what they were going to do when the man next to them dropped. 'Troop Sergeant, what are you going to do when the Troop Commander drops? Company Second-in-Command, what are you going to do when I drop? What are you going to do, Marine McGillicuddie, when you drop? Are you going to scream like a Dervish and unnerve the man next to you, or are you going to die quietly like a soldier?' Needless to say, they all burst out laughing. 'See yon McGillicuddie: he'll be screamin' afore he's shot!' This was exactly the effect I'd hoped to achieve. So they understood the worst potentialities, but if they could laugh at them now, then they would be all the more able to cope with them when their time came. 'War is a game to be played with a smiling face,' said Winston Churchill. How right he was.

In this way I tried to breed a cheerful brotherhood of constructive cynics: optimistic sceptics; men who, when you gave them their orders, would say, 'nice plan, boss - looks a good place to start - but, of course, we know THAT won't happen; but we do know what you are trying to achieve and why, and we will somehow make it work for you.' And so we went to war.[68]

Transferred to the *Canberra* (Cunard being reluctant to expose their flagship to further danger) Lawrence's accommodation was a world away from the pleasant surroundings of Chelsea, where the Scots Guards had previously been based on ceremonial duties. The *Canberra* was in San Carlos Water, known as 'Bomb Alley' and one of the worst spots in the Falklands; Lawrence was on the top deck, one of the worst spots on the *Canberra*:

Every time the ship lurched with the waves, a cupboard door with a broken latch swung open and the automatic light inside the cupboard swung on. Then, as the ship wallowed again, the cupboard door swung shut. This went on all through the night. It was like sleeping in some wretched Third World discotheque.

Outside, meanwhile, the weather was getting progressively colder. There were enormous blue and turquoise icebergs floating around, and flotillas of penguins in the middle of nowhere. It was like something out of a Jules Verne movie – spectacular, but also dream-like.[69]

Ken Millar, nominally an operational reinforcement to an augmented medical unit, ended up as medic to the 2nd Battalion, Scots Guards, something to do, he assumed, 'with my having the ability to speak Jockinese.' He was introduced to Lawrence during the transfer of his battalion by sea from San Carlos to Bluff Cove on HMS *Fearless*. Angus Smith, the Padre, introduced them:

We briefly chatted on such schoolmasters that we might have had in common (not many, as he is substantially younger than I am), then went our separate ways. I did not see him again for several years, as when he was wounded he was evacuated by helicopter direct to the field hospital. Next time we met was at a meeting of the Tumbledown Dining Club some ten years later, when he hailed me across the room with 'Hey! It's the Old Fettesian Doctor!'

Such encounters were not uncommon; although Gardiner rarely met any other OFs in the Royal Marines, Fettes' military tradition, although smaller in scale and less gung-ho than in the late nineteenth and early twentieth centuries, ensured that that the school was well-represented in the Falklands, especially by infantry officers.

Since the Falklands, it has been popular in some quarters to denigrate the British victory as that of a high-tech NATO member over an impoverished but proud third world country. This is grossly unfair on both participants. The British land forces had to fight an old-fashioned series of battles across open and inhospitable terrain, foot-slogging their way towards Port Stanley with rifle and pack and without the main battle tanks or tactical bombers which would have made their task easier in Germany. Gardiner's 45 Commando were famous for 'yomping' across the unforgiving landscape:

The unusual achievement, if there was one, was that we remained a fully fit fighting body of men carrying about 120lb each, in what was something like Rannoch Moor in mid-winter: bleak, windswept, rocky, boggy, cold and wet; without any tents, buildings, woods, or hedges; indeed without any cover at all, except our groundsheet bivouacs and our sleeping bags. And on several occasions we didn't even have those. And we often went short of food. For young men in these conditions, burning calories in prolific quantities, this was no small matter. It was all we could do to stop some Marines eating the cardboard boxes that the rations didn't turn up in. When I saw myself in a mirror after the campaign, I found my skin was stretched across my ribcage and my legs were like a ballet dancer's.[70]

'In these circumstances,' Gardiner told the pupils of the Fettes Historical Society in a well-attended lecture, 'you live off nicotine, caffeine and adrenaline – and they're all brown.' (He added for the benefit of modern education's increasingly paranoid health regime that 'if an officer can keep his troops alive long enough to die of lung cancer, that's doing pretty well.') This was the kind of low-tech hard military graft which belied the boasts of the Ministry of Defence about superior British technology, especially in the form of the Harrier jump jet. In fact, the Argentines were able to deploy a variety of western-made aircraft, many of which were faster than the agile but relatively slow Harrier. Duncan Ferguson, on HMS *Arrow* which, with *Alacrity* and *Glamorgan*, was tasked with bombarding enemy positions on shore, was on the receiving end of Argentine technology in the shape of the combat-proven Israeli Dagger fighter:

Four Argentinian Dagger aircraft, undetected by our radar and when sighted assumed to be British Sea Harriers suddenly started to spit fire and release bombs. For me as an engineer it wasn't at all comforting to know that the operations teams of all three ships had been caught napping, I was merely grateful that the sailor manning Arrow's *port 20mm Oerlikon disregarded the order to check fire and by opening fire certainly saved our lives. The Argentinian pilot had sighted on the 4 Exocet missiles in front of the bridge, but swerved because of the tracer aimed at him and he hit us instead with eleven 30mm cannon shells in a line from the funnel back to the flight deck.*

Fortunately only one man was injured and the bomb bounced over the ship and exploded harmlessly between ourselves and Alacrity. *All three ships were let off lightly with a warning, but from that day none of us on* Arrow *doubted, down to the most junior seaman, that we were at war and that the Argentinians were determined and courageous pilots.*

Arrow had indeed been fortunate, as she was during the landings when an Exocet whistled over the flight-deck, but *Sheffield*, notoriously, was not. When she was hit, *Arrow* went to her aid, only to have to pull away because of danger from torpedoes (which turned out to be because a British ship was busy launching them against 'phantom submarines'). *Arrow* returned to take on and feed the battered survivors:

After a long and harrowing afternoon we took on some 230 men from Sheffield *and come face to face with not only death, but with the sight and smell of burning flesh, and the unbelievable horror of the loss of a Royal Navy ship.* Arrow *was a different ship from then on. It was touching to see our ship's company give up their bunks, clothes, sweets, cigarettes and sympathy to the smoke-blackened survivors who outnumbered them by some 50 souls.*

Because of the danger from air raids, Ferguson, like everyone on board, slept in his clothes with lifejacket, gas mask and anti-flash kit to hand. He saw the subsequent loss of *Antelope*, which blew up whilst an unexploded bomb went off whilst being defused; having lost friends on two ships, *Arrow's* crew 'were bitterly resolved to avenge that loss' and shelled the Argentine camps at Goose Green and Mount Kent 'with a rare hatred.' *Arrow* was to spend two weeks in 'Bomb Alley' supporting the British ground troops and diverting enemy missiles with Verey pistols, flares and 'any visible weapon that came to hand', but she survived intact.

Just as their pilots were proving to be dangerous professionals, so too the Argentine ground troops were more capable than their recent function of torturing fellow-citizens might suggest. As Fettesians fighting Italy during the Second World War knew, the fact that a country is ruled by comic-opera fascists whose main victims are the civilian population does not make its army's bullets any less deadly. Robert Lawrence, arriving by landing craft as his predecessors had done at D-Day, knew he was in for a hard fight as he made his way towards Tumbledown:

...the troops the Paras had fought and captured at Goose Green, in the Argentinians' outer ring of defence, were mostly teenage conscripts. The troops we had to face at Tumbledown, however, were extremely well-trained and well-equipped marines in their mid-twenties, who had had recent fighting experience in the Argentinian civil war. They had had years of aggression. People like me, on the other hand, only weeks previously had been doing the Changing of the Guard at Buckingham Palace – not exactly the greatest experience for fighting a war in some godforsaken little island in the middle of nowhere.[71]

Just how well-equipped the Argentine army actually was became apparent when Lawrence discovered a box of night-sights in captured enemy tents – 'third-generation IWSs, the absolute top grade, more advanced than the ones we had ourselves.' Nonetheless, there were differences between the two forces. Ian Gardiner found that the Argentines resembled the Iranians with whom he had fought in Oman in their unfortunate relationships between ranks. Whereas in the British forces, the 'beasting' stopped after training, beating soldiers was unknown and officers said 'please' and 'thank you', the Argentinian army seemed to work on a basis of bullying and feat. This had the tactically undesirable result that 'when the fear of the approaching enemy eventually superseded their fear of their superiors, they broke and ran.[72]

Nonetheless, Gardiner found that the Argentines could inflict plenty of damage when able to do so. The Marines were tasked with the taking of the peaks of Two Sisters, which resulted in a 'ding-dong battle':

Of course, the attack did not go to plan. There were no enemy on the lower reaches of the mountain, but it was stoutly defended at the top. On one occasion, I gave my own position as the target for the mortars because we were that close to the enemy. Machine guns, anti-tank weapons and artillery came crashing down in among us as we tried to bury ourselves like moles in the peaty, wet, rocky surface. We lost two men wounded to artillery fire. The battle tends to stop while you are under artillery fire, and it takes a major effort to get it moving again. Being shelled is deafening, terrifying, shocking and quite the loudest noise I have ever heard. Nevertheless, both in Oman and the South Atlantic, I was left feeling surprised at the number of people it didn't kill. Its chief effect is an assault on the mind. Our own anti-tank weapons, also without night sights but skilfully directed by use of flash lights and radio, fired missiles in over our heads to smash resoundingly into the positions in front of us.

Over the next few hours, my Marines worked their way forwards up the hill under machine gun and artillery fire, supported by our anti-tank weapons. It was like fighting in a built-up area, the rocks were so large. There were some quite personal battles fought at close range against an enemy shooting at us from behind the rocks in the dark. Throughout the battle, I kept on thinking how depressingly familiar our grandfathers and their grandfathers would have found it.[73]

The anti-tank weapons – cumbersome MILAN missile launchers – had been roundly cursed by the Marines during their 'yomp', when a three-hour march took twice the time because of them, as Gardiner told the Scots at War Trust in an interview: 'a piece of rock or a small stream that a man in normal fighting order would never have noticed became a major obstacle to a man carrying his own kit plus a 30 pound weight round of MILAN ammunition.' However, their value became apparent at Two Sisters:

While 2 Troop were moving up, I decided to see what the MILAN could do and invited them to have a go. It would mean firing over our heads and we were nearer to the target than we were to him, but it would fill the gap before the artillery arrived. The round was fired. It is an extraordinary thing having a MILAN rocket fired over your head. We could see it coming towards us, quite slowly, it seemed, making a curious spluttering noise, quite unlike what I expected. It sounded almost friendly. We all involuntarily ducked but it must have passed about 30 feet above us, and when it hit, it produced a most satisfactory bang.[74]

Gardiner was decorated for his role in the capture of Two Sisters, but had a narrow escape:

From now until 36 hours later we underwent intermittent shelling, and the intermittent nature of this shelling added greatly to the danger and uncertainty. They were only using two guns, but over the period, some 40 or 50 shells landed on the ridge among our positions, and the saddle between us and the rest of the unit became heavily cratered with many more … During a lull, I got out to have a pee. I hadn't finished when I heard the dreaded whistle. The shell hit the ground at the same time I did. A healthy chunk of rock landed on my back. I measured the distance afterwards. It was nineteen paces.

Another OF was to be less fortunate. Lawrence and the Scots Guards pressed forward to Tumbledown, the last peak before Port Stanley, where they would fight one of the last, and most famous, battles of the Falklands campaign. Whereas many Fettesians had tended to be rather reticent about describing their intimate thoughts and experiences in battle, Robert Lawrence was extremely frank about what he had seen, done and felt at Tumbledown, and it is worth quoting him at length:

I was really going to go for it. Yes, I told myself, what the fuck, I am really going to go for it now… Not far down the gully, I collected a rifle with an IWS on it, saw some Argentinians moving position across the back of Tumbledown, and picked off about four of them. I then radioed to James Dalrymple's platoon, who were joining Left Flank to add fire protection, and asked them to put some fire down on the Argentinian machine-gun post, so that we could see where it was. I also hoped their fire would keep the Argentinians' heads down while we came into the attack.

The minute we started leading our assault in, however, the machine-gun post saw us coming, and switched its fire on to us. We hit the ground at about the time Mark's platoon was coming up level with us, and then tried to return fire. I began crawling forward on my own for about forty or fifty feet, and remember feeling desperately scared. There were bullets flying everywhere – from James's platoon on my left, from the Argentinians ahead, and from my own guys behind, and the bullets were all ricocheting off the rocks. This is it, I thought. This is the end. And, as I continued to crawl along, I tried to make myself disappear into the ground, face right down in the dirt.[75]

Sheltering behind a rock, Lawrence hoped to destroy the machine-gun post with a phosphorous grenade, but discovered that its pin was too stiff to be removed by one man. He had to crawl back under fire to his corporal, who helped him extract the pin; Lawrence then crawled back again, yelled an order to his men to reduce their fire, and threw the grenade into the enemy position, which blew up.

I took off, and screamed at my men to follow me. In that instant, my one sudden thought was, are they going to follow me, or will I be left to run off on my own? But when I glanced round, there was this unbelievably fantastic sight of every man getting up and running in. I remember thinking at that moment that this was life on a knife edge. Amazing. Fantastic. Nothing would ever bother me again from that moment on. If I got back to London and found that my flat had burned down, it would be a totally insignificant event in comparison to this experience.

The other thing that occurred to me was that people in real life don't die in real life the way they do on television. If a man is shot, a bit of him might come off, but he doesn't drop immediately. He just carries on coming. It takes an enormous amount to kill a man. Usually he has to be shot three or four times before he dies.[76]

Just how much it took to kill a man Lawrence discovered in a terrible way when he ran out of ammunition and had to kill an enemy soldier with a broken bayonet. 'Stabbing a man to death is not a clean way to kill somebody, and what made it doubly horrific was that at one point he started screaming "*Please…*" in English to me,' Lawrence wrote, 'But had I left him he could have ended up shooting me in the back.'[77]

He took the dead soldier's rifle, shot a sniper and collected his rifle too, and pressed on. He hoped to keep going to get to the Argentine supply area at the far end of Tumbledown, and soon found himself gazing down at the lights of Port Stanley, which would soon be liberated:

I turned to Guardsman McEntaggart as we went along and, for some inexplicable reason, suddenly cried out, 'Isn't this fun?'

Seconds later, it happened. I felt a blast in the back of my head that felt more as if I'd been hit by a train than a bullet. It was a high velocity bullet, in fact, travelling at a speed of around 3800 feet per second… at the time, all I knew was that my knees had gone and I collapsed, totally paralysed, to the ground.[78]

With five pints of blood lost and 45 per cent of his brain shot away, Lawrence was flown to a converted refrigeration plant at Fitzroy used as a field hospital, where the severity of his injuries led to his being placed at the back of the queue. He was also denied anaesthetic. However, slowly and agonisingly, he was treated by the medical services for wounds which would have killed people in earlier wars. Lawrence came to feel that the system was not adequately looking after the long-term wounded – especially not those who had severe and untelegenic injuries. He and his father would spend much of the eighties causing trouble for the authorities on this issue. Whilst they succeeded in drawing attention to an issue which the triumphalist politicians would have preferred to ignore, several other Scots Guards, including some Old Fettesians, felt hurt by what Lawrence conceded was 'very stroppy' behaviour.

Along with R. deG. Hanson, whose diving experience was put to use in salvage work, Ken Millar was one of several OFs to return to the islands after the war to command Port Stanley hospital.

Work was usually pretty routine, but on one occasion I happened to be the on-call doctor for emergencies and received a shout from the HQ that there was a serious casualty to be extracted from a Japanese fishing boat some distance offshore. Next thing I knew, I was about 100 kms offshore in a Sea King helicopter, hovering about 30 metres above this fishing vessel – which was shifting a fair amount in all directions in the swell – with the strop at the end of the winch cable under my arms. When I got to the deck of the vessel, I said to the RAF Loadmaster (who had gone down first) 'That was good; I've never done that before.' He went a bit white, and asked if I could keep quiet about this omission in my previous experience, as apparently no-one was meant to do it without proper training, especially in the middle of the ocean. Not everything in what some perceive as the rigid and hierarchical military is always quite as one might expect. The casualty was not as seriously injured as we had expected; however, the military nursing staff at the hospital had got themselves fully set up to deal with a serious spinal injury and were not to be denied their fun. When it became obvious that the casualty needed no more than standard care, they grabbed me and thrust me into a Stryker frame (a device in which a spinal patient is held completely helpless which allows the nurses to turn him over without risking further injury). I have never before or since been completely surrounded by feisty young women and at the same time been totally unable to defend myself against their ministrations. I hope there are no photographs! [79]

He also reflected on the conflict after the twenty-fifth anniversary:

On attending the 25th Anniversary Parade in London in 2007, and on the previous night a Scots Guards all ranks regimental reunion, I felt there was a mixture of great pride at the achievement of the military mission and unquenchable sorrow at the cost in life, limb and sanity. I seldom talk of it, but it will always be with me.

It was also with Fettes College, where a rumour flew round that the sixth-form boys were going to get call-up papers, for a long time too. Summer camp in 1982 featured an exercise over 'sovereignty', a word never previously mentioned by the CCF.[80] A highlight of the autumn term in 1983 was a sermon in chapel by the Revd David Cooper, Chaplain of 2 Para, who spoke of his war experiences and 'left us with the sobering thought that those men who did not shirk their day to day responsibilities in normal Army life were those who, in his opinion, had best been able to cope with the rigours of the Falklands.'[81] Prince Andrew, a Falklands veteran who had flown helicopters during the war, inspected the CCF in 1989 and was given a 'smart parade' and a present for his new daughter, Princess Eugenie.[82]

The Duke of York visits Fettes in 1989, accompanied by Contingent Commander Andrew Murray and reforming Headmaster Malcolm Thynne

Such visits were rather of a piece with the traditional Fettes understanding of war, as were the summer 1985 rides in a naval Wessex helicopter (the type which attacked the Argentine submarine *Santa Fe*) and visit to HMS *Invincible,* which meant a great deal to the cadets.[83]

Invincible was sailed up the Firth of Forth by Captain C.H. Layman, DSO, whose daughter Alexandra was a pupil at the school; she recalls feeling uneasy at an exchange visit to Fettes in the late eighties by the pupils of an Argentine boarding school, whose parents were, presumably, associated with the fascist regime.[84]

The Cameron family had lived in Argentina for more than half a century, and whilst earlier generations had boarded ships immediately to join the British Army, those at Fettes in the eighties had more divided loyalties. Roderick Cameron, a devout Christian, wrote in 1984 of his feelings about 'I vow to thee, my country', a Fettes favourite, in an article illustrated by G. Lamb with a drawing of an Argentine flag merging into a Union Jack and jet aeroplanes merging into doves:

I first came across this hymn at my prep school in Argentina, where we sang it on Founder's Day and on other important occasions which merited some sort of national anthem. The first words 'I vow to thee, my country' are sufficiently ambiguous to satisfy both the torn allegiance of the British community and the easily offended Argentine national pride…

This is my favourite hymn because it comforts me when I suspect myself of being guilty of what other people call 'narrow-minded selfish national pride'; because it reminds me of my Christian nationality when perhaps I'm getting carried away with my purely 'earthly' feelings; because it makes me think that though I may love my country and you may love yours, and though those two nations may be involved in a bloody war, isn't it wonderful that we may come together in worship, in the fellowship of one Christian nation and in the love of one sole sovereign; because it gives me hope that our petty conflicts may be solved through the 'ways of gentleness' and the paths of peace.[85]

As Ian Gardiner wrote in 2007, the conflict had much more significance than 'two bald men fighting over a comb', because it not only liberated the Falklanders but also showed the USSR that the notion of a 'degenerate, spineless Britain' was wrong – more importantly, Britons' view of their own country's decline was reversed.[86]

The military Fettes of the eighties was, in many respects, a thoroughly different beast from its earlier incarnation, with pieces like this suggesting a greater awareness of the complexity of world affairs. The OTC had been one of the few non-sporting, non-musical games in town when it was founded, but its successor the CCF had many competitors for the pupils' attentions, not least other pupils in skirts and the thrills of the Commodore (computer) Society. For all the changes, though, there were lines of continuity; Lt Corvi and the new RSM, Willie Ross, had taken cadets to the range in 'fairly wet, midge-ridden conditions' and adventurous (formerly, it was noted, arduous) training still taught 'how to cope with the discomfort, people and smells of rough living.'[87]

For all the individualistic decadence of the eighties, these experiences, and the hard fighting of the Falklands, would hardly have been unfamiliar to the last survivors of the original Fettes OTC, and nor would the hardiness of those teenagers who took part in the school's increasingly tough adventures. 'It has been the custom of in the past for each generation to denigrate their successors,' wrote Raymond Scott of the cross-channel swimmers: 'If this team is a sample of the rising generation, we need have no fears for the future. I am very proud to be associated with such as they.'[88]

NOTES

[1] See *Fettesian*, September 1980

[2] Ibid., 1983

[3] Ibid., 1988

[4] See Philp, ch. 8

[5] Ibid., September 1980

[6] Ibid., 1982

[7] Ibid., 1983

[8] Ibid., 1984

[9] Ibid.

[10] *Fettesian*, 1988

[11] Ibid., 1989

[12] Ibid., 1983

[13] Ibid.

[14] Ibid., 1984

[15] Ibid., September 1980

[16] Email to the author, 15 September 2009

[17] *Fettesian*, 1984

[18] Ibid., 1985

[19] Ibid., 1987

[20] Ibid., 1981

[21] Ibid., 1985

[22] Ibid., 1982

[23] Ibid., 1986

[24] Ibid., 1987

[25] Ibid., 1982

[26] Ibid., 1989

[27] Ibid., 1986

[28] Ibid., 1987

[29] Willy Inglis, email to the author, 14 April 2010

[30] *Fettesian*, September 1980

[31] Ibid., 1981

[32] Ibid., 1988

[33] Ibid., 1989

[34] Ibid., 1986

[35] Ibid., 1988

[36] Ibid., 1989

[37] Ibid., 1984

[38] Ibid.

[39] Ibid., 1985

[40] Ibid.

[41] Ibid., 1989

[42] Ibid., 1982

[43] Ibid.

[44] Ibid.

[45] Ibid., 1987

[46] Ibid., 1986

[47] Ibid.

[48] Ibid., 1985

[49] Ibid., 1987

[50] Ibid.

[51] Ibid., 1994

[52] Ibid., 1985

[53] Ibid.

[54] Ibid., 1984

[55] Ibid.

[56] Ibid., 1985

[57] Ibid., 1989

[58] Lawrence & Lawrence, p. 15

[59] *Fettesian*, 1982

[60] Ibid.,

[61] Millar

[62] *Fettesian*, 1984

[63] Francis Salvesen, *Journal of a Student at Arms* (Warrior Enterprises, Bristol, 1989)

[64] Email to the author, 2 January 2010

[65] *Fettesian*, 1982, pp. 4-5

[66] Brig. Ian Gardiner, Interview with Scots at War Trust, 2004 (http://www.scotsatwar .org.uk/printerv/igardiner.htm accessed 25 December 2009)

[67] Lawrence & Lawrence, p. 17

[68] Ian Gardiner, 'Chain of Command', *The Scotsman*, 17 June 2007

[69] Lawrence & Lawrence, p. 18

[70] Gardiner (2007)

[71] Lawrence & Lawrence, p. 29

[72] Gardiner (2006) p. 153

[73] Gardiner (2007)

[74] Gardiner (2004)

[75] Lawrence & Lawrence, pp. 34-5

[76] Ibid., pp. 35-6

[77] Ibid., p. 38

[78] Ibid., p. 39

[79] Millar, op. cit.

[80] *Fettesian*, 1982

[81] Ibid., 1984

[82] Ibid., 1989

[83] Ibid., 1985

[84] Email to the author, 12 November 2009

[85] *Fettesian*, 1984

[86] Gardiner (2007)

[87] Ibid., 1986

[88] Ibid., 1986

Chapter Twenty-One

'Whoops, my cynicism is showing again'

Fettes in the New World Order

Kuwait and the Peace Dividend

After the rhapsodic close to the eighties, with the somewhat unexpected collapse of communism, many expected the nineties to be a decade of peace. However, Fettesians would continue to serve in Northern Ireland, but also return to the Middle East for the first time in decades, and revisit, in the former Yugoslavia, the kind of sinister ethnic politics that a previous generation had uncovered at Belsen. What infuriated many who served in the nineties was the politicisation and parsimony applied to the forces, a process which continues to the present day.

The first of the decade's conflicts was in the Middle East. In 1990, third former Gayle Young was in Saudi Arabia when news came through that Iraq had invaded Kuwait. From her house in Riyadh, Gayle got a close-up view of 'good-looking US Marines' flown in to protect Saudi Arabia, and was amused to see that the locals were 'dumbfounded' by the sight of American female soldiers. Gayle was evacuated in time for the start of term and wrote a report on what she had seen for the *Fettesian* – possibly its first ever 'war story' from a girl.[1]

OF Army medic Ken Millar had had high hopes of the end of the Cold War, and had been looking forward to a pleasant posting in Germany. He had been promoted to Colonel to be the 'boss doctor' in the 3rd Armoured Division, with its Headquarters on the banks of the Möhnesee. Included within the Division were the Royal Scots, 'so old friends appeared once again in the sights of my partying rifle.' He recalls ruefully that:

As we were not at war with anyone, and as the Berlin Wall had suddenly come down, I reckoned I would have a peaceful couple of years in a nice house with lots of non-military things to keep me from doing any proper work. Unfortunately one Saddam Hussein had obviously heard of my plans, and decided that it would be bad for my soul to have any relaxation at all – so he invaded Kuwait. As can be imagined, the decision that the UK was going to participate in his forcible ejection back into Iraq caused a certain upswing in the level of work! Half way through getting the bits of my Division that would be involved in the operation sorted out, I got a call from MOD telling me that I had to get my little pink body across the Channel (by yesterday, if not sooner) as they needed a more senior, post-command, Staff College trained doctor to be the medical whipping boy in the Joint HQ at High Wycombe which was allegedly pulling the whole business together. So away from the nice house and into a Portakabin (occasionally, when I was allowed to sleep) and away from the Bonnie Banks of the Möhnesee to a troglodyte existence some 300 feet underground. I had no sight of daylight at all, as it was midwinter and I started in the bunker at 5.00 am and finished when I had finished – usually not before 8.00 pm.

Although much of what Millar did at High Wycombe was classified, he does write that:

The work was intense, urgent and always carried with it the concern that if we missed out on some small detail, it would be the soldier in the field who would suffer. I did, however, develop (and still retain) a healthy degree of cynicism in relation to the motivation of some military officers and career civil servants in relation to the effective deployment of our Service personnel into harm's way. It was my observation that some (but, I hasten to add, by no means all) had more interest in making personal career moves than ensuring the safety and comfort of those at the sharp end. I never actually made it to the Middle East – I was well and truly stuck in a huge, bombproof, airless hole in the ground in Buckinghamshire.

Several Old Fettesians did serve in Kuwait, including Brig Ian Durie (artillery), Lt-Col C.J. Haig (transport), Maj E.F.R. Scroggie (King's Own Scottish Borderers), Maj R.M.D. Young (Territorial) and Capt P. Macfarlane (Queen's Royal Irish Hussars).[2]

Durie, the third generation of his family to serve and the commander of the Divisional Artillery Group, was a familiar figure at the front as he strode about visiting his men, armed with a traditional Scots cromach (crook) and a powerful personal faith. The task of Durie's gunners – armed both with traditional artillery and the new Multiple Launch Rocket System, known to the troops as the Grid Square Removal System because of its ability completely to destroy everything in a square kilometre – was to deliver the overwhelming firepower which would both support the tank and motorised infantry thrust and shatter the reserve Iraqi units. A devout Christian who later took holy orders, Durie discussed the morality of the events with a magazine several years later:

I was a brigadier, commanding a division of artillery. It was huge and very powerful. It was over a third of the strength of the British division and it must have killed hundreds and possibly thousands of people under my commands. It did seem to me intellectually to be right, but I prayed about it every day once we were in Saudi Arabia, saying, 'Lord, is this right?' One day in answer to that prayer the Lord brought the words of Psalm 131 to my mind: 'I have stilled and quietened you like a weaned child with its mother.' I knew as these words came into my mind that that was the answer to my prayer. God was saying, 'You get on with what you've got to do and I'll get on with what I have to do.' We were about to do something that the British army hadn't attempted since the end of the Second World War: a major offensive with an armed force – and an armed force of a strength and power that nobody had ever handled in battle.[3]

So effective was the onslaught that the Iraqis surrendered in droves – as Capt Macfarlane and the tanks crashed through the enemy lines in the aftermath of the artillery bombardment, one of Maj Scroggie's tasks was to keep order among the vast numbers of prisoners. Justin Holt, having gone through the arduous training necessary to transfer from the Royal Navy to the Royal Marines in 1989-90, was with 40 Commando in Norway when the First Persian Gulf War broke out at the end of 1990. The Marines watched the conflict unfold on television, 'feeling pretty useless' but were soon deployed to Iraqi Kurdistan where their mountain training could be put to good use. Operation Haven was based on what for the British government was a novel idea of providing a humanitarian space for the persecuted Kurds to survive the winter until they could return home. [4]

Whether or not they expected to be sent to the Middle East, young Fettesians still joined the armed forces; Willy Inglis met plenty in the course of the nineties:

I went to Sandhurst in September 1990 and was commissioned into the Scots Guards. Charles MacLean Bristol was at Sandhurst with me – he was a contemporary at Fettes. Many other OFs were in the Scots Guards, including Johnny Clavering and Patrick Gascoigne. Paddy Stewart Blacker joined 5 years after me... I did bump into Justin Holt who had joined the Marines after Fettes while working in Northern Ireland; I met up with Richard Inman in Yorkshire and briefly saw Richard Determeyer and Christopher Butler in Colchester – they were all my vintage at Fettes. I did the Junior Division of Staff College with Johnny Biggart and I also saw Peter MacFarlane briefly in Germany when he was 2ic of the Royal Dragoon Guards.[5]

Once again, here we have Ian Hay's Prince's St on the morning of a rugby international. Despite the continuing enthusiasm of many Fettesians, and the fact that what the first President Bush optimistically called a 'new world order' was obviously shaky, this was the era of the 'Peace Dividend' cutbacks. Her Majesty was expected to do without some of the military resources which had previously defended West Germany from the Red Menace, and the taxpayer would reap rewards in the form of decreased demand from the Treasury. Ken Millar was somewhat cynical about how this impacted on the real work of the forces, especially their medical services. After the Gulf War he returned to Germany to 'manage' the medical 'contribution' to this process:

When I say 'contribution to the Peace Dividend', what I really mean is the piecemeal destruction of the Army Medical Services by the financiers which delivered many of the difficulties extant today – not that we didn't try to point that out at the time, but of course it was seen as far more important to retain the mounted band of the Life Guards and the vast array of other ceremonial accoutrements than it was to ensure that the remaining deployable Army had a viable medical organisation as part of the package – whoops, my cynicism is showing again. No-one had apparently listened to Henry Kissinger when he said: 'The only dividend from peace is peace itself'. Well, they know now. Apart from those matters, while at MOD on this occasion I had much to do with our excursion into the Former Yugoslavia, and the medical support for that expedition – or should I say series of expeditions, as I seemed to be involved in them off and on over the next few years.

Millar's contemporary Ian McCoubrey, a medic with the RAF, had served in the UK and in Germany, Hong Kong, Ascension Island and the USA, serving as senior medical officer on a number of stations and at the RAF College Cranwell, at HQ Strike Command, on the British Defence Staff in Washington, and in the MoD. His experiences in the nineties would drive him out of the RAF:

I was the last commanding officer of Princess Alexandra's RAF Hospital, Wroughton, and coincidentally the last medical officer ever to command an RAF station. I had been sent there to oversee the £33 million expansion under Plan A. Five months into my tour along came Plan B, to close the hospital and station by the end of the following year.

Despite the cutbacks of the mid-90s, I was promoted to Air Commodore after closing Wroughton. However, I believed that the changes resulting from the cuts had made the Defence Medical Services non-viable. The career opportunities had also shrunk significantly. I therefore resigned and sought my fortune elsewhere.[6]

Millar was later to contribute to an increasingly popular aspect of modern military activity, helping to design a Diploma which recognised the peculiar expertise involved in delivering medical assistance in disasters – war, terrorism, industrial accidents, fire, famine, earthquake, tsunami, flood and pestilence. That work evolved into the Diploma in the Medical Care of Catastrophes, in which he remains an examiner today. It also indirectly led to the formation of the Faculty of Conflict and Catastrophe Medicine, and has seen the publication of several books on the subject, to one of which Millar contributed.[7]

This humanitarian aspect of military life was one which the British armed services were increasingly to focus; there is something faintly reminiscent of the imperial Fettesians' reports of bringing football, medicine and justice to remote villages in the BBC's coverage of uniformed personnel helping to reconstruct war zones, help refugees or alleviate the results of natural disasters. As a troop commander in Operation Haven, for instance, Justin Holt found himself as de facto mayor and police chief of part of Iraqi Kurdistan which might suffer from stray marauders from the Republican Guard – a role which would not have been unfamiliar to a district officer or subaltern a hundred years earlier. He found it a 'tremendous' experience; although 40 Commando had not taken part in the hundred-hour war in which Kuwait was liberated, he felt that the Marines were 'doing something equally of value' and got to know the country and Kurds well.

The school looks at war
At Fettes itself during the nineties, the *Fettesian* looked at war almost entirely on a cultural basis; there was relatively little about the specific conflicts of the period. The editor of the *Fettesian* in 1993, whilst accepting that the justifiable transition from a narrow classical curriculum meant that

the Victorian parodies of Tennyson or translations of Greek epics which appeared in the 1880s were no longer submitted for publication, lamented that the modern youth lacked 'the Victorians' obvious enthusiasm for intellectual gymnastics and their desire to see their work in print.'[8]

They certainly weren't writing excitable essays or poems in the grand style eulogising the force of British arms or the glories of the Empire. The 1990 school performance of *Oh What a Lovely War* was both well received and viewed through what was increasingly becoming the standard lens through which the 1914–18 war was refracted. The review reflected the modern interpretation of the Great War as pure tragedy:

Despite raised eyebrows, the school this year put on a production of Oh What a Lovely War. *This musical dealt with various aspects of First World War life, in the High Command, on the Home Front, and in the trenches. Its mocking tone, however, raised the question of whether anything amusing could or should be found in the carnage which produced ten million dead. Yet as the immortal Figaro once said, 'Je me presse de rire de tout, de peur d'obligé d'en pleurer.' (I force myself to laugh at everything, for fear of having to weep.) The musical did highlight the hypocrisy of those in command and showed the stark contrast between playful humour and harsh reality; its use of comic relief intensified rather than trivialised the hardship and the pain.*[9]

The cast discarded the conventional ending and read the 246 names of the school's war dead over a stunned silence. Young literary historians were encouraged to develop their ideas; in 1994 the *Fettesian* carried an essay on the liberation of Auschwitz from the point of view of a soldier in the Soviet Army, a detailed and well-researched piece by fourth-former Zoe Green, and in 1997 it featured a disturbing short story entitled 'A Touch of Evil' about Stalin's childhood. That year's school play, *Agamemnon*, was produced by Brendan Butler (a former paratrooper) and presented through the filter of 1939, with cast in thirties costumes, military uniforms, and white masks in honour of the classical tradition. The production included slide-projection of images of the war interspersed with more recent conflicts in Africa. Reviewer Kirsty Bennett of the sixth form had no doubt as to the effectiveness and importance of what some in the audience found uncomfortable:

The play confronted the horrors and waste of war, which was its aim, and an aim that was certainly fulfilled. The focal point was the Second World War. Despite this happening over fifty years ago, the horrors have not stopped. The world does not seem to have learnt any lessons from the experience – a point that should be openly stressed… Many were offended or upset by the slides and felt that there was an unnecessary dwelling on the disgusting, but we are of course still living in a century where there are people who lost loved ones in the war – surely this is a demonstration of the human tendency to sweep such troubles away and ignore what does not directly affect us.[10]

The *Scotsman* clearly agreed with Kirsty; when the play was taken to the Fringe along with *The Prime of Miss Jean Brodie*, it published an admiring review praising the young actors' 'understanding and power.'[11] Similarly, a trip to the battlefields of the Great War in 1999 prompted reflections of a type which, although by now familiar, would probably have seemed a bit morbid to earlier generations:

The rain spatters down and taps like falling drawing pins on the roof of the bus. Somewhat appropriately, the battlefields and graveyards of northern France are bleakly framed by gathering clouds, driving monstrously over the land where millions of men fought and died for their country. Trudging round a corner brings forth, with spine creeping coldness, the tremendous scale of bloody destruction: desolate uniform ranks; rings of roses hanging on stark, white crosses; not a blade of grass to offend the military order; endless stories behind each of the men that guard their own graves. Nothing distinguishes the thousands of soldiers. Rows and rows that seem to march into the horizon and beyond. Nothing seems to make clear what the fighting and dying was for. Nothing makes sense to me… My great grandfather killed in the Battle of the Somme almost exactly 82 years ago, the forceful reminder of the personal loss initiating a complex mixture of feelings welling up inside me. The endless military formations of white crosses have a greater significance, each apparently anonymous grave symbolizing the life of an individual young man, a brother, a husband and father – their ultimate sacrifice for our freedom and peace. At the going down of the sun, and in the morning, we shall remember them.[12]

The attitudes which led to the magazine's vaguely anti-war tone also found expression in an article published in 1997 which questioned the CCF itself. Upper sixth-former Katherine Shiffner quoted a survey which showed that of 383 pupils, 312 felt they would rather be doing something other than cadets.[13]

As Katherine pointed out, following the Dunblane massacre of 1996, when sixteen pupils and a teacher were killed by a crazed gunman, the idea of an organisation which 'encourages violence' was somewhat suspect. Although she accepted the CCF's argument that it did not exist to 'produce war-mongering adolescents but to train them into a responsible attitude towards war', she pointed out that the 'opportunities' associated with it – camping, the development of leadership qualities and self-awareness, and expeditions to climb mountains – were not intrinsically military. The Ministry of Defence subsidised cadet activities (at the bargain rate for the taxpayer of 0.005% of the armed services budget) but Katherine observed that many of these would go on anyway if the Corps did not exist, and that pupils would enjoy them more because they weren't linked to conscription into a military institution. Jeremy Morris, former cavalry officer turned French master, equally shrewdly observed that 'it is by making the cadets suffer that they learn to empathise with other soldiers.' Officer Commanding Andrew Murray had no objections to the CCF being made voluntary, believing that after an initial decrease in numbers people would soon come back to it, realising it was more fun than any alternative. 'It is not corrupting on the whole because its main aim is to teach pupils to handle power responsibly,' Katherine conceded, 'It certainly is not sexist, because in the past five years three of its under-officers have been female.'

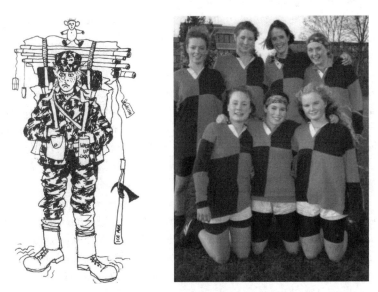

Equality: a female cadet, as depicted in the Fettesian, *and the Fettes team which won Scotland's first recorded schoolgirl rugby match, beating the Academy 17-0*

In fact, the amount of directly military activities outside Fettes available for CCF activities went down with the 'peace dividend' in the nineties, and, apart from the odd trip to British bases in Germany, the cadets stuck to the familiar round of shooting at Bisley, camping at Lochgilphead and climbing in the highlands and islands – all of which were still popular and valued opportunities for many youngsters. The CCF reports in the issue of the *Fettesian* which carried Katherine Shiffner's article were written by her fellow-pupils and were full of enthusiasm. That year's inspecting officer had been accompanied by an old girl, Flt–Lt Elizabeth Holland, who had attended Fettes in the eighties and was a member of the RAF's shooting team. The RAF section had enjoyed camp at RAF Marham, where they flew in Bulldogs and constructed rafts as well as taking part in a night exercise which 'exposed the primitive natures of some.' The Army section's new fourth-formers were delighted to get to wear camouflage uniforms and face-paint, but were less pleased to discover that they were required to wash it off again afterwards. The weekly routine of the CCF continued as it had always done. In 1999, RSM Willie Ross described his job in the school magazine:

In the morning I have to do my security check to make sure everything's still there. The place has been broken into twice when I've been here. The most serious was the break-in at the range when two rifles were stolen. The police tracked them down somewhere in Pilton; they'd been abandoned because the bolts were missing…

If I ever get stressed with my job, it would be on Wednesday afternoons. It's when you plan things to happen and they don't. For example last Wednesday when I asked who didn't want to go on the overnight exercise the number of people who stepped to one side, it was horrendous. What's wrong with them? They've no sense of adventure. You cannot force anyone to do overnight exercise because you can't force anyone to hold or fire weapons. That's totally against the rules!

During a Wednesday afternoon I might encounter any number of dangers. I've been accidentally shot at twice by Fettesians! There's been a few more serious accidents, though. A girl had a cadet G. P. blank shot next to her ear and is deaf in that ear as a result. I go back to the stores at 3.30 on Wednesday and it is a shambles; pullovers and shirts back on the shelves unfolded. Mind you when I was younger I wasn't so law-abiding myself.[14]

Although the amount of equipment available to the CCF had gone down, the increased activity of the armed services in the 'Blair Wars' of the late nineties meant that the military was often in the news and cadets could see it in training for campaigns further afield. At Lochgilphead in 1999, during the Kosovo campaign, the cadets were subject to practice photo-recce flights by the RAF, and air cadets at Brüggen in Germany saw at first hand the preparations for the air war. In 1994, those Fettesians able to avail themselves of the opportunities could dive in the Red Sea or explore the Nepalese jungle. For the school, one of the most meaningful events was the ascent of Mount Fettes in 1995, the school's 125th anniversary. The peak had been named by Charles Douglas, the founder's great-nephew and a somewhat eccentric explorer, who surveyed the mountains and glaciers of New Zealand in the late nineteenth century equipped with little more than a dog, a swag, a pipe (he found heavy smoking no barrier to his activities – his inability to swim was equally irrelevant) and a few books. After paying their respects at his grave, the rather more safety-conscious Fettes team made their way to Alpine Lodge at Christmas Flats, where heavy rain and the narrow-minded attitude of a local restaurant towards the legal drinking age dampened spirits a little. Armed with ice-axes and roped together, they set off up the Zircon Glacier on 2 April, reaching the 8,000 ft peak that same day. Fiona O'Reilly described her experience:

After a couple of hours we eventually reached the bottom of the peak. To this point we had climbed a couple of thousand feet. We had a break for a snack and got ready for the most difficult part – the 150 feet to the summit. I was getting really excited and couldn't believe that we were actually approaching the top.

The climb was now extremely steep so Alex and I were guided up on ropes. Sean would get the rope ready and shout 'On belay' then I would start up after shouting 'Climbing!' The use of our crampons and ice-axes was vital at this point but at least we knew that if we slipped the rope would still hold us up. Progress was very slow and near the top I began to get scared again, not just because of the danger but because of the fear of failing, knowing how important it was to everyone that we make it to the top.

The last 20 feet or so freaked me out. I don't know why – I'm not scared of heights or anything but I just couldn't see anything at all because of the cloud. I was also the last one to climb up and therefore had to undo the slings around the rocks – quite difficult to do when balancing on the edge of a mountain. The final step onto the summit was pure exhilaration – we'd made it! I didn't know whether to laugh or cry. This what all those training weekends were for – a day's climb. But it was an important day's climb.[15]

Like their thirties predecessors, they buried a biscuit tin to mark their presence, and managed to return safely, despite one of the boys managing to drive a crampon into Fiona's leg and the non-appearance of the helicopter which was intended to take them from base camp back to Alpine Lodge (the Fettes flag made a useful point on which to home in when it finally arrived). Although Andrew Murray, Willie Ross and Den Mather were all in attendance, the actual ascent was made by the pupils themselves.

Fettes Peak in New Zealand and the Fettes pupils who climbed it in April 1995

Many of these activities did not come cheap, but the CCF still provided adventure and challenges for the less well off. In that year, Quentin Rae captained the Scottish shooting VIII at Bisley and shot as an Atheling in Canada, where Bruce Benson spent a summer after winning a place on the International air Cadet Exchange. Charlotte Hills parachuted at Netheravon, two naval cadets learned seamanship on the three-masted sailing ship STS *Sir Winston Churchill* (which rammed HMS *Wilton* at Dartmouth), and many air and army cadets got helicopter rides. Shooting remained a major part of the life of the school, and Andrew Murray encouraged piping at camp – Prince Philip was piped in at Cultybraggan by Niall Rowantree, and, in the spirit of Scots warriors (if not modern tactics), a dawn attack was heralded by the pipes. Alison Shanley described the modern CCF camp for the *Fettesian* in 1997:

Day one: departure

Some of the senior NCOs took delight in carrying the sacred SA80s for a precious few seconds; when the highlight of your day is holding a rifle you know that something must be wrong. The enthusiastic cadets marched to the coach, loaded their luggage and looked out of the windows with eager faces; the rest of us fell asleep dreaming of the tortures we had let ourselves in for. Why oh why did I sign up for army camp?

Day two: escape and evasion

I spent the night in a tiny billet listening to other people snoring and watching underwear being thrown across the room in an attempt to wake the snoring culprits. Our first activity was, appropriately, escape and evasion. The thought crossed my mind of escape from the whole idea of camp, running back to Edinburgh and evading being caught. Unfortunately, I was put in charge of a group so it would possibly have noticed if I had disappeared. Every now and again the group stopped to wait for their unfit NCO. I, of course, was slowing down on purpose to ensure that we were not being attacked from behind – it was nothing to do with the fact that I hadn't done any exercise for over two months! The final destination was reached way after all the rest of the groups. But another cadet entertained us by telling us tales of how she had gone skinny dipping in the lake.

Day three: battle techniques; the march and shoot

The RSM told us how to carry out a successful ambush, Mr. Murray educated us on battle drills and formations and Mr. Morris waxed lyrical on how to secure a camp and building bashas. All the while all I could concentrate on was the march and shoot to come. I couldn't run 20m without getting out of breath. How I supposed to run 6km? However I made it to the end and was surprised to find I had enjoyed myself. But if it hadn't been for the encouraging words of my NCO Andrew Clements and the tolerance and patience of the rest of my group, I would've given up long before.

Day four: shooting

The first activity took place in an old converted house. A 'hostage' had been taken and we had to walk through the house spotting and in the 'eliminating' the various terrorists before they shot us. In the second shooting event, we had to walk up the valley firing at targets which suddenly appeared in front of us. In the afternoon we were visited by a brigadier. On the way back the boys decided not to allow girls in the 4-tonner as they were doing some 'male bonding', or rather 'bondage', according to John Alexander's slip of the tongue.

Day five: abseiling and mountain biking

As we set out on our cycling routes we were given various orders, the most important being issued by Mr. Murray: 'Don't cycle into any trees or canals!' We *abseiled off the cliffs and trusted in Mr. Alexander's reassuring words of 'Just step off the cliff' while we looked down at a 30m drop. The hero of the day was Mr. Morris as it took real courage to do an abseil which two years ago had nearly killed him. The last time he was encouraged by the pupils to do an abseil at Lochgilphead he turned upside down and nearly fell out of his harness! This evening we dined in style of the NCOs dinner. Jamie Woodward made an excellent president of the meal, introducing games, rules and forfeits. I dare not mention the name of the two respectable NCOs who were made to stand in the corner, one with a peach in her mouth for letting slip some rather insulting words.*

Day six: overnight exercise

It had been explained to us that a terrorist group rejoicing in the name of the SNOGS were occupying the surrounding reservoirs and driving tourists away. We occupied our area in an old farm and the enemy continued to attack us throughout the night. Overnight was to be our final activity of camp. The next day was spent packing and saying final goodbyes to the clean billets and terrifying drill hall as we well turned-out soldiers marched proudly home.[16]

Modern cadet activities – sub-aqua and
the REME Section

Fettes in the New World Order

Although there had been school trips to the Cold War USSR, the fall of communism opened almost the entire Eastern bloc for easy travel, and Fettes educational visits in the nineties included Prague and, more exotically, Siberia. 'Why waste half your summer holiday in a desolate country full of exiled criminals and unwanted intellectuals?' the intrepid travellers were asked.[17]

The reason, Sarah-Louise Skinner (the first of several sixth-formers to write up Siberian odysseys) recorded, was obvious; to demonstrate Fettesian resilience to appalling food, biting insects, heavy drinking and starkly rugged landscapes. In other respects these trips were presumably different from staying in Scotland. The winners of the Iain Macleod Award (a subsidy for interesting travel) went along the former Iron Curtain in 1991, though to read between the lines of the report is to see none-too-subtle admissions of a vaguely justifiable drinking tour ('we drank in the western atmosphere and large measures of international friendliness'[18]). Old fears died hard; Dr Alla Tsytovich from Russia, speaking to the European Society about the August coup which temporarily overthrew Mikhail Gorbachev, told the assembled throng that she had to be careful about what she said in case there were KGB members present in disguise.[19]

The newly-wealthy of Eastern Europe sent increasing numbers of their children to Fettes; Bulgarians, Romanians and especially Russians were added to the school's already international clientele. This enabled the *Fettesian* to run a series of articles in which pupils from around the world compared various aspects of their home countries with Scotland. In a piece on religion, one cynic from Dubai wrote that Christianity was illegal there. 'Apparently the penalty for being caught is having an arm or finger cut off,' he continued, 'It's not all good, though.'[20]

Interestingly but perhaps not surprisingly, the survey on education showed that study was both more traditional and taken more seriously abroad, with the British system of choice of subjects regarded as odd.[21] Equally unsurprisingly, Scottish food was regarded as unhealthy, bland and stodgy, even by other north Europeans, though one pupil said that Fettes food shared a 'mystical quality' with Polish cuisine – the issue of 'what's actually in it?'[22]

The presence of the Slavs gave the same kind of frisson to the Political Society that Africans had provided in the apartheid era; when Peter Riddell of the Times spoke in the aftermath of one of Tony Blair's military campaigns, he 'tactfully told the Eastern Europeans among the audience that the war in Kosovo was not the result of British propaganda inflating the whole affair and that had the Serbs allowed greater coverage on the ground the media could have given more balanced and factual reports.'[23]

The Fettes European Society (which was originally to be called 'La Societe des Etudes Europeennes', a name rejected as too pretentious) was set up in 1990 for the '1992-minded among us.'[24]

It hosted speakers on the Enlightenment, the French Revolution and the Single Market, though these often had to battle against the school's notorious clanking radiators and the perils of unfamiliar technology (twenty minutes were wasted hunting for an adaptor for a cassette-recorder for a Professor Larkin). Head Girl Camilla Stack spent a year in Novgorod helping to teach English. Like many previous Fettesians, she 'had high hopes of changing the world' but 'came home feeling that I had given rather less than I took away.'[25] Unlike previous generations of young Fettesians who had been to the USSR on school trips, she was able fully to experience the Russian way of life in all its eccentric glory, and was fascinated by national characteristics such as women's obsession with looking like glamorous soap opera stars and the 'unlimited hospitality' which 'puts us Brits to shame.'

Soldiers who had spent decades looking at the communist countries through gunsights suddenly found themselves visiting them. Ken Millar, based from the mid-nineties in Chester with HQ, Army Medical Services (Territorial Army) was one of those British officers who was sent to Eastern Europe to assessing the readiness or otherwise of the armies there to join NATO – 'I think my name probably came up in the pub the Generals drink in.' He was posted to Romania with the usual badinage about watching out for Dracula, avoiding going out at night and carrying garlic, which he countered with a serious demeanour and an absolute conviction that what he had been tasked with was a highly important matter and not to be joked about. 'That, of course, was just my own grandiosity and pomposity,' he admits, 'I should have been sensible enough to realise that I was merely being sent to demonstrate a willingness to look – the decision to admit Romania or otherwise (at that time) having almost certainly already been made, and definitely not being dependant on their ability to demonstrate that they could deliver shining examples of field medical care (or otherwise).'

However, despite his rejection of all the Bram Stoker allusions, he was met at Bucharest Airport by one Colonel Vlad, 'who certainly looked as if he could have been a descendant of the Impaler of that name' and made an unasked detour to visit 'Dracula's Castle'. As if this was not odd enough, his interpreter, a Lieutenant Colonel, 'insisted on holding my hand at every available opportunity, and fluttering his eyelashes at me' which Millar decided to accept as a local custom. What Millar witnessed in Romania hardly inspired him to fast-forward the country's application to the 'big boys' club' even had that been the real purpose of his mission:

It had not been many years since Ceausescu had been ousted, and the evidence of the Communist ethos was everywhere. Urbanisation, with ghastly utilitarian concrete boxes, had been the message, which had resulted in the virtual destruction of traditional rural villages. Ceausescu's vast palace dominated the centre of Bucharest, of course. The levels of pollution were extreme; all the rivers seemed to consist of viscous brown liquid, there was a permanent level of smog, and bed sheets and towels were grey, rather than white after laundering in the said polluted water. The extremes of material wealth were also very evident; large black Mercedes with deeply tinted windows flashing past on one side of the road while oxcarts driven by what can only be described as peasants crawled at the other showed the inevitable capitalist (and probably criminal) reaction to years of totalitarian rule.

Romanian pupils would soon be at Fettes – some whose parents were eyewitnesses to and even participants in the revolution – as the country modernised. The school itself plunged enthusiastically into the post-imperial international outlook. In the mid-nineties, Fettes also set up a link with the Ying-Hao School in Guangdong, China, which saw a stream of diligent mathematics enthusiasts head west, and, along with the influx of eastern Europeans, necessitated the development of English as a Foreign Language. A more localised exchange was conducted with Fettes' modern comprehensive neighbour Broughton, which whose pupils relations were not always very good. Alison Warner of Broughton wrote an analysis of the differences between the schools for the Fettesian, and observed that, whilst much was similar, Fettes' rules (for instance on contact between the sexes) seemed to her very old-fashioned, the power of prefects 'an unsettling experience and hard to accept' and the restricted boarding school lifestyle, with obedience to rules on smoking, drinking and curfew-breaking strictly enforced, rather odd. As she perceptively pointed out, 'discipline is one of the reasons why parents pay large sums of money to send their children to Fettes' but just as many pupils there were misbehaving in the usual teenage fashion as they were at Broughton.[26]

Many principals of independent schools must wish they could broadcast this obvious fact from the rooftops, but the bourgeois fantasy that thousands of pounds can purchase the virtue and innocence of children persists to this day. Sarah Winter and Gillian Burns, who went from Fettes to Broughton, found the latter relaxed, friendly and well-equipped. It was probably coincidental that their piece appeared alongside an article by a pupil from the Outer Hebrides, which noted that alcohol was a national problem and that schoolchildren on Lewis were worse than their Edinburgh equivalents, stashing bottles of vodka in cisterns to keep themselves in a reality more pleasant than driechness relieved only by midges.

In an interesting blast from the school's Corinthian past, fourth-former Louise Lamont won the Young Sportswriter of the Year competition organised by the *Daily Record* with a rousing open letter to Malcolm Bradbury, who had recently condemned the media's obsession with the cult of the body.[27] She wittily and knowledgeably defended the role of sport in society, despite by her own admission being 'someone who would rather watch TV than walk to the shops.' Some of her points might have come as a bit of a surprise to the school's Victorian athletes – the thought of female Rangers fans at Fettes pining for Ally McCoist in tartan shorts would probably have caused Clem Cotterill spontaneously to combust – but in general Louise was a chip off the big Fettes block.

We can learn from their strengths and reflect the acceptance of authority, discipline and tolerance most people in sport display. It may teach some to abide by the rules when Ooh-ah Cantona is sent off the pitch for foul play. When we see Krajicek and Sampras jog up to the net and shake hands, despite one having just beaten the other, we might try to be better winners or (in my case) losers, the next time we land on the hotel in Mayfair. Sport in this way is needed by our population who are constantly scolded for their poor morals. It is certainly needed more than heated debates on early Vorticism.

The *Fettesian* also carried an interesting analysis of the schoolboy rebel without a cause: 'nobody ever understands them, so they must spend their time explaining themselves to people who don't want to know and trying to get themselves recognised.'[28] The piece concluded that:

The rebels are an essential part of society, for without them we would never be made aware of our own obvious character weaknesses. Who else is going to point out the flaws in Fettesian society and make clear exactly what we are doing wrong? Without these realistic, intellectual, tragically misunderstood and generally superior pupils, Fettes might collapse under the strain of all the rest of us and our superficial incomprehension.

More than one Fettesian of sixties vintage would have seen this as a reasonable enough description of the young Tony Blair. A school play in 1998, *From Fettes With Love*, combined the Bond epic with Tony Blair's rise to power and a host of female pupils clad in improvised chocolate-and-magenta bikinis. This did not mean that the school was a political hotbed; although its Amnesty International group was going strong, most pupils weren't members, and when asked in a survey why this was 'girls tended to look rather guilty and offer some kind of justification, whilst the boys preferred not to think about the problem. Their response was inevitably "Dunno."'[29]

Fettesians and the Peace Process

One of the great achievements of the nineties was the slow and painful crawl towards peace in Northern Ireland. After his time in Kurdistan, Justin Holt joined other OFs, mostly infantry officers, serving there, just before the IRA and CLMC ceasefires of 1994. He remembered that the paramilitaries were 'still a worthy adversary' with whom a 'cat and mouse game' was frequently played. His Royal Marines performed some of the more exotic tasks of the conflict, boarding suspect vessels in Carlingford and Belfast Loughs, secretly swabbing the decks of fishing-boats owned by known 'players' to pick up explosive residues, conducting 'hot extractions' of compromised troops and lurking offshore at night to watch the homes of questionable individuals. At his disposal were the fast patrol launches *Grey Fox* and *Grey Wolf*, which carried radar and could move at 30 knots. On a night patrol on Lough Neagh Holt realised that *Grey Wolf* was being slowly circled by the bailiff boat of the Lough Neagh Fishermen's Co-operative Society. He sent several Marines out in an inflatable to get in behind the bailiff boat and board it from the rear, which they duly did, returning with the appropriate form signed by the boardees certifying that the operation had been conducted with all due concern for legal procedures. Rather to his surprise, Holt found himself repeatedly summoned to see his superiors and tell the story of what happened; Fr Oliver Kennedy, leader of the fishermen, was apparently outraged at the Marines' improper actions, but Holt had seen nothing untoward and was mystified. Only much later, whilst having a drink in Poole with some of the men who had been there that night, did he discover that the boarding party had put the bailiff boat's crew down on the deck with guns at their heads and warned them in no uncertain terms not to give the Royal Marines any trouble on the Lough.

What the public, and many serving soldiers, did not realise at the time was that the paramilitaries had been looking for ways out of their pointless conflict. Although Sinn Fein would later claim that their strategy, formulated in the late eighties and early nineties, was to pursue peace, this was probably not out of any sense of altruism or achievement. A united Ireland was – thanks in large part to the antics of Irish republicans – further away than ever. The British government could not be seen to be giving in to terrorists, the loyalists were more, not less opposed to unity than they had been in 1969, and the Irish Republic, roaring ahead as a model European economy, had no desire to be saddled with a million and a half people with no apparent redeeming features. As the Roman Catholic community in Northern Ireland sickened of the conflict, the votes won by the IRA's political wing fell to 78,921 in 1992 – only ten per cent, and Gerry Adams, godfather of West Belfast, lost his seat. Southern Irish Catholics, with whom Sinn Fein and the IRA hoped to unite, had ceased bothering to conceal their distaste for the criminality of some of their Northern cousins, and opinion polls showed that Irish unity was not considered an important issue. The military situation had also become distinctly unfavourable; penetrated by British intelligence, many republican attacks were being aborted, and when the IRA succeeded in mounting an attack, as at Enniskillen or Warrington, the response, even among many die-hard nationalists, was revulsion. Meanwhile, working-class loyalists' increasingly vindictive revenge attacks on republican communities – which were cynically 'justified' with reference to 'Bomber' Harris' terrorising of German civilians in the Second World War – made many question whether or not the 'patriot game' was worth it.

The ceasefires of 1994 were followed by a jerky pantomime in which the British and Irish governments, the White House, the Northern Irish political parties and the paramilitaries attempted to hammer out some kind of deal. Although the initial credit must go to the premier of that time, John Major, there is no doubt that the British politician most associated with the peace process was Tony Blair.

That Tony Blair would occupy 10 Downing St was not always as obvious as his cheerleaders in the media subsequently claimed. As late as 1993, Dr John Curtice could tell the Political Society that a Labour victory was 'possible' but the party still had to overcome the weakening of their electoral base and 'their image of incompetence.' In 1991 the *Fettesian* carried interviews with Tony Blair and Tilda Swinton, both conducted by the enterprising Imogen Gassert. She enjoyed the then Labour Employment spokesman's cheeky frankness about his schooldays, and was impressed by his diplomatic stance on public schools – though he was indeed to look at their charitable status once in power, as he admitted in the interview – and self-deprecating comment that a recent assessment of him as 'the brightest of a new generation' in Parliament was 'a terrible exaggeration'.

Themes which would become prominent when he became leader of his party in 1994 were already in evidence. The 'New Age' man who made time for his children and wanted to see more women in politics, the impatience with amateurism in British business and in Parliament, the casual clothes, the relaxed, reasonable approach which led a staunchly Tory member of the Political Society to comment that if the rest of the 'Labour crowd' were like this they might be all right – all came out in the 1991 visit to his alma mater.[30] (Blair also got a flattering large photograph with his interview – but then so did Shona Mackilligin, a sixth-former who won a *Cosmopolitan* competition to become a model, a career she didn't pursue as she wanted to be a lawyer[31]).

Blair' predecessor as Labour leader, John Smith, gave a very well-received talk to the Political Society in 1994; a letter confirming a follow-up interview for the school magazine arrived on the day his death was announced. Mark Peel, the Head of Politics, wrote the only obituary ever to appear in the *Fettesian* of someone who had been neither pupil nor teacher at the school, noting:

The overwhelmingly favourable reaction that his visit engendered among young and old alike helps to explain the universal sense of grief that greeted the news of his passing. In their lamentations for the lost leader the British public have shown that for all the efforts of the political image makers, their attachment to men of vision and depth remains cast iron. It is a lesson that we at Fettes would do well to pay heed to as we endeavour to prepare future generations for a higher calling.[32]

Of Scotland's famous schools, only Glasgow High had educated Prime Ministers – the rather short-lived Campbell-Bannerman and Bonar Law. All this changed in May 1997 and Fettes gave a cautious welcome to the new PM, with Ralph McClelland and Katherine Shiffner writing in the *Fettesian*:

As it will be well-night impossible for you not to know, this year an OF was elected with an overwhelming majority. 'Tony' seems to be distinctly lukewarm about his private school background in spite of the favourable publicity that Fettes has received in his name. But does the school influence its pupils' futures as much as its pupils' futures influence the school?... The prospect of a demon-eyed Mr Blair turning Fettes College into a state-run educational commune is not one we need to worry about (at least, not until he is re-elected in five years' time).[33]

A survey carried out by Zoe Green for the *Fettesian* suggested that the new Prime Minister was quite popular; 47 per cent of pupils questioned said they would have voted Labour in the 1997 elections, though 19 per cent were unaware that they had won it. Although unable to identify senior Tories David Mellor and Malcolm Rifkind, most pupils knew who Gerry Adams and Alex Salmond were.[34]

Answering a questionnaire on wider aspects of life, many pupils predictably named Nelson Mandela as the politician who inspired them most, though Blair got some support for his 'boyish charms' and one wag said he liked John Major, who 'cured my insomnia.' The school's mock election, however, saw a convincing win for the Conservatives; this was gleefully reported by the *Sunday Telegraph*, which announced 'Blair school set for Tory Landslide.'[35]

It was noted that the Assisted Places Scheme, which Blair was pledged to abolish, helped 8 per cent of Fettes pupils, and it was this which counted against him more than anything else. The 'Vive-La' jocularly focused on one of Blair's highly-embellished schoolboy tales:

> *The news has gone out from Cape Wrath to Cape Finisterre*
> *That Britain has got a Fettesian Prime Minister*
> *As a schoolboy his life was a series of dramas*
> *But don't mention that business about the Bahamas.*[36]

Headmaster Malcolm Thynne (himself a reformer) was unstinting in his praise; speaking on Founder's Day, he put Blair in the context of his distinguished Fettes political predecessors and told the assembled pupils and parents that 'the remarkable achievement of Tony Blair in pushing ahead with the modernisation of the Labour Party and in becoming Prime Minister in a landslide victory is a matter of great pleasure and pride for the whole school.'[37]

Blair devoted an enormous amount of time to trying to solve the problems of Northern Ireland, and now that the lustre of his early success has faded it is all too easy to forget what an extraordinary impact he had, thanks in part to the 'creative ambiguity' which is now held against him. The public-school charm and messianic zeal were turned on the squabbling politicians of the province over a decade of breakthroughs and false starts. Blair made his position clear from the start; Unionists need not fear a united Ireland in their lifetimes, but republicans were welcome to talk to him if they behaved themselves. Blair's breezy style was more popular in Ulster than the patrician grandeur of the Conservatives, although some Unionists were uncomfortable with 'the way he keeps grinning all the time' and were disconcerted by the even greater informality of Mo Mowlam, his Northern Ireland Secretary. Their Good Friday Agreement of 1998 represented an enormous breakthrough, providing a platform on which to build a workable future. It was undermined by Sinn Fein's inability to abandon their old habits, or, more importantly, their weapons; in 2006, David Trimble, who felt London concessions to Sinn Fein had led to his party's destruction by Ian Paisley's Democratic Unionists, criticised this aspect of the peace process at the Fettes Political Society.[38]

Trimble's resignation as First Minister in protest over this issue had been organised through the offices of Old Fettesian Sir Josias Cunningham (Sir Knox's nephew). As Unionist President, Sir Josias – universally respected as an honourable and moderate figure – persuaded his party that the power-sharing devolved coalition could be tolerated because the republicans would behave themselves, and persuaded Blair to suspend it when it emerged that they couldn't. Old Fettesian General John de Chastelain would ultimately supervise the decommissioning of terrorist weapons; in an interview with the school magazine, lavishly illustrated with photos of the loyalist murals which impressed the pupils when they visited Ulster, he explained the difficulties with his role:

Our task is to attempt to verify the decommissioning of paramilitary arms. That has involved, first of all, attempting to gain the confidence of each of the paramilitary groups with which we deal. We've had to convince them that what we do will be fair and will be seen to be so, and that the act of decommissioning will be conducted in such a way as not to imply surrender or defeat – since no-one's surrendered and no-one's been defeated.[39]

The general was to be immortalised in the 1998 'Vive-la' – long before his mission was accomplished:

I'm bass, I'm soprano; together we're charming
And just like de Chastelain we're very disarming.[40]

Tony Blair, as seen in the Fettesian *in 1991, and John de Chastelain at Founder's Day in 1995*

Decommissioning was a slow and painful process, costing Trimble dearly and causing Blair enormous frustration. His position was hardly helped when the political parties of the Irish Republic announced that they would not, following their general election, form a coalition with Sinn Fein, who they regarded as a bunch of fanatical northern criminals, and declared a cordon sanitaire of the type used in Belgium against the extremist Vlaams Blok. If their fellow Catholic-nationalists in the Republic they aspired to join were unwilling to work with Sinn Fein, Blair was going to have his work cut out persuading the Protestant Unionists they had spent thirty years shooting at to do so. Yet within a year of the Fettes Political Society meeting at which Trimble understandably condemned Blair's over-flexibility, the Prime Minister had made progress again.

As politics lecturer and Trimble adviser Professor Paul Bew put it, 'Once again, when we thought the old maestro was fading, his capacity to seduce, politically speaking, is phenomenal.' Ian Paisley, the 'abominable no-man' had been cajoled into sharing power with Martin McGuinness. Blair spent his Christmas holidays on the phone to Paisley (with whom he discussed religious issues in a way no previous leader could) and the republicans, who had finally decommissioned their weapons in 2005.

The British Army formally ended Operation Banner, its military deployment in Northern Ireland, in 2007, although unrest still sporadically erupted. Old Fettesian Caroline Graham-Brown was one of the last to be deployed there, in her first posting as an officer in the REME. As Battalion Group Engineer for 2 Royal Regiment of Fusiliers in Belfast, she had responsibility for the Ardoyne Shop Fronts – 'a nasty area indeed, and we saw many a riot there.'[41] She was also site commander for a number of hilltop watchtower demolitions, which she described as 'a great experience.' The removal of these strange metal 'castles' which peppered the border badlands was one of the great images of the end of the conflict.

Blair's Wars

Ulster peacemaking apart, Blair would, in fact, go down in history for having taken Britain to war more often than any Prime Minister for decades, and other Fettesians would be there, as they always had been, in uniform. Unlike the previous political high achievers, Blair had had no contact with the armed services; even the pacifist Sir John Simon had joined the Royal Flying Corps in 1917, and the Tory OFs had excellent war records. Tony Blair had disapproved of the Corps and his long-haired rock-star ambitions at Oxford were not those of a traditional Fettesian, whilst the Labour policies on which he was originally elected in 1983 were deeply anti-military.

Blair's intellectual justifications for his shift from pacifist to war leader would have been surprisingly familiar to the Victorians, rooted as they appeared to be in a sense of progress and duty. The late twentieth century version of this idea, known in America as neoconservatism, was a breezily confident philosophy based on the notion that the future had been seen, and it worked. Such a republic of virtue was a template for all mankind and could, indeed should, be exported using the righteous might of the US armed forces. As he formed his own opinions, the post-Fettes Tony Blair was surely unaware of the debates of the American right-wing literary intelligentsia, yet he was to become their European poster boy. Just as many American 'neocons' had started off as post-war radicals, then became disillusioned with the failures of a society which appeared to lack the internal cohesion and international confidence to survive, so too Blair was to reject almost all of the policy platform on which he was first elected in Michael Foot's Labour Party. A Fettesian of the fifties, Norman Cameron, noted that:

The idea that such a place would produce a very successful Labour Prime Minister would have seemed fantasy in 1959. Of course, what he did to the Labour Party's policies would also have seemed like fantasy, though much more consistent with attitudes of Fettes parents!

Most significantly for his foreign policy, Blair rejected the guilt-ridden left-wing mantra about British imperialism. 'Century upon century it has been the destiny of Britain to lead other nations,' he told a meeting in Manchester during the 1997 election campaign, 'We are a leader of nations or nothing.'[42]

Like Orwell, he wanted to reclaim the Union Jack for the left, and, having shorn British nationalism of its embarrassing racialist components, restore a sense of positive patriotism and purpose. An early Fettesian of liberal imperialist leanings would have found surprisingly little in Blair's vision with which to disagree. As a rebel in his schooldays against what he (like many others) saw as Fettes' reactionary fustiness, Blair could legitimately argue that he wanted a world in which freedom genuinely reigned, and was frequently frustrated by the left's idea that leaving dictatorial regimes to get on with bullying their own people was a progressive position. Like Mrs Thatcher, with whom he shared a remarkably wide range of ideas, Blair had been appalled by what was widely seen as the cynical pragmatism displayed by the Tories during the Bosnian war of the early nineties. On a visit to Yugoslavia in the late seventies, Sir Sandy Glen was told by an old partisan general that Tito had recently said 'there is no party and soon there will be no country.' Glen had proof of this when Milosevic – to whom he referred, along with Croatia's Tudjman, as 'evil' – invited him in the eighties to the unveiling of a memorial to the Chetnik leader Mihailovic. Although Glen felt Milhailovic had been let down in some respects by the British, he refused to attend on the grounds that 'this was the formal rebirth of a Greater Serbian creed.'[43]

He was not happy to be proved right when, as communism waned, Milosevic and Tudjman whipped up nationalist passions, war broke out and 'ethnic cleansing' became the latest euphemism for mass murder. As the Serbs, closely followed in murderousness by the Croats, slaughtered, raped and robbed all around them, the west played for time or bleated platitudes. With the terrible object lesson of the Srebrenica massacre of 1995 in mind, Blair was determined that Britain would, wherever possible, intervene to prevent such atrocities recurring.

In 1997, Maj Jeremy Morris, who after a career in the armed forces now ran modern languages at Fettes and was adjutant of the CCF, 'was asked to volunteer for Bosnia just after the Dayton Peace Accords were signed, because a lot of multi-national formations were being used, and there was a requirement for linguists to act as liaison officers (low-octane Edward Spears).'[44]

In the former Yugoslavia, he served at the British base in Banja Luka (the 'capital' of the Republika Srpska) and later acted as liaison officer to the French Division Salamandre at Mostar. One of the most tragic towns in Bosnia, Mostar was attacked by the Serbs, which was agony enough, but its Croats treacherously turned upon their Bosniak neighbours and intensive close-quarter fighting killed thousands, smashed an ancient cultural gem and sent the historic bridge tumbling into the Neretva river. 'Bits of it were fascinating, some was hairy and vile; a lot was boring and the food was memorably disgusting,' wrote Maj Morris. In his time there, the two remaining ethnic factions (the Serbs had been pushed out by this point) conducted noisy demonstrations with women and children to the fore so that any trigger-happy types on the other side would hand them a propaganda victory. The Croats took advantage of the Muslim custom of burying the dead quickly by booby-trapping cemeteries and even graves with explosives. 'I came back here in Jan '98,' wrote Morris, 'and it took me some time to get back to normal.'

Because of the well-attested horrors of Bosnia, Blair was one of the driving forces in forcing action in Kosovo in 1999, when the Serb armed forces were driven out from a region they saw as their spiritual homeland but which was, inconveniently, largely inhabited by Albanian-speakers. Given what the Serbs had done to the relatively innocuous Bosniaks, a terrible purge of the widely-disliked Albanians was only too possible; the net result of Blair's involvement was the creation of a new Republic of Kosovo, in effect a colony of the UN and EU. He – unlike the nervous Bill Clinton, who hoped the whole thing might be dealt with by air strikes, or better still just go away – was convinced that it was the threat of a ground invasion which called the bluff of Serbian leader Slobodan Milosevic.[45]

British forces were also sent into Sierra Leone and supported President Clinton in Operation Desert Fox, the 1998 punishment raids on Iraq. Justin Holt, by now a major, was involved at a staff level in the planning for British interventions in East Timor, Sierra Leone and Kosovo, and other OFs such as Matthew Wells were posted all over the world. The Fettesian in uniform might no longer be patrolling an empire, but the one-time cheeky schoolboy in Downing St would still send him or, increasingly, her, overseas to show the flag in the cause of national honour and international progress.

Fettes in the New Scotland

One of Blair's changes was not widely anticipated in the early nineties. The Political Society was told in 1992 (by Alex Salmond, no less) that Scotland as yet lacked the confidence to govern itself [46], and in 1993 that Scottish devolution was impossible (admittedly by Lord Fraser, a Tory peer). [47] As the decade closed, the entire Celtic Fringe had been devolved. Louise Lamont, by 1999 in the fifth form, wrote an essay for the Scottish Office at the time of the devolution referendum. If she was any measure, Fettes was ablaze with political excitement:

There is a girl in my dormitory who worships the Scottish National Party (a close second in her favorite topics of conversation after her private theories about Area 51. While the non-Scottish girls are rehearsing their proposals to Leo or deciding whether they should put that grey cardigan over that top, she is writing to the SNP women's forum or fixing posters of Sean Connery about her bed. Whether the faith she puts in devolution is justified or not, what can be universally admired by others is her keen interest in Scotland's recent momentous events and her determination to understand how devolution will affect her in the future…

The growing awareness of national identity among my generation, aroused less appropriately by Hollywood rather than by political manifestos, and the pride we can take from the knowledge that Scotland is not a land of haggis-scoffing, whisky-swigging, eightsome-reeling, orange wig-wearers are touching emotions one would be hard pressed to uncover in any other nations' children. Of course it is easier to influence children who are begging to be filled with opinions and cynics might claim this is simply brainwashing used by fading adults, just to throw the torch to others before they die. But we do have the capacity to decide what we believe in, and many choose to support and identify with Scotland rather than seek employment elsewhere. This means we could support or oppose devolution and independence depending on what we believed was best for Scotland. This strong national identity and pride is a potential long lasting fuel and power for Scotland (lead free, naturally) as we, the future administrative makeup of a new and uncertain Scotland, bear responsibility for our nation and need to be driven by an overwhelming love of our country (not one which fringes on racism or xenophobia) to cultivate a confidence that will drive Scotland through the millennium and into its unknown but exciting future.[48]

NOTES

[1] *Fettesian*, 1990

[2] *Industria*, 1991

[3] Jenny Taylor, 'Lethal Compassion', *ThirdWay*, September 2003

[4] In conversation with the author, June 2010

[5] Email to the author, 14 April 2010

[6] Email to the author, 18 December 2008

[7] A. Hopperus Buma et al., eds. *Conflict and Catastrophe Medicine – A Practical Guide* (London, Springer, 2009) 2nd Ed.

[8] *Fettesian*, 1993

[9] Ibid., 1990

[10] Ibid., 1994

[11] Quoted in Ibid., 1994

[12] Ibid., 1999

[13] Ibid., 1997

[14] Ibid., 1999

[15] Ibid., 1995

[16] Ibid., 1997

[17] Ibid., 1992

[18] Ibid., 1992

[19] Ibid., 1992

[20] Ibid., 1996

[21] Ibid., 1995

[22] Ibid., 1997

[23] Ibid., 1999

[24] Ibid., 1990

[25] Ibid., 1996

[26] Ibid., 1993

[27] Ibid., 1998

[28] Ibid., 1999

[29] Ibid., 1998

[30] Ibid., 1991

[31] Ibid., 1998

[32] Ibid., 1994

[33] Ibid., 1997

[34] Ibid.

[35] Quoted in Ibid.

[36] Ibid.

[37] Ibid.

[38] Ibid., 2006

[39] Ibid., 2002

[40] Ibid., 1998

[41] Email to the author, 21 June 2010

[42] Quoted in Con Coughlin, *American Ally: Tony Blair and the War on Terror* (New York, HarperCollins, 2006) p. 7

[43] Glen (2002) p. 155

[44] Jeremy Morris, email to the author, 9 November 2009

[45] See Coughlin, Ch. 4

[46] *Fettesian*, 1992

[47] Ibid., 1993

[48] Ibid., 1999

Chapter Twenty-Two

'A pimple on the enormous American military bottom'

Fettes Warriors in the New Century

We emerged from a meeting to discover the world had changed
The 1993 'Vive-la', referring to the school's attempt to recruit new
pupils from the Middle East, had mentioned a peril not unfamiliar to
Victorian OFs, revived by the Rushdie affair and the aftermath of the
first Gulf War:

> *In search of new pupils – well-mannered, not rowdy,*
> *The Headmaster's off to the prep schools of Saudi*
> *Though to sign up the son of a sheikh can't be bad,*
> *A suspension might cause an Islamic Jihad.*[1]

Also in the early nineties, Tam Dalyell MP told the Political Society that
the war in Kuwait had been misguided because it had not addressed the
real issues, and had, indeed, exacerbated the problems of the region.[2]

A variety of attacks and protests through the nineties had kept these
issues in the public eye, but this did not diminish the shock value of what
was about to happen. On 11 September 2001 Chris Collister, a new
member of staff at Fettes, was called into the Common Room to see the
unfolding events in New York on the television normally used for sports
broadcasts. Headmaster Michael Spens was preparing for a meeting of
the Senior Management Team when Deputy Head Judy Campbell – a
New Yorker – came in and told him that an aeroplane had hit one of the
twin towers. Thinking it had been an accident, they went ahead with the
meeting, only to emerge, as the Headmaster put it, 'to discover that the
world had changed.' (In retrospect, he pondered if perhaps they might
have been more sensitive to Mrs Campbell, who was presumably
wondering what on earth was happening to her home city.) Rosha
Fitzhowle, later one of the most talented singers of her generation at
Fettes, a primary school child at the time, remembers a football match on

television being interrupted in time for the second aircraft crash and the towers' collapse, much to the bewilderment of the watching children. Tasos Aidonis, the Resident Tutor in Carrington House, remembered that one boy was exulting that the American capitalists had had their come-uppance, 'but he wasn't a Muslim, he was just a bit strange.' Much of the school was glued to the news for around 24 hours, but it quickly emerged that there were no friends or relations among the dead or missing. Head of Politics Mark Peel spoke about the attacks in a chapel address which concluded:

Thus as the trumpet sounds once again, let our prayer be that the battle is not only against the terrorists, but also against the hand that feeds them. For it is only by fighting poverty and injustice, and extending the ideal of freedom to the downtrodden in Africa and Asia, that Isaiah's vision of a new city emerging from the rubble to become a beacon for the world can be well and truly fulfilled.[3]

Britain had already experienced a surreal horror that year; the outbreak of foot and mouth disease on the country's farms in February saw the deployment of the armed forces to assist the Ministry of Agriculture, Fisheries and Food in a mass cull of tens of thousands of animals. In his last operational responsibility before he retired, Ken Millar was 'head of shed' for the military medical cover as the countryside lit up with the slaughtered livestocks' funeral pyres:

Much of this job involved ensuring that the unpleasant environment in which many very young Service personnel could be working had the least possible effect on their health. Such problems as the possibility of infectious abortion had to be borne in mind with a young and fecund population suddenly working on farms; the effect the sights, sounds and smells of mass destruction of animals could have on mental health; the many other infectious diseases connected with farm animals and the nature of the farmyards, not all of which were necessarily icons of good hygiene practice. And, of course, I had to spend quite a lot of time convincing the great and the not very good that Foot and Mouth disease was not per se a health risk to human handlers. So the only time in my service that I actually dealt with the huge numbers of dead which might have been expected had World War Three erupted was right at the end — and they were cattle and sheep!

Funeral pyres and terrorism apart, Fettes had entered the new century with an optimistic host of innovations, many of which were pushed

845

forward by the modern-minded Headmaster Michael Spens. In 2000 it was announced that a sports centre-cum-health club was to be built and an eight-day timetable introduced; a few years later the International Baccalaureate was introduced (more or less divorcing the school from the entire Scottish assessment system) and Craigleith, a specialised boarding-house for the upper sixth, was erected on the former site of the CCF huts. These changes affected the life of the school in a variety of ways, chiefly by reinforcing cosmopolitan feel which had been developing for decades and especially since the end of the Cold War. Although there were those who worried that the various changes would break down the vertical pillars which held the school together and that ancient institutions such as the CCF might suffer. In practice, this did not happen; whilst there was a noticeable decline in certain aspects of Fettes' military culture, others revived and were even strengthened, partly because of events in the outside world.

'Army Barmy'

Fettes' increased interest in military life was undoubtedly based on a general trend in British popular culture; it was noticed that 'army barmy' teenage boys once again knew the difference between a Sten gun and an MP40, thanks to the spread of computer games about the Second World War such as *Call of Duty* and *Medal of Honor* (themselves based on films such as *Saving Private Ryan*) which took the place of seventies war comics in instructing the young. Plays at Fettes regularly revisited the past: *Fear and Misery in the Third Reich*, *Ring Around the Moon* and, once again, *Journey's End*. The First World War became a popular part of the third-form history curriculum, especially in the lessons where old rifles and helmets were dug out. Unlike British society in general, which often lived in ignorance of Armistice Day (a *Daily Express* report in November 2000 suggested that between 25 and 50 per cent of teenagers had no idea what it was, some imagining that it was connected to Guy Fawkes[4]) Fettes never ceased to honour both its dead and its veterans, and to educate the present generation about war. However, the military heritage was given much greater prominence in the twenty-first century.

To take one year as an example, in 2003 a plaque was unveiled in the school chapel to honour Lt Hector Maclean, the OF who won a posthumous Victoria Cross on the North-West Frontier. After an address by Andrew Murray, the Officer Commanding of the CCF, the Very Rev Dr James Harkness, a Fettes Governor and former Church of Scotland

Moderator and Chaplain-General to HM Forces, dedicated the plaque in prayer with the words: 'May all who look on this memorial in days to come find new faith in their God and King, and new strength for their duty to Him, their Queen and their Country.'[5]

A 'Fettes Pals' Battalion' of pupils visited the Western Front, where the muddy trenches and claustrophobia-inducing dugouts of Sanctuary Wood were very popular (some pupils complained that their clean shoes were getting dirty – 'how long would *they* have lasted?' asked *Fettesian* reporter Oliver Hunt scornfully). The pupils conducted a quiet ceremony after the Menin Gate Last Post, laying a wreath and reading the Act of Remembrance. Oliver, who found the whole experience deeply moving and was impressed with the 'magnificent and highly emotive' memorials, hoped that 'the names on the walls of the Menin Gate would approve of what I was asked to read out.'[6]

Alastair Armstrong organised a trip to Berlin, visiting sites associated with the Third Reich and the Cold War – which for twenty-first century pupils were almost as distant as the trenches of 1914. It was noticeable that whilst the *Fettesian* reports of these trips (written by pupils aged 13 or 14) were dignified, sensitive and well-written, they lacked any sense of triumph – in keeping with attitudes to war in contemporary Britain. Indeed, Oliver Hunt said of the Thiepval Memorial that 'it looked properly imperial and thus particularly suitable, as the First World War was really the end of the British Empire' (so pervasive had the emphasis on loss in remembrance become that one Fettes history master snapped in exasperation, 'The last time I checked we won two world wars, no matter what Richard Curtis says'). The 2003 *Fettesian* also carried the text of Andrew Murray's Remembrance Sunday sermon to the school, during which he addressed OF veterans with the words:

Sirs, we wish to acknowledge all that you have seen your country through with your singularity of aim and purpose. We know in our thoughts the memories you must hold of those you knew of those you knew who 'did not grow old.'[7]

Addressing the school, he continued with a distillation of Moses' message to Israel in Deuteronomy:

You thought that the wilderness years were bad. They were, but they were not the real test. That will come when you experience, not slavery, but freedom, not poverty, but affluence. This is when you may forget everything that was fought for.

You will start thinking of yourself, not others. You will put present pleasure above the responsibilities to the future. When that happens you will be at risk.

2003 also marked Andrew Murray's retirement after many years at the helm, or rather the controls since he was an air cadet officer. The Biennial CCF inspection was carried out by Air Commodore David Walker, the Air Officer Commanding Training Group, and visited by low-flying Tornado fighters from RAF Leuchars in Murray's honour. Maj Jeremy Morris reviewed the Army Section's year:

Autumn and summer field days continue to generate as much excitement as ever, as well as providing a realistic practical test of how thoroughly the lessons have been absorbed. Judging by some of the sagging bashas and burnt mess tins, a lot remains to be done. Just when will Fettesians learn that sleep on manoeuvres is a priority, and that tired, dozy cadets who have tried to stay awake all night are a liability the following morning? Our inspection concluded with the final exercise and was blessed with good weather. Precisely what the Inspecting Officer made of the keen but dishevelled cadets we have yet to discover…

As we embark on the next phase of the Army Section's development, we can be confident that our numbers are holding up and morale is sound. Whether or not a glittering military career beckons, if nothing else, cadets are being furnished with a lifetime's material for campfire yarns and a healthy appreciation of home comforts.[8]

The RAF Section, led by Flt-Lt Chris Rose (a science master who took his love of aircraft to the extreme of building one in his house in the school grounds; structural rearrangements were necessary to get it out) was able to use the new technology of the health club to his advantage – its CCTV spotted an un-named cadet rearranging orienteering pegs. Andrew Murray's retirement message mentioned the challenges facing the twenty-first century cadets:

To have commanded the CCF at Fettes College for twenty years has been an extraordinary privilege and something I will look back on with immense gratitude. The CCF is an integral part of school life which affords the pupils yet another arena of wonderful opportunities, with activities to experience, responsibilities to grasp and skills to learn, adding a whole dimension to the forward momentum of growing up.

While the structure of the CCF in the school has remained much the same, that of the Services has seen changes in this period. The Army in Scotland has undergone several organisational changes, while simultaneously the Services have been imposing increased financial strictures and stringent qualifications regarding outdoor pursuits and shooting; these have inevitably imposed increasing pressure on the CCF and its officers. No longer do we have a Royal Navy base at Rosyth and the RAF at Turnhouse; such proximity for time aboard and flying was a boon.[9]

Despite these lost facilities (air cadets now had to make the four-hour return trip to Leuchars if they wanted to fly, and often did so only to be told on arrival that the weather prohibited it; small wonder that numbers dropped off) he summed up all that was best about the modern cadet movement:

There have been annual camps at Lochgilphead, Cultybraggan and Warcop; RAF camps at stations the length and breadth of Great Britain; overseas camps in Germany, Gibraltar and Cyprus; sub aqua diving camps on Skye, Mull and at Oban; overseas expeditions to Greenland, Norway, Zanskar, Nepal, Ecuador, Kenya, Russia and New Zealand; West Coast sailing cruises to the Hebrides and Adventurous Training Camps in the Central Highlands at Blair Atholl, Newtownmore, Tyndrum and Bridge of Orchy...

There is a host of memories that clamour to be told. Again space constrains me to mention a mere handful: the Land Rover stuck up to its axles in a bog and the Army recovery vehicle becoming stuck too; a night sail up the Minch to Harris; a visit to the RN section by the Duke of York, piped by Alasdair Macleod; a night exercise manoeuvre in which a marine outflanking move across a loch was executed; the Pipe Band playing in Grand Central Station and outside the UN Building in New York; two pupils standing on the summit of Mount Fettes in New Zealand; NCOs' dinner nights at Lochgilphead; pipers playing on the bridge of a destroyer returning to Rosyth; landing on the Queen's Lawn in a helicopter; a dawn advance led by pipers; the Duke of Edinburgh piped into camp by Niall Rowantree, and the overall spontaneity and quality of Fettes College CCF cadets over the years.

Lt Matt Leary, an Old Fettesian tank officer who talked to the cadets in 2008, was not sure about how well the modern CCF prepared people for the realities of modern Army training. He described the programme at Sandhurst as 'extremely unpleasant'.[10] As a junior recruit, the object was 'to beat the civvy out of you' with only four hours' sleep per night.

At intermediate level, some leadership skills were developed, but only the seniors were actually treated like officers, 'so they aren't scared of their NCOs when they join their regiments.' He summed up the experience by saying:

There are 28 pretty crap weeks and then 14 pretty decent ones, and then you become an officer. And then you realise how little you know about the Army.

Fettes cadets on exercise in 2006

Carrying On

Given contemporary regulations on health and safety, not to mention child welfare, the extent to which the CCF could prepare people for the sheer scale of the modern army's 'beasting' was open to question. Lt-Col Andrew Alexander, who succeeded Murray at the helm of the CCF, noted that modern health and safety regulations require cadets on exercise to get at least seven hours' uninterrupted sleep, which put paid to night patrols, dawn raids and other capers which had been the bread and butter of the traditional camp. In any case, the number of other demands on pupils' attention was increasing exponentially. In addition to the CCF's camps and increasingly non-military expeditions, in 2003 there were also language trips, an art trip, choir tour of North America, and Duke of Edinburgh-type treks to Baffin Island and the French Alps. The Science, Historical, Political and Shakespeare Societies were still going strong, the Christian Fellowship and Paramecium also flourished, and there were novelties such as the Aeronautical Society, Chaplain's

Marbles and Conker Championships, and bell-ringing. Gap year reports were by former pupils who had, as they put it, 'humbling' experiences doing voluntary work in less developed parts of the world. Sarah Hammond worked in wildlife conservation in Costa Rica, Mariana Ranken taught in a school in a poor part of Brazil, and Julie Gray did the same thing in Vanuatu (though after repeated blank looks she tended to tell people that she was going to Fiji). As one of the only white people on the island, Julie found herself an object of, to put it mildly, curiosity:

Everywhere we go people gape and stare; small children have been known to burst into tears and run away when they see us! The first lessons were awkward. The students hid under their desks when I spoke to them, and would run out of the room if they got a question wrong.[11]

Sarah also found her efforts in hacking a trail through the jungle for the use of children looked at with disapproval by locals, who did not like the idea of 'gringas' doing such physical work, whilst Mariana's pupils stared it her in disbelief and asked why she was so white (a Victorian OF would doubtless have had an answer to this, but she did not). It was not just white Fettesians who encountered racial curiosity: on several occasions, Asian students on Fettes school trips were subjected to petty and irritating delays by presumably racist passport control staff in Eastern Europe. Gap years, although offering plenty of opportunities for sightseeing and leisure, were genuinely hard work, and most of those who took part in them did not fail to comment on the deeply distressing nature of the toilet facilities in foreign parts. Most Fettesians, of course, did not do anything so exotic or public-spirited – they either went straight to university or used their year out to try to make money in order to pay for their degrees. The school magazine published 'a more down to earth perspective' by Fiona Anderson in which she gave an engagingly frank message to her successors:

Over the past year I have had four different jobs: all involving humiliation and coming quickly to terms with the fact that, despite having three rather good A-levels, I am, at age 18 and straight out of school, the lowest form of life in the world of temporary work...[12]

Sir Tommy Macpherson, Scotland's most highly-decorated war veteran and an Old Fettesian of 1934, would have been delighted by all of this.

Addressing the school on Founder's Day in 2002, he described the tough ways of the old school and the advantages this had given him in life:

Amenities, home comforts? Well, virtually none. There was no heating in any of the houses except Kimmerghame, which was new and considered rather soft, and the recognition marks of a Fettesian boy during the winter outside the School were the enormous red chilblains on his fingers. The result of this, which we all took as perfectly normal, was that those of us who went straight from Fettes into the Second World War and encountered various conditions of winter campaigns and so on thought that these were only minor discomforts compared to what we had at Fettes – great advantage, Headmaster: treat 'em rough! [13]

Carpeted, centrally-heated, beating- and fagging-free Fettes was hardly the grim institution of Sir Tommy's memories; treating children roughly was no longer accepted pedagogical doctrine, thanks in part to the increased power of mothers in the educational marketplace. The Guest of the Day was, of course, exaggerating for comic effect, and was quick to note that the place was in many respects more civilised than it had been before. Nonetheless, Fettes still made considerable demands of its pupils. Cadet activity, compulsory camping and, although fagging had been abolished, performing duties in houses were only some of the ways in which pupils were pushed beyond their comfort zones. A 2001 essay by fifth-former Tim Macdonald took the form of a report on Fettes by an observer from classical Sparta:

The upbringing of Fettesian children was remarkably similar to the way in which we conduct the raising of children. As we do, unlike any other race of the Greeks, they educated both boys and girls in rigorous physical training, making them chase fast-moving animals, called Steeples, over distances of fifty miles or more. We do not yet know what these creatures were. Military training, as in modern day Sparta, was also highly emphasised. Youths would have to spend lengthy periods camping in the wilderness surrounding the city, much like our krypteia, and the time of this 'overnight' expedition was always deliberately chosen to be under the most adverse weather conditions possible. Soldiers were highly trained in fighting on the land, at sea, and at making martial music to rally troops into battle. [14]

As they flailed about looking for some new way of dealing with the nation's apparently ungovernable youth, politicians lighted on these character-building aspects of the cadet movement as a panacea. Gordon

Brown, who had not previously shown a great deal interest in military matters, announced that:

The cadet forces are perhaps the most under-utilised [organisations] *in reaching their full potential of civic utility, particularly in offering opportunities for self-development, initiative, character building and leadership among young people, many of whom are forced by circumstances into blind alleys.*[15]

The education union Voice (formerly the Professional Association of Teachers) went so far as to demand a Corps in every school, both to instil discipline and to counter left-wing 'anti-forces feeling' spread by unpatriotic, left-wing staff – admittedly, not a burning concern at Fettes, but one which had become a real issue in the wider world.[16]

One reason why there was anti-forces feeling (beyond the sneering at their own country which Orwell identified as a trait of the 'pansy left') was the policy of Gordon Brown and his predecessor following the attack on the World Trade Center. Although Blair's wars of liberal intervention in the late nineties could be seen as successful – Milosevic finally got some payback for the murderous rampages of 1993, and Kosovan children are named Tonibler in the Prime Minister's honour – the twenty-first century wars in Afghanistan and Iraq were much more controversial. They evoked the shadows of Suez and the nineteenth century retreat from Kabul, drip-fed an apparently endless stream of casualties through the streets of Wootton Bassett, and tied Britain to an unpopular American president. They also sent Old Fettesians back to the haunts of their great-grandfathers.

Back to the Frontier, back to Iraq

Fettes began its military career with old boys in combat on the North-West Frontier in the 1870s; almost a century and a half later, they would be back again, and others would have served, often with distinction, in Iraq (though Maj Jeremy Morris, who had been recalled from the teaching staff to go to the former Yugoslavia, did write that 'I am too old and smelly, fortunately, to be called up for Iraq and Afghanistan'[17]). Justin Holt's 40 Commando was in Oman when the attack on Afghanistan was announced: at the thought of the British Army's first large-scale combat operations since 1991 'we were all pretty excited.'[18]

The Marines went out one company at a time to Bagram airfield, where they supported special forces. Aware of the much greater world

*Fettesians about to lay wreaths on the school war memorial,
Remembrance Sunday, 2005*

attention on the region in 2002 – previous British forces had been able to 'butcher and bolt' with little coverage in the press – Holt found himself involved in 'smoke and mirrors' exercises with the media. *Guardian* journalist Rory Carroll, he recalled, 'stumbled upon' an operation to clear the caves in which the terrorists were lurking, and was promised an exclusive if he kept quiet about it until the Marines had finished. Carroll duly produced an optimistic piece which suggested that Britain was on course for success.[19]

In fact, as Holt was quoted in Carroll's article as saying, there was a lot more going on than mopping up the remnants of a vanquished regime. It soon became apparent that al-Qaida operatives were moving backwards and forwards across the border, as troublemakers had done for centuries, except this time the British were on the other side of it. There were also tough Chechen veterans fighting alongside the Afghans and their Arab sympathizers. Although Holt's men were moved on in May 2002, he would soon be back in Afghanistan.

Tony Blair's sense of history may have infuriated that department at his old school – his comments that the USA had stood alongside Britain when she faced the Blitz alone, whereas in fact the Empire and exiled European armies were her allies and America was making a fortune as a neutral arms supplier provoked particular outrage – but he was completely sincere in his belief that he should go to war alongside President Bush. Although the *Fettesian* no longer printed their letters, it was believed at the school that as many as 30 Old Fettesians were serving in Afghanistan and Iraq at any one time. *Industria*, the magazine of the Friends of Fettes College, reported in 2003 that:

Jonathan Biggart (J-C78) and his tank squadron joined Justin Holt (S83) and his Royal Marines to fight side-by-side in the Iraq conflict. They pine for cold showers at Fettes.[20]

They were, in fact, part of the initial attack, and took part in the capture of Basra, Iraq's second-largest city. After intensive firearms training in the Mojave Desert and mountain work in the Sierra Nevada, 40 Commando was combat-ready and knew of its role by December 2002. Justin Holt and his colleagues were aware of the political controversy, and one troop commander had doubts about the legality of the operation. Most, however, were convinced that it was a worthwhile operation, and accepted that 'when the decision was made, it was probably irreversible – we just wanted to get on with it.'[21]

There was, he recalled, a general feeling, based on the precedent of 1991, that it would be 'a short, sharp affair'. This view was not wholly naïve. The Royal Marines and their American equivalents practiced invasion techniques, first in Cyprus and then in Kuwait, in readiness for a 'pretty audacious' amphibious seizure of the oil installation at al-Faw. The mission statement was to capture and control the oil installations, both to prevent an environmental catastrophe (Saddam Hussein might set fire to the refineries and flood the Gulf with oil) and to ensure Iraq's economic future. It was audacious because British defence doctrine has, for decades, been to avoid opposed landings, but al-Faw's strategic value, and the fact that the Iranians had captured it during the eighties, ensured that it would be well defended. The Marines, who would be taking the target with the US Navy SEALs and Polish special forces, carried out three practice assaults on a full-size mock-up of the target in Kuwait before attacking by sea and air on 19 March. The attack would coincide with attempts to decapitate the Iraqi government in Baghdad (which failed) and be supported by the USAF in the shape of A-10 tank-busting jets and an AC-130 gunship. The refineries were rigged to explode and had to be taken.

When Holt's A Company arrived in their Chinooks, they found that 42 Commando had taken casualties and that B and C Companies were fighting against Iraqis in trenches and bunkers who had survived the initial bombardment. Holt's men cleared a route south-east from the refinery's metering station, taking up position between al-Faw town and the military installations. 'It was probably the most violently executed operation you could imagine in terms of completely paralysing the Iraqi defences, destroying them and then taking the installations intact.' With no-one lost from 40 Commando, it was a complete success. By this point the Marines had had no sleep for a day and a half, and were astonished to discover local civilians attempting to turn up to work or simply to loot. Those attempting to help themselves to weapons in the Iraqi army barracks were turned away, but other items were freely removed. A portable loudspeaker system informed the locals in Arabic that the Marines had come to liberate them, but this did not convince diehard Ba'athists in al-Faw town, who attempted to fight A Company when Holt – with only 105 men – was ordered to take it. Fedayeen riflemen on rooftops made progress through the town slow, especially with the heavy packs carried by the Marines and the fierce heat, but A Company sustained no casualties and killed seven of the defenders. After dark, Holt organized an assault on the Ba'ath party building whose extreme shock and violence was designed to intimidate the enemy into surrender. He eschewed air or artillery attack on the grounds that civilian casualties would be inevitable as well as unwelcome. Using explosives, Holt's men blasted their way into the building, killing six Iraqi gunmen, though unfortunately three Marines had to be evacuated after suffering burns when a gas canister exploded. The following day a local official asked for a ceasefire. '40 Commando had achieved its objectives and held them on its own,' said Holt, matter-of-factly, when describing the events for this book.[22]

Basra was attacked several days later, and it was here that Holt found himself next to Maj Jonathan Biggart, commanding C Squadron, the Royal Scots Dragoon Guards. Progress into Basra had been held up by tanks, but these proved no match for Biggart's more modern Challenger IIs, which defeated 14 of the Soviet-supplied Iraqi T-55s on the outskirts of the city with no losses. Operation James, the taking of Basra, was nonetheless a hard fight – advancing into the sunrise, without the advantages of either surprise or momentum which had served them so well at al-Faw, 40 Commando was less confident than it had been before. Biggart's tanks, however, came into their own again, laying waste to armoured vehicles and bunkers, and between them the Marines and Dragoon Guards were able to take the suburb of Abu al-Khasib. Once the whole city had been cleared, and the majority of the fighters had been killed or captured or had run away, the British found themselves in charge of a vast area whose population was greater than that of Northern Ireland and even more heavily armed. It was, moreover, an extremely excited population, divided between those (often in the business community) who wanted to work with the new arrivals, residual party people stirring up trouble and still in possession of weapons, and a large number of enthusiastic looters. Arms searches risked alienating potential sympathizers, so Holt – in effect the colonial administrator of Abu al-Khasib – adopted a twin-track policy of amiable high-visibility 'hearts and minds' patrols by day and targeted snatch squads to capture particularly important Ba'athists by night.

Unlike his Victorian forebears, Holt had no manual or training for being a colonial governor (his only clear instruction from his colonel was not to behave like God[23]) so, like the other British and American officers in this position, had to make it up as he went along. He established what became known as a 'drop-in centre' in an office building, which was used both as a security base and as a point of contact between the British and the Iraqis. He encouraged the locals to set up a council to advise him and to act as a mouthpiece for popular opinion, which was not always favourable. Although things were improving – the Shia population of Abu al-Khasib could celebrate religious festivals which the Sunni-dominated regime had banned, and local policemen were working with the Marines – shortages disappointed a public which seems to have imagined that the invasion would be accompanied by a mixture of humanitarian aid and consumer goods, both in abundance.

In retrospect, the Americans who ran the invasion - and, as Lt Leary reminded the cadets, 'Britain is just a pimple on the enormous American military bottom' – had not given enough thought to this. Maj Holt's next posting to Afghanistan would reflect the discussions which subsequently took place about how to rebuild a post-conflict society. Still, as he told Mike Rossiter, he did manage to make a difference in at least one case. Free, if rationed, petrol was provided by the coalition forces for key services in the town, and when a garage-owner tried to sell it at sky-high prices, much to the locals' anger, Holt told him that he would 'let the crowd lynch him if he didn't stop profiteering.'[24] The Victorians would have been proud. Holt would later be awarded the MBE for his service in Iraq.

Not all of the OFs in Iraq were fighting. Catherine Philp, one of the eighties 'Fettesiennes', described her experiences as a journalist in Iraq to the pupils on Founder's Day in 2009. Her job had dangers which the military types tended to avoid – specifically, setting off, unarmed, down roads without knowing exactly what lay ahead. A few days after the fall of Baghdad, she was trying to get to Saddam Hussein's home town of Tikrit in time for its capture by Americans:

Suddenly, about half an hour before we expected to reach Tikrit, the village we were driving through erupted into gunfire. Now, I knew that when you drive into oncoming gunfire, you have to keep going. It's called the kill zone, and the faster you drive through it, the faster the guns, and the bullets, are behind you. If you turn back, you're just dragging out your time in the kill zone, and multiplying your chances of getting hit.

Nobody, however, had told my staff this. Leo, my translator, started screaming at the driver to turn back and I started screaming at him to go forward. The poor man was paralyzed. Eventually he plumped for my suggestion and hit the accelerator, but not before Leo was halfway out the back door of the car, declaring he was quitting and swearing wretchedly at me in Kurdish. We slid onto the bridge over the river Tigris moments later – with a shot-out tyre – under the incredulous gaze of American Marines – who don't mention venture down roads they don't know either.[25]

She also recounted her experiences of what happened when she was injured in a road accident on the road to Baghdad:

Anyone who thought the war in Iraq was lost before it began, that this was an implacable clash of civilizations, should have been there that day on a desert road through the Sunni Triangle, in the midst of an American invasion, and seen the dozens of cars and ordinary people in them who stopped to try and help an injured westerner. Perhaps ungratefully, I wasn't quite ready to be carted off to an Iraqi hospital so my colleague, Steve, hitched a ride back up the road to an encampment of American tanks to get help. I was drifting in and out of foggy consciousness by the time my photographer yelled, 'Here come the Marines!'

The next part of the journey was in a military ambulance. About fifteen minutes in, we heard the crack of gunfire and the convoy shuddered to a sudden halt. The marines started piling out the back, pulling on their rifles and I was left, strapped down to a stretcher, with the paramedic who just pumped me full of a Marine-sized dose of morphine. He pulled off his body armor and laid it over me like a blanket. Then he whipped off his helmet and wedged it neatly between my head and the side of the ambulance. 'Never tell my wife I did this,' he said.

'Uh, is this ambulance not armoured?' I squeaked. Of course it wasn't. People aren't meant to shoot at ambulances.

'It's Kevlar, sweetie,' he said. 'It just slows them down.'

Then he started to move towards the door and it dawned on me that he was about to jump out and join the firefight too. At the last moment he turned back, pulled his pistol from its holster, and put it in my hands. Then he jumped out into the bright light, the ambulance door banging behind him.

OK, this was indeed frightening, more so than the unknown road, mostly because I was now alone, strapped down to a stretcher, and unable to do anything about the bullets flying outside. As I lay there with the unfamiliar weight of a pistol in my hand, I began to fret that if I did have to use it, I was more likely to shoot one of my returning rescuers than any marauding fedayeen.

But I had one kernel of comfort that stayed with me as the gunfire crackled, right through to the moment, twenty minutes later, when they all came back alive. A complete stranger, a man who less than an hour before had picked me of the desert and put me into it onto a stretcher, had walked into gunfire without a shred of armour, risking his own life for the chance that in doing so, he might save mine.

Unfortunately, the successes and optimism of the invasion period were not entirely accurate pointers to the future. It is now known that the Americans had not thought through exactly what would happen once they had overthrown the Ba'ath regime: they seem to have hoped that, as with the liberation of Western Europe in 1944 and, better still, the collapse of communism in East-Central Europe in 1989, liberal capitalism would be welcomed with open arms.

Fettes' military connections, but minimal Islamic population, gave the school an outlook which was largely pro-forces and opposed to those who were fighting them but politicians were regarded with scepticism. A Labour Party speaker at the Fettes Political Society, who explained the real benefits liberation had brought to Kurdistan, was informed by a pupil in the audience with a parent in Basra that the British forces were profoundly disillusioned and wanted to get out of there. The Kimmerghame House play in 2007, *The Which Blair Project*, might have been an amateur piece of knockabout farce, but it caught the attention of the press with greater success than the grand unveiling of the school's new facilities because of a perception that it was an attack on Fettes' most famous alumnus. When sixth-former Matty Hand (the son of an RAF officer serving in Iraq) playing Blair ad-libbed that he had organized the invasion of a rival school because they 'had a giant laser to blow up the world in ten minutes, or, er, something', the line might have been lost on many of the younger pupils but not on journalists, who decided that this was 'savage satire' of the highest order.[26]

As the bemused Headmaster, not used to taking calls about school drama, put it, the play was 'schoolboy tomfoolery', but such was Blair's sullied reputation that even a production with a comedy donkey called George Best and a Russian spy masquerading as the school chaplain could be dignified as a work worthy of Weimar Berlin.

A scene from The Which Blair Project, which the press mistakenly interpreted as hard-hitting satire

The military situation which gave the play its backdrop, however, did not depress Justin Holt, who admits to being 'optimistic by nature':

There was a dark period in 2006-7, which was worse for the Americans than for us. But they will persevere in order not to be defeated. They will push on and take the pain – they can absorb it – and it would be more unpopular to give in. There have been advances in human rights, women's rights and education, and the alternative to success is pretty bleak. To the Americans' credit they learn very quickly, then adapt.[27]

Lt Matt Leary, who had been serving in Iraq in this period, recalled it as a seriously tough posting. Thanks to the 'enormous' roadside bombs, only Challenger tanks and Warrior armoured fighting vehicles could go into Basra during the 'hotter' periods, and 'confusion reigns supreme most of the time.' Although the tanks offered protection, the regiment still suffered casualties when men poked their heads out of the hatches and were sniped at. Although battles were rare – he estimated that many people had spent six months in Iraq and seen 15 minutes' worth of straight fighting – they were intense. After one encounter, one of Leary's men exclaimed. 'Fucking hell, boss, that was a hell of a firefight. I didn't think we were going to get out of that alive. Thanks for sorting it out.' This meant a great deal to Leary and would, he said, stay with him for the rest of his life.

Other aspects of service in Iraq were brought home to the cadets in this talk. In the fierce heat, with the weight of body armour, the British troops were drinking two litres of water per hour to remain hydrated. The 'warfare and welfare' aspect of the officer's role had not gone away, despite the supposedly greater sophistication of modern British society; some soldiers required 'pretty simple parenting.' Lt Leary recounted one tale of having to sort out the problems caused by one soldier who had managed not only to get a girl pregnant, but also her mother. The young Fettesians were impressed with what they were told but horrified to discover that Lt Leary was paid £29,000 per year, which, taking into account all he had to do, worked out at £3.00 per hour. This is, perhaps, one of the reasons why the armed services' intake from Fettes was not as substantial in modern times as it had been in the decades after the school's birth.

Returning from Basra in mid-2003, Lt-Col Justin Holt initially found other postings 'pretty tedious after all that excitement.' He taught about counter-insurgency and peace support at the Defence Academy, training majors on the Intermediate Land Staff Course, and worked on the Naval Battle Staff. A 2006 Defence Academy trip to France to retrace the route of the Royal Marine 'Cockleshell Heroes' who attacked Bordeaux Harbour in 1942, was interesting but hardly the kind of fearsome challenge the Commandos had faced in Iraq. However, he eventually found himself back in Afghanistan, where he worked for the Post-Conflict Reconstruction (now Stabilisation) Unit, a government body which was set up to 'enhance the capacity for self-governance' of fragile states after the failure of rebuilding in Iraq. Going out as a 'semi-civilian' stabilisation adviser, he worked in Musa Qala in Northern Helmand, an 'iconic' town which had been captured by the British in 2002, returned to its people in 2006, recaptured by the Taliban in February 2007 and then taken from them in a major battle ten months later. A problem with the British concept of stabilization, however, was that, as Holt put it:

People respected tough leaders, but weren't interested in capable technocrats who could run a council and handle money. People felt cheated if there weren't hangings and floggings… it's a pretty brutal place by our standards.[28]

Although Tony Blair might consider the (eventual and relative) stability of Ulster as a great success, the systems in place there were not really a model for Afghanistan. 'There are,' says Holt, 'almost six centuries between Northern Helmand and Northern Ireland.' Accordingly, he had to work with the controversial ex-Taliban commander Mullah Salaam, who he described as 'a very charismatic man who had natural authority' but whose cultural preferences were mediaeval. In an echo of Herzen's nineteenth century fear of future tyrants being like 'Genghis Khan with the telegraph' Holt referred to the situation as resembling thirteenth century England, but with mobile phones, machine guns and opium. Like his forebears, Holt used a mixture of firmness, cultural tact and efficiency to establish his credentials: he grew a beard to reassure the locals that he was trustworthy, ensured that officials were paid, established literacy courses and, in an incident which made the British press, even arrested the governor's son (one of his 27 offspring by five wives) for trying to spring one of his associates from prison. Mullah Salaam said that he would rather the British had shot his son than imprisoned him; it would have been less insulting.[29]

Local corruption also hampered his efforts – reconstruction work was subject to repeated sub-contraction and extortion, which slowed progress and raised doubts in the public's eyes about the benefits of change. One policy was to pay $200 to those who could identify Taliban fighters, a remarkable sum in a country where doctors make $70 and teachers $60 per month. Progress was slow, and when the British handed the area over to the US Marines Mullah Salaam was swiftly replaced by the less piratical and slightly more staidly bourgeois figures of Niamatullah, a teacher, and Akbar Khan, a policeman and shopkeeper.

Oliver Blake, who on graduating from Sandhurst had been serving with the Light Dragoons (leading their victorious Alpine Race team and enjoying 'diving, sailing and cavalry excess in the mess') was posted to Afghanistan in 2007. His duties were more straightforwardly military than Justin Holt's:

Our days were varied - sometimes spent reassuring locals, on other occasions conducting snap vehicle checks for drugs and weapons, sometimes fighting as part of deliberate raids and always desperately trying to avoid IEDs. During this time we were also launched on other specific missions often moving through the desert by night ready for daytime activity against Terry Taliban.

On one such occasion my troop were operating in the area of Basharan and my vehicle was being pinned down by sniper fire. I used the radio to contact my Troop Cpl's wagon to suggest that he might like to get a sighting onto the insurgent and perhaps be so kind as to direct some accurate fire as I was unable to poke my head out of the turret for fear of losing it. The reply came, 'Mustang 10 this is Mustang 12, watch my tracer out.' I expected the usual machine gun tracer onto the confirmed position, which in turn would direct all other friendly fire in the right direction. I was a little shocked to see an entire wall disappear under a cloud of dust, 'Mustang 10, Mustang 12, enemy destroyed, out,' - he had indeed used tracer.....of the 30mm kind! [30]

This kind of weaponry – armoured vehicles mounting automatic cannon – would have been as credible to the Victorian OF as a flying saucer. There was still continuity, however; the British hoped in both 1887 and 2007 that their combination of superior technology and sophisticated training would bring some semblance of order. Above all, the ferocity of the fighting was exactly the same. Ollie Blake's most challenging week came when the Light Dragoons led a company of Welsh Guards up the Shamalan Canal as part of Phase One Operation Panchay Palang:

It took 7 hours to cover a few kilometres coming under fire from 18 separate ambushes many of which were initiated by Rocket Propelled Grenades. What followed was a week of aggressive and difficult fighting.

On one occasion our boys were able to react to an emergency call at 0430 in the morning as one of the Royal Tank Regiment Viking vehicles had veered into the canal. They were extracted – two had drowned and were resuscitated by our incredible medics. The helicopters swooped in and they were repatriated to a German hospital within 12 hours and survived.

Later that day we were ambushed with small arms fire from 360 degrees. In the middle of an orders group each man had to dash back to his turret – the longest run I have ever completed in the shortest amount of time – certainly quicker than the Fettes Mile! Returning fire, we soon won the firefight but had to call the American Black Hawks in again as one of the Welsh Guards Captains had taken a bullet to the knee.

I have rarely felt more relieved than on day 7 when I fired up the satellite radio only to be greeted by a friendly Black Watch voice on the other end – my old housemate from university!... Jumping off my turret at the end of the canal, a firm hand shake with Andy Colquhoun and then the characteristic and comforting tones of a fellow Scot as their Intelligence Sgt gave me the most thorough and useful int brief of my entire tour. We have much to be proud of for our Scottish soldiers are amongst the finest in the world.

Despite the incredible array of modern equipment, from satellites to helicopters, this last experience of the joy of contact with fellow-Scots is one which goes back to the earliest Fettesians, and indeed beyond, when Sir William's in-laws were making their way in India.

Ollie Blake and his troop in Afghanistan

Controversy

Unlike the situation in the past, it was comparatively rare for those serving on the frontier to write back to, or visit, the school (though books like *The Junior Officers' Reading Club* were popular among some of the boys). The politics of the 'War on Terror', however, were eagerly discussed. Political Society meetings in 2000 included three Scottish socialist radicals, Tommy Sheridan, Dennis Canavan and Tam Dalyell, all of whom denounced Blair's 'shallowness'. When the fighting started, the gloves came off. In 2002, George Galloway – who was as impressed with the pupils as they were with him – told the society that Blair's relationship with America was 'not shoulder to shoulder but lips to behind.'[31] (To be fair, other speakers with higher standing in the Labour Party defended the war policy). What came later was to damage Blair's standing even further; the attack on Afghanistan was understandable, but that on Iraq was so shrouded in controversy that the Prime Minister would soon be labelled a 'war criminal'. The fact that the secular, pan-Arab socialist totalitarianism of Iraq was nothing to do with the mediaeval superstition of the Islamists was glossed over, especially in the USA, where the public was encouraged to see a connection between '9/11' and Saddam Hussein (rather than Saudi Arabia, the actual home of the terrorists). Above all, the public believed it had been lied to and that the war was unwinnable.

This was discussed in the school more vigorously than any military issue since the sixties or possibly even the thirties. The 2003 *Fettesian* carried an article by Peter Grant and Caitlin McKenna arguing the cases for and against the invasion of Iraq. Peter deployed a battery of information illustrating the range of crimes committed by the Ba'ath regime and its non-compliance with the United Nations, concluding with Jefferson's 'The tree of liberty must be refreshed from time to time with the blood of patriots and tyrants.'[32] Caitlin denounced President Bush as an environmental criminal who had raped Alaska for oil and was exploiting September 11 for political advantage, had misled the world about weapons of mass destruction, did not care about human rights when they were abused by America's fascist allies in South America, had wrecked the Iraqi infrastructure and was himself in violation of UN rules. The tragedy of the Iraq war was that neither participant said anything that was actually untrue. The upper sixth intellectuals of the Paramecium also vigorously debated the issue, with, apparently, a strong 'I hate America' tendency emerging, with sceptics (mostly girls) viewing the 'War on Terror' with suspicion as a neoconservative plot, and pro-American boys adopting a more gung-ho attitude.[33]

Very occasional war-related cultural pieces began to reappear in the *Fettesian*, including a short story about a soldier in Iraq who sees a veiled girl shot by comrades who are panicking over whether she might be a suicide bomber (she is). The Pipe Band, however, had other concerns, beginning its annual report on an understandably grumpy note:

One event marred an otherwise gleamingly productive year for the Pipe Band: a non-event. The failed tour to the States, cancelled because of some scrap over non-

existent weaponry in a nondescript faraway country was disappointing, particularly after much hard work and cash had been put in by teachers, pupils and parents.[34]

It would be fanciful to suggest that the increased interest in Scottish nationalism at Fettes was due to the same disillusionment with the British imperial project which gradually seeped into post-Suez Scotland. Revive it did, however, under the leadership of 'dynasties' such as the Torrances, Wilkies and Ansells; in mock elections the SNP scored highly, the Pipe Band was regarded as one of the treasures of the school, and Burns Supper became a central point of the calendar. In the school magazine in 2005, one of the boys provocatively attacked the National Bard as an outdated figure who, as a 'serial adulterer and often abusive drunk' and a 'lazy, indifferent misogynist' would be wholly unacceptable in modern society.[35] Rona Wilkie, a talented folk-musician, Gaelic-speaker, debater and SNP stalwart, fought back with a defence of the great man which pointed out that for all his faults, he was still important in modern century Scotland:

Burns created a realistic picture of the rural Scotland in which he lived – one full of mice, drunks, adulterous men, hatred of the English and superstition. This picture is still relevant to Scotland, as superstition still exists, we have the highest number of binge drinkers in Europe, sex outside marriage is commonly accepted – as are multiple marriages – and there are still tensions, largely confined to football, between Scotland and her southern neighbour; we also still have mice.[36]

Rona went on to put Burns in his proper place as a pillar of the Enlightenment:

This is probably most evident in his 'A Man's a Man for a' that'. In an international school like ours surely the lyrics 'man to man the world o'er shall brothers be for a'that' should strike a chord. Yes, it is true that 'culture and historical importance' are part of the attraction of Burns, but a line like that overcomes all, including simple verse, and is more relevant today than it has ever been. Burns was both a nationalist and an internationalist; this is the key.

Of course, schools being what they are, of much greater importance that academic year was a mumps outbreak which inspired impressive literary contributions by James Angus (in the spirit of Defoe's *Journal of the Plague Year*) and Katherine Reeves (in the style of *Bridget Jones's Diary*) both of which showed that there were still plenty of young intellectuals at Fettes and that the Victorians did not have a monopoly on good teenage writing. The school's cultural output, whilst showing some real quality, never returned to the militaristic fervour which had characterised it a century earlier. It has been decades since anything remotely tub-thumping has appeared in the *Fettesian* or featured in an art exhibition or drama production. The modern celebration was of community, and in the late noughties adventurous pupils, especially those taking the International Baccalaureate, could go as a group to help out in a less well-to-do country. This did not begin entirely auspiciously; on the first such trip, to Costa Rica in 2007, the pupils' baggage went astray and they were without a change of clothes for a week. One girl, after enduring this stoically for a while, eventually said plaintively, 'I'm not a materialist, really I'm not, but I do like to change my underwear after four days.' On a trip to Vietnam in 2010, the Fettesians' work in a remote village attracted the attention of the media, which led in turn to exhortations from Hanoi to the local party cadre to get to work and stop being shown up as slackers by this crowd of imperialists. Sadly, Lucas Von Hoff, the charismatic young teacher who organised this increasingly popular aspect of Fettes life, died shortly before this book was completed, but his name lives on in a school award for public service.

Celebration

With so many of its former pupils serving in trouble-spots around the world, Fettes had been extraordinarily fortunate. During Operation Banner, the thirty years of the Troubles in Northern Ireland, terrorists killed around a thousand British military and police personnel; 179 were killed on Operation Telic (Iraq) and to date 300 have been killed on Operation Herrick (Afghanistan). 225 had been lost in the Falklands, around 500 in Malaya and a thousand in Korea. In total, over 2,750 British servicemen and women had been killed since the end of the Second World War, with 1968 being the only year (and the first for centuries) in which none died. As it neared the centenary of the establishment of its cadet contingent and the 150th anniversary of the foundation of the cadet movement, Fettes had been luckier than many other schools, in having suffered so few fatalities since 1945 – five serving officers, of whom three were killed in accidents and two in combat, the last in Rhodesia, though Robert Lawrence's survival in the Falklands was a close-run thing. Despite the presence of several OFs in harm's way in Iraq, none were lost, and the school's last casualties there, buried at Amara or commemorated on the Basra Memorial, remain the eight who were killed fighting the Turks in 1916-17. There was, accordingly, little gloom attached to the anniversary celebrations, which largely consisted of special CCF parades and chapel services. The CCF entered its second century in surprisingly good health; despite the changes within the school, it did not become rudderless; in particular, the creation of Craigleith sixth form house did not decapitate the organization, and not only did the NCOs remain but a number continued to apply for Army scholarships – four winning them in 2009. That September, 2/Lt Christopher Murphy, an Old Fettesian in the Tayforth Officer Training Corps, received the Duke of Westminster's Sword at the Royal Military Academy Sandhurst as the top student on the Territorial Army Commissioning Course. As drum-major of the school's pipe band, he had led the combined Scottish schools' pipers and drummers out of Edinburgh Castle in the 2006 Beating Retreat. Now a philosophy student at St Andrew's, he was taking part in the latest model of officer training, the Military Leadership Development Programme, which included a 'module' at Garelochhead, Exercise Summer Leader, where weather, hills, bogs and midges added spice to an already testing environment and physically demanding course. He wrote afterwards that:

Sandhurst is an impressive place, with standards held so high that barely a giraffe could reach them. The testing is formal and exacting, demanding thorough preparation. Ex Summer Leader provided exactly that; the morale crippling conditions of Garelochhead were a hard place to learn the skills required of an Infantry Platoon Commander. However, such extreme training conditions made my life a lot easier when it came to the testing phase at Sandhurst. Being able to soldier on through wind and rain on the west coast of Scotland made the flat fields of the South seem positively comfortable! [37]

His CO wrote proudly that:

Not everyone who aspires to a TA Commission makes the grade and this 'testing ground' can bear testament to the fact, although most leave confident that they could attempt anything! Finishing top on one of the flagship courses run at the world renowned centre of excellence for leadership is an achievement that 2nd Lt Murphy is clearly very proud of.

Murphy himself was characteristically modest about his achievement:

Upon being told I was going to be awarded the Duke of Westminster's Sword I was stunned; speechless. I had worked as hard as I could, but nonetheless I didn't feel like I had done anything particularly more deserving than everyone else on the course. That said, I was of course thrilled, and felt an enormous sense of achievement.

Walking up the steps of Old College behind my colleagues was an awesome moment, with the hairs on the back of my neck standing erect, I knew I had done myself proud, but I also had a deep feeling of humility in recognising that I was only one of nearly eighty people to gain the Queen's Commission that day.

I was extremely conscious that I could not have achieved this award without the teamwork, loyalty and friendship of my colleagues. In short, I felt surprised, proud and thankful.

This was very much part of the Fettes tradition of self-effacing pride in the nation's military traditions and each generation's capacity to contribute to them. A Victorian OF at Sandhurst might have considered his observations that the OTC gave students 'an edge in the increasingly competitive graduate job market' and had 'furthered my skills in leadership and management' rather odd, but they were part of the modern conception of how the Army ought to be marketed. Equally, another Old Fettesian in Tayforth, Andrew Collister, was stunned to hear how relaxed the Victorian regime at Sandhurst had been; in his experience, modern officers in training went to bed at one and rose at five, having slept on the floor rather than disturb the pristine beauty of their regulation-made beds, and elaborate mess dinners had been replaced by a brief scoff during which notes were written up. Both Murphy and Collister were members of the Tayforth team which won the Royal Armoured Corps competition Exercise Utopian Vagabond in February 2010; on this occasion, they did enjoy a splendid mess dinner with much merriment, but it was followed early the next morning with an 'adrenaline-pumping' assault course.

At Fettes, the most elaborate event organized for the anniversaries was the unveiling in 2008 of a plaque in St George's Memorial Church in Ypres, where many British schools commemorate their war dead. A party of third-formers, led by historians John Fern and Charlie du Vivier (leader of the Royal Navy cadets at Fettes) toured the battlefields and met up with a smaller group composed of Old Fettesians and adult staff, mostly connected with the CCF, in the town where so many of their predecessors had served and thirty had been killed. Andrew Murray and his successor as Contingent Commander, Andrew Alexander, carried the flags of the Corps into the little church, the poetry of OF John Humphreys was read, and the Chaplain, David Campbell, preached a brief sermon. He had, he said, been searching for the right words for the occasion, and had found them at the vast British cemetery at Tyne Cot. Only one OF, one-time head boy Lt Peter Alexander MC, is buried there, so many of those who fell in the Salient having no known grave, so it was by his headstone that a third-former Luke Bridges poppies on behalf of the school. Also lost for words, the boy simply said, 'Thank you.' This, said the Chaplain, was the most appropriate tribute of all. The names of all those from Fettes who had died at Ypres were read out in order of age, beginning with 46-year-old Capt James Brack Boyd and ending with 2/Lt John Murray, who had been only 19 – little older than Ross Turner and Sam Cooper, the sixth-form pipers who accompanied the pilgrimage – when he was killed at Passchendaele in 1917. By special arrangement with the local officials, Fettes took part in the Last Post ceremony that night. RSM Willie Ross, who Ollie Blake remembered as 'a huge influence in inspiring me to go on to join the regular army – a great man', read the Act of Remembrance, and two pupils laid a wreath. The bugles of the Last Post Association were accompanied by the two Fettes pipers, one of whom said afterwards that it was the most important thing he had ever done.

Fettes sixth-formers at the Somme in 2011, taking part in a virtually universal British school ritual of battlefield pilgrimage

In the anniversary years, Fettes' serving military alumni were being kept busy. Lt-Col Jonathan Biggart, taking time off from training for Afghanistan in the huge Army ranges in Canada, was proudly receiving a Classical Brits award for the best album of the year on behalf of the band of his Royal Scots Dragoon Guards, of which he was Commanding Officer. 'Spirit of the Glen: Journey' was recorded whilst the regiment was on duty in Basra. The regiment subsequently marched down the Royal Mile in Edinburgh, accompanied by one of their tanks, after having guarded the Queen at Holyrood. Lt-Col Justin Holt, after Afghanistan, was posted to as liaison with the US forces in Washington DC, where he shared his expertise in counter-insurgency and marrying troops with civilian specialists. He was later given the less glamorous task of managing the coronial process for operational deaths. Capt Caroline Graham-Brown of the Royal Engineers was based in England with 527 Specialist Team at 64 Works Group RE in Nottingham; in this capacity, she was the lead designer for the Barker Crossing in Workington in November 2009, providing a fixed link between local communities on either side of the River Derwent who had been severed by severe floods which wrecked all the existing bridges. In 2010, following in the footsteps of Justin Holt, she joined the Provincial Reconstruction Team in Helmand delivering designing the stabilisation projects intended to create a viable infrastructure. 'It's really interesting work and I am really enjoying the new role,' she wrote.[38]

Nor were older generations idle. Robert Lawrence MC had founded an extraordinary organisation, Global Adventure Plus, which aimed to motivate and encourage injured ex-servicemen through demanding but rewarding challenges. One of the first to take part was a Scots Guard who had been on Tumbledown with Lawrence in 1982 and had suffered seven years' Post-Traumatic Stress Disorder; he found a new sense of purpose in a trek through the Himalayas. Sir Tommy Macpherson published a popular memoir of his adventures in the Second World War, and a memorial was unveiled in Rhyl to Norman MacQueen, the Fettesian Spitfire pilot killed in the defence of Malta. Ian Gardiner published both memoirs and observations on military history, as well as acerbic newspaper articles on such Blairite irritations as meaningless airport security checks ('If you felt so inclined, you could pass through the process as clean as a whistle and then go and buy a bottle of Johnny Walker...this process will equip you with a weapon of proven ferocity'[39]). A one-time President of the Old Fettesians, he remains a popular speaker at the school's Historical Society, where his talks on Oman and the Falklands are greatly appreciated.

Brigadier Ian Gardiner telling the Fettes History Society about his service in Oman

The bewildering complexity of modern military life, and the relatively lower pay which so shocked the pupils, clearly did not deter these and the dozens of other modern Fettesians from pursuing fulfilling careers with the armed services. Maj Jeremy Morris, long-serving modern languages teacher at Fettes and a leading figure in the CCF, also reflected positively on his time in the Army, and its importance in his role with the cadets:

It has always been a pleasure to pass on authentic military experience, either at school or in the field and to add a touch of realism to training. I am glad to have given pupils a steer towards, or away from, the Services when they have asked. I would like to think that maybe some nugget of experience which I passed on may have helped those who signed up, come home safely. I am sure I have been a better teacher as a result of my time in the Army, especially with the Queen's Royal Irish Hussars, than I would have been otherwise.[40]

As the cadet movement celebrated its 150th anniversary in 2010, Fettes Corps having marked its centenary in 2008, there was no shortage of encouraging voices for the patriotic, military-minded Fettesian. The world which had created the cadet movement had changed – fears of France and later Germany, and the need for trained lads to serve the Empire, had gone the way of the music-halls and Hansom cabs so familiar to the first cadets – and, in some ways, there had been a reversion to some of the attitudes of Sir William Fettes' day. Specifically, whilst the public might shed a sentimental tear over 'our brave boys', there was a marked reluctance to pay higher taxes to ensure that they were well-equipped, and a great many people were reluctant to see their offspring embark on such a dangerous and poorly-paid career. There were accusations in Scotland that the Army was trying to recruit boys from the poorest areas, leading some teachers in the grittier types of comprehensive to refuse forces liaison teams access to their schools. The powerful play *Black Watch* reinforced the notion of tough, but possibly misled, working-class Jocks, led by English-accented officers from the eccentric highland gentry, being sent to fight Westminster's wars in far-away lands of which they knew little. The right wing also grumbled about the services being hidebound by political correctness and being required to act more like social workers than warriors. These views were, of course, exaggerations – plenty of people who were neither mad aristocrats nor embittered unemployed were joining the services, which had always had a broader role than simply the killing of foreigners. Capt Caroline Graham-Brown, with her M.Eng. degree sponsored by the Royal Engineers, is not (her sex apart) an unimaginable figure from any point in the school's past. Her role in Afghanistan, and indeed on the River Derwent, is also in keeping with the activities of OFs in the forces and in other agencies from the school's earliest days. Ken Millar's judgment on his career could stand for so many Fettesian professional soldiers from the Victorian days onward:

I had a great time in the Army; I have no regrets whatsoever over my decisions to join in the first place, to remain for a full career or to move away from clinical medicine. The variety of jobs I was given was very broad, and at every new appointment I was able to bring my accumulated experience to bear on a new challenge. I met, and had the privilege of working with, some exceptional individuals in all ranks from Private upwards, and was enormously lucky in having many people as subordinate and supporting staff on whom I could rely for industry, perception and loyalty – which loyalty I can only hope I returned at least in part. As with, I reckon, most jobs there were times when there was more cloud than sunshine – but the black humour of the soldier carried us through. I have no regrets either about leaving when I did – it was the right time for me to do so. I do not miss the Army, but I do miss the people; almost without exception they represented all that is great about our different National characteristics – the Scots, the English, the Welsh and the Irish all being subtly (or not so subtly) different but all making a cohesive and inimitable contribution to our United Kingdom.

OF war reporter Catherine Philp, referring to her experiences in Iraq, summed up her own reasons why she did her job to the pupils of Fettes on Founder's Day 2009:

...for all its other bleakness this is the extraordinary fact of war, and the reason I keep going back. Not just because there are stories that must be told, voices that must be given to the voiceless, and atrocities that might otherwise go unwitnessed. But because in war, the best, and worst of humanity is on offer. The darkness and the light. And you never know which you'll find along the road.

War will never stop fascinating humanity, and not only the male of the species. Although the numbers of OFs joining up have declined since their Victorian peak, Fettes probably sends an above-average number of young people into the armed services. Thanks to the failure of humanity to evolve in the direction envisaged by the optimistic philosophers of Sir William Fettes' youth, there is no doubt that the state will continue to have need of them. In terms of the duty, in its broadest sense, which the first Headmaster so cherished, Fettes College will still 'Carry On.' Just as Fettes pupils first saw combat in Afghanistan, it is perhaps appropriate to end with the observations of Ollie Blake, who served there in the twenty-first century:

I look back on my time in the Army with the happiest of memories shared with the most phenomenal, loyal, happy and dedicated bunch of soldiers. There is no doubt that Fettes prepared me for war in many ways – physically, emotionally and intellectually. But perhaps the most important lesson that Fettes taught me was the value in life of camaraderie and of friendship - with such support anything can be achieved.

NOTES

1 *Fettesian*, 1993

2 *Fettesian*, 1991

3 *Fettesian*, 2002

4 Suzanna Chambers & Edward Black, 'Lest we forget?' *Daily Express*, 12 November 2000

5 *Fettesian*, 2003

6 Ibid.

7 Ibid.

8 Ibid.

9 Ibid.

10 Lt Matt Leary, talk to Fettes CCF, 23 February 2008

11 *Fettesian*, 2003

12 Ibid.

13 Ibid., 2002

14 Ibid., 2001

15 Quoted in Robert Chesshyre, 'The young guns of the Army Cadet Force', *Daily Telegraph*, 12 November 2009

16 Graeme Paton, 'Army cadets should be established in all schools', *Daily Telegraph*, 30 July 2008

17 Email to the author, 6 November 2009

18 In conversation with the author, June 2010

19 Rory Carroll, 'Perilous fight against shadowy enemy', *Guardian*, 9 April 2002

20 *Industria*, 2003

21 In conversation with the author, June 2010

22 In conversation with the author, July 2010

23 Quoted in Mike Rossiter, *Target Basra* (London, Bantam, 2008) p. 348

24 Ibid., p. 349

25 *Fettesian*, 2009

26 Auslan Cramb, 'Tony Blair's Old School satirises the ex-PM', *Daily Telegraph*, 12 November 2007

27 In conversation with the author, June 2010

28 Ibid.

29 Magnus Linklater, 'Scottish troops trying to keep the peace in Afghanistan', Times, 9 July 2008

30 Email to the author, 3 May 2011

31 Ibid., 2002

32 Ibid., 2003

33 Ibid.

34 Ibid.

35 Ibid., 2005

36 *Fettesian*, 2005

37 Army press release accessed 9 August 2010

38 Email to the author, 24 April 2010

39 Ian Gardiner, 'Air Security? Lethal weapons can be found on the other side of checks', *Scotsman*, 5 June 2008

40 Email to the author, 6 November 2009

Bibliography

Jack Alexander, *McCrae's Battalion* (Edinburgh, Mainstream, 2003)

S. Allen & A. Carswell, *The Thin Red Line: War, Empire & Visions of Scotland* (Edinburgh, NMS, 2004)

Leo Amery (ed.), *The Times History of the War in South Africa*, Vol. II (London, Sampson Low, Marston, 1900-9)

Henry William Auden, *A Minimum of Greek* (Toronto, Morang & Co., 1906)

H.H. Austin, *With MacDonald in Africa* (London, Edward Arnold, 1903)

A.A.S. Barnes, *On Active Service with the Chinese Regiment* (London, Grant Richards, 1902)

Corelli Barnett, *Britain And Her Army* (London, Weidenfeld & Nicholson, 2000)

Andy Beckett, *When the Lights went out* (London, Faber & Faber, 2010)

James Boswell, *Journal of a Tour to the Hebrides with Samuel Johnson, LL.D* (New York, Viking Press, 1936, first published 1775)

Paul Brickhill, *The Great Escape* (London, Cassell ed., 2000)

Michael Burleigh, *Earthly Powers* (London, Harper Perennial, 2006)

Michael Byrne (ed.) *Collected Poems and Songs of George Campbell Hay* (Edinburgh, University Press, 2003)

Tim Carroll, *The Great Escape from Stalag Luft III* (Edinburgh, Mainstream, 2004)

Miranda Carter, *Anthony Blunt: His Lives* (London, Pan, 2001)

Henry Chancellor, *James Bond: the man and his world* (London, John Murray, 2005)

Winston Churchill, *The Story of the Malakand Field Force*, (London, 1897)

Anthony Clayton, *The British Officer* (Pearson, London, 2006)

Lord Cockburn, *Memorials of His Time* (Edinburgh, Black, 1856)

Bryan Cooper, *The Tenth (Irish) Division in Gallipoli* (London, Jenkins, 1918)

Gordon Corrigan, *Mud, Blood and Poppycock* (London, Cassell, 2004)

Mary Cosh, *Edinburgh: the Golden Age* (Edinburgh, Birlinn, 2003)

Con Coughlin, *American Ally: Tony Blair and the War on Terror* (New York, HarperCollins, 2006)

Robert Cowley (ed.) *No End Save Victory*, (New York, Putnam, 2001)

John Darwin, *Britain and Decolonisation* (London, Palgrave, 1988)

Saul David, *Zulu: the Heroism & Tragedy of the Zulu War of 1879* (London, Viking, 2004)

Saul David, *Victoria's Wars* (London, Viking, 2006)

T.M. Devine, *The Scottish Nation 1700-2000* (London, Penguin, 1999)

T.M. Devine, *Scotland's Empire* (London, Penguin, 2007)

Clive Dewey, *Anglo-Indian Attitudes: the Mind of the Indian Civil Service* (London, Hambledon, 1993)

A. Dougan, *Through the Crosshairs* (New York, Carroll & Graf, 2006)

Sir J.E. Edmonds, *Military Operations, France & Belgium 1914* (London, Macmillan, 1937)

Elie Parish Church Guild, *Rev. W.N. Monteith* (booklet, 2008)

Cyril Falls, *The First World War* (London, Longman, 1967)

Robert Farquharson, *For Your Tomorrow* (London, Trafford, 2004)

Thomas Fegan, *The Baby Killers: German Air Raids on Britain in the First World War* (Barnsley, Pen & Sword, 2002)

Niall Ferguson, *The Pity of War* (London, Penguin, 1998)

Niall Ferguson, *Empire: how Britain made the modern world* (London, Allen Lane, 2003)

Nigel Fisher, *Iain Macleod* (London, Andre Deutsch, 1973)

Ian Gardiner, *In the Service of the Sultan* (Barnsley, Pen & Sword, 2006)

A.I.R. Glasfurd, *Rifle and Romance in the Indian Jungle,* (London, John Lane, 1905)

Alexander Glen, *Young Men in the Arctic* (London, Faber & Faber, 1935)

Alexander Glen, *Footholds against a Whirlwind* (London, Hutchinson, 1975)

Alexander Glen, *Target Danube* (Lewes, Book Guild, 2002)

James Grant, *Old and New Edinburgh*, (Cassell, Edinburgh, 1886) Vol III

John Guest, *Broken Images – a Journal* (London, Longman, 1949)

Ronnie Guild, *Own Tales* (Edinburgh, 2008)

Nick Hammond, *Venture into Greece* (London, William Kimber, 1983)

Robert Hardie, *The Burma-Siam Railway* (London, IWM, 1983)

Maitland Hardyman, *A Challenge* (London, Allen & Unwin, 1919)

Ian Harvey, *Talk of Propaganda* (London, Falcon, 1947)

Ian Harvey, *To fall like Lucifer* (London, Sidgwick & Jackson, 1971)

Max Hastings, *Bomber Command: The Myth and Reality of the Strategic Bombing Offensive* (New York, Dial Press, 1979)

Ian Hay, *The First Hundred Thousand* (London, Blackwood, 1915)
Ian Hay, *All in it: K(1) Carries On* (New York, Houghton Mifflin, 1917)
Ian Hay, *The Oppressed English*, (New York, Doubleday, Page & Co., 1917)
Ian Hay, *Arms and the Men* (London, HMSO, 1950)
Howard Hensman, *A History Of Rhodesia* (Edinburgh, Blackwood, 1900)
Vernon Hesketh-Prichard, *Where Black Rules White* (New York, Charles Scribner, 1900)
Vernon Hesketh-Prichard, *Through the Heart of Patagonia* (New York, Appleton, 1902)
Vernon Hesketh-Prichard, *Sniping in France* (London, Hutchinson, 1920)
Tom Hickman, *The Call-up: A History of National Service* (London, Headline, 2004)
Gertrude Himmelfarb, *The Roads To Modernity* (New York, Random House, 2004)
Eric Hobsbawm, *Nations and Nationalism since 1780* (Cambridge, 1990)
Eric Hobsbawm & Terence Ranger (eds), *The Invention Of Tradition* (Cambridge University Press, 1983)
Warren Hope, *Norman Cameron: his Life, Work & Letters* (London, Greenwich Exchange, 2000)
John Humphries, *A Lifetime of Verse* (Bicester, Dogma, 2006)
J. Forsyth Ingram, *The Story of an African City* (Maritzburg, Coetzer, 1898)
C.L.R. James, *Beyond a Boundary* (London, Hutchinson, 1963)
Lawrence James, *Warrior Race – a History of the British at War* (London, Little, Brown, 2001)
Andrew Jeffrey, *This Present Emergency* (Mainstream, Edinburgh, 1992)
Stephen Jeffery-Poulter, *Peers, queers, and commons: the struggle for gay law reform from 1950 to the present* (London, Routledge, 1991)
C.A. Jenkins, *Days of a Dogsbody* (London, Harrap, 1946)
Roy Jenkins, *The Chancellors* (London, Macmillan, 1998)
Paul Johnson, *The Suez War* (London, MacGibbon & Kee, 1957)
Paul Johnson, *Modern Times* 2nd Ed., (London, Phoenix, 1999)
Dr Samuel Johnson, *A Journey to the Western Isles of Scotland* (London, 1775)
Sandy Johnstone, *Spitfire into War* (London, Grafton, 1988)
Denis Judd & Keith Surridge, *the Boer War* (Palgrave Macmillan, New York, 2003)
John Keegan, *The Battle for History* (London, Pimlico, 1997)
Paul Kennedy, *The Realities Behind Diplomacy* (London, Fontana, 1981)
Paul Kennedy, *The Rise and Fall of the Great Powers* (Fontana, London 1989)
Heinz Knocke, *I Flew for the Führer* (London, Cassell ed., 2003)
Keith Kyle, *Suez: Britain's End of Empire in the Middle East* (London, I.B. Tauris, 2003)
David Kynaston, *Austerity Britain* (London, Bloomsbury, 2008)
John Laffin, *Raiders* (Stroud, Sutton, 1999)
J. Lawrence & R. Lawrence, *When the fighting is over: Tumbledown* (London, 22 Books, 1987)
A. Lawrie & J. Mackay Thompson, *Old Fettesians who served in His Majesty's Forces at home and abroad during the Great War* (Edinburgh, 1920)
Alexia Lindsay et al., *William Fettes* (Edinburgh, Fettes College, 1996)
Robert Bruce Lockhart, *Memoirs of a British Agent* (London, Putnam, 1932)
Robert Bruce Lockhart, *Retreat from Glory* (London, Putnam, 1934)
Robert Bruce Lockhart, *Return to Malaya* (London, Putnam, 1936)
Robert Bruce Lockhart, *My Scottish Youth*, (London, Putnam, 1937)
Robert Bruce Lockhart, *Comes the Reckoning* (London, Putnam, 1947)
Robert Bruce Lockhart, *Friends, Foes & Foreigners* (London, Putnam, 1957)
Stephen H. Louden, *Chaplains in Conflict* (Avon Books, London, 1996)
Ursula Low, *Fifty Years with John Company: from the letters of General Sir John Low of Clatto, Fife 1822-1858* (London, John Murray, 1936)
Callum MacDonald & Jan Kaplan, *Prague in the shadow of the swastika: A history of the German occupation* (Vienna, Facultas Verlags- und Buchhandels AG, 2001)
H.F. MacDonald (ed.) *A Hundred Years of Fettes* (Edinburgh, Constable, 1970)
Ian Mackenzie, *Brief Encounters: A Fettes Memoir* (privately published, 2002)
R.J. Mackenzie, *Almond of Loretto* (London, Constable, 1905)
J.D. Mackie, *a History of Scotland* (London, Penguin, 1964)
Fitzroy Maclean, *Eastern Approaches* (London, Jonathan Cape, 1949)
Norman MacMillan, *The Royal Air Force in the Second World War*, Vol. II (London, Harrap, 1944)
Tommy Macpherson & Richard Bath, *Behind Enemy Lines* (Edinburgh, Mainstream 2010)
Magnus Magnusson, *The Clacken and the Slate* (London, Collins, 1974)
J.A. Mangan, *The Games Ethic and Imperialism* (London, Frank Cass, 1998)
J.A. Mangan, *Athleticism in the Victorian & Edwardian Public School* (London, Routledge, 2000)
Andrew Marr, *A History of Modern Britain* (London, Pan, 2009)

Karl Marx & Frederick Engels, *the Communist Manifesto* (London, 1848)

E. McCamley & W. Dunbar (eds) *Belfast Royal Academy* (Belfast, 2010)

W.K. M'Clure, *Italy in North Africa* (London, Constable, 1913)

Helen McCorry, *The Thistle at War* (Edinburgh, NMS, 1997)

D.B.McDowell, *A Brief History of Collyer's* (Horsham, 2002)

David McKittrick & David McVea, *Making Sense of the Troubles* (London, Penguin, 2000)

Andy McSmith, *No such thing as Society: a history of Britain in the 1980s* (London, Constable, 2010)

William J. Mills, *Exploring Polar Frontiers* (Santa Barbara, ABC CLIO, 2003)

Norval Mitchell, *Sir George Cunningham* (Edinburgh, Blackwood, 1968)

R. Morris, *Aboard HMS May Island* (Save the Wemyss Ancient Caves Society, 2006)

H.G. Newman, *Old Fettesians who served in H.M. Forces during the War 1939-45* (Edinburgh, Fettes 1948)

Ian Nimmo, *Scotland at War*, (Edinburgh, Scotsman Publications, 1989)

D. N. Panigrahi, *India's partition: the story of imperialism in retreat* (London, Routledge, 2004)

Edward Pearce, *The Lost Leaders* (London, Little, Brown, 1997)

Mark Peel, *The Land of Lost Content* (Durham, Pentland, 1996)

Robert Philp, *A Keen Wind Blows* (London, James & James, 1998)

Mark Postlethwaite, *Hampden Squadrons in Focus* (London, Red Kite, 2003)

Alfred Price, *Spitfire Mark I/II Aces* (London, Osprey, 1996)

H. R. Pyatt (ed.) *Fifty Years of Fettes* (Edinburgh, Constable, 1931)

Harold Pyman, *Call To Arms* (London, Leo Cooper, 1971)

J.D.R. Rawlings, *The History of the Royal Air Force* (London, Temple Press, 1984)

Andrew Rawnsley, *Servants of the People: the inside story of New Labour* (London, Penguin, 2001)

Cecil Reddie, *Abbotsholme* (London, Allen, 1900)

John Rentoul, *Tony Blair, Prime Minister* (London, Little, Brown, 2001)

Angelique Richardson, *Love and Eugenics in the Late Nineteenth Century* (Oxford, OUP, 2003)

William Robertson, *A History of Scotland* (London, 1759)

Charles Rollings, *Prisoners of War* (London, Ebury, 2007)

Theodore Roosevelt, *The Rough Riders* (New York, Collier, 1899)

W.C.A. Ross, *The Royal High School* (Edinburgh, Oliver & Boyd, 1934)

Mike Rossiter, *Target Basra* (London, Bantam, 2008)

Cornelius Ryan, *A Bridge Too Far* (London, Hamish Hamilton, 1974)

Francis Salvesen, *Journal of a Student at Arms* (Warrior Enterprises, Bristol, 1989)

T.E. Sandall, *A History of the 5th Batt. Lincolnshire Regt.* (Oxford, Blackwell, 1923)

Dominic Sandbrook, *Never Had it So Good: A History of Britain from Suez to the Beatles* (London, Abacus, 2006)

Walter Schellenberg, *Invasion 1940* (Little, Brown, London, 2001)

Victoria Schofield, *Afghan frontier: feuding and fighting in Central Asia* (London, I.B. Tauris, 2003)

Robin Scott-Elliott, *The Way Home* (Leicester, Troubador, 2007)

R.E. Scouller, *The Armies of Queen Anne* (Oxford, OUP, 1966)

William Seymour, *British Special Forces* (London, Sidgwick & Jackson, 1985)

G. Sparrow & J.N.MacB. Ross, *On Four Fronts with the Royal Naval Division* (London, Hodder & Stoughton, 1918)

Edward Spiers, *Haldane– Army Reformer* (Edinburgh, University Press, 1980)

G.W. Steevens, *With Kitchener to Khartum* (New York, Dodd, Mead & Co., 1911)

A.T.Q. Stewart, *Belfast Royal Academy: The First Century 1785-1885* (Belfast, 1985)

Hew Strachan, *The Outbreak of the First World War* (Oxford, OUP, 2004)

D.R. Thorpe, *Selwyn Lloyd*, (Jonathan Cape, London, 1989)

Alex von Tunzelmann, *Indian Summer: The Secret History of the End of an Empire* (London, Picador, 2008)

Alwyn Turner, *Crisis? What Crisis? Britain in the 1970s* (London, Aurum, 2009)

Graham Walker, *A History of the Ulster Unionist Party*, (Manchester, MUP, 2004)

P.J. Waller, *Town, City & Nation* (Oxford, OUP, 1983)

Gabriel Warburg, *Islam, Sectarianism and Politics in Sudan since the Mahdiyya* (London, Hurst, 2003)

Clive Whitehead, *Colonial Education* (London, I.B. Taurus, 2003)

E.H. Wilcox, *Russia's Ruin* (New York, Scribner, 1919)

J.M. Winter, *The Great War and the British People* (London, Macmillan, 1986)

Marguerite Wood, 'The Notebook of Sir William Fettes, Bart.', *Book of the Old Edinburgh Club*, 1953

M. Young & R. Stamp, *Trojan Horses* (London, Bodley Head, 1989)

Index

Ackroyd, Ronald 782
Adam, Alexander 3-4
Adam, A.R. 241
Adam, Norman Macleod 130
Adam, P. 'Sarge' 27, 28, 136
Adam, W.B. 122, 141, 150, 156, 159, 163, 165, 168, 171-5, 179, 225, 254-268, 282-4
Adams, N.V.M. 433, 485
Adams, Ord 152
Adamson, W.C. 240
Addison, J.V.G.P. 795
Afghanistan, Afghans 43, 47, 51, 65, 69, 101, 111-2, 307, 666, 853-7, 861-5
Ahlers, P. 141
Air Training Corps 397-9
Airey, W.M. 383
Aitken, 'Bill' 688
Aitken, G. 679
Alabaster, Denys 514
Alexander, Andrew 826, 850, 870,
Alexander, J.M. 668
Alexander, Peter 223, 870
Allan, James 716
Allsebrook, A.J. 441-2
Allsebrook, P.W. 505, 511, 668
Almond, Hely 40-1, 114
Alston, Tim 712
Amnesty International 793, 831
Anderson, Bobby 480
Anderson, Charles 224
Anderson, Edward (Teddie) 224, 236-8, 269-70, 276
Anderson, Eric 698, 700
Anderson, Fiona 851
Anderson, Herbert (Bertie) 224, 226-8
Anderson, H.E.C. 117
Anderson, John Kerr 98
Anderson, Mathew 214
Anderson, Robert 589, 597, 599
Anderson, Ronald 224
Angus, James 866
ANZAC 231, 244-5
Appeasement 358-60, 371-2
Arabs 251, 309, 447, 661, 663
Artbuthnot, John Campbell 45, 48
Arbuthnott, David 402, 411-2, 417

Arbuthnott, John Viscount 414, 789
Argentina 79, 121, 238, 306, 427, 609, 669, 798, 810
Armistice Day 1918 150, 230
Arniston House 698-700, 740-1, 777-8
Arnold, Thomas 33-4, 39
Ashcroft, Alec 176, 180, 284-6, 294, 332, 361, 384-6, 404-5, 407, 413-4, 417, 421, 435, 522, 602-4
Atbara, Battle of 84
Atkinson, Miles 172, 230
Auden, H.W. 41-2, 57-8, 123
Auld, J.H. 288
Austerity, post-war 576-7
Ayre, Andrew 704
Baden-Powell, Robert 39
Backhouse, Colin 480
Bain, Mickey 585, 589
Barnard, Andrew 784
Barnes, Arthur 51, 56-7, 100-104
Barnwell, Frank & Harold 235-6, 357
Barr, Leslie 'Chappie' 698, 713, 747
Barr, A. Lyle 483, 489, 605-6
Barton, Bertie 222
Barton, Charles, Robert & Thomas 255-7
Batmanghelidj, Fereydoon 669
Beament, Tib 576, 585, 587-8, 593
Beamish, G.C. 379-80, 397, 411, 416-7, 436, 553-4
Beaumont, Thomas 222
Bedell-Sivright, David 'Darkie' 244, 246-7
Belfast 298-9, 383, 763, 794, 837
Belfast (Royal) Academy 3, 7-8, 188
Bell, Malcolm 186
Bennett, Kirsty 819
Benson, Bruce 824
Berlin 13, 339, 469, 606-7, 615, 641-2, 645, 723, 847
Betts-Brown, Andrew 715-6
Biggart, Jonathan 817, 855-6, 871
Bisley 2, 129, 132, 323, 391, 698, 712, 760, 780, 783, 824
Black, James 222
Black, Stewart 566
Blaikie, James Adrian 63-5, 687

Blair, Tony 687-700, 730, 740-1, 788, 823, 827, 831-40, 853-4, 859, 862-5
Blake, Ollie 862-4, 870, 874
Bleakley, Bob 714-6
Blelloch, J.N.H. 576
Boase, Edgar 214
Boer War 90-102
Bohuslav-Kroupa, A.F. 113-4
Bolshevism 294, 294-8
Bombing, British 303, 409, 436-7, 467-71
Bombing, German 152-7, 379-90
Bond, James 542-4
Borrowman, A.P.R. 464
Bowden, Charles 111, 126
Bowden, Sydney 91, 502
Boxer Rebellion 94, 102-4
Boxing 318, 371, 519, 581-2, 633
Boyes, Mark 797
Braine, Hector 535
Britain, Battle of 405, 412, 438-9
British Honduras (Belize) 648
Britton, Allan 435-6
Brough, James 150
Broughton, John 781
Brown, Brian 535
Brown, David Cassels 513-4
Brown, Gordon 47, 853
Brown, James Hardie (father & son) 470
Brownlee, Fergus 759
Bryson, Lucy 793
Buchan, John 87, 548
Buchan, Lindsay 711, 714, 716, 720
Buchan, Paddy 464
Buchanan, Alan 204
Buchanan-Smith, George 537, 716, 718, 753, 793
Budberg, Moura 550
Burma, Burmese 45, 50, 67-8, 86, 117, 349, 493, 495, 510, 537, 571
Burns, Gillian 830
Burns, Robert 6-7, 9-10
Burtinshaw, R.J.G. 567
Butler, Brendan 819
Cadet Movement 109-10, 127-137, 296, 343-4, 706, 748, 783, 849, 853, 867, 872
Cairns, C.N. 504
Cameron, David 626, 657

Cameron, Ian 468-9
Cameron, J.R. 504, 538
Cameron, Norman (inter-war pupil, poet) 310, 323, 367, 459,
Cameron, Norman (post-war pupil) 588, 838
Cameron, Roderick 810
Campbell, David 870
Campbell, Duncan 63
Campbell, Hamish 601
Campbell, J.R. 467-8
Campbell Swinton, Alan 111
Camels 65, 249-50
Canada 57-8, 220, 304, 349, 435, 518-22, 637
Cardwell, Edward 30-1
Cargill, Featherston 88-9
Carmichael, D.S. 511
Carrington House 49, 168-9, 287, 323, 334, 372, 381, 384, 386, 411, 416, 507, 514-5, 531, 553-4
Carruthers, A.G.H. & R.A. 86
Casement, J.M. 259
Caskie, Donald 511
Castel Rosso 465-6
Cattenach, K.D.H. 480, 668
Catto, E.M. 668
Catto, W.E. 330-1, 367
Cavalry (regiments) 115-7, 350-2, 374, 640, 862-3
Censorship 268-70
Centenary of Fettes College 736-9
Certificate A 128, 133, 188, 343, 346, 371, 392, 584, 631, 714, 716
Ceylon 48, 74-5, 313, 352, 436
Changi Gaol 510, 523, 526, 528, 535
Chenevix-Trench, Anthony 445, 528, 532, 534, 536, 743, 768, 772, 776
Chetwynd, Walter 150
China, Chinese 56, 86, 94, 102-4, 118, 341, 437, 829
Chree, George 214
Christian, Roger 648
Churchill, Winston 72, 212, 241, 297, 303, 327, 360, 411, 433, 456, 465, 475, 553, 607, 612, 618, 626, 720-1
Civil Defence Section 709-10
Clark, Bill 605, 607-8

Clark, Neville 244, 728, 776, 785
Classical curriculum 41-4, 168
Clavering, Douglas 726-7
Clavering, Johnny 816
Clegg, Barry 581-2, 585-6, 590-3
Cleland, J.R. 668
Clift, Cecil 214
Clubb, Lindsay 711-2
Cochrane, Cameron 776, 792
Cochrane, Fiona 779
Cockburn, Henry, Lord 4, 9-10, 15
Collister, Andrew 869
Collister, Chris 844
Colquhon, Patric 716
Combined Cadet Corps 584-601, 622, 623, 630, 638, 698, 702-14, 735, 738-9, 743-54, 779-85, 795-6, 809, 820-4, 848-50, 868-9, 872
Communism 295, 297-8, 316, 365, 369-70, 552-3, 562-4, 757,
Connery, Sean 544, 840
Cook, G. 666
Cook, Walter 32, 51, 66
Cooke-Taylor, Charles 503
Cooper, Clifford 516-8, 538
Cooper, Kenneth 675
Cooper, Patrick Ashley 352
Cooper, Sam 870
Cormack, John 700
Coronel, Battle of 259
Cotterill, Clement 24, 40-1, 248, 830
Cowie, J.D. 393, 409, 487, 489, 494, 531-2, 606
Craig, Robert 431
Craig-Adams, Michael 433-6
Crete 441, 443-4
Crichton-Miller, Donald 578-9
Crimean War 27-8
Cumming, A.R.H. 391-2, 435
Cunningham, D. 504
Cunningham, Sir George 306, 351, 664-5, 679
Cunningham, Sir Josias 835
Cunningham, Sir Knox 298, 329, 699-70, 713, 722, 739, 761-3
Currie, Hugh 674
Currie, I.R. 435
Currie, J.D. 503
Currie, Sir William 289, 471, 667
Cyprus 646-8

Dalyell, Tam 438, 844
Daniels, Tim 585, 638-9
Dann, F.E.T. 467
Dardanelles Campaign 235, 241-9
Davidson, F.C. 306
Davidson, Richard 703
Davis, Alastair 225
Day, Michael 448
De Valera, Eamon 299, 301
Debating, school 111-2, 137-9, 329-30, 336-7, 701, 721, 723, 866
De Chastelain, John 751, 835-6
Dewar, Hewan 432
Dick, Colin 464
Dick, David 494
Dickson, Alan 185
Dillon, George 36, 50-1, 67-9
Disarmament 343, 345, 358, 618
Donald, Alan 640
Donald, Pippa 794
Donald, Robin 388, 393, 407, 408, 412-3
Doughty, Bill 448
Douglas, Charles 21, 823
Douglas, R.H. 711
Douglas, Rob 707
Dowell, Gordon 699, 708, 711,
Downie, R.G. 493
Drysdale, G.R. 503
Duff, Alan 48-9
Duke, D.A. 347, 534
Duncan, A.B. 306
Duncan, G.R. 431
Dundas, Harry (Viscount Melville) 6, 8, 10, 12, 13
Dundas, W.F. 504
Dunford, Hugh 717, 730
Dunkirk 383, 394, 411, 431
Dunlop, Jonathan 746-7, 749
Dunn-Pattison, R.P. 253
Dunnett, Stephen 601
Durham, Robin 745
Durie, Ian 815-6
Durie. T.P. 646
Easter Rebellion 1916 254-7
Eccles, Chris 784
Eden, Sir Anthony 341, 676-8
Edinburgh Academy 4, 41, 46, 57, 110, 127, 131, 139, 279, 317, 323,
Edinburgh (Royal) High School 3-4, 8, 16, 110, 689, 703
Egypt 55, 80, 309, 354, 675-9

El Alamein, Battle of 412, 448, 450, 496

Elandslaagte, Battle of 92-4

Elie (Fife) 47, 150-2, 321-2, 348, 594, 794

Ellis, Jack 424

Enlightenment 2-8, 866

Esplen, Bill 469

European Communities/Institutions 616, 670, 675, 771, 827

Evers, Richard 391, 415, 417

Fairweather, David 395, 398-9, 401, 406, 411

Falklands War 797-810

Farmar, William 503

Fawcett, A.M. 250-254

Ferguson, David Whigham 642

Ferguson, Duncan 798, 803-4

Ferguson, Graeme 449

Ferguson, Ian 354

Ferguson, Jock 782

Ferguson, John 587, 588, 710, 760, 767

Ferguson, Malcolm 680

Festeubert, Battle of 210-1, 224

Fet-Lor Club 331-3, 340, 544, 580, 719, 754

Fettes, Maria (Malcolm) 6, 14, 19

Fettes Peak/Mount Fettes (New Zealand) 21, 355, 823-4

Fettes, Sir William 2-8, 11-13, 18-21

Fettes, William (son) 13, 15

Field, Charles 240

Findlay, Arthur, 118n

Findlay, Charles 84

Findlay, Ian 463

Finlay, G.L.F. 432, 504

Finlayson, James 491, 493, 494

Fleming, Charles 44, 50, 90, 524

Fleming, Ian 542, 544, 548, 555, 558, 573

Fleming, Sarah 582

Foch, Ferdinand 227

Foot, John 781

Fortune, Caroline 780

Founder's Day 131, 140, 165, 289, 302, 343, 386, 414, 443, 511, 571, 576, 578, 619, 664, 667, 679, 690, 692, 717, 720, 728-9, 737, 740, 762, 768-9, 788-9, 834, 836, 852, 858, 874

Fox, Alastair 701, 707

Franklin, J.M. 674

Franklin, T.B. 129, 131-5, 146

Fraser, Hugo 735, 739-40

Fraser, Michael 721, 739, 770

Fraser, Patrick 435

French Revolutionary Wars 7-17

Fyfe, Neil 712

Gaitskell, Hugh 577, 612, 677-8

Gallie, Alexander Knox 440, 447

Gallie, George Holmes 464

Gallie, Henry Holmes 73

Gallie, Robert 431

Galloway, R. M. 243

Galloway, George 864

Gardiner, Ian 757-9, 764, 799-810, 871-2

Gassert, Imogen 833

Geddes, Willie 380, 386, 387, 390, 394, 395, 399, 424, 426, 440

Germany, Germans 122-5, 141, 147, 153, 187, 267, 284, 288, 330, 339, 359, 362-3, 365, 367-8, 375, 396, 408-9, 463, 488, 504, 517-9, 521, 531, 549, 576-7, 595, 605-6, 608, 637, 639-46, 748, 760, 780, 796-7, 814-5

Giants, prevalence of references to 44

Gilchrist, W.M. 287, 536

Giles, Henry 317-8, 392, 594

Gilroy, Tony 644

Glasfurd, A.I.R. 116-7

Glen, Sandy 355-6, 367, 544, 553-61, 768, 772

Glencorse House 40-1, 109, 111, 130, 141, 163, 302, 382, 416, 584, 631, 728

Goldschmidt, 'Froggy' 114

Goodbody, Desmond 472

Goodbody, Douglas 480

Good Schools Guide 791-2

Gordon, Charles 82-3

Gordon, Lindsay 475

Gordon, R.H. 123, 239, 308

Graham, Ian 445-6, 508, 537

Graham-Brown, Caroline 837, 871, 873

Grahame, Clementina 20

Grant, Sir Alfred Hamilton 43, 307

Grant, D.J. 348, 365, 386

Gray, Charles 324, 350, 374-5, 506

Gray, Julie 851

Gray, Wingate 204, 309

Gray-Buchanan, Cecil 245

Great Escape 514-8

Greaves, Rob 799-800

Greece (modern; for ancient, see Classical Curriculum) 248, 441, 463, 561-4, 607, 646

Greenaway, I.F. 480

Griffiths, Neil 'Gurkha' 763-6

Guest, John 333-4, 383, 426, 432, 447, 451, 458-9

Guild, Ronnie 425-6, 492, 494-6, 600-1, 604-5, 670, 704-5, 710, 737-8

Gulf War (1990-1) 814-6, 844

Gunn, Alistair 514-8

Guthrie, Colin 416

Haig, C.J. 815

Haig, Douglas 127, 188, 212, 230

Haiti 52-3, 100, 543

Haszlakiewicz, M.J. 712, 760

Haldane, R.B. (army reform) 127-9, 136

Hall, Kenneth 380, 382

Hamilton, Ian 708

Hamilton, Jock 466-7, 501

Hamilton Fyfe, Henry 46-7, 140, 147, 268, 284, 297, 314

Hammond, Nicholas 466-7, 561-4, 692, 720

Hanbury, Sir Cecil 366

Hanson, R. de G. 727, 808

Hardie, Robert 157, 162, 166, 445, 524-30, 533, 536

Hardyman, Maitland 149, 151, 244-5, 271-3, 295-6

Harkness, James 846-7

Harrison, A.J.R. 674

Harvey, Alan 301-2, 310, 325, 426, 462-3

Harvey, Ian 320, 340, 361, 367, 395-6, 583, 617, 620-1, 762, 789-90

Haugh, David 610

Hay, George Campbell 363-4, 373-4, 427-8, 506, 653, 770, 787

Hay, Ian (John Hay Beith) 30, 129, 176, 180, 185, 189, 214-6, 230, 256-7, 269, 293, 316, 347, 603

Heard, William 27, 41, 179-80, 285

Heatley, James 706

Hebeler, Bernard Armstrong 97

Hendy, Ronald 138, 299-300

881

Herdman, Nigel 711, 748-9
Herford, Bernard & Geoffrey 243, 259
Heron, Alastair 623
Herriot, Allan 375, 428, 564
Herzberg, Charles 387, 518-23
Hesketh-Prichard, Vernon 36-7, 39, 52-4, 199, 206-7, 215-20, 268, 316, 545-8
Hill, Octavia 109-10
Hills, Joe 705, 775, 779
Hinshelwood, Thomas 238
Hodge, Sandy 442-3, 492-3
Holt, Justin 816, 818, 831-2, 840, 853-7, 861-2, 871
Hooper, J.G.D. 369-70
Hope, John Deans 99
Hudson, A.W. 177
Hudson, Norman 442
Hughes, Robin 687
Humble, Richard 357-8, 471, 769
Humphries, John 379-80, 383, 391-2, 393-4, 402, 404-5, 410, 413, 415-7, 429, 469, 472, 534, 604, 606, 685
Hunter, Andrew 709-10
Hunter, Colin 493, 510
Hunter, Jimmy 485
Hunter, Murray 346, 368-9, 447, 450-2
Hunter-Blair, R.S. 32, 82
Hutchins, C.D.M. 504, 505, 530
Hutchinson, A.O. 430
Imperial Yeomanry 96, 98, 115, 117
India, Indians 6, 31, 43, 47-50, 55, 56, 65-73, 98, 115-8, 121, 139, 306-8, 312, 313, 348-9, 350-2, 426, 427, 445 494-6, 510, 663-7, 691, 784
Indonesian Confrontation 725-7
Inglis, J. 504
Inglis, Willy 785, 816-7
Iraq, Iraqis 254, 374, 814-6, 855-61
Ireland (pre-1922), Irish 11, 29, 112, 139, 254-7, 298-301, 329
Ireland, J.D. 435
Irvine, Neil 467, 474, 478-81, 489-90,
Irvine Robertson, A. 432
Isandlwana see Blaikie
Italy, Italians 26, 39, 139-40, 224, 363, 366, 374, 409-10, 439,

456-67, 497, 505-6, 509, 511, 570
Jackson, Alyster 42-3, 302, 320, 322, 324, 326, 329, 340, 366-8, 426-7, 433, 457, 661
Jackson, Neil, 709
James, C.L.R. 34, 38
Jamieson, Donald 731
Jamieson, Douglas 358
Jardine, Allan 744-5, 750-2
Jeff, John 628, 630, 631, 634, 640, 641-2, 644-5, 653, 655, 656-7
Jenkins, Charles 304-5, 326-7
Jenkins, K.F. 352
Jenkins, Roy 327, 358-9, 371
Jerusalem 252-3, 432, 451, 471, 661
Johnson, Christopher 609-10
Johnson, J.M.H. 514
Johnson, Samuel 3, 11, 53
Johnston, G.A.B. 436
Johnston, G.C.N. 355
Johnston, Stephen 523
Johnstone, Alan 460
Johnstone, Sandy 405-6
Jones, Hugh 442
Journey's End 319, 408, 740-2, 846
Jutland, Battle of 166, 259
Keith, Lindsay 700, 701, 714
Keith, R.F. 472
Kenion, J.M. 330-1
Kennedy, John F. 700-1
Kenya 311-2, 453, 649-50, 654, 655-6, 667, 679-84, 688, 691
Ker, Andrew 589
Kidston, Adrian 487
Kilpatrick, David 586-7
Kimmerghame House 130, 285, 301-2, 323, 390-1, 399, 480, 698, 717-8, 747, 852, 859-60
King, Andrew 204
King, John 691
Kipling, Rudyard 56, 96, 99, 146, 547
Kirk, Bingham 379, 384, 469, 471, 606
Kirkness, James 383
Kirkwood, Gordon 703
Kirsop, James 703, 704, 710-11
Kitchener, Lord 84, 92, 97, 114, 188, 212
Knight, R.J. 423
Knocke, Heinz 514-5
Korean War 604, 608, 610-3, 640

Kuwait 814-6
Lamb, Lindsay 444
Lamont, Louise 830-1, 840-1
Lang, Charlie 650-3, 659, 674-5
Laslett, H.C.R. 504
Latham, Arthur 58
Lawder, K.M. 259
Lawrence, Christopher 754-5
Lawrence, Robert 754-6, 794, 798, 800, 804, 806-8, 871
Layman, Alexandra 780, 810
Learmont, John 687, 796
Leary, Matt 849-50, 857, 861
Leckie, James 464
Leckie, Roy 784
Lee, William 26-7
Le Maitre, Sir Alfred 135, 141, 152, 158, 166-7
Le Queux, William 125-6
Leresche, Charles 354
Libya 39, 139-40, 441, 514
Lice 209
Liddell, Hamish 380, 383, 390, 408, 411, 412, 423, 453, 605
Liebenthal, L.G. 243
Lindsay, Alexia 286-7, 382
Lindsay, Sandy 214, 286-7
Lloyd, Arthur 200, 220
Lloyd, Selwyn 162, 177, 179, 180, 286, 320, 473, 476, 482, 484, 489-91, 547, 617-9, 621, 675-9, 722, 738, 788-9
Lockerby, William 448
Lockhart, Sir Robert Bruce 37-8, 49, 75-7, 101, 110, 136, 284, 296-7, 300, 315-6, 333, 339, 350-3, 359, 402-3, 548-52, 619-20, 659, 739, 789
Lodge, Jerry 286-7, 329, 381, 411-2, 507
Logan, W.D. 430
Loos, Battle of 151, 152, 211-2
Loretto College 36, 40, 78, 114, 136, 172, 173, 280, 322, 331, 504, 553, 628, 787
Lorimer, William 787-8
Lowles, Ian 708
Lumber Camps 174-5
Lumsden, J.M.A. 428, 459
Lyon, Francis H. 259, 297
Lyons, M.C. 391, 393, 400-1, 416
MacAlpine, George 711-2, 744, 746, 782
MacDonald, Allen 313

MacDonald, A.R. 668
MacDonald, Colin 688
MacDonald, H. 'Jock' 253-4
MacDonald, H.F. 'Freddy' 301, 384, 400, 415, 428, 435, 496, 617, 735, 739, 742
Macdonald, Roddy 725-6, 748
Macdonald, Tim 852
Macfarlane, P. 815, 816, 817
MacGibbon, James 369, 373, 552-3
MacGregor, Donald 288, 503
MacGregor, Douglas 416, 627, 635
MacIldowie, Edward 213-4
Macindoe, Gourlay 311
Macindoe, R.C.B. 243
Macintosh, Angus 627, 631, 645
MacIntyre, Alastair 619
MacIntyre, Duncan 691
MacIntyre, Ian 615
Mackay, Eric 484-6, 512-3
Mackie, Alexander 223
Mackenzie, Alan 523, 537
Mackenzie, Charles 486-7
Mackenzie, Ian (pre-WW1 pupil) 225
Mackenzie, Ian (WW2 pupil) 386, 416
Mackenzie, J.D. 504
Mackenzie, Kenneth 186, 229
Mackenzie, Moir 300-1
Mackenzie Stuart, Amanda 699, 738
Mackenzie Stuart, Jack 371-2, 379-82, 384, 386, 389, 392, 394, 411, 770-1
MacKinnon, N. 504, 505
Mackintosh, Donald 222-3, 227, 228, 276
Maclaren, Alastair 393, 402, 413
Maclay, Joe 158, 471
Maclean, Charles 691
Maclean, Sir Fitzroy 556
Maclean, Hector 56, 72-3,
Maclean, Lachlan Loudon 360
Maclean, Ranald 571, 596
Maclean, Raymond 745
Maclean, W.A. 200
Maclellan, Joseph 272
Macleod, Iain 366-7, 431, 473, 477, 617-8, 621, 679-86, 687-8, 698, 722, 738-9
Macleod, K.G. 300, 503
Macleod, Kirsty 793

Macleod, J. 504
Macleod, Rhoderick 367, 608, 663, 679-84
MacNair-Smith, James 306
Macnaughtan, Neil 628, 630, 632, 633, 641-6
Macphail, Alasdair 692
Macpherson, Archie 506
Macpherson, D.S.R. 186
Macpherson, G.P.S. 'Phil' 160, 163, 167-8, 179, 280, 285
Macpherson, Niall (Lord Drumalbyn) 670, 690, 789-90
Macpherson, Sir Tommy 372, 505-6, 509, 511-2, 535, 536, 568-71, 851-2
Macpherson, Sir William 121, 186, 231, 291, 292
MacQueen, Norman 448, 871
Macrae, R.I. 441, 444
MacVean, Neil 98, 109
Mair, Amanda 778-9
Mair, M.J. 677
Malaya 75-7, 352-3, 445, 493, 523, 650-3, 659, 673-5
Malcolm (family) 6-7
Mallinson, Robin 627, 635, 648-50, 655-6, 667
Malta 68, 435, 444, 448, 709
Mangan, J.A. 34, 38, 56
Marshall, Fred 79
Marshall, William 186
Masque, Centenary 736-7
Mather, Denholm 783-4, 824
Mathew, Grant 622
McCallum, A.D.D. 423
McCallum, Ian 464
McCallum, Kenneth 55, 423, 427, 460-2, 463-4, 496-7
McCallum, Malcolm 480
McClelland, Ralph 834
McCollum, David 719, 731
McCowan, H. 243
McGillycuddy, Richard 255, 464
McGillivray, Duncan 471
McGlashan, Donald 759
McGlashan, John 501, 506-7, 530, 531-2, 535, 536
McIntosh, Ian 696-7, 740
McKean, Charles 700-1
McKee, Ian 688-90, 692-3, 726
McKellar, A. 493
McKenna, Caitlin 865
McKerron, R.G. 508

McLennan, Raymond 794-5, 796-7
M'Clure, W.K. 39, 139-40
McMurray, David 699
McNeil, Jane 777
McNeill, H.M. 460
McWilliam, C.D. 399
McWilliam, D.S.D. 439-40, 668
Memorial Brass (19th century) 65, 89-90, 97-8
Mesopotamia 235, 254 (for post-WW1, see Iraq)
M'Ewen, Bruce 58
Mhor, Fergus 781
Mieklejohn, Matthew 93, 136-7
Millar, Ken 724, 759-60, 795, 801-2, 808-9, 814-5, 817-8, 828-9, 845, 873-4
Millar, N.G. 413
Miller, Archibald 238, 241
Miller, Iain 798
Miller, James Innes 246-7
Miller, John 493
Miller, Keith 745
Miller, T.A.G. 241-2
Milman, Kenneth 429, 431, 579
Milne, Kenneth 439
Mitchell, D.D. 511
Mitchell, J.H. 223
Mitchell, W.B. 216
Mitchell-Innes, Cecil 86
Mitchell-Rose, Colin 713
Mitchison, C.G.F. 763
M'Leod, Duncan 84-5
M'Neill, Tennant 308-9
Moir, J.M. 504
Moir, R.G. 523
Moncrieff, Dick 332-3
Moncrieff, Harry 431-2
Moncrieff, Francis & Norman 291
Monteith, Hugh 152
Monteith, John 152
Monteith, Patrick 214
Montieth, William 124, 150-2
Moñypenny, David 95
Moodie, Oliver 502-3
Moore, I.A.H. 321, 325
Moredun House 111, 226, 227, 276, 322-3, 384, 720, 721, 721
Morison, R.R. 468
Morris, Jeremy 821, 825, 826, 839, 848, 853
Morrison, Angus 753, 767, 770
Morrison, A.J.M. 458

Morrison, G. 321, 325, 340, 346, 365
Morrison, T.H. 436
Mosley, Sir Oswald 362, 366, 661
Mudie, Sir Francis 665-6
Muirhead, John Spencer 113
Muirhead, J.P. 468
Mure, Mary 752-3
Murphy, Christopher 868-9
Murray, Andrew 783, 784, 809, 821, 824, 825, 847-8
Murray, Andy 730
Murray, J. 223
Naiff, John 537
National Defence Force 295
National Socialism 339, 361-2, 367-8, 396-7, 410
Newman, H.G. 286, 408, 443, 603, 670
Newsom, A.W. 367, 472
Newton, Lovell 503
Nicholson, W.I. 225
Nigeria 58-9, 88-9, 310-1, 668, 671-4, 682-5, 687-8, 691, 754
Nimmo, Bill & Jimmy 472
Nimmo, Geordie 493
Nimmo, Patrick 439
Norie, E.W.M. 72, 102, 117
Normand, Christopher 576-8, 584, 594-5, 598-9, 610, 612-3, 616, 627-9, 633-4, 635, 636, 639-40, 647-8, 654-6, 676-7
Normand, Dick 373, 474, 488, 502
Normand, Jim 87
Normand, L.P. 686
Normand, Pat 91, 92-3, 95-6, 502
Normand, W.G. 358, 383-4
North, Mike 637-8
North-West Frontier see Afghanistan
Northern Ireland 298-9, 383, 700, 755, 760-7, 794, 831-2, 835-7, 862
Norway 432-3, 433-5, 474, 489, 514-5, 554-5, 557-8, 783
Nuclear Weapons 491, 537, 565, 612, 614-5, 638, 642, 643, 701, 709-10, 795
Officers' Training Corps 126, 127-136, 166, 167, 168-174, 231, 276, 279, 290-1, 316-8, 320-5, 328, 342-8

Ogilvie, Will 77-9

Ogilvy, David 620, 728-9
Oman 757-8
Orchard, David 788
O'Reilly, Fiona 823-4
Orwell, George 56, 340, 551, 838, 853
Outside Service 716, 717, 753, 793
Oxenham, Sian 784
Pacifism 318-9, 330-1, 342-5, 372, 614-5, 715-6, 730, 735, 742-3
Palestine 309-10, 351, 660-3
Park, Sam 391, 393, 399
Park, Sandy 399, 493
Park, William 248
Parker, Chris 593-4
Parker, Ronald 414
Passchendaele, Battle of 148, 200, 223-4, 870
Paterson, Robert 200-1
Patten, Charles 249
Pearse, J.F.W. 675
Peel, Mark 787, 833, 845
Philp, Catherine 858-9, 874
Philp, Robert 42, 700, 717, 792
Pig-sticking 350-1
Pipe band 134, 172, 294, 322, 324, 588, 730, 744-5, 751-2, 849, 865-6, 868
Polo 49, 72, 86, 351-2
Ponsford, Jim 298, 571-2
Potter, Alex 783-4
Potter, Harry 574n
Potts, Alexander 27, 34, 41, 43-4
Potts, Charles 449-50, 668
Potts, David 421
Prentice, W.D.R. 352
Preston, Eric 357
Preston, George 566, 638
Prophit, G.C. 310
Prosser, D.P.B. 504
Purves, Alec 504
Purves, Andrew 749
Purves, Trina 777, 780
Purves, Walter 249
Purves, W.D.C.L. 351
Pyatt, H.R. 44, 168-9, 280, 290, 302-3, 329, 358, 388, 508, 553-4
Pyman, George 566
Pyman, Sir Harold English 'Pete' 325, 328, 352, 429, 448-9, 473, 475, 482-4, 489-91, 512, 613, 641-2, 663, 705
Quiggin, P.V.M. 668

Raasay 503-4
Race 42-3, 51-7, 74-6, 101, 125-6, 314, 352-4, 410, 529, 659, 683, 702
Rae, Bruce 488, 601
Rae, Douglas 368, 373, 504, 507, 520, 531, 532,
Rae, Ian 475
Rae, Quentin 824
Raeburn, A.S. 430
Raeburn, G.F. 504, 505
Ranken, Mariana 851
Rankin, John 654, 680-2
Read, Eric 259
Reddie, Cecil 39, 123, 287
Reeves, Katherine 867
Reeves, Tony 781, 784, 791
Reid, Jimmy 768, 788
Reilly, Sidney 550-2
Reid, Harry 705
Remembrance 1-2, 288-292, 536, 601-4, 730, 847-8, 854, 870
Rettie, Archibald 259
Rettie, William 213
Rew, David 96
Rhind, Birnie 290
Rhodesia 667, 668, 670, 683, 685, 686-7
Richards, E.G. 447, 449, 457-8, 474, 488, 496
Riehle, August 434-5
Ring, Donald 669
Ritchie, Robert 354
Roberts, Bob 699
Roberts, Gordon 457
Robertson, A. Irvine 432, 510
Robertson, J.B. 440
Robertson, William 3, 5, 7
Robinson, Kenneth 118
Romania 313, 556-7, 828-9
Rose, A.W. 354
Rose, Chris 848
Rose, Walter 373, 446
Ross, James MacBean 150, 190, 193, 197, 200, 201, 206, 209, 220, 223-4, 241-3, 247, 248, 269, 270-1, 273-4
Ross, Willie 690, 766, 782, 811, 822, 824, 870
Ross, W.L.N.L. 669
Rounthwaite, D.C. 668
Rowantree, Niall 824, 849
Rowlatt, Sir Frederick 55
Roy, Donald 566-7

Royal Visits 622-3, 738-9
Rugby School 33-4
Russell, Bill 722
Russell, J.C. 357
Russia, Russians (also USSR) 27-8, 37, 56, 58, 65, 112, 113, 121, 124, 187, 223, 224, 241, 254, 296-8, 328, 367, 369-71, 456, 469, 472, 490, 501, 548-53, 560-1, 563, 564, 601, 606, 608, 613, 641-3, 677, 701, 735, 771, 826-8
Ryden, Nick 697
St Nazaire Raid 566-8
Sale, Geoffrey 392, 393, 399, 407
Salonica 248-9
Salvesen, Eric 85
Salvesen, Francis 795, 796
Sanders, Neil 714
Sanders, Sir Robert 692
Sanderson, A.N. 703-4
Sanderson, G.B. 524, 534
Sanderson, K.W.B. 356
Sanderson, W.R. 383, 471
Sandhurst 31-4, 40, 215, 227, 304, 324, 425, 593, 610, 715, 735, 739-40, 754-6, 796, 816, 849-50, 868-9
Schulze, Douglas (Miller) 49-50
Schoolhouse (College East and West) 155, 415, 680, 701, 753, 777
Scotland, Scots 2-13, 17-21, 26-7, 34, 46-8, 53, 71, 78, 147, 154-5, 230, 235, 248, 293-5, 311, 329, 339-40, 362-4, 373-4, 385, 474, 532, 619, 660, 723, 736, 757, 767-71, 787-8, 840-1, 867, 873
Scott, D.B.H. 313, 534
Scott, Freddie 424-6, 477-80, 482, 489, 490, 660-2
Scott, H.M. 469
Scott, J.H. 309-10
Scott, J.M. 286, 304, 355, 435
Scott, Michael 464
Scott, Raymond 811
Scott, Sir Walter 7, 11, 17, 18
Scouts 397, 716
Scroggie, A.U.R. 768
Scroggie, E.F.R. 815-6
Sellar, W.C. 50, 155-6, 158-9, 162-3, 168, 174-5, 177, 180-1, 320, 772

Shah, Z.A. 688
Shanley, Alison 824-5
Sharp, Sir Richard 510, 523, 525-7, 529, 533-4
Sharp, William 577, 588, 639, 670, 668, 671-4, 682-5, 687-8, 691
Shaw, George 96
Shaw, J.D.R. 469-70
Shaw, Ronnie 413, 627
Shennan, Chris 716
Shiffner, Katherine 820, 822, 834
Shooting (school) see Bisley
Simon, Sir John 37, 138, 167, 289, 327, 358-9, 371, 396, 422-3, 837
Simonett, J.F. 769
Simpson, David 354
Singapore 68, 75-6, 351, 353-4, 445-6, 502, 523, 526, 534, 688-93, 726
Skinner, Sarah-Louise 826-7
Skrine, P.R.H. 448
Sloane Rangers 791-2
Smith, David 480
Smith, G.G. 97-8
Smith, J.M. 102, 121
Smith, W.A. 446
Smyth, J.B.A. 387, 395, 465-6
Sniping see Hesketh-Prichard
Social Darwinism see Race
Somme, Battle of the 148, 165-6, 172, 200, 212-6, 230, 820, 870
Souter, David 441, 444
Souter, Ian 441
South Africa 63-5, 90-102, 114, 115, 189, 214, 358, 508, 701, 786-7,
Spanish Flu 279-81
Sparling, S.J. 243
Sport 33-41, 49-50, 54, 86, 87, 95, 116, 158-9, 160-1, 166, 168, 186, 248, 280, 300-1, 352, 359, 379-80, 424, 425, 429, 505, 536, 545, 580-2, 588, 644, 649, 669, 689, 730, 736, 791, 821
Stack, Camilla 828
Stanion, Vernon 437
Steel, William 531
Stephen, Sir A. Murray 135
Stewart, Alastair 468-9
Stewart, Herbert 186
Stewart, Ian 395, 402, 406, 411, 436
Stewart, James 201

Storey, C.B.C. 96
Storey, J.H. 239
Stout, Tommy 132, 243
Strikes 285, 288, 293-6, 471, 767-8
Stuart-Menteth, James 464
Sub-Aqua Section 749, 783
Sudan, Sudanese 50, 57, 83-5, 87-8, 92, 119, 308-9, 351, 691
Sutcliffe, Ian 579
Sutherland, Alfred 265-6
Sutherland, G.D.McK. 534
Sutherland, Malcolm 784
Sutton, Chris 771
Swan, N.S. 666-7
Swanson, Joe 487-8
Swinton, Tilda 777, 833
Talbot, Keith 723
Tel-el-Kebir, Battle of 80-2, 94
Tennant, H.C.L. 680
Terris, Sylvia 779-80
Thaw, Alastair 784
Thompson, Edmund Peel 186-7
Thompson, Harold 252
Thompson, John Mackay 177-8
Thomson, Arthur 488
Thomson, Hamish 585
Thomson, Ian 325, 431
Thomson, Jenny 780
Thomson, William (colonial official) 58-9
Thomson, William (soldier) 97, 98
Thomson, William (sailor) 446
Thorpe, D.R. 676, 678, 696, 788
Timbs, Basil 593
Tindall, R.M.H. 480
Tippett, Sir Michael 286
Trimble, David 835-6
Turnbull, Ronald 564-6
Turner, Ross 870
Uganda 87-8, 668, 669, 787
Underwood, Desmond 211-2
Urquhart, John 593
Vawdrey, Daniel 'Gents' 195-6, 198-9, 202, 203, 205, 207-8, 210-1, 219-20, 269, 406-7
VE-Day 412, 416, 487
Vietnam 660, 701-3, 727-8, 730, 867
Vive-la 94, 128-9, 131, 139, 285, 298, 327, 350, 355, 358, 500, 577, 618, 621, 665, 679, 722, 737-8, 760, 762, 768, 770, 779, 788, 789, 790, 834, 836, 844

VJ-Day 416-7, 533
Von Hoff, Lucas 867
Waddell, A.N.A. 491-2, 668, 692
Waddell, Alan 627
Waddell, Herbert 481-2, 603
Wadsworth, Edward 176
Wait, W.E. 48-9
Wallace, Frederick 187
War Memorial, school 1-2, 227, 266, 290-2, 414, 415-6, 601, 602-3, 854
Warden, W.E. 225, 238
Ware, Fabian 374
Watling, R.G. 352
Watson, Ronald 442
Watt, B.M. 357, 467
Watt, D.M. 36, 46, 47, 70-2,
Watt, G.M. 240-1
Watt, L. M. 149-50, 229,
Watters, Ruaridh 738, 749
Waugh, Evelyn 554
Waugh, K.A. 514
Waugh, W.G. 464
Weatherill, Edward 245-6
Webster, Robin 586, 595, 597
Weekes, David 793
Weekes, Victoria 794
Wells, Matthew 840
Weston Smith, I. 514
Weston Smith, J. 656
Whigham, Robert 170, 296, 343, 345, 603
Whittle, Charles 678, 721, 740
Whyte, David 559
Whyte, E.R. 241
Wilcox, E.H. 297
Wiley, Struan 644
Wilkie, Rona 866
Williams, Morris Meredith 176, 292
Williamson, Archibald 503
Williamson, Bruce 767
Williamson, Ian 311
Williamson, Ronnie 456-7, 543
Wilson, C.A.K. 666
Wilson, Douglas 436
Wilson, Harold 699, 738, 757
Wilson, K.P. 163, 177,
Wilson, Nicol 702
Wilson, N.A. 87-8
Wilson, W.R. 289
Winter, Sarah 830
Wolfenden, J.C. 252-3
Wood, Peter 468

Wright, Ronald Selby 687, 737, 783
Wright, Victoria 784
Wylie, Gordon 611-2
Yates, Gar 588, 610, 616, 637, 657
Yeo, John 40
Young, E.T. 243
Young, Gayle 814
Young, J.E. 185
Young, R.B. 357
Young, R.M.D. 815
Younie, John 348, 361, 406, 470-1
Ypres 152, 170, 185, 202-4, 223, 319-20, 325, 404, 431, 869-70

Full casualty lists with notes on places of burial are available from the Fettes College History Department on request.